Cost Accounting
A Data Analytics Approach

Cost Accounting
A Data Analytics Approach

Margaret H. Christ
University of Georgia

D. Kip Holderness Jr.
West Virginia University

Vernon J. Richardson
University of Arkansas and Baruch College

Mc
Graw
Hill

COST ACCOUNTING: A DATA ANALYTICS APPROACH, 2024 RELEASE

1 2 3 4 5 6 7 8 9 LWI 29 28 27 26 25 24

ISBN 978-1-266-65401-5 (bound)
MHID 1-266-65401-1 (bound)
ISBN 978-1-266-65609-5 (loose-leaf)
MHID 1-266-65609-X (loose-leaf)

Portfolio Manager: *Noelle Bathurst*
Product Developers: *Steven Rigolosi and Michael McCormick*
Marketing Manager: *Nate Anderson*
Content Project Managers: *Pat Frederickson and George Theofanopoulos*
Manufacturing Project Manager: *Sandy Ludovissy*
Designer: *David W. Hash*
Content Licensing Specialist: *Brianna Kirschbaum*
Cover Image: Windfarms credit: *Mischa Keijser/Image Source/Getty Images*; Columns credit: *Kubko/Shutterstock*
Design elements: (justice scale) *K3Star/Shutterstock*; (app) *PureSolution/Shutterstock*; (business icon) *miakievy/ DigitalVision Vectors/Getty Images*
Compositor: *Straive*

All credits appearing on page or at the end of the book are considered to be an extension of the copyright page.

Library of Congress Cataloging-in-Publication Data

Names: Christ, Margaret H., author. | Holderness, D. Kip, Jr., author. |
  Richardson, Vernon J., author.
Title: Cost accounting : a data analytics approach / Margaret H. Christ,
  University of Georgia, D. Kip Holderness Jr., West Virginia University,
  Vernon J. Richardson, University of Arkansas and Baruch College.
Description: New York, NY : McGraw Hill, [2024] | Includes index. |
  Audience: Ages 18+
Identifiers: LCCN 2023049855 (print) | LCCN 2023049856 (ebook) | ISBN
  9781266654015 (paperback) | ISBN 9781266656576 (epub)
Subjects: LCSH: Business planning—Data processing. | Decision making—Data
  processing. | Organizational effectiveness—Data processing. |
  Accounting—Data processing.
Classification: LCC HD30.28 .C537 2024 (print) | LCC HD30.28 (ebook) |
  DDC 657/.42—dc23/eng/20231213
LC record available at https://lccn.loc.gov/2023049855
LC ebook record available at https://lccn.loc.gov/2023049856

mheducation.com/highered

Dedications

For Adam, Kate, Eloise, and James, with love.

—Margaret Christ

To Carolyn, who is and will ever be my favorite.
Thank you for your unwavering love and support
when I decide to do the impractical.

—Kip Holderness

To my most amazing son, Daniel, who has a zest
for life and is the hardest worker I know. Love you,
Danny!

—Vern Richardson

About the Authors

Margaret H. Christ is the J. M. Tull Chair in Accounting in the Terry College of Business at the University of Georgia. Her research focuses on accounting innovation, including data analytics and other accounting technologies, and how they impact organizational risk, management control systems, and employee behavior. She has served as an editor for *The Accounting Review, The Journal of Management Accounting Research,* and *Accounting Horizons* and serves on several editorial boards. Dr. Christ teaches accounting analytics using a case-based curriculum that focuses on data analytics, visualization, and automation and their uses in a variety of accounting contexts. She also works with the Ernst and Young Academic Resource Center to develop and disseminate educational materials on the analytics mindset. Her teaching cases have won several awards from the AAA and Institute of Management Accounting, including the 2020 Innovation in Accounting Education Award.

D. Kip Holderness Jr. is Associate Professor of Accounting at West Virginia University. He teaches cost, management, and forensic accounting, and he works extensively with doctoral students conducting various research projects. Dr. Holderness's research focuses primarily on the impact of fraud and employee deviance on individuals and organizations and on improving detection methods. He also examines the effects of personality and generational differences in the workplace. He has published in practitioner and academic journals in the areas of fraud and forensics, auditing, managerial accounting, information systems, and accounting education. Dr. Holderness has received numerous research grants from the Institute for Fraud Prevention and the Institute of Management Accountants.

Vernon J. Richardson is Distinguished Professor of Accounting and the G. William Glezen Chair in the Sam M. Walton College of Business at the University of Arkansas and Visiting Professor at Baruch College. He received his BS, Master of Accountancy, and MBA from Brigham Young University and his PhD in accounting from the University of Illinois at Urbana–Champaign. Dr. Richardson is a member of the American Accounting Association and has served as president of the American Accounting Association Information Systems section. He previously served as an editor of *The Accounting Review* and is currently an editor at *Accounting Horizons.* He is also a co-author of McGraw Hill's *Accounting Information Systems, Introduction to Data Analytics for Accounting, Introduction to Business Analytics, Data Analytics for Accounting,* and *Financial Statement Analysis* textbooks. His accounting analytics textbooks won the AAA's 2022 Innovation in Accounting Education Award.

Data-Driven Insights: Guiding Students and Shaping Future Leaders

From the Authors

The role of management accountants is to analyze data to help organizations make effective business decisions. Thanks to an ever-increasing amount of data generated by companies, the opportunities for management accountants to provide data-driven insights have never been greater. We believe that students can prepare for an accounting career not only by understanding the methods and procedures of cost accounting but also by learning how to examine and analyze data, interpret the results, and share insight with others in their organizations.

In addition to providing a strong foundation in cost accounting, *Cost Accounting: A Data Analytics Approach* offers a valuable framework that will help students use and analyze data and provide value to their organizations. This framework, which we call the AMPS model, is composed of four steps:

1. **A**sk the Question
2. **M**aster the Data
3. **P**erform the Analysis
4. **S**hare the Story

Throughout the text, the AMPS model helps students approach management accounting topics in a data-driven way. These topics include, but are not limited to, cost analysis, cost-volume-profit analysis, budgeting, variance analysis, and strategy maps. The model is reinforced as students complete labs in each chapter that require them to use common workplace tools (such as Excel®, Tableau®, and Power BI®) to analyze data, interpret results, and make effective business decisions.

The text explains important data analytics skills—such as sensitivity analysis, regression analysis, and goal-seek analysis—and asks students to apply these skills in a host of decision-making contexts. Students also learn how to create data visualizations to become effective communicators within their organizations.

In writing this book, we've incorporated input from hundreds of instructors through detailed development reviews, in-depth focus groups, and intensive panels to ensure that it includes the cost and management accounting topics that today's instructors and students need. Our focus on real-world applications, and on the integration of data analytics tools and decision making, sets our book apart while preparing today's students to become tomorrow's accounting leaders.

Margaret Christ
Kip Holderness
Vern Richardson

Key Features

Management Accounting and Data Analytics

Information is a strategic asset of any firm, and the way a business accesses, analyzes, and uses information to inform critical business decisions can give it a unique competitive advantage. Management accounting exists to address management's questions and to facilitate decision making. To this end, management accountants must be able to identify, transform, and analyze appropriate data, and then provide salient, real-time reporting and data visualizations to management. To help students develop these essential business skills, we integrate data analytics skills in every chapter of this text.

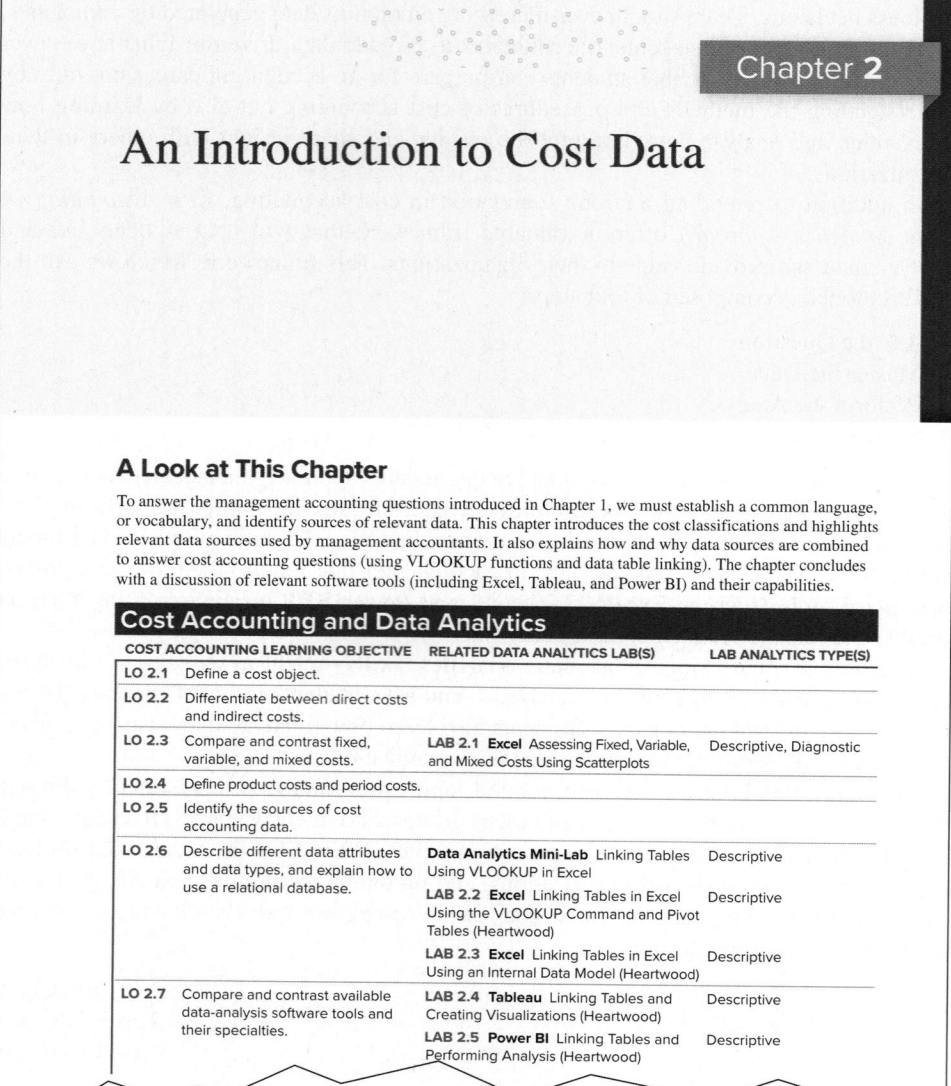

Chapter **2**

An Introduction to Cost Data

A Look at This Chapter

To answer the management accounting questions introduced in Chapter 1, we must establish a common language, or vocabulary, and identify sources of relevant data. This chapter introduces the cost classifications and highlights relevant data sources used by management accountants. It also explains how and why data sources are combined to answer cost accounting questions (using VLOOKUP functions and data table linking). The chapter concludes with a discussion of relevant software tools (including Excel, Tableau, and Power BI) and their capabilities.

Cost Accounting and Data Analytics

COST ACCOUNTING LEARNING OBJECTIVE	RELATED DATA ANALYTICS LAB(S)	LAB ANALYTICS TYPE(S)
LO 2.1 Define a cost object.		
LO 2.2 Differentiate between direct costs and indirect costs.		
LO 2.3 Compare and contrast fixed, variable, and mixed costs.	**LAB 2.1 Excel** Assessing Fixed, Variable, and Mixed Costs Using Scatterplots	Descriptive, Diagnostic
LO 2.4 Define product costs and period costs.		
LO 2.5 Identify the sources of cost accounting data.		
LO 2.6 Describe different data attributes and data types, and explain how to use a relational database.	**Data Analytics Mini-Lab** Linking Tables Using VLOOKUP in Excel	Descriptive
	LAB 2.2 Excel Linking Tables in Excel Using the VLOOKUP Command and Pivot Tables (Heartwood)	Descriptive
	LAB 2.3 Excel Linking Tables in Excel Using an Internal Data Model (Heartwood)	Descriptive
LO 2.7 Compare and contrast available data-analysis software tools and their specialties.	**LAB 2.4 Tableau** Linking Tables and Creating Visualizations (Heartwood)	Descriptive
	LAB 2.5 Power BI Linking Tables and Performing Analysis (Heartwood)	Descriptive

Hands-on Learning with Labs and Mini-Labs

In *Cost Accounting: A Data Analytics Approach,* data analytics is not a footnote to the cost accounting curriculum. Instead, it is an integral part of every chapter, guiding students from accounting and data analytics concepts, to step-by-step practice and application, to independent analysis, interpretation, and data-driven decision making. To provide students with hands-on practice, each chapter provides not only an introductory Data Analytics Mini-Lab within the chapter but also full-length end-of-chapter labs that offer decision-making context, ask specific management questions, and walk students through the process of analyzing the data and presenting the results to decision makers. The labs are supported by an extensive library of author-created videos in Connect.

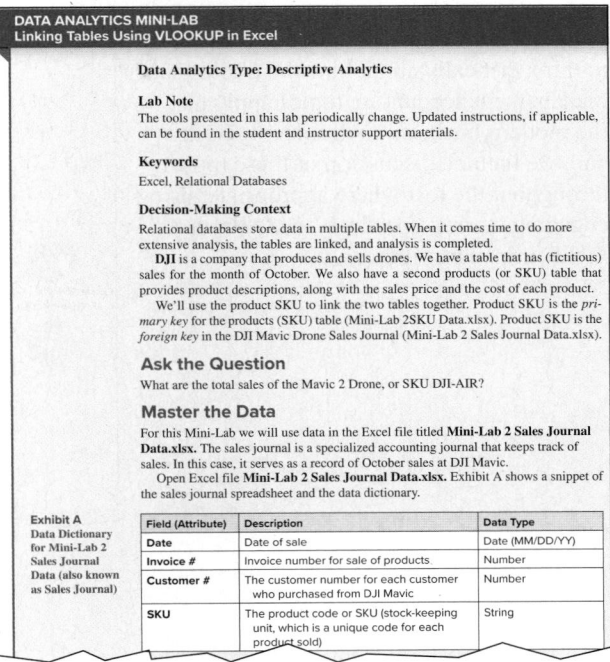

DATA ANALYTICS MINI-LAB
Linking Tables Using VLOOKUP in Excel

Data Analytics Type: Descriptive Analytics

Lab Note
The tools presented in this lab periodically change. Updated instructions, if applicable, can be found in the student and instructor support materials.

Keywords
Excel, Relational Databases

Decision-Making Context
Relational databases store data in multiple tables. When it comes time to do more extensive analysis, the tables are linked, and analysis is completed.
DJI is a company that produces and sells drones. We have a table that has (fictitious) sales for the month of October. We also have a second products (or SKU) table that provides product descriptions, along with the sales price and the cost of each product.
We'll use the product SKU to link the two tables together. Product SKU is the *primary key* for the products (SKU) table (Mini-Lab 2SKU Data.xlsx). Product SKU is the *foreign key* in the DJI Mavic Drone Sales Journal (Mini-Lab 2 Sales Journal Data.xlsx).

Ask the Question
What are the total sales of the Mavic 2 Drone, or SKU DJI-AIR?

Master the Data
For this Mini-Lab we will use data in the Excel file titled **Mini-Lab 2 Sales Journal Data.xlsx.** The sales journal is a specialized accounting journal that keeps track of sales. In this case, it serves as a record of October sales at DJI Mavic.
Open Excel file **Mini-Lab 2 Sales Journal Data.xlsx.** Exhibit A shows a snippet of the sales journal spreadsheet and the data dictionary.

Exhibit A
Data Dictionary for Mini-Lab 2 Sales Journal Data (also known as Sales Journal)

Field (Attribute)	Description	Data Type
Date	Date of sale	Date (MM/DD/YY)
Invoice #	Invoice number for sale of products	Number
Customer #	The customer number for each customer who purchased from DJI Mavic	Number
SKU	The product code or SKU (stock-keeping unit, which is a unique code for each product sold)	String

Contemporary Management Accounting Topics: Ethics, ESG, and Human Dimensions of Management Accounting

A variety of important new and emerging issues that organizations face today can impact management decision making. For example, many companies have prioritized sustainability efforts and sustainability reporting, using their management accounting system to accumulate, analyze, and report sustainability information for internal decision makers and external stakeholders. In addition, in performing their jobs, management accountants (and all other types of accountants) must exhibit a strong degree of integrity and adhere to a strict code of ethics. They must understand and respect customers', suppliers', and employees' right to privacy and make sure that they collect, use, and maintain data ethically. They must also be aware of, and work with, their companies' commitments to various ESG (environmental, social, and governance) goals. Finally, management accountants must understand the human dimensions of accounting decisions, ensuring that processes and procedures provide the right incentives to the workforce.

From the Field

Accounting students need exposure to contemporary issues and should be prompted to think critically about how the traditional management accounting topics apply in the modern business environment. To this end, we include discussion of these topics throughout the text where appropriate, using engaging stories, anecdotes, and "From the Field" mini case studies.

ENVIRONMENTAL, SOCIAL, GOVERNANCE

ETHICS

FROM THE FIELD

Tracing Costs to Remove the Need for Allocation

Allocation always involves some element of guesswork. Traced costs are directly attributed to jobs or products, which removes the need for allocation. Therefore, one way to improve the accuracy of cost information is to increase the number of costs that are traced, which allows companies to reclassify indirect costs as direct costs.

Consider labor costs. In some industries such as accounting, legal services, and consulting, employees track their time in 15-minute increments, which are then traced to specific jobs. Tracing labor decreases indirect costs and provides more accurate cost information.

In many cases, tracing labor costs may not be practical, even though companies can do so. Consider a supervisor who oversees dozens of employees who work on separate projects. In this case, the cost of tracing supervisor labor may outweigh the benefits of more accurate cost data.

Thinking Critically

Companies have greatly increased tracing of the environmental costs of providing goods and services in the past several years. How might the specific identification of environmental costs have altered company behavior as it pertains to companies' ESG efforts? How will these efforts be impacted by ESG reporting regulations?

Jurisdictions that have relatively low corporate tax rates are known as *tax havens*. The British Virgin Islands, the Cayman Islands, and Bermuda are among the most popular international locations for multinational corporations looking to minimize their tax liability. In the United States, the state of Delaware is an attractive choice for incorporation because Delaware-based companies can avoid corporate taxes even while doing business across state lines.

Some question the ethical considerations of organizations relying heavily on tax havens to reduce their tax liability. Research shows that tax havens cost governments between $500 billion and $600 billion (per year) in lost corporate tax revenue. It is estimated that in 2021 U.S. Fortune 500 companies held $2.6 trillion in profits in offshore tax havens, allowing them to avoid over $700 billion in U.S. federal income taxes.

Career-Readiness Focus

The introduction to each chapter shows how the chapter concepts relate to specific career skills. Markers throughout the text show where these career-readiness concepts are taught and reinforced. In addition, each chapter concludes with a recent job posting for a company looking to hire an accountant with the skills taught in that chapter. These materials help students see the direct connection between the skills learned in this course and the skills used in the real world of modern business.

Chapter Concepts and Career Skills

Learning About . . .	Helps with These Career Skills
Cost objects	Defining a company's costs
Direct vs. indirect costs	Determining which costs are tracked directly and which costs are not tracked directly
Fixed, variable, and mixed costs	Determining a firm's pricing and marketing strategies
Product vs. period costs, and prime vs. conversion costs	Understanding the nature of costs and how they impact the accounting for costs overall
Cost accounting data sources	Recognizing and using data from various sources to address management questions
Relational databases	Understanding how databases link attributes of different customers, sales transactions, vendors, payroll, employees, and suppliers to each other using tables and primary and foreign keys
Analytics software tools, including Excel, Tableau, and Power BI	Matching the most applicable software tool to the management accounting task

Tools and Resources

AMPS Model

To help develop an analytics mindset, our textbook centers on the AMPS model of data analytics that serves as the framework for each chapter:

- **Ask the Question:** Management has questions that relate to the achievement of the organization's goals. Students learn how to ask the right questions that can be answered with data to improve decision making.
- **Master the Data:** The sources of management accounting data are described, and the basics of data preparation are considered.
- **Perform the Analysis:** Each chapter and lab emphasize the use of the appropriate data analytics techniques to answer management's specific questions. Four broad categories of data analytics are covered:
  - **Descriptive Analytics:** counts, summaries, totals, averages, cost breakdowns
  - **Diagnostic Analytics:** variances, cross-tabulations, conditional formatting
  - **Predictive Analytics:** correlation, regression, time series forecasting
  - **Prescriptive Analytics:** what-if analysis, goal-seek (break-even) analysis, cash flow analysis
- **Share the Story:** To make effective data-driven decisions, and to communicate results to key stakeholders, management must clearly understand accounting data and the results of data analysis. Each chapter emphasizes data reporting, creating visualizations, and developing dashboards that can help managers make effective decisions.

Progress Checks

Progress Check questions posed following each major section of each chapter encourage students to consider and apply the concepts presented.

> **⊘ PROGRESS CHECK**
>
> 10. From which enterprise system does a company's cost accounting system receive aggregate and detailed revenue information? How might the company use this information to determine which products are most profitable at the company?
> 11. How does an understanding of the macroeconomy and industry performance help a company project future performance?

In-Chapter Data Analytics Mini-Labs

The in-chapter Data Analytics Mini-Labs illustrate how management accountants can answer managers' questions via the AMPS model. These labs move students from concepts to hands-on practice with the tools that modern businesses use to help them make profit-maximizing decisions. Each Mini-Lab serves as an introduction to the data analytics that students will work with in greater detail in the full-length labs at the end of each chapter.

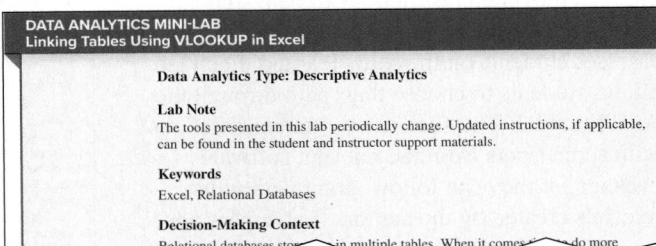

DATA ANALYTICS MINI-LAB
Linking Tables Using VLOOKUP in Excel

Data Analytics Type: Descriptive Analytics

Lab Note
The tools presented in this lab periodically change. Updated instructions, if applicable, can be found in the student and instructor support materials.

Keywords
Excel, Relational Databases

Decision-Making Context
Relational databases store ... in multiple tables. When it comes ... do more

Focus on Building Skills with Excel®, Tableau®, and Power BI®

Students learn how to conduct business analytics using three software tools that are widely used by businesses today: Excel, Tableau, and Power BI.

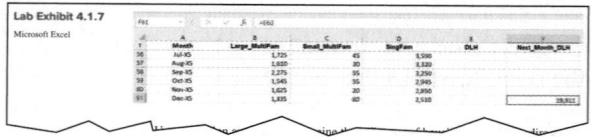

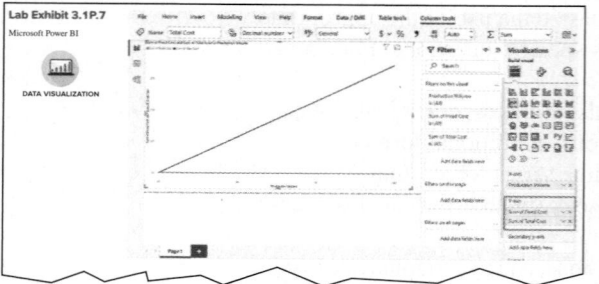

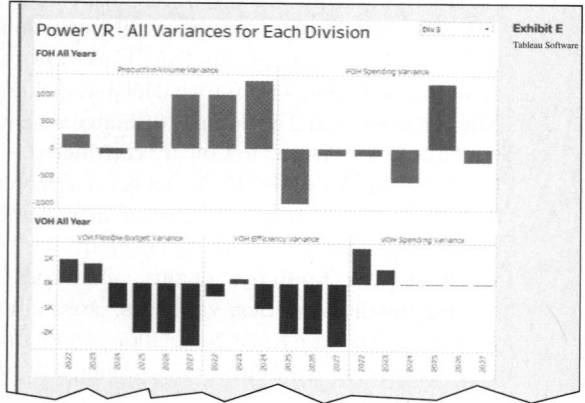

Data Analytics Labs

To provide students with hands-on experience in data analysis techniques and skills, each chapter includes approximately *five* detailed labs that require them to use Excel, Tableau, and/or Power BI. Each lab asks students to bring together their knowledge of cost accounting and data analytics to ask and answer questions, and to present their findings to decision makers. Each lab has two versions. The first provides step-by-step instructions to help students learn the relevant techniques, while the second assesses students on the skills learned. Each lab allows students to choose their path through the AMPS model: They can use written instructions with screenshots from the relevant software package, or they can follow along with video tutorials created by the authors. Lab assessment is conducted primarily in Connect through the use of auto-graded questions, including multiple-choice questions, algorithmic questions, and other objective questions.

CHAPTER 2 LABS

LAB 2.1 **Excel** Assessing Fixed, Variable, and Mixed Costs Using Scatterplots

LAB 2.2 **Excel** Linking Tables in Excel Using the VLOOKUP Command and Pivot Tables

LAB 2.3 **Excel** Linking Tables in Excel Using an Internal Data Model

LAB 2.4 **Tableau** Linking Tables and Creating Visualizations

LAB 2.5 **Power BI** Linking Tables and Performing Analysis

Lab 2.1   Excel

Assessing Fixed, Variable, and Mixed Costs Using Scatterplots

Data Analytics Types: Descriptive Analytics, Diagnostic Analytics

Lab Note: The tools presented in this lab periodically change. Updated instructions, if applicable, can be found in the student and instructor support materials.

Keywords

Scatterplot, Visualization, Cost Behavior

Decision-Making Context

Cheap Drones is trying to determine its cost behavior to make sure its products are profitable.

It is important for managers to understand their cost behavior, which is the relationship between cost and behavior. Variable cost changes in proportion to the change in cost drivers, but variable cost per unit is constant within the relevant range. Fixed cost does not change in total, but fixed cost per unit decreases within the relevant range. Mixed cost increases as activity increases but not to proportion.

Later chapters will use more sophisticated methods to explain cost behavior. This lab focuses on developing a basic understanding of cost behavior with scatterplots, a common type of data visualization.

Required

Determine the cost behavior for each input cost and the total cost of each drone produced.

Practical Examples from Real-World Companies

Throughout the text, management accounting concepts are introduced via examples from a host of real-world companies and industries. In addition, each chapter includes at least one lab using data from **Heartwood Cabinets**, a fictional business adapted from a real manufacturing company, to provide continuity and to allow students to work with the cost accounting aspects of the many operations of a single company.

PRODUCT COSTS AND PERIOD COSTS

Companies also classify costs as either product costs or period costs. **Product costs** are all costs that are incurred to produce goods and services for customers. What gets categorized as product costs differs substantially between companies. For service companies, such as the **Boston Consulting Group**, product costs may include the materials used to provide consulting services, but many service companies have no product costs. For retailers such as **TJ Maxx** and **Target**, product costs consist of inventory purchased for resale in their stores. For manufacturing companies such as **Tesla** and **Apple**, product costs consist of all costs incurred to produce goods: namely, direct materials, direct labor, and manufacturing overhead. Companies often use the terms **prime costs** to refer to direct materials and direct labor and **conversion costs** to refer to direct labor and manufacturing overhead.

Period costs are recorded as expenses on the income statement when they occur. Any cost that is not a product cost is a period cost. In contrast, product costs are recorded as part of an asset in inventory. Exhibit 2.4 provides some examples of product costs and period costs at Tesla and **Heartwood Cabinets**.

End-of-Chapter Exercises and Problems

In-chapter and end-of-chapter progress checks, exercises, and problems are essential to each chapter. The end-of-chapter assessments include real-world application questions with a special emphasis on data analytics skills and tools. Each chapter also provides multiple-choice and discussion questions as well as exercises and problems to reinforce learning. Adapted CMA exam questions are also included and called out with an icon.

CMA

Problems   connect

1. (LO4.4) Web Bytes allocates manufacturing overhead on the basis of direct labor hours. Web Bytes had the following cost information:

   Estimated direct labor hours: 10,000 hours

   Actual direct labor hours: 12,000 hours

   Estimated manufacturing overhead costs: $18,000

   Actual manufacturing overhead costs: $24,000

   Required

   a. What is Web Bytes' predetermined overhead rate?

   b. What is Web Bytes' applied overhead for the year?

   c. What is the amount of overapplied or underapplied overhead for the year?

2. (LO4.1, 4.3, 4.6) Dashing Diva has the following costs for April.

Direct labor	$20,000.00
Direct materials	$15,000.00
Factory utilities	$8,000.00
Accounting services	$12,000.00
Direct marketing	$17,000.00
Production supervisor salaries	$6,000.00
Factory equipment depreciation	$13,000.00

   Required

   a. What are the total production costs?

   b. What are the total manufacturing overhead costs?

   c. Dashing Diva produced Job #123 with the following actual costs: $1,500 of direct materials, $1,800 of direct labor, and $1,000 of manufacturing overhead. Dashing Diva allocates manufacturing overhead at a rate of 80% of direct labor costs. Under a normal costing system, what was Dashing Diva's recorded cost for Job #123?

3. (LO4, 4.6) Jackson Mills has the following cost information:

CMA

21. (LO5.2) When using activity-based costing techniques, which one of the following departmental activities would be expected to use machine hours as a cost driver to allocate overhead costs to production?

   a. Plant cafeteria

   b. Machine setups

   c. Material handling

   d. Robotics painting

CMA

22. (LO5.2) A company is considering the implementation of an activity-based costing and management program. The company:

   a. should focus on manufacturing activities and avoid implementation with service-type functions.

   b. will probably find a lack of software in the marketplace to assist with the related recordkeeping.

   c. will likely gain added insights into causes of cost.

   d. will likely use fewer cost pools than it did under more traditional accounting methods.

23. (LO5.2, 5.3) The Chocolate _____ specializes in chocolate baked go___

A complete course platform

Connect enables you to build deeper connections with your students through cohesive digital content and tools, creating engaging learning experiences. We are committed to providing you with the right resources and tools to support all your students along their personal learning journeys.

65%
Less Time Grading

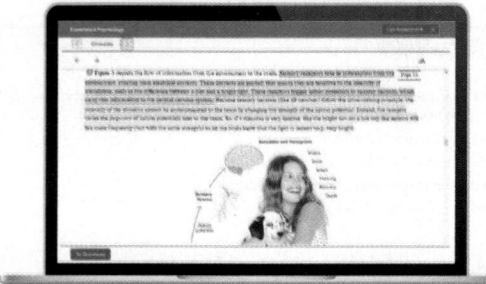

Laptop: Getty Images; Woman/dog: George Doyle/Getty Images

Every learner is unique

In Connect, instructors can assign an adaptive reading experience with SmartBook® 2.0. Rooted in advanced learning science principles, SmartBook® 2.0 delivers each student a personalized experience, focusing students on their learning gaps, ensuring that the time they spend studying is time well spent. **mheducation.com/highered/connect/smartbook**

Study anytime, anywhere

Encourage your students to download the free ReadAnywhere® app so they can access their online eBook, SmartBook® 2.0, or Adaptive Learning Assignments when it's convenient, even when they're offline. And since the app automatically syncs with their Connect account, all of their work is available every time they open it. Find out more at **mheducation.com/readanywhere**

> *"I really liked this app—it made it easy to study when you don't have your textbook in front of you."*
>
> Jordan Cunningham, a student at *Eastern Washington University*

Effective tools for efficient studying

Connect is designed to help students be more productive with simple, flexible, intuitive tools that maximize study time and meet students' individual learning needs. Get learning that works for everyone with Connect.

Education for all

McGraw Hill works directly with Accessibility Services departments and faculty to meet the learning needs of all students. Please contact your Accessibility Services Office, and ask them to email **accessibility@mheducation.com**, or visit **mheducation.com/about/accessibility** for more information.

Affordable solutions, added value

Make technology work for you with LMS integration for single sign-on access, mobile access to the digital textbook, and reports to quickly show you how each of your students is doing. And with our Inclusive Access program, you can provide all these tools at the lowest available market price to your students. Ask your McGraw Hill representative for more information.

Solutions for your challenges

A product isn't a solution. Real solutions are affordable, reliable, and come with training and ongoing support when you need it and how you want it. Visit **supportateverystep.com** for videos and resources both you and your students can use throughout the term.

Updated and relevant content

Our new Evergreen delivery model provides the most current and relevant content for your course, hassle-free. Content, tools, and technology updates are delivered directly to your existing McGraw Hill Connect® course. Engage students and freshen up assignments with up-to-date coverage of select topics and assessments, all without having to switch editions or build a new course.

Connect® for *Cost Accounting*

SmartBook® is the market-leading adaptive study resource that is proven to strengthen memory recall, increase retention, and boost grades. SmartBook 2.0 identifies and closes knowledge gaps through a continually adapting reading and questioning experience that helps students master the key concepts in each chapter.

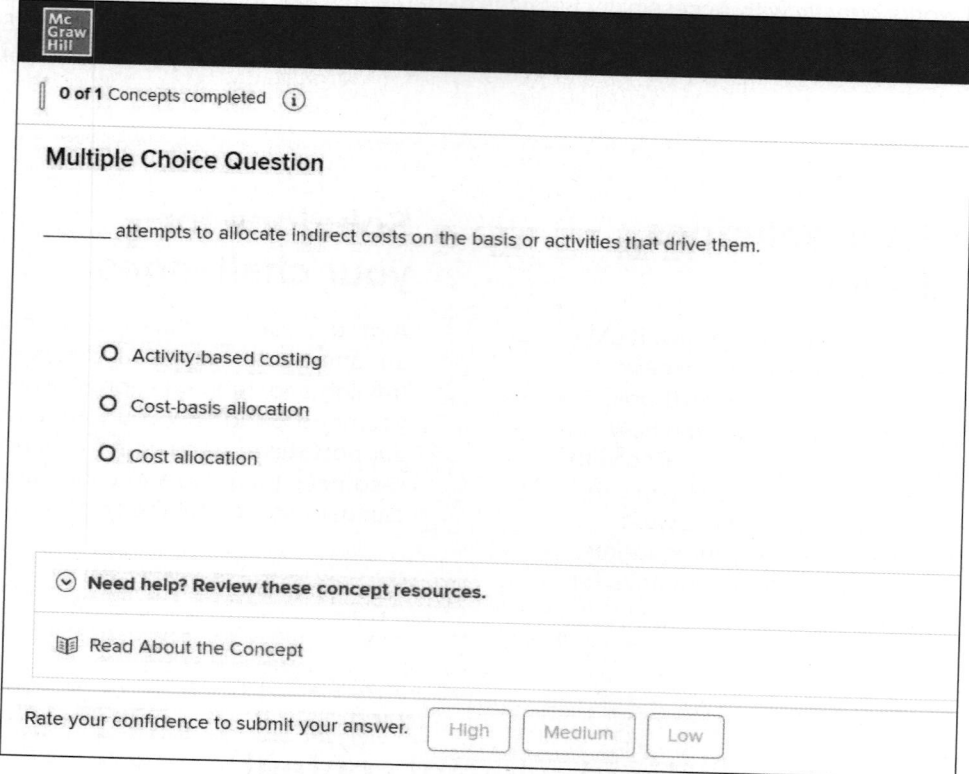

Exercises/Problems: Selected exercises and problems from the text are available for assignment in Connect to ensure students are building an analytical skill set.

> Download the SkyDio Drone Sales Journal dataset in Excel. Note the sales price and cost of each sale.
>
> **Required:**
>
> In Excel, calculate the gross margin (Sales Price − Cost) for each line of the invoice. Use a pivot table to determine the following. It may be helpful to perform this project after completing Lab 1.3 Excel, Lab 1.3 Tableau, or Lab 1.3 Power BI.
>
> | Question | Answer |
> |---|---|
> | a. What are the total sales for SKU SK2-CIK? | |
> | b. What is the total cost for all sales of SKU SKY-BAT? | |
> | c. What is the total gross margin for SKU SK2-BEA? | |
> | d. Which product (SKU) had the highest sales during the month? | |
> | e. Which product (SKU) had the lowest cost of sales during the month? | |
> | f. Which product (SKU) had the highest gross margin during the month? | |

Labs with Lab Assessments: While the labs require students to work outside of Connect in Excel, Tableau, and/or Power BI, Connect allows students to upload their results and answer analytical questions designed to reinforce the concepts and techniques taught in each chapter.

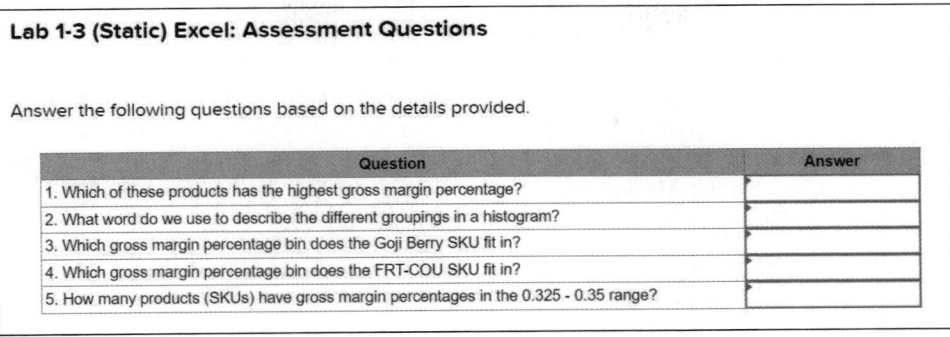

Lab Help Videos: Help videos for each lab provide step-by-step tutorials that walk students through the assigned analysis tasks in Excel, Tableau, and Power BI.

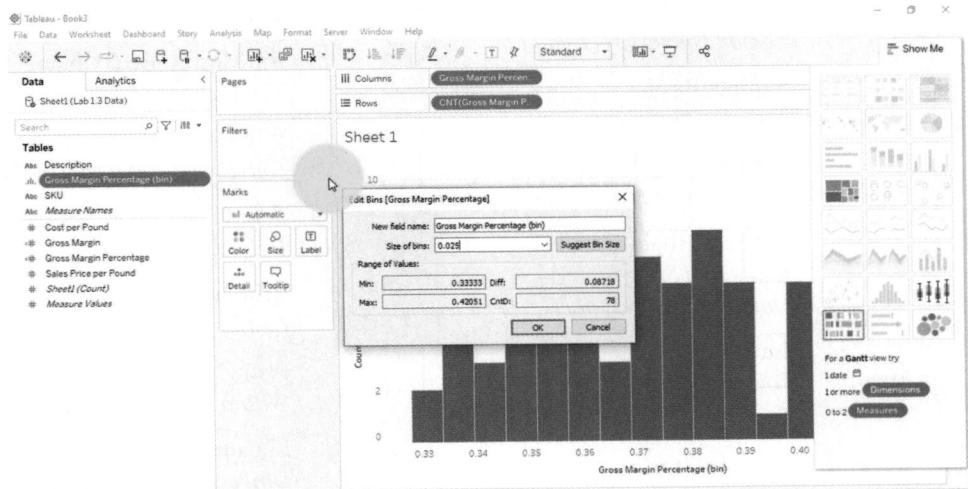

Acknowledgments

Enormous thanks to the awesome team at McGraw Hill, including Rebecca Olson, Noelle Bathurst, Steven Rigolosi, Michael McCormick, Nate Anderson, Kelsey Darin, Pat Frederickson, George Theofanopolous, Betsy Blumenthal, and Isabella Carpenter.

We also appreciate the work of Bailey Cahill, Miranda Hugie, and Caylee Whiteford.

We are grateful for the assistance of the following instructors who helped us develop and review the assessment content and additional resources: Emily Bello, Michael Casey, Chad Hugie, Alyssa Ong.

Thank you to our intensive review panel:

Sanaz Aghazadeh
Louisiana State University–Baton Rouge

Jace Garrett
Clemson University

Amelia Hart
University of Tennessee

Michael Majerczyk
Georgia State University

Kari Olsen
Utah Valley University

Paige Patrick
University of Illinois–Chicago

Thank you to the following instructors who provided feedback during the development process:

Sanaz Aghazadeh
Louisiana State University–Baton Rouge

Pat Albers
University of Wisconsin–Green Bay

Michael Alles
Rutgers University

Kwadwo Asare
Bryant University

Frank Badua
Lamar University–Beaumont

Sudipta Basu
Temple University

Jeremiah Bentley
University of Massachusetts–Amherst

Rebecca Bogie
Louisiana State University–Shreveport

Isaac Bonaparte
Towson University

Travis Brodbeck
Siena College

Ann Brooks
Wake Forest University–Winston-Salem

James Cannon
Utah State University

Sandra Cereola
Saint Anselm College

Yunshil Cha
University of New Hampshire

Suzanne Chaille
Saint Martin's University

Bih Horng (Bea) Chiang
The College of New Jersey

Willie (Jongwoon) Choi
University of Wisconsin–Madison

Toni Clegg
Delta College

Brittany Cord
Luther College

Paul Croitoru
Wilbur Wright College

Louann Cummings
University of Findlay

Alan Czyzewski
Indiana State University

Janet Dausey
Northeast Wisconsin Technical College–Green Bay

Bill Davenport
Lewis-Clark State College

Patricia Davis
Keystone College

Holly Dexter
West Virginia University–Parkersburg

Richard Dippel
Webster University

Carleton Donchess
Bridgewater State University

Jennifer Dosch
Metro State University–Minneapolis

George Drymiotes
Texas Christian University

Adam du Pon
Georgia Southern University

Augustine Duru
American University

Michael Eames
Santa Clara University

Sarah Engle
Portland State University

Qintao Fan
University of Oregon–Eugene

Andrew Felo
Susquehanna University

Wanda Fisher
Coastal Carolina Community College

Judith Flaxman
Temple University

Jean Fonkoua
Iowa Western Community College

Jace Garrett
Clemson University

Michael Gauci
Florida Atlantic University

Xin Geng
Berry College

Daniel Gibbons
Waubonsee Community College

Andrea Gouldman
Weber State University

Marina Grau
Houston Community College–West Loop Center

Kay Guess
Samford University

Sanjay Gupta
Valdosta State University

Heidi Hansel
Kirkwood Community College–Cedar Rapids

Lizhong Hao
University of Portland

Dave Harr
American University

Amelia Hart
University of Tennessee

Haihong He
California State University–Los Angeles

Youngwon Her
California State University–Northridge

Andrew Hildebrand
Lebanon Valley College

Dave Hinrichs
Lehigh University

Mike Hoppe
Wake Technical Community College

Surya Janakiraman
The University of Texas–Dallas

Vicki Jobst
Benedictine University

Cindy Johnson
University of Arkansas–Little Rock

Nikole Johnson
Iowa Central Community College

Stacy Johnson
Iowa Central Community College

David Jordan
Northeastern Illinois University

Ramadevi Kannan
*Owens Community
College–Perrysburg*

Carl Keller
Missouri State University

Kaimee Kellis
University of Oklahoma

Anne Kenner
Eastern Florida State College

Hyunpyo Kim
Shippensburg University

Brian Knox
Boise State University

Wikil Kwak
University of Nebraska–Omaha

Tricia Lackmeyer
Rose State College

Lydia Lafleur
*Louisiana State University–Baton
Rouge*

Sabrina Landa
Central Washington University

Brian Lazarus
Harford Community College

Picheng Lee
Pace University–NYC

Wee Meng Eric Lee
University of Northern Iowa

Miriam Lefkowitz
Brooklyn College

Dana Leland
*State University of New York–Empire
State College*

Marc Lewis
Central Connecticut State

Haijin Lin
University of Houston–Houston

Qianhua Ling
Marquette University

Harrison Liu
The University of Texas–San Antonio

Xiang (Samantha) Liu
*California State University–San
Bernardino*

Lorraine Magrath
Troy University

Michael Majerczyk
Georgia State University

Gilberto Marquez-Illescas
University of Rhode Island–Kingston

Jason Matthews
University of Georgia

Jeff McGowan
Saint Mary's College

Connie McKnight
University of Central Arkansas

Reynard McMillian
Tennessee State University

Christopher Mingyar
Mount Aloysius College

Tim Mitchell
University of Massachusetts–Amherst

Pam Neely
*State University of New
York–Brockport*

Phillip Njoroge
University of Colorado

Kari Olsen
Utah Valley University–Orem

John Palmer
*California State University–Long
Beach*

Shanshan Pan
University of Houston–Clear Lake

Paige Patrick
University of Illinois–Chicago

Valarie Pepper
Delaware State University

Michael Petersen
North Dakota State University

Debra Petrizzo-Wilkins
Curry College

Jenice Prather-Kinsey
University of Alabama–Birmingham

Santhosh Ramalingegowda
University of Georgia

Robert Rankin
Texas A&M University–Commerce

Jason Rasso
University of South Carolina

Jill Roberts
Campbellsville University

Paulette Rodriguez
The University of Texas–El Paso

Lyle Rupert
Hendrix College

Susan Sadowski
University of Maryland–Global Campus

Robert Sagedy
Rowan University

Savita Sahay
Rutgers University

Paul San Miguel
Midwestern State University–Texas

Margaret Shackell-Dowell
Ithaca College

Haeyoung Shin
University of Houston–Clear Lake

John Simms
University of St. Thomas

Philip Slater
Forsyth Technical Community College

Neal Smith
Northern Arizona University–Flagstaff

Mohsen Souissi
Fayetteville State University

Marc Sperling
Aurora University

Bryan Stikeleather
University of South Carolina

Huey-Lian Sun
Morgan State University

Jason Swartzlander
Bluffton University

Brian Sweeney
Drake University

Mollie Sweet
Northwest Nazarene University

Scott Swenson
Washington State University

Ivo Tafkov
Georgia State University

William Thomas
University of North Carolina at Pembroke

Todd Thornock
University of Nebraska–Lincoln

Kristen Thornton
Missouri State University

Sebastian Tideman
Syracuse University

Ian Van Deventer
Spalding University

Christine VanNamee
Mohawk Valley Community College

Inna Voytsekhivska
Western Michigan University–Kalamazoo

Christine Wayne
Harper College

Kimberly Webb
Texas Wesleyan University

Amber Whisenhunt
Northeastern State University

Biyu Wu
University of Nebraska–Lincoln

Di Wu
*California State
University–Bakersfield*

Li Xu
Washington State University

Dimitri Yatsenko
University of Wisconsin–Whitewater

Yan Zhang
*New Mexico State University–Las
Cruces*

Lin Zheng
IUPUI

Ying Zhou
University of Connecticut

Janet Zlojutro
Northwestern Michigan College

Brief Table of Contents

Table of Contents

Chapter 1

Strategic Management Questions and the Role of Management Accountants

A Look at This Chapter

Companies like **Pepsi** exist to create value. Management makes many strategic decisions about how the company can best create that value. Such decisions might include which markets or customers to target, which products or services to develop and offer, and how to maximize profits. To make these decisions, management needs accurate and meaningful information.

Management accountants help management make data-driven decisions about the company's direction. They support management by using a structured approach that includes identifying and articulating the questions that are important for strategic decision making, finding appropriate data to address them, analyzing the data, and communicating the results of the analysis and data-driven insights to management.

This chapter describes the types of strategic questions that managers must consider as they strive to make the company successful, and the important role that management accountants play in this effort. It also introduces the AMPS data analytics model as a systematic means of supporting data-driven decision making at the company.

Cost Accounting and Data Analytics

COST ACCOUNTING LEARNING OBJECTIVE	RELATED DATA ANALYTICS LAB(S)	LAB ANALYTICS TYPE
LO 1.1 Describe why companies exist and how they create value.		
LO 1.2 Describe the role of management accountants in facilitating data-driven decision making.		

Cost Accounting and Data Analytics *(continued)*

COST ACCOUNTING LEARNING OBJECTIVE	RELATED DATA ANALYTICS LAB(S)	LAB ANALYTICS TYPE
LO 1.3 Explain the use of the AMPS data analytics model as a foundation for addressing management accounting questions.	**LAB 1.1 Excel** Assessing the Profitability of a Small Business	Descriptive
	LAB 1.2 Excel Working with Data in Excel: Ranges and Tables	Descriptive
	LAB 1.3 Excel Assessing Product (SKU) Profitability with Pivot Tables	Descriptive
	LAB 1.3 Tableau Assessing Product (SKU) Profitability	Descriptive
	LAB 1.3 Power BI Assessing Product (SKU) Profitability	Descriptive
LO 1.4 Illustrate the types of strategic management questions and how management accountants address them using data analytics.	**Data Analytics Mini-Lab** Assessing Customer Profitability in Excel	Descriptive
LO 1.5 Summarize the differences between management accounting and financial accounting.		
LO 1.6 Understand the importance of ethics in data analysis and decision making.		

Chapter Concepts and Career Skills

Learning About . . .	Helps with These Career Skills
Value creation at companies	• Understanding the value-enhancing activities that companies use to create value
The AMPS analytics model	• Using data to address strategic management questions and communicate the results of data analysis
Four general types of strategic management questions	• Categorizing management questions to help determine the type of analysis required
The difference between management accounting and financial accounting	• Understanding the differences between careers in management accounting and careers in financial accounting

Cost Problems with Tesla's Solar Roof

Management accountants use data to address management's questions. Perhaps Elon Musk, the CEO of **Tesla**, should have asked different or better questions to determine the right cost for its solar roofs, which the company sells to homeowners and bills as a "fully integrated solar and energy storage system." Tesla recently admitted that it had underestimated the complexity of roof installations and has made "significant mistakes" in calculating installation costs. As a result, it increased the price of a solar roof by an overwhelming 70 percent.[1] Could management accountants have performed more or better analysis to help Tesla avoid this mistake?

[1]Isobel Asher Hamilton, "Elon Musk Said Tesla Made 'Significant Mistakes' Calculating How Much Its Solar Roof Should Cost, Leading to Massive Price Hikes," *Business Insider,* April 27, 2021, www.businessinsider.com/elon-musk-tesla-solar-roof-price-mistakes-calculating-cost-2021-4 (accessed April 30, 2021).

The sustainable nature of solar energy and other renewable energy solutions is extremely important to a huge demographic swath of potential customers. This is just one reason why it is so important to get the costs and prices right from the beginning.

Hilda Weges/Alamy Stock Photo

COMPANIES CREATE VALUE

LO 1.1

Describe why companies exist and how they create value.

The purpose of a for-profit company is to create value by designing, manufacturing, selling, or trading products and services to customers at a price greater than the cost of creating and distributing those products and services. To create value, management makes many strategic decisions to achieve its goal of maximizing long-term profits, including the following:

- Which product or service to sell.
- Which customers to target.
- Which employees to hire.
- How to best produce its products or services.
- Which price to charge its customers.

CAREER SKILLS

Learning about value creation at companies supports this career skill:

- Understanding the value-enhancing activities that companies use to create value

Management accountants play a very important role in strategic decision making by delivering data-driven insights to executives and other decision makers. **EY,** the public accounting and consulting firm once known as Ernst & Young, argues that its professionals and its new hires need an *analytics mindset.* EY believes that accountants should support management decision making by:

- **Asking the right questions:** identifying and articulating relevant strategic management questions.
- **Finding, extracting, transforming, and loading relevant data:** locating appropriate data to address these strategic management questions and preparing those data for analysis.
- **Applying appropriate data analytics techniques:** analyzing the data in a way that will most directly address the questions asked.
- **Interpreting and sharing the results of the data analysis with stakeholders:** making sense of the results and communicating those data-driven insights to decision makers.[2]

Management is then able to make more informed decisions that create more value for the company. A company creates value by taking inputs (such as raw materials, talented workers, buildings, and equipment) and producing a more valuable output (such as iPhones, microprocessor chips, and completed architectural plans). Consider a college or university

[2]Ernst & Young Foundation, EY Academic Resource Center (EYARC), *The Analytics Mindset* (2017), https://www.ey.com/en_us/about-us/ey-foundation-and-university-relations/academic-resource-center (accessed September 6, 2023).

as an example. Universities admit students (as inputs) and use their resources (curriculum, faculty, buildings, computers) to create (or process) a job-ready, educated graduate (the output). Arguably, the school creates value, as shown in Exhibit 1.1. If it is not creating value in one form or the other, it probably will not survive.

Exhibit 1.1
Universities Create Value by Admitting, Preparing (Processing), and Placing Job-Ready Graduates

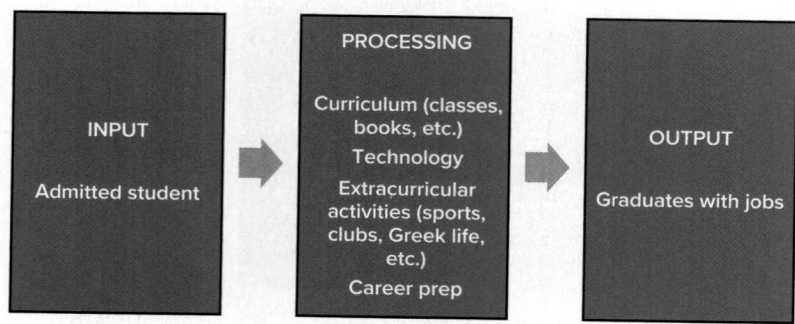

Apple creates value by designing a must-have iPhone. **Amazon** creates value by delivering products to your doorstep within a day or two and enhances the customer experience by providing information about these products through customer reviews and by facilitating convenient payment processes and delivery possibilities. **Netflix** creates value by providing online streaming of films and television series to its subscribers for a price greater than the cost of producing them. **Bank of America** creates value by offering auto, personal, business, and mortgage loans to its customers.

Business Value and Business Processes

business value
All the items, events, and interactions that determine a company's financial health and well-being.

business process
A coordinated, standardized set of activities conducted by both people and equipment to accomplish a specific task, such as invoicing a customer.

Let's continue our discussion by examining **business value**, which refers to all the items, events, and interactions that determine a company's financial health and well-being. This value may come from the company's suppliers, customers, employees, or information systems. Although we can measure business value in a variety of ways, a common business value metric is the increase in long-term profitability (or profit margin), which incorporates the revenues associated with the activity and the cost of producing that activity.

To consider how value is created, we begin by looking at the specific activities, or business processes, a company performs. A **business process** is a coordinated, standardized set of activities conducted by both people and equipment to accomplish a specific task. Examples of business processes include the following:

- **Amazon** accepts orders for products.
- **KPMG** delivers a service, such as offering tax advice to a client.
- **TruGreen** bills a customer for herbicide sprayed on the customer's lawn.
- **Tesla** produces an electric vehicle to sell in China.
- **Fulton Homes** writes a contract with a customer to build a house using a 3-D printer.
- **eBay** advertises a product to potential consumers.
- **Toyota** procures parts.
- **DoorDash** pays independent contractors for deliveries (work performed).
- **Procter & Gamble** addresses customer complaints, sometimes with refunds.
- The **Boston Consulting Group** summarizes financial options for management decision making.

Companies perform thousands, perhaps millions, of business processes each day. The managers' challenge is to identify the processes that create the most value at the lowest cost. To do so, they often use a value chain to identify which processes create value.

The Value Chain

To evaluate the effectiveness of each of its business processes in creating value, a company can use Michael Porter's value chain analysis.[3] A **value chain** is a chain of critical business processes that create business value at a company. A product passes through all activities of the chain in order, and the product is expected to gain some value with each activity.

It is important not to confuse the concept of the value chain with the actual cost of performing the activities. The *cost* of an activity represents the resources expended by the company to conduct that activity. The *value* of an activity is reflected in the price that consumers are willing to pay for the result of the company's activities. Consider a specific example: cutting a rough diamond. Although cutting a diamond may have a very low cost to a company, this cutting activity adds much of the value to the end product because a cut diamond is much more valuable than a rough diamond. And a well-cut diamond adds more value than a diamond cut poorly.

value chain
A chain of critical business processes that create business value at a company.

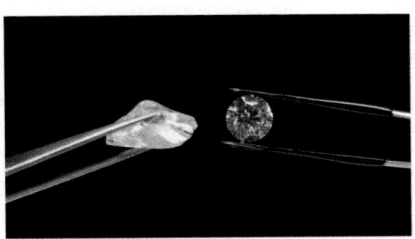

REUTERS/Alamy Stock Photo

primary activities
Value chain activities that directly create value for the company and its customers: inbound logistics, operations, outbound logistics, marketing and sales activities, and service activities.

The value chain illustrated in Exhibit 1.2 shows both primary activities and support activities. **Primary activities** are the value chain activities that directly create value for the company and its customers. They include the following five activities:

Primary Activities: Inbound Logistics → Operations → Outbound Logistics → Marketing and Sales → Service

Support Activities: Procurement | Information Technology | Human Resource Management | Infrastructure

Exhibit 1.2
The Value Chain

1. *Inbound logistics* are the activities associated with receiving and storing raw materials and other partially completed materials, and distributing those materials to manufacturing divisions when and where they are needed.
   - At **Tesla**, inbound logistics might include receiving car batteries and tires ready for installation in a new car.

Mariusz Burcz/Alamy Stock Photo

[3]Michael E. Porter, *Competitive Advantage: Creating and Sustaining Superior Performance* (New York: Free Press, 1998).

2. *Operations* are the activities that transform inputs into finished goods and services.
   - At Tesla, operations include the activities on the assembly line to assemble the various car parts into a finished automobile.
3. *Outbound logistics* are the activities that warehouse and distribute the finished goods to customers.
   - At Tesla, outbound logistics include delivery of cars to its dealerships and sometimes directly to customers.
4. *Marketing and sales activities* identify the needs and wants of customers to attract them to and then buy the company's products.
   - At Tesla, marketing and sales activities include advertising campaigns, the company's salespersons, the company website, and Elon Musk's social media posts.
5. *Service activities* provide support to customers after the products and services are sold to them. Service activities include warranty repairs, parts, instruction manuals, and phone or Internet support.
   - At Tesla, service activities include making warranty repairs, updating car software, and providing battery-charging stations for its cars throughout the world.

As Exhibit 1.2 shows, these five primary activities are sustained by four **secondary activities** (also known as **supporting activities**):

secondary activities (supporting activities)
Value chain activities that support the five primary value chain activities. The four secondary activities are procurement, information technology, human resource management, and infrastructure.

1. *Procurement* activities involve purchasing inputs such as raw materials, supplies, and equipment.
   - At Tesla, procurement includes purchasing and procuring tires, computer consoles, door locks, and other car components.
2. *Information technology* (IT) activities include all of the technologies to support value-creating activities. These technologies include research and development (R&D) to develop new products or to determine how to produce products at a lower cost.
   - At Tesla, IT activities include designing new cars and writing and testing the self-driving software.
3. *Human resource (HR) management* activities include recruiting, hiring, training, and compensating employees.
   - At Tesla, HR activities include hiring and retaining the right number of trained employees to design, assemble, and test the vehicles.
4. **Infrastructure** activities are all of the activities needed to support the primary activities of the company, including the CEO and the finance, accounting (including management accounting), and legal departments.
   - At Tesla, infrastructure includes the management accountants who assess the costs of production.

infrastructure
The activities needed to support a company's activities, including the CEO and the finance, accounting, and legal departments.

Examining the value chain allows managers to identify the activities that add value and those that do not. This analysis helps them maximize the value created by the primary activities while minimizing the cost of performing them. If specific activities don't create value, then management may look to outsource them or otherwise minimize their cost. Management accountants support the CEO and other decision makers as they work to make each primary activity more effective and efficient. They do so by providing data-driven insights that likely help to create additional value for the organization.

cost advantage (cost leadership)
A corporate strategy in which a company offers its goods and services to customers at prices lower than its competitors', thereby stimulating demand and generating higher profits through higher sales volume.

Different companies pursue different strategies to create value. **Cost advantage** (also called **cost leadership**) is a corporate strategy in which the company offers its goods and services to customers at prices lower than its competitors', thereby stimulating demand and generating higher profits through higher sales volume. An alternative cost-leadership strategy requires the firm to have a lower cost structure than its competitors, thereby allowing it to sell its goods at or slightly below an industry-average price. A successful cost leadership strategy creates value by allowing the firm to offer its goods and services at slightly lower prices (thereby stimulating higher sales volume) and leveraging its lower cost structure (thereby realizing a higher profit margin per unit sold).

Perhaps the best-known firm that adheres to the cost-leadership strategy is **Walmart**. "Everyday low prices (EDLP)" is the cornerstone mantra of Walmart's corporate strategy. It signals to customers that everything for sale at Walmart is priced at the lowest price that Walmart can offer. To generate sustainable profits with its cost-leadership strategy, Walmart relies on selling higher volumes than its competitors. Also, Walmart has structured its operations to function with low levels of inventory, thereby minimizing the costs associated with holding higher inventory levels.

Product differentiation is a corporate strategy in which the company seeks to offer products or services that are distinct from those offered by competitors and valued by customers. Firms with a product-differentiation focus tend to have higher cost structures, attributable to higher expenditures in R&D, product development, warranties, or other customer-centric costs. Product-differentiation strategies seek to create products that are distinct in some way that customers highly value, allowing the products to be sold at prices higher than competitors' products. **Apple** is an excellent example of a company that follows a product-differentiation strategy. Apple never competes on price. Rather, its products tend to sell at higher price points to customers who value the distinctive features found only in Apple products.

product differentiation
Corporate strategy in which the company seeks to offer products or services that are distinct from those offered by competitors and valued by customers.

Which Management Questions Do Management Accountants Address?

Because businesses exist to create and sustain business value, management has the responsibility to assess both the revenues and costs of current performance and possible opportunities. Throughout this book, we discuss the management questions that require input from management accountants. These questions include, but are not limited to, the following:

- Which specific data sources will help answer management's questions? (Chapter 2)
- What is the company's cost profile? At what point does the company break even on new and existing products and services? (Chapter 3)
- How are costs allocated to various jobs, and how are those costs evaluated? (Chapter 4)
- What are the appropriate cost drivers for allocating indirect costs, such as overhead? (Chapter 5)
- How are support activities and supporting department costs allocated? (Chapter 6)
- How are costs allocated to products in a process-based manufacturing system? (Chapter 7)
- How is performance measured in centralized (vs. decentralized) organizations? (Chapter 8)
- How does a company use budgets to plan for future sales and production in an upcoming period? (Chapter 9)
- When results differ from budgets (and they always do), why do they differ and what can the company do to capitalize on strengths or address deficiencies? (Chapters 10 and 11)
- How will the organization most effectively measure and monitor performance across multiple strategic goals? (Chapter 12)
- What information should the company consider when making strategic decisions? (Chapter 13)
- How should the company evaluate potential capital investments and allocate resources to competing projects? (Chapter 14)

✓ PROGRESS CHECK

1. How do managers create business value for their company? How do management accountants assist in those efforts?
2. If a business process isn't creating value, what should the company do?

LO 1.2

Describe the role of management accountants in facilitating data-driven decision making.

THE EVOLVING ROLE OF MANAGEMENT ACCOUNTANTS IN FACILITATING DATA-DRIVEN DECISION MAKING

To address management's questions, management accountants use data from many sources. Increasingly, management accountants use their accounting- and business-specific knowledge to serve as data analysts, analyzing relevant financial and nonfinancial data. These activities are possible because management accountants understand what the accounting and related data provide, how transactions are measured, and how the company evaluates performance.

The Explosion of Available Data to Address Management Questions

As Exhibit 1.3 shows, in recent years the availability of data has rapidly increased. So has the development of high-powered and easy-to-use data analysis tools. Because of these trends, the job of a management accountant is evolving from one primarily focused on data collection and summarization to one that includes meaningful data analysis and interpretation. As mentioned earlier in this chapter, **EY** expects its accountants to develop an analytics mindset, which means they need to ask the right questions, find and extract pertinent data that might help them address those questions, run the appropriate analyses, and then communicate the results to decision makers. Indeed, "[a]nalytics is at the heart of every business decision."[4] This text works to develop your analytics mindset and prepare you for the new and evolving role of the management accountant and accounting data analyst.

The Role of Management Accountants

management accountant

An accountant who analyzes accounting-related data to help an organization make effective business decisions.

A **management accountant** is an accountant who analyzes accounting-related data to help an organization make effective business decisions. Management accountants add value to this process because they have a deep knowledge of the costs associated with the production and distribution of the company's products or services, as well as the factors that can increase or decrease those costs and impact the company's profitability. For this reason, management accountants are particularly well suited to identifying the specific business questions that need to be addressed and interpreting and communicating the output from data analysis.

data scientist

A person employed to acquire, maintain, curate, access, manipulate, and statistically test data to address business questions.

A **data scientist** is a person employed to acquire, maintain, curate, access, manipulate, and statistically test data to address business questions. Data scientists maintain the data, create specific datasets to address specific questions, and know where the datasets are stored and how to access them. While they are usually adept in programming and data manipulation, they usually do not know or understand the business context or the language of business.

Because decision makers and data scientists do not necessarily speak with the same vocabulary, it may be difficult for decision makers to communicate with data scientists. For example, what specific knowledge is needed to support a decision on how to minimize the costs at a factory in Malaysia? As Exhibit 1.4 illustrates, the management accountant serves as an expert interpreter between the decision maker and the data scientist. Management accountants not only understand the decisions that management is making

---

[4]Ernst & Young Foundation, E&Y Academic Resource Center (EYARC), *The Analytics Mindset* (2017), http://aaahq.org/Education/Webinars/6-7-17-EY-Academic-Resource-Center-An-Overview-of-Analytics-Mindset-Competencies-and-Case-Offerings (accessed January 22, 2021).

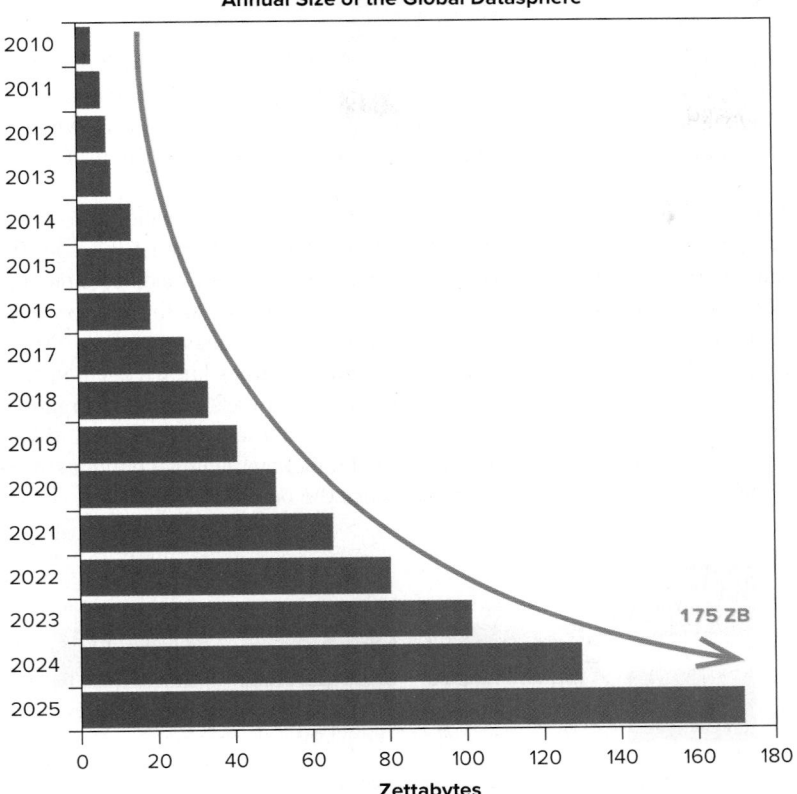

Annual Size of the Global Datasphere

175 ZB

Zettabytes

Exhibit 1.3
Data Growth Since 2010

Source: David Reinsel, John Gantz, and John Rydning, "The Digitization of the World: From Edge to Core" (IDC White Paper #US44413318, November 2018), p. 6, www.seagate.com/files/www-content/our-story/trends/files/idc-seagate-dataage-whitepaper.pdf (accessed January 22, 2021).

Management

Management accountant

Data scientist

Decision maker

Expert interpreter

Developer

Exhibit 1.4
Management Accountant as Interpreter Between the Decision Maker and Data Scientist

and what is needed to evaluate those decisions, they are also intimately familiar with the characteristics of the data and have a working knowledge of data quality, statistical tools, and programming.

Information Value Chain: Going from Data to Knowledge

"Data are widely available; what is scarce is the ability to extract wisdom from them."
—**HAL VARIAN**, UC Berkeley and Chief Economist, **Google**

data
Raw facts that describe an event and have little meaning on their own.

information
Data organized in a way that is useful to the user in a given context.

context
The setting surrounding the data; the event, statement, or situation in which the data can be fully understood and evaluated.

information value chain
The events and processes from the collection of data and information to an ultimate business decision.

knowledge
Understanding of or familiarity with information gained through learning.

decision
A conclusion reached after consideration of knowledge gained.

Although an enormous amount of data is available to management accountants, some data are not useful to decision makers. Indeed, **data** are raw facts that describe an event and have little meaning on their own. However, data may serve as an input to **information**, which is data organized in a way that is useful to the user in a given context. **Context** is the setting surrounding the data—the event, statement, or situation in which the data can be fully understood and evaluated. In other words, information is useful, organized data with context.

The events and processes from the collection of data and information to the ultimate business decision comprise the **information value chain** (Exhibit 1.5). To get from data to information, data are often processed (aggregated, transformed, calculated, sorted, manipulated, and/or analyzed) in some way and then combined with the appropriate business context (such as time of year, location, or specific business need) to turn the data into information. Some of the information ultimately becomes knowledge helpful in making decisions. **Knowledge** is an understanding of or familiarity with information gained through learning, and **decisions** are conclusions reached after consideration of knowledge gained. By applying the insights derived from data, management accountants work on all aspects of the information value chain and enhance the organization's value.

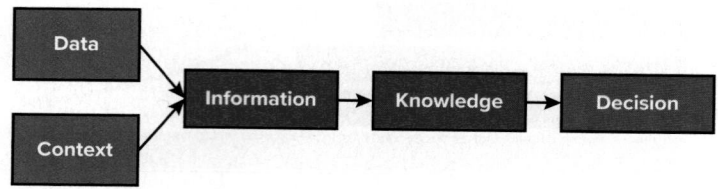

| Data Scientist | ----- Management Accountant ----- | Management |

Exhibit 1.5
The Information Value Chain

Let's apply all these terms to an example. The price of each vehicle sold in each transaction at the local **Honda** dealership is data. At the end of the day or year, the dealership will have a lot of data, but it is impossible to make effective decisions based simply on those individual data points. However, if the data are summarized—perhaps counted or summed—and organized by salesperson, by product, and by department, the dealership can determine (1) which salesperson is the most successful, (2) which car model is selling best, (3) the average discount on the manufacturer's suggested retail price, and so on. This is useful information that helps the dealership make decisions about inventory, salespeople, discounts, and many other factors.

As Exhibit 1.5 shows, converting the data and its related context into information and ultimately knowledge is the responsibility of the management accountant. Management accountants provide this knowledge to managers, who then make the final decision.

✓ PROGRESS CHECK

3. Which individual is more likely to know which data are most appropriate for addressing business questions: the data scientist or the management accountant?

4. What specific skills are unique to the data scientist?

THE AMPS DATA ANALYTICS MODEL: THE FOUNDATION FOR ADDRESSING MANAGEMENT QUESTIONS

Information is a strategic asset for any company. The way a company accesses, analyzes, and uses information to inform critical business decisions can give it a unique competitive advantage.

The AMPS Data Analytics Model

To create information and knowledge, management accountants must develop the analytics mindset articulated by **EY** as the ability to:

- Ask the right questions;
- Find, extract, transform, and load relevant data;
- Apply appropriate data analytics techniques; and
- Interpret and share the results with stakeholders.[5]

Closely related to the analytics mindset is the use of a data analytics framework. **Data analytics** is the process of evaluating data with the purpose of drawing conclusions to address all types of questions, including accounting questions. We call this framework the **AMPS data analytics model** (or **AMPS model**), which is an acronym for:

1. **A**sk the question
2. **M**aster the data
3. **P**erform the analysis
4. **S**hare the story

Note how each component of the analytics mindset corresponds to each component of the AMPS framework. In each chapter of this textbook, we use the AMPS model to identify the question and appropriate data sources, to explain the appropriate type of data analysis to use, and to communicate the results by sharing the story, often in the form of a data visualization.

Exhibit 1.6 summarizes the AMPS model.

LO 1.3

Explain the use of the AMPS data analytics model as a foundation for addressing management accounting questions.

CAREER SKILLS

Learning about the AMPS analytics model supports this career skill:

- Using data to address strategic management questions and communicate the results of data analysis

data analytics
The process of evaluating data with the purpose of drawing conclusions to address all types of questions, including accounting questions.

AMPS data analytics model (AMPS model)
A framework for addressing management accounting questions and performing data analytics. It includes four steps: (1) **A**sk the question, (2) **M**aster the data, (3) **P**erform the analysis, and (4) **S**hare the story.

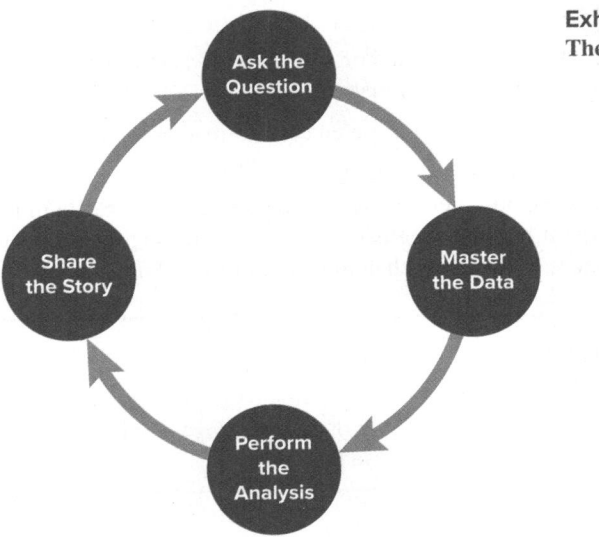

Exhibit 1.6
The AMPS Model

[5]Ernst & Young Foundation, E&Y Academic Resource Center (EYARC), *The Analytics Mindset* (2017), http://aaahq.org/Education/Webinars/6-7-17-EY-Academic-Resource-Center-An-Overview-of-Analytics-Mindset-Competencies-and-Case-Offerings (accessed March 29, 2023).

Illustration of the AMPS Model

To illustrate how the AMPS model might be applied, let's assume that **Cisco** (a producer of popular Wi-Fi network routers used in homes and businesses) is trying to decide whether to manufacture its most basic and cheapest router product or to outsource the manufacturing process to a third party.

Ask the Question

Will Cisco be more profitable if it outsources its low-end router product or if it manufactures that router itself?

Master the Data

Data sources that Cisco management can use to inform its decision making include:

- Relevant cost data for producing the router internally from the cost accounting system.
- Projections of the per-unit cost of outsourcing the manufacture of routers to another company.

Perform the Analysis

Perform *what-if analysis* to compare the costs under each of the two potential scenarios.

- Will Cisco be more profitable if it outsources some or all of its low-end routers to other producers?

Perform *sensitivity analysis* to assess if the decision to outsource depends on the number of routers to be manufactured.

- What cost is the point of indifference between the two alternatives? That is, at what point will management see no benefit in one alternative over the other?

Note: We discuss what-if analysis and sensitivity analysis in much greater detail throughout this book.

Share the Story

Use visualizations, written reports, and/or in-person presentations to communicate findings to management or other decision makers.

- The management accountant might use an easy-to-read graph to summarize the financial implications of outsourcing versus not outsourcing.

In every lab in this textbook, we walk through each step of the AMPS model. We begin by asking the relevant questions and conclude with communicating the results to management. Let's now look more closely at each component of the AMPS model.

> ### 🔍 LAB CONNECTION
>
> **LAB 1.1 Excel** uses the AMPS model to determine the profitability of a lawn-mowing business under a few different scenarios. It also reviews basic Excel skills. (Appendix A provides a basic tutorial on how to use Excel.)

The AMPS Model, Step 1: <u>A</u>sk the Question

The first step in the AMPS model is *Ask the question*. Running a business is all about asking and answering questions. Here are some questions that decision makers might ask:

1. Is it more profitable to produce an item in the United States or in the Philippines?
2. How much overhead should we apply to each one of the **Android** apps that we've built and must maintain?
3. As our fixed and variable costs change with the service we provide, how is our break-even point affected?
4. If employee health insurance rates continue to increase, can we maintain the company's profitability?
5. Which line of tools is more profitable to offer at stores in Georgia?

Generally, the more specific the question, the better. For example, it is hard to answer a question like "How can **Aldi** grow its net income?" but easier to address a question like "How do we sell more of our highest-margin snack-food offerings at Aldi store #359 in Fayetteville, Arkansas?" Narrowing the scope of the question sets up the management accountant to find the necessary data, perform the analysis, and address the question at hand.

In data analysis, the axiom "Your data won't speak unless you ask them the right data analysis questions"[6] refers to the expertise that management accountants offer by asking questions that the data can answer. Given management accountants' knowledge of business processes and their understanding of which data are available to address the question, they are in a perfect position to perform data analysis.

Types of Management Questions

In management accounting in general, there are four common types of questions, each with its own appropriate data analytics techniques:

1. What happened? What is happening? (descriptive analytics)
2. Why did it happen? Why is it different from what we expected? (diagnostic analytics)
3. Will it happen in the future? What is the probability something will happen? Is it forecastable? (predictive analytics)
4. What should we do based on what we expect will happen? How do we optimize our performance based on potential constraints? (prescriptive analytics)

Specific management accounting questions that line up with the four analytics types include the following:

1. **Descriptive analytics: "What happened?" and "What is happening?"**
   a. Did we make a profit last year?
   b. Did return on assets improve or decline over the past year?
   c. Did the airline's on-time departures improve this past month?
   d. Which product is the most profitable for the company?
2. **Diagnostic analytics: "Why did it happen?" and "Why is it different from what we expected?"**
   a. Why did labor expenses increase over the past year as compared to prior years?
   b. Why did sales, general, and administrative expenses increase relative to the industry?
   c. Why did our cost structure (fixed and variable costs) change over the past year?
3. **Predictive analytics: "Will it happen in the future? What is the probability something will happen? Is it forecastable?"**
   a. What is the chance the company will go bankrupt?
   b. Can we predict future sales for this company?
   c. What is the forecast for future cash flows? Will they meet our expected cash needs?
   d. What is our expected profitability over the next five years?

CAREER SKILLS

Learning about the four general types of strategic management questions helps with this career skill:

• Categorizing management questions to help determine the type of analysis required

---

[6]B. Calzon, "Your Data Won't Speak Unless You Ask It the Right Data Analysis Questions," *Datapine,* February 2022, www.datapine.com/blog/data-analysis-questions/ (accessed March 29, 2023).

4. **Prescriptive analytics: "What should we do based on what we expect will happen?" and "How do we optimize our performance based on potential constraints?"**
   a. Should we offer a discount next month to reduce inventory?
   b. Should the company rent or lease its headquarters building?
   c. Should the company make its products or outsource to other manufacturers?
   d. How can revenues be maximized (or costs be minimized) if there is a trade war with another country?

We revisit each of these question types throughout the text to match the available data to the appropriate data analytics methods.

Management Questions about Environmental, Social, and Governance Goals

ENVIRONMENTAL, SOCIAL, GOVERNANCE

Increasingly, management questions relate to environmental, social, and governance (ESG) goals. Attention to these questions reflects a growing commitment to ESG issues by companies, organizations, governments, and individuals across the globe. By focusing on ESG goals, managers recognize how their company contributes to changes in environmental, economic, and social conditions, as well as how those changes might affect the company's ability to continue operations. For example, when applying the AMPS model, management may ask the following ESG-related questions:

1. How can we cost-effectively help to reduce environmental degradation, inequality, and poverty in the communities in which we operate?
2. How can we reduce carbon emissions and ultimately make our operations carbon neutral without charging our customers more?

Companies measure and monitor their progress against their ESG goals and often report progress to stakeholders in annual ESG reports. Exhibit 1.7 summarizes the focus of the individual ESG goals and provides examples of each.

Exhibit 1.7
ESG Goals and Examples

Goal	Focus	Example Goals
Environmental	The organization's environmental impact(s) and risk-management practices.	• Reduce the company's carbon footprint. • Add no pollutants to the water supply. • Source only sustainable raw materials.
Social	An organization's relationships with its stakeholders. Social goals often focus on humane practices for employees as well as the organization's impact on the communities in which it operates. Commitment to social issues is especially important and complicated for organizations that conduct business with nations that do not have the same environmental or social standards.	• Pay fair wages to all employees. • Do not conduct business with third parties that violate human rights (for example, by using child labor or making people work in sweatshops).
Governance	How a company is led and managed.	• Ensure that management and the board of directors reflect the demographics of the company and its stakeholders.

The AMPS Model, Step 2: <u>M</u>aster the Data

After asking the question, management accountants start to consider appropriate data that could be used to answer it. This second step is the "M" in the AMPS model, which stands for *Master the Data*. We use the word "master" to convey the idea that not all datasets are equal. Some are of high quality; others are useless. Some are well organized, while others are a mess. In any two sets of data reporting on similar phenomena, different words may be used to mean the same thing, and abbreviations may vary wildly. "Mastering" the data means truly understanding what data you are working with and how to get the best results from them.

In particular, management accountants need to understand the trade-offs between *relevant data* (data that directly address the question at hand) and *reliable data* (data with fewer errors or bias). For example, you might be able to get data on last month's operations, but they may not have been audited, or they may have errors in them. The key here is ensuring that the data exhibit a high level of **data integrity**, meaning that they are accurate, valid, and consistent over time. Management accountants also need to know whether the data are considered to be facts (for example, marketing expenses for the past month) or opinions (for example, customer reviews on **Amazon** and other websites).

data integrity
A term that refers to the overall accuracy, validity, and consistency of data used and stored over time.

Management accountants must also work to understand the trade-offs between data that are well organized and structured (such as a financial statement or a spreadsheet) and data that are not well organized (such as Facebook posts and Instagram pictures). They must also understand if the data are internal or external to the company. If it will *cost* money to acquire and process data, does the cost justify the potential *value* provided by using the data?

Additional traits of the data also need to be considered. For example, we need to know the format and type of each dataset. Are the data *alphanumeric* (text)? Are the data *categorical* (blood type A, B, AB, or O) or *numerical* (1,253)? How will the data be accessed and from what source? Are there errors in the dataset, or are any data missing? Chapter 2 addresses potential sources of management accounting data as well as the specific aspects of data.

ⓠ LAB CONNECTION

LAB 1.2 Excel starts to build your data and analysis skills by asking you to work with data in Excel, with an emphasis on the differences between ranges and tables.

The AMPS Model, Step 3: <u>P</u>erform the Analysis

The third step in the AMPS model is *Perform the analysis*. We can use many different analytics techniques to analyze the data. Different types of questions require different analytics types. Part of the accountant's task is to match the question to the correct data and right type of analytics in a way that most effectively addresses the question.

Exhibit 1.8 defines the four analytics types and provides examples of analytics techniques used in each (by software tool). This exhibit provides an overview of the techniques you'll be learning in this book and this course. Don't worry about trying to understand or memorize all of the techniques now; we'll return to these concepts many times throughout the book as we determine the best tools to use to address management's questions.

Data Analytics Type and Definition	Questions Accountants Try to Address	Example Analytics Techniques in Software Tools
Descriptive analytics Characterizes, summarizes, and organizes features and properties of the data to facilitate understanding.	• What happened? • What is happening?	**Excel:** Counts, totals, sums, averages, pivot tables, percentage change **Tableau/Power BI:** Histograms, graphs, charts, basic visualizations, heat maps
Diagnostic analytics Investigates the underlying cause or why actual performance differed from expectations.	• Why did it happen? • Why is it different from what we expected?	**Excel:** Conditional formatting, pivot tables, correlations, variances, computations **Tableau/Power BI:** Pivot tables (cross-tabulations), scatterplots
Predictive analytics Identifies patterns in historical data and assesses likelihood or probability of future outcomes.	• Will it happen in the future? • What is the probability something will happen? • Is it forecastable?	**Excel:** Time series (forecast sheet), regression analysis **Tableau/Power BI:** Time series, line graphs, single-variable regressions, trend lines
Prescriptive analytics Identifies the best possible options given constraints or changing conditions.	• What should we do based on what we expect will happen? • How do we optimize our performance based on potential constraints?	**Excel:** What-if analysis, goal-seek analysis, cash flow analysis, sensitivity analysis (data table), optimization **Tableau/Power BI:** histograms, graphs, charts, basic visualizations, heat maps

Exhibit 1.8
Data Analytics Types, Definitions, and Techniques for Addressing Management Accounting Questions

descriptive analytics
Analytics that characterizes, summarizes, and organizes features and properties of the data to facilitate understanding.

diagnostic analytics
Analytics performed to investigate an underlying cause or why actual performance differed from expectations.

predictive analytics
Analytics that identifies patterns in historical data to forecast future activity.

prescriptive analytics
Analytics that identifies best possible options given constraints or changing conditions.

FROM THE FIELD

The Importance of Working Expertly in Microsoft Excel

Several analytics software tools are available and useful for accountants, including Excel, Alteryx, Tableau, Power BI, Python, and R. Of these, the most used and useful tool for the vast majority of accountants is Microsoft Excel. Feeling comfortable in Excel will make you ready for your first internship and first accounting job, and will serve as a jumping-off point to more sophisticated tools. Chapter 2 provides additional discussion of the various data analysis tools available.

Thinking Critically

If you've already started or completed an internship, was a working knowledge of Excel expected? Do you feel that if you know how to perform an analysis in Excel, it will be easier to learn how to perform the same analysis in a different software tool?

The AMPS Model, Step 4: Share the Story

Once we've performed the analysis, we move to the fourth and final step in the AMPS model: *Share the story*. It is important to share the story—that is, answer the question—by interpreting what the results might suggest to decision makers and communicating the results in an easily accessible way. One way to communicate results is through the use of **visualizations**, such as graphs, charts, infographics, or other images, that might help management more easily and fully grasp the content being communicated. Another option is a **dashboard**, which is a graphical summary of various measures tracked by a company.

Increasingly, data visualizations are preferred to written content to communicate results. Indeed, studies have shown that 91 percent of people prefer visual content over written content.[7] For example, Facebook photos have an interaction rate of 87 percent, compared to 4 percent or less for other types of posts, such as links or text.[8] In addition, the brain processes images 60,000 times faster than it processes text, and 90 percent of information transmitted to the brain is visual.[9] Increasingly, data visualizations, rather than written reports, are used to communicate the results of the analysis to stakeholders.

Should results present a moment in time, or should they be updated occasionally or regularly? If you are providing a one-time analysis to a decision-making committee, you might choose to present **static data**, which remain unchanged. If the analysis needs to be done daily, weekly, or continuously, you might choose to present **dynamic data** that are updated on a regular basis.

Different visualizations are used for different purposes. Exhibit 1.9 summarizes some common purposes for data visualization as well as five corresponding business questions and common visualization types: bar charts, pie charts, histograms, line graphs, and scatterplots. Exhibit 1.10 shows samples of these five basic visualization types. Because management accountants must be adept at communicating results effectively, we will work with data visualizations throughout this book.

In Chapter 2, we introduce software tools that specialize in visualizations, specifically Tableau and Power BI. There, we explore the types of visualizations that are most helpful to management accountants and decision makers. Appendix F provides a fuller explanation of available visualizations to share the story.

DATA VISUALIZATION

visualization
The representation of information as a graph, chart, or other type of image.

dashboard
A graphical summary of various measures tracked by a company.

static data
Data that remain unchanged.

dynamic data
Data that change over time.

Purpose of Visualization		Common Visualization Type (See Exhibit 1.10)
Comparison of values	Which company sold more cars last year, **Toyota** or **Tesla**?	Bar chart (Panel A) or column chart
Composition of values	What proportion of sales comes from each of the five divisions at **J.B. Hunt**?	Pie chart (Panel B)
Distribution of values	How many days on average did it take **Wayfair** to fulfill a set of 20,000 orders?	Histogram (Panel C)
Trends of values over time	How has **Google**'s ad revenue changed over the last five years?	Line graph (Panel D)
Relationships between values	What is the relationship between advertising expense and sales revenue at **Costco**?	Scatterplot (Panel E)

Exhibit 1.9
Purposes of Data Visualization, Business Examples, and Visualization Types

The Human Element: Data Visualizations

The ethical use of visualizations is essential. Visualizations are powerful ways to communicate information, and unethical analysts can manipulate them to promote some preferred decision or outcome over another. Some techniques for presenting results in a biased way include changing the scale, using color inappropriately, and highlighting one finding over another.

[7]Zohar Dayan, "Visual Content: The Future of Storytelling," *Forbes,* April 2, 2018, www.forbes.com/sites/forbestechcouncil/2018/04/02/visual-content-the-future-of-storytelling/?sh=6517bfbe3a46 (accessed January 14, 2021).

[8]Hannah Whiteoak, "Six Reasons to Embrace Visual Commerce in 2018," *Pixlee,* www.pixlee.com/blog/six-reasons-to-embrace-visual-commerce-in-2018/ (accessed January 14, 2021).

[9]Harry Eisenberg, "Humans Process Visual Data Better," *Thermopylae Sciences + Technology,* September 15, 2014, www.t-sciences.com/news/humans-process-visual-data-better#:~:text=Visualization%20works%20from%20a%20human,to%20the%20brain%20is%20visual (accessed January 14, 2021).

Exhibit 1.10
Common Types of
Data Visualization

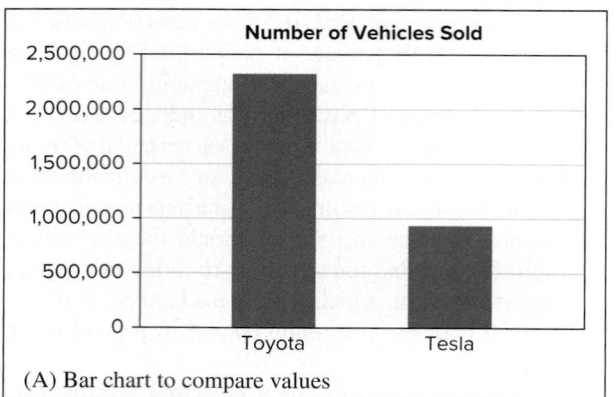

(A) Bar chart to compare values

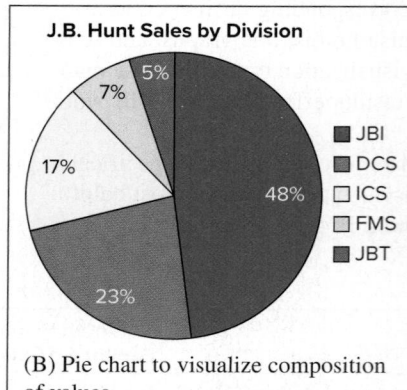

(B) Pie chart to visualize composition of values

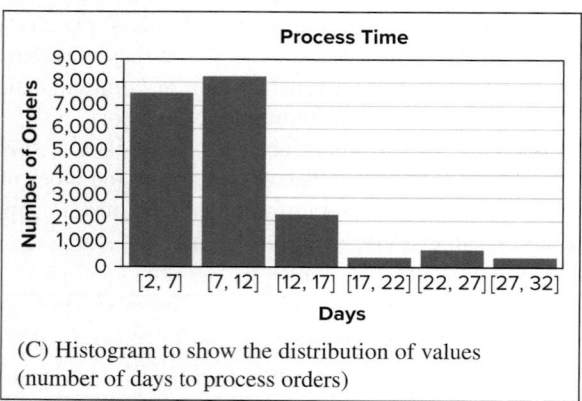

(C) Histogram to show the distribution of values (number of days to process orders)

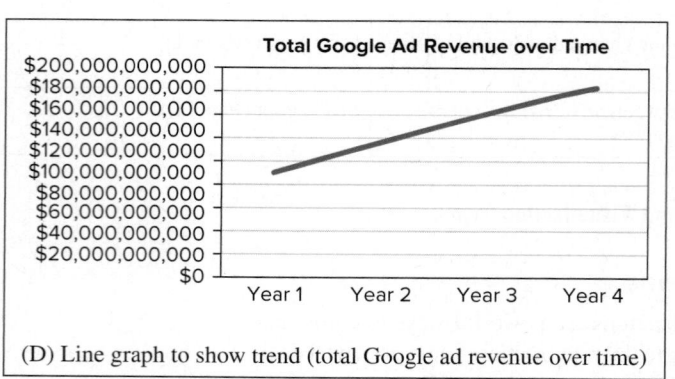

(D) Line graph to show trend (total Google ad revenue over time)

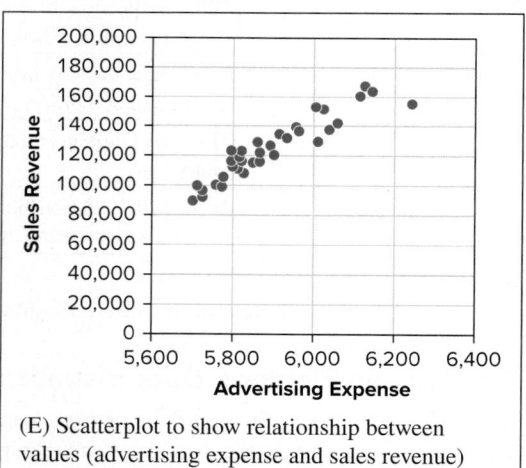

(E) Scatterplot to show relationship between values (advertising expense and sales revenue)

The fact that visualizations can be biased highlights the fact that management accountants are people who face personal incentives that can lead to biases and errors in data visualizations.

The Cyclical, Recursive Nature of the AMPS Model

After completing all the steps of the AMPS model, the management accountant and the decision maker often are more knowledgeable and better able to ask deeper, more refined questions, suggesting that the AMPS model is best viewed as cyclical, or recursive, in nature (Exhibit 1.11).

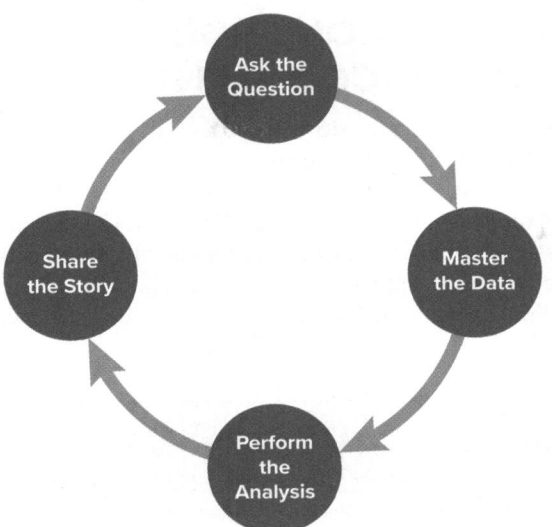

We can also view data analytics as successively peeling off the layers of an onion. By peeling off the first layer of the onion, you see the second layer, which allows for a deeper look into the organization, which may necessitate a deeper look into the third layer, and so on.

Often, the AMPS model must be performed multiple times. The management team may need to refine the question (*Ask the question*); consider different, perhaps complementary data sources that better match the refined question (*Master the data*); perform additional analytics (*Perform the analysis*); and retell the story in each iteration (*Share the story*) before the issue/problem/challenge can finally be addressed with some confidence.

Some consider the primary role of management accountants to be one of planning and control in decision making. **Planning** refers to the actions taken to understand and identify the problem or opportunity facing the company (*Ask the question*), obtain information to address the question (*Master the data*), and analyze the past in order to make decisions about the future (*Perform the analysis* and *Share the story*). **Control** refers to the actions taken to implement the decisions, evaluate performance based on those decisions, and learn from feedback to tweak (or change) subsequent actions. The recursive nature of the AMPS model is consistent with the control process.

planning
The actions taken to understand and identify the problem or opportunity facing the company, obtain information to address the question, and analyze the past in order to make decisions about the future.

control
The actions taken to implement decisions, evaluate performance based on those decisions, and learn from feedback to tweak (or change) subsequent actions.

(Q) LAB CONNECTION

LAB 1.3 Excel provides an example of using the AMPS model to perform descriptive analytics. Specifically, it uses pivot tables to summarize revenue and costs for various products. It will also help you review basic Excel skills. (Appendix A also provides a basic tutorial on how to use Excel.)

LABS 1.3 TABLEAU and **1.3 POWER BI** use two other software tools to perform descriptive analytics. (Appendices B and C provide basic tutorials on Tableau and Power BI, respectively.)

✓ PROGRESS CHECK

5. If a company wants to track its actual daily sales as compared to its sales targets, would it use a dynamic report or a static report? Explain.

6. Why is the AMPS model considered to be recursive or cyclical? Once you've completed the AMPS model, why start all over?

STRATEGIC QUESTIONS ADDRESSED BY MANAGEMENT ACCOUNTANTS

Although management accountants do not address all of a company's strategic questions, they do specialize in questions regarding performance (revenues and costs) and control measures (monitoring, measuring, and correcting actual results to make sure that the goals and plans of a business are achieved). Exhibit 1.12 provides a sample of typical strategic questions addressed by management accountants, along with potential data analytics and cost accounting techniques. Again, there's no need to memorize the specific techniques in the third column; all of these techniques are introduced and explained in later chapters.

Analytics Type and the Types of Questions Addressed	Example Management Accounting Questions by Analytics Type	Specific Cost Accounting and Data Analytics Techniques That Can Be Used to Answer the Question
Descriptive analytics summarizes activity or analyzes master data based on certain attributes to address these questions: • What happened? • What is happening?	How many board feet of decking product did we produce last week, and at what cost?	Summary statistics (sums, totals, averages, medians, bar charts, histograms)
	How much did Job #304 cost?	Computation of job order Costing and/or process costing
	What was the segment margin for the West Coast and Midwest regions last quarter?	Key performance indicators (KPIs) tracking performance
	Which products are the most profitable for the company?	Pivot tables analyzing cross-tabulations of performance
Diagnostic analytics detects correlations and patterns of interest and compares them to a benchmark to address these questions: • Why did it happen? • What are the reasons for past results? • Why are the results different from what we expected? • What are the root causes of past results?	Why is segment margin higher on the West Coast than in the Midwest?	Price, rate, usage, quantity, and overhead variance analysis
	What is driving the labor rate variance?	Conditional formatting
	Why did our rate of production defects go down this month compared to last month?	Evaluation of production statistics based on past performance
	What is the level of fixed and variable costs of our primary products? Are they different from the industry's or our competition's?	Regression analysis Estimating cost behavior
Predictive analytics identifies common attributes or patterns that may be used to forecast future activity to address these questions: • Will it happen in the future? • What is the probability something will happen? • Is it forecastable?	What is the level of expected sales in the next month, quarter, and year (to help plan our production)?	Sales forecasting: • Time series • Competitor and industry performance • Macroeconomic forecasts
	What is the correct level of overhead to allocate to various jobs?	Regression analysis
	What are the appropriate cost drivers for allocating overhead?	Regression analysis to forecast the appropriate level of indirect (overhead) costs to be applied to jobs or processes

Exhibit 1.12

Management Accounting Questions and Cost Accounting/Data Analytics Techniques by Analytics Type

Analytics Type and the Types of Questions Addressed	Example Management Accounting Questions by Analytics Type	Specific Cost Accounting and Data Analytics Techniques That Can Be Used to Answer the Question
Prescriptive analytics recommends action based on previously observed actions to address these questions: • What should we do based on what we expect will happen? • How do we optimize our performance based on potential constraints?	Should the company lease or own its headquarters office building? Should the company manufacture its products or outsource to other producers?	Differential analysis
	What is the expected return for an investment in a new piece of factory equipment?	Cash flow (capital budgeting) analysis
	What level of sales will allow the company to break even on a product?	Goal-seek analysis
	How can revenues be maximized (or costs be minimized) if there is a trade war with another country?	What-if scenario analysis
	If we can reduce our fixed (or variable) costs, what will our resulting profit be?	Sensitivity analysis (cost-volume-profit analysis)

Exhibit 1.12 *(Continued)*

Let's now use the following Data Analytics Mini-Lab to show how descriptive analytics can be used to identify a company's most profitable customers, an important analysis commonly conducted by management accountants and salespeople. Working this Mini-Lab will give you valuable experience in working with key Excel features, including pivot tables.

DATA ANALYTICS MINI-LAB
Assessing Customer Profitability in Excel

Data Analytics Type: Descriptive

Lab Note: The tools presented in this lab periodically change. Updated instructions, if applicable, can be found in the student and instructor support materials.

Keywords
Gross Margin, Excel, Pivot Table

Decision-Making Context
Merchandising companies sell products to customers. They make money by selling the products for more than what they paid. In this Mini-Lab, we compute the gross margin for each sale and then identify the company's most profitable customers. This analysis allows merchandising companies to focus their efforts on selling more products to those customers, which in turn helps them make more profits overall.

   Fancy Fruits is a fictitious mail-order business that sells exotic fruit from around the world to customers throughout the United States. The company keeps a sales journal that records each sale and its related sales and cost details.

gross margin
Net sales minus the cost of goods sold. Gross margin is the amount of revenue a company retains after deducting the direct costs of producing a good or service.

Ask the Question

Which customers are the most profitable?

Master the Data

This sales journal is for March 1–4, 2025. The sales journal provides a list of all individual sales (in addition to other data) for the four-day period.

Open the Excel file titled **Mini-Lab 1 Data.xlsx**. Exhibit A shows a snippet of the spreadsheet. The data dictionary follows.

Exhibit A

Microsoft Excel

	A	B	C	D	E	F	G	H	I
1	Invoice #	Customer #	Zip Code	Date of Sale	SKU	Description	Quantity (Pounds)	Sales	Cost
2	3021	2001	67510	3/1/2025	FRT-APL	Apple	15	25.52	16.36
3	3021	2001	67510	3/1/2025	FRT-GOR	Goji berry	5	5.92	3.71
4	3021	2001	67510	3/1/2025	FRT-OLV	Olive	35	53.92	33.26
5	3021	2001	67510	3/1/2025	FRT-REN	Red currant	5	7.12	4.26
6	3022	2091	67621	3/1/2025	FRT-FII	Fig	35	84.37	54.26
7	3023	2025	67511	3/1/2025	FRT-JUR	Juniper berry	50	65.02	43.01
8	3023	2025	67511	3/1/2025	FRT-PAY	Papaya	35	37.12	22.06
9	3023	2025	67511	3/1/2025	FRT-BAN	Banana	5	2.52	1.56
10	3023	2025	67511	3/1/2025	FRT-PEO	Persimmon	35	69.67	43.06
11	3024	2079	66401	3/1/2025	FRT-SAM	Satsuma	50	34.52	22.01
12	3024	2079	66401	3/1/2025	FRT-MII	Miracle fruit	15	30.77	18.01
13	3024	2079	66401	3/1/2025	FRT-CHI	Chico fruit	15	26.27	15.46
14	3024	2079	66401	3/1/2025	FRT-DUA	Durian	25	54.27	33.01
15	3024	2079	66401	3/1/2025	FRT-BAN	Banana	35	17.52	10.86
16	3025	2099	66710	3/1/2025	FRT-SAM	Satsuma	30	20.72	13.21
17	3025	2099	66710	3/1/2025	FRT-ELR	Elderberry	25	60.27	38.01
18	3025	2099	66710	3/1/2025	FRT-NAC	Nance	5	5.92	3.61
19	3025	2099	66710	3/1/2025	FRT-BAN	Banana	45	22.52	13.96

Data Dictionary

invoice
A list of goods sent or services provided.

Invoice #	Invoice number for each sale of fruit
Customer #	Customer number making purchase
Zip Code	Zip code of customer making purchase
Date of Sale	Date of invoice
SKU	Fancy Fruits' SKU (stock-keeping unit, a unique code for each type of fruit sold)
Description	Description of each fruit sold
Quantity (Pounds)	Total weight of each type of fruit sold
Sales	Total sales price of product sold
Cost	Total cost of product sold

Perform the Analysis

Analysis Task #1: Compute the Gross Margin of Each Sale

First, we need to compute the gross margin of each sale.

1. Start by going to cell J1. Insert the title "Gross Margin". Also insert a bottom border. (Appendix A provides a brief Excel tutorial if you need a refresher.)

   In cell J2, we'll compute the gross margin on each line item sold. To do so, we must subtract the cost in cell I2 from the sales in cell H2 by inserting the formula =H2-I2 and hitting Enter (Exhibit B).

Exhibit B

Microsoft Excel

	H	I	J	K
1	Sales	Cost	Gross Margin	
2	25.52	16.36	=H2-I2	
3	5.92	3.71		
4	53.92	33.26		
5	7.12	4.26		
6	84.37	54.26		

2. Copy the gross margin formula from cell J2 down to cells J3:J194.

3. Highlight Column J by clicking on Column J. Right-click and select **Format Cells**. Select the **Number** tab and select **Number**. Also set **Decimal places** to **2**. Click **OK**.

Analysis Task #2: Calculate Profitability by Customer

To determine the profitability of each customer, we need to compute the gross margin for each customer. To do so, we will use a pivot table.

1. In the menu, select **Insert > Pivot Table**. A dialog box will open, as shown in Exhibit C.

Exhibit C

Microsoft Excel

Create PivotTable   ?   ✕

Choose the data that you want to analyze
  ⦿ Select a table or range
      Table/Range: Sheet1!$A$1:$J$194
  ◯ Use an external data source
        Choose Connection...
        Connection name:
      ◯ Use this workbook's Data Model
Choose where you want the PivotTable report to be placed
  ⦿ New Worksheet
  ◯ Existing Worksheet
      Location:
Choose whether you want to analyze multiple tables
  ☐ Add this data to the Data Model

                              OK   Cancel

2. In the dialog box, select the **Table/Range** that includes the account titles and all of the data ($A$1:$J$194). Select **New Worksheet**, then click **OK**. The empty pivot table will open up in a new worksheet, ready for the next step, as follows:

Inputs into Pivot Table
Columns:
Rows: [Customer #]
ΣValues: [Gross Margin]

3. Drag [**Customer #**] from **FIELD NAME** into the **Rows**. Drag [**Gross Margin**] from **FIELD NAME** into $\sum$**Values** fields in the pivot table. The $\sum$values will default to **Sum of Gross Margin**. The resulting pivot table will look like Exhibit D.

Exhibit D

Microsoft Excel

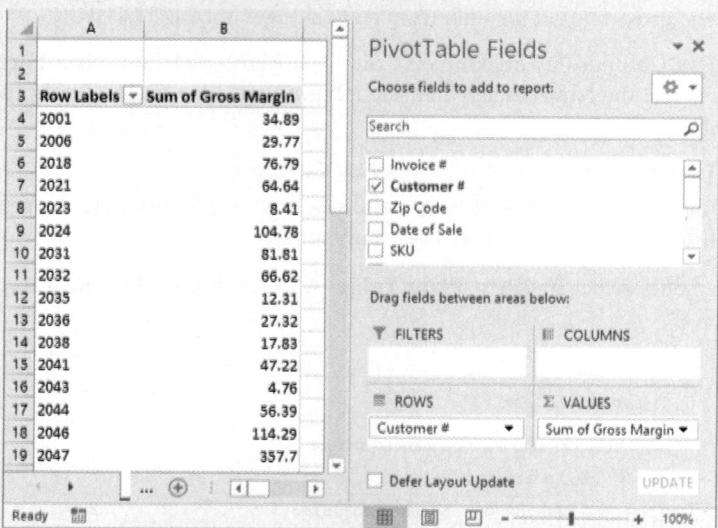

4. (Optional Step) Highlight cell A3 and insert the title "Customer Number".

Analysis Task #3: Sort Total Gross Margin by Customer

1. Our last analysis task is to sort gross margin from highest to lowest to find the most profitable customer. To do this, select one of the numbers in Column B and select **Data > Sort**. To get the most profitable customers on top, select **descending**.

2. Select the numbers in Column B. Right-click and select **Format Cells**. Select the **Number** tab and select **Number**. Also set **Decimal places** to **2**. Click **OK**.

3. The pivot table will now appear as shown in Exhibit E.

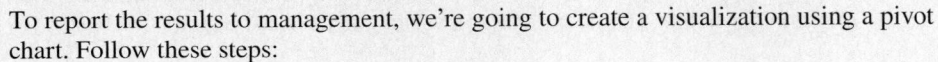

Exhibit E

Microsoft Excel

Row Labels	Sum of Gross Margin
2047	357.70
2088	212.23
2072	139.01
2081	137.78
2100	135.47
2060	118.74
2064	115.33
2087	114.85
2046	114.29
2086	107.41
2024	104.78
2063	96.45
2031	81.81
2018	76.79
2051	69.83
2032	66.62
2021	64.64
2079	64.00
2099	58.56
2044	56.39
2041	47.22
2067	44.94
2048	41.12
2074	38.18
2068	36.62

Share the Story

To report the results to management, we're going to create a visualization using a pivot chart. Follow these steps:

DATA VISUALIZATION

1. Select a cell in the pivot table.
2. Select **PivotTable Analyze > Tools > PivotChart**.
3. Select **Clustered Column**.
4. Click **OK**.

The resulting pivot chart will resemble Exhibit F.

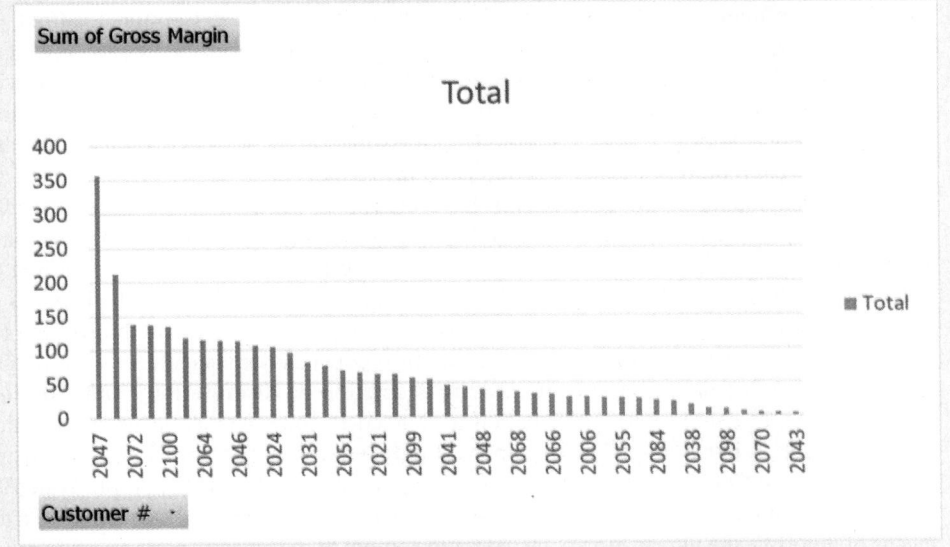

Exhibit F
Profitability by Customer ID

Microsoft Excel

We can report the results regarding Fancy Fruits' most profitable customers to the sales department and to company management. To keep these customers engaged and satisfied, Fancy Fruits could send additional advertising emails to them, enhance the customer service provided to them, or give them discounts on future purchases.

Mini-Lab Assessment

1. Why would Fancy Fruits be interested in computing gross margin by customer? How will this information help the company's managers in their subsequent marketing?

2. In this Mini-Lab, we computed gross margin by customer. Why might a company wish to compute gross margin percentage (gross margin/sales) for each customer instead?

3. How are pivot charts different from pivot tables? How does a visualization complement a table?

 PROGRESS CHECK

7. Explain how management accountants can use diagnostic analytics to address the question "Why did it happen?"

8. How could a management accountant use prescriptive analytics to address the question of whether a company should lease or purchase its headquarters building?

DIFFERENCES BETWEEN MANAGEMENT ACCOUNTING AND FINANCIAL ACCOUNTING

LO 1.5

Summarize the differences between management accounting and financial accounting.

Recall from your financial accounting courses that the goal of financial accounting is to report financial performance to external stakeholders such as investors, lenders, regulators, customers, and suppliers. Many rules and standards exist to make it easier to compare information across companies. In general, financial accounting information is considered **mandatory information** that is required by law or regulation. It is often required for compliance purposes and must be audited by an independent, external auditor. Financial accounting information is usually produced at the lowest possible cost to comply with regulations (for example, the requirements of the Securities and Exchange Commission, Internal Revenue Service, State Banking Commission, and State Tax Commission) and other parties that require it (banks, bondholders, investors).

mandatory information
Information that is required by law or regulation to be generated or provided.

In contrast, management accountants have complete freedom to compile whatever information is needed to answer managers' questions or help them meet company goals. Management accountants do not need to follow predefined rules or work according to standards established by laws or regulations. The only real standard is that the benefits of the information produced by management accountants must be greater than the cost of producing that information. Because the information produced by management accountants is produced for internal purposes only, it is considered to be **discretionary information**. Managers simply decide what information they need to track and build an information system to track it. For example, management at **Apple** may want an activity-based costing (ABC) system to figure out the true cost of making a product, such as the Apple Watch™.

discretionary information
Information that is produced for management but is not required for compliance purposes.

The final difference between management accounting and financial accounting is the means of reporting the information obtained (or the output of the analysis performed) to users. In financial accounting, the output is in the form of financial statements—the balance sheet, the income statement, the statement of cash flows, and the statement of stockholders' equity.

All of the financial statements are available to external parties, such as investors. In management accounting, the output is in the form most useful for decision makers, whether in the form of a written report, a visualization, an individualized dashboard, or some other format.

Management accountants often pursue a professional designation to demonstrate mastery of their trade. Two common management accounting designations are the **Certified Management Accountant (CMA)**, which is granted by the **Institute of Management Accountants (IMA)**, and the **Chartered Global Management Accountant (CGMA)**, which is granted by the **American Institute of Certified Public Accountants (AICPA)** and the **Chartered Institute of Management Accountants (CIMA)**. These professional accounting organizations support the management accounting profession through research, practice development, education, knowledge sharing, and advocacy for the best and most ethical business practices in management accounting and finance. To ensure that management accountants are properly trained, those who pursue the CMA or CGMA designations must show their mastery of management accounting by completing required training and passing an examination. In very broad terms, a Certified Public Accountant (CPA) is more associated with financial accounting and auditing, and a CMA is more associated with management accounting.

At the end of most chapters in this text, you will find questions that are adapted from the CMA exam. They will help you test your knowledge and practice your skills while familiarizing you with the types of questions you will find on the CMA exam.

Exhibit 1.13 summarizes the differences between management accounting and financial accounting.

CMA

Information Characteristic	Management Accounting	Financial Accounting
Purpose of information	Address management's questions to help create business value and/or meet company goals	Primarily for compliance purposes Communicate financial performance to investors, regulators, lenders (banks or bondholders), suppliers, and customers
Prescribed rules/standards for measurement and reporting	None, but general guidance is provided by the Institute of Management accountants (IMA)	Extensive (including SEC, FASB, GAAP)
Audit performed to verify information	No audit performed by independent, external auditors	Audit performed by independent, external auditors
Type of information provided	Discretionary	Mandatory (required)
Information production costs	Benefit of information must exceed the cost of producing information	Minimize cost of compliance
Primary users	Management/company employees at many different levels	External users (investors, regulators, lenders such as banks or bondholders, suppliers, customers)
Primary source(s) of data (further addressed in Chapter 2)	Cost accounting system Financial reporting system A variety of other company information systems (see Exhibit 2.8 for a more complete discussion)	Financial reporting system
Reporting output	Individualized reporting to meet the specific needs of management (the "S" in the AMPS model, *Share the story*)	Common output for all: Financial statements including balance sheet, income statement, statement of cash flows, and statement of stockholders' equity

Exhibit 1.13
The Differences Between Management Accounting and Financial Accounting

PROGRESS CHECK

9. Why does management accounting have no rules or standards, but financial accounting has many standards?

10. Why is the submission of financial statements to the SEC considered mandatory rather than discretionary?

LO 1.6

Understand the importance of ethics in data analysis and decision making.

ETHICS

Institute of Management Accountants (IMA)
Professional accounting organization that focuses on research, practice development, education, knowledge sharing, and advocacy for the best and most ethical business practices in management accounting and finance.

Certified Management Accountant (CMA)
Certification offered to management accountants by the Institute of Management Accountants.

conflict of interest
A situation in which employees have a competing personal or financial interest that makes it challenging to fulfill their duties fairly.

HUMAN DIMENSIONS OF MANAGEMENT ACCOUNTING: ETHICAL DATA ANALYSIS AND STRATEGIC DECISION MAKING

As we've seen, management accountants provide information and analysis to help managers make strategic, data-driven decisions. In performing their jobs, they (and all other types of accountants) must exhibit a strong degree of integrity and adhere to a strict code of ethics. What can happen if the accountant does not maintain confidentiality, does not exhibit integrity, or lacks credibility? Consider the following examples, which breach professional codes of conduct.

- *Lack of competence*: What can happen if a management accountant makes errors? How can those errors affect the company?
  - See this chapter's opening story: **Tesla** misestimated the cost of the solar roof, which ultimately led to a 70% increase in price.
- *Lack of training:* What can happen if a management accountant is not fully trained on new software and data analytics techniques?
  - Many of the sourcing problems **Hershey Foods** experienced in 2000 could have been avoided if the company had provided more training on new software.[10]
- *Conflict of interest or lack of integrity*: What can happen if a management accountant has a **conflict of interest**—that is, a competing personal or financial interest that makes it challenging to fulfill their duties fairly?
  - Conflicts of interest may cause management accountants to unfairly sway decision making toward an individual or business.[11]
- *Lack of confidentiality:* What can happen if a management accountant uses confidential information for unethical or illegal advantage?
  - Breaches of confidentiality can lead to costly lawsuits.
- *Biased reporting*: What can happen if a management accountant manipulates visualizations or other reports so that the decision maker is biased towards a certain conclusion?
  - Biased reporting can lead the company to make wrong and costly decisions.
- *Giving in to political pressure*: What can happen if a supervisor or co-worker favors a certain analytics outcome over another one, and then pressures the management accountant accordingly?
  - Giving in to political pressure can lead to many bad outcomes, including higher costs and lower revenues and profits.

---

[10]ICFAI Center for Management Research, "ERP Implementation Failure at Hershey Foods Corporation," Case study #908-001-1 (2008), https://kopisusa.com/wp-content/uploads/ERP_Implementation_Failure_Hershey_Foods.pdf (accessed April 30, 2021).

[11]Examples of conflict of interest are summarized here: "What Is a Conflict of Interest?," EVERFI, https://everfi.com/blog/workplace-training/conflicts-of-interest-at-work/?rd=workplaceanswers.com&rp=%2Fresources%2Fblog%2Fconflicts-of-interest-workplace-examples (accessed April 30, 2021).

To emphasize the importance of ethics in management accounting, in 2017 the Institute of Management Accountants issued its Statement of Ethical Professional Practice, reproduced in Exhibit 1.14. It emphasizes four overarching ethical principles:

- Competence
- Confidentiality
- Integrity
- Credibility

IMA Statement of Ethical Professional Practice

Effective July 1, 2017

Members of IMA shall behave ethically. A commitment to ethical professional practice includes overarching principles that express our values and standards that guide member conduct.

Principles

IMA's overarching ethical principles include: Honesty, Fairness, Objectivity, and Responsibility. Members shall act in accordance with these principles and shall encourage others within their organizations to adhere to them.

Standards

IMA members have a responsibility to comply with and uphold the standards of Competence, Confidentiality, Integrity, and Credibility. Failure to comply may result in disciplinary action.

I. COMPETENCE

1. Maintain an appropriate level of professional leadership and expertise by enhancing knowledge and skills.
2. Perform professional duties in accordance with relevant laws, regulations, and technical standards.
3. Provide decision support information and recommendations that are accurate, clear, concise, and timely. Recognize and help manage risk.

II. CONFIDENTIALITY

1. Keep information confidential except when disclosure is authorized or legally required.
2. Inform all relevant parties regarding appropriate use of confidential information. Monitor to ensure compliance.
3. Refrain from using confidential information for unethical or illegal advantage.

III. INTEGRITY

1. Mitigate actual conflicts of interest. Regularly communicate with business associates to avoid apparent conflicts of interest. Advise all parties of any potential conflicts of interest.
2. Refrain from engaging in any conduct that would prejudice carrying out duties ethically.
3. Abstain from engaging in or supporting any activity that might discredit the profession.
4. Contribute to a positive ethical culture and place integrity of the profession above personal interests.

IV. CREDIBILITY

1. Communicate information fairly and objectively.
2. Provide all relevant information that could reasonably be expected to influence an intended user's understanding of the reports, analyses, or recommendations.
3. Report any delays or deficiencies in information, timeliness, processing, or internal controls in conformance with organization policy and/or applicable law.
4. Communicate professional limitations or other constraints that would preclude responsible judgment or successful performance of an activity.

Exhibit 1.14
IMA Statement of Ethical Professional Practice

Chartered Global Management Accountant (CGMA) Certification issued by AICPA and CIMA, together as the Association of International Certified Professional Accountants, to management accountants.

The Chartered Institute of Management Accountants (CIMA) A global professional accounting body based in the United Kingdom that offers training and education in the field of management accounting.

American Institute of Certified Public Accountants (AICPA) A professional organization that represents certified public accountants (CPAs) in the United States.

Careers in Management Accounting

In each chapter, we will highlight careers and key roles and responsibilities of the management accountant across a set of companies.

Exhibit 1.15 reproduces a job posting from a site like **Indeed.com** or **LinkedIn**. This post is from a staffing company looking for a Senior Cost Accountant for a manufacturing company. The key roles and responsibilities for the cost accountant are highlighted with annotations. We will begin examining cost accounting in more detail in Chapter 2. Each chapter in this book concludes with a job listing to illustrate how the skills you are learning in this course will help you in your career.

Job Title:

Sr. Cost Accountant, Manufacturing Company

Job Summary:

A **SR. COST ACCOUNTANT** is needed to fill an immediate opening for an industry-leading manufacturing company with regional offices across North America.

This role supports both the finance organization and the firm's manufacturing operations with financial and analytical reporting. The role will primarily be based in the U.S., covering regional manufacturing facilities in Southern Texas, Colorado, and the Pacific Northwest. A successful senior cost accountant will work closely with other senior members of the accounting organization across North America.

Candidate Requirements:

- Master's degree in finance or accounting (or other related business fields)
- 8+ years in prior cost accounting roles within finance and/or accounting
- Active CPA
- Confident and innovative problem solver with strong analytical skills
- Ability to work effectively in a team environment
- Experience working closely with product teams and departments including Operations and IT
- Clear communicator with exceptional written and verbal skills
- Ability to gather and analyze detailed financial data resulting in clear, concise, and actionable recommendations to decision makers within the business

Responsibilities of the Job:

- Prepare monthly inventory reports for related organizations, including regional factories across North America
- Complete various internal- and external-facing financial analyses as needed for decision making, including actual vs. plan budget, manufacturing costs, inventory, and expense logs.
- Track standard costs, budgets, and forecasts, and resolve any significant variances.
- Support new factory start-up activities including accounting for non-recurring costs, monitoring actual utilization of factory assets relative to expectations, and training new employees on factory and product cost details.
- Set up new raw material, packaging, and related items; create and maintain production bills of materials; maintain periodic cost rolls and updates.
- Analyze actual production costs and the effects that changes in manufacturing methods, raw materials, product design, or services provided would have on costs.

Starting Salary Range: $100,000–140,000 (including benefits and annual incentive bonus)

Annotations (left margin callouts):

- Strong analytical and problem-solving skills desired.
- Sharing the story (communicating results) is an important component of the job.
- Track inventory transactions
- Compare actual to expected costs.

Exhibit 1.15
Senior Cost Accountant Position at a Manufacturing Company

⊘ PROGRESS CHECK

11. The competence standard in the IMA Statement of Ethical Professional Practice specifies the need to "maintain an appropriate level of professional leadership and expertise." Why is it important for management accountants to maintain their level of expertise?
12. If management accountants feel they know what is best for the company, why is it a problem to promote their preferred solution over another?

Key Takeaways: The Role of Management Accountants in Addressing Strategic Management Questions

Companies exist to create value. Management makes many operational and strategic decisions about how the company can best create value. Management accountants increasingly serve as a liaison, or interpreter, between management and data scientists, gaining access to appropriate datasets and analyzing them to address management's questions by providing data-driven insights.

We introduced the AMPS model as a systematic means of supporting data-driven decision making. When management accountants follow this four-step structured approach, they provide a major service to management. Let's summarize this chapter's key takeaways using the AMPS model:

Ask the Question

- **What question(s) does management want to answer?**

Management accountants identify and articulate the questions that are important for management decision making. Among other decisions, managers must determine how to achieve financial goals and how various investments will influence outcomes.

Master the Data

- **Which data are appropriate to address management's questions?**

"Mastering" the data means truly understanding and getting the most from the data you are working with. It also means finding data that have integrity, meaning they are accurate, valid, and consistent over time. Two key aspects of data integrity are reliability (exhibiting data integrity) and relevance (addressing the question at hand).

Perform the Analysis

- **Which analytics are performed to address management questions?**

The type of analysis performed depends on the question being asked. **Descriptive analytics** characterizes, summarizes, and organizes features and properties of the data to answer the questions "What happened?" and "What is happening?" **Diagnostic analytics** investigates an underlying cause or why actual performance differed from expectations, addressing the questions "Why did it happen?" and "Why is it different from what we expected?" **Predictive analytics** identifies patterns in historical data to forecast future activity, addressing the questions "Will it happen in the future?" "What is the probability something will happen?" and "Is it forecastable?" **Prescriptive analytics** identifies the best options given constraints or changing conditions, addressing the questions "What should we do based on what we expect will happen?" and "How do we optimize our performance based on potential constraints?"

Share the Story

■ **How are the results of analytics shared with stakeholders?**

Management accountants use written reports, visualizations, dashboards, and in-person presentations to communicate results of the analysis to management.

Key Terms

AMPS data analytics model (AMPS model)

business process

business value

Certified Management Accountant (CMA)

conflict of interest

context

control

cost advantage (cost leadership)

dashboard

data

data analytics

data integrity

data scientist

decision

descriptive analytics

diagnostic analytics

discretionary information

dynamic data

firm infrastructure

information

information value chain

Institute of Management Accountants (IMA)

knowledge

management accountant

mandatory information

planning

predictive analytics

prescriptive analytics

primary activities

product differentiation

secondary activities (supporting activities)

static data

value chain

visualization

 ## ANSWERS TO PROGRESS CHECKS

1. To create business value, management makes many strategic decisions, including which product or service to sell, which customers to target, which employees to hire, and how to best produce its products or services to achieve its goal of creating value. Management accountants help determine management's informational needs by identifying their questions. Then they use data and other means to answer those questions.

2. If a business process isn't creating value, the company should decide if it can do without that process. If the process is necessary, the company should attempt to minimize the cost of performing it. For example, can it be outsourced to other companies at a lower cost?

3. Management accountants not only understand the decisions that management needs to make and what information/knowledge managers need in order to make those decisions, they also are intimately familiar with the characteristics of the data and have a working knowledge of data quality, statistical tools, and programming. Management accountants speak the language of business and are more likely than data scientists to know which data are most appropriate for addressing business questions.

4. The data scientist is a person employed to acquire, maintain, curate, access, manipulate, and statistically test data to address business questions. Data scientists maintain the data, create specific datasets to address specific questions, and know where the datasets are stored and how to access them. While they are usually adept in programming and data manipulation, they do not usually know or understand the business context or the language of business.

5. Because the company needs to access updated sales on a daily basis, a dynamic dashboard that updates on a continuous basis will be the most appropriate way to communicate results.

6. After completing all steps of the AMPS model, the management accountant and the decision maker often are more knowledgeable and better able to ask deeper, more refined questions, which can lead to better and better answers. In other words, the AMPS model

is cyclical. As soon as you've shared the story, new questions will arise, and the steps in the AMPS model will begin anew.

7. Diagnostic analytics is performed to investigate an underlying cause that cannot be determined by simply looking at the descriptive data. Diagnostic analytics employs techniques such as detecting correlations and patterns of interest and comparing them to a benchmark to explain why something has occurred.

8. Prescriptive analytics identifies the best possible options given constraints or changing conditions. To help management decide whether to lease or buy/own its headquarters building, management accountants will look at the costs associated with both options. They may also consider some qualitative implications of leasing or owning a headquarters building that may not be addressed in the costing analysis.

9. Management accounting needs to meet only the needs of management and therefore has no external standards imposed on it. In contrast, because many external parties rely on the financial statements, financial accounting has extensive rules and standards.

10. The law requires submission of financial statements to the SEC for compliance purposes. Because this information is required to be disclosed, it is considered mandatory information.

11. To advise management effectively, management accountants must maintain their credentials and expertise by receiving appropriate training to enhance their knowledge and skills. The world changes (as do laws and regulations), and management accountants must keep up with those changes.

12. Decision makers need to see the results of analysis based on criteria they deem most important. Although management accountants may have a reason for preferring a specific alternative, they should not push one solution over another. Only after presenting the unbiased results to the decision maker should they offer their opinions and insights regarding what they consider to be the best alternative.

Multiple-Choice Questions   Mc Graw Hill connect

1. (LO1.3) Which component of the AMPS model addresses the question of the best way for management accountants to communicate their analyses with decision makers?
   a. Ask the question
   b. Master the data
   c. Perform the analysis
   d. Share the story

2. (LO1.5) Which of the following is discretionary information that a company's accountants must provide?
   a. The break-even level of a new product
   b. The annual report submitted to shareholders detailing financial performance
   c. The federal tax return
   d. Sales information as part of the sales tax return

3. (LO1.1) Which of the following value chain activities is a primary activity?
   a. Procurement
   b. Inbound logistics
   c. Human resources management
   d. Information technology

4. (LO1.2) What requires context to create information?
   a. Knowledge
   b. Data
   c. Facts
   d. Data stores

5. (LO1.4) The analysis of variances (for example, actual performance is different from budgeted performance) is most often associated with which type of analytics?
   a. Descriptive analytics
   b. Diagnostic analytics
   c. Predictive analytics
   d. Prescriptive analytics

6. (LO1.4) Summary statistics are most often associated with which type of analytics?
   a. Descriptive analytics
   b. Diagnostic analytics
   c. Predictive analytics
   d. Prescriptive analytics

7. (LO1.4) Time series analysis is most often associated with which type of analytics?
   a. Descriptive analytics
   b. Diagnostic analytics
   c. Predictive analytics
   d. Prescriptive analytics

8. (LO1.6) Which of the following is not one of the four overarching ethical principles mentioned in the 2017 IMA Statement of Ethical Professional Practice?
   a. Competence
   b. Honesty
   c. Confidentiality
   d. Credibility

9. (LO1.3) Which questions aim to more clearly understand why net income is decreasing when revenues are increasing?
   a. What happened? What is happening?
   b. Why did it happen? What are the root causes of past results?
   c. Will it happen in the future? What is the probability something will happen? Is it forecastable?
   d. What should we do based on what we expect will happen? How do we optimize our performance based on potential constraints?

10. (LO1.3) What type of visualization is used to track overtime labor on a continuous, real-time basis?
    a. Dashboard with static display
    b. Dashboard with dynamic display
    c. Conditional formatting
    d. Bar chart for the past 10 months

11. (LO1.3) Which management accounting question will require predictive analytics?
    a. Why did labor expenses increase over the past year as compared to prior years?
    b. Should the company rent or lease its headquarters building?
    c. Can we forecast future sales for this company?
    d. Why did our cost structure (fixed and variable costs) change over the past year?

12. (LO1.3) Which management accounting question will require prescriptive analytics?
    a. Why did the company perform worse this year than last year?
    b. Should the company manufacture its product, or should it outsource production to an outside contractor?
    c. Can we forecast future sales, earnings, and cash flows for this company?
    d. Which level of sales will allow us to break even?

13. (LO1.2) A _____ is a person who analyzes accounting-related data to help an organization make effective business decisions.
    a. management accountant
    b. financial accountant
    c. data scientist
    d. computer programmer

14. (LO1.2) A _____ is a person employed to acquire, maintain, curate, access, manipulate,
and statistically test data to address business questions.
    a. management accountant
    b. financial accountant
    c. data scientist
    d. computer programmer

15. (LO1.2) If a manager is a decision maker, and a data scientist is a developer, then what
is a management accountant?
    a. An interpreter
    b. An expert at investments
    c. An intermediary
    d. A broker

16. (LO1.5) Which of the following is mandatory information that a company's accountants
are required to maintain?
    a. The cost drivers used to allocate overhead
    b. The calculation of the difference between actual and budgeted performance
    c. The product price that should be charged to maximize profits
    d. The amount of dividends paid to shareholders

17. (LO1.5) Which organization sponsors the certification of a management accountant as
a CMA?
    a. Institute of Management Accountants
    b. Institute of Certified Public Accountants
    c. American Institute of Management Accountants
    d. Association of Certified Management Accountants

18. (LO1.5) Which statement about management accounting is true?
    a. Management accounting information must be audited by an external auditor.
    b. Management accounting works to minimize the cost of compliance with regulatory
       entities.
    c. One source of management accounting data is a cost accounting system.
    d. One common output of management accounting is the income statement.

19. (LO1.3) Performing a regression falls into which of the following components of the
AMPS model?
    a. Ask the question
    b. Master the data
    c. Perform the analysis
    d. Share the story

20. (LO1.3) Which data visualization is used to evaluate trends of values over time?
    a. Bar chart
    b. Pie chart
    c. Scatterplot
    d. Line graph

Discussion Questions

1. (LO1.1) Describe the primary activities in the value chain for your college or university. In your opinion, which primary activities create the most value?

2. (LO1.1) Describe the primary activities in the value chain for an accounting firm that issues audit reports. In your opinion, which primary activities create the most value?

3. (LO1.1) Give five examples of business processes at **Tesla**. How do they create business value for Tesla and its shareholders?

4. (LO1.1) Describe where the management accounting role fits in the supporting activities of the firm in the value chain.

5. (LO1.1) Why are marketing and sales activities considered to be primary value chain activities? How do those activities create value?

6. (LO1.1) In a manufacturing company, which primary value chain activity is supported by procurement?

7. (LO1.2) What is the difference between the roles of the management accountant and the role of the data scientist? Are both roles needed?

8. (LO1.3) Describe the AMPS model (or AMPS data analytics model). How is it used to summarize the data analytics process?

9. (LO1.3) What does *recursive* mean? Why is the AMPS model considered to be recursive? What exactly is repeated?

10. (LO1.3) What is the difference between descriptive analytics and diagnostic analytics?

11. (LO1.3) Why would you want to perform descriptive analytics before predictive analytics?

12. (LO1.3) Some argue that a picture is worth a thousand clicks. Argue for and against the use of data visualizations when sharing the story.

13. (LO1.4) Why do descriptive analytics techniques use counts, totals, sums, and averages to help address the question "What happened?"

14. (LO1.4) Identify three or four strategic management questions that might be addressed by a management accountant using prescriptive analytics.

15. (LO1.5) Management needs management accounting information to address strategic questions. Why, then, is this information considered to be discretionary?

16. (LO1.5) Why is mandatory information produced even if the benefit to management is smaller than the cost to produce it? What potentially is the cost of noncompliance?

17. (LO1.6) Why is presenting results in a neutral way (not favoring one conclusion over another) consistent with an ethical approach to management accounting? When, if ever, should a management accountant depart from that approach?

18. (LO1.6) Why is accountant competence consistent with an ethical approach to management accounting? If the accountant isn't competent (for example, hasn't been trained, has inadequate expertise), what is the accountant's duty?

ETHICS

Brief Exercises   Mc Graw Hill connect

1. (LO1.1) Order the following primary value chain activities in the correct sequence.
   a. Marketing and sales activities
   b. Service activities
   c. Operations
   d. Outbound logistics
   e. Inbound logistics

2. (LO1.1) Match each primary value chain activity with its definition.

Definition	Primary Value Chain Activity (Marketing and sales activities, Service activities, Operations, Outbound logistics, Inbound logistics)
a. The activities that transform inputs into finished goods and services (for example, turning wood into furniture)	
b. The support of customers after the products and services are sold to them (for example, warranty repairs, parts, and instruction manuals)	
c. The activities that warehouse and distribute finished goods to customers	
d. Identification of customers' needs and wants to help attract them to the company's products and then buy them	
e. The activities associated with receiving and storing raw materials and other partially completed materials, and distributing those materials to manufacturing divisions when and where they are needed	

3. (LO1.1) Match the examples of the supporting value chain activities to the correct term.

Example Activities	Supporting Value Chain Activity (Infrastructure, Human resource management, Technology, Procurement)
a. Attorneys writing contracts with suppliers	
b. Purchasing and installing supply chain software to help managers evaluate supply chain performance	
c. Purchasing raw materials to use in the manufacturing process	
d. Determining the cost of one square foot of decking board product	
e. Hiring new production-line workers	

4. (LO1.2) Indicate whether each of the following tasks is most likely to be performed by a manager, a management accountant, or a data scientist.
   a. Serve as a liaison between other professionals
   b. Help management make effective decisions
   c. Write scripts to extract data from databases
   d. Make decisions for the organization that are expected to maximize business value
   e. Create specific datasets to address specific questions
   f. Match management's questions to the data that might help to answer those questions
   g. Acquire, maintain, curate, access, manipulate, and statistically test data

5. (LO1.3) Link the components of the analytics mindset with the components of the AMPS model.

Analytics Mindset Component	AMPS Model Component (Ask the question, Master the data, Perform the analysis, or Share the story)
a. Extract, transform, and load relevant data	
b. Apply appropriate data analytics techniques	
c. Interpret and share the results	
d. Ask the right questions	

6. (LO1.3) To *Master the data,* a component of the AMPS model, we need to determine whether each type of data is categorical, alphanumeric, or numerical. Match each data item to its data type.

Data Item	Data Type (Categorical, Alphanumeric, or Numerical)
a. Item product number	
b. Sale or return (Yes or no)	
c. Product name	
d. In stock (Yes or No?)	
e. Item price	

7. (LO1.3) Match each management accounting task with the correct step in the AMPS model (*Ask the question, Master the data, Perform the analysis,* or *Share the story*).

Management Accounting Task	AMPS Model Component
a. Gather datasets that show budgeted projections of the sales price per unit and related costs of production and marketing for the new product	
b. Evaluate the break-even level of sales for a new product	
c. Report the break-even level of sales using visualizations in a written report	
d. Ask management accounts to determine the break-even level of sales for a newly proposed product	

8. (LO1.3) Match each analytics type (descriptive, diagnostic, predictive, and prescriptive) with the management accounting question.

Management Accounting Question	Analytics Type
a. Why did it happen?	
b. Will it happen in the future?	
c. What should we do, based on what we expect will happen?	
d. What happened?	

9. (LO1.5) Label each of the following information items created by accountants as either discretionary information or mandatory information.
   a. Tax return to the Internal Revenue Service
   b. Break-even analysis for the firm
   c. A summary of the firm's fixed costs versus variable costs
   d. Financial statements that help banks continuously monitor a firm's financial condition
   e. Costs of leasing versus buying a new mainframe computer
   f. Employee terminations submission to the U.S. Department of Labor to determine the level of unemployment insurance that a company is required to carry

10. (LO1.5) Classify each of the following information items created by accountants as the result of either financial accounting or management accounting.
   a. Information provided to auditors to help them complete their audit of financial statements
   b. Production budget
   c. The allocation of costs to different jobs
   d. Financial statements for shareholder use
   e. The product price that maximizes profits for the company
   f. Evaluation of different potential planning scenarios based on customer demand

11. (LO1.2) Match the following components of the information value chain to their definitions.

Definition	Component of the Information Value Chain (Data, Context, Information, Decision, Knowledge)
a. The setting surrounding the data; the event, statement, or situation in which the data can be fully understood and evaluated	
b. Data organized in a way that is useful to the user in a given context	
c. Understanding of or familiarity with information gained through learning	
d. Raw facts that describe an event and have little meaning on their own	
e. A conclusion reached after consideration of knowledge gained	

12. (LO1.3) Match the components of the AMPS model to a variety of management accounting tasks.

Management Accounting Task	AMPS Model Component (Ask the question, Master the data, Perform the analysis, or Share the story)
a. Decide which management question to emphasize to help management assess possible strategies	
b. Run a regression analysis to evaluate the impact of advertising	
c. Extract data from the accounting system and prepare it for analysis in a pivot table	
d. Clean the data and get the datasets ready for analysis	
e. Identify the reporting period for the upcoming budget to be produced	
f. Publish financial results using visualizations	
g. Analyze how profits will change if fuel prices increase in the coming year	

13. (LO1.3) Match the components of the AMPS model to the management accounting task of proposing a budget for the next period.

Management Accounting Task	AMPS Model Component (Ask the question, Master the data, Perform the analysis, Share the story)
a. Find appropriate past data to help create the budget for the next period	
b. Use prediction techniques to forecast next period's budget	
c. Share the budget with management in written form and using visualizations	
d. Clean the past data and make sure all parts of the data are relevant for analysis	
e. Provide budget presentation to all interested parties	
f. Compare the budgeted company sales projections to industry sales projections	

14. (LO1.4) Match each management accounting question to the correct data analytics type.

Management Accounting Question	Data Analytics Type
a. Which product mix will allow us to maximize profits?	
b. Why did the product costs differ from the amount budgeted?	
c. How many car batteries did we produce last week and last month?	
d. What do we expect car battery sales to be next quarter?	

15. (LO1.4) Match each management accounting question to the correct data analytics type.

Management Accounting Question	Data Analytics Type (Descriptive, Diagnostic, Predictive, Prescriptive)
a. What should we do if the inputs for our products increase in price?	
b. Why did sales, general, and administrative expenses increase relative to our closest competitor?	
c. Which product is the most profitable one for our company?	
d. What is our expected profitability over the next five years?	

16. (LO1.4) Match each data analytics technique with the correct type of data analytics.

Data Analytics Technique	Data Analytics Type (Descriptive, Diagnostic, Predictive, Prescriptive)
a. Computing total sales by product over the past quarter	
b. Determining the difference between budgeted performance and actual performance	
c. Considering the break-even level of products sold for a new product based on expected performance	
d. Creating sales forecasts	
e. Evaluating production statistics based on comparison with past performance	
f. Identifying percentage changes from last period to this period	

17. (LO1.6) Match each example of ethical behavior to the related standard in the IMA Statement of Ethical Professional Practice (competence, confidentiality, integrity, or credibility).

Example of Ethical Behavior	Standard in the IMA Statement of Ethical Professional Practice (Competence, Confidentiality, Integrity, or Credibility)
a. Mitigate conflicts of interest.	
b. Communicate information fairly and objectively.	
c. Maintain an appropriate level of professional leadership and expertise by enhancing knowledge and skills.	
d. Refrain from using confidential information for unethical or illegal advantage.	
e. Report any delays or deficiencies in information, timeliness, processing, or internal controls in conformance with organization policy and/or applicable law.	
f. Contribute to a positive ethical culture.	

Problems   McGraw Hill connect

1. (LO1.4) Management is asking you to determine which of your company's products is most profitable in Arizona. This information will help determine the company's marketing plans, and ultimately its production plans.

   Required

   Using the four components of the AMPS model, explain each step in addressing management's question. The first answer has been completed for you.

AMPS Model Component	Detailed Steps in Determining Which Product Is Most Profitable
a. Ask the question	Which of our products sold in Arizona is the most profitable?
b. Master the data	
c. Perform the analysis	
d. Share the story	

2. (LO1.4) Management is asking you to determine the break-even level of sales for a new product (in units sold).

   Required

   Using the four components of the AMPS model, explain each step a cost accountant would use in addressing management's question. The first answer has been completed for you.

AMPS Model Component	Detailed Steps in Determining the Break-even Level of Sales
a. Ask the question	How many units need to be sold to break even?
b. Master the data	
c. Perform the analysis	
d. Share the story	

3. (LO1.3) Download the SkyDio Drone SKU dataset. Note the sales price and cost of each SKU (product). Use Excel to address the following questions. You may want to complete the Excel tutorial in Appendix A before attempting this problem.

   Required

   a. Which SKU has the highest sales price? (*Hint:* Use =MAX() function to calculate.)

   b. What is the highest cost of any SKU? (*Hint:* Use =MAX() function to calculate.)

   c. Which SKU has the lowest sales price? (*Hint:* Use =MIN() function to calculate.)

   d. What is the lowest cost of any SKU? (*Hint:* Use =MIN() function to calculate.)

   e. What is the average sales price of the SKUs offered for sale (round to two digits)? (*Hint:* Use =AVERAGE() function to calculate.)

   f. What is the median cost of the SKUs offered for sale? (*Hint:* Use =MEDIAN() function to calculate.)

4. (LO1.3) Download the DJI Mavic Drone SKU dataset. In Excel, calculate the gross margin (Sales Price − Cost) and gross margin percentage [(Sales Price − Cost)/Sales Price] for each SKU (product). You may want to complete the Excel tutorial in Appendix A before attempting this problem.

   Required

   a. Which SKU has the highest gross margin? (*Hint:* Use =MAX() function to calculate.)

   b. Which SKU has the highest gross margin percentage? (*Hint:* Use =MAX() function to calculate.)

   c. Which SKU has the lowest gross margin? (*Hint:* Use =MIN() function to calculate.)

d. Which SKU has the lowest gross margin percentage? (*Hint:* Use =MIN() function to calculate.)

e. What are the average and median gross margins of the SKUs offered for sale? (*Hint:* Use =AVERAGE() and =MEDIAN() functions to calculate.)

f. What are the average and median gross margin percentage of the SKUs offered for sale (round to three digits)? (*Hint:* Use =AVERAGE() and =MEDIAN() functions to calculate.)

5. (LO1.3) Download the DJI Mavic Drone Sales Journal dataset in Excel. Note the sales price and cost of each sale. In Excel, calculate the gross margin (Sales Price − Cost) for each sale. Use a pivot table to determine the following. It may be helpful to perform this problem. After completing Lab 1.3 Excel, Lab 1.3 Tableau, or Lab 1.3 Power BI.

Required

a. What are the total sales for SKU DJI-AIR?

b. What is the total gross margin for sales of SKU DJI-MMC?

c. Which product (SKU) had the highest sales during the month?

d. Which product (SKU) had the lowest gross margin during the month?

6. (LO1.3) Download the SkyDio Drone Sales Journal dataset in Excel. Note the sales price and cost of each sale. In Excel, calculate the gross margin (Sales Price − Cost) for each line of the invoice. Use a pivot table to determine the following. It may be helpful to perform this problem. After completing Lab 1.3 Excel, Lab 1.3 Tableau, or Lab 1.3 Power BI.

Required

a. What are the total sales for SKU SK2-CIK?

b. What is the total cost for all sales of SKU SKY-BAT?

c. What is the total gross margin for SKU SK2-BEA?

d. Which product (SKU) had the highest sales during the month?

e. Which product (SKU) had the lowest cost of sales during the month?

f. Which product (SKU) had the highest gross margin during the month?

7. (LO1.3) Download the SkyDio Drone Sales Journal dataset in Excel. Note the sales price and cost of each sale. In Excel, calculate the gross margin (Sales Price − Cost) for each line of the invoice. Use a pivot table to determine the following. It may be helpful to perform this problem after completing Lab 1.3 Excel, Lab 1.3 Tableau, or Lab 1.3 Power BI.

Required

a. What is the total gross margin earned from customer 3022?

b. What are the total sales for customer 3000?

c. What is the total cost of sales for customer 3039?

d. Which customer bought the most during the month?

e. Which customer bought the least during the month?

f. What was the total amount of customer sales for the month?

ETHICS

8. (LO1.6) Santos Romero, a management accountant at PAM Transportation, has been around a long time. In fact, he's been around so long that he believes he knows what has made and will continue to make the company successful and profitable. Given that there are no external standards to follow in management accounting, he would like to pick and choose which specific data to show management in a way that highlights his preferred outcome.

Required

a. Is Santos's approach ethical or not ethical? Explain.

b. How can Santos provide management with various scenarios without emphasizing his preferred outcome? If he does show various scenarios, what type of analytics has he used to identify the possible outcomes (descriptive, diagnostic, predictive, or prescriptive)? Explain.

9. (LO1.5) Consider the chapter's opening story regarding the increased cost and increased price for **Tesla**'s solar roof.

Required

Using the AMPS model, explain how Tesla could have avoided the following problems in each of these four areas:

a. What is the appropriate question to determine the cost of a solar roof?

b. What data would you use?

c. Because the type of question leads to the appropriate analytics techniques, which analytics technique fits the question you asked?

d. Which type(s) of visualization would be effective in presenting your findings to Elon Musk and the Tesla management team?

10. (LO1.3) The following data visualization summarizes the relationship between total monthly profit margin and labor cost per lawn.

DATA VISUALIZATION

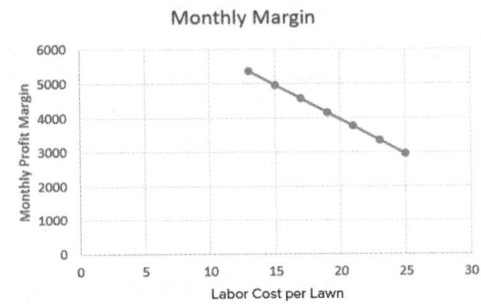

Microsoft Excel

Required

a. What does the data visualization tell us about the relationship between labor cost per lawn mowed and monthly (profit) margin (the extent to which revenues exceed expenses)?

b. Is using the data visualization above better or worse than showing the same data in the following tabular format? Explain.

Labor Cost per Lawn	Monthly Margin
13	5350
15	4950
17	4550
19	4150
21	3750
23	3350
25	2950

11. (LO1.1) Consider the value chain in Exhibit 1.2 as a guide and apply it to **Apple**.

Required

a. Give examples of the primary activities that Apple uses to create value with its iPhone product.

b. In which supporting activity will management accountants be most useful? Why?

12. (LO1.3) Recall the axiom, "Your data won't speak unless you ask them the right data analysis questions." What does this axiom mean in terms of matching the right question with the available data?

Now assume you are the CEO of **Chipotle** (an American chain of fast casual restaurants), and you are trying to decide whether to add a drive-through component to all your stores to increase sales and profits. What question would you ask to address this question, and which data would you seek to address this question directly? (Assume you can find and use any available data to answer this question.)

13. (LO1.1) Consider the information value chain in Exhibit 1.5.

Required

Imagine and improvise context for each of the following eight data items that will allow you to convert them from data into information. What additional contextual information might be needed to evaluate the data?

   a. The gross margin of the new drone product is 40%.
   b. The salespeople are demanding a 10% raise.
   c. The accountant found 123 errors in the journal entries.
   d. The product can no longer be manufactured in Vietnam due to export restrictions.
   e. Profits at **Netflix** increased by 2.1%.
   f. Sales at **Chipotle** are expected to increase next year.
   g. Sales returns at **Dillard's** fell by 2% in January.
   h. Inventory of last year's Kubota model increased by 7% in May.

14. (LO1.3) **Chipotle** has a goal of maximizing its profits over the next five years.

Required

For each of the following general sets of question types, imagine/improvise specific questions to support Chipotle's goal.

   a. What happened? What is happening?
   b. Why did it happen? What are the root causes of past results?
   c. Will it happen in the future? What is the probability something will happen? Is it forecastable?
   d. What should we do based on what we expect will happen? How do we optimize our performance based on potential constraints?

15. (LO1.5) Consider the Senior Cost Position at HT Group in Exhibit 1.15 from the perspective of the AMPS model. Use specific items from "Key Roles and Responsibilities" and "The Ideal Candidate" in your response.

   Which characteristics of the job position are consistent with each component of the AMPS model? Are some components emphasized over others?

Lab 1.1 Excel

Assessing the Profitability of a Small Business

Data Analytics Type: Descriptive Analytics

Keywords

Developing Excel Skills, Assessing Profitability

Decision-Making Context

You have been approached by a friend who is retiring from his lawn-mowing business. He asks you if you would like to take over his business. He is not trying to make money on the sale of the business. Instead, he is concerned with (1) taking care of his existing customers and (2) having someone take over the existing contracts on equipment he has purchased.

He currently mows 50 yards each week and charges $50 per yard. In addition to mowing the lawns himself, he has 2 people working for him. He has the following equipment:

Truck: He has 1 truck he purchased. The amount he still owes is $20,000 and the payment is $300/month.

Mowers: He has 3 new riding mowers on which he owes $3,000 each. He makes a $100 monthly payment for each mower.

Other Equipment: All other equipment is paid for and in good working order, and he is willing to sell all of it to you for $2,000 (and you think it will last 20 mowing months). He thinks it will cost you $100/month to maintain the truck, mowers, and other equipment.

You have a degree in landscape architecture and design, and you have been the groundskeeper at a golf course for the last 5 years. You believe with your knowledge and entrepreneurial ideas you could improve greatly on your friend's business model.

In summary, your costs are:

- Truck payment: $300/month
- Mowers payment: $300/month
- Other equipment: $2,000 to purchase now (will last approximately 20 months); this is the equivalent of $100/month in depreciation.

Lab Note: The tools presented in this lab periodically change. Updated instructions, if applicable, can be found in the student and instructor support materials.

depreciation
The reduction in value of an asset as time passes, due to use, wear and tear, or obsolescence.

- Chief mower makes $15/hour; staff worker makes $10/hour. Each staff person has the capacity to mow 1 yard/hour. (Average labor cost is $13/yard in Scenario 1 or $25 per yard in Scenario 2.)
- Equipment maintenance: $100/month
- Insurance: $300/month
- Fuel: $3/gallon; one gallon will be sufficient for 1 yard.
- Supplies, such as trimmer line, etc.: $1.50/lawn
- Advertising: $50/month, but if you do $300/month in advertising, you can potentially triple your number of contracts.
- Owner (you) will spend time doing quality control, marketing, and planning for the future.

Required

Assess whether this mowing business could be profitable if you mow 200 lawns per month.

Ask the Question

What is the profit on each lawn if the mowing business mows 200 lawns per month? What is the profit in sum total?

Master the Data

For this lab you will use data in the Excel file titled **Lab 1.1 Data.xlsx**. As you complete this lab, various assumptions will be made about cost and revenue data.

Perform the Analysis

Open the data file and browse its contents.

Analysis Task 1: Set Up the Two Scenarios on the Spreadsheet

We will assess the revenues, costs, and margins by first estimating the profit margin per lawn and then by comparing two different scenarios.

1. In cells C4 and D4, insert the number 200, representing the number of lawns you will mow each month. See Lab Exhibit 1.1.1.
2. In cells C6 and D6, insert the number 50, representing the revenue for each lawn.
3. In cell A10, type the word "Truck". In cell B10, insert the number 300, representing the monthly truck payment. To get the cost per unit, insert this formula in cell C10: =$B$10/C4. Make sure to use an absolute reference to cell B10 ($B$10) so that Excel will always refer to the cell with the truck's monthly payment. See again Lab Exhibit 1.1.1.

Lab Exhibit 1.1.1

Microsoft Excel

	A	B	C	D
1	Base Scenario			
2			Scenario 1	Scenario 2
3			Per Lawn	Per Lawn
4	Assumption: Total Lawns Serviced Each Month		200	200
5				
6	Revenue		50	50
7				
8	Costs			
9				
10	Truck	Monthly 300	=$B10/C4	

4. Copy the contents of cell C10 to cell D10.
5. In cell A11, type the word "Mowers". In cell B11, insert the number 300, representing the monthly truck payment. To get the cost per unit, insert this formula in cell C11: =$B$11/C4. Copy the result to cell D11. The resulting spreadsheet should resemble Lab Exhibit 1.1.2.

	A	B	C	D
1	Base Scenario		Scenario 1	Scenario 2
2			Per Lawn	Per Lawn
3				
4	Assumption: Total Lawns Serviced Each Month		200	200
5				
6	Revenue		50	50
7				
8	Costs			
9		Monthly		
10	Truck	300	1.50	1.50
11	Mowers	300	1.50	1.50

6. In cell A12, type the words "Other Equipment". In cell B12, insert the number 100, representing the monthly depreciation. To get the cost per unit (yard), insert this formula in cell C12: =$B$12/C4. Copy the result to cell D12.
7. In cell A13, type the words "Labor (Average $13/yard or $25/yard)". In cell C13, insert the number 13, representing the labor cost per lawn in Scenario 1. In cell D13, insert the number 25, representing the labor cost per lawn in Scenario 2.
8. In cell A14, type the word "Maintenance". In cell B14, insert the number 100, representing the monthly equipment maintenance. To get the cost per yard mowed, insert this formula in cell C14: =$B$14/C4. Copy the result to cell D14.
9. In cell A15, type the word "Insurance". In cell B15, insert the number 300, representing the monthly insurance payment. To get the cost per lawn, insert this formula in cell C15: =$B$15/C4. Copy the result to cell D15. The resulting spreadsheet should resemble Lab Exhibit 1.1.3.

	A	B	C	D
1	Base Scenario		Scenario 1	Scenario 2
2			Per Lawn	Per Lawn
3				
4	Assumption: Total Lawns Serviced Each Month		200	200
5				
6	Revenue		50	50
7				
8	Costs			
9		Monthly		
10	Truck	300	1.50	1.50
11	Mowers	300	1.50	1.50
12	Other Equipment	100	0.50	0.50
13	Labor (Average $13/yard or $25/yard)		13.00	25.00
14	Maintenance	100	0.50	0.50
15	Insurance	300	1.50	1.50

10. In cell A16, type the word "Fuel". In both cells C16 and D16, insert the number 3, representing the fuel cost for each of the two scenarios.

11. In cell A17, type the word "Supplies". In both cells C17 and D17, insert the number 1.50, representing the supplies cost for each of the two scenarios.
12. In cell A18, type the word "Advertising". In cell B18, insert the number 50, representing the monthly advertising payment. To get the advertising cost per lawn, insert this formula in cell C18: =$B$18/C4. Copy the result to cell D18. The resulting spreadsheet should resemble Lab Exhibit 1.1.4.

Lab Exhibit 1.1.4

Microsoft Excel

	A	B	C	D
1	Base Scenario		Scenario 1	Scenario 2
2			Per Lawn	Per Lawn
3				
4	Assumption: Total Lawns Serviced Each Month		200	200
5				
6	Revenue		50	50
7				
8	Costs			
9		Monthly		
10	Truck	300	1.50	1.50
11	Mowers	300	1.50	1.50
12	Other Equipment	100	0.50	0.50
13	Labor (Average $13/yard or $25/yard)		13.00	25.00
14	Maintenance	100	0.50	0.50
15	Insurance	300	1.50	1.50
16	Fuel		3.00	3.00
17	Supplies		1.50	1.50
18	Advertising	50	0.25	0.25

13. Insert a single border at the bottom of cells C18:D18, as shown in Lab Exhibit 1.1.5.

Lab Exhibit 1.1.5

Microsoft Excel

	A	B	C	D
1	Base Scenario		Scenario 1	Scenario 2
2			Per Lawn	Per Lawn
3				
4	Assumption: Total Lawns Serviced Each Month		200	200
5				
6	Revenue		50	50
7				
8	Costs			
9		Monthly		
10	Truck	300	1.50	1.50
11	Mowers	300	1.50	1.50
12	Other Equipment	100	0.50	0.50
13	Labor (Average $13/yard or $25/yard)		13.00	25.00
14	Maintenance	100	0.50	0.50
15	Insurance	300	1.50	1.50
16	Fuel		3.00	3.00
17	Supplies		1.50	1.50
18	Advertising	50	0.25	0.25

Analysis Task 2: Calculate Cost and Margin per Lawn and in Total

1. In cell A19, type the words "Cost per Lawn". In cell C19, insert this formula: =SUM(C10:C18). In cell D19, insert the formula =SUM(D10:D18) to calculate the total cost of each scenario.

2. In cell A21, type the words "Margin per Lawn". In cell C21, insert this formula: =C6-C19. In cell D19, insert the formula =D6-D19 to calculate the total margin per lawn of each scenario.
3. In cell A23, type the words "Total Monthly Margin". In cell C23, insert this formula: =C21*C4, and in cell D19, insert the formula =D21*D4 to calculate the total monthly margin of each scenario.
4. The final spreadsheet should resemble Lab Exhibit 1.1.6.

	A	B	C	D
1	Base Scenario		Scenario 1	Scenario 2
2			per Lawn	per Lawn
3				
4	Assumption: Total Lawns Serviced Each Month		200	200
5				
6	**Revenue**		$50	$50
7				
8	**Costs**			
9		Monthly		
10	Truck	300	1.50	1.50
11	Mowers	300	1.50	1.50
12	Other Equipment	100	0.50	0.50
13	Labor (Average $13/lawn or $25/lawn)		13.00	25.00
14	Maintenance	100	0.50	0.50
15	Insurance	300	1.50	1.50
16	Fuel		3.00	3.00
17	Supplies		1.50	1.50
18	Advertising	50	0.25	0.25
19	Cost per Lawn		23.25	35.25
20				
21	Margin per Lawn		26.75	14.75
22				
23	Total Monthly Margin		5350.00	2950.00

Lab Exhibit 1.1.6

Microsoft Excel

Share the Story

We note that a big difference between the two scenarios is the cost of labor for each lawn. It would be good to know how profitability changes based on the price of labor, which will allow us to assess how profitable the mowing business could be. To conduct this assessment, we will evaluate profitability using Excel's data table for the labor rate from $13 (low end) to $25 (high end) per lawn.

DATA VISUALIZATION

1. Input "Labor Cost per Lawn" in cell B27.
2. Input 13 in cell B28, 15 in cell B29, 17 in cell B30, 19 in cell B31, 21 in cell B32, 23 in cell B33, and 25 in cell B34.
3. In cell C27, insert =C23. This command tells the data table which cell to compute based on the inputs.
4. Highlight cells B27:C34 and select **Data > What-If Analysis > Data Table**.

5. In **Column input cell**, input $C$13, as shown in Lab Exhibit 1.1.7. This tells the data table which input will vary.

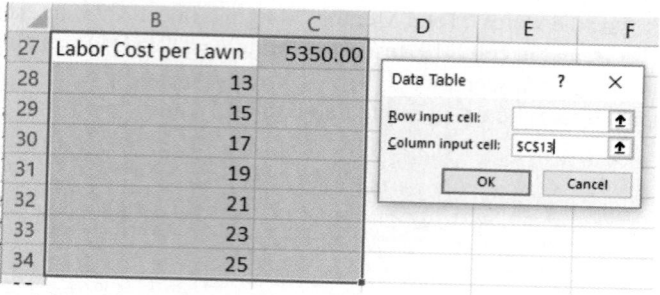

	B	C	D	E	F
27	Labor Cost per Lawn	5350.00			
28	13				
29	15				
30	17				
31	19				
32	21				
33	23				
34	25				

Data Table ? ✕
Row input cell: [   ] ↑
Column input cell: [$C$13] ↑
OK   Cancel

6. Select **OK**.
7. Copy the cells to another area of the spreadsheet and replace the header of the second column with the words "Monthly Margin" to arrive at the result shown in Lab Exhibit 1.1.8.

Labor Cost per Lawn	Monthly Margin
13	5350
15	4950
17	4550
19	4150
21	3750
23	3350
25	2950

8. Highlight cells B28:C34, insert a scatterplot, and label the horizontal axis as Labor Cost per Lawn to arrive at the visualization shown in Lab Exhibit 1.1.9. Label the vertical axis as "Monthly Profit Margin". You might use this visualization in a brief written report or as part of a PowerPoint presentation.

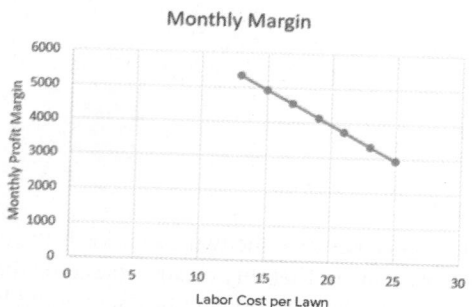

Assessment

1. Take a screenshot of the completed spreadsheet, paste it into a Word document named "Lab 1.1 Submission.docx", and label the screenshot Submission 1.
2. Take a screenshot of the scatterplot showing labor cost per lawn and monthly margin, paste it into the same Word document, and label the screenshot Submission 2.
3. Answer the questions in Connect and upload your Lab 1.1 Submission.docx via Connect if assigned.

Assessing the Profitability of a Small Business

Apply the same steps in Lab 1.1 to the **Lab 1.1 Data.xlsx** dataset with two modifications. The same scenarios exist as before, with labor costing either $13/lawn or $25/lawn. Assume that your mowing business will mow 350 lawns per month rather than 200 lawns per month. Also assume that the cost for advertising increases from $50 to $300 per month. Label these two new scenarios Scenario 3 (with labor costing $13/lawn) and Scenario 4 (with labor costing $25/lawn).

Ask the Question

What is the profit on each lawn if the mowing business mows 350 lawns per month? What is the business's total profit per month?

Required

1. Assess whether this mowing business will be profitable if you mow 350 lawns per month.
2. Show a visualization of the change in monthly margin based on a range of labor costs per lawn.

Assessment

1. Take a screenshot of the completed spreadsheet, paste it into a Word document named "Alt Lab 1.1 Submission.docx", and label the screenshot Submission 3.
2. Take a screenshot of the visualization showing labor cost per lawn and monthly margin, paste it into the same Word document, and label the screenshot Submission 4.
3. Answer the questions in Connect and upload your Alt Lab 1.1 Submission.docx via Connect if assigned.

Lab 1.2   Excel

Lab Note: The tools presented in this lab periodically change. Updated instructions, if applicable, can be found in the student and instructor support materials. All Lab Exhibits are available within the eBook and in Connect.

Working with Data in Excel: Ranges and Tables

Data Analytics Type: Descriptive Analytics

Keywords

Range, Table, Pivot Table

Decision-Making Context

In Excel, there are three primary ways to organize data: a range, a table, and a pivot table. There are advantages to all three. In this lab, we explore how and why to work with data in range and table formats.

Required

Use Excel to determine which data-organization technique is most useful for each data type.

Ask the Question

What are the various ways of organizing the data to facilitate analysis?

Master the Data

For this lab you will use data in the Excel file titled **Lab 1.2 Data.xlsx**. The dataset contains information about sales transactions to different customers. There are 132 unique transactions but 150 rows—this is because some of the transactions included multiple products. The data dictionary follows.

Data Dictionary

Table	Attribute Name	Description	Data Type
Sales_Transactions	Sales_Order_ID	Unique identifier for each individual sales order	String (text)
Sales_Transactions	Sales_Order_Date	Date each sales order was placed	Date
Sales_Transactions	Sales_Employee_ID	Unique identifier for the employee who was responsible for taking the sales order	String (text)
Sales_Transactions	Customer_ID	Unique identifier for the customer who placed the sales order	String (text)
Sales_Transactions	Product_Code	Unique identifier for the product sold on the order	String (text)
Sales_Transactions	Sales_Order_Quantity_Sold	Quantity of each product sold on the transaction	Numerical
Sales_Transactions	Product_Sale_Price	Price of the product on the day it was sold	Numerical

Perform the Analysis

Analysis Task #1: Discover How Excel Interacts with Range Data

1. Navigate to the **Sales_Transactions_Range** worksheet tab. Although these data resemble a table (with organized columns and rows and clearly marked headings), they are formatted as a range in Excel. A range of data in Excel is the default when entering data. Even if the columns have headings, the data are still organized as a range.
2. In this range of data, add a column to calculate the amount of the invoice for each line item by multiplying Sales_Order_Quantity_Sold by Product_Sale_Price.
3. In cell H1, type in the heading "Invoice Amount".
4. In cell H2, type in a formula multiplying 12 and 105 by referencing the cells F2 and G2, as shown in Lab Exhibit 1.2.1. The formula is =F2*G2.
5. Click **Enter** to see the result of the formula. Notice that once you click **Enter**, the result of the formula (12*105) appears, and the active cell moves to the cell below, H3.
6. Copy the results of the formula down the rest of the column. To do so, place your cursor in the bottom right of cell H2 (the cell with the formula in it that you would like to copy) and double-click the **plus sign (+)**, as shown in Lab Exhibit 1.2.2.
7. Once the formula is copied all the way down the column, click into any of the cells with the new formula in Column H to see that Excel not only copied the formula all the way down the column but also adjusted the cell references in the formula to reflect each shift down one row, as shown in Lab Exhibit 1.2.3.

Lab Exhibit 1.2.3 illustrates the Excel technique called **relative referencing**. If you were to copy a formula to the left or right, or to the cell above or below, then the references will adjust *relative* to the direction you copied the cell.

Data Tip

Absolute and Relative References

Relative referencing is useful, but sometimes you will want to always reference the same cell you initially referenced, rather than automatically shifting the reference relative to where the formula is copied. In these instances, you can override Excel's default of relative referencing by using **absolute references**. An absolute reference "locks" the cell reference in place. To lock a cell into place, select the cell reference that you wish to lock and press F4 on your keyboard (or FN + F4 on a laptop). Doing so will change the formatting of the cell reference in the formula so that it has dollar signs to the left of the column and row references. If you continue clicking F4, it functions as a toggle key. You will see the dollar signs shift; when the dollar sign is only next to the row reference, then the column will still shift relative to where you copy the formula, but the row will be locked. When the dollar sign is only next to the column reference, then only the column is locked. The last time you click F4, you will shift out of all absolute references.

In this formula, cell F2 is absolutely referenced for columns and rows:

=$F$2*G2

In this formula, cell F2 is absolutely referenced for just the row:

=F$2*G2

In this formula, cell F2 is absolutely referenced for just the column:

=$F2*G2

Analysis Task #2: Discover How Excel Interacts with Table Data.

Repeat the same steps in the Sales_Transactions_Table tab to see how Excel interacts with data formatted as a table differently than how it works with data in a range. We will also perform a few steps to gain general familiarity with the functions provided in an Excel table.

1. Click into the **Sales_Transactions_Table** worksheet tab. This set of data appears different because of the blue shading, which is typically Excel's default format for tables (although when you connect to external data, Excel defaults to a green format). Also notice that each heading has a drop-down arrow next to it because Excel tables default to providing a method for filtering the data based on every column in the table.

2. Click the drop-down button next to the **Product_Code** header, unselect **(Select All)**, and select **2003**. Then click **OK** (Lab Exhibit 1.2.4). These actions will filter the results so that only the sales transactions that include product 2003 appear.

3. Return to the same filter and select <u>Clear Filter From "Product_Code"</u> to restore the table to show all the records (Lab Exhibit 1.2.5). When a column is filtered, the filter icon replaces the down arrow. This icon helps users of the table determine whether the data have been filtered or not.

4. Another default of tables is the Total Row. From the **Table Design** tab (in the **Table Style Options** section of the ribbon), place a checkmark next to **Total Row**, as shown in Lab Exhibit 1.2.6.

5. Scroll to the bottom of the Excel spreadsheet to see the new Total Row. Excel defaulted to providing a sum of the Product_Sale_Price, as shown in Lab Exhibit 1.2.7.

6. Click into the cell to the left of the sum of Product_Sale_Price (cell F151, the total cell for Sales_Order_Quantity_Sold). A drop-down arrow will appear. Click it and select **Sum**, as shown in Lab Exhibit 1.2.8.

    This default in **Tables** is available for every column. However, Excel tables don't adjust the options for the type of data in each column, so be careful not to select a summary value that doesn't make sense for a column's data type.

7. Scroll back to the top of the dataset to create a new column. Replicate the steps taken in the **Sales_Transactions_Range** tab to add a column to calculate the amount of the invoice for each line item by multiplying Sales_Order_Quantity_Sold by Product_Sale_Price.

8. In cell H1, type in the heading "Invoice Amount". Then click **Enter**. Notice that Excel immediately formatted the entire column to fit into the table.

9. In cell H2, type in a formula multiplying 12 and 105 by referencing cells F2 and G2, as shown in Lab Exhibit 1.2.9.

    There are a few interesting things to note here. Even though you are referencing cells F2 and G2, the formula presents column headers as the references in the formula. This format is excellent for making reports and tables more understandable for people who did not create them.

10. Click **Enter** to see the result of the formula. Another great aspect of working with Excel tables has just revealed itself: The formula automatically copied all the way down the table.

Share the Story

You have now worked with Excel data in ranges and in tables, and you've learned how Excel interacts differently with data depending on the format in which they are stored. At some point in your career, you will likely have to train new employees or interns; showing them what you just learned in this lab will be very helpful.

Assessment

1. Return to the **Sales_Transactions_Range** worksheet tab. Take a screenshot of the data, including the new column for Invoice Amount. Label it "Screenshot 1" and paste it into a Microsoft Word document titled "Lab 1.2 Submission.docx".
2. Return to the **Sales_Transactions_Table** worksheet tab. Take a screenshot of the data, including the new column for Invoice Amount. Label it "Screenshot 2" and paste it into your Word document.
3. Answer the questions in Connect and upload your Lab 1.2 Submission.docx via Connect if assigned.

Alternate Lab 1.2 Excel—On Your Own

Working with Data in Excel: Ranges and Tables

Keywords

Range, Table, Pivot Table

Apply the same steps in Lab 1.2 to the **Alt Lab 1.2 Data.xlsx** dataset. These data are purchasing data rather than sales data, so instead of working with Sales_Order_Quantity_Sold, you will work with Quantity_Purchased, and instead of working with Products, you will work with Raw_Materials.

Required

1. Create a new column in the **Purchase_Orders_Range** tab for PO Amount and copy it down the column. Keep in mind that the columns are in a different order than they were in the first dataset.
2. Create a new column in the **Purchase_Orders_Table** for PO Amount and ensure it copies down automatically.

Assessment

1. Return to the **Purchase_Orders_Range** spreadsheet. Take a screenshot of the data, including the new column for Invoice Amount. Label it "Screenshot 1" and paste it into a Microsoft Word document titled Alt Lab 1.2 Submission.docx.
2. Return to the **Purchase_Orders_Table** spreadsheet. Take a screenshot of the data, including the new column for Invoice Amount. Label it "Screenshot 2" and paste it into your Word document.
3. Answer the questions in Connect and upload your Alt Lab 1.2 Submission.docx via Connect if assigned.

gross margin
Net sales minus the cost of goods sold. Gross margin is the amount of revenue a company retains after deducting the direct costs of producing a good or service.

SKU
Stock-keeping unit, a unique code for each product sold.

Assessing Product (SKU) Profitability with Pivot Tables

Data Analytics Type: Descriptive Analytics

Keywords

SKU, Product Profitability, Inventory Management

Decision-Making Context

Merchandising companies sell products to customers. They make money by selling the products for more than what they paid. In this lab, we compute the gross margin for each product to identify the company's most profitable products. This analysis allows merchandising companies to focus their efforts on selling the most profitable products, which in turn helps them make more profits.

Required

1. Create a histogram of the gross margin percentages using bins of 0.025 size.
2. Create a list of SKUs in the highest 0.025 bin (from 0.40 to 0.425).
3. Create a histogram visualization.

Ask the Question

Which products (SKUs) are the most profitable to sell?

Master the Data

Fancy Fruits is a fictitious mail-order business that sells exotic fruit from around the world to customers throughout the United States. The company keeps a price list for each product. We will work from this price list to find the items that are most profitable per dollar of sales. This is the data dictionary:

Data Dictionary	
SKU	Fancy Fruits' SKU (unique code for each fruit product sold)
Description	Description of each fruit sold
Sales price per pound	Total sales price per pound of product
Cost per pound	Total cost of product sold per pound of product

Open Excel file **Lab 1.3 Data.xlsx**, which includes the Fancy Fruits price list. A snippet of the spreadsheet appears in Lab Exhibit 1.3E.1.

Perform the Analysis

Analysis Task #1: Compute the Gross Margin and Gross Margin Percentage for Each Product (SKU)

1. We first need to compute the gross margin for each SKU. A SKU, or stock-keeping unit, is an alphanumeric identification that tracks the inventory of a particular product.

2. Go to cell E1 and insert the title "Gross Margin". Also insert a bottom border. In cell E2, we'll compute the gross margin on each line item sold. To do so, we must subtract the cost in cell D2 from the sales in cell C2. Insert the formula =C2-D2 and hit **Enter** (Lab Exhibit 1.3E.2). Next, copy that formula down for every sale below from cell E3:E82.
3. We also need to compute the gross margin percentage, which is the percent of every dollar of sales that is gross margin. Go to cell F1 and insert the title "Gross Margin Percentage". To compute the gross margin percentage, go to cell F2 and enter =E2/C2 as shown in Lab Exhibit 1.3E.3.
4. Then copy that formula down for every sale below from cell F3:F82.

Analysis Task #2: Sort the Gross Margin Percentages into Buckets Using Excel's Data Analysis ToolPak

1. To share the story, it is important to be able to visualize the results. To do so, we will plot the gross margin percentages using a histogram to see the frequency of gross margin percentages in each bin.
2. Insert in cell I1 the word "Bins". Also insert a bottom border. Insert the following bins beginning in cell I2 and continuing through cell I6: 0, 0.35, 0.375, 0.40, and 0.425, as shown in Lab Exhibit 1.3E.4.
3. We will need the Data Analysis ToolPak to use the **Histogram** tool. If you haven't installed the Data Analysis ToolPak, Appendix D at the end of this textbook provides instructions for installing the ToolPak. Once the Data Analysis ToolPak is installed, go to **Data > Analysis > Data Analysis > Histogram**, as shown in Lab Exhibit 1.3E.5.
4. For **Input Range**, input $F$1:$F$82 to get all of the gross margin percentage possibilities.
5. For **Bin Range**, input $I$1:$I$6 to get all of the bin possibilities.
6. Select **Labels**, as we have included the labels in our bin range. Steps 4–6 are shown in Lab Exhibit 1.3E.6.
7. Select **OK** to get the result that is shown in Lab Exhibit 1.3E.7.

Analysis Task #3: Sort the Gross Margin Percentages into Buckets Using a Pivot Table

1. We'll now work on the second requirement: Get a list of SKUs in the highest 0.025 bin (from 0.40 to 0.425). We could sort the gross margin percentages from lowest to highest and copy the 24 SKUs in that range. A second, more sophisticated way to get that list is to use a pivot table.
2. To do so, first click in the table itself and then click on **Insert > Pivot Table** after clicking on one cell of the data.
3. Drag **[Gross Margin Percentage]** from **FIELD NAME** into the **Rows** field and **[SKU]** from **FIELD NAME** into the $\sum$**Value**s field in the pivot table. The $\sum$Values will default to "Count of SKU". The resulting pivot table will resemble Lab Exhibit 1.3E.8.
4. Right-click on one of the numbers under Row Labels in column A and select **Group**.
5. Insert 0.325 for **Starting at:**, 0.425 for **Ending at:**, and 0.025 for **By:** in the **Grouping** dialog box, as shown in Lab Exhibit 1.3E.9.
6. Select **OK** to get the result shown in Lab Exhibit 1.3E.10.
    Note that the counts of SKUs in each bin are the same as those shown in the histogram in Lab Exhibit 1.3E.12.
7. The second requirement asks us to get a detailed listing of the products that are in the 0.4 to 0.425 gross margin percentage range. To do so, all we need to do is double-click on cell B7 with the 23 under **Count of SKU**. Double-clicking on it will give us the list of the products in the 0.4 to 0.425 range, as shown in Lab Exhibit 1.3E.11.

Share the Story: Visualizing the Histogram Using a Pivot Chart

It is important to visualize the counts of products in each percentage bin. To visualize, highlight any cell in the pivot table, then click **Pivot Chart** and select **Clustered Column** to see the visualization as shown in Lab Exhibit 1.3E.12.

The histogram gives us a good illustration of the distribution of the gross margin percentages.

We can share the story by reporting our findings to the sales staff and company management to identify the inventory items (fruits) that are most profitable. Potentially, the company could send additional advertising emails to its customers promoting these high-gross-margin products. The company might also stop purchasing and selling some of the items with the lowest gross margin percentages to concentrate on sales of products with a higher gross margin percentage.

Assessment

1. Take a screenshot of your detailed listing of fruit products sold from the 0.4 to 0.425 gross margin percentage range, paste it into a Word document named "Lab 1.3 Excel Submission.docx", and label the screenshot Submission 1.
2. Take a screenshot of your histogram as a pivot chart, paste it into the same Word document, and label the screenshot Submission 2.
3. Answer the questions in Connect and upload your Lab 1.3 Excel Submission.docx via Connect if assigned.

Lab 1.3   Tableau

Assessing Product (SKU) Profitability

Data Analytics Type: Descriptive Analytics

Keywords
Customer Profitability, Inventory Management, Customer Relationship Management

Decision-Making Context
Merchandising companies sell products to customers. They make money by selling the products for more than what they paid. In this lab, we compute the gross margin for each product to identify the company's most profitable products. This analysis allows merchandising companies to focus their efforts on selling the most profitable products, which in turn helps them make more profits.

Required
1. Create calculated fields for the gross margin and gross margin percentage.
2. Create a histogram to visualize the distribution of gross margin percentage across SKUs.
3. Adjust the automated bin size to .025.
4. Create a list of SKUs in the highest bin.

Ask the Question
Which products (SKUs) are the most profitable to sell?

Master the Data
Fancy Fruits is a fictitious mail-order business that sells exotic fruit from around the world to customers throughout the United States. The company keeps a price list for each product. We will work from this price list to find the items that are most profitable per dollar of sales. This is the data dictionary:

Data Dictionary

SKU	Fancy Fruits' SKU (unique code for each fruit product sold)
Description	Description of each fruit sold
Sales price per pound	Total sales price per pound of product
Cost per pound	Total cost of product sold per pound of product

---

1. Open Tableau. Then open **Lab 1.3 Data.xlsx**.
2. Click **Sheet 1** to begin working with the data (Lab Exhibit 1.3T.1).

Perform the Analysis

Analysis Task #1: Compute the Gross Margin and Gross Margin Percentage for Each Product (SKU)

1. Right-click below the variable names and select **Create Calculated Field . . .** (Lab Exhibit 1.3T.2).

Lab Note: The tools presented in this lab periodically change. Updated instructions, if applicable, can be found in the student and instructor support materials. All Lab Exhibits are available within the eBook and in Connect.

gross margin
Net sales minus the cost of goods sold. Gross margin is the amount of revenue a company retains after deducting the direct costs of producing a good or service.

SKU
Stock-keeping unit, a unique code for each product sold.

2. Name your new calculated field "Gross Margin".
3. Gross Margin is calculated by subtracting the Cost per pound field from the Sales Price per Pound field. Type in **Sales Price per Pound – Cost per pound** (Lab Exhibit 1.3T.3). Tableau will automatically configure the words into references to the fields in the dataset.
4. Create a second calculated field. Name your new calculated field "Gross Margin Percentage", which is the percent of every dollar of sales that is gross margin. It is calculated by dividing Gross Margin by Sales Price per Pound. Type in **Gross Margin / Sales Price per Pound**. Tableau will automatically configure the words into references to the fields in the dataset (Lab Exhibit 1.3T.4). Click **OK**.

DATA VISUALIZATION

Analysis Task #2: Create a Histogram

1. To get started, we want to create a histogram to display the distribution of gross margin percentage across SKUs.
   Double-click **Gross Margin Percentage** to begin working with the measure. Notice that Tableau defaults to displaying the value as an aggregate measure (SUM) in a bar chart.
2. To change this default visualization to a histogram, select histogram from the **Show Me** menu, as shown in Lab Exhibit 1.3T.5.
3. The histogram will default to very narrow bins.
4. To change the bin size, select the new **Gross Margin Percentage (bin)** dimension, and then select **Edit** from the menu (Lab Exhibit 1.3T.6).
5. Change the **Size of bins** to **0.025**, then click **OK**, as shown in Lab Exhibit 1.3T.7.

Analysis Task #3: Access a List of SKUs in the Highest Bin

1. We'll now work on the next requirement: Get a list of SKUs in the highest 0.025 bin (from 0.40 to 0.425). To do so, we can sort the gross margin percentages from lowest to highest and copy the 24 SKUs in that range.
   Right-click on **Sheet 1**, then click <u>**Rename**</u> to rename the sheet (Lab Exhibit 1.3T.8).
2. Rename the sheet "Histogram".
3. Open a new sheet by clicking on the icon shown in Lab Exhibit 1.3T.9.
4. Name this new sheet "Tabular Data."
5. Double-click **SKU** to get a unique list of all of the SKUs in the dataset, and then double-click **Gross Margin Percentage**.
6. Double-click **Description** to make the tabular data more interesting and intuitive to interpret.

Analysis Task #4: Create a Dashboard Summarizing the Analysis Performed

1. We can create a dashboard to view both of our charts in the same pane. Click the icon shown in Lab Exhibit 1.3T.10 to create a new dashboard.
2. Drag and drop each Sheet (**Histogram** and **Tabular Data**) to the **Dashboard** pane (Lab Exhibit 1.3T.11).
3. Click the histogram sheet to make it active, and select the **Use as Filter** button. This will allow you to click any of the bars in the histogram to activate that bin as a filter for the entire dashboard (Lab Exhibit 1.3T.12).
4. Click the bin with the highest percentages in it to filter the Tabular Data list (Lab Exhibit 1.3T.13).
5. When in the tabular graphic, you can also sort your results by clicking the sort buttons in the menu (Lab Exhibit 1.3T.14).

Share the Story

With the histogram and the dashboard, we can share the story by reporting our findings to the sales staff and company management to identify the inventory items (fruits) that are most profitable. Potentially the company could send additional advertising emails to our customers promoting these high-gross-margin products. The company might also stop purchasing and selling some of the items with the lowest gross margin percentages to concentrate on sales of products with a higher gross margin percentage.

Assessment

1. Take a screenshot of your histogram, paste it into a Word document named "Lab 1.3 Tableau Submission.docx", and label the screenshot Submission 1.
2. Take a screenshot of your dashboard, paste it into the same Word document, and label the screenshot Submission 2.
3. Answer the questions in Connect and upload your Lab 1.3 Tableau Submission.docx via Connect if assigned.

Lab 1.3 Power BI

Lab Note: The tools presented in this lab periodically change. Updated instructions, if applicable, can be found in the student and instructor support materials. All Lab Exhibits are available within the eBook and in Connect.

gross margin
Net sales minus the cost of goods sold. Gross margin is the amount of revenue a company retains after deducting the direct costs of producing a good or service.

SKU
Stock-keeping unit, a unique code for each product sold.

Assessing Product (SKU) Profitability

Data Analytics Type: Descriptive Analytics

Keywords

Customer Profitability, Inventory Management, Customer Relationship Management

Decision-Making Context

Merchandising companies sell products to customers. They make money by selling the products for more than what they paid. In this lab, we compute the gross margin for each product to identify the company's most profitable products. This analysis allows merchandising companies to focus their efforts on selling the most profitable products, which in turn helps them make more profits.

Required

1. Create calculated fields for the gross margin and gross margin percentage.
2. Create a histogram to visualize the distribution of gross margin percentage across SKUs.
3. Adjust the automated bin size to .025.
4. Create a list of SKUs in the highest bin.

Ask the Question

Which products (SKUs) are the most profitable to sell?

Master the Data

Fancy Fruits is a (fictitious) mail-order business that sells exotic fruit from around the world to customers throughout the United States. The company keeps a price list for each product. We will work from this price list to find the items that are most profitable per dollar of sales. The data dictionary explains which data are included in the dataset.

Data Dictionary

SKU	Fancy Fruits' SKU (unique code for each fruit product sold)
Description	Description of each fruit sold
Sales price per pound	Total sales price per pound of product
Cost per pound	Total cost of product sold per pound of product

---

1. Open Power BI Desktop. From Power BI Desktop, click **Home > Get Data > Excel Workbook,** then browse to the location where you have saved the file **Lab 1.3 Data. xlsx,** and click **Open.**

2. In the **Navigator** window, check the box next to **Sheet 1** and click **Load** to begin working with the data.

Perform the Analysis

Analysis Task #1: Compute the Gross Margin and Gross Margin Percentage for Each Product (SKU)

1. In the Ribbon, click **Home > Modeling > New Column** to create a new calculated field.
2. Name your new calculated field "Gross Margin". Gross Margin is calculated by subtracting the Cost per pound field from the Sales Price per Pound field. Type in **Gross Margin = Sheet1[Sales Price per Pound] – Sheet 1[Cost per pound]** as shown in Lab Exhibit 1.3P.1.
3. Create a second calculated field. Name your new calculated field "Gross Margin Percentage", which is the percent of every dollar of sales that is gross margin. It is calculated by dividing Gross Margin by Sales Price per Pound. Type in **Gross Margin Percentage = Sheet1[Gross Margin]/Sheet1[Sales Price per Pound]**.

Analysis Task #2: Create a Histogram

DATA VISUALIZATION

1. To get started, we want to create a histogram to display the distribution of gross margin percentage across SKUs.
2. Right-click **Gross Margin Percentage** in your **Fields** pane and choose **New Group** (as shown in Lab Exhibit 1.3P.2).
3. The histogram will default to very narrow bins. Change the **Bin size** to .025, then click **OK**, as shown in Lab Exhibit 1.3P.3.
4. Next, create the histogram. Click the blank area on your page and then click the **Stacked Column Chart** icon in the **Visualizations** pane. Resize the chart to fill the left side of the page.
5. Check the box next to **Gross Margin Percentage (bins)** to add it to the axis.
6. Check the box next to **Gross Margin Percentage** to add it to the Values. It will default to a Sum, so click the drop-down next to **Gross Margin Percentage** in the Values area and select **Count** to change the aggregate value.

Analysis Task #3: Access a List of SKUs in the Highest Bin

1. We'll now work on the next requirement: Get a list of SKUs in the highest 0.025 bin (from 0.40 to 0.425). To do this, we can sort the gross margin percentages from lowest to highest and copy the 24 SKUs in that range.
2. Click the blank area on your page and then click the **Matrix** icon in the **Visualizations** pane. Resize the chart to fill the right side of the page.
3. Click **SKU** to get a unique list of all of the SKUs in the dataset as rows.
4. Drag **Description** to the **Values** box to make the tabular data more interesting and intuitive to interpret.
5. Click **Gross Margin Percentage** to show the values.
6. Click the bin with the highest percentages in it to filter the Tabular Data list (see Lab Exhibit 1.3P.4).
7. Remember that you can also sort your results by clicking the sort buttons in the menu.

Share the Story

We share the story with the sales staff and company management to identify the products (SKUs) that are most profitable. The company may want to emphasize the marketing of these products in the future.

Assessment

1. Take a screenshot of page 1 with the histogram and the table, paste it into a Word document named "Lab 1.3 Power BI Submission.docx", and label the screenshot Submission 1.
2. Take a screenshot of your dashboard, paste it into the same Word document, and label the screenshot Submission 2.
3. Answer the questions in Connect and upload your Lab 1.3 Power BI Submission.docx via Connect if assigned.

Alternate Lab 1.3—On Your Own

Assessing Product (SKU) Profitability

Apply the same steps in Lab 1.3 Excel (or Lab 1.3 Tableau or Lab 1.3 Power BI) to the **Alt Lab 1.3 Data.xlsx** dataset using your tool of choice.

Open Excel file **Alt Lab 1.3 Data.xlsx** and follow similar directions to those in Lab 1.3 Excel above.

ThrustMaster is a fictitious company that sells game controllers, joysticks, and steering wheels for PCs and for Xbox, Nintendo, and PlayStation consoles. A summary of the price list of its products by SKU is included in the Excel spreadsheet.

Required

1. Draw a histogram of the gross margin percentages using bins of 0.025 size. Use bins 0.425, 0.45, 0.475, 0.5.
2. Get a list of SKUs in the highest 0.025 bin (from 0.475 to 0.5).

gross margin
Net sales minus the cost of goods sold. Gross margin is the amount of revenue a company retains after deducting the direct costs of producing a good or service.

Assessment

1. Take a screenshot of your detailed listing of gaming products sold from the 0.475 to 0.5 gross margin percentage range, paste it into a Word document named "Alt Lab 1.3 Submission.docx", and label the screenshot Submission 1.
2. Take a screenshot of your histogram as a pivot chart, paste it into the same Word document, and label the screenshot Submission 2.
3. Answer the questions in Connect and upload your Alt Lab 1.3 Submission.docx via Connect if assigned.

Chapter 2

An Introduction to Cost Data

A Look at This Chapter

To answer the management accounting questions introduced in Chapter 1, we must establish a common language, or vocabulary, and identify sources of relevant data. This chapter introduces the cost classifications and highlights relevant data sources used by management accountants. It also explains how and why data sources are combined to answer cost accounting questions (using VLOOKUP functions and data table linking). The chapter concludes with a discussion of relevant software tools (including Excel, Tableau, and Power BI) and their capabilities.

Cost Accounting and Data Analytics

COST ACCOUNTING LEARNING OBJECTIVE		RELATED DATA ANALYTICS LAB(S)	LAB ANALYTICS TYPE(S)
LO 2.1	Define a cost object.		
LO 2.2	Differentiate between direct costs and indirect costs.		
LO 2.3	Compare and contrast fixed, variable, and mixed costs.	**LAB 2.1 Excel** Assessing Fixed, Variable, and Mixed Costs Using Scatterplots	Descriptive, Diagnostic
LO 2.4	Define product costs and period costs.		
LO 2.5	Identify the sources of cost accounting data.		
LO 2.6	Describe different data attributes and data types, and explain how to use a relational database.	**Data Analytics Mini-Lab** Linking Tables Using VLOOKUP in Excel	Descriptive
		LAB 2.2 Excel Linking Tables in Excel Using the VLOOKUP Command and Pivot Tables (Heartwood)	Descriptive
		LAB 2.3 Excel Linking Tables in Excel Using an Internal Data Model (Heartwood)	Descriptive
LO 2.7	Compare and contrast available data-analysis software tools and their specialties.	**LAB 2.4 Tableau** Linking Tables and Creating Visualizations (Heartwood)	Descriptive
		LAB 2.5 Power BI Linking Tables and Performing Analysis (Heartwood)	Descriptive

Chapter Concepts and Career Skills

Learning About . . .	Helps with These Career Skills
Cost objects	• Defining a company's costs
Direct vs. indirect costs	• Determining which costs are tracked directly and which costs are not tracked directly
Fixed, variable, and mixed costs	• Determining a firm's pricing and marketing strategies
Product vs. period costs, and prime vs. conversion costs	• Understanding the nature of costs and how they impact the accounting for costs overall
Cost accounting data sources	• Recognizing and using data from various sources to address management questions
Relational databases	• Understanding how databases link attributes of different customers, sales transactions, vendors, payroll, employees, and suppliers to each other using tables and primary and foreign keys
Analytics software tools, including Excel, Tableau, and Power BI	• Matching the most applicable software tool to the management accounting task

Mike Mareen/Shutterstock

What Is the Cost of Tesla's New Cybertruck?

What does it cost to build **Tesla**'s new Cybertruck? Can Tesla use its existing plants to assemble another product (beyond Models 3, X, S, Y)? As it prepares to manufacture the new Cybertruck, can Tesla save money on tooling? Will its cost structure change from its current products, including its mix of fixed and variable costs, or direct and indirect costs?[1]

In this chapter, we introduce and explain the cost accounting terminology necessary to evaluate and categorize costs, which enables companies to determine profitability (total revenues minus total costs). We also identify the internal and external data sources that may be useful in addressing management's questions about cost, revenue, and profitability.

Throughout this book we use many companies to illustrate management accounting principles. One company that we will refer to in either the text or labs of every chapter is **Heartwood Cabinets**, which was founded in 1965 in the southeastern United States. What started as a small family business has grown into a multinational company with over $1 billion in annual revenue. Heartwood sells cabinets in hundreds of sizes, styles, and finishes, allowing consumers to customize cabinets to fit their needs. Heartwood cabinets can be purchased through major big-box retailers or directly from the company's website. Over the past 20 years, Heartwood has become the go-to supplier for many homebuilders and has expanded rapidly during recent home-building booms.[2]

---

[1]Frank Markus, "Cybercurrency: What the Tesla Cybertruck Will Really Cost to Build," *MotorTrend,* January 20, 2020, www.motortrend.com/news/tesla-cybertruck-electric-pickup-will-cost-build/ (accessed June 8, 2021).
[2]Heartwood Cabinets is a real company, but for purposes of confidentiality we have changed its name.

DEFINING COST AND THE COST OBJECT

A **cost** is the monetary value of the resources used or sacrificed to achieve a certain objective, such as the production of a product or the delivery of a service. For example, **Tesla** incurs costs to manufacture its Cybertruck, and **Apple** incurs costs in designing and manufacturing the iPhone. Enormous hospitals and individual doctors' offices incur costs in providing medical care, and your local landscaper incurs costs to mow lawns and trim trees.

Understanding costs is fundamental to making strategic decisions. For example, managers may need to decide whether to purchase a new factory or invest in increasing the efficiency of existing facilities, or they may wonder which products and services are most profitable. Managers may also examine costs to determine whether to undertake an advertising campaign to attract new customers, or to improve customer loyalty by focusing on customer service or product quality.

All of these decisions require management accountants to analyze cost objects. A **cost object** is anything for which a measurement of costs is wanted or needed. Management accountants can identify very large cost objects (such as divisions, departments, and production processes) or granular cost objects (such as specific products, services, or customers). The choice of cost object depends on the information that is required or requested by management. Exhibit 2.1 provides examples of various cost objects for Tesla and **Heartwood Cabinets**.

Type of Cost Object	Cost Object Examples at Tesla	Cost Object Examples at Heartwood Cabinets
Product	Cybertruck	Bathroom vanities
Process	Assembly	Gluing
Service	Warranty service	Reworking returned items
Department	Charging stations (setting up and maintaining Tesla charging stations around the world)	Wood procurement for raw materials
Customer	**AT&T** needing vehicles to service its network	**Fulton Homes** (Arizona home builders) needing cabinets for its homes

Exhibit 2.1
Examples of Cost Objects at Tesla and Heartwood Cabinets

✓ PROGRESS CHECK

1. What is an example of a cost object at **Apple**?
2. Who is interested in tracking, accumulating, and assigning costs for the production of a **Tesla** Cybertruck? How will they use this cost information?

DIRECT COSTS AND INDIRECT COSTS

How do companies assign costs to cost objects? The answer is determined by an important cost classification: direct vs. indirect costs.

Direct costs are costs that can be identified as belonging to a specific cost object. The process of identifying and assigning direct costs to the relevant cost objects is known as

cost tracing
The process of identifying and assigning direct costs to the relevant cost objects.

direct materials
Materials that are traced to a product or job and tracked by the accounting system.

direct labor
Employee labor (hands-on, touch labor) involved in producing goods or delivering services.

indirect costs
Costs related to a cost object but not easily or clearly traceable to it.

manufacturing overhead
Indirect costs that are essential to the manufacturing of goods.

cost allocation
The process of assigning indirect costs to the relevant cost objects.

cost tracing. Common examples of direct costs include the **direct materials** (tangible components of a finished product) and **direct labor** used to construct a finished product or deliver a service. Sales commissions are another type of direct cost. Most of the primary activities in the value chain that we discussed in Chapter 1—inbound logistics, operations, outbound logistics, marketing and sales activities, and service activities—incur direct costs.

For example, if **Tesla** is trying to determine its direct costs for the Cybertruck, it can sum the direct costs traced to manufacturing and preparing each Cybertruck. These direct costs likely include the costs of the battery, the engine, the tires, and the wages of laborers who work on the Cybertruck assembly line.

Indirect costs are related to a cost object but not easily or clearly traceable to it. Indirect costs at Tesla include production supervisor salaries, quality control costs, insurance costs, the costs of development and tooling, and depreciation. For example, a production supervisor's salary is an indirect cost because Tesla does not trace the number of minutes the supervisor spends on each vehicle. Indirect costs that are essential to the manufacturing of goods are known as **manufacturing overhead**. Because it is difficult to trace most of the value-chain supporting activities (firm infrastructure, human resource management, technology, and procurement) to the cost object directly, the costs of these activities are usually considered indirect costs.[3]

Because indirect costs are not traced to specific cost objects, accountants must estimate how much indirect cost to assign to specific cost objects (such as the different car models at Tesla) through the process of **cost allocation**.

FROM THE FIELD

Companies Decide Whether or Not to Trace Costs

Indirect costs are indirect because companies choose not to trace them. Companies could track each minute of a supervisor's time and make it a direct cost. They could also track every gram or ounce of indirect materials. In many but not all cases, it's just not worth the cost and effort to do so. Furniture manufacturing requires small amounts of glue whose cost isn't tracked, but jewelers do track the cost of the tiny diamonds they use in making jewelry. The decision to track or not to track is often based on a cost-benefit analysis.

Thinking Critically

Think about **Heartwood Cabinets**. Which costs of manufacturing cabinets might its accountants choose not to track?

Challenges of Allocating Indirect Costs

Indirect costs are not traced to cost objects for one of two reasons. First, a company may lack the technical ability to trace indirect costs to cost objects. For example, if an employee procures raw materials and parts (such as tires and batteries) for multiple **Tesla** car models, Tesla may not have systems in place to determine exactly how much of the employee's time (and associated salary) was spent for each part. Alternatively, a company may decide that tracing costs is not economically feasible. For example, even if **Heartwood Cabinets** could measure the amount of glue spent on each individual cabinet, the company may decide that doing so is a poor use of company resources.

---

[3]For a review of these terms, see Chapter 1.

One of the key jobs of the management accountant is to assist in the allocation of indirect costs, a topic we discuss in more detail in Chapters 4 and 5. If indirect costs are not correctly allocated to cost objects, then management may decide certain products are less (or more) profitable than they truly are, leading to faulty decision making.

FROM THE FIELD

The Importance of Allocating Indirect Costs Correctly

BY VERNON J. RICHARDSON

A few years ago, I was asked to testify in Arkansas state court regarding the appropriate allocation of indirect costs (overhead) to cigarettes. Some state regulators were alleging that the company was selling cigarettes below its costs, which is against Arkansas state law. After examining the company's allocation practices, I realized that the company was not using the appropriate method to allocate indirect costs to the cost objects (in this case, cigarettes and other products the company distributed).

While the state suggested that the indirect costs should be allocated on the basis of sales dollars for the products warehoused and distributed by the company (which would result in an abnormally high cost of cigarettes), I argued that there were many other more appropriate ways to allocate costs beyond sales dollars. Cigarettes are relatively lightweight, and they are arguably easier and lighter to transport than the other two primary products the company distributed, gallon water jugs and chocolate candy bars.

Thinking Critically

Which cost driver would you use to allocate overhead to cigarettes?

cost accumulation
The collection of cost data in an accounting system.

cost assignment
The process of (1) tracing direct costs to a cost object or (2) allocating indirect costs to a cost object.

Cost accumulation refers to the collection of cost data in an accounting system. **Cost assignment** is the process of (1) tracing direct costs to a cost object or (2) allocating indirect costs to a cost object. Exhibit 2.2 summarizes how accountants accumulate and assign direct and indirect costs, using the Tesla Cybertruck as an example. Actual direct costs are assigned to cost objects via cost tracing, while estimated indirect costs are allocated to cost objects.

Exhibit 2.2 Accumulation and Assignment of Direct and Indirect Costs for a Tesla Model

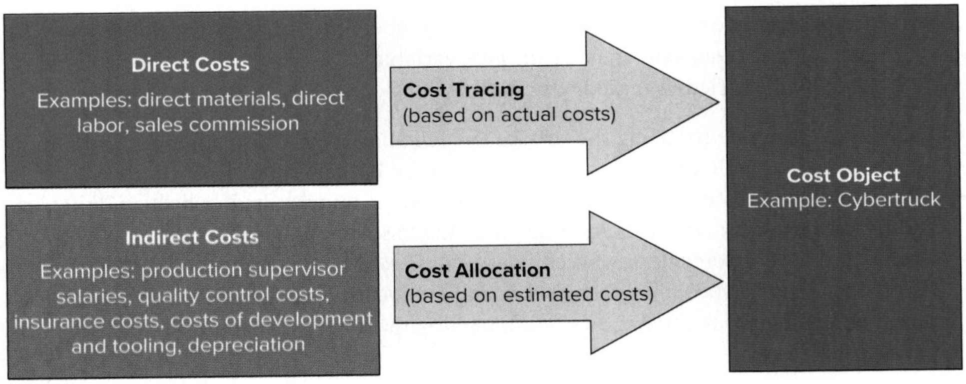

✓ PROGRESS CHECK

3. What is the difference between cost accumulation and cost assignment?
4. Should all costs that are traceable be considered direct costs? Why or why not?

LO 2.3

Compare and
contrast fixed,
variable, and mixed
costs.

VARIABLE, FIXED, AND MIXED COSTS

Now that we understand cost objects and how costs are allocated to cost objects, we turn our attention to how companies categorize the costs that are assigned to cost objects. We will discuss two such categorizations: variable vs. fixed costs, and product vs. period costs. These categorizations have important ramifications for company strategy as well as financial reporting in the financial statements.

The first categorization, variable vs. fixed costs, describes how costs vary with the production of goods and services.

variable cost

A cost that changes with
production volume.

Variable costs change based on the number of units of the cost object produced. Total variable cost increases in proportion to change of activity (such as the number of units produced). For each unit produced, there is a corresponding increase in the total variable cost.

The following costs are usually classified as variable costs:

- Raw materials: all raw materials, such as wood, grains, and minerals, used to produce the product.
- Direct labor: the cost of the labor to produce the product.
- Production/manufacturing supplies: the supplies required to create the product, such as glue and nails.
- Sales commissions: bonus compensation based on each salesperson's total sales in a period (usually based on the number of units sold).

fixed cost

A cost that does not
change with production
volume.

In contrast, **fixed costs** do not change with the number of units of a cost object produced. As a result, increasing production decreases per-unit fixed costs because a company's fixed costs are spread out among a greater number of units. The following costs are usually classified as fixed costs:

- Rent: rental payments for use of real estate, such as a warehouse or a retail store.
- Depreciation: the gradual charging of expense for the use of a tangible asset, such as a machine.
- Insurance: periodic payment for insurance coverage.
- Salaries of some employees: some office employees receive fixed compensation, regardless of the number of hours worked.

mixed costs

A cost that has both
fixed and variable
components.

Mixed costs include both fixed and variable components. Chapter 3 explains how to disaggregate mixed costs into their fixed and variable cost components. The following costs are usually classified as mixed costs:

- Utilities: a fixed rate for using the service (which allows for a base amount), and then an additional variable charge for any usage over the base amount.
- Mobile phone: a fixed rate for using a base amount of minutes and/or data, and then an additional variable charge for any usage over the base amount.
- Credit card fees: a percentage of credit card sales, paid to the credit card company (some merchants, especially when processing debit cards, pay a flat fee per transaction plus a percentage of the transaction total, making those fees a mixed cost rather than pure variable cost).

CAREER SKILLS

Learning about
fixed, variable, and
mixed costs sup-
ports this career
skill:

- Determining a
  firm's pricing
  and marketing
  strategies

Why is it important to differentiate between variable and fixed costs? As production increases, per-unit costs decrease, which has important ramifications for production and firm profitability. This idea forms the basis of cost-volume-profit analysis, which is discussed in detail in Chapter 3.

Exhibit 2.3 provides examples of variable, fixed, and mixed costs associated with production cost objects at **Tesla** and **Heartwood Cabinets**.

Type of Cost Associated with Production Cost Object	Tesla (Production of Cybertrucks)	Heartwood Cabinets (Production of Bathroom Vanities)
Variable costs	Car batteries installed in Cybertrucks Tires Video dashboard	Cost of wood used in vanities Hinges Door handles
Fixed costs	Factory insurance	Factory equipment depreciation
Mixed costs	Utilities (for example, electricity usage at the plant)	Mobile phone bills (cell phones for production supervisors)

Exhibit 2.3
Examples of Variable, Fixed, and Mixed Costs at Tesla and Heartwood Cabinets

CAREER SKILLS

Learning about product, period, prime, and conversion costs supports this career skill:

• Understanding the nature of costs and how they impact the accounting for costs overall

✓ **PROGRESS CHECK**

5. Would a touchscreen installed in each **Tesla** Cybertruck be considered a fixed cost or a variable cost?

6. Is the cost of **Walmart** inventory an example of a fixed cost or a variable cost? Is the property tax on a Walmart distribution center a fixed cost or a variable cost?

PRODUCT COSTS AND PERIOD COSTS

Companies also classify costs as either product costs or period costs. **Product costs** are all costs that are incurred to produce goods and services for customers. What gets categorized as product costs differs substantially between companies. For service companies, such as the **Boston Consulting Group**, product costs may include the materials used to provide consulting services, but many service companies have no product costs. For retailers such as **TJ Maxx** and **Target**, product costs consist of inventory purchased for resale in their stores. For manufacturing companies such as **Tesla** and **Apple**, product costs consist of all costs incurred to produce goods: namely, direct materials, direct labor, and manufacturing overhead. Companies often use the terms **prime costs** to refer to direct materials and direct labor and **conversion costs** to refer to direct labor and manufacturing overhead.

Period costs are recorded as expenses on the income statement when they occur. Any cost that is not a product cost is a period cost. In contrast, product costs are recorded as part of an asset in inventory. Exhibit 2.4 provides some examples of product costs and period costs at Tesla and **Heartwood Cabinets**.

LO 2.4
Define product costs and period costs.

product costs
Costs incurred to create a product or service intended for sale to customers.

prime costs
Direct material costs and direct labor costs as part of product costs.

conversion costs
Direct labor and manufacturing overhead costs incurred to convert raw materials into a finished product.

Type of Cost	Tesla (Production of Cybertrucks)	Heartwood Cabinets (Production of Bathroom Vanities)
Product cost	Touchscreen for dashboard Tires for each Cybertruck Factory maintenance worker's salary Property (or real estate) taxes on the factory Plant insurance	Hinges for cabinet doors Assembly worker's salary Wood components used in cabinet construction Factory equipment depreciation Glue, screws, and nails
Period cost	Property (or real estate) taxes on the sales office	Salesperson commission Sales office depreciation

Exhibit 2.4
Examples of Product Costs and Period Costs at Tesla and Heartwood Cabinets

period costs
Costs that are recorded as expenses on the income statement when they occur. Any cost that is not a product cost is a period cost.

product costs (or **inventoriable costs**)
Costs assigned to goods that were either purchased or manufactured for resale and recorded as inventory.

cost of goods sold
The accumulated total of the costs of acquiring or manufacturing the product plus any shipping charges; recognized when inventory is sold.

Why is it important to differentiate between product and period costs? This distinction is important because these costs differ in how they are consumed, and thus when they are recorded on the financial statements as an expense. When companies incur product costs, they are purchasing or producing assets that will produce a future benefit. For example, Tesla may incur $50,000 in costs to produce a Cybertruck. While cost is certainly incurred during production, Tesla does not experience any decrease in resources. Instead, the company has converted direct materials, direct labor, and overhead into a more valuable resource—inventory. For this reason, product costs are often called **inventoriable costs**. When are product or inventoriable costs consumed? From the company's viewpoint, inventory is consumed when it is sold. At that point, it no longer has value to the company, and product costs are expensed as **cost of goods sold**. Chapter 4 provides greater detail regarding how costs flow through a company's accounting information system.

Because companies must record the value of inventory in their financial statements, an individual product is the most commonly used cost object in most companies. Exhibit 2.5 summarizes how Heartwood assigns product costs to an individual cabinet. Notice that the cost of a cabinet includes direct costs, indirect costs, variable costs, and fixed costs.

Exhibit 2.5
Heartwood's Allocation of Product Costs to Individual Cabinet

Cost	Prime/ Conversion	Variable/ Fixed	Example(s)	Direct/ Indirect	Traced/ Allocated
Direct materials	Prime	Variable	Wood, hinges, door pulls	Direct	Traced
Direct labor	Both	Variable	Assembly labor	Direct	Traced
Manufacturing overhead	Conversion	Variable	Indirect labor, glue, electricity	Indirect	Allocated
Manufacturing overhead	Conversion	Fixed	Factory rent	Indirect	Allocated

Period costs differ substantially from product costs because they represent resources that are not converted into inventory. Instead, they are consumed in the period in which they are incurred. Consider the cost of Tesla's accounting department. Is the accounting department essential to the business? Absolutely! However, accountants generally are not producing goods and services for customers (except in an accounting firm). Instead, the cost of accountants' labor is consumed immediately. As a result, the accounting department is expensed as a selling, general, and administrative expense (SG&A) in the period it is incurred.

This categorization may seem familiar to you. All income statements prepared according to GAAP are presented in a way that segregates product costs and period costs. Consider the excerpt from Tesla's annual report in Exhibit 2.6. All product costs are listed above the gross profit line item as "Total cost of revenues." All period costs are presented below gross profit under the heading "Operating Expenses."

If you're having trouble determining whether a cost is a product cost or a period cost, a good rule of thumb (in a manufacturing facility) is that all costs incurred in the company's factory or production facility are product costs.

In millions of USD or shares as applicable, except per share data	Q4-2020	Q1-2021	Q2-2021	Q3-2021	Q4-2021
STATEMENT OF OPERATIONS (unaudited)					
REVENUES					
Automotive sales	9,034	8,705	9,874	11,672	15,339
Automotive leasing	280	297	332	385	628
Total automotive revenue	9,314	9,002	10,206	12,057	15,967
Energy generation and storage	752	494	801	806	688
Services and other	678	893	951	894	1,064
Total revenues	**10,744**	**10,389**	**11,958**	**13,757**	**17,719**
COST OF REVENUES					
Automotive sales	6,922	6,457	7,119	8,150	10,689
Automotive leasing	148	160	188	234	396
Total automotive cost of revenues	7,070	6,617	7,307	8,384	11,085
Energy generation and storage	787	595	781	803	739
Service and other	821	962	986	910	1,048
Total cost of revenues	8,678	8,174	9,074	10,097	12,872
Gross profit	**2,066**	**2,215**	**2,884**	**3,660**	**4,847**
OPERATING EXPENSES					
Research and development	522	666	576	611	740
Selling, general and administrative	969	1,056	973	994	1,494
Restructuring and other	–	(101)	23	51	–
Total operating expenses	1,491	1,621	1,572	1,656	2,234
INCOME FROM OPERATIONS	**575**	**594**	**1,312**	**2,004**	**2,613**

Exhibit 2.6
Tesla Income Statement Illustrating Product and Period Costs

Source: https://tesla-cdn.thron.com/static/WIIG2L_TSLA_Q4_2021_Update_O7MYNE.pdf?xseo=&response-content-disposition=inline%3Bfilename%3D%22tsla-q4-and-fy-2021-update.pdf%22

✓ **PROGRESS CHECK**

7. Why are **Tesla** Cybertruck batteries considered a product cost instead of a period cost?
8. Why is direct labor considered both a prime cost and a conversion cost?
9. Are commissions paid to salespeople better classified as product expenses or period costs? Are they considered a prime cost, a conversion cost, both, or neither?

A Summary of Cost Classification

It is important for management to understand the company's cost behavior, which is the relationship between cost and activity. Total variable cost changes in proportion to the change in cost drivers, but variable cost per unit is constant within the relevant range. Total fixed cost is constant as activity increases, but fixed cost per unit decreases within the relevant range. A mixed cost increases as activity increases, but not in proportion to the activity.

To summarize our discussion so far, Exhibit 2.7 provides examples of the different costs that **Tesla** or **Heartwood Cabinets** may have. Notice that our cost classifications (fixed/variable, product/period, direct/indirect) overlap and must be evaluated independently.

Cost Classification at Tesla and/or Heartwood Cabinets	Variable or Fixed Cost?	Product or Period Cost?	Prime or Conversion Cost?	Direct or Indirect Cost?
Salaries/Wages				
Factory supervisor salary	Fixed	Product	Conversion	Indirect
Hourly production wages for workers on the assembly line	Variable	Product	Both	Direct
CEO salary	Fixed	Period	Neither	Indirect
Materials				
Vehicle tires (Tesla) or cabinet hinges (Heartwood)	Variable	Product	Prime	Direct
Supplies (such as glue or adhesives) used in the production process but not directly traceable	Variable	Product	Conversion	Indirect
Other Costs				
Factory repair and maintenance	Variable	Product	Conversion	Indirect
Factory building rent	Fixed	Product	Conversion	Indirect
Interest payments on company debt	Fixed	Period	Neither	Indirect
Manufacturing equipment depreciation	Fixed	Product	Conversion	Indirect
Development and tooling	Fixed	Product	Conversion	Indirect
Product advertising and marketing	Variable	Period	Neither	Indirect

Exhibit 2.7
Cost Classifications and Examples of Relevant Company Costs

Q LAB CONNECTION

LAB 2.1 Excel uses scatterplots to help you determine whether an input cost is fixed, variable, or mixed (that is, both fixed and variable).

LO 2.5

Identify the sources of cost accounting data.

COST ACCOUNTING SYSTEMS AND DATA SOURCES

A **cost accounting system** is a system designed to aggregate, monitor, and report information about revenues, costs, and profitability to management through the use of forms, processes, controls, and reports. For example, for manufacturers, a cost accounting system tracks the flow and costs of inventory continually through the various stages of production, helping management accountants cost out jobs and assess profitability. Cost accounting systems may include costs already incurred (**actual costs**), predicted or forecasted costs (**budgeted costs**), or estimated costs per unit of output that normally occur during the production of a product or performance of a service (**standard costs**).

Cost accounting systems use internal and external data sources as inputs to assess the monetary value of revenues earned (the inflow of assets usually in the form of cash or accounts receivable) and costs (resources sacrificed).

Internal Sources of Cost Accounting–Related Data

The data that record business activities and track expenditures come from many different sources. Companies frequently manage a single, large integrated database that creates, stores, and maintains the data that are generated during day-to-day business operations, including data regarding sales, purchasing, accounts payable, and manufacturing. This database includes customer, supplier, and inventory listings, as well as employee information.

Internal databases can be relatively small and held on a desktop, or they can be quite large. When companies outgrow smaller databases, they may choose to implement an **enterprise system**, also known as an **enterprise resource planning (ERP) system**. Enterprise systems integrate applications from throughout the functional areas of the business (such as manufacturing, accounting, finance, and human resources) into one system. Three of the most widely used enterprise systems are **SAP**, **Workday**, and **Oracle**.

Management accountants use the diverse sets of data maintained in the enterprise system to address many of management's questions, often using descriptive analytics. Five principal business information systems available within a company contain much of the data needed for robust data analytics:

- Financial reporting systems (FRS), also known as accounting systems.
- Manufacturing (production) systems (MS).
- Human resource management (HRM) systems.
- Customer relationship management (CRM) systems.
   ○ Point-of-sale (POS) systems.
- Supply chain management (SCM) systems.

The integration of the systems helps the company track and integrate its financial and nonfinancial information. Such integrated systems not only address business transactions but can also integrate information from these various systems regarding ESG initiatives. For example, in addition to tracking the company's level of carbon emissions, a company's manufacturing system and financial reporting system can track the cost of potential remediation. HRM systems can track employee pay to ensure a living wage is paid, and supply chain management systems can track potential violations of human rights by overseas (or even domestic) vendors.

Let's now look at these systems in more detail, explaining how they might be used in a cost accounting system. We'll then explain how the inputs from the various enterprise systems combine to form a company's cost accounting system (see Exhibit 2.8).

Financial Reporting Systems (FRS)

Financial reporting systems (FRS), or **accounting systems**, capture and measure financial transactions and communicate financial performance to interested parties. These systems are used to record journal entries and detailed transactions, maintain general ledgers,

cost accounting system
The system that aggregates, monitors, and reports information about revenues, costs, and profitability to management through the use of forms, processes, controls, and reports.

actual costs
Costs already incurred.

budgeted costs
Predicted or forecasted costs.

standard costs
The estimated costs per unit of output that normally occur during the production of a product or performance of a service.

ENVIRONMENTAL, SOCIAL, GOVERNANCE

Enterprise system or **enterprise resource planning (ERP) system**
Business management software that integrates applications from throughout the functional areas of the business (such as manufacturing, accounting, finance, and human resources) into one system.

Financial reporting system (FRS) or accounting system
An information system that captures and measures financial transactions and communicates financial performance to interested parties.

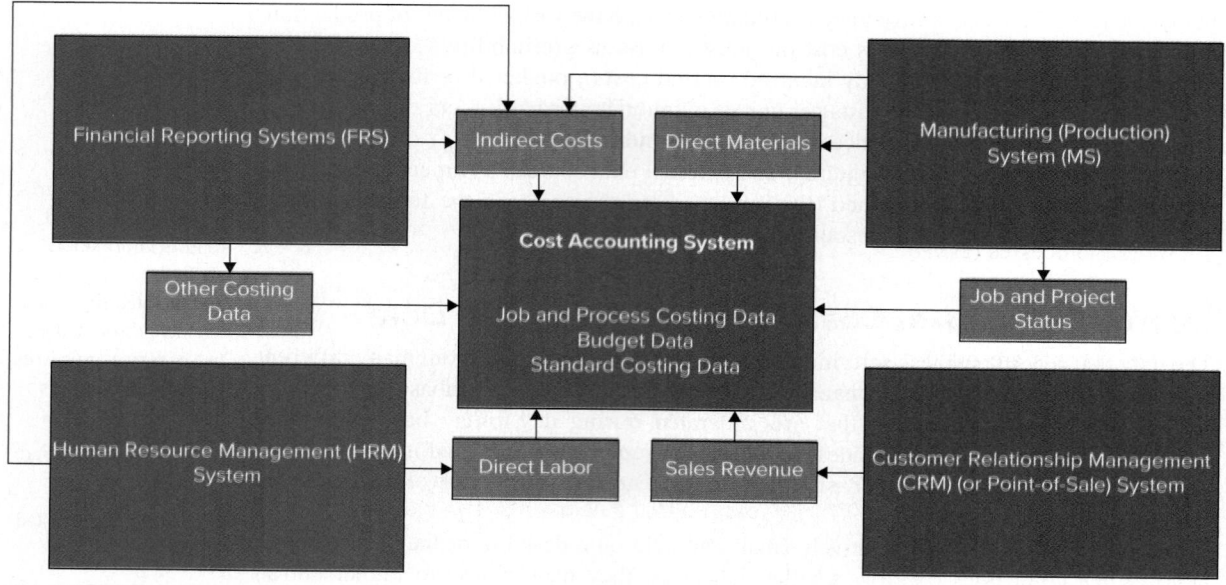

Exhibit 2.8
Inputs from Various Company Enterprise Systems Form a Manufacturing Company's Cost Accounting System

and generate financial statements. The detailed transaction data captured in the financial reporting system are the primary inputs into a cost accounting system.

As an input into a cost accounting system, the financial reporting system contributes cost information on indirect costs and other period costs, as shown in Exhibit 2.8.

Manufacturing (Production) Systems

Cost accounting systems may use data regarding manufacturing or production in **manufacturing (production) information systems (MS)**. In a factory, *manufacturing processes* are the steps by which raw materials and other inputs are transformed into finished goods. The data about these manufacturing processes are maintained in the manufacturing system, and they are particularly important to cost accountants, who seek to understand costs and the profitability of goods produced.

For example, cost accountants will be most interested in data included in the MS about the following:

- The costs of various inputs into the manufacturing system, including the cost of raw materials.
- Production quality (defect rates) and variances in that quality.
- Job and project status.

As an input into a cost accounting system, the MS information contributes cost information on direct materials (raw materials) and job and project status, as shown in Exhibit 2.8.

Human Resource Management (HRM) Systems

A **human resource management (HRM) system** is an information system for managing all interactions with past, current, and potential employees. Data maintained in the HRM system may include the following:

- Employee payroll and compensation.
- Employee timecards to track time on specific jobs or projects.
- Employee recruiting data and leads.
- Employee training (current and desired certifications).

manufacturing (production) information system (MS)
A system that tracks the steps by which raw materials and other inputs are transformed into finished goods.

human resource management (HRM) system
An information system for managing all interactions with past, current, and potential employees.

- Employee benefits (stock options, bonuses, health insurance).
- Employee annual reviews (prior- and current-year reviews, rating received).
- Employee absenteeism.
- Employee career progression (prior and current roles).
- Employee satisfaction and sentiment survey results.

Cost accountants need data from the HRM system—including the payroll wages and salaries of employees involved in the production or service process (as direct labor) and supporting processes (as indirect labor), as well as timecard data—to determine costs for various jobs or processes (as shown in Exhibit 2.8).

Human Dimensions of HRM Data In addition to their cost allocation responsibilities, cost accountants are often responsible for helping their companies design and evaluate performance incentive systems, such as bonuses for meeting certain production targets or for minimizing costs. HRM systems can track employees' performance compared to those targets, as well as the incentive payments distributed to employees, to make sure the given incentives are aligned with outcomes. Data from the HRM system are critical in determining whether current incentives are leading to the desired employee behaviors.

Customer Relationship Management (CRM) Systems

A **customer relationship management (CRM) system** is an information system for managing all interactions with past, current, and potential customers. CRM systems might include data related to:

- Customer contact history:
  - What happened in the interaction? What was the customer asked about or what was decided?
  - Does the customer have any interest in new products or services?
- Customer sales order history from point-of-sale (POS) systems.
- Customer payment history (any outstanding accounts receivable); how well (quickly) are customers paying their bills?
- Potential (as opposed to current) customers.

> **customer relationship management (CRM) system**
> An information system for managing all interactions with past, current, and potential customers.

While CRM systems do not have direct cost implications, they do serve as critical inputs to the revenue-generating and budgeting processes that we will learn in later chapters. Therefore, detailed sales revenue data are maintained to help accountants calculate the profitability of each job and/or each customer (as shown in Exhibit 2.8).

FROM THE FIELD

Walmart's Enormous Data Collection Efforts

Walmart collects vast amounts of data necessary to make more informed, better business decisions. With the emergence of e-commerce and the potential for omnichannel sales, the amount of data available to collect and analyze has grown tremendously. Every hour, Walmart collects 2.5 petabytes of unstructured data from 1 million customers. It also collects extensive customer data on over 145 million Americans.

Thinking Critically

Why is it important for Walmart to determine what customers buy via e-commerce versus what they buy at retail stores? How might this information affect Walmart's operations? Why would a management accountant be interested in these data? For example, perhaps fulfillment costs are different at each location, in which case a management accountant might recommend different pricing online as compared to store pricing.

point-of-sale (POS) system
A system that captures transactional data regarding sales, inventory, and payment method at the point of sale.

Point-of-Sale (POS) Systems   One specific type of CRM system used in retail stores and restaurants is a **point-of-sale (POS) system**, which captures transactional data regarding sales, inventory, and payment method at the point of sale (whether the sale takes place on an app, via a website, or in a bricks-and-mortar store). The company, and its cost accountants, can use POS data internally to analyze its costs at a granular level; it can also supply the data automatically to key suppliers and business partners. For example, **Walmart** employs a system called Retail Link, an Internet-based tool that allows its suppliers to access Walmart's point-of-sale data. Retail Link captures every sale recorded at the point of checkout at a Walmart store, and the relevant sales and inventory data—by item, store, and date—are automatically shared with suppliers. In other words, Retail Link contains records of every sale of every individual item at every Walmart store, every hour of the day. Suppliers use the data to identify buying patterns, predict trends, and manage inventory.[4] By better predicting future demand for products, Walmart and its partners can work to make sure that the right products are in the right place at the right time.

Supply Chain Management (SCM) Systems

supply chain
The flow of goods, services, and information from the initial source to final delivery of product to customers.

A company's **supply chain** is the flow of goods, services, and information from the initial source to final delivery of product to customers. **Supply chain management (SCM) systems** coordinate the flow of goods and services from initial product to final customer delivery, usually across multiple companies.

A supply chain system might include data related to:

supply chain management (SCM) system
The system that coordinates the flow of goods and services from original production to final customer delivery, usually across multiple companies.

- Active vendors (their contact info, where payment should be made, how much should be paid).
- The orders made to date (how much was ordered, when the orders are made) and the cost of those orders.
- Demand schedules for which components of the final product are needed (when and where).
- Transportation status and schedules.
- The current location of the product in the supply chain.

Because Walmart is a merchandiser and sells goods provided by its vendors, it will manage its relationships with them with a supply chain management system rather than a manufacturing system. However, for a manufacturing company such as **Tesla**, the MS is the heart of its information systems.

CAREER SKILLS
Learning about cost accounting data sources supports this career skill:

• Recognizing and using data from various sources to address management questions

Inputs from Individual Enterprise Systems into a Cost Accounting System

As Exhibit 2.8 illustrates, the various enterprise systems all contribute cost information to the cost accounting system. The cost accounting system is the central repository of cost information, and it receives data inputs from the financial reporting system, the manufacturing system, the HRM system, the CRM system, and the supply chain management system, as follows:

- The financial reporting system contributes information about the amounts paid for indirect costs for each cost object.

---

[4]Sharon Shichor, "Walmart's Retail Link® Point-of-Sale Data," 18 Knowledge, March 16, 2017, https://18knowledge.com/blog/walmarts-retail-link-point-of-sale-data/ (accessed March 23, 2022).

- The HRM system contributes information on direct labor (as reflected by the arrow from the HRM system to direct labor) and indirect labor costs (as reflected by the arrow from the HRM system to indirect costs).
- The manufacturing system reports on the status of various processes and jobs, contributing information on direct materials (as reflected by the arrow from the MS to direct materials) and indirect materials (as reflected by the arrow from the MS to indirect costs).
- The CRM system contributes information on sales revenues to help assess profitability at the customer level, product level, and company level to help evaluate whether business value was created, as reflected by the arrow from the CRM system to sales revenue and on to the cost accounting system. The CRM is also used to help predict production budgets (which are discussed in Chapter 9).

External Data Sources of Cost Accounting–Related Data

External sources of data may be available to help managers analyze situations and answer questions. Some common types of external data are macroeconomic statistics, industry-level reports, and competitor data (including financial statements of publicly traded companies).

Macroeconomic Data

Macroeconomic data provide context for firm performance by summarizing the economy as a whole. Macroeconomic data are generally useful for forecasting a firm's future performance, especially its future revenues. The following types of macroeconomic data are often useful:

1. Gross domestic product (GDP)—as a measure of the performance of the economy as a whole.
2. Housing market starts and house prices—generally regarded as key measures of economic performance.
3. Consumer Price Index (CPI)—as a measure of inflation.
4. Unemployment numbers—as a measure of labor availability.
5. Labor availability and current and expected future labor costs—might help companies predict how much labor will cost in the future.

Access to basic macroeconomic data for the countries where the company is doing business is an important part of the cost accountant's data toolkit.

Exhibit 2.9 provides an example of how **Walmart** might use macroeconomic data to assess the overall performance of the economy and to plan various aspects of its operations.

Macroeconomic Data	Potential Use of Macroeconomic Data by Walmart's Management Accountants
Gross domestic product (GDP) Housing market starts and housing prices	• Assess overall performance of the economy • Determine if customers have available funds to make essential purchases and discretionary purchases at Walmart • Determine how much of each product to order and to hold in inventory
Consumer Price Index (CPI)	• Assess if costs are increasing overall, including the costs of providing products to Walmart customers
Unemployment numbers and labor availability	• Assess whether there will be people available to hire and the wage rate for new employees

Exhibit 2.9
Potential Uses of Macroeconomic Data at Walmart

Macroeconomic data are particularly important for multinational companies such as **McDonald's**, which must understand key macro factors in other countries that may be economically very different from the United States. Exhibit 2.10 shows a novel example of measuring whether different countries' currencies are overvalued or undervalued based on a common standard, the price of a Big Mac. *The Economist* (a magazine) has published the Big Mac Index since 1986 as an informal means of comparing the price of a Big Mac across countries. As Exhibit 2.10 shows, in June 2022, the British pound was 13.8% undervalued as compared to the U.S. dollar.

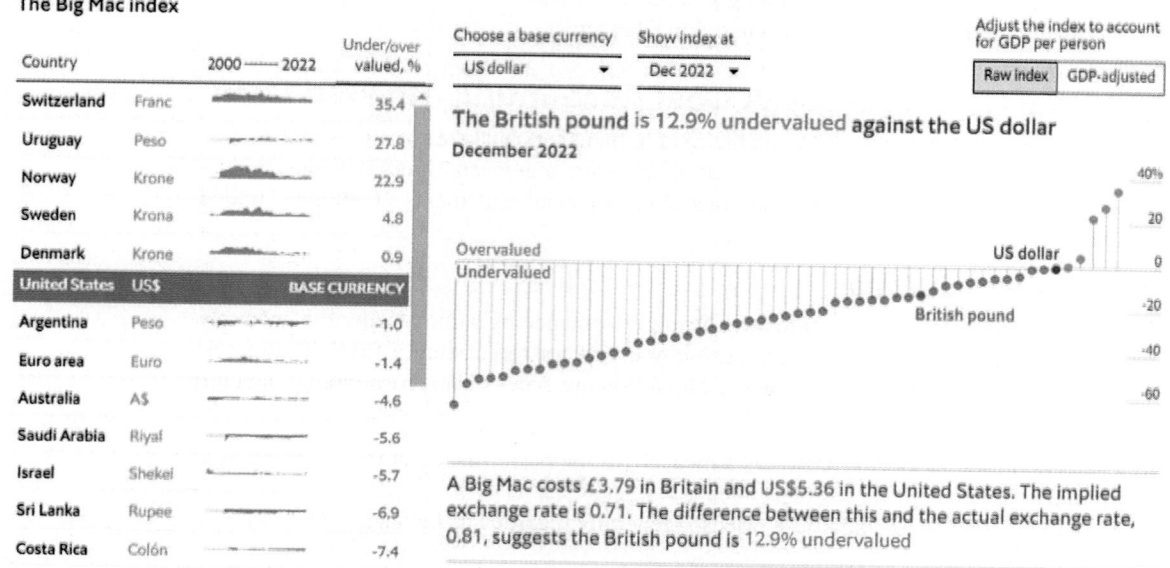

Exhibit 2.10
The Big Mac Index

Source: www.economist.com/big-mac-index. Accessed 10/10/2022.

Industry-Level Reports and Competitor Data

The better a company understands the costs of its industry and its closest competitors, the greater the likelihood that it will achieve or maintain profitability. Industry consortia often capture and report performance that can be used as benchmarks for evaluating industry members' performance. Exhibit 2.11 is an example of a retail industry report across different industries. It was prepared by retail supplier **NPD**, which helps industry members "measure, predict, and improve performance across all (retail) channels." NPD tracks point-of-sale data from 600,000 retail locations, and it conducts more than 12 million retail consumer surveys each year to assist retailers in their decision making. Note the four portions of the figure, which summarize Accelerating, Maintaining, Improving, and Declining industries. In the period shown here (the second quarter of 2022, as compared to the first quarter of 2022), the toy and auto industries were accelerating, the beauty industry was maintaining, the sports equipment industry was improving, and the apparel, housewares, and footwear industries (among others) were declining.

Business intelligence is often used to understand and evaluate competitor performance, new products, and opportunities and threats. In addition, a basic understanding of competitors' financial statements will go a long way toward evaluating and benchmarking against their performance.

Shifting Momentum
Year-over-year Q1 and Q2 industry shifts

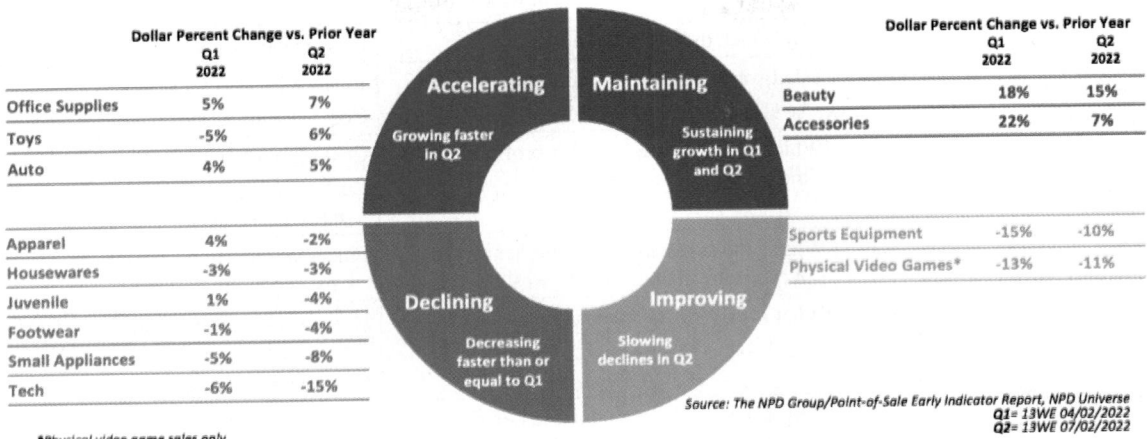

Dollar Percent Change vs. Prior Year	Q1 2022	Q2 2022
Office Supplies	5%	7%
Toys	-5%	6%
Auto	4%	5%
Apparel	4%	-2%
Housewares	-3%	-3%
Juvenile	1%	-4%
Footwear	-1%	-4%
Small Appliances	-5%	-8%
Tech	-6%	-15%

Dollar Percent Change vs. Prior Year	Q1 2022	Q2 2022
Beauty	18%	15%
Accessories	22%	7%
Sports Equipment	-15%	-10%
Physical Video Games*	-13%	-11%

Source: The NPD Group/Point-of-Sale Early Indicator Report, NPD Universe
Q1= 13WE 04/02/2022
Q2= 13WE 07/02/2022

*Physical video game sales only

Exhibit 2.11
Example of Retail Industry Data

Source: www.npd.com/news/thought-leadership/2022/retail-momentum-ups-and-downs/ (accessed October 10, 2022).

Examples of Data Sources Needed to Answer Management Questions

In Chapter 1, we identified a set of management questions according to analytics type. Exhibit 2.12 lists those same questions but now includes potential data sources that can be used to answer those questions. The specific data and analytics techniques are discussed throughout this text.

Ethical Data Collection and Use

ETHICS

As management accountants use data from internal enterprise systems and external information systems, and as they attempt to extract all possible value from these data, they must also work to ensure that they are using the data ethically and for the intended purpose. Specifically, companies must respect customers', suppliers', and employees' right to privacy and make sure that they collect, use, and maintain data ethically.

To provide guidance on the ethical use of data, the Institute of Business Ethics suggests that companies answer the following six questions as they consider how to create value from data while still protecting the privacy of stakeholders:[5]

1. **How does the company use data, and to what extent is it integrated into firm strategy?** What is the purpose of the data? Are they accurate and reliable? Will their use benefit the customer or the employee?
2. **Does the company send a privacy notice to individuals when their personal data are collected?** Is the request to use the data clear? Do individuals agree to the terms and conditions of use of their personal data?

[5]S. White, "6 Ethical Questions about Big Data," *Financial Management,* June 2016, www.fm-magazine.com/news/2016/jun/ethical-questions-about-big-data.html (accessed June 2021).

Analytics Type	Example Management Accounting Questions	Primary Data Sources
Descriptive analytics summarizes activity or analyzes master data based on certain attributes to address these questions: • What happened? • What is happening?	How many board feet of decking product did we produce last week, and at what cost?	Manufacturing systems Cost accounting systems
	How much did Job #304 cost?	Cost accounting systems
	What was the segment margin for the West Coast and Midwest regions last quarter?	Financial reporting systems Cost accounting systems
	Which products are the most profitable for the company?	Cost accounting systems Customer relationship management (CRM) systems
Diagnostic analytics detects correlations and patterns of interest and compares them to a benchmark to address these questions: • Why did it happen? • What are the reasons for past results? • Can we explain why it happened? • What are the root causes of past results?	Why is the segment margin higher on the West Coast than in the Midwest?	Financial reporting systems Cost accounting systems
	What is driving the labor rate variance?	Human resource management (HRM) systems Cost accounting systems
	Why did our rate of production defects go down this month compared to last month?	Manufacturing systems
	What is the level of fixed and variable costs of our primary products? Are they different from the industry's or our competition's?	Cost accounting systems Industry and competitor data
Predictive analytics identifies common attributes or patterns that may be used to forecast similar activity to address these questions: • Will it happen in the future? • What is the probability something will happen? • Is it forecastable?	What is the level of expected sales for the company in the next month, quarter, and year (to help plan our production)?	Cost accounting systems Financial reporting systems Industry and competitor data Macroeconomic data
	What is the correct level of overhead to allocate to the various jobs? Which are the appropriate cost drivers for allocating overhead?	Cost accounting systems Manufacturing systems
Prescriptive analytics recommends action based on previously observed actions to address these questions: • What should we do based on what we expect will happen? • How do we optimize our performance based on potential constraints?	Should the company lease or own its headquarters office building?	Cost accounting systems
	Should the company manufacture its own products or outsource to other producers?	Manufacturing systems
	What is the expected return to an investment on a new piece of factory equipment?	Cost accounting systems Manufacturing systems
	What level of sales will allow us to break even on a product?	Cost accounting systems Customer relationship management (CRM) systems
	How can revenues be maximized (or costs be minimized) if there is a trade war with another country? If we can reduce our fixed (or variable) costs, what will our resulting profit be?	Cost accounting systems Customer relationship management (CRM) systems

Exhibit 2.12
Examples of Data Sources Needed to Address Management Questions

3. **Does the company assess the risks linked to the specific type of data it uses?** Has the company considered the risks of data use or possible data breaches of potentially sensitive data?
4. **Does the company have safeguards in place to mitigate the risks of data misuse?** Are preventive controls on data access in place, and are they effective? Are penalties established and enforced for data misuse?
5. **Does the company have the appropriate tools to manage the risks of data misuse?** Is the feedback from these tools evaluated and measured? Does internal audit regularly evaluate these tools?
6. **Does the company conduct appropriate due diligence when sharing data with or acquiring data from third parties?** Do third-party data providers follow similar ethical standards in the acquisition and transmission of the data?

The answers to these questions will help the company evaluate its gathering and use of data, and ensure its use of data is ethical.

⊘ PROGRESS CHECK

10. From which enterprise system does a company's cost accounting system receive aggregate and detailed revenue information? How might the company use this information to determine which products are most profitable at the company?
11. How does an understanding of the macroeconomy and industry performance help a company project future performance?

STORING AND ACCESSING COST DATA USING RELATIONAL DATABASES

LO 2.6

Describe different data attributes and data types, and explain how to use a relational database.

Most large organizations store data in **databases**, which are structured datasets that can be accessed by authorized users via a computer system or network. Databases store and track characteristics of different entities, including details about customers, sales transactions, vendors, employees, and suppliers. These characteristics are called **attributes** or **fields**. For example, attributes of a customer might include customer ID, customer name, and customer address. Attributes of a sale might include invoice number, date, product sold, and who bought it.

Attributes can be composed of words, dates, numbers, or some combination of these. The possible set of values that each attribute can possess is called its **data type**. The following are some common data types:

- *String, text, short text, or alphanumeric.* A *string* of characters is a collection of one or more characters that can be letters, numbers, or a combination. However, the numbers are not meaningful values that can be used in calculations. For example, a record locater for an airline trip is often a six-digit code with letters and numbers, such as X2YAZ7.
- *Number.* The number data type is reserved for numeric data. Any characters that are stored as numbers can be used in calculations. An example of a number in accounting is the amount of the sale, such as $3.95.

database
Structured datasets that can be accessed by authorized users via a computer system or network.

attribute or **field**
A descriptor in a dataset, such as customer ID, customer name, or customer address for a customer dataset.

data type
A set of possible values that a variable (or attribute) can possess.

- *Date.* The date data type represents a string of characters that are formatted in a traditional date format, such as mm/dd/yyyy or mm/dd/yy.
- *Geographic.* Geographic data are typically linked with their latitude and longitude numbers so that they can be linked to and represented in maps. Geographic data can include attributes for state, city, and/or country. The two-digit code for Arizona is AZ, and for Arkansas it is AR.

Exhibit 2.13 provides examples of potential data types for attributes of a specific sales transaction and customer.

Exhibit 2.13
Data Types and Attributes

Data Type	Attributes of Sales Transaction	Attributes of Customer
String, text, short text, or alphanumeric	Name of product sold	Customer name
Number	Amount of sale	Cumulative sales to date
Date	Date of sale	Date of last sale
Geographic	Store location/address	Customer location/address

relational database

Database that stores and facilitates access to datasets that are related to one another.

table

Data organized into columns (fields) and rows (records).

fields

The columns in a table that contain descriptive information about the observations in the table. This term is used interchangeably with *attributes* in practice.

record

Each row (or observation) in a table. Each record corresponds to a unique instance of what is being described in the table.

primary key

A column in a relational database that functions as a unique identifier for a record.

Some smaller businesses could store all data about every transaction in a single massive Excel spreadsheet, but it would be very hard to use. Instead, most organizations use **relational databases**, which store data in separate tables and facilitate access to datasets that are related to one another. A relational database is composed of tables, fields, and records.

- **Tables**: Data organized into columns (fields) and rows (records).
  - **Fields** (attributes) are the columns that contain descriptive information about the observations in the table. In Exhibit 2.14, the fields in each column of the Transaction Table are Transaction ID, Date, Amount, and Customer ID.
  - **Records** are the rows of the database, with each observation corresponding to a record, or unique instance, of what is being described in the table. In Exhibit 2.14, the records in each row of the Transaction Table are for each Sale transaction.

Every table includes a field (or combination of fields) that functions as a unique identifier for the record. This field is called the **primary key**. For example, at your school, there is probably a database containing data about every student. It probably includes a student ID number field that serves as the primary key because the student ID number uniquely identifies each student. In a cost accounting context, examples of primary keys include a customer number (or customer ID), transaction ID, vendor ID, product number, employee ID number, or Social Security number.

Exhibit 2.14 shows two tables from a CRM (customer relationship management) system. The Customers Table, on the right, lists every customer and contains a unique list of attributes about each one, including Customer_ID, Business_Name, Customer_Address, Customer_City, Customer_State, and Customer_Zip. The primary key for the Customers Table is Customer_ID. No two customers will have the same Customer_ID. The Transaction Table, on the left, contains a unique listing of every transaction that has ever been made between the company and its customers. It includes several attributes about each transaction, including Transaction_ID, Date, Amount, and the customer involved (Customer_ID). The primary key for the Transaction Table is Transaction_ID. No two transactions will be assigned the same Transaction_ID.

You may notice that the Transaction Table does not include any data about the customers involved in the transactions, except their Customer_ID number. What happens if management has questions about whether to increase sales in certain states? There is no way to determine the total amount of sales made in Louisiana, Wisconsin, or any other state using

Transaction Table

Transaction_ID	Date	Amount	Customer_ID
20062	11/22/2024	27.32	2001
20168	12/27/2024	38.2	2001
20383	3/4/2025	99.77	2002
20564	4/28/2025	53.67	2002
20140	12/20/2024	46.47	2004
20310	2/11/2025	38.36	2004

Foreign Key

Customers Table

Customer_ID	Business_Name	Customer_Address	Customer_City	Customer_St	Customer_Zip
2001	Beverage Distributors	3221 SE 14th Street	Des Moines	IA	50320
2002	Deep Ellum Brewing Company	2823 St Louis Street	Dallas	TX	75226
2003	Schatz Distributing Co.	3140 S. 28th Steet	Kansas City	KS	66106
2004	Arkansas Craft Distributors	1515 E. 4th Street	Little Rock	AR	72202

Primary Key

Exhibit 2.14

Transaction and Customers Tables from a CRM

Microsoft Excel

the data stored in the Transaction Table. Therefore, to answer management's question, we need to join the data in these two tables. Doing so allows us to use the data from both tables, even though they are stored in separate datasets.

For two tables to be joined, there must be a common field in both tables. In Exhibit 2.14, Customer_ID is the common field in the two tables. This common field, sometimes called a **foreign key**, *relates* the Transaction Table to the Customers Table so that the company can look up the details about a customer from a given transaction in the Customers Table. In other words, foreign keys create relationships between two tables so that users of the database can look up details of the record based on the primary key/foreign key relationship.

In Exhibit 2.14, the color coding and lines drawn between the two tables show how the tables interact. In the Customers Table, Customer_ID is the *primary key* because it uniquely identifies every customer in the table. The Customer_ID field also exists in the Transaction Table so that the two tables can be linked.

In the Transaction Table, Customer_ID is not the primary key. Instead, it is a foreign key because it facilitates a look-up relationship.

Looking at the Customer_ID foreign key in the Transaction Table and the Customer_ID primary key in the Customers Table, we determine that Beverage Distributors participated in two transactions in 2024, Deep Ellum participated in two different transactions in 2025, and Arkansas Craft Distributors participated in two transactions during 2024 and 2025.

Unlike primary keys, foreign keys are not required in every table. However, when a foreign key exists, it must contain matching data in the related table. In other words, if we assume that the Customers Table in Exhibit 2.14 is a complete list of customers, then we would not include any Customer_ID in the Transaction Table that is not contained in the Customers Table (that is, any Customer_ID other than 2001, 2002, 2003, or 2004). If a new customer initiates a transaction, we need to record the relevant customer data in the Customers Table first. The new customer is associated with the next sequential number in the primary key field—in this case, Customer_ID 2005. We could then add Customer_ID 2005 to a transaction in the Transaction Table.

The following Data Analytics Mini-Lab teaches you how to use the VLOOKUP function to link tables in Excel.

foreign key
A column (or group of columns) that exists to create relationships between two tables in a relational database.

CAREER SKILLS

Learning about relational databases supports this career skill:

• Understanding how databases link attributes of different customers, sales transactions, vendors, payroll, employees, and suppliers to each other using tables and primary and foreign keys

---

🔍 LAB CONNECTIONS

LAB 2.2 Excel uses Excel commands, such as VLOOKUP, INDEX, and MATCH, to link tables from various data sources. Linking tables using primary and foreign keys is critical to the use of relational databases.

LAB 2.3 Excel uses Excel's internal data model to demonstrate how tables are linked to each other using primary and foreign keys to provide inputs into a company's cost accounting system.

PROGRESS CHECK

12. What is the purpose of a primary key?

13. Why must the data in a foreign key field match the data in its related primary key field? (*Hint:* Look at Exhibit 2.14. Why is it critical that the Customer IDs in the Transaction Table match the Customer IDs in the Customers Table?)

DATA ANALYTICS MINI-LAB
Linking Tables Using VLOOKUP in Excel

Data Analytics Type: Descriptive Analytics

Lab Note

The tools presented in this lab periodically change. Updated instructions, if applicable, can be found in the student and instructor support materials.

Keywords

Excel, Relational Databases

Decision-Making Context

Relational databases store data in multiple tables. When it comes time to do more extensive analysis, the tables are linked, and analysis is completed.

DJI is a company that produces and sells drones. We have a table that has (fictitious) sales for the month of October. We also have a second products (or SKU) table that provides product descriptions, along with the sales price and the cost of each product.

We'll use the product SKU to link the two tables together. Product SKU is the *primary key* for the products (SKU) table (Mini-Lab 2SKU Data.xlsx). Product SKU is the *foreign key* in the DJI Mavic Drone Sales Journal (Mini-Lab 2 Sales Journal Data.xlsx).

Ask the Question

What are the total sales of the Mavic 2 Drone, or SKU DJI-AIR?

Master the Data

For this Mini-Lab we will use data in the Excel file titled **Mini-Lab 2 Sales Journal Data.xlsx.** The sales journal is a specialized accounting journal that keeps track of sales. In this case, it serves as a record of October sales at DJI Mavic.

Open Excel file **Mini-Lab 2 Sales Journal Data.xlsx.** Exhibit A shows a snippet of the sales journal spreadsheet and the data dictionary.

Exhibit A
Data Dictionary for Mini-Lab 2 Sales Journal Data (also known as Sales Journal)

Field (Attribute)	Description	Data Type
Date	Date of sale	Date (MM/DD/YY)
Invoice #	Invoice number for sale of products	Number
Customer #	The customer number for each customer who purchased from DJI Mavic	Number
SKU	The product code or SKU (stock-keeping unit, which is a unique code for each product sold)	String

◢	A	B	C	D
1	Date	Invoice #	Customer #	SKU
2	10/1/2025	8001	3009	DJI-AIR
3	10/2/2025	8002	3036	DJI-AC2
4	10/2/2025	8002	3018	DJI-DSC
5	10/3/2025	8003	3079	DJI-AIF
6	10/3/2025	8004	3015	DJI-AC2
7	10/3/2025	8005	3051	MAV-AR2
8	10/3/2025	8006	3035	DJI- OM5
9	10/3/2025	8007	3055	DJI--SMC
10	10/3/2025	8007	3082	DJI-FLP
11	10/3/2025	8008	3061	DJI-MMC
12	10/3/2025	8009	3095	MAV-2II
13	10/3/2025	8009	3036	MAV-AI2

Exhibit A   (*continued*)

Microsoft Excel

Open Excel file **Mini-Lab 2 SKU Data.xlsx.** Exhibit B shows a snippet of the spreadsheet of the SKU table and the data dictionary.

Field (Attribute)	Description	Data Type
SKU	The product code or SKU (stock-keeping unit, which is a unique code for each product sold)	String
Description	Product (SKU) description	String
Sales Price	Product sales price	Number
Cost	Cost of product	Number

Exhibit B
Data Dictionary for Mini-Lab 2 SKU Data (also known as Product Table)

Microsoft Excel

◢	A	B	C	D
1	SKU	Description	Sales Price	Cost
2	DJI-AC2	DJI Action 2	519	311
3	DJI- OM5	DJI OM 5	159	96
4	DJI-AIR	DJI AIR 2S	999	616
5	DJI-DSC	DJI Action 2 Dual-Screen Cor	519	315
6	DJI-2PC	DJI Action 2 Power Combo	399	239
7	DJI-OM4	DJI OM 4 SE	119	72
8	DJI-PO2	DJI Pocket 2	439	270
9	OSM-P11	Osmo Pocket	299	182
10	OSM-A11	Osmo Action	199	125
11	DJI-FLP	DJI OM Fill Light Phone Clam	59	36
12	DJI-P2D	DJI Pocket 2 Do-It-All Handle	99	59
13	DJI-AIF	DJI Air 2S Fly More Combo	1749	1082

Perform the Analysis

Analysis Task #1: Link the Tables Using the Primary Key and the Foreign Key

1. In cell E1 of the Sales Journal Table, insert the title "Description". In cell F1, insert the title "Sales Price". In cell G1, insert the title "Cost".

2. To link tables, we need a primary key and a foreign key. We identify SKU as the primary key of the Product (SKU) Table.

3. To link tables, we'll use the VLOOKUP function in Excel. VLOOKUP is used when you need to find things in a table or a range. In this case, we'll look inside a table. To perform VLOOKUP, we need to input certain information to tell Excel where to look and which data to access. We call these input items "Arguments" (see Exhibit C). In cell E2, we need to look up the appropriate description for the SKU listed in cell D2.

    a. The **Lookup_value** is the foreign key. We are trying to get relevant information from the product table to put in the sales journal. In this case, we are trying to find information for the DJI Mavic 2 Drone. Its SKU is DJI-AIR, which is in cell D2. To be able to copy this cell to other rows and other columns, we need to input $D2 in the **Lookup_value**, as shown in Exhibit C.

    b. **Table_array**: We highlight the full product table in the separate spreadsheet file DJI Mavic Drone SKU table.xlsx, with the first column in the array as the primary key SKU in the Products table, or as written, '[Mini-Lab 2 SKU Data.xlsx]Sheet1'!$A$2:$D$25. (Note that only the latter part of this expression is readable in Exhibit C.)

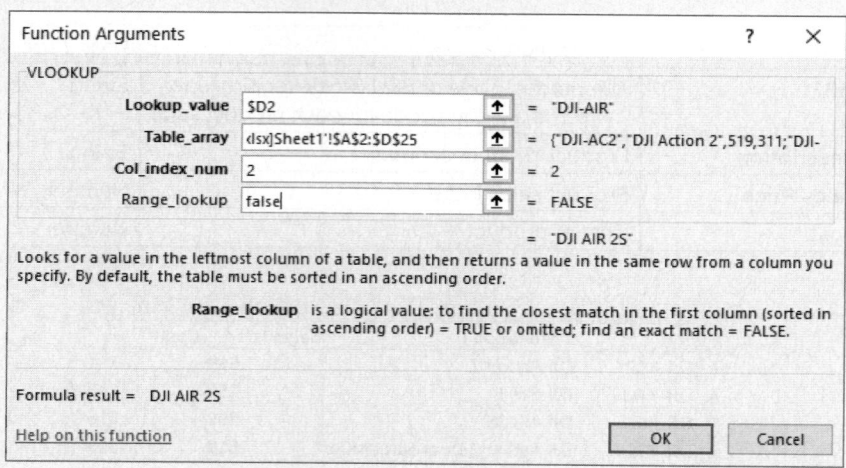

    c. For **Col_index_num** in this column, we are trying to get the description, so we need to highlight the second column of the array, or **2**. See again Exhibit C.

    d. For **Range_lookup**, we want an exact match, so we set this to **false**.

    e. The final form of the formula in cell E2 is =VLOOKUP($D2,'[Mini-Lab 2 SKU Data.xlsx]Sheet1'!$A$2:$D$25,2,FALSE). These formulas may seem complicated. For now, focus on entering them into your spreadsheet. As you gain experience with Excel, you will learn how to write these formulas on your own.

    f. The final form of the formula in cell F2 is =VLOOKUP($D2,'[Mini-Lab 2 SKU Data.xlsx]Sheet1'!$A$2:$D$25,3,FALSE). Note that we only change the column index number from "2" to "3" to get the sales price.

    g. The final form of the formula in cell G2 is =VLOOKUP($D2,'[Mini-Lab 2 SKU Data.xlsx]Sheet1'!$A$2:$D$25,4,FALSE). Note that we only change the column index number from "2" to "4" to get the product cost.

    h. Copy the results of cells E2:G2 to cells E3:G230.

Analysis Task #2: Calculate Sales of the DJI Mavic 2 Drones

To calculate the total sales of the DJI Mavic 2 Drone, we will create a pivot table and accumulate the total sales.

1. In the menu, select **Insert** then **PivotTable**. A dialog box will open, as shown in Exhibit D.

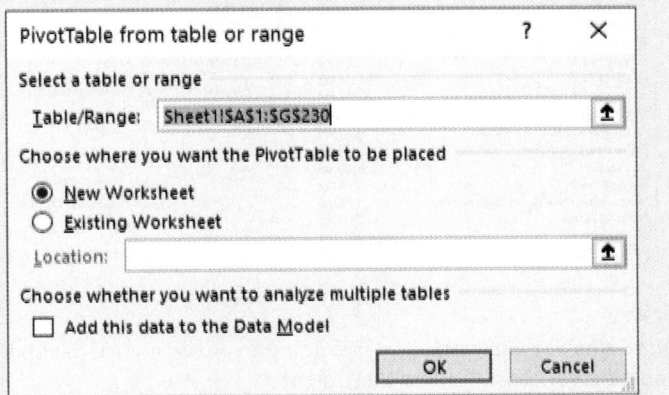

Exhibit D

Microsoft Excel

2. In the dialog box, select the **Table/Range:** that includes the account titles and all of the data ($A$1:$G$230). Select **New Worksheet**, then click **OK**. The empty pivot table will open up in a new worksheet, ready for the next step, as shown in Exhibit E.

Exhibit E

> **Inputs into Pivot Table**
>
> **Columns:**
>
> **Rows:** [Description]
>
> **Values:** [Sales]

3. Drag **[Description]** from **PivotTable Fields** into the **Rows**, and drag **[Sales Price]** from **PivotTable Fields** into **Values** in the pivot table. The **Values** will default to Sum of Sales Price. The resulting pivot table will look like Exhibit F.

4. (Optional Step) Highlight cell A3 and insert the title "Customer Number".

Exhibit F

Microsoft Excel

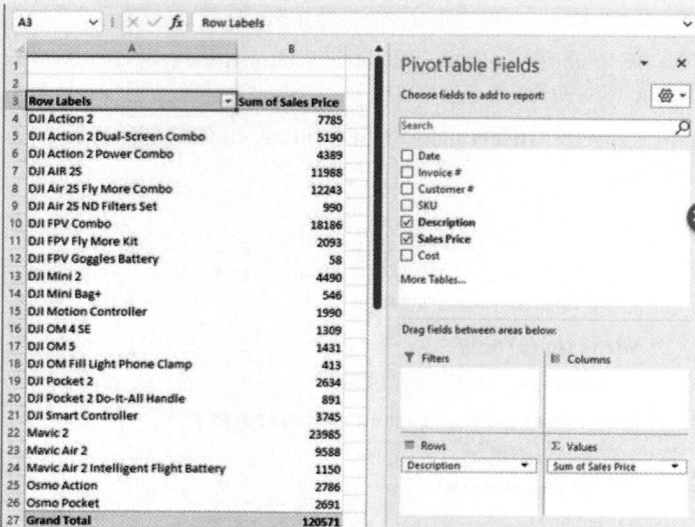

DATA VISUALIZATION

Share the Story

To report the results to management, we're going to create a visualization of all product sales, using a pivot chart. Follow these steps:

1. Select a cell in the pivot table.

2. Select **PivotTable Analyze**, then **Tools**, then **PivotChart**.

3. Select **Clustered Column**.

4. Select **OK**.

The resulting pivot chart will resemble Exhibit G.

Exhibit G
Total Sales by
SKU Description

Microsoft Excel

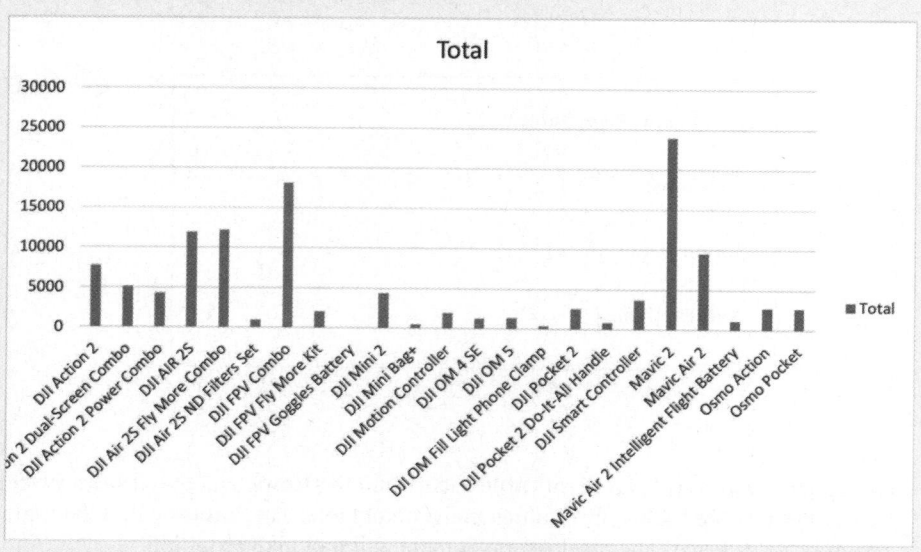

We can use the data visualization to report the results of DJI Mavic's products to the sales department and to company management.

Mini-Lab Assessment

1. How would you calculate DJI Mavic's most profitable product? What data would you need? What else would you need to compute?

2. How do visualizations help you explain the results of your analysis? Would it be helpful to sort the results, perhaps from highest to lowest, or from lowest to highest? Explain.

3. The sales journal also includes customer numbers. Why does it make sense that customer number would be a foreign key in a sales journal to get access to customer data?

ANALYZING COST DATA USING DATA-ANALYSIS SOFTWARE TOOLS

LO 2.7

Compare and contrast available data-analysis software tools and their specialties.

When accountants want to answer management's questions, they must access the data from the systems and transform them into a useable and useful form. Sometimes this process is as simple as asking the company's data scientist or database administrator for the specific data needed—but before you ask for it, you need to know what is available. Sometimes the data that you request are already aggregated, formatted, and ready for analysis. But more frequently you will retrieve raw data, which you will need to transform before you can analyze them. For this reason, organizations are increasingly investing in self-serve analytics tools that can access data items from sources and databases directly.

Many data-analysis software tools are available, but in this book we work with three general-purpose software tools to conduct data analysis: Microsoft Excel, Tableau Desktop (which we call simply "Tableau"), and Power BI. It is possible to create and store data in Excel, but it is far preferable to store data in a relational database and simply connect to it in Excel when you wish to perform data analysis. Excel is a powerful tool for exploring data and performing data analysis; it allows you to create pivot table reports, charts, and graphs and perform fairly advanced data analysis. Excel also offers some powerful business intelligence tools that allow you to connect to external data and transform them for ease of use.

While Tableau and Power BI are also powerful software tools for data analysis, their biggest advantage over Excel is data visualization. Tableau and Power BI almost always default to showing the data in a visual format instead of a numerical or tabular format. This feature makes them particularly useful for exploring data, identifying trends and outliers, and presenting the results in visualizations or dashboards when sharing the story with decision makers.

Unlike Excel, Tableau and Power BI do not allow you to input (or create) raw data. When working in Tableau, you need to create a connection to an existing data source outside of Tableau (for example, connecting to Excel or to a database). Exhibit 2.15 summarizes several components of the AMPS model and the data acquisition, preparation, analysis, and visualization tools that are useful for each component. Data acquisition and preparation tools access needed data from a variety of sources and databases. Data analysis tools analyze the data using descriptive, diagnostic, predictive, and/or prescriptive analytics. Data visualization tools may be used to either *Perform the analysis* or *Share the story* in an accessible way.

Each software tool has its own set of quirks, advantages, and opportunities. Please be aware that some of the functionality of Excel for Windows is not available on Excel for Mac. For example, in forecasting future performance, Excel for Windows has a forecast sheet (with forecasting capabilities), while Excel for Mac does not. Power BI is part of Microsoft Office, but it works only on the Windows platform. In contrast, Tableau works

CAREER SKILLS

Learning about analytics software tools supports this career skill:

• Matching the most applicable software tool to the management accounting task

DATA VISUALIZATION

Exhibit 2.15
Analysis and Visualization Software Tools by AMPS Model Component and Data Analysis Specialty

AMPS Model Component	Data Acquisition and Preparation Tools	Data Analysis Tools	Data Visualization Tools
Master the data	• Excel (basic) • Alteryx • SQL (Structured Query Language) • Tableau Prep (Tableau) • Power Query (Power BI)		
Perform the analysis		• Excel (basic analysis) • SAS, SPSS, Stata (advanced analysis) • R and Python (advanced analysis)	• Excel (basic) • Tableau Desktop (advanced) • Power BI (advanced)
Share the story			• Excel (basic) • Tableau Desktop (advanced) • Power BI (advanced)

on both Mac and Windows computers. Also, you can effortlessly run a regression in Excel, but in Power BI you'll have to input complex code to perform a regression.

You will learn about the benefits and limitations of each software package as you work with them. Exhibit 2.16 provides a summary of characteristics of each of the software tools used in this text.

	Software Tool		
Tool Characteristic	**Excel**	**Tableau (Tableau Prep and Tableau Desktop)**	**Power BI (and Power Query)**
Data source	Input and store data Access external data sources	Access external data sources (including Excel files)	Access external data sources (including Excel files)
Statistical tools	Broad choice of statistical tools (including regression and hypothesis testing)	Limited choice	Limited choice
Visualization creation	Basic	Advanced	Advanced
Dashboard creation	Limited	Advanced	Advanced
Platforms	Excel for Windows more functional than Excel for Mac	Available on Windows and Mac	Windows only (not available on Mac)
Total number of rows and columns in a worksheet	1,048,576 rows by 16,384 columns	No limitations	No limitations

Exhibit 2.16
Characteristics of Software Tools Emphasized in This Textbook

Throughout this course, you will find some labs that ask you to work through a data analytics problem in Excel followed by analytics labs that ask you to work through the same problem in Tableau or Power BI. The use of different software tools to accomplish a similar task will teach you flexibility and show that you can apply the same structured, critical thinking. The labs will also help you develop your own preferences in identifying the software tool that best meets your analysis and communication needs.

> ### (Q) LAB CONNECTIONS
>
> **LAB 2.4 Tableau** shows you how to link tables to each other in Tableau using primary and foreign keys. These links allow analysts to evaluate all data that are linked together.
>
> **LAB 2.5 Power BI** shows you how to link tables in Power BI, again using primary and foreign keys as links. These links allow analysts to evaluate all data that are linked together.

Careers in Management Accounting

Exhibit 2.17 reproduces a Cost Accountant job listing from a staffing and recruiting firm posted on a site like **Indeed.com** or **ZipRecruiter.com**. Notice the database skills required

Job Title

Cost Accountant/Controller, Global Manufacturing Company

Job Summary

An active and growing global manufacturing company is seeking a Cost Accountant/Controller to join their accounting department. Candidates should have experience working with complex, large data sets, combining data from multiple sources, and calculating profit margins. The person in this role will be responsible for preparing budget reports and undertaking cost analyses. Our ideal candidate should have excellent analytical skills and be able to create detailed reports to recommend cost savings and budgeting solutions for our company.

Salary and Details

Up to $115,000 a year
Full-time and partially remote

Required Qualifications and Skills

- Proven work experience in one of the following roles: Accountant, Cost Accountant, Cost Analyst (2 years)
- Thorough knowledge of accounting procedures and Generally Accepted Accounting Principles (GAAP)
- ERP systems (1 year)
- BS degree in Accounting, Finance, or another relevant field (MBA or CPA preferred)
- Excellent analytical skills with an attention to detail
- Proven ability to correctly manage confidential information — *Importance of data ethics, especially regarding data security*
- Fluent in bookkeeping/accounting software (QuickBooks or similar) and Microsoft Excel, especially advanced skills like VLOOKUPs and pivot tables — *Experience with Excel, VLOOKUP, and pivot tables, as shown in the Data Analytics Mini-Lab*
- Ability to work independently and manage high-priority project deadlines

Responsibilities

- Plan and record operations costs, purchases of raw materials, and other variable costs
- Determine salaries, insurance, rent, and other fixed costs — *Determine fixed and variable costs*
- Perform audits and reviews of standard and actual costs
- Prepare company-wide and division cost forecasts and budgeting reports
- Create and maintain an expenses database for gathered cost information — *Ability to build and access database and accumulate data*
- Construct systems to track data accumulation
- Analyze and report profit margins
- Manage month-end and year-end closing
- Analyze key reports in order to recommend savings measures and cost-effective solutions

Exhibit 2.17
Cost Accountant Job Opportunity

for the job in addition to the importance of understanding fixed and variable costs, as emphasized in this chapter (see yellow highlights). The materials in this chapter clearly constitute a valuable skill set for management accountants.

 PROGRESS CHECK

14. Why would management accountants perform some analysis in Excel and other analysis in Tableau or Power BI? What are the advantages of each?

15. What are some challenges of using Excel on a Mac (as compared to using Excel on a Windows-based computer)?

Key Takeaways: An Introduction to Cost Data

In this chapter, we introduced cost classifications and explained the internal and external sources of data that management accountants use. We also explained the elements of relational databases and provided an overview of key software tools that management accountants use.

Using the AMPS model, let's review how the information in this chapter can be used to address important managerial questions:

Ask the Question

■ **What question(s) does management want to answer?**
To address management questions, we need appropriate terminology regarding costs. For example, when we ask, "What will be the cost to build a **Tesla** Cybertruck?" we need to understand the different cost classifications to address the question at hand and report the results to management.

Master the Data

■ **Which data are appropriate to address management's questions?**
We described the various internal and external cost accounting data sources, including financial reporting systems, manufacturing (production) systems, human resource management systems, customer relationship management systems, point-of-sale systems, and supply chain management systems, as well as macroeconomic data and industry-level reports and competitor data. We also described how linking these various systems (or tables) is facilitated by relational databases that contain primary and foreign keys.

Perform the Analysis

■ **Which analytics are performed to address management questions?**
We introduced the different software tools used to access, analyze, and visualize accounting data. While some tools, such as Excel, emphasize general-purpose analysis, others (such as Tableau and Power BI) emphasize visualizations. We will work with all three of these tools throughout this text.

Share the Story

■ **How are the results of the analytics shared with stakeholders?**
Understanding the data attributes and characteristics being reported will ultimately help us determine the appropriate means of visualizing data and communicating results.

Key Terms

actual costs

attribute or field

budgeted costs

conversion costs

cost

cost accounting (costing) system

cost accumulation

cost allocation

cost assignment

cost of goods sold

cost object

cost tracing

customer relationship management (CRM) system

data type

database

direct costs

direct labor

direct materials

enterprise system or enterprise resource planning (ERP) system

fields

financial reporting system (FRS) or accounting system

fixed cost

foreign key

human resource management (HRM) system

indirect costs

manufacturing overhead

manufacturing (production) information system (MS)

mixed costs

period costs

point-of-sale (POS) system

primary key

prime costs

product costs

product costs (or inventoriable costs)

record

relational database

standard cost

supply chain

supply chain management (SCM) system

table

variable cost

⊘ ANSWERS TO PROGRESS CHECKS

1. Apple Music, Apple Care, the Apple Watch and iPhone, and the App Store are all examples of cost objects at Apple.

2. Tesla decision makers will assess the costs that accrue to its Cybertruck model to monitor the types and levels of costs to bring the Cybertruck to market, to identify the break-even point, and to set the price that the company should charge for a Cybertruck.

3. Cost accumulation is the collection of cost data in an accounting system. Cost assignment is the process of (1) tracing direct costs to a cost object or (2) allocating indirect costs to the cost object.

4. It is not worth the cost/effort to directly trace every cost. Management accountants decide whether to trace costs based on a cost-benefit analysis.

5. Because there is a touchscreen in every Tesla Cybertruck, the cost of the touchscreen is considered a variable cost. It varies with the amount of Cybertrucks produced.

6. Walmart inventory is a variable cost because it is based on volume. In contrast, the property taxes at its distribution center are a fixed cost.

7. Because the Tesla car batteries are a component of the final product, they are a product cost.

8. Direct labor is a prime cost (as a direct cost) as well as a conversion cost that converts direct materials into a finished product.

9. Sales commissions are considered period costs (as opposed to product costs) because they are not part of the product cost. Because they are not product costs, they are neither prime nor conversion costs.

10. The cost accounting system gets revenue information from the CRM system, which tracks orders and identifies who purchased what products. Managers could pair detailed revenue information with cost information (which would come from either the manufacturing system or financial reporting system) to determine which products are most profitable.

11. Companies do business in an economy and in the context of competition. Assessing how the overall economy and industry are performing (and are expected to perform in the future) assists managers in determining the company's prospects.

12. A primary key uniquely identifies each record in a table.

13. A foreign key creates the relationship between two tables in a relational database.

14. Excel is a general-purpose analysis tool. Tableau and Power BI are used primarily for visualization, to communicate the results of the analysis to decision makers in an easy-to-understand way.

15. Some of the functionality of Excel for Windows is not available on Excel for Mac. For example, to forecast future performance, Excel for Windows has a forecast sheet with the ability to perform time series analysis, while Excel for Mac does not have this capability.

Multiple-Choice Questions   Mc Graw Hill connect

1. (LO2.2) The salary of a factory supervisor is considered to be a(n) _____ cost that requires _____ of costs to the cost object.
   a. direct; tracing
   b. direct; allocation
   c. indirect; tracing
   d. indirect; allocation

2. (LO2.3) Whereas a _____ cost of a cost object changes in proportion to the changes in its volume, a _____ cost of a cost object does not change regardless of the volume produced.
   a. fixed; variable
   b. variable; fixed
   c. variable; mixed
   d. mixed; fixed

3. (LO2.1) What is the monetary value of the resources used or sacrificed to achieve a certain objective, such as the production of a product or the delivery of a service?
   a. Sales price
   b. Cost
   c. Variable cost
   d. Cost object

4. (LO2.2) Suppose that manufacturing overhead is allocated to a cost object. It is implied that overhead is a _____ cost.
   a. direct
   b. product
   c. period
   d. prime

5. (LO2.2) What is the correct order for cost tracing?
   a. Cost Incurred → Cost Accumulation → Cost Assignment → Cost Object
   b. Cost Incurred → Cost Tracing → Cost Accumulation → Cost Object
   c. Cost Incurred → Cost Assignment → Cost Accumulation → Cost Object
   d. Cost Incurred → Cost Tracing → Cost Object → Cost Accumulation

6. (LO2.3) Which type of cost includes a fixed rate for using a base amount, and then an additional variable charge for any usage over a base amount?
   a. Fixed cost
   b. Variable cost
   c. Amalgamated cost
   d. Mixed cost

7. (LO2.4) Advertising a line of products on social media is considered which type of cost?
   a. Direct cost
   b. Product cost
   c. Period cost
   d. Inventoriable cost

8. (LO2.4) The tires and installation for a **Tesla** Model Y are considered which types of cost?
    a. Product and prime costs
    b. Direct and period costs
    c. Variable and conversion costs
    d. Variable and period costs

9. (LO2.5) The _____ is the estimated costs per unit that normally occur during the pro-duction of a product or performance of a service.
    a. standard cost
    b. budgeted cost
    c. actual cost
    d. cost object

10. (LO2.5) The enterprise system that captures financial transactions and communicates financial performance to interested parties is a _____ system.
    a. manufacturing information
    b. human resource management
    c. financial reporting
    d. supply chain

11. (LO2.5) The system that includes budgets and standard costs is the _____ system.
    a. costing
    b. human resource management
    c. customer relationship management
    d. supply chain

12. (LO2.5) Which type of analytics addresses the management accounting question "Is the level of fixed and variable costs of our primary products different from the industry's?"
    a. Descriptive analytics
    b. Diagnostic analytics
    c. Predictive analytics
    d. Prescriptive analytics

13. (LO2.7) The software package that is known more for data analysis than for visualization is:
    a. Tableau.
    b. Excel.
    c. Power BI.
    d. Access.

14. (LO2.6) The unique identifier in a relational table is the _____ key.
    a. primary
    b. secondary
    c. foreign
    d. unique

15. (LO2.6) The columns in a table that contain descriptive information about the observa-tions in the table are called:
    a. fields.
    b. records.
    c. tables.
    d. primary keys.

16. (LO2.6) _____ exist to create relationships between two tables so that users of the database can link up the details from multiple databases.
    a. Foreign keys
    b. Primary keys
    c. Unique keys
    d. Linking keys

17. (LO2.6) Linking tables in a relational database requires:

    a. a primary key and a foreign key, each in a different table.

    b. a foreign key in each table.

    c. a primary key in one table.

    d. a primary key and a foreign key, both in the same table.

18. (LO2.7) Which analytics software tool works only on a Windows computer, and not on a Mac?

    a. Power BI

    b. Tableau

    c. Excel

    d. Python

ETHICS

19. (LO2.5) Which of the following questions regarding the ethical collection and use of data is *not* suggested by the Institute of Business Ethics?

    a. How does the company use data, and to what extent is it integrated into firm strategy?

    b. Does the company send a privacy notice to individuals when their personal data are collected?

    c. Do the data used by the company include personally identifiable information?

    d. Does the company conduct appropriate due diligence when sharing data with or acquiring data from third parties?

CMA

20. (LO2.5) Enterprise resource planning (ERP) systems integrate:

    a. financial and nonfinancial information from an organization's business processes.

    b. financial information among different organizations only.

    c. financial and human resources systems only.

    d. financial and nonfinancial information from an organization's accounting processes.

Discussion Questions

1. (LO2.1) Why is important to assign costs to a specific cost object, such as a product, process, service, department, or customer? What does this assignment accomplish?

2. (LO2.1) What is the difference between cost tracing and cost allocation when costs are assigned? Why are there different ways to assign costs?

3. (LO2.2) Explain the difference between direct costs and indirect costs. What is the accounting treatment of each?

4. (LO2.3) Why is it important when assessing profitability to understand the fixed and variable components of a product's cost structure?

5. (LO2.4) Explain how product costs ultimately show up as inventory (on the balance sheet) first and then as cost of goods sold (on the income statement). What is the order of events? How do product costs differ from period costs?

6. (LO2.4) Direct labor is both a prime cost and a conversion cost. Why is direct labor a component of both?

7. (LO2.5) Why does the Institute of Business Ethics suggest that companies conduct due diligence regarding ethical practices of third-party data providers? Why is that due diligence important?

8. (LO2.6) Why is a centralized, shareable database preferable to many individual spreadsheets?

9. (LO2.6) What is the difference between primary keys and foreign keys? Why are they important for linking tables from different databases?

10. (LO2.6) What is the difference between a field and a record in a table?

11. (LO2.6) How do foreign keys work? Are they required in each table? Are they unique to each record?

12. (LO2.7) What do data acquisition and preparation tools do? Name a few of the available software tools to perform data acquisition and preparation.

13. (LO2.7) In which situations would a management accountant use Power BI or Tableau instead of Excel?

14. (LO2.7) What is the difference between data acquisition tools and data visualization tools? What is the function of each in terms of facilitating data analysis and reporting on the findings?

15. (LO2.7) The job listing provided in the chapter mentions the VLOOKUP skill (see Exhibit 2.17). Given the formation of a cost accounting system (as shown in Exhibit 2.8), why would VLOOKUP be an important skill for a management accountant to develop?

Brief Exercises   Mc Graw Hill connect

1. (LO2.2) Classify each of the following product costs as either direct or indirect for the **Hershey's** chocolate factory that makes Hershey's Kisses™.
   a. Foil to wrap Hershey's Kisses
   b. Factory supervisor
   c. Factory security (annual fee)
   d. Chocolate
   e. Sugar
   f. Factory building rent
   g. Equipment depreciation (straight-line)

2. (LO2.3) Classify each of the following costs as either variable costs (V) or fixed costs (F) for **Hershey's** chocolate factory.
   a. Rent
   b. Chocolate
   c. Direct labor costs (hourly)
   d. Salaries
   e. Insurance
   f. Sugar

3. (LO2.2) Classify each of the following costs as direct labor (DL), direct materials (DM), indirect labor (IL), or indirect materials (IM) for the manufacture of the **Tesla** Cybertruck.
   a. Maintenance labor
   b. Maintenance parts
   c. Janitorial work
   d. Assembly (labor) of the Cybertruck
   e. Touchscreens for the Cybertruck
   f. Tires for the Cybertruck
   g. Factory supervisor salary

4. (LO2.4) Classify each of the following costs as either period cost or product cost for the manufacture of a **Tesla** Cybertruck.
   a. Maintenance labor
   b. Maintenance parts
   c. Advertising on the Web
   d. Assembly (labor) of the Cybertruck
   e. Costs of branding
   f. Tires for the Cybertruck
   g. Factory supervisor salary

5. (LO2.4) Classify each of the following costs as either product costs or period costs.
    a. Product advertising
    b. Direct labor
    c. Direct materials
    d. Office rent
    e. Indirect labor
    f. Selling expenses

6. (LO2.4) Classify each of the following costs of services as direct, indirect, selling, or general and administrative for a consulting company, where the cost object is the consulting engagement.
    a. Marketing/bidding on new consulting jobs
    b. Wages paid to consultants performing consulting work
    c. Human resources department to manage existing and hire new consultants
    d. Office maintenance manager salary
    e. Supplies used by consultants on consulting jobs
    f. Wages paid for administrative staff to directly support consulting work

7. (LO2.5) For each of the following management accounting questions, explain which enterprise system(s) or other data source(s) can provide the data that are needed to address the question(s).
    a. What is driving the materials quantity variance?
    b. What is our competitors' cost structure (fixed and variable costs)? How does our cost structure compare?
    c. How many workers are available to fill our open positions, and what wage rate will we need to pay?
    d. How many of each product should we order from our suppliers?
    e. Who are our most profitable customers? Which products are they buying?

8. (LO2.1, 2.2, 2.3, 2.4, 2.5) Match each type of data required for a cost accounting system to the enterprise system that is the source of those data.

Cost Accounting Data Need	Enterprise System Choose from: • Financial reporting (accounting) systems (FRS) • Manufacturing (and/or production) system (MS) • Human resource management system (HRMS) • Customer relationship management system (CRMS) • Supply chain management system (SCMS)
a. Point-of-sale data	
b. Direct labor	
c. Status of incoming raw materials	
d. Indirect labor	
e. Potential cost drivers	
f. Financial statements	

9. (LO2.6) Classify each of the relational database terms as database, fields, foreign key, primary key, records, or table.
    a. Columns that contain descriptive characteristics
    b. Observations shown in each row
    c. Unique identifier
    d. Facilitates linking of tables or databases to one another

e. Data organized like a spreadsheet with columns and rows

f. Structured dataset accessed by many potential users

10. (LO2.6) Classify each of these data types as string, date, number, or geographic.

a. Customer's zip code

b. Last transaction data

c. Customer age

d. Customer name

e. Total customer purchases to date

11. (LO2.7) Match the characteristics shown to the three software tools primarily considered in this text (Excel, Tableau, Power BI).

Characteristic	Software Tool: Excel, Tableau Desktop, or Power BI (May have more than one answer)
a. Works only on Windows computers	
b. Functionality the same on Windows and Mac computers	
c. Defaults to a visual format	
d. General-purpose analysis tool	
e. Part of Microsoft Office	
f. Has different functionality in Windows-based and Mac-based computers	
g. Emphasizes visualization	

12. (LO2.7) Match the software tools (Alteryx, Excel, Power BI, Python, Tableau Desktop, Tableau Prep) with their descriptions.

Description of Software Tool	Software Tool (Alteryx, Excel, Power BI, Python, Tableau Desktop, Tableau Prep)
a. Similar to Tableau Prep, but also assists in advanced data preparation	
b. Usually considered the best software tool for visualizations (in addition to Power BI)	
c. Multipurpose tool for basic data preparation, business analysis, and data visualizations	
d. Requires knowledge of programming to perform business analytics	
e. Works directly with Tableau Desktop as a data-preparation tool	
f. Microsoft product that goes beyond Microsoft Excel for reporting and visualizing data	

13. (LO2.7) Match the software tool to its primary data analytics task (data preparation, data analysis, or data visualization).

Software Tool	Data Analytics Task (Data preparation, data analysis, or data visualization)
a. Alteryx	
b. Power BI	
c. SPSS	
d. Tableau Prep	
e. SQL	

14. (LO2.7) Given the linked tables below from a relational database, answer the following questions.

    a. What are the total sales for Customer 2002?

    b. What is the business name of the customer for Transaction_ID 20310?

    c. What are the Transaction_IDs for Customer 2002?

    d. Where is the customer located that was involved with Transaction_ID 20168?

Transaction Table

Transaction_ID	Date	Amount	Customer_ID
20062	11/22/2024	27.32	2001
20168	12/27/2024	38.2	2001
20383	3/4/2025	99.77	2002
20564	4/28/2025	53.67	2002
20140	12/20/2024	46.47	2004
20310	2/11/2025	38.36	2004

Foreign Key

Customers Table

Customer_ID	Business_Name	Customer_Address	Customer_City	Customer_St	Customer_Zip
2001	Beverage Distributors	3221 SE 14th Street	Des Moines	IA	50320
2002	Deep Ellum Brewing Company	2823 St Louis Street	Dallas	TX	75226
2003	Schatz Distributing Co.	3140 S. 28th Steet	Kansas City	KS	66106
2004	Arkansas Craft Distributors	1515 E. 4th Street	Little Rock	AR	72202

Primary Key

Microsoft Excel

15. (LO2.7) Given the linked tables below from a relational database, answer the following questions.

    a. Which Transaction_IDs are for Arkansas Craft Distributors?

    b. What are the dates of the transactions for Customer 2004?

    c. What is the business name of the customer for Transaction_ID 20383?

    d. Where is the customer located that was involved with Transaction_ID 20310?

Transaction Table

Transaction_ID	Date	Amount	Customer_ID
20062	11/22/2024	27.32	2001
20168	12/27/2024	38.2	2001
20383	3/4/2025	99.77	2002
20564	4/28/2025	53.67	2002
20140	12/20/2024	46.47	2004
20310	2/11/2025	38.36	2004

Foreign Key

Customers Table

Customer_ID	Business_Name	Customer_Address	Customer_City	Customer_St	Customer_Zip
2001	Beverage Distributors	3221 SE 14th Street	Des Moines	IA	50320
2002	Deep Ellum Brewing Company	2823 St Louis Street	Dallas	TX	75226
2003	Schatz Distributing Co.	3140 S. 28th Steet	Kansas City	KS	66106
2004	Arkansas Craft Distributors	1515 E. 4th Street	Little Rock	AR	72202

Primary Key

Microsoft Excel

Problems   connect

1. (LO2.1, 2.2, 2.3, 2.4) Match the following cost classifications to their definition.

Cost Term Definitions	Cost Classification (Actual cost, cost allocation, cost object, cost tracing, fixed cost, prime cost, or variable cost)
a. Costs that do not change regardless of the number of units (or volume) of the cost object produced	
b. The process of assigning direct costs to the relevant cost objects due to a direct linkage	
c. All direct manufacturing costs, including direct material costs and direct labor costs	
d. Cost that changes in proportion to changes in the number of units produced (volume)	
e. Anything for which a measurement of costs is wanted or needed	
f. The process of assigning indirect costs to the relevant cost objects	

2. (LO2.5) Match the appropriate enterprise system data source for each type of cost accounting and related data.

Cost Accounting and Related Data	Enterprise System Choose from: • Financial reporting (accounting) systems (FRS) • Manufacturing (and/or production) system (MS) • Human resource management system (HRMS) • Customer relationship management system (CRMS) • Supply chain management system (SCMS)
a. Details on returns transactions	
b. Employee satisfaction and sentiment survey results	
c. Customer satisfaction data	
d. Active vendors (their contact info, where payment should be made, how much should be paid)	
e. Past orders by customers	
f. General ledger	

3. (LO2.6) Imagine a table listing direct and indirect parts (materials) used in production. Classify each type of data produced as database, field, foreign key, primary key, records, or table.

Data Produced	Database Characteristic (Database, field, foreign key, primary key, records, or table)
a. Line-by-line listing of parts	
b. List of contacts with various attributes maintained on an iPhone	
c. Cost of part	
d. Listing of all direct and indirect parts and their characteristics	
e. Part number (unique)	
f. Product that typically uses a specific part	

4. (LO2.2, 2.3) Companies incur many costs to perform their business processes. Cost accountants will classify them in certain ways to understand them.

Required

Classify each company cost as a fixed cost or variable cost, and as a direct cost or indirect cost.

Company Cost	Fixed Cost or Variable Cost?	Direct Cost or Indirect Cost?
a. Factory insurance		
b. Hourly production wages for employees working on assembly line		
c. Product marketing commissions		
d. Equipment repair		
e. Rent on factory building		
f. Factory maintenance		
g. Direct materials		
h. Business licenses		

5. (LO2.4) Companies incur many costs to perform their business processes. Cost accountants will classify them in certain ways to understand them.

Required

Classify the following company cost as period cost or product cost, and as prime cost and/or conversion cost.

Company Costs	Period Cost or Product Cost?	Prime Cost and/or Conversion Cost?
a. Factory insurance		
b. Hourly production wages for employees working on assembly line		
c. Product marketing commissions		
d. Equipment repair		
e. Rent on factory building		
f. Corporate office maintenance		
g. Direct materials		
h. Business licenses		

6. (LO2.6) Data types detail the possible set of values that each attribute can possess. Label each of the following attributes with the correct data type (alphanumeric, date, number, or geographic).

Attribute	Data Type (Alphanumeric, date, number, or geographic)
a. Supplier name	
b. Supplier address	
c. Supplier ID number	
d. Supplier location	
e. Supplier contact number	

7. (LO2.6) Review the following exhibit and then answer the questions that follow.

Transaction Table

Transaction_ID	Date	Transaction_Type	Amount	CustomerID
1	1/1/2025	Return	-27.32	1001
2	1/1/2025	Sale	38.2	1001
3	1/1/2025	Sale	99.77	1002
4	1/1/2025	Return	-53.67	1002
5	1/1/2025	Return	-46.47	1002
6	1/2/2025	Sale	38.36	1003

Foreign Key

Customers Table

customerID	FirstName	LastName	City	State	Phone_Number
1001	Paula	George	Oklahoma City	Oklahoma	405-205-4800
1002	Terry	Herman	Austin	Texas	512-471-3333
1003	Edna	Orgeron	Baton Rouge	Louisiana	225-578-2184

Primary Key

Microsoft Excel

a. How much did Edna spend on her transaction?

b. If the company needed to contact the customer who participated in Transaction 4, what phone number should it use?

c. What is the purpose of a foreign key? Does the Customers Table have a foreign key?

8. (LO2.5) Cost accountants use a number of internal and external data sources to perform their work. For each of the following internal and external data sources, propose one management accounting question the data may be able to address.

a. Macroeconomic data

b. Financial reporting system

c. Industry data

d. Customer relationship management system

e. Supply chain management system

f. Human resource management system

9. (LO2.7) Refer to the job listing for the Cost Accountant position advertised in Exhibit 2.17. Which of the necessary skills for this position are discussed in this chapter? How do you think this course will prepare you for a job like this one? In which courses, life experiences, or on-the-job training will you learn and develop the other skills?

10. (LO2.6) Summarize monthly sales and compute the percentage change from one month to the next.

Required

a. Open the file **Daily Company Sales.xlsx** in Excel.

b. Use a pivot table to sum sales by month.

    i. Take a screenshot of sales by month, paste it into a Word document named "Problem 2-10 SS.docx", and label it Submission 1.

    ii. What are the July monthly sales?

    iii. What are the November monthly sales?

c. Calculate the percentage change in sales from one month as compared to the previous month as (Current Month minus Previous Month)/Previous Month.

    i. Take a screenshot of the percentage change from the previous month, paste it into your Word document named "Problem 2-10 SS.docx" from Requirement b, and label it Submission 2.

    ii. What is the percentage change in monthly sales from May to June? (Round to 2 decimal points.)

    iii. What is the percentage change in monthly sales from November to December? (Round to 2 decimal points.)

d. In Connect, upload your Problem 2-10 SS.docx if assigned.

11. (LO2.6) Summarize sales by month, by sales region (regions 1–4), and by both month and region.

Required

a. Open the file **Daily Company Sales.xlsx** in Excel.

b. Use a pivot table to sum sales by month.

    i. Take a screenshot of sales by month, paste it into a Word document named "Problem 2-11 SS.docx", and label it Submission 1.

    ii. What are the January monthly sales?

    iii. What are the February monthly sales?

c. Use a pivot table to sum sales by region.

    i. Take a screenshot of sales by region, paste it into your "Problem 2-11 SS.docx" Word document, and label it Submission 2.

    ii. What are the total sales for region 3?

    iii. What are the total sales for region 1?

d. Use a pivot table to sum sales by both month and region. (*Hint:* In the pivot table, put month in the rows and region in the columns.)

    i. Take a screenshot of sales by month and region, paste it into your "Problem 2-11 SS.doc" Word document, and label it Submission 3.

    ii. What are the December sales for region 2?

    iii. What are the April sales for region 3?

e. In Connect, upload your Problem 2-11 SS.docx if assigned.

ETHICS

12. (LO2.1, 2.2, 2.3, 2.4, 2.5) Consider the following hypothetical situation. Divya Patel, the new plant manager of Garden Scapes Manufacturing Plant Number 7, wonders about the classification of its product and period costs. Product costs are held in inventory until they are sold. Once the inventory is sold, the expense of the inventory will be shown on the income statement as the cost of goods sold. However, period costs are expensed on the income statement as they are incurred.

    Required

    a. Imagine that you are in a job similar to Divya's. If you believe that certain costs are unclearly classified and you needed the income statement to report higher income so that you can receive bonus pay in the current period, would you classify those costs as product costs or as period costs? How would your decision impact subsequent periods?

    b. In your view, is it ethical to change cost classifications to maximize reported income? Would it be ethical to change your accounting methods each period to maximize your chances of getting a bonus?

ETHICS

13. (LO2.5) Personally identifiable information is any information that permits an individual's identity to be directly or indirectly inferred. Suppose that **Sleep Number Mattresses** uses personally identifiable income information and a credit score to determine whether to extend credit to its customers, and this information is maintained in its customer relationship management (CRM) system.

    Required

    a. Why might the company need to use personally identifiable information to decide whether to extend credit to a customer?

    b. If such information is used, what ethical responsibility does the company have to keep that information secure and private?

ETHICS

14. (LO2.5) As discussed in the chapter, the Institute of Business Ethics suggests that companies consider six questions that will allow a company to create value from data use and analysis while protecting the privacy of stakeholders. How do you think **Sleep Number Mattresses** will answer the first two questions, summarized below, when gathering and collecting data from its current and potential customers?

    Required

    a. How does the company use data, and to what extent are data collection and analysis integrated into firm strategy? Are the data accurate and reliable? Will data collection primarily benefit customers and/or employees?

    b. How should Sleep Number Mattresses advise its customers when their personal data are collected? How should it request to use customers' private data? Do they agree to the terms and conditions of use of their personal data?

15. (LO2.7) Consider the Cost Accountant job position at **Archon Resources** (Exhibit 2.17).

    Required

    a. Why is it important for the cost accountant to determine the level of fixed and variable costs?

    b. Explain why the cost accountant needs to have the VLOOKUP skill in working with data.

    c. Why is the quality of "Integrity, with an ability to handle confidential information" an important ethical consideration for cost accountants?

    d. Given this chapter's discussion of available enterprise systems, why does a cost accountant need to "collect cost information and maintain an expenses database" and "construct data accumulation systems"?

Lab 2.1　Excel

Assessing Fixed, Variable, and Mixed Costs Using Scatterplots

Data Analytics Types: Descriptive Analytics, Diagnostic Analytics

Lab Note: The tools presented in this lab periodically change. Updated instructions, if applicable, can be found in the student and instructor support materials.

Keywords

Scatterplot, Visualization, Cost Behavior

Decision-Making Context

Cheap Drones is trying to determine its cost behavior to make sure its products are profitable.

It is important for managers to understand their cost behavior, which is the relationship between cost and behavior. Variable cost changes in proportion to the change in cost drivers, but variable cost per unit is constant within the relevant range. Fixed cost does not change in total, but fixed cost per unit decreases within the relevant range. Mixed cost increases as activity increases but not to proportion.

Later chapters will use more sophisticated methods to explain cost behavior. This lab focuses on developing a basic understanding of cost behavior with scatterplots, a common type of data visualization.

Required

Determine the cost behavior for each input cost and the total cost of each drone produced.

Ask the Question

What is the cost behavior of each of the four input costs and the total cost for the manufacture of drones?

Master the Data

For this lab you will use data in the Excel file titled **Lab 2.1 Data.xlsx**. Open the file and browse the production and cost data from 10/1/2027 and 9/30/2028. Note that there is no production (or related costs) on 12/25/2027.

DATA VISUALIZATION

Data Dictionary

Date	Date of production
Units Produced	The number of drones produced on that day of production
Input Cost A	The cost of input A
Input Cost B	The cost of input B
Input Cost C	The cost of input C
Input Cost D	The cost of input D
Total Cost (A+B+C+D)	Total cost of production (including inputs A, B, C, and D)

Perform the Analysis

Analysis Task #1: Create Scatterplots to Determine Nature of Cost

1. Highlight cells B1:B367 and holding the Control key, highlight cells C1:C367 to highlight both columns of data.
2. From the Excel menu, select **Insert > Charts > Scatter**. This will plot input cost A on the Y-axis and units of production on the X-axis. The resulting plot will resemble Lab Exhibit 2.1.1.

Lab Exhibit 2.1.1

Microsoft Excel

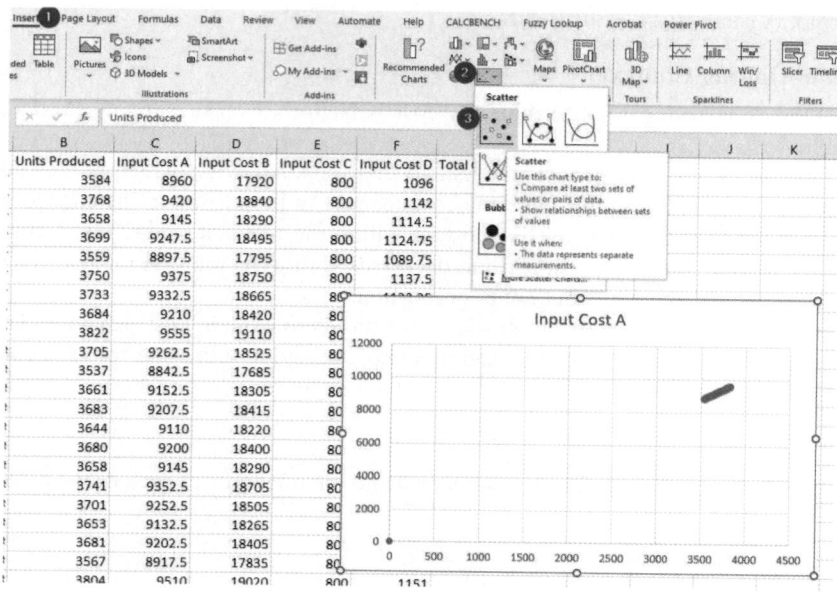

3. Click on **Chart Design > Chart Layouts > Quick Layout > Layout 9**. We note that the input cost A (y) is a variable cost as it costs $2.50 for every unit of production (x). We will discuss R^2 in later chapters.
4. Label the Y-axis as "Input Cost A" by double-clicking on the Y-axis and replacing the text. Label the X-axis as "Units Produced" by double-clicking on the X-axis and replacing the text. The resulting plot will be as shown in Lab Exhibit 2.1.2.

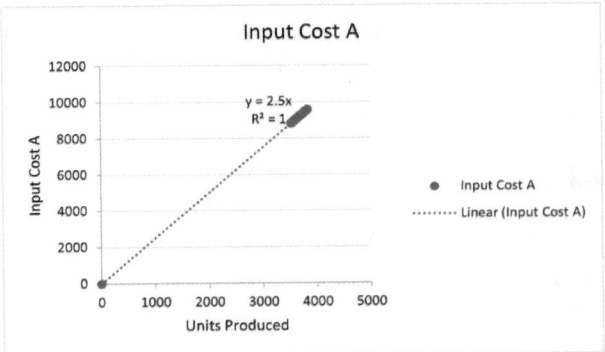

5. To evaluate input cost B, repeat steps 1–4 above by highlighting cells B1:B367 and holding the Control key, highlighting cells D1:D367 to highlight both columns of data. Then repeat steps 2–4 above. The resulting plot suggests that input cost B is a variable cost because it costs $5 for every unit of production (x).

6. To evaluate input cost C, repeat steps 1–4 above by highlighting cells B1:B367 and holding the Control key, highlighting cells E1:E367 to highlight both columns of data. Then repeat steps 2–4 above. The resulting plot suggests that input cost C is a fixed cost, as it costs $800 daily regardless of the level of production.

7. To evaluate input cost D, repeat steps 1–4 above by highlighting cells B1:B367 and holding the Control key, highlighting cells F1:F367 to highlight both columns of data. Then repeat steps 2–4 above. The resulting plot suggests that input cost D is a mixed cost, as it costs $0.25 for every unit of production (x) and $200 regardless of the level of production, as shown in Lab Exhibit 2.1.3.

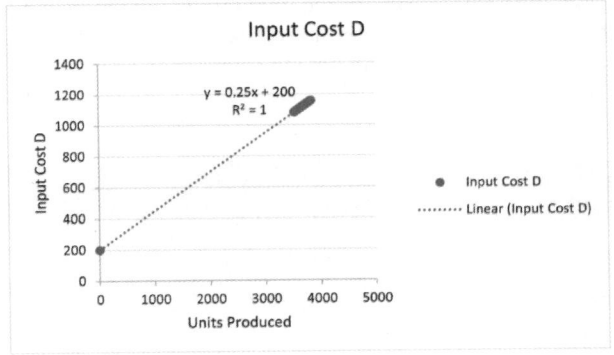

Analysis Task #2: Analyze the Cost Behavior of All Input Costs (or Total Costs)

1. In cell G2, sum all of the input costs, as shown in Lab Exhibit 2.1.4. Copy the result from cell G2 to cells G3:G367 to get total cost for each day.

	A	B	C	D	E	F	G
1	Date	Units Produced	Input Cost A	Input Cost B	Input Cost C	Input Cost D	Total Cost (A+B+C+D)
2	10/1/2027	3584	8960	17920	800	1096	=sum(C2:F2)

2. To evaluate total cost, repeat Steps 1–4 above by highlighting cells B1:B367 and holding the Control key, also highlighting cells G1:G367 to highlight both columns of data. Then create the scatterplot for total cost, as shown in Lab Exhibit 2.1.5.

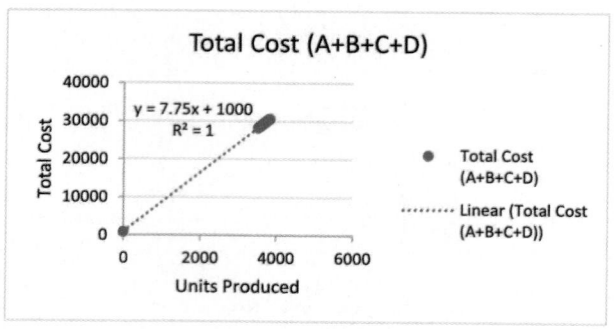

Share the Story

As a result of this analysis, Cheap Drones learns that its total production costs are a mixed cost, with $1,000 in total fixed costs and variable costs of $7.75 per unit produced.

To present this information to management, we could also sum up the costs for each input cost (input costs A, B, C, and D) as shown in the following table:

Cost	Variable Cost per Unit Produced	Total Fixed Costs
Input Cost A	$2.50 per unit produced	
Input Cost B	$5.00 per unit produced	
Input Cost C		$ 800
Input Cost D	$0.25 per unit produced	$ 200
Total Cost (A+B+C+D)	$7.75 per unit produced	$1,000

Assessment

1. Take a screenshot of the scatterplot of the total production costs and paste it into a Word document named "Lab 2.1 Submission.docx".
2. Answer the questions in Connect and upload your Lab 2.1 Submission.docx via Connect if assigned.

Alternate Lab 2.1   Excel—On Your Own

Assessing Fixed, Variable, and Mixed Costs Using Scatterplots

Keywords

Scatterplot, Visualization, Cost Behavior

Apply the same analysis steps used in Lab 2.1 to the Excel file **Alt Lab 2.1 Data.xlsx**.

Required

Determine the cost behavior for each input cost and the total cost of the other drone produced by Cheap Drones.

Assessment

1. Take a screenshot of the scatterplot of the total production costs and paste it into a Word document named "Alt Lab 2.1 Submission.docx".
2. Answer the questions in Connect and upload your Alt Lab 2.1 Submission.docx via Connect if assigned.

Linking Tables in Excel Using the VLOOKUP Command and Pivot Tables (Heartwood)

Data Analytics Type: Descriptive Analytics

Lab Note: The tools presented in this lab periodically change. Updated instructions, if applicable, can be found in the student and instructor support materials. All Lab Exhibits are available within the eBook and in Connect.

Keywords

VLOOKUP, Primary Key, Foreign Key

Decision-Making Context

Heartwood Cabinets makes custom cabinets. The company maintains different relational databases for its sales (Rev) transactions and its customers. As part of a marketing campaign, Heartwood wants to look more in depth at the type of products sold to each customer, and its managers have asked for your help. To answer their questions, we'll use the Excel VLOOKUP function to pull descriptive attributes from Heartwood's Customer table into the Rev sales transaction table.

Ask the Question

What is the name of the customer who purchased the most from Heartwood during the month of March?

Master the Data

For this lab you will use data in the Excel file titled **Lab 2.2 Data.xlsx**. The dataset contains information about revenue transactions with different customers.

Data Dictionary

Worksheet Tab/Table	Attribute Name	Primary or Foreign Key?	Required? (Y = Yes, N = No)	Description	Data Type
Rev	Job No.	Primary key	Y	Unique identifier for each individual job order	Numerical
Rev	Month		Y	Month each job order was placed	Date
Rev	Revenue		Y	Sales amount	Numerical
Rev	CustNo	Foreign key	Y	Customer number	Numerical
Cust	CustNo	Primary key	Y		
Cust	First		Y	Unique identifier for each individual customer	String (text)
Cust	Last		Y	Last name for the customer	String (text)

Worksheet Tab/Table	Attribute Name	Primary or Foreign Key?	Required? (Y = Yes, N = No)	Description	Data Type
Cust	Address		N	Street address for the customer	String (text)
Cust	City		N	City in which the customer lives	String (text)
Cust	State		N	State in which the customer lives	String (text)
Cust	Zip		N	Zip code associated with the customer's address	String (text)
Cust	Country		N	Country in which the customer lives	String (text)
Cust	Phone		N	Customer phone number	String (text)

As the data dictionary shows, the Rev table has the CustNo, but not the customer name. We'll have to look up the customer name from the Customer worksheet tab (or table).

Perform the Analysis

Analysis Task #1: Use the VLOOKUP Command

1. We will add a new column to the Rev table. In cell E1, insert the text "Customer Last Name", as shown in Lab Exhibit 2.2.1.

   In cell E2, we will create a VLOOKUP function. To link tables, we'll use the VLOOKUP function in Excel. VLOOKUP is used when you need to find things in a table or a range. In this case, we'll look inside a table. To perform VLOOKUP, we'll need to input certain information to tell Excel where to look and which data to access. To use the VLOOKUP function in Excel, we need to supply four pieces of information, or "arguments," as follows:

   - *Cell_reference:* The cell in the current table that has a match in the related table. In this case, it is a reference to the row's corresponding CustNo. Excel will match that CustNo with the corresponding primary key in the related table (referenced in the next argument, *Table_array*).
   - *Table_array:* An entire table reference to the table that contains the descriptive data that you wish to be returned. In this case, it is the entire Cust (Customer) table.
   - *Column_number:* The number of the column (not the letter!) that contains the descriptive data that you wish to be returned. In this case, Last (customer last name) is in the third column of the Cust table, so we type **3**.
   - *True or false:* There are two types of VLOOKUP functions, true and false. TRUE is for looking up what Excel calls "approximate" data. This option is useful for looking up tax rates based on income buckets or discount rates based on buckets corresponding with dates by which the customer pays. In our case, we'll use FALSE. A FALSE VLOOKUP will return matches only when there is an exact match between the two tables. Whenever data are relational, structured data, a perfect match should be easily discoverable.

   Because the ranges of data are not only formatted as tables but also named properly, it will be relatively easy to use the VLOOKUP function.

2. Type in the VLOOKUP function shown at the top of Lab Exhibit 2.2.2 (using cell references will be easier than typing manually).
3. Click **Enter**. The formula should copy all the way down, exhibiting the benefits of working with Excel tables instead of ranges.

Analysis Task #2: Analyze Data Using a Pivot Table

One of the benefits of using VLOOKUP functions to add descriptive attributes to the Rev table is to analyze the sales data more thoroughly using a pivot table.

1. Create a pivot table using your new Rev table. To do so, select **Insert > PivotTable** and click **OK**.
2. Ensure that Customer Last Name is available in **PivotTable Fields**. You may need to click **Refresh** from the **PivotTable Analyze** tab on the ribbon to see the new attribute.
3. To get revenues by customer, insert **Customer Last Name** in the **Rows** field and **Revenue Total** in the **Values** field. The resulting pivot table is shown in Lab Exhibit 2.2.3.
4. We can now sort the data by right-clicking any cell in the pivot table in the **Sum of Revenue Total** column, then selecting **S̲ort > S̲ort Largest to Smallest**.

Share the Story

Using VLOOKUP, we've retrieved the data from one table into another to add descriptive attributes to the Transaction table. Connecting the data from the two different tables allows us to find the name of the customer who purchased the most product from Heartwood Cabinets during the time period. The results suggest that Reese purchased the most from Heartwood during the month of March.

This information may convince Heartwood to market its products to Reese more heavily because Reese seems to like our products. The analysis also gives the full range of customers, from those buying a great deal of product to those who buy very little. Such data might help the company evaluate its sales strategy to various customer types in the future.

Assessment

1. Return to the pivot table that you created. Take a screenshot of the pivot table and field list, ensuring that the new field for Customer Last Name is available. Next, paste it into a Word document named "Lab 2.2 Submission.docx", and label the screenshot Submission 1.
2. Answer the questions in Connect and upload your Lab 2.2 Submission.docx via Connect if assigned.

Alternate Lab 2.2   Excel—On Your Own

Linking Tables in Excel Using the VLOOKUP Command and Pivot Tables (Heartwood)

Keywords

VLOOKUP, Primary Key, Foreign Key

Use the same general procedures in Lab 2.2 with the Excel file **Alt Lab 2.2 Data.xlsx**.

Required

1. Use VLOOKUP to get the customer last name for each sale.
2. Use a pivot table to calculate the Sum of Quantity Sold for each customer.
3. Calculate the sum of quantity sold by customer last name using a pivot table.
4. Within the pivot table, sort the pivot table by the Sum of Quantity Sold from high to low by right-clicking on a number in the Quantity Sold column of the pivot table, then selecting **Sort > Sort Largest to Smallest**.

Assessment

1. Take a screenshot of the final pivot table (including the pivot table fields) with the sum of quantity sold by customer last name sorted by the Sum of Quantity Sold from high to low. Next, paste it into a Word document named "Alt Lab 2.2 Submission.docx", and label the screenshot Submission 1.
2. Answer the questions in Connect and upload your Alt Lab 2.2 Submission.docx via Connect if assigned.

Linking Tables in Excel Using an Internal Data Model (Heartwood)

Data Analytics Type: Descriptive Analytics

Lab Note: The tools presented in this lab periodically change. Updated instructions, if applicable, can be found in the student and instructor support materials. All Lab Exhibits are available within the eBook and in Connect.

Keywords

Linking, Data Types, Primary Keys, Foreign Keys

Decision-Making Context

Heartwood Cabinets makes custom cabinets. The company maintains different relational databases for its sales (Rev) transactions, its customers, and its components of the costs of production by job order. As part of its analysis, Heartwood wants to determine which jobs performed were most profitable for the company. To conduct this analysis, we'll use Excel's powerful business intelligence tools to create relationships between tables in Excel so that we can pull data from related tables into pivot tables for analysis. In this lab, we will link five relational data tables to assess job profitability.

Ask the Question

Based on an analysis of costs and revenues, which jobs performed were most profitable for the company?

Master the Data

For this lab you will use data in the Excel file **Lab 2.3 Data.xlsx**.

The dataset contains information about customers (Cust), revenues by cabinet job (Rev), direct materials (DM), direct labor (DL), and overhead applied (OH). The company has 22 sales transactions, and many costs are incurred for each of those transactions. We need to assess both the revenues and the job costs to assess each transaction's profitability. The data dictionary follows.

Data Dictionary

Table	Attribute Name	Primary or Foreign Key?	Required? (Y = Yes, N = No)	Description	Data Type
Rev	Job No.	Primary key	Y	Unique identifier for each individual job order	Numerical
Rev	Month		Y	Month each sales order was placed	Date
Rev	Revenue Total		Y	Sales amount	Numerical
Rev	CustNo	Foreign key	Y	Customer number	Numerical

Table	Attribute Name	Primary or Foreign Key?	Required? (Y = Yes, N = No)	Description	Data Type
Cust	CustNo	Primary key	Y		
Cust	First		Y	Unique identifier for each individual customer	String (text)
Cust	Last		Y	Last name for the customer	String (text)
Cust	Address		N	Street address for the customer	String (text)
Cust	City		N	City in which the customer lives	String (text)
Cust	State		N	State in which the customer lives	String (text)
Cust	Zip		N	Zip code associated with the customer's address	String (text)
Cust	Country		N	Country in which the customer lives	String (text)
Cust	Phone		N	Customer phone number	String (text)
DL	Emp ID	Primary key	Y	Unique identifier for each employee	Numerical
DL	Employee Name		Y	Employee name	String (text)
DL	DL Charge		Y	Direct labor charged	Numerical
DL	Job No.	Foreign Key	Y	Each individual job order charged	Numerical
DM	Requisition Number	Primary key	Y	Unique identifier for each material's requisition	Numerical
DM	DM Charge		Y	Direct materials charged to each job	Numerical
DM	Job No.	Foreign key	Y	Each individual job order charged	Numerical
OH	OH Transaction Number	Primary key	Y	Unique identifier for overhead application transaction number	Numerical
OH	OH Charge		Y	Overhead applied to each job	Numerical
OH	Job No.	Foreign key	Y	Each individual job order charged	Numerical

Perform the Analysis

Analysis Task #1: Link the Tables

1. The internal data model is easiest using Excel tables. To create Excel tables, either select **Insert > Table** or press **Ctrl-T**. Go to each of the five workshop tabs (Rev, Cust, DL, DM, and OH), select a cell in the range, and create the table using either **Insert > Table** or **Ctrl-T** using all the cells of the table (including the headers).
2. Next, in the **Table Design** tab, name the respective tabs as "Rev", "Cust", "DL", "DM", and "OH" (Lab Exhibit 2.3.1).
3. Next, from the **Data** tab in the ribbon, click **Relationships**, as shown in Lab Exhibit 2.3.2.
4. In the pop-up window, click **New . . .** , as shown in Lab Exhibit 2.3.3.

5. The first relationship we will build is between the Rev table and the DL table. As shown in Lab Exhibit 2.3.4, select **DL** as the **Table:** and **Job No.** as the **Column (Foreign):**. Then, select **Rev** as the **Related Table:** and **Job No.** as the **Related Column (Primary):**. Click **OK** to enforce the relationship.

6. Click **New...** again to build the relationship between the Rev table and the DM table. Follow similar steps as above, relating **Job_No.** under **Column (Foreign):** to **Job_No.** under **Related Column (Primary):** as shown in Lab Exhibit 2.3.5. Select **OK**.

7. Click **New...** again to build the relationship between the Rev table and the OH table. Follow similar steps as above, relating **Job_No.** under **Column (Foreign):** to **Job_No.** under **Related Column (Primary):**. See Lab Exhibit 2.3.6. Select **OK**.

8. Click **New...** again to build the relationship between the Cust table and the Rev table. Follow similar steps as above, relating **Custno** to **CustNo**, noting that the Cust table should have the primary key and the Rev table should have the foreign key (Lab Exhibit 2.3.7). Select **OK**.

9. **Manage Relationships** should now appear as shown in Lab Exhibit 2.3.8.

While it doesn't appear that anything special has occurred between the tables in Excel, once we create a pivot table, we will see a difference.

Analysis Task #2: Create a Pivot Table and Assess Costs by Job Number

We will use pivot tables to calculate the costs for each job.

1. From any of the tables, create a pivot table by selecting **PivotTable** from the **Insert** tab on the ribbon.

2. In the box that pops up, select **Add this data to the Data Model**. Then click **OK**, as shown in Lab Exhibit 2.3.9.

3. In the **All** section of **PivotTable Fields**, expand the **Rev** table, place a check mark next to **Job No.** (Lab Exhibit 2.3.10), and drag it to the **ROWS** field of the pivot table.

4. Next, place a check mark next to **Revenue Total**. Expand the DM table and place a check mark next to **DM Charged**. Then expand the DL table and place a check mark next to **DL Charged**. Finally, expand the OH table, and place a check mark next to **OH Charged**. These should all default to sums in the **Values** field. The resulting pivot table resembles Lab Exhibit 2.3.11.

Analysis Task #3: Calculate Profitability by Job

The next step is to calculate profitability by job. There are two possibilities. We can cut and paste values into a different worksheet tab and calculate Revenues less Direct Materials, Direct Labor, and OH, or we can use Power Pivot to do that. Steps 1–3 below use Power Pivot.

1. To use Power Pivot in Excel, go to **Files > Options > Add-Ins** and enable **Microsoft Power Pivot for Excel** by choosing **COM Add-ins** from the drop-down, clicking **Go**, and checking the box beside **Microsoft Office Power Pivot**. In the ribbon, click on **Power Pivot > Measures > New Measure....**

2. In **Table Name:** choose **Rev**. In **Measure name:** enter the title as "Profitability by Job". We'll now find the relevant piece from each of the tables and take revenues minus each of the three expenses, using the formula =Rev[Sum of Revenue Total]-DL[Sum of DL Charged]-DM[Sum of DM Charged]-OH[Sum of OH Charged], and then select **OK**, as shown in Lab Exhibit 2.3.12.

3. We now go back to the original pivot table, look in the Rev table, and find the Power Pivot Measure we just created, **Profitability by Job**. Put a check mark next to it and ensure that it is in the **Values** field. This will show the profitability by job.

Share the Story

After linking tables, we are able to combine the data and determine the revenue and respective costs to determine profitability by job. This information will help management decide the jobs it will offer and the price it charges for each type of job.

Assessment

1. Take a screenshot of the final pivot table (including profitability by job), paste it into a Word document named "Lab 2.3 Submission.docx", and label the screenshot Submission 1.
2. Answer the questions in Connect and upload your Lab 2.3 Submission.docx via Connect if assigned.

Alternate Lab 2.3   Excel—On Your Own

Linking Tables in Excel Using an Internal Data Model (Heartwood)

Keywords

Linking, Data Types, Primary Keys, Foreign Keys

Apply the same steps in Lab 2.3 to the **Alt Lab 2.3 Data.xlsx** dataset. Build the relationships in Excel so that you can create a pivot table using all the tables.

Required

Using the same relationships as in Lab 2.2, link the tables to be able to compute profitability by job.

Assessment

1. Take a screenshot of the final pivot table (including profitability by job), paste it into a Word document named "Alt Lab 2.3 Submission.docx", and label the screenshot Submission 1.
2. Answer the questions in Connect and upload your Alt Lab 2.3 Submission.docx via Connect if assigned.

Linking Tables and Creating Visualizations (Heartwood)

Data Analytics Type: Descriptive Analytics

Lab Note: The tools presented in this lab periodically change. Updated instructions, if applicable, can be found in the student and instructor support materials. All Lab Exhibits are available within the eBook and in Connect.

Keywords

Linking, Data Types, Primary Keys, Foreign Keys, Tableau

Decision-Making Context

Heartwood Cabinets makes custom cabinets. The company maintains different relational databases for its sales (Rev) transactions, its customers, and its components of the costs of production by job order. As part of its analysis, Heartwood wants to determine which jobs performed were most profitable for the company. To conduct this analysis, we'll use Tableau. While Tableau is a great tool for exploratory analysis and visualizations, it also makes it easy to connect related tables.

Ask the Question

Based on an analysis of costs and revenues, which customers were most profitable for the company?

Master the Data

For this lab you will use data in the Excel file titled **Lab 2.4 Data.xlsx**.

Perform the Analysis

Analysis Task #1: Open and Prepare Tableau for Data Analysis

1. Open Tableau and connect to Excel file **Lab 2.4 Data.xlsx**, as shown in Lab Exhibit 2.4.1.

The data set contains information about customers (Cust), revenues by cabinet job (Rev), direct materials (DM), direct labor (DL), and overhead applied (OH). The company has 22 sales transactions, and many costs are incurred for each of those transactions. We need to assess both the revenues and the job costs to assess each transaction's profitability. The data dictionary follows.

Data Dictionary

Worksheet Tab/Table	Attribute Name	Primary or Foreign Key?	Required? (Y = Yes, N = No)	Description	Data Type
Rev	Job No.	Primary key	Y	Unique identifier for each individual job order	Numerical
Rev	Month		Y	Month each job order was placed	Date
Rev	Revenue		Y	Sales amount	Numerical
Rev	CustNo	Foreign key	Y	Customer number	Numerical

Worksheet Tab/Table	Attribute Name	Primary or Foreign Key?	Required? (Y = Yes, N = No)	Description	Data Type
Cust	CustNo	Primary key	Y		
Cust	First		Y	Unique identifier for each individual customer	String (text)
Cust	Last		Y	Last name for the customer	String (text)
Cust	Address		N	Street address for the customer	String (text)
Cust	City		N	City in which the customer lives	String (text)
Cust	State		N	State in which the customer lives	String (text)
Cust	Zip		N	Zip code associated with the customer's address	String (text)
Cust	Country		N	Country in which the customer lives	String (text)
Cust	Phone		N	Customer phone number	String (text)
DL	Emp ID	Primary key	Y	Unique identifier for each employee	Numerical
DL	Employee Name		Y	Employee name	String (text)
DL	DL Charge		Y	Direct labor charged	Numerical
DL	Job No.	Foreign Key	Y	Each individual job order charged	Numerical
DM	Requisition Number	Primary key	Y	Unique identifier for each materials requisition	Numerical
DM	DM Charge		Y	Direct materials charged to each job	Numerical
DM	Job No.	Foreign key	Y	Each individual job order charged	Numerical
OH	OH Transaction Number	Primary key	Y	Unique identifier for overhead application transaction number	Numerical
OH	OH Charge		Y	Overhead applied to each job	Numerical
OH	Job No.	Foreign key	Y	Each individual job order charged	Numerical

Analysis Task #2: Link the Tables in Tableau

1. The first relationship we will build is between the Rev table and the DL table. Drag over **Rev** as the first table and then **DL** as the second table. They will connect to each other. You'll then have to identify the relationship. Select **Job No.** in each as the foreign and primary keys, as shown in Lab Exhibit 2.4.2.

2. In similar fashion, drag the **DM** table from the left and connect it with the **Rev** table with the **Job No.** in each. Do the same with the **OH** table (to the **Rev** Table) with **Job No.** in each. Finally, connect the **Cust** table to the **Rev** Table (with **Cust No.** or **Custno** in each). The final diagram should appear as shown in Lab Exhibit 2.4.3.

Analysis Task #3: Calculate Customer Profitability

We will now view and calculate profitability by customer last name. First, we need to calculate profitability. Click on **Sheet 1** at the bottom left to begin the analysis.

1. First, we need to calculate profitability. Click **Analysis**, then **Create Calculated Field....**

120

2. Title the Calculation "Profit". We are trying to calculate the profit by subtracting direct materials (DM), direct labor (DL), and overhead (OH) from the revenues. To do so, in the calculation field, type in sum([Revenue Total])-sum([DM Charged])-sum([DL Charged])-sum([OH Charged]) and select **OK**. Because some customers have more than one job, we must calculate the total, or sum, for each customer.
3. Drag **Last** (or **Last1**) from the **Tables** area to the **Rows** shelf.
4. Drag **Revenue Total** from the Rev table, **DM Charged** from the DM table, **DL Charged** from the DL table, **OH Charged** from the **OH** table, and **Profit** from **Measure Names** to the **Columns** shelf. The shelf should appear as shown in Lab Exhibit 2.4.4.
5. We want the resulting visualization to show the non-null values. We can create this visualization by using the filter above the **Marks** shelf. Drag **Profit** under **Measure Names** to the **Filters** area. A dialog box will open. Deselect (if needed) the box that says **Include Null Values**.
6. The final visualization should appear as shown in Lab Exhibit 2.4.5. To show the individual values of each data bar, click on **Label** and then **Show Mark Labels**.

DATA VISUALIZATION

Share the Story

We have combined tables from relational databases and linked primary and foreign keys to connect them. We also used Tableau to create a visualization that helps us evaluate profitability. We note that Heartwood did not make profit from two of its customers, Sanchez and Schellman. The company may choose to investigate those jobs performed, and those specific customers in particular, to see if it can improve profitability. Perhaps it makes sense for Heartwood to drop those types of jobs or negotiate increased prices with certain customers.

Assessment

1. Take a screenshot of the complete profitability analysis by customer, paste it into a Word document named "Lab 2.4 Submission.docx", and label the screenshot Submission 1.
2. Answer the questions in Connect and upload your Lab 2.4 Submission.docx via Connect if assigned.

Alternate Lab 2.4   Tableau—On Your Own

Linking Tables and Creating Visualizations (Heartwood)

Keywords

Linking, Data Types, Primary Keys, Foreign Keys, Tableau

Apply the same steps in Lab 2.4 to the **Alt Lab 2.4 Data.xlsx** dataset. This dataset contains similar tables regarding the revenues and costs of the various jobs performed for customers. Evaluate the profitability of each job performed.

Assessment

1. Take a screenshot of the complete profitability analysis by customer, paste it into a Word document named "Alt Lab 2.4 Submission.docx", and label the screenshot Submission 1.
2. Answer the questions in Connect and upload your Alt Lab 2.4 Submission.docx via Connect if assigned.

Lab 2.5   Power BI

Linking Tables and Performing Analysis (Heartwood)

Data Analytics Type: Descriptive Analytics

Keywords

Power BI, Data Relationships

Decision-Making Context

Heartwood Cabinets makes custom cabinets. The company maintains different relational databases for its sales (Rev) transactions, its customers, and its components of the costs of production by job order. As part of its analysis, Heartwood wants to determine which jobs performed were most profitable for the company. To conduct this analysis, we'll use Power BI to link five relational data tables to assess job profitability.

Ask the Question

Based on an analysis of costs and revenues, which customers were most profitable for the company?

Master the Data

For this lab you will use data in the Excel file **Lab 2.5 Data.xlsx** to create data relationships between datasets.

Perform the Analysis

Analysis Task #1: Prepare Power BI for Data Analysis

Open Power BI and connect to Excel file **Lab 2.5 Data.xlsx**, as shown in Lab Exhibit 2.5.1.

The dataset contains information about customers (Cust), revenues by cabinet job (Rev), direct materials (DM), direct labor (DL), and overhead applied (OH). The company has 22 sales transactions, and many costs are incurred for each of those transactions. We need to assess both the revenues and the job costs to assess each transaction's profitability. The data dictionary follows.

Data Dictionary

Worksheet Tab/Table	Attribute Name	Primary or Foreign Key?	Required? (Y = Yes, N = No)	Description	Data Type
Rev	Job No.	Primary key	Y	Unique identifier for each individual job order	Numerical
Rev	Month		Y	Month each job order was placed	Date
Rev	Revenue		Y	Sales amount	Numerical
Rev	CustNo	Foreign key	Y	Customer number	Numerical
Cust	CustNo	Primary key	Y		

Worksheet Tab/Table	Attribute Name	Primary or Foreign Key?	Required? (Y = Yes, N = No)	Description	Data Type
Cust	First		Y	Unique identifier for each individual customer	String (text)
Cust	Last		Y	Last name for the customer	String (text)
Cust	Address		N	Street address for the customer	String (text)
Cust	City		N	City in which the customer lives	String (text)
Cust	State		N	State in which the customer lives	String (text)
Cust	Zip		N	Zip code associated with the customer's address	String (text)
Cust	Country		N	Country in which the customer lives	String (text)
Cust	Phone		N	Customer phone number	String (text)
DL	Emp ID	Primary key	Y	Unique identifier for each employee	Numerical
DL	Employee Name		Y	Employee name	String (text)
DL	DL Charge		Y	Direct labor charged	Numerical
DL	Job No.	Foreign Key	Y	Each individual job order charged	Numerical
DM	Requisition Number	Primary key	Y	Unique identifier for each materials requisition	Numerical
DM	DM Charge		Y	Direct materials charged to each job	Numerical
DM	Job No.	Foreign key	Y	Each individual job order charged	Numerical
OH	OH Transaction Number	Primary key	Y	Unique identifier for overhead application transaction number	Numerical
OH	OH Charge		Y	Overhead applied to each job	Numerical
OH	Job No.	Foreign key	Y	Each individual job order charged	Numerical

Analysis Task #2: Power BI Automatically Links the Tables

Put a check mark next to all five tables (**Cust**, **DL**, **DM**, **OH**, and **Rev**) as shown in Lab Exhibit 2.5.2 and select **Load**. The various tables will form relationships between them automatically, which we can check within the menu item **Modeling**, then **Manage Relationships**. This is a really nice feature of Power BI.

Analysis Task #3: Calculate Profitability as a New Measure

Within the **Modeling** menu item, click on **New Measure**. We will calculate profitability as revenues less the expenses of direct materials (DM Charged), direct labor (DL Charged), and overhead applied (OH Charged). In the equation editor, insert the following equation: Profit = sum(Rev[Revenue Total])-sum(OH[OH Charged])-sum(DL[DL Charged])-sum(DM[DM Charged]). Then click **Enter**.

Because some customers ordered more than one job, we must calculate the total, or sum, for each customer. This is the reason for the additional summations needed.

Analysis Task #4: Build a New Table

We'll now build the table by selecting the table icon, ▦, in the **Visualizations** tab. In the **Fields** area, select **Last** from the Cust Table, then **Revenue Total** from the Rev table, **DL Charged** from the DL table, **DM Charged** from the DM table, **OH Charged** from the OH table, and finally our new measure **Profit** in the Cust table. Depending on what was selected when we formed the **Profit** measure, it may be found in a different table. The resulting table is as shown in Lab Exhibit 2.5.3. You may need to change the view to be able to see the table better. To do so, select **View**, **Page**, **View**, **Actual Size**.

Share the Story

DATA VISUALIZATION

The table is complete, but we choose to create two additional visualizations to communicate the story with decision makers, especially because Power BI is particularly strong in visualizations. In the **Visualizations** area, choose the downward arrow next to **Profit** and select **Conditional formatting** and then **Data bars**, as shown in Lab Exhibit 2.5.4. When the dialog box opens, select **OK**.

Note the data bars that explain the relative profit associated with each customer, as shown in Lab Exhibit 2.5.5. Experiment with this visualization for a few minutes and see if you can figure out how to sort by profit.

The second visualization shows the makeup of revenue for each customer. In the **Visualizations** area, select ▥ (the stacked bar chart) to see the DM, DL, OH, and Profit components of each dollar of revenues by customer.

Assessment

1. Sort the stacked column chart ascending by last name. Take a screenshot of your stacked column chart, paste it into a Word document named "Lab 2.5 Submission. docx", and label the screenshot Submission 1.
2. Answer the questions in Connect and upload your Lab 2.5 Submission.docx via Connect if assigned.

Alternate Lab 2.5   Power BI—On Your Own

Linking Tables and Performing Analysis (Heartwood)

Apply the same steps in Lab 2.5 to the **Alt Lab 2.5 Data.xlsx** dataset, which contains similar tables regarding the revenues and costs of the various jobs performed for customers.

Required

Evaluate the profitability of each job performed.

Assessment

1. Sort the stacked column chart ascending by last name. Then take a screenshot of your stacked column chart, paste it into a Word document named "Alt Lab 2.5 Submission. docx", and label the screenshot Submission 1.
2. Answer the questions in Connect and upload your Alt Lab 2.5 Submission.docx via Connect if assigned.

Chapter 3

Cost Behavior and Cost-Volume-Profit Analysis

A Look at This Chapter

This chapter takes a detailed look at a company's *cost structure,* or its relative mix of fixed and variable costs. It discusses techniques used to estimate fixed costs and variable costs. It also introduces a framework that uses the relationship between costs, production volume, and profitability to help companies understand their business and make strategic decisions. Finally, it explains two important costing approaches, absorption costing and variable costing, and how to account for each approach in a company's financial statements.

Cost Accounting and Data Analytics

COST ACCOUNTING LEARNING OBJECTIVE		RELATED DATA ANALYTICS LABS	LAB ANALYTICS TYPES
LO 3.1	Distinguish between a fixed cost and a variable cost.	**LAB 3.1 Power BI and Tableau** Using Graphs to Display Costs	Diagnostic, Predictive
LO 3.2	Estimate fixed and variable costs using the high-low method.	**LAB 3.2 Excel** Estimating Cost Behavior Using the High-Low Method	Diagnostic, Predictive
LO 3.3	Estimate fixed and variable costs using regression analysis.	**LAB 3.3 Excel** Estimating Cost Behavior Using Regression Analysis	Diagnostic, Predictive
LO 3.4	Define contribution margin and explain its usefulness.		
LO 3.5	Use cost-volume-profit (CVP) analysis to calculate break-even point and target profit.	**Data Analytics Mini-Lab** Using CVP Analysis in Excel to Analyze Strategy	Diagnostic, Predictive
		LAB 3.4 Excel Conducting Cost-Volume-Profit Analysis Under Different Assumptions	Diagnostic, Predictive
		LAB 3.5 Excel Conducting Cost-Volume-Profit Analysis with Multiple Products	Diagnostic, Predictive

Cost Accounting and Data Analytics (*continued*)

COST ACCOUNTING LEARNING OBJECTIVE	RELATED DATA ANALYTICS LABS	LAB ANALYTICS TYPES
LO 3.6 Explain operating leverage and how it influences a company's profitability.		
LO 3.7 Compare and contrast absorption costing and variable costing.	**LAB 3.6 Excel** Comparing and Contrasting Absorption Costing and Variable Costing (Heartwood Cabinets)	Descriptive, Diagnostic, Predictive

Chapter Concepts and Career Skills

Learning About . . .	Helps with These Career Skills
Fixed costs and variable costs	• Budgeting and managing overhead and unit costs to maximize profitability • Estimating costs for future periods
Regression analysis	• Using software packages and large amounts of data to inform decision making
Contribution margin	• Understanding the links between revenue and operating income
Cost-volume-profit analysis	• Making decisions regarding product pricing, cost of production, production levels, and profitability
Break-even point	• Identifying the sales volume at which a company becomes profitable
Operating leverage	• Understanding how the mix of a company's fixed and variable costs influences profitability

Karen Hovsepyan/Alamy Stock Photo

The Atlanta Falcons: Cutting Prices to Increase Revenue per Fan

For many sports fans, enjoying a meal or snack during the game is an important part of the game-day experience. For many teams, game-day concessions are a significant revenue source. Because attendees of major sporting events are unable to easily purchase food elsewhere, it is easy to understand why food prices tend to be so high in a stadium. Fans are essentially a captive audience.

When the **Atlanta Falcons** opened their new stadium in 2017, the team made a significant change to concession pricing. It decided to adopt a "street pricing" model instead of adding the high surcharge that is common at sporting-event concessions. For instance, the Falcons cut the price of a hot dog from $4 to $2. Although the team made less money on each hot dog sold, it found that average fan spending per game increased 16%. In addition, the Falcons saw attendance increase at their stadium even as average NFL attendance at other stadiums declined.

In this chapter, we discuss how companies can use a cost-volume-profit framework to analyze these types of business decisions. The Falcons sacrificed profit margin on concessions to increase overall profits through increased sales volume. The organization's strategy demonstrates a sound understanding of the relationship between cost, sales volume, and profit. Other NFL teams took note of the Falcons' success and began to follow suit.

Source: Andrew Beaton and Rachel Bachman, "Big Seats and $2 Hot Dogs: How the Super Bowl Host Made Football Better to Watch," *The Wall Street Journal*, February 3, 2019.

COST CHANGES WITH PRODUCTION VOLUME

Recall from Chapter 2 that costs can be categorized as either fixed costs or variable costs. In this chapter, we examine these costs in detail. When a firm increases its output of a good or service, it naturally incurs additional costs. However, not all of the firm's costs will necessarily change. Let's use **Heartwood Cabinets**, a cabinet manufacturer, as an example. As Heartwood produces cabinets, it has capacity-related costs for its workshop and equipment, such as equipment depreciation and rent on its manufacturing facility. These are **fixed costs**, meaning they do not change with production volume. Heartwood will incur the same cost for its facility and equipment whether it produces 100 or 10,000 cabinets. Importantly, fixed costs are *fixed* only when we are considering the total number of units produced. On a *per-unit* basis, the fixed cost per unit declines with each additional unit produced as costs are spread among more units.

In contrast, when Heartwood wants to produce one additional cabinet, it will have to purchase more materials such as wood. The wood is a **variable cost** because the total cost for wood changes with the production volume of cabinets. Importantly, variable costs are *variable* only when we are considering the total number of units produced. If considered on a *per-unit* basis, the variable cost per unit is constant with each additional unit produced.

Some costs have both a fixed component and a variable component. These costs are known as **mixed costs**. For example, a production worker making wooden cabinets could be paid a set salary (a fixed cost to the firm) yet could also earn a bonus for each completed cabinet (a variable cost to the firm). This employee's salary is a mixed cost because part of the employee's pay depends on production volume while the other part does not. Exhibit 3.1 provides some examples of fixed, variable, and mixed costs at Heartwood Cabinets.

LO 3.1

Distinguish between a fixed cost and a variable cost.

CAREER SKILLS

Learning about fixed costs and variable costs supports these career skills:

- Budgeting and managing overhead and unit costs to maximize profitability
- Estimating costs for future periods

fixed cost
A cost that does not change with production volume.

variable cost
A cost that changes with production volume.

mixed cost
A cost that has both fixed and variable components.

Type of Cost Associated with Production Cost Object	Heartwood Cabinets (Production of Vanities)
Fixed costs	• Factory equipment depreciation • Lease costs for manufacturing facility
Variable costs	• Cost of wood used in vanities • Paint • Indirect materials such as glue
Mixed costs	• Mobile phone bills (cell phones for production supervisors) • Some utilities

Exhibit 3.1
Fixed, Variable, and Mixed Costs at Heartwood Cabinets

relevant range
The level of production volume over which variable costs remain constant per unit and fixed costs remain constant in total.

Importantly, costs are considered fixed or variable within a **relevant range**, which is the range of production volume over which variable costs remain constant per unit and fixed costs remain constant in total. Within a relevant range, as production volumes increase or decrease, we assume that total fixed costs and per-unit variable costs per unit do not change. Outside the relevant range, companies are far less certain that these same cost behaviors will persist. For example, Heartwood may have a machine that can produce up to 10,000 units. The fixed cost for the machine for the volume range of 0 to 10,000 units will not change. However, if Heartwood wants to produce 12,000 units, it will need to purchase a second machine. This purchase will change the level of fixed costs for the production range between 10,000 and 20,000 units because two machines will be needed. Variable costs can also change outside a relevant range. For example, at some point, direct labor may increase as production workers start working overtime.

Companies track and estimate costs for many reasons, such as producing regular budgets and determining the profitability of a new product or production facility. We know that total costs can be broken down into fixed and variable components. Therefore, we can write a total cost equation as follows:

$$\text{Total Costs} = \text{Fixed Costs} + (\text{Variable Costs per Unit} * \text{Units})$$
$$y = a + bx$$

This equation may look familiar. It is the basic equation for a line that you may recognize from an algebra class: $y = a + bx$. We have simply adapted the equation to costs, such that:

y = Total costs
a = Fixed costs
b = Variable costs per unit
x = Units (volume)

Total costs can be visualized using a graph, as seen in Exhibit 3.2. The fixed costs are represented by the Y-intercept of the line (that is, where the total cost line crosses the Y-axis) while variable costs are represented by the slope (or steepness) of the line.

Exhibit 3.2
Graphing Fixed, Variable, and Total Costs

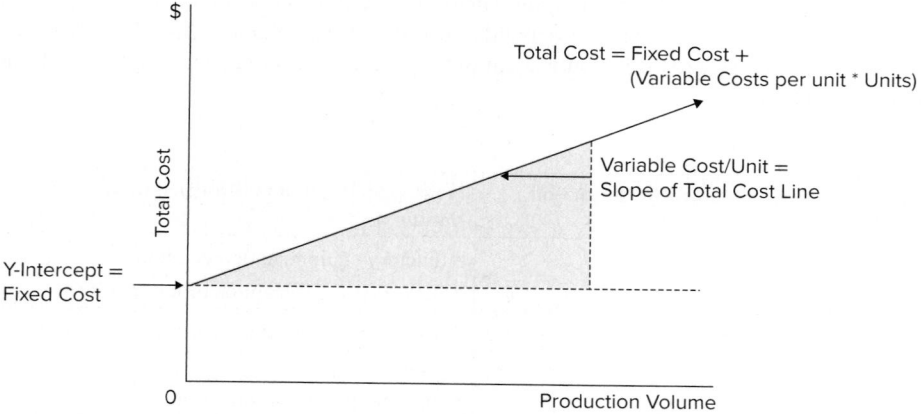

LAB CONNECTION

LAB 3.1 TABLEAU AND POWER BI use software visualization tools to graph fixed, variable, and mixed costs.

1. What determines whether a cost is considered fixed or variable?
2. Why is relevant range important to understanding cost behavior?

THE HIGH-LOW METHOD: A SIMPLE APPROACH TO COST ESTIMATION

LO 3.2

Estimate fixed and variable costs using the high-low method.

In many cases, it is easy to distinguish between fixed costs and variable costs. However, when detailed cost data are unavailable, we can use a company's total costs to estimate the fixed and variable components. Let's use a simple example to illustrate how this can be accomplished. Exhibit 3.3 provides cost information for a call center that assists customers with technical support for various appliances. It shows cost information for 15 recent months.

Month	Number of Calls	Total Costs
1	481	$21,294
2	**325**	**$19,149**
3	359	$20,079
4	388	$20,147
5	425	$20,612
6	482	$22,229
7	336	$19,595
8	**571**	**$29,964**
9	474	$20,449
10	447	$21,462
11	416	$20,594
12	328	$17,792
13	401	$21,157
14	392	$21,047
15	410	$20,285

Exhibit 3.3
Customer Support Costs

A simple approach to estimating the fixed and variable cost components in Exhibit 3.3 is the **high-low method**, which uses the highest and the lowest volume points to approximate the cost equation.

To use the high-low method, start by identifying the highest volume data point and its associated total cost. Then, identify the lowest volume data point and its associated total cost. Note that the highest and lowest volume data are not necessarily the highest and lowest cost data. These two data points are boldfaced in Exhibit 3.3. To estimate the variable cost per unit (or in this case, per call), we must find the slope of the line connecting these two data points. We calculate the slope by finding the difference

high-low method
A method that estimates fixed costs and variable costs by deriving a cost function from the highest and lowest production data points.

between the two identified total costs and dividing by the difference between the two volume levels, as follows:

$$\text{Variable Cost per Unit} = \frac{\left(\begin{array}{c}\text{Total Cost for Highest} \\ \text{Volume Data Point}\end{array} - \begin{array}{c}\text{Total Cost for Lowest} \\ \text{Volume Data Point}\end{array}\right)}{(\text{Highest Volume Data Point} - \text{Lowest Volume Data Point})}$$

$$\text{Variable Cost per Unit} = \frac{(\$29{,}964 - \$19{,}149)}{(571 - 325)}$$

Variable Cost per Unit = $43.96 (rounded)/call

This solution provides an estimate of the slope of the total cost line, which represents the variable cost per unit. Now that we have estimated the variable cost per unit, we can turn to estimating the fixed cost. To do so, we can use either of the points we used to identify the slope of the line. We simply plug one of these data points into our equation and solve for fixed costs. Recall the equation for total costs:

Total costs = Fixed Costs + (Variable Costs per Unit * Units)

We can rearrange this equation to solve for fixed costs as follows:

Fixed Costs = Total Cost − (Variable Cost per Unit * Units)

In our example:

Fixed Costs = $29,964 − ($43.96/call * 571 calls)
Fixed Costs = $4,862.84

Note: If you use the low data point (325, $19,149), you will arrive at the same solution for fixed costs, though rounding may cause small differences. It is a good way to check your work.

Now that we have estimated fixed and variable costs, we can write a total cost equation for the data set in Exhibit 3.3:

Total Costs = $4,862.84 in fixed costs + $43.96 variable cost per call

One of the primary reasons for deriving a cost formula is to estimate costs for future periods. For example, we can use our cost formula to estimate customer service costs for a future period when 400 service calls are anticipated, as follows:

Total Costs = Fixed Costs + (Variable Costs per Unit * Units)
Total Costs = $4,862.84 + ($43.96 * 400)
Total Costs = $22,446.84

Notice that 400 service calls is within the relevant range because it falls within the range of the data used to perform our calculation. When we try to predict costs based on volumes that differ drastically from available data, our predictions are less likely to be accurate because of changing cost behavior.

Although the high-low method can help us conceptually understand the fixed and variable components of a firm's total costs, it is rarely if ever be used in practice. Why? A firm's success may depend on the accuracy of its cost estimates. After all, cost information is critical for determining a firm's strategy and marketing efforts. How many firms would feel comfortable with an estimate that uses only two data points?

Exhibit 3.4 demonstrates the cost equation we just created if the cost per call is unrounded. Notice that the line perfectly fits our data only for the highest and lowest call volumes.

The high-low method ignores all other data points! This problem is particularly trouble-some in this example, where it appears that the month with the highest number of calls is an anomaly, or an **outlier** (a data point that differs significantly from other points in a data set). The line does not appear to fit the data very well. Almost all of the data points lie below the line.

outlier
A data point that differs significantly from other points in a data set.

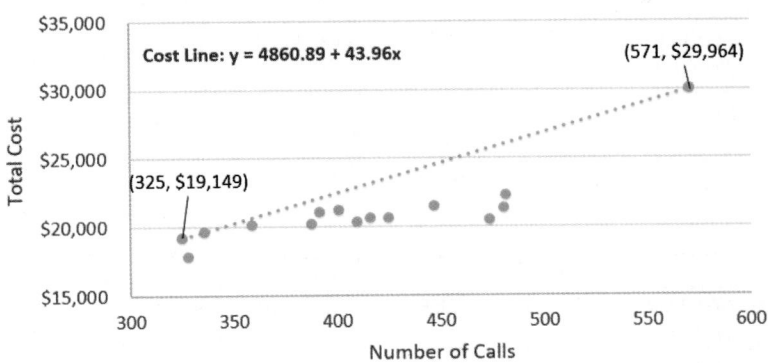

Exhibit 3.4
Customer Support Costs: High-Low Method

Microsoft Excel

The next section introduces regression analysis, which accounts for all data observa-tions rather than only two data points. Generally, the more data we use to create estimates, the more accurate our cost estimates will be. For this reason, regression analysis is the superior tool for estimating costs.

 LAB CONNECTION

LAB 3.2 EXCEL asks you to practice using the high-low method to estimate fixed and variable costs.

LO 3.3

Estimate fixed and variable costs using regression analysis.

✓ **PROGRESS CHECK**

3. How does the high-low method estimate fixed and variable costs?
4. What is the major drawback of using the high-low method?

REGRESSION ANALYSIS: A BETTER APPROACH TO COST ESTIMATION

Regression analysis is a statistical method used to estimate the relationship between out-come variables (also known as **dependent variables**) and predictor variables (also known as **independent variables**). Simple linear regression uses a single independent variable, while multiple linear regression uses more than one independent variable.

Independent variables can be continuous (such as number of orders) or dichotomous (yes/no—whether or not an order was shipped overnight). As it relates to cost estimation, regression analysis allows us to estimate the relationship between total costs (the depend-ent variable) and production volume (a continuous, independent variable). Regression analysis has many advantages, including providing statistical measures of how well an estimated cost line fits the underlying data.

regression analysis
A statistical method used to estimate the relation-ship between indepen-dent and dependent variables, or predictor and outcome variables.

dependent variable
A variable that depends on another (independent) variable. Usually denoted as Y in statistical models. Sometimes called an *out-come variable.*

independent variable
A variable that does not depend on another. Usually denoted as X in statistical models. Sometimes called a *pre-dictor variable.*

The equation for total costs remains the same whether we use the high-low method or regression analysis: Total Costs = Fixed Costs + (Variable Costs per Unit * Units). The primary difference is that, in running a regression analysis, we use a statistical software package to calculate estimates of fixed and variable costs. Using the customer service data from Exhibit 3.3 in a regression analysis provides the Excel output shown in Exhibit 3.5.

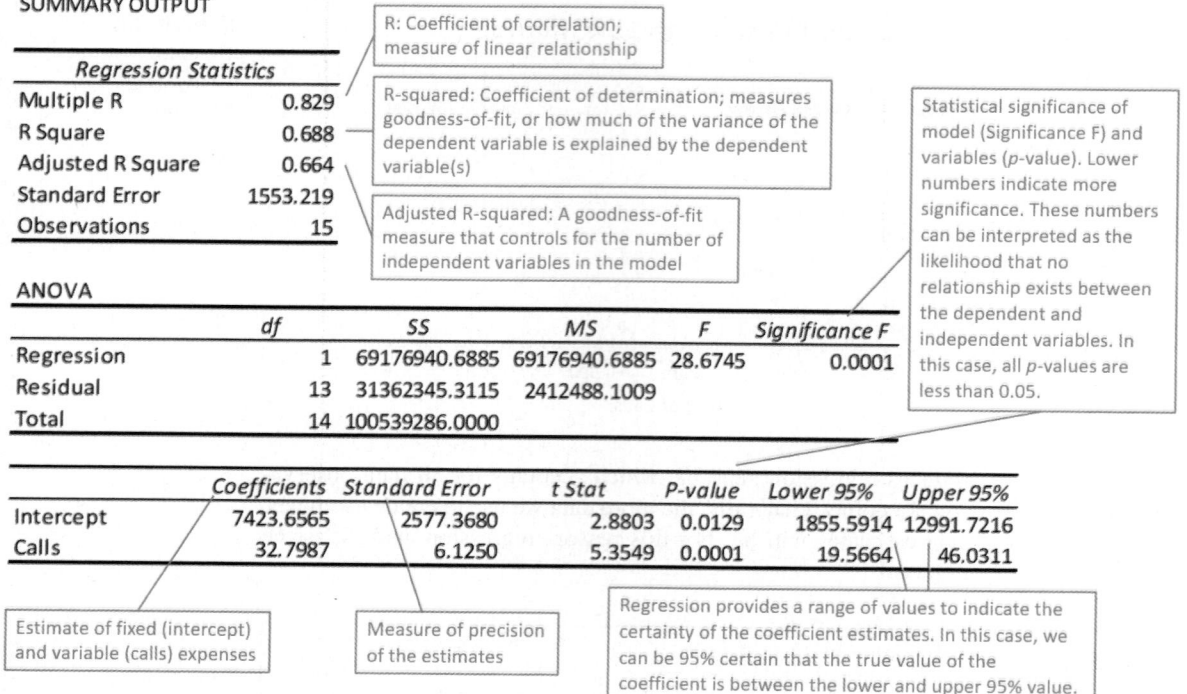

SUMMARY OUTPUT

Regression Statistics

Multiple R	0.829
R Square	0.688
Adjusted R Square	0.664
Standard Error	1553.219
Observations	15

R: Coefficient of correlation; measure of linear relationship

R-squared: Coefficient of determination; measures goodness-of-fit, or how much of the variance of the dependent variable is explained by the dependent variable(s)

Adjusted R-squared: A goodness-of-fit measure that controls for the number of independent variables in the model

Statistical significance of model (Significance F) and variables (*p*-value). Lower numbers indicate more significance. These numbers can be interpreted as the likelihood that no relationship exists between the dependent and independent variables. In this case, all *p*-values are less than 0.05.

ANOVA

	df	SS	MS	F	Significance F
Regression	1	69176940.6885	69176940.6885	28.6745	0.0001
Residual	13	31362345.3115	2412488.1009		
Total	14	100539286.0000			

	Coefficients	Standard Error	t Stat	P-value	Lower 95%	Upper 95%
Intercept	7423.6565	2577.3680	2.8803	0.0129	1855.5914	12991.7216
Calls	32.7987	6.1250	5.3549	0.0001	19.5664	46.0311

Estimate of fixed (intercept) and variable (calls) expenses

Measure of precision of the estimates

Regression provides a range of values to indicate the certainty of the coefficient estimates. In this case, we can be 95% certain that the true value of the coefficient is between the lower and upper 95% value.

Exhibit 3.5
Excel Output

Microsoft Excel

R

The coefficient of correlation. R is a measure of the linear relationship between independent and dependent variables.

correlation

A statistical term describing the extent to which variables move together.

R-squared

The coefficient of determination. R-squared describes the proportion of variation in the dependent variable that can be explained by changes in the independent variables.

While this output may seem complicated, we can quickly look through it to assess the strength of the linear relationship between calls and total costs, and to construct our cost equation. A couple of items are noteworthy. First, we will not cover every item on the output, as many are beyond the scope of this text, but you can find additional information about regression analysis in Appendix F. Second, the terms on the Excel output differ slightly from those generally used by statisticians.

R (labeled Multiple R in the output) is the coefficient of correlation. **Correlation** is a statistical term describing the extent to which variables move together. It can range from −1 to 1. R describes the strength of the linear relationship between the independent and dependent variables. A value of 1 indicates a *perfect positive correlation,* meaning that the independent and dependent variables move in the same direction. A value of −1 indicates a *perfect negative correlation,* meaning that the independent and dependent variables move in opposite directions. An R of 0 signifies that there is no linear relationship between the independent and dependent variables. In this case, R = 0.83, which indicates a positive correlation. This makes sense, as we expect the costs of running a call center to increase with the number of calls.

R-squared (labeled R square in the output) is a goodness-of-fit measure that can range from 0 to 1. R-squared is sometimes called the *coefficient of determination* because it tells us how much of the variation of our dependent variable is explained by changes in our independent variables. In this case, R-squared is 0.69. One drawback of R-squared is that mechanically, R-squared will always increase with addition of new independent variables, even if the model hasn't improved. As a result, **adjusted R-squared** is a more commonly used measure of goodness-of-fit because it controls for the number of independent variables used in the regression model. For this reason, we will use adjusted R-squared to measure how well the data fit the model. In this case, call volume explains $0.66 = 66\%$ of the variance in total costs (see Adjusted R Square in Exhibit 3.5).

The bottom portion of the regression output provides estimates for fixed and variable costs based on our data. We find these in the Coefficients column of the regression output. The estimated fixed cost, or intercept, is $7,423.66, while the estimated cost per call is $32.80. Are these good estimates? We can look in a couple of places to answer that question.

First, a *p*-value describes the statistical significance of the variable. In this case, it is the probability that a variable is unrelated to the independent variable. For instance, the *p*-value of 0.0001 for the Calls variable indicates that there is a 0.01% likelihood that there is no linear relationship between the number of calls and total costs, or that the observed relationship is a result of chance. A high *p*-value would indicate no linear relationship between variables, in which case the variable would not be useful for predicting costs. Statisticians generally consider a *p*-value of 0.05 to be **statistically significant**, but other cutoffs can be used instead.

Second, we can look at the **standard error** of these coefficients as an indicator of the precision of the estimates. For example, the standard error for the cost of Calls is $5.13 (rounded). The smaller the standard error, the more precise our coefficient estimate.

Finally, notice the 95% **confidence interval** provided for the Intercept and Calls. This number helps us understand the precision of the estimate. The regression analysis indicates that the cost per call is $32.80, but this is only an estimate, and the true cost per call is unknown. However, we can say with 95% certainty that the true cost per call lies between $19.57 and $46.03.

Like the high-low method, regression analysis provides us with a cost equation, which is the formula for the line that best fits the data points. Compare the cost line from regression analysis, as shown in Exhibit 3.6, with the cost line derived from the high-low method.

adjusted R-squared
A modified version of R-squared that accounts for the number of independent variables in a model.

statistical significance
A result is considered statistically significant if its occurrence is unlikely to have occurred by chance.

standard error
A measure of the precision of an estimate.

confidence interval
A range of values that describes the precision of an estimate.

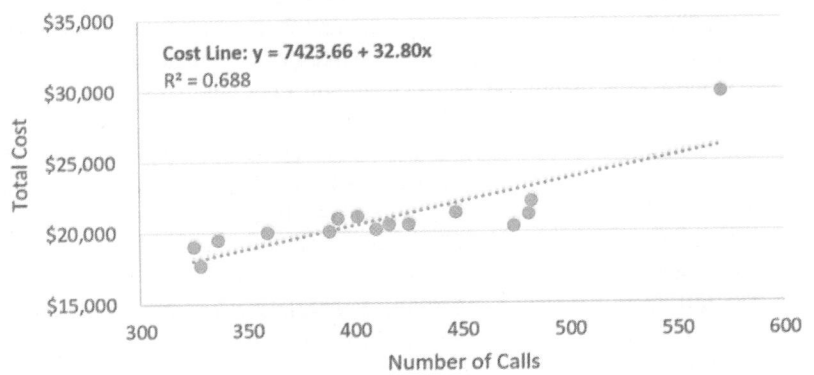

Customer Support Costs - Linear Regression

Exhibit 3.6
Customer Support Costs: Linear Regression

Microsoft Excel

Notice that the regression-derived line fits the data better. That is, the data points are closer to the line. Why? Regression analysis uses all data points rather than just two data points. The outlier still influences the cost line, but it is one data point out of many used to estimate costs rather than one of two. We may consider investigating the outlier to determine whether to remove it from this analysis. For instance, if we discover that costs were abnormally high in one period because of legal costs related to a lawsuit, but that such costs are unlikely to occur in the near future, we may choose to omit the data point from analysis, or we could choose to use the data after removing abnormal legal costs.

Our regression-derived cost line allows us to estimate total costs for a given number of calls. Let's use 400 calls so that we can compare our new estimate with our previous estimate based on the high-low method. Here are the calculations based on the regression analysis:

$$\text{Total Costs} = \text{Fixed Costs} + (\text{Variable Costs per Unit} * \text{Units})$$
$$= \$7{,}423.66 + (\$32.80 * 400)$$
$$= \$20{,}543.66$$

Notice that our regression-based estimate suggests higher fixed costs and lower variable costs than the cost estimate derived from the high-low method. Again, the total cost estimate is probably more accurate using regression because it considers all data points.

 LAB CONNECTION

LAB 3.3 EXCEL uses Microsoft Excel to estimate cost behavior with regression analysis.

⊘ PROGRESS CHECK

5. Why is regression analysis preferred over the high-low method when estimating a total cost equation?
6. What are the benefits of regression analysis?

CONTRIBUTION MARGIN: A MEASURE FOR ANALYSIS AND DECISION MAKING

Now that we have an understanding of fixed and variable costs, as well as the tools to estimate their values, we can use our knowledge of cost behavior to analyze a variety of managerial decisions. The key concept to facilitate our analysis is a performance measure called **contribution margin**. In simple terms, contribution margin is calculated as revenue minus all variable costs. Contribution margin can be calculated on a per-unit basis or for a company as a whole. When we calculate contribution margin, we include *all* variable costs, meaning both variable product costs and variable period costs. Recall from Chapter 2 that **product costs** are costs that are included in inventory, while **period costs** are not. We include all variable costs because our focus is on the cost behavior and not on GAAP-related financial reporting.

Conceptually, contribution margin is the amount of revenue available to cover fixed costs and increase **operating income**, which is a firm's income from regularly occurring operations. The following simplified contribution margin income statement can help you understand the relationship between revenue, contribution margin, operating income, and fixed and variable costs:

contribution margin
Revenue minus all variable costs. Contribution margin is the amount of revenue available after variable costs that can be used to cover fixed costs and contribute to profits.

Simplified Contribution Margin Income Statement
Revenue
− Variable Costs
= Contribution Margin
− Fixed Costs
= Operating Income

Contribution margin is a key reference point to aid in operational, marketing, and strategic decisions. We can use contribution margin for a variety of analyses, such as:

- Examining firm and product profitability.
- Evaluating production options.
- Examining product and service pricing.

 PROGRESS CHECK

7. What is the definition of contribution margin?
8. Why does contribution margin group together both period costs and product costs?

COST-VOLUME-PROFIT (CVP) ANALYSIS: APPLYING CONTRIBUTION MARGIN

Using contribution margin, we can create a framework for analyzing decisions. This framework, the **cost-volume-profit (CVP) framework**, recognizes that decisions about product pricing, production cost, production levels, and profitability goals are all interrelated. The CVP framework builds on the total cost equation by introducing revenue into the equation, which can be represented in several different ways, as follows:

$$\text{Operating income} = \begin{array}{c} \text{Revenue} - \text{Variable Costs} - \text{Fixed Costs} \\ \text{or} \\ \text{Total Contribution Margin} - \text{Fixed Costs} \\ \text{or} \\ [(\text{Sales price per unit} - \text{Variable cost per unit}) * \text{Units}] - \text{Fixed Costs} \\ \text{or} \\ (\text{Contribution margin per unit} * \text{Units}) - \text{Fixed Costs} \end{array}$$

At the per-unit level, there are five key variables in the CVP framework:

1. Operating income
2. Sales price per unit
3. Variable cost per unit
4. Volume
5. Fixed costs

Using these factors, we can examine how changes in sales price, sales volume, and cost affect operating income.

Exhibit 3.7 provides a graphical illustration of the CVP framework. We explain some of the key terms in this graph, such as the break-even point, in the next section.

CVP analysis can be used to answer a host of questions, including:

- What is a company's profit or loss at a given volume?
- How will changes in product inputs affect profitability?
- How many additional units must be sold to increase operating income by 10%?
- How might automation, which shifts variable costs to fixed costs, affect profitability?

@ **LAB CONNECTION**

LABS 3.4 EXCEL AND 3.5 EXCEL provide detailed examples of the types of problems that can be solved with the CVP framework.

product costs
Costs incurred to create a product or service intended for sale to customers.

period costs
Costs that are recorded as expenses on the income statement when they occur. Any cost that is not a product cost is a period cost.

operating income
Income from regularly recurring operations.

LO 3.5

Use cost-volume-profit (CVP) analysis to calculate break-even point and target profit.

CAREER SKILLS

Learning about cost-volume-profit analysis supports this career skill:
- Making decisions regarding product pricing, cost of production, production levels, and profitability

cost-volume-profit (CVP) framework
A framework that describes the relationship between operating costs, production volume, and operating income. The CVP framework allows for several useful analyses examining how changes in revenue, costs, or cost structure affect profitability.

Exhibit 3.7
The CVP Framework

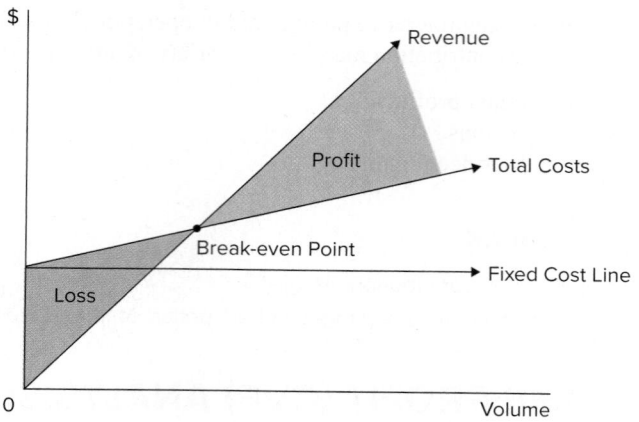

We can think of contribution margin on a per-unit basis or as a total amount. On a per-unit basis, firms benefit from knowing how many revenue dollars from each additional unit sold can be used to cover fixed costs or contribute to profit. Companies can also use total contribution margin to determine a **break-even point**, or the point at which a firm's operating income equals $0 or the contribution margin equals fixed costs. We derive this conclusion from our previous calculation of operating income:

break-even point
The point at which operating income is zero, or at which fixed costs are equal to the contribution margin.

$$\text{Operating Income} = \text{Total Contibution Margin} - \text{Fixed Costs}$$
$$0 = \text{Total Contribution Margin} - \text{Fixed Costs}$$
$$\text{Fixed Costs} = \text{Total Contribution Margin}$$
$$\text{or}$$
$$\text{Fixed Costs} = \text{Contribution Margin/Unit} * \text{Units}$$

Break-even analysis is an important tool for companies considering new product lines or businesses because it identifies the volume at which the company becomes profitable. Here we will use a sample company, Man's Best Friend (MBF) Inc., to illustrate a few examples of break-even analysis.

MBF sells dog beds, and it sold 10,000 beds last year. Below is a summary of its financial data, arranged according to the simplified contribution margin income statement:

	Per unit	Total	% of Sales
Revenue	$ 50.00	$ 500,000	100%
(Variable Costs)	$ (10.00)	$ (100,000)	20%
Contribution Margin	$ 40.00	$ 400,000	80%
(Fixed Costs)	$ (16.00)	$ (160,000)	32%
Net Operating Income	$ 24.00	$ 240,000	48%

Microsoft Excel

We can use contribution margin to calculate the break-even point in a variety of ways.

Break-Even Point in Units or Revenue

First, we can calculate break-even point in units as follows:

$$\text{Break-Even Point in Units} = \text{Fixed Costs/Contribution Margin per Unit}$$
$$= \$160,000/\$40$$
$$= 4,000 \text{ units}$$

That is, MBF can break even, or have an operating income of $0, by selling 4,000 units.

Companies often use a metric known as the **contribution margin ratio**, which is the ratio of contribution margin to sales (or contribution margin divided by sales). Using the contribution margin ratio allows us to quickly calculate the break-even point in terms of sales dollars, as follows:

$$\text{Break-Even Point in Revenue} = \text{Fixed Costs/Contribution Margin Ratio*}$$
$$= \$160,000/80\%$$
$$= \$200,000$$

contribution margin ratio
Contribution margin divided by sales. It tells us how many cents in each dollar are available to cover fixed costs and contribute to profits.

Note: Contribution margin ratio = Contribution margin/Sales

MBF can break even with sales of $200,000.

Target Profit Point in Units or Revenue

Companies' ultimate goal is not to break even but rather to make a profit. We can adapt the CVP framework to compute the number of sales units or total sales revenue that must be achieved to generate a specific profit. For this analysis, we make a slight adjustment to the above two formulas. Essentially, we are looking for the point at which contribution margin covers the company's fixed costs as well as the target profit. Let's assume that MBF has a target profit of $300,000.

$$\text{Target Profit Point in Units} = (\text{Fixed Costs} + \text{Target Profit})/\text{Contribution Margin per Unit}$$
$$= (\$160,000 + \$300,000)/\$40$$
$$= 11,500 \text{ units}$$

MBF can achieve a profit of $300,000 by selling 11,500 units.

We can also use the contribution margin ratio to calculate the target profit point in revenue:

$$\begin{array}{l}\text{Target Profit Point}\\ \text{in Revenue}\end{array} = (\text{Fixed Costs} + \text{Target Profit})/\text{Contribution-Margin Ratio}$$

$$= (\$160,000 + \$300,000)/80\%$$

$$= \$575,000$$

MBF can achieve a profit of $300,000 with revenue of $575,000.

Accounting for Income Taxes

Taxes increase the amount of revenue that a company must generate to earn a desired profit. Within the CVP framework, we can alter our formulas to account for the effect of income taxes. Specifically, we know that

$$\text{After-Tax Profit} = \text{Pretax Profit} * (1 - \text{Tax Rate})$$

Let's assume MBF wants to earn a profit of $300,000 after taxes, and the tax rate is 40%. We can calculate the required unit sales with the following equations:

$$\text{Target After-Tax Profit Point in Units} = \frac{\text{Fixed Costs} + \dfrac{\text{Target After-Tax Profit}}{(1 - \text{Tax Rate})}}{\text{Contribution Margin per Unit}}$$

$$= \frac{\$160,000 + \dfrac{\$300,000}{(1 - 0.40)}}{\$40}$$

$$= \frac{\$160,000 + \$500,000}{\$40}$$

$$= 16,500 \text{ units}$$

To achieve $300,000 in after-tax profit, we first calculate that MBF must earn a pretax profit of $500,000 = $300,000/(1 − 0.4). MBF can earn this profit by selling 16,500 units.

We can use a similar formula to calculate the revenue that will result in $300,000 of after-tax profit:

$$\text{Target After-Tax Profit Point in Revenue} = \frac{\text{Fixed Costs} + \dfrac{\text{Target After-Tax Profit}}{(1 - \text{Tax Rate})}}{\text{Contribution Margin Ratio}}$$

$$= \frac{\$160,000 + \dfrac{\$300,000}{(1 - 0.40)}}{0.80}$$

$$= \$825,000$$

Margin of Safety

margin of safety
A measure of how much revenue or how many units a company is producing above and beyond the break-even point.

Finally, companies can use break-even analysis to calculate their **margin of safety**, which is a measure of revenue or sales units above and beyond the break-even point. This is an important figure for many companies because it measures how close companies are to flipping from a profit to a loss.

$$\text{Margin of Safety (in Units)} = \text{Sales Units} - \text{Break-Even Units}$$
$$= 10,000 - 4,000$$
$$= 6,000$$

or

$$\text{Margin of Safety (in Revenue)} = \text{Revenue} - \text{Break-Even Revenue}$$
$$= \$500,000 - \$200,000$$
$$= \$300,000$$

MBF's margin of safety indicates little risk of generating a loss. It currently exceeds the break-even point by 6,000 units, or $300,000 in revenue.

margin of safety ratio
The proportion of sales that exceeds the break-even point.

The **margin of safety ratio** represents the proportion of sales that exceeds the break-even point. It can be calculated using sales units or revenues as follows:

$$\text{Margin of Safety Ratio} = 6,000 \text{ units}/10,000$$
$$= 0.60$$

MBF's margin of safety ratio indicates that 60% of current sales are unnecessary to achieve the break-even point.

FROM THE FIELD

The Importance of Break-Even Analysis

In this era of high-tech startups, it may seem that break-even analysis is unimportant. **Amazon, Facebook,** and **Tesla,** for example, were all billion-dollar companies for several years before they were able to turn a profit. Other valuable companies, including **Zillow, Pinterest, Lyft,** and **Uber,** are in similar situations today.

However, the reality is that break-even analysis is essential for all companies. Many entrepreneurs and small business owners know the risks of starting and running a business, and they use break-even analysis to determine whether they can survive long enough to become profitable. Large companies perform the same analysis. Cash infusions from investors simply allow the companies listed above to survive for a longer time period before turning a profit.

Thinking Critically

Consider the current state of the economy. How do economic expansions and recessions affect the patience of investors and the amount of time companies have to generate profits? How do these realities affect a company's decision to go public?

(Q) LAB CONNECTION

LAB 3.4 EXCEL shows how revenue, price, and volume affect company profitability. In that lab, you will practice solving for break-even point and target income, and you will see how cost structure affects profitability.

Multiproduct Setting: An Expanded CVP Framework

We can use the CVP framework in a multiproduct setting by expanding it to include the sales price per unit and variable cost per unit for each product or service. Consider how the CVP framework would look for MBF if the company sold two products, a regular dog bed and a premium dog bed:

$$\text{Operating income} = \begin{aligned}&\left[\left(\begin{array}{c}\text{Sales price per unit} \\ \text{of regular beds}\end{array} - \begin{array}{c}\text{Variable cost per unit} \\ \text{of regular beds}\end{array}\right) \times \text{Regular Units}\right] \\ &+ \left[\left(\begin{array}{c}\text{Sales price per unit} \\ \text{of premium bed}\end{array} - \begin{array}{c}\text{Variable cost per unit} \\ \text{of premium bed}\end{array}\right) \times \text{Premium units}\right] \\ &- \text{Fixed Costs}\end{aligned}$$

sales mix
In a multiproduct setting, the ratio of each product's sales to total sales.

composite unit
A hypothetical unit that combines a company's various products using each product's proportion of sales. A composite unit is sometimes called a weighted-average unit. Companies can use a firm's composite unit to determine the average sales price, expense, and contribution margin of the firm's average unit sold.

We can add an unlimited number of products or services to the equation. As we add more products or services to the CVP framework, we see the importance of sales mix in multiproduct settings. **Sales mix** is the ratio of each product or service's sales relative to total sales. This sales mix ratio can be represented as a percentage of sales dollars. For example, regular beds may account for 60% of MBF's sales. Alternatively, the sales-mix ratio could also be represented on a unit basis. For example, MBF may sell 2 regular beds for every premium bed, which equates to a 2-to-1 sales mix. Knowledge of a company's sales mix allows us to calculate information for a **composite unit** (that is, a weighted-average unit), including contribution margin per unit, which is necessary for our CVP calculations. We calculate contribution margin per composite unit by dividing total contribution margin by total number of sales units.

Note that when we apply a sales mix to the CVP framework, we must assume the sales mix is constant in order to solve our equation for profits. We could alter our sales-mix assumption, but we will then need to solve for profits again under the new assumption (because the composite contribution margin will change).

In the following Mini-Lab, we use data analytics to determine how MBF can use the CVP framework to analyze budgeted financial performance for the upcoming year in a multiproduct setting.

DATA ANALYTICS MINI-LAB
Using CVP Analysis in Excel to Analyze Strategy

Data Analytics Types: Diagnostic Analytics, Predictive Analytics

Lab Note: The tools presented in this lab periodically change. Updated instructions, if applicable, can be found in the student and instructor support materials.

Keywords

Excel, CVP Analysis

Decision-Making Context

We have discussed the types of analyses that we can perform within the CVP framework. Now let's apply what we have learned to a new strategy that Man's Best Friend (MBF) Inc. is considering. MBF is planning to introduce a premium dog bed to sell next quarter in addition to the company's regular dog bed. Introducing new products has important ramifications for company performance, and management accountants can use CVP to advise management about these types of decisions. We'll work through the process step by step, using the AMPS data analytics model.

Ask the Question

How will the introduction of a premium dog bed affect MBF's financial performance? Specifically, determine expected (1) operating income, (2) break-even units, (3) target revenue to generate $300,000 in operating income, and (4) the margin of safety in units.

In addition, consider how performance may change based on changing sales mixes.

Master the Data

Open Excel file **Mini-Lab 3 Data.xlsx**. As summarized in Exhibit A, sales for the upcoming year are expected to be 8,000 units for the regular bed and 4,000 units for the premium beds. A regular bed will sell for $50 and have a variable cost of $10, while the premium bed will sell for $80 and have a variable cost of $25. The expanding product line will require additional machinery and plant capacity, which will increase fixed costs to $260,000.

The first step in mastering the data is preparing a spreadsheet in Excel. In Exhibit A, fill in the gray cells with the correct Excel formulas to assist in your CVP analysis. Three formulas are provided to get you started. (*Hint:* If you get stuck, see Exhibit D. Don't simply copy the formulas. Make sure you know what they mean and how they generate the required information.)

Exhibit A

Microsoft Excel

◢	A	B	C	D	E	F
1			MBF Inc.			
2		Regular		Premium		Composite
3	Sales (units)	8000		4000		=SUM(B3:D3)
4	Rev/unit	50		80		
5	Var Cost/unit	10		25		
6	Cont. Margin/unit	=B4-B5				
7	Total Cont. Margin	=B6*B3				
8	Fixed Costs					-260000
9	Operating Income					

Perform the Analysis

To use the CVP framework in a setting with multiple products, MBF must determine its *composite,* or weighted-average, contribution margin per item. After preparing the formulas, we know that the contribution margins for the regular dog bed and premium dog bed are $40 and $55, respectively, as shown in Exhibit B. On average, what is the contribution margin for one dog bed? The answer depends on the sales mix.

MBF expects to sell 8,000 regular beds and 4,000 premium beds, which is a 2:1 ratio. We calculate composite contribution margin by combining the contribution margin of MBF's products using this 2:1 ratio. Alternatively, we can calculate composite contribution margin by calculating the total contribution margin across all units (total contribution margin for regular beds + total contribution margin for premium beds) and dividing by the total number of units (12,000). You can see the required formula in cell F6 in Exhibit B.

Exhibit B

Microsoft Excel

	A	B	C	D	E	F
1			MBF Inc.			
2		Regular		Premium		Composite
3	Sales (units)	8,000		4,000		12,000
4	Rev/unit	$	50	$	80	$ 60
5	Var Cost/unit	$	10	$	25	$ 15
6	Cont. Margin/unit	$	40	$	55	$ 45
7	Total Cont. Margin	$	320,000	$ 220,000		$ 540,000
8	Fixed Costs					$ (260,000)
9	Operating Income					$ 280,000

Averaged across all units, the composite contribution margin is $45, as shown in Exhibit C. Now that we know MBF's composite unit contribution margin, we can use the formulas discussed previously to analyze MBF's data. We can also use the CVP analysis to provide insight about MBF's break-even point, target points, and margin of safety.

Exhibit C

Microsoft Excel

					MBF Inc.		
		Regular		Premium		Composite	
Sales (units)		8,000		4,000		12,000	
Rev/unit	$	50	$	80	$	60	
Var Cost/unit	$	10	$	25	$	15	
Cont. Margin/unit	$	40	$	55	$	45	
Total Cont. Margin	$	320,000	$ 220,000		$	540,000	
Fixed Costs					$	(260,000)	
Operating Income					$	280,000	

First, let's determine expected operating income for MBF. We can see in Exhibit C that operating income = $280,000.

Use formulas in Excel to complete the analysis, as shown in Exhibit D.

Exhibit D

Microsoft Excel

	A	B	C	D	E	F
1		MBF Inc.				
2		Regular		Premium		Composite
3	Sales (units)	8000		4000		=SUM(B3:D3)
4	Rev/unit	50		80		=(B4*$B$3+D4*$D$3)/$F$3
5	Var Cost/unit	10		25		=(B5*$B$3+D5*$D$3)/$F$3
6	Cont. Margin/unit	=B4-B5		=D4-D5		=(B6*$B$3+D6*$D$3)/$F$3
7	Total Cont. Margin	=B6*B3		=D6*D3		=B7+D7
8	Fixed Costs					-260000
9	Operating Income					=SUM(F7:F8)
10						
11	Breakeven Units	=ROUNDUP(-F8/F6,0)				
12	Target Profit Point	=(30000+-F8)/(F6/F4)				
13	Margin of safety	=F3-B11				

In Exhibit E, we see that MBF earned $280,000 in operating income. With this cost structure and sales mix, MBF would have to sell 5,778 dog beds to break even. Note that these dog beds are composite units. To calculate the number of regular and premium dog beds, we must use the assumed 2:1 sales mix, resulting in break-even sales of 3,852 regular dog beds and 1,926 deluxe dog beds.

The target revenue necessary to earn $300,000 in operating income is $746,666.67. Finally, we see that the margin of safety is 6,222 dog beds, meaning that MBF sells 6,222 beds above and beyond the number needed to break even.

Exhibit E

Microsoft Excel

	Regular	Premium	Composite
	MBF Inc.		
Sales (units)	8,000	4,000	12,000
Rev/unit	$ 50	$ 80	$ 60
Var Cost/unit	$ 10	$ 25	$ 15
Cont. Margin/unit	$ 40	$ 55	$ 45
Total Cont. Margin	$ 320,000	$ 220,000	$ 540,000
Fixed Costs			$ (260,000)
Operating Income			$ 280,000
Breakeven Units	5,778		
Target Profit Point	$386,666.67		
Margin of safety	6,222		

Sensitivity analysis is a useful tool to determine how changes in assumptions, in this case sales mix, will alter financial performance. Let's examine operating income by altering the sales volume and sales mix according to the numbers in Exhibit F.

DATA VISUALIZATION

Exhibit F

Microsoft Excel

Operating Income at Various Sales Mixes					
			Regular Units		
$ 280,000	6,000	7,000	8,000	9,000	10,000
Premium Units 6,000	$ 310,000	$ 350,000	$ 390,000	$ 430,000	$ 470,000
5,000	$ 255,000	$ 295,000	$ 335,000	$ 375,000	$ 415,000
4,000	$ 200,000	$ 240,000	$ 280,000	$ 320,000	$ 360,000
3,000	$ 145,000	$ 185,000	$ 225,000	$ 265,000	$ 305,000
2,000	$ 90,000	$ 130,000	$ 170,000	$ 210,000	$ 250,000

Observe how the *heat map* in Exhibit F uses color to help us interpret how product volume affects profitability. Now examine the boldfaced figures on the diagonal from upper left to lower right. Each of these cells represents sales of 12,000 units, but with differing sales mixes. The heat map also helps us determine how, as a higher proportion of our sales come from premium units, operating income increases. As cells range in color from red to green, revenues increase.

Share the Story

As a result of your analysis, you have determined the following:

- Expected operating income: $280,000
- Expected break-even units: 5,778 units
- Target revenue to generate $300,000 in operating income: $746,667
- Margin of safety: 6,222 units

As you present these results to others in the company, you may wish to use a data visualization like that shown in Exhibit G.

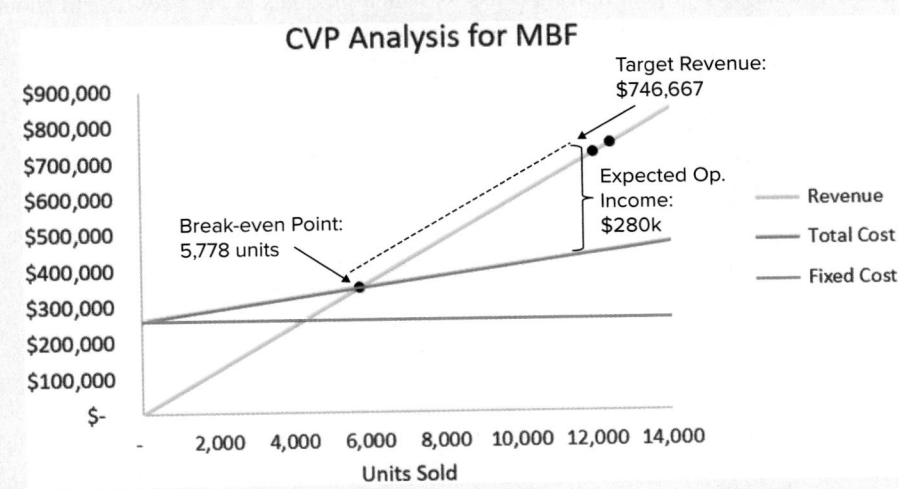

Exhibit G

Microsoft Excel

When compared with the results of the previous period (shown earlier in this chapter), it appears that operating income will increase by $40,000 after the introduction of the premium bed. However, there is a fair amount of uncertainty involved with introducing a new product and altering a company's product mix, and the additional fixed

DATA VISUALIZATION

cost will increase MBF's break-even point. The use of CVP analysis provides MBF management with insight into the potential risks and rewards inherent in adding product offerings.

Mini-Lab Assessment

1. We know that MBF expects to sell 12,000 beds in a 2:1 regular-to-premium-bed ratio. How is the break-even analysis affected if the ratio is instead 3:1?

2. Consider Exhibit G. How would a 3:1 regular-to-premium-bed ratio affect the slope of the revenue line, the total cost line, and the fixed cost line?

3. Given our knowledge of the profitability of the different types of dog beds, what are some recommendations you could make for MBF management to increase company profitability?

 LAB CONNECTION

LAB 3.5 EXCEL expands your understanding of cost-volume-profit analysis by examining a setting with multiple products. This setting makes CVP analysis slightly more complicated, but it is very useful in the field because most companies sell more than one product.

Constrained Resources: How Contribution Margin Can Guide Decisions

Contribution margin can help managers assess which products or services a firm should emphasize, keep, or discontinue. Consider the following example of a plastic molding company that sells two products used in the automotive industry, KG1 and BC2:

	KG1	BC2
Revenue	$20	$40
Variable cost	$ 5	$20
Contribution margin	$15	$20
Machine hours	1	2
Contribution margin/Machine hour	$15	$10

All things equal, firms prefer to sell products with higher contribution margins. Because each unit sold of BC2 brings in $5 more in contribution margin than each unit sold of KG1, the company should emphasize BC2. This is the appropriate analysis if the firm does not face **constraints**, or resource limitations, in producing its products.

However, companies often face constraints, including shortages of specific materials, machine hours, or skilled labor. The key principle when facing constrained resources is to maximize contribution margin per unit of constrained resource. In this example, machine hours are the constraint, and so the company should maximize contribution margin per machine hour. Producing and selling KG1 will provide 50% more contribution margin

constraint
Any limitation of resource that impedes production of a good or service.

per hour than producing and selling BC2 ($15 vs. $10). As the number of products and production processes expands, this type of analysis can get complicated. Just remember the principle of maximizing contribution margin per unit of constrained resource to guide your analysis.

 PROGRESS CHECK

9. How can contribution margin be used to determine break-even point?
10. When resources are constrained, how can contribution margin aid decision making?

COST STRUCTURE AND OPERATING LEVERAGE

A company's **cost structure** is its relative mix of fixed and variable costs. Cost structure is determined by a company's industry and strategy. For instance, **Delta**, **United**, and other airlines have a very high proportion of fixed costs. Depreciation on airplanes, employee salaries, and even fuel are relatively constant regardless of how many passengers are on an airplane. Until recent changes were implemented to airlines' snack menus to protect those prone to allergic reactions, variable costs for an additional passenger amounted to little more than peanuts. In contrast, retailers like **Costco** and restaurants like **McDonald's** and **Starbucks** have a higher proportion of variable costs. For these companies, inventory may be the single highest cost of doing business.

Operating leverage is a measure of a company's cost structure. Companies with higher relative fixed costs have high operating leverage. A firm's degree of operating leverage is calculated as follows:

$$\text{Degree of Operating Leverage} = \text{Contribution Margin/Operating Income}$$

Increasing operating leverage increases the risks and rewards associated with changes in sales. Let's consider an example. **Unifiller Systems** produces machinery that can automate several processes in bakeries. For instance, it produces a machine that can ice or decorate seven cakes in a minute. Let's assume that a local baker plans to build a bakery and is deciding between one of two business models. The baker can choose a labor-intensive model that makes use of highly skilled cake decorators and limited machines, or the baker can use a machine-intensive model that relies heavily on automation and very little on direct labor, as follows:

LO 3.6

Explain operating leverage and how it influences a company's profitability.

cost structure
The relative proportion of a company's fixed costs and variable costs.

operating leverage
A measure of a company's relative fixed expenses to variable expenses, calculated as contribution margin/ divided by operating income.

	Labor-intensive bakery	Machine-intensive bakery
Sales	$100,000	$100,000
Variable costs	$ 50,000	$ 10,000
Contribution margin	$ 50,000	$ 90,000
Fixed costs	$ 10,000	$ 50,000
Operating income	$ 40,000	$ 40,000
Degree of operating leverage	1.25	2.25

CAREER SKILLS

Learning about operating leverage supports this career skill:

• Understanding how the mix of a company's fixed and variable costs influences profitability

In either case, $100,000 in sales and $40,000 in operating income are expected, but the operating leverage is substantially different between the two scenarios. Why does this matter? Changes in sales have a much greater influence on the profitability of companies with higher operating leverage. Notice that the labor-intensive bakery's degree of operating leverage is 1.25 ($50,000/$40,000 = 1.25) while that of the machine-intensive bakery is 2.25 ($90,000/$40,000). This means that for every 1% change in sales, operating income will increase by 1.25% for the labor-intensive bakery and 2.25% for the machine-intensive bakery. Now consider the following table, which shows a 10% increase in sales in both scenarios, with the associated higher variable costs.

	Labor-intensive bakery	Machine-intensive bakery
Sales (10% increase)	$110,000	$110,000
Variable costs	$ 55,000	$ 11,000
Contribution margin	$ 55,000	$ 99,000
Fixed costs	$ 10,000	$ 50,000
Operating income	$ 45,000	$ 49,000

A 10% increase in sales leads to a 12.5% increase in operating income for the labor-intensive bakery and a 22.5% increase in operating income for the machine-intensive bakery. Before we replace all workers with robots, we should note that the same conclusion holds for a decrease in sales. That is, the machine-intensive bakery would have a more significant decrease in operating income than the labor-intensive bakery because a larger proportion of its costs are fixed and do not change with production volumes.

Human Dimensions of Automation: Using Automation to Shift Variable Costs to Fixed Costs

As automation becomes a viable strategy in various industries, managers have the opportunity to invest more in machinery and technology, effectively shifting variable costs (in the form of labor) to fixed costs. For example, **Miso Robotics** is building robots to work in the food industry, and you may have seen a robot cleaning the floors of local grocery stores. Or perhaps you have seen restaurants that encourage customers to order via kiosks or a phone app rather than ordering from an employee. Automation has the potential to alleviate worker shortages as well as assist employees by relieving them of repetitive or even dangerous tasks.

Moley Robotics/Cover Images/AP Images

By using robots that can perform basic tasks in a kitchen, restaurants can shift variable costs in the form of direct labor to fixed costs in the form of increased depreciation and maintenance.

Source: https://www.bbc.com/news/business-59651334

Sensitivity Analysis

Once we understand the cost-volume-profit framework, it's easy to understand how small changes in input costs, volume, operating leverage, and price can impact a variety of company objectives. CVP-based **sensitivity analysis** is the systematic examination of how these changes influence objectives such as a company's break-even point, profit, contribution margin, and margin of safety. Mastering the CVP framework, predicting what will happen if various events occur, and recommending what strategies should be implemented to improve operations is an important function of management accountants.

sensitivity analysis
A what-if prescriptive analytics technique that evaluates outcomes based on uncertainty regarding inputs.

 PROGRESS CHECK

11. How does cost structure relate to operating leverage?
12. What is the primary effect of increased operating leverage?

COMPARING ABSORPTION COSTING AND VARIABLE COSTING

Let's now compare two cost-classification approaches and their effect on the income statement and balance sheet.

LO 3.7

Compare and contrast absorption costing and variable costing.

Absorption Costing Income Statement	Variable Costing Income Statement
Revenue	Revenue
– Variable Cost of Goods Sold	– Variable Cost of Goods Sold
– Fixed Manufacturing Overhead (for units sold only)	– Variable Selling, General, and Administrative Expenses
= Gross Margin	**= Contribution Margin**
– Variable Selling, General, and Administrative Expenses	– Fixed Manufacturing Overhead (total)
– Fixed Selling, General, and Administrative Expenses	– Fixed Selling, General, and Administrative Expenses
= Operating Income	**= Operating Income**

Exhibit 3.8
Comparison of Absorption Costing and Variable Costing Income Statements

Gross margin emphasizes profitability after product costs are deducted.
Contribution margin emphasizes profitability after variable costs are deducted.

The first cost classification approach is **absorption costing**. You are probably familiar with the absorption costing income statement because it is the format required by GAAP (see the left side of Exhibit 3.8). On a traditional, GAAP-based income statement, costs are categorized as either product costs or period costs. Subtracting product costs from revenue allows companies to quickly identify their gross margin. Gross margin minus a company's period costs results in operating income. This useful approach is fundamental to financial reporting because it allows for a simple comparison of information across firms.

absorption costing
GAAP-based costing approach requiring capitalization of all production costs, including direct materials, direct labor, and manufacturing overhead.

variable costing
Managerial costing approach that categorizes product and period costs based on their cost behavior being variable or fixed.

variable costing income statement
Income statement that categorizes costs as variable costs or fixed costs and emphasizes contribution margin.

contribution margin income statement
Income statement that categorizes costs as variable costs or fixed costs and emphasizes gross margin.

The second cost classification approach is **variable costing** (see the right side of Exhibit 3.8). An income statement prepared with this approach is called a **variable costing income statement** or a **contribution margin income statement**. Does the variable costing income statement look familiar? It should. It is identical to our earlier calculation of operating income, and it is the basis for CVP analysis, which we have used extensively in this chapter. Variable costing is more useful from a managerial perspective because it rearranges the income statement according to cost behavior, which is beneficial for firms' internal strategic decision making. Revenue minus variable costs equals a company's contribution margin. Subtracting fixed costs from contribution margin results in a company's operating income.

When comparing these two income statements, it may be difficult to understand how variable costing and absorption costing differ. After all, it appears that both formats use the same costs (albeit in a different order).

To understand the difference, we must consider how each method treats fixed manufacturing overhead. Recall from Chapter 2 that product costs are capitalized (that is, categorized as inventory), and they are not expensed until units are sold. In contrast, period costs are expensed as they are incurred. Under both methods, direct materials, direct labor, and variable manufacturing overhead are considered product costs and capitalized. However, there is an important difference between how the two methods define fixed manufacturing overhead. That is, absorption and variable costing use different calculations for manufacturing overhead. The following summary is useful:

	Absorption Costing	Variable Costing
Direct materials	Product cost	Product cost
Direct labor	Product cost	Product cost
Variable manufacturing overhead	Product cost	Product cost
Fixed manufacturing overhead	Product cost	Period cost

Under absorption costing, fixed manufacturing overhead is considered a product cost because, in accordance with GAAP, inventory must "absorb" all manufacturing costs. In other words, inventory under absorption costing includes fixed manufacturing overhead and thus "costs" more relative to variable costing. How are profits affected? The answer depends on a company's production and sales levels. Let's walk through a short example. MaiTie Company is a fictional company that produces tie racks. The company has $10,000 in fixed manufacturing overhead, which equates to $2.00 ($10,000/5,000 produced units) of fixed manufacturing overhead per unit at current production levels. Exhibit 3.9 shows the differences between absorption costing and variable costing. Because the primary difference between the two relates to how they treat fixed manufacturing overhead, fixed manufacturing overhead costs are highlighted.

Under variable costing, each unit costs only $12 because inventory does not include the cost of fixed manufacturing overhead. The fixed manufacturing overhead costs ($10,000) are expensed as a period cost. Under absorption costing, each unit costs $14, which includes fixed manufacturing overhead. Fixed manufacturing costs of $10,000 ($2 per unit * 5,000 units) are expensed as cost of goods sold.

If a firm sells every unit it produces, then income and ending inventory balances will be equivalent regardless of whether the firm uses absorption costing or variable costing. (See Exhibit 3.9.) Notice that although the $10,000 of fixed manufacturing costs appears in different places on the income statements, the entire amount is expensed in the current period under each method. Thus, there is no difference in operating income or inventory between methods.

Finished Good Inventory		
Beginning Inventory		500
Units Produced		5,000
Units Sold		5,000
Ending Inventory		500

Sales		
Sales Price per unit	$	36

Variable Costs		
Variable Mfg Costs	$	12
Variable SG&A per unit	$	3

Fixed Costs		
Fixed Mfg Costs	$	10,000
Fixed SG&A Costs	$	3,000

Variable Costing Income Statement	
Sales	**$ 180,000**
Variable Costs	
Variable Cost of Goods Sold	$ 60,000
Variable SG&A per unit	$ 15,000
Total Variable Costs	$ 75,000
Contribution Margin	**$ 105,000**
Fixed Costs	
Fixed Mfg Costs	$ 10,000
Fixed SG&A Costs	$ 3,000
Total Fixed Costs	$ 13,000
Operating Income	**$ 92,000**

Absorption Costing Income Statement	
Sales	**$ 180,000**
Cost of Goods Sold	
Variable Mfg Costs	$ 60,000
Fixed Mfg Costs	$ 10,000
Total Cost of Goods Sold	$ 70,000
Gross Margin	**$ 110,000**
SG&A Expenses	
Variable SG&A	$ 15,000
Fixed SG&A Costs	$ 3,000
Total Fixed Costs	$ 18,000
Operating Income	**$ 92,000**

Per unit product cost	Variable Costing	Absorption Costing
Variable Mfg Costs	$ 12.00	$ 12.00
Fixed Mfg Overhead		$ 2.00
Total	$ 12	$ 14

Variable Costing Inventory Value		
	units	value
Change in inventory	-	$ -

Absorption Costing Inventory Value		
	units	value
Change in inventory	-	$ -

Exhibit 3.9
Comparison of Income and Inventory Balance Between Absorption Costing and Variable Costing When Production Equals Sales

Microsoft Excel

The method used to calculate income and inventory starts to become important when companies produce a different number of units than they sell.

Let's examine Exhibit 3.10 to determine what happens when MaiTie Company produces more units than it sells. In this example, MaiTie produces 5,000 units, but it manages to sell only 4,000 units. Under variable costing, fixed manufacturing costs are expensed in the current period, so the entire $10,000 cost reduces income. Notice that under absorption costing, only $8,000 of fixed manufacturing costs are incurred in the current period.

Finished Good Inventory		
Beginning Inventory		500
Units Produced		5,000
Units Sold		4,000
Ending Inventory		1,500

Sales		
Sales Price per unit	$	36

Variable Costs		
Variable Mfg Costs	$	12
Variable SG&A per unit	$	3

Fixed Costs		
Fixed Mfg Costs	$	10,000
Fixed SG&A Costs	$	3,000

Variable Costing Income Statement	
Sales	**$ 144,000**
Variable Costs	
Variable Cost of Goods Sold	$ 48,000
Variable SG&A per unit	$ 12,000
Total Variable Costs	$ 60,000
Contribution Margin	**$ 84,000**
Fixed Costs	
Fixed Mfg Costs	$ 10,000
Fixed SG&A Costs	$ 3,000
Total Fixed Costs	$ 13,000
Operating Income	**$ 71,000**

Absorption Costing Income Statement	
Sales	**$ 144,000**
Cost of Goods Sold	
Variable Mfg Costs	$ 48,000
Fixed Mfg Costs	$ 8,000
Total Cost of Goods Sold	$ 56,000
Gross Margin	**$ 88,000**
SG&A Expenses	
Variable SG&A	$ 12,000
Fixed SG&A Costs	$ 3,000
Total Fixed Costs	$ 15,000
Operating Income	**$ 73,000**

Per unit product cost	Variable Costing	Absorption Costing
Variable Mfg Costs	$ 12.00	$ 12.00
Fixed Mfg Overhead		$ 2.00
Total	$ 12	$ 14

Variable Costing Inventory Value		
	units	value
Change in inventory	1,000	$ 12,000

Absorption Costing Inventory Value		
	units	value
Change in inventory	1,000	$ 14,000

Exhibit 3.10
Comparison of Income and Inventory Balance Between Absorption Costing and Variable Costing When Production Does Not Equal Sales

Microsoft Excel

What happened? Under absorption costing, fixed costs are included in inventory as product costs. The cost of inventory is not expensed until it is sold. Because MaiTie sold only 4,000 units, only $8,000 of fixed manufacturing costs are expensed in the current period ($2.00 of fixed overhead per unit * 4,000 units). How does MaiTie account for the remaining $2,000 portion of fixed manufacturing overhead that was incurred during the period? While the $2,000 cost was incurred, it is considered a product cost and included in inventory. As such, it cannot be expensed until the remaining units are sold. The result is that under absorption costing, MaiTie can report lower cost of goods sold and higher inventory values, as compared to variable costing. The higher inventory value is solely due to the fixed manufacturing overhead ($2.00 of fixed overhead per unit * 1,000 unsold units).

ENVIRONMENTAL, SOCIAL, GOVERNANCE

This phenomenon can encourage managers to overproduce inventory in order to increase net income. This tactic is short-sighted, however. Why? First, if inventory levels decrease (and what goes up must certainly come down eventually), companies will show lower income under absorption costing than under variable costing because they will expense all of the current period's fixed overhead as well as that portion from a previous period that was included in inventory. Second, there are significant long-term costs associated with holding too much inventory, such as storage, shrinkage, and obsolescence. The use of variable costing prevents these problems from occurring.

While it may seem difficult to compare operating income under absorption costing and variable costing, just remember that the difference has everything to do with fixed manufacturing overhead. All inventory costs must be expensed eventually, but the timing of those expenses depends on a company's costing method.

 LAB CONNECTION

LAB 3.6 EXCEL is useful for understanding key differences between absorption costing and variable costing. It asks you to construct income statements using both cost methods, identifying how changes in production can be used to affect GAAP income even when sales remain constant.

 PROGRESS CHECK

13. What is the difference between gross margin and contribution margin?
14. What causes differences in operating income between variable costing and absorption costing?

Careers with CVP Responsibilities

CVP analysis is very helpful to organizations. Management accounts can use CVP analysis to help organizations understand how profitability will be impacted by a host of factors, including sales price, the quality of inputs, the purchase of new machinery, and advertising campaigns.

Exhibit 3.11 reproduces a job posting from a site like **LinkedIn.com** or **ZipRecruiter .com** for a Senior Strategy and Financial Planning Analyst at an infant and children's accessories business like **Yinibini**, **Goldbug**, or **Lovevery**. Take a look at the analyses that can be accomplished using the CVP framework, which are highlighted in yellow. CVP analysis is clearly a valuable skill set for management accountants.

Job Title:

Senior Strategy and Financial Planning Analyst

Job Summary:

The senior strategy and financial planning analyst position will have responsibility for partnering with sales and product teams and aligning with operations and finance to perform analysis of margin, profitability, and inventory in support of company strategies.

> These terms are synonymous with CVP analysis.

Candidate Requirements:

- Bachelor's degree in Finance, Accounting, Economics, or related field
- 3+ years of experience in financial analysis and modeling, preferably in a corporate environment
- Strong analytical and problem-solving skills, including experience working with large data sets and interpreting complex financial data to provide actionable insights
- Expertise in Microsoft Excel and financial modeling software, including building dashboards
- Strong communication skills, with the ability to present complex financial information in a clear and concise manner
- Self-starter with the ability to work independently and manage multiple projects simultaneously
- Ability to collaborate effectively with cross-functional teams
- Detail-oriented with a strong focus on accuracy and quality

> Management accountants need to be comfortable with data and data analytics tools.

Responsibilities and Roles:

- Collaborate across business units and partner with strategic leads to conduct managerial analysis that will support strategic decision making
- Work to uncover new business by identifying areas of sales and margin opportunity
- Develop and maintain reports and databases on sales, margin, and profitability analyses
- Work collaboratively with vendors and sellers to understand product cost analysis, retail selling results, SKU, and price elasticity analyses
- Report on and analyze key performance indicators to identify trends and opportunities for improvement, including analyses to understand intersection of product mix, account costs, operating costs, and product cost improvements
- Track sales and profit for new programs and proposals against desired metrics
- Conduct research and analysis on industry trends, competitive landscape, and other relevant factors to support decision making and identify opportunities

> CVP analysis is useful to decision makers throughout an organization.

> CVP analysis provides insight that affects company strategy.

Additional Details:

- Salary Range: $90,000–110,000
- This role reports to the Chief Strategy Officer and senior financial leadership team

Exhibit 3.11
Job Opportunity: Senior Strategy and Financial Planning Analyst

Key Takeaways: The CVP Framework, Management Accounting, and Data Analytics

In this chapter, we presented techniques for estimating cost behavior and provided a cost-volume-profit framework for analysis. The CVP framework is derived from the variable costing or contribution margin income statement, which classifies costs primarily on the basis of whether they are fixed or variable. The framework allows management to understand and predict how changes in various costs and sales volume will affect company performance, and it is very useful when determining company strategy. We also discussed how the variable costing income statement differs from the GAAP-based absorption costing income statement, which primarily classifies costs as either product costs or period costs. Management accountants must understand the differences between these two presentation styles.

Using the AMPS model, let's review how the information in this chapter can be used to address important managerial questions:

Ask the Question

■ **What question(s) does management want to answer?**

Cost behavior and CVP analysis serve as a foundation for many strategic decisions. Organizations must determine which products to offer and at what price. They must also determine how to achieve financial goals and how various investments will influence outcomes.

Master the Data

■ **Which data are appropriate to address management's questions?**

Data are pulled primarily from prior-period financial data gathered from an organization's cost accounting system, as well as pro forma (forecasted) financial statements that reflect an organization's future strategies. This information is often presented using absorption costing because GAAP requires absorption costing. In addition, variable costing allows for important analyses via the CVP framework. For this reason, management accountants often create variable costing income statements to better understand company data and cost behavior.

Perform the Analysis

■ **Which analytics are performed to address management questions?**

Management accountants use descriptive analytics to understand financial results and generate financial reports using variable or absorption costing. CVP analysis is also frequently used for predictive and prescriptive analytics in the form of sensitivity analysis and pro forma financial statements. CVP analysis, which is a form of sensitivity analysis, can be used to determine what might happen under various strategic assumptions.

Share the Story

■ **How are the results of the analytics shared with stakeholders?**

CVP analysis is a powerful tool for management accountants. It can be used to quantitatively display how organizational strategy is likely to affect real performance, allowing decision makers to quickly sift through various ideas and provide value to the organization.

Key Terms

absorption costing
adjusted R-squared
break-even point
composite unit
constraint
contribution margin
contribution margin
  income statement
contribution margin
  ratio

correlation
cost structure
cost-volume-profit
  (CVP) framework
dependent variable
fixed cost
high-low method
independent
  variable
margin of safety

margin of safety ratio
mixed cost
operating income
operating leverage
outlier
period costs
product costs
R regression analysis
relevant range

R-squared
sales mix
sensitivity analysis
standard error
statistical
  significance
variable cost
variable costing
variable costing
  income statement

✓ ANSWERS TO PROGRESS CHECKS

1. A cost is fixed if it remains the same regardless of changes in production volume. A cost is variable if it changes based on production volume.

2. The relevant range allows us to assume a cost-behavior pattern in which fixed costs remain constant and variable costs are constant on a per-unit basis. It allows for the reasonable estimation of cost by assuming a consistent cost-behavior pattern over a range of production levels.

3. The high-low method uses two data points to estimate variable and fixed costs. It calculates the difference between costs at the highest activity level and lowest activity level to estimate variable costs, and then uses that result to determine fixed costs.

4. The biggest drawback to the high-low method is that it produces estimates based on only two data points, while ignoring all other data.

5. Regression analysis is preferred over the high-low method because it takes into account all data points instead of just two data points. Including more data points in the analysis improves the accuracy of the cost estimation of variable costs and fixed costs.

6. Regression analysis includes all data observations in the analysis and provides statistical measures of how well an estimated cost line fits the underlying data.

7. Contribution margin is the amount of sales dollars available to cover fixed costs and contribute to profits. It is the amount of sales dollars remaining after paying all variable costs, resulting in dollars left to contribute to fixed costs or to profits.

8. GAAP income statements group costs depending on whether they are product costs or period costs. In contrast, a contribution margin income statement groups costs by behavior—that is, whether they are variable or fixed.

9. The break-even point occurs when a firm has an operating income of $0, meaning that sales are sufficient to cover all variable and fixed costs. Break-even point in units can be determined by dividing fixed costs by contribution margin per unit. The break-even point in dollars can be determined by dividing fixed costs by the contribution margin ratio.

10. When resources are limited, contribution margin can be used to optimize resource usage by prioritizing products or services based on contribution margin per unit of constrained resource.

11. Cost structure is the relative mix of a company's fixed costs and variable costs. Operating leverage is a measure of cost structure, such that higher operating leverage equates to a higher proportion of fixed costs.

12. Increasing operating leverage amplifies a company's risk and reward of changes in sales. As operating leverage increases, changes in sales have a greater effect on operating income.

13. Gross margin applies to absorption costing and is equal to sales minus cost of goods sold. Contribution margin applies to variable costing and is equal to sales minus all variable costs.

14. Differences in operating income between variable costing and absorption costing arise solely due to fixed manufacturing overhead. Absorption costing capitalizes fixed manufacturing overhead and can create differences in the timing of expense recognition based on inventory levels.

Multiple-Choice Questions · **connect**

1. (LO3.1) A water utility charges homeowners $0.03 per gallon of water, in addition to a monthly service fee. A customer's water bill can accurately be classified as a:
   a. fixed cost.
   b. variable cost.
   c. mixed cost.
   d. standard cost.

2. (LO3.1) Geormetician Inc. purchased machinery from Grey Star, which has guaranteed that the machine will last 10 years. Depreciation for the machinery is best classified as a:
   a. fixed cost.
   b. variable cost.
   c. mixed cost.
   d. standard cost.

3. (LO3.1) Within a relevant range:
   a. fixed costs per unit are constant.
   b. total variable costs are constant.
   c. increased production does not require the purchase of additional machinery.
   d. total cost per unit increases.

4. (LO3.1) Qualytics Company purchased machinery from Easy Bit, which has guaranteed that the machine will last 10 years. Within the relevant range, as Qualytics increases production:
   a. per-unit variable cost increases.
   b. per-unit total costs remain constant.
   c. total fixed costs increase.
   d. per-unit fixed costs decrease.

5. (LO3.2, 3.3) To estimate costs using prior data, regression analysis is preferable to the high-low method because:
   a. regression analysis is not influenced by data outliers.
   b. regression analysis makes use of more data.
   c. regression analysis is computationally simpler.
   d. regression analysis emphasizes data that are more recent.

6. (LO3.2, 3.3) Which of the following is *not* an advantage of using regression analysis instead of the high-low method to estimate costs?
   a. Regression is likely more accurate because it uses more data points in the calculations.
   b. Regression uses simpler calculations.
   c. Regression provides an estimate of fixed costs.
   d. Regression can be used to predict future costs.

7. (LO3.3) In a regression analysis examining the effect of customer visits on total office costs, R is 0.12. Interpret R.
   a. There is a strong positive correlation between customer visits and total office costs.
   b. There is a strong negative correlation between customer visits and total office costs.
   c. There is little or no linear relationship between customer visits and total office costs.
   d. There is a curvilinear relationship between customer visits and total office costs.

8. (LO3.3) Which of the following describes the precision of an estimate in a regression analysis?

a. Correlation

b. Standard error

c. Coefficient

d. Margin of safety

9. (LO3.3) Snack Pantry regresses total costs on units produced. Results of the regression indicate a statistically significant coefficient of 2.5 on the units-produced variable. How should this result be interpreted?

a. Each unit costs an average of $2.50 to produce.

b. Each unit has an average variable cost of $2.50.

c. Each unit has an average fixed cost of $2.50.

d. Each unit has an average labor cost of $2.50.

10. (LO3.4) Which of the following is not used in CVP analysis?

a. Fixed cost per unit

b. Variable cost per unit

c. Total operating income

d. Revenue per unit

11. (LO3.4) Which of the following equations is incorrect?

a. Contribution margin – Fixed costs = Operating income

b. Contribution margin per unit + Variable cost per unit = Sales price

c. (Contribution margin per unit * Units) – Fixed cost per unit = Sales price

d. Revenue – Variable costs – Operating income = Fixed costs

12. (LO3.4) Which of the following costs is deducted from revenue to calculate contribution margin?

a. Depreciation

b. Hourly wages for the sales department

c. Rent for production facility

d. Production supervisor salary

13. (LO3.5) All things equal, how will the purchase of additional production equipment affect a company's break-even point?

a. The break-even point will increase.

b. The break-even point will decrease.

c. The break-even point will remain the same.

d. The answer depends on the price of the production equipment.

14. (LO3.5) Trader Mo's is a furniture company. The company has decided to alter its strategy by selling its automated production equipment and producing furniture using skilled labor instead. However, in the short term, the company is unable to cut fixed costs due to contractual obligations related to production equipment. In the short term, how will this change in strategy affect the break-even point?

a. The break-even point will increase.

b. The break-even point will decrease.

c. The break-even point will remain the same.

d. We cannot answer this question without knowing the average selling price of the furniture.

15. (LO3.5) The break-even point is the point at which _____ is equal to zero.

a. revenue

b. gross margin

c. contribution margin

d. operating income

16. (LO3.5) Gouda Vibes Company must increase profitability this year to avoid bankruptcy. Gouda Vibes can sell all units produced, but it faces a production constraint: a shortage of skilled labor. To maximize profit, Gouda Vibes should produce:

    a. products that have the highest contribution margin.

    b. products that have the highest sales price.

    c. products that use the least amount of skilled labor.

    d. products that have the highest contribution margin per hour of skilled labor.

17. (LO3.6) Operating leverage is a measure of:

    a. a company's cost structure.

    b. a company's profitability.

    c. a company's competitiveness.

    d. a company's strategy.

18. (LO3.6) All things equal, which of the following will decrease a company's operating leverage?

    a. Purchasing production equipment

    b. Hiring supervisors who work on salary

    c. Increasing production

    d. Automating production to decrease direct labor

19. (LO3.7) When companies sell more units than they produce, operating income will be highest under:

    a. absorption costing.

    b. variable costing.

    c. standard costing.

    d. mixed costing.

20. (LO3.7) Which of the following is considered a period cost under variable costing?

    a. Direct materials

    b. Direct labor

    c. Variable manufacturing overhead

    d. Fixed manufacturing overhead

Discussion Questions

1. (LO3.1, 3.5) Explain how increased automation may affect break-even analysis, margin of safety, and operating leverage.

2. (LO3.2, 3.3) Why is regression analysis superior to the high-low method for producing cost models?

3. (LO3.2, 3.3) Explain the effect of data outliers on the high-low method and regression.

4. (LO3.3) Explain why companies should be cognizant of relevant range when using regression analysis to predict future costs.

5. (LO3.1, 3.6) Identify companies at opposite ends of the cost structure spectrum (relatively high versus relatively low fixed costs). How does cost structure alter firm strategy?

6. (LO3.4, 3.5) Explain how changes in product mix affect CVP analysis in a multiproduct setting. What strategies might companies use to alter product mix?

7. (LO3.4, 3.5) How do the quality and price of raw materials and direct labor influence break-even point and target-profit analysis?

8. (LO3.6) Under what conditions might a company wish to increase its degree of operating leverage?

9. (LO3.6) Explain how outsourcing production can affect a company's cost structure and operating leverage.

10. (LO3.6) How are a company's cost structure and break-even point related?

11. (LO3.7) What are the drawbacks of absorption costing?

12. (LO3.7) How might absorption costing lead to unethical behavior on the part of managers?

13. (LO3.7) How might companies design incentive packages for managers to counteract the drawbacks of absorption costing?

14. (LO3.7) Briefly explain the differences between an absorption costing income statement and a variable costing income statement.

15. (LO3.7) When calculating product cost per unit, why does absorption costing include fixed manufacturing overhead cost?

ETHICS

Brief Exercises   Mc Graw Hill connect

1. (LO3.1, 3.4) Food Orchard sells a single product. It has total sales of $250,000 (10,000 units), a variable cost of $15 per unit, and fixed costs of $125,000. What is contribution margin per unit?

2. (LO3.1, 3.2) SpeakerSoft Inc. uses the high-low method to estimate production costs. Per the company's analysis, variable costs are $12.95 per unit, while fixed costs are $13,500. If SpeakerSoft expects to produce 3,000 units next month, what are projected production costs?

3. (LO3.1, 3.3) SpeakerSoft Inc. uses regression analysis to estimate production costs. Per the company's regression output, units produced have a regression coefficient of $13.80, while the intercept coefficient is $15,000. If SpeakerSoft expects to produce 4,000 units next month, what are projected production costs?

4. (LO3.4) Consider the following information for FestiveFood Co.:

Sales (units)	500
Revenue	$60,000.00
Variable costs	$20,000.00
Fixed costs	$ 10,000.00
Operating income	$30,000.00

If FestiveFood increases sales price by 10% but sales volume remains the same, what is the effect on contribution margin? Will contribution margin increase or decrease, and by what percent?

5. (LO3.4) Nature Mart has after-tax income of $30,000, a tax rate of 40%, fixed costs of $15,000, and a contribution margin ratio of 50%. What is Nature Mart's total revenue?

6. (LO3.4) Lifestyle Colors Co. has operating income of $75,000, fixed costs of $12,000, a contribution margin of $4.50 per unit, and a contribution margin ratio of 0.6. What is Lifestyle Colors' variable cost per unit?

7. (LO3.4) Sell Squad Co. has a contribution margin of 0.75, a sales price per unit of $9.75, and total variable costs of $19,500. What are total unit sales for Sell Squad?

8. (LO3.4) Venture Bliss Co. spends 36% of its revenue on variable costs. It has an average fixed cost per unit of $4.00, a sales price per unit of $8.00, and total variable costs of $18,000. What is Venture Bliss's operating income?

9. (LO3.4) Investify Co. has revenue of $198,000 over 24,000 units. Contribution margin per unit is $6.60 and fixed costs are $70,000. What is the tax rate for Investify if after-tax net income is $51,272?

10. (LO3.4) Hagle Inc. saw a 10% increase in sales last year. Selling price per unit, variable cost per unit, and total fixed costs remained constant. Determine whether the following items increased (I), decreased (D), remained the same (R), or cannot be determined (C).

    a. Total sales

    b. Contribution margin per unit

    c. Margin of safety

    d. Break-even point

11. (LO3.5) Heal Quick Co. has revenue of $13,500 over 4,320 units, a contribution margin of $2.50 per unit, and fixed costs of $25,000. What is the break-even point in revenue for Heal Quick?

12. (LO3.5) Nexa Bull Co. has revenue of $11.00 per unit. Variable costs are 35% of revenue and total fixed costs are $31,000. What is the break-even point in units for Nexa Bull?

13. (LO3.5) Nutrilix Co. earns an average of $20.00 in revenue per unit and spends an average of $7.20 per unit on variable costs. Fixed costs are $25,000. How much revenue must Nutrilix generate in order to achieve operating income of $50,000?

14. (LO3.5) Pharm Nest Co. has a contribution margin ratio of 50% and per-unit revenue of $50.00. The tax rate is 25% and fixed costs are $65,000. How many units must Pharm Nest sell in order to generate after-tax profits of $150,000?

15. (LO3.5) Gadget Gazette Co. has revenue of $30.00 per unit. Variable costs are 30% of revenue and total fixed costs are $84,000. Current sales generate revenue of $150,000. What is the margin of safety in units for Gadget Gazette?

16. (LO3.5) Classify the following changes with regard to how they will change the break-even point (in number of units). Use the following classifications: Increase (I), Decrease (D), Remained the same (R), or Cannot be determined (C).

    a. Increase in selling price

    b. Decrease in variable cost per unit

    c. Increase in fixed costs

    d. Automation alters the mix of variable costs to fixed costs

17. (LO3.6) Phelps Co. has current sales of $200,000, operating income of $40,000, and a degree of operating leverage of 1.5. If sales increase by $40,000, what will operating income be?

18. (LO3.6) Zennit Co. has current sales of $30,000, variable costs of $6,000, and fixed costs of $14,000. What is Zennit's degree of operating leverage?

19. (LO3.6) Couture Engine Co. has current sales of $800,000, variable costs of $200,000, and a 1.6 degree of operating leverage. What must sales be in order to increase operating income to $562,500?

20. (LO3.7) Absorption costing incentivizes the overproduction of goods. What is the most likely effect of overproduction of goods in the current period on each of the following? Use the following classifications: Increase (I), Decrease (D).

    a. Inventory

    b. Spoilage

    c. Operating income

    d. Future operating income

Problems ![McGraw Hill] connect

1. (LO3.1, 3.4, 3.5) Maine Outfitters produces boots for outdoor enthusiasts. Average cost information for its boots follows:

Selling price per unit	$	75
Variable cost per unit		
Direct material	$	25
Direct labor	$	10
Manufacturing overhead	$	7.50
Marketing	$	2.50
Annual fixed costs	$300,000	

Required

a. What is the break-even point in units?

b. How many units must Maine Outfitters sell in order to earn $150,000 in operating income?

c. Assume Maine Outfitters is subject to a 25% tax rate. How many units must the company sell in order to earn $180,000 in after-tax income?

d. Assume Maine Outfitters is currently selling 20,000 units. Calculate the company's margin of safety in sales dollars.

2. (LO3.1, 3.2) Maui Cream Co. is a restaurant that provides catering services. The table below tracks the number of orders and total catering travel costs for Maui Cream Co. for each month during the past year. Tourist season is denoted by a 1 in the Tourist Season column. Use the table and the high-low method to evaluate the effect of orders on total cost, then answer the following questions.

Maui Cream Co.			
Month	**Orders**	**Tourist Season**	**Total Cost**
January	61	0	$ 1,720
February	81	0	$ 2,120
March	85	0	$2,200
April	69	1	$ 2,156
May	85	1	$2,370
June	62	1	$ 1,740
July	93	1	$2,546
August	58	1	$ 1,428
September	98	0	$2,300
October	81	0	$ 2,444
November	79	0	$2,080
December	88	0	$ 2,612

Required

a. Using the high-low method, estimate the variable travel cost per order.

b. What is the monthly fixed travel cost for Maui Cream Co.?

c. Estimate the travel cost for next month assuming Maui Cream Co. expects 80 orders.

3. (LO3.1, 3.3) Maui Cream Co. is a restaurant that provides catering services. Below is the regression output to analyze the effect of number of orders and busy season on total catering travel costs. Tourist season is a binary variable set equal to 1 in the tourist season. Use the regression output to answer the following questions.

SUMMARY OUTPUT

Regression Statistics	
Multiple R	0.91
R Square	0.82
Adjusted R Square	0.78
Standard Error	172.06
Observations	12

ANOVA

	df	SS	MS	F	Significance F
Regression	2	1216882.40	608441.20	20.55	0.00
Residual	9	266452.27	29605.81		
Total	11	1483334.67			

	Coefficients	Standard Error	t Stat	P-value	Lower 95%	Upper 95%
Intercept	109.76	351.96	0.31	0.76	−686.42	905.94
Orders	25.95	4.23	6.14	0.00	16.39	35.51
Tourist Season	33.72	106.90	0.32	0.76	−208.10	275.55

Required

a. What is the coefficient of correlation?

b. What amount of variation in travel costs is explained by the independent variables of orders and tourist season?

c. According to the regression output, which independent variable(s) are statistically significant?

4. (LO3.1, 3.3) White Space Services provides basic and advanced Internet installation. To better understand costs, White Space Services has regressed total monthly costs on the number of basic and advanced installations. Use the regression output to answer the following questions.

SUMMARY OUTPUT

Regression Statistics	
Multiple R	0.49
R Square	0.24
Adjusted R Square	0.19
Standard Error	1945.48
Observations	34

ANOVA

	df	SS	MS	F	Significance F
Regression	2	36092314.77	18046157.38	4.77	0.02
Residual	31	117331391.23	3784883.59		
Total	33	153423706.00			

	Coefficients	Standard Error	t Stat	P-value	Lower 95%	Upper 95%
Intercept	260.37	1965.44	0.13	0.90	−3748.18	4268.91
Basic	56.76	30.49	1.86	0.07	−5.42	118.94
Advanced	97.64	55.07	1.77	0.09	−14.67	209.95

Required

a. What is the coefficient of correlation?

b. What amount of variation in costs is explained by the model? (Use the metric that controls for number of independent variables.)

c. According to the regression output, which independent variable(s) are statistically significant at is $p = 0.1$?

d. According to the regression output, what is the total cost estimate for a month with 250 basic installations and 100 advanced installations?

5. (LO3.3) Fruitzy produces batches of flavored sodas and uses regression analysis to better understand costs. Fruitzy has regressed total weekly costs on the number of batches of each soda flavor. Use the regression output to answer the following questions.

SUMMARY OUTPUT	
Regression Statistics	
Multiple R	0.80
R Square	0.64
Adjusted R Square	0.59
Standard Error	12719.46
Observations	24

ANOVA

	df	SS	MS	F	Significance F
Regression	3	5752957226.03	1917652408.68	11.85	0.00
Residual	20	3235690875.43	161784543.77		
Total	23	8988648101.46			

	Coefficients	Standard Error	t Stat	P-value	Lower 95%	Upper 95%
Intercept	25404.59	52624.33	0.48	0.63	−84367.84	135177.02
Lemon	99.88	188.33	0.53	0.60	−292.97	492.73
Strawberry	245.28	100.44	2.44	0.02	35.78	454.79
Grape	239.68	48.42	4.95	0.00	138.69	340.68

Required

a. What amount of variation in costs is explained by the model? (Use the metric that controls for the number of independent variables.)

b. According to the regression output, which flavor has the highest variable cost?

c. According to the regression output, which independent variable has the highest level of significance?

d. According to the regression output, what is the total cost estimate for a week in which Fruitzy produces 150 lemon batches, 250 strawberry batches, and 350 grape batches?

6. (LO3.4) All Or Muffin Company has the following financial information:

Revenue	$1,800,000
Variable Costs	$ 630,000
Contribution Margin	$1,170,000
Fixed Costs	$ 430,000
Operating Income	$ 740,000
Taxes	$ 199,880
Net Income	$ 540,200

Microsoft Excel

Required

a. What is All Or Muffin's contribution margin ratio?

b. What is All Or Muffin's tax rate?

c. If All Or Muffin increases sales price by 10% and maintains current unit sales, what will All Or Muffin's net income be?

d. If All Or Muffin increases unit sales by 10%, what will All Or Muffin's net income be?

7. (LO3.4, 3.5) The Pet Mansion Company has the following financial information:

Sales (units)	8,000
Revenue	$1,600,000
Variable Costs	$ 384,000
Fixed Costs	$ 66,120
Operating Income	$1,149,880

Microsoft Excel

Required

a. What is The Pet Mansion's contribution margin ratio?

b. What is The Pet Mansion's break-even point in units?

c. The Pet Mansion has the opportunity to switch suppliers to gain higher-quality inputs to production. Doing so will increase variable costs by 10% and increase unit sales by 10%. If The Pet Mansion switches suppliers, what will The Pet Mansion's contribution margin ratio be?

d. If The Pet Mansion switches suppliers, what will The Pet Mansion's break-even point in units be?

8. (LO3.5) Pawxie Vibe Company has sales of 20,000 units and the following per-unit financial information:

Revenue	$	4.80
Variable Costs	$	1.20
Contribution Margin	$	3.60
Fixed Costs	$	2.40
Operating Income	$	1.20

Microsoft Excel

Required

a. Assuming a tax rate of 25%, what is current net income?

b. Pawxie Vibe has a target operating income of $37,500. How many units must it sell to reach that target?

c. Pawxie Vibe predicts that it can cut fixed advertising expenses by $10,000, resulting in a reduction in unit sales of 10%. What will operating income be if Pawxie Vibe cuts $10,000 of advertising expenses?

9. (LO3.4, 3.5) Pupzy Company units have a sales price of $1,875.00 and a variable cost of $562.50. Fixed costs are $550,000 and Pupzy's tax rate is 40%.

Required

a. What is Pupzy's contribution margin ratio?

b. Pupzy wants after-tax net income of $300,000. How much revenue must Pupzy generate in order to achieve this net income?

c. Pupzy has the opportunity to switch to a new, more efficient supplier. Doing so will decrease variable cost per unit by 15%. However, the switch will also require an additional $60,000 in fixed costs. If Pupzy makes the switch, what is Pupzy's new contribution margin ratio?

d. If Pupzy makes the switch to the new supplier, how much revenue must Pupzy generate to generate $300,000 in after-tax net income?

10. (LO3.4, 3.5) Shield Panda Company has sales of 2,500 units and the following financial information:

Revenue	$135,000.00
Variable Costs	$ 54,000.00
Contribution Margin	$ 81,000.00
Fixed Costs	$ 45,000.00
Operating Income	$ 36,000.00

Microsoft Excel

Required

a. What is Shield Panda's break-even point in units?

b. Shield Panda projects an increase in sales of 25% next year. What will be Shield Panda's break-even point in units next year?

c. What will be Shield Panda's margin of safety next year in units?

d. Calculate Shield Panda's margin of safety ratio for next year.

11. (LO3.5) Agri Bucket Company has the following financial information:

Unit Sales	70,000
Revenue	$2,800,000
Variable Costs	$1,946,000
Contribution Margin	$ 854,000
Fixed Costs	$ 90,000
Operating Income	$ 764,000
Net Income	$ 550,080

Microsoft Excel

Required

a. What is Agri Bucket's break-even point in units?

b. What is Agri Bucket's income-tax rate?

c. What is Agri Bucket's margin of safety?

d. What must Agri Bucket's revenue be for it to earn $750,000 in net income?

12. (LO3.6) Agro Market has the following financial information:

Unit Sales	10,000
Revenue	$ 5,000,000
Variable Costs	$ 1,250,000
Contribution Margin	$ 3,750,000
Fixed Costs	$ 750,000
Operating Income	$ 3,000,000

Microsoft Excel

Required

a. What is Agro Market's degree of operating leverage?

b. A 10% increase in sales will generate what percent increase in operating income?

c. Agro Market has determined a way to reconfigure its production line to reduce labor costs. Doing so will save Agro Market 20% on its per-unit variable costs. If Agro Market reconfigures its production line, what will be the change in Agro Market's operating income?

d. If Agro Market reconfigures its production line, what will be Agro Market's degree of operating leverage?

e. If Agro Market reconfigures its production line, a 10% increase in sales will generate what percent increase in operating income?

13. (LO3.6) Study Volt has the following financial information:

Unit Sales	86,000
Revenue	$ 8,600,000
Variable Costs	$ 2,150,000
Contribution Margin	$ 6,450,000
Fixed Costs	$ 1,800,000
Operating Income	$ 4,650,000

Microsoft Excel

Required

a. What is Study Volt's degree of operating leverage?

b. A 10% increase in sales will generate what percent increase in operating income?

c. To deal with an industry-wide labor shortage, Study Volt has decided to increase automation on its production line. Doing so will decrease variable costs by 60% but will increase fixed costs by $2,000,000. Assuming constant sales, if Study Volt reconfigures its production line, what will be the change in Study Volt's operating income?

d. If Study Volt reconfigures its production line, what will be Study Volt's degree of operating leverage?

e. If Study Volt reconfigures its production line, a 10% increase in sales will generate what percent increase in operating income?

14. (LO3.5) Nutri Eazy has the following financial information:

Unit Sales	150,000
Revenue	$ 210,000
Variable Costs	$ 825,000
Contribution Margin	$ 1,275,000
Fixed Costs	$ 300,000
Operating Income	$ 975,000

Microsoft Excel

Required

a. What is Nutri Eazy's break-even point in units?

b. Nutri Eazy currently pays a fee of $1.50 in advertising costs to a marketing company for each item sold. Nutri Eazy has been offered a new contract by the marketing company in which Nutri Eazy pays a flat fee of $210,000, regardless of how many units are sold. If Nutri Eazy changes the marketing contract to include the fixed fee, what is the new break-even point in units?

c. If Nutri Eazy changes the marketing contract to include the fixed fee, how will operating income change?

d. At what level of sales units will Nutri Eazy will be indifferent between the per-unit and fixed-fee contracts? In other words, at what level of sales units will operating income be identical?

15. (LO3.5) The Lace Connection has the following financial information:

Unit Sales	25,000
Revenue	$ 5,000,000
Variable Costs	$ 3,750,000
Contribution Margin	$ 1,250,000
Fixed Costs	$ 850,000
Operating Income	$ 400,000

Microsoft Excel

Required

a. How many units must The Lace Connection sell in order to generate $600,000 in operating income?

b. The Lace Connection is considering updating its production line to increase quality. The change will require more machinery and automation, which will result in savings of 25% of variable costs and an increase of $1,175,000 in fixed costs. Assuming no change in unit sales, what will operating income be if The Lace Connection updates the production line?

c. If The Lace Connection updates the production line, how many units must it sell in order to generate $600,000 in operating income?

d. At what level of sales units will The Lace Connection be indifferent between updating and not updating the production line? In other words, at what level of sales units will operating income be identical (rounded to the nearest whole number)?

16. (LO3.7) Chassen Company, a cracker and cookie manufacturer, has the following unit costs for June.

Variable manufacturing cost	Variable marketing cost	Fixed manufacturing cost	Fixed marketing cost
$5.00	$3.50	$2.00	$4.00

A total of 100,000 units were manufactured during June, of which 10,000 remain in ending inventory. The 10,000 units are the only finished goods inventory at month-end.

Required

a. Using the absorption costing method, what will Chassen's finished goods inventory value be?

b. Using the variable costing method, what will Chassen's finished goods inventory value be?

c. How much higher will Chassen's operating income be under absorption costing than variable costing?

CMA

17. (LO3.7) Dremmon Corporation reports the following information from the last fiscal year:

	Units
Beginning inventory of finished goods	100
Production during the year	700
Sales	750
Ending inventory of finished goods	50
Per unit	
Product selling price	$200
Variable manufacturing cost	90
Fixed manufacturing cost (based on units produced)	20
Budgeted selling and administrative costs (all fixed)	$45,000

Assume product costs are consistent between periods and that all units in ending inventory were produced in the last fiscal year.

Required

a. Prepare a basic absorption costing income statement, showing Dremmon's operating income.

b. Under absorption costing, by how much did Dremmon's ending inventory balance decrease?

c. Prepare a basic variable costing income statement, showing Dremmon's operating income.

d. Under variable costing, by how much did Dremmon's ending inventory balance decrease?

Lab 3.1   Power BI

Using Graphs to Display Costs

Data Analytics Types: Diagnostic Analytics, Predictive Analytics

Lab Note: The tools presented in this lab periodically change. Updated instructions, if applicable, can be found in the student and instructor support materials.

Keywords

Fixed Cost, Variable Cost, Production Volume, Total Cost, Line Graph

Decision-Making Context

Elite Eyewear manufactures blue-light-blocking eyeglasses to sell to retailers around the United States. Managers keep data about the fixed and variable costs for different production amounts in an Excel spreadsheet, and they would like to use a visualization to illustrate how total cost changes as production volume increases. They have asked their management accounting team to use Power BI to create this visualization.

Ask the Question

How does total cost change as production volume increases?

Master the Data

1. For this lab you will use data in the Excel file titled **Lab 3.1 Data.xlsx**.

    Review the data set, which contains information about the fixed and variable costs for each production volume.

Data Dictionary

Worksheet Tab/Table	Attribute Name	Description	Data Type
Product Cost Data	Production Volume	Number of units produced	Numerical
Product Cost Data	Fixed Cost	Fixed cost for production	Currency
Product Cost Data	Variable Cost	Variable cost per unit produced	Currency

2. After you review the Excel data, you will need to close it to import it into Power BI. Import the data from **Lab 3.1 Data.xlsx** into Power BI using the **Get Data** command (Lab Exhibit 3.1P.1). Select **Excel Workbook** and then **Connect** (Lab Exhibit 3.1P.2). Then select the **Product Cost Data** worksheet and click **Load** (Lab Exhibit 3.1P.3).

Lab Exhibit 3.1P.1

Microsoft Power BI

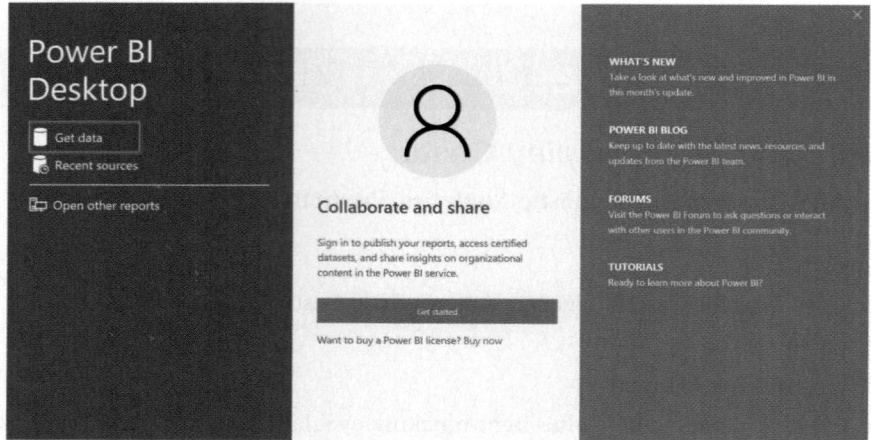

Lab Exhibit 3.1P.2

Microsoft Power BI

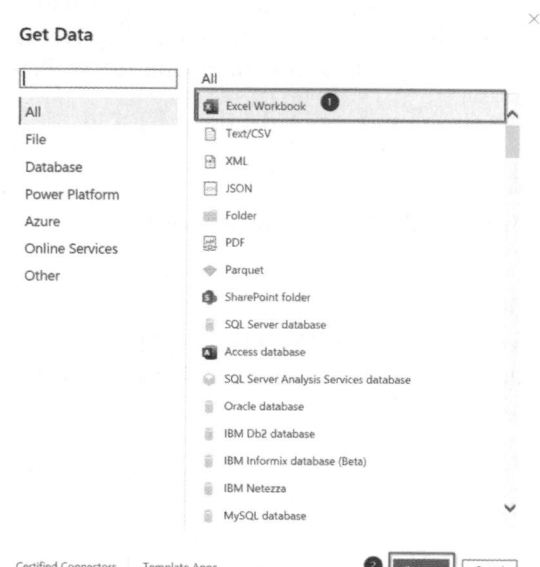

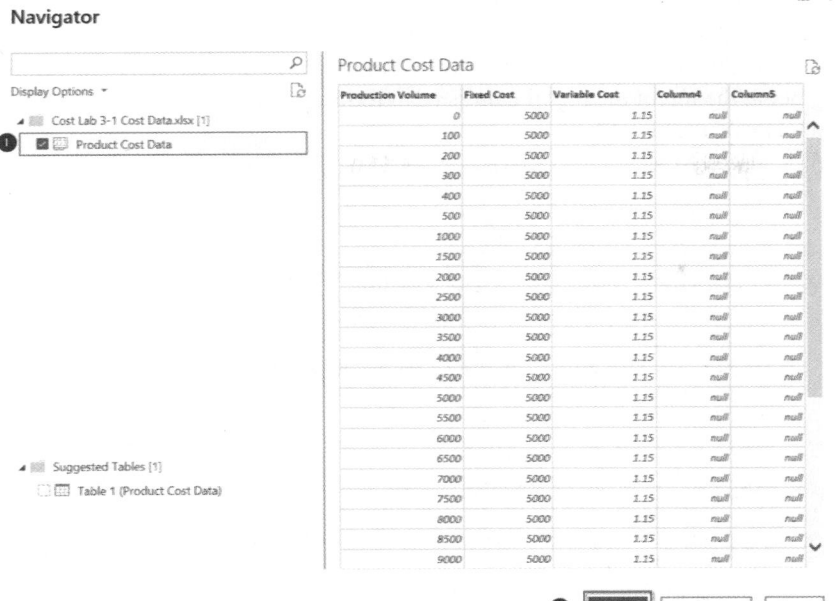

Navigator

Product Cost Data

Production Volume	Fixed Cost	Variable Cost	Column4	Column5
0	5000	1.15	null	null
100	5000	1.15	null	null
200	5000	1.15	null	null
300	5000	1.15	null	null
400	5000	1.15	null	null
500	5000	1.15	null	null
1000	5000	1.15	null	null
1500	5000	1.15	null	null
2000	5000	1.15	null	null
2500	5000	1.15	null	null
3000	5000	1.15	null	null
3500	5000	1.15	null	null
4000	5000	1.15	null	null
4500	5000	1.15	null	null
5000	5000	1.15	null	null
5500	5000	1.15	null	null
6000	5000	1.15	null	null
6500	5000	1.15	null	null
7000	5000	1.15	null	null
7500	5000	1.15	null	null
8000	5000	1.15	null	null
8500	5000	1.15	null	null
9000	5000	1.15	null	null

Display Options ▾

▲ Cost Lab 3-1 Cost Data.xlsx [1]
☑ Product Cost Data

▲ Suggested Tables [1]
Table 1 (Product Cost Data)

Load Transform Data Cancel

Lab Exhibit 3.1P.3

Microsoft Power BI

Perform the Analysis

Analysis Task #1: Begin Data Visualization

1. On the report canvas, select the icon for the **Line Chart** visualization (Lab Exhibit 3.1P.4).
2. Drag the **Production Volume** field to the **X-axis**. Your screen should look like Lab Exhibit 3.1P.4.

DATA VISUALIZATION

Lab Exhibit 3.1P.4

Microsoft Power BI

3. You will want to show the total cost on the Y-axis, but first you have to calculate total cost.

Analysis Task #2: Calculate Total Cost

1. Calculate total cost by creating a new column. Navigate to the **Modeling** tab and select the icon for **New Column** (Lab Exhibit 3.1P.5). This will open the formula builder at the top of the report canvas (Lab Exhibit 3.1P.6). Enter the following formula to calculate total cost:

   `Total Cost = [Fixed Cost]+([Production Volume]*[Variable Cost]).`

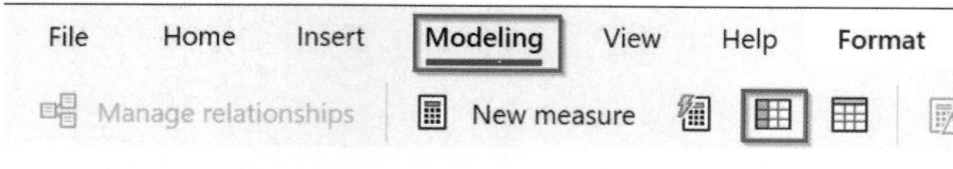

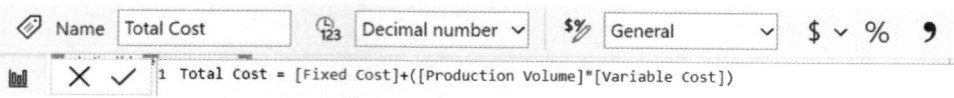

Analysis Task #3: Complete the Data Visualization

1. Drag the (new) **Total Cost** field to the **Y-axis** option. You will now see a line graph for the total cost at each production volume (the dark blue line in Lab Exhibit 3.1P.7).
2. Add the **Fixed Cost** field to the **Y-axis** option next to show the constant fixed cost for all production volumes. (See the light blue line in Lab Exhibit 3.1P.7.)

DATA VISUALIZATION

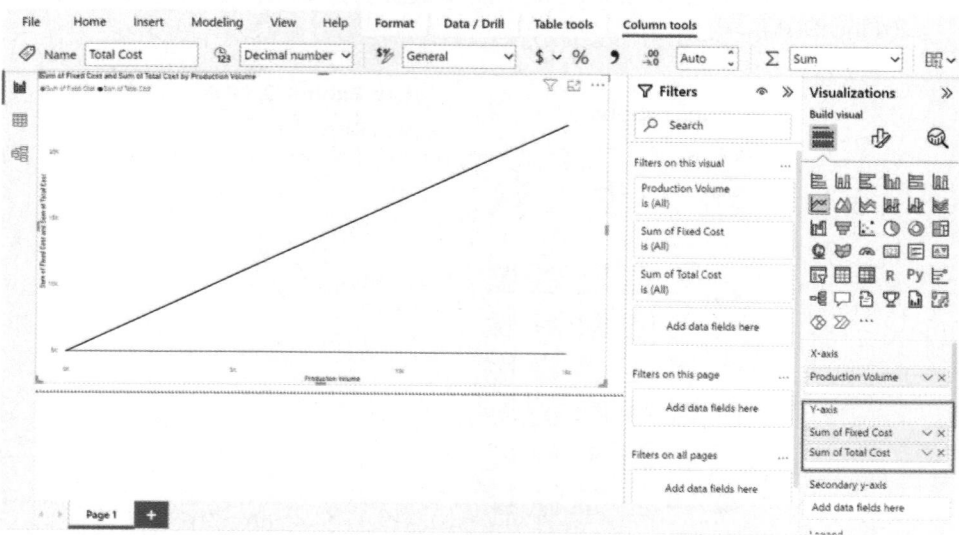

3. Format the visualization by navigating to the **Format Visual** menu (the paint brush icon in the **Visualizations** pane, Lab Exhibit 3.1P.8).

   a. You can change the line style by navigating to the **Lines** option and applying the settings to the Sum of Fixed Cost series. For **Line Style**, select **Dotted**.

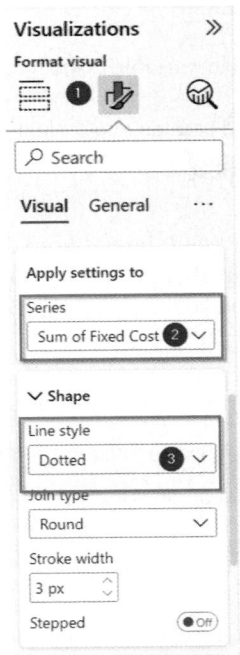

Lab Exhibit 3.1P.8

Microsoft Power BI

b. You can format the title from the **Title** option. Select the **paint brush** icon from the **Visualizations** pane, select **General**, and then select **Title**. Change the **Text** title to "Costs by Production Volume" (Lab Exhibit 3.1P.9).

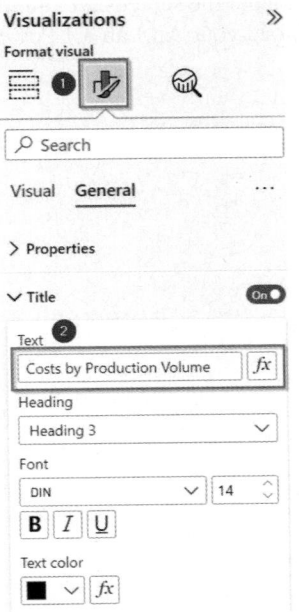

Lab Exhibit 3.1P.9

Microsoft Power BI

Share the Story

Our analysis and our line graph demonstrate that variable costs increase with production, but fixed costs remain constant.

You have now loaded data into Power BI and created and formatted a line graph visualization. You also created a new field by calculating a new column.

Assessment

1. Take a screenshot of your visualization. Paste it into a Word document named "Lab 3.1 Power BI Submission.docx" and label the screenshot Submission 1.
2. Answer the questions in Connect and upload your Lab 3.1 Power BI Submission.docx via Connect if assigned.

Alternate Lab 3.1   Power BI—On Your Own

Using Graphs to Display Costs

Keywords

Fixed Cost, Variable Cost, Production Volume, Total Cost, Line Graph

Apply the same steps in Lab 3.1 Power BI to the **Alt Lab 3.1 Data.xlsx** data set and create a line graph in Power BI to show the total cost for each unit of production.

Required

When formatting your visualization, select different data colors than the default options.

Assessment

1. Take a screenshot of your visualization. Paste it into a Word document named "Alt Lab 3.1 Power BI Submission.docx" and label the screenshot "Submission 1".
2. Answer the questions in Connect and upload your Alt Lab 3.1 Power BI Submission .docx via Connect if assigned.

Using Graphs to Display Costs

Data Analytics Types: Diagnostic Analytics, Predictive Analytics

Lab Note: The tools presented in this lab periodically change. Updated instructions, if applicable, can be found in the student and instructor support materials.

Keywords

Fixed Cost, Variable Cost, Production Volume, Total Cost, Line Graph

Decision-Making Context

Elite Eyewear manufactures blue-light-blocking eyeglasses to sell to retailers around the United States. Managers keep data about the fixed and variable costs for different production amounts in an Excel spreadsheet, and they would like to use a visualization to illustrate how total cost changes as production volume increases. They have asked their management accounting team to use Tableau to create this visualization.

Ask the Question

How does total cost change as production volume increases?

Master the Data

For this lab you will use data in the Excel file **Lab 3.1 Data.xlsx**.

Review the data set, which contains information about the fixed and variable costs for each production volume.

Data Dictionary

Worksheet Tab/Table	Attribute Name	Description	Data Type
Product Cost Data	Production Volume	Number of units produced	Numerical
Product Cost Data	Fixed Cost	Fixed cost for production	Currency
Product Cost Data	Variable Cost	Variable cost per unit produced	Currency

After you review the Excel data, you will need to close it to import it into Tableau. Import the data into Tableau using the **Connect to Data** command (Lab Exhibit 3.1T.1). The **Product Cost Data** worksheet should automatically import because it is the only worksheet.

Lab Exhibit 3.1T.1

Tableau Software

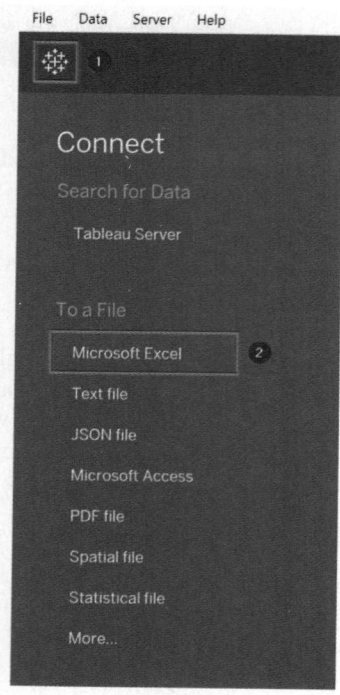

Perform the Analysis

Analysis Task #1: Calculate Total Cost

1. Open **Sheet 1**.
2. You will want to show the total cost on the Y-axis, but first you have to calculate total cost.
3. To calculate total cost, go to the **Analysis** tab and click on **Create Calculated Field...** (Lab Exhibit 3.1T.2). Name the new variable "Total Cost". Enter the following formula, shown in Lab Exhibit 3.1T.3, to calculate total cost:

Total Cost = [Fixed Cost]+([Production Volume]*[Variable Cost]).

Lab Exhibit 3.1T.2

Tableau Software

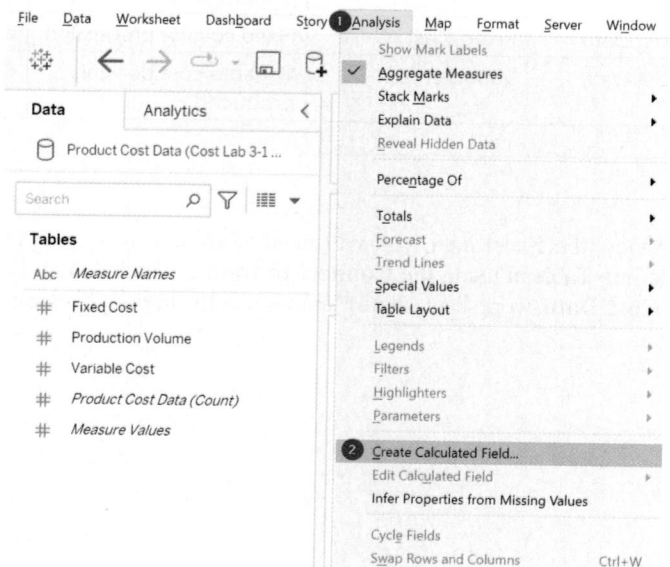

Total Cost   ✕

[Fixed Cost]+([Production Volume]*[Variable Cost])

▶

The calculation is valid.   Apply   OK

Analysis Task #2: Begin Data Visualization

1. Drag the (new) **Total Cost** field to the **Rows** shelf. Drag the **Production Volume** field to the **Columns** shelf. Change the Production Volume field to a dimension by right-clicking on the **Production Volume** field (pill) and then clicking on **Dimension** (Lab Exhibit 3.1T.4).

DATA VISUALIZATION

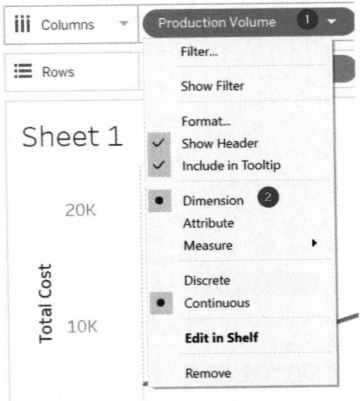

2. Change **Marks** type to **Line**. This will change the visualization to a line graph (Lab Exhibit 3.1T.5).

3. Drag **Measure Values** from the tables into **Marks** (Lab Exhibit 3.1T.6). Then remove **Product Cost Data**, **Production Volume**, and **Variable Cost** from **Measure Values** by right-clicking on the pill and selecting **Remove** (Lab Exhibit 3.1T.7).

Lab Exhibit 3.1T.6

Tableau Software

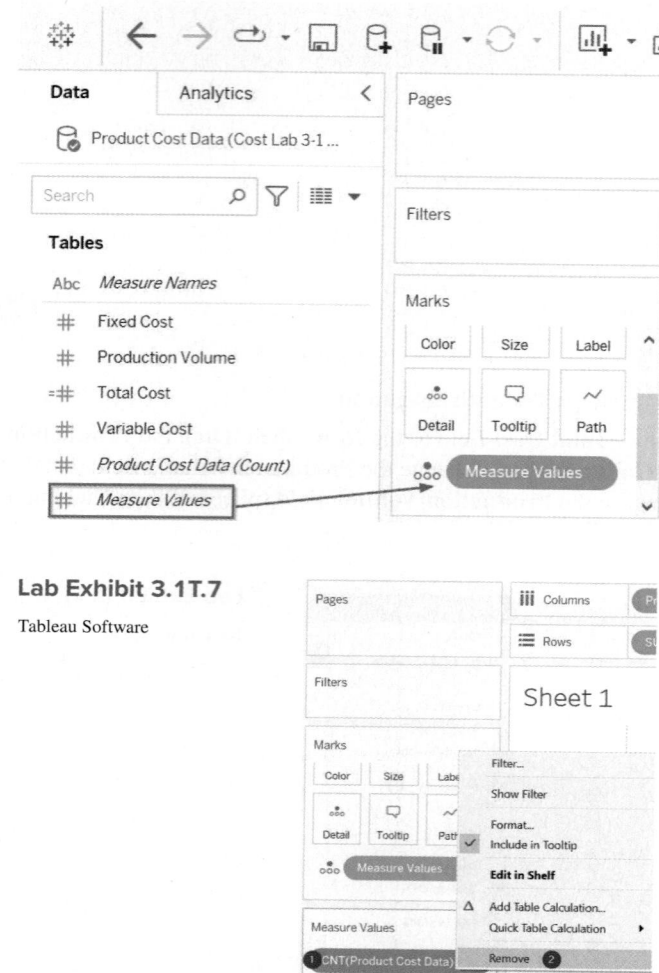

Lab Exhibit 3.1T.7

Tableau Software

4. Change Total Cost from measure to attribute by clicking the drop-down and selecting **Attribute** (Lab Exhibit 3.1T.8).

Lab Exhibit 3.1T.8

Tableau Software

5. To get both Total Cost and Fixed Cost on the same graph, drag the **Measure Values** field to the **Rows**. Then remove **Total Cost** from **Rows** (Lab Exhibit 3.1T.9).

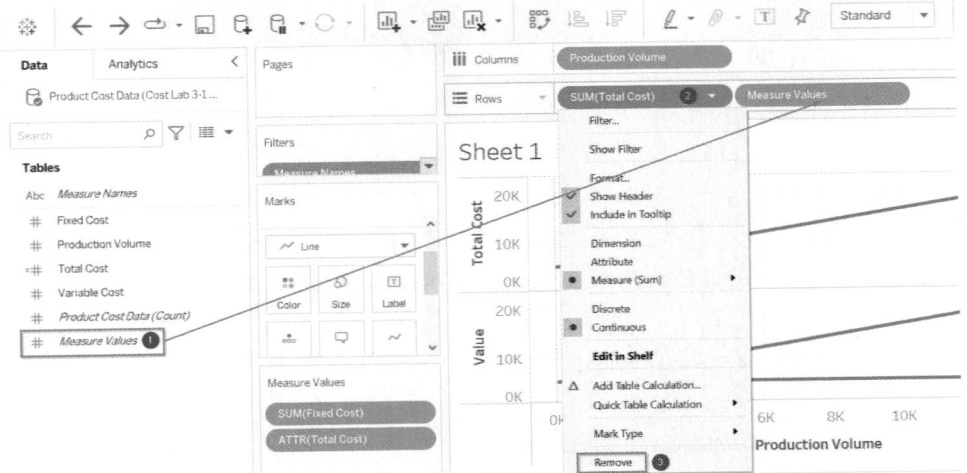

Lab Exhibit 3.1T.9

Tableau Software

Analysis Task #3: Format the Data Visualization

1. To change the color of the lines on the graph, drag **Measure Names** in **Marks** into the **Color** box (Lab Exhibit 3.1T.10).

Lab Exhibit 3.1T.10

Tableau Software

2. Format the title by clicking on the title and changing the name to "Cost by Production Volume". Change the label of the Y-axis by clicking on the current label and changing the axis title at the bottom of the **Edit Axis...** menu that pops up (Lab Exhibit 3.1T.11).

Lab Exhibit 3.1T.11

Tableau Software

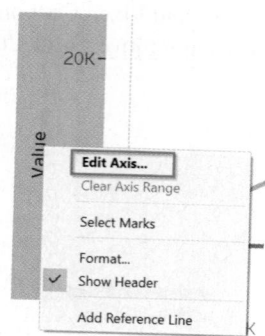

3. **Title** the axis "Total Costs", as shown at the bottom of Lab Exhibit 3.1T.12.

Lab Exhibit 3.1T.12

Tableau Software

Edit Axis [Measure Values]   ✕

General   Tick Marks

Range

- ◉ Automatic   ☑ Include zero
- ○ Uniform axis range for all rows or columns
- ○ Independent axis ranges for each row or column
- ○ Fixed

Automatic ▾	Automatic ▾
0	23,541.7519182

Scale

- ☐ Reversed
- ☐ Logarithmic
  - ◉ Positive   ○ Symmetric

Axis Titles

Title

Total Cost

Share the Story

Our analysis demonstrates that costs increase with production. Specifically, as production increases, variable costs increase. In contrast, fixed costs remain constant as production increases, assuming that production remains within the relevant range.

You have now loaded data into Tableau and created and formatted a line graph visualization. You also created a new field by creating a calculated field.

Assessment

1. Take a screenshot of your visualization. Paste it into a Word document named "Lab 3.1 Tableau Submission.docx" and label the screenshot Submission 1.
2. Answer the questions in Connect and upload your Lab 3.1 Tableau Submission.docx via Connect if assigned.

Alternate Lab 3.1   Tableau—On Your Own

Using Graphs to Display Costs

Keywords

Fixed Cost, Variable Cost, Production Volume, Total Cost, Line Graph

Apply the same steps in Lab 3.1 Tableau to the **Alt Lab 3.1 Data.xlsx** data set and create a line graph in Tableau to show the total cost for each unit of production.

When formatting your visualization, select different data colors than the default options.

Assessment

1. Take a screenshot of your visualization. Paste it into a Word document named "Alt Lab 3.1 Tableau Submission.docx" and label the screenshot Submission 1.
2. Answer the questions in Connect and upload your Alt Lab 3.1 Tableau Submission.docx via Connect if assigned.

Estimating Cost Behavior Using the High-Low Method

Data Analytics Types: Diagnostic Analytics, Predictive Analytics

Keywords

High-Low Method, Mixed Costs

Decision-Making Context

Managers need to understand their cost structure—their relative mix of fixed costs and variable costs—in order to understand their business and implement strategy. Sometimes they must estimate the fixed and variable components of total costs. They can accomplish this task through analyses such as the high-low method and regression.

Toothweb LCC is a small company that creates custom websites for dentists and orthodontists. The company has been in business for five years, and the owners have limited data available to determine the company's cost structure.

Required

1. Use the high-low method to estimate Toothweb's fixed expenses and variable expenses.
2. Use the high-low method to estimate future total costs.

Ask the Question

Toothweb LLC expects to create 40 websites next month. What are expected costs for next month?

Master the Data

For this lab you will use data in the Excel file titled **Lab 3.2 Data.xlsx**.

Data Dictionary

Quarter	3-month period; Q1 represents the first quarter of the company's existence
Dental Web	The number of websites produced for dental offices in a given month
Ortho Web	The number of websites produced for orthodontics offices in a given month
Total Web	The sum of dental and orthodontics websites in a given month
Total Costs	The total costs of running Toothweb in a given month

---

Perform the Analysis

Analysis Task #1: Identify High and Low Production

1. Open Excel file **Lab 3.2 Data.xlsx**.
2. Browse the spreadsheet very quickly to make sure there isn't any obvious error in the Excel file.

3. In cells H2 and H3, enter the highest and lowest number of websites for the past 8 quarters (Q13–Q20) (Lab Exhibit 3.2.1). Be sure to use cell references, not numbers. For example, in cell H3, use =D16.
4. In cells I2 and I3, enter the total costs associated with the highest and lowest number of websites for the past 8 quarters, again using cell references (Lab Exhibit 3.2.2).

Analysis Task #2: Calculate Costs

1. In cell H5, calculate the variable cost per website, which is the slope of the cost line; Variable cost = (High cost – Low cost)/(High websites – Low websites). Lab Exhibit 3.2.3 shows the correct formula: =(I2-I3)/(H2-H3).
2. In cell H6, calculate the fixed cost of running Toothweb. Given that Total Costs = Fixed Costs + (Variable Costs per Unit * Units), we can rearrange this formula to solve for fixed costs: Fixed Costs = Total Cost – (Variable Cost per Unit * Units). Lab Exhibit 3.2.4 shows the correct formula: =I2-(H5*H2). Using either the high or low data point, solve for fixed costs.
3. In cell H8, estimate the total costs for next quarter. Toothweb estimates that the company will create 40 websites next quarter. Recall that Total Costs = Fixed Costs + (Variable Costs per Unit * Units). As Lab Exhibit 3.2.5 shows, the formula is =H6+40*H5.

Analysis Task #3: Graph Your Results

DATA VISUALIZATION

1. Graph your results. Select cells D14:E21. Click **Insert**, then click the **Scatter** drop-down menu, and then click the first scatter option (Lab Exhibit 3.2.6).
2. Now we will plot a line between the high and low points. Right-click the chart and click **Select Data....** Click **Add**. Type "High Low" under **Series name**. Next, click the box under **Series X values**. While holding the Ctrl key, click the high and low website values (cells D14 and D16). Now click the box under **Series Y values**. While holding the Ctrl key, click the corresponding total cost values (cells E14 and E16). Click **OK** on the two open menus. See Lab Exhibits 3.2.7 and 3.2.8.
3. Click the chart. Near the upper right corner of the chart, click the chart element icon (it appears as a green +). Hover over **Trendline**, and then click the arrow that appears to the right of it. Click **More Options....** Click **High Low** and **OK** (Lab Exhibit 3.2.9). In the **Format Trendline** menu, click **Display Equation on chart** (Lab Exhibit 3.2.10). The equation should match your calculated variable and fixed costs.
4. Repeat this exercise, using the data from all available quarters (Q1–Q20) rather than just the last 8 quarters, to see how the inclusion of additional data alters the estimate for next quarter's total costs.

Share the Story

DATA VISUALIZATION

Based on our analysis of the past 20 quarters, Toothweb's estimated costs for next month are $59,912.60, based on 40 projected websites.

The high-low method can be used to estimate a company's cost structure, or a company's relative mix between fixed costs and variable costs. This information is helpful for managers as they forecast costs. In addition, managers can use a scatterplot to visualize how costs will change at various levels of production, as shown in Lab Exhibit 3.2.11.

Assessment

1. Take a screenshot of the table following Analysis Task #3, paste it into a Word document named "Lab 3.2 Submission.docx," and label the screenshot Submission 1.
2. Answer the questions in Connect and upload your Lab 3.2 Submission.docx via Connect if assigned.

Estimating Cost Behavior Using the High-Low Method

Keywords

High-Low Method, Mixed Costs

Apply the same steps in Lab 3.2 to the **Alt Lab 3.2 Data.xlsx** data set. The dataset Alt Lab 3.2 Data.xlsx includes total cost information for 15 individual websites (A–O), as well as the number of webpages contained in each site. Use the high-low method to estimate the fixed and variable costs for Toothweb on a per-website basis.

Assessment

1. Take a screenshot of your visualization. Paste it into a Word document named "Alt Lab 3.2 Submission.docx" and label the screenshot Submission 1.
2. Answer the questions in Connect and upload your Alt Lab 3.2 Submission.docx via Connect if assigned.

Estimating Cost Behavior Using Regression Analysis

Data Analytics Types: Diagnostic Analytics, Predictive Analytics

Lab Note: The tools presented in this lab periodically change. Updated instructions, if applicable, can be found in the student and instructor support materials. All Lab Exhibits are available within the eBook and in Connect.

Keywords

Regression, Mixed Costs

Decision-Making Context

Managers need to understand their cost structure, or their relative mix of fixed expenses and variable expenses, in order to understand their business and implement strategy. At times, managers must estimate the fixed and variable components of total costs. They can accomplish this task through analyses such as the high-low method and regression.

Toothweb LCC is a small company that creates custom websites for dentists and orthodontists. The company has been in business for five years, and the owners have limited data available to determine the company's cost structure.

Required

1. Use regression analysis to estimate the company's fixed expenses and variable expenses.
2. Analyze regression output to compare regression models.

Ask the Question

Toothweb LLC expects to create 40 websites next month. What are expected costs for next month?

Master the Data

For this lab you will use data in the Excel file titled **Lab 3.3 Data.xlsx**.

Data Dictionary

Quarter	3-month period; Q1 represents the first quarter of the company's existence
Dental Web	The number of websites produced for dental offices in a given month
Ortho Web	The number of websites produced for orthodontics offices in a given month
Total Web	The sum of dental and orthodontics websites in a given month
Total Costs	The total costs of running Toothweb in a given month

Perform the Analysis

Analysis Task #1: Use Regression to Analyze Cost Data

1. Open Excel file **Lab 3.3 Data.xlsx**.
2. Quickly browse the spreadsheet to make sure there isn't any obvious error in the Excel file.

3. We will be using regression analysis for this lab. To run the regression, we make sure our Analysis ToolPak is loaded, by looking at **Data > Analysis** and seeing if the **Data Analysis** add-in has been installed (Lab Exhibit 3.3.1).

　　If it has not yet been added, go to **File > Options > Add-ins > Manage: > Excel Add-ins > Go...** (Lab Exhibit 3.3.2). Then select the **Analysis ToolPak** and then **OK** (Lab Exhibit 3.3.3).

4. Click the **Data** tab in Excel. At the far right of the ribbon, click **Data Analysis**. Under **Analysis Tools**, click **Regression**. Click **OK** (Lab Exhibit 3.3.4).

5. Click the box to the right of **Input Y Range**. Select E1:E21. This column represents the dependent variable. Click the box to the right of **Input X Range**. Select D1:D21. This column represents the independent variable. Click the box to the left of **Labels** to alert the program that the top row does not contain numerical data for the analysis. Click **OK**. See Lab Exhibit 3.3.5. The regression output will open in a new sheet.

Analysis Task #2: Interpret Regression Results

1. Lab Exhibit 3.3.6 reproduces the regression results. Identify **Multiple R**, which measures the strength of the linear relationship between the independent and dependent variables. R is 0.92.

2. Identify **R Square**, which is the coefficient of determination. This is a measure of fit, and it tells us the amount of variation in total costs that are explained by changes in the number of websites. R square is 0.84. Always remember to use Adjusted R Square instead if you have multiple independent variables!

3. Evaluate the regression output by checking **Significance F** of the model (1.20305E-08), the **P-value** of the **Intercept** (0.017909537) and of **Total Web** (1.20305E-08). Note that these numbers are written in scientific notation. We can convert them to a standard notation by moving the decimal point 8 places to the left. Low p-values (less than 0.1 or 0.05) indicate statistical significance.

4. Identify the fixed and variable cost estimates. On the regression output, the fixed cost estimate is the **Intercept Coefficient** (10401.87). The variable cost estimate (cost per website) is the **Total Web Coefficient** (1179.13).

　　For more information on interpreting statistical output, see Appendix F.

5. Use the regression output to estimate the total costs for next quarter. Toothweb estimates that the company will create 40 websites next quarter. Recall that Total Costs = Fixed Costs + (Variable Costs per Unit * Units). The formula, as shown in Lab Exhibit 3.3.7, is =B17+40*B18. Excel returns a total cost estimate of $57,567.20 after the formula is input.

Analysis Task #3: Graph the Data

DATA VISUALIZATION

1. Return to the Excel sheet with the raw data. We are going to graph the cost equation. Select cells D1:E21. Click **Insert**, click the **Scatter** drop-down menu, and then click the **Scatter** icon (Lab Exhibit 3.3.8).

2. Click the chart. Near the upper-right corner of the chart, click the chart element icon (it appears as a green +). Hover over **Trendline**, and then click the arrow that appears to the right of it. Click **More Options...** (Lab Exhibit 3.3.9). In the **Format Trendline** menu, click **Display Equation on chart** and **Display R-squared value on chart** (Lab Exhibit 3.3.10). The resulting equation should match the output from the regression.

3. Toothweb wants to determine how cost estimates differ if multiple regression analysis using two independent variables (Dental Web and Ortho Web) is used, rather than simple regression analysis using a single combined independent variable (Total Web). Repeat this exercise to estimate Toothweb's total costs for a quarter in which the company creates 25 Dental websites and 15 Orthodontics websites. (*Hint:* When repeating Step 5 of Analysis Task #1, select columns B and C as the X range.)

Share the Story

Based on our multiple regression analysis (which projects 25 Dental websites and 15 Orthodontics websites), Toothweb's estimated costs for next month are $53,843.65.

Regression analysis can be used to estimate a company's cost structure, which can assist managers in estimating costs. Regression analysis is a powerful tool that makes use of all data points in the data set. Note that the results of a *simple* regression can easily be graphed, as shown in Lab Exhibit 3.3.11. Multiple regression is more difficult to graph because it requires more than two dimensions.

Assessment

1. Take a screenshot of the table following Analysis Task #3, name it "Lab 3.3 Submission.docx", and label the screenshot Submission 1.
2. Answer the questions in Connect and upload your Lab 3.3 Submission.docx via Connect if assigned (using all quarters' data).

Alternate Lab 3.3   Excel—On Your Own

Estimating Cost Behavior Using Regression Analysis

Keywords

Regression, Mixed Costs

Perform multiple regression analysis to determine how production and how a specific manager affect production costs. To do so, apply the same steps listed in Lab 3.3 to the **Alt Lab 3.3 Data.xlsx** data set.

This data set contains production cost information for Mountaineer Pepperoni Rolls. The company is trying to determine fixed and variable costs of production using regression analysis. In addition, the company wants to determine how costs differ when Karl is the production manager on duty.

Data Dictionary

Week	Week number for the previous 52 weeks
Production	Number of rolls produced in a given week
Karl Mgr	An indicator variable set to "1" if Karl is managing production that week, "0" if not
Total Production Cost	Weekly production cost

Assessment

1. Take a screenshot of the regression output, paste it into a Word document named "Alt Lab 3.3 Submission.docx", and label the screenshot Submission 1.
2. Answer the questions in Connect and upload your Alt Lab 3.3 Submission.docx via Connect if assigned.

Conducting Cost-Volume-Profit Analysis Under Different Assumptions

Data Analytics Types: Diagnostic Analytics, Predictive Analytics

Keywords

CVP Analysis, Fixed Costs, Variable Costs

Decision-Making Context

The CVP framework helps managers understand the relationship between revenues, costs, volume, and profitability. Using the CVP framework, managers can analyze how changes in prices, product inputs, and volume will change financial performance.

ProSports is a manufacturer of sports equipment. Data for ProSports' basketball division are presented in a contribution margin income statement, also known as a variable costing income statement. Recall that when using variable costing, all variable costs are subtracted from revenues to calculate contribution margin. Then, all fixed costs are subtracted from contribution margin to calculate operating income.

In this lab, we will use goal-seek analysis within the CVP framework. *Goal-seek analysis* is a what-if prescriptive analytics technique that tells us the required input needed to reach a desired outcome, output, or result.

Required

1. Use Excel to create a contribution margin income statement.
2. Use CVP analysis to analyze and estimate a company's profitability.
3. Use goal-seek analysis to solve CVP problems.

Ask the Question

How do changes in prices, product inputs, and cost structure affect ProSports' profitability?

Master the Data

For this lab you will use data in the Excel file titled **Lab 3.4 Data.xlsx**. Quickly review the sheet to gain an understanding of ProSports' financial information.

Perform the Analysis

Analysis Task #1: Calculate Basic Financial Data

1. In this lab, we will perform multiple CVP analyses. Excel's goal-seek function is a very helpful tool for these analyses. To use goal seek, we must populate our income statement with formulas rather than numbers. In cell D6, calculate Total Sales by multiplying sales price per unit by sales volume (number of units). In cell C11, calculate variable cost per unit by adding variable manufacturing cost per unit and SG&A expenses per unit. In cell D12, calculate Total Variable Costs by multiplying total sales by variable Cost per unit. Lab Exhibit 3.4.1 shows the formulas, and Lab 3.4.2 shows the results.
2. In cell C14, calculate Unit Contribution Margin by subtracting variable Cost per unit from Sales price per unit. In cell D15, calculate Total Contribution Margin by subtracting total variable costs from total sales. In cell D20, calculate Total Fixed Costs by adding fixed manufacturing costs and fixed SG&A costs. In cell D22, calculate

Operating Income by subtracting total fixed costs from total contribution margin. Lab Exhibit 3.4.1 shows the formulas, and Lab Exhibit 3.4.2 shows the results.

3. Identify current units and operating income. This will be the baseline position against which we will compare future changes. Copy these cells to a new area on your sheet or to a new sheet so that you can refer back to it later.

Analysis Task #2: Calculate the Break-Even Point and Target Profit Point Using Goal Seek

1. Companies often perform break-even analysis to determine how many units they need to sell (assuming a constant cost structure) to generate $0 in operating income. To perform this analysis using Goal Seek, click the **Data** tab, then **What-If Analysis**, then **Goal Seek...** (Lab Exhibit 3.4.3).

2. Calculate the break-even point using Goal Seek. In the **Goal Seek** window, enter D22 next to **Set cell**, enter 0 next to **To value**, and enter $C$5 next to **By changing cell**. This tells Excel to change volume until we have achieved $0. Click **OK**. See Lab Exhibit 3.4.4. For the output generated by Excel, see Lab Exhibit 3.4.5.

3. Goal seek can also be used to calculate target profit. Calculate how many units must be sold in order to make $250,000 in operating income. To do so, repeat Step 2, but enter 250000 next to **To value** (as shown in Lab Exhibit 3.4.6). For the output generated by Excel, see Lab Exhibit 3.4.7.

Analysis Task #3: Perform Additional Analysis Under the CVP Framework

1. To see how different assumptions or actions can change profitability, it is helpful to replicate our spreadsheet to see operating income under two conditions at once. To do so, highlight and copy Columns A–D to Columns F–I.

2. Label cell G24 "Change in Operating Income". In cell G25, enter the following calculation: =I22-D22.

3. Refer to the baseline condition. Assume that the company has found a less-expensive supplier who can provide similar-quality raw materials at $1 less in variable manufacturing costs per unit. Calculate the change in operating income under the new conditions. Change the variable cost per unit in cell H11 to $14. Lab Exhibit 3.4.8 shows how this change in variable cost affects profitability. As cell G25 indicates, there is a $10,000 negative change in operating income.

4. Now assume that rather than shift suppliers, the company can reduce variable manufacturing costs by $1 per unit through increased automation, which will require a new machine. The new machine will increase fixed manufacturing costs by $20,000. Calculate the number of units the company must sell in order to be indifferent between the baseline condition and increasing automation. To do so, update the contribution margin income statement by reducing the variable manufacturing cost by $1 per unit and increasing fixed manufacturing costs by $20,000. Then, set the new sales volume equal to the baseline sales volume with a formula (in cell H5, use =C5, as shown in Lab Exhibit 3.4.9).

Now use goal seek to set the change in operating income equal to zero while altering sales volume. In the **Goal Seek** dialog box, set cell G25 to 0 (meaning that there's no difference in operating income between the two conditions) by changing cell C5, sales volume. See Lab Exhibit 3.4.10.

At 20,000 units, ProSports will have equivalent operating income with either the baseline or changed cost structure (see Lab Exhibit 3.4.11). You will notice that operating income is more sensitive to changes in sales volume in the changed condition. This is due to increased operating leverage (that is, a higher proportion of fixed costs). Unless ProSports expects to sell more than 20,000 units, it should not invest in increased automation.

Share the Story

By using a CVP framework, we have analyzed how changes in sales price, costs, and volume at ProSports affect profitability. In addition, we have seen how companies can use CVP analysis to determine the break-even point and the target-profit point for goods and services. Finally, we've seen how CVP can be a useful tool for what-if analysis because it allows companies to determine profitability under various circumstances.

Assessment

1. Take a screenshot of your spreadsheet output following Step 4 above. Paste it into a Word document named "Lab 3.4 Submission.docx" and label the screenshot Submission 1.
2. Answer the questions in Connect and upload your Lab 3.4 Submission.docx via Connect if assigned.

Alternate Lab 3.4   Excel—On Your Own

Conducting Cost-Volume-Profit Analysis Under Different Assumptions

Keywords

CVP Analysis, Fixed Costs, Variable Costs

Apply the same steps in Lab 3.4 to the **Alt Lab 3.4 Data.xlsx** data set. The data set Alt Lab 3.4 Data.xlsx includes information needed to construct a contribution margin income statement for ProSports' Snorkel Division.

Assessment

1. Take a screenshot of your spreadsheet output. Paste it into a Word document named "Alt Lab 3.4 Submission.docx" and label the screenshot Submission 1.
2. Answer the questions in Connect and upload your Alt Lab 3.4 Submission.docx via Connect if assigned.

Conducting Cost-Volume-Profit Analysis with Multiple Products

Data Analytics Types: Diagnostic Analytics, Predictive Analytics

Lab Note: The tools presented in this lab periodically change. Updated instructions, if applicable, can be found in the student and instructor support materials. All Lab Exhibits are available within the eBook and in Connect.

Keywords

Cost-Volume-Profit, Excel, Prediction

Decision-Making Context

The CVP framework helps managers understand the relationship between revenues, costs, volume, and profitability. Using the CVP framework, managers can analyze how changes in prices, product inputs, and volume will change financial performance. This lab extends the CVP framework to examine a setting with multiple products.

ProSports is a manufacturer of sports equipment. Data for ProSports' basketball and football products are presented in a contribution margin income statement, also known as a variable costing income statement. Recall that when using variable costing, all variable costs are subtracted from revenues to calculate contribution margin. Then, all fixed costs are subtracted from contribution margin to calculate operating income.

In this lab, we will use goal-seek analysis within the CVP framework. Goal-seek analysis is a what-if prescriptive analytics technique that that tells us the required input needed to reach a desired outcome, output, or result.

Required

1. Use Excel to create a contribution margin income statement with multiple products.
2. Use CVP analysis to analyze and estimate a company's profitability.
3. Use goal-seek analysis to solve CVP problems.

Ask the Question

How do changes in prices, product inputs, and cost structure affect ProSports' profitability in a multiproduct setting?

Master the Data

Open Excel file **Lab 3.5 Data.xlsx**. Quickly review the sheet to gain an understanding of ProSports' financial information.

Perform the Analysis

Analysis Task #1: Calculate Basic Financial Data

1. In this lab, we will perform multiple CVP analyses. Excel's goal-seek function is a very helpful tool for these analyses. To use goal seek, we must populate our income statement with formulas rather than numbers. In the spreadsheet, you will need to use formulas to populate all gray cells. In columns C and D (for each product), calculate Sales Volume by multiplying the total sales volume by the sales mix. Calculate Variable cost per unit by adding variable manufacturing costs and variable SG&A expenses per unit for each product. Calculate Unit Contribution Margin by subtracting variable cost per unit from sales price per unit for each product. Lab Exhibit 3.5.1 shows the formulas, and Lab 3.5.2 shows the results.
2. Now we need to calculate values for a composite unit (Column E). Conceptually, a composite unit is a weighted-average unit. When performing CVP analysis with multiple products, we assume that product mix remains constant. Calculate a composite

unit's sales price, variable cost, and contribution margin by summing the product of each product's sales mix and unit data. For instance, if our sales mix is divided equally between two products, the composite sales price would be one-half of the first product's price plus one-half of the second product's price. Lab Exhibit 3.5.3 shows the formulas to input, and Lab Exhibit 3.5.4 shows the results.

3. To complete the contribution margin income statement, we need to complete Column F. Calculate Total Sales by multiplying the composite sales price per unit by the total sales volume. Calculate Total Variable Costs by multiplying composite cost per unit by sales volume. Calculate Total Contribution Margin by subtracting total variable costs from total sales. Calculate Total Fixed Costs by adding fixed manufacturing costs and fixed SG&A costs. Calculate Operating Income by subtracting total fixed costs from total contribution margin. All formulas are shown in Lab Exhibit 3.5.5. The completed income statement in Lab Exhibit 3.5.6 will represent current sales projections, which we will use as the baseline against which we will compare proposed changes.

Analysis Task #2: Calculate the Break-Even Point and Target Profit Point Using Goal Seek

1. To see how different assumptions or actions can change profitability, it is helpful to replicate our spreadsheet to see operating income under two conditions at once. To do so, highlight and copy Columns A–F and to Columns H–M.

2. Label cell I25 "Change in Operating Income". In Cell G26, enter the following calculation: =F23-M22.

3. Perform break-even analysis using Goal Seek. Click the **Data Tab**, then **What-if Analysis**, then **Goal Seek...**. Input the values shown in Lab Exhibit 3.5.7. Because companies cannot sell partial units, the convention is to round units up to the nearest whole number. To break even, SportPro must sell 10,715 total units (see Lab Exhibit 3.5.8). When we look at individual product lines in the Sales Volume row, that equates to 5,358 units for both basketballs and footballs.

4. Lab Exhibit 3.5.9 shows a comparison between the baseline and break-even conditions. Recall that the margin of safety is the number of units or the sales amount that surpasses break-even. In this case, comparing the break-even and baseline conditions results in a margin of safety of 9,286 units (which can be calculated by subtracting cell L6 from E6) or $325,000 (calculated by subtracting M7 from F7).

5. Repeat the goal-seek analysis to calculate how many units must be sold to achieve a target profit of $300,000. To do so, repeat Step 1, but enter 300000 next to **To value**. The results are shown in the Sales Volume row of Lab Exhibit 3.5.10: The company must sell a total of 25,000 units.

Analysis Task #3: Perform Additional Analysis Under the CVP Framework

1. Refer to the baseline condition. Assume that the company has the opportunity to increase spending on general advertising. Fixed SG&A costs would increase by $20,000, and total sales would increase by 20%. Product mix would not change. Calculate how the increased advertising expense would change operating income. Also, the company found a less-expensive supplier who can provide similar-quality raw materials at $1 less in variable manufacturing costs per unit. Calculate the change in operating income under the new conditions. Lab Exhibit 3.5.11 shows the results: Operating income increases by $64,000 (see cell I26).

2. Now assume that rather than general advertising, the $20,000 spent on advertising would focus on basketball products. Total sales would increase by 20%, but the sales mix would shift to 80% basketball and 20% football. Calculate the change in operating income under the new conditions (relative to the baseline condition). You will notice that the results are more favorable with the product mix. Why? Basketballs

have a higher contribution margin than footballs. Assuming units sold stays constant, a higher proportion of basketballs sold will increase profitability. See cell I26 in Lab Exhibit 3.5.12.

Share the Story

By using a CVP framework, we have analyzed how changes in sales price, costs, and volume at ProSports affect profitability. The use of composite units enables ProSports to use CVP analysis in a multiple-product setting to determine the break-even point and target-profit point. In addition, ProSports can use the CVP framework for what-if analysis, which can be used to determine profitability under various circumstances.

Assessment

1. Take a screenshot of your spreadsheet output. Paste it into a Word document named "Lab 3.5 Submission.docx" and label the screenshot Submission 1.
2. Answer the questions in Connect and upload your Lab 3.5 Submission.docx via Connect if assigned. For each question, start from or compare to the baseline condition.

Alternate Lab 3.5 Excel—On Your Own

Conducting Cost-Volume-Profit Analysis with Multiple Products

Keywords

Cost-Volume-Profit, Excel, Prediction

Apply the same steps in Lab 3.5 to the **Alt Lab 3.5 Data.xlsx** data set. The data set Alt Lab 3.5 Data.xlsx includes information needed to construct a contribution margin income statement with multiple products for ProSports' snorkel and fins products.

Assessment

1. Take a screenshot of your spreadsheet output. Paste it into a Word document named "Alt Lab 3.5 Submission.docx" and label the screenshot Submission 1.
2. Answer the questions in Connect and upload your Alt Lab 3.5 Submission.docx via Connect if assigned. Compare proposed changes to the original, baseline data supplied in the spreadsheet.

Lab Note: The tools presented in this lab periodically change. Updated instructions, if applicable, can be found in the student and instructor support materials. All Lab Exhibits are available within the eBook and in Connect.

Comparing and Contrasting Absorption Costing and Variable Costing (Heartwood)

Data Analytics Types: Descriptive Analytics, Diagnostic Analytics, Predictive Analytics

Keywords

Absorption Costing, Excel, Ethics Variable Costing

Decision-Making Context

Both variable costing and absorption costing are commonly used by companies. Variable costing groups costs by behavior (variable vs. fixed), while absorption costing (which is required by GAAP) classifies costs as product or period. Management accountants must be able to calculate product costs using each cost system, and the calculation differs slightly depending on whether variable or absorption costing is used. Both variable and absorption costing include direct materials, direct labor, and variable manufacturing overhead as product costs. Absorption costing also includes fixed manufacturing costs, while variable costing does not.

These two cost systems have important differences that show up in the income statement and balance sheet. Management accountants must know and understand these differences and their implications.

Heartwood Cabinets has a manufacturing plant that manufactures kitchen islands with butcher block tops. Let's assume for the purpose of this lab that the plant manager's bonus is contingent on net income. In this lab, you will review projected annual sales and cost data for the Heartwood plant. Your task is to construct variable costing and absorption costing income statements to estimate the plant's profitability.

Required

1. Demonstrate how to account for product and period costs under both variable costing and absorption costing.
2. Use Excel to create a variable costing income statement and an absorption costing income statement.
3. Understand how changes in production can alter income and inventory under both costing systems.

Ask the Question

How can managers affect GAAP net income by altering production?

Master the Data

Open Excel file **Lab 3.6 Data.xlsx**. Quickly review the sheet to gain an understanding of the Heartwood plant's financial information.

Perform the Analysis

Analysis Task #1: Calculate Product Costs

1. Review projected beginning and ending inventory. You will notice that the company intends to produce and sell the same number of units this year. Review sales and cost information. Cost information is grouped by cost behavior.

2. Calculate the product cost for one unit for both variable and absorption costing. Make sure to use formulas, as we will later determine how changes in production can alter costs. Set cell B24 equal to B12 (Lab Exhibit 3.6.1). Press the F4 key until you see a "$" in front of the B only. This locks the B column in the formula and facilitates copying our formula to other cells. First, copy the formula from cell B24 to cells B25 and B26. Next, we will copy the product costs from the variable costing column to the absorption costing column (Lab Exhibit 3.6.2). This can be accomplished by selecting and copying cells B24:B26, and then pasting to cell C24.

   Absorption costing includes fixed manufacturing costs as a product cost. Calculate the per-unit allocation of fixed manufacturing costs. In cell C27, divide the fixed manufacturing costs by the units produced, using the formula =B18/B4, as shown in Lab Exhibit 3.6.3.
3. Use the **SUM** function to calculate the total per-unit product cost under each costing system (Lab Exhibit 3.6.4). You'll notice that absorption costing has a higher per-unit product cost (Lab Exhibit 3.6.5).
4. Calculate the total product costs in cells B32 and C32 by multiplying the per-unit product cost by the total units produced. Use the formula =B4*C28, as shown at the bottom of Lab Exhibit 3.6.6.
5. Calculate total period costs under each costing system. Both systems include variable and fixed SG&A costs. Variable costing also includes fixed manufacturing costs. *Note:* Make sure that variable SG&A expenses are multiplied by units sold, not units produced. Use the formulas shown in Lab Exhibits 3.6.7 and 3.6.8:
   - Variable costing: Enter =B15*B5+B18+B19 in cell B35.
   - Absorption costing: Enter =B15*B5+B19 in cell C35.
6. Calculate total costs by adding total product and total period costs. Notice that these costs are equivalent under both cost systems. The only difference between variable and absorption costing is how they account for fixed manufacturing costs (see Row 27 in Lab Exhibit 3.6.9).

Analysis Task #2: Create Variable and Absorption Income Statements

1. Use the formulas in Lab Exhibit 3.6.10 to fill out the variable costing income statement. Variable cost of goods sold represents the product cost for all units sold (not produced). It sometimes appears as variable manufacturing costs on the income statement.
2. Use the formulas in Lab Exhibit 3.6.11 to fill out the absorption costing income statement. Again, ensure that cost of goods sold is linked to units sold rather than units produced.
3. Finally, determine how inventory changes as a result of projected production and sales. In cells F24 and J24, enter =B6-B3 to determine how units have changed. In cells G24 and K24, multiply the change in units by the per-unit product cost (cell B28 or C28) to determine how the total inventory value has changed. Lab Exhibit 3.6.12 shows the formulas to enter.

Analysis Task #3: Determine How Changes in Production Affect Financial Statements Under Variable Costing and Absorption Costing

1. With our spreadsheet set up, we can now determine how changes in production alter net income and inventory levels under these two costing systems. Change production levels to reflect Heartwood producing 1,200 kitchen islands but selling only 1,000. How are income and inventory affected? You'll notice that income and inventory are higher under absorption costing than variable costing. Why? The fixed manufacturing costs are not expensed until the islands are sold. The extra 200 units in inventory increase the inventory value and will not be expensed until they are sold in future periods (Lab Exhibit 3.6.13).

   Taken to the extreme, if Heartwood produces 2,000 units and sells 1,000 units, half of the $250,000 in fixed manufacturing costs are included as inventory, which increases the inventory account on the balance sheet and increases income by $125,000. In contrast, if Heartwood produces fewer units than it sells, absorption costing income and inventory will be lower than variable costing income and inventory.

2. Assume that the plant manager of Heartwood will receive a bonus if operating income is $6,000,000 for the year. The manager believes it unlikely that sales will be higher than 1,000 units but understands that increasing production can temporarily increase GAAP income. Use Goal Seek to calculate how many units must be produced to achieve $6,000,000 in income (without selling more units). The inputs are shown in Lab Exhibit 3.6.14. The answer is 1,667 kitchen islands.

3. Consider the following. Is it illegal for a company to produce more units than it sells? Is it ethical? What problems may arise from this practice? How can companies prevent these issues? Is increased island inventory likely to be impaired due to damage, shrinkage, or obsolescence? How would your answers change if the company in question produced pharmaceutical products?

Share the Story

ETHICS

Cost accountants must be familiar with both variable costing and absorption costing, how they differ, and how production levels influence income and inventory under both cost systems. Our analysis demonstrates how managers can alter income through increased production using absorption costing, which is required by GAAP, even when sales remain constant. In contrast, variable costing is not influenced by production levels. Cost accountants who understand these issues can help companies prevent and detect managers' overproduction of products to report higher profits.

Assessment

1. Take a screenshot of your final spreadsheet output. Paste it into a Word document named "Lab 3.6 Submission.docx" and label the screenshot Submission 1.
2. Answer the questions in Connect and upload your Lab 3.6 Submission.docx via Connect if assigned. For each question, start from or compare to a sales and production level of 1,000 units.

Alternate Lab 3.6   Excel—On Your Own

Comparing and Contrasting Absorption Costing and Variable Costing (Heartwood)

Keywords

Absorption Costing, Excel, Ethics, Variable Costing

Apply the steps from Lab 3.6 to the **Alt Lab 3.6 Data.xlsx** data set. The data set Alt Lab 3.6 Data.xlsx includes production and cost information about Heartwood's deluxe kitchen island line.

Assessment

1. Take a screenshot of your final spreadsheet. Paste it into a Word document named "Alt Lab 3.6 Submission.docx" and label the screenshot Submission 1.
2. Answer the questions in Connect and upload your Alt Lab 3.6 Submission.docx via Connect if assigned. For each question, start from or compare to a sales and production level of 500 units.

Chapter 4

Job Costing

A Look at This Chapter

This chapter describes a cost system used to track and categorize costs for specific jobs or products. It defines a job-cost system and describes the flow of costs from the start of the production process to the sale of the product. It also discusses manufacturing overhead and how it is estimated and assigned to products.

Cost Accounting and Data Analytics

COST ACCOUNTING LEARNING OBJECTIVE	RELATED DATA ANALYTICS LABS	LAB ANALYTICS TYPE(S)
LO 4.1 Explain the importance of tracking costs.		
LO 4.2 Define job costing and categorize job costs.		
LO 4.3 Explain the flow of job costs through the accounting system.		
LO 4.4 Determine manufacturing overhead application rates.	**LAB 4.1 Excel** Using Linear Regression in Forecasting (Heartwood)	**Predictive**
	LAB 4.2 Excel Seasonal Forecasting	**Predictive**
	LAB 4.3 Excel Determining Application Base and Overhead Rate	**Descriptive, Predictive**
LO 4.5 Make adjusting entries for underapplied or overapplied manufacturing overhead.		
LO 4.6 Compute the costs of a job.	**Data Analytics Mini-Lab** Using Data to Estimate Job Costs	**Descriptive**
	LAB 4.4 Excel Calculating Job Costs	**Descriptive**
	LAB 4.5 Tableau/Power BI Visualizing Job-Cost Data	**Descriptive, Diagnostic**

Chapter Concepts and Career Skills

Learning About...	Helps with These Career Skills
Job costing	• Tracking costs for unique jobs and orders, and following these costs through the financial statements • Determining the profitability of unique products and services • Determining pricing and marketing strategies
Direct materials and direct labor	• Understanding how direct costs affect product costs • Understanding how and why different products are targeted to different markets
Overhead application rates and applied manufacturing overhead	• Understanding how company activities affect indirect product costs and how companies track and account for costs • Estimating the indirect costs of providing unique products and services • Understanding how production costs flow through financial statements and how to correct errors caused by inaccurate estimates

Image Source/Getty Images

Would You Pay $10,000 for a Bicycle?

The growing popularity of bicycles for recreation, exercise, competition, and commuting has fueled growth and advancements in the industry. To a novice, bicycles look largely the same. They have a frame, two wheels, and pedals. But those characteristics tell you little about the features that can make them function very differently from other bikes and why their prices vary so widely. Companies such as **Huffy** mass-produce bicycles that can be purchased for as little as $100 and may prefer to account for costs using process costing (see Chapter 7). In contrast, companies such as **Cannondale** and **Specialized** produce bicycles to customer specifications with unique or customized features, which makes job costing more appropriate. These customized bicycles can command prices of more than $10,000. What justifies a $10,000 price tag? Some bikes are made with steel, while others are made with carbon or titanium, which are much more costly. The materials and specialized options also influence the amount of labor needed to construct a bike.

In this chapter, we discuss the importance of tracking costs for calculating the cost of unique products and services. Cannondale and Specialized can use a job-costing system to track the production costs of bicycles that vary in the materials used and labor involved. They can then use this cost information to inform their product pricing and to analyze product profitability and business operations.

Source: Cassandra Brooklyn, "These Bikes Are the SUVs of the Cycling World," *The Wall Street Journal*, March 25, 2021.

THE IMPORTANCE OF TRACKING COSTS

As discussed in Chapter 1, companies exist to create value. To quantify value creation, managers must be able to identify and understand the costs of producing products and services.

Generating cost information often entails using estimates, which implies some degree of inaccuracy. One of the most important reasons for understanding costs is to help managers make pricing decisions. What are the consequences of inaccurate cost information? If a company sets prices too high because of inaccurate cost information, it might lose customers to competitors that have a better understanding of their production costs. On the flip side, if a company sets prices too low because of inaccurate cost information, the company may not make sufficient profit to continue operations. In extreme cases, businesses may unknowingly set prices below costs. In this case, the harder the company works, the faster it loses money.

In competitive settings where companies are price takers, an understanding of costs informs companies whether they can make sufficient profits to continue doing business, and whether they should discontinue certain products or services.[1] Understanding costs also informs companies about how to market their products and how to incentivize sales staff to increase sales of high-margin products.

Many companies adopt **cost-plus pricing**, in which they charge customers a certain percentage above their costs for goods and services. This strategy is common for companies that contract with government agencies to provide goods and services. The approach makes sense, as it allows owners to earn a reasonable return on their time and assets.

Several types of cost systems are used to track the costs of producing goods and services. These systems carefully track product costs (discussed in Chapter 2) so that companies can determine their profitability. Management accountants can help companies determine which cost system is most appropriate for their particular circumstances.

This chapter discusses **job costing**, also called **job-order costing**. Companies use job costing to assign costs to unique products. This method works especially well for companies that produce goods and services that are customized and produced in low volumes. Activity-based costing (discussed in Chapter 5) builds on job costing but assigns costs in a more targeted way on the basis of cost-driving activities. Activity-based costing is more appropriate for companies that have high amounts of overhead costs and that produce goods and services with varying levels of complexity and in different volumes. **Process costing** (discussed in Chapter 7) is a costing system that accumulates cost by production process. It is ideal for companies that produce mass quantities of the same product (such as breakfast cereal or oil).

✓ PROGRESS CHECK

1. Why is it important for companies to understand their costs?
2. What incentives do firms have to control costs under a cost-plus contract? What is one potential drawback of using cost-plus pricing?

AN INTRODUCTION TO JOB COSTING

A **job-costing system** is a simple costing system in which all production costs are accumulated by job. A **job** is a broad term used to refer to a customized order, a specific batch of products, or an individualized product or service that is created for a specific customer.

---

[1]Price-takers are companies that do not have sufficient market share to influence purchase prices. Rather, they must accept prevailing market prices.

manufacturing overhead (MOH)
Indirect costs that are essential to the manufacturing of goods.

direct materials
Materials that are traced to a product or job and tracked by the accounting system.

indirect materials
Materials that are not traced to a product or job and whose costs are included in manufacturing overhead.

direct labor
Employee labor (hands-on, touch labor) involved in producing goods or delivering services.

indirect labor
Labor used to provide a product or service that is not traced to a specific product or job; the efforts of the workers who are involved with the production process but who don't provide touch labor. Indirect labor costs are included in manufacturing overhead.

Job costing does not apply only to manufacturing. Many service offerings, such as producing a tax return or preparing a lawsuit, fit well within the framework of a job-costing system.

Here are a few more examples of businesses or business activities in which a job-costing system can be used:

• Home construction.
• Production of custom-built cabinets, tables, and chairs.
• Computer system installation.
• Production of a movie by a major film studio.
• Legal services provided by attorneys.
• Catered meals.
• Business consulting projects.
• Financial statement audits.
• Medical procedures.

As you can see, job costing is used across a variety of settings. The common features are that the jobs are unique and made to order.

Categorizing Job Costs

Whatever the product being produced or service being offered, job costs follow a very similar cost flow. The three major components of a product or service cost are:

1. Direct materials,
2. Direct labor, and
3. Manufacturing overhead.

The first two factors, direct materials and direct labor, are fairly intuitive and easy to understand. In a manufacturing setting, they constitute the use of materials and human efforts to create a product. In a service setting, they are the supplies used along with human efforts to deliver a service. The third factor of production is **manufacturing overhead (MOH)**, which is the cost of indirect materials, indirect labor, and all other indirect production costs. The concept of manufacturing overhead can be a bit difficult to grasp, so let's expand our discussion of what goes into manufacturing overhead by discussing direct and indirect costs.

Recall the **Heartwood Cabinets** company from prior chapters. To think about job costs, let's consider how Heartwood produces a standard kitchen cabinet. **Direct materials** are the materials that are traced to a product or job and tracked by the accounting system. At Heartwood, direct materials include various types of wood as well as hardware, such as hinges and knobs. In contrast, **indirect materials** are those materials that are not traced to a product or job. Examples of indirect materials used to make cabinets are the glue and screws used to attach various pieces and the polyurethane used to protect the finished product. Although we know glue is used in production, it is impractical to determine the exact amount of glue used in each cabinet. Because Heartwood does not trace actual amounts of glue to individual cabinets, glue is categorized as an indirect material, and the cost of glue is assigned to the manufacturing overhead account.

Direct labor is all production labor that is traced to a specific product or job. It refers to the human efforts—hands-on, touch labor—that are directly involved with the work of making the product or job. The time a carpenter spends on a cabinet is considered direct labor. In contrast, **indirect labor** represents the effort of the workers who are involved with the production process of a product or job but who don't provide touch labor. For example, any Heartwood supervisor who oversees carpenters while they make cabinets, but who does not perform any of the actual production work, is providing indirect labor.

The supervisor is also likely overseeing the production process of multiple products or jobs, which may make it difficult to trace indirect labor to individual cabinets. For this reason, Heartwood assigns indirect labor costs to the manufacturing overhead account.

What determines whether production costs are direct or indirect? Management makes this distinction through a cost-benefit analysis. If management traces a cost to individual jobs, either because it is easy to do so or because it is deemed necessary, then it is a direct cost. For example, if Heartwood decides to trace the number of screws used to make specific cabinets, then screws will be categorized as a direct cost rather than an indirect cost. In contrast, if management determines that the cost of tracing a particular cost outweighs the benefit, then that cost is categorized as an indirect production cost. The sophistication of a company's cost accounting system may make it easier to trace costs and thus may influence management's cost classifications.

In sum: Manufacturing overhead includes indirect materials, indirect labor, and all other indirect production costs. Examples of these other indirect costs at Heartwood are the rent on manufacturing buildings, depreciation and maintenance on production equipment, and factory utilities. Manufacturing overhead can be considered a catch-all account for all production costs other than direct materials and direct labor.

FROM THE FIELD

Determining the Cost of Knee Surgery

Manufacturing overhead can be extremely difficult to calculate. Consider a hospital operating room. Nurses and technicians are often considered indirect labor. In addition, many types of hospital personnel work to facilitate and prepare for operations. Other overhead costs of an operating room include the depreciation on dozens of different machines as well as the operating facility.

After pushback on the rising price of surgeries, **Gundersen Health Systems** spent 18 months reviewing the cost of knee surgeries. It required experts to track every minute of time spent by medical staff and detailed the use of equipment and facilities. The experts found that the list price of a knee surgery was five times higher than the cost of the surgery—far more than anyone suspected. From a practical perspective, it is likely that knee surgeries were bearing the costs of other types of surgeries and procedures. Overall, the lack of detailed cost information within the health care industry distorts the true cost of procedures and is one reason for the unsustainable rise in medical costs over the past several years.

Thinking Critically

The health care industry is known for high rates of technological advancement. Why do you think hospitals have been slow to adopt technologies that can better track costs?

Remember from Chapter 2 that not all indirect costs at Heartwood or any other company are *product costs* (that is, costs that are incurred to provide goods and services to customers and that are included in inventory as manufacturing overhead). Some indirect costs, such as advertising costs and executive salaries, are considered *period costs* because they are immediately expensed. Period costs are not included in the cost of inventory. Only costs that are used to produce goods or services are product costs. A good rule of thumb is that if the cost occurs in the factory, it is generally a product cost. Consider electricity and other utilities. Heartwood categorizes utilities used in its factory as manufacturing overhead, which is a product cost. Utilities in the office building used by the accounting and human resource departments are period costs.

Now that we have a better understanding of manufacturing costs, let's consider how companies account for manufacturing costs within an organization.

CAREER SKILLS

Learning about direct materials and direct labor supports these career skills:

- Understanding how direct costs affect product costs

- Understanding how and why different products are targeted to different markets

LO 4.3

Explain the flow of job costs through the accounting system.

TRACKING JOB COSTS

As you learned in Chapter 2, companies can get data from several reliable sources. The information used to track production costs comes from a company's financial reporting, manufacturing, and human resource management systems. As an example, let's consider the production processes of Ever Ring, a fictitious company that makes tungsten wedding bands. Ever Ring maintains a stockpile of raw tungsten and nickel used to make rings. These minerals are the company's direct materials or raw materials inventory. Ever Ring begins to manufacture a batch of rings based on budgeted customer demand. Producing rings requires direct materials (tungsten and nickel) and direct labor. For each batch of rings, there is also a portion of manufacturing overhead costs, which consist of indirect materials, indirect labor, factory utilities, and equipment depreciation.

work-in-process

A temporary account to record the cost of jobs as they are being completed.

The costs of these three factors of production (direct materials, direct labor, and manufacturing overhead) are accumulated by job in a **Work-in-Process** inventory account, which is a temporary account to record the cost of jobs as they are being completed. When the batch of rings is completed, the total cost of that job is transferred from work-in-process inventory to finished goods inventory. When sold, the costs of production are then transferred to the Cost of Goods Sold or Cost of Sales accounts. Exhibit 4.1 summarizes the process.

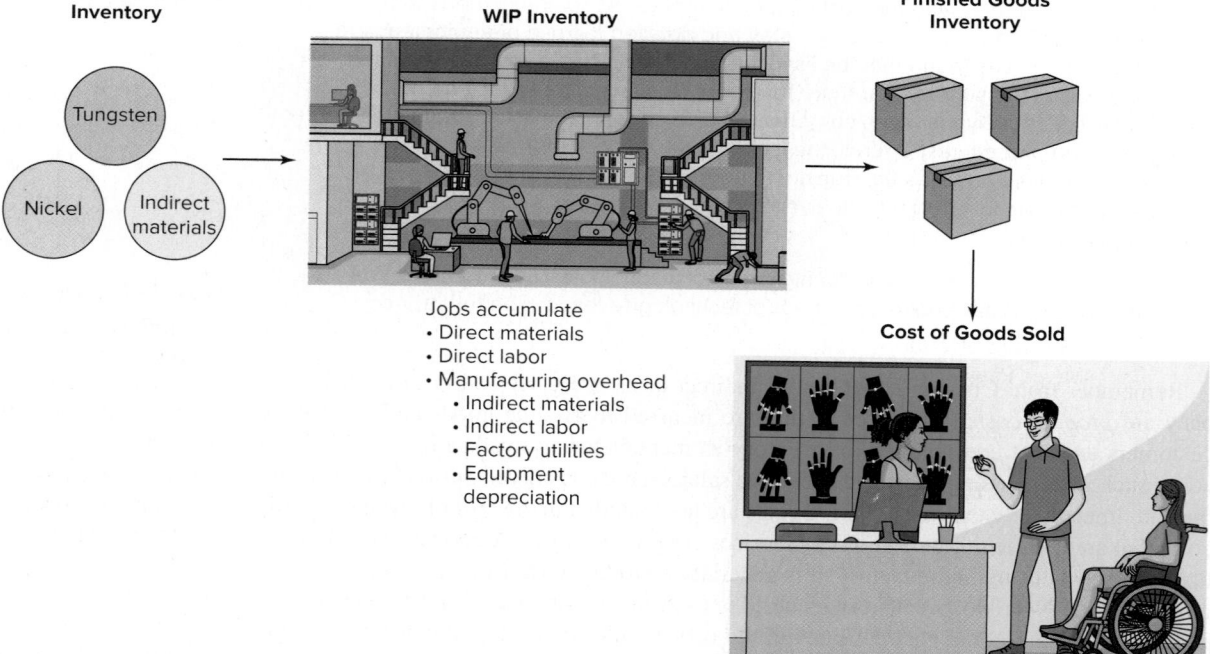

Exhibit 4.1
Production Flow for Ever Ring

Now that we have visualized Ever Ring's production process, we can better understand how the company accounts for production costs within its accounting system. After all, accounting systems are designed to reflect the realities of a company's processes. Exhibit 4.2 represents the tracking of costs through Ever Ring's production process.

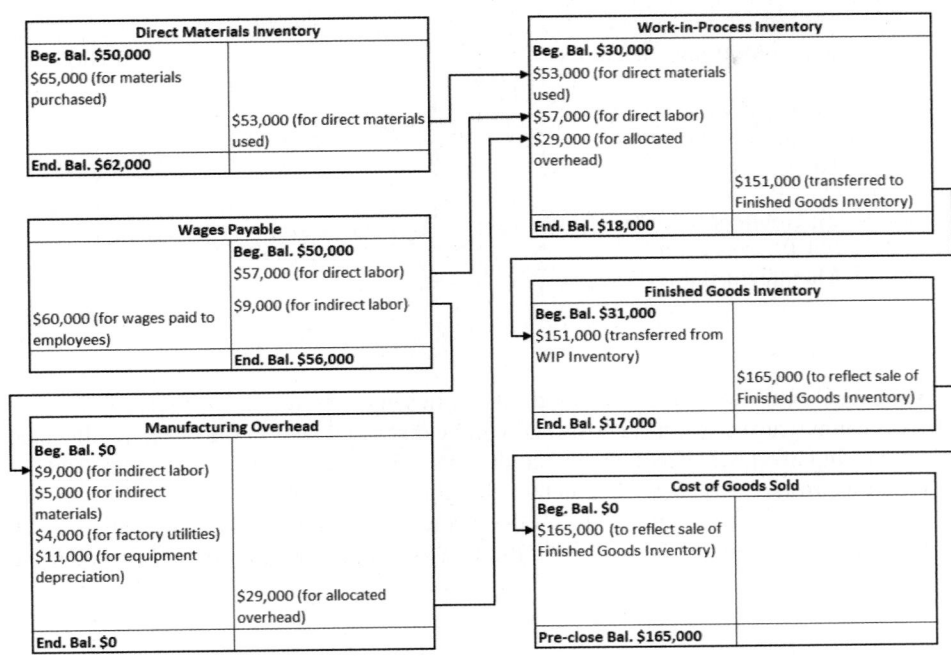

Exhibit 4.2
Tracking Costs through Ever Ring's Job-Costing System

As you can see, indirect labor costs and indirect materials are accumulated in the Manufacturing Overhead account, along with factory utilities and equipment depreciation. Note that all of the debits to the manufacturing overhead account represent **actual manufacturing overhead**, or the *actual* amounts spent on items categorized as manufacturing overhead. To record these transactions, Ever Ring will use the following journal entries:

actual manufacturing overhead
The actual costs of indirect materials, indirect labor, and all other indirect production costs.

To incur indirect (supervisor) labor:

Manufacturing Overhead	9,000	
Wages Payable		9,000

To record the purchase of indirect materials:

Manufacturing Overhead	5,000	
Accounts Payable		5,000

To account for factory utilities:

Manufacturing Overhead	4,000	
Utilities Payable		4,000

To record depreciation on factory equipment:

Manufacturing Overhead	11,000	
Accumulated Depreciation		11,000

Direct material, direct labor, and *applied* manufacturing overhead costs flow to the work-in-process account via the following entries:

To record the use of direct materials:

Work-in-Process Inventory	53,000	
Direct Materials Inventory		53,000

To record the use of direct labor:

Work-in-Process Inventory	57,000	
Direct Labor		57,000

To record the application of overhead:

Work-in-Process Inventory	29,000	
Manufacturing Overhead		29,000

allocated manufacturing overhead
The amount of overhead assigned to each job based on a predetermined overhead rate and the actual amount of overhead application base incurred.

Allocated manufacturing overhead, or applied manufacturing overhead, is an estimate of manufacturing overhead costs and will be discussed later in the chapter. Allocated manufacturing overhead is recorded by crediting the Manufacturing Overhead account.

When a product or job is completed, the cost of that job flows out of the Work-in-Process account to a Finished Goods Inventory account. When the job is sold, those costs are included in Cost of Goods Sold. These transactions are recorded as follows:

To record the completion of Work-in-Process Inventory:

Finished Goods Inventory	151,000	
Work-in-Process Inventory		151,000

To record the sale of Finished Goods Inventory:

Cost of Goods Sold	165,000	
Finished Goods Inventory		165,000

Management ensures that Ever Ring's accounting system carefully tracks this information because this information is necessary for creating financial statements. All costs that flow through the production system are used to create Ever Ring's Cost of Goods Manufactured Schedule (Exhibit 4.3), which eventually feeds into the Cost of Goods Sold on Ever Ring's income statement.

Large companies may be tracking hundreds or even thousands of jobs each day. A good accounting system is critical for a company to track and understand its costs. To keep track of these costs, companies use a job-cost sheet, which is stored electronically within a company's cost accounting system and feeds into the cost accounting system. A **job-cost sheet** details when a job was started and completed, basic information about the job, and all production costs associated with the job. Production-cost data come from purchase requisition and employee time tickets, which are also stored within the cost accounting system. Exhibit 4.4 provides an example of a job-cost sheet for Ever Ring.

job-cost sheet
Details when a job was started and completed, basic information about the job, and all production costs associated with the job.

Exhibit 4.3
Cost of Goods
Manufactured
Schedule

Cost of Goods Manufactured Schedule

Direct materials		
Beginning direct materials Inventory	$ 50,000	
Add: direct materials purchases	$ 65,000	
Total direct materials to account for	$115,000	
Less: Ending Direct Materials Inventory	$ (62,000)	
Direct materials used in production		$ 53,000
Direct labor		$ 57,000
Manufacturing overhead		
Indirect labor	$ 9,000	
Indirect materials	$ 5,000	
Factory utilities	$ 4,000	
Equipment depreciation	$ 11,000	
Total manufacturing overhead costs		$ 29,000
Total manufacturing costs for the period		$139,000
Add: Beginning Work-in-Process Inventory		$ 35,000
Total manufacturing costs to account for		$174,000
Less: Ending Work-in-Process Inventory		$ (23,000)
Cost of Goods Manufactured		$151,000
Add: Beginning Finished Goods Inventory		$ 31,000
Total Finished Goods Inventory to account for		$182,000
Less: Ending Finished Goods Inventory		$ (17,000)
Cost of Goods Sold		$165,000

Job Costing within a Service Company

Job costing in a service company differs in several ways from job costing in a manufacturing company. For example, service companies do not have a Finished Goods Inventory account because, unlike products, services cannot be stockpiled. Service companies also use different account names than manufacturing companies. For instance, service companies may use a Supplies account rather than Raw Materials or Direct Materials because they use little if any raw materials inventory. In addition, Service Contracts in Process may be used instead of Work-in-Process Inventory, and Cost of Completed Contracts may replace Cost of Goods Sold. Despite these differences, job costing within a service company follows the same steps as job costing within a manufacturing company to track the costs of individual jobs.

✓ **PROGRESS CHECK**

  6. Describe how inventory costs flow through a company's accounting system, from the purchase of raw materials to the sale of finished goods.

  7. Explain the purpose of a job-cost sheet.

Exhibit 4.4
Sample Job-Cost Sheet for Ever Ring

Microsoft Excel

Job Cost Sheet

Job Number	442
Description	Tungsten Rings Model 104
Date Started	5-Jan
Date completed	18-Jan
Number of units	60

Direct materials

Date	Requisition #	Quantity	Unit Price	Cost
6-Jan	10235	25	$ 10.00	$250.00
11-Jan	10239	28	$ 12.00	$336.00
				$586.00

Direct labor

Date	Time Card #	Hours	Hourly Rate	Cost
6-Jan	144	6	$ 23.00	$138.00
12-Jan	159	8	$ 38.00	$304.00
				$442.00

Manufacturing overhead

Date	Allocation base	Quantity	Application rate	Cost
6-Jan	Direct labor hours	6	$ 20.00	$120.00
12-Jan	Direct labor hours	8	$ 20.00	$160.00
				$280.00

Cost Summary

Cost item	Amount
Direct materials	$ 586.00
Direct labor	$ 442.00
Manufacturing overhead	$ 280.00
Total cost	$ 1,308.00
Unit cost	$ 21.80

LO 4.4

Determine manufacturing overhead application rates.

actual costing
The process of calculating costs by summing actual direct materials, actual direct labor, and actual manufacturing overhead.

normal costing
The process of calculating costs by summing actual direct materials, actual direct labor, and estimated manufacturing overhead.

MANUFACTURING OVERHEAD: APPLICATION AND ANALYSIS

As noted previously, job costs are determined using *allocated manufacturing overhead* (also known as *applied manufacturing overhead*). But why? Why not use *actual* manufacturing overhead costs?

In theory, companies could use actual manufacturing overhead costs, a process known as **actual costing**. Under actual costing, costs are calculated by summing actual direct materials, actual direct labor, and actual manufacturing overhead. However, actual costing is seldom used. Unlike direct materials and direct labor, for which the costs for each job are known at the time of production, indirect costs are difficult to trace to individual jobs at the time of production and may not even be known until after the end of a reporting period. For example, a firm may be unable to trace electricity usage to individual jobs. Furthermore, the cost of the electricity will not be known until the company receives a bill from the power company. Can a company wait until it knows all costs with certainty before it bills customers? Usually, it cannot. As a result, firms commonly use an *estimate* of manufacturing overhead, along with actual direct materials and direct labor, to determine the cost of jobs. In fact, this practice is so common that it is known as **normal costing**.

In a normal costing system, companies apply overhead to jobs using a **predetermined overhead rate**. This rate is based on two estimates:

1. The first estimate is the total manufacturing overhead costs for a reporting period. This is the numerator of the predetermined overhead rate.
2. The second estimate is the **allocation base** (also called the **application base**). This is the denominator of the predetermined overhead rate.

The predetermined overhead rate is therefore calculated as:

$$\text{Predetermined overhead rate} = \frac{\text{Estimated total overhead costs}}{\text{Estimated allocation base}}$$

Organizations can choose from a variety of allocation bases, and companies commonly use either direct labor hours, direct labor costs, or machine hours as an allocation base. Ideally, a company's allocation base should be associated with the company's overhead costs. An allocation base that is associated with production costs is known as a **cost driver**.

Consider a company with significant overhead costs tied to labor costs (for example, significant supervisor costs). Although company management could select any allocation base to apply manufacturing overhead, the use of a cost driver as an allocation base will result in more accurate cost information. In this case, direct labor hours is probably the most appropriate application base because an increase in direct labor hours inherently leads to additional supervisor (that is, indirect labor) costs. Similarly, companies with significant machine-related costs (for example, maintenance and depreciation) often choose machine hours as their application base. Service companies with significant transportation costs may use miles driven as an application base.

Let's consider Ever Ring again. As part of its annual budgeting process for the subsequent year, Ever Ring estimates $1,500,000 in total manufacturing overhead. Ever Ring's managers have decided to allocate overhead on the basis of direct labor hours, and they estimate that in the subsequent year, factory employees will work a total of 75,000 direct labor hours.

$$\begin{aligned}\text{Predetermined overhead rate} &= \frac{\text{Estimated total overhead costs}}{\text{Estimated allocation base}}\\[6pt] &= \frac{\$1,500,000}{75,000 \text{ direct labor hours}}\\[6pt] &= \$20.00 \text{ per direct labor hour}\end{aligned}$$

Using these two estimates, a predetermined overhead rate is created. Ever Ring will allocate $20 of manufacturing overhead for each direct labor hour used. Notice in the job-cost sheet in Exhibit 4.4 that Job Number 442 used 14 direct labor hours. As a result, $280 in manufacturing overhead (14 direct labor hours * $20 overhead/hour) was applied to the job.

Department Overhead Rates

Many companies have multiple manufacturing departments and choose to allocate overhead from each department individually. That is, every manufacturing department has a predetermined overhead rate. In this case, each department selects an allocation base that is most appropriate for that department. Each department may use the same allocation base, such as direct labor hours. Alternatively, companies may choose different allocation bases for each department, such as machine hours for a department that relies heavily on automation and direct labor hours for a department that relies more on direct labor.

predetermined overhead rate
The rate used to allocate estimated overhead costs to specific jobs or activities.

allocation base or application base
The basis on which costs are assigned to cost objects. Allocation bases include direct labor hours, direct labor costs, and machine hours. Ideally, allocation bases should be cost drivers.

cost driver
A variable that has a causal relationship with costs, such that more or less of the cost driver will result in more or less cost.

ETHICS

Let's assume that Ever Ring has two departments: molding and polishing. Expected manufacturing overhead in the molding department is $800,000, and management has decided to allocate overhead for the molding department using an application base of 50,000 direct labor hours. In addition, management has decided to allocate $700,000 in expected polishing manufacturing overhead using an application base of 25,000 direct labor hours. Let's calculate predetermined overhead rates for each department.

$$\text{Predetermined overhead rate} = \frac{\text{Estimated total overhead costs}}{\text{Estimated allocation base}}$$

Molding predetermined overhead rate:

$$\frac{\$800,000}{50,000 \text{ direct labor hours}} = \$16.00 \text{ per direct labor hour}$$

Polishing predetermined overhead rate:

$$\frac{\$700,000}{25,000 \text{ direct labor hours}} = \$28.00 \text{ per direct labor hour}$$

Now let's assume that Job Number 442 requires 8 direct labor hours in the molding department and 6 direct labor hours in the polishing department. How much manufacturing overhead will be applied to this job?

(8 molding hours × $16.00/hour) + (6 polishing hours × $28.00/hour) = $296.00

This change in how Ever Ring allocates manufacturing overhead has no effect on companywide profitability. After all, the company still has a total of $1,500,000 in applied overhead expenses. However, it does affect the profitability of individual jobs. In this case, this new allocation method shifts overhead expenses from other jobs to Job Number 442, making it less profitable. The profitability of individual jobs can influence the pay and promotion of employees, and companies should carefully consider how their choice of allocation affects employees. If overhead is applied on an arbitrary basis, employees may perceive the results to be unfair. The use of cost drivers as application bases helps to mitigate this concern because when cost drivers are used, overhead costs are more likely to be allocated to the products and services that consume overhead resources.

When working with applied overhead, it is important to remember that predetermined rates are based on two estimates (estimated overhead costs and estimated allocation base). These estimates are determined using historical information and forecasts, but they are estimates nonetheless. As a result, companies can be nearly certain that their estimates are incorrect. Why, then, go to all the trouble of estimating overhead when it is bound to be incorrect? Company strategy depends on cost information, and overhead can constitute a significant portion of a product's cost. A company cannot wait until the end of the year to gather perfect indirect cost information. Instead, management accountants seek to provide good estimates that approximate actual overhead costs. Fortunately, it is relatively simple to correct errors in overhead at the end of the year, as we discuss in the next section.

CORRECTING FOR UNDERAPPLIED OR OVERAPPLIED MANUFACTURING OVERHEAD

At the end of each accounting period, companies must reconcile the Manufacturing Overhead account. To do so, they review overhead transactions and ensure that all manufacturing overhead is appropriately applied to inventory.

Let's examine Ever Ring's Manufacturing Overhead account, as shown in Exhibit 4.5. The debit side of the Manufacturing Overhead account tracks Ever Ring's *actual* incurred overhead costs. Every time Ever Ring incurs an expense that is classified as manufacturing overhead, the actual expense is recorded as a debit in the Manufacturing Overhead account. These actual costs come from indirect materials, indirect labor, and other indirect costs such as rent, utilities, and equipment depreciation.

The credit side of the account tracks overhead costs that Ever Ring *applies* to work-in-process inventory. Note that applied overhead is estimated, not actual. Ever Ring credits the Manufacturing Overhead account when overhead is applied to individual jobs, which, for Ever Ring, corresponds to a predetermined rate applied with each direct labor hour. Applied overhead costs are eventually included in Cost of Goods Sold after inventory is completed and sold to customers. In this case, actual overhead is equal to applied overhead, so no adjustment needs to be made to Manufacturing Overhead.

Manufacturing Overhead	
Beg. Bal. $0	
$9,000 (for indirect labor)	
$5,000 (for indirect materials)	
$4,000 (for factory utilities)	
$11,000 (for equipment depreciation)	
	$29,000 (for applied overhead)
End. Bal. $0	

Exhibit 4.5
Ever Ring's Manufacturing Overhead Account

In practice, because allocation is based on estimates, the Manufacturing Overhead account rarely has a zero balance. To reconcile the Manufacturing Overhead account, companies must determine whether overhead is underapplied or overapplied. Manufacturing overhead is *underapplied* when there is a debit balance in the account, or when insufficient overhead is applied to inventory. Overhead is *overapplied* when there is a credit balance in the account, or when a company has applied more overhead to inventory than is accurate. In either case, companies can make an adjustment to reconcile the account and ensure that inventory is properly costed.

To illustrate this concept, let's look at another example of Ever Ring's year-end manufacturing overhead account, as shown in Exhibit 4.6. In this example, we assume that actual utilities are lower than anticipated (all other entries remain the same).

Exhibit 4.6
Overapplied
Manufacturing
Overhead at Ever
Ring

Manufacturing Overhead	
Beg. Bal. $0	
$9,000 (for indirect labor)	
$5,000 (for indirect materials)	
$3,000 (for factory utilities)	
$11,000 (for equipment depreciation)	
	$29,000 (for applied overhead)
	End. Bal. $1,000

Ever Ring has a $1,000 credit in the Manufacturing Overhead account at the end of the year (meaning that Ever Ring has applied more overhead than the company incurred). How will this affect a company's financial statements if left uncorrected? An overapplication of manufacturing overhead means that work-in-process inventory is overvalued. As Ever Ring completes goods, the overapplication of overhead will also result in overvalued finished goods inventory. When Ever Ring sells this inventory, cost of goods sold will be inflated and net income will be understated.

Companies generally use one of two common approaches to dispose of overapplied overhead.

Option 1: Adjust Cost of Goods Sold

The first option is simply to adjust the Cost of Goods Sold account as follows.

Manufacturing Overhead	1,000	
COGS		1,000

This entry has the effect of zeroing out the $1,000 credit in the Manufacturing Overhead account and decreasing Cost of Goods Sold (expenses are typically recorded as debits and are thus decreased by credits). This adjustment will also flow through to the income statement and increase net income by $1,000 (see t-accounts below).

Manufacturing Overhead		Cost of Goods Sold	
Beg. Bal. $0		**Beg. Bal. $0**	
DR $9,000 (for indirect labor)		DR $165,000 (To reflect sale of inventory)	
DR $5,000 (for indirect materials)			CR $1,000 (adjusting entry)
DR $3,000 (for factory utilities)			
DR $11,000 (for equipment Depreciation)			
	CR $29,000 (for applied overhead)		
DR $1,000 (adjusting entry)			
End. Bal. $0		**Pre-close Bal. $164,000**	

This approach to correcting a misapplication of manufacturing overhead assumes that all inventory has been completed and sold. In reality, some of the overstated inventory is still in the production process (work-in-process inventory), some is completed but unsold (finished goods inventory), and the remainder has been completed and sold (cost of goods sold). Companies use this first approach to disposing of overapplied overhead when managers deem the amount of work-in-process and finished goods inventory to be immaterial. In this case, management knows that the adjusting entry will result in slight inaccuracies in the financial statements that won't affect decision making, which is likely the case for a $1,000 adjusting entry.

Option 2: Adjust Inventory Accounts Proportionally

The second option is to adjust the inventory accounts proportionally. This second option requires Ever Ring to analyze the ending balances of the Work-in-Process Inventory, Finished Goods Inventory, and Cost of Goods Sold accounts and prorate the adjusting entry.

Ever Ring's account balances at year-end show $18,000 in Work-in-Process Inventory, $17,000 in Finished Goods Inventory, and $165,000 in Cost of Goods Sold. In using Option 2, Ever Ring will add up the total cost in the three inventory accounts and get a total of $200,000 (= $18,000 + $17,000 + $165,000). It can then determine the proportion of the total represented in each account by dividing its balance by the $200,000 total, as follows:

Work-in-Process Inventory	$18,000/$200,000 = 9%
Finished Goods Inventory	$17,000/$200,000 = 8.5%
Cost of Goods Sold	$165,000/$200,000 = 82.5%

The $1,000 adjusting entry is then divided among these three accounts using these calculated proportions as follows:

Manufacturing Overhead	1,000	
Work-in-Process Inventory		90 ($1,000 * 9%)
Finished Goods Inventory		85 ($1,000 * 8.5%)
Cost of Goods Sold		825 ($1,000 * 82.5%)

This second approach to disposing of overapplied overhead is used when company management deems that a significant amount of inventory overstatement has not yet been completed or sold. In this case, a simpler adjustment involving only cost of goods sold may mislead users of the financial statements.

Manufacturing Overhead	
Beg. Bal. $0	
$9,000 (for indirect labor)	
$5,000 (for indirect materials)	
$3,000 (for factory utilities)	
$11,000 (for equipment depreciation)	
	$29,000 (for allocated overhead)
$1,000 (adjusting entry)	
End. Bal. $0	

Work-in-Process Inventory	
Beg. Bal. $30,000	
$53,000 (for direct materials used)	
$57,000 (for direct labor)	
$29,000 (for allocated overhead)	
	$151,000 (transferred to Finished Goods Inventory)
	$90 (adjusting entry)
End. Bal. $17,910	

Finished Goods Inventory	
Beg. Bal. $31,000	
$151,000 (transferred from WIP Inventory)	
	$165,000 (to reflect sale of Finished Goods Inventory)
	$85 (adjusting entry)
End. Bal. $16,915	

Cost of Goods Sold	
Beg. Bal. $0	
$165,000 (to reflect sale of Finished Goods Inventory)	
	$825 (adjusting entry)
Pre-close Bal. $164,175	

With either approach, the effect of the overapplied overhead is attenuated. The adjustment decreases the expense recognized on the income statement and increases reported income.

What would happen if Ever Ring underapplied manufacturing overhead? For this example, we will assume that factory utilities are $6,000 rather than the $4,000 we previously recorded in Exhibit 4.2. In this case, the debits and credits will be reversed. Let's examine what the adjusting entries will look like in the case of a $2,000 underapplication of overhead (Exhibit 4.7).

Exhibit 4.7
Underapplied
Manufacturing
Overhead at
Ever Ring

Manufacturing Overhead	
Beg. Bal. $0	
$9,000 (for indirect labor)	
$5,000 (for indirect materials)	
$6,000 (for factory utilities)	
$11,000 (for equipment depreciation)	
	$29,000 (for allocated overhead)
End. Bal. $2,000	

Option 1: Close manufacturing overhead to COGS.

Cost of Goods Sold	2,000	
Manufacturing Overhead		2,000

Option 2: Prorate adjusting entry.

Work-in-Process Inventory	180 (2,000 * 9%)	
Finished Goods Inventory	170 (2,000 * 8.5%)	
Cost of Goods Sold	1,650 (2,000 * 82.5%)	
Manufacturing Overhead		2,000

Human Dimensions: Predetermined Overhead Rates

The adjusting entries discussed above ensure that the financial statements are fairly presented. However, by the time these adjusting entries take place, companies typically have actual overhead cost information, and they could theoretically adjust the costs of all goods and services provided during the year by substituting the actual overhead rate for the predetermined overhead rate. Some companies do just that to analyze how individual products, services, and even customers provide value to the company. However, companies seldom use this method to reconcile manufacturing overhead, opting instead for one of the two methods described above. Why?

One reason is that using a predetermined overhead rate provides a *fixed standard* of cost. Managers and other employees are often evaluated based on the profitability of their divisions. If companies change cost information at the end of the year, they may create a "moving goal post" for managers, which may be viewed as unfair and significantly impact employee morale. This is a good example of how management accountants must weigh the costs and benefits of various accounting methods, as well as how those methods will affect employee behavior.

 PROGRESS CHECK

8. Why is applied overhead used to determine job costs instead of actual overhead?

9. How can overapplied or underapplied overhead be reconciled at the end of a reporting period?

DETERMINING A JOB'S COST

We've discussed the various costs that go into a product or service. Now let's pull everything together to determine a specific product's cost. Consider the following specific information related to the production of a custom kitchen island at **Heartwood Cabinets**.

LO 4.6
Compute the costs of a job.

Cost of raw materials	$350
Direct labor cost per hour	$20/hour
Hours used in production	15 hours
Predetermined overhead rate	$10 per direct labor hour

Note that the predetermined overhead rate is the rate used by the company on all jobs and that it uses direct labor hours as the application base. The predetermined overhead rate is based on the estimated total overhead for the company within the reporting period and the estimated total direct labor hours.

As Exhibit 4.8 shows, to determine the product cost for the island, we add up the three product cost categories. First, the materials cost is $350. Second, the direct labor cost is the $20 per hour rate multiplied by the 15 actual hours incurred, for a total of $300 in direct labor cost. Third, the predetermined overhead rate of $10 per direct labor hour (DLH) is multiplied by the 15 actual hours incurred, for a total of $150. We now add up the three costs, $350 + $300 + $150, and get a total product cost of $800.

Exhibit 4.8
Determining the Cost of a Job (Custom Kitchen Island) at Heartwood Cabinets

Cost of island:	
Direct materials	$350
Direct labor	300 (15 hours * $20/hour)
Applied manufacturing overhead	150 (15 hours * $10/DLH application rate)
Total cost of island	$800

This same process will be repeated for other jobs completed by Heartwood. The raw materials cost and direct labor cost will change with each product. The total applied overhead cost will also change based on the direct labor hours actually incurred, but the same predetermined overhead rate will be used. The firm will then be able to determine its product costs as it completes orders. At the end of the period, the manufacturing overhead account will be reconciled by comparing the amount of overhead applied to the amount of overhead actually incurred.

Why is it so important to understand and track product costs? In the United States alone, tens of thousands of companies declare bankruptcy every year. Many of these companies are founded on good ideas and sell desirable goods and services, but they are managed by people who do not understand their company's costs.

Consider some of the decisions a company makes that are influenced by product cost data:

- What products should we sell?
- Can we compete in a new market?
- Should we outsource production to another country where labor is less costly?
- Should we relocate a factory to be closer to raw materials?
- What type of sales discounts and promotions can we offer to customers?
- Should we hire more workers or ask our current workers to work overtime?

ENVIRONMENTAL, SOCIAL, GOVERNANCE

FROM THE FIELD

How Will ESG Initiatives Affect Product Costs?

In recent years, many companies, including **General Motors**, are increasing their environmental efforts by asking global suppliers to commit to carbon neutrality, social responsibility programs, and sustainable procurement practices.[2]

How will these initiatives affect product costs? Will direct materials increase because sustainable inputs are more expensive? Who will provide oversight to determine whether suppliers are following through on their promises? Will oversight increase overhead costs, and who will bear the costs of these initiatives—suppliers, producers, or customers? These types of initiatives will need to be analyzed and supported by management accountants.

Thinking Critically

How might companies' increased emphasis on ESG initiatives positively and negatively affect profits?

It's easy to imagine how poor-quality cost information can lead to poor decision making. By leveraging basic cost accounting knowledge and expertise in data analytics, management accountants are in the ideal position to provide insight to companies and help them succeed.

Let's now work through the following Mini-Lab to see how we calculate cost information for unique jobs, and how we can use data to improve company decision making.

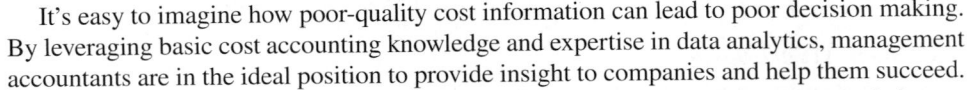

DATA ANALYTICS MINI-LAB
Using Data to Estimate Job Costs

Data Analytics Type: Descriptive Analytics

Lab Note: The tools presented in this lab periodically change. Updated instructions, if applicable, can be found in the student and instructor support materials.

Keywords

Excel, Job Costing, Regression Analysis

Decision-Making Context

In a job-costing system, we calculate the cost of a job by summing up all direct costs (for example, direct materials and direct labor), along with the estimated overhead, associated with each job.

Consider Spruce Mountain Advisors (SMA), a fictitious small firm that provides financial advice and estate planning services. SMA has two partners and two part-time staff. The partners perform all financial services for SMA clients and are paid $125 per hour. Their time is considered direct labor, and each hour is billed to a particular job. SMA has no direct materials. It does, however, have significant overhead costs. The part-time staff members take care of all administrative functions and assist the partners with various tasks. The part-timers' time is not traced to particular jobs. Rather, it is considered overhead. Office supplies and office rent are also included in overhead costs.

Historically, SMA has applied $35 per partner in overhead to each job. SMA's presence in the market has grown in the past few years, and so have its billable hours. SMA estimates an average of 450 billable hours per month in the foreseeable future.

Ask the Question

A local business, Winsome Gardens, has asked for a quote for financial services. SMA estimates that the job will require 100 billable hours. Before providing a quote, SMA must estimate the total cost of the job.

SMA has always applied $35 in overhead per partner hour to each job. Now, the company has decided to use the last two years' cost data to assess the relationship between partner hours and overhead costs.

Required

1. Determine an overhead application rate using regression analysis.
2. Assess the reasonableness of the traditional $35/partner overhead application rate.
3. Estimate the cost to provide financial services to Winsome Gardens.

Master the Data

Exhibit A displays overhead cost data compiled for the previous 24 months, along with the monthly partner hours. These data can found in the file titled **Mini-Lab 4 Data.xlsx**

Notice that an average of 450 monthly billable hours represents a significant increase over previous months.

Exhibit A

Microsoft Excel

Month	Partner hours	Overhead costs	Month	Partner hours	Overhead costs
Jan 'X1	330	10606	Jan 'X2	330	11074
Feb 'X1	423	13117	Feb 'X2	327	11515
Mar 'X1	338	10787	Mar 'X2	316	10681
Apr 'X1	337	11535	Apr 'X2	424	11857
May 'X1	341	11735	May 'X2	327	10690
Jun 'X1	405	13592	Jun 'X2	344	10416
Jul 'X1	341	11346	Jul 'X2	310	9273
Aug 'X1	304	10380	Aug 'X2	374	11071
Sep 'X1	304	10734	Sep 'X2	422	13513
Oct 'X1	320	10013	Oct 'X2	388	13267
Nov 'X1	321	9471	Nov 'X2	396	12109
Dec 'X1	398	12627	Dec 'X2	362	12047

Perform the Analysis

Regressing overhead costs on partner hours results in the statistical output displayed in Exhibit B.

Let's interpret the regression results. The model is highly significant, indicated by a high F-statistic of 52.23 and low Significance F (extremely close to zero). Our goodness-of-fit measure, R Square, is 0.70, indicating that 70% of the variation in overhead costs is explained by partner hours. The intercept indicates that $2,423 of overhead costs are fixed, and each partner hour increases overhead costs by $25.38.

SUMMARY OUTPUT					
Regression Statistics					
Multiple R	0.84				
R Square	0.70				
Adjusted R Square	0.69				
Standard Error	670.28				
Observations	24				
ANOVA					
	df	*SS*	*MS*	*F*	*Significance F*
Regression	1	23463712.76	23463712.76	52.23	3.05727E-07
Residual	22	9884027.24	449273.97		
Total	23	33347740			

	Coefficients	*Standard Error*	*t Stat*	*P-value*	*Lower 95%*	*Upper 95%*
Intercept	2423.01	1248.88	1.94	0.07	-167.00	5013.02
Partner hours	25.38	3.51	7.23	0.00	18.10	32.67

Exhibit B

Microsoft Excel

If we graph the relationship between partner hours and costs (as in Exhibit C), we can see how accurate our cost estimates are by comparing the traditional $35 per partner hour application rate and the cost function defined by our regression.

DATA VISUALIZATION

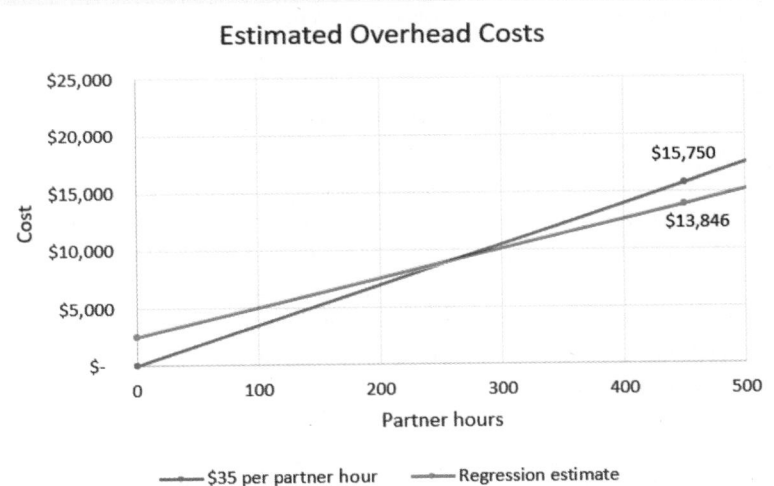

Estimated Overhead Costs

$15,750

$13,846

———— $35 per partner hour   ———— Regression estimate

Exhibit C

Microsoft Excel

Should SMA allocate $25.38 (per the regression) of overhead per partner hour or the traditional $35 per partner hour? Which overhead estimate is correct? The answer is that neither is "correct." Both are estimates, and the true cost is unknown. The application of $25.38 of overhead per partner hour is probably more accurate on an hourly basis, but it doesn't account for the fixed overhead costs that SMA must cover. The data suggest that SMA's historical estimate of $35 is reasonable, but we can see from the graph that as billable hours increase or decrease from approximately 250 hours, the difference between the estimates will diverge.

What is SMA's cost to provide 100 hours of service to Winsome Gardens? Each hour adds $125 in direct labor costs plus an overhead application. We can use Excel to quickly calculate the cost of the Winsome Gardens job using both overhead application estimates. The total cost is estimated as follows:

$$\text{Total cost estimate} = \text{Direct labor costs} + \text{Overhead costs}$$

$$\text{Total cost estimate} = (\text{Partner hours} * \text{Direct labor cost/hour})$$
$$+ (\text{Partner hours} * \text{Overhead allocation/hour})$$

Exhibit D shows the results of this calculation.

Exhibit D

Microsoft Excel

Winsome Garden Cost Estimate				
	Partner Hours	Direct Labor Cost per Hour	Overhead Allocation per Hour	Total Cost Estimate
$35 per partner hour	100	$ 125.00	$ 35.00	$ 16,000.00
Regression estimate	100	$ 125.00	$ 25.38	$ 15,038.00

Share the Story

Our regression analysis allows us to determine a variable overhead application rate of $25.38 per partner hour. However, that rate does not include fixed overhead, which should be charged in some form to the cost of a job. An analysis of the traditional $35.00 rate appears reasonable, as it reasonably approximates the cost function determined by the regression output at SMA's current level of billable hours.

Exhibit E presents the estimated costs of the Winsome Gardens job using both overhead application rates.

Exhibit E

Microsoft Excel

Winsome Gardens Cost Estimate			
	Direct Labor	Allocated Overhead	Total Cost Estimate
$35 per partner hour	$ 12,500	$ 3,500	$16,000.00
Regression estimate	$ 12,500	$ 2,538	$15,038.00

DATA VISUALIZATION

When reporting these results to management, you may want to consider adding a data visualization, such as Exhibit F, to clearly demonstrate the direct labor and overhead components of the cost estimate.

Exhibit F

Microsoft Excel

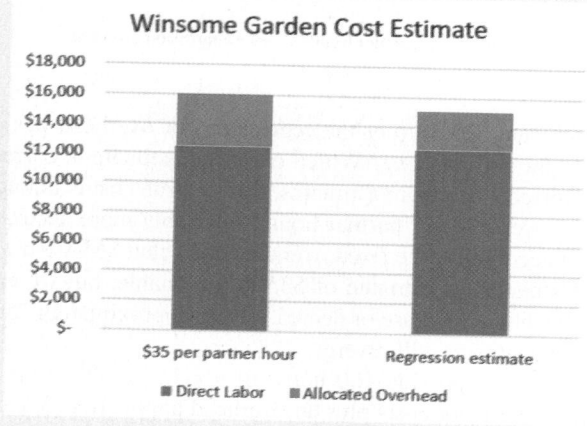

Mini-Lab Assessment

1. SMA has a request for service from Starlight Theater and is trying to estimate the cost of providing services that will require 350 partner hours. What is the total cost estimate under each of the two cost functions discussed in this Mini-Lab?
2. SMA is considering tracing the time of part-time staff to individual jobs. How will this change in process affect the mix of direct costs and overhead costs?
3. Notice in Exhibit F that overhead is a relatively small component of total production costs. As overhead costs increase, it becomes more important for companies to be thoughtful and strategic as they allocate these costs to individual jobs. What company factors may increase overhead costs as a proportion of total costs?

Management accountants must be proficient at dealing with ambiguity. Estimates are inherently ambiguous. When it comes to overhead, "true" costs are difficult to ascertain because total overhead costs are not traced to specific jobs, and a company's total overhead costs are not known with certainty at the time that it determines application rates.

Despite the natural inaccuracies of estimates, they are extremely useful. We estimated cost information for Spruce Mountain Advisors (SMA) in the Mini-Lab, but the price that SMA charges its customers depends on the market. Better knowledge of costs helps companies determine whether or not they can compete in the market, and which services provide greater profits.

How can companies improve their overhead estimates? There are several options. First, they can gather more data to develop better estimates. In addition, companies can trace more costs to individual jobs, which will reduce the need for estimates because fewer costs will be categorized as overhead costs. Rather, they will be direct costs charged to specific jobs. Management accountants should consider the time and energy necessary to improve estimates. In the Mini-Lab, we found that the simple $35 per partner hour application rate was reasonable. SMA might consider that rate "good enough" and spend its time generating more revenue rather than gathering more cost data.

(Q) LAB CONNECTIONS

Company strategy depends on cost information. Now that we have discussed how companies use job costing to calculate costs for individual jobs, you will put what you have learned into practice by working through **LAB 4.4 EXCEL** and **LAB 4.5 TABLEAU/POWER BI**. Notice that the process of calculating costs remains constant despite various industry differences and regardless of the software used to aggregate cost data.

(✓) PROGRESS CHECK

10. What three types of costs must be included when calculating the cost of a product or service?
11. Why must management accountants consider the cost and benefits of gathering data that can be used to improve cost information?

Careers with Job Costing Responsibilities

Management accountants use job costing to track the costs of distinct goods and services. This cost information is central to corporate strategy.

Exhibit 4.9 is adapted from a job posting from a job recruiting site like **Indeed.com** or **ZipRecruiter.com**. This posting might be applicable to a Senior Cost Accounting Manager at a staffing company such as **Robert Half, LHH, Insight Global**, or **Lucas Group/Korn Ferry**. Notice the emphasis placed on a candidate's ability to understand cost information, as highlighted in yellow. Perhaps just as important, management accountants must communicate this information effectively to others within the organization.

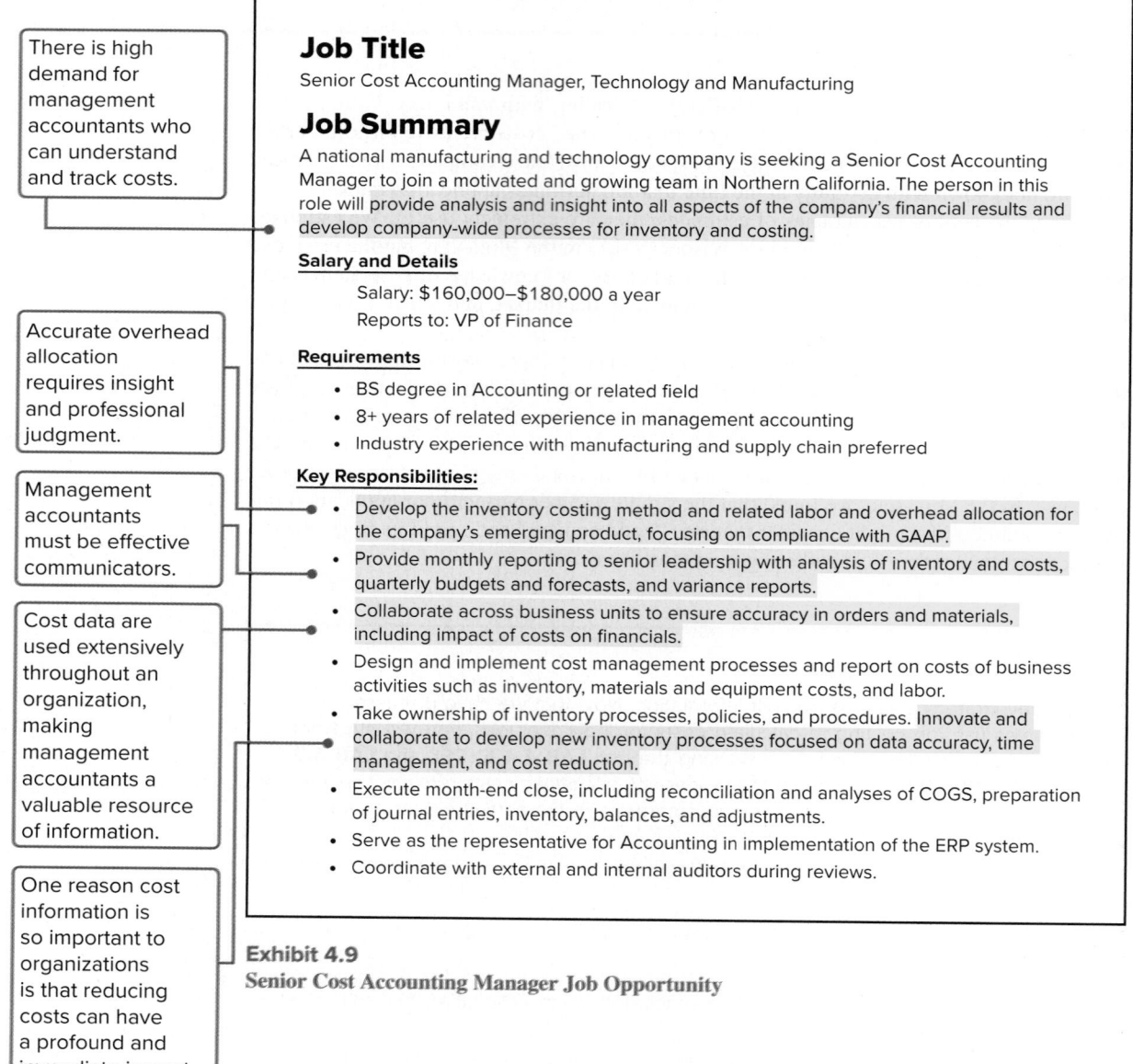

There is high demand for management accountants who can understand and track costs.

Accurate overhead allocation requires insight and professional judgment.

Management accountants must be effective communicators.

Cost data are used extensively throughout an organization, making management accountants a valuable resource of information.

One reason cost information is so important to organizations is that reducing costs can have a profound and immediate impact on profitability.

Job Title

Senior Cost Accounting Manager, Technology and Manufacturing

Job Summary

A national manufacturing and technology company is seeking a Senior Cost Accounting Manager to join a motivated and growing team in Northern California. The person in this role will provide analysis and insight into all aspects of the company's financial results and develop company-wide processes for inventory and costing.

Salary and Details

Salary: $160,000–$180,000 a year

Reports to: VP of Finance

Requirements

- BS degree in Accounting or related field
- 8+ years of related experience in management accounting
- Industry experience with manufacturing and supply chain preferred

Key Responsibilities:

- Develop the inventory costing method and related labor and overhead allocation for the company's emerging product, focusing on compliance with GAAP.
- Provide monthly reporting to senior leadership with analysis of inventory and costs, quarterly budgets and forecasts, and variance reports.
- Collaborate across business units to ensure accuracy in orders and materials, including impact of costs on financials.
- Design and implement cost management processes and report on costs of business activities such as inventory, materials and equipment costs, and labor.
- Take ownership of inventory processes, policies, and procedures. Innovate and collaborate to develop new inventory processes focused on data accuracy, time management, and cost reduction.
- Execute month-end close, including reconciliation and analyses of COGS, preparation of journal entries, inventory, balances, and adjustments.
- Serve as the representative for Accounting in implementation of the ERP system.
- Coordinate with external and internal auditors during reviews.

Exhibit 4.9
Senior Cost Accounting Manager Job Opportunity

KEY TAKEAWAYS: JOB COSTING AND DATA ANALYTICS

Understanding the cost of a product or a service is critical for business operations, analysis, and strategy. In this chapter, we discussed how costs are classified and used to determine the cost of a product or service offering. We presented a job-costing system, which is used to track costs for unique products and services, and we showed how costs flow through the accounting system and how they affect the financial statements. We explained how to account for manufacturing overhead, which inevitably involves estimates in a normal costing system. Finally, we considered how companies apply estimated overhead to jobs and how they reconcile the manufacturing overhead to correct for inaccurate estimates.

Let's review how the information in this chapter can be used to address important managerial questions:

Ask the Question

■ **What question(s) does management want to answer?**

Management must understand the costs of providing goods and services to customers. Understanding cost information not only forms the basis for determining which products and services a company can offer, but also indicates which offerings have the potential for sustained profitability. Unfortunately, determining costs accurately can prove difficult because overhead costs are not immediately known.

Master the Data

■ **Which data are appropriate to address management's questions?**

Data are primarily provided by an organization's cost accounting system, which can track direct materials and direct labor with relative ease. Managers use forecasted information to estimate overhead costs, which they then allocate to products on a predetermined basis.

Perform the Analysis

■ **Which analytics are performed to address management questions?**

Management accountants use **descriptive** and **diagnostic analytics** to calculate product costs in a job-costing system. Costs are calculated by summing direct material, direct labor, and applied manufacturing overhead. Management uses **predictive** and **prescriptive analytics** to estimate future costs and to develop accurate overhead application rates.

Share the Story

■ **How are the results of the analytics shared with stakeholders?**

The product costs generated by management are a central component in a company's financial statements. Work-in-process inventory, finished goods inventory, and cost of goods sold all depend on accurate data produced by a company's cost accounting system. As shown in this chapter, management accountants must compile and share detailed cost information with others for companies to successfully plot future strategy.

Key Terms

actual costing	cost driver	job	normal costing
actual manufacturing overhead	cost-plus pricing	job (order) costing or job-costing system	predetermined overhead rate
allocation base or application base	direct labor		process costing
	direct materials	job-cost sheet	work-in-process
applied manufacturing overhead	indirect labor	manufacturing overhead (MOH)	
	indirect materials		

ANSWERS TO PROGRESS CHECKS

1. In-depth knowledge of cost information is the basis of many strategic decisions. It informs companies about which products and services they should provide, and where they are unable to compete. Costs also inform decisions about marketing, sales, incentive structures, and strategy.

2. Cost-plus pricing guarantees a company a specific percentage of profits above and beyond costs. Companies that are competing for business using a cost-plus contract are incentivized to set prices that are low enough to win the contract. However, there is little or no incentive to cut costs after winning the contract because there is a direct correlation between costs and profits.

3. Job costing is used by companies that create a number of unique or customized products. Process costing is used by companies that create mass quantities of identical products.

4. Direct costs are traced to the production of a product or service. In contrast, indirect costs are not traced to a specific product because management believes the cost of tracing indirect costs outweighs the benefits of doing so. Both types of costs are important to the production of a product, but they vary in how they are accounted for. Direct costs are assigned to a specific job, while indirect costs are included in overhead, and an application of overhead is assigned to a job to approximate the indirect costs.

5. All indirect costs are included in manufacturing overhead. These include the costs of indirect materials, indirect labor, and other indirect production costs such as equipment depreciation, utilities, and rent for a manufacturing facility.

6. The purchase of raw materials is recorded in a company's Raw Materials Inventory or Direct Materials Inventory account. Raw materials, along with direct labor and manufacturing overhead, are combined to create work-in-process inventory. When work-in-process inventory is completed, inventory costs are transferred to the Finished Goods Inventory account. When finished goods are sold, costs are transferred to the Cost of Goods Sold account.

7. A job-cost sheet contains important information about an individual job, including when it was started and completed, and all associated production costs.

8. The actual costs of overhead may not be determinable when a job is completed. Businesses often need cost information in order to price out products or perform profitability analyses. To help with these activities, management accountants can use an estimated overhead rate to apply overhead to jobs. At the end of the reporting period, the overhead account and connected inventory accounts can be adjusted if overhead was overapplied or underapplied.

9. Underapplied or overapplied overhead can be reconciled at the end of the reporting period by either (1) adjusting the difference directly to the Cost of Goods Sold account or (2) prorating the needed adjustment to the Work-in-Process Inventory, Finished Goods Inventory, and Cost of Goods Sold accounts. The proration can be based on the value in each account or on the activity level of the overhead application base in each account.

10. Direct materials, direct labor, and applied overhead are always included in calculating the cost of a product or service.

11. Unlike financial accountants, management accountants have a great deal of freedom when it comes to gathering and presenting information. All companies have limited resources, and the benefits of gathering information should always outweigh the costs. For example, if management determines that overhead costs are 95% accurate with a simple estimate, the costs of refining the overhead estimate with expensive, sophisticated information systems may outweigh the benefits of greater accuracy.

Multiple-Choice Questions

1. (LO4.2) Which of the following products or services is least appropriate for a job-costing system?

   a. Furniture

   b. Soft drinks

   c. Medical services

   d. Interior design consultations

2. (LO4.1, 4.2) Which of the following is NOT included as a production cost in a job-costing system?

   a. Production machine maintenance

   b. Marketing

   c. Indirect materials

   d. Factory utilities

3. (LO4.4) All of the following are reasons why companies are likely to use applied, rather than actual, overhead for job costing EXCEPT:

   a. companies have difficulty tracing supervisor labor costs.

   b. companies have significant amounts of indirect costs.

   c. companies face a delay when gathering indirect cost data.

   d. companies decide not to trace certain materials costs.

4. (LO4.5) Correcting an overapplication of overhead will result in increased:

   a. finished goods inventory.

   b. work-in-process inventory.

   c. cost of goods sold.

   d. net income.

5. (LO4.4) Nature Meadow Company analyzes indirect costs and determines that 85% of its costs are related to machine maintenance and depreciation. Which of the following is the most appropriate application base?

   a. Direct labor hours

   b. Direct labor costs

   c. kWh (kilowatt hours) of electricity consumed

   d. Machine hours

6. (LO4.2) Job costing is most likely to be used by companies that produce:

   a. jewelry.

   b. paint.

   c. bottled water.

   d. breakfast cereals.

7. (LO4.1, 4.3) In job costing, costs are accumulated by a specific cost object. Which of the following is NOT a cost object in job costing?

   a. An individual client

   b. A customized order

   c. An individualized service

   d. Monthly factory production costs

8. (LO4.1, 4.2) Which of the following information is not contained on a job cost sheet?
   a. Direct labor hours
   b. Amount of direct materials purchased
   c. Direct labor rates
   d. Applied overhead rates

9. (LO4.3) Which of the following represents a credit to the Manufacturing Overhead account?
   a. The application of overhead
   b. The use of indirect materials
   c. The use direct labor
   d. The use of supervisor labor

10. (LO4.6) Snack Mart uses a normal costing system and applies overhead at a rate of $10 per direct labor hour. During the year, the company had the following data:

    Actual direct labor costs: $80,000

    Actual direct labor hours: 3,000 hours

    Estimated direct labor hours: 3,500 hours

    Actual direct materials: $30,000

    Actual manufacturing overhead: $25,000

    Prior to any adjusting entries to manufacturing overhead, what are the total production costs for Snack Mart for the year?
    a. $135,000
    b. $140,000
    c. $145,000
    d. $150,000

11. (LO4.4) Given the following information about Nibbles N Scribbles Co., what was Nibbles N Scribbles' predetermined application rate for manufacturing overhead (MOH)?

    MOH application base: machine hours (MHs)

    Estimated MHs: 10,000 hours

    Actual MHs: 12,000 hours

    Estimated overhead costs: $48,000

    Actual overhead costs: $50,000
    a. $4.00/machine hour
    b. $4.17/machine hour
    c. $4.80/machine hour
    d. $5.00/machine hour

12. (LO4.6) Study Volt Inc. underapplied manufacturing overhead during the quarter. Assuming no adjusting entry is made, which of the following will be overstated?
    a. Net income
    b. Finished goods inventory
    c. Work-in-process inventory
    d. Cost of goods sold

13. (LO4.6) Zen Craft applies overhead at a rate of $4.50 per direct labor hour. Zen Craft's overhead was underapplied during the year. Which of the following statements is correct?
    a. Actual total overhead must be higher than estimated total overhead.
    b. Actual total overhead must be lower than estimated total overhead.
    c. Zen Craft had fewer direct labor hours than anticipated during the year.
    d. None of these statements is correct.

14. (LO4.5) Bake It Easy incurred more overhead costs than it applied. Prior to any adjusting entries, which of the following statements must be true?

    a. The overhead application rate was higher than the actual overhead rate.

    b. The manufacturing overhead account has a debit balance.

    c. Net income is overstated.

    d. Bake It Easy produced more goods than anticipated.

15. (LO4.3) Regal Furnishers used $10,000 worth of indirect materials in production in June. The journal entry made to record this transaction should include a $10,000 debit to:

    a. Work-in-Process Inventory.

    b. Accounts Payable.

    c. Raw Materials.

    d. Manufacturing Overhead.

16. (LO4.6) Under a normal costing system, which of the following is NOT included when computing the cost of a job?

    a. Direct materials

    b. Direct labor

    c. Sales commission

    d. Applied overhead

17. (LO4.5) Shield Bunny had the following information:

    Allocation base: Direct labor hours (DLH)

    Estimated DLH: 20,000 hours

    Actual DLH: 25,000 hours

    Estimated overhead cost/DLH: $5/DLH

    Actual overhead cost/DLH: $4/DLH

    Assuming no adjusting entry to manufacturing overhead, which of the following statements is true?

    a. There will be a debit balance in the Manufacturing Overhead account.

    b. There will be a credit balance in the Manufacturing Overhead account.

    c. There will be a zero balance in the Manufacturing Overhead account.

    d. The balance in the Manufacturing Overhead account cannot be calculated with the given information.

18. (LO4.1, 4.2) Chic Lab produces furniture. Under a job-costing system, which of the following is most likely to be considered indirect labor during the construction of a chair?

    a. Significant labor used to shape and cut wood

    b. Moderate labor used to assemble wood

    c. Minimal labor used to stain the chair

    d. Moderate labor used to closely supervise the production of chairs

19. (LO4.1, 4.2) Alfredough caters meals for large corporate functions. Under a job-costing system, which of the following is most likely to be considered indirect materials for Alfredough's orders?

    a. Cost of meat used during preparation of food

    b. Cost of fruit used during preparation of food

    c. Cost of vegetables used during preparation of food

    d. Cost of salt used during preparation of food

20. (LO4.2, 4.3) Under a job-costing system, a company that uses two distinct processes to produce inventory must use the same allocation base for each production process.

    a. True

    b. False

21. (LO4.2) In practice, items such as wood screws and glue used in the production of school desks and chairs would most likely be classified as
    a. direct labor.
    b. factory overhead.
    c. direct materials.
    d. period costs.

Discussion Questions

1. (LO4.1) Describe how accurate cost information can provide a competitive advantage to a company.
2. (LO4.1) What are the potential consequences of inaccurate cost information?
3. (LO4.2) Describe how inaccurate overhead allocations, if not corrected, can affect a company's financial statements.
4. (LO4.2) Describe the process of generating predetermined overhead rates.
5. (LO4.2) Explain why companies typically use applied overhead rather than actual overhead.
6. (LO4.3) Explain how financial statements are impacted if overhead allocation rates are too low and no adjusting entries are made to correct manufacturing overhead.
7. (LO4.4) Describe the principles and factors that should guide management's selection of a manufacturing overhead application base.

ETHICS

8. (LO4.4) Describe how the selection of allocation bases can be used to favor one division or product over another. What ethical considerations should be considered when determining allocation bases?
9. (LO4.4) Explain the conditions under which a company may choose to use different application bases for different production processes, even if only one type of product is made.
10. (LO4.4) Explain why companies estimate an overhead application rate when any such estimate is unlikely to be correct.
11. (LO4.5) Describe the two methods of correcting overapplied or underapplied overhead and explain how management decides which method to use.
12. (LO4.5) Describe why writing off all overapplied or underapplied overhead to cost of goods sold leads to inaccurate cost information.
13. (LO4.6) Explain the factors that management should consider when determining whether or not to trace production costs.
14. (LO4.6) Explain why and how a company could recategorize overhead costs as direct costs.
15. (LO4.6) Explain how overhead costs are affected when companies replace direct labor with machine labor.
16. (LO4.6) Explain the role that estimates play in the calculation of job costs.

Brief Exercises   connect

1. (LO4.3, 4.5) During the year, the total actual cost of inventory produced for The Wood Legacy was $1,500,000 (assume no beginning or ending inventory balances). Actual manufacturing overhead was $300,000. Direct materials incurred during the year were $900,000, and direct labor costs were $350,000. The Wood Legacy uses a normal costing system and applies overhead at a rate of 100% of direct labor costs. The Wood Legacy's adjusting entry to manufacturing overhead at the end of the year would have been a _____ (debit or credit) entry of $_____ to Manufacturing Overhead.

2. (LO4.1, 4.6) CreativeCubicle uses a normal costing system and applies overhead on the basis of machine hours. CreativeCubicle has compiled the following information:

Actual direct labor costs: $300,000

Actual direct labor hours: 25,000 hours

Estimated machine hours: 14,000 hours

Actual direct materials: $750,000

Actual machine hours: 15,000 hours

Actual MOH: $235,000

Estimated MOH: $210,000

Prior to any adjusting entries to manufacturing overhead, what are the total production costs for CreativeCubicle for the year?

3. (LO4.4) Calculate Sneakerzy's predetermined overhead application rate given the following information:

Overhead application base: Direct labor hours

Estimated direct labor hours: 18,000

Actual direct labor hours: 22,000

Estimated MOH: $165,600

Actual MOH: $188,000

4. (LO4.1, 4.4) High Icon underapplied inventory by $12,000 during the year. The company had the following information:

Overhead application base: Machine hours

Estimated machine hours: 10,000

Actual machine hours: 14,000

Estimated overhead: $190,000

What were the actual overhead costs for the year for High Icon?

5. (LO4.4) Solar Nexus overapplied inventory by $43,250 in May. The following information was compiled from Solar Nexus's cost accounting system:

Overhead application base: Machine hours

Estimated machine hours: 40,000

Actual overhead: $432,500

Estimated overhead: $346,000

Calculate actual machine hours for Solar Nexus in May.

6. (LO4.3) In January, Fine Furnish used 4,000 pounds of a bonding agent, X2P, for its products. The cost of X2P is $0.015 per pound. Fine Furnish classifies X2P as indirect materials and records the cost of X2P in an account called "Indirect Materials." What is the journal entry that Fine Furnish should use to record the use of X2P in January?

7. (LO4.6) Quest API applies manufacturing overhead at a rate of $2.75 per machine hour. Total production costs per Quest API's normal costing system were $194,000 for November. Direct materials and direct labor costs were $65,000 and $85,000, respectively. How many machine hours were used during November?

8. (LO4.6) In December, Dwellify used $130,000 of direct materials in production. Dwellify's costs for direct labor average $12.50 per hour, and total production costs were $204,800. In addition, Dwellify applies manufacturing overhead at a rate of $4.50 per direct labor hour. How many direct labor hours did Dwellify use in December?

9. (LO4.6) Insomniacs Inc. reported the following information:

Predetermined overhead application rate: $8.30/machine hour

Actual overhead rate: $8.50/machine hour

Estimated machine hours: 30,000

Actual machine hours: 32,000

If Insomniacs Inc. does not use an adjusting entry to correct manufacturing overhead, what will be the effect on net income (assuming no beginning or ending inventory balances)?

Insomniacs Inc.'s net income will be _____ (overstated or understated) by $_____.

10. (LO4.5) Andromics determined that it must make an adjusting entry to correct a $16,000 underapplication of manufacturing overhead. Andromics had the following ending balances:

   Raw materials inventory: $6,500

   Work-in-process inventory: $175,000

   Finished goods inventory: $135,000

   Cost of goods sold: $490,000

   Assuming that Andromics has determined that the amount of the correction is material and cannot all be written off to cost of goods sold, what journal adjusting entry must be made to correct the underapplication?

11. (LO4.5) Alpha Heal applies overhead at a rate of $6 per direct labor hour. Applied overhead during the year amounted to $56,000, while actual overhead amounted to $52,000. Alpha Heal had the following ending balances:

   Work-in-process inventory: $32,000

   Finished goods inventory: $18,000

   Cost of goods sold: $70,000

   Assuming that Alpha Heal has determined that the amount of the correction is immaterial, what journal adjusting entry must be made to correct the misapplication of overhead?

12. (LO4.5) Stratify Co. made the following adjusting entry at the end of the last quarter:

| Cost of Goods Sold | $12,700 | |
| Manufacturing Overhead | | $12,700 |

This journal entry means that manufacturing overhead was _____ (overstated or understated). Without this adjusting entry, net income would be _____ (overstated or understated).

13. (LO4.2, 4.3) Hackersome has the following costs for August.

Sales consulting services	$35,000
Administrative building rent	$5,000
Factory electricity	$500
Administrative building utilities	$600
Advertising	$3,000
Factory maintenance	$14,000
Factory equipment depreciation	$25,000
Direct labor	$30,000
Indirect labor	$12,000
Direct materials	$10,500
Accounting services	$4,000

What are Hackersome's total production costs for August?

14. **(LO4.4)** Boots N Beyond had the following cost information for July:

	Estimated	Actual
Overhead costs	$130,000	$125,000
Direct labor hours	40,000	42,000
Machine hours	8,000	8,500

Boots N Beyond uses direct labor hours to apply manufacturing overhead. What is Boots N Beyond's overhead application rate?

15. **(LO4.4, 4.6)** Hypercraft has two production departments, Cutting and Sewing. The Cutting department applies costs based on direct labor hours while the Sewing department applies costs based on machine hours. Hypercraft had the following cost information for October:

	Cutting	Sewing
Estimated overhead	$54,000	$64,600
Direct labor hours	2,400	950
Machine hours	30	170

Hypercraft received and completed order #225 in October, which had the following information:

Direct materials: $6,000

Direct labor: $15,500

Cutting department direct labor hours: 200 hours

Sewing department machine hours: 20 hours

Hypercraft uses a normal costing system. What is the cost of order #225?

16. **(LO4.4)** Using the following budget data for Valley Corporation, which produces only one product, calculate the company's predetermined factory *variable* overhead application rate.

Units to be produced: 11,000

Units to be sold: 10,000

Indirect materials, varying with production: $1,000

Indirect labor, varying with production: $10,000

Factory supervisor's salary, incurred regardless of production: $20,000

Depreciation on factory building and equipment: $30,000

Utilities to operate factory machines: $12,000

Security lighting for factory: $2,000

Selling, general, and administrative expenses: $5,000

17. **(LO4.2, 4.4)** Patterson Corporation expects to incur $70,000 of factory overhead and $60,000 of general and administrative costs next year. Direct labor costs at $5 per hour are expected to total $50,000. If factory overhead is to be applied per direct labor hour, how much overhead will be applied to a job incurring 20 hours of direct labor?

Problems   connect

1. (LO4.4) Web Bytes allocates manufacturing overhead on the basis of direct labor hours. Web Bytes had the following cost information:

   Estimated direct labor hours: 10,000 hours

   Actual direct labor hours: 12,000 hours

   Estimated manufacturing overhead costs: $18,000

   Actual manufacturing overhead costs: $24,000

   Required

   a. What is Web Bytes' predetermined overhead rate?

   b. What is Web Bytes' applied overhead for the year?

   c. What is the amount of overapplied or underapplied overhead for the year?

2. (LO4.1, 4.3, 4.6) Dashing Diva has the following costs for April.

Direct labor	$20,000.00
Direct materials	$15,000.00
Factory utilities	$8,000.00
Accounting services	$12,000.00
Direct marketing	$17,000.00
Production supervisor salaries	$6,000.00
Factory equipment depreciation	$13,000.00

   Required

   a. What are the total production costs?

   b. What are the total manufacturing overhead costs?

   c. Dashing Diva produced Job #123 with the following actual costs: $1,500 of direct materials, $1,800 of direct labor, and $1,000 of manufacturing overhead. Dashing Diva allocates manufacturing overhead at a rate of 80% of direct labor costs. Under a normal costing system, what was Dashing Diva's recorded cost for Job #123?

3. (LO4.4, 4.6) Jackson Mills has the following cost information:

	Estimated	Actual
Overhead costs	$100,000	$125,000
Direct labor hours	40,000	50,000
Machine hours	32,000	25,000

   Required

   a. If Jackson Mills uses direct labor hours as an application base, what is the predetermined overhead rate for the year?

   b. If Jackson Mills uses direct labor hours as an application base, how much manufacturing overhead is applied to jobs during the year?

   c. If Jackson Mills uses direct labor hours as an application base, and Job #486 uses 40 direct labor hours, how much overhead is applied to Job #486?

   d. If Jackson Mills uses machine hours as an application base, what is the predetermined overhead rate for the year?

   e. If Jackson Mills uses machine hours as an application base, how much manufacturing overhead is applied to jobs during the year?

f. If Jackson Mills uses machine hours as an application base, and Job #486 uses 16 machine hours, how much overhead is applied to Job #486?

g. What journal entry would Jackson Mills make to apply overhead to Job #486 if Jackson Mills uses machine hours as an application base and Job #486 uses 16 machine hours?

4. (LO4.4, 4.6) Jacobs Molding Company has separate application rates for each of its two departments, Mixing and Assembly. In the Mixing Department, Jacobs uses machine hours to allocate costs. In the Assembly Department, direct labor costs are used to allocate costs. The following estimates were provided by Jacobs' management at the beginning of the year:

	Mixing	Assembly
Estimated overhead costs	$60,000	$90,000
Estimated direct labor costs	$600,000	$750,000
Estimated direct labor hours	25,000	30,000
Estimated machine hours	24,000	45,000

Required

a. What is the Mixing Department's predetermined application rate per unit of application base?

b. What is the Assembly Department's predetermined application rate per unit of application base?

c. Jacobs recorded 20 machine hours in the Mixing Department and direct labor costs of $1,500 in the Assembly Department for Job #357. How much manufacturing overhead is applied to Job #357?

5. (LO4.4, 4.6) Smithson Electric provides residential and business electric repair services. While direct labor and materials costs are traced to individual customers, administrative labor and transportation costs are considered overhead and applied as a percentage of direct labor costs.

At the beginning of the year, Smithson estimates $10,000 of overhead costs and $50,000 of direct labor costs. Actual costs for the year are $12,000 for overhead and $48,000 for direct labor. Ending balances for WIP Inventory, Finished Goods Inventory, and Cost of Goods Sold are $4,000, $15,000, and $141,000 respectively.

Required

a. What is Smithson's predetermined overhead rate (rounded to the nearest percent)?

b. The Jackson account accumulated $5,000 in direct labor costs and $3,300 in direct materials for the year. What is the amount of overhead charged to the Jackson account?

c. Using the data from part b above, what is the total cost for Jackson?

d. If Smithson determines that any overapplication or underapplication of manufacturing overhead can be written off to cost of goods sold at the end of the year, what journal entry should be used to reconcile overhead?

e. If Smithson determines that writing off all overapplied or underapplied manufacturing overhead to cost of goods sold could significantly affect the company's financial statements, what journal entry should be used at the end of the year to reconcile overhead?

6. (LO4.5) Glenway Enterprises applies manufacturing overhead at a rate of $4/MH (machine hour), and it used 57,000 MH during the year. At the end of the year, Glenway learns that actual overhead costs incurred were $210,000. Ending balances are $800, $200, and $9,000 for Work-in-Process inventory, Finished Goods Inventory, and Cost of Goods Sold, respectively.

Required

a. By what amount is Glenway's manufacturing overhead overapplied or underapplied?

b. Assume the amount of overapplied overhead is deemed immaterial by Glenway management. What is the adjusting entry to manufacturing overhead?

c. Assume the amount of overapplied overhead is deemed material by Glenway management. What is the adjusting entry to manufacturing overhead?

7. (LO4.4) The Spice Saga has two production departments, Assembly and Finishing. The following information was used to calculate overhead application rates:

	Assembly	Finishing	Total
Estimated overhead	$800,000	$400,000	$1,200,000
Direct labor hours	50,000	30,000	80,000
Machine hours	16,000	8,000	24,000

Overhead information for Job #687 is as follows:

	Assembly	Finishing	Total
Direct labor hours	100	125	225
Machine hours	30	18	48

Required

a. Assume that The Spice Saga uses direct labor hours to apply overhead in both production departments. How much overhead will be applied to Job #687?

b. Assume that The Spice Saga uses machine hours to apply overhead in both production departments. How much overhead will be applied to Job #687?

c. Assume that The Spice Saga uses direct labor hours to apply overhead in the Finishing Department and machine hours to apply overhead in the Assembly Department. How much overhead will be applied to Job #687?

8. (LO4.2, 4.3) Chefly applies manufacturing overhead at a rate of $15 per direct labor hour. During June, 10,000 hours of direct labor were incurred. Chefly also recorded the following transactions in June:

- $20,000 of indirect materials (categorized on the books as raw materials) were used in production.
- $15,000 of indirect labor (paid on account) were used in production.
- $100,000 of direct materials were used in production.

Required

a. What is the journal entry to record the use of direct materials?

b. What is the journal entry to record the use of indirect labor?

c. What is the journal entry to record the application of manufacturing overhead for the month of June?

9. (LO4.2, 4.3, 4.5) Olive You applies manufacturing overhead at a rate of $0.40 per kilowatt hour (kWh) of electricity. Olive You's production facility used 125,000 kWh of electricity during January. The following information is provided about Olive You's production in January:

- Olive You overapplied overhead by $1,350 during the month. The company writes off overapplied or underapplied overhead to cost of goods sold only.
- $736,000 of inventory was completed during January.
- $700,000 of inventory was sold during January.

Required

a. What is the journal entry to record the application of manufacturing overhead for the month of January?

b. What is the journal entry to record the completion of WIP inventory during January?

c. What is the journal entry to record the sale of inventory during January?

d. What is the journal entry to write off the overapplication of overhead in January?

10. (LO4.5) Style Loop has compiled overhead costs from the past several years in order to determine how various application bases correlate with the firm's total manufacturing overhead costs. Use the following correlation output as you answer the questions below. Assume all correlation coefficients are statistically significant.

	Actual Overhead Costs	Direct Labor Costs	Direct Labor Hours	Machine Hours
Actual overhead costs	1.00			
Direct labor costs	0.82	1.00		
Direct labor hours	0.91	0.95	1.00	
Machine hours	0.67	0.55	0.42	1.00

Required

a. What is the correlation between overhead costs and machine hours?

b. What is the correlation between direct labor costs and direct labor hours?

c. Based only on the correlation data, which allocation base is the most suitable for applying manufacturing overhead?

11. (LO4.5) Dapperfy has three production departments: Assembly, Sanding, and Painting. Dapperfy has compiled actual overhead cost information for each completed job for the past two years in order to examine how four overhead application bases could be used to apply overhead in the future. Use the following correlation output as you answer the questions below. Assume all correlation coefficients are statistically significant.

	Assembly Department Overhead Costs	Sanding Department Overhead Costs	Painting Department Overhead Costs	Direct Labor Costs	Direct Labor Hours	Machine Hours	Kilowatt Hours
Assembly Department overhead costs	1.00						
Sanding Department overhead costs	0.70	1.00					
Painting Department overhead costs	0.75	0.91	1.00				
Departmental direct labor costs	0.95	0.72	0.79	1.00			
Departmental direct labor hours	0.82	0.75	0.82	0.90	1.00		
Departmental machine hours	0.43	0.92	0.99	0.52	0.57	1.00	
Departmental kilowatt hours	0.36	0.96	0.94	0.44	0.48	0.89	1.00

Required

a. What is the correlation between overhead costs in the Sanding Department and departmental machine hours?

b. Based only on the correlation data, which allocation base is the most suitable for applying manufacturing overhead in the Assembly Department?

c. Based only on the correlation data, which allocation base is the most suitable for applying manufacturing overhead in the Sanding Department?

d. Based only on the correlation data, which allocation base is the most suitable for applying manufacturing overhead in the Painting Department?

12. (LO4.6) Style Lab uses a normal costing system to calculate order costs. Style Lab allocates manufacturing overhead costs to its orders at the rate of 25% of direct labor costs. Use the following information to answer the questions below.

	Order #1466	Order #1467	Order #1468
Direct materials	$1,538	$3,449	$10,817
Direct labor	$1,250	$2,114	$4,994

Required

a. What is the total cost of order #1466?

b. What is the total cost of order #1467?

c. What is the total cost of order #1468?

13. (LO4.6) Ad Spot provides advertising services to local businesses. It is calculating customer profitability for the previous year. Ad Spot uses a normal costing system to calculate the costs of servicing clients. Ad Spot applies manufacturing overhead costs to its clients at a rate of 10% of direct labor costs. Use the following information to answer the questions below.

	McDowell	Jones	Yang	Bernanke
Revenue	$12,500	$15,435	$11,800	$6,000
Direct materials	$4,414	$7,144	$4,360	$4,864
Direct labor	$3,265	$4,518	$5,334	$1,120
Direct labor hours	172	251	314	63

Required

a. What was the total cost of providing service to McDowell last year?

b. What was the total cost of providing service to Bernanke last year?

c. What is the sales profit percentage for the Jones account?

d. How much profit did Ad Spot generate from the Yang account?

14. (LO4.4, 4.6) Tuxedough applies manufacturing overhead on the basis of machine hours. Tuxedough has compiled the following information for the prior year:

Estimated overhead costs:	$1,800,000
Actual overhead costs:	$1,750,000
Estimated machine hours:	64,000 hours
Actual machine hours:	75,000 hours

Required

a. Under a normal costing system, what is Tuxedough's overhead application rate?

b. What is the total applied overhead for last year?

c. To close out underapplied or overapplied overhead to cost of goods sold at the end of the year, Tuxedough would have made a _____ (debit or credit) entry of $_____ to Manufacturing Overhead.

d. With perfect hindsight, what overhead application rate could Tuxedough have used so that all incurred overhead was applied to inventory without the need for an adjusting entry?

15. (LO4.1, 4.3, 4.5) Glamly uses a normal costing system and applies manufacturing overhead to jobs at a rate of 110% of direct labor costs. The company had no beginning or ending raw materials or work-in-process inventory in January. In addition, the company has the following costs for February.

Direct labor	$84,000
Direct materials	$27,000
Factory utilities	$10,000
Advertising expenses	$23,000
Production supervisor salaries	$18,000
Factory equipment depreciation	$20,000
Factory rent	$25,000
Janitorial services for production facility	$18,000
Indirect materials	$5,000

Required

a. Prior to any adjusting entries, what is the total amount debited to Manufacturing Overhead in February?

b. Prior to any adjusting entries, what is the total amount credited to Manufacturing Overhead in February?

c. Glamly makes an adjusting entry at the end of February to account for any inaccurate application of overhead. Assuming that the overhead estimate is immaterial, what adjusting entry will Glamly make?

Lab 4.1 Excel

Lab Note: The tools presented in this lab periodically change. Updated instructions, if applicable, can be found in the student and instructor support materials.

Using Linear Regression in Forecasting (Heartwood)

Data Analytics Type: Predictive Analytics

Keywords

Regression Analysis, Forecasting, Direct Production Costs

Decision-Making Context

Heartwood Cabinets has a small subsidiary that installs completed cabinets in homes. The subsidiary is located in the Southeast region of the United States. To determine overhead rates for the upcoming year, Heartwood must estimate direct labor hours. Managers have historically used their intuition and experience to predict labor hours. However, management is considering a data-driven approach to this estimate, and it is curious about which factors may influence direct labor hours.

Required

1. Use regression analysis to estimate the direct labor hours for Heartwood's upcoming year.
2. Analyze regression output.

Ask the Question

Heartwood uses direct labor hours as an application base for allocating manufacturing overhead. As such, Heartwood must estimate direct labor hours for the upcoming year. Based on an analysis of direct labor hours and housing starts, are housing starts correlated with direct labor hours? Can housing starts be used to predict future direct labor hours?

Master the Data

For this lab you will use data in the Excel file titled **Lab 4.1 Data.xlsx**.

The data file contains eight years of regional housing start data, along with three years of labor data for the Heartwood Cabinets Installation Subsidiary.

Perform the Analysis

Analysis Task #1: Install the Analysis ToolPak

1. Open Excel file **Lab 4.1 Data.xlsx**.
2. Quickly browse the spreadsheet to make sure there isn't any obvious error in the Excel file.
3. The data do not easily fit on a single screen. To make it easier to view the data, click **View**, and then **Freeze Panes**, and then select **Freeze Top Row** (Lab Exhibit 4.1.1).

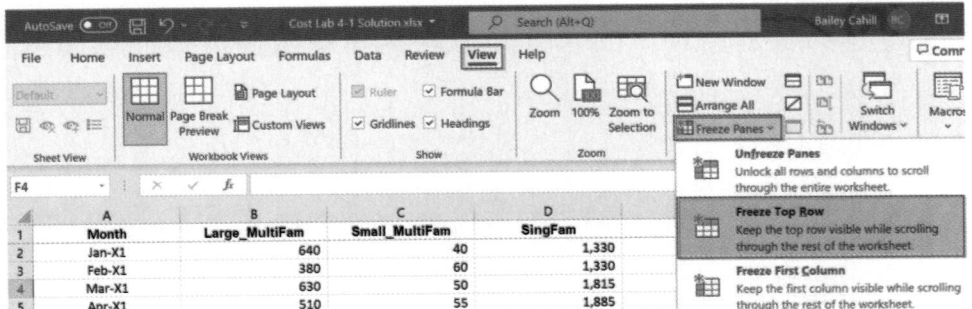

Lab Exhibit 4.1.1

Microsoft Excel

4. We will be using regression for this lab. To run the regression, we need to make sure the Analysis ToolPak is loaded, by looking at **Data > Analysis** and seeing if the Data Analysis Add-In has been installed (Lab Exhibit 4.1.2). For more information on how to install the ToolPak, see Appendix D.

Lab Exhibit 4.1.2

Microsoft Excel

If it has not yet been added, go to **File > Options > Add-ins > Manage: > Excel Add-ins > Go...**. Select the **Analysis ToolPak** and then select **OK** (Lab Exhibit 4.1.3).

Analysis Task #2: Perform Regression Analysis

1. Click the **Data** tab in Excel. At the far right of the ribbon, click **Data Analysis**. Under **Analysis Tools**, click **Regression**. Click **OK** (Lab Exhibit 4.1.4).

Lab Exhibit 4.1.3

Microsoft Excel

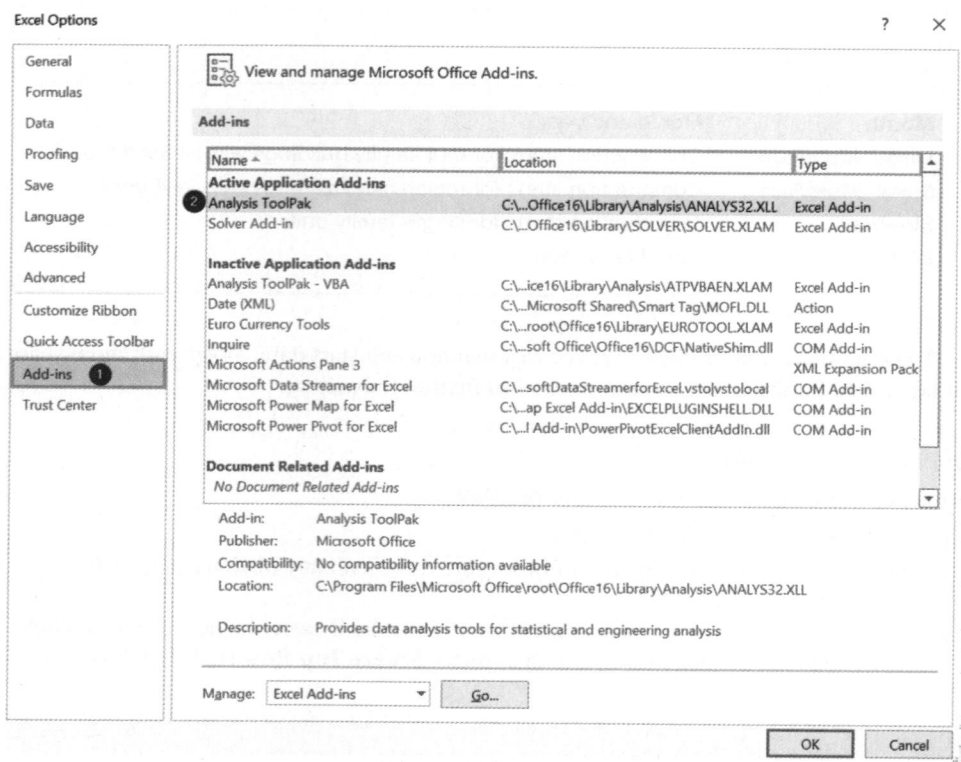

Lab Exhibit 4.1.4

Microsoft Excel

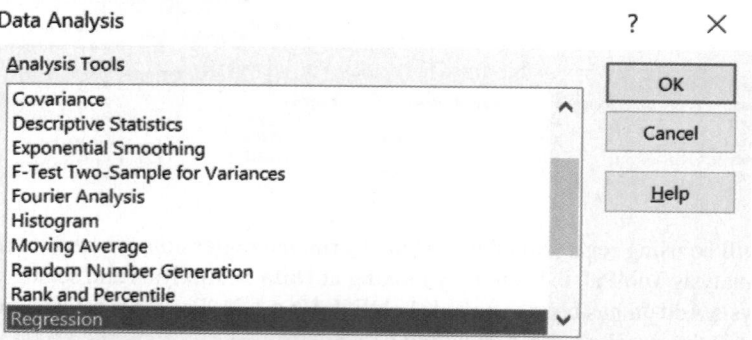

2. Heartwood wants to examine whether housing start data from the past three years ('X6–'X8) can be used to predict direct labor hours in January of 20X9. Click the box to the right of **Input Y Range:** and then select E62:E97. This column represents the dependent variable. Click the box to the right of **Input X Range:** and select B62:D97. These columns will serve as independent variables. Make sure that the **Labels** box does not contain a check mark so that the numerical values in the top row will be used in the analysis. These requirements are shown in Lab Exhibit 4.1.5. Click **OK**.

Because we do not have labels, independent variables will be labeled as X Variable 1, 2, and 3. These are presented in the same order as they are included in the spreadsheet, so X Variable 1 is Large_MultiFam, X Variable 2 is Small_MultiFam, and X Variable 3 is SingFam. The regression output will open in a new sheet.

Regression   ? ✕

Input

Input Y Range: $E$62:$E$97   ⬆   [OK]

Input X Range: $B$62:$D$97   ⬆   [Cancel]

☐ Labels   ☐ Constant is Zero   [Help]

☐ Confidence Level: 95 %

Output options

○ Output Range: ⬆

◉ New Worksheet Ply: [   ]

○ New Workbook

Residuals

☐ Residuals   ☐ Residual Plots

☐ Standardized Residuals ☐ Line Fit Plots

Normal Probability

☐ Normal Probability Plots

3. Evaluate the regression output, which is shown in Lab Exhibit 4.1.6. (For detailed guidance, see Appendix F.)

	A	B	C	D	E	F
1	SUMMARY OUTPUT					
2						
3	*Regression Statistics*					
4	Multiple R	0.255228421				
5	R Square	0.065141547				
6	Adjusted R Square	-0.022501433				
7	Standard Error	5970.367475				
8	Observations	36				
9						
10	ANOVA					
11		*df*	*SS*	*MS*	*F*	*Significance F*
12	Regression	3	79481181.06	26493727.02	0.743260292	0.534200444
13	Residual	32	1140649209	35645287.79		
14	Total	35	1220130390			
15						
16		*Coefficients*	*Standard Error*	*t Stat*	*P-value*	*Lower 95%*
17	Intercept	9629.32829	8395.18218	1.147006472	0.259882965	-7471.098217
18	X Variable 1	1.513593621	5.013651701	0.30189445	0.764685922	-8.698880702
19	X Variable 2	-43.89197658	47.63387449	-0.921444603	0.363713543	-140.9190038
20	X Variable 3	2.410129845	2.155474291	1.118143629	0.271829857	-1.98042761

Using the coefficients in the output, the line that best fits the data is:

$$DLH = 9{,}629 + 1.51 * (Large\_MultiFam) - 43.89 * (Small\_MultiFam) + 2.41 * (SingFam)$$

However, notice that Adjusted R Square (the coefficient of determination) is negative, indicating that the independent variables do not explain *any* of the variance in the dependent variable. The significance of the model (0.534) as a whole, as well as the intercept and variables, is not statistically significant.

Analysis Task #3: Adjust the Regression Model

1. Heartwood decides to adjust the model. Managers believe that housing starts are a leading indicator for installation labor hours. They believe that for Heartwood's jobs, cabinetry installation does not occur in the month of the housing start. Instead, it occurs in the month *following* the housing start.

   To examine this hypothesis, add a new column to the right of the data (Column F) and label it "Next_Month_DLH", as shown in Lab Exhibit 4.1.7. The idea is that December 'X5 housing starts will predict January 'X6 direct labor hours, so these data should be in the same row.

   In cell F61, enter "=E62". Copy the formula down the remainder of the column. One way to do this is to double-click the bottom-right corner of the green rectangle in cell F61 (see again Lab Exhibit 4.1.7).

Lab Exhibit 4.1.7

Microsoft Excel

F61		× ✓ fx	=E62			
	A	B	C	D	E	F
1	**Month**	**Large_MultiFam**	**Small_MultiFam**	**SingFam**	**DLH**	**Next_Month_DLH**
56	Jul-X5	1,725	45	3,590		
57	Aug-X5	1,610	30	3,320		
58	Sep-X5	2,275	55	3,250		
59	Oct-X5	1,545	55	2,945		
60	Nov-X5	1,625	20	2,850		
61	Dec-X5	1,335	60	2,510		19,811

2. Use regression analysis to determine the influence of housing starts on the direct labor hours of the following month. Next_Month_DLH should be used as the dependent variable. We can still use 36 months of data, but the X and Y ranges must be shifted upwards by one row to avoid errors related to missing data. Make sure that only rows 61–96 are included in the Y and X ranges, as shown in Lab Exhibit 4.1.8.

Lab Exhibit 4.1.8

Microsoft Excel

Regression   ? ✕

Input

Input Y Range: $F$61:$F$96 ⬆

Input X Range: $B$61:$D$96 ⬆

☐ Labels   ☐ Constant is Zero

☐ Confidence Level: 95 %

OK

Cancel

Help

Output options

◯ Output Range: ⬆

⦿ New Worksheet Ply:

◯ New Workbook

Residuals

☐ Residuals   ☐ Residual Plots

☐ Standardized Residuals   ☐ Line Fit Plots

Normal Probability

☐ Normal Probability Plots

3. Evaluate the new regression output, which is shown in Lab Exhibit 4.1.9.

   Determine the model fit and the coefficient of determination. Is Heartwood correct in thinking that housing starts are a good predictor of the subsequent month's installation labor?

	A	B	C	D	E	F
1	SUMMARY OUTPUT					
2						
3	*Regression Statistics*					
4	Multiple R	0.51206551				
5	R Square	0.262211087				
6	Adjusted R Square	0.193043376				
7	Standard Error	5303.886177				
8	Observations	36				
9						
10	ANOVA					
11		*df*	*SS*	*MS*	*F*	*Significance F*
12	Regression	3	319931715.7	106643905.2	3.790946448	0.019637783
13	Residual	32	900198674.6	28131208.58		
14	Total	35	1220130390			
15						
16		*Coefficients*	*Standard Error*	*t Stat*	*P-value*	*Lower 95%*
17	Intercept	-7089.104859	7682.326375	-0.922781006	0.363027166	-22737.49161
18	X Variable 1	11.44352063	4.584903886	2.495912873	0.01790885	2.104377028
19	X Variable 2	26.42266135	43.28008102	0.610503971	0.545839939	-61.73597879
20	X Variable 3	1.872306613	1.872557457	0.999866042	0.324876546	-1.941968108

Determine which variable(s) are significant. What is the model that best fits the data? If you need help, review Analysis Task #2, Step 3, and use the following form: $Y = \text{Intercept} + \beta_1 X_1 + \beta_2 X_2 + \beta_3 X_3$, where each X is a dependent variable and each β is the corresponding regression coefficient.

Use housing start data from Row 97 (Dec 'X8) to predict direct labor hours for January 'X9. Assuming you choose to use all variables in the model, predicted labor hours would be calculated as follows:

$$\text{Labor hours} = \text{Intercept} + (\beta_1 * \text{Large\_MultiFam}) + (\beta_2 * \text{Small\_MultiFam}) + (\beta_3 * \text{SingFam})$$

Lab Exhibit 4.1.10 illustrates how this can be done in Excel.

	A	B	C	D	E	F
13	Residual	32	900198674.6	28131208.58		
14	Total	35	1220130390			
15						
16		*Coefficients*	*Standard Error*	*t Stat*	*P-value*	*Lower 95%*
17	Intercept	-7089.104859	7682.326375	-0.922781006	0.363027166	-22737.49161
18	X Variable 1	11.44352063	4.584903886	2.495912873	0.01790885	2.104377028
19	X Variable 2	26.42266135	43.28008102	0.610503971	0.545839939	-61.73597879
20	X Variable 3	1.872306613	1.872557457	0.999866042	0.324876546	-1.941968108
21						
22		Month	Large_MultiFam	Small_MultiFam	SingFam	
23		Dec-X8	1,095	75	2,630	
24						
25		Jan X9 hours:	12,347.42	=B17+B18*C23+B19*D23+B20*E23		

Consider what other factors may play a role in influencing labor hours. Also, what other uses might this type of regression analysis have at Heartwood?

Share the Story

Managers frequently have to make estimates. Because these estimates can have serious consequences for a company's financial health and performance, managers should use available data and tools to improve the accuracy of estimates. One important tool is regression analysis that uses historical data to predict the future.

Regression analysis can help management predict sales, costs, and other helpful information. Effective analysis requires intuition and trial and error as management looks for meaningful relationships within data.

In this lab, we have shown that housing starts are correlated with direct labor hours and can therefore be used to predict future direct labor hours. We also found that large, multifamily housing units can be used to estimate future labor hours. Heartwood can use these data to help plan for future direct labor needs.

Assessment

1. Take a screenshot of the multiple regression output following Analysis Task #3, Step 3; paste it into a Word document named "Lab 4.1 Submission.docx"; and label the screenshot Submission 1.
2. Answer the questions in Connect using your new regression output and upload your Lab 4.1 Submission.docx via Connect if assigned.

Alternate Lab 4.1   Excel—On Your Own

Using Linear Regression in Forecasting (Heartwood)

Keywords

Regression Analysis, Forecasting, Direct Production Costs

Heartwood Cabinets has gathered two more years of historical direct labor data, and it wants to determine how the regression analysis will change when adding the additional data to the analysis.

Required

Perform multiple regression analysis to determine how housing start data affect direct labor hours *in the following month* for the Heartwood Cabinets Installation Subsidiary. You can do so by replicating Analysis Tasks #2 and #3 in Lab 4.1. Use the **Alt Lab 4.1 Data.xlsx** dataset. Be sure to include all five years of data, and create an additional column to look at the effect of housing starts on labor in the subsequent month.

Data Dictionary

Month	Month and year
Large_MultiFam	Construction starts for multifamily buildings with at least 5 units
Small_MultiFam	Construction starts for multifamily buildings with 2–4 units
SingFam	Construction starts for single-family units
DLH	Direct labor hours

The data file contains eight years of regional housing start data, along with five years of labor data for Heartwood.

Assessment

1. Take a screenshot of the regression output, paste it into a Word document named "Alt Lab 4.1 Submission.docx", and label it Submission 1.
2. Answer the questions in Connect and upload your Alt Lab 4.1 Submission.docx via Connect if assigned.

Seasonal Forecasting

Data Analytics Type: Predictive Analytics

Keywords

Forecasting, Scatterplots, Excel

Decision-Making Context

Boardwalk FroYo is a (fictitious) small lakefront frozen yogurt shop in northern Ohio. To determine overhead rates for the upcoming year, Boardwalk must estimate manufacturing overhead costs. Boardwalk has decided to estimate costs on a monthly basis, and it knows that costs vary substantially based on seasonal trends. Boardwalk would like to incorporate these seasonal trends into its cost estimates.

Required

Use Excel's forecasting tool with Exponential Triple Smoothing (ETS), a forecasting tool that accounts for the seasonality of data, to incorporate seasonality into overhead cost forecasts.

Ask the Question

Boardwalk FroYo is estimating monthly manufacturing overhead costs for next year. Management has noticed that overhead costs are dependent on the season, and it wants to determine whether seasonality can be incorporated into its forecast of overhead costs. How does the inclusion of seasonality affect Boardwalk FroYo's forecasts?

Master the Data

For this lab you will use data in the Excel file **Lab 4.2 Data.xlsx**.

Data Dictionary

Month	Month and year
MOH	Total monthly manufacturing overhead costs

Perform the Analysis

Analysis Task #1: Create a Scatterplot

1. Open Excel file **Lab 4.2 Data.xlsx**.
2. Quickly browse the spreadsheet to make sure there isn't any obvious error in the Excel file.
3. Create a scattergraph to examine your data for seasonal trends. To do so, select cells A2:B73. Then click **Insert > Scatter (in the Charts Area) > Scatter with Straight Lines and Markers** (Lab Exhibit 4.2.1). Notice the seasonal or cyclical pattern of the data. The highest and lowest costs for each year are June and December respectively.

Lab Note: The tools presented in this lab periodically change. Updated instructions, if applicable, can be found in the student and instructor support materials. All Lab Exhibits are available within the eBook and in Connect.

DATA VISUALIZATION

Analysis Task #2: Forecast Overhead Costs

1. Now let's determine how well historical data can forecast overhead costs. We will do so by forecasting costs for 2018 by using data from 2015–2017. Then we can compare forecasted and actual cost data from 2018.

    Create a new column with the heading "Forecast". In cell C38, enter this formula: =FORECAST.ETS(). Then click the **fx** button to bring up the **Function Arguments** box that will provide details on the function arguments (Lab Exhibit 4.2.2). ETS stands for *exponential triple smoothing*. ETS is helpful because it allows for the incorporation of seasonal patterns in forecasting.

2. Enter the following parameters for the function, as shown in Lab Exhibit 4.2.3. For **Target_date**, enter the cell (A38) that contains January 2018, as that is the date for which we are forecasting. For **Values**, enter cells B2:B37. These are the data upon which the forecast is based. For **Timeline**, select cells A2:A37 to indicate the period that corresponds to the data. **Seasonality** indicates how many periods are in a cycle. For monthly data, enter 12. If you are examining quarterly data, 4 should be used. The remaining arguments can be left blank. The formula result is an estimate of 859, as shown in the lower right of Lab Exhibit 4.2.3.

    Note: Be sure to use dollar signs to lock the cells for **Values** and **Timeline**. You can do so by highlighting the cells and clicking **F4**.

3. Click **OK**. Now copy the formula from cell C38 through cell C49. This will provide forecasts for each month of 2018 (as shown in Lab Exhibit 4.2.4).

4. Create another column labeled "Margin". We are going to determine a 95% confidence interval for our forecast. In cell D38, enter this formula: =FORECAST.ETS .CONFINT(). As shown in Lab Exhibit 4.2.5, use the same values for this cell that you used in Step 2. For **Confidence_level**, enter 0.95. You should get an answer of 70 (**Formula result = 70.24500126**). This means that, assuming 2018 follows the same general pattern as years 2015–2017, we can be 95% confident that the actual January 2018 cost value will fall between the range of 70 above and 70 below our estimate of 859. Copy the formula through the remainder of 2018.

5. Because we want to graph our forecasts and confidence interval, we will create two new columns. As shown in Lab Exhibit 4.2.6, label Columns E and F "Upper" and "Lower" respectively to indicate the upper and lower bounds of our confidence interval. In cell E38, enter this formula: =C38+D38. In cell F38, enter this formula: =C38-D38. Copy these formulas for the remainder of 2018.

6. To make graphing easier, cut and paste the Margin column so that it appears to the right of the Lower column. To do so, right-click the letter of the column and select the appropriate option.

Analysis Task #3: Update the Scatterplot

1. Select cells A1:E49. Click **Insert > Scatter (in the Charts area) > Scatter with Straight Lines and Markers** (refer back to Lab Exhibit 4.2.1). Lab Exhibit 4.2.7 displays the results. Use the legend to interpret the data. Notice that the confidence interval widens as we forecast further into the future. This makes sense, as it is far easier to predict next month's costs than it is to predict costs 12 months in the future. Also notice that the actual 2018 overhead costs are within the confidence interval and that the forecast appears reasonable.

2. Now that we have learned how to forecast using seasonal trends, and that the output creates reasonable estimates, use Boardwalk FroYo 2015–2020 cost data to graph 2021 forecasted manufacturing overhead costs. Re-perform Analysis Tasks #2 and #3 to include all available data. You will need to delete your previous forecast information.

Share the Story

Time series data often display various trends, including seasonal trends. These trends can be incorporated into forecasts to improve a company's decision making. Regression analysis can be used to predict sales, costs, and other helpful information. Effective analysis requires intuition and trial and error as management looks for meaningful relationships within data.

For Boardwalk FroYo, accounting for seasonality greatly improves forecasting ability and allows management to better anticipate demand. In addition, we have seen how graphing forecasts with upper and lower confidence intervals provides a useful data visualization for presenting the probability range for manufacturing costs (see Lab Exhibit 4.2.8).

Assessment

1. Take a screenshot of your screen following Analysis Task #3, paste it into a Word doc labeled "Lab 4.2 Submission.docx", and label the screenshot Submission 1.
2. Answer the questions in Connect using your new forecasted values and upload your Lab 4.2 Submission.docx via Connect if assigned.

Alternate Lab 4.2   Excel—On Your Own

Seasonal Forecasting

Keywords

Forecasting, Scatterplots, Excel

Doc Ocs, a fictitious company, sells polarized sunglasses for deep-sea fishermen. Doc Ocs has compiled quarterly data on manufacturing overhead costs for 10 years. Doc Ocs knows that costs tend to be slightly higher in the summer months and lower during the winter months. Doc Ocs would like to use historical data to forecast next year's overhead costs.

Required

Use exponential triple smoothing in Excel to forecast overhead costs by replicating Lab 4.2 using the **Alt Lab 4.2 Data.xlsx** dataset.

Note: You must adjust your formulas for quarterly rather than monthly data.

Data Dictionary

Quarter	Quarter and year. Q1 ends 3/31, Q2 ends 6/30, etc.
MOH	Total quarterly manufacturing overhead costs

Assessment

1. Take a screenshot of your final result, paste it into a Word document named "Alt Lab 4.2 Submission.docx", and label the screenshot Submission 1.
2. Answer the questions in Connect and upload your Alt Lab 4.2 Submission.docx via Connect if assigned.

Lab Note: The tools presented in this lab periodically change. Updated instructions, if applicable, can be found in the student and instructor support materials. All Lab Exhibits are available within the eBook and in Connect.

Determining Application Base and Overhead Rate

Data Analytics Types: Descriptive Analytics, Predictive Analytics

Keywords

Overhead Rates, Correlation, Cost Drivers, Excel

Decision-Making Context

Hearth Inc. is a fictitious company that produces kitchen gadgets. As part of the annual budgeting process, Hearth management has forecasted overhead costs with several potential application bases that could be used for overhead application. However, management is not sure which application base is most appropriate.

Required

1. Calculate potential overhead rates for Hearth Inc. to be used in the upcoming year.
2. Use Excel's Correlation function to determine the suitability of various overhead application bases.

Ask the Question

How does Hearth calculate a predetermined overhead rate to be used during the upcoming year? How can Hearth use a correlation matrix to determine which application base is the most suitable for the company?

Master the Data

For this lab you will use data in the Excel file titled **Lab 4.3 Data.xlsx**.

Data Dictionary

Annual OH Costs	Annual overhead costs
DLH	Direct labor hours
DL Costs	Direct labor costs in dollars
MH	Machine hours

The spreadsheet provides a forecast for these figures for the upcoming year, as well as the actual figures for the past 10 years.

Perform the Analysis

Analysis Task #1: Install the Analysis ToolPak

1. Open Excel file **Lab 4.3 Data.xlsx**.
2. Quickly browse the spreadsheet to make sure there isn't any obvious error in the Excel file.

3. We will be using correlations for this lab. To use Excel's correlation function, make sure the Analysis ToolPak is loaded, by looking at **Data > Analysis** and seeing if the Data Analysis Add-In has been installed (Lab Exhibit 4.3.1).

If it has not yet been added, go to **File > Options > Add-ins > Manage: > Excel Add-ins > Go...** and select the **Analysis ToolPak**. Then select **OK** (Lab Exhibit 4.3.2). For more information, see Appendix D.

Analysis Task #2: Computer Overhead Application Rate

1. Management has provided an estimate for annual manufacturing overhead costs. In addition, management has identified three potential cost drivers that could serve as application bases for the upcoming year: direct labor hours, direct labor costs, and machine hours. Label cell A3 "Predetermined Overhead Rate", as shown in Lab Exhibit 4.3.3.

2. Calculate predetermined overhead rate by dividing annual OH costs by each potential application base. For example, in cell C3, enter =$B$2/C2. Using F4 to lock cell B2 will enable you to copy the formula to cells D2 and E2 without making changes. Copy the formula to calculate all three potential predetermined overhead rates. (See again Lab Exhibit 4.3.3.)

3. The predetermined rate can be used to calculate applied overhead on individual jobs. Label cell A5 "Job #111", as shown in Lab Exhibit 4.3.4. Let's assume that Job #111 uses 20 direct labor hours, $300 in direct labor costs, and 10 machine hours. In cells C6 through E6, calculate the applied overhead for Job #111 using each predetermined overhead rate by multiplying application base units by the predetermined overhead rate. Lab Exhibit 4.3.4 shows the formula in cell E6: =E3*E5.

This same process can be used to calculate total applied overhead for the year by multiplying the total number of application base units by the predetermined overhead rate. Enter the formulas in cells C6 and D6.

Analysis Task #3: Evaluate Allocation Bases

1. Management often uses intuition to determine which application base to use. For instance, a company may elect to use machine hours if much of its overhead costs are related to machine depreciation and maintenance. A company may use direct labor hours if much of its overhead costs are related to factory supervisors who oversee direct labor. In general, management should select an application base that is a cost driver, such that when the application base increases, overhead increases in a reasonably predictable way.

Assume that Hearth Inc. isn't sure which application base is most suitable. One way to determine suitability is to examine previous years' data. Accordingly, Hearth has compiled the actual overhead costs and application base units.

Highlight cells B8:E18, as shown in Lab Exhibit 4.3.5.

2. On the **Data** tab, select **Data Analysis > Correlation**. Click **OK** (Lab Exhibit 4.3.6).

3. **Input Range:** should contain your highlighted cells, B8:E18. The data should be **Grouped By: Columns**. Make sure that you indicate that you have **Labels in First Row** by checking the box. For **Output Range:** select cell G3 (Lab Exhibit 4.3.7).

4. Interpret the output, which is shown in Lab Exhibit 4.3.8. Correlations range from −1 to 1. A correlation of −1 indicates a perfect negative correlation, such that when one variable increases, the other decreases. A correlation of 1 is a perfect positive correlation, indicating that variables move in the same direction. By examining Column H, we can see how these three potential application bases are correlated with actual overhead costs in previous years. Based on the output, what is the most appropriate allocation base? Why? Notice that both direct labor hours and direct labor costs have high correlations. A high value in cell I6 indicates that these variables are highly correlated, which makes sense. As the company uses more direct labor hours, direct labor costs

are increasing at a relatively consistent ratio. Machine hours are only moderately coordinated with overhead costs. (For more information on interpreting Excel output, see Appendix F.)

Share the Story

The process for calculating the predetermined overhead application rate is relatively straightforward and highly useful. Companies can use correlations to help determine which application base to use for overhead.

In this lab, we learned how Hearth can calculate overhead rates by dividing overhead costs by the appropriate allocation base. We also learned that correlations can be used to determine whether application bases are cost drivers.

A predetermined overhead rate allows companies to estimate manufacturing overhead throughout the year. Better estimates lead to better cost information, which in turn leads to better decision making. Companies can choose from many different possible application bases, and management should use both data and intuition to select an appropriate application base.

Assessment

1. Take a screenshot of the dataset following Analysis Task #3, paste it into a Word document named "Lab 4.3 Submission.docx", and label the screenshot Submission 1.
2. Answer the questions in Connect and upload your Lab 4.3 Submission.docx via Connect if assigned.

Alternate Lab 4.3 Excel—On Your Own

Determining Application Base and Overhead Rate

Keywords

Overhead Rates, Correlation, Cost Drivers, Excel

Required

Replicate the tasks in Lab 4.3 using the **Alt Lab 4.3 Data.xlsx** dataset. The dataset contains data from PipeDream LLC, a fictitious manufacturer of plumbing tools.

Data Dictionary

Annual OH Costs	Annual overhead costs
DLH	Direct labor hours
DL Costs	Direct labor costs in dollars
MH	Machine hours

The spreadsheet provides a forecast for these figures for the upcoming year, as well as the actual figures for the past 10 years.

Assessment

1. Take a screenshot of the correlation output following Analysis Task #3, paste it into a Word document named "Alt Lab 4.3 Submission.docx," and label the screenshot Submission 1.
2. Answer the questions in Connect and upload your Alt Lab 4.3 Submission.docx via Connect if assigned.

Calculating Job Costs

Data Analytics Type: Descriptive Analytics

Keywords

Job Costing, VLOOKUP, Direct Costs, Excel

Decision-Making Context

MAC Consulting Services is a fictitious consulting firm that specializes in real estate services. MAC uses a job-costing system. MAC has significant direct labor costs, but direct material costs are minimal given the nature of the business. Frank Roberts, owner of MAC, would like to compute monthly costs for his clients to aid in future client selection. As such, he has compiled a list of the month's direct materials and direct labor transactions.

Required

1. Use Excel's VLOOKUP tool to calculate labor costs.
2. Calculate total job costs by summing direct materials, direct labor, and overhead.

Ask the Question

What are the total job costs for the Brown account during the past month?

Master the Data

For this lab you will use data in the Excel file titled **Lab 4.4 Data.xlsx**.

Lab Note: The tools presented in this lab periodically change. Updated instructions, if applicable, can be found in the student and instructor support materials. All Lab Exhibits are available within the eBook and in Connect.

Data Dictionary

Transactions Worksheet

Transaction	Transaction number, listed sequentially
Account	The client for each transaction
Cost Type	Indicates direct materials (supplies) or direct labor. For each transaction, employees are required to list either the cost of supplies or the number of hours worked.
Employee	MAC employee who performed worked or used supplies
Hours	Number of hours worked, if the transaction is for labor
Supply Cost	Cost of supplies, if the transaction is for supplies

Wage Rates Worksheet

Employee	MAC employee who entered the transaction
Wages	Hourly wage

Perform the Analysis

Analysis Task #1: Prepare the Spreadsheet for Analysis

1. Open Excel file **Lab 4.4 Data.xlsx**.
2. Quickly browse the spreadsheet to make sure there isn't any obvious error in the Excel file.
3. To calculate job costs, a company needs to combine actual direct materials, actual direct labor, and applied overhead. In the Transactions worksheet, we have employees and hours, but we must use the Wage Rates worksheet to find the direct labor rate for each employee. We could create a formula that references the Wage Rates worksheet. Instead, we will add a column so that all necessary data are on the transactions worksheet. We will use the VLOOKUP function for this task. VLOOKUP is useful because it looks up a specified name in a table and returns values from that table, which we can then use for additional analysis.

    Insert a new Column E and label it "Wages", as shown in Lab Exhibit 4.4.1.
4. In cell E2, enter =VLOOKUP(), and click the **Fx** button to see the **Function Arguments** dialog box (Lab Exhibit 4.4.2). The **Lookup_value** indicates what Excel should search for in the table. In this case, we are looking for an employee named Campbell, so enter D2. The **Table_array** indicates where Excel should look for "Campbell". We want Excel to search for "Campbell" in the Wage Rates worksheet between cells A2:B4. Use the **F4** function key to lock the table so that it doesn't change when you copy the formula down. The **Col_index_num** is the column number in the table that should be returned. The wage is in the second column of our data, so enter 2. For the **Range_lookup**, enter FALSE, which indicates that only exact matches should be returned. If we have a value that is not in the table, Excel will give us an error message and let us know that there is a problem in the data. If you entered the formula correctly, you should have a value of $50 (**Formula result = 50**), indicating Campbell's wage rate.
5. Select Column E and change the format to **Accounting** number format to indicate that the column represents dollars. Then copy the formula down to the end of the data in Row 115. See Lab Exhibit 4.4.3.
6. Insert a new Column G and label it "Wage Cost". Multiply Wages by Hours to calculate wage cost using the formula =E2*F2 (Lab Exhibit 4.4.4). Copy the formula down Column G.

Analysis Task #2: Calculate Job Costs

1. Now we can create a separate table to total the cost of each job, or, in this case, client. Starting in Column L, create the following column labels: Job, Labor, Supplies, Overhead, and Total Job Costs. See Lab Exhibit 4.4.5. Note that Labor refers to direct labor and Supplies refers to direct materials. All other costs to provide consulting services are considered Overhead. In cell L2, enter "Brown".
2. Use the **SUMIF** function to sum all direct labor costs for the Brown account. We use this formula to sum values that meet our specified criteria. In cell L2, enter this formula: =SUMIF(B:B,K2,G:G). This formula instructs Excel to search Column B for "Brown". For rows that contain "Brown", Excel will sum wage costs from Column G. Use the **SUMIF** function to sum supply costs for the Brown account as well. Lab Exhibit 4.4.6 shows the formula in cell M2.
3. To calculate overhead, you must know MAC's predetermined overhead rate, which is determined by management as part of the budgeting process. MAC's predetermined overhead rate is $10 per direct labor hour. Use the **SUMIF** function to calculate the hours worked on each account, and then multiply the total by $10/hour. To do

so, enter the following formula in cell N2: =SUMIF(B:B,K2,F:F). Total up Labor, Supplies, and Overhead to calculate total job costs for Brown for the month, using the formula shown in cell O2 in Lab Exhibit 4.4.7. Total costs should be $8,599.75 (see cell O2 in Lab Exhibit 4.4.10).

4. Now calculate the total monthly job costs for MAC's remaining clients. One way to determine unique accounts is to highlight Column B and click **Filter** on the **Data** tab (Lab Exhibit 4.4.8). Then click the drop-down menu arrow to **Account** at the top of Column B (Lab Exhibit 4.4.9). Add these accounts to your new table and copy your formulas down to total job costs (Lab Exhibit 4.4.10).

Share the Story

To use job costing, companies must assign and total costs by a job, project, or client. Direct materials and direct labor are calculated by summing all transactions related to a job, while overhead is assigned based on a predetermined overhead rate. Job costing provides useful information to management about the costs and profitability of specific jobs, projects, and customers.

In this lab, we learned how to track the job costs of various clients. Service organizations such as MAC Consulting often do not track direct materials. Instead, service organizations sum direct labor and overhead costs to assign costs to a client or job. Using this process, we determined that the total job costs for the Brown account were $8,599.75.

Assessment

1. Take a screenshot of your data following Analysis Task #2, paste it into a Word document named "Lab 4.4 Submission.docx", and label the screenshot Submission 1.
2. Answer the questions in Connect and upload your Lab 4.4 Submission.docx via Connect if assigned.

Alternate Lab 4.4   Excel—On Your Own

Calculating Job Costs

Keywords

Job Costing, VLOOKUP, Direct Costs, Excel

Alt Lab 4.4 Data.xlsx is a dataset that contains another month's worth of cost data for MAC Consulting Services (see Lab 4.4).

Required

Calculate total monthly job costs for all of MAC's clients. To do so, replicate the relevant steps in Lab 4.4 using the **Alt Lab 4.4 Data.xlsx** dataset.

Note: For this dataset, MAC has changed how it allocates overhead. For this dataset, overhead is calculated as 5% of direct labor costs.

Data Dictionary

Transactions Worksheet

Transaction	Transaction number, listed sequentially
Account	The client for each transaction
Cost Type	Indicates direct materials (supplies) or direct labor. For each transaction, employees are required to list either the cost of supplies or the number of hours worked.
Employee	MAC employee who performed work or used supplies
Hours	Number of hours worked, if the transaction is for labor
Supply Cost	Cost of supplies, if the transaction is for supplies

Wage Rates Worksheet

Employee	MAC employee who entered the transaction
Wages	Hourly wage

Assessment

1. Take a screenshot of your data following Analysis Task #2, paste it into a Word document named "Alt Lab 4.4 Submission.docx", and label the screenshot Submission 1.
2. Answer the questions in Connect and upload your Alt Lab 4.4 Submission.docx via Connect if assigned.

Visualizing Job Cost Data

Data Analytics Types: Descriptive Analytics, Diagnostic Analytics

Lab Note: The tools presented in this lab periodically change. Updated instructions, if applicable, can be found in the student and instructor support materials. All Lab Exhibits are available within the eBook and in Connect.

Keywords

Data Visualization, Job Costing, Production Costs

Decision-Making Context

MC Gaming is a fictitious company that designs and manufactures several lines of gaming consoles, handheld games, and learning devices. It has received very positive reviews on its latest line of gaming systems. MC Gaming would like to become more efficient and profitable overall. The CFO and CEO have called on you to evaluate the manufacturing processes, costs, and profitability of each of the company's devices.

Required

1. Use Tableau to summarize costs by gaming console.
2. Calculate total job costs by summing direct materials, direct labor, and overhead.
3. Identify which products are the costliest to produce and any anomalies that require attention.

Ask the Question

Which gaming console has the greatest scrap costs for MC Gaming?

Master the Data

The data are contained in separate tables (Excel worksheets). For this lab you will use data in the Excel file **Lab 4.5 Data.xlsx**. You will need to upload the data to Tableau and join the tables appropriately to perform the analysis. Importantly, you will notice that you will be required to pivot some of your Production table so that it can be joined to the other tables correctly.

Data Dictionary

Production Worksheet

JobNumber	Unique identifier for a production run
ProductCode	Unique code to identify the gaming console
BatchSize	Number of gaming consoles that can be produced in a single production run
CompletedUnits	Number of gaming consoles that were actually produced during the production run
WS-XXX	Labor minutes spent at a given workstation during the production run

Materials Cost

ProductName	Full name for the product type
ProductCode	Unique identifier for the product type
Materials Cost	Standard cost for materials used to prepare 1 batch of 100 units of a product type (that is, materials cost for 1 production run)

Workstation Labor Cost	
Workstation1	Unique code to identify each workstation. Labeled as Workstation1 because the field Workstation already exists in one of the related tables (specifically, the Production table)
Labor Cost Per Hour	Hourly wage for employee(s) associated with each workstation. For this example, each workstation has just one employee.

Perform the Analysis

Analysis Task #1: Import the Data

1. Open Excel file **Lab 4.5 Data.xlsx**.
2. Quickly browse the spreadsheets to make sure there isn't any obvious error in the Excel file.
   a. Your Production spreadsheet should contain 158 rows of data (including headers).
   b. You should notice that the Production spreadsheet identifies each individual production run and provides detail about the number of minutes spent at each workstation to complete that particular batch. Time at workstations might be different for each production run (and may differ from standards) due to problems such as mechanical breakdowns or inefficient labor.
3. Import the data to Tableau.
4. Drag the Production worksheet to the **Preview** pane, as shown in Lab Exhibit 4.5T.1.

Analysis Task #2: Join Tables

1. First, we want to join the Production and Workstation Labor Cost worksheets. However, the tables share no matching fields (which appear as a column in the data view but appear as rows in Excel). To join these two tables, we need matching fields, so we'll need to pivot the Production data so that there is a record for each job/workstation combination.
   a. Click on the Production label.
      i. Highlight all of the columns in the Production data that have a workstation label as a header (e.g., Ws-702, Ws-832, etc.). See Lab Exhibit 4.5T.2.
      ii. Right-click on those columns and select **Pivot**. Pivoting creates a new row for each job number/workstation combination.
      iii. Rename the two new columns that have been added to Production Data. Name the first "Workstation" and the second "Labor Minutes", as shown in Lab Exhibit 4.5T.3.
   b. Now you should be able to join the Production and Workstation Labor Cost worksheets using the Workstation field. Drag the Workstation Labor Cost worksheet to the **Preview** pane, as shown in Lab Exhibit 4.5T.4.
   c. Join the tables using the Workstation fields in each worksheet by expanding the drop-down menu under each table and selecting "Workstation" (Lab Exhibit 4.5T.5).
   d. Following the steps listed above, drag the Materials Cost worksheet to the data view. Join it to the Production table using the Product Code field (Lab Exhibit 4.5T.6).
2. Once you have joined the tables, the Data view should appear as shown in Lab Exhibit 4.5T.7.

Analysis Task #3: Visualize Total Job Costs by Workstation

DATA VISUALIZATION

1. Select Sheet 1 to begin your visualization (see Lab Exhibit 4.5T.8). To calculate job costs, a company needs to combine actual direct materials, actual direct labor, and applied overhead. In the Production table, we have the minutes spent at each workstation, but we do not have the labor rates to apply to that time in this table.

To calculate labor cost, we will create a calculated field using the Labor Cost per Hour field from the Workstation Labor Cost table and the Labor Minutes field from the Production table. To create a calculated field, click on the **Analysis** tab at the top of the screen. Select **Create Calculated Field...** (Lab Exhibit 4.5T.9). Then, as shown in Lab Exhibit 4.5T.10, change the name of the new variable at the top of the pop-up to "Labor Cost". Then type the following calculation into the window:

[Labor Minutes] * ([Labor Cost Per Hour]/60)

Note: Because the Workstation Labor Cost table reports Labor Cost as an hourly wage, you'll need to divide it by 60 before you apply it to the minutes worked at each workstation.

The new Labor Cost variable will appear beneath your tables, as shown in Lab Exhibit 4.5T.11.

2. MC Gaming calculates overhead rates at $0.05 per workstation minute. We can add this calculated field using steps that are similar to those listed above.

Click on the **Analysis** tab at the top of the screen. Select **Create Calculated Field...**. Change the name of the new variable at the top of the pop-up to "Applied MOH". Then, as shown in Lab Exhibit 4.5T.12, type the following calculation into the window:

[Labor Minutes]*.05

3. Materials Costs for each production run are reported in the Materials Cost table. Importantly, while we want the sum of labor time and overhead across workstations, materials costs are already calculated as the costs for an entire batch (which includes all workstations). This will affect how we write our next formula.

To calculate Total Cost, you will create another calculated field. Click on the **Analysis** tab at the top of the screen. Select **Create Calculated Field...**. Label this new field "Total Cost" and, as shown in Lab Exhibit 4.5T.13, input the following formula:

SUM([Labor Cost]) + SUM([Applied MOH]) +
AVG([Materials Cost (Materials Cost)])

Note: When we pivot the data in Step 1 of Analysis Task #2, each Job Number has 20 rows, one for each workstation, instead of one row containing all the workstation data. When we join the Materials Cost table to the Production table, we use Product Code to form the relationship. This means that every time the Product Code appears, the Materials Cost associated with that code will be added. We need the Materials Cost only once for each Job Number, but because each Job Number has 20 rows, it gets added 20 times. This is why we take the average of the Materials Cost to find the Total Cost.

You may also notice the formula requires "[Materials Cost (Materials Cost)]". This is to call the Materials Cost values, not the entire table.

4. We want to create a column chart with the Total job cost on the Y-axis (**Rows**) and the Job Number on the X-axis (**Columns**). You should also show the cost as the **Data Labels** above each column by clicking **Show Mark Labels** in the **Analysis** menu (Lab Exhibit 4.5T.14). We also want to see only one product, so click and drag **Product Code** to the **Filters** pane (Lab Exhibit 4.5T.15) and select **GS3** and then **OK** (Lab Exhibit 4.5T.16). Format Total Cost to be displayed as currency. Click **Format...** from the drop-down on the **Total Cost** pill (Lab Exhibit 4.5T.17) and select "Currency (Standard)" (Lab Exhibit 4.5T.18). Right-click on Sheet 1, select **Rename**, and change the title of the sheet and visualization to "GS3 Total Cost by Workstation". See Lab Exhibit 4.5T.19.

Analysis Task #4: Use Data Visualization to Look for Anomalies

1. One of the benefits of visualization is that it allows you to see issues and anomalies. Create a visualization that shows the amount of scrapped cost for each job number. The *scrapped cost* is the cost of not producing the total batch capacity for a job. This can be calculated by creating a new calculated field. Click on the **Analysis** tab at the top of the screen. Select **Create Calculated Field....** Change the name of the new variable at the top of the pop-up to "Scrapped Cost". Then, as shown in Lab Exhibit 4.5T.20, type the following calculation into the window:

   ([Materials Cost (Materials Cost)]/[Batch Size])*([Batch Size]-[Completed Units])

2. Follow Lab Exhibit 4.5T.21 for this step. First, drag **Job Number** to the **Columns** shelf. Second, drag **Scrapped Cost** to the **Rows** shelf. Scrapped Cost should sum automatically. Third, drag **Product Name** to the **Color** box in **Marks**. Fourth, sort the scrapped costs in descending order, which will show the jobs with the most scrapped costs first. **Format** Scrapped Costs to show as currency. (For a reminder of how to do this, see Lab Exhibits 4.5T.17 and 4.5T.18.) This chart should reveal that most of the jobs that have scrapped costs are associated with Game Station NextGen. Title this visualization and sheet "Scrapped Cost by Job Number".

3. Next, consider the possibility that there may be inefficiencies at specific workstations by creating a visualization that identifies outliers for time spent at each workstation. Use the circle views visualization again. Drag **Workstation** to the **Columns** shelf and **Labor Minutes** to the **Rows** shelf. Then select the **circle views** icon on the right side of the screen under **Show Me**. Your screen should resemble Lab Exhibit 4.5T.22.

4. To show each production run separately, drag **Job Number** to the **Detail** box in **Marks** (Lab Exhibit 4.5T.23).

5. It will be helpful to see which product type was produced during each production run, which will help us determine if outliers occur more often when certain gaming systems are being produced. So, drag **Product Name** to the **Color** box in **Marks**. Change the title of this visualization and sheet to "Labor Minutes Outlier Analysis." See Lab Exhibit 4.5T.24.

Share the Story

Job costing requires companies to track direct materials and direct labor. In addition, companies must allocate overhead using a predetermined overhead rate. Understanding costs can improve decision making, as costs can inform company strategy.

To use job costing, companies must assign and total costs by a job, project, or client. Direct materials and direct labor are calculated by summing all transactions related to a job, while overhead is assigned based on a predetermined overhead rate. Job costing provides useful information to management about the costs and profitability of specific jobs, projects, and customers.

Using powerful visualization tools also allows companies to find insights, investigate anomalies, and identify opportunities. From our analysis, we determined that Game Station NextGen has the most scrapped costs at MC Gaming.

Assessment

1. Take screenshots of the data visualizations you produced and copy them to a Word document titled "Lab 4.5 Tableau Submission.docx".
2. Answer the questions about your visualizations in Connect and upload your Lab 4.5 Tableau Submission.docx via Connect if assigned.

Calculating Job Costs

Keywords

Data Visualization, Job Costing, Production Costs

Alt Lab 4.5 Data.xlsx is a dataset that contains MC Gaming's cost data for the first three quarters of 2023.

Required

Replicate the analysis tasks from Lab 4.5 Tableau to gain insights into MC Gaming's job costs using the **Alt Lab 4.5 Data.xlsx** dataset.

Note: For this dataset, Materials Costs and Hourly Labor Rates have increased. In addition, MC Gaming has changed how it allocates overhead. For this dataset, overhead is calculated as 9% of direct labor costs.

Data Dictionary

Production Worksheet

JobNumber	Unique identifier for a production run
ProductCode	Unique code to identify the gaming console
BatchSize	Number of gaming consoles that can be produced in a single production run
CompletedUnits	Number of gaming consoles that were actually produced during the production run
WS-XXX	Labor minutes spent at a given workstation during the production run

Materials Cost

ProductName	Full name for the product type
ProductCode	Unique identifier for the product type
Materials Cost	Standard cost for materials used to prepare 1 batch of 100 units of a product type (that is, materials cost for 1 production run)

Workstation Labor Cost

Workstation1	Unique code to identify each workstation. Labeled as Workstation1 because the field Workstation already exists in one of the related tables (specifically, the Production table)
Labor Cost Per Hour	Hourly wage for employee(s) associated with each workstation. For this example, each workstation has just one employee.

Assessment

1. Take screenshots of the data visualizations you produced and copy them to a Word document titled "Alt Lab 4.5 Tableau Submission.docx".
2. Answer the questions about your visualizations in Connect and upload your Alt Lab 4.5 Tableau Submission.docx via Connect if assigned.

Lab Note: The tools presented in this lab periodically change. Updated instructions, if applicable, can be found in the student and instructor support materials. All Lab Exhibits are available within the eBook and in Connect.

Visualizing Job Cost Data

Data Analytics Types: Descriptive Analytics, Diagnostic Analytics

Keywords

Data Visualization, Job Costing, Production Costs

Decision-Making Context

MC Gaming is a fictitious company that designs and manufactures several lines of gaming consoles, handheld games, and learning devices. It has received very positive reviews on its latest line of gaming systems. MC Gaming would like to become more efficient and profitable overall. The CFO and CEO have called on you to evaluate the manufacturing processes, costs, and profitability of each of the company's devices.

Required

1. Use Power BI to summarize costs by gaming console.
2. Calculate total job costs by summing direct materials, direct labor, and overhead.
3. Identify which products are the costliest to produce and any anomalies that require attention.

Ask the Question

Which gaming console has the greatest scrap costs for MC Gaming?

Master the Data

The data are contained in separate tables (Excel worksheets). For this lab you will use data in the Excel file **Lab 4.5 Data.xlsx**. You will need to upload the data to Power BI and join the tables appropriately to perform the analysis. Importantly, you will notice that you will be required to pivot some of your Production table so that it can be joined to the other tables correctly.

Data Dictionary

Production Worksheet

JobNumber	Unique identifier for a production run
ProductCode	Unique code to identify the gaming console
BatchSize	Number of gaming consoles that can be produced in a single production run
CompletedUnits	Number of gaming consoles that were actually produced during the production run
WS-XXX	Labor minutes spent at a given workstation during the production run

Materials Cost

ProductName	Full name for the product type
ProductCode	Unique identifier for the product type
Materials Cost	Standard cost for materials used to prepare 1 batch of 100 units of a product type (that is, materials cost for 1 production run)

Workstation Labor Cost

Workstation1	Unique code to identify each workstation. Labeled as Workstation1 because the field Workstation already exists in one of the related tables (specifically, the Production table)
Labor Cost Per Hour	Hourly wage for employee(s) associated with each workstation. For this example, each workstation has just one employee.

Perform the Analysis

Analysis Task #1: Import the Data

1. Open Excel file **Lab 4.5 Data.xlsx**.
2. Quickly browse the spreadsheets to make sure there isn't any obvious error in the Excel file.
   a. Your Production spreadsheet should contain 158 rows of data (including headers).
   b. You should notice that the production spreadsheet identifies each individual production run and provides detail about the number of minutes spent at each workstation to complete that particular batch. Time at workstations might be different for each production run (and may differ from standards) due to problems such as mechanical breakdowns or inefficient labor.
3. Import the data to Power BI by selecting **Get data** from the opening menu, as shown in Lab Exhibit 4.5P.1.
4. From the **Get Data** menu, select **Excel Workbook** and then **Connect** (Lab Exhibit 4.5P.2).
5. Select the Excel workbook **Lab 4.5 Data.xlsx**.
6. From the **Navigator**, select the following worksheets, as shown in Lab Exhibit 4.5P.3:
   a. Materials Cost
   b. Production
   c. Workstation Labor Cost
   Then select **Load**.

Analysis Task #2: Combine Data from Related Tables

You will need to merge several tables in Power BI to be able to analyze the data. The Production table lists each job (or batch) completed. While it contains data about the schedule and number of units completed, it does not contain any cost data. We will merge data from the Materials Cost table and the Overhead table into the Production table. This task is relatively straightforward because overhead and materials cost are constant for each batch of a specific product type.

1. Click on the **Transform data** icon at the top of your screen (Lab Exhibit 4.5P.4).
2. The **Power Query Editor** opens. Click on the **Production** table in the pane on the left to activate this table. Then select **Merge Queries** at the upper right, as shown in Lab Exhibit 4.5P.5.
3. The **Merge** wizard opens. The Production table should be active at the top.
   a. In the drop-down box in the middle of the screen, select the **Materials Cost** table to merge with the Production table (Lab Exhibit 4.5P.6).
   b. Click to activate **ProductCode** in both tables because this is the common attribute that links these tables.
   c. Check the **Join Kind** to make sure it is matching every record from the Production table to a single record in the Materials Cost table (Left Outer).
   d. Click **OK**.

4. Data from the Materials Cost table are now merged into the Production table, as evidenced by the new Materials Cost column at the end of the table (see Lab Exhibit 4.5P.7). Click on the double-sided arrow to expand the column and select the attributes from the Materials Cost table that you'd like to add to the Production table.

5. When the Column tool window opens, you can select the attributes you want to include.

   a. For simplicity, include only the new attribute—in this case, Materials Cost (Lab Exhibit 4.5P.8).

   b. Uncheck the **Use original column name as prefix** option. Now the new attribute will be included in the Production table simply as "Materials Cost". If you left this option checked, the new attribute would be named "Materials Cost per Batch. Materials Cost", which allows you to see which table it originated from, which is helpful when you are dealing with a lot of data from many different sources—sometimes with the same attribute names. However, we won't need that information for this analysis.

   c. Click **OK**.

6. We want to join the Production and Workstation Labor Cost worksheets. However, the tables share no matching fields (which appear as a column in the data view but appear as rows in Excel). To join these tables, we need matching fields, so we'll need to unpivot the Production data so that there is a record for each job/workstation combination. Follow along with Lab Exhibit 4.5P.9 as you complete the following steps.

   a. Click on the **Production** label at left.

      i. Highlight all of the columns in the Production data that have a workstation label as a header by holding the **Ctrl** key (for example, WS-101, WS-201, WS-270, etc.).

      ii. Right-click on those columns and select **Unpivot Columns**. Unpivoting creates a new row for each job number/workstation combination.

      iii. Rename the two new columns that have been added to Production data. Name the first "Workstation" and the second "Labor Minutes", as shown in Lab Exhibit 4.5P.10.

   b. Repeat Steps 2–5 to merge Workstation from the Workstation Labor Cost table into the Production table. The actions in Lab Exhibits 4.5P.11 through 4.5P.13 should be familiar from Steps 2–5.

7. Return to the **Home** tab and click **Close & Apply** (Lab Exhibit 4.5P.14).

   This takes you back to the **Reports** screen, and you'll see that in the **Fields** pane on the right, the **Production** table now includes the **Materials Cost** and the **Workstation** attributes (Lab Exhibit 4.5P.15).

Analysis Task #3: Visualize Total Job Costs by Workstation

1. To calculate job costs, a company needs to combine actual direct materials, actual direct labor, and applied overhead. To calculate labor cost, we will create a calculated field using the Labor Cost per Hour and the Labor Minutes fields from the Production table. Make sure to click on the Production table header in the **Data** pane to access the fields.

   To create a calculated field, click on the **Modeling** tab at the top of the screen. Select the icon for **Create New Column** (Lab Exhibit 4.5P.16). Then, as shown in Lab Exhibit 4.5P.17, change the name of the attribute to "Labor Cost". Then type the following calculation into the window:

$$\text{[Labor Minutes]}*(\text{[Labor Cost Per Hour]}/60)$$

   Change the value display to **Currency** and set decimal places to 2.

Note: Because the Workstation Labor Cost table reports Labor Cost as an hourly wage, you'll need to divide it by 60 before you apply it to the minutes worked at each workstation.

The new **Labor Cost** variable will appear under the **Production** table heading (see Lab Exhibit 4.5P.18).

2. MC Gaming calculates overhead rates at $0.05 per workstation minute. We can add this calculated field using steps similar to those listed above.

Click on the **Modeling** tab at the top of the screen. Select the icon for **Create New Column**. Change the name of the attribute to "Applied MOH". Then, as shown in Lab Exhibit 4.5P.19, type the following calculation into the window:

$$[\text{Labor Minutes}] * .05$$

Change the value display to **Currency** with two decimal places.

3. Materials Costs for each production run are reported in the Materials Cost table. Importantly, while we want the sum of labor time and overhead across workstations, materials costs are already calculated as the costs for an entire batch (which includes all workstations). This will affect how we write our next formula.

Click on the **Modeling** tab at the top of the screen. Select the icon for **Create New Column**. Change the name of the attribute to "Total Cost" and, as shown in Lab Exhibit 4.5P.20, use the following formula:

$$[\text{Labor Cost}]+[\text{Applied MOH}]+([\text{Materials Cost.1}]/20)$$

Change the value display to **Currency** with two places.

Note: When we unpivot the data in Step 6 of Task #2, each Job Number has 20 rows, one for each workstation, instead of one row containing all the workstation data. When we join the Materials Cost table to the Production table, we use Product Code to form the relationship. This means that every time the Product Code appears, the Materials Cost associated with that code will be added. We need the Materials Cost only once for each Job Number, but because each Job Number has 20 rows, it gets added 20 times. This is why we divide Materials Cost by 20 to find the Total Cost.

4. Drag **Total Cost** and **Job Number** to the report canvas, as shown in Lab Exhibit 4.5P.21. Select the **Clustered Column Chart** icon in the **Visualizations** pane and ensure that **Sum of Total Cost** is on the **Y-axis** and **JobNumber** is on the **X-axis**.

5. You should also show the cost as the **Data Labels** above each column. Do so by selecting the option shown in Lab Exhibit 4.5P.22. We also want to see only one product, so filter by **Product Code** and select GS3 (Lab Exhibit 4.5P.23). Change the title of the visualization to "GS3 Total Cost by JobNumber". See Lab Exhibit 4.5T.24.

Analysis Task #4: Use Data Visualization to Look for Anomalies

1. One of the benefits of visualization is that it allows you to see issues and anomalies. Create a visualization that shows the amount of scrapped cost for each job number. The *scrapped cost* is the cost of not producing the total batch capacity for a job. This can be calculated by creating a new calculated field. First, make sure you have the Production table highlighted. Click on the **Modeling** tab at the top of the screen. Select the icon for **Create New Column**. Change the name of the attribute to "Scrapped Cost". Then, as shown in Lab Exhibit 4.5P.25, type the following calculation into the window:

$$([\text{Materials Cost.1}]/[\text{BatchSize}])*([\text{BatchSize}]-[\text{CompletedUnits}])$$

Change the value display to **Currency** with two decimal places.

2. For this step, follow along with Exhibit 4.5P.26. Create a **Clustered Column Chart** by selecting that icon, and then drag **Job Number** and **Scrapped Cost** to the report canvas. Ensure **JobNumber** is on the **X-axis** and **Sum of Scrapped Cost** is on the **Y-Axis**. Scrapped Cost should sum automatically. Drag **Product Name** to the **Legend**. Sort the scrapped costs in descending order, which will show the jobs with the most scrapped costs first. To do this, you must first format the X-axis as categorical data, following the steps shown in Lab Exhibits 4.5P.27 and 4.5P.28. This resulting chart, shown in Lab Exhibit 4.5P.29, should reveal that most of the jobs that have scrapped costs are associated with Game Station NextGen. Change the title of this visualization to "Scrapped Cost by Job Number and Product Name".

3. Next, consider the possibility that there may be inefficiencies at specific workstations by creating a visualization that identifies outliers for time spent at each workstation. Use the circle views visualization again. As shown in Lab Exhibit 4.5P.30, drag **Workstation** and **Sum of Labor Minutes** to the report canvas. **Workstation** should be on the **X-Axis** and **Sum of Labor Minutes** on the Y-axis. Select the **scatter chart** icon on the **Visualizations** pane. You can see the result on the left side of Lab Exhibit 4.5P.30.

4. To show each production run separately, drag **JobNumber** to the **Legend**, as shown in Lab Exhibit 4.5T.31.

5. Sort by JobNumber to ensure all data points are shown on the visualization (Lab Exhibit 4.5P.32).

6. It will be helpful to see which product type was produced during each production run, which will help us determine if outliers occur more often when certain gaming systems are being produced. So, as shown in Lab Exhibit 4.5P.33, drag **Product Name** to **Filters**. Change the title of this visualization and sheet to "Labor Minutes Outlier Analysis."

Share the Story

Job costing requires companies to track direct materials and direct labor. In addition, companies must allocate overhead using a predetermined overhead rate. Understanding costs can improve decision making, as costs can inform company strategy.

To use job costing, companies must assign and total costs by a job, project, or client. Direct materials and direct labor are calculated by summing all transactions related to a job, while overhead is assigned based on a predetermined overhead rate. Job costing provides useful information to management about the costs and profitability of specific jobs, projects, and customers.

Using powerful visualization tools also allows companies to find insights, investigate anomalies, and identify opportunities. From our analysis, we determined that Game Station NextGen has the most scrapped costs at MC Gaming.

Assessment

1. Take screenshots of the data visualizations you produced and copy them to a Word document titled "Lab 4.5 Power BI Submission.docx".

2. Answer the questions about your visualizations in Connect and upload your Lab 4.5 Power BI Submission.docx via Connect if assigned.

Calculating Job Costs

Keywords

Data Visualization, Job Costing, Production Costs

Alt Lab 4.5 Data.xlsx is a dataset that contains MC Gaming's cost data for the first three quarters of 2023.

Required

Replicate the analysis tasks from Lab 4.5 Power BI to gain insights into MC Gaming's job costs using the **Alt Lab 4.5 Data.xlsx** dataset.

Note: For this dataset, Materials Costs and Hourly Labor Rates have increased. In addition, MC Gaming has changed how it allocates overhead. For this dataset, overhead is calculated as 9% of direct labor costs.

Data Dictionary

Production Worksheet

JobNumber	Unique identifier for a production run
ProductCode	Unique code to identify the gaming console
BatchSize	Number of gaming consoles that can be produced in a single production run
CompletedUnits	Number of gaming consoles that were actually produced during the production run
WS-XXX	Labor minutes spent at a given workstation during the production run

Materials Cost

ProductName	Full name for the product type
ProductCode	Unique identifier for the product type
Materials Cost	Standard cost for materials used to prepare 1 batch of 100 units of a product type (that is, materials cost for 1 production run)

Workstation Labor Cost

Workstation1	Unique code to identify each workstation. Labeled as Workstation1 because the field Workstation already exists in one of the related tables (specifically, the Production table)
Labor Cost Per Hour	Hourly wage for employee(s) associated with each workstation. For this example, each workstation has just one employee.

Assessment

1. Take screenshots of the data visualizations you produced and copy them to a Word document named "Alt Lab 4.5 Power BI Submission.docx".
2. Answer the questions about your visualizations in Connect and upload your Alt Lab 4.5 Power BI Submission.docx via Connect if assigned.

Chapter 5

Two-Stage Cost Allocations and Activity-Based Costing

A Look at This Chapter

This chapter builds on the job-order system by refining the process of overhead allocation through the use of overhead cost pools. First, it examines the use of two-stage cost allocations within a job-order cost system. Second, it describes the use of an activity-based costing system, which makes several improvements to the two-stage cost allocation process. Two-stage costing systems carefully analyze the cost drivers and business activities that result in increased overhead costs, leading to cost data that better reflect the accurate cost of providing goods and services.

Cost Accounting and Data Analytics

COST ACCOUNTING LEARNING OBJECTIVE		RELATED DATA ANALYTICS LAB(S)	LAB ANALYTICS TYPES
LO 5.1	Explain how two-stage costing works.	**Data Analytics Mini-Lab** Using Data to Analyze Allocation Bases	Descriptive, Predictive
		LAB 5.1 Excel Using Two-Stage Costing to Address a Hidden Cost Driver Difference (Heartwood)	Diagnostic, Predictive
		LAB 5.2 Excel Using Two-Stage Costing to Address a Hidden Cost Driver Difference	Diagnostic, Predictive
LO 5.2	Describe how activity-based costing improves cost information.	**LAB 5.3 Power BI/Tableau** Identifying Potential Cost Drivers and Creating Dashboards	Diagnostic, Predictive
LO 5.3	Explain the mechanics of activity-based costing.	**LAB 5.4 Excel** Estimating Activity-Based Costing Drivers with Regression Analysis	Diagnostic, Predictive
LO 5.4	Demonstrate how time-driven activity-based costing allocates overhead.	**LAB 5.5 Excel** Estimating Time-Driven Activity-Based Costing Drivers	Diagnostic, Predictive

Chapter Concepts and Career Skills

Learning About . . .	Helps with These Career Skills
Two-stage cost allocations	• Identifying allocation bases that are cost drivers
Activity-based costing	• Identifying which activities influence the cost of providing goods and services • Analyzing how business activities provide value to customers
When companies should use two-stage costing	• Recognizing that increased information comes at a cost • Conducting a cost-benefit analysis

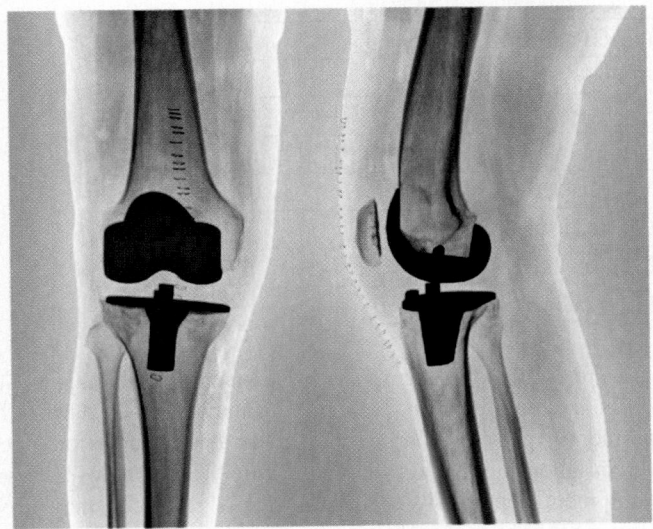

Zephyr/Getty Images

Determining the Cost of Knee Surgery

Knee-replacement surgery was first performed in 1968. Over the past several decades, the surgery has become safer and more common. In the United States, more than half a million knee-replacement surgeries are performed each year, using a highly standardized operating procedure. Despite this standardization, there is substantial variation in the cost of performing knee surgeries. Why? The cost of running an operating room is several thousand dollars per hour, and the cost of the hospital room in which patients recover from the surgery is also significant. Historically, medical professionals and hospital personnel have found it very difficult to predict how long surgery and recovery will take, and time is an important cost driver of medical costs.

A time-driven activity-based costing system allows medical care providers to use patients' data to estimate the cost of surgeries with greater reliability and accuracy than traditional cost systems do. Researchers have found that several patient-level attributes can predict surgery time and recovery time. For example, the length of knee replacement surgery varies reliably with a patient's health, age, race, and gender. Specifically, men require 4.9 more minutes of operating time than women do, but less recovery time in the hospital. Using a sophisticated activity-based costing system provides administrators with a better understanding of these costs and how they should be allocated to individual patients.

Sources: R. Balakrishnan, A. J. Pugely, and A. S. Shah, "Modeling Resource Use with Time Equations: Empirical Evidence," *Journal of Management Accounting Research* 29, no. 1 (2017), pp. 1–12.

LO 5.1

Explain how two-stage costing works.

TWO-STAGE COST ALLOCATION

Better cost information leads to better decision making. Gathering data about direct costs is relatively easy because direct costs are traced to **cost objects**, which are any units or items to which costs are assigned, such as a job, a product, or a customer. Gathering data about indirect costs such as manufacturing overhead is far more difficult because indirect costs are not traced to cost objects, and therefore we do not know how much indirect cost should

cost object
Anything for which a measurement of costs is wanted or needed.

allocation base
The basis on which costs are assigned to cost objects. Allocation bases include direct labor hours, direct labor costs, and machine hours. Ideally, allocation bases should be cost drivers.

cost driver
A variable that has a causal relationship with costs, such that more or less of the cost driver will result in more or less cost.

be assigned to individual cost objects. For this reason, companies use an **allocation base** to allocate indirect costs to cost objects using a predetermined overhead rate. For example, companies may allocate manufacturing overhead to cost objects on the basis of direct labor hours or machine hours. Or they may allocate manufacturing overhead as a percentage of direct labor costs or as a set amount per unit produced.

In Chapter 4, we discussed the importance of selecting an allocation base that is a cost driver. Recall that a **cost driver** is a variable that has a causal relationship with costs, such that more of the cost driver or less of the cost driver results in more cost or less cost. However, using a single allocation base to allocate indirect costs ignores the reality that different types of overhead costs have different cost drivers. Consider the following potential sources of manufacturing overhead in a typical manufacturing facility:

Manufacturing Overhead Components
Rent on production facilities
Property taxes on production facilities
Utilities
Supervisor labor
Quality control labor
Maintenance labor
Equipment depreciation
Indirect materials
Janitorial labor

CAREER SKILLS
Learning about two-stage cost allocations supports this career skill:
• Identifying allocation bases that are cost drivers

Although all of these costs are included in a company's financial statements as manufacturing overhead, they differ in terms of how they are consumed or used during the production process. For example, direct labor hours are generally a cost driver for supervisor labor (because more direct labor hours lead to increased supervisor costs), but they may have little effect on equipment depreciation. Similarly, units produced may drive the cost of quality control but probably have no effect on the rent or property taxes on the production facilities.

The following Data Analytics Mini-Lab demonstrates how companies can use data to determine the cause-effect relationship between allocation bases and indirect costs.

DATA ANALYTICS MINI-LAB
Using Data to Analyze Allocation Bases

Data Analytics Types: Descriptive, Predictive

Lab Note: The tools presented in this lab periodically change. Updated instructions, if applicable, can be found in the student and instructor support materials.

Keywords
Allocation Bases, Cost Drivers

Decision-Making Context
Ideally, allocation bases should be cost drivers, meaning that the allocation bases used to assign indirect costs should influence those indirect costs.

Nonno's Pizza Ovens (a fictional company) recently began producing portable pizza ovens. These ovens are constructed from stainless steel, and they can reach a temperature of nearly 1,000 degrees, providing backyard enthusiasts with the opportunity to bake Neapolitan-style pizzas in minutes.

Ask the Question

Nonno's produces several oven models. They come in different sizes and use various fuel sources. Historically, Nonno's has allocated overhead costs based on direct labor hours. However, management believes that it's time to reevaluate the company's cost data to determine if direct labor hours is a cost driver for Nonno's indirect costs.

Required

1. Produce a correlation matrix to identify potential cost drivers for Nonno's indirect costs.
2. Use regression analysis to examine the statistical significance of Nonno's cost drivers.
3. Make a recommendation to Nonno's management for appropriate cost drivers.

Master the Data

Open the Excel file titled **Mini-Lab 5 Data.xlsx** (reproduced in Exhibit A). You will see Nonno's production and costs for the previous 12 months. In addition to monthly production, direct labor hours, and machine hours, Nonno's collects data for three sources of indirect cost: indirect materials, maintenance, and indirect labor.

	A	B	C	D	E	F	G
1		Production (units)	Direct Labor Hours	Machine Hours	Indirect Materials	Maintenance	Indirect Labor
2	January	8,000	3,433	996	$ 20,544	$ 20,169	$ 40,132
3	February	8,200	2,015	978	$ 21,074	$ 21,281	$ 22,931
4	March	7,700	2,692	959	$ 19,835	$ 20,101	$ 30,877
5	April	8,100	1,804	985	$ 21,036	$ 20,084	$ 19,086
6	May	8,800	2,256	974	$ 23,223	$ 21,068	$ 24,703
7	June	8,600	1,907	970	$ 21,638	$ 20,622	$ 19,814
8	July	9,400	2,166	980	$ 24,036	$ 21,315	$ 22,461
9	August	10,100	2,829	972	$ 25,361	$ 20,597	$ 30,864
10	September	10,100	2,745	992	$ 26,321	$ 21,209	$ 31,869
11	October	10,500	2,524	938	$ 27,594	$ 19,904	$ 29,985
12	November	10,000	3,155	960	$ 25,050	$ 20,410	$ 32,749
13	December	9,900	3,278	960	$ 24,305	$ 19,277	$ 33,370

Exhibit A

Microsoft Excel

Perform the Analysis

Analysis Task #1: Perform Correlation Analysis

1. On the **Data** menu, select **Data Analysis > Correlation** (Exhibit B). Click **OK**. This lab requires Excel's Analysis ToolPak. If you do not have the Analysis ToolPak installed, see the instructions in Appendix D.

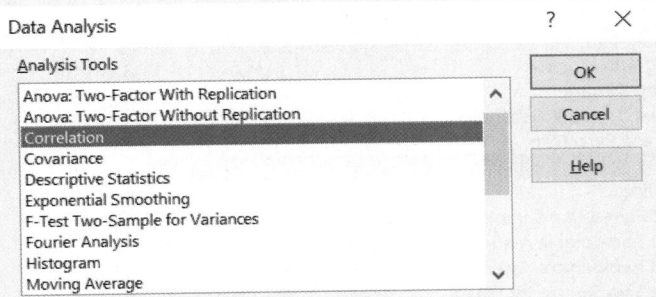

Exhibit B

Microsoft Excel

2. The **Input Range** should be $B$1:$G$13. Because we have included labels in our selection, make sure to check the box next to **Labels in First Row**. The **Output Range** should be $A$15 (Exhibit C). Click **OK**.

Exhibit C

Microsoft Excel

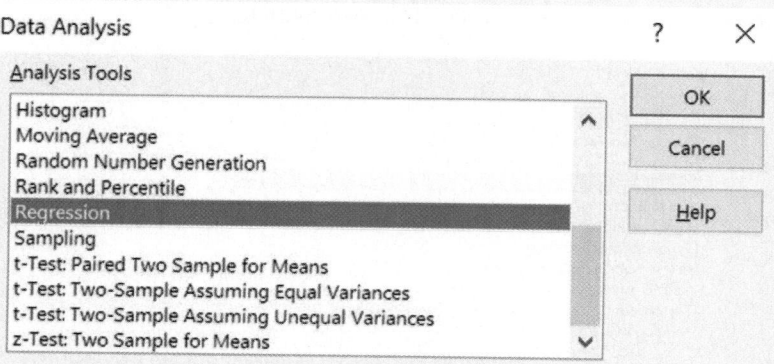

3. Highlight the highest correlation between each potential cost driver and each indirect cost (Exhibit D).

Exhibit D

Microsoft Excel

	Production (units)	Direct Labor Hours	Machine Hours	Indirect Materials	Maintenance	Indirect Labor
Production (units)	1.000					
Direct Labor Hours	0.320	1.000				
Machine Hours	-0.408	-0.074	1.000			
Indirect Materials	0.978	0.239	-0.390	1.000		
Maintenance	-0.064	-0.466	0.481	0.014	1.000	
Indirect Labor	0.253	0.966	-0.034	0.214	-0.404	1.000

The highlighted cells are likely cost drivers. However, the correlation analysis in Excel does not provide the statistical significance of these correlations. To determine if the highlighted correlations are significant, we will run regressions to determine how our allocation bases (that is, production units, direct labor hours, and machine hours) affect indirect costs. In other words, which allocation bases are cost drivers?

Analysis Task #2: Use Regression Analysis to Verify Potential Cost Drivers

1. On the **Data** menu, select **Data Analysis > Regression** (Exhibit E). Click **OK**.

Exhibit E

Microsoft Excel

2. The **Y range** is the indirect cost category we're analyzing. Select indirect materials data ($E$1:$E$13) for our first regression. The **X range** will include all potential cost drivers ($B$1:$D$13). Click the box next to **Labels** to include labels, and send the regression output to a new worksheet. See Exhibit F.

Exhibit F

Microsoft Excel

Regression	? ✕

Input

Input Y Range: `$E$1:$E$13` ⬆

Input X Range: `$B$1:$D$13` ⬆

☑ Labels ☐ Constant is Zero

☐ Confidence Level: `95` %

OK

Cancel

Help

Output options

○ Output Range: ⬆

◉ New Worksheet Ply:

○ New Workbook

Residuals

☐ Residuals ☐ Residual Plots

☐ Standardized Residuals ☐ Line Fit Plots

Normal Probability

☐ Normal Probability Plots

3. Perform the same regression analysis twice more, changing the **Y range** for the other two indirect cost categories (maintenance and indirect labor). The results of the regressions are shown in Exhibits G, H, and I.

SUMMARY OUTPUT FOR INDIRECT MATERIALS

Regression Statistics	
Multiple R	0.98
R Square	0.96
Adjusted R Square	0.95
Standard Error	566.25
Observations	12

ANOVA

	df	SS	MS	F	Significance F
Regression	3	66296010.98	22098670.33	68.92	4.67E-06
Residual	8	2565081.47	320635.184		
Total	11	68861092.45			

	Coefficients	Standard Error	t Stat	P-value	Lower 95%	Upper 95%
Intercept	-1309.28	12073.79	-0.11	0.92	-29151.48	26532.93
Production (units)	2.55	0.20	12.83	1.29E-06	2.09	3.01
Direct Labor Hours	-0.38	0.33	-1.16	0.28	-1.14	0.38
Machine Hours	2.44	11.61	0.21	0.84	-24.34	29.21

Exhibit G

Microsoft Excel

Exhibit H

Microsoft Excel

SUMMARY OUTPUT FOR MAINTENANCE

Regression Statistics	
Multiple R	0.71
R Square	0.51
Adjusted R Square	0.32
Standard Error	522.54
Observations	12

ANOVA

	df	SS	MS	F	Significance F
Regression	3	2240155.65	746718.5494	2.73	1.13E-01
Residual	8	2184377.27	273047.1585		
Total	11	4424532.92			

	Coefficients	Standard Error	t Stat	P-value	Lower 95%	Upper 95%
Intercept	-2149.64	11141.84	-0.19	0.85	-27842.76	23543.48
Production (units)	0.22	0.18	1.20	0.26	-0.20	0.64
Direct Labor Hours	-0.62	0.30	-2.03	0.08	-1.32	0.08
Machine Hours	22.87	10.71	2.13	0.07	-1.84	47.57

Indirect Labor SUMMARY OUTPUT FOR INDIRECT LABOR

Regression Statistics	
Multiple R	0.97
R Square	0.94
Adjusted R Square	0.91
Standard Error	1890.04
Observations	12

ANOVA

	df	SS	MS	F	Significance F
Regression	3	418429310.59	139476436.9	39.04	4.00E-05
Residual	8	28577901.66	3572237.707		
Total	11	447007212.25			

	Coefficients	Standard Error	t Stat	P-value	Lower 95%	Upper 95%
Intercept	-3694.77	40300.29	-0.09	0.93	-96627.40	89237.86
Production (units)	-0.36	0.66	-0.55	0.60	-1.90	1.17
Direct Labor Hours	11.46	1.10	10.41	6.27E-06	8.93	14.00
Machine Hours	5.99	38.75	0.15	0.88	-83.36	95.35

Exhibit I

Microsoft Excel

4. Large *t*-stats and small *p*-values[1] (highlighted in yellow) indicate significant relationships between independent variables (allocation bases) and dependent variables (indirect cost categories). For more information on interpreting the output of regression analyses, see Chapter 3 and Appendix E. Notice that the results of the regression analyses support the correlations identified in Exhibit B. Regression analysis suggests that units produced is a cost driver for indirect materials, machine hours is a cost driver for maintenance, and direct labor hours is a cost driver for indirect labor. Clearly, direct labor hours is not a suitable cost driver for all indirect costs.

[1]In Exhibits G and I, the *p*-value is listed in scientific notation: for example, 6.27E-06. The "E-06" means to move the decimal point in 6.27 six places to the left. Therefore, the *p*-value here is 0.00000627, which is a tiny value.

Share the Story

Our correlation and regression analyses allowed us to determine that direct labor hours are not a good cost driver for all indirect costs at Nonno's Pizza Ovens. Instead, our analysis suggests that units produced drive indirect materials cost, machine hours drive maintenance costs, and direct labor hours drive indirect labor costs.

A job-order costing system that allocates indirect costs on the basis of a single allocation base is prone to error because it ignores the fact that overhead costs have different cost drivers. This issue can be addressed through the use of two-stage cost allocation.

Mini-Lab Assessment

1. Based on regression analysis, how does the production of a single unit influence indirect materials cost (that is, by what amount)?
2. Based on regression analysis, how does the use of a machine hour influence the cost of maintenance?
3. Direct labor hours has a statistically significant effect on maintenance costs. Why isn't direct labor hours a good cost driver for maintenance costs? What does our regression analysis tell us about the relationship between direct labor hours and machine hours?

Two-stage cost allocation improves cost information by improving the cause-effect relationship between allocation bases and indirect costs. In the first stage, total manufacturing overhead is subdivided into various pools based on distinct cost drivers. In the second stage, costs from each cost pool are allocated to individual cost objects. Many companies, such as **Coca-Cola** and **UPS**, have greatly benefited from two-stage cost systems that provide a better understanding of costs. Let's now use an example to illustrate the use of a two-stage cost allocation within a job-order cost system, and then let's examine how it compares with a job-order cost system that uses a single-stage cost allocation for manufacturing overhead.

two-stage cost allocation
A method of cost allocation that first allocates costs to cost pools, and then allocates costs from cost pools to cost objects.

Comparison of Single- and Two-Stage Overhead Cost Allocations

Skyrite is a fictitious company that produces and sells two models of drones. It produces approximately 4,000 photography drones and 1,000 racing drones per month. Table 5.1 summarizes information regarding manufacturing overhead and production at Skyrite.

Let's first examine overhead cost allocations using a single-stage allocation, shown in Exhibit 5.1. In this case, all $500,000 of manufacturing overhead is allocated to units using a single allocation base, which for Skyrite is direct labor hours. The predetermined overhead rate (labeled as POR in Exhibits 5.1 and 5.2) is $62.50 per direct labor hour, or DLH ($500,000 overhead/8,000 direct labor hours). Overhead is then allocated to each drone on the basis of direct labor hours per unit. As reported in the Skyrite Monthly Production Information in Table 5.1, the photography drone requires 1.5 DLH and the racing drone requires 2.0 DLH. Therefore, each photography drone is allocated $93.75 in overhead, while each racing drone is allocated $125 in overhead.

Single-stage cost allocations can lead to distorted costs because they fail to account for the fact that manufacturing overhead costs have various cost drivers. Let's examine Skyrite's manufacturing overhead costs in greater detail. After some investigation,

Table 5.1
Manufacturing Overhead and Production at Skyrite

Skyrite Manufacturing Overhead Costs	
Indirect materials	$100,000
Quality control costs	$ 50,000
Indirect labor	$150,000
Equipment maintenance	$150,000
Equipment depreciation	$ 50,000
Total Monthly Overhead (MOH)	**$500,000**

Skyrite Monthly Production Information					
	Monthly Units	Direct Labor Hours/Unit	Monthly Direct Labor Hours (DLH)	Machine Hours/Unit	Monthly Machine Hours (MH)
Photography drone	4,000 units	1.5 hours	6,000 hours	0.5 hour	2,000 hours
Racing drone	1,000 units	2.0 hours	2,000 hours	3.0 hours	3,000 hours
Total	5,000 units		8,000 hours		5,000 hours

Exhibit 5.1
Single-Stage Overhead Allocation

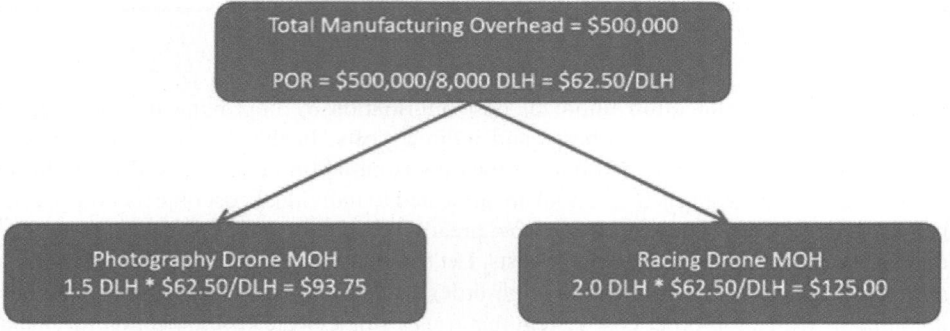

DLH = Direct labor hours
MOH = Manufacturing overhead
POR = Predetermined overhead rate

Skyrite management learns that both types of drones use approximately equal indirect materials and require similar quality-control costs. Thus, it makes sense to allocate these costs ($100,000 + $50,000 = $150,000, based on Table 5.1) on the basis of units produced. Indirect labor ($150,000) consists primarily of supervisors overseeing direct labor, so it makes sense to allocate indirect labor on the basis of direct labor hours. Equipment maintenance and depreciation ($150,000 + $50,000 = $200,000) are related to the use of machinery used during the manufacturing process, so it makes sense to allocate these costs on the basis of machine hours.

The first stage of a two-stage allocation, shown in Exhibit 5.2, is to subdivide the total manufacturing overhead costs into cost pools based on allocation bases. A **cost pool** is any grouping or category of costs. Companies can use as many cost pools as they desire. In this example, Skyrite will use three cost pools: one each for manufacturing overhead cost driven by (1) units produced, (2) direct labor hours, and (3) machine hours. Notice that the sum of manufacturing overhead in the cost pools is equal to total manufacturing overhead for the company (MOH = $500,000). Rather than calculating a single predetermined

cost pool
A grouping or category of costs.

overhead rate for total overhead, Skyrite must calculate a predetermined overhead rate for each cost pool. In this case, the allocation rates are calculated as follows (refer again to Table 5.1 to understand where these numbers come from):

- Unit-related MOH: $150,000 (Indirect materials + Quality control costs)/5,000 units produced = $30.00/Unit
- Direct labor hour–related MOH: $150,000 (Indirect labor)/8,000 DLH = $18.75/ Direct labor hour
- Machine hour–related MOH: $200,000 (Equipment maintenance + Equipment depreciation)/5,000 MH = $40.00/Machine hour

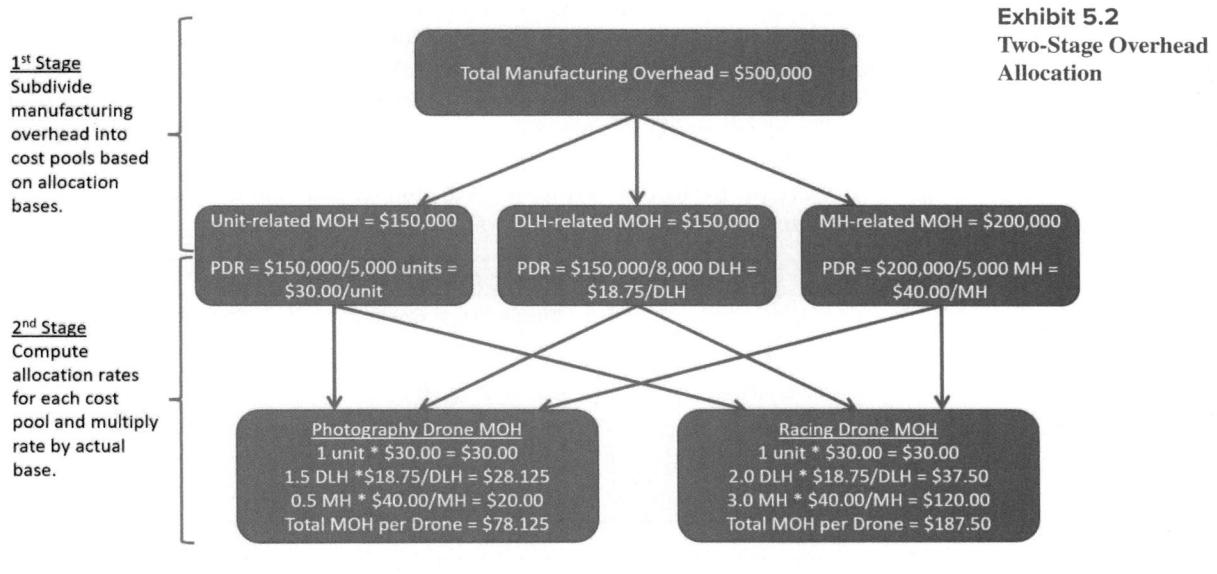

Exhibit 5.2
Two-Stage Overhead Allocation

DLH = Direct labor hours
MH = Machine hours
MOH = Manufacturing overhead
POR = Predetermined overhead rate

In the second stage of a two-stage overhead allocation, overhead is allocated to units based on Skyrite's predetermined overhead rates, as shown in the last row of Exhibit 5.2. Note that we are computing the cost allocation for one unit, so the allocation for unit-related overhead is the same for both drone types ($30.00), while overhead allocations from the other two cost pools differ between drone types. Also note that the numbers we are using to calculate DLH and MH come from the yellow-highlighted boxes in Table 5.1 and the 1st Stage row of Exhibit 5.2.

Using a two-stage overhead allocation, we calculate the manufacturing overhead cost of a photography drone to be $78.125, while the overhead cost of a racing drone is $187.50. Compare these overhead estimates with those calculated using a single-stage allocation:

Per-Unit Overhead Cost per Drone		
	Single-stage allocation	Two-stage allocation
Photography drone	$ 93.75	$ 78.125
Racing drone	$125.00	$187.50

overcosted

When a product is over-costed, a company's cost system has assigned (allocated) more cost to a good or service than is accurate.

Which cost data are correct? The answer is most likely that neither set is correct. Both single-stage and two-stage allocations are estimates. However, two-stage costing produces better estimates because it is less susceptible to the cost distortions resulting from assigning costs that are not caused by allocation bases. With either allocation method, all $500,000 in overhead costs are assigned to the units. In this case, a cost comparison across allocation methods, conducted by Skyrite's management accountants, shows that under a single-stage allocation, overhead costs are distorted. Specifically, photography drones are **overcosted** under a single-stage allocation, meaning that they were allocated more cost than is accurate. Another way to think about overcosted products is that they are cheaper to produce than the company realizes. In contrast, racing drones are **undercosted**, meaning that they were allocated less cost than is accurate. Under a single-stage allocation, photography drones were essentially subsidizing the racing drones by assuming less than their fair share of cost.

undercosted

When a product is undercosted, a company's cost system has assigned (allocated) less cost to a good or service than is accurate.

Why is inaccurate cost information a problem? Assume that because of the way Skyrite allocates indirect costs to drones, the company believes it can produce a racing drone for $650 (including direct costs). In this case, the company may be happy to sell the product for $700. What if, unbeknownst to Skyrite, a more accurate cost of a racing drone is $712.50? In this case, the harder Skyrite works to produce and sell racing drones, the faster the company loses money, as Table 5.2 shows.

Table 5.2
Skyrite Profitability Based on Single-Stage and Two-Stage Costing

Calculated Racing Drone Profitability		
	Single-Stage Costing	**Two-Stage Costing**
Revenue	$700.00	$700.00
Less: Direct materials	$375.00	$375.00
Direct labor	$150.00	$150.00
Allocated indirect costs	$125.00	$187.50
Profit	**$ 50.00**	**$ (12.50)**

Clearly, better cost information leads to better decisions. With accurate cost information, Skyrite will have a better understanding of which products can compete effectively in the market, which may lead it to drop product lines whose costs are higher than competitors'. Skyrite may also choose to focus on products that have higher margins, perhaps putting more marketing effort into more profitable products.

That said, gathering more accurate cost information requires considerable time and resources, and companies must determine whether the value of more accurate information is worth the company resources necessary to obtain that information. At many companies, a single allocation rate may provide cost data that are sufficiently accurate for their purposes.

🔍 LAB CONNECTION

LAB 5.1 EXCEL and **LAB 5.2 EXCEL** use Excel to help you learn the steps of two-stage costing and why two-stage allocations can improve cost information.

✓ PROGRESS CHECK

1. Why does a two-stage costing system use multiple manufacturing overhead allocation bases?

2. Two-stage overhead allocations are based on the premise that overhead costs should be allocated according to cost drivers. What are some examples of overhead costs for which there are no good cost drivers?

ACTIVITY-BASED COSTING

LO 5.2

Describe how activity-based costing improves cost information.

As we've seen, a two-stage allocation of overhead costs can generate improved cost information by improving the cause-effect relationship between cost driver and indirect costs. **Activity-based costing** relies on this same premise, but to a much greater degree. Activity-based costing is a two-stage costing system that assigns indirect costs to activities, and then allocates activity costs to cost objects such as jobs or products.

Indirect Costs in an Activity-Based Costing System

Let's first consider indirect costs. Under GAAP, the cost of inventory must include the cost of all indirect manufacturing costs, or manufacturing overhead. Therefore, the only indirect costs considered by a job-order cost system are manufacturing overhead costs. However, many *nonmanufacturing costs* can be attributed to specific cost objects as well. For instance, some products incur extensive warranty expenses or require above-average advertising expenses. Activity-based costing uses a more holistic approach to indirect costs, and considers both indirect manufacturing and indirect nonmanufacturing costs when assigning the total cost of a cost object. Importantly, *all* indirect costs should be assigned to cost objects based on a cause-effect relationship, such that the cost object that causes the cost or uses the resources should bear the cost of those resources.

Companies that use activity-based costing usually avoid assigning indirect costs to cost objects in the absence of a cause-effect relationship. For instance, companies may not be able to attribute rent on a production facility to a particular job. GAAP requires this rent to be included in the cost of inventory, and so it is often assigned to cost objects using an arbitrary overhead rate. However, because activity-based costing focuses on the cause-effect relationship between cost drivers and indirect costs, companies using activity-based costing typically choose to expense these types of costs as a period expense.

activity-based costing
A two-stage costing system that assigns indirect costs to activity cost pools, and then allocates activity costs to the other cost objects such as jobs or products.

Activity Cost Pools in an Activity-Based Costing System

In a job-order cost system, two-stage costing assigns indirect costs to cost pools and then allocates costs to units to determine unit-level costs. Activity-based costing refines the idea of cost pools by assigning costs to specific activities. An **activity** is any event or task performed for a specific purpose during the course of operations. In activity-based costing systems, cost pools are often called **activity cost pools**.

Activity-based costing recognizes that many activities contribute to the cost of an object. These activities include processing purchase orders, designing products, setting up machines, repairing equipment, and handling consumer complaints. Instead of thinking about these activities as strictly fixed costs or strictly variable costs, activity-based costing views activities on a fixed/variable continuum, as Exhibit 5.3 shows.

Activity cost pools can be related to activities taking place at the unit level, batch level, product line-level, or facility level. Each level of activity has a corresponding level of costs. **Unit-level costs** are incurred in the production of individual goods and services. They are tied to production volume, and they rise with each unit produced. Costs related to direct materials used in production or indirect materials are examples of unit-level costs. **Batch-level costs** are incurred on a group of jobs or products. These might include setting up equipment for a production run or placing purchase orders.

activity
Any event or task performed for a specific purpose during the course of operations.

activity cost pool
A grouping or category of costs associated with performing an activity or task.

unit-level costs
Costs incurred in the production of goods and services that increase with each additional unit of production.

batch-level costs
Costs associated with batch-level activities, or tasks performed for a group of jobs or products.

Exhibit 5.3
Activities Levels

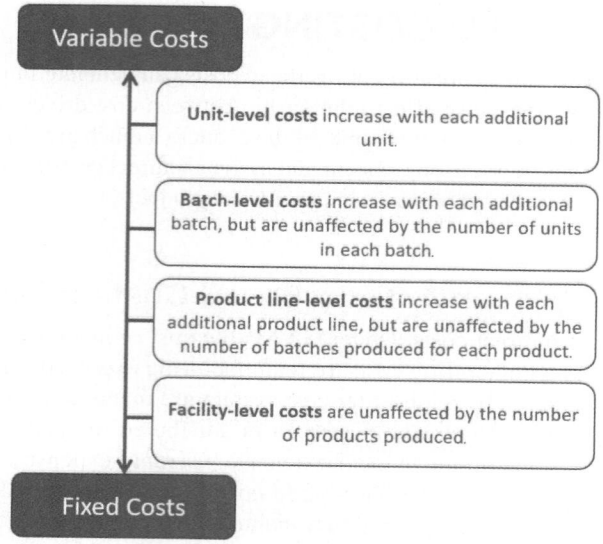

product line-level costs

Costs associated with producing a line of products or services.

facility-level costs

The broader set of overhead costs that relate to all of the firm's products or jobs.

Product line-level costs, or product-line costs, are associated with producing a line of products or services. They increase with each product or SKU offered by a firm. Product engineering costs and the costs of patenting a product design are examples of product-line costs. **Facility-level costs**, or facility-support costs, are the broader set of indirect costs that relate to all the firm's products or services. They are "true" fixed costs, and they include many administrative tasks such as security as well as building depreciation and factory rent.

It is important to understand the fixed and variable nature of various activities. As an example, consider product-line costs such as engineering a new product or acquiring a patent on a new product. These costs can be significant. They are variable in the sense that each new product will require additional product-line costs. However, they are fixed in the sense that they do not change with the number of batches of the new product produced.

Companies that implement activity-based costing may have dozens of activities and activity cost pools. Each activity cost pool should have a cost driver that aligns with that level of activity cost pool. For instance, all unit-level costs should have a unit-level cost driver, as these costs rise and fall with the number of units produced. Similarly, batch and product-line costs should have batch and product-line cost drivers, respectively.

Importantly, unit-level, batch-level, and product-line costs are all allocated as product costs in an activity-based cost system. In contrast, costs associated with facility-level activities generally are not allocated to individual jobs or products. Instead, they are kept separate because the causal link between facility-level activities and individual units is weak and would require a more arbitrary basis for allocating costs (just as we sometimes allocate overhead costs to products under job-order costing).

Let's walk through an example to see how these different levels of costs work in practice. Consider **Panera Bread**, which makes a variety of pastries and desserts (among other tasty items). Assume that we've been tasked with grouping the following costs into activity cost pools:

Even without specialized knowledge of baking, we can probably group these costs by level, as shown in Exhibit 5.4. Costs that are driven by the number of units produced will be

Costs	Level
Indirect materials (for example, yeast)	
Indirect labor—bakery security	
Indirect labor—production supervisor	
Depreciation on production equipment	
Lease on bakery facility	
Designing a recipe	
Determining nutritional information	
Quality control	
Custodial services	

classified as unit-level costs. These costs include indirect materials, indirect labor, and perhaps depreciation on production equipment (assuming that each unit decreases the life of the asset). Quality control (such as taste testing) and custodial services do not need to be performed for every unit. Instead, these costs are likely to occur during or after every batch. The number of product lines drives some of these costs, as each new product requires a recipe and nutritional information. Finally, facility-level costs are grouped together in a separate cost pool. Why? There is no good cost driver for these costs. There is a weak causal link between these costs and individual units, and there is little (if anything) managers can do to manage these costs.

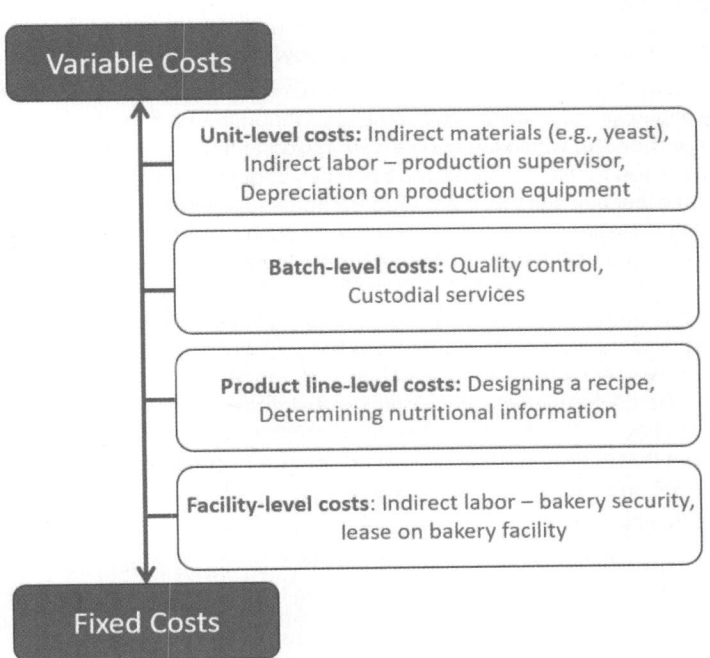

Exhibit 5.4
Activity Levels
for Panera Bread
Example

Often, companies have some costs that span multiple cost pools. Indirect labor costs are a good example. An engineer may spend much of her time evaluating batches of product to determine if certain quality standards are met, but she may also spend time designing new products. While her varied activities may increase the difficulty of using activity-based costing, the objective remains the same: We want to subdivide all indirect costs into activity cost pools that behave similarly.

Activity-Based Costing Informs Company Strategy

Although an activity-based costing system is more complicated than a traditional costing system, remember that it relies on a strong causal relationship between cost drivers and indirect costs. This cause-effect relationship is key because it leads to important strategic decisions.

For starters, identifying relevant cost drivers helps management determine which activities can be minimized to save costs. For instance, if **Panera** can create goods in bigger batches, it could reduce batch costs while producing the same number of goods.

Alternatively, if a company has significant product-level costs, management should consider minimizing the number of different products it sells. This approach has been used with great success by **Chick-fil-A**, which is known for efficiency partly because the company sells a far smaller variety of products than its competitors. Low-cost airlines use a similar strategy. By minimizing the type of aircraft used in their fleets, **Southwest**, **Ryanair**, and **Easyjet** need fewer spare parts than competitors, which reduces storage costs and downtime for maintenance.

Management often evaluates a company's business activities by comparing the cost of an activity with the value the activity adds for the customer. This analysis, known as **activity-based management**, requires the accurate cost data provided by activity-based costing.

activity-based management
A method of using activity-based costing information to evaluate how a company's activities provide value to customers. Companies can improve operations and customer satisfaction by focusing resources on activities that provide value to customers.

FROM THE FIELD

Using Activity-Based Costing to Reduce Downtime

One of the authors of this text once had the opportunity to tour a manufacturing facility of a major pharmaceutical company. During the tour, the author saw several large rooms in which chemicals were mixed to make medicine tablets and was surprised to learn that between batches of different medicines, employees dressed in hazmat suits worked 40 to 50 hours to sanitize these mixing rooms. Given the risks of cross-contamination of pharmaceuticals (it's literally a life-and-death situation), it makes sense for the company to incur the considerable time and expense.

One way to cut down on cleaning expenses (a batch-level cost) is to combine batches of the same drug or structure production to minimize the number of times the company switches back and forth between drugs. However, given the size and complexity of large companies, many of these insights go unnoticed because companies do not have accurate information about cost drivers. This is precisely the type of information that activity-based costing can provide to companies—information that leads to insight and improved strategic decisions.

Thinking Critically

It is likely that production workers noticed the inefficiencies resulting from switching between medications. What steps can companies take to encourage employees to pass on cost-saving ideas to decision makers?

🔍 LAB CONNECTION

LAB 5.3 POWER BI/TABLEAU asks you to use data visualization software to identify potential cost drivers and create dashboards that companies can use to monitor those cost drivers.

✓ PROGRESS CHECK

3. What are the four levels of costs in an activity-based costing system?
4. Why aren't facility support costs always allocated to jobs or products under activity-based costing?

DETERMINING A JOB'S COST USING ACTIVITY-BASED COSTING

Now that you understand the basics of activity-based costing, we will discuss the mechanics of cost allocation under an activity-based costing system. You will notice that the two-stage process for activity-based costing is the same as the two-stage process used in some job-order cost systems, except that activity-based costing uses a wider variety of indirect costs, and cost pools are more closely related to the activities that influence an organization's indirect costs. Here we will illustrate the cost allocation process by using data from a Brazilian division of **Heartwood Cabinets** as summarized in Exhibit 5.5.

Overhead Costs	
Employee wages	$ 500,000
Machine maintenance	$ 300,000
Factory administration	$ 200,000
Total	$1,000,000

	Resource Consumption by Activity				
	Quality Control (Unit level)	Equipment Setup (Batch level)	Custom Product Design (Product level)	Facility-Supporting (Facility level)	Total
Employee wages	60%	25%	10%	5%	100%
Machine maintenance	50%	30%	10%	10%	100%
Factory administration	20%	40%	30%	10%	100%

First-stage allocations—Allocate indirect costs to activity pools based on resource consumption

	Activity Cost Pools				
	Quality Control (60%)	Equipment Setup (25%)	Custom Product Design (10%)	Facility Support (5%)	Total
Employee wages	$300,000	$125,000	$ 50,000	$25,000	$ 500,000
Machine maintenance	$150,000	$ 90,000	$ 30,000	$30,000	$ 300,000
Factory administration	$ 40,000	$ 80,000	$ 60,000	$20,000	$ 200,000
Total	$490,000	$295,000	$140,000	$75,000	$1,000,000

Exhibit 5.5
Heartwood Activity-Based Costing Data

LO 5.3

Explain the mechanics of activity-based costing.

Stage 1: Grouping Costs by Cost Pool

Heartwood has determined that its total indirect costs are $1,000,000 (see the yellow highlights in Exhibit 5.5): indirect employee wages of $500,000, machine maintenance of $300,000, and other factory-related administrative overhead of $200,000. The first-stage allocation for activity-based costing involves determining how to subdivide total indirect costs to various activity cost pools. Heartwood has determined that it has four activity cost pools. Referring to Exhibit 5.5, we see that the activities that Heartwood has identified are quality control, equipment setup, custom product design, and facility support. Quality control is a unit-level cost, equipment setup is a batch-level cost, and custom product design is a product-line cost.

This process may seem somewhat complicated because the sources of our indirect costs (employee wages, machine maintenance, and factory administration) do not align perfectly with the cost pools. For example, indirect employee labor supports various activities. How does management know how to assign these costs to activity cost pools? Activity-based costing requires a significant amount of investigation, usually in the form of employee surveys and other analysis, to determine how activities consume company resources, and how the cost of these resources (that is, indirect costs) should be grouped. For this reason, allocating the cost of firm resources to activity cost pools is the most difficult aspect of using an activity-based costing system. At Heartwood, management determines that for employee wages, 60% is spent on quality control, 25% is spent setting up equipment, 10% is spent designing custom products, and the remaining 5% supports the facility. We must therefore divide the $500,000 in total employee wages into the four cost pools based on these relative proportions. In Exhibit 5.5, the allocations are shown in the "Employee Wages" row under the heading "First-stage allocations—Allocate indirect costs to activity pools based on resource consumption."

We use the same process to subdivide our other indirect costs into the most appropriate activity cost pools. After completing the first-stage allocations, we calculate the total amount allocated to each cost pool. The four activity cost pool totals are as follows (see the final row of Exhibit 5.5):

Quality control:	$ 490,000
Equipment setup:	$ 295,000
Custom product design:	$ 140,000
Facility support:	$ 75,000
Total:	$1,000,000

Notice that the total amount of indirect costs ($1,000,000) has not changed. Rather, we have subdivided the total indirect costs into smaller activity cost pools such that there is an improved cause-effect relationship between indirect costs and the cost drivers causing the costs to be incurred (with the exception of facility-level costs).

FROM THE FIELD

Tracing Costs to Remove the Need for Allocation

Allocation always involves some element of guesswork. Traced costs are directly attributed to jobs or products, which removes the need for allocation. Therefore, one way to improve the accuracy of cost information is to increase the number of costs that are traced, which allows companies to reclassify indirect costs as direct costs.

Consider labor costs. In some industries such as accounting, legal services, and consulting, employees track their time in 15-minute increments, which are then traced to specific jobs. Tracing labor decreases indirect costs and provides more accurate cost information.

In many cases, tracing labor costs may not be practical, even though companies can do so. Consider a supervisor who oversees dozens of employees who work on separate projects. In this case, the cost of tracing supervisor labor may outweigh the benefits of more accurate cost data.

Thinking Critically

Companies have greatly increased tracing of the environmental costs of providing goods and services in the past several years. How might the specific identification of environmental costs have altered company behavior as it pertains to companies' ESG efforts? How will these efforts be impacted by ESG reporting regulations?

ENVIRONMENTAL, SOCIAL, GOVERNANCE

Stage 2: Allocating Costs to Cost Objects

The second-stage allocation assigns costs from each activity cost pool to cost objects. Recall that a cost object can be any job, product, or customer to which a company wants to assign costs. This process should seem familiar, as it is identical to the process used in job-order costing.

To complete second-stage allocations, we must first calculate the application rates for each activity. Consider Exhibit 5.6, which provides information about each cost pool and the associated cost drivers. First, we estimate the total activity level of each cost driver for the reporting period. Then, we calculate the overhead application rates by dividing each cost pool's total allocated overhead from first-stage allocations by the estimated cost driver level. For example, the quality-control labor cost pool has $490,000 allocated from first-stage allocations. For the reporting period, we estimate that 20,000 direct labor hours will be worked. (Note: All estimated cost driver amounts in Exhibit 5.6 are given, not calculated.) We divide $490,000 by 20,000 to get an application rate of $24.50 of quality-control costs per direct labor hour. We repeat this same process for equipment setups ($196.67 per equipment setup) and custom product design ($800 per custom product design). Notice that we do not allocate the facility-level cost pool.

Activity Cost Pool	Cost Pool Amount (Last Row of Exhibit 5.5)	Activity Cost Driver	Estimated Cost Driver Amount (Given, not calculated here)	Overhead Allocation Rate
Quality control	$490,000	Direct labor hours	20,000	$24.50 per direct labor hour
Equipment setup	$295,000	Number of equipment setups	1,500	$196.67 per setup
Custom product design	$140,000	Number of custom product designs	175	$800 per custom design
Facility support	$ 75,000	None. Not allocated	N/A*	N/A

Exhibit 5.6
Calculation of Allocation Rates

*N/A = not applicable.

Now that we have the overhead application rates, we can assign costs to a specific job and see how the costs are applied. Consider a customer who orders a set of customized cabinets (Job #102). The completion of the order required 120 direct labor hours and 4 equipment setups due to the nature of this customer's particular custom design. The indirect costs applied are calculated as follows:

Job #102 Indirect Costs

Quality control: 120 direct labor hours * $24.50 per direct labor hour = $2,940
Equipment setup: 4 equipment setups * $196.67 per setup = $786.68
Custom product design: 1 custom design * $800 per custom design = $800
Total applied overhead: $4,526.68

Compare this application of overhead to another customer's order. Job #103 required the same amount of direct labor hours, but it was for a standard set of cabinets (that is, no custom design) that required only 2 equipment setups. The overhead applied is as follows:

Job #103 Indirect Costs

Quality control: 120 direct labor hours * $24.50 per direct labor hour = $2,940
Equipment setup: 2 equipment setups * $196.67 per setup = $393.34
Custom product design: 0 custom design * $800 per custom design = $0
Total applied overhead: $3,333.34

The activity-based costing system recognizes that the custom order requires extra work to design the product and requires more equipment setups than the standard order. A traditional job-order system using a single overhead application rate would have treated these two orders the same, based on direct-labor hours. The activity-based costing system offers a more accurate application of indirect costs based on more activities taking place for one job compared to another.

Note that these calculations provide only the allocation of indirect costs. To calculate the total cost of a job, traced costs such as direct materials and direct labor need to be added to these indirect costs. Exhibit 5.7 shows a summary diagram of activity-based costing for **Heartwood**'s Brazilian subsidiary.

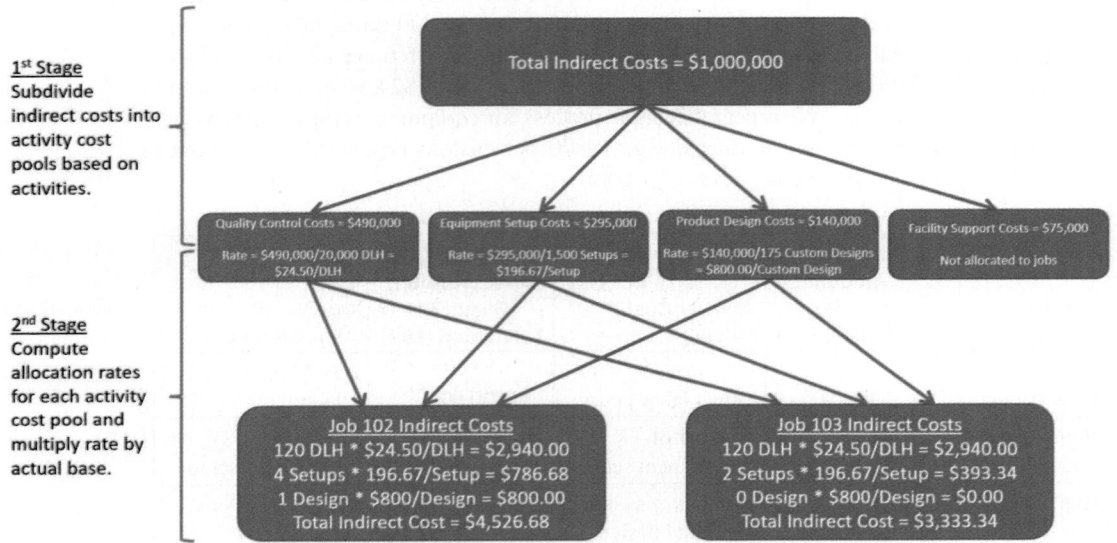

DLH = Direct labor hours worked

Exhibit 5.7
Diagram of Activity-Based Costing

Activity-Based Costing for Services

The principles of activity-based costing also apply to services, and they are often used to determine the profitability of customers. Let's consider GrabBag, a fictitious food delivery company. GrabBag operates in a single city and delivers food made by local restaurants to the homes of their customers (much like **DoorDash** and **Uber Eats**).

Activity-based costing allows GrabBag to determine the profitability of individual customers. In the first stage of activity-based costing, GrabBag management must determine how to group the company's service costs by activity. GrabBag estimates that the company has $180,000 in monthly indirect costs, and it has grouped these costs by activity as follows:

Activity Cost Pool	Account Maintenance	Delivery Preparation	Transportation	Total
Indirect costs	$5,000	$25,000	$150,000	$180,000

In stage 2 of activity-based costing, GrabBag must determine allocation rates for each cost pool. It does so by determining the appropriate cost driver for each pool:

- *Account maintenance* involves tracking customer information and billing customers monthly. Management has determined that these costs are the same for all customers, so the number of customers is the appropriate cost driver.

- *Delivery preparation* involves the direct costs associated with employees interacting with restaurants. These costs are incurred on a per-delivery basis, so management has decided that number of deliveries is the appropriate cost driver for this cost pool.
- *Transportation costs* include direct labor for delivery personnel, along with vehicle maintenance and fuel. Management has decided that miles driven is the appropriate cost driver for this cost pool.

By dividing indirect costs by the number of cost drivers in each cost pool, GrabBag can determine the allocation rates for each activity cost pool as follows:

Activity Cost Pool	Cost Pool Amount	Activity Cost Driver	Estimated Cost Driver Amount	Cost Allocation Rate
Account maintenance	$ 5,000	Number of customers	800	$6.25
Delivery preparation	$ 25,000	Number of deliveries	5,000	$5.00
Transportation	$150,000	Delivery miles	60,000	$2.50

With this information, GrabBag can examine the cost of individual customers. Let's examine three customers (Amir, Daniels, and Gonzales), the cost drivers associated with each customer's account, and the total cost of servicing each customer.

Activity Cost Pool	Cost Driver	Amir	Daniels	Gonzales
Account maintenance	Number of Customers	1 * $6.25	1 * $6.25	1 * $6.25
Delivery preparation	Number of deliveries	4 * $5.00	25 * $5.00	10 * $5.00
Transportation	Delivery miles	13.6 * $2.50	205 * $2.50	43 * $2.50
	Total cost	$60.25	$643.75	$163.75

As the table shows, Mr. Amir has 4 deliveries a month and requires a total of 13.6 miles for those deliveries. Based on the calculated cost allocation rates, GrabBag determines that the total cost of servicing the Amir account is $60.25. We can use the same process to calculate the cost of servicing the Daniels account ($643.75) and the Gonzales account ($163.75). This information is important to GrabBag because it provides information about individual customers' profitability. GrabBag may even discover that it loses money servicing certain customers. This information can also inform GrabBag's strategy regarding how to price its services. For example, GrabBag may charge more to customers that require more miles, or create rewards programs to attract more profitable customers.

Which Companies Should Implement Activity-Based Costing?

Activity-based costing has intuitive appeal as an improved costing system. It has the potential to more accurately reflect the cost of a job or product by taking into account the unique activities involved with completing that job or product. Hundreds of companies have successfully implemented activity-based costing to better understand and control their costs. These companies include many in the automotive industry, including **Ford**, **Chrysler**, and **Toyota**, which have used the more accurate cost information provided by activity-based costing to eliminate or improve costly production processes and increase efficiency. Similar results have been achieved by **Safety-Kleen**, which provides recycling and other environmental services, and **Pratt & Whitney**, which produces aircraft engines. So, if activity-based costing yields better cost information than other cost systems, why don't all companies use it?

The choice to implement activity-based costing is based primarily on a cost-benefit analysis. Activity-based costing requires significant resources in terms of time and money, and the benefits may not outweigh the increased costs of implementation. Companies that have little variety in production processes or products, or that have few indirect costs, likely have little need for an activity-based costing system. For these companies, the cost information provided by job-order costing is good enough, and better cost information isn't worth the expense of implementing activity-based costing. In contrast, a company is more likely to adopt activity-based costing if it has diverse products or services, complex production processes, and/or large amounts of indirect costs. Under these conditions, the risk of distorted cost allocations increases, and companies have an increased need for better cost information.

The primary challenge to implementing activity-based costing is gathering the data necessary to complete the first-stage allocation, which is precisely what can cause activity-based costing to be a costly endeavor. These data include cost information for activities, as well as cost driver data. Companies often have more data available than they realize, and technological advances have made it easier than ever for companies to gather data. As discussed in Chapter 2, companies can use data from financial reporting systems, manufacturing systems, human resource systems, and other systems to better understand their costs. However, activity-based costing often requires companies to gather and generate new data, particularly detailed data about how employees devote their time to various activities.

Another challenge with an activity-based costing system is the need to meet GAAP reporting requirements. Activity-based costing information is meant to be used internally and does not conform to GAAP. Recall that when calculating product costs under activity-based costing, companies can include period costs such as warranty expense or marketing as a product cost and exclude facility-level product costs such as factory rent. Consequently, companies that use activity-based costing must adjust activity-based costing numbers for reporting purposes to comply with GAAP. Alternatively, companies that use activity-based costing can keep two sets of accounting records—one for activity-based costing analysis and another for financial reporting. Although the benefit of improved costing data for decision making and analysis makes activity-based costing appealing, the need to maintain multiple costing systems for external reporting and internal analysis can discourage the adoption of activity-based costing. Ultimately, companies must weigh the expense of implementing activity-based costing against the benefits of more accurate cost information.

The Human Side of Activity-Based Costing

Large companies can track dozens or even hundreds of activities in an activity-based costing system, and companies must estimate how resources are being used for each activity. Creating these estimates often involves asking employees to complete surveys to report how their time is spent. Designing and administering these surveys, as well as processing and analyzing the gathered data, can take tremendous amounts of time and energy. A 10- to 15-minute survey may not seem too onerous for a given employee, but consider the time required to conduct quarterly or monthly surveys across hundreds or even thousands of employees in a large organization. These surveys take employees away from their primary job responsibilities. In addition, employees may not complete the survey, leading to insufficient or unrepresentative data. Even when the surveys are completed, employee estimates of time spent are prone to error. For example, when asked to complete a report of how they spent their time, employees often report having worked at **full capacity** (100% of time spent working on productive activities). However, employees are rarely 100% efficient, and it's more realistic to assume some lower **practical capacity** (85–90% of time spent working on productive activities).

 LAB CONNECTION

LAB 5.4 EXCEL demonstrates how to use regression analysis to estimate activity-based costing drivers.

> ⊘ **PROGRESS CHECK**
>
> 5. Why does an activity-based costing system use multiple indirect cost allocation bases?
> 6. What are the first-stage allocations in an activity-based costing system?
> 7. What are the second-stage allocations in an activity-based costing system?
> 8. Which types of firms will most benefit from an activity-based costing system?

TIME-DRIVEN ACTIVITY-BASED COSTING

To help improve the time-consuming and costly nature of implementing activity-based costing, Robert Kaplan (an accounting professor at Harvard) and Steven Anderson (founder of **Acorn Systems**, a software and consulting firm) developed **time-driven activity-based costing (TDABC)**. TDABC is becoming increasingly popular in practice. It has some clear advantages over activity-based costing because it is far less costly to implement than traditional activity-based costing. As we've discussed, traditional activity-based costing requires enormous amounts of employee time and energy to estimate the resources consumed by various activities, and employees often overestimate their productivity, which can distort cost information. In contrast, TDABC relies solely on management to estimate how long it takes employees to perform various activities. Because employees do not need to be regularly surveyed to gather this information, TDABC frees up significant employee time.

Let's consider a customer service department with $450,000 in indirect costs. The service department has four tasks: (1) processing customer orders, (2) expediting shipping for rush orders, (3) registering new customers, and (4) performing customer credit checks. In a traditional activity-based costing system, the department will use employee surveys to determine how much time employees spend on these activities. These estimates will then be used to determine allocation rates. TDABC forgoes the need for such surveys and can be implemented using just two estimates supplied by management.

The first estimate is the cost of resources (that is, the indirect costs) per unit of time. For instance, management may estimate that the employees in the customer service department can reasonably work 10,000 hours per year (based on practical capacity). With this estimate, management can calculate that the cost of the customer service department is $0.75 per minute ($450,000 indirect costs/10,000 hours/60 minutes).

Next, to determine overhead application rates, management must estimate how long it takes to complete activities. These estimates can be based on experience or observation, and they don't have to be exact so long as they are reasonable. For the customer service department, assume management estimates the duration of each activity as follows:

1. Processing customer orders: 6 minutes
2. Expediting shipping: 30 minutes
3. Registering new customers: 20 minutes
4. Performing credit checks: 75 minutes

With this information, we can compute time-driven activity cost driver rates by multiplying the cost of capacity ($0.75 per minute) by the unit time estimates for each activity. The time-driven activity cost driver rates are as follows:

1. Processing customer orders: 6 minutes * $0.75 per minute = $4.50 per customer order
2. Expediting shipping: 30 minutes * $0.75 per minute = $22.50 per expedited item
3. Registering new customers: 20 minutes * $0.75 per minute = $15.00 per new customer
4. Performing credit checks: 75 minutes * $0.75 per minute = $56.25 per credit check

---

LO 5.4

Demonstrate how time-driven activity-based costing allocates overhead.

time-driven activity-based costing (TDBAC)
A form of activity-based costing that allocates indirect costs on the basis of the time required to perform various tasks or activities.

We can now use these rates to apply overhead to different jobs. For example, how much indirect cost is applied for a returning customer who placed one order for which 3 items required expedited shipping (that is, rush orders)? Assume that because of the returning customer's payment history, no credit check was necessary. The indirect costs will be applied as follows:

1. Processing customer orders: 1 order * $4.50 per customer order = $4.50
2. Expediting shipping: 3 items * $22.50 per expedited item = $67.50
3. Registering new customers: Not applicable. Returning customer.
4. Performing credit checks: Not applicable. No credit check necessary.

Total = $72.00 total indirect costs

Contrast this example with a new customer who places two regular orders and for whom a credit check is required. What are the allocated indirect costs in this situation? We calculate them as follows:

1. Processing customer orders: 2 orders * $4.50 per customer order = $9.00
2. Expediting shipping: 0 * $22.50 per expedited item = $0.00
3. Registering new customers: 1 new customer * $15.00 per new customer = $15.00
4. Performing credit checks: 1 credit check * $56.25 per credit check = $56.25

Total = $80.25 total indirect costs

We can observe that the time-driven activity-based system has the ability to recognize differences in the activities that drive indirect costs, similar to the original activity-based system. However, time-driven activity-based costing is implemented at a significantly reduced cost relative to traditional activity-based costing systems.[2]

 LAB CONNECTION

LAB 5.5 EXCEL provides an example of how companies can estimate overhead costs using time-driven activity-based costing (TDABC).

 PROGRESS CHECK

9. What is the primary benefit of TDABC over traditional activity-based costing?
10. What are the two key estimates used in time-driven activity-based costing?

Jobs with Activity-Based Costing Responsibilities

Understanding activity-based costing and other advanced costing methods is a valuable skill set for management accountants. For example, **Amazon** depends on accurate cost information not only to produce accurate financial statements but also to drive strategic decisions.

Exhibit 5.8 is adapted from a job posting from a recruiting site like **LinkedIn** or **Indeed.com**. This posting is for as a Finance Analytics Manager at a worldwide online retailer like Amazon, **Walmart**, or **Target**. Read the posting to better understand how companies depend on good cost information and sound analytic skills throughout their organization. This is particularly true for companies that have complex operations that span multiple industries.

[2]For more information about how time-driven activity-based costing overcomes some of the challenges of traditional activity-based costing, see Robert S. Kaplan and Steven R. Anderson, "Time-Driven Activity-Based Costing," *Harvard Business Review,* November 2004, https://hbr.org/2004/11/time-driven-activity-based-costing.

Job Title

Finance Analytics Manager, Transportation Controllership

Job Summary

The Transportation Controllership division seeks a Finance Analytics Manager for Financial Reporting and Advanced Analytics. The Transportation Controllership group is a global finance team responsible for Financial Reporting activities, establishing Financial Control Frameworks and Advance Analytics for the transportation sector of a global company. This group manages all aspects of the transportation space, including warehouse activities, domestic shipments and deliveries, imports, and outbound processing. This group works closely with the transportation business units and technology teams to continually refine and adjust to the company's rapid expansion. Experience in this team opens up several career opportunities across the company.

In this role, the Finance Analytics Manager will rely on a combination of critical thinking, project management, and advanced analytical skills in order to succeed. This role provides an opportunity to think on your feet, expand your understanding of our key business problems and performance indicators, become a company-wide problem-solver, and ensure successful reporting and automation processes.

This role will be responsible for logistics costing data sets for one of the world's largest companies. The ideal candidate will combine excellent business analysis skills with the ability to derive actionable cost measures for consumption across the company.

Requirements

- MBA, CPA, or advanced degree in Accounting, Economics, Finance, Engineering, or other fields with analytical focus
- Seven or more years of experience in a corporate finance role; analytics experience a plus
- Self-starter who is curious, interested in fast-paced learning, and focused on optimizing the customer experience
- Experience with business forecasting, financial modeling, and problem solving
- Strong communication skills with an emphasis on clear writing and presentation to explain technical information and data findings to a broad audience
- Experience leading teams or projects with proven results
- Ability to manage and interpret data, create executive-level reports, and coordinate with executive leadership to enact data-driven decisions

Key Roles and Responsibilities

- Interpret company data and use key business knowledge to build financial models, draw conclusions, and make recommendations to meet stated metrics, drive improvements, and influence global executive leadership.
- Deliver regular financial reporting and updates on KPIs by working with large data sets and creating visualizations and outputs of forecasts, budgets, and other key plans.
- Partner with operations and finance groups to support and inform key business needs.
- Communicate data (via written reports or presentations) in a clear, concise, and unambiguous manner and adjust formats and delivery style for various audiences to clearly articulate complex finance issues.
- Support the department in hiring, developing, and mentoring peers and team members. Encourage and seek out diverse perspectives in all activities.
- Utilize reports, data, and other metrics to consistently work toward improvement of finance tools for all internal teams.

Sidebar annotations:

High growth and complex transportation costs increase the need for good cost data.

Understanding cost data and data analytics can lead to additional career opportunities.

Management accountants are problem solvers. They need good communication skills to work with people in other departments who have different backgrounds.

Activity-based costing provides important cost insights that are not possible to understand without sophisticated analysis and data.

The ability to communicate well in a variety of settings is critical for management accountants. This is precisely why "sharing the story" is a critical component of the AMPS model.

Notice the impact of management accounting. Information provided by management accountants is used throughout the organization.

Data analytics helps management accounts to "persuade with data" or use data to inform decision makers of the appropriate strategies to take. Data analytics can also help to determine if strategies are effective.

Exhibit 5.8
Transportation Analytics Manager Job Opportunity

Key Takeaways: Two-Stage Costing and Activity-Based Costing

As companies become more complex, traditional job-order costing using a single allocation base is likely to produce inaccurate cost information, which can lead to ineffective and costly business decisions. Two-stage job-order costing improves the link between the causes and effects of costs by linking allocation bases or cost drivers with indirect costs. Two-stage costing creates multiple cost pools, allocating the costs of each cost pool using an allocation base that drives indirect costs.

Activity-based costing is a more advanced two-stage costing system that companies can use to apply all indirect costs (not just manufacturing overhead) to cost objects. The cost pools used in activity-based costing recognize that cost-driving activities occur at the unit, batch, product-line, and facility levels. By improving the causal relationship between activities and indirect costs, two-stage costing helps companies identify areas for improvement in their processes, products, and services. Management can improve profitability by reducing or eliminating costly activities that do not provide value to customers.

The primary advantage of two-stage and activity-based costing is that these systems can provide more accurate indirect cost information than a single-stage cost system. However, successful implication of these advanced cost systems can require considerable company resources. Management accountants can help companies determine whether the benefits of two-stage and activity-based costing outweigh the costs.

Let's use the AMPS model to summarize how the information in this chapter can be used to address important managerial questions:

Ask the Question

- **What question(s) does management want to answer?**

Indirect costs can be a significant component in the overall cost of a product or service. Management must understand not only the cost of providing goods and services but also the activities that influence these costs.

Master the Data

- **Which data are appropriate to address management's questions?**

A company's cost accounting system provides important inputs for a two-stage costing system. In addition, activity-based costing requires significant additional data, often obtained through surveys, regarding how employees throughout an organization use their time and resources to complete various activities.

Perform the Analysis

- **What analytics are performed to address management questions?**

Two-stage costing can be used during **descriptive analytics** to understand indirect costs. Activity-based costing is a form of **diagnostic analytics** because it seeks to understand how cost objects use a company's resources. Diagnostic analytics may include correlation and regression analysis as shown in this chapter's mini-lab. **Predictive analytics** can be used to determine how changes in activities will affect profitability. Management accountants can also perform **prescriptive analytics** to provide management with actionable directives that will improve company performance.

Share the Story

- **How are the results of the analytics shared with stakeholders?**

Two-stage costing is an important tool for management accountants. Management accountants may need to prepare reports to demonstrate to others how imprecise allocations can distort cost information and lead to poor strategic decisions.

Key Terms

activity

activity cost pool

activity-based costing

activity-based management

allocation base

batch-level costs

cost driver

cost object

cost pool

facility-support costs

full capacity

overcosted

practical capacity

product-line costs

time-driven activity-based costing (TDBAC)

two-stage cost allocation

undercosted

unit-level costs

⊘ ANSWERS TO PROGRESS CHECKS

1. Two-stage allocations use multiple overhead allocation bases to improve the causal link between allocation bases and incurred overhead costs. Cost pools increase management's ability to choose cost drivers for overhead costs. The result is more accurate overhead cost information.

2. Some costs, such as factory rent and some utilities, may not have adequate cost drivers. For example, while electricity costs may be reasonably caused by machine hours, fixed utility costs such as Internet access do not have the same cause-effect relationship with any allocation base. As a result, some overhead costs are still allocated somewhat arbitrarily. That said, a two-stage allocation has less arbitrary allocation costs than a single-stage allocation because of the use of multiple cost pools.

3. The four levels of costs are unit-level costs, batch-level costs, product line-level costs, and facility-level costs.

4. Often, facility-level costs aren't allocated to jobs or products because there is little or no link between the consumption of facility-level costs (such as factory insurance) and individual jobs or products.

5. An activity-based costing system uses multiple overhead allocation bases to improve the causal link between costs that are incurred and costs that are assigned or allocated to a job. Multiple overhead allocation bases allow overhead to be broken down into several cost pools and then assigned to jobs based on which activities the job requires.

6. First-stage allocations in an activity-based costing system involve assigning total overhead costs to cost pools. Cost pools are groupings of cost related to an activity. All costs in a cost pool should behave similarly, such that a cost driver can reasonably predict all costs in the cost pool through a cause-effect relationship.

7. Second-stage allocations in an activity-based costing system apply overhead costs to cost objects, which are jobs, products, or services. The activity-based costing system uses multiple overhead application rates to more accurately reflect the costs incurred for a job or product based on the activities involved in its production. Overhead rates can be applied on a unit level, batch level, product-line level, or facility level.

8. Firms with a diverse set of product offerings will benefit from using an activity-based costing system. Not all jobs or products require the same use of resources. An activity-based costing system improves the allocation of overhead based on the activities that give rise to costs being incurred. Firms with a single product have little need to differentiate how resources are consumed. Firms with diverse products have a much greater need for more accurate cost information.

9. The primary benefit of TDABC is that it does not require as much time and expense to perform first-stage allocations because it depends on management estimates of time-based metrics rather than those reported by employees throughout the organization.

10. The two key estimates used in time-driven activity-based costing are (1) an estimate of the cost of resources per unit of time and (2) estimates of time needed to complete an activity.

Multiple-Choice Questions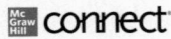

1. (LO5.1) Fably Inc. is a specialty clothing shop that employs dozens of tailors and several supervisors who oversee the tailors' work in the production facility. Supervisor labor is considered manufacturing overhead. Which of the following allocation bases is most likely to be the cost driver of supervisor labor?
   a. Direct labor hours
   b. Machine hours
   c. Units produced
   d. Square footage

2. (LO5.1) The Glow Company produces motion-sensor LED candles. The company has considerable manufacturing overhead costs, including a number of employees who meticulously examine the quality of the candles before they are shipped to customers. Which of the following allocation bases is most likely to be the cost driver of quality control?
   a. Direct labor hours
   b. Machine hours
   c. Units produced
   d. Square footage

3. (LO5.1) Using a traditional job-order cost system with a single allocation base may result in the undercosting of a product or service. Undercosting a product or service can result in:
   a. overstated product efficiency.
   b. overstated product market share.
   c. understated product profitability.
   d. undercosting all products and services.

4. (LO5.1) Crimson Box produces two products. Per the company's traditional job-costing system, Basic Box and Premium Box cost $30 and $50 to produce, respectively. Recently, Crimson Box implemented a two-stage allocation system, which indicated a cost of $25 for the Basic Box and $65 for the Premium Box. The implementation of a two-stage cost allocation revealed that Basic Box was:
   a. undercosted.
   b. overcosted.
   c. cross-costed.
   d. inefficient.

5. (LO5.1) Crimson Box produces two products. Per the company's traditional job-costing system, Basic Box and Premium Box cost $30 and $50 to produce, respectively. Recently, Crimson Box implemented a two-stage allocation system, which indicated a cost of $25 for the Basic Box and $65 for the Premium Box. When Crimson Box implements two-stage cost allocation, how are manufacturing overhead costs affected?
   a. Total manufacturing overhead costs increase.
   b. Total manufacturing overhead costs decrease.
   c. Total manufacturing overhead costs are unchanged.
   d. Total manufacturing overhead costs increase, but product costs remain the same.

6. (LO5.1, 5.2) Activity-based costing differs from two-stage job-order costing in that it attempts to establish a cause-effect relationship between cost drivers and indirect costs.
   a. True
   b. False

7. (LO5.2) Which of the following cost systems is least likely to conform to GAAP?
   a. Traditional job-order costing
   b. Two-stage job-order costing

c. Activity-based costing

d. Process costing

8. (LO5.2) Which of the following indirect costs can be included as a product cost under activity-based costing but should not be included as a product cost according to GAAP?

a. Machine depreciation

b. Factory rent

c. Supervisor labor

d. Advertising expenses

9. (LO5.2) Which of the following indirect costs is not included as a product cost under activity-based costing but should be included as a product cost according to GAAP?

a. Machine depreciation

b. Factory rent

c. Supervisor labor

d. Advertising expenses

10. (LO5.2) Under activity-based costing, which of the following costs are not allocated to individual products and services?

a. Marketing costs

b. Warranty costs

c. Facility-level costs

d. Indirect labor costs

11. (LO5.2) The costs of testing a new product and obtaining a patent are examples of:

a. unit-level costs.

b. batch-level costs.

c. product-line costs.

d. facility-level costs.

12. (LO5.2) Big T's Apparel produces custom t-shirts. Big T's uses activity-based costing and has determined that it is willing to sell t-shirts for $12 each for orders of 100 shirts or more and $15 each for orders of fewer than 100 shirts. This pricing strategy is likely the result of Big T's analysis of:

a. unit-level costs.

b. batch-level costs.

c. product-line costs.

d. facility-level costs.

13. (LO5.2) In an activity-based costing system, costs are allocated to jobs and products based on:

a. resource usage.

b. simplicity.

c. profit margins.

d. historic costs.

14. (LO5.2) Which of the following levels of cost is most susceptible to changes in production volume?

a. Unit-level

b. Batch-level

c. Product-line

d. Facility-level

15. (LO5.2) Which of the following is the chief difficulty of implementing and maintaining an activity-based costing system?

a. Allocating costs from cost pools to jobs and products

b. Determining activity cost pools

c. Allocating costs to activity cost pools

d. Allocating traced costs to products

16. (LO5.3) Practical capacity typically means that workers are using _____ of their time productively.
    a. 65%–70%
    b. 75%–80%
    c. 85%–90%
    d. 95%–100%

17. (LO5.3) Which of the following factors indicates that a company should not implement activity-based costing?
    a. Minimal overhead costs
    b. Complex products
    c. Extensive product variety
    d. Excessive profits

18. (LO5.3) At highly productive companies, most employees are able to work at full capacity.
    a. True
    b. False

19. (LO5.4) Relative to traditional activity-based costing, time-driven activity-based costing is easier to implement because it removes the need to:
    a. estimate the resources used by activities.
    b. query employees about how they spend their time.
    c. allocate indirect costs.
    d. identify activity cost pools.

20. (LO5.2, 5.3, 5.4) Unlike traditional activity-based costing, time-driven activity-based costing relies on estimates from management rather than more detailed information from employees throughout the organization.
    a. True
    b. False

CMA

21. (LO5.2) When using activity-based costing techniques, which one of the following departmental activities would be expected to use machine hours as a cost driver to allocate overhead costs to production?
    a. Plant cafeteria
    b. Machine setups
    c. Material handling
    d. Robotics painting

CMA

22. (LO5.2) A company is considering the implementation of an activity-based costing and management program. The company:
    a. should focus on manufacturing activities and avoid implementation with service-type functions.
    b. will probably find a lack of software in the marketplace to assist with the related recordkeeping.
    c. will likely gain added insights into causes of cost.
    d. will likely use fewer cost pools than it did under more traditional accounting methods.

CMA

23. (LO5.2, 5.3) The Chocolate Baker specializes in chocolate baked goods. The firm has long assessed the profitability of a product line by comparing revenues to the cost of goods sold. However, Barry White, the firm's new accountant, wants to use an activity-based costing system that takes into consideration the cost of the delivery person. Listed below are activity and cost information relating to two of The Chocolate Baker's major products.

	Muffins	Cheesecakes
Revenue	$53,000	$46,000
Cost of goods	$26,000	$ 21,000

Delivery Activity		
Number of deliveries	150	85
Average length of delivery	10 minutes	15 minutes
Cost per hour for delivery	$20.00	$20.00

Under activity-based costing, which one of the following statements is correct?

a. The muffins are $2,000 more profitable.
b. The cheesecakes are $75 more profitable.
c. The muffins are $1,925 more profitable.
d. The muffins have a higher profitability as a percentage of sales and, therefore, are more advantageous.

Discussion Questions

1. (LO5.1) Describe how companies create cost pools in a job-order cost system that uses two-stage cost allocations.
2. (LO5.1) Assume that a company allocates overhead on the basis of machine hours, and it uses the same overhead rate for all machines in the factory. Under what circumstances would this practice distort the overhead assigned to specific products?
3. (LO5.1, 5.2) Explain why two-stage cost systems improve the cause-effect relationship between allocation base and indirect costs, compared to a single-stage cost system.
4. (LO5.1, 5.2) Why should allocation bases be cost drivers?
5. (LO5.1) In the context of the allocation of indirect costs, explain what is meant by one product subsidizing another, and explain how this phenomenon can affect a company.
6. (LO5.1) Describe the circumstances under which a company may opt for a job-order cost system with single-stage allocations for indirect costs rather than two-stage allocations.
7. (LO5.2) Describe the type of companies for which activity-based costing would not be worth the cost of implementation.
8. (LO5.3) Describe why companies group activities together based on the level of costs associated with those activities.
9. (LO5.2) Employees often provide services that their employer could categorize into multiple activities. How does an activity-based costing system account for this division of labor?
10. (LO5.3) Activity-based costing relies on survey data from employees regarding how they use their time. Why might this information be inaccurate?
11. (LO5.2) Explain how a company with better cost information may outperform companies with inaccurate cost information, even when underlying costs are the same.
12. (LO5.3) Consider a clothing manufacturer. Identify costs at the unit level, batch level, product line-level, and facility-support level that are common in the industry.
13. (LO5.3) Explain why many companies that use activity-based costing do not allocate facility-level indirect costs.
14. (LO5.4) Explain the primary advantage of time-driven activity-based costing over traditional activity-based costing.
15. (LO5.4) What are the ethical concerns related to management estimating how long it takes to perform various activities in a time-driven activity-based costing system?

ETHICS

Brief Exercises

1. (LO5.3) HiFly runs a flight school and uses an activity-based costing system. Flight hours are often used as an allocation base. Lessons can range from 30 minutes to 120 minutes of flight time. HiFly uses various aircraft. Classify the following costs as unit level, batch level, product line-level, or facility level.

a. Aircraft maintenance (maintenance scheduled is based on flight time)
b. Aircraft hangar rental
c. Aircraft depreciation
d. Aircraft insurance
e. Pilot certification (pilots must be certified for each aircraft type they fly)
f. Aircraft safety inspection (performed after each flight lesson)

2. (LO5.3) Butter Tint produces jewelry boxes and uses an activity-based costing system. Classify the following costs as unit level, batch level, product line-level, or facility-level.
   a. Indirect materials such as wood glue
   b. Machine setups
   c. Packing/shipping costs
   d. Factory insurance
   e. Product design costs
   f. Warranty costs

3. (LO5.1) Touristica has the following budgeted cost information:

Budgeted manufacturing overhead	$720,000
Budgeted production (units)	18,500
Budgeted direct labor hours	2,400

Cost Pool	Total Cost	Allocation Base
Cost Pool 1	$400,000	Unit
Cost Pool 2	$320,000	Direct labor hour
Total	$720,000	

Assume Touristica uses two-stage allocation to assign overhead costs to cost objects. What is the allocation rate of Cost Pool 2 (rounded to the nearest penny)?

4. (LO5.1) Weekend Lab has the following budgeted cost information:

Budgeted manufacturing overhead	$400,000
Budgeted production (units)	25,000
Budgeted direct labor hours	18,000

Cost Pool	Total Cost	Allocation Base
Cost Pool 1	$ 100,000	Unit
Cost Pool 2	$300,000	Direct labor hour
Total	$400,000	

Weekend Lab uses two-stage allocation to assign overhead costs to cost objects. How much overhead cost is allocated to Job 123, which is an order for 50 units and uses 15 hours?

5. (LO5.1) Thrill Engine has the following budgeted cost information:

Budgeted manufacturing overhead	$36,000
Budgeted machine hours	20,000
Budgeted direct labor hours	5,000

Cost Pool	Total Cost	Allocation Base
Machine-related MOH	$20,000	Machine hour
Labor-related MOH	$ 16,000	Direct labor hour
Total	$36,000	

Thrill Engine has historically used traditional job-order costing, applying all overhead on the basis of machine hours. The company is now considering using two-stage allocation to assign overhead costs to jobs using the two cost pools listed above.

Job 226 uses 80 machine hours and 80 direct labor hours. Assuming that two-stage allocation yields more accurate cost allocations, a single-stage allocation of overhead using machine hours as the allocation base results in Job 226 being _____ (over-costed/undercosted) by _____.

6. (LO5.1) HyperLens has the following budgeted cost information:

Budgeted manufacturing overhead	$1,928,500
Budgeted machine hours	8,000
Budgeted direct labor hours	4,200
Budgeted units	40,000

Cost Pool	Total Cost	Allocation Base
Machine-related MOH	$772,800	Machine hour
Labor-related MOH	$ 44,500	Direct labor hour
Unit-related MOH	$ 146,000	Unit
Total	$963,300	

HyperLens uses two-stage allocation with three cost pools to assign overhead costs to orders. What is the per-unit allocation rate for unit-related manufacturing overhead?

7. (LO5.1) Zen Detour has the following budgeted cost information:

Budgeted manufacturing overhead	$704,000
Budgeted machine hours	5,000
Budgeted direct labor hours	3,500
Budgeted units	20,000

Cost Pool	Total Cost	Allocation Base
Machine-related MOH	$352,500	Machine hour
Labor-related MOH	$ 73,500	Direct labor hour
Unit-related MOH	$278,000	Unit
Total	$704,000	

Zen Detour uses two-stage allocation with three cost pools to assign overhead costs to orders. How much overhead cost is allocated to Order #0221, which used 2 machine hours and 1.5 direct labor hours and produced 48 units?

8. (LO5.2, 5.3) Photo Saga uses activity-based costing and has come up with the following allocation rates:

Activity	Driver	Rate	
Process order	Sales order	$ 18.00	per order
Packing and shipping	Item shipped	$ 3.00	per item
Billing	Sales order	$ 4.00	per order
Product customization	Customized order	$120.00	per customized order

Job 924 is a custom order for 12 items. How much indirect cost should be allocated to Job 924?

9. (LO5.3) Artica uses activity-based costing and has developed the following allocation rates:

Activity	Driver	Rate	
Process order	Sales order	$ 4.50	per order
Quality check	Item checked	$ 1.25	per item
Modification	Item modified	$ 8.25	per modified item
Packing and shipping	Order shipped	$12.00	per shipped order

Hetic, one of Artica's clients, recently ordered 100 items from Artica, of which 25 were modified (which incurs additional cost). How much indirect cost should be allocated to the Hetic order?

10. (LO5.2, 5.3) Silver Company is a catering company that uses activity-based costing and has developed the following allocation rates:

Activity	Driver	Rate	
Receive request	Event	$350.00	per event
Plan an event	Event	$400.00	per event
Invite guests	Guest	$ 12.00	per guest
Billing	Event	$ 25.00	per event

Silver Company recently catered an event for 50 guests. How much indirect cost should be allocated to the event?

11. (LO5.4) Photo Factory is a photography studio that uses time-driven activity-based costing. Photo Factory estimates that one minute of time uses $1.85 in resources. It has developed the following time estimates for its activities:

Activity	Driver	Estimated minutes
Photo appointment	Photo session	45
Digital editing	Photos edited	10
Printing/packaging	Photos printed	0.5
Rush order	Rush order	45

Photo Factory recently did work for a client named Jones. The job consisted of editing 10 photos and printing 250 photos. The order was expedited. How much indirect cost should be allocated to the client?

12. (LO5.4) Shine Capsule, which provides lighting for concerts and music festivals, uses time-driven activity-based costing. Shine Capsule estimates that one minute of time uses $6.50 in resources, and it has developed the following time estimates for its activities:

Activity	Driver	Estimated minutes
Equipment packing and unpacking	Event	350
Equipment setup	Number of stages	240
Light optimization	Number of light towers	15

Shine Capsule was recently hired to help with the Mountain Music Festival. The event had three stages, each with 6 light towers. How much indirect cost should be allocated to the event?

13. (LO5.4) Gold Sense, which uses time-driven activity-based costing, estimates that one minute of time uses $1.35 in resources, and it has developed the following time estimates for its activities:

Activity	Driver	Estimated minutes
Process order	Sales order	6
Packing and shipping	Item shipped	2
Billing	Sales order	5
Customization	Customized item	7.5

Gold Sense recently fulfilled an order for 15 items, 5 of which were customized. How much indirect cost should be allocated to the order?

14. (LO5.3) Amber Allure is implementing an activity-based costing system. The company has gathered information about overhead costs, and it used employee surveys to determine how resources are consumed by various activities as follows:

Overhead Costs	
Supervisor labor	$ 750,000
Machine maintenance	$ 450,000
Indirect materials	$ 225,000
Factory lease and insurance	$ 125,000
Total	$1,550,000

	Resource Consumption by Activity				
	Unit Production	Quality Control	Design Improvement	Facility Support	Total
Supervisor labor	40%	50%	5%	5%	100%
Machine maintenance	70%	30%	0%	0%	100%
Indirect materials	75%	10%	10%	5%	100%
Factory lease and insurance	20%	0%	0%	80%	100%

What is the total amount of cost allocated to the quality control cost pool?

15. (LO5.3) Bling Fuel is implementing an activity-based costing system. The company has gathered information about overhead costs, and it used employee surveys to determine how resources are consumed by various activities as follows:

Indirect Costs	
Indirect labor	$ 115,000
Indirect materials	$ 310,000
Product design	$ 80,000
Equipment depreciation	$ 120,000
Factory lease	$ 145,000
Total	$ 770,000

	Resource Consumption by Activity					
	Production	Quality Control	Patent Filing	Marketing	Facility Support	Total
Indirect labor	45%	20%	10%	20%	5%	100%
Indirect materials	60%	25%	0%	15%	0%	100%
Product design	0%	10%	10%	80%	0%	100%
Equipment depreciation	50%	0%	0%	0%	50%	100%
Factory lease	0%	0%	0%	0%	100%	100%

What is the total amount of cost allocated to the Marketing cost pool?

PROBLEMS

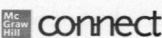

CMA

1. (LO5.3) Atmel Inc. manufactures and sells two products. Consider the following data regarding these products.

	Product A	Product B
Units produced and sold	30,000	12,000
Machine hours required per unit	2	3
Receiving orders per product line	50	150
Production orders per product line	12	18
Production runs	8	12
Inspections	20	30

Total budgeted machine hours are 100,000. The budgeted overhead costs are shown below.

Receiving costs	$450,000
Engineering costs	300,000
Machine setup costs	25,000
Inspection costs	200,000
Total budgeted overhead	$975,000

Required

a. The cost driver for receiving costs is the number of receiving orders per product line. Using activity-based costing, what is the receiving cost per unit for Product A?

b. The cost driver for engineering costs is the number of production orders per product line. Using activity-based costing, what is the engineering cost per unit for Product B?

CMA

2. (LO5.2, 5.3) Smart Electronics manufactures two types of gaming consoles, Models M-11 and R-24. Currently, the company allocates overhead costs based on direct labor hours; the total overhead cost for the past year was €80,000. Additional cost information for the past year is presented below.

Product Name	Total Direct Labor Hours Used	Units Sold	Direct Costs per Unit	Selling Price per Unit
M-11	650	1,300	€10	€90
R-24	150	1,500	€30	€60

Recently, the company lost bids on a contract to sell Model M-11 to a local wholesaler and was informed that a competitor offered a much lower price. Smart Electronics' controller believes that the cost reports do not accurately reflect the actual manufacturing costs and product profitability for these gaming consoles. He also believes that there is enough variation in the production process for Models M-11 and R-24 to warrant a better cost-allocation system. Given the nature of the electronic gaming market, setting competitive prices is extremely crucial. The controller has decided to try activity-based costing and has gathered the following information.

	Number of Setups	Number of Components	Number of Material Movements
M-11	3	17	15
R-24	7	33	35
Total activity cost	€20,000	€50,000	€10,000

The number of setups, number of components, and number of material movements have been identified as activity-cost drivers for overhead.

Required

a. Using Smart Electronics' current costing system, calculate the gross margin per unit for Model M-11 and for Model R-24. Assume no beginning or ending inventory. Show your calculations.

b. Using activity-based costing, calculate the gross margin for Model M-11 and for Model R-24. Assume no beginning or ending inventory. Show your calculations.

c. Describe how Smart Electronics can use the activity-based costing information to formulate a more competitive pricing strategy. Be sure to include specific examples to justify the recommended strategy.

d. Identify and explain two advantages and two limitations of activity-based costing.

3. (LO5.1) Harper Manufacturing determines allocation rates as part of its annual budgeting process, which takes place 1 month before the beginning of the year. The company reports the following manufacturing overhead information as part of its budgeting process:

Budgeted MOH	$ 15,000,000
Budgeted production (units)	25,000,000
Budgeted direct labor hours	40,000

Cost Pool	Total Cost	Allocation Base
Cost Pool 1	$ 6,000,000	Unit
Cost Pool 2	$ 9,000,000	Direct labor hour
Total	$15,000,000	

Required

a. Assuming that Harper uses a traditional job costing system with a single allocation base (units), what is the predetermined overhead rate for the upcoming year?

b. Assume Job 189 comprises 36 units and 2 direct labor hours. If Harper uses a traditional job costing system with a single allocation base (units), what is the total manufacturing overhead allocated to the job?

c. Now assume that Harper uses a two-stage job costing system with the two cost pools listed above. What are the predetermined overhead rates for each cost pool for the upcoming year?

d. Assume Job 189 comprises 36 units and 2 direct labor hours. If Harper uses a job-costing system with the two cost pools listed above, what is the total allocated manufacturing overhead to the job?

4. (LO5.1) Brew Shack is a small brewery that is trying to better understand its costs. The company, which currently uses traditional job-order costing, allocates overhead costs using a single cost driver. The company is considering using two-stage allocation to assign overhead costs to batches of product. It gathers the following estimates:

Budgeted MOH	$48,000
Budgeted machine hours	20,000
Budgeted direct labor hours	5,000

Cost Pool	Total Cost	Allocation Base
Machine-related MOH	$30,000	Machine hour
Labor-related MOH	$ 18,000	Direct labor hour
Total	$48,000	

One batch of Pumpkin Moon Ale uses 4 machine hours and 1.5 direct labor hours.

Required

a. Assuming that Brew Shack allocates manufacturing overhead costs on the basis of machine hours, what amount of overhead is allocated to a batch of Pumpkin Moon Ale?

b. Assuming that Brew Shack allocates manufacturing overhead costs on the basis of direct labor hours, what amount of overhead is allocated to a batch of Pumpkin Moon Ale?

c. Assuming that Brew Shack uses two-stage allocation with the two cost pools indicated above, what amount of overhead is allocated to a batch of Pumpkin Moon Ale?

5. (LO5.1) Munch Lab produces and sells gourmet gift baskets. The company currently uses traditional job-order costing that allocates indirect costs based on the budgeted production of baskets. Munch Lab is considering using two-stage allocation to assign overhead costs to batches of product. Management gathers the following estimates:

Budgeted MOH	$240,000
Budgeted machine hours	1,000
Budgeted direct labor hours	16,000
Budgeted baskets	40,000

Cost Pool	Total Cost	Allocation Base
Machine-related MOH	$ 30,000	Machine hour
Labor-related MOH	$ 180,000	Direct labor hour
Unit-related MOH	$ 30,000	Basket
Total	$240,000	

Job 314 is an order for 10 gift baskets. The job requires 2 hours of labor and 15 minutes of machine time.

Required

a. Assuming that Munch Lab allocates all indirect costs on the basis of gift baskets, how much indirect cost will be allocated to Job 314?

b. Assuming that Munch Lab uses two-stage allocation to allocate indirect costs using the three cost pools listed above, how much indirect cost will be allocated to Job 314?

c. Assuming that two-stage costing is more accurate than single-stage costing, under a single-stage costing system, Job 314 would be _____ (undercosted/overcosted) by _____.

6. (LO5.3) Finagle Industries uses an activity-based costing system and has determined the following allocation rates:

Activity	Driver	Rate	
Process order	Sales order	$ 8.00	per order
Packing and shipping	Item shipped	$ 5.00	per item
Billing	Sales order	$ 3.00	per order
Product customization	Customized order	$140.00	per customized order

Required

Use the table above to answer the following questions:

a. Job 124 is a standard order that contains 14 items. What is the indirect cost allocation for Job 124?

b. Job 125 is a customized order that contains 3 items. What is the indirect cost allocation for Job 125?

c. Job 126 is a customized order that contains 23 items. What is the indirect cost allocation for Job 126?

7. (LO5.3) Chow Maine sells earthen dishes. It ships products throughout the United States, though occasionally orders are picked up at the manufacturing facility. Chow Maine uses an activity-based costing system and has determined the following allocation rates:

Activity	Driver	Rate	
Process order	Sales order	$ 3.50	per order
Quality check	Item checked	$ 0.75	per item
Modification	Item modified	$ 9.50	per modified item
Packing and shipping	Order shipped	$13.00	per shipped order

Required

Use the table above to answer the following questions:

a. Job 0208 is an order for 23 items, 6 of which required modification. The order is shipped. What is the indirect cost allocation for Job 0208?

b. Job 0209 is an order for 114 items, none of which required modification. The order is shipped. What is the indirect cost allocation for Job 0209?

c. Job 0210 is an order for 6 items, all of which required modification. The order is picked up at the manufacturing facility. What is the indirect cost allocation for Job 0210?

8. (LO5.3) Black Tie is an event-planning organization. It meets with the client to determine the scope of the engagement before planning and running the event. Black Tie has developed an activity-based costing system with the following allocation rates:

Activity	Driver	Rate	
Receive request	Event	$300.00	per event
Plan an event	Event	$850.00	per event
Invite guests	Guest	$ 52.00	per guest
Billing	Event	$ 15.00	per event

Required

Use the table above to answer the following questions:

a. The Malphus event was a wedding for 200 guests. What is the indirect cost allocation?

b. The Liu event was a graduation and included 40 guests. What is the indirect cost allocation?

c. The Vanderfall event was an anniversary party for 150 guests. What is the indirect cost allocation?

9. (LO5.4) Sweet Hues Industries has adopted a time-driven activity-based costing system. Its management estimates that an indirect cost rate of $1.50 per minute reasonably reflects the cost of company resources.

Management has estimated the amount of time that each activity uses as follows:

Activity	Driver	Estimated Minutes
Process order	Sales order	5
Packing and shipping	Item shipped	3
Billing	Sales order	2
Rush order	Rush order	60

Required

a. Job 226 is a standard order that contains 93 items. What is the indirect cost allocation for Job 226?

b. Job 227 is a standard order that contains 18 items. What is the indirect cost allocation for Job 227?

c. Job 228 is a rush order that contains 2 items. What is the indirect cost allocation for Job 228?

10. (LO5.4) The Accounts Payable department at Pelletize Grillz uses a time-driven activity-based costing system. The company estimates that each minute of time in the Accounts Payable department uses $3.15 worth of resources. Pelletize Grillz, which is very cautious with new vendors, implements an extensive quality-control check on all items received for the first six months of using a new vendor. Management believes that after six months, the quality control check is no longer needed.

Management has estimated the amount of time that each activity uses as follows:

Activity	Driver	Estimated Minutes
Process invoice	Invoice	12
Set up new vendor	First order from new vendor	25
Quality control	Units received in first 6 months with a new vendor	2

Required

a. Invoice 0246 is an invoice for 18 items from a vendor who has worked with Pelletize Grillz for over a year. What is the indirect cost allocation for Job 0246?

b. Invoice 0247 is an invoice for 30 items from a vendor who has worked with Pelletize Grillz for the past 4 months. What is the indirect cost allocation for Job 0247?

c. Invoice 0248 is an invoice for 25 items from a vendor who has not worked with Pelletize Grillz previously (in other words, this is the vendor's first invoice). What is the indirect cost allocation for Job 0248?

11. (LO5.4) Tru Photo is a photo studio that has adopted a time-driven activity-based costing system. Tru Photo's management estimates that an indirect cost rate of $2.40 per minute reasonably reflects the cost of company resources.

Management has estimated the amount of time that each activity uses as follows:

Activity	Driver	Estimated Minutes
Photo appointment	Photo session	60
Digital editing	Photos edited	5
Printing/packaging	Photos printed	0.5
Rush order	Rush order	30

Required

a. After the Jones family photo session, Tru Photo edited 13 photos and printed 30 photos. The Jones family did not request that the order be expedited. What is the indirect cost allocation for the Jones family?

b. After the Ong family photo session, Tru Photo printed 50 photos, and the order was expedited. The session required no digital editing. What is the indirect cost allocation for the Ong family?

c. The Festa family photo session resulted in 18 photos that were digitally edited. Tru Photo expedited the order, which included 25 photos. What is the indirect cost allocation for the Festa family?

12. (LO5.3) Grecko Inc. has the following indirect costs:

Overhead Costs	
Supervisor labor	$ 1,250,000
Machine maintenance	$ 1,500,000
Indirect materials	$ 300,000
Factory lease and insurance	$ 450,000
Total	$3,500,000

While implementing an activity-based costing system, Grecko decides to use the following activity cost pools: Production, Quality Control, Design Improvement, and Facility Support.

Grecko has gathered data to estimate how indirect cost categories relate to activity cost pools as follows:

| | Resource Consumption by Activity | | | | |
	Unit Production	Quality Control	Design Improvement	Facility Support	Total
Supervisor labor	60%	30%	5%	5%	100%
Machine maintenance	70%	30%	0%	0%	100%
Indirect materials	75%	5%	10%	10%	100%
Factory lease and insurance	0%	0%	0%	100%	100%

Required

Use the template below to determine the total amount of indirect cost in each activity cost pool:

| | Activity Cost Pools | | | | |
	Unit Production	Quality Control	Design Improvement	Facility Support	Total
Supervisor labor					
Machine maintenance					
Indirect materials					
Factory lease and insurance					
Total					

13. (LO5.3) Spice Gram produces hot sauce and has the following indirect costs:

Indirect Costs	
Indirect labor	$355,000
Indirect materials	$ 150,000
Product design	$ 45,000
Equipment depreciation	$ 135,000
Factory lease	$ 120,000
Total	$805,000

Spice Gram has identified the following activities for its activity-based costing system: Production, Quality Control, Patent Filing, Marketing, and Facility Support. Production is a unit-level cost, Quality Control is a batch-level cost, Patent Filing and Marketing are product-level costs, and facility-level costs are aggregated in a Facility-Support pool.

Spice Gram has gathered data to estimate how indirect cost categories relate to activity cost pools as follows:

| | Resource Consumption by Activity | | | | | |
	Production	Quality Control	Patent Filing	Marketing	Facility Support	Total
Indirect labor	55%	15%	5%	20%	5%	100%
Indirect materials	70%	25%	0%	5%	0%	100%
Product design	0%	5%	20%	75%	0%	100%
Equipment depreciation	40%	0%	0%	0%	60%	100%
Factory lease	0%	0%	0%	0%	100%	100%

Required

Use the template below to determine the total amount of indirect cost in each activity cost pool:

	Activity Cost Pools					
	Production	Quality Control	Patent Filing	Marketing	Facility Support	Total
Indirect labor						
Indirect materials						
Product design						
Equipment depreciation						
Factory lease						
Total						

14. (LO5.3) Shutter Spark is a printing company that specializes in photo printing. Shutter Spark has the following indirect costs:

Indirect Costs	
Indirect materials	$3,750,000
Indirect labor	$1,560,000
Utilities and insurance	$1,250,000
Depreciation	$1,040,000
Total	$7,600,000

Shutter Spark uses the following cost pools in its activity-based costing system: Album Printing, Batch Setup, Product Design, and Facility Support.

Shutter Spark uses employee surveys to estimate how indirect cost categories relate to activity cost pools. The company has gathered the following data:

	Resource Consumption by Activity				
	Album Printing	Batch Setup	Product Design	Facility Support	Total
Indirect materials	95%	0%	5%	0%	100%
Indirect labor	40%	30%	25%	5%	100%
Utilities and insurance	50%	10%	10%	30%	100%
Depreciation	50%	0%	0%	50%	100%

Required

Use the template below to determine the total amount of indirect cost in each activity cost pool:

	Activity Cost Pools				
	Album Printing	Batch Setup	Product Design	Facility Support	Total
Indirect materials					
Indirect labor					
Utilities and insurance					
Depreciation					
Total					

15. (LO5.3) Nomadist Inc. publishes a travel magazine. Nomadist has the following activity cost pools and estimated cost drivers for the year:

Activity	Cost Pool	CostDriver	Number of Cost Drivers	Allocation Rate
Copy editing	$ 3,375	# of pages	1,500	_____ per page
Photography	$ 5,000	# of photos	180	_____ per photo
Advertisement design	$ 12,500	# of advertisements	400	_____ per advertisement
Printing	$30,000	# of printed copies	18,000	_____ per copy
Distribution	$ 4,200	# of printed copies	18,000	_____ per copy
Total	$ 55,075			

Required
a. Calculate allocation rates for each activity cost pool by filling in the Allocation Rate column.
b. Use your answer above to assign costs to three monthly issues of Nomadist's travel magazine by completing the table below.

Activity	Cost Driver	March	April	May
Copy editing	# of pages	150	160	140
Photography	# of photos	25	28	32
Advertisement design	# of advertisements	45	40	30
Printing	# of printed copies	1,700	1,750	1,900
Distribution	# of printed copies	1,700	1,750	1,900
Total cost allocation				

16. (LO5.3) The Adventure Studio creates escape room scenarios that are then sold to escape rooms around the United States. Through extensive research, the Adventure Studio has found a number of activities that influence the cost of producing escape room scenarios. These activities and the associated cost drivers are displayed below:

Activity	Cost Pool	Cost Driver	Number of Cost Drivers	Allocation Rate
Scenario design	$250,000	Scenario	8	_____ per scenario
Prop production	$ 120,000	Props	160	_____ per prop
Film clip production	$ 130,000	Film clips	32	_____ per film clip
Total	$500,000			

Required
a. Calculate allocation rates for each activity cost pool by filling in the Allocation Rate column.
b. Use your answer above to assign costs to three escape room scenarios created by The Adventure Studio by completing the table below.

Activity	Cost Driver	Haunted Food Truck	Zombie Wedding	8th Grade Algebra
Scenario design	Scenario	1	1	1
Prop production	Props	25	20	16
Film clip production	Film clips	4	5	7
Total cost allocation				

17. (LO5.2, 5.3) Wanderica makes software for managing real estate portfolios. Wanderica is implementing activity-based costing in one of its departments, which has the following indirect costs and allocation base data:

Activity Cost Pool	Cost Pool Total	Cost Driver	# of Cost Drivers
Customer service	$ 310,250	# of customer requests	5,000
Process orders	$ 616,750	# of orders	400
Feature design	$2,231,500	# of new features	1,200
Debug software	$ 436,500	# of patches	1,800

Required

a. Determine allocation rates for each cost driver listed above.

b. Calculate cost allocations for each of the following customers (BiG6, SanTech, and Coastal), based on their usage of Wanderica's resources.

Activity	Cost Driver	BiG6	SanTech	Coastal
Customer service	# of customer requests	14	30	17
Take customer orders	# of orders	4	3	7
Design new features	# of new features	18	25	35
Debug software	# of batches	30	10	28
Total cost allocation				

Lab 5.1 Excel

Using Two-Stage Costing to Address a Hidden Cost Driver Difference (Heartwood)

Data Analytics Types: Diagnostic Analytics, Predictive Analytics

Lab Note: The tools presented in this lab periodically change. Updated instructions, if applicable, can be found in the student and instructor support materials.

Keywords

Cost Drivers, Overhead Allocation, Excel

Decision-Making Context

Heartwood Cabinets has been making cabinets for customers for many years. Although the design of a basic cabinet has changed very little over time, cabinet door styles change over time as customers seek unique and elaborate doors.

Heartwood Cabinets uses several automated CNC routers to cut designs into cabinet doors, and the company purchases new routers as necessary. Customers have recently requested doors with elaborate scrollwork. As a result, Heartwood purchased a new SkillCut router that can cut with finer precision than Heartwood's other routers. The new router is significantly more expensive than Heartwood's other routers.

Historically, Heartwood has allocated manufacturing overhead on the basis of machine hours. However, a management accounting intern has suggested that the company consider a two-stage allocation for manufacturing overhead. The intern suspects that indirect costs associated with the new router are significantly higher than those associated with Heartwood's other routers.

Required

Use data to determine whether the intern is correct. Compare in detail the costs of a scrollwork cabinet door (which requires the SkillCut router) with the costs of a traditional shaker-style cabinet door that uses a basic CNC router.

Ask the Question

What indirect costs are associated with the new SkillCut router? How does a single-stage allocation, which treats all machine hours as if they cost the same amount, distort indirect costs when SkillCut machine hours are more expensive? The term "hidden difference" is sometimes used to refer to a setting where one category of cost driver (for example, machine hours) should be split into multiple cost drivers because they are associated with different costs.

Master the Data

Data Dictionary

The data include the manufacturing overhead costs for January.

Router Costs	Monthly machine hours, depreciation, and maintenance costs
Finishing Department	Monthly indirect costs from the finishing department. The finishing department finishes cabinet doors by sanding down rough edges. It then paints the doors or finishes them with polyurethane. All finishing department labor is indirect labor because it is not traced to individual doors.
Other information	The bottom of the spreadsheet provides the number of hours it takes to complete a cabinet door, as well as the direct materials and direct labor required for each door.

Perform the Analysis

Analysis Task #1: Calculate Allocation Rates

1. Open Excel file **Lab 5.1 Data.xlsx**.
2. Browse the spreadsheet very quickly to make sure it doesn't contain any obvious error.
3. We will first calculate an allocation rate under a single-stage allocation such that all manufacturing overhead is assigned on the basis of machine hours. In cell B10, calculate total overhead costs by adding total router costs with finishing department costs. The formula is =G7+J7 (see Lab Exhibit 5.1.1).

	A	B		C	D	E	F	G	H	I	J
1	January '25 Manufacturing Overhead										
2											
3		Router A		Router B	Router Costs Router C	Router D	SkillCut		Total			Finishing Department
4	Machine Hours	160		160	160	160	160		800		Labor	$ 15,000
5	Depreciation	$ 5,000	$	4,500	$ 6,000 $	4,500 $	15,000 $		35,000		Sanding supplies	$ 500
6	Maintenance	$ 2,400	$	2,000	$ 2,100 $	2,300 $	4,200 $		13,000		Paint	$ 5,000
7	Total Router Costs	$ 7,400	$	6,500	$ 8,100 $	6,800 $	19,200 $		48,000		Poly	$ 2,000
8											Total	$ 22,500
9	Single-stage allocation											
10	Total Overhead Costs	=G7+J7										

Lab Exhibit 5.1.1

Microsoft Excel

4. Use formulas to assign total machine hours and the allocation rate in cells B11 and B12, respectively. The formula for Total MH in cell C11 is =G4, and the formula for Allocation Rate in cell C12 is =B10/B11 (see Lab Exhibit 5.1.2).

	A	B		C	D	E	F	G	H	I	J
1	January '25 Manufacturing Overhead										
2											
3		Router A		Router B	Router Costs Router C	Router D	SkillCut		Total			Finishing Department
4	Machine Hours	160		160	160	160	160		800		Labor	$ 15,000
5	Depreciation	$ 5,000	$	4,500	$ 6,000 $	4,500 $	15,000 $		35,000		Sanding supplies	$ 500
6	Maintenance	$ 2,400	$	2,000	$ 2,100 $	2,300 $	4,200 $		13,000		Paint	$ 5,000
7	Total Router Costs	$ 7,400	$	6,500	$ 8,100 $	6,800 $	19,200 $		48,000		Poly	$ 2,000
8											Total	$ 22,500
9	Single-stage allocation											
10	Total Overhead Costs	$ 70,500										
11	Total MH			800 G4								
12	Allocation Rate	$		88.125 B10/B11								

Lab Exhibit 5.1.2

Microsoft Excel

5. Next we calculate allocation rates using a two-stage allocation. First, we need to subdivide total overhead costs into two pools—the first associated with the older, basic routers and the second associated with the new SkillCut router. Management assigns all manufacturing overhead based on machine hours, so we will assume that finishing department costs should be assigned to the two cost pools based on their proportion of total machine hours as well. Input the formulas as shown in Lab Exhibit 5.1.3.

Two-stage allocation			
Total Overhead Costs	$	70,500	=G7+J7
Basic Router Pool	$	46,800	=SUM(B7:E7)+((SUM(B4:E4)/G4)*J7)
Basic Router MH			
Basic Router Rate			
SkillCut Router Pool	$	23,700	=F7+(F4/G4*J7)
SkillCut Router MH			
SkillCut Router Rate			

6. Next, calculate allocation rates for each pool by dividing costs in each pool by machine hours for each pool. Input the additional formulas as shown in Lab Exhibit 5.1.4.

Two-stage allocation			
Total Overhead Costs	$	70,500	=G7+J7
Basic Router Pool	$	46,800	=SUM(B7:E7)+((SUM(B4:E4)/G4)*J7)
Basic Router MH		640	=SUM(B4:E4)
Basic Router Rate	$	73.13	=B16/B17
SkillCut Router Pool	$	23,700	=F7+(F4/G4*J7)
SkillCut Router MH		160	=F4
SkillCut Router Rate	$	148.13	=B19/B20

Analysis Task #2: Calculate Production Costs

1. In Row 29, we will allocate overhead costs by multiplying machine hours by the appropriate allocation rate. Be sure to change the rate based on the type of cabinet door (shaker or scrollwork) and the allocation method (single- or two-stage). In cell E29, add the formula shown in the lower-right corner of Lab Exhibit 5.1.5: =E26*$B$21.

	A	B	C	D	E
14	Two-stage allocation				
15	Total Overhead Costs	$ 70,500			
16	Basic Router Pool	$ 46,800			
17	Basic Router MH	640			
18	Basic Router Rate	$ 73.13			
19	SkillCut Router Pool	$ 23,700			
20	SkillCut Router MH	160			
21	SkillCut Router Rate	$ 148.13			
22					
23					
24					
25		1-Stage Shaker	1-Stage Scrollwork	2-Stage Shaker	2-Stage Scrollwork
26	Machine Hours	0.05	0.05	0.05	0.05
27	Direct Materials	$ 15.00	$ 16.00	$ 15.00	$ 16.00
28	Direct Labor	$ 2.00	$ 2.00	$ 2.00	$ 2.00
29	Allocated Overhead	$ 4.41	$ 4.41	$ 3.66	=E26*$B$21

2. In Row 30, cell E30, calculate total production costs by adding together direct materials, direct labor, and allocated overhead. Use the **SUM** function as shown in the lower-right corner of Lab Exhibit 5.1.6: =SUM(E27+E28+E29).

	A	B	C	D	E
25		1-Stage Shaker	1-Stage Scrollwork	2-Stage Shaker	2-Stage Scrollwork
26	Machine Hours	0.05	0.05	0.05	0.05
27	Direct Materials	$ 15.00	$ 16.00	$ 15.00	$ 16.00
28	Direct Labor	$ 2.00	$ 2.00	$ 2.00	$ 2.00
29	Allocated Overhead	$ 4.41	$ 4.41	$ 3.66	$ 7.41
30	Total Cost	$ 21.41	$ 22.41	20.66	=SUM(E27+E28+E29)

Lab Exhibit 5.1.6

Microsoft Excel

Analysis Task #3: Create a Chart to Display Production Costs

1. Select cells A27:E29. Insert a stacked bar chart by selecting **Insert**, then the **column chart** icon, and then the **2-D bar** column, as shown in Lab Exhibit 5.1.7.

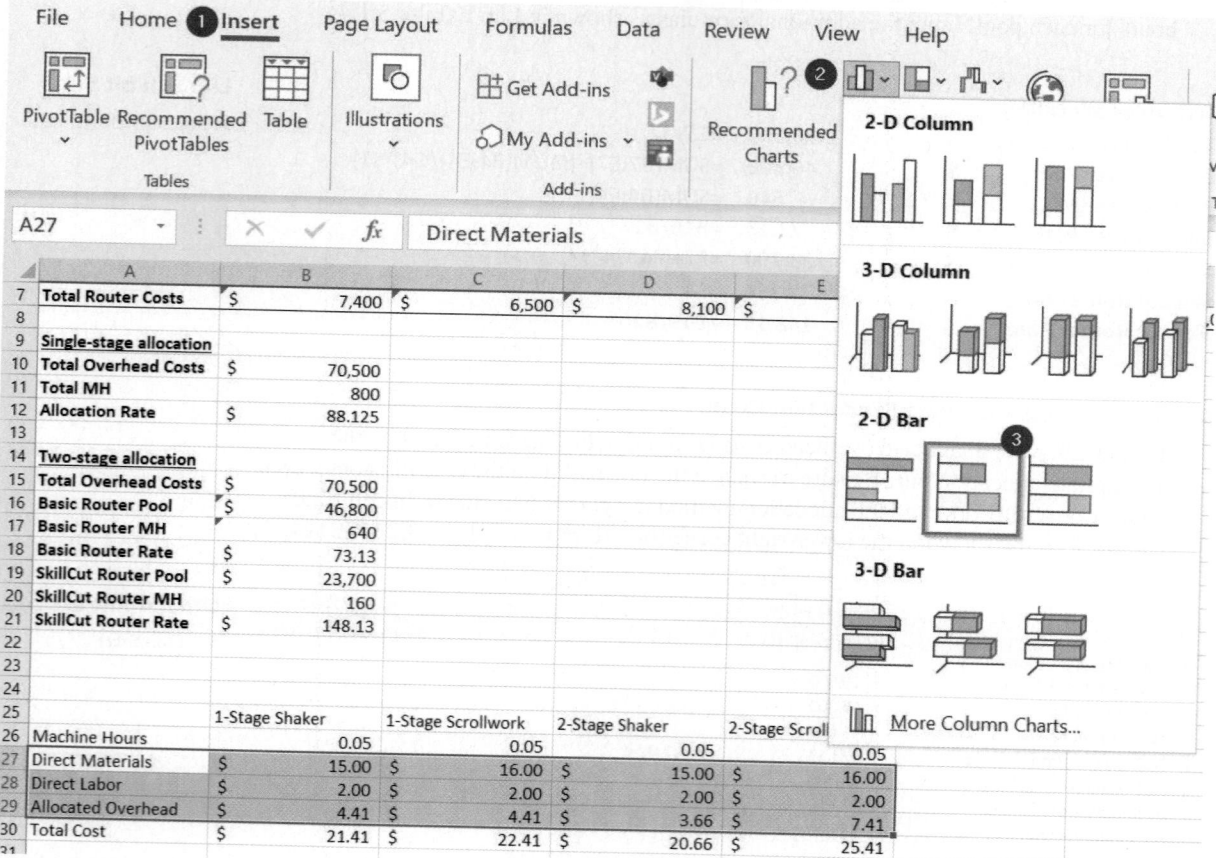

Lab Exhibit 5.1.7

Microsoft Excel

2. Change the chart title to "Production Costs".
3. Right-click on the chart and choose **Select Data...** (see Lab Exhibit 5.1.8).

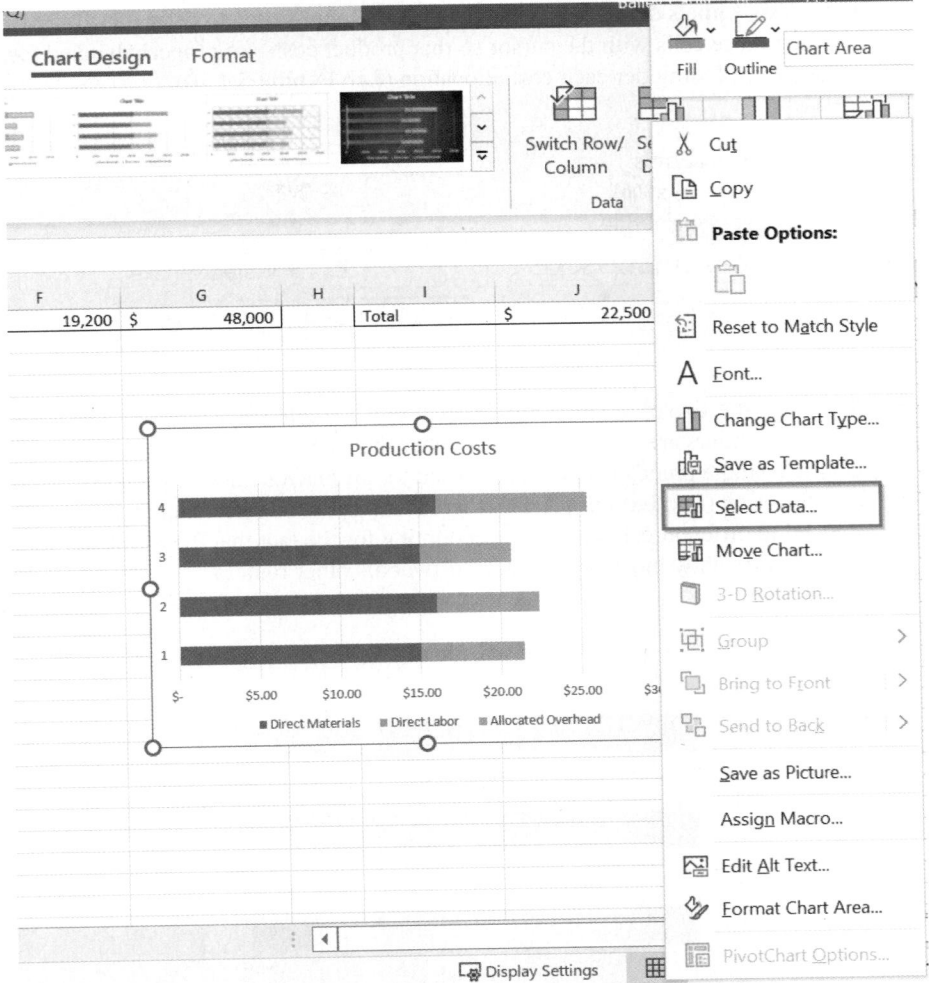

Lab Exhibit 5.1.8

Microsoft Excel

4. On the **Horizontal (Category) Axis Labels**, select **1** and then select **Edit** (Lab Exhibit 5.1.9).

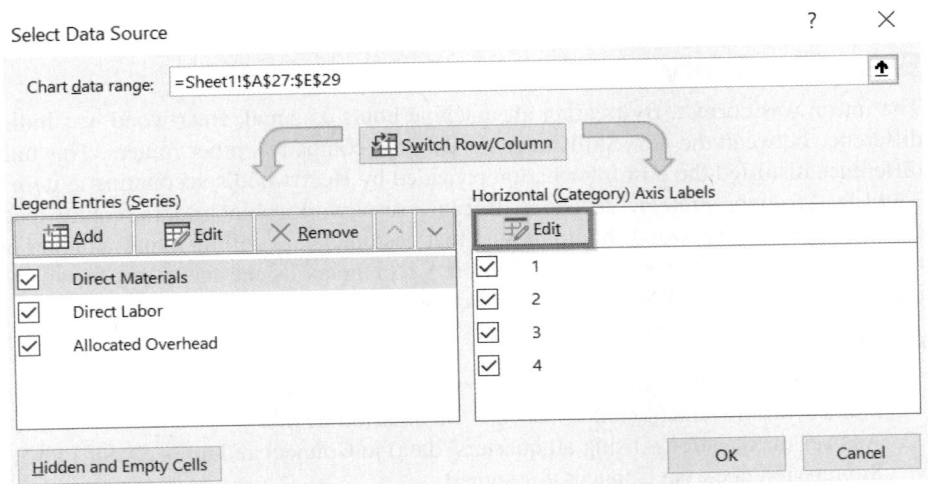

Lab Exhibit 5.1.9

Microsoft Excel

5. In the **Axis Labels** dialog box, change the **Axis label range** to cells B25:E25 by selecting those cells with the cursor so that product costs are properly labeled for each cabinet door under each cost allocation (Lab Exhibit 5.1.10).

Lab Exhibit 5.1.10

Microsoft Excel

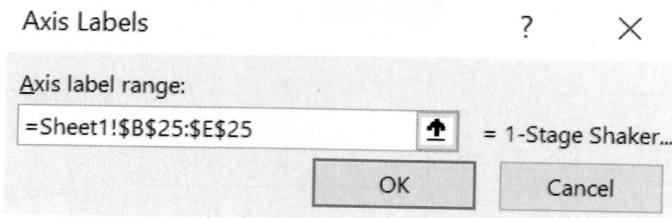

6. Notice that the size of the gray box is equal under single-stage allocation because all machine hours are treated the same under the single-stage cost allocation. This is because a single predetermined rate is used for all machine hours. Under two-stage cost allocation (Lab Exhibit 5.1.11), there is a significant difference in the overhead assigned to different cabinet doors, accounting for the fact that the SkillCut router incurs significantly more costs than Heartwood's other routers.

DATA VISUALIZATION

Lab Exhibit 5.1.11

Microsoft Excel

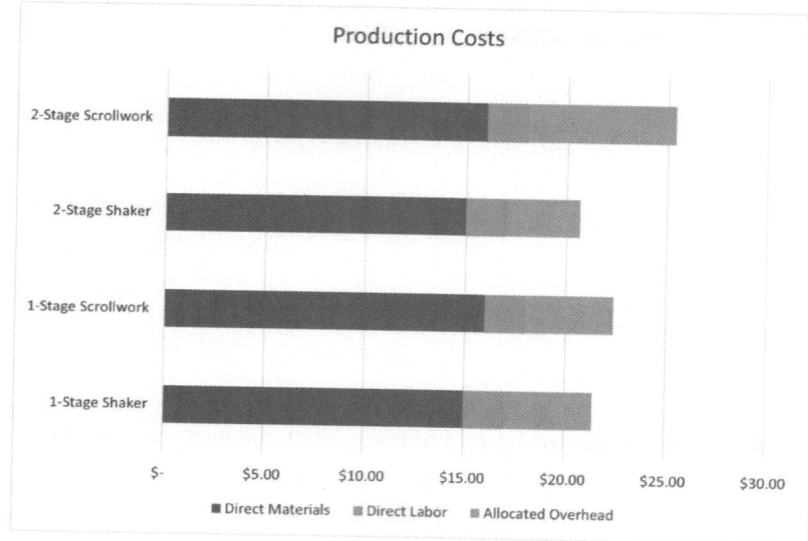

Share the Story

The intern was correct. By treating all machine hours as equal, Heartwood was hiding a difference between the new SkillCut router and the company's other routers. This hidden difference distorted the cost information provided by Heartwood's accounting system and could lead to poor strategic decisions. Because scrollwork cabinet doors require specialized machinery, Heartwood should be sure that customers are willing to pay a higher price to offset higher costs. The graph in Exhibit 5.1.11 helps us see the extent to which the indirect cost distortion affected total production costs.

Assessment

1. Take a screenshot of the bar chart following Step 6 of Analysis Task #3 and paste it into a Word document named "Lab 5.1 Submission.docx".
2. Answer the questions (using all quarters' data) in Connect and upload your Lab 5.1 Submission.docx via Connect if assigned.

Using Two-Stage Costing to Address a Hidden Cost Driver Difference (Heartwood)

Keywords

Cost Drivers, Overhead Allocation, Excel

The intern at **Heartwood** has another critical insight! Because of the intricacy of the scrollwork in a cabinet door, the intern has suggested that scrollwork doors might require extra time to be sanded and finished. Internal analysis confirms the intern's beliefs. Although scrollwork doors account for only about 20% of total router hours, they account for 50% of the finishing department's costs.

Required

Apply the same steps in Lab 5.1 to the **Alt Lab 5.1 Data.xlsx** dataset. This dataset includes manufacturing overhead information for February. As you calculate the production of doors under the single- and two-stage allocation processes, make sure to assign half of the finishing department's cost to each cost pool.

Assessment

1. Take a screenshot of the output and paste it into a Word document named "Alt Lab 5.1 Submission.docx".
2. Answer the questions in Connect and upload your Alt Lab 5.1 Submission.docx via Connect if assigned.

Lab 5.2   Excel

Using Two-Stage Costing to Address a Hidden Cost Driver Difference

Data Analytics Types: Diagnostic Analytics, Predictive Analytics

Keywords

Cost Drivers, Overhead Allocation, Excel

Decision-Making Context

True History is a fictitious company that builds small-scale models depicting historical events including sports games, battles, and even personal experiences as described by its customers.

Historically, True History has allocated all manufacturing overhead using a single allocation base: direct labor hours. True History is investigating how the two-stage allocation of overhead costs would affect its accounting system. As such, the company wants to analyze last year's cost data to determine allocation rates for the upcoming year.

Required

1. Calculate overhead rates using single- and two-stage allocation.
2. Apply overhead to specific jobs using single- and two-stage allocation and determine how single-stage allocation can distort product costs.

Ask the Question

Traditional job-order costing systems allocate manufacturing overhead using a single allocation base or cost driver. How will the implementation of two-stage cost allocation affect product costs for True History? Two-stage cost allocations often indicate "hidden drivers," which are cost drivers that are ignored in a single-stage allocation.

Master the Data

Data Dictionary

The data include manufacturing overhead and production data for the previous year's production at True History.

Month	Month of the year
Production	Monthly production in units
Direct labor hours	Monthly direct labor hours
Machine hours	Monthly machine hours
Depreciation	Monthly depreciation expense
Maintenance	Monthly machine maintenance expense
Indirect Labor	Monthly indirect labor expense
Factory rent	Monthly factory rent
Total MOH	Monthly manufacturing overhead expense
Other information	The bottom of the spreadsheet provides information about Job 894 that will be needed to calculate allocated manufacturing overhead

Perform the Analysis

Analysis Task #1: Calculate Allocation Rates.

1. Open Excel file **Lab 5.2 Data.xlsx**.
2. Browse the spreadsheet very quickly to make sure it doesn't contain any obvious error.
3. We will first calculate an allocation rate under a single-stage allocation such that all manufacturing overhead is assigned on the basis of direct labor hours. In cells B17:B19, use formulas to calculate total overhead costs by dividing total manufacturing overhead costs by total direct labor hours. The formulas are shown in Lab Exhibit 5.2.1, as follows:

   Cell B17: =J14

   Cell B18: =C14

   Cell B19: =B17/B18

4. Now we calculate allocation rates using a two-stage allocation. First, we need to subdivide total overhead costs into three cost pools. Management has decided to use a production pool to aggregate production-related costs. These costs include the indirect materials. Management has determined that the maintenance expense of the machines should be in a machine pool, and indirect labor should be in a direct labor pool. Management has identified cost drivers for all these pools, as displayed on the spreadsheet in cells A22, A26, and A29.

   Management has determined that depreciation and factory rent should be included in the production pool, even though the relationship between these costs and the cost driver is not very strong. These costs must be allocated on some basis so that all costs are properly recorded on the company's financial statements.

   Use the formulas shown in Lab Exhibit 5.2.2 to subdivide total manufacturing overhead into cost pools, ensuring that all costs are accounted for.

5. Next, calculate allocation rates for each pool by dividing costs in each pool by each pool's cost driver. Use the formulas shown in Lab Exhibit 5.2.3.

Analysis Task #2: Calculate Production Costs

1. In Rows 36–38, we will allocate overhead costs by multiplying our allocation rates by each cost driver, depending on whether we use single- or two-stage allocation. Sum allocation costs in Row 39 to determine total allocated manufacturing overhead for Job 894. Use the **Sum** function, as shown in Lab Exhibit 5.2.4.

   Notice how our hidden drivers (machine hours and units produced, as shown in Lab Exhibit 5.2.4) affect product costs in ways that are not evident using single-stage costing.

Analysis Task #3: Create a Chart to Display Production Costs

1. Select cells A36:C38. From the main menu, select **Insert**. Next, choose the bar graph icon and then the icon for a stacked column chart (Lab Exhibit 5.2.5).
2. Right-click on the chart and choose **Select Data...**. Then select **Switch Row/Column**, as shown in Lab Exhibit 5.2.6.
3. Under **Horizontal (Category) Axis Labels**, select **1** and then select **Edit**. Next, change the **Axis label range** to cells B32:C32 by selecting the appropriate cells with the cursor so that product costs are properly labeled (Lab Exhibit 5.2.7).
4. Double-click the **Chart Title** and change it to "Job 894 MOH Costs". Left-click on the chart, select the plus sign (**+**), and select **Data Labels** to display the allocated amounts for each cost pool. The resulting data visualization appears in Lab Exhibit 5.2.8.
5. Notice how different methods of allocation can drastically change allocated overhead. If two-stage costing is accurate, then our data suggest that Job 894 is undercosted by $232.38, calculated as the $556.01 cost under a two-stage cost system minus $323.63 under the single-stage cost system. This cost distortion could have significant consequences for True History's strategic decisions.

DATA VISUALIZATION

Share the Story

Two-stage allocation provides more accurate data than single-stage allocation because it helps companies identify hidden cost drivers that affect product costs. In this lab, True History found that the same job cost $323.63 under a single-stage cost system and $556.01 under a two-stage cost system. Simple data visualization helps us see the extent to which the indirect cost distortion affected total production costs.

Assessment

1. Take a screenshot of the table following step 5 of Analysis Task #3 and paste it into a Word document named "Lab 5.2 Submission.docx".
2. Answer the questions (using all quarters' data) in Connect and upload your Lab 5.2 Submission.docx via Connect if assigned.

Alternate Lab 5.2   Excel—On Your Own

Using Two-Stage Costing to Address a Hidden Cost Driver Difference

Keywords

Cost Drivers, Overhead Allocation, Excel

Apply the same steps in Lab 5.2 to the **Alt Lab 5.2 Data.xlsx** dataset, which contains a new year's worth of data. In addition, management has decided that depreciation and factory rent should be assigned to the machine pool rather than the production pool. Make sure you change your spreadsheet accordingly. Your task is to calculate the total cost allocation to Job 1262.

Assessment

1. Take a screenshot of the output and paste it into a Word document named "Alt Lab 5.2 Submission.docx".
2. Answer the questions in Connect and upload your Alt Lab 5.2 Submission.docx via Connect if assigned.

Identifying Potential Cost Drivers and Creating Dashboards

Data Analytics Types: Diagnostic Analytics, Predictive Analytics

Lab Note: The tools presented in this lab periodically change. Updated instructions, if applicable, can be found in the student and instructor support materials. All Lab Exhibits are available within the eBook and in Connect.

Keywords

Management Accounting, Cost Drivers, Overhead Allocation

Decision-Making Context

Overhead costs are indirect costs that are generally hard to trace to an individual product. They include taxes, advertising, rent, office supplies/equipment, business-related travel, insurance, business permits, maintenance and repair of equipment, utilities (electricity, telephone), professional assistance (accountant, attorney, consultant), and any other costs related to the overall operation of the business. We must allocate those costs to adequately price, compute cost, and evaluate the overall profitability of each product for sale.

Many corporations use activity-based costing to allocate overhead costs. Activity-based costing (ABC) is a cost system that assumes that the best way to assign indirect costs to products is based on the products' demand for resource-consuming activities, which are called cost drivers.

In one sense, we are trying to make indirect costs come as close to direct costs as we can in order to see if we would make different decisions based on that cost allocation.

This lab asks you to use scatterplots and correlations to assess candidate drivers before additional analysis is performed.

Required

1. Using scatterplots and correlations, assess potential cost drivers of overall overhead costs that can be used to help allocate overhead.
2. Create a dashboard to evaluate all three scatterplots and the correlation matrix.

Ask the Question

How can we use scatterplots to assess potential cost drivers of activities that may help allocate overhead appropriately?

Master the Data

Office Depot delivers bulk paper products to its customers. It incurs various indirect costs, including car maintenance, tires, oil changes, gasoline, car insurance, and car property tax, that it would like to allocate to each delivery. If managers can more accurately allocate these indirect, or overhead, costs, then the business can more accurately charge its customers for their deliveries. Managers would like to estimate cost drivers as part of an activity-based costing system. Office Depot does an intense analysis of overhead costs. After the managers identify the drivers of overhead costs, they can develop a formula to allocate the overhead based on those cost drivers.

The analysis calculates total overhead costs over 122 delivery days and considers four potential cost drivers that the company believes may be associated with the overhead costs. These potential cost drivers include the number of deliveries made, the number of miles driven, the total delivery time, and the combined weight of delivery for the day.

We are trying to prepare the data for analysis. Here is the data dictionary.

Data Dictionary

Delivery Day	Indicates delivery day (total cost was estimated from days 1 to 122)
Total Overhead Cost	The total indirect costs incurred for that delivery day
Deliveries	The number of deliveries made that day
Miles	The number of miles to make all deliveries that day
Time (Minutes)	The delivery time (in minutes) it takes to make all deliveries that day
Weight	Combined weight of all deliveries made that day

Open Power BI and import the **Lab 5.3 Data.xlsx** workbook through the **Get Data** command, as shown in Lab Exhibit 5.3P.1.

We're now ready to perform the analysis.

Perform the Analysis

Analysis Task #1: Calculate the Potential Cost Drivers

Using the variables in the dataset, we need to calculate our overhead cost per delivery as well as our three potential cost drivers: miles per delivery, time per delivery, and weight per delivery.

1. To start calculating overhead cost per delivery, click on **Modeling** and then select the **New column** icon (Lab Exhibit 5.3P.2). This will open the formula builder at the top of the report canvas. Enter the following formula to calculate total cost:

   `Overhead Cost Per Delivery = [Total Overhead Cost]/[Deliveries]`

   Click the **check mark** to the left of the formula bar to save the new column (Lab Exhibit 5.3P.3).

2. Following the directions in Step 1, calculate miles per delivery. Enter the following formula to calculate total cost:

   `Miles per Delivery = [Miles]/[Deliveries]`

   Click the check mark to the left of the formula bar to save the new column.

3. Following the directions in Step 1, calculate time per delivery. Enter the following formula to calculate total cost:

   `Time per Delivery = [Delivery Time (Minutes)]/[Deliveries]`

   Click the check mark to the left of the formula bar to save the new column.

4. Following the directions in Step 1, calculate the weight per delivery. Enter the following formula to calculate total cost:

   `Weight per Delivery = [Weight of delivery (lbs)]/[Deliveries]`

   Click the check mark to the left of the formula bar to save the new column.

Analysis Task #2: Create the Scatterplots for Each Possible Cost Driver

DATA VISUALIZATION

1. Double-click on Page 1 and replace the label with "Scatter Plot Miles and OH Cost". To do so, select **Rename Page** and then input "Scatter Plot Miles and OH Cost" (see Lab Exhibits 5.3P.4 and 5.3P.5).

2. To create the first scatterplot, assessing the relationship between Miles per Delivery and Overhead Cost per Delivery, drag **Miles per Delivery** and **Overhead Cost per Delivery** onto the **report canvas**. These will appear with the aggregated sum value of each, as shown in Lab Exhibits 5.3P.6 and 5.3P.7.

3. To view the individual observations in the scatterplot, select the **Scatter Chart** icon in the **Visualizations** pane (Lab Exhibit 5.3P.8). Make sure Miles per Delivery is on the X-axis and Overhead Cost per Delivery is on the Y-axis. Click the drop-down next to the variables and select **Don't summarize** to disaggregate the values (Lab Exhibit 5.3P.9). The resulting scatterplot is shown in Lab Exhibit 5.3P.10.

4. Follow the same procedure as above on a new page titled "Page 1", replacing the label with "Scatter Plot Time and OH Cost" and dragging **Time per Delivery** and **Overhead Cost per Delivery** to the report canvas. To view the individual observations in the scatterplot, click the drop-down and select **Don't summarize** to disaggregate the values. The resulting scatterplot is shown in Lab Exhibit 5.3P.11.

5. Follow the same procedure as above on a new page titled "Page 1", replacing the label with "Scatter Plot Weight and OH Cost" and dragging **Weight per Delivery** and **Overhead Cost per Delivery** to the report canvas. To view the individual observations in the scatterplot, click the drop-down and select **Don't summarize** to disaggregate the values. The resulting scatterplot is shown in Lab Exhibit 5.3P.12.

Analysis Task #3: Calculate the Correlation Between Potential Cost Drivers and Overhead Costs

DATA VISUALIZATION

1. Next we'll calculate the correlations for each of the potential cost drivers with the overhead cost per delivery. To do so, open another worksheet. Label it "Page 1" and title it "Correlations".

   To calculate the correlation between overhead cost per delivery and time per delivery, click on **Modeling** and then select the **Quick measure** icon, as shown in Lab Exhibit 5.3P.13. The calculation window will open. Select **Correlation coefficient** (under mathematical operations) from the **Calculation** drop-down menu. Calculate the correlation by entering the inputs shown in Lab Exhibit 5.3P.14 and then select **Add**.

   Change the title of the formula to "Correlation Cost and Time" in the formula bar after clicking **Add** on the **Quick Measure** window, as shown in Lab Exhibit 5.3P.15.

2. To calculate the correlation between overhead cost per delivery and miles per delivery, click on **Modeling** and then select the **Quick measure** icon (see Lab Exhibit 5.3P.13). The calculation window will open. Select **Correlation coefficient** from the **Calculation** drop-down. Calculate the correlation by entering the inputs shown in Lab Exhibit 5.3P.16 and then selecting **Add**.

   Change the title of the formula to "Correlation Cost and Miles" in the formula bar after clicking **Add** on the **Quick Measure** window.

3. To calculate the correlation between overhead cost per delivery and weight per delivery, click on **Modeling** and then select the **Quick measure** icon. The calculation window will open. Select **Correlation coefficient** from the **Calculation** drop-down menu. Calculate the correlation by entering the inputs as shown in Lab Exhibit 5.3P.17 and then selecting **Add**.

   Change the title of the formula to "Correlation Cost and Weight" in the formula bar after clicking **Add** on the **Quick Measure** window.

4. Drag the new variables—the **Correlation Cost and Miles** variable, the **Correlation Cost and Time** variable, and the **Correlation Cost and Weight** variable—to the report canvas (Lab Exhibit 5.3P.18), and then select the **Multi Row Card** icon in the **Visualization** pane (Lab Exhibit 5.3P.19).

The result should resemble Lab Exhibit 5.3P.20.

We note a reasonably high correlation between overhead cost per delivery and miles per delivery (0.61), as well as between overhead cost per delivery and time per delivery (0.87), suggesting they may be appropriate cost drivers. However, there is a much lower correlation between overhead cost per delivery and weight per delivery (0.06), suggesting that weight per delivery may not be an appropriate cost driver.

Analysis Task #4: Create a Dashboard of All Individual Scatterplots

1. We now have all of the individual scatterplots and the correlation table. To view them all together, create a new page titled "Page 1" and label it "Combination of Potential Cost Drivers".
2. Copy each of the visualizations from all four pages and paste them into the new combination page. The dashboard allows us to view all of the scatterplots and correlations at one time.

Share the Story

We have now developed a formula for overhead costs that we can use to apply overhead to subsequent deliveries. This formula will help us in costing out subsequent deliveries.

Assessment

1. Take a screenshot of the final dashboard and paste it into a Word document named "Lab 5.3 Power BI Submission.docx".
2. Answer the questions in Connect and upload your Lab 5.3 Power BI Submission.docx via Connect if assigned.

Alternate Lab 5.3   Power BI—On Your Own

Identifying Potential Cost Drivers and Creating Dashboards

Keywords

Management Accounting, Cost Drivers, Overhead Allocation

Apply the same steps in Lab 5.3 to the **Alt Lab 5.3 Data.xlsx** dataset to evaluate the scatterplots and correlations between total overhead cost and potential cost drivers (including customer call minutes, customer complaints, average workers, and company sales).

Required

1. Using scatterplots and correlations, assess potential cost drivers of overall overhead costs that can be used to help allocate overhead.
2. Create a dashboard to evaluate all three scatterplots and the correlation matrix.

Open Excel file **Alt Lab 5.3 Data.xlsx** and perform the analysis.

Data Dictionary

Customer Service Months	The number of the month for the overhead costs
Total Overhead Cost	The total overhead cost for the service month
Customer Call Minutes	The number of minutes spent on customer calls during the month
Customer Complaints	The number of customer complaints filed during the month
Average Workers	The number of average workers during the month
Company Sales	The gross dollar amount of company sales during the month

---

Assessment

1. Take a screenshot of the final dashboard and paste it into a Word document named "Alt Lab 5.3 Power BI Submission.docx".
2. Answer the questions in Connect and upload your Alt Lab 5.3 Power BI Submission .docx via Connect if assigned.

Identifying Potential Cost Drivers and Creating Dashboards

Data Analytics Types: Diagnostic Analytics, Predictive Analytics

Keywords

Management Accounting, Cost Drivers, Overhead Allocation

Decision-Making Context

Overhead costs are indirect costs that are generally hard to trace to an individual product. They include taxes, advertising, rent, office supplies/equipment, business-related travel, insurance, business permits, maintenance and repair of equipment, utilities (electricity, telephone), professional assistance (accountant, attorney, consultant), and any other costs related to the overall operation of the business. We must allocate those costs to adequately price, compute cost, and evaluate the overall profitability of each product for sale.

Many corporations use activity-based costing to allocate overhead costs. Activity-based costing (ABC) is a cost system that assumes that the best way to assign indirect costs to products is based on the products' demand for resource-consuming activities, which are called cost drivers.

In one sense, we are trying to make indirect costs come as close to direct costs as we can in order to see if we would make different decisions based on that cost allocation.

This lab asks you to use scatterplots and correlations to assess candidate drivers before additional analysis is performed.

Required

1. Using scatterplots and correlations, assess potential cost drivers of overall overhead costs that can be used to help allocate overhead.
2. Create a dashboard to evaluate all three scatterplots and the correlation matrix.

Ask the Question

How can we use scatterplots to assess potential cost drivers of activities that may help allocate overhead appropriately?

Master the Data

Office Depot delivers bulk paper products to its customers. It incurs various indirect costs, including car maintenance, tires, oil changes, gasoline, car insurance, and car property tax, that it would like to allocate to each delivery. If managers can more accurately allocate these indirect, or overhead, costs, then the business can more accurately charge its customers for their deliveries. Managers would like to estimate cost drivers as part of an activity-based costing system. Office Depot does an intense analysis of overhead costs. After the managers identify the drivers of overhead costs, they can develop a formula to allocate the overhead based on those cost drivers.

The analysis calculates total overhead costs over 122 delivery days and considers four potential cost drivers that the company believes may be associated with the overhead costs. These potential cost drivers include the number of deliveries made, the number of miles driven, the total delivery time, and the combined weight of delivery for the day.

We are trying to prepare the data for analysis. Here is the data dictionary.

Data Dictionary

Delivery Day	Indicates delivery day (total cost was estimated from days 1 to 122)
Total Overhead Cost	The total indirect costs incurred for that delivery day
Deliveries	The number of deliveries made that day
Miles	The number of miles to make all deliveries that day
Time (Minutes)	The delivery time (in minutes) it takes to make all deliveries that day
Weight	Combined weight of all deliveries made that day

Open Tableau and connect to Excel file **Lab 5.3 Data.xlsx**. We're now ready to perform the analysis.

Perform the Analysis

Analysis Task #1: Calculate the Potential Cost Drivers

1. Click on **Sheet 1** at the bottom left of the Tableau screen. Using the variables in the dataset, we'll need to calculate our overhead cost per delivery as well as our three potential cost drivers: miles per delivery, time per delivery, and weight per delivery.
2. To calculate overhead cost per delivery, click on **Analysis > Create Calculated Field...**. Calculate the overhead cost per delivery by inputting the formula [Total Overhead Cost]/[Deliveries], as shown in Lab Exhibit 5.3T.1. Then select **OK**.
3. To calculate miles per delivery, click on **Analysis > Create Calculated Field...**. Calculate the miles per delivery by inputting the formula [Miles]/[Deliveries], as shown in Lab Exhibit 5.3T.2. Then select **OK**.
4. To calculate time per delivery, click **Analysis > Create Calculated Field...**. Calculate the time per delivery by inputting the formula [Delivery time (Minutes)]/[Deliveries], as shown in Exhibit 5.3T.3. Then select **OK**.
5. To calculate the weight per delivery, click **Analysis > Create Calculated Field...**. Calculate the weight per delivery by inputting the formula [Weight of delivery (lbs)/[Deliveries], as shown in Lab Exhibit 5.3T.4. Then select **OK**.

Analysis Task #2: Create the Scatterplots for Each Possible Cost Driver

1. Double-click on Sheet 1 and replace the label with "Scatterplot Miles and OH Cost".
2. To create the first scatterplot, assessing the relationship between Miles per delivery and Overhead Cost per delivery, drag **Miles per delivery** to the **Columns** and **Overhead Cost per delivery** to the **Rows**, as shown in Lab Exhibit 5.3T.5. These will show up with the aggregated sum value of each.
3. To view the individual observations in the scatterplot, click on **Analysis > Aggregate Measures** to uncheck the aggregate measure of each variable, as shown in Lab Exhibit 5.3T.5a.
4. Follow the same procedure as above on a new spreadsheet titled Sheet 2, replacing the label with "Scatterplot Time and OH Cost" and dragging the **Time per Delivery** to the **Columns** and **Overhead Cost per delivery** to the **Rows**. To view

DATA VISUALIZATION

the individual observations in the scatterplot, click on **Analysis > Aggregate Measures** to uncheck the aggregate measure of each variable. Lab Exhibit 5.3T.6 shows the results.

5. Follow the same procedure as above on a new spreadsheet titled Sheet 3, replacing the label with "Scatterplot Weight and OH Cost" and dragging the **Weight per Delivery** to the **Columns** and **Overhead Cost per Delivery** to the **Rows**. To view the individual observations in the scatterplot, click on **Analysis > Aggregate Measures** to uncheck the aggregate measure of each variable. Lab Exhibit 5.3T.7 shows the results.

Analysis Task #3: Calculate the Correlation Between Potential Cost Drivers and Overhead Costs

1. Next we'll calculate the correlations for each of the potential cost drivers with the overhead cost per delivery. To do so, open another worksheet, Sheet 4, and label it "Correlations".

   To calculate the correlation between Overhead Cost per Delivery and Time per Delivery, click on **Analysis > Create Calculated Field...**. Calculate the correlation by inputting the formula corr([Overhead Cost per Delivery],[Time per Delivery]), as shown in Lab Exhibit 5.3T.8. Then select **OK**.

2. To calculate the correlation between Overhead Cost per Delivery and Miles per Delivery, click on **Analysis > Create Calculated Field...**. Calculate the correlation by inputting the formula corr([Overhead Cost per Delivery],[Miles per Delivery]), as shown in Lab Exhibit 5.3T.9. Then select **OK**.

3. In similar fashion, calculate the correlation between Overhead Cost per Delivery and Weight per Delivery. Label the calculation "Correlation Cost and Weight" and calculate the correlation as above using the Overhead Cost per Delivery and Weight per Delivery variables, as shown in Lab Exhibit 5.3T.10. The formula is corr([Overhead Cost per Delivery],[Weight per Delivery]).

4. Drag the new variables—the **Correlation Cost and Miles** variable, the **Correlation Cost and Time** variable, and the **Correlation Cost and Weight** variable—to the **Rows** shelf. Then click on **Show Me** and select the **Text Table** icon, as shown in Lab Exhibit 5.3T.11.

   The result should resemble Lab Exhibit 5.3T.12.

We note reasonably high correlations between overhead cost per delivery and miles per delivery (.6060), as well as between overhead cost per delivery and time per delivery (.8747), suggesting they may be appropriate cost drivers. However, there is a much lower correlation between overhead cost per delivery and weight per delivery (.0567), suggesting weight per delivery may not be an appropriate cost driver.

Analysis Task #4: Create a Dashboard of All Individual Scatterplots

1. We now have all of the individual scatterplots and the correlation table. To view them all together, click on the **Dashboard** icon at the bottom of the page and label it "Dashboard of Potential Cost Drivers".

2. From the **Sheets** area, drag each of the sheets to the dashboard and organize as you desire. The dashboard allows us to view all of the scatterplots and correlations at one time. Lab Exhibit 5.3T.13 shows what your final dashboard might look like.

Share the Story

We have now developed a formula for overhead costs that we can use to apply overhead to subsequent deliveries. This formula will help us in costing out subsequent deliveries.

1. Take a screenshot of the final dashboard, paste it into a Word document named "Lab 5.3 Tableau Submission.docx", and label the screenshot Submission 1.
2. Answer the questions in Connect and upload your Lab 5.3 Tableau Submission.docx via Connect if assigned.

Alternate Lab 5.3   Tableau—On Your Own

Identifying Potential Cost Drivers and Creating Dashboards

Keywords

Management Accounting, Cost Drivers, Overhead Allocation

Apply the same steps in Lab 5.3 to the **Alt Lab 5.3 Data.xlsx** dataset to evaluate the scatterplots and correlations between total overhead cost and potential cost drivers (including customer call minutes, customer complaints, average workers, and company sales).

Required

1. Using scatterplots and correlations, assess potential cost drivers of overall overhead costs that can be used to help allocate overhead.
2. Create a dashboard to evaluate all the scatterplots and the correlation matrix.

Open Excel file **Alt Lab 5.3 Data.xlsx** and perform the analysis.

Data Dictionary

Customer Service Months	The number of the month for the overhead costs
Total Overhead Cost	The total overhead cost for the service month
Customer Call Minutes	The number of minutes spent on customer calls during the month
Customer Complaints	The number of customer complaints filed during the month
Average Workers	The number of average workers during the month
Company Sales	The gross dollar amount of company sales during the month

---

Assessment

1. Take a screenshot of the final dashboard and paste it into a Word document named "Alt Lab 5.3 Tableau Submission.docx".
2. Answer the questions in Connect and upload your Alt Lab 5.3 Tableau Submission.docx via Connect if assigned.

Lab Note: The tools presented in this lab periodically change. Updated instructions, if applicable, can be found in the student and instructor support materials. All Lab Exhibits are available within the eBook and in Connect.

Estimating Activity-Based Costing Drivers with Regression Analysis

Data Analytics Types: Diagnostic Analytics, Predictive Analytics

Keywords

Management Accounting, Cost Drivers, Overhead Allocation

Decision-Making Context

Overhead costs are indirect costs that are generally hard to trace to an individual product. They include taxes, advertising, rent, office supplies/equipment, business-related travel, insurance, business permits, maintenance and repair of equipment, utilities (electricity, telephone), professional assistance (accountant, attorney, consultant), and any other costs related to the overall operation of the business. We must allocate those costs to adequately price, compute cost, and evaluate the overall profitability of each product for sale.

Many corporations use activity-based costing to allocate overhead costs. Activity-based costing (ABC) is a cost system that assumes that the best way to assign indirect costs to products is based on the products' demand for resource-consuming activities, which are called cost drivers.

In one sense, we are trying to make indirect costs come as close to direct costs as we can in order to see if we would make different decisions based on that cost allocation.

This lab asks you to use regression analysis to derive the cost drivers used in ABC and derive a costing formula using the cost drivers to allocate overhead.

Required

1. Using regression analysis, choose from several potential cost drivers to identify the cost drivers that are significant predictors of overall overhead costs that can be used to help allocate overhead.
2. Derive the formula for allocating overhead.
3. Compare estimated overhead per delivery to actual overhead per delivery using a scatterplot.

Ask the Question

How can we use regression analysis to find cost drivers and derive a formula for allocating overhead?

Master the Data

Office Depot delivers bulk paper products to its customers. It incurs various indirect costs, including car maintenance, tires, oil changes, gasoline, car insurance, and car property tax, that it would like to allocate to each delivery. If managers can more accurately allocate these indirect, or overhead, costs, then the business can more accurately charge its customers for their deliveries. Managers would like to estimate cost drivers as part of an activity-based costing system. Office Depot does an intense analysis of overhead costs. After the managers identify the drivers of overhead costs, they can develop a formula to allocate the overhead based on those cost drivers.

The analysis calculates total overhead costs over 122 delivery days and considers four potential cost drivers that the company believes may be associated with the overhead costs. These potential cost drivers include the number of deliveries made, the number of miles driven, the total delivery time, and the combined weight of delivery for the day.

We are trying to prepare the data for analysis. Here is the data dictionary.

Data Dictionary

Delivery Day	Indicates delivery day (total cost was estimated from days 1 to 122)
Total Overhead Cost	The total indirect costs incurred for that delivery day
Deliveries	The number of deliveries made that day
Miles	The number of miles to make all deliveries that day
Time (Minutes)	The delivery time (in minutes) it takes to make all deliveries that day
Weight	Combined weight of all deliveries made that day

Open Excel file **Lab 5.4 Data.xlsx**. We're now ready to perform the analysis.

Perform the Analysis

Analysis Task #1: Calculate the Potential Cost Drivers

1. Because we are trying to apply the overhead cost to each delivery, we need to calculate the cost, miles, time, and weight for each delivery made during the day.

    We begin by adding titles. Add the following titles to the cells as shown in Lab Exhibit 5.4.1.

Cell	Title
G1	Overhead Cost per Delivery
H1	Miles per Delivery
I1	Time per Delivery
J1	Weight per Delivery

    Also add a bottom border by highlighting cells G1:J1. Use the **bottom border** icon, which is outlined in red near the top of Lab Exhibit 5.4.2.

Follow along with Lab Exhibit 5.4.3 for Steps 2 through 6.

2. In cell G2, calculate the average overhead cost per delivery by taking total overhead cost (in cell B2) and dividing by the number of deliveries (in cell C2).
3. In cell H2, calculate the average miles per delivery by taking total miles (in cell D2) and dividing by the number of deliveries (in cell C2).
4. In cell I2, calculate the average time per delivery by taking total delivery time (in cell E2) and dividing by the number of deliveries (in cell C2).
5. In cell J2, calculate the average weight per delivery by taking total weight of delivery (in cell F2) and dividing by the number of deliveries (in cell C2).
6. In cells G2:J2, be sure the formulas are entered as shown in Lab Exhibit 5.4.3. Then copy the same formulas to cells G3:J123.
7. After entering these formulas, your cells should match Lab Exhibit 5.4.4.
8. We'll now format the accounts. Highlight columns G:J, right-click on those columns, and select **Format Cells**.

9. Under **Category**, select **Number**. Also indicate two decimal places, as shown in Lab Exhibit 5.4.5.
10. The results should match Lab Exhibit 5.4.6.

Analysis Task #2: Perform Regression Analysis

Regression analysis uses mathematics and statistics to determine which of several variables has an impact on an outcome and the size of that impact.

Regression analysis helps answer the following questions: Which factors matter most in predicting the outcome? Which factors can we ignore?

In this case, we are trying to figure out which cost drivers are associated with the outcome, or total overhead costs.

We can think about this situation in terms of an algebraic equation in which y is the dependent variable and x represents the independent variables, where $y = f(x)$. In other words, we will run an equation where y, or Overhead cost per delivery, $= f(\text{cost drivers})$, where the dependent variable is total overhead costs for that delivery day and the independent variables are these three potential cost drivers:

Miles per Delivery	The number of miles for each delivery
Time per Delivery (Minutes)	The time (in minutes) it takes to make each delivery
Weight per Delivery	The weight of each delivery

Using regression analysis, we can assess which cost drivers impact the overhead cost, along with the size of that impact. We do so by looking at those cost drivers that are statistically related to overhead cost. Once we find that information, we can derive a formula to allocate overhead to future deliveries.

1. To run the regression, make sure the Analysis ToolPak is loaded by looking at **Data > Analysis** and seeing if the Data Analysis ToolPak has been installed (Lab Exhibit 5.4.7).
2. If the Data Analysis ToolPak has not yet been added, go to **File > Options > Add-Ins** and select the Analysis ToolPak. Then select **OK** (Lab Exhibit 5.4.8).
3. To perform the regression, select **Data > Analysis > Data Analysis**. A dialog box will open. Select **Regression**, as shown in Lab Exhibit 5.4.9.
4. A dialog box will open. Select **Regression** and click **OK**. We need to select the dependent variable (or Y Range). Our dependent variable is overhead cost per delivery, so enter $G$1:$G$123 in the **Input Y Range**.
5. Next, we need to select our independent variable (or X Range). Our cost drivers (miles per delivery, time per delivery, and weight per delivery) are our independent variables, so enter $H$1:$J$123 in the **Input X Range**.
6. Because we highlighted the labels in the data range, click on **Labels**. Also select **New Worksheet Ply** to get the results in a new worksheet.
   The completed **Regression** dialog box should match Lab Exhibit 5.4.10.
7. Now select **OK** to get the regression results shown in Lab Exhibit 5.4.11.

There are many things to note about the regression. The first is that the regression did better than chance at predicting overhead costs. We note that the Significance F result is extremely small, suggesting there is an extremely small probability that the overhead costs can be better explained by a model that has no cost drivers than by a model that has cost drivers. This is exactly the situation we want and suggests that we will be able to identify cost drivers to explain total overhead costs.

In fact, there are two cost drivers, miles per delivery and time per delivery, that seem to explain overhead costs. This conclusion is based on the t-Stat that is greater than two for both of these cost drivers, suggesting we have found two cost drivers that impact overhead costs per delivery. We also note that weight per delivery did not have a t-Stat greater than two, suggesting it does not impact overhead costs per delivery. (For more information on interpreting regression output, see Appendix E.)

Analysis Task #3: Perform Regression Analysis with the Refined Set of Cost Drivers

We will work to develop a formula to apply to future deliveries. We will now rerun the regression with just the two cost drivers that have been shown to impact total overhead cost: miles per delivery and time per delivery.

1. To rerun the regression, select **Data> Analysis > Data Analysis > Regression** (Lab Exhibit 5.4.12).
2. In the **Regression** dialog box, select the dependent variable (or Y Range) as overhead cost per delivery by entering $G$1:$G$123 in the **Input Y Range**.
3. Next, we need to select our independent variable (or X Range). Our cost drivers (miles per delivery, time per delivery) are our independent variables, so enter $H$1:$I$123 in the **Input X Range**.
4. Again, because we highlighted the labels in the data range, click on **Labels**. Also, select **New Worksheet Ply** to get the results in a new worksheet.
   The completed **Regression** dialog box should match Lab Exhibit 5.4.13.
5. Now select **OK** to get the regression results shown in Lab Exhibit 5.4.14.

Analysis Task #4: Apply the Cost Overhead

With these regression results, we are ready to create our formula to estimate overhead costs based on our two cost drivers. The intercept gives us the base cost for each delivery of $13.352. Because the coefficient on miles per delivery is 0.465, the cost per mile is $0.465. And because the coefficient on time per delivery is 1.924, the cost per minute is $1.924.

So, if we know how many miles the delivery took and how many minutes it took to make the delivery, we can estimate and apply the overhead costs using this formula:

$$\text{Estimated overhead costs} = \$13.352 + (\$0.465 * \text{Miles}) + (\$1.924 * \text{Minutes})$$

To see how well our estimate does at explaining the overhead costs, we'll compare actual overhead costs to our estimated overhead costs using a scatterplot.

1. Go to cell K1 (on the Data sheet) and insert the title "Estimated Overhead Costs". Then go to cell L1 and insert the title "Actual Overhead Costs" and insert a bottom border under cells K1:L1, as shown in Lab Exhibit 5.4.15.
2. Next, insert the formula "=13.352+(0.465*H2)+(1.924*I2)" into cell K2 and copy to all cells K3:K123. See again Lab Exhibit 5.4.15.
   This formula applies the formula to the cost drivers to calculate the estimated overhead costs.
3. Also copy G2:G123 to L2:L123, which puts the estimated costs next to the actual overhead costs per delivery. Placing these columns side by side facilitates creating a graph of the two variables.
4. To graph these variables, highlight cells K1:L123 and go to **Insert > Charts > Scatter or Bubble Chart > Scatter**, as shown in Lab Exhibit 5.4.16.
5. Modify the title of the scatterplot to read "Actual vs. Estimated Overhead Costs". Lab Exhibit 5.4.17 shows the result.

DATA VISUALIZATION

The result suggests that at least for this dataset, there seems to be a pretty good correlation between actual and estimated overhead costs per delivery.

Share the Story

We have now developed a formula for overhead costs that can be used to apply overhead to subsequent deliveries. This formula will help us cost out overhead for subsequent deliveries.

1. Take a screenshot of the regression output, paste it into a Word document named "Lab 5.4 Submission.docx", and label the screenshot Submission 1.
2. Take a screenshot of the scatterplot, paste it into a Word document named "Lab 5.4 Submission.docx", and label the screenshot Submission 2.
3. Answer the questions in Connect and upload your Lab 5.4 Submission.docx via Connect if assigned.

Alternate Lab 5.4   Excel—On Your Own

Estimating Activity-Based Cost Drivers with Regression Analysis

Apply the same steps in Lab 5.4 to the **Alt Lab 5.4 Data.xlsx** dataset to perform cost driver analysis for the service call center at Thrustmaster, which sells game controllers, joysticks, steering wheels for PCs, and XBOX, Nintendo, and PlayStation consoles.

Thrustmaster is trying to understand its overhead allocation for the call center that supports its sales. It believes that by understanding the overhead costs and their respective cost drivers, it will be in a better position to allocate overhead to the various products that require more service. Thrustmaster is considering these four potential cost drivers:

1. Customer Call Minutes
2. Customer Complaints
3. Average Workers
4. Company Sales

Required

1. Using regression analysis, choose the cost drivers that are significant predictors of overall overhead costs and can therefore be used to allocate overhead.
2. Derive the formula for allocating overhead.
3. Compare total estimated overhead to total actual overhead using a scatterplot.

Open Excel file **Alt Lab 5.4 Data.xlsx**.

Data Dictionary

Customer Service Months	The number of the month for the overhead costs
Total Overhead Cost	The total cost for the service month
Customer Call Minutes	The number of minutes spent on customer calls during the month
Customer Complaints	The number of customer complaints filed during the month
Average Workers	The number of average workers during the month
Company Sales	The gross dollar amount of company sales during the month

Assessment

1. Take a screenshot of the regression output, paste it into a Word document named "Alt Lab 5.4 Submission.docx", and label the screenshot Submission 1.
2. Take a screenshot of the scatterplot, paste it into a Word document named "Alt Lab 5.4 Submission.docx", and label the screenshot Submission 2.
3. Answer the questions in Connect and upload your Alt Lab 5.4 Submission.docx via Connect if assigned.

Estimating Time-Driven Activity-Based Costing Drivers

Data Analytics Types: Diagnostic Analytics, Predictive Analytics

Lab Note: The tools presented in this lab periodically change. Updated instructions, if applicable, can be found in the student and instructor support materials. All Lab Exhibits are available within the eBook and in Connect.

Keywords

Management Accounting, Cost Drivers, Overhead Allocation

Decision-Making Context

Overhead costs are indirect costs that are generally hard to trace to an individual product. They include taxes, advertising, rent, office supplies/equipment, business-related travel, insurance, business permits, maintenance and repair of equipment, utilities (electricity, telephone), professional assistance (accountant, attorney, consultant), and any other costs related to the overall operation of the business. We must allocate those costs to adequately price, compute cost, and evaluate the overall profitability of each product for sale.

Many corporations use activity-based costing to allocate overhead costs. Activity-based costing (ABC) is a cost system that assumes that the best way to assign indirect costs to products is based on the products' demand for resource-consuming activities, which are called cost drivers.

Time-driven activity-based costing (TDABC) is a modified form of activity-based costing that relies on management's estimates rather than employee surveys to allocate overhead costs to jobs. In this lab, we evaluate a phone repair shop called **CPR Cell Phone Repair**. Using its knowledge and expertise, management estimates that each repair takes 60 minutes to complete, and it has calculated that each minute of repair time costs $0.55 in indirect costs (depreciation on repair facility and equipment, utilities, insurance, indirect parts, and so on). Thus, internally, CPR records the cost to repair each phone at $33.

However, management is interested in determining which factors increase or decrease the amount of time it takes to repair a phone. Does the age or brand of the phone matter? Does the type of problem increase or decrease repair time? More accurate cost information could lead CPR to charge more or less to customers based on these factors, allowing CPR to focus on more profitable repair jobs.

Required

1. Using regression analysis, choose from several potential drivers of repair time to derive the time required based on the characteristic of each repair.
2. Derive the formula for estimating time to repair based on just those characteristics that are significant determinants of time to repair.
3. Compare estimated to actual time to repair using a scatterplot.
4. Explain how overhead costs should be allocated based on estimated time to repair.

Ask the Question

How can we use regression analysis to find the time to make each repair and derive a formula for allocating overhead?

Master the Data

CPR Cell Phone Repair repairs phones. To establish its job costing and time-driven activity-based costing, it tracked the time it took to make 1,000 repairs based on various characteristics.

For this lab you will use data in the Excel file titled **Lab 5.5 Data.xlsx**.

To understand the data needed for analysis, consider this data dictionary:

Data Dictionary

Job No.	The number of job repair at CPR Cell Phone Repair numbered from 1 to 1,000
Total Time (min)	The time spent on each repair in minutes
Water Damage	Equals 1 if the phone had water damage; 0 otherwise
Cracked Screen (Minor)	Equals 1 if the phone had a minor cracked screen; 0 otherwise
Cracked Screen (Major)	Equals 1 if the phone had a major cracked screen; 0 otherwise
Software Update Needed	Equals 1 if the phone required software update; 0 otherwise
Under Warranty	Equals 1 if the phone is currently under warranty; 0 otherwise
Age of Phone (yrs)	Equals the age of the phone in number of years
iPhone/Android	Equals 1 if iPhone; 0 if Android

Perform the Analysis

Analysis Task #1: Perform Regression Analysis to Assess Cost Drivers

Through regression analysis, we can assess which characteristics of the repairs impact the amount of time it takes to complete the repair. We can then derive a time-driven formula to allocate overhead to future deliveries.

1. To run the regression, we make sure the Analysis ToolPak is loaded by looking at **Data > Analysis** and seeing if the Data Analysis ToolPak has been installed (Lab Exhibit 5.5.1).

   If it has not yet been added, go to **File > Options > Add-ins > Manage: Excel Add-ins > Go...** and select the **Analysis ToolPak** and the **Solver Add-in**. Then select **OK** (Lab Exhibits 5.5.2 and 5.5.3).

2. To perform the regression, select **Data > Data Analysis**. A dialog box will open (Lab Exhibit 5.5.4).

For Steps 3–5, follow along with Lab Exhibit 5.5.5.

3. Select **Regression** and click **OK**. We need to select the dependent variable (or Y Range). Our dependent variable is Total time (min), so enter $B$1:$B$1001 in the **Input Y Range**.

4. Next, we need to select our independent variable (or X Range). The potential characteristics that affect the amount of time to repair include water damage, cracked screen (minor), cracked screen (major), software update needed, under warranty, age of phone, and whether the phone is an iPhone or Android. These are our independent variables, so enter $C$1:$I$1001 in the **Input X Range**.

5. Because we highlighted the labels in the data range, click on **Labels**. Also select **New Worksheet Ply:** to get the results in a new worksheet. The completed **Regression** dialog box should match Lab Exhibit 5.5.5.
6. Now select **OK** to get the regression results shown in Lab Exhibit 5.5.6.

There are many things to note about the regression. The first is that the regression does better than chance at predicting overhead costs. The Significance F result is very small, suggesting there is an extremely small probability that the time to repair can be explained by none of the characteristics instead of a model that has these characteristics. This is exactly the situation we want and suggests that we will be able to identify the characteristics of phone repair that contribute to overhead.

In fact, the first six characteristics—water damage, cracked screen (minor), cracked screen (major), software update needed, under warranty, and age of phone—have a t-Stat that is greater than two, suggesting we have found the cost drivers that impact the time for repair. We also note that whether the phone was an iPhone or Android did not have a t-Stat greater than two, suggesting it does not impact the time to repair. (For more information on interpreting regression output, see Appendix F.)

Analysis Task #2: Run Another Regression Using the Refined Set of Cost Drivers

Now we will rerun the analysis without the insignificant iPhone/Android independent variable. The other six variables have been shown to impact total repair time.

1. To rerun our regression, select **Data > Data Analysis > Regression** (Lab Exhibit 5.5.7).

For Steps 2–4, follow along with Lab Exhibit 5.5.8.

2. In the **Regression** dialog box, we again select the dependent variable (or Y Range) as Total time (min), so enter $B$1:$B$1001 in the **Input Y Range**.
3. Next, we select our independent variable (or X Range). The characteristics that affect the amount of time to repair are water damage, cracked screen (minor), cracked screen (major), software update needed, under warranty, and age of phone; they have shown to be significant determinants of the time to repair, so enter $C$1:$H$1001 in the **Input X Range**.
4. Again, because we highlighted the labels in the data range, click on **Labels**. Also select **New Worksheet Ply:** to get the results in a new worksheet.
   The completed Regression dialog box should match Lab Exhibit 5.5.8.
   Now select **OK** to get the regression results shown in Lab Exhibit 5.5.9.

Analysis Task #3: Estimate the Time to Repair Based on Various Characteristics

With these regression results, we are ready to estimate the time to repair a phone based on its various characteristics.

1. In cell J1, insert the title "Estimated Time to Repair".
2. In cell J2, insert this equation:

$$=24.66+(12.2 * C2)+(10.70 * D2)+(23.77 * E2)+(7.0 * F2)+(9.38 * G2)+(3.45 * H2)$$

   and then click **Enter**.
3. Copy the results of cell J2 to cells J3:J1001.
4. In cell K1, insert the title "Actual Time to Repair".
5. Copy Column B2:B1001 to Column K2:K1001.
6. To graph the data, highlight cells J1:K1001 and go to **Insert > Charts > Scatter or Bubble Chart > Scatter** (Lab Exhibit 5.5.10).

Modify the title of the scatterplot to "Actual vs. Estimated Time to Repair". Your results should resemble Lab Exhibit 5.5.11.

The result suggests that at least for this dataset, there seems to be a pretty good correlation between actual and estimated time to repair.

Share the Story

With an estimated time to repair, we are in a position to allocate overhead dollars. Assuming there is an overhead cost of $0.54/minute of repair, overhead can be allocated to the specific repair jobs and total costs, and overall profitability can be determined.

We have now developed a formula for allocating overhead costs based on the specifics of each repair job, which will help CPR in costing out the repairs.

Assessment

1. Take a screenshot of the regression output, paste it into a Word document named "Lab 5.5 Submission.docx", and label the screenshot Submission 1.
2. Take a screenshot of the scatterplot, paste it into a Word document named "Lab 5.5 Submission.docx", and label the screenshot Submission 2.
3. Answer the questions in Connect and upload your Lab 5.5 Submission.docx via Connect if assigned.

Alternate Lab 5.5   Excel—On Your Own

Estimating Time-Driven Activity-Based Costing Drivers

Keywords

Management Accounting, Cost Drivers, Overhead Allocation

Apply the same steps in Lab 5.5 to the **Alt Lab 5.5 Data.xlsx** dataset to perform a time-to-repair analysis for a competitor phone repair company, PhoneDoctors.

Required

1. Using regression analysis, choose from several potential drivers of repair time to derive the time required based on the characteristic of each repair.
2. Derive the formula for estimating time to repair based on just those characteristics that are significant determinants of time to repair.
3. Compare estimated to actual time to repair using a scatterplot.
4. Explain how overhead costs should be allocated based on estimated time to repair.

Open Excel file **Alt Lab 5.5 Data.xlsx** and perform the analysis. The data dictionary for PhoneDoctors data is as follows:

Data Dictionary

Job No.	The number of job repair at PhoneDoctors numbered from 1 to 1,000
Total Time (min)	The time spent on each repair in minutes
Water Damage	Equals 1 if the phone had water damage; 0 otherwise

Cracked Screen (Minor)	Equals 1 if the phone had a minor cracked screen; 0 otherwise
Cracked Screen (Major)	Equals 1 if the phone had a major cracked screen; 0 otherwise
Software Update Needed	Equals 1 if the phone required software update; 0 otherwise
Under Warranty	Equals 1 if the phone is currently under warranty; 0 otherwise
Age of Phone (yrs)	Equals the age of the phone in number of years
iPhone/Android	Equals 1 if iPhone; 0 if Android

Assessment

1. Take a screenshot of the regression output, paste it into a Word document named "Alt Lab 5.5 Submission.docx", and label the screenshot Submission 1.
2. Take a screenshot of the scatterplot, paste it into a Word document named "Alt Lab 5.5 Submission.docx", and label the screenshot Submission 2.
3. Answer the questions in Connect and upload your Alt Lab 5.5 Submission.docx via Connect if assigned.

Chapter 6

Cost Allocation: Support-Department Costs and Joint Product Costing

A Look at This Chapter

One of the primary functions of a management accountant is to determine production costs. This chapter continues our discussion of allocating overhead. Allocating certain overhead costs, such as support-department costs and joint product costs, can be difficult because it is not always clear which products should bear the cost of production. This chapter discusses three methods of assigning overhead costs from support departments to production departments. In addition, it explains various methods of allocating the costs of joint-production processes to product lines. Finally, it describes how to evaluate product decisions related to joint products.

Cost Accounting and Data Analytics

COST ACCOUNTING LEARNING OBJECTIVE	RELATED DATA ANALYTICS LABS	LAB ANALYTICS TYPES
LO 6.1 Define shared support services.		
LO 6.2 Allocate support-department costs using the single-rate method and the dual-rate method.		
LO 6.3 Allocate multiple support-department costs using the direct, step-down, and reciprocal methods.	Data Analytics Mini-Lab Estimating the Cost Savings of Shared Services	Predictive, Prescriptive
	LAB 6.1 Excel Allocating Support-Department Costs with the Direct Method	Descriptive, Diagnostic
	LAB 6.2 Excel Allocating Support-Department Costs with the Step-Down Method	Descriptive, Diagnostic
	LAB 6.3 Excel Allocating Support Department Costs with the Reciprocal Method	Descriptive, Diagnostic

Cost Accounting and Data Analytics (*continued*)

COST ACCOUNTING LEARNING OBJECTIVE	RELATED DATA ANALYTICS LABS	LAB ANALYTICS TYPES
LO 6.4 Define and explain joint product costs.		
LO 6.5 Calculate joint product costs using various methods, and evaluate product decisions to process further or sell as is.	**LAB 6.4 Excel** Allocating Joint Costs Using Various Methods (Heartwood)	Descriptive, Diagnostic
	LAB 6.5 Power BI/Tableau Using Trend Analysis to Identify Joint Product Opportunities	Diagnostic, Predictive

Chapter Concepts and Career Skills

Learning About . . .	Helps with These Career Skills
Allocating support-department costs to production departments	• Identifying cost drivers • Identifying strategies that decrease costs
Allocating joint product costs to product lines	• Identifying cost drivers • Identifying which products generate the greatest value for a firm
Additional processing costs to convert products into high-value products	• Identifying optimal product mixes

APFootage/Alamy Stock Photo

Who's Going to Pay for That?

The Blue Angels and the Thunderbirds are the U.S. military's top flight-demonstration squadrons. Hundreds of millions of people have seen their air shows at sporting and other events. The cost of operating their aircraft is considerable. In addition to the labor costs of pilots and maintenance crew, the jets require significant amounts of fuel and maintenance. Some estimate the cost of operating this group of jets at $60,000 per hour or more.

Many major sporting events feature flyovers of military aircraft. While the flyovers are exhilarating, they are also costly. Who should bear the cost of these flyovers? Many politicians have argued that the cost should be borne by those organizing or attending the sporting events. Others argue that the cost should be paid for with funds earmarked for military training. After all, pilots require flight time to maintain their skills, and it's just as easy to log flight hours while flying over a stadium as it is to fly over any other part of the country. Both sides have valid arguments—it can be difficult to know how costs should be divided between or allocated to different parties.

Companies often face similar decisions when trying to allocate costs between cost objects, whether those cost objects are clients, product lines, or products. For example, how should the costs of a human resources department be split among the departments that use its services? If two distinct products share production processes, how should production costs be allocated between the products? Management accountants must use sound judgment to allocate costs appropriately.

Source: Dan Lamothe, "Pentagon Plans to Dispatch Blue Angels and Thunderbirds in Coronavirus Tribute," *The Washington Post,* April 22, 2020.

LO 6.1

Define shared
support services.

WHAT ARE SHARED SUPPORT SERVICES?

We tend to think of companies and organizations in terms of outputs—that is, the products or services they market and sell. For example, **Nike** makes athletic apparel, **Caterpillar** makes construction and mining equipment, and **DoorDash** facilitates online food ordering and delivery. Within organizations, the departments that produce goods and services are known as **production departments**.

production departments

Departments that produce goods or services that are sold to consumers.

Support departments, also known as service departments, often work behind the scenes to provide services that make the production of goods and services possible. These services include accounting, human resources, custodial services, and employee cafeterias. They also can include legal services, information technology, or a motor pool to provide vehicles for company employees. While they may be less visible than production departments, support departments are vital to a company's success.

support departments

Departments that facilitate and support production departments but do not produce goods or services that are sold to consumers. Also known as service departments.

For example, **Heartwood Cabinets** relies on its accounting department to track costs, analyze data, and compile financial information. The accounting department is a support department that is necessary for efficient operations. Accounting isn't considered a production department because accountants don't produce the cabinets that Heartwood sells to its customers (and Heartwood probably prefers that the accounting professionals stay away from any heavy machinery).

support services

All services provided by support departments that facilitate and support production departments.

Support services are all services provided by support departments that facilitate and support production departments. Companies have largely adopted the practice of sharing support services across production departments, and the benefits of doing so are considerable. For example, a single, companywide human resources (HR) staff tends to be more efficient and knowledgeable than multiple HR departments each serving a distinct production department. Sharing support-department services across the organization eliminates duplicate work, saves costs, and improves process consistency.

Who should bear the cost of these support services? Some companies choose not to allocate support-department costs to production departments and instead account for the costs at the organizational level. Most companies, however, choose to allocate support-department costs to the production departments that use those services.

How should these costs be divided and assigned to production departments? We answer this question in the following sections. How companies allocate support-department costs is important because the allocation method affects each production department's reported profitability, which has important ramifications for company strategy.

✓ PROGRESS CHECK

1. What is the difference between production departments and support departments?
2. Think about colleges and universities. What are some examples of support departments at a college or university?

LO 6.2

Allocate support-department costs using the single-rate method and the dual-rate method.

ALLOCATING COSTS FROM A SINGLE SUPPORT DEPARTMENT

Allocating support-department costs to production departments allows companies to identify and understand the full cost of providing goods and services. It also helps them budget for planning purposes and offers insight into how production departments performed.

In addition, for companies that must comply with GAAP, all production costs, including the cost of services provided by support departments, must be included in inventory. In the following sections, we discuss several different methods of allocation. Remember that for each method, all support-department costs should be allocated to production departments.

First, let's consider a scenario in which a company with a single support department must allocate costs to multiple production departments. For this example, we will evaluate the (fictitious) Stokes Marketing Agency, which offers two main services to customers: market research and public relations. The market research department determines the target markets for various products and services by communicating with consumers through surveys, interviews, and focus groups. The public relations department aligns marketing efforts with the company's desired image. Stokes Marketing Agency considers each of these departments as production departments. Stokes Marketing Agency also has a human resources support department that provides services to market research and public relations. The HR department has the following budgeted costs.

Stokes Marketing Agency: HR Department Budgeted Costs

Fixed costs:	$120,000
Variable costs:	$ 60,000 ($40 * 1,500 hours)
Total costs:	$180,000

Management's budgeted and actual usage of HR services across production departments is as follows:

Production Department	Budgeted Usage	Actual Usage
Market Research	900 hours	1,000 hours
Public Relations	600 hours	500 hours

How should Stokes Marketing Agency allocate HR costs to its production departments? Two common methods for companies with a single support department are the single-rate method and the dual-rate method.

The Single-Rate Method

As its name implies, the **single-rate method** allocates all support-department costs (both fixed and variable) to cost objects using a single rate. To calculate this rate for the Stokes Marketing Agency, we divide total budgeted HR costs of $180,000 ($120,000 fixed costs + $60,000 variable costs) by an allocation base. In this case, the company allocates HR costs on the basis of HR hours. By dividing total costs by the 1,500 hours that the HR department expects (that is, budgets) to provide to market research and public relations, we calculate an allocation base of $120 per hour (= $180,000/1,500).

While allocation rates are determined using budgeted costs and allocation bases (see Chapter 4 for a review), the cost allocation is a function of the *actual* usage of resources. As Exhibit 6.1 shows, $120,000 is allocated to market research while $60,000 is allocated to public relations (based on 1,000 hours and 500 hours of actual usage, respectively). Notice that all $180,000 of support-department costs are allocated to production departments.

single-rate method
A cost-allocation method that allocates all support-department costs (both fixed and variable) to cost objects using a single rate.

Exhibit 6.1
Single-Rate
Allocation of
Support-Department
Costs

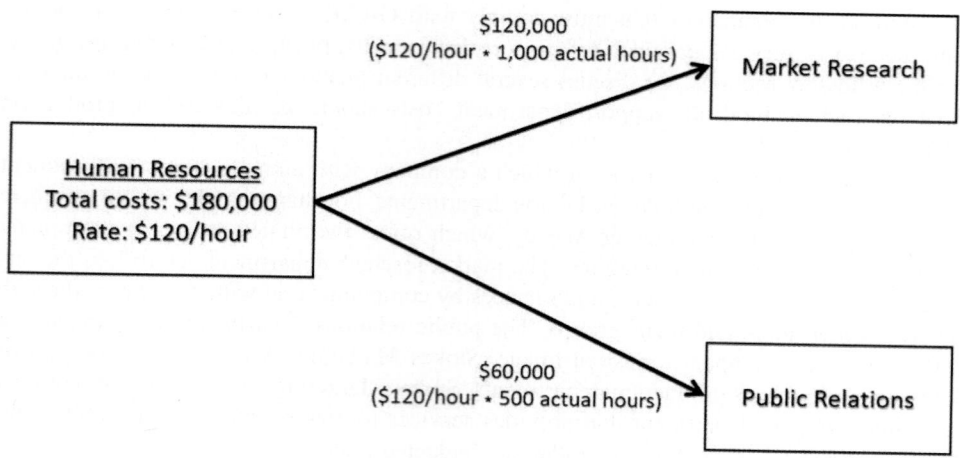

The Dual-Rate Method

dual-rate method
A cost-allocation method that uses two rates (one for fixed costs and one for variable costs) to allocate support-department costs to cost objects.

The **dual-rate method** differs from the single-rate method by distinguishing between the fixed and variable costs of the support department, and allocating fixed and variable costs separately.

Recall that rates are calculated using budgeted allocation bases. The support-department costs are then allocated to market research and public relations based on actual usage, just as in the single-rate method. The variable cost rate is $40/hour ($60,000 variable costs/1,500 budgeted hours). The fixed cost rate is $80/hour ($120,000 variable costs/1,500 budgeted hours). Unlike variable costs, fixed costs are not allocated based on actual usage. Instead, these costs are allocated based on *budgeted* usage, as Exhibit 6.2 shows. Again, notice that all support-department costs have been allocated to production departments.

Exhibit 6.2
Dual-Rate Allocation
of Support-
Department Costs

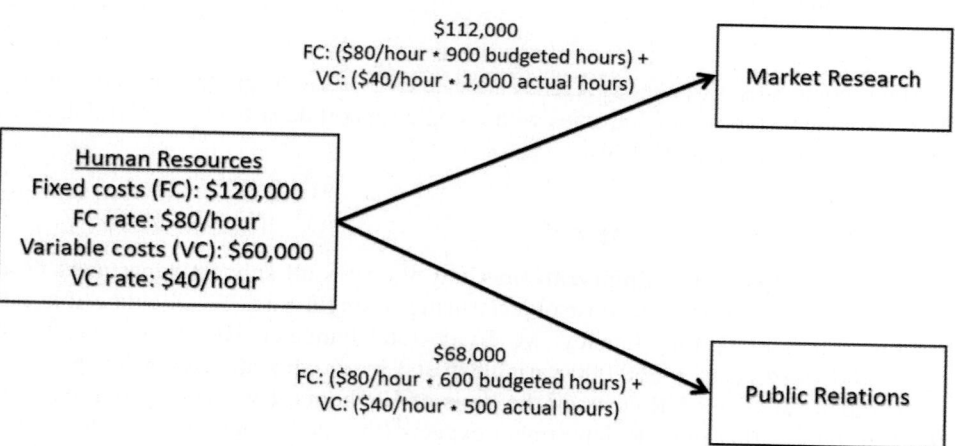

Companies can use either the single-rate or dual-rate method to allocate the costs of a single support department to production departments. The single-rate method is quantitatively simpler. However, because all HR costs are treated as variable (that is, production departments are "charged" $120 per hour of HR service), the production departments may limit their use of HR services. While this decision may decrease the departments' cost of human resources, much of that cost is fixed. Thus, a single rate does not reflect the realities of support-department costs. The dual-rate method is theoretically superior, but as explained in Chapter 3, it can be difficult to distinguish between fixed costs and variable costs. Companies must weigh the costs and benefits of each method to determine how to account for support-department costs.

✓ PROGRESS CHECK

3. Describe the difference between the single-rate method and the dual-rate method of allocating support-department costs.
4. What are an advantage and a disadvantage of the single-rate method of allocating support-department costs?

ALLOCATING COSTS FROM MULTIPLE SUPPORT DEPARTMENTS

The previous section discussed a scenario in which the Stokes Marketing Agency had a single support department. In reality, most companies have several support departments. Furthermore, in addition to serving the needs of production departments, support departments often provide services to other support departments, which complicates the allocation process. In this section, we explain how companies allocate budgeted support-department costs when support departments provide services to other support departments as well as to production departments.

To better illustrate the following allocation methods, we make a couple of simplifying assumptions. First, we assume that support-department allocations are based on *budgeted* (rather than actual) support-department costs, as this method is most commonly used in practice. Second, we assume that companies use the single-rate method to allocate costs to production departments.

For this discussion, let's assume that Stokes Marketing has two support departments, human resources and custodial services. Human resources takes care of employment benefits and payroll, while custodial services cleans and maintains company facilities. Total annual costs for the human resources department are $180,000, and the annual cost of custodial services is $120,000. The HR department provides support services to custodial services (another support department), market research, and public relations. Custodial services provides support services for HR, market research, and public relations. Exhibits 6.3 and 6.4 illustrate this arrangement and provide additional information about Stokes Marketing resources.

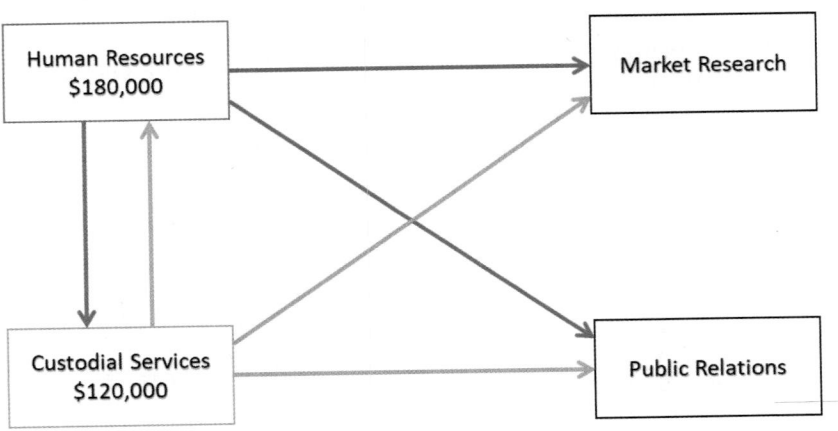

LO 6.3

Allocate multiple support-department costs using the direct, step-down, and reciprocal methods.

CAREER SKILLS

Learning about allocating support-department costs to production departments supports these career skills:

- Identifying cost drivers
- Identifying strategies that decrease costs

Exhibit 6.3
Support Structure within Stokes Marketing Agency

Exhibit 6.4
Stokes Marketing
Agency Resources

	Support Departments		Production Departments		
	Human Resources	Custodial Services	Market Research	Public Relations	Total
HR: Number of employees	3	10	20	10	43
CS: Square footage	300	200	700	500	1,700
Costs to allocate	$180,000	$120,000	$–	$–	$300,000

HR = Human Resources; CS = Custodial Services

In this section, we discuss three different methods of allocating support-department costs to production departments:

1. The direct method.
2. The step-down method.
3. The reciprocal method.

Under all three methods, Stokes Marketing must allocate all $300,000 of support-department costs (the costs of providing HR and custodial services; see Exhibit 6.4) to production departments using an allocation base. Ideally, an allocation base is causal in nature, such that an increase in the allocation base should result in an increase in the associated cost. In other words, the allocation base should be a cost driver. Recall that a **cost driver** is a variable that has a causal relationship with costs, such that more or less of the cost driver will result in more or less cost. At Stokes Marketing, HR expenses are allocated to departments based on the number of employees in each department. This is a logical allocation base that is causal in nature because HR costs tend to be highly correlated with the number of employees in a department. Custodial service costs are allocated based on square footage. Stokes Marketing believes that larger offices require more custodial services than smaller offices do.

The difference between allocation methods relates to how costs are allocated between support departments—that is, how HR costs are allocated to custodial services and vice versa.

The Direct Method

We know that HR and custodial services provide services to each other. The **direct method** makes a simplifying assumption that makes allocation easier. Specifically, the direct method ignores any cross-departmental support that support departments provide to each other. Instead, the costs for each support department are allocated directly to production departments, as shown in Exhibit 6.5.

cost driver
A variable that has a causal relationship with costs, such that more or less of the cost driver will result in more or less cost.

direct method
A method of allocating support-department costs to production departments. Under the direct method, no support costs are allocated between support departments.

Exhibit 6.5
Allocation of Stokes
Marketing Agency's
Support Departments
Using the Direct
Method

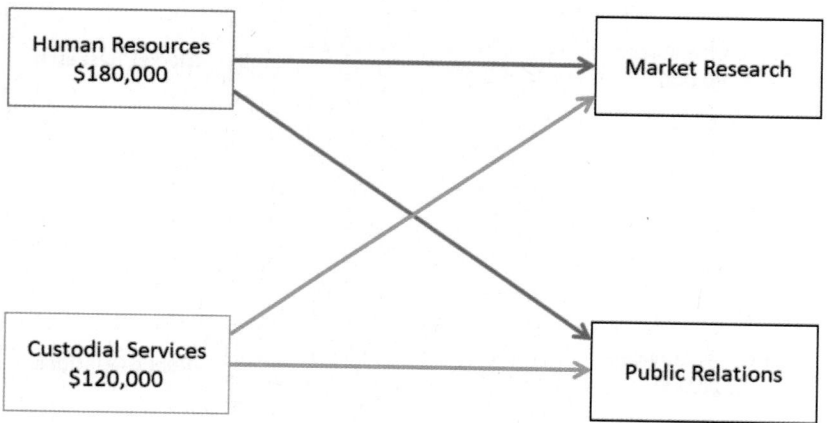

To determine how much cost should be allocated from support departments to production departments, we allocate based on the use of support-department resources. HR allocates its $180,000 annual costs based on employee head count. As Exhibit 6.4 shows, Stokes Marketing has a total of 40 employees who are not in the HR department (support departments never allocate costs to their own department). The direct method does not allocate costs from one support department to another, so HR costs are not allocated to the custodial services department even though HR provides services to custodial services employees. Instead, two-thirds of HR costs, or $120,000, is allocated to the market research department (20 market research employees/30 total employees in market research or public relations) while the other one-third, $60,000, is allocated to public relations (10/30 employees). These proportions are multiplied by $180,000 of HR support costs to determine allocation amounts, as shown in Exhibits 6.6 and 6.7.

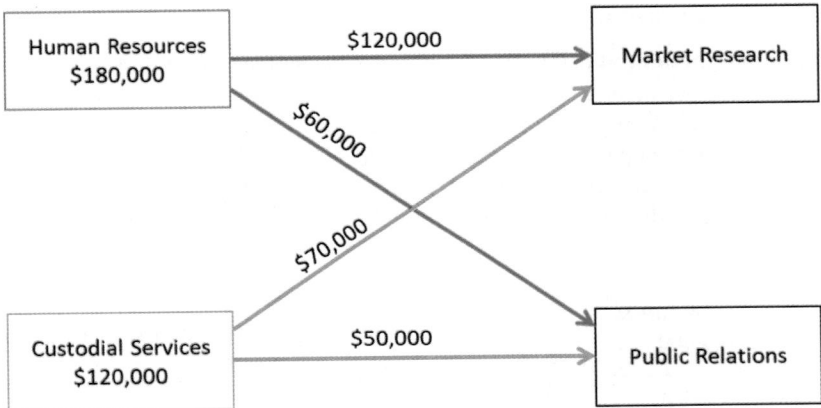

Exhibit 6.6
Cost Allocation of Stokes Marketing Agency's Support Departments Using the Direct Method

| | Support Departments | | Production Departments | | |
	Human Resources	Custodial Services	Market Research	Public Relations	Total
HR: Number of employees	3	10	20	10	43
CS: Square footage	300	200	700	500	1,700
Costs to allocate	$ 180,000	$ 120,000	$ −	$ −	$ 300,000
Allocation of HR costs	$(180,000)	$ −	$120,000	$ 60,000	−
Allocation of CS costs	$ −	$(120,000)	$ 70,000	$ 50,000	−
Total cost allocation	$ −	$ −	$190,000	$110,000	$ 300,000

Exhibit 6.7
Breakdown of Cost Allocations for Stokes Marketing Agency's Support Departments Using the Direct Method

Notice that the employees in the custodial services (CS) department are ignored for these calculations because HR will not allocate costs to the custodial services department. This doesn't mean that there are no employees in the HR department—Exhibit 6.7 shows that the HR department has three employees. Rather, it indicates that support departments *never* allocate costs to their own department.

Similarly, Stokes Marketing allocates custodial services costs on the basis of square footage. This cost driver makes logical sense because a larger space generally requires more custodial services. Stokes Marketing operates out of a facility that has 1,500 square feet. As Exhibits 6.6 and 6.7 show, $70,000 is allocated to market research ($120,000 * [700 sq. ft./1,200 sq. ft.]) and $50,000 is allocated to public relations ($120,000 * [500 sq. ft./1,200 sq. ft.]). We ignore the square footage of the human resources department and use 1,200 square feet as the denominator in our calculations because, under the direct method, custodial services allocates costs only to production departments. If costs have been correctly allocated, then all support-department costs will have been allocated to production departments.

The process of allocating support-department costs is critical for evaluating production department profitability. For example, allocating support-department costs to the market research department will reduce its reported profitability by $190,000 (see the final row of Exhibit 6.7), but relative to ignoring support-department costs, it will provide a better picture of the costs of running the department.

Are these cost allocations an accurate depiction of reality? Because costs are not allocated between support departments, they are not. However, the allocations are likely sufficiently accurate to facilitate good decision making. Companies that use the direct method believe any slight inaccuracies are more than offset by the ease of calculating allocations using this simplified method.

The Step-Down Method

The **step-down method**, illustrated in Exhibit 6.8, is another simplified approach to allocating support-department costs. It differs from the direct method by allowing some (but not all) cost allocations between support departments. To use the step-down method, companies rank support departments. Higher-ranked support departments allocate costs to lower-ranked support departments as well as to production departments, but lower-ranked support departments do not allocate costs to higher-ranked support departments.

step-down method
A method of allocating support-department costs to production departments. In this method, support departments are ranked. Higher-ranked support departments allocate costs to lower-ranked support departments as well as to production departments, but lower-ranked support departments do not allocate costs to higher-ranked support departments.

Exhibit 6.8
Allocation of Stokes Marketing Agency's Support Departments Using the Step-Down Method

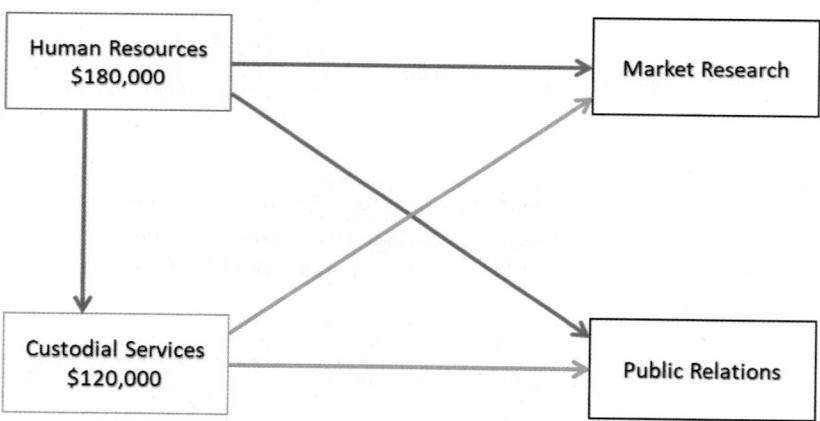

The ranking is usually determined by the percentage of costs incurred to support other support departments. For Stokes Marketing, 25 percent of HR resources are expended on custodial services (10/40 employees—notice that we include in the denominator employees from all departments other than the HR department because a support department never allocates costs to itself). Meanwhile, only 20 percent of custodial services resources are expended on the HR department (300/1,500 sq. ft.). Consequently, HR will allocate to custodial services, but custodial services will not allocate to HR. Note that changing the criteria for ranking can change the rank order as well as the total allocation to production departments.

HR allocates costs based on employees. Because HR allocates costs to all other departments (including custodial services), the total number of employees in all three departments is used to determine proportions. Specifically:

- $45,000 ($180,000 * [10/40 employees]) is allocated to custodial services.
- $90,000 ($180,000 * [20/40 employees]) is allocated to market research.
- $45,000 ($180,000 * [10/40 employees]) is allocated to public relations.

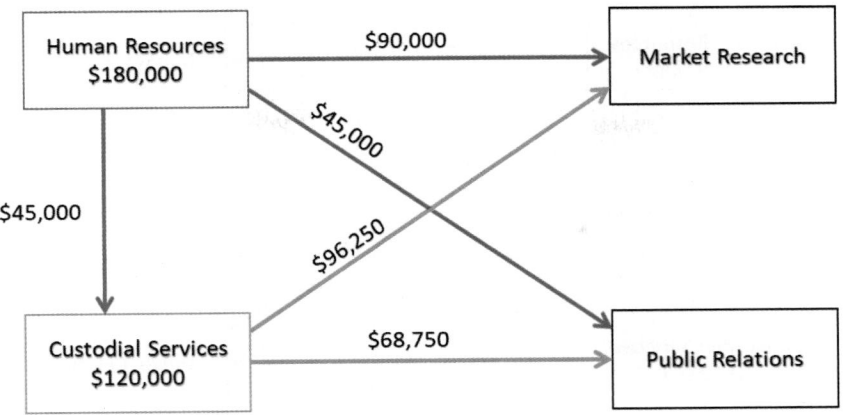

Exhibit 6.9
Cost Allocation of
Stokes Marketing
Agency's Support
Departments Using
the Step-Down
Method

Exhibit 6.9 summarizes these allocations.

Because all HR costs are allocated, Stokes Marketing can "step down" to the next-ranked support department, and the HR department is excluded from subsequent calculations.

Next, the company allocates custodial services costs to the production departments. Because the custodial services department has been allocated $45,000 from the HR department, the total amount to allocate to the production department is now $165,000 (the original $120,000 + the $45,000 allocation from the HR department). Stokes Marketing allocates $96,250 to market research ($165,000 * [700 sq. ft./1,200 sq. ft.]) and $68,750 to public relations ($165,000 * [500 sq. ft./1,200 sq. ft.]). As a check figure, notice in Exhibits 6.9 and 6.10 that all $300,000 in support-department costs have been allocated to production departments.

	Support Departments		Production Departments		
	Human Resources	**Custodial Services**	**Market Research**	**Public Relations**	**Total**
HR: Number of employees	3	10	20	10	43
CS: Square footage	300	200	700	500	1,700
Costs to allocate	$ 180,000	$ 120,000	$ −	$ −	$300,000
Allocation of HR costs	$(180,000)	$ 45,000	$ 90,000	$ 45,000	−
Allocation of CS costs	$ −	$(165,000)	$ 96,000	$ 68,000	−
Total cost allocation	$ −	$ −	$186,250	$113,750	300,000

Exhibit 6.10
Breakdown of Cost
Allocations for Stokes
Marketing Agency's
Support Departments
Using the Step-Down
Method

It's important to note that companies can use different criteria to rank support departments. It's possible that Stokes Marketing prefers to allocate custodial services costs before HR costs. The mechanics of calculating allocation amounts are identical, but switching the order of allocation can change the results. Exhibits 6.11 and 6.12 summarize the allocations when custodial services allocates to other departments first, followed by the allocation from human resources.

Exhibit 6.11
Cost Allocation of Stokes Marketing Agency's Support Departments Using the Step-Down Method, with Different Ranking

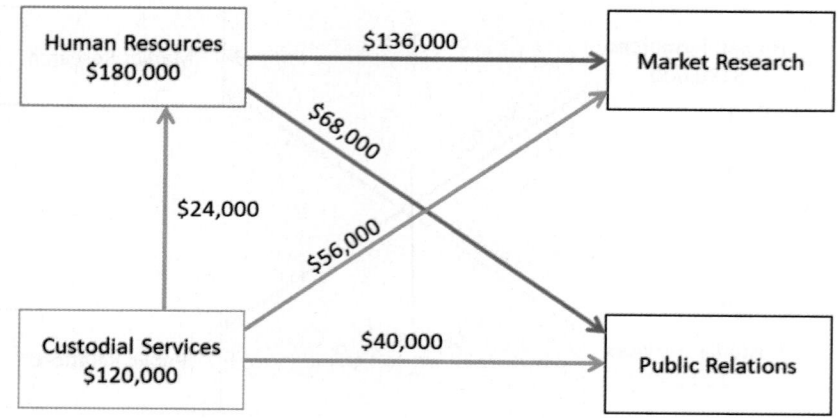

Exhibit 6.12
Breakdown of Cost Allocations for Stokes Marketing Agency's Support Departments Using the Step-Down Method, with Different Ranking

	Support Departments		Production Departments		
	Human Resources	Custodial Services	Market Research	Public Relations	Total
HR: Number of employees	3	10	20	10	43
CS: Square footage	300	200	700	500	1,700
Costs to allocate	$ 180,000	$ 120,000	$ –	$ –	$300,000
Allocation of HR costs	$(204,000)	$ –	$136,000	$ 68,000	–
Allocation of CS costs	$ 24,000	$(120,000)	$ 56,000	$ 40,000	–
Total cost allocation	$ –	$ –	$192,000	$108,000	300,000

The Reciprocal Method

reciprocal method
A method of allocating support-department costs in which all support departments allocate costs to other support departments as well as to production departments.

The **reciprocal method** provides the most accurate representation of the reality of cost flows because it allows all support departments to allocate to other support departments. To determine how much cost should be allocated from each support department, we must first determine the total cost of the support departments. In our example, the cost of human resources is $180,000, plus 20 percent of the cost of custodial services. Why? The HR department uses 20 percent of Stokes Marketing square footage (300/1,500 sq. ft.). Similarly, the cost of custodial services is $120,000 plus 25 percent of the cost of human resources (10/40 employees). We can record these costs in equation form as follows:

$$H = 180{,}000 + 0.2C$$
$$C = 120{,}000 + 0.25H$$

where H is Human Resources and C is Custodial Services.

We can then solve for this system of equations by solving for one equation and plugging the solution into the other, as follows:

$$H = 180{,}000 + 0.2C$$
$$C = 120{,}000 + 0.25H$$

Step 1:   Plug the cost of Human Resources (H) equation into the cost of Custodial Services (C) equation. Replace the "H" with $180,000 + 0.2C.

$$C = 120,000 + 0.25(180,000 + 0.2C)$$

Step 2:   With the inputs of H in the C equation, solve for C using the proper order of operations.
- Multiply 0.25 by the values in the parentheses.

$$C = 120,000 + 45,000 + 0.05C$$

- Sum the $120,000 and the $45,000.

$$C = 165,000 + 0.05C$$

- Subtract 0.05C from each side.

$$0.95C = 165,000$$

- Now divide both sides by 0.95 to get

$$C = \$173,684.21 \text{ (rounded to 2 decimals)}$$

Step 3:   Plug the solved value of C into the original equation to solve for H:

$$H = 180,000 + 0.2C$$
$$H = 180,000 + 0.2(173,684.21)$$

- Multiply 0.2 by 173,684.21.

$$H = 180,000 + 34,736.84$$

- Sum 180,000 and 34,736.84.

$$H = \$214,736.84 \text{ (rounded to 2 decimals)}$$

Our results provide the amount of cost that must be allocated from each support department to ensure that all costs are appropriately allocated to production departments.

- HR allocates costs as follows:
  $53,684.21 to custodial services ($214,736.84 * [10/40 employees])
  $107,368.42 to market research ($214,736.84 * [20/40 employees])
  $53,684.21 to public relations ($214,736.84 * [10/40 employees])
- Custodial services allocates as follows:
  $34,736.84 to human resources ($173,684.21 * [300/1,500 sq. ft.])
  $81,052.63 to market research ($173,684.21 * [700/1,500 sq. ft.])
  $57,894.74 to public relations ($173,684.21 * [500/1,500 sq. ft.])

Exhibit 6.13 summarizes all of these allocations.

Notice that the amount allocated from human resources is equal to $180,000 of department costs plus the costs allocated from custodial services ($34,736.84). Similarly, the allocation from custodial services to other departments is equal to department costs plus costs allocated from HR. As illustrated in Exhibits 6.13 and 6.14, when all calculations are complete, the $300,000 of support-department costs have been completely allocated from support departments to production departments.

Exhibit 6.13
Allocation of Stokes
Marketing Agency's
Support Departments
Using the Reciprocal
Method

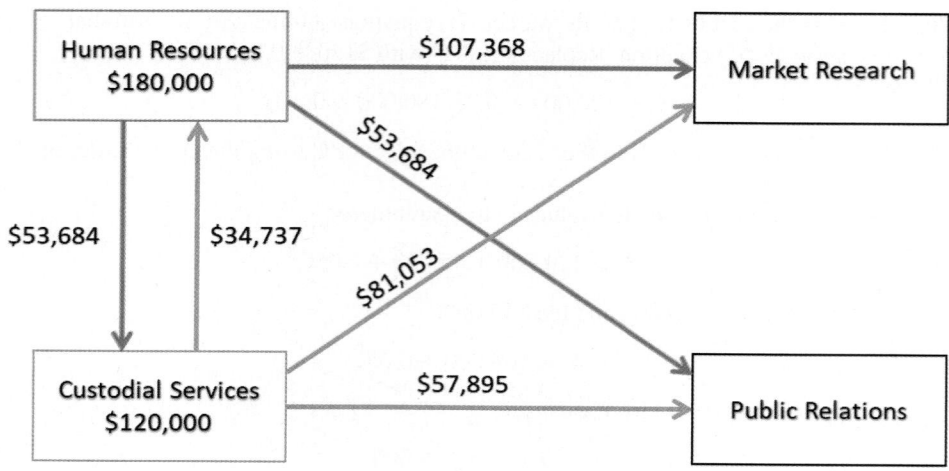

Exhibit 6.13
Allocation of Stokes Marketing Agency's Support Departments Using the Reciprocal Method

Exhibit 6.14
Breakdown of Cost Allocations for Stokes Marketing Agency's Support Departments Using the Reciprocal Method

	Support Departments		Production Departments		
	Human Resources	Custodial Services	Market Research	Public Relations	Total
HR: Number of employees	3	10	20	10	43
CS: Square footage	300	200	700	500	1,700
Costs to allocate	$ 180,000.00	$ 120,000.00	$ –	$ –	$300,000.00
Allocation of HR costs	$(214,736.84)	$ 53,684.21	$107,368.42	$ 53,684.21	$ –
Allocation of CS costs	$ 34,736.84	$(173,684.21)	$ 81,052.63	$ 57,894.74	$ –
Total cost allocation	$ –	$ –	$188,421.05	$111,578.95	$300,000.00

Benefits and Drawbacks of the Methods

All three methods of allocating support-department costs have benefits and drawbacks. The core trade-off between methods is the accuracy of cost numbers and the complexity of the costing system. Often, firms can benefit from making simplifying assumptions to ease the accounting workload without significant loss of information. In our example, total allocation to market research ranges from $186,250 to $192,000 between allocation methods—a relatively narrow window of values.

Sometimes, though, a more refined, complex system can provide value in decision making. The reciprocal method is theoretically the most accurate (though note that no method is likely to result in perfect allocations). However, that accuracy comes at a cost: The allocations quickly become computationally complex. In fact, if more than two support departments are included, the solution may require matrix algebra. Fortunately, software is available to perform these difficult calculations.

We have discussed three methods of allocating support-department costs to production departments. Let's now take a step back and examine why companies use support departments or shared services in the first place, and let's see how management accountants can use data analytics to provide important input into the decision of whether to create a support department or not. We illustrate this process in the following Data Analytics Mini-Lab.

DATA ANALYTICS MINI-LAB
Estimating the Cost Savings of Shared Services

Data Analytics Types: Predictive, Prescriptive

Lab Note: The tools presented in this lab periodically change. Updated instructions, if applicable, can be found in the student and instructor support materials.

Keywords
Support Departments, Monte Carlo Simulation, Excel

Decision-Making Context
Rayburn School District is a collection of eight schools for K–12 students. While the schools are located in the same county, each school currently has an independent IT specialist who maintains technological equipment for teachers, staff, and students. The school superintendent is considering creating a centralized IT office that will house all IT support personnel, who would then provide IT assistance for the entire school district.

Ask the Question
What are the expected cost savings from creating an IT support department that services the entire district, relative to each school having its own IT specialist?

Required
1. Determine the number of IT employees needed in both a decentralized setting and a centralized setting.
2. Estimate weekly costs in both a decentralized setting and a centralized setting.
3. Use a Monte Carlo simulation to generate 100 sample weeks of data.
4. Estimate weekly cost savings in IT labor costs from creating an IT support department that services the entire school district.

Master the Data
Open Excel file **Mini-Lab 6 Data.xlsx**. As Exhibit A shows, at the top left of the screen, you will see the minimum, maximum, and average weekly IT specialist hours for the eight schools in the district. You will also notice a number of assumptions beginning in row 14. Full-time IT employees are expected to work up to 40 hours a week, for which they receive $1,000. Every additional hour of labor costs $35. If a school's average IT hours exceed 50 hours, then the school hires a second IT specialist, and it hires a third specialist if expected hours exceed 100 hours. Finally, you will notice a box starting in Column I that we will use to calculate summary statistics, which are explained later in this Mini-Lab.

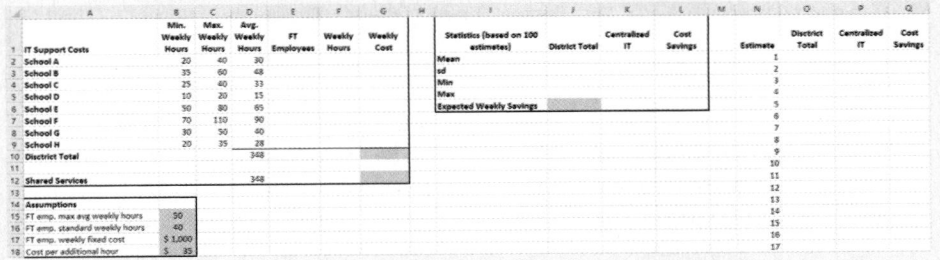

Exhibit A

Microsoft Excel

Perform the Analysis
Analysis Task #1: Calculate Weekly Labor Costs for IT Specialists

1. In cell E2, insert the following formula to calculate the number of full-time employees needed in each school: =ROUNDUP(D2/$B$15,0). Your screen should match Exhibit B. Remember, an IT employee is expected to work a maximum amount of 50 hours per week. If average hours exceed 50, the school will hire another IT specialist rather than rely on overtime hours.

Exhibit B

Microsoft Excel

	A	B	C	D	E	F	G
		Min. Weekly Hours	Max. Weekly Hours	Avg. Weekly Hours	FT Employees	Weekly Hours	Weekly Cost
1	IT Support Costs						
2	School A	20	40	=ROUNDUP(D2/$B$15,0)			
3	School B	35	60	ROUNDUP(number, **num_digits**)			
4	School C	25	40	33			
5	School D	10	20	15			
6	School E	50	80	65			
7	School F	70	110	90			
8	School G	30	50	40			
9	School H	20	35	28			
10	District Total			348			
11							
12	Shared Services			348			
13							
14	Assumptions						
15	FT emp. max avg weekly hours	50					
16	FT emp. standard weekly hours	40					
17	FT emp. weekly fixed cost	$ 1,000					
18	Cost per additional hour	$ 35					

2. In cell F2, insert this formula: =RANDBETWEEN(B2,C2), which will randomly select a number of hours between the minimum and maximum weekly hours. With this formula, each number within the range has the same likelihood of being selected. Your screen should now match Exhibit C; you can see the formula at the top of the screen.

Exhibit C

Microsoft Excel

HYPERLINK   ✕ ✓ *fx*   =RANDBETWEEN(B2,C2)

	A	B	C	D	E	F	G
		Min. Weekly Hours	Max. Weekly Hours	Avg. Weekly Hours	FT Employees	Weekly Hours	Weekly Cost
1	IT Support Costs						
2	School A	20	40	30	1	B2,C2)	
3	School B	35	60	48			

3. In cell G2, insert this formula: =E2*$B$17+$B$18*MAX(0,F2-(E2*$B$16)). This is the trickiest formula, so think carefully about what it is doing. Labor costs for IT are $1,000 for the first 40 hours per worker, and $35 per hour thereafter. The MAX formula indicates that if the weekly hours exceed the 40-hours-per-employee

threshold, then additional direct labor costs are incurred. If not, then the cost is
fixed at $1,000 per employee. Your screen should now match Exhibit D.

Exhibit D

Microsoft Excel

| T.DIST.2T | ▼ : | × ✓ | fx | =E2*$B$17+$B$18*MAX(0,F2-(E2*$B$16)) |

▲	A	B	C	D	E	F	G
1	IT Support Costs	Min. Weekly Hours	Max. Weekly Hours	Avg. Weekly Hours	FT Employees	Weekly Hours	Weekly Cost
2	School A	20	40	30	1	28	E2*$B$16))
3	School B	35	60	48			
4	School C	25	40	33			
5	School D	10	20	15			
6	School E	50	80	65			
7	School F	70	110	90			
8	School G	30	50	40			
9	School H	20	35	28			
10	District Total			348			
11							
12	Shared Services			348			
13							
14	Assumptions						
15	FT emp. max avg weekly hours	50					
16	FT emp. standard weekly hours	40					
17	FT emp. weekly fixed cost	$ 1,000					
18	Cost per additional hour	$ 35					

4. Copy formulas from cells E2:G2 through Rows 3–9. In Row 10, sum up Columns
   E–G. *Note:* Your numbers will be different from those shown in Exhibit E because
   our formulas are randomly generating numbers based on our formulas. For the
   Shared Services row (Row 12), cells D12 and F12 should be set equal to cells D10
   and F10 respectively, while cells E12 and G12 should have the same formulas as
   cells E2 and G2 respectively.

Exhibit E

Microsoft Excel

▲	A	B	C	D	E	F	G
1	IT Support Costs	Min. Weekly Hours	Max. Weekly Hours	Avg. Weekly Hours	FT Employees	Weekly Hours	Weekly Cost
2	School A	20	40	30	1	27	$ 1,000
3	School B	35	60	48	1	36	$ 1,000
4	School C	25	40	33	1	25	$ 1,000
5	School D	10	20	15	1	20	$ 1,000
6	School E	50	80	65	2	63	$ 2,000
7	School F	70	110	90	2	95	$ 2,525
8	School G	30	50	40	1	32	$ 1,000
9	School H	20	35	28	1	27	$ 1,000
10	District Total			348	10	325	10,000
11							
12	Shared Services			348	7	325	$ 8,575

Analysis Task #2: Use a Monte Carlo Simulation to Generate 100 Sample Weeks of Data

1. We now have one week's worth of data for IT costs. If we press F9, Excel will
   select new random numbers and we can generate another week's worth of data.
       A *Monte Carlo simulation* is a model that uses random variables to
   generate probabilities of various outcomes. We will now use our Excel

spreadsheet to conduct a simple Monte Carlo simulation, generating 100 weeks' worth of cost data.

Set cell O2 equal to cell G10, and set cell P2 equal to cell G12. Next, enter a formula in cell Q2 to find the cost savings between decentralized and centralized IT services. As Exhibit F shows, the formula is =Income-P2.

Exhibit F

Microsoft Excel

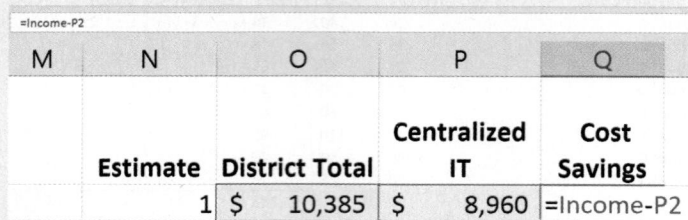

	=Income-P2			
M	N	O	P	Q
			Centralized	**Cost**
	Estimate	District Total	IT	Savings
	1	$ 10,385	$ 8,960	=Income-P2

2. Next, highlight cells N2:Q101, which will contain the data of the 100 income estimates. In the **Data** tab, click **What-If Analysis** > **Data Table** (see Exhibit G). In the **Data Table** dialog box (Exhibit H), leave **Row input cell** blank. Enter any blank cell, such as S2, for **Column input cell**. Click **OK**. This action will generate 100 random estimates from your simulation.

Exhibit G

Microsoft Excel

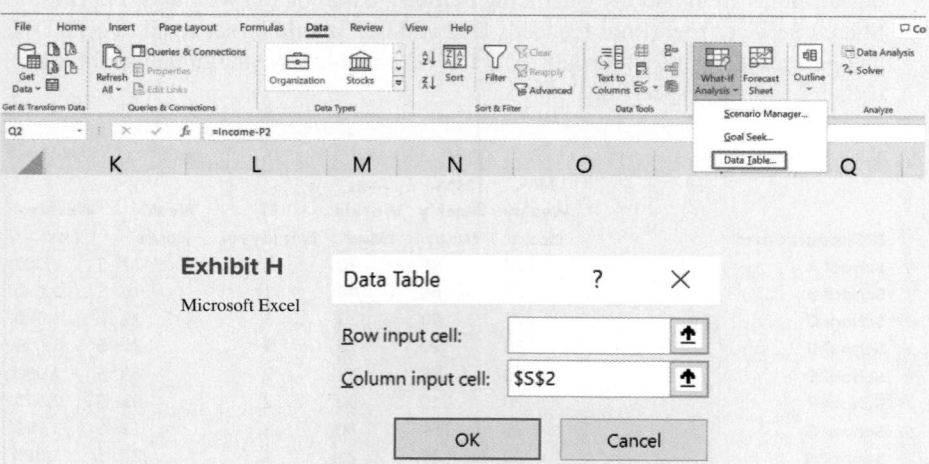

Exhibit H

Microsoft Excel

Analysis Task #3: Generate Summary Statistics from the Monte Carlo Simulation

1. Use the formulas shown in Exhibit I to generate the mean, standard deviation, minimum, and maximum of the District Total, Centralized IT costs, and Cost Savings. In addition, calculate the expected weekly savings by subtracting the centralized IT costs from the district total.

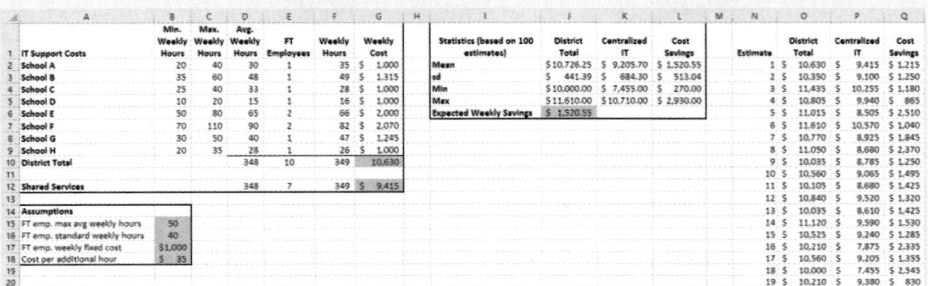

Exhibit I

Microsoft Excel

	Statistics (based on 100 estimates)	District Total	Centralized IT	Cost Savings
1				
2	Mean	=AVERAGE(O2:O101)	=AVERAGE(P2:P101)	=AVERAGE(Q2:Q101)
3	sd	=STDEV(O2:O101)	=STDEV(P2:P101)	=STDEV(Q2:Q101)
4	Min	=MIN(O2:O101)	=MIN(P2:P101)	=MIN(Q2:Q101)
5	Max	=MAX(O2:O101)	=MAX(P2:P101)	=MAX(Q2:Q101)
6	Expected Weekly Savings	=J2-K2		

The resulting spreadsheet should be similar to Exhibit J.

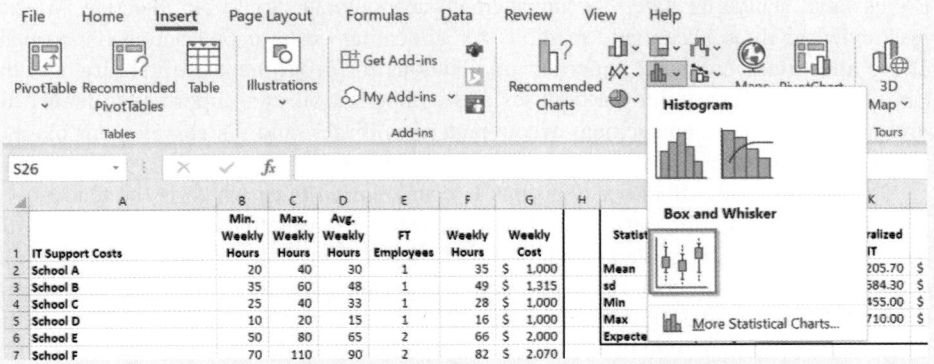

Exhibit J

Microsoft Excel

2. Finally, select cells O1:P101, and select **Insert > Histogram > Box and Whisker** to graphically present the range of costs between a decentralized IT department and a centralized IT department for the Rayburn School District (Exhibit K).

Exhibit K

Microsoft Excel

Share the Story

We can use the results of our Monte Carlo simulation to illustrate the labor cost savings that could result if IT specialists were grouped together in a centralized support department rather than each school having its own IT specialist. While your results will differ based on the random nature of the analysis, the cost savings are likely to be between $1,300 and $1,500 per week. A box-and-whisker plot such as the one shown in Exhibit L can help illustrate the difference in costs between a decentralized and a centralized IT function.

DATA VISUALIZATION

Exhibit L

Microsoft Excel

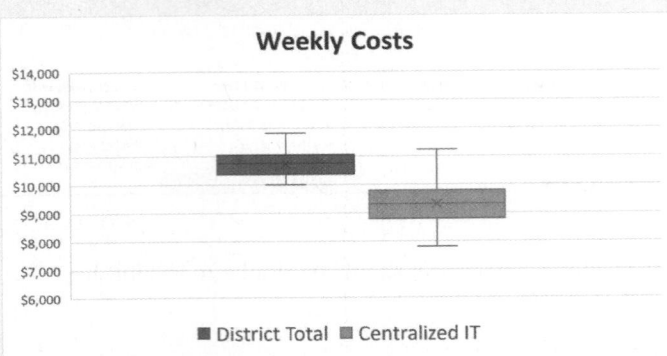

Mini-Lab Assessment

1. Examine the data. Why do labor costs decrease when the school district uses a centralized IT department?
2. How will an increase in the number of estimates generated by the Monte Carlo simulation affect your output?
3. What are some possible reasons why the Rayburn School District should not use a centralized IT function?

Human Dimensions: Cost Allocation Methods and Confirmation Bias

Professional standards state that management accountants should be objective. We have just reviewed three acceptable methods for allocating costs to production departments. These allocations can have important implications for department profitability, and they can ultimately affect employee bonuses and compensation. It's important to realize that everyone (including management accountants) has biases, and it's easy for our biases to affect our decisions.

One bias that can affect our decisions is *confirmation bias,* which is the tendency for individuals to search for and interpret new evidence in a way that confirms their existing beliefs, while ignoring evidence that does not support their beliefs. In the context of allocating support-department costs to production departments, management accountants must be careful to select the most appropriate cost allocation method, rather than the method that is most consistent with their preconceived notions.

🔍 LAB CONNECTION

LAB 6.1 EXCEL, LAB 6.2 EXCEL, and **LAB 6.3 EXCEL** all use different methods to allocate support-department costs. These labs all use the same company so that you can compare cost allocations across methods. In addition, they provide a more complex setting than that demonstrated in the chapter, as the company has three support departments and three production departments. As you will see, adding departments makes the reciprocal method exponentially more difficult, and you can use software to assist you in your calculations.

5. Explain the similarities between the direct, step-down, and reciprocal methods of allocating support-department costs.

6. How do the direct, step-down, and reciprocal methods of allocating support-department costs differ with respect to how costs are allocated between support departments?

7. Why would a company choose to use the direct method over the reciprocal method?

WHAT ARE JOINT COSTS?

We have discussed how management accountants can help companies determine how to allocate support-department costs to production departments. Similar issues arise when a company is trying to determine its **joint costs**, which are production costs that are shared between multiple product lines.

LO 6.4
Define and explain joint product costs.

joint costs
Production costs that are shared between multiple product lines.

S.Borisov/Shutterstock

Consider the production of coconuts, which are an important raw material for many companies, including **Vita Coco**, **Baker's Angel**, and **Ulta Beauty**. As a food source, coconuts are used in the production of not only coconut meat but also coconut water, milk, oil, cream, butter, flakes, and sugar. In addition, coconut oil and coconut vinegar are valuable raw materials in the cosmetics and skin-care industries.

Before coconuts can be used in any manufacturing process, they must be planted, cultivated, and harvested. They may also need to be shipped to a manufacturing facility, sanitized, and sorted based on size, type, and other qualities. Finally, husks must be removed, and the coconut water must be separated from the meat. Only then can the coconuts be used to produce various products.

All of these steps require significant labor and equipment costs. If a company produces several coconut-based products, which product lines should bear these costs? These costs are joint costs because they cannot be attributed to any single product line. Instead, they are required for the production of *all* the company's coconut-based products, and they should be shared among all product lines that use coconuts during production. **Joint products** are the products that result from a single production process.

At some point in production, known as the **split-off point**, joint production processes are complete, and companies begin to produce distinct products. In our coconut example,

joint products
Products that result from a single production process.

split-off point
The point of production at which joint production processes are complete and subsequent costs can be traced to unique product lines.

separable cost
Any cost incurred after the split-off point in a production process. Separable costs are assigned to specific products rather than allocated to multiple products.

the split-off point occurs when coconut water and meat are separated from the coconut husk. The company can then use the coconut water and meat as inputs to create products for consumers. The costs of converting these raw inputs into sellable goods are known as **separable costs**. Separable costs are production costs that are directly traceable to individual production lines rather than shared by multiple product lines. Exhibit 6.15 summarizes these cost flows.

Exhibit 6.15
The Flow of Joint Costs

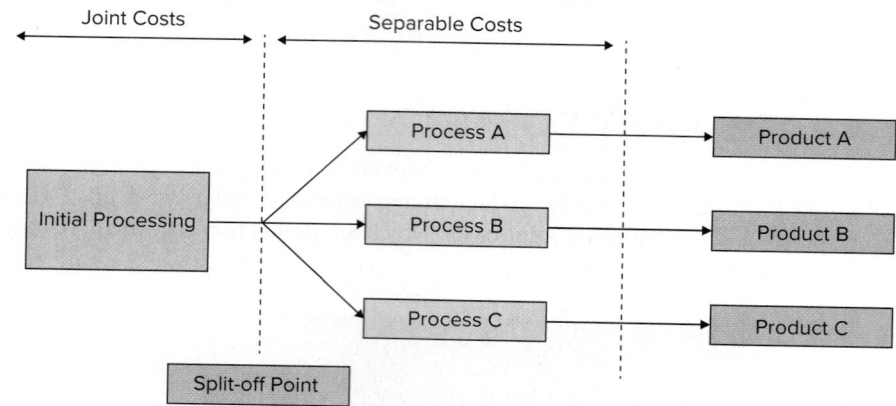

PROGRESS CHECK

8. Describe the difference between joint costs and separable costs.
9. Explain how a company determines a split-off point during production.
10. Consider the cost of educating university students. Universities often track education expenses by major or program. However, most incoming students do not know what their major will be when they start college. In a university setting, what are joint costs? What is the split-off point for educating university students? In other words, at what point are costs traceable to specific majors?

LO 6.5

Calculate joint product costs using various methods, and evaluate product decisions to process further or sell as is.

by-products
Incidental products that are created during a manufacturing process. In the context of joint product processes, they have minimal economic value.

ALLOCATING JOINT PRODUCT COSTS

To better understand joint and separable costs, let's consider the (fictitious) Island Processors Company, which harvests and processes coconuts. As part of this process, it removes the husks of the coconuts in order to gather coconut water and coconut meat. Coconut water and meat are joint products because they are the result of a joint production process. Coconut husks are a by-product of this process. **By-products** are incidental products that are created during a manufacturing process, and in joint product processes, they have minimal economic value. Although husks have some commercial value, they are not a core product and do not provide significant value to the firm. Joint costs for Island Processors are $50,000 per month.

Each month, Island Processors can produce 20,000 pounds of coconut water and 80,000 pounds of coconut meat. Coconut water and coconut meat can be sold as is (that is, without any further processing) for $2.50 and $3.00 per pound, respectively.

Island Processors can process both coconut water and coconut meat further, though it does not have to do so. Coconut water can be processed further to produce 20,000 pounds of a frozen dessert called Coconut Ice. This process costs $20,000, and the company can sell Coconut Ice for $2.75 per pound. Coconut meat can be processed further to produce coconut milk. This process includes adding ingredients such as water. The process costs $150,000, and it will result in 100,000 pounds of coconut milk, which sells for $5.00 per pound. Exhibit 6.16 summarizes this information.

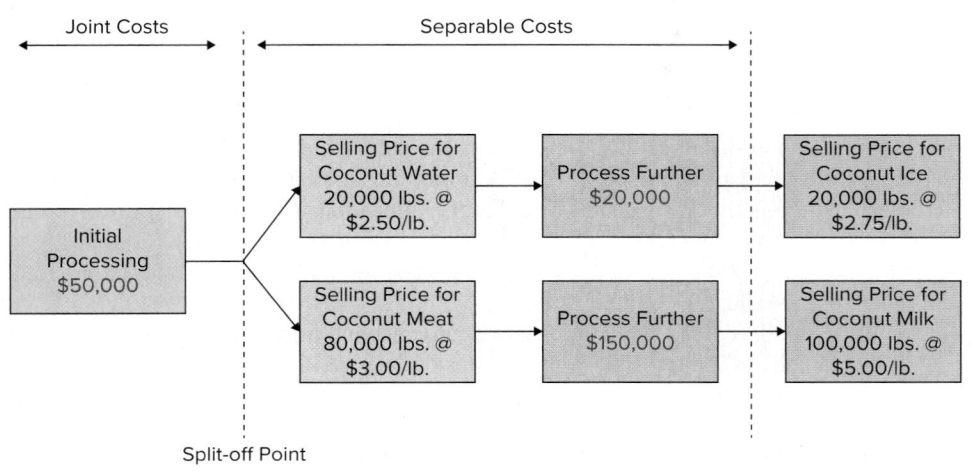

Exhibit 6.16
The Flow of Costs for Island Processors

How should Island Processors divide the $50,000 in joint production costs to its joint products? Which product line should bear these costs? The answers are important for several reasons. First, although these decisions do not alter the profitability of the firm as a whole, they can change the reported profitability of individual products, which can affect the company's future strategic decisions. Companies should also consider the ethical implications of tying employees' compensation to joint costs over which the employees have no control and the effect such practices will have on performance and morale. Finally, U.S. GAAP requires that all product costs (including joint costs) be included as inventory.

ETHICS

In the following sections, we explain four common methods used to allocate joint costs:

1. Physical units method.
2. Sales value at split-off method.
3. Net realizable value method.
4. Constant gross margin method.

Allocating Joint Costs: Physical Units Method

The first method is the simplest. The **physical units method** is based on some quantifiable measurement of products at the split-off point. Output can be based on weight, volume, or number of units produced—but a consistent metric must be used across products. That's why Island Processors uses pounds to measure both coconut water and coconut meat, even though coconut water is frequently measured in fluid ounces or liters. For Island Processors, there are 100,000 pounds of joint products at the split-off point: 20,000 pounds of coconut water and 80,000 pounds of coconut meat. To calculate the allocation rate, we divide $50,000 in joint costs by 100,000 pounds of product to get $0.50 of joint costs per pound.

We then use this rate to allocate to each product line. Island Processors allocates $10,000 ($0.50/lb. * 20,000 lbs.) to coconut water and $40,000 ($0.50/lb. * 80,000 lbs.) to coconut meat. Notice that all $50,000 in joint costs have been allocated to joint products, which provides a useful check figure.

physical units method
A method of allocating joint costs such that all product lines are allocated joint costs on the basis of a consistent physical measurement such as quantity, weight, length, or volume.

In addition, notice that we use physical units at the split-off point for our calculations. Additional processing can sometimes result in greater or fewer physical units. For Island Processors, processing coconut meat into coconut milk increases output from 80,000 to 100,000 pounds. The increase in production weight is unrelated to the joint costs that we are allocating to product lines. Instead, it is related to the additional processing required for coconut milk.

Allocating Joint Costs: Sales Value at Split-off Method

sales value at split-off method
A method of allocating joint costs such that joint costs are prorated to product lines based on each product line's sales value at the split-off point.

The second method of allocating joint costs is the **sales value at split-off method**. The mechanics of calculating product-line allocations are similar to the physical measure method, but this method uses sales value as the allocation base. At the split-off point, Island Processors can generate $50,000 in revenue from coconut water (20,000 lbs. * $2.50/lb.) and $240,000 in revenue from coconut meat (80,000 lbs. * $3.00/lb.), for a total sales value of $290,000. (See Exhibit 6.16.)

By dividing joint costs by sales value, we can calculate a joint cost allocation rate of $0.1724 (rounded) in joint costs for each dollar of sales ($50,000/$290,000). Under this method, Island Processors can calculate the allocation amount by multiplying the sales value of each product by the allocation rate. In this case, Island Processors will allocate $8,620 in joint costs to coconut water ($50,000 sales value * $0.1724) and $41,376 to coconut meat ($240,000 sales value * $0.1724).

Notice that all $50,000 in joint costs have been allocated (with a slight difference in the figures shown due to rounding the joint cost allocation rate to four decimals). In addition, note that we do not use final sales value (after additional processing of products). Instead, we use sales value at the split-off point.

Allocating Joint Costs: Net Realizable Value Method

net realizable value (NRV) method
A method of allocating joint costs such that joint costs are prorated to product lines based on each product line's net realizable value, which is calculated as revenue minus separable costs.

The third method of allocating joint costs is the **net realizable value method**. Net realizable value (NRV) is calculated as:

$$NRV = \text{Revenue generated from final sales price} - \text{Separable costs}$$

Why would a company choose to use the NRV method rather than the sales value at split-off method? The NRV method is used primarily when there is no market for products at the split-off point. Instead, companies must process units further before they are able to sell them. Though uncommon, companies may also choose the NRV method to account for the total revenue that a further-processed unit will generate. But what is the final sales price? In our example, Island Processors has the option to produce various products with the same inputs. The NRV method requires companies to determine the extent to which they will continue to refine and process products to produce more valuable products. Specifically, Island Processors must determine whether to produce coconut water or coconut ice, and whether to produce coconut meat or coconut milk. (Again, see Exhibit 6.16.) Let's consider each choice in turn.

We have already determined that coconut water has a sales value of $50,000 (20,000 lbs. * $2.50/pound) at the split-off point, or without any additional processing. Should Island Processors instead produce coconut ice? Coconut ice can generate revenue of $55,000 (20,000 lbs. * $2.75/pound), but it requires an additional $20,000 of processing. Because the additional $5,000 revenue is less than the additional processing costs, Island Processors should produce coconut water rather than coconut ice. Note that the $50,000 initial process costs are a sunk cost and should not be considered when determining whether to process a product further.

Now let's examine the decision to produce coconut meat or coconut milk. As Exhibit 6.16 shows, coconut milk can generate revenues of $240,000 (80,000 lbs. * $3/lb.) without any further processing. However, if Island Processors is willing to incur additional processing costs of $150,000, the company could generate $500,000 (100,000 lbs. * $5/lb.) in revenue for coconut milk. Because the additional $260,000 in revenue is more than the additional processing costs, Island Processors should produce coconut milk. Exhibit 6.17 updates company information to reflect which products Island Processors will produce based on profitability.

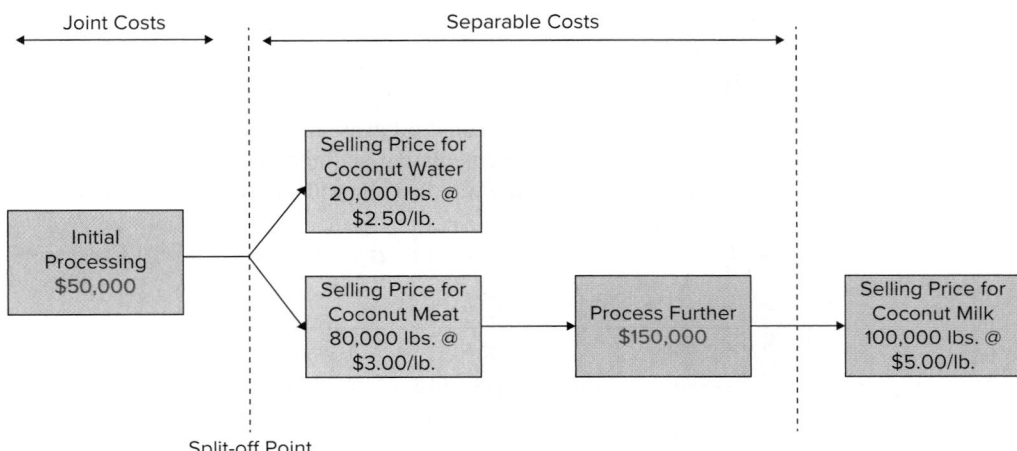

Exhibit 6.17
The Flow of Costs for Island Processors Using the Net Realizable Value Method

Now that we have determined that Island Processors should produce coconut water and coconut milk, we determine total NRV by adding $50,000 for coconut water ($50,000 revenue – $0 separable costs) and $350,000 for coconut milk ($500,000 revenue – $150,000 separable costs), for a total of $400,000.

To calculate the allocation rate for the net realizable value method, we divide $50,000 in joint costs by $400,000, which is the total NRV of all joint products. The allocation rate is $0.125 for each dollar of NRV. Under this method, Island Processors allocates $6,250 to coconut water ($50,000 NRV * $0.125) and $43,750 to coconut milk ($350,000 NRV * $0.125).

FROM THE FIELD

Balancing Processing Decisions with Expected Profitability

Companies often face the decision to sell products in their current form or further process these products to create more valuable products. Consider **Heartwood Cabinets**, which owns several forests and manufacturing facilities around the world. Heartwood can sell raw timber (that is, cut trees) with relatively low effort and costs. However, Heartwood has found that processing timber into more valuable lumber (boards and planks) generates additional profit, even after accounting for additional processing costs. Similarly, Heartwood has found that further processing of lumber into cabinets can increase company profits, as can additional processing in the form of painting or staining these cabinets.

At every step in the process, Heartwood must focus on the relevant revenues and costs of processing products. For example, in deciding whether to paint cabinets, Heartwood must determine whether the additional revenue generated from painted cabinets (relative to unpainted cabinets) is higher than the cost of painting those cabinets. All previous manufacturing costs, including both joint and separable costs, occurred in the past and are irrelevant to this decision.

Thinking Critically

Which revenues and costs are relevant to Heartwood's decision to paint cabinets? Some relevant costs are difficult to quantify, such as how the effect of a wider product selection may influence customer perceptions and how these perceptions may affect future sales.

Allocating Joint Costs: Constant Gross Margin Method

constant gross margin method
A method of allocating joint costs such that all product lines are allocated the amount of joint costs necessary to produce the company-wide gross margin.

gross profit
Profit minus cost of goods sold (which includes both separable and joint costs).

gross margin
Gross profit divided by revenue.

The final method of allocating joint costs, the **constant gross margin method**, is fundamentally different from the others. Rather than calculating and applying a constant allocation rate, this method applies joint costs in such a way that all product lines have identical gross profit margins.

The first step under this method is to calculate **gross profit** for Island Processors, as follows:

Revenue	$550,000*
− Separable costs (coconut milk)	−150,000
− Joint costs	−50,000
= Gross profit	$350,000

*$50,000 from coconut water + $500,000 from coconut milk

Gross margin is equal to gross profit divided by revenue, so Island Processors has a gross margin of approximately $350,000/$550,000 = 63.64 percent.

Under the gross margin method, we ensure that all product lines report the company-wide gross margin. Gross profit for each product line is calculated by multiplying revenue by 63.64 percent. Note that rounding may cause slight differences in calculation:

	Coconut Water	Coconut Milk	Total
Revenue	$50,000	$500,000	$550,000
− Separable costs	0	150,000	150,000
− Joint costs	?	?	50,000
= Gross profit (Revenue * 63.64%)	$31,818.18	$318,181.82	$350,000.00

Because we know the revenue, separable costs, and a predetermined gross profit for each product, we can calculate joint cost allocations algebraically. Joint costs are equal to revenue minus gross profit minus separable costs. Thus, Island Processors allocates $18,181.82 to coconut water and $31,818.18 to coconut milk, as follows:

	Coconut Water	Coconut Milk	Total
Revenue	$50,000	$500,000	$550,000
− Separable costs	0.00	150,000	150,000
− Joint costs	18,181.82	31,818.18	50,000
= Gross profit (Revenue * 63.64%)	$31,818.18	$318,181.82	$350,000.00

Notice that in each allocation method, all $50,000 in joint costs are allocated to product lines. Note that because joint costs are a plug figure to ensure a constant gross profit, it is possible for the joint costs of a product to be *negative* for a particular product line.

Joint Costs and By-products

As mentioned above, Island Processors generates coconut husks as by-products. Coconut husks are not very profitable. For this example, let's assume they can be sold for $2,000 without any additional processing. Should we allocate joint costs to by-products, and how can Island Processors account for the value of coconut husks?

It's important to note that we never allocate joint costs to by-products. Unlike joint products, by-products are not part of the company's core business. Thus, the net realizable value of processing and selling coconut husks is $2,000.

There are two ways that Island Processors can account for the revenue from selling husks. We'll illustrate this process by using the constant gross margin method to allocate joint costs to Island Processors, this time accounting for coconut husks as a by-product.

Method 1

The $2,000 of proceeds from coconut husks are categorized as a distinct product and added to the company's revenues. In this case, notice that the constant gross margin method only considers the gross margin of the joint products when allocating joint costs (that is, it does not include the $2,000 of gross profit from the coconut husks). The calculation of gross margin is identical to our previous calculation without by-products.

Revenue of joint products	$550,000
− Separable costs (coconut milk)	−150,000
− Joint costs	−50,000
= Gross profit	$350,000

Gross margin is $350,000/$550,000 = 63.64 percent.

	Coconut Water	Coconut Milk	Coconut Husks	Total
Revenue	$50,000	$500,000	$2,000	$552,000
Separable costs	0.00	150,000	0.00	150,000
Joint costs	18,181.82	31,818.18	0.00	50,000
Gross profit	$31,818.18	$318,181.82	$2,000.00	$352,000.00
Gross margin	63.64%	63.64%	100.00%	

Notice that because coconut husks have no separable costs or joint costs, the by-product has a gross margin of 100 percent. Only joint products have a constant gross margin.

Method 2

The $2,000 of proceeds can be deducted from the joint costs allocated to the joint products. If Island Processors adopts this second method of approaching by-products, then instead of allocating $50,000 of joint costs to products, the company would allocate $48,000 of joint costs ($50,000 joint costs − $2,000 by-product net realizable value). All allocations will then be reallocated with the new net joint cost amount.

Revenue of joint products	$550,000
− Separable costs (coconut milk)	−150,000
− Joint costs	− 48,000
= Gross profit	$352,000

Gross margin is $352,000/$550,000 = 64.00 percent.

	Coconut Water	Coconut Milk	Coconut Husks	Total
Revenue	$50,000	$500,000	$ 0	$550,000
− Separable costs	0	150,000	0	150,000
− Joint costs	18,000	30,000	0	48,000
Gross profit	$32,000	$320,000	$ 0	$352,000
Gross margin (= Gross profit/Revenue)	64.00%	64.00%	0.00%	

Under this second method, the revenues and costs for coconut husks are not reported.

ENVIRONMENTAL, SOCIAL, GOVERNANCE

FROM THE FIELD

From Cars to Charcoal Briquettes

Companies often overlook by-products because they are not core products and not very profitable. Henry Ford is known for his assembly-line-produced vehicles. Less known is the fact that each original Model T Ford used about 100 board feet of wood for the interior. The process created an incredible amount of scrap wood and sawdust. Mr. Ford was an early environmentalist, and he was determined to find a way to reduce the wood waste generated during production.

The result was that the **Ford Motor Company** invented the now-ubiquitous charcoal briquette. In the mid-1900s, the Ford Motor Company turned seemingly worthless piles of sawdust into nearly 100 tons of charcoal briquettes a day!

Managers can create value by finding a use for by-products. Thinking about by-products as valuable assets not only may generate revenue for a company but also may lower the company's environmental impact.

Thinking Critically

What other companies have found unique uses for overlooked by-products? How does the use of by-products relate to the idea of recycling for both companies and individuals?

Which Method Should Companies Use to Allocate Joint Costs?

Most professionals agree that the sales value at split-off method should be used if sales data are available. Why? It provides a strong causal relationship between the costs allocated to products and the economic benefit received from those products, and it doesn't require any information about further processing or future profitability. The net realizable value method is a good alternative when sales value at split-off data are not available. It can be argued that these methods are "fair" because products bear costs based on the revenue they generate.

However, there are other ways of evaluating what's fair. For instance, the constant gross margin method levels the playing field by maintaining equal profitability for all products. While this method does not reflect economic reality, higher joint costs are assigned to products with the greatest ability to bear those costs. The physical measure method may also be considered fair because costs are allocated based on usage. Many companies use this method because of its simplicity, although it ignores the economic benefits received by different products.

Ultimately, the assignment of these costs is arbitrary and does not change a company's overall profitability. That said, these cost allocations change the reported profitability of product lines and can affect both strategy and employee morale as managers argue about the most equitable way to assign costs to products.

LAB CONNECTION

LAB 6.4 EXCEL demonstrates how companies determine whether or not to process joint products further to increase revenue. It allows you to practice allocating joint costs using each method discussed above.

LAB 6.5 POWER BI/TABLEAU provides insight into the process of determining which joint products companies decide to produce using various market factors such as forecasted demand, market power, and production capabilities.

PROGRESS CHECK

11. Describe how companies decide whether or not to further process a product line.
12. What is the primary difference between the constant gross margin method and other joint-cost allocation methods?
13. How do joint products differ from by-products?

Careers in Management Accounting: Jobs with Cost Allocation Responsibilities

As we've discussed in this chapter, cost allocations can be challenging because they determine the reported performance of individual jobs and products, which affect company strategy and are critical to a company's success. Management accountants need to have a firm grasp on cost data, and they must be able to communicate their understanding of data to others in their organization.

Exhibit 6.18 illustrates a job posting from a site like **ZipRecruiter.com** or **Indeed.com** for a cost analyst at a management consulting firm like **Accenture**, **Booz Allen Hamilton**, or **Deloitte**. Read the posting to better understand how companies value management accounting knowledge and data analytics tools.

This description perfectly matches a management accountant with data analytics skills.

Cost data are critical to company strategy.

Excel skills are a must for management accountants.

Notice that companies are looking for employees who can share results in various ways. Data visualizations can be an effective way to share analyses and solutions with others.

Monte Carlo simulations and joint cost analysis are advanced techniques that companies use to analyze costs.

Tableau and Power BI skills can set you apart from other job candidates.

Job Title

Cost Analyst, Management Consulting

Job Summary

Put your analytical skills to use in a fast-paced cutting-edge industry as a Cost Analyst for a leading management consulting firm. This role utilizes financial and statistical analysis to advise on millions of dollars of project investment in the aerospace field. You will interact with subject matter experts and coordinate with engineers and project managers to analyze cost data connected to technology, development, and performance. Analysts will utilize a wide range of tools and skills including financial modeling using Excel and other programs, advanced data analysis, statistical regression, and data science to provide insights and support for the full project team.

Salary and Details

Range is $85,000 to $100,000 with additional compensation benefits including education assistance, health care, retirement plan, commuter support, and childcare benefits.

Required Qualifications

- Bachelor's degree in finance, accounting, or related business field
- Two or more years of experience with a focus on financial analysis and estimation
- Experience with applying statistical analysis for cost forecasting
- Advanced Excel skills including experience with complex logic
- Experience using cost estimating software and tools

Additional Skills and Experience

The ideal candidate will have experience

- Working in collaborative or cross-functional teams
- Managing, analyzing, and summarizing historical cost data from multiple sources
- Creating or presenting clear and concise reports based on detailed data analysis
- Working with governmental departments
- Using various software and programming languages including Visual Basic for Applications (VBA), Python, R, Monte Carlo Simulation Software, Joint Confidence Level Software
- Using additional applications for project management and visualization, including Microsoft Project, Power BI, and Tableau

Responsibilities

The Cost Analyst is responsible for performing analyses, creating cost models, managing financial data, and reporting on results to the full team, including project leadership. You will work with clients as part of a team to create cost estimates based on data, estimates, and project requirements and specs. The role requires you to create cost/risk analyses and various types of projections and models, utilizing simulation software along with strong analytical skills. You will have opportunities to use statistics, operational mathematics, data science, scripting and coding, engineering, and economics as you learn and grow in this exciting consulting role.

Exhibit 6.18
Cost Analyst Job Opportunity

KEY TAKEAWAYS: SUPPORT-DEPARTMENT COSTS AND JOINT PRODUCT COSTING

In this chapter, we continued our discussion of allocating overhead costs that cannot be traced to individual products. We examined how to assign overhead costs from support departments and joint-production processes. We also discussed how to allocate overhead from shared support services using the direct, step-down, and reciprocal methods. We used these cost-allocation techniques to address how companies can better assign indirect costs to departments that are responsible for those costs. We also learned how to allocate costs for joint products using several allocation base methods and how to evaluate product decisions related to joint products.

Let's use the AMPS model to summarize how the information in this chapter can be used to address important managerial questions:

Ask the Question

■ **What question(s) does management want to answer?**

Indirect costs can be a significant component of producing a product or service. When multiple cost objects (that is, production departments or product lines) use the same resources, management accountants must understand how to properly allocate joint and separable costs.

Master the Data

■ **Which data are appropriate to address management's questions?**

The cost information used to allocate support-department costs primarily comes from an organization's financial reporting and human resource management systems. Companies pull data from their financial reporting and manufacturing systems to calculate joint product costs.

Perform the Analysis

■ **Which analytics are performed to address management questions?**

We use **descriptive analytics** and **diagnostic analytics** to determine how costs should be allocated to production departments and product lines as well as the reason for these allocations. Once companies determine costs, they can undertake **predictive analytics** to determine how costs can be reduced as well as **prescriptive analytics** to identify which actions might improve company performance and efficiency.

Share the Story

■ **How are the results of the analytics shared with stakeholders?**

A firm's strategy depends on sound cost data, and accurately allocating indirect costs can be difficult. Management accountants play a major role in a firm's strategy by providing reports and data visualizations to managers of an organization that summarize key information about the challenges companies face as well as potential solutions.

Key Terms

by-products	gross margin	physical units method	separable cost
constant gross margin method	gross profit		single-rate method
	joint costs	production departments	split-off point
cost driver	joint products	reciprocal method	step-down method
direct method	net realizable value (NRV) method	sales value at split-off method	support departments
dual-rate method			support services

✓ ANSWERS TO PROGRESS CHECKS

1. Production departments produce goods and services for sale to customers. Support departments help ensure efficient and effective operations by providing necessary services to other departments within an organization.

2. Support services do not generate sales; rather, they support the production of goods and services. Universities are in the business of providing education, or teaching classes. They also generate revenue by providing housing and food to students. Academic advising, counseling, and information technology are all examples of support services.

3. The single-rate method uses a single rate to allocate all support-department costs (both fixed costs and variable costs). Under the single-rate method, all costs are allocated on the basis of actual hours. The dual-rate method requires companies to calculate separate rates for fixed costs and variable costs. Under the dual-rate method, fixed costs are allocated on the basis of budgeted hours, and variable costs are allocated on the basis of actual hours.

4. An advantage of the single-rate method is that it is computationally simple, compared to the dual-rate method. A disadvantage is that it does not accurately reflect the realities of support-department costs.

5. Under all three methods, all support-department costs are allocated to production departments. In addition, all of these methods use cost drivers to allocate costs to the departments that use support-department resources.

6. Under the direct method, no support-department costs are allocated to other support departments. Under the step-down method, support-department costs are ranked, and costs can only be allocated from higher-ranked support departments to lower-ranked departments. Under the reciprocal method, all support departments allocate costs to all other support departments.

7. In cost accounting, there is always a trade-off between the complexity or cost of obtaining information and the accuracy of that information. Although the direct method may yield less-accurate costs, it's considerably simpler than the reciprocal method. For many companies, especially those without significant support-department costs, the direct method provides cost numbers that are "close enough," and it isn't worth the cost or trouble to obtain more accurate cost data from other methods.

8. Joint costs arise from products that share the same production process up to a split-off point. Separable costs can be traced to a specific product because they are not shared by multiple product lines.

9. The split-off point is the point of production at which joint production processes are complete. To identify the split-off point, companies must identify when individual product lines begin their distinct or separate manufacturing processes.

10. For students with undeclared majors, undergraduate recruiting costs, the cost of processing applications, and student orientation costs are all examples of joint costs. These are costs incurred by the organization that cannot be directly attributed to specific majors. The split-off point for universities is the point at which students declare a major or apply for specific programs. After the split-off point, universities can assign the costs of educating and supporting students in specific majors.

11. To determine whether a product should be processed further, a company must use cost-benefit analysis. If additional production costs for a given product are greater than the additional revenue to be gained, then the product should be sold as is.

12. The constant gross margin method allocates joint costs in such a way that all product lines can report an identical gross margin. The calculations involved are very different from the other methods, which prorate joint costs across product lines.

13. While both joint products and by-products are the results of a common manufacturing process, they differ in two ways. First, the creation of joint products is a primary purpose of a joint manufacturing process, while by-products are an incidental (and sometimes undesirable) result of the process. In addition, by-products have significantly lower economic value than joint products.

Multiple-Choice Questions

1. (LO6.1) Which of the following is not a reason for sharing support services?
   a. Increased efficiency
   b. Increased expertise
   c. Improved consistency
   d. Improved ability to customize shared services to groups and departments

2. (LO6.1) Which of the following departments is least likely to be considered a support department?
   a. Motor pool
   b. Cafeteria
   c. Information technology department
   d. Assembly department

3. (LO6.2) When allocating the costs of a single support department to production departments, the dual-rate method determines an allocation rate for *variable costs* by using the _____ usage of support-department resources, and it allocates costs by multiplying this rate by the _____ usage of support-department resources.
   a. actual, actual
   b. actual, budgeted
   c. budgeted, actual
   d. budgeted, budgeted

4. (LO6.2) The dual-rate method of allocating support-department costs relies on categorizing costs as either:
   a. fixed or variable.
   b. inventoriable or non-inventoriable.
   c. recurring or unique.
   d. product or period.

5. (LO6.2) When allocating the costs of a single support department to production departments, the dual-rate method determines an allocation rate for *fixed costs* by using the _____ usage of support-department resources, and it allocates costs by multiplying this rate by the _____ usage of support-department resources.
   a. actual, actual
   b. actual, budgeted
   c. budgeted, actual
   d. budgeted, budgeted

6. (LO6.3) In which of the following allocation methods does the order of allocation (that is, which support department allocates first) affect cost allocations?
   a. Direct method
   b. Single-rate method
   c. Step-down method
   d. Reciprocal method

7. (LO6.3) Which of the following allocation methods ignores the cost of services provided by one support department to another?
   a. Direct method
   b. Single-rate method
   c. Step-down method
   d. Reciprocal method

8. (LO6.3) Which of the following methods provides the simplest support-department cost allocations?

a. Direct method

b. Equitable method

c. Step-down method

d. Reciprocal method

9. (LO6.3) Which of the following methods provides the most accurate support-department cost allocations?

a. Direct method

b. Equitable method

c. Step-down method

d. Reciprocal method

10. (LO6.3) Which of the following methods provides support-department cost allocations that are 100% accurate?

    I. Direct method

    II. Step-down method

    III. Reciprocal method

a. None of these

b. III only

c. I and III

d. II and III

11. (LO6.3) Which of the following methods is sometimes used to allocate production-department costs to support departments?

    I. Direct method

    II. Step-down method

    III. Reciprocal method

a. None of these

b. III only

c. I and III

d. II and III

12. (LO6.4) Costs used in a single production process that produces multiple products, but that cannot be attributed to individual products, are:

a. sunk costs.

b. separable costs.

c. joint costs.

d. combination costs.

13. (LO6.4) Separable costs are costs that occur after the _____ and can be attributed to specific products.

a. split-off point

b. midpoint

c. completion point

d. separable point

14. (LO6.5) Which of the following statements regarding joint products and by-products is true?

a. Joint products are more profitable than by-products.

b. Joint costs are typically allocated to by-products.

c. Joint production processes always yield joint products and by-products.

d. There are always more joint products than by-products.

15. (LO6.5) Which joint-product allocation method ignores revenue?

   a. Physical units method

   b. Sales value at split-off method

   c. Net realizable value method

   d. Constant gross margin method

16. (LO6.5) Which joint-product allocation method can sometimes cause negative costs to be allocated to products?

   a. Physical units method

   b. Sales value at split-off method

   c. Net realizable value method

   d. Constant gross margin method

17. (LO6.5) Which joint-product allocation method best assigns costs based on the causal relationship between costs and economic benefit received?

   a. Physical units method

   b. Sales value at split-off method

   c. Net realizable value method

   d. Constant gross margin method

18. (LO6.5) Which of the following joint-cost allocation methods affects overall company profitability?

   I. Physical units method

   II. Sales value at split-off method

   III. Net realizable value method

   IV. Constant gross margin method

   a. None of these

   b. I and II

   c. III and IV

   d. I, II, III, and IV

19. (LO6.5) Which of the following joint-cost allocation methods are affected by separable costs?

   I. Physical units method

   II. Sales value at split-off method

   III. Net realizable value method

   IV. Constant gross margin method

   a. I and III

   b. I and II

   c. III and IV

   d. I, II, III, and IV

20. (LO6.5) In which of the following joint-cost allocation methods is the profitability of one product most influenced by the separable costs of other products?

   a. Physical units method

   b. Sales value at split-off method

   c. Net realizable value method

   d. Constant gross margin method

21. (LO6.1, 6.3) Wilcox Industrial has two support departments, the Information Systems Department and the Personnel Department, and two manufacturing departments, the Machining Department and the Assembly Department. The support departments service each other as well as the two production departments. Company studies have

CMA

shown that the Personnel Department provides support to a greater number of departments than the Information Systems Department. If Wilcox uses the step-down method of departmental allocation, which one of the following cost allocations will not occur?

a. The Personnel Department will be allocated to the Information Systems Department.

b. The Information Systems Department will be allocated to the Personnel Department.

c. The Personnel Department will be allocated to the Assembly Department.

d. The Personnel Department will be allocated to the Assembly Department and the Machining Department.

22. (LO6.1, 6.3) Render Inc. has four support departments (maintenance, power, human resources, and legal) and three operating departments. The support departments provide services to the operating departments as well as to the other support departments. The method of allocating the costs of the support departments that *best* recognizes the mutual services rendered by support departments to other support departments is the:

a. direct allocation method.

b. dual-rate allocation method.

c. step-down allocation method.

d. reciprocal allocation method.

23. (LO6.4) In a production process where joint products are produced, the primary factor that will generally distinguish a joint product from a by-product is the:

a. relative total sales value of the products.

b. relative total volume of the products.

c. relative ease of selling the products.

d. accounting method used to allocate joint costs.

Discussion Questions

1. (LO6.1) Why do companies create support departments to provide companywide services?

2. (LO6.1) Why do most companies allocate support-department costs to production departments?

3. (LO6.2, 6.3) There are various methods of allocating support-department costs. Explain why companies may sacrifice accuracy for convenience.

4. (LO6.2) The single-rate method may discourage managers of production departments from using support-department services. How will this decision affect a company's costs in the short term and in the long term?

5. (LO6.3) For companies that have multiple support departments, describe how support-department allocation methods differ with regard to how costs are allocated between support departments.

6. (LO6.3) Under the step-down method of allocating support-department costs, support departments are ranked to determine the order in which costs are allocated to production departments. Explain why the order in which support departments are ranked can affect the allocation of support-department costs to production departments.

7. (LO6.3) Why is the reciprocal method theoretically superior to the direct and step-down methods of support-department cost allocation?

8. (LO6.4) Explain how companies determine the split-off point in a production process.

9. (LO6.5) Managers can select from many methods for allocating joint costs. If managers' desire to allocate joint costs to products is based on each product's ability to cover those costs, which method should be selected? Explain your answer.

10. (LO6.5) Managers can select from many methods for allocating joint costs. If managers desire to reduce competition within the firm between employees working on different products, which method should be selected? Explain your answer.

11. (LO6.5) Explain the difference between joint products and by-products.

12. (LO6.5) Explain why production costs that occur after the split-off point are allocated to individual joint products rather than shared between joint products.

13. (LO6.5) Managers' compensation is often tied to the profitability of the product lines over which they have control. Explain why joint-cost allocation methods may have a significant effect on managers' compensation even though they have no effect on company profitability.

14. (LO6.5) Ultimately, regardless of joint-cost allocation method, a company's overall costs do not change. Explain how the choice of joint-cost allocation method might influence the morale of employees and the cooperation between production departments.

15. (LO6.5) What ethical considerations must a manager consider when determining how to allocate joint costs among departments?

ETHICS

Brief Exercises   connect

1. (LO6.1, 6.2) Golden Martini has two production departments, Bottling and Packaging. Both departments are serviced by a single support department—information technology (IT). Support-department costs are allocated to production departments on the basis of service-department hours. The IT department has fixed costs of $450,000. In addition, the IT department incurs a rate of $40 per hour in variable costs. Budgeted and actual IT department hours in each production department are as follows:

Production Department	Budgeted Hours	Actual Hours
Bottling	1,500	1,200
Packaging	4,500	5,000
Total	6,000	6,200

Required

If a single-rate cost allocation method is used, what amount of IT services cost will be allocated to the Bottling department?

2. (LO6.1, 6.2) The Bling Club has two production departments, Smelting and Repair. Both production departments are serviced by a single support department, machine maintenance. Service-department costs are allocated on the basis of service-department hours. The maintenance department has fixed costs of $140,000. In addition, the maintenance department incurs a rate of $30 per hour in variable costs. Budgeted and actual maintenance department hours in each production department are as follows:

Production Department	Budgeted Hours	Actual Hours
Smelting	2,000	1,800
Repair	2,500	3,000
Total	4,500	4,800

Required

If a single-rate cost allocation method is used, what amount of maintenance services cost will be allocated to the smelting department?

3. (LO6.1, 6.2) Style Cycle has two production departments, Frames and Tires, that are both serviced by a single support department, Engineering Services. Service-department costs are allocated on the basis of service-department hours. The Engineering Services department has fixed costs of $35,000. In addition, the engineering services department incurs a rate of $45 per hour in variable costs. Budgeted and actual maintenance department hours in each production department are as follows:

Production Department	Budgeted Hours	Actual Hours
Frames	1,800	2,000
Tires	3,000	3,000
Total	4,800	5,000

Required

If a dual-rate cost allocation method is used, what amount of engineering services cost will be allocated to Frames based on actual usage?

4. (LO6.1, 6.3) Antique Charm has two support departments, Machine Maintenance (MM) and Human Resources (HR). MM costs for the year total $300,000 and are allocated according to the number of budgeted machine hours expected for each department. HR costs for the year total $150,000 and are allocated based on employee head count. Use the data below to answer the following question.

	Support Departments		Production Departments		
	Machine Maintenance	Human Resources	Furniture	Décor	Total
MM: Machine hours	200	—	18,000	2,000	20,200
HR: Number of employees	20	8	40	40	104
Costs to allocate	$300,000	$150,000	$–	$–	$450,000

Required

Using the direct method, what amount of MM costs will be allocated to the Furniture department?

5. (LO6.1, 6.3) Amber Envy has two support departments, Engineering Services (ES) and Human Resources (HR). Engineering costs for the year total $500,000 and are allocated according to the number of budgeted labor hours expected for each department. HR costs for the year total $200,000 and are allocated based on employee head count. Use the data below to answer the following question.

	Support Departments		Production Departments		
	Engineering Services	Human Resources	Candles	Lotion	Total
ES: Labor hours	500	—	1,200	400	2,100
HR: Number of employees	18	10	46	56	130
Costs to allocate	$500,000	$200,000	$–	$–	$700,000

Required

Using the direct method, what amount of engineering costs will be allocated to the Lotion department?

6. (LO6.1, 6.3) Tidal Splash has two support departments, Engineering Services (ES) and Human Resources (HR). ES costs for the year total $1,800,000 and are allocated

according to the number of budgeted labor hours expected for each department. HR costs for the year total $240,000 and are allocated based on employee head count. Use the data below to answer the following question.

	Support Departments		Production Departments		
	Engineering Services	Human Resources	Boards	Slides	Total
ES: Labor hours	600	–	6,000	9,000	15,600
HR: Number of employees	4	3	10	14	31
Costs to allocate	$1,800,000	$240,000	$–	$–	$2,040,000

Required

Using the step-down method, what amount of engineering costs will be allocated to the Boards department if ES allocates prior to HR?

7. (LO6.1, 6.3) Lit Treasures has two support departments, Machine Maintenance (MM) and Human Resources (HR). MM costs for the year total $45,000 and are allocated according to the number of budgeted machine hours expected for each department. HR costs for the year total $95,000 and are allocated based on employee head count. Use the data below to answer the following question.

	Support Departments		Production Departments		
	Machine Maintenance	Human Resources	Sparklers	Rockets	Total
MM: Machine hours	1000	–	$25,000	30,000	56,000
HR: Number of employees	10	4	5	25	44
Costs to allocate	$45,000	$95,000	$–	$–	$140,000

Required

Using the step-down method, what amount of MM costs will be allocated to the Sparklers department if HR allocates prior to the MM department?

8. (LO6.1, 6.3) Craftism has two support departments, Information Technology (IT) and Custodial Services (CS). IT allocates costs on the basis of labor hours, while CS allocates on the basis of square footage. Craftism allocates support-department costs to production departments using the reciprocal method. Craftism reports the following data:

	Support Departments		Production Departments		
	Information Technology	Custodial Services	Macramé	Knitting	Total
IT: Labor hours	200	500	2,000	2,500	5,200
CS: Square footage	600	500	800	1,600	3,500
Costs to allocate	$250,000	$350,000	$–	$–	$600,000

Required

Identify the two equations that should be used to determine the total costs allocated from the support departments.

9. (LO6.1, 6.3) Arts Vibe has two support departments: Machine Maintenance (MM) and Human Resources (HR). MM allocates costs on the basis of machine hours, while HR allocates on the basis of employee head count. Arts Vibe allocates support-department

costs to production departments using the reciprocal method. Arts Vibe reports the following data:

	Support Departments		Production Departments		
	Machine Maintenance	Human Resources	Abstract	Impressionism	Total
MM: Machine hours	50	30	200	$270	550
HR: Number of employees	2	2	8	15	27
Costs to allocate	$50,000	$75,000	$–	$–	$125,000

Required

Identify the two equations that should be used to determine the total costs allocated from the support departments.

10. (LO6.4, 6.5) Biochem incurs $180,000 in joint costs to produce 34,000 gallons of RX1 and 46,000 gallons of RX2. RX1 is sold for $4.00 per gallon, while RX2 is sold for $6.00 per gallon. Biochem allocates joint costs using the physical units method.

Required

Determine the reported profit per gallon for RX1.

11. (LO6.4, 6.5) Jack's Lumber produces lumber from pine forests. Processing one batch creates two joint products—Grade A lumber and Grade B lumber—at a cost of $275,000. During production, 200,000 board feet of Grade A lumber are produced and can be sold at a price of $2.00 per board foot. In addition, one batch produces 300,000 board feet of Grade B lumber, which can be sold at $1.25 per board foot. Jack's Lumber accounts for joint costs using the sales value at split-off method.

Required

Determine the total profit per batch for Grade A lumber.

12. (LO6.4, 6.5) Sunny Inc. uses a joint production process costing $50,000 to produce 60,000 pounds of sunflower oil and 20,000 pounds of sunflower meal. Sunflower oil can be sold for $1.75/pound. Alternatively, Sunny can spend $60,000 to process oil further to produce 40,000 pounds of sunflower cream, which can be sold for $8.00/pound. Sunflower meal can be sold for $1.00 per pound. Sunny can spend $30,000 to process meal into 15,000 pounds of sunflower flour, which can be sold for $1.50 per pound.

Required

Determine the total profit for Sunny Inc.'s products, assuming the company chooses which products to produce based on maximizing profit.

13. (LO6.4, 6.5) Florange Growers uses a joint production process costing $75,000 to produce 20,000 pounds of orange juice and 5,000 pounds of pulp. Juice can be sold for $2.00/pound or processed further to make 2,000 pounds of an essential oil. The separable cost to produce the oil is $50,000, and oil can be sold for $100 per pound. Pulp can be sold for $0.50 per pound or processed further to produce 15,000 pounds of pelletized feedstock at a cost of $3,600. These pellets can be sold for $1.25 per pound. Florange Growers uses the net realizable value method to allocate joint costs.

Required

Determine the total joint-cost allocation for each of Florange's products, assuming the company chooses which products to produce based on maximizing profit.

14. (LO6.4, 6.5) Palm Life uses a joint production process costing $120,000 to produce 50,000 pounds of palm oil and 30,000 pounds of pulp. Palm oil can be sold for $3.00/pound or processed further to make 30,000 pounds of cosmetics products.

The separable cost to produce the cosmetics is $40,000, and cosmetics can be sold for $7.00 per pound. Pulp can be sold for $0.40 per pound or processed further to produce 25,000 pounds of fuel at a cost of $8,000. Fuel can be sold for $0.50 per pound.

Required

Determine the total joint-cost allocation for each of Palm Life's products, assuming the company chooses which products to produce based on maximizing profit. Palm Life uses the net realizable value method to allocate joint costs.

15. (LO6.4, 6.5) Hobby Hub has joint production costs of $50,000. The production process creates two products and a by-product. The following financial information for the latest period has been compiled:

	Revenue	Allocated Joint Costs	Separable Costs	Profit
Product A	$40,000	$ 18,000	$10,000	$ 12,000
Product B	$50,000	$ 31,000	$ 5,000	$ 14,000
Total	$90,000	$49,000	$15,000	$26,000

Required

Determine the net realizable value of Hobby Hub's by-product during the period.

16. (LO6.1, 6.3) Adam Corporation manufactures computer tables and has the following budgeted indirect manufacturing cost information for next year.

	Support Departments		Operating Departments		
	Maintenance	Systems	Machining	Fabrication	Total
Budgeted overhead	$360,000	$95,000	$200,000	$300,000	$955,000
Support work furnished					
From Maintenance		10%	50%	40%	100%
From Systems	5%		45%	50%	100%

Required

If Adam Corporation uses the step-down method, beginning with the Maintenance Department, to allocate support-department costs to production departments, what is the total overhead (rounded to the nearest dollar) for the Machining Department to allocate to its products?

17. (LO6.4, 6.5) Tempo Company produces three products from a joint process. The three products are sold after further processing as there is no market for any of the products at the split-off point. Joint costs per batch are $315,000. Other product information is shown below.

	Product A	Product B	Product C
Units produced per batch	20,000	30,000	50,000
Further processing and marketing cost per unit	$ .70	$3.00	$ 1.72
Final sales value per unit	$5.00	$6.00	$7.00

Required

If Tempo uses the net realizable value method of allocating joint costs, how much of the joint costs will be allocated to each unit of Product C?

Problems ![Mc Graw Hill] connect

1. (LO6.1, 6.2) Nicabrew has two production departments that each produce one beverage: Pinolillo and Cacao. The Maintenance department is a support department that provides services to both production departments. Support-department costs are allocated to the Pinolillo and Cacao departments on the basis of service-department hours. The Maintenance department has fixed costs of $200,000. In addition, the Maintenance department incurs a rate of $25 per hour in variable costs. Budgeted and actual Maintenance department hours in each production department are as follows:

Production Department	Budgeted Hours	Actual Hours
Pinolillo	2,500	3,000
Cacao	1,500	1,600
Total	4,000	4,600

Required

a. If a single-rate cost allocation method is used, what amount of maintenance cost will be budgeted for each production department?

b. If a single-rate cost allocation method is used, what amount of maintenance cost will be allocated to each department based on actual usage?

c. If a dual-rate cost allocation method is used, what amount of maintenance cost will be budgeted for each department?

d. If a dual-rate cost allocation method is used, what amount of maintenance cost will be allocated to each department based on actual usage?

2. (LO6.1, 6.3) Posh Bakery has two support departments, Machine Maintenance (MM) and Human Resources (HR). MM costs for the year total $500,000 and are allocated according to the number of budgeted machine hours expected for each department. HR costs for the year total $200,000 and are allocated based on employee head count. Use the data below to allocate support-department costs to Posh Bakery's two production departments: Pies and Cakes.

	Support Departments		Production Departments		
	Machine Maintenance	Human Resources	Pies	Cakes	Total
MM: Machine hours	2,000	–	15,000	5,000	22,000
HR: Number of employees	20	7	40	40	10
Costs to allocate	$500,000	$200,000	$–	$–	$700,000

Required

Prepare a schedule that allocates service-department costs using the direct method. Compute the total amount of support costs allocated to each operating department: Pies and Cakes.

3. (LO6.1, 6.3) Posh Bakery has two support departments, Machine Maintenance (MM) and Human Resources (HR). MM costs for the year total $500,000 and are allocated according to the number of budgeted machine hours expected for each department. HR costs for the year total $200,000 and are allocated based on employee head count. Use the data below to allocate support-department costs to Posh Bakery's two production departments: Pies and Cakes.

	Support Departments		Production Departments		
	Machine Maintenance	Human Resources	Pies	Cakes	Total
MM: Machine hours	2,000	–	15,000	5,000	22,000
HR: Number of employees	20	7	4	40	107
Costs to allocate	$500,000	$200,000	$–	$–	$700,000

Required

Prepare a schedule that allocates service-department costs using the step-down method. Posh Bakery has decided to allocate MM costs first. Compute the total amount of support costs allocated to each operating department: Pies and Cakes.

4. (LO6.1, 6.3) Posh Bakery has two support departments, Machine Maintenance (MM) and Human Resources (HR). MM costs for the year total $500,000 and are allocated according to the number of budgeted machine hours expected for each department. HR costs for the year total $200,000 and are allocated based on employee head count. Use the data below to allocate support-department costs to Posh Bakery's two production departments: Pies and Cakes.

| | Support Departments | | Production Departments | | |
	Machine Maintenance	Human Resources	Pies	Cakes	Total
MM: Machine hours	2,000	–	15,000	5,000	22,000
HR: Number of employees	20	7	40	40	107
Costs to allocate	$500,000	$200,000	$–	$–	$700,000

Required

Prepare a schedule that allocates service-department costs using the step-down method. Posh Bakery has decided to allocate human resources costs first. Compute the total amount of support costs allocated to each operating department: Pies and Cakes.

5. (LO6.1, 6.3) Posh Bakery has two support departments, Machine Maintenance (MM) and Human Resources (HR). MM costs for the year total $500,000 and are allocated according to the number of budgeted machine hours expected for each department. HR costs for the year total $200,000 and are allocated based on employee head count. Use the data below to allocate support-department costs to Posh Bakery's two production departments: Pies and Cakes.

| | Support Departments | | Production Departments | | |
	Machine Maintenance	Human Resources	Pies	Cakes	Total
MM: Machine hours	2,000	–	15,000	5,000	22,000
HR: Number of employees	20	7	40	40	107
Costs to allocate	$500,000	$200,000	$–	$–	$700,000

Required

Prepare a schedule that allocates service-department costs using the reciprocal method.

a. Identify the equations that should be used to determine the costs that should be allocated by the support departments.

b. Compute the total amount of support costs allocated to each operating department: Pies and Cakes.

6. (LO6.1, 6.3) Williams Electric Corp. has two support departments, Human Resources (HR) and Information Technology (IT). HR costs for the year total $300,000 and are allocated based on employee count. IT costs for the year total $420,000 and are allocated according to the number of hours that employees are logged onto the computer network. Use the data below to allocate support-department costs to Williams Electric Corp.'s two production departments: Interior and Exterior.

	Support Departments		Production Departments		
	Human Resources	Information Technology	Interior	Exterior	Total
HR: Number of employees	5	20	35	45	105
IT: Network hours	40,000	12,000	45,000	15,000	112,000
Costs to allocate	$300,000	$420,000	$–	$–	$720,000

Required

Prepare a schedule that allocates support-department costs using the direct method. Compute the total amount of support costs allocated to each operating department: Interior and Exterior.

7. (LO6.1, 6.3) Williams Electric Corp. has two support departments, Human Resources (HR) and Information Technology (IT). HR costs for the year total $300,000 and are allocated based on employee count. IT costs for the year total $420,000 and are allocated according to the number of hours that employees are logged on to the computer network. Use the data below to allocate support-department costs to Williams Electric Corp.'s two production departments: Interior and Exterior.

	Support Departments		Production Departments		
	Human Resources	Information Technology	Interior	Exterior	Total
HR: Number of employees	5	20	35	45	105
IT: Network hours	40,000	12,000	45,000	15,000	112,000
Costs to allocate	$300,000	$420,000	$–	$–	$720,000

Required

Prepare a schedule that allocates service-department costs using the step-down method. Williams Electric has decided to allocate HR costs first. Compute the total amount of support costs allocated to each operating department: Interior and Exterior.

8. (LO6.1, 6.3) Williams Electric Corp. has two support departments, Human Resources (HR) and Information Technology (IT). HR costs for the year total $300,000 and are allocated based on employee count. IT costs for the year total $420,000 and are allocated according to the number of hours that employees are logged on to the computer network. Use the data below to allocate support-department costs to Williams Electric Corp.'s two production departments: Interior and Exterior.

	Support Departments		Production Departments		
	Human Resources	Information Technology	Interior	Exterior	Total
HR: Number of employees	5	20	35	45	105
IT: Network hours	40,000	12,000	45,000	15,000	112,000
Costs to allocate	$300,000	$420,000	$–	$–	$720,000

Required

Prepare a schedule that allocates service-department costs using the step-down method. Williams Electric has decided to allocate IT costs first. Compute the total amount of support costs allocated to each operating department: Interior and Exterior.

9. (LO6.1, 6.3) Williams Electric Corp. has two support departments, Human Resources (HR) and Information Technology (IT). HR costs for the year total $300,000 and are allocated based on employee count. IT costs for the year total $420,000 and are allocated according to the number of hours that employees are logged on to the computer network. Use the data below to allocate support-department costs to Williams Electric Corp.'s two production departments: Interior and Exterior.

| | Support Departments | | Production Departments | | |
	Human Resources	Information Technology	Interior	Exterior	Total
HR: Number of employees	5	20	35	45	105
IT: Network hours	40,000	12,000	45,000	15,000	112,000
Costs to allocate	$300,000	$420,000	$–	$–	$720,000

Required

Prepare a schedule that allocates service-department costs using the reciprocal method.

a. Identify the equations that should be used to determine the costs that should be allocated by the support departments.

b. Compute the total amount of support costs allocated to each operating department: Interior and Exterior.

10. (LO6.4, 6.5) Tactile Inc. uses a joint production process to produce two bonding agents, Holdtight and Tilelock, used in the masonry industry. Joint costs are $30,000 per batch. The joint production process produces 40,000 pounds of Holdtight, which can be sold for $1.50 per pound, and 60,000 pounds of Tilelock, which can be sold for $2.00 per pound. Holdtight can be processed further to produce 30,000 pounds of Holdtight Plus at a cost of $20,000. Holdtight Plus sells for $2.50 per pound. Tilelock can be processed further to produce 50,000 pounds of Tilelock Plus at a cost of $40,000. Tilelock Plus sells for $4.00 per pound. Tactile uses the physical units method to allocate joint costs.

Required

a. What proportion of joint costs should be allocated to Holdtight and Tilelock?

b. Determine how the joint costs should be allocated to each product by using the physical units method.

11. (LO6.4, 6.5) Tactile Inc. uses a joint production process to produce two bonding agents, Holdtight and Tilelock, used in the masonry industry. Joint costs are $30,000 per batch. The joint production process produces 40,000 pounds of Holdtight, which can be sold for $1.50 per pound, and 60,000 pounds of Tilelock, which can be sold for $2.00 per pound. Holdtight can be processed further to produce 30,000 pounds of Holdtight Plus at a cost of $20,000. Holdtight Plus sells for $2.50 per pound. Tilelock can be processed further to produce 50,000 pounds of Tilelock Plus at a cost of $40,000. Tilelock Plus sells for $4.00 per pound. Tactile uses the sales value at split-off method to allocate joint costs.

Required

a. What proportion of joint costs should be allocated to Holdtight and Tilelock?

b. Determine how the joint costs should be allocated to each product by using the sales value at split-off method.

12. (LO6.4, 6.5) Tactile Inc. uses a joint production process to produce two bonding agents, Holdtight and Tilelock, used in the masonry industry. Joint costs are $30,000 per batch. The joint production process produces 40,000 pounds of Holdtight, which can be sold for $1.50 per pound, and 60,000 pounds of Tilelock, which can be sold for $2.00 per pound. Holdtight can be processed further to produce 30,000 pounds of Holdtight Plus at a cost of $20,000. Holdtight Plus sells for $2.50 per pound. Tilelock can be

processed further to produce 50,000 pounds of Tilelock Plus at a cost of $40,000. Tilelock Plus sells for $4.00 per pound. Tactile uses the net realizable value method to allocate joint costs.

Required

a. Determine which products should be produced. In other words, should products be sold as is, or should they be processed further?

b. What proportion of joint costs should be allocated to Holdtight and Tilelock?

c. Determine how the joint costs should be allocated to each product by using the net realizable value method.

13. (LO6.4, 6.5) Tactile Inc. uses a joint production process to produce two bonding agents, Holdtight and Tilelock, used in the masonry industry. Joint costs are $30,000 per batch. The joint production process produces 40,000 pounds of Holdtight, which can be sold for $1.50 per pound, and 60,000 pounds of Tilelock, which can be sold for $2.00 per pound. Holdtight can be processed further to produce 30,000 pounds of Holdtight Plus at a cost of $20,000. Holdtight Plus sells for $2.50 per pound. Tilelock can be processed further to produce 50,000 pounds of Tilelock Plus at a cost of $40,000. Tilelock Plus sells for $4.00 per pound. Tactile uses the constant gross margin method to allocate joint costs.

Required

a. Determine which products should be produced. In other words, should products be sold as is, or should they be processed further?

b. What is the company's gross margin?

c. Determine how the joint costs should be allocated to each product by using the constant gross margin method.

14. (LO6.4, 6.5) Deep Sea Drilling extracts oil from the seabed. Each week, oil is extracted and processed at a cost of $100,000. From this process, Deep Sea Drilling produces 50,000 gallons of Product A, which sells for $1.00 per gallon, and 30,000 gallons of Product B, which sells for $1.25 per gallon. Each of these products can be processed further into more valuable products. Product A can be processed to produce 50,000 gallons of petroleum for an additional $40,000 in costs, while Product B can be processed into 25,000 gallons of diesel for an additional $30,000 in costs. Petroleum can be sold for $2.50 per gallon, and diesel sells for $3.00 per gallon. Deep Sea Drilling allocates joint costs using the physical units method.

Required

a. What proportion of joint costs should be allocated to Product A and Product B?

b. Determine how the joint costs should be allocated to each product by using the physical units method.

15. (LO6.4, 6.5) Deep Sea Drilling extracts oil from the seabed. Each week, oil is extracted and processed at a cost of $100,000. From this process, Deep Sea Drilling produces 50,000 gallons of Product A, which sells for $1.00 per gallon, and 30,000 gallons of Product B, which sells for $1.25 per gallon. Each of these products can be processed further into more valuable products. Product A can be processed to produce 50,000 gallons of petroleum for an additional $40,000 in costs, while Product B can be processed into 25,000 gallons of diesel for an additional $30,000 in costs. Petroleum can be sold for $2.50 per gallon, and diesel sells for $3.00 per gallon. Deep Sea Drilling allocates joint costs using the sales value at split-off method.

Required

a. What proportion of joint costs should be allocated to Product A and Product B?

b. Determine how the joint costs should be allocated to each product by using the sales value at split-off method.

16. (LO6.4, 6.5) Deep Sea Drilling extracts oil from the seabed. Each week, oil is extracted and processed at a cost of $100,000. From this process, Deep Sea Drilling produces 50,000 gallons of Product A, which sells for $1.00 per gallon, and 30,000 gallons of Product B, which sells for $1.25 per gallon. Each of these products can be processed further into more valuable products. Product A can be processed to produce 50,000 gallons of petroleum for an additional $40,000 in costs, while Product B can be processed into 25,000 gallons of diesel for an additional $30,000 in costs. Petroleum can be sold for $2.50 per gallon, and diesel sells for $3.00 per gallon. Deep Sea Drilling allocates joint costs using the net realizable value method.

    Required

    a. Determine which products should be produced. In other words, should products be sold as is, or should they be processed further?

    b. What proportion of joint costs should be allocated to Product A and Product B?

    c. Determine how the joint costs should be allocated to each product by using the net realizable value method.

17. (LO6.4, 6.5) Deep Sea Drilling extracts oil from the seabed. Each week, oil is extracted and processed at a cost of $100,000. From this process, Deep Sea Drilling produces 50,000 gallons of Product A, which sells for $1.00 per gallon, and 30,000 gallons of Product B, which sells for $1.25 per gallon. Each of these products can be processed further into more valuable products. Product A can be processed to produce 50,000 gallons of petroleum for an additional $40,000 in costs, while Product B can be processed into 25,000 gallons of diesel for an additional $30,000 in costs. Petroleum can be sold for $2.50 per gallon, and diesel sells for $3.00 per gallon. Deep Sea Drilling allocates joint costs using the constant gross margin method.

    Required

    a. Determine which products should be produced. In other words, should products be sold as is, or should they be processed further?

    b. What is the company's gross margin?

    c. Determine how the joint costs should be allocated to each product by using the constant gross margin method.

18. (LO6.4, 6.5) Sonimad Sawmill Inc. (SSI) purchases logs from independent timber contractors and processes the logs into the following three types of lumber products:

    - Studs for residential building (walls, ceilings).

    - Decorative pieces (fireplace mantels, beams for cathedral ceilings).

    - Posts used as support braces (mine support braces, braces for exterior fences around ranch properties).

    These products are the result of a joint sawmill process that involves removing bark from the logs, cutting the logs into a workable size (ranging from 8 to 16 feet in length), and then cutting the individual products from the logs, depending on the type of wood (pine, oak, walnut, or maple) and the size (diameter) of the log. The joint process results in the following costs and output of products for a typical month.

Joint production costs:	
Materials (rough timber logs)	$ 500,000
Debarking (labor and overhead)	50,000
Sizing (labor and overhead)	200,000
Product cutting (labor and overhead)	250,000
Total joint costs	$1,000,000

Product yield and average sales value on a per-unit basis from the joint process are as follows.

Product	Monthly Output	Fully Processed Sales Price
Studs	75,000	$ 8
Decorative pieces	5,000	100
Posts	20,000	20

The studs are sold as rough-cut lumber after emerging from the sawmill operation without further processing by SSI. Also, the posts require no further processing. The decorative pieces must be planed and further sized after emerging from the SSI sawmill. This additional processing costs SSI $100,000 per month and normally results in a loss of 10% of the units entering the process. Without this planning and sizing process, there is still an active intermediate market for the unfinished decorative pieces, where the sales price averages $60 per unit.

Required

a. Based on the information given for Sonimad Sawmill Inc., allocate the joint processing costs of $1,000,000 to each of the three product lines using the

   1. Relative sales value method at split-off.

   2. Physical output (volume) method at split-off.

   3. Estimated net realizable value method.

b. Prepare an analysis for Sonimad Sawmill Inc. to compare processing the decorative pieces further, as it presently does, with selling the rough-cut product immediately at split-off. Recommend which action the company should take, and be sure to provide all calculations.

Lab 6.1   Excel

Allocating Support-Department Costs with the Direct Method

Data Analytics Types: Descriptive Analytics, Diagnostic Analytics

Lab Note: The tools presented in this lab periodically change. Updated instructions, if applicable, can be found in the student and instructor support materials.

Keywords

Support Departments, Direct Method, Excel

Decision-Making Context

Located in a large city, LRW is a CPA firm with three divisions (that is, production departments). Each division provides a distinct accounting service: Audit, Tax, and Consulting. LRW also has three support departments that are available to assist these divisions. The Information Technology Department provides technical support, the Travel Service Department handles all travel arrangements, and the Office of Research and Analysis conducts in-depth analysis on a host of company issues.

For management to better understand costs, support-department costs must be allocated to LRW's divisions. LRW partners have determined that the cost of Information Technology will be allocated to divisions based on employee count. The cost of the Travel Service Department will be allocated on the basis of employee business trip count, and the Office of Research and Analysis costs will be allocated based on the number of requests received for analysis. Support departments provide services to one another, in addition to the divisions.

LRW has decided to allocate support-department costs to divisions using the direct method.

Required

Use Excel to create a template for allocating support-department costs using the direct method.

Ask the Question

How much support-department cost should be allocated to each of LRW's divisions using the direct method of allocation for the month of March?

Master the Data

In March, the Information Technology Department had costs of $800,000. Information Technology Department costs are allocated based on the number of employees serviced in each department. A total of 400 employees were serviced in March.

The Travel Service Department had March costs of $100,000 and allocates costs based on the number of business trips arranged, which totaled 800 in March.

Costs for the Office of Research and Analysis were $1,300,000 in March. These costs are allocated based on the number of research requests received by the office, which totaled 500 in March.

This summary information is provided in **Lab 6.1 Data.xlsx**.

Perform the Analysis

Analysis Task #1: Create a Cost-Allocation Template

1. Open Excel file **Lab 6.1 Data.xlsx**.
2. You have been provided with raw data related to support-department costs, as well as the allocation bases used to allocate those costs. By creating a cost-allocation template, we can visually display the amount that each support department allocates to other departments.

   To complete the cost allocation template, add the following titles in cells A7, A8, and A9, respectively: Allocation of IT costs, Allocation of TS costs, Allocation of RA costs (see Lab Exhibit 6.1.1). IT stands for Information Technology, TS stands for Travel Service, and RA stands for Research and Analysis.

Lab Exhibit 6.1.1

Microsoft Excel

	A
1	Summary Data for March
2	Support Department
3	IT: Number of employees
4	TS: Number of trips
5	RA: Number of requests
6	Costs to Allocate
7	Allocation of IT costs
8	Allocation of TS costs
9	Allocation of RA costs

3. Finally, in cell A10, add the title "Total Cost Allocation" (see Lab Exhibit 6.1.2). This row will help us determine that all support-department costs have been allocated to production departments, as well as the total support-department cost allocated to each production department.

Lab Exhibit 6.1.2

Microsoft Excel

	A
1	Summary Data for March
2	Support Department
3	IT: Number of employees
4	TS: Number of trips
5	RA: Number of requests
6	Costs to Allocate
7	Allocation of IT costs
8	Allocation of TS costs
9	Allocation of RA costs
10	Total Cost Allocation

Analysis Task #2: Determine Detailed Allocations from Each Support Department

1. Recall that with the direct method, support departments do not allocate costs to other support departments. Rather, support departments allocate all costs directly to production departments based on usage.

   In cell B7, enter the formula =-B$6, which reflects that the total cost that should be allocated from the IT department is $800,000. Using this formula format will enable us to copy the formula to other cells in subsequent steps. In cells C7 and D7, enter zero to reflect that no IT costs are allocated to other support departments. After you have made these entries, your screen should resemble Exhibit 6.1.3.

	A	B	C	D
1	Summary Data for March	Support Departments		
2	Support Department	Information Technology	Travel Service	Research and Analysis
3	IT: Number of employees	8	5	15
4	TS: Number of trips	10	10	10
5	RA: Number of requests	20	5	5
6	Costs to Allocate	$ 800,000.00	$ 100,000.00	$ 1,300,000.00
7	Allocation of IT costs	$ (800,000.00)	$ -	$ -

Lab Exhibit 6.1.3

Microsoft Excel

2. For Information Technology (IT) costs, which are allocated on the basis of employees, we must determine the total number of relevant employees that will be used for allocation. In this case, we use the total number of employees in the Audit (120), Tax (150), and Consulting (110) departments, or a total of 380 employees. Notice that the number of employees in the IT department is ignored because a support department never allocates costs to itself. In addition, employees in the Travel Service Department and Office of Research and Analysis are ignored because in the direct method, support-department costs are not allocated to other support departments.

   To determine how much cost to allocate to production departments, we will divide the number of employees in each production department by the total number of relevant employees using the formula shown in cell E7 in Lab Exhibit 6.1.4. Copy this formula to cells F7 and G7. The formula is:

$$=E3/SUM(\$E\$3:\$G\$3)*-\$B\$7$$

	A	B	C	D	E	F	G
1	Summary Data for March	Support Departments			Production Departments		
2	Support Department	Information Technology	Travel Service	Research and Analysis	Audit	Tax	Consulting
3	IT: Number of employees	8	5	15	120	150	110
4	TS: Number of trips	10	10	10	150	130	500
5	RA: Number of requests	20	5	5	100	125	250
6	Costs to Allocate	$ 800,000.00	$ 100,000.00	$ 1,300,000.00	$ -	$ -	$ -
7	Allocation of IT costs	$ (800,000.00)	$ -	$ -	=E3/SUM($E3:$G3)*-B7		

Lab Exhibit 6.1.4

Microsoft Excel

3. In cell H7, sum cells B7:G7 as shown in Lab Exhibit 6.1.5. If all IT costs have been allocated to other departments, the total in cell H7 should be zero.

	A	B	C	D	E	F	G	H
1	Summary Data for March	Support Departments			Production Departments			
2	Support Department	Information Technology	Travel Service	Research and Analysis	Audit	Tax	Consulting	Total
3	IT: Number of employees	8	5	15	120	150	110	408
4	TS: Number of trips	10	10	10	150	130	500	810
5	RA: Number of requests	20	5	5	100	125	250	505
6	Costs to Allocate	$ 800,000.00	$ 100,000.00	$ 1,300,000.00	$ -	$ -	$ -	$ 2,200,000.00
7	Allocation of IT costs	$ (800,000.00)	$ -	$ -	$252,631.58	$315,789.47	$231,578.95	=SUM(B7:G7)

Lab Exhibit 6.1.5

Microsoft Excel

4. We will use the same process to allocate costs from the Travel Service Department and Office of Research and Analysis. Copy the formula from cell B7 to cells C8 and D9 to reflect that all support-department costs should be allocated from the Travel Service Department and Office of Research and Analysis. Enter zeros in relevant cells to indicate that no costs are allocated between support departments, as shown in Lab Exhibit 6.1.6.

Lab Exhibit 6.1.6

Microsoft Excel

D9		✕ ✓ fx	=-D$6	

	A	B	C	D
1	**Summary Data for March**		**Support Departments**	
2	**Support Department**	**Information Technology**	**Travel Service**	**Research and Analysis**
3	**IT: Number of employees**	8	5	15
4	**TS: Number of trips**	10	10	10
5	**RA: Number of requests**	20	5	5
6	**Costs to Allocate**	$ 800,000.00	$ 100,000.00	$ 1,300,000.00
7	**Allocation of IT costs**	$ (800,000.00)	$ -	$ -
8	**Allocation of TS costs**	$ -	$(100,000.00)	$ -
9	**Allocation of RA costs**	$ -	$ -	$ (1,300,000.00)

5. Copy the formula from cell E7 to E8, then double-click the formula. Notice that the formula correctly uses cells E4:G4 to prorate the number of trips taken by each production department. However, it multiplies these allocations by the total IT costs rather than Travel Service costs, as shown in Lab Exhibit 6.1.7.

Lab Exhibit 6.1.7

Microsoft Excel

	A	B	C	D	E	F	G
1	Summary Data for March		Support Departments			Production Departments	
2	Support Department	Information Technology	Travel Service	Research and Analysis	Audit	Tax	Consulting
3	IT: Number of employees	8	5	15	120	150	110
4	TS: Number of trips	10	10	10	150	130	500
5	RA: Number of requests	20	5	5	100	125	250
6	Costs to Allocate	$ 800,000.00	$ 100,000.00	$ 1,300,000.00	$ -	$ -	$ -
7	Allocation of IT costs	$ (800,000.00)	$ -	$ -	$252,631.58	$315,789.47	$231,578.95
8	Allocation of TS costs	$ -	$(100,000.00)	$ -	=E4/SUM($E4:$G4)*-$B$7		

Change $B$7 to $C$8 to correct the formula (as shown in Lab Exhibit 6.1.8), and then copy the formula from cell E8 to cells F8 and G8.

Lab Exhibit 6.1.8

Microsoft Excel

	A	B	C	D	E	F	G
1	Summary Data for March		Support Departments			Production Departments	
2	Support Department	Information Technology	Travel Service	Research and Analysis	Audit	Tax	Consulting
3	IT: Number of employees	8	5	15	120	150	110
4	TS: Number of trips	10	10	10	150	130	500
5	RA: Number of requests	20	5	5	100	125	250
6	Costs to Allocate	$ 800,000.00	$ 100,000.00	$ 1,300,000.00	$ -	$ -	$ -
7	Allocation of IT costs	$ (800,000.00)	$ -	$ -	$252,631.58	$315,789.47	$231,578.95
8	Allocation of TS costs	$ -	$(100,000.00)	$ -	=E4/SUM($E4:$G4)*-$C$8		

6. Use the same steps to allocate Research and Analysis costs to production departments, ensuring that the formula references the appropriate cells, as shown in Lab Exhibit 6.1.9. For example, the formula in cell G9 should be =G5/SUM($E5:$G5)*-$D$9.

Lab Exhibit 6.1.9

Microsoft Excel

	A	B	C	D	E	F	G	H
1	Summary Data for March		Support Departments			Production Departments		
2	Support Department	Information Technology	Travel Service	Research and Analysis	Audit	Tax	Consulting	Total
3	IT: Number of employees	8	5	15	120	150	110	408
4	TS: Number of trips	10	10	10	150	130	500	810
5	RA: Number of requests	20	5	5	100	125	250	505
6	Costs to Allocate	$ 800,000.00	$ 100,000.00	$ 1,300,000.00	$ -	$ -	$ -	$ 2,200,000.00
7	Allocation of IT costs	$ (800,000.00)	$ -	$ -	$252,631.58	$315,789.47	$231,578.95	$ -
8	Allocation of TS costs	$ -	$(100,000.00)	$ -	$ 19,230.77	$ 16,666.67	$ 64,102.56	
9	Allocation of RA costs	$ -	$ -	$ (1,300,000.00)	$273,684.21	$342,105.26	=G5/SUM($E5:$G5)*-$D$9	

7. Copy the formula in cell H7 to cells H8 and H9 to determine that all support-department costs have been allocated to production departments. Each of these cells should have a value of zero. See Lab Exhibit 6.1.10.

Lab Exhibit 6.1.10

Microsoft Excel

H9 · : × ✓ fx =SUM(B9:G9)

	A	B	C	D	E	F	G	H
1	Summary Data for March		Support Departments			Production Departments		
2	Support Department	Information Technology	Travel Service	Research and Analysis	Audit	Tax	Consulting	Total
3	IT: Number of employees	8	5	15	120	150	110	408
4	TS: Number of trips	10	10	10	150	130	500	810
5	RA: Number of requests	20	5	5	100	125	250	505
6	Costs to Allocate	$ 800,000.00	$ 100,000.00	$ 1,300,000.00	$ -	$ -	$ -	$ 2,200,000.00
7	Allocation of IT costs	$ (800,000.00)	$ -	$ -	$252,631.58	$315,789.47	$231,578.95	$ -
8	Allocation of TS costs	$ -	$(100,000.00)	$ -	$ 19,230.77	$ 16,666.67	$ 64,102.56	$ -
9	Allocation of RA costs	$ -	$ -	$ (1,300,000.00)	$273,684.21	$342,105.26	$684,210.53	$ -

8. Now, in Row 10, we will sum Rows 6–9 for Columns B–G to determine that there are no unallocated costs in any support department, as shown in Lab Exhibit 6.1.11. In addition, this process will provide the total support-department costs that have been allocated to each production department.

Lab Exhibit 6.1.11

Microsoft Excel

	A	B	C	D	E	F	G
1	Summary Data for March		Support Departments			Production Departments	
2	Support Department	Information Technology	Travel Service	Research and Analysis	Audit	Tax	Consulting
3	IT: Number of employees	8	5	15	120	150	110
4	TS: Number of trips	10	10	10	150	130	500
5	RA: Number of requests	20	5	5	100	125	250
6	Costs to Allocate	$ 800,000.00	$ 100,000.00	$ 1,300,000.00	$ -	$ -	$ -
7	Allocation of IT costs	$ (800,000.00)	$ -	$ -	$252,631.58	$315,789.47	$231,578.95
8	Allocation of TS costs	$ -	$(100,000.00)	$ -	$ 19,230.77	$ 16,666.67	$ 64,102.56
9	Allocation of RA costs	$ -	$ -	$ (1,300,000.00)	$273,684.21	$342,105.26	$684,210.53
10	Total Cost Allocation	$ -	$ -	$ -	$545,546.56	$674,561.40	=SUM(G6:G9)

9. Finally, copy the formula from cell H6 to cell H10 to ensure that all $2,200,000 of support-department costs have been allocated, as shown in Lab Exhibit 6.1.12.

	A	B	C	D	E	F	G	H
1	Summary Data for March		Support Departments			Production Departments		
2	Support Department	Information Technology	Travel Service	Research and Analysis	Audit	Tax	Consulting	Total
3	IT: Number of employees	8	5	15	120	150	110	408
4	TS: Number of trips	10	10	10	150	130	500	810
5	RA: Number of requests	20	5	5	100	125	250	505
6	Costs to Allocate	$ 800,000.00	$ 100,000.00	$ 1,300,000.00	$ -	$ -	$ -	$ 2,200,000.00
7	Allocation of IT costs	$ (800,000.00)	$ -	$ -	$252,631.58	$315,789.47	$231,578.95	$ -
8	Allocation of TS costs	$ -	$(100,000.00)	$ -	$ 19,230.77	$ 16,666.67	$ 64,102.56	$ -
9	Allocation of RA costs	$ -	$ -	$(1,300,000.00)	$273,684.21	$342,105.26	$684,210.53	$ -
10	Total Cost Allocation	$ -	$ -	$ -	$545,546.56	$674,561.40	$979,892.04	=SUM(B10:G10)

Share the Story

To understand their costs, companies allocate support-department costs to production departments. To perform this allocation, they can use several different methods, including the direct method. Creating a cost-allocation template can save managers time because it can be used each period with new data.

Our analysis shows that under the direct method, $545,546.56 is allocated to Audit, $674,561.40 is allocated to Tax, and $979,892.04 is allocated to Consulting. The sum equals the total amount to be allocated, $2,200,000.

Assessment

1. Take a screenshot of the dataset following Analysis Task #2, paste it into a Word document, and label the document "Lab 6.1 Submission.docx".
2. Answer the multiple-choice questions in Connect based on the results of your analysis and upload your Lab 6.1 Submission.docx via Connect if assigned.

Alternate Lab 6.1   Excel—On Your Own

Allocating Support-Department Costs with the Direct Method

Keywords

Support Departments, Direct Method, Excel

Required

Given April summary data for LRW, replicate the assignment in Lab 6.1 using the **Alt Lab 6.1 Data.xlsx** dataset.

Assessment

1. Take a screenshot of the worksheet following Analysis Task #2, paste it into a Word document, and label it "Alt Lab 6.1 Submission.docx".
2. Answer the multiple-choice questions in Connect and upload your Alt Lab 6.1 Submission.docx via Connect if assigned.

Allocating Support-Department Costs with the Step-Down Method

Data Analytics Types: Descriptive Analytics, Diagnostic Analytics

Lab Note: The tools presented in this lab periodically change. Updated instructions, if applicable, can be found in the student and instructor support materials. All Lab Exhibits are available within the eBook and in Connect.

Keywords

Support Departments, Step-Down Method, Excel

Decision-Making Context

Located in a large city, LRW is a CPA firm with three divisions (that is, production departments). Each division provides a distinct accounting service: Audit, Tax, and Consulting. LRW also has three support departments that are available to assist these divisions. The Information Technology Department provides technical support, the Travel Service Department handles all travel arrangements, and the Office of Research and Analysis conducts in-depth analysis on a host of company issues.

For management to better understand costs, support-department costs must be allocated to LRW's divisions. LRW partners have determined that the cost of Information Technology will be allocated to divisions based on employee count. The cost of the Travel Service Department will be allocated on the basis of employee business trip count, and the Office of Research and Analysis costs will be allocated based on the number of requests received for analysis. Support departments provide services to one another, in addition to the divisions.

LRW has decided to allocate support-department costs to divisions using the step-down method. LRW uses the following order when allocating support-department costs: (1) Office of Research and Analysis, (2) Information Technology Department, (3) Travel Service Department.

Required

Use Excel to create a template for allocating support-department costs using the step-down method.

Ask the Question

How much support-department cost should be allocated to each of LRW's divisions using the step-down method of allocation for the month of March?

Master the Data

In March, the Information Technology Department had costs of $800,000. Information Technology Department costs are allocated based on the number of employees serviced in each department. A total of 400 employees were serviced in March.

The Travel Service Department had March costs of $100,000 and allocates costs based on the number of business trips arranged, which totaled 800 in March.

Costs for the Office of Research and Analysis were $1,300,000 in March. These costs are allocated based on the number of research requests received by the office, which totaled 500 in March.

This summary information is provided in **Lab 6.2 Data.xlsx**.

Open Excel file **Lab 6.2 Data.xlsx**.

Perform the Analysis

Analysis Task #1: Create a Cost-Allocation Template

1. You have been provided with raw data related to support-department costs, as well as the allocation bases used to allocate those costs. By creating a cost-allocation template, we can visually display the amount that each support department allocates to other departments.

    To complete the cost allocation template, add the following titles in cells A7, A8, and A9, respectively: Allocation of IT costs, Allocation of TS costs, Allocation of RA costs (see Lab Exhibit 6.2.1). IT stands for information technology, TS stands for travel service, and RA stands for research and analysis.

2. Finally, in cell A10, add the title "Total Cost Allocation" (see Lab Exhibit 6.2.2). This row will help us determine that all support-department costs have been allocated to production departments, as well as the total support-department cost allocated to each production department.

Analysis Task #2: Determine Detailed Allocations from Each Support Department

1. Recall that with the step-down method, the company ranks support departments. Higher-ranked support departments allocate costs to lower-ranked support departments, but lower-ranked support departments do not allocate costs to higher-ranked support departments. This method makes creating the Excel template for these problems more difficult because fewer formulas can be copied. However, the effort expended to create the template becomes more valuable as time goes on and the template is used across periods.

    LRW uses the following order when allocating support-department costs: (1) Office of Research and Analysis, (2) Information Technology Department, (3) Travel Service Department.

    Based on these ranks, we will start with the Office of Research and Analysis. The total costs that must be allocated from Research and Analysis are found in cell D6. In cell D9, enter the formula =-D$6, as shown in Lab Exhibit 6.2.3.

2. Next, we must determine the proportion of Research and Analysis costs that should be allocated to other departments, based on usage. Because Research and Analysis has the highest rank, it can allocate costs to all other departments (both support departments and production departments). Remember that a support department never allocates costs to itself. Thus, the relevant number of requests (the allocation base) is 500, which is the sum of requests in all departments other than Research and Analysis.

    In cell B9, enter the formula =B5/SUM($B5,$C5,$E5,$F5,$G5)*-$D$9" (see Lab Exhibit 6.2.4). This formula calculates the IT department's proportion of total relevant requests and multiplies it by the total support-department costs that must be allocated from the Office of Research and Analysis.

    Copy this formula in cell B9 (press Ctrl+c) and paste it (press Ctrl+v) for all other departments in Row 9. Lab Exhibit 6.2.5 shows the results.

3. In cell H9, sum cells B9:G9, as shown in Lab Exhibit 6.2.6. If all Research and Analysis costs have been allocated to other departments, the total in cell H9 should be zero.

4. Next, we must allocate Information Technology costs. The total cost to be allocated from IT includes the original costs ($800,000) *plus* costs allocated to IT from other support departments. As shown in Lab Exhibit 6.2.7, in cell B7, enter the formula =-(B6+B9).

5. The amount calculated in cell B7 is the IT allocation that must be allocated to production departments, as well as lower-ranked support departments (Travel Service), but *not* to higher-ranked support departments (Research and Analysis). For this reason, enter zero in cell D7 for the Office of Research and Analysis.

In cell C7, enter this formula: =C3/SUM($C3,$E3,$F3,$G3)*-$B$7 (see Lab Exhibit 6.2.8). This formula may look complicated, so let's consider what it's calculating. We are multiplying the IT allocation in cell B7 by the Travel Service share of relevant employees. To calculate the correct proportion, we must exclude employees in the Office of Research and Analysis, as we do not allocate support-department costs to higher-ranked support departments under the step-down method.

6. Copy the formula from cell C7 to all production departments and the Travel Service Department on Row 7, as shown in Lab Exhibit 6.2.9. In addition, use the formula =SUM(B7:G7) in cell H7 to sum the row to ensure that all IT costs have been allocated to other departments.

7. Next, we must determine the total costs that must be allocated from the Travel Service Department. In cell C8, use the formula =-(C6+C7+C9) to sum all Travel Service costs, including those allocated from other support departments. You can see this formula in the formula bar of Lab Exhibit 6.2.10.

8. Because the Travel Service Department is the lowest-ranked support department, it does not allocate costs to other support departments. Enter zero in cells B8 and D8.

    Travel Service costs must be allocated on a prorated basis to production departments only. In cell E8, enter this formula: =E4/SUM($E4,$F4,$G4)*-$C$8, as shown in Lab Exhibit 6.2.11. This formula multiplies total costs from the Travel Service Department by the Audit Division's share of business trips, which is the basis for Travel Service costs.

    Copy the formula from cell E8 to cells E9:E10. In addition, use the sum function in cell H8 to ensure that all costs from IT have been allocated, as shown in Lab Exhibit 6.2.12. The sum should be zero.

9. For each department, sum Rows 6–9 to determine total allocations to production departments, and to ensure that no support-department costs are unallocated. In addition, copy the formula from H6 to H10 to verify that all $2,200,000 in support-department costs have been allocated (see Lab Exhibit 6.2.13).

Share the Story

To understand their costs, companies allocate support-department costs to production departments. To perform this allocation, they can use several different methods, including the step-down method. Creating a cost-allocation template can save managers time because it can be used each period with new data.

Our analysis shows that under the step-down method, $549,417.08 is allocated to Audit, $677,625.54 is allocated to Tax, and $972,957.38 is allocated to Consulting.

Assessment

1. Take a screenshot of the dataset following Analysis Task #2, paste it into a Word document, and label it "Lab 6.2 Submission.docx".
2. Answer the multiple-choice questions in Connect based on the results of your analysis and upload your Lab 6.2 Submission.docx via Connect if assigned.

Alternate Lab 6.2   Excel—On Your Own

Allocating Support-Department Costs with the Step-Down Method

Keywords

Support Departments, Step-Down Method, Excel

Required

Given May summary data for LRW, replicate the assignment in Lab 6.2 using the **Alt Lab 6.2 Data.xlsx** dataset.

Assessment

1. Take a screenshot of the worksheet following Analysis Task #2, paste it into a Word document, and label it "Alt Lab 6.2 Submission.docx".
2. Answer the multiple-choice questions in Connect and upload your Alt Lab 6.2 Submission.docx via Connect if assigned.

Allocating Support-Department Costs with the Reciprocal Method

Data Analytics Types: Descriptive Analytics, Diagnostic Analytics

Lab Note: The tools presented in this lab periodically change. Updated instructions, if applicable, can be found in the student and instructor support materials. All Lab Exhibits are available within the eBook and in Connect.

Keywords

Support Departments, Reciprocal Method, Excel

Decision-Making Context

Located in a large city, LRW is a CPA firm with three divisions (that is, production departments). Each division provides a distinct accounting service: Audit, Tax, and Consulting. LRW also has three support departments that are available to assist these divisions. The Information Technology Department provides technical support, the Travel Service Department handles all travel arrangements, and the Office of Research and Analysis conducts in-depth analysis on a host of company issues.

For management to better understand costs, support-department costs must be allocated to LRW's divisions. LRW partners have determined that the cost of Information Technology will be allocated to divisions based on employee count. The cost of the Travel Service Department will be allocated on the basis of employee business trip count, and the Office of Research and Analysis costs will be allocated based on the number of requests received for analysis. Support departments provide services to one another, in addition to the divisions.

LRW has decided to allocate support-department costs to divisions using the reciprocal method.

Required

1. Use Excel to create a template for allocating support-department costs using the reciprocal method.
2. Use Excel's Solver function to solve the simultaneous equations required for calculating allocation amounts under the reciprocal method.

Ask the Question

How much support-department cost should be allocated to each of LRW's divisions using the reciprocal method of allocation for the month of March?

Master the Data

In March, the Information Technology Department had costs of $800,000. Information Technology Department costs are allocated based on the number of employees serviced in each department. A total of 408 employees were serviced in March.

The Travel Service Department had March costs of $100,000 and allocates costs based on the number of business trips arranged, which totaled 810 in March.

Costs for the Office of Research and Analysis were $1,300,000 in March. These costs are allocated based on the number of research requests received by the office, which totaled 505 in March.

This summary information is provided in **Lab 6.3 Data.xlsx**.

Open Excel file **Lab 6.3 Data.xlsx**.

Perform the Analysis

Analysis Task #1: Create a Cost-Allocation Template

1. This exercise requires Excel's Solver add-in. If you don't already have the Solver add-in installed, install it now. Click **File** at the top left of the screen (Lab Exhibit 6.3.1), and then click **Options** at the bottom left of the screen (Lab Exhibit 6.3.2). Click **Add-ins > Go...** (Lab Exhibit 6.3.3). Make sure **Solver Add-in** is selected and click **OK** (Lab Exhibit 6.3.4).

2. The use of the reciprocal method is made a little easier if we create a second table with support-service data converted into percentages.

   We will create this second table in Rows 11–13. As we convert cost data to percentages, we need to consider how support departments allocate costs to other departments.

   A support department never allocates costs to itself. To reflect the fact that support departments do not allocate costs to themselves, enter 0% in cells B11, C12, and D13, as shown in Exhibit 6.3.5.

3. Costs are allocated to other departments based on the usage of resources. Under the reciprocal method, support departments allocate costs to all other departments, including other support departments. Thus, for allocation purposes, the relevant total for the allocation base relates to the total usage by all *other* departments, and we must subtract out the usage of the allocation base by the support department that is allocating costs.

   To illustrate this idea, consider the Information Technology Department, which allocates costs according to the number of employees in those departments. There are 408 total employees in the company. However, since the IT department does not allocate costs to itself, the relevant number of employees is 400 (408 total employees less the 8 employees in the IT department).

   In cell C11, enter the formula =C3/($H3-$B$3), which represents the Travel Service Department's proportion of employees that are not in the IT department (see Lab Exhibit 6.3.6).

4. Copy the formula from cell C11 to cells D11:G11. In cell H11, sum cells B11:G11 to verify that 100% of relevant employees are accounted for. The result should resemble Lab Exhibit 6.3.7.

5. Use this same process to determine the proportions that should be used to allocate Travel Service costs, which are allocated on the basis of the number of trips used by other departments. Copy the formula from cell C11 to cell B12. In the formula, change $B$3 to $C$4, as shown in Lab Exhibit 6.3.8. We do this because we want to exclude all trips taken by the Travel Service Department. These 10 trips are not relevant because the Travel Service Department cannot allocate costs to itself.

6. Copy the formula from cell B12 to all other departments (except Travel Service). Sum the percentages in cell H12 to verify that we have accounted for 100% of the relevant trips. See Lab Exhibit 6.3.9.

7. Finally, repeat the process to determine the relevant usage proportions for the Office of Research and Analysis. In cell B13, enter the formula =B5/($H5−$D$5), as shown in Lab Exhibit 6.3.10. Notice that this formula excludes data requests from the Office of Research and Analysis in the denominator. We do this because the Office of Research and Analysis cannot allocate costs to itself.

8. Copy the formula from cell B13 to all other departments (except Research and Analysis). Sum the percentages in cell H13 to verify that we have accounted for 100% of the relevant data requests. See Lab Exhibit 6.3.11.

9. Set cell B14 equal to cell B6 by using the formula =B6. Copy the formula to cells C14:H14 so that Row 14 replicates Row 6 (Lab Exhibit 6.3.12).

Analysis Task #2: Use the Solver Function to Determine Total Costs for Each Department

1. Under the reciprocal method, all support departments can allocate to other support departments. The difficult part of this method is determining how much in costs will be allocated from each support department. It's not simply the amount listed in the "Costs to Allocate" row because this amount doesn't include additional costs from other support departments.

    Fortunately, we can use Excel's **Solver** function to determine these amounts. First, we must set up cost equations in Row 23 (see Lab Exhibit 6.3.13). This row will contain the total amount of cost for each department.

    The cost of the Information Technology Department is $800,000, plus a prorated portion of the costs of each support department. In cell B23, enter this formula: =B14+B11*$B$24+B12*$C$24+B13*$D$24, as shown in Lab Exhibit 6.3.13.

    Notice that for calculating the proportion of support-department costs, we reference Row 24. Although this row is empty, it will contain each department's total cost after allocation.

2. Copy the formula from cell B23 to cells C23:G23. In addition, use the sum formula =SUM(B23:G23) in cell H23, as shown in Lab Exhibit 6.3.14.

3. In cell H24, sum cells B24:G24, as shown in Lab Exhibit 6.3.15.

4. In cell H25, sum cells E24:G24, which will be the total costs allocated to production departments (Lab Exhibit 6.3.16). Our template is now set up to enable the use of the **Solver** function.

5. On the **Data** tab, click **Solver** (Lab Exhibit 6.3.17). Set the **Set Objective:** field to cell $H$25 (the sum of costs allocated to production departments) with a **Value of** $2,200,000 (the total of support-department costs for the period) by setting **By Changing Variable Cells:** to cells $B$24:$G$24 (Lab Exhibit 6.3.18).

6. Next, we must add constraints to the **Subject to the Constraints:** field. In the **Solver Parameters** dialog box, click **Add** (see Lab Exhibit 6.3.19).

    Then, in the **Add Constraint** dialog box, under **Cell Reference:**, set cell B23 equal to cell B24 (under **Constraint:**), as shown in Lab Exhibit 6.3.20.

7. Repeat this step (set Row 23 equal to Row 24) for Columns C–G. Then click **OK**. The result is shown in Lab Exhibit 6.3.21. At the bottom of the **Solver Parameters** dialog box, click **Solve**.

8. In the **Solver Results** dialog box, click **OK** (Lab Exhibit 6.3.22).

9. If the formulas and parameters are entered correctly, the **Solver** function will find a solution such that all support-department costs will be allocated to production departments. Row 24 will contain the total costs of support departments (original cost plus costs allocated from other support departments) and production departments (total costs allocated from support departments). Lab Exhibit 6.3.23 shows the final output.

Analysis Task #3: Determine Detailed Allocations from Each Support Department

1. We can use the Solver solution to obtain detailed support-department cost allocations. In cell B15, enter =-B24 (Lab Exhibit 6.3.24). This amount is represented as a negative number because it's an allocation out of the Information Technology Department.

2. In cell C15, enter the formula =$B$24*C11 to calculate the prorated allocation from Information Technology to Travel Service (Lab Exhibit 6.3.25). Copy the formula from cell C15 to cells D15:G15.

3. Use these same steps to calculate allocation amounts for the Travel Service Department and the Office of Research and Analysis. Ensure that allocations from a department to other departments are indicated with a negative number. Your output should resemble Lab Exhibit 6.3.26.

4. In Row 18, sum Rows 15–17 to ensure all support-department costs have been allocated (the totals in Columns B–D should be zero). The formula =SUM(D14:D17) is shown in the formula bar in Lab Exhibit 6.3.27. This step also provides the total allocations to the production departments, as shown in Row 18 of Lab Exhibit 6.3.27.

In Column H, sum Columns B–G for Rows 15–18 as an additional verification that all support-department costs have been allocated to production departments (see Lab Exhibit 6.3.28).

Share the Story

To understand their costs, companies allocate support-department costs to production departments. They can use a number of methods to perform this allocation, including the reciprocal method. Creating a cost-allocation template can save managers time because it can be used each period with new data. Using the **Solver** function enables managers to solve equations that would be difficult to solve using other methods such as a system of equations or matrix algebra.

Our analysis shows that under the direct method, $546,444.33 is allocated to Audit, $674,141.31 is allocated to Tax, and $979,414.36 is allocated to Consulting.

Assessment

1. Take a screenshot of the dataset following Analysis Task #3, paste it into a Word document, and label it "Lab 6.3 Submission.docx".
2. Answer the multiple-choice questions in Connect based on the results of your analysis and upload your Lab 6.3 Submission.docx via Connect if assigned.

Alternate Lab 6.3   Excel—On Your Own

Allocating Support-Department Costs with the Reciprocal Method

Keywords

Support Departments, Reciprocal Method, Excel

Required

Given June summary data for LRW, replicate the assignment in Lab 6.3 using the **Alt Lab 6.3 Data.xlsx** dataset.

Assessment

1. Take a screenshot of the worksheet following Analysis Task #3, paste it into a Word document, and label it "Alt Lab 6.3 Submission.docx".
2. Answer the multiple-choice questions in Connect and upload your Alt Lab 6.3 Submission.docx via Connect if assigned.

Allocating Joint Costs Using Various Methods (Heartwood)
Data Analytics Types: Descriptive Analytics, Diagnostic Analytics

Lab Note: The tools presented in this lab periodically change. Updated instructions, if applicable, can be found in the student and instructor support materials. All Lab Exhibits are available within the eBook and in Connect.

Keywords
Joint Cost Allocation, Excel

Decision-Making Context
Heartwood Cabinets owns forests and sawmills in many countries. In Malaysia, Heartwood has a sawmill conveniently located near several sustainable hardwood forests. Each day, trucks bring loads of logs into the sawmill. The logs are scanned by a machine called an optimizer, which can identify defects (such as knots) inside the log. A computer then determines how the log should be cut in order to avoid defects, maximize the selling value of the cut lumber, and minimize waste.

Hardwoods are graded by the National Hardwood Lumber Association. Grading designation depends on board dimensions and number of defects in each board, as follows:

Grade	Minimum Board Width	Minimum Area Free of Defects
First and Seconds (FAS)	6″	83.33%
Select (SEL)	4″	83.33%
No. 1 Common (1C)	3″	66.67%
No. 2 Common (2C)	3″	50%

Heartwood's Malaysian sawmill can sell each grade of lumber after cutting without any further processing. Alternatively, Heartwood can transport the lumber to one of the company's cabinet manufacturing facilities, where the lumber will be processed further and used in the production of cabinets.

The sawmill produces approximately 100,000 board feet per day of hardwood. Because all grades of wood are produced from the same milling process, FAS, SEL, 1C, and 2C are joint products. The milling process also produces sawdust. This by-product is converted into fuel pellets at the sawmill, and it can be sold for a nominal profit.

Required
Use Excel to create a template for allocating joint costs using the following methods: (1) physical units method, (2) sales value at split-off method, (3) net realizable value method, and (4) constant gross margin method.

Ask the Question
How should Heartwood Cabinets allocate sawmill expenses to milled lumber for October 31st production?

Master the Data
Excel lab file **Lab 6.4 Data.xlsx** contains cost information for October 31st, along with templates that can be used to calculate joint-cost allocations.

Data Dictionary

Joint Costs	Production costs for the day
Joint Products	The different products, in this case different grades of milled wood, produced from Heartwood's milling process, listed in order from highest to lowest quality
Quantity	Number of board feet (*Note:* Assume further processing does not result in any loss or gain of quantity.)
AS IS Selling Price/Unit	Selling price per board foot
Separable Costs/Unit	Separable costs per board foot. Separable costs are all attributable to further processing.
Processed Selling Price/Unit	Selling price per board foot if units are processed further

Open Excel file **Lab 6.4 Data.xlsx**.

Perform the Analysis

Analysis Task #1: Calculate Joint Costs Using the Physical Units Method

1. The physical units method is the simplest method of calculating joint-cost allocations. Under this method, costs are allocated based on prorated units at the split-off point. In other words, the allocation rate is calculated as joint costs/quantity, and this rate is then multiplied by each joint product's relative share of the total.

    To calculate the allocation to the FAS product, enter the formula =$A$12/$C$7*C3 in cell C12 (Lab Exhibit 6.4.1).
2. Copy this formula into cells C13:C15 to determine cost allocations to Heartwood's other joint products. Next, in cell C16 sum the joint-product allocation amounts to ensure that all joint costs have been allocated to joint products (Lab Exhibit 6.4.2).

Analysis Task #2: Calculate Joint Costs Using the Sales Value at Split-off Method

1. The sales value at split-off method is very similar to the physical units method. The difference is that cost allocations are based on sales value at split-off rather than a production quantity.

    To use this method, we must determine sales value at split-off. In cell G2, enter "Sales Value at Split-off". Then calculate sales value by multiplying quantity in Column C by AS IS Selling Price/Unit in Column D. To do so, in cell G3 enter the formula =C3*D3 (as shown in Lab Exhibit 6.4.3).
2. Copy this formula for all joint products, and sum the sales value in cell G7. Lab Exhibit 6.4.4 shows the result.
3. To calculate the allocation to FAS, enter the formula =$A$12/$G$7*G3 in cell D12 (Lab Exhibit 6.4.5).
4. Copy this formula into cells D13:D15 to determine cost allocations to Heartwood's other joint products. Next, sum the joint-product allocation amounts to ensure that all joint costs have been allocated to joint products. Lab Exhibit 6.4.6 shows the results.

Analysis Task #3: Calculate Joint Costs Using the Net Realizable Value Method

1. The net realizable value method is mechanically similar to the two previous methods, but allocations are based on net realizable value, which is calculated as the final sales price minus separable costs. How do we know if Heartwood will sell lumber as is or process it further as cabinets? We will assume that Heartwood wants to maximize profit. If processing a product further increases profitability, then Heartwood will do so.

In cell H2, enter "Processing Decision". We will use the **IF** function in Excel to indicate whether or not products should undergo further processing.

2. In cell H3, enter the formula =IF(F3-E3> D3,"Process Further", "Sell as is"). This formula tells Excel to compare the incremental value of processing units further (F3-E3) to the sales prices at split-off (D3). If the incremental value is greater, the cell will return "Process Further". If not, the cell will return "Sell as is". Copy this formula for the remaining joint products (Lab Exhibit 6.4.7).

3. Label cell I2 "Net Realizable Value", as shown in Lab Exhibit 6.4.8. If the company should process a product further, net realizable value is calculated as (Processed Selling Price [Column F] – Separable Costs [Column E]) * Quantity (Column C). If the company should sell as is, net realizable value is set equal to sales value at split-off (Column G). Use formulas to calculate net realizable value for each joint product, and sum net realizable value in cell G7. In Lab Exhibit 6.4.8, those formulas appear in Column J, but be sure to input them in Column I. For example, in cell I3, enter the formula =(F3-E3)*C3.

4. To calculate the allocation to the FAS product, enter the formula =$A$12/$I$7*I3 in cell E12 (Lab Exhibit 6.4.9).

5. Copy this formula into cells E13:E15 to determine cost allocations to Heartwood's other joint products. Next, sum the joint-product allocation amounts to ensure that all joint costs have been allocated to joint products. The results are shown in Lab Exhibit 6.4.10.

Analysis Task #4: Calculate Joint Costs Using the Constant Gross Margin Method

1. The constant gross margin method is calculated differently from the other three methods. This method assumes that all joint products have an identical gross margin, which is calculated as gross profit divided by revenue. Joint costs are allocated in such a way that a constant gross margin is achieved across all joint products.

   To use this method, we must determine companywide gross margin. Use formulas to determine the revenue for each joint product. This revenue is calculated as quantity multiplied by selling price (which is determined by whether the company sells products at the split-off point or processes them further). Then sum revenue for all products. Lab Exhibit 6.4.11 shows the formulas and Lab Exhibit 6.4.12 shows the results.

Exhibit 6.4.11

Microsoft Excel

	A	B
19	Constant Gross Margin Method	Revenue
20	FAS	=C3*F3
21	SEL	=C4*F4
22	1C	=C5*F5
23	2C	=C6*D6
24	Total	=SUM(B20:B23)

Exhibit 6.4.12

Microsoft Excel

	A	B	C	D	E	F
19	Constant Gross Margin Method	Revenue	Separable Costs	Joint Costs	Gross Profit	Gross Margin
20	FAS	$375,000.00				
21	SEL	$437,500.00				
22	1C	$525,000.00				
23	2C	$240,000.00				
24	Total	$1,577,500.00				

2. Use formulas to calculate separable costs for each product. Remember that for this particular sawmill, no separable costs are incurred if products are sold at the split-off point. Sum separable costs for the company. Lab Exhibit 6.4.13 shows the formulas and Lab Exhibit 6.4.14 shows the results.

Exhibit 6.4.13

Microsoft Excel

	A	C
19	**Constant Gross Margin Method**	**Separable Costs**
20	FAS	=C3*E3
21	SEL	=C4*E4
22	1C	=C5*E5
23	2C	0
24	**Total**	=SUM(C20:C23)

Exhibit 6.4.14

Microsoft Excel

	A	B	C	D	E	F
19	**Constant Gross Margin Method**	**Revenue**	**Separable Costs**	**Joint Costs**	**Gross Profit**	**Gross Margin**
20	FAS	$375,000.00	$ 150,000.00			
21	SEL	$437,500.00	$ 192,500.00			
22	1C	$525,000.00	$ 270,000.00			
23	2C	$240,000.00	$ -			
24	**Total**	$1,577,500.00	$ 612,500.00			

3. Set cell D24 equal to cell A12 to account for total joint costs. Enter the formula =B24-C24-D24 in cell E24 to calculate gross profit, and divide gross profit by revenue to calculate gross margin in cell F24 using the formula =E24/B24. Lab Exhibit 6.4.15 shows the formulas and Lab Exhibit 6.4.16 shows the results.

Exhibit 6.4.15

Microsoft Excel

	D	E	F
18			
19	**Joint Costs**	**Gross Profit**	**Gross Margin**
20			
21			
22			
23			
24	=A12	=B24-C24-D24	=E24/B24
25			

Exhibit 6.4.16

Microsoft Excel

	D	E	F
18			
19	**Joint Costs**	**Gross Profit**	**Gross Margin**
20			
21			
22			
23			
24	$ 500,000.00	$465,000.00	29.48%

4. Gross margin for each joint product will be set equal to the companywide gross margin. By multiplying the companywide gross margin by each joint product's revenue, we can calculate gross profit. Lab Exhibit 6.4.17 shows the formulas and Lab Exhibit 6.4.18 shows the results.

	E	F
18		
19	**Gross Profit**	**Gross Margin**
20	=B20*F20	=$F$24
21	=B21*F21	=$F$24
22	=B22*F22	=$F$24
23	=B23*F23	=$F$24
24	=B24-C24-D24	=E24/B24

Exhibit 6.4.17

Microsoft Excel

	E	F
18		
19	**Gross Profit**	**Gross Margin**
20	$110,538.83	29.48%
21	$128,961.97	29.48%
22	$154,754.36	29.48%
23	$70,744.85	29.48%
24	$465,000.00	29.48%

Exhibit 6.4.18

Microsoft Excel

5. At long last, we're ready to allocate joint costs. We know that revenue minus separable costs minus joint costs equals gross profit. We can rearrange this equation as follows:

$$\text{Revenue} - \text{Separable costs} - \text{Gross profit} = \text{Joint costs}$$

In cell D20, enter the formula =B20-C20-E20 to calculate FAS joint-cost allocations. Copy this formula into cells D21:D23 to determine allocations for the remaining joint products (Lab Exhibit 6.4.19).

6. Use formulas in cells F12:F15 to reference calculated allocation amounts. Sum allocations to ensure that all joint costs have been allocated. Compare allocation amounts under the different methods. Lab Exhibit 6.4.20 shows the formulas and Lab Exhibit 6.4.21 shows the results.

	F
10	
11	**Constant Gross Margin Method**
12	=D20
13	=D21
14	=D22
15	=D23
16	=SUM(F12:F15)

Exhibit 6.4.20

Microsoft Excel

Exhibit 6.4.21

Microsoft Excel

	F
10	
11	**Constant Gross Margin Method**
12	$114,461.17
13	$116,038.03
14	$100,245.64
15	$169,255.15
16	$500,000.00

7. Heartwood's production process creates sawdust as a by-product, which Heartwood uses to produce fuel pellets. The sale of these pellets cuts down on waste and generates $1,400 per day. Heartwood accounts for this profit by reducing the allocation amount by $1,400. Change cell A12 to "=A3-1400" to reflect this policy, as shown in Lab Exhibit 6.4.22. If our formulas are correct, then allocation amounts under each method should automatically update. See Lab Exhibit 6.4.23 for the final results.

Share the Story

To understand their costs, companies allocate support-department costs to production departments. The method used to calculate allocations does not affect company profitability, but it can have a significant effect on the reported profitability of product lines or departments. Effective managers must know how to calculate joint-cost allocations and understand their impact on reported profitability. Our analysis shows how cost allocations can differ between the physical units method, sales value at split-off method, net realizable value method, and constant gross margin method. These varying allocation amounts can affect strategic decisions. For instance, while FAS may appear very profitable when assigned $62,325 in joint costs (per the physical units method), the joint costs allocated to FAS can balloon to nearly twice as much under different methods, which may lead companies to emphasize other products, even though the allocations have no bearing on overall firm profit. Without a deep understanding of how allocation methods affect product costs, companies may make poor decisions.

Assessment

1. Take a screenshot of the Excel spreadsheet following Analysis Task #4, paste it into a Word document, and label it "Lab 6.4 Submission.docx".
2. Answer the multiple-choice questions in Connect using the results of your analysis and upload Lab 6.4 Submission.docx via Connect if assigned.

Alternate Lab 6.4   Excel—On Your Own

Allocating Joint Costs Using Various Methods (Heartwood)

Keywords

Joint Cost Allocation, Excel

Required

Replicate the assignment from Lab 6.4 using the **Alt Lab 6.4 Data.xlsx** dataset.

This dataset contains cost information for November 15th, along with templates that can be used to calculate joint-cost allocations. Remember that Heartwood has $1,400 in by-product profits per day, which will reduce the amount of joint costs that must be allocated to joint products.

Data Dictionary

Joint Costs	Production costs for the day
Joint Products	The different products, in this case different grades of milled wood, produced from Heartwood's milling process, listed in order from highest to lowest quality
Quantity	Number of board feet (*Note:* Assume further processing does not result in any loss or gain of quantity.)
AS IS Selling Price/Unit	Selling price per board foot
Separable Costs/Unit	Separable costs per board foot. Separable costs are all attributable to further processing.
Processed Selling Price/Unit	Selling price per board foot if units are processed further

---

Assessment

1. Take a screenshot of the worksheet following Analysis Task #4, paste it into a Word document, and label it "Alt Lab 6.4 Submission.docx".
2. Answer the multiple-choice questions in Connect and upload Alt Lab 6.4 Submission.docx via Connect if assigned.

Using Trend Analysis to Identify Joint Product Opportunities

Data Analytics Types: Diagnostic Analytics, Predictive Analytics

Keywords

Power BI, Forecasting, Joint Products

Decision-Making Context

Joint products are products that result from a single production process. For companies that harvest or mine natural resources, or that produce foodstuffs, raw materials can be used to produce a wide variety of products. To determine which products to produce, managers must forecast the demand for various products and decide how to allocate resources.

Power BI can be used to analyze data and forecast sales, which can provide useful information to managers.

Required

1. Use Power BI to analyze agriculture data.
2. Use Power BI to forecast future demand for various products based on trends of past data.

Ask the Question

How can we use Power BI to help forecast demand for potential products?

Master the Data

Alberta Dairy is a (fictitious) large dairy farm. In addition to owning several large herds of cattle, Alberta has several manufacturing facilities that produce a wide variety of dairy-based products.

Alberta Dairy can produce and sell raw milk, or it can process milk further to produce cheeses, yogurt, evaporated and condensed milk, and other products. To determine which products to produce, Alberta must perform a detailed analysis of product demand, as well as the profitability of each product.

Our task in this lab is to analyze countrywide agriculture data to get a better understanding of the demand for dairy-based products, which will serve as an important input as management determines which joint products to produce.

Data Dictionary

Year	The year of analysis
Other variables	Average per-person annual consumption in pounds of each dairy-based product

Open Power BI and connect to Excel file **Lab 6.5 Data.xlsx**. We're now ready to perform the analysis.

Perform the Analysis

Analysis Task #1: Graph Existing Demand Trends

DATA VISUALIZATION

1. Click on **Page 1** at the bottom left of the Power BI screen (Lab Exhibit 6.5P.1). Our dataset has various products. We will combine several products to create categories, and we'll do so by creating new variables.
2. To calculate total cheese and dry products, click on **Modeling > New Measure...**, as shown in Lab Exhibit 6.5P.2.
3. We create "Total Cheese Products" and "Total Dry Products" variables by using the formulas shown below in Lab Exhibit 6.5P.3 and 6.5P.4 and selecting **OK**. The formulas are:

Total Cheese Products = 'Per capita Dairy Consumption'[American Cheese]
+ 'Per capita Dairy Consumption'[Cottage Cheese]
+ 'Per capita Dairy Consumption'[Non-American Cheese]

Total Dry Products = 'Per capita Dairy Consumption'[Dry butter-milk]
+ 'Per capita Dairy Consumption'[Dry skim milk]
+ 'Per capita Dairy Consumption'[Dry whey]
+ 'Per capita Dairy Consumption'[Dry whole milk]

4. Click and drag **Fluid Milk**, **Total Cheese Products**, and **Total Dry Products** to the report canvas. Each variable should appear in a separate visualization. Click and drag **Year** to each visualization. The result should resemble Lab Exhibit 6.5P.5.
5. Select the icon for **line chart** as the Visualization type (Lab Exhibit 6.5P.6).
6. In all three visualizations, change the **X-Axis** to **Year**. Leave Fluid Milk, Total Cheese Products, and Total Dry Products in the **Y-Axis** in their respective visualizations. An example is shown in Lab Exhibit 6.5P.7.
7. Notice the data trends. As the line graphs in Lab Exhibit 6.5P.8 show, the consumption of Fluid Milk and Dry Products is decreasing, while the consumption of cheese products is increasing.

Analysis Task #2: Create a Visualization to Examine Year-over-Year Percent Change in Consumption

DATA VISUALIZATION

1. Create a new page. Click and drag **Year**, **Fluid Milk**, **Total Cheese Products**, and **Total Dry Products** to the report canvas. All the variables should be in the same visualization (Lab Exhibit 6.5P.9). Title the new page "% Change in Consumption".
2. Change the Visualization type to **line chart**.
3. Change the **X-Axis** to **Year**, leaving the other variables in the **Y-Axis** (Lab Exhibit 6.5P.10).
4. Click on the drop-down arrow next to **Sum of Fluid Milk**. Select **Show Value As > Percent of grand total** (Lab Exhibit 6.5P.11). Use this same step to calculate year-over-year changes for the other two products.
5. Notice that the graph (shown in Lab Exhibit 6.5P.12) has far more variability than the previous graph.

Analysis Task #3: Use Existing Data to Forecast Future Demand

1. Click back to the **Dairy Consumption** page.
2. Navigate to the **Analytics** tab of the **Visualizations** pane by selecting the icon shown in Lab Exhibit 6.5P.13.
3. Turn on **Forecast** for all three visualizations (see the bottom of Lab Exhibit 6.5P.14). You should now see the forecasted consumption for each of your three products in gray, as shown in Lab Exhibit 6.5P.15.
4. Now let's refine our forecast options. Expand the **Options** drop-down. Lab Exhibit 6.5P.15 shows the default options.
5. Select 5 periods for the **Forecast length** (as shown in Lab Exhibit 6.5P.16). Ensure the options reflect that we do not ignore the most recent data by entering 0 for **Ignore the last**. If we had seasonal data (monthly or quarterly), we could choose whether or not to include the seasonal trend in the forecast. Finally, change the **Confidence interval** to 99%. This widens the range of the estimate. Based on our data, we expect the actual future consumption to fall within this range 99 times out of 100. Click **Apply**. Repeat this step for all three visualizations.

Share the Story

We have now used Power BI to forecast annual consumption of various dairy products. The managers of Alberta Dairy will consider this information as they determine which joint products to produce in the future. For example, it appears from the data that fluid milk consumption is decreasing, while cheese consumption is increasing. This trend may encourage Alberta Dairy to invest more heavily in cheese production in order to be ready for future demand.

Assessment

1. Take a screenshot of the final Dairy Consumption worksheet, paste it into a Word document named "Lab 6.5 Submission.docx", and label the screenshot Submission 1.
2. Answer the questions in Connect and upload your Lab 6.5 Submission.docx via Connect if assigned.

Alternate Lab 6.5   Power BI—On Your Own

Using Trend Analysis to Identify Joint Product Opportunities

Keywords

Power BI, Forecasting, Joint Products

Apply the same steps in Lab 6.5 to the **Alt Lab 6.5 Data.xlsx** dataset. The Alt Lab 6.5 dataset contains countrywide data for various potato products from 1975 to 2026, including fresh potatoes and a variety of processed potatoes. For this lab, do not combine categories of products. Instead, analyze each of the five types of potatoes (fresh, canned, chipped, dehydrated, and frozen) separately, using the same steps as in Lab 6.5.

Required

1. Use Power BI to analyze agriculture data.
2. Use Power BI to forecast future demand for various products based on trends of past data.

Open Excel file **Alt Lab 6.5 Data.xlsx** and perform the analysis.

Data Dictionary

Year	The year of analysis
Fresh	Annual fresh potatoes, pounds per person
Canning	Annual canned potatoes, pounds per person
Chipping	Annual chipped potatoes, pounds per person
Dehydrating	Annual dehydrated potatoes, pounds per person
Freezing	Annual frozen potatoes, pounds per person
Processing, total	Annual processed potatoes, pounds per person. Includes the four categories described immediately above
All potatoes	Annual potatoes, pounds per person. Includes processed and fresh potatoes

Assessment

1. Take a screenshot of the final dashboard, paste it into a Word document named "Alt Lab 6.5 Submission.docx", and label the screenshot Submission 1.
2. Answer the questions in Connect and upload your Alt Lab 6.5 Submission.docx via Connect if assigned.

Lab Note: The tools presented in this lab periodically change. Updated instructions, if applicable, can be found in the student and instructor support materials. All Lab Exhibits are available within the eBook and in Connect.

Using Trend Analysis to Identify Joint Product Opportunities

Data Analytics Types: Diagnostic Analytics, Predictive Analytics

Keywords

Tableau, Forecasting, Joint Products

Decision-Making Context

Joint products are products that result from a single production process. For companies that harvest or mine natural resources, or that produce foodstuffs, raw materials can be used to produce a wide variety of products. To determine which products to produce, managers must forecast the demand for various products and decide how to allocate resources.

Tableau can be used to analyze data and forecast sales, which can provide useful information to managers.

Required

1. Use Tableau to analyze agriculture data.
2. Use Tableau to forecast future demand for various products based on trends of past data.

Ask the Question

How can we use Tableau to help forecast demand for potential products?

Master the Data

Alberta Dairy is a (fictitious) large dairy farm. In addition to owning several large herds of cattle, Alberta has several manufacturing facilities that produce a wide variety of dairy-based products.

Alberta Dairy can produce and sell raw milk, or it can process milk further to produce cheeses, yogurt, evaporated and condensed milk, and other products. To determine which products to produce, Alberta must perform a detailed analysis of product demand, as well as the profitability of each product.

Our task in this lab is to analyze countrywide agriculture data to get a better understanding of the demand for dairy-based products, which will serve as an important input as management determines which joint products to produce.

Data Dictionary

Year	The year of analysis
Other variables	Average per-person annual consumption in pounds of each dairy-based product

---

Open Tableau and connect to Excel file **Lab 6.5 Data.xlsx**. We're now ready to perform the analysis.

Perform the Analysis

Analysis Task #1: Graph Existing Demand Trends.

DATA VISUALIZATION

1. Click on **Sheet 1** at the bottom left of the Tableau screen (Lab Exhibit 6.5T.1). Our dataset has various products. We will combine several products to create categories, and we'll do so by creating new variables.
2. To calculate total cheese and dry products, click on **A**nalysis **> Create** **C**alculated Field..., as shown in Lab Exhibit 6.5T.2. **Aggregate Measures** is checked by default.
3. We create "Total Cheese Products" and "Total Dry Products" variables by using the formulas shown in Lab Exhibits 6.5T.3 and 6.5T.4 and selecting **OK**. The formulas are:

Total Cheese Products = [American Cheese] + [Cottage Cheese]
+ [Non-American Cheese]

Total Dry Products = [Dry butter-milk] + [Dry skim milk] + [Dry whey]
+ [Dry whole milk]

4. Now we will examine consumption of various products over time. Rename Sheet 1 "Dairy Consumption". **Year** is currently categorized as numeric data. Right-click on **Year**, then select **Change Data Type > Date** (Lab Exhibit 6.5T.5).
5. Select **Year** as the Columns, and set **Fluid Milk**, **Total Cheese Products**, and **Total Dry Products** as the Rows. Tableau creates the line graph shown in Lab Exhibit 6.5T.6. Notice the data trends. Consumption of Fluid Milk and Dry Products is decreasing, while consumption of cheese products is increasing.

Analysis Task #2: Create a Visualization to Examine Year-over-Year Percent Change in Consumption

DATA VISUALIZATION

1. Right-click on the **Dairy Consumption** tab and select **Duplicate**, as shown in Lab Exhibit 6.5T.7. Label the new tab and worksheet "% Change in Consumption".
2. Right-click on **SUM(Fluid Milk)**. Select **Quick Table Calculation > Percent of Total**, as shown in Lab Exhibit 6.5T.8. Use this same step to calculate year-over-year changes for the other two products also.
3. Tableau generates the graph shown in Lab Exhibit 6.5T.9. Notice that this graph has far more variability than the previous graph.

Analysis Task #3: Use Existing Data to Forecast Future Demand

1. Left-click on **Dairy Consumption**.
2. Under the **Analytics** tab, drag **Forecast** to the worksheet to forecast future consumption, as shown in Lab Exhibit 6.5T.10.
   You should now see forecasted consumption for each of your three products (Lab Exhibit 6.5T.11).
3. Now let's refine our forecast options. Right-click any forecast line, then click **Forecast > Forecast Options...**, as shown in Lab Exhibit 6.5T.12. All three forecast lines will be updated simultaneously.
4. The **Forecast Options** window opens. For the **Forecast Length**, select **Exactly** and enter 5 years, as shown in Lab Exhibit 6.5T.13. Change the options so that we do not ignore the most recent data. To do so, select 0 next to **Ignore last**. If we had seasonal data (monthly or quarterly), we could choose whether or not to include the seasonal trend in the forecast. Finally, change the confidence interval in **Show prediction intervals** to 99%. This widens the range of the estimate. Based on our data, we expect the actual future consumption to fall within this range 99 times out of 100. Click **OK**. Lab Exhibit 6.5T.14 shows the final result.

Share the Story

We have now used Tableau to forecast annual consumption of various dairy products. The managers of Alberta Dairy will consider this information as they determine which joint products to produce in the future. For example, it appears from the data that fluid milk consumption is decreasing, while cheese consumption is increasing. This trend may encourage Alberta Dairy to invest more heavily in cheese production in order to be ready for future demand.

Assessment

1. Take a screenshot of the final Dairy Consumption worksheet, paste it into a Word document named "Lab 6.5 Submission.docx", and label the screenshot Submission 1.
2. Answer the questions in Connect and upload your Lab 6.5 Submission.docx via Connect if assigned.

Alternate Lab 6.5   Tableau—On Your Own

Using Trend Analysis to Identify Joint Product Opportunities

Keywords

Tableau, Forecasting, Joint Products

Apply the same steps in Lab 6.5 to the **Alt Lab 6.5 Data.xlsx** dataset. This dataset contains countrywide data for various potato products from 1975 to 2026, including fresh potatoes and a variety of processed potatoes. For this lab, do not combine categories of products. Instead, analyze each of the five types of potatoes (fresh, canned, chipped, dehydrated, and frozen) separately, using the same steps as in Lab 6.5.

Required

1. Use Tableau to analyze publicly available data from the U.S. Department of Agriculture.
2. Use Tableau to forecast future demand for various products based on trends of past data.

Open Excel file **Alt Lab 6.5 Data.xlsx** and perform the analysis.

Data Dictionary

Year	The year of analysis
Fresh	Annual fresh potatoes, pounds per person
Canning	Annual canned potatoes, pounds per person
Chipping	Annual chipped potatoes, pounds per person
Dehydrating	Annual dehydrated potatoes, pounds per person
Freezing	Annual frozen potatoes, pounds per person
Processing, total	Annual processed potatoes, pounds per person. Includes the four categories described immediately above
All potatoes	Annual potatoes, pounds per person. Includes processed and fresh potatoes

---

Assessment

1. Take a screenshot of the final dashboard, paste it into a Word document named "Alt Lab 6.5 Submission.docx", and label the screenshot Submission 1.
2. Answer the questions in Connect and upload your Alt Lab 6.5 Submission.docx via Connect if assigned.

Chapter 7

Process Costing

A Look at This Chapter

Companies use job costing to track the costs of unique products and services. For companies that produce high volumes of identical products, process costing provides a simpler way to track and understand costs. While both job costing and process costing track the same cost components (direct materials, direct labor, and manufacturing overhead), the calculation of individual unit costs is very different. Process costing determines costs by totaling all product costs and dividing them by the units produced during the period.

Cost Accounting and Data Analytics

COST ACCOUNTING LEARNING OBJECTIVE	RELATED DATA ANALYTICS LABS	LAB ANALYTICS TYPES
LO 7.1 Describe when process costing should be used.		
LO 7.2 Explain the concept of equivalent units.		
LO 7.3 Summarize the five steps of process costing to assign costs to completed and partially completed units.	**Data Analytics Mini-Lab** Analyzing How Process Costing Estimates Affect Financial Statements	Descriptive, Predictive
	LAB 7.1 Excel Assigning Costs to Inventory Accounts Using the Weighted-Average Method (Heartwood)	Descriptive, Diagnostic
	LAB 7.2 Excel Assigning Costs to Inventory Accounts Using the FIFO Method (Heartwood)	Descriptive, Diagnostic
	LAB 7.3 Excel Process Costing with Multiple Production Processes	Descriptive, Diagnostic

Cost Accounting and Data Analytics *(continued)*

COST ACCOUNTING LEARNING OBJECTIVE	RELATED DATA ANALYTICS LABS	LAB ANALYTICS TYPES
	LAB 7.4 Excel Boosting Net Income with Process Costing	Descriptive, Diagnostic, Prescriptive
	LAB 7.5 Tableau Identifying Anomalies and Trends with Data Visualizations	Descriptive, Diagnostic, Prescriptive
	LAB 7.5 Power BI Identifying Anomalies and Trends with Data Visualizations	Descriptive, Diagnostic, Prescriptive
LO 7.4 Explain the factors that determine whether a company should use the weighted-average or FIFO method of process costing.		

Chapter Concepts and Career Skills

Learning About . . .	Helps with These Career Skills
Process costing	• Identifying product costs and how they change over time
Equivalent units	• Understanding how production costs affect a company's financial statements
Different process costing methods	• Understanding how small choices in accounting can affect reported financial performance

Viktor Gladkov/Alamy Stock Photo

Process Costing for Mass-Produced Items

Bubblegum is a great example of a mass-produced homogeneous product. If you buy a bucket of **Dubble Bubble** bubblegum, you would probably find it disconcerting if one piece looked slightly different from the others. *How It's Made,* a popular TV documentary series, often shows the production processes used for popular mass-produced items such as bubblegum, gummy bears, baseball bats, frozen pizzas, crackers, and hot dogs. *How It's Made* videos on **YouTube** have been viewed hundreds of millions of times! The manufacturing plant in the bubblegum episode features machines that can each produce 54,000 pieces of bubblegum per hour. Tracking and calculating the cost of each individual unit—in this case, each piece of bubblegum—using a job-order cost system would be difficult and very inefficient. Fortunately, we can use a costing method called *process costing* to more easily determine the cost of each unit.

Source: "How It's Made–Bubblegum," *Discovery UK,* www.youtube.com/watch?v=2kttVyakHN4&t=33s&ab_channel=DiscoveryUK.

WHAT IS PROCESS COSTING?

One of the primary responsibilities of management accountants is to track the costs of goods and services. As discussed in Chapter 4, when companies offer customizable products and services, it makes sense to track these products separately. **Job-costing** systems (Exhibit 7.1), also known as **job-order costing** systems, provide companies with cost information about individual jobs, allowing them to make strategic decisions about pricing and strategy based on those jobs.

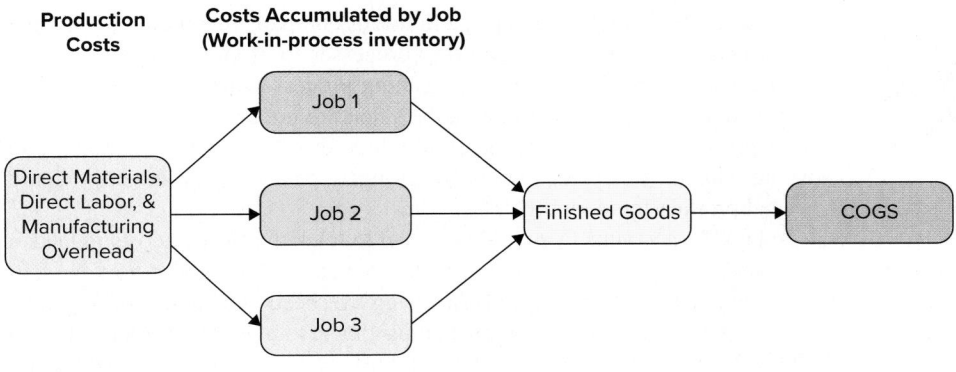

Exhibit 7.1
Job Costing

job (order) costing
A costing system in which all production costs are accumulated by job.

process costing
A costing system in which all production costs are accumulated by process.

direct materials
Materials that are traced to a product or job and tracked by the accounting system.

direct labor
Employee labor (hands-on, touch labor) involved in producing goods or delivering services.

manufacturing overhead (MOH)
Indirect costs that are essential to the manufacturing of goods.

   Process costing is another common costing system used to record and assign costs to products, but it is used by companies that mass-produce identical items such as **Sherwin-Williams** paint, **Lay's** potato chips, and **Clorox** cleaning products. Process costing tracks the same production costs as a job-order costing system: **direct materials**, **direct labor**, and **manufacturing overhead**. However, job costing and process costing differ according to the basis that each system uses to accumulate costs. Job-order costing accumulates costs by job, while process costing accumulates costs by manufacturing processes. Because companies that use process costing produce identical units, process costing uses total production costs for a specific batch or time period, and then simply divides these costs by the number of units produced to determine per-unit product costs.

   Process costing, summarized in Exhibit 7.2, works well for companies that produce commodities or similar items. Why? First, these companies do not typically allow for

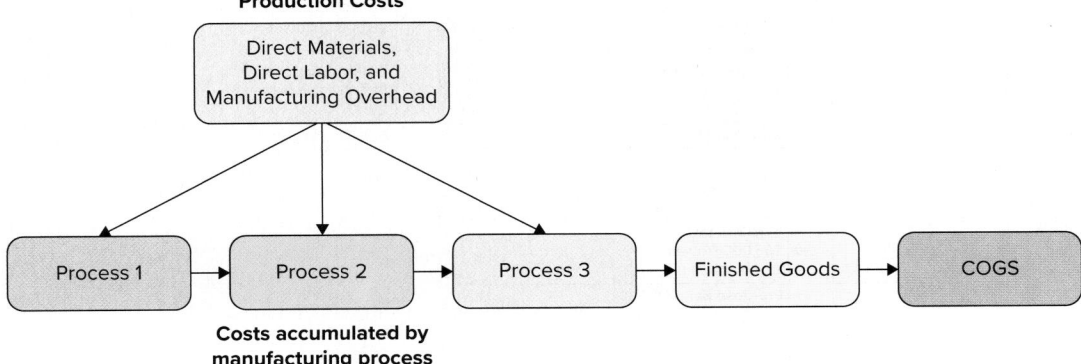

Exhibit 7.2
Process Costing

Joshua Resnick/Shutterstock

customization, nor do they know who will be purchasing the final product. Thus, it doesn't make sense to account for product costs on a job basis. Second, tracking costs for each item simply isn't feasible given the sheer quantity of units produced. Consider the resources that would be required for companies to track the cost of each individual carton of ice cream, box of cereal, container of laundry detergent, or tube of toothpaste. Each hour of direct labor, for example, would need to be prorated and assigned to hundreds or thousands of individual items. Process costing is a far more efficient system of cost accounting for mass-produced items.

Consider Peak Apple Company, a fictitious company that produces caramel apples. Peak uses three manufacturing processes to produce its very popular product. First, apples go through a cleaning process to prepare them for further processing and to discard any apples that are not up to standard. Second, apples go through a coating process in which different types of caramel and nuts are added. Finally, the apples go through a packaging process to prepare the final product for shipping.

Exhibit 7.3 displays the accounts that would be used to track the flow of costs in Peak's process costing system. The production processes are shaded in blue. Notice how the factors of production—materials, labor, and manufacturing overhead—are added during each stage of production (cleaning, coating, and packaging), as resources are needed for each part of the manufacturing process. Rather than tracing and allocating these production costs to individual jobs (as is done in a job-costing system), they are instead traced and

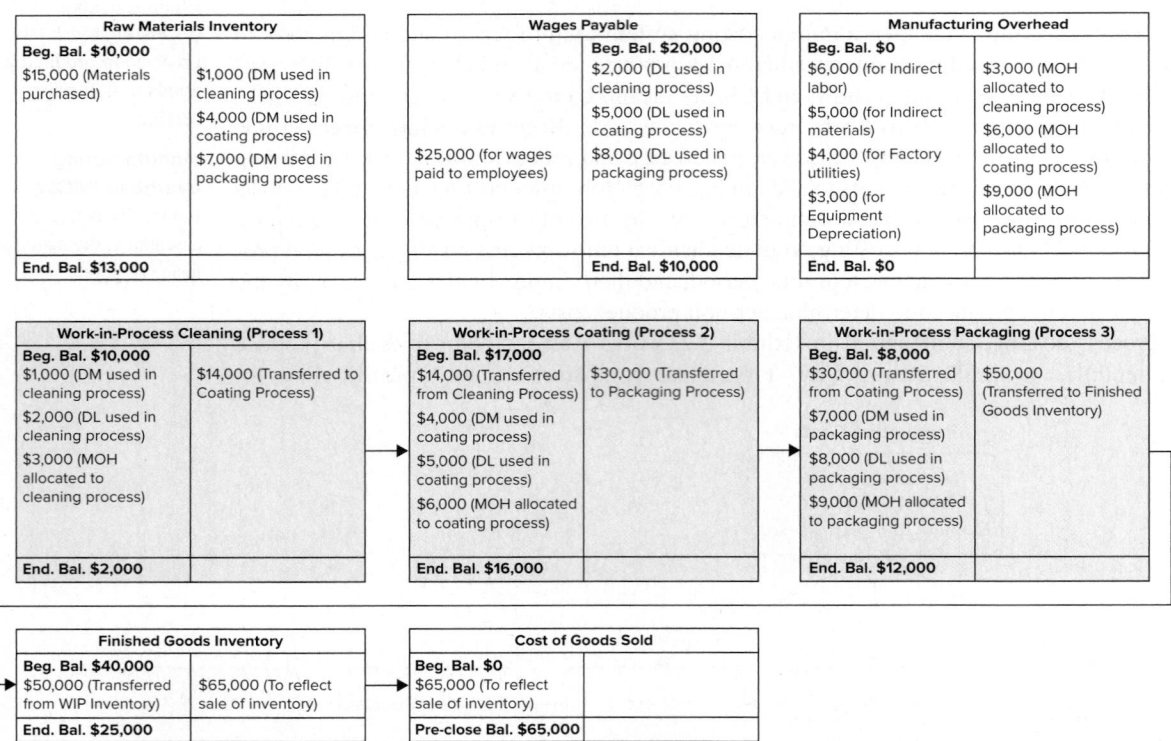

Exhibit 7.3

Tracking Costs Through Peak Apple Company's Process Costing System

DL = direct labor; DM = direct materials; MOH = manufacturing overhead allocated individual production processes. Production costs are transferred from one process to another as work is completed. As in a job costing system, production costs in a process-costing system are eventually transferred from work-in-process inventory to finished goods inventory when production is complete and finally expensed as cost of goods sold when sold. Though the number of processes can vary by company, the flow of cost through a process-costing system will follow this general pattern.

Journal entries in a process-costing system are very similar to those in a job-order system. Below are some examples of journal entries that Peak Apple would make to record the cost flows displayed in Exhibit 7.3:

Raw Materials Inventory	$15,000	
Accounts Payable		$15,000

To record the purchase of raw materials

Work-in-Process—Cleaning	$1,000	
Raw Materials		$1,000

To record the use of direct materials in the cleaning process

Work-in-Process—Coating	$5,000	
Wages Payable		$5,000

To record direct labor costs in the coating process

Work-in-Process—Packaging	$9,000	
Manufacturing Overhead		$9,000

To record the application of overhead in the packaging process

Work-in-Process—Packaging	$30,000	
Work-in-Process—Coating		$30,000

To record the cost of goods transferred from the coating process to the packaging process

Finished Goods Inventory	$50,000	
Work-in-Process—Packaging		$50,000

To record the transfer of goods from the packaging process to finished goods

An accounting challenge arises with process costing because some units are only partially completed when an accounting reporting period ends. In other words, goods that are undergoing one of the manufacturing processes may not be fully produced at the end of an accounting reporting period. This situation is very common for items that are produced on assembly lines continuously, and it is unavoidable for products that require large amounts of time to process. Parmesan cheese, for instance, may take 1 to 3 years to process. Other products, such as **Colavita** balsamic vinegar, may require even longer processing times before they are ready for consumption.

Partially completed products are important because accounting standards require that costs be assigned to the income statements in the period in which they occur and to balance sheets as of a given date. Companies can easily account for total production costs, but determining how much of those costs should be assigned to items that are in process can be challenging.

PROGRESS CHECK

1. What types of products are commonly associated with process-costing systems?
2. Compare and contrast how costs flow through a process-costing system and a job-order costing system.

LO 7.2

Explain the concept of equivalent units.

ASSIGNING COSTS TO PARTIALLY COMPLETED UNITS

As noted at the start of this chapter, process costing divides total production costs by the number of units to determine production costs per unit:

$$\text{Cost per unit} = \frac{\text{Total production cost}}{\text{Total units produced}}$$

CAREER SKILLS

Learning about equivalent units supports this career skill:

• Understanding how production costs affect a company's financial statements

The numerator in this equation is relatively straightforward: Companies simply sum all direct materials, direct labor, and manufacturing overhead costs for each period. Identifying the denominator (total units produced) is more complicated because it can be difficult to determine how many units are produced each period due to partially completed units.

To determine the total units produced, accountants use **equivalent units of production**, which is the number of completed physical units that are equivalent to a company's partially completed units. In process costing, equivalent units are calculated by multiplying the number of incomplete units by their degree of completion (expressed as a percentage). To illustrate this concept, consider 5 glasses of water that are 60 percent full.

equivalent units of production
The number of completed physical units that are equivalent to a company's partially completed units.

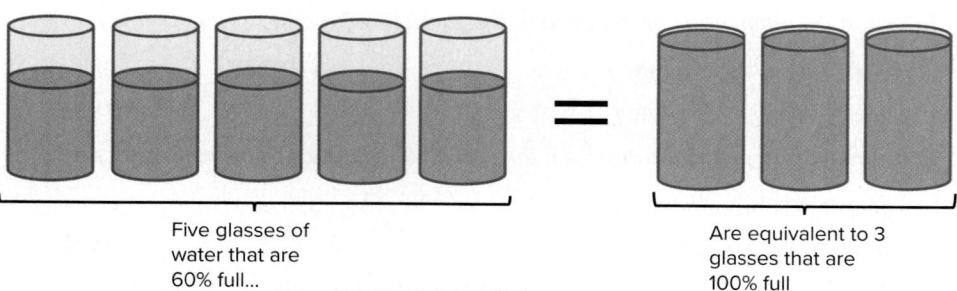

Five glasses of water that are 60% full...

Are equivalent to 3 glasses that are 100% full

We could determine that we have three equivalent units by multiplying 5 glasses by 60 percent. Similarly, if a company has 10 units that are 50 percent complete, the company would report five equivalent units. In other words, the work performed on these 10 partially completed units is equivalent to the work needed to complete five units. The use of equivalent units allows companies to determine total units produced, which is then used to calculate a per-unit production cost.

With an understanding of equivalent units, we are ready to discuss the mechanics of process costing.

 PROGRESS CHECK

3. Why do partially completed units necessitate equivalent units of production?
4. How do equivalent units facilitate the calculation of per-unit production cost?

STEPS IN PROCESS COSTING

Accounting for process costing is relatively straightforward. Process costing requires five steps:

1. Measuring physical units of production.
2. Computing equivalent units of production.
3. Summing production costs.
4. Calculating cost per equivalent unit.
5. Assigning costs to completed and in-process units.

LO 7.3

Summarize the five steps of process costing to assign costs to completed and partially completed units.

These steps are used in the two process costing methods that we will examine: the weighted-average method and the first-in, first-out (FIFO) method. The primary difference between these methods relates to the granularity with which the costs of completed units are tracked. The **weighted-average method** is primarily concerned with work done to date. It combines costs and units produced in a period with the costs and units in beginning work-in-process inventory. The **first-in, first-out (FIFO) method** is primarily concerned with work done in a specific period, and therefore it clearly distinguishes between the units and production costs of each period. As a result, the FIFO method provides more accurate cost information about the costs and units produced in each period.

To illustrate these process costing methods, we will examine process costing for Silver Spoons Creamery, which uses a single production process to produce its ice cream. All raw ingredients are added at the beginning of the process, and Silver Spoons' slow-churn process requires several hours to complete.

weighted-average method
A process-costing method that combines costs and units produced in a period with the costs and units in beginning work-in-process inventory.

first-in, first-out (FIFO) method
A process-costing method that does not mix production costs or units between periods. As a result, the FIFO method provides very accurate cost information about the costs and units produced in each period.

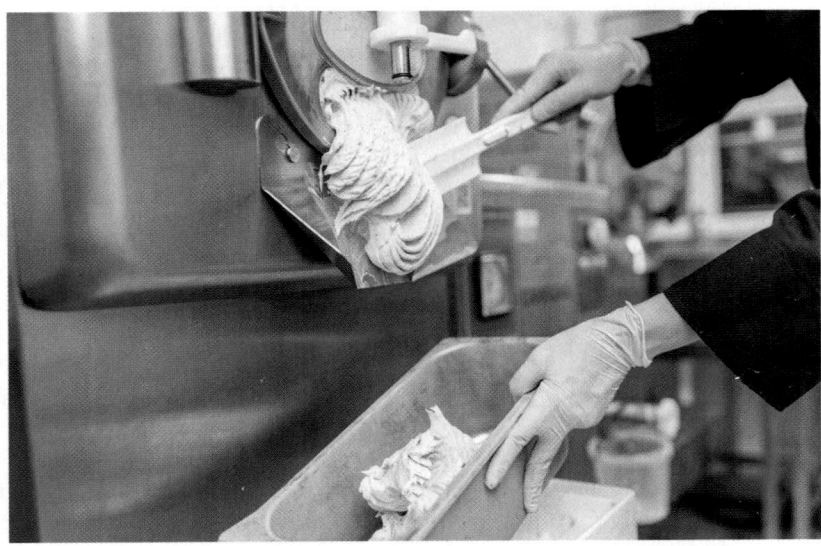

RossHelen/Shutterstock

Weighted-Average Method

Let's assume that Silver Spoons uses the weighted-average method of process costing, which means that all costs and units in beginning work-in-process (those that were partially completed at the end of the previous period) are combined with the costs and units produced in the current period.

Step 1: Measuring Physical Units of Production

The first step in process costing involves tracking the physical units of production. In this step, accountants evaluate what is taking place in the production process.

At the beginning of this month, Silver Spoons Creamery had 10,000 partially completed units in production. These units were started in the prior month. This month, Silver Spoons began production on 90,000 additional units of ice cream. Adding these units together, we know that we need to account for 100,000 units, and these units can be in one of two places: Either they were completed and transferred out of production during the period or they are still undergoing processing at the end of the month (ending work-in-process inventory). An important formula is derived from the physical flow of physical units through the production process:

> Beginning work-in-process inventory + Units started during the period
> = Units transferred out + Ending work-in-process inventory

You can see this relationship in Column B (Step 1) of Exhibit 7.4. Comparing units to account for and units accounted for helps ensure that no physical units have been overlooked.

	A	B	C	D
1				
2		**Step 1**	**Step 2**	
3			**Equivalent Units**	
			Direct	Conversion
4	*Flow of units (Steps 1-2)*	Physical Units	Materials	Costs
5	WIP, beginning	10,000		
6	Started during period	90,000		
7	**Total Units to Account for**	100,000		
8				
9	Completed and transferred out	85,000	85,000	85,000
10	WIP, ending[a]	15,000	15,000	6,000
11	**Total Units Accounted for**	100,000	100,000	91,000
12	[a]Ending WIP 100% complete with respect to direct materials and 40% with respect to conversion costs			

Exhibit 7.4
Weighted-Average Method: Calculating Total Units

Microsoft Excel

Step 2: Computing Equivalent Units of Production

The next step is to determine equivalent units of production. Companies often report equivalent units separately for direct materials and conversion costs because these costs behave differently. **Conversion costs** are the costs incurred to transform raw materials into a finished product. They are the sum of direct labor costs and manufacturing overhead costs. Often, all direct materials costs are added at the beginning of the period, while conversion costs are uniformly added during production. This system is appropriate for the production process of Silver Spoons Creamery. All ice cream ingredients are added at the beginning of the batch, and conversion costs (direct labor and manufacturing overhead) are incurred uniformly during the churning process.

Let's use Exhibit 7.4 to explain how to calculate equivalent units for Silver Spoons Creamery. Recall that the weighted-average method of process costing combines the costs

conversion costs
Direct labor and manufacturing overhead costs incurred to convert raw materials into a finished product.

and units from beginning work-in-process with those units that were started this period. In other words, the weighted-average method focuses on equivalent units and costs that are completed *to date,* or at the end of the period, and does not differentiate between units started in the prior period or started in the current period.

Of the 100,000 units to account for, 85,000 units were transferred out this period. That means that *to date,* these 85,000 units are 100 percent complete in terms of both direct materials and conversion costs. As a result, equivalent units are equal to physical units for these units. Toward the bottom of Exhibit 7.4, Row 10 indicates that the remaining 15,000 units are only partially complete. It is generally up to managers to estimate the completion percentage for these units. Because we are using the weighted-average method, we are concerned only with how much work has been completed *to date.* As footnote *a* indicates, these 15,000 units are 100 percent complete with respect to direct materials (because ingredients are added at the beginning of production) but only 40 percent complete with respect to conversion costs. Therefore, the equivalent units of production completed for these 15,000 units are 15,000 (15,000 * 100%) and 6,000 (15,000 * 40%), as shown in Columns C and D of Row 10. We sum equivalent units to determine the total number of equivalent units completed *to date,* for both direct materials and conversion costs. These totals are 100,000 and 91,000 respectively, as shown in cells C11 and D11 of Exhibit 7.4.

 PROGRESS CHECK

5. What are conversion costs, and how do they behave differently than direct materials costs?
6. Explain the concept of equivalent units of production, and how equivalent units are calculated.

Step 3: Summing Production Costs

Step 3 is straightforward (Exhibit 7.5, Row 18). For both direct materials and conversion costs, we simply sum the beginning work-in-process production costs with those added during the current period. Where does this cost information come from? A company's accounting information system tracks production costs in beginning work-in-process, as well as production costs added during each period. Step 3 totals these production costs and provides a useful check figure that will be referenced later. Ultimately, all production costs must be either assigned to work-in-process inventory or transferred out of the production process. These costs are important inputs for a company's financial statements. Ending work-in-process inventory will be reported on the balance sheet. In the case of Silver Spoons Creamery, costs transferred out will be recorded as finished goods inventory and, when sold, will increase cost of goods sold on the income statement.

Step 4: Calculating Cost per Equivalent Unit

Cost per equivalent unit of production is the assigned value for the cost of materials, labor, and overhead to each equivalent unit of production. To calculate cost per equivalent unit, we divide all production costs (for each cost category) that have been incurred *to date* by the number of equivalent units produced *to date* calculated in Step 2 (see Exhibit 7.5, Row 20). For direct materials, we divide $188,000 in total costs by 100,000 units (from Row 11 of Exhibit 7.4). For conversion costs, we divide $138,750 in total costs by 91,000 units. As Row 20 of Exhibit 7.5 shows, each unit of ice cream costs Silver Spoons Creamery $1.88 in direct materials and $1.52 in conversion costs.

cost per equivalent unit of production
The assigned value for the cost of materials, labor, and overhead to each equivalent unit of production.

	A	B	C	D
14		Total Costs	Direct Materials	Conversion Costs
15	*Flow of Costs (Steps 3-5)*			
16	WIP, beginning	$ 33,000	$ 18,000	$ 15,000
17	Costs added during period	$ 293,750	$ 170,000	$ 123,750
18	**Total costs to account for (Step 3)**	$ 326,750	$ 188,000	$ 138,750
19				
20	Cost per equivalent unit **(Step 4)**		$ 1.88	$ 1.52
21				
22	Costs assigned to transferred-out units	$ 289,402	$ 159,800	$ 129,602
23	Costs assigned to WIP, ending	$ 37,348	$ 28,200	$ 9,148
24	**Total costs accounted for (Step 5)**	$ 326,750	$ 188,000	$ 138,750

Exhibit 7.5
Weighted-Average Method: Summing Production Costs

Microsoft Excel

Step 5: Assigning Costs to Completed and In-Process Units

The final step in process costing is to assign costs to completed and in-process units. Notice that the two cost categories, transferred-out units and ending work-in-process (Rows 22 and 23 of Exhibit 7.5) match the equivalent unit categories discussed in Step 2. To calculate costs, we simply multiply equivalent units in each category by the relevant cost per equivalent unit calculated in Step 4.

Continuing with our Silver Spoons example, we calculated that 85,000 equivalent units of production were transferred out during the period. Each unit had a cost per equivalent unit of $1.88 for direct materials and $1.52 in conversion costs. Thus, the costs transferred out for these units is $159,800 (85,000 equivalent units * $1.88) plus $129,602 (85,000 equivalent units * $1.52—your answer may vary slightly due to rounding). By summing direct materials and conversion costs, we calculate that $289,402 worth of inventory was transferred from work-in-process to finished goods during the period (Exhibit 7.5, Row 22).

Using the same process, we calculate that $37,348 in cost remains in ending work-in-process. As shown in Exhibit 7.5, Row 23, this rounded total represents $28,200 in direct materials (15,000 equivalent units * $1.88) and $9,148 in conversion costs (6,000 equivalent units * $1.52). As a final check figure, notice that total production costs in Step 5 (Row 24) match costs to account for calculated in Step 3 (Row 18), signifying that all production costs have been accounted for.

Ⓠ **LAB CONNECTION**

LAB 7.1 EXCEL provides you with a template for the weighted-average method of process costing and walks you through the five steps outlined in this section.

 PROGRESS CHECK

7. What are the five steps of process costing?
8. Why must companies track the costs of both completed units and work-in-process units?
9. Why are equivalent units tracked separately for direct materials and conversion costs?

FIFO Method

To demonstrate the differences between the FIFO and weighted-average methods, we will now walk through the five steps of process costing for Silver Spoons Creamery using the FIFO method. The FIFO method assumes that in any period of production, the first units to be completed are those that were in beginning work-in-process. This assumption is logical for most companies and certainly for Silver Spoons Creamery. Beginning work-in-process contains those units that are partially churned, which will certainly be the first units completed during the current production period.

Recall that the weighted-average method combines the equivalent units and production costs of units in beginning work-in-process with those completed during the current period. In other words, because no distinction is made between units that were started during the last period and the current period, the weighted-average method focuses on equivalent units and costs *to date*. In contrast, the FIFO method tracks equivalent units and production costs for each period separately. Thus, FIFO focuses on the equivalent units produced and production costs incurred *this period*. As we outline the five steps of process costing using the FIFO method, we will point out where and how these two methods differ.

CAREER SKILLS

Learning about different process costing methods supports this career skill:

• Understanding how small choices in accounting can affect reported financial performance

Step 1: Measuring Physical Units of Production

The process of tracking physical units of production using the FIFO method is very similar to the weighted-average method. Silver Spoons Creamery must account for 100,000 physical units of product. Notice in Row 12 of Exhibit 7.6 that while 85,000 units are completed, the FIFO method tracks separately those completed units that were begun last period and completed this period (10,000 units, Row 10) and those units that were started and completed during the current period (75,000 units, Row 11). Why? To the extent that production costs vary between periods, the units that were begun in the prior period will have different production costs than those started and completed

	A	B	C	D
			Step 2	
2		Step 1	Equivalent Units	
3			Direct	Conversion
4	Flow of units (Steps 1-2)	Physical Units	Materials	Costs
5	WIP, beginning	10,000		
6	Started during period	90,000		
7	**Total Units to Account for**	100,000		
8				
9	Completed and transferred out			
10	From WIP, beginning[a]	10,000	-	2,000
11	Started and completed	75,000	75,000	75,000
12	Total completed and transferred out	85,000	75,000	77,000
13	WIP, ending[b]	15,000	15,000	6,000
14	**Total Units Accounted for**	100,000	90,000	83,000
15	[a]Beginning WIP 100% complete with respect to direct materials and 80% with respect to conversion costs			
16	[b]Ending WIP 100% complete with respect to direct materials and 40% with respect to conversion costs			

Exhibit 7.6
FIFO Method: Calculating Total Units

Microsoft Excel

during the current period. Similar to the weighted-average method, we record 15,000 units in ending work-in-process inventory (Row 13).

Step 2: Computing Equivalent Units of Production

Next we must determine equivalent units of production. We now have three categories of equivalent units: (1) those started in the prior period and completed in the current period, (2) those started and completed during the current period, and (3) those started in the current period that remain incomplete at the end of the period. As we calculate equivalent units, remember that the FIFO method focuses only on the work completed *this period.* In other words, it excludes any work done previously.

To calculate equivalent units for beginning work-in-process units, we must determine how much work was performed *this period* to finish these units. Reviewing footnote *a* in Row 15 of Exhibit 7.6, we see that production managers have estimated that the units in beginning work-in-process were 100 percent complete with respect to direct materials and 80 percent complete with respect to conversion costs. So how much work was performed to complete these units *this period?* Because all ice cream ingredients are added at the beginning of the process and the process began in the prior period, no additional direct materials must be added during the current period. Thus, zero equivalent units are required for direct materials (cell C10). Similarly, because beginning work-in-process units underwent 80 percent of the churning process in the prior period, only 2,000 equivalent units (10,000 physical units * 20%) of production were required for these units to be completed *this period* (cell D10).

By definition, units that are started and completed during the current period are 100 percent completed this period. For this category, equivalent units always equal physical units (cells C11 and D11).

We treat ending work-in-process units identically regardless of whether we use the weighted-average or FIFO method. Footnote *b* in Row 16 indicates that at the end of the current period, production managers estimated these units were 100 percent complete with respect to direct materials and 40 percent complete with respect to conversion costs. Because these units were started this period, all work was performed *this period.* We therefore have 15,000 equivalent units for direct materials (15,000 units * 100%) and 6,000 units for conversion costs (15,000 * 40%), as shown in cells C13 and D13.

Summing equivalent units for each cost category reveals 90,000 equivalent units for direct materials and 83,000 units for conversion costs (cells C14 and D14). These FIFO totals differ from the weighted-average totals. Why? FIFO focuses on equivalent units *this period,* while the weighted-average method focuses on equivalent units *to date.*

ETHICS

FROM THE FIELD

Using Equivalent Units to Manipulate Reported Earnings

The calculations for equivalent units depend on management's estimates of percentage completion for direct materials and conversion costs. With thousands of in-process items in various stages of completion, management may be able to overestimate completion units without being challenged by auditors.

Why does this matter? Overestimating completion can shift cost of goods sold from current periods to future periods, which can increase current-period income. In other words, these estimates can be used to manipulate reported earnings. The Securities and Exchange Commission (SEC) investigated **Rynco Scientific Corporation,** a manufacturer of contact lenses, over this issue. As a result of the investigation, Rynco agreed to restate its financial statements.

Thinking Critically

How much leeway do managers have when providing estimates in the financial statements? Are auditors in a good position to challenge managers on these estimates?

Step 3: Summing Production Costs

Step 3 using the FIFO method is straightforward (Exhibit 7.7). We simply sum the beginning work-in-process production costs (Row 20) with those added during the current period (Row 21). The total costs to account for are shown in Row 22. Note that this step is identical in both process-costing methods.

	A	B	C	D
			Direct	Conversion
18		Total Costs	Materials	Costs
19	Flow of Costs (Steps 3-5)			
20	WIP, beginning	$ 33,000	$ 18,000	$ 15,000
21	Costs added during period	$ 293,750	$ 170,000	$ 123,750
22	**Total costs to account for (Step 3)**	$ 326,750	$ 188,000	$ 138,750
23				
24	Cost per equivalent unit **(Step 4)**		$ 1.89	$ 1.49
25				
26	Costs assigned to transferred-out units			
27	Costs from WIP, beginning	$ 33,000	$ 18,000	$ 15,000
28	Costs to complete WIP, beginning	$ 2,982	$ -	$ 2,982
29	Total costs for WIP, beginning	$ 35,982	$ 18,000	$ 17,982
30	Cost of started and completed units	$ 253,489	$ 141,667	$ 111,822
31	Total costs transferred out	$ 289,471	$ 159,667	$ 129,804
32	Costs assigned to WIP, ending	$ 37,279	$ 28,333	$ 8,946
33	**Total costs accounted for (Step 5)**	$ 326,750	$ 188,000	$ 138,750

Exhibit 7.7
FIFO Method: Summing Production Costs

Microsoft Excel

Step 4: Calculating Cost per Equivalent Unit

To calculate cost per equivalent unit using the FIFO method, we divide production costs added *this period* by the equivalent units of production *this period* (the total equivalent units calculated in Step 2: See Exhibit 7.6, Row 14). As shown in Exhibit 7.7, Row 24, for direct materials we calculate a cost of $1.89 per equivalent unit ($170,000 in current period costs divided by 90,000 equivalent units). For direct materials, we calculate a $1.49 cost per equivalent unit ($123,750 divided by 83,000 units).

Step 5: Assigning Costs to Completed and In-Process Units

Finally, we must assign costs to completed and in-process units. Refer back to Step 2. Notice that we have three categories of units: (1) units started in the prior period and completed in the current period, (2) units started and completed during the period, and (3) units started but incomplete by the end of the period.

First, we determine the costs transferred out from our beginning work-in-process units. In the prior period, $33,000 in costs were used to partially complete these units (Exhibit 7.7, cell B27). To this total, we add all costs that were added to complete these units. No additional direct materials were needed, as all ingredients were added in the prior period (cell C28). However, these units required an additional $2,982 in conversion costs to complete (cell D28). We calculate these conversion costs by multiplying the 2,000 equivalent units produced *this period* to complete beginning work in process by $1.49 of conversion costs per unit, for a total of $2,982 (cell B28). The total cost to produce these 10,000 units in beginning work-in-process is therefore $35,982 (cell B29). (*Note:* The numbers reported in the Excel spreadsheet are rounded.)

Next, we calculate the costs of the units started and completed this period. These 75,000 units (from Exhibit 7.6, Row 11) cost $1.89 and $1.49 (rounded) in direct materials and conversion costs, respectively, for a total of $253,489 (Exhibit 7.7, cell B30). We add these costs to the costs of our beginning work-in-process units, and we find that $289,471 in costs were transferred out of production (cell B31). For many companies, these costs would be transferred out to another manufacturing process. In the case of Silver Spoons Creamery, which has only a single production process, these costs are transferred to finished goods inventory.

Finally, we must calculate the costs assigned to ending work-in-process inventory. These costs and units will become beginning work-in-process in the next period, and the same five steps of process costing will be used again. To calculate these costs, we multiply the equivalent units produced *this period* (15,000 equivalent units for direct materials and 6,000 equivalent units for conversion costs—see Exhibit 7.6, Row 13) by the relevant cost per equivalent unit. We calculate these units by the cost per equivalent unit and calculate $28,333 in direct materials and $8,946 in conversion costs (Exhibit 7.7, Row 32). Thus, Silver Spoons has a total of $37,279 in ending work-in-process (cell B32).

It's always a good idea to compare the total costs accounted for in Step 5 (Row 33) with the total costs to account for calculated in Step 3 (Row 22). Doing so gives us some assurance that our calculations are correct. Here, the numbers in Row 22 match those in Row 33.

Exhibit 7.8 provides a brief summary of the process costing steps under the weighted-average and FIFO methods of process costing, and how the two methods differ.

Step	Weighted-Average Method	FIFO Method
Step 1: Measuring physical units of production	Determine how many units are: 1) completed. 2) in ending WIP.	Determine how many units are: 1) started in the previous period and completed in the current period. 2) started and completed in the current period. 3) in ending WIP.
Step 2: Computing equivalent units of production	Determine how many units are completed *to date.*	Determine how many units are completed *this period*. Beginning WIP % complete is ignored.
Step 3: Summing production costs	Sum production costs in beginning WIP and current production costs.	Sum production costs in beginning WIP and current production costs.
Step 4: Calculating cost per equivalent unit	Divide total costs by equivalent units.	Divide current period costs by equivalent units.
Step 5: Assigning costs to completed and in-process units	For each of the categories listed in Step 1, multiply equivalent units by the cost per equivalent unit calculated in Step 4.	For each of the categories listed in Step 1, multiply equivalent units by the cost per equivalent unit calculated in Step 4. For the units started in the previous period and completed in the current period, add current-period production costs.

Exhibit 7.8
Comparison of Weighted-Average and FIFO Methods of Process Costing

LAB CONNECTION

LAB 7.2 EXCEL provides you with a template for the FIFO method of process costing and walks you through the five steps outlined in this section. Pay particular attention to how the steps differ between the weighted-average and FIFO methods.

Process Costing with Multiple Production Processes

In some cases, companies have multiple production processes. How does this affect accounting for product costs with process costing? Let's examine Silver Spoons Creamery again. This time we'll assume that prior to the churning process discussed above, the raw ingredients undergo a quality-control process.

When companies have multiple production processes, process costing is used to calculate the distinct costs of *each* production process. In our example, Silver Spoons calculates production costs (both direct materials and conversion costs) for the first production process, quality control of raw ingredients. When a batch of raw ingredients completes the quality-control process, the production costs of that process are transferred to the second production process, churning. The churning process continues to track all **transferred-in costs**, which represent the combined production costs of all previous processes, as well as the direct materials and conversion costs accumulated in the churning process. Exhibit 7.9 demonstrates how Silver Spoons will track production costs using the weighted-average method of process costing for the churning process in a setting with a previous production process.

transferred-in costs
Total production costs (both direct materials and conversion costs) accumulated in prior production processes.

	B	C	D	E
	Step 1		**Step 2**	
			Equivalent Units	
		Transferred-in	Direct	Conversion
4 Flow of units (Steps 1-2)	Physical Units	Costs	Materials	Costs
5 WIP, beginning	10,000			
6 Started during period	90,000			
7 Total Units to Account for	100,000			
8				
9 Completed and transferred out	85,000	85,000	85,000	85,000
10 WIP, ending[a]	15,000	15,000	15,000	6,000
11 Total Units Accounted for	100,000	100,000	100,000	91,000
12 [a]Ending WIP 100% complete with respect to direct materials and 40% with respect to conversion costs				
13				
14	Total Costs	Transferred-in Costs	Direct Materials	Conversion Costs
15 Flow of Costs (Steps 3-5)				
16 WIP, beginning	$ 38,000	$ 5,000	$ 18,000	$ 15,000
17 Costs added during period	$ 338,750	$ 45,000	$ 170,000	$ 123,750
18 Total costs to account for (Step 3)	$ 376,750	$ 50,000	$ 188,000	$ 138,750
19				
20 Cost per equivalent unit (Step 4)		$ 0.5000	$ 1.8800	$ 1.5247
21				
22 Costs assigned to transferred-out units	$ 331,902	$ 42,500	$ 159,800	$ 129,602
23 Costs assigned to WIP, ending	$ 44,848	$ 7,500	$ 28,200	$ 9,148
24 Total costs accounted for (Step 5)	$ 376,750	$ 50,000	$ 188,000	$ 138,750

Exhibit 7.9
Weighted-Average Process Costing for the Churning Process When Previous Processes Exist

Microsoft Excel

To calculate production costs with multiple production costs, we use the same five steps discussed earlier. Calculating physical units (Step 1) does not change with additional production processes. Steps 2–4 use the same calculations as those discussed previously. However, companies with prior production processes must add a new column (Column C in Exhibit 7.9) to track costs accumulated during earlier production processes. For the purpose of calculating equivalent units (Step 2), it's important to note that transferred-in costs are always 100 percent complete (and thus not addressed by the footnote in Row 12) because these costs occurred in a previous production process.

Notice in Step 3 that the direct materials and conversion costs for the churning process are identical to those calculated in Exhibit 7.5, where we assumed no earlier production processes. We see in cell C16 that beginning work-in-process had a total of $5,000 in quality-control costs that were previously transferred into the churning process. Similarly, we see in cell C17 that $45,000 of quality-control costs were transferred into the churning process during the period. Therefore, a total of $50,000 in quality control costs (cell C18) must be accounted for.

In Step 4, we determine the transferred-in cost per equivalent unit by dividing the $50,000 in quality-control costs by 100,000 equivalent transferred-in units, which in this case equals $0.50 per unit. Step 5 is calculated as discussed earlier, by multiplying equivalent units by the cost per equivalent unit. For companies with multiple production departments, we must perform this calculation for transferred-in costs in addition to direct materials and conversion costs. In this example, 85,000 equivalent units have been transferred out (Row 9). By multiplying by the cost per equivalent unit, we can determine the cost of these transferred-out units. As cell B22 shows, that cost is $331,902 (85,000 equivalent units * $0.50 for transferred-in costs, $1.88 for direct materials, and $1.5247 for conversion costs, with those costs per equivalent unit coming from Row 20). The remaining $44,848 of production cost (cell B23) is categorized as ending work-in-process on the balance sheet.

 LAB CONNECTION

Some companies use multiple production processes during production. **LAB 7.3 EXCEL** demonstrates how process costing can be adapted to account for multiple processes. In addition, it demonstrates how to adapt process costing for processes that do not add costs at the beginning of production or uniformly throughout a process.

 PROGRESS CHECK

10. How does the calculation of equivalent units differ between the weighted-average and FIFO methods of process costing?

11. When calculating equivalent units, the weighted-average method ignores the percentage of completion for beginning work-in-process units. How does the FIFO method differ from the weighted-average method in this regard?

ETHICS

Human Dimensions of Process Costing: Manipulating Earnings with Process Costing

We have discussed how to use process costing to calculate product costs and how these costs affect a company's financial statements. However, it's important to remember that there is an element of judgment in process costing as it relates to how "complete" ending work-in-process is at the end of each accounting period. Whenever estimates are involved, managers have the opportunity to manipulate earnings, and these estimates can have a profound impact on earnings and inventory values.

The following Mini-Lab provides a simplified example demonstrating how managers can use slight changes in accounting estimates to hit predefined earnings targets. For a more detailed analysis of the effect of accounting estimates on financial statements, complete Lab 7.4.

DATA ANALYTICS MINI-LAB
Analyzing How Process Costing Estimates Affect Financial Statements

Data Analytics Types: Descriptive, Predictive

Lab Note: The tools presented in this lab periodically change. Updated instructions, if applicable, can be found in the student and instructor support materials.

Keywords
Allocation Bases, Cost Drivers

Decision-Making Context
LifeSeife is a (fictitious) producer of hand soap that has just completed its first month of operations. LifeSeife uses process costing. During the month, LifeSeife started production on 50,000 units of soap and completed 30,000 units, all of which were sold to customers. The company incurred $400,000 of production costs. In addition, LifeSeife generated $560,000 in revenue and incurred $50,000 of Sales, General, and Administrative (SG&A) expenses for the month.

LifeSeife's general manager estimates that ending work-in-process units are approximately 50 percent complete. To motivate the manager's performance, LifeSeife's owners have implemented a bonus plan whereby the manager can earn additional compensation if operating income is $220,000 or more for the month.

Ask the Question
Based on the information above, is LifeSeife performing well financially? How does the manager's estimate of the completion for ending work-in-process units affect LifeSeife's income statement and balance sheet?

Required
1. Determine the cost per equivalent unit for a unit of hand soap.
2. Calculate operating income.
3. Calculate the cost of ending work-in-process inventory.
4. Use Excel's Goal Seek to determine what estimate of completion for ending work-in-process will result in the manager qualifying for a bonus.

Master the Data
Open the Excel file titled **Mini-Lab 7 Data.xlsx**, which is reproduced in Exhibit A. You will see a simplified template for process costing as well as a simplified income statement and balance sheet. Your task is to complete the spreadsheet by entering information in all cells that are shaded blue. With the exception of cell B9 (% completion for Ending WIP units), all blue cells should be calculated by using the formulas shown in Column D of Exhibit B. (*Note:* You will input those formulas into Column C.)

Exhibit A

Microsoft Excel

	A	B	C	D	E	F	G
2		Physical Units	Equivalent Units			Income Statement	
3	**Total Units to Account for**	50,000				Revenue	$ 560,000
4						COGS	
5	Units completed during the period	30,000				Gross Margin	
6	Ending WIP units	20,000				SG&A Expenses	$ 50,000
7	Total Units Accounted for	50,000				Operating Income	
8							
9	% completion for Ending WIP units						
10						**Balance Sheet**	
11	**Production costs to Account for**	$ 400,000				Ending WIP	
12							
13	**Cost per equivalent Unit**						
14							
15	Costs transferred out						
16	Costs in Ending WIP						
17	**Total Production Costs Accounted for**						

Exhibit B

Microsoft Excel

	A	B	C	D
2		Physical Units	Equivalent Units	
3	**Total Units to Account for**	50,000		
4				
5	Units completed during the period	30,000	30,000	=B5
6	Ending WIP units	20,000	10,000	=B6*B9
7	Total Units Accounted for	50,000	40,000	=SUM(C5:C6)
8				
9	% completion for Ending WIP units	50.00%		
10				
11	**Production costs to Account for**	$ 400,000		
12				
13	**Cost per equivalent Unit**	$ 10.00	=B11/C7	

Perform the Analysis

Analysis Task #1: Calculate Cost per Equivalent Unit

1. In this simplified mini-lab, all production costs (direct materials and conversion costs) have been combined into a single total. To calculate cost per equivalent unit, we must first determine how many equivalent units were produced during the month. This is LifeSeife's first month of operations. Thus, all completed units were completed during the month, and equivalent units should be set equal to physical units. Accordingly, set cell C5 equal to B5.
2. Set cell B9 equal to 50% to indicate that ending work-in-process units are 50% complete.
3. Equivalent units in ending work-in-process (cell C6) are calculated by multiplying the physical units in cell B6 by the % completion estimate in cell B9.

4. Calculate total equivalent units in cell C7 by summing cells C5 and C6.
5. Finally, calculate cost per equivalent unit (Row 13) by dividing production costs in cell B11 by the total equivalent units in cell C7.

Analysis Task #2: Calculate Costs Transferred Out and Costs in Ending Work-in-Process

1. To determine the total costs transferred out in cell B15, multiply the equivalent units completed in cell C5 by the cost per equivalent unit in cell B13. See Exhibit C for the correct formula. LifeSeife sold all completed units this period, so these costs will be expensed in the current period as Cost of Goods Sold.
2. We will use this same process to calculate the total production costs in ending work-in-process (cell B16). Multiply the equivalent units in ending work-in-process in cell C6 by the cost per equivalent unit in cell B13. This total will be categorized as an asset on the balance sheet, and it will not be expensed until the units are sold in a future period.
3. Add costs transferred out to costs in ending WIP (cell B17) to ensure that all $400,000 of production costs have been accounted for.

	A	B	C
2		Physical Units	Equivalent Units
3	**Total Units to Account for**	50,000	
4			
5	Units completed during the period	30,000	30,000
6	Ending WIP units	20,000	10,000
7	Total Units Accounted for	50,000	40,000
8			
9	% completion for Ending WIP units	50.00%	
10			
11	**Production costs to Account for**	$ 400,000	
12			
13	**Cost per equivalent Unit**	$ 10.00	=B11/C7
14			
15	Costs transferred out	300,000	=C5*B13
16	Costs in Ending WIP	100,000	=C6*B13
17	**Total Production Costs Accounted for**	400,000	=SUM(B15:B16)

Exhibit C

Microsoft Excel

Analysis Task #3: Calculate Operating Income and the Ending Work-in-Process Inventory Balance

1. Recall that revenue minus COGS equals gross margin, and gross margin minus SG&A expenses equals operating income. As shown in Exhibit D, set COGS in cell G4 equal to cell B15 because all completed units were sold to customers, then use formulas to complete the income statement and calculate operating income. The formulas are shown in Exhibit D. You will input them into the blue-shaded area to the left of each formula.
2. Set the Ending Work-in-Process inventory balance in cell G11 equal to B16.

	A	B	C	D	E	F	G	H
1								
2		Physical Units	Equivalent Units			Income Statement		
3	Total Units to Account for	50,000				Revenue	$ 560,000	
4						COGS	$ 300,000	=B15
5	Units completed during the period	30,000	30,000	=B5		Gross Margin	$ 260,000	=G3-G4
6	Ending WIP units	20,000	10,000	=B6*B9		SG&A Expenses	$ 50,000	
7	Total Units Accounted for	50,000	40,000	=SUM(C5:C6)		Operating Income	$ 210,000	=G5-G6
8								
9	% completion for Ending WIP units	50.00%						
10						Balance Sheet		
11	Production costs to Account for	$ 400,000				Ending WIP	100,000	=B16
12								
13	Cost per equivalent Unit	$ 10.00	=B11/C7					
14								
15	Costs transferred out	300,000	=C5*B13					
16	Costs in Ending WIP	100,000	=C6*B13					
17	Total Production Costs Accounted for	400,000	=SUM(B15:B16)					

Exhibit D

Microsoft Excel

Analysis Task #4: Determine How Changes in Accounting Estimates Affect the Financial Statements

1. Change the % completion in cell B9 for Ending WIP units from 50% to 40%. Notice how this change affects our data. Because fewer equivalent units are produced, the cost per equivalent unit increases. As a result, a greater proportion of costs are transferred out and fewer costs remain in ending WIP. This has the effect of decreasing operating income from $210,000 to $194,211 (Exhibit E).

Exhibit E

Microsoft Excel

	A	B	C	D	E	F	G
1							
2		Physical Units	Equivalent Units			Income Statement	
3	Total Units to Account for	50,000				Revenue	$ 560,000
4						COGS	$ 315,789
5	Units completed during the period	30,000	30,000			Gross Margin	$ 244,211
6	Ending WIP units	20,000	8,000			SG&A Expenses	$ 50,000
7	Total Units Accounted for	50,000	38,000			Operating Income	$ 194,211
8							
9	% completion for Ending WIP units	40.00%					
10						Balance Sheet	
11	Production costs to Account for	$ 400,000				Ending WIP	84,211
12							
13	Cost per equivalent Unit	$ 10.53					
14							
15	Costs transferred out	315,789					
16	Costs in Ending WIP	84,211					
17	Total Production Costs Accounted for	400,000					

2. Now change the % completion in cell B9 to 60%. Notice that with this change, a greater proportion of production costs are included in ending WIP as an asset rather than in Cost of Goods Sold as an expense. As a result, operating income and ending WIP inventory increase, as Exhibit F shows. (Compare these numbers to those shown in Exhibit E.)

Exhibit F

Microsoft Excel

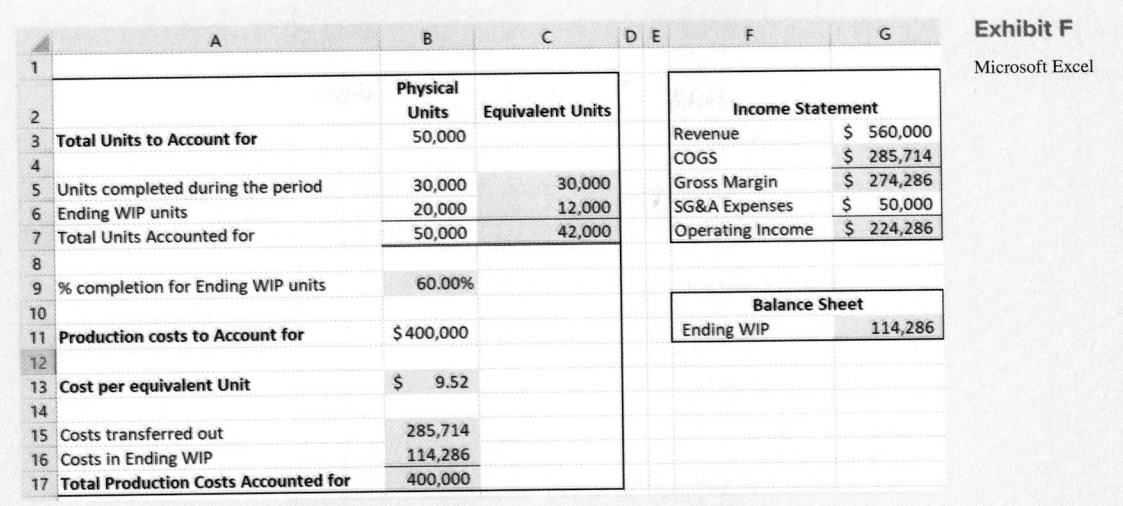

	A	B	C	D	E	F	G
1							
2		Physical Units	Equivalent Units			Income Statement	
3	Total Units to Account for	50,000				Revenue	$ 560,000
4						COGS	$ 285,714
5	Units completed during the period	30,000	30,000			Gross Margin	$ 274,286
6	Ending WIP units	20,000	12,000			SG&A Expenses	$ 50,000
7	Total Units Accounted for	50,000	42,000			Operating Income	$ 224,286
8							
9	% completion for Ending WIP units	60.00%					
10						Balance Sheet	
11	Production costs to Account for	$ 400,000				Ending WIP	114,286
12							
13	Cost per equivalent Unit	$ 9.52					
14							
15	Costs transferred out	285,714					
16	Costs in Ending WIP	114,286					
17	Total Production Costs Accounted for	400,000					

3. The manager can earn a bonus by achieving $220,000 in operating income during the month. On the **Data** tab, select **What-if Analysis > Goal Seek** (Exhibit G).

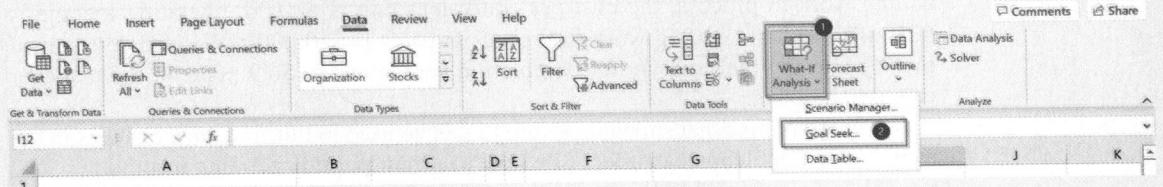

Exhibit G

Microsoft Excel

4. In the **Goal Seek** window, set operating income in cell G7 to $220000 (the target income) by changing the estimated percentage completion for Ending WIP units in cell B9 (see Exhibit H). Click **OK**. The result will indicate that an estimate of 56.9 percent will result in operating income that merits a bonus (see Exhibit I).

Exhibit H

Microsoft Excel

Goal Seek   ?   ✕

Set cell: $G$7

To value: 220000

By changing cell: $B$9

OK   Cancel

Exhibit I

Microsoft Excel

	A	B	C	D	E	F	G
1							
2		Physical Units	Equivalent Units			Income Statement	
3	Total Units to Account for	50,000				Revenue	$ 560,000
4						COGS	$ 290,000
5	Units completed during the period	30,000	30,000			Gross Margin	$ 270,000
6	Ending WIP units	20,000	11,379			SG&A Expenses	$ 50,000
7	Total Units Accounted for	50,000	41,379			Operating Income	$ 220,000
8							
9	% completion for Ending WIP units	56.90%					
10						Balance Sheet	
11	Production costs to Account for	$400,000				Ending WIP	110,000
12							
13	Cost per equivalent Unit	$ 9.67					
14							
15	Costs transferred out	290,000					
16	Costs in Ending WIP	110,000					
17	Total Production Costs Accounted for	400,000					

Share the Story

Our analysis has illustrated how changes in estimates can affect both the income statement and the balance sheet. Using an estimate of 50 percent completion for ending work-in-process, the cost per equivalent unit is $10.00, operating income is $210,000, and the ending work-in-process balance is $100,000. We also determined that by altering the estimate for completion percentage to 56.9 percent, the manager can earn a bonus.

A line graph like that shown in Exhibit J can be used to illustrate how changes in the estimate of completion can affect LifeSeife's current-period operating income.

Exhibit J

Microsoft Excel

DATA VISUALIZATION

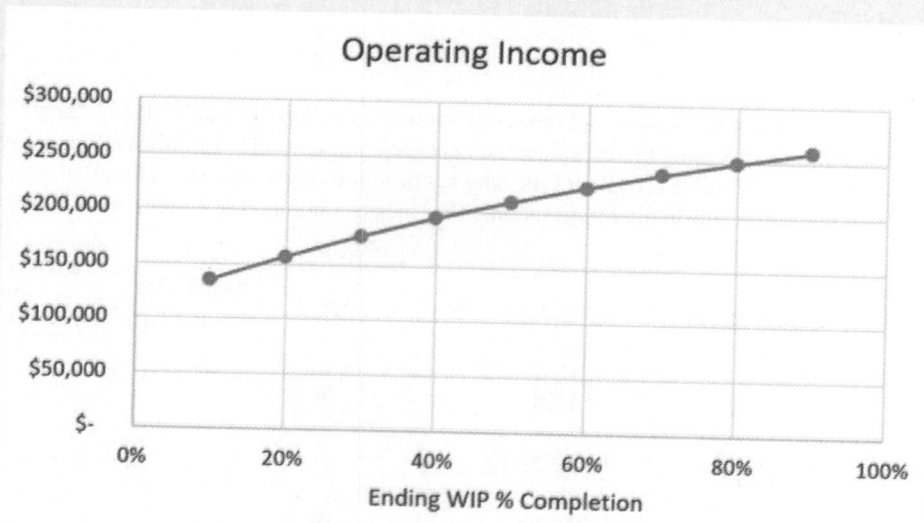

Mini-Lab Assessment

1. What is the equivalent cost per unit if LifeSeife estimates that ending work-in-process inventory is 20 percent complete?
2. What completion percentage estimate would yield operating income of $240,000?
3. Consider how easy it would be for a manager to change an estimate. What is the likelihood that auditors are sufficiently familiar with LifeSeife's operations to know whether the original 50 percent estimate is appropriate? What policies or procedures can LifeSeife put in place to prevent this type of earnings manipulation?

ENVIRONMENTAL, SOCIAL, GOVERNANCE

(Q) LAB CONNECTIONS

LAB 7.4 EXCEL demonstrates how managers can adjust process costing estimates to "fudge the numbers." It shows how altering completion estimates for ending work-in-process units can be used to shift costs between periods.

LAB 7.5 TABLEAU and **LAB 7.5 POWER BI** use basic data-visualization techniques to trace processing costs across time and between different manufacturing facilities. The resulting information provides insight to managers as they consider strategic decisions for the future.

CHOOSING A PROCESS COSTING METHOD

LO 7.4

Explain the factors that determine whether a company should use the weighted-average or FIFO method of process costing.

The choice of process costing method is largely a matter of preference. Theoretically, companies should choose the method that best reflects the reality of the business. However, companies are free to use either method. While it is possible for companies to change methods of process costing, they rarely do so.

The primary advantage of the FIFO method is that changes in production costs between periods are more apparent. Because these costs exclude any units from prior periods, they can be easily compared with prior-period costs to view trends in production costs. When companies use the weighted-average method and merge costs between periods, they muddy the waters and make comparisons more difficult.

The FIFO method also allows us to easily determine how the costs of units started and completed during the period differ from the beginning work-in-process units completed during the period. Refer back to Exhibits 7.6 and 7.7. For units started and completed during the period, production costs were approximately $1.89 and $1.49 per equivalent unit. What about the units from beginning work-in-process? By dividing the total costs for beginning work-in-process units (see Row 29 of Exhibit 7.7) by the 10,000 physical units in beginning work-in-process (cell B5 of Exhibit 7.6), we calculate a cost of approximately $1.80 for direct materials and $1.7982 for conversion costs (see Exhibit 7.10). These numbers indicate an increase in direct materials and a decrease in conversion costs between

Exhibit 7.10
Calculating Per-Unit
Costs Using the FIFO
Method

	Total Costs	Direct Materials	Conversion Costs
Cost of beginning WIP units	$ 3.5982	$ 1.8000	$ 1.7982
Cost of started and completed units	$ 3.3799	$ 1.8889	$ 1.4910

periods. Management must determine whether these changes are significant and what steps may be taken to address them.

Identifying such trends is very important. Consider the experience of **Heartwood Cabinets**. During the COVID-19 pandemic, the global economy experienced record-setting increases in lumber prices, which is the most expensive raw material for Heartwood. The FIFO method makes such cost increases apparent more quickly than the weighted-average method. In other words, using the FIFO method will help Heartwood's management respond more quickly to the higher costs, perhaps by increasing the price of completed cabinets.

Another important consideration in deciding which process-costing method to use is its effect on net income. In times of inflation, the FIFO method will result in higher profits because lower-cost units will be the first to be expensed as cost of goods sold. The opposite holds true in times of deflation, when the FIFO method will result in lower profits than the weighted-average method. However, it is important to remember that these effects on net income are temporary. Once inventory has been reduced to zero, a company's total profit will be identical under either method.

 PROGRESS CHECK

12. How does the choice of process costing method affect companies' decision making and reporting?

13. How does the FIFO method increase reported income in times of inflation, relative to the weighted-average method?

Jobs with Process Costing Responsibilities

Process costing is typically associated with manufacturing rather than service industries. It requires substantial expertise regarding both tracking the costs of manufacturing processes and determining how to make those processes more efficient.

Exhibit 7.11 is a job posting from a site like **ZipRecruiter.com** or **Indeed.com**. This posting is for a Cost Analyst at a full-production winery and bottling facility like **Rack & Riddle**, **Summerland Wines**, or **Purple Wine & Spirits**. Read the posting to better understand what companies value in a management accountant who will use process costing.

Job Title

Cost Accountant & Financial Analyst, reporting to the CFO/Controller

Job Summary

We are seeking a skilled financial analyst and cost accountant at our swiftly growing full-service wine production facility. This role supports the CFO with operations analysis, supports inventory management, and oversees the company's cost accounting. In this position, you will be responsible for conducting analysis of constraints, variances, and costing standards, as well as developing systems to provide costing information. This position also assists in the implementation of our ERP system.

The ideal candidate will have a deep understanding of cost accounting principles as well as experience with manufacturing and operational analysis. This role engages with and collaborates across all levels of the organization including winemaking teams, production line managers, and the executive team.

Skills/Qualifications

- Bachelor's degree in accounting, finance, or related field
- Three or more years' experience in a cost accounting or finance role, including experience with job costing or process costing
- Deep understanding of managerial accounting, finance, budgeting, and cost control
- Technical proficiency with cost analysis, inventory reconciliation, and month-end close processes
- Independent thinker with excellent decision-making skills, clear judgment, and the ability to learn new tools and programs quickly
- Advanced skills in Microsoft Office Suite, including deep knowledge of Excel programs and other accounting programs
- Experience working with large databases
- Ability to summarize data to prepare detailed reports
- Strong written and verbal communication skills, including presentation skills and business writing

Responsibilities:

- Create and maintain reports analyzing pricing and profitability for products and services
- Manage information on the controls for reporting systems and data accumulation
- Analyze and report on effects on product cost based on changes in materials, design, or manufacturing methods
- Analyze manufacturing costs to create quarterly reports on budget costs versus actual production costs and review for inaccuracies
- Apply overhead costs as required by GAAP
- Report and analyze margins by product and production lines, periodic variances, and process constraint

Management accountants are experts in analyzing and interpreting data.

Management accountants often report to the CFO, and many CFOs have management accounting experience.

Management accountants provide insight to decision makers throughout an organization.

Management accountants have expertise in all of these areas.

Process costing is common for the bottling industry because of the uniformity of products as well as the production processes used with these types of products.

Management accountants are valued for their communication skills.

Good analysis leads to good strategic decisions.

Exhibit 7.11
Cost Analyst Job in the Wine Industry

Key Takeaways: Process Costing

In this chapter, we expanded our cost-flow model beyond job-order costing to another costing method called process costing. While the general flow of costs is very similar in both costing methods, the calculation of individual unit costs is very different. With process costing, we typically are determining the cost of a homogeneous product—that is, a uniform or identical product—and we accumulate costs by department or significant process instead of by individual job or unit.

We can use the AMPS model to summarize how the information in this chapter is used to address important managerial questions:

Ask the Question

■ **What question(s) does management want to answer?**

While process costing differs from job costing and activity-based costing, the underlying importance of cost information remains the same. Management depends on accurate cost information to determine strategy.

Master the Data

■ **Which data are appropriate to address management's questions?**

Production cost information used in process costing is gathered from an organization's accounting information system. This information includes labor rates for employees, the cost of raw materials, and indirect manufacturing costs.

Perform the Analysis

■ **Which analytics are performed to address management questions?**

Management accountants use **descriptive analytics** to determine the costs of products. They use **diagnostic analytics** to determine why product costs change between accounting periods, and they use **predictive analytics** to determine how costs will change if various actions are taken.

Share the Story

■ **How are the results of the analytics shared with stakeholders?**

Company decision makers sometimes struggle to understand the seemingly complicated system of process costing. One of a management accountant's primary roles is to effectively communicate financial data so that the company makes sound strategic decisions.

Key Terms

conversion costs	equivalent units of production	manufacturing overhead (MOH)	transferred-in costs
cost per equivalent unit of production	first-in, first-out (FIFO) method	process costing	weighted-average method
direct labor			
direct materials	job (order) costing		

✓ ANSWERS TO PROGRESS CHECKS

1. Process costing is used when products are homogeneous—that is, when products are uniform and identical in their production. Furthermore, with process costing, the end customer is usually not identifiable, so costs are accumulated by production process rather than by customer or job.

2. Process costing gathers costs by production process or department, which creates multiple work-in-process accounts along the production process. Factors of production—materials, labor, and overhead—can be added to each work-in-process account. Job-order costing typically has only a single work-in-process account to which all costs are added.

3. Companies use equivalent units of production to deal with partially completed units. Companies that manufacture mass-produced items commonly have products in various states of completion. The concept of equivalent units enables companies to more easily quantify partially completed output.

4. Determining product costs is one of the primary duties of managerial accountants. Under process costing, product costs are determined by dividing total production costs by total units produced. Equivalent units help accountants determine the total units in this equation.

5. Conversion costs are the costs incurred to transform raw materials into a finished product. They are the sum of direct labor costs and manufacturing overhead costs. Typically they are assumed to be incurred uniformly during a production process. In contrast, direct materials are often assumed to be incurred at the beginning of a production process.

6. The concept of equivalent units is used in process costing to equate a number of incomplete units to an equivalent number of completed units. It is the number of completed physical units that are equivalent to a company's partially completed units. Equivalent units are calculated by multiplying the number of incomplete units by their degree of completion (expressed as a percentage).

7. The five steps of process costing are:
   1. Measuring physical units of production
   2. Computing equivalent units of production
   3. Summing production costs
   4. Calculating cost per equivalent unit
   5. Assigning costs to completed and in-process units

8. Companies must track the costs of completed units and work-in-process units for reporting and strategic reasons. The cost of completed units is used to compute finished goods inventory on the balance sheet as well as cost of goods sold on the income statement. The cost of work-in-process units shows up on the balance sheet. In addition, understanding costs assists companies in making strategic decisions about production inputs, processes, and pricing strategies.

9. Companies track direct materials and conversion costs separately because, generally, these costs behave differently. Direct materials costs are often all added at the beginning of the process. Conversion costs are usually assumed to be added uniformly throughout the process. If these costs were to behave identically, then equivalent units would be the same in the two cost categories. For example, if raw materials were assumed to be added uniformly throughout a production process (as conversion costs are assumed to be), then the process of calculating equivalent units and production cost per equivalent unit would mirror that of conversion costs.

10. The weighted-average method focuses on units produced and costs added to production *to date*. In contrast, the FIFO method focuses on units produced and costs added to production *this period*. Because the weighted-average method merges beginning work-in-process units with those that are started and completed during the period, these units are combined as transferred-out units. The FIFO method keeps these units distinct and reports them separately.

11. The weighted-average method is concerned with the equivalent units done to date. All completed units are assumed to be 100 percent completed in the current period. While this assumption isn't precisely accurate, it is nonetheless a component of the weighted-average method. The FIFO method is concerned with the equivalent units completed this period. Thus, the FIFO method must account for the work performed during the period to complete those units begun in the prior period (that is, beginning work-in-process).

12. The FIFO method treats the costs of each production period distinctly, whereas the weighted-average method combines the cost of units across periods. Thus, FIFO better reflects current production costs and provides better comparability between periods. Process costing methods also affect income. In periods of inflation, FIFO results in higher

net income because older goods cost less than newer goods and are the first to be expensed when units are sold.

13. During inflationary periods, production costs rise. FIFO assumes that products produced earlier (when production costs were lower) are finished and sold before products produced later. Lower production costs equate to lower cost of goods sold and increased net income.

Multiple Choice Questions   Mc Graw Hill connect

1. (LO7.1) Which of the following products is most likely to be accounted for using process costing rather than job costing?
   a. Paint
   b. Furniture
   c. Hand-made jewelry
   d. Sculptures

2. (LO7.1) All of the following products are suitable for process costing except:
   a. cereal.
   b. gasoline.
   c. fruit punch.
   d. portraits.

3. (LO7.1) Under process costing, all of the following are production costs except:
   a. direct materials.
   b. advertising and marketing.
   c. direct labor.
   d. manufacturing overhead.

4. (LO7.1) Under process costing, why are direct materials tracked separately from conversion costs?
   a. Conversion costs are generally higher than direct materials.
   b. Costs for direct materials are generally higher than conversion costs.
   c. Direct materials are generally incurred at a different pace than conversion costs.
   d. Conversion costs include all traced costs.

5. (LO7.1) Process costing is often used by companies that produce highly customized products.
   a. True
   b. False

6. (LO7.2) In general, when calculating equivalent units, it is easier to estimate the percentage completion for:
   a. direct materials.
   b. conversion costs.

7. (LO7.2) Under the weighted-average method of process costing, beginning work-in-process completion estimates can be ignored because these units are always grouped together with units that are started and completed during the period.
   a. True
   b. False

8. (LO7.2) Canvas Engine generally produces 5,000 units per month. During March, Canvas started 4,000 units but finished only 1,000. Canvas Engine uses process costing to account for product costs. For the purpose of assigning production costs in March, Canvas Engine must divide production costs by:
   a. average monthly units completed.
   b. units completed in March.
   c. units started in March.
   d. March equivalent units.

9. (LO7.3) Which of the following costs are not considered conversion costs?

a. Direct materials

b. Direct labor

c. Factory rent

d. Factory utilities

10. (LO7.3) Which of the following categories of costs is considered only when a company has multiple production processes?

a. Production costs

b. Direct materials

c. Conversion costs

d. Transferred-in costs

11. (LO7.3) Which method of process costing considers the costs incurred by the end of an accounting period?

a. Weighted-average method

b. FIFO method

12. (LO7.3) Which method of process costing divides *total* production costs by equivalent units to calculate cost per equivalent unit?

a. Weighted-average method

b. FIFO method

13. (LO7.3) Which method of process costing subdivides completed units into those units started in the previous period and those units started in the current period?

a. Weighted-average method

b. FIFO method

14. (LO7.3) Which method of process costing considers only the costs incurred during an accounting period to determine equivalent cost per unit?

a. Weighted-average method

b. FIFO method

15. (LO7.3) The calculation for the equivalent units of transferred-in costs is equivalent to the calculation for the equivalent units of:

a. direct materials that are 100 percent complete.

b. direct materials that are 50 percent complete.

c. conversion costs that are 50 percent complete.

d. conversion costs that are 0 percent complete.

16. (LO7.2, 7.3) In April, True Colors Paint Co. has ending work-in-process inventory that is 30 percent complete with respect to conversion costs. True Colors uses the weighted-average method of process costing. When calculating May's equivalent units of production for these units, what percentage will True Colors Paint Co. use (assuming that all of April's ending work-in-process was completed in May)?

a. 0 percent

b. 30 percent

c. 70 percent

d. 100 percent

17. (LO7.2, 7.3) In April, True Colors Paint Co. has ending work-in-process inventory that is 30 percent complete. True Colors uses the FIFO method of process costing. When calculating May's equivalent units of production for these units, what percentage will True Colors Paint Co. use (assuming that all of April's ending work-in-process was completed in May)?

a. 0 percent

b. 30 percent

    c. 70 percent

    d. 100 percent

18. (LO7.4) Hobby Capsule accounts for costs using process costing. Hobby Capsule has significant changes in production costs across time, and it seeks to respond to these changes as soon as possible. Which process-costing method is most appropriate for Hobby Capsule?

    a. Weighted-average method

    b. FIFO method

19. (LO7.4) Which process-costing method will provide a lower reported net income during times of inflation?

    a. Weighted-average method

    b. FIFO method

20. (LO7.4) Which process-costing method will provide higher reported production costs during times of inflation?

    a. Weighted-average method

    b. FIFO method

Discussion Questions

1. (LO7.1) What types of products are more suitable for process costing than job costing?

2. (LO7.2) Explain why process costing is generally not used for customizable products.

3. (LO7.1) Describe how process costing differs from job costing in terms of which costs are considered product costs.

4. (LO7.1) Describe how process costing differs from job costing in terms of how production costs are accumulated.

5. (LO7.2) What are equivalent units and why are they necessary when using process costing?

6. (LO7.2) Explain why direct materials are tracked separately from conversion costs in a process-costing system.

7. (LO7.3) Briefly describe the five steps of process costing.

8. (LO7.3) Process costing results in an assignment of production costs to costs transferred out and ending work-in-process. How does this assignment manifest in a company's financial statements?

9. (LO7.2, 7.3) The weighted-average method of accounting is concerned with equivalent units completed and costs added by the end of the current period. In contrast, the FIFO method is concerned with equivalent units completed and costs added during the current period. How does this distinction affect the five steps of process costing?

10. (LO7.2, 7.3) Step 4 of process costing involves computing equivalent cost per unit. Under the weighted-average method, total production costs are divided by equivalent units. Under the FIFO method, only current-period costs are divided by equivalent units. Explain why this is the case.

ETHICS

11. (LO7.3) Explain how completion estimates can be used to shift expenses from one period to the next.

12. (LO7.3) What steps might a company take to ensure that managers are not manipulating the percent completed for partially completed units in order to affect net income?

ETHICS

13. (LO7.4) Explain how reported net income can be affected by a company's choice to use the weighted-average or FIFO method of accounting in periods of inflation or deflation.

14. (LO7.4) What is the primary advantage of the FIFO method?

15. (LO7.4) Explain how the FIFO method of process costing can make companies more responsive to changes in production costs than the weighted-average method can.

Brief Exercises ![Mc Graw Hill] connect

1. (LO7.1) Categorize each of the following products according to whether job costing or process costing is more appropriate.

Product	Job Costing or Process Costing?
a. Cereal	
b. Jewelry	
c. Oil	
d. Tabasco sauce	
e. Automobiles	
f. Mustard	
g. Yarn	
h. Custom-made furniture	
i. Wedding dresses that are not custom-made	

2. (LO7.2) In January, Pinnacle Paintball company has 500 units in beginning WIP, and the company began production on an additional 1,300 units during the month. Ending WIP was 250 units. Pinnacle uses the weighted-average method of process costing. How many units were completed during January?

3. (LO7.2, 7.3) During March, Skyflower Fireworks had 800 units in beginning WIP, and it started an additional 2,600 units during the month. Skyflower completed 3,000 units in March. Skyflower uses the FIFO method of process costing.

   a. How many units were both started and completed during the month (that is, 100 percent of production was undertaken during March)?

   b. How many units remain in ending WIP at the end of the month?

4. (LO7.2, 7.3) The Still Safe Company began production on 32,000 units during the month. Still Safe completed 35,000 units, and it had 2,500 units in ending WIP. Still Safe uses the weighted-average method of process costing. How many units were in beginning WIP for the month?

5. (LO7.2, 7.3) The Monacle Peanut Butter Company uses the FIFO method of process costing to account for production costs. During November, Monacle started 2,900 units. In addition, 8,500 units were completed, including 3,800 units that were completed in their entirety during the month. Monacle has 1,500 units in ending WIP. What is the total number of units in beginning WIP on November 1?

6. (LO7.2, 7.3) The Bacchus Grape Preserves Company had 30,000 units in beginning WIP in July. Bacchus began production on an additional 175,000 units during the month and completed 160,000 units. Bacchus uses the weighted-average method of process costing. How many units were in ending work-in-process inventory at the end of July?

7. (LO7.2, 7.3) The Nauvoo Brick Company had 10,000 units in beginning WIP in October. Nauvoo began production on an additional 60,000 units during the month. Ending WIP was 14,000 units at the end of October. The Nauvoo Brick Company uses the weighted-average method of process costing. How many units were completed during October?

8. (LO7.2, 7.3) During January, Far North Maple Syrup Company had 108,000 units in beginning WIP, and it started an additional 364,000 units during the month. Far North

completed 402,000 units in January. Far North uses the FIFO method of process costing.

   a. How many units were both started and completed during the month (that is, 100 percent of production was undertaken during January)?

   b. How many units remain in ending WIP at the end of the month?

9. (LO7.2, 7.3) Bee Sweet Candy Company began production on 17,000 units during the month. Bee Sweet completed 28,750 units during the month, and it had 1,850 units in ending WIP. Bee Sweet Candy Company uses the weighted-average method of process costing. How many units were in beginning WIP for the month?

10. (LO7.2, 7.3) Boss Vase uses the FIFO method of process costing to account for production costs. During February, Boss Vase started 13,500 units. During the month, 19,500 units were completed, including 14,600 units that were started in February. Boss has 1,200 units in ending WIP. What is the total number of units in beginning WIP on February 1?

11. (LO7.2, 7.3) En Garde Fencing Company completed 27,500 units in September, of which 22,000 were also started in September. En Garde had 40,000 units in ending work-in-process. En Garde uses the FIFO method of process costing. How many units were in beginning work-in-process in September?

12. (LO7.2, 7.3) The Nunya Beeswax Company used the weighted-average method of process costing and calculated that for December, the company had 300 equivalent units for direct materials and 280 equivalent units for conversion costs.

   Nunya also reported the following information for process costs in December:

	Total	Direct Materials	Conversion Costs
Equivalent units		300	280
Beginning WIP costs	$ 3,200	$ 1,400	$ 1,800
Costs added during December	$22,000	$10,000	$12,000

What is the cost per equivalent unit for direct materials and conversion costs for units completed in December?

13. (LO7.2, 7.3) Brite Candles Inc. uses the FIFO method of process costing and calculated that for December, the company had 20,050 equivalent units for direct materials and 23,000 equivalent units for conversion costs.

	Total	Direct Materials	Conversion Costs
Equivalent units		20,050	23,000
Beginning WIP costs	$ 5,500	$ 1,900	$ 3,600
Costs added during December	$340,800	$220,000	$120,800

What is the cost per equivalent unit for direct materials and conversion costs for a unit completed in December?

14. (LO7.2, 7.3) Bings Jar Company uses the FIFO method of process costing. With regard to direct materials, the company calculated 9,000 equivalent units in February and reported an $8.50 equivalent cost per unit. Direct materials costs in January for February's beginning work-in-process inventory were $14,000. How many dollars of additional direct materials costs did Bings incur during February?

15. (LO7.2, 7.3) Valley Mills Flour Company uses the weighted-average method of process costing. With regard to direct materials, the company calculated 11,500 equivalent units in April and reported a $13.25 equivalent cost per unit. Direct materials costs in March for April's beginning work-in-process inventory were $25,000. How many dollars of direct materials costs did Valley Mills Flour Company incur during April?

16. (LO7.4) Young Co. produces wagons and uses the FIFO method of process costing to account for production costs. In the most recent quarter, Young reported direct materials cost per equivalent unit of $224. Young has experienced significant decreases in raw materials prices over the past several months, and it expects the trend to continue. If Young were to recalculate direct materials cost per equivalent unit under the weighted-average method, how would the new cost compare to the reported $224 per unit (higher, lower, or equal)? Why?

17. (LO7.2, 7.3) Mack Inc. uses a weighted-average process costing system. Unlike most manufacturing processes, Mack Inc. has a process for which both direct materials and conversion costs are incurred evenly during the production process. During the month of October, the following costs were incurred:

Direct materials: $39,700
Conversion costs: $70,000

The work-in-process inventory as of October 1 consisted of 5,000 units, valued at $4,300, that were 20 percent complete. During October, 27,000 units were transferred out. Inventory as of October 31 consisted of 3,000 units that were 50 percent complete. What is Mack's weighted-average inventory cost per unit completed in October?

18. (LO7.2, 7.3) Colt Company uses a weighted-average process cost system to account for the cost of producing a chemical compound. As part of production, Material B is added when the goods are 80 percent complete. Beginning work-in-process inventory for the current month was 20,000 units, 90 percent complete. During the month, 70,000 units were started in process, and 65,000 units were completed. There were no lost or spoiled units. If the ending inventory was 60 percent complete, what are the total equivalent units for Material B for the month?

19. (LO7.2, 7.3) San Jose Inc. uses a weighted-average process costing system. All materials are introduced at the start of manufacturing, and conversion cost is incurred evenly throughout production. The company started 70,000 units during May and had the following work-in-process inventories at the beginning and end of the month.

May 1:   30,000 units, 40 percent complete
May 31: 24,000 units, 25 percent complete

What are the total equivalent units used to assign costs for May for direct materials and conversion costs?

20. (LO7.2, 7.3) During December, Krause Chemical Company had the following selected data concerning the manufacture of Xyzine, an industrial cleaner.

CMA

Production Flow	Physical Units	
Completed and transferred to the next department	100	
Add: Ending work-in-process inventory	10	(40% complete as to conversion)
Total units to account for	110	
Less: Beginning work-in-process inventory	20	(60% complete as to conversion)
Units started during December	90	

All material is added at the beginning of processing in this department, and conversion costs are added uniformly during the process. The beginning work-in-process inventory had $120 of raw material and $180 of conversion costs incurred. Materials added during December were $540, and conversion costs of $1,484 were incurred. Krause uses the weighted-average process-costing method. What are the total conversion costs transferred out in December?

Problems   📖 connect

1. (LO7.1, 7.2, 7.3) TruVu is a manufacturer of contact lenses and uses the weighted-average method of process costing. TruVu's production facility produces millions of lenses every month. Direct materials are all added at the beginning of production and conversion costs are incurred uniformly during production.

   In March, TruVu had 40,000 units in beginning work-in-process and began production on another 2,200,000 units. At the end of the month, TruVu had 60,000 units in ending work-in-process that were 75 percent complete with respect to conversion costs.

   TruVu incurred $65,000 of direct materials costs and $75,000 of conversion costs in February for March's beginning work-in-process units. TruVu incurred an additional $3,000,000 in direct materials costs and $1,400,000 in conversion costs in March.

   Required

   (Do not round your intermediate calculations. Round your final answer to 2 decimals.)

   a. Why are contact lenses a good candidate for process costing?

   b. What are the equivalent units of production for direct materials in March?

   c. What are the total costs transferred out of production and the total cost of ending work-in-process inventory?

2. (LO7.2, 7.3) LozzaMozza produces artisan cheese wheels and uses the weighted-average method of process costing. Direct materials are all added at the beginning of production and conversion costs are incurred uniformly during production.

   In September, LozzaMozza had 5,000 units in beginning work-in-process and began production on another 35,000 units. At the end of the month, LozzaMozza had 8,000 units in ending work-in-process that were 40 percent complete with respect to conversion costs.

   LozzaMozza incurred $12,000 of direct materials costs and $3,000 of conversion costs in August for September's beginning work-in-process units. LozzaMozza incurred an additional $80,000 in direct materials costs and $15,000 in conversion costs in September.

   Required

   (Do not round your intermediate calculations. Round your final answer to 2 decimals.)

   a. What are the equivalent units of production for direct materials in September?

   b. What is September's cost per equivalent unit for conversion costs?

   c. What are the total costs transferred out of production and the total cost of ending work-in-process inventory?

3. (LO7.2, 7.3) Woodshed Inc. produces toothpicks and uses the weighted-average method of process costing. Woodshed tracks production costs on a weekly basis. Direct materials are all added at the beginning of production and conversion costs are incurred uniformly during production.

   In Week 11, Woodshed Inc. had 13,000 units in beginning work-in-process and began production on another 50,000 units. Woodshed Inc. completed 48,000 units during Week 11. Ending work-in-process units were 30 percent complete with respect to conversion costs.

   Woodshed Inc. incurred $1,500 of direct materials costs and $2,500 of conversion costs in Week 10 for Week 11's beginning work-in-process units. Woodshed Inc. incurred an additional $5,000 in direct materials costs and $7,500 in conversion costs in Week 11.

   Required

   (Do not round your intermediate calculations. Round your final answer to 2 decimals.)

   a. What are the equivalent units of production for conversion costs in Week 11?

   b. What is Week 11's total production cost per equivalent unit?

   c. What are the total costs transferred out of production and the total cost of ending work-in-process inventory?

4. (LO7.2, 7.3) Memphis Blues produces jeans and uses the weighted-average method of process costing. Direct materials are all added at the beginning of production and conversion costs are incurred uniformly during production.

In December, Memphis Blues had 50,000 units in beginning work-in-process and began production on another 400,000 units. Memphis Blues completed 420,000 units during December. Ending work-in-process units were 70 percent complete with respect to conversion costs.

In addition, Memphis Blues reported the following cost information for December:

	Direct Materials	Conversion Costs
Beginning WIP costs	$ 250,000	$100,000
Costs added in the current period	$2,250,000	$800,000

Required

(Do not round your intermediate calculations. Round your final answer to 2 decimals.)

a. What is the December cost per equivalent unit for direct materials?

b. What is the December cost per equivalent unit for conversion costs?

c. What are the total costs transferred out of production and the total cost of ending work-in-process inventory?

5. (LO7.2, 7.3) LaserCat produces laser pointers used to distract and entertain pets. LaserCat accounts for production costs using the weighted-average method of process costing. All direct materials are assumed to be added at the beginning of the period, while conversion costs are added uniformly throughout production. LaserCat had 7,500 units in beginning work-in-process on January 1. In addition, LaserCat completed 22,000 units during January and had 8,000 units in ending work-in-process at the end of the month.

Management estimates that beginning work-in-process inventory was 100 percent complete for direct materials and 60 percent complete for conversion costs. Ending work-in-process inventory is estimated to be 100 percent complete for direct materials and 20 percent complete for conversion costs.

Costs incurred during December for January's beginning WIP units totaled $8,000 for direct materials and $3,500 for conversion costs. During January, production costs included $30,000 in direct materials and $18,000 for conversion costs.

Required

(Do not round your intermediate calculations. Round your final answer to 2 decimals.)

a. How many units were started in January?

b. What is the January total production cost per equivalent unit?

c. What are the total costs transferred out of production and the total cost of ending work-in-process inventory?

6. (LO7.2, 7.3) Venture Kayaks produces plastic kayaks for outdoor enthusiasts. Venture Kayaks accounts for production costs using the weighted-average method of process costing. All direct materials are assumed to be added at the beginning of the period, while conversion costs are added uniformly throughout production. Venture Kayaks started production on 500 units in July. In addition, Venture Kayaks completed 540 units during July and had 60 units in ending work-in-process at the end of the month.

Management estimates that beginning work-in-process inventory was 100 percent complete for direct materials and 50 percent complete for conversion costs. Ending work-in-process inventory is estimated to be 100 percent complete for direct materials and 80 percent complete for conversion costs.

In addition, Venture Kayaks reported the following cost information for July:

	Direct Materials	Conversion Costs
Beginning WIP costs	$ 12,500	$ 5,000
Costs added in the current period	$80,000	$55,000

Required

(Do not round your intermediate calculations. Round your final answer to 2 decimals.)

a. How many units were in beginning work-in-process inventory on July 1?

b. What is the July total production cost per equivalent unit?

c. What are the total costs transferred out of production and the total cost of ending work-in-process inventory?

7. (LO7.2, 7.3) Long Island Rum accounts for production costs using the FIFO method of process costing. Direct materials are all added at the beginning of production and conversion costs are incurred uniformly during production.

In August, Long Island Rum had 8,500 units in beginning work-in-process that were 30 percent complete with respect to conversion costs. The company began production on another 13,500 units in August and had 4,000 units in ending work-in-process that were 75 percent complete with respect to conversion costs.

Long Island Rum incurred $160,000 of direct materials costs and $30,000 of conversion costs in July for August's beginning work-in-process units. Long Island Rum incurred an additional $250,000 in direct materials costs and $180,000 in conversion costs in August.

Required

(Do not round your intermediate calculations. Round your final answer to 2 decimals.)

a. What are the equivalent units of production for direct materials in August?

b. What is the total per-unit production cost for a unit completed in its entirety in August?

c. What are the total costs transferred out of production and the total cost of ending work-in-process inventory?

8. (LO7.2, 7.3) Star Solar Panels accounts for production costs using the FIFO method of process costing. Direct materials are all added at the beginning of production and conversion costs are incurred uniformly during production.

In September, Star Solar Panels had 7,000 units in beginning work-in-process that were 45 percent complete with respect to conversion costs. The company began production on another 37,000 units in September, and it had 12,500 units in ending work-in-process that were 60 percent complete with respect to conversion costs.

Star Solar Panels reported the following production cost information for September:

	Direct Materials	Conversion Costs
Beginning WIP costs	$ 48,000	$ 19,000
Costs added in the current period	$960,000	$260,000

Required

(Do not round your intermediate calculations. Round your final answer to 2 decimals.)

a. What are the equivalent units of production for direct materials in September?

b. What is September's cost per equivalent unit for conversion costs?

c. What are the total costs transferred out of production and the total cost of ending work-in-process inventory?

9. (LO7.2, 7.3) HE Double Inc. produces hockey sticks and uses the FIFO method of process costing. HE Double Inc. tracks production costs on a weekly basis. Direct materials are all added at the beginning of production and conversion costs are incurred uniformly during production.

In April, HE Double Inc. had 10,000 units in beginning work-in-process and began production on another 35,000 units. HE Double Inc. completed 35,500 units during April. Beginning work-in-process units were 50 percent complete with respect to conversion costs on April 1 and ending work-in-process units were 80 percent complete at the end of the month with respect to conversion costs.

HE Double Inc. incurred $45,000 of direct materials costs and $15,000 of conversion costs in March for April's beginning work-in-process units. HE Double Inc. incurred an additional $145,000 in direct materials costs and $120,000 in conversion costs in April.

Required

(Do not round your intermediate calculations. Round your final answer to 2 decimals.)

a. What are the equivalent units of production for conversion costs in April?

b. What is April's total production cost per equivalent unit?

c. What are the total costs transferred out of production and the total cost of ending work-in-process inventory?

10. (LO7.2, 7.3) HiFiber produces fiber-optic cable and uses the FIFO method of process costing. Direct materials are all added at the beginning of production and conversion costs are incurred uniformly during production.

In October, HiFiber had 2,000 units in beginning work-in-process that were 10 percent complete with respect to conversion costs. HiFiber completed 86,000 units during October, and there were 10,000 units in ending work-in-process inventory (25 percent complete for conversion costs) at the end of October.

HiFiber reported the following cost information for October production:

	Direct Materials	Conversion Costs
Beginning WIP costs	$ 150,000	$ 10,000
Costs added in the current period	$8,000,000	$4,500,000

Required

(Do not round your intermediate calculations. Round your final answer to 2 decimals.)

a. How many units were started in October?

b. What is the total production cost for a unit produced in October?

c. What are the total costs transferred out of production and the total cost of ending work-in-process inventory?

11. (LO7.2, 7.3) ChowBella produces pasta noodles and accounts for production costs using the FIFO method of process costing. All direct materials are assumed to be added at the beginning of the period, while conversion costs are added uniformly throughout production. ChowBella had 40,000 units in beginning work-in-process on November 1. In addition, ChowBella completed 390,000 units during November and had 50,000 units in ending work-in-process at the end of the month.

Management estimates that beginning work-in-process inventory was 100 percent complete for direct materials and 40 percent complete for conversion costs. Ending work-in-process inventory was estimated to be 100 percent complete for direct materials and 90 percent complete for conversion costs.

Costs incurred during October for November's beginning WIP units totaled $150,000 for direct materials and $52,000 for conversion costs. During November, production costs included $1,250,000 in direct materials and $1,500,000 for conversion costs.

Required

(Do not round your intermediate calculations. Round your final answer to 2 decimals.)

a. What is the average production cost of a unit produced entirely during November?

b. What is the average production cost of a unit started in October and completed in November?

c. What are the total costs transferred out of production and the total cost of ending work-in-process inventory?

12. (LO7.2, 7.3) Shroom and Board produces mushrooms that are sold to grocery stores throughout the Southeast United States. Shroom and Board accounts for production costs using the FIFO method of process costing. All direct materials are assumed to be added at the beginning of the period, while conversion costs are added uniformly throughout production. Shroom and Board started production of 24,500 units in July. During July, 25,000 units were completed, while 1,000 units remained in ending work-in-process.

Management estimates that beginning work-in-process inventory was 100 percent complete for direct materials and 60 percent complete for conversion costs. Ending work-in-process inventory was estimated to be 100 percent complete for direct materials and 30 percent complete for conversion costs.

The company reported the following production costs for July:

	Direct Materials	Conversion Costs
Beginning WIP costs	$ 3,500	$ 2,500
Costs added in the current period	$60,000	$60,000

Required

(Do not round your intermediate calculations. Round your final answer to 2 decimals.)

a. How many units were in beginning work-in-process inventory on July 1?

b. What is the total production cost per equivalent unit for units produced entirely in July?

c. What are the total costs transferred out of production and the total cost of ending work-in-process inventory?

13. (LO7.2, 7.3) BigSmoker Inc. produces hardwood pellets for barbecue aficionados. BigSmoker uses the weighted-average method of process costing. All direct materials are assumed to be added at the beginning of the period, while conversion costs are added uniformly throughout production. BigSmoker had 20,000 units in beginning work-in-process inventory on February 1. During February, production was started on an additional 320,000 units. Ending WIP at the end of February was 40,000 units.

Management estimates that beginning work-in-process inventory was 100 percent complete for direct materials and 25 percent complete for conversion costs. Ending work-in-process inventory was estimated to be 100 percent complete for direct materials and 75% complete for conversion costs.

Costs incurred during January for February's beginning WIP units totaled $120,000 for direct materials and $50,000 for conversion costs.

During February, production costs included $2,200,000 in direct materials and $1,500,000 for conversion costs.

Required

(Do not round your intermediate calculations. Round your final answer to 2 decimals.)

a. How many units were completed in February?

b. What are BigSmoker's equivalent units for direct materials?

c. What are BigSmoker's equivalent units for conversion costs?

d. What are the total costs to account for?

e. What is the cost per equivalent unit for direct materials?

f. What is the cost per equivalent unit for conversion costs?

g. What is the cost of producing a complete unit in the current period?

h. What is the cost of direct materials transferred out of production during the period?

i. What are the total conversion costs transferred out of production during the period?

j. What are the total conversion costs in ending WIP at the end of the period?

14. (LO7.2, 7.3) BigSmoker Inc. produces hardwood pellets for barbecue aficionados. BigSmoker uses the FIFO method of process costing. All direct materials are assumed to be added at the beginning of the period, while conversion costs are added uniformly throughout production. BigSmoker had 20,000 units in beginning work-in-process inventory on February 1. During February, production was started on an additional 320,000 units. Ending WIP at the end of February was 40,000 units.

Management estimates that beginning work-in-process inventory was 100 percent complete for direct materials and 25 percent complete for conversion costs. Ending work-in-process inventory was estimated to be 100 percent complete for direct materials and 75 percent complete for conversion costs.

Costs incurred during January for February's beginning WIP units totaled $120,000 for direct materials and $50,000 for conversion costs.

During February, production costs included $2,200,000 in direct materials and $1,500,000 for conversion costs.

Required

(Do not round your intermediate calculations. Round your final answer to 2 decimals.)

a. How many units were completed in February?

b. What are BigSmoker's equivalent units for direct materials?

c. What are BigSmoker's equivalent units for conversion costs?

d. What are the total costs to account for?

e. What is the cost per equivalent unit for direct materials?

f. What is the cost per equivalent unit for conversion costs?

g. What is the average production cost of a unit started in January and completed in February?

h. What is the cost of producing a complete unit in the current period?

i. What is the cost of direct materials transferred out of production during the period?

j. What are the total conversion costs in ending WIP at the end of the period?

15. (LO7.2, 7.3, 7.4) Big Air Boards produces skateboards and accounts for production costs using the FIFO method of process costing. All direct materials are assumed to be added at the beginning of the period, while conversion costs are added uniformly throughout production. Big Air Boards had 22,000 units in beginning work-in-process on December 1. In addition, Big Air Boards completed 23,000 units during December and had 5,000 units in ending work-in-process at the end of the month.

Management estimates that beginning work-in-process inventory was 100 percent complete for direct materials and 50 percent complete for conversion costs. Ending work-in-process inventory was estimated to be 100 percent complete for direct materials and 40 percent complete for conversion costs.

Costs incurred during November for December's beginning WIP units totaled $50,000 for direct materials and $35,000 for conversion costs. During December, production costs included $300,000 in direct materials and $150,000 for conversion costs.

Required

(Do not round your intermediate calculations. Round your final answer to 2 decimals.)

a. What is the average production cost of a unit produced entirely during December?

b. What is the average production cost of a unit started in November and completed in December?

c. Management believes the changes in production costs are a result of inflationary pressures. How would production costs under the weighted-average method of process costing compare with those you calculated? Would costs under the weighted-average method be lower or higher? Why?

> **LAB 7.1** **Excel** Assigning Costs to Inventory Accounts Using the Weighted-Average Method (Heartwood)
>
> **LAB 7.2** **Excel** Assigning Costs to Inventory Accounts Using the FIFO Method (Heartwood)
>
> **LAB 7.3** **Excel** Process Costing with Multiple Production Processes
>
> **LAB 7.4** **Excel** Boosting Net Income with Process Costing
>
> **LAB 7.5** **Tableau** Identifying Anomalies and Trends with Data Visualizations
>
> **LAB 7.5** **Power BI** Identifying Anomalies and Trends with Data Visualizations

Lab 7.1 Excel

Lab Note: The tools presented in this lab periodically change. Updated instructions, if applicable, can be found in the student and instructor support materials.

Assigning Costs to Inventory Accounts Using the Weighted-Average Method (Heartwood)

Data Analytics Types: Descriptive Analytics, Diagnostic Analytics

Keywords

Process Costing, Production Costs, Weighted-Average Method

Decision-Making Context

Heartwood Cabinets has a small manufacturing plant in Florida that uses a single manufacturing process to produce a standard bathroom vanity, which is later sold by home-improvement retailers across the United States. The plant uses process costing to assign costs to products. For this lab, assume that Heartwood Cabinets uses the weighted-average method of process costing.

Both job costing and process costing can be used to track and record the cost of inventory. Process costing often seems more daunting than job costing because it requires a greater number of steps. However, the steps are relatively straightforward, and process costing is very efficient for companies that produce large quantities of identical units.

Required

1. Use Excel to create a weighted-average process-costing template.
2. Calculate WIP inventory and costs transferred out for Heartwood Cabinets.

Ask the Question

Heartwood is compiling month-end financial data. Given cost information for March, how much cost should be assigned to month-end work-in-process inventory, and how much cost should be transferred out of production?

Master the Data

Heartwood had 3,000 units in beginning work-in-process inventory on March 1. Costs incurred during February for these units totaled $160,000 for direct materials and $35,000 for conversion costs.

During March, 15,000 additional units were started and 16,000 units were completed. Costs added to the process in March totaled $860,000 in direct materials and $720,000 in conversion costs. The production manager estimates that ending work-in-process inventory is 100 percent complete with respect to direct materials and 25 percent complete with respect to conversion costs.

You have been provided a template for the weighted-average method of process costing. Open Excel file **Lab 7.1 Data.xlsx**.

Perform the Analysis

Analysis Task #1: Trace the Flow of Units

1. Use the information provided above to complete Step 1 of the process-costing process (measuring physical units of production; see Learning Objective 7.3). To the extent possible, use formulas rather than values so that you may use your template for future months of data. Lab Exhibit 7.1.1 shows the formulas for this step. Ensure that total units accounted for in cell B11 equals total units to account for in cell B7. Lab Exhibit 7.1.2 shows what the spreadsheet will look like after you've entered the formulas.

	A	B
1		
2		**Step 1**
3		
4	*Flow of units (Steps 1-2)*	Physical Units
5	WIP, beginning	3000
6	Started during period	15000
7	**Total Units to Account for**	=SUM(B5:B6)
8		
9	Completed and transferred out	16000
10	WIP, ending[a]	=B11-B9
11	**Total Units Accounted for**	=B7

Lab Exhibit 7.1.1

Microsoft Excel

	A	B
1		
2		**Step 1**
3		
4	*Flow of units (Steps 1-2)*	Physical Units
5	WIP, beginning	3,000
6	Started during period	15,000
7	**Total Units to Account for**	18,000
8		
9	Completed and transferred out	16,000
10	WIP, ending[a]	2,000
11	**Total Units Accounted for**	18,000

Lab Exhibit 7.1.2

Microsoft Excel

2. The next step is to compute equivalent units of production (Step 2 of the process-costing process). We will do so in Rows 9–11. The weighted-average method focuses on the work completed *to date,* regardless of whether it was started in February or March. All 16,000 units transferred out were completed *to date,* so set cells C9 and D9 equal to B9 (equivalent units equal physical units). For the units in ending work-in-process, we look at footnote *a* to determine how much work was completed by the end of the period. The footnote indicates that ending work-in-process (WIP) was 100 percent complete with respect to direct materials and 25 percent complete with respect to conversion costs. We multiply these percentages by the physical units to determine equivalent units. Use the SUM function to determine the total equivalent units of production for both direct materials and conversion costs. Lab Exhibit 7.1.3 shows the formulas for this step. After you input the formulas, the spreadsheet should resemble Lab Exhibit 7.1.4.

Lab Exhibit 7.1.3

Microsoft Excel

	A	B	C	D
1				
2		Step 1	Step 2	
3			Equivalent Units	
4	Flow of units (Steps 1-2)	Physical Units	Direct Materials	Conversion Costs
5	WIP, beginning	3000		
6	Started during period	15000		
7	Total Units to Account for	=SUM(B5:B6)		
8				
9	Completed and transferred out	16000	=B9	=B9
10	WIP, ending[a]	=B11-B9	=B10*1	=B10*0.25
11	Total Units Accounted for	=B7	=SUM(C9:C10)	=SUM(D9:D10)

	A	B	C	D
1				
2		Step 1	Step 2	
3			Equivalent Units	
			Direct	Conversion
4	Flow of units (Steps 1-2)	Physical Units	Materials	Costs
5	WIP, beginning	3,000		
6	Started during period	15,000		
7	Total Units to Account for	18,000		
8				
9	Completed and transferred out	16,000	16,000	16,000
10	WIP, ending[a]	2,000	2,000	500
11	Total Units Accounted for	18,000	18,000	16,500
12	[a]Ending WIP 100% complete with respect to direct materials and 25% with respect to conversion costs			

Lab Exhibit 7.1.4

Microsoft Excel

Analysis Task #2: Trace the Flow of Costs

1. Next, enter cost information from beginning work-in-process as well as costs added to production. This information is provided above. To complete Step 3 of the process-costing process (summing production costs), sum costs for each cost category. Lab Exhibit 7.1.5 shows the formulas for this step. After you input the formulas, your spreadsheet should resemble Lab Exhibit 7.1.6.

	A	B	C	D
14		Total Costs	Direct Materials	Conversion Costs
15	Flow of Costs (Steps 3-5)			
16	WIP, beginning	=SUM(C16:D16)	160000	35000
17	Costs added during period	=SUM(C17:D17)	860000	720000
18	Total costs to account for (Step 3)	=SUM(B16:B17)	=SUM(C16:C17)	=SUM(D16:D17)

	A	B	C	D
			Direct	Conversion
14		Total Costs	Materials	Costs
15	Flow of Costs (Steps 3-5)			
16	WIP, beginning	$ 195,000	$ 160,000	$ 35,000
17	Costs added during period	$ 1,580,000	$ 860,000	$ 720,000
18	Total costs to account for (Step 3)	$ 1,775,000	$ 1,020,000	$ 755,000

Lab Exhibit 7.1.6

Microsoft Excel

2. To calculate cost per equivalent unit (Step 4 of the process-costing process), divide costs added to production *to date,* cells C18 and D18, by the equivalent units of production completed *to date,* cells C11 and D11. Lab Exhibit 7.1.7 shows the formulas for this step. After you input the formulas, your spreadsheet should resemble Lab Exhibit 7.1.8.

	A	B	C	D
1				
2		Step 1	Step 2	
3			Equivalent Units	
4	Flow of units (Steps 1-2)	Physical Units	Direct Materials	Conversion Costs
5	WIP, beginning	3000		
6	Started during period	15000		
7	Total Units to Account for	=SUM(B5:B6)		
8				
9	Completed and transferred out	16000	=B9	=B9
10	WIP, endingª	=B11-B9	=B10*1	=B10*0.25
11	Total Units Accounted for	=B7	=SUM(C9:C10)	=SUM(D9:D10)
12	ªEnding WIP 100% complete with respec			
13				
14		Total Costs	Direct Materials	Conversion Costs
15	Flow of Costs (Steps 3-5)			
16	WIP, beginning	=SUM(C16:D16)	160000	35000
17	Costs added during period	=SUM(C17:D17)	860000	720000
18	Total costs to account for (Step 3)	=SUM(B16:B17)	=SUM(C16:C17)	=SUM(D16:D17)
19				
20	Cost per equivalent unit (Step 4)		=C18/C11	=D18/D11

Lab Exhibit 7.1.8

Microsoft Excel

	A	B	C	D
1				
2		**Step 1**	**Step 2**	
3			**Equivalent Units**	
4	*Flow of units (Steps 1-2)*	Physical Units	Direct Materials	Conversion Costs
5	WIP, beginning	3,000		
6	Started during period	15,000		
7	**Total Units to Account for**	18,000		
8				
9	Completed and transferred out	16,000	16,000	16,000
10	WIP, ending[a]	2,000	2,000	500
11	**Total Units Accounted for**	18,000	18,000	16,500
12	[a]Ending WIP 100% complete with respect to direct materials and 25% with respect to conversion costs			
13				
14		Total Costs	Direct Materials	Conversion Costs
15	*Flow of Costs (Steps 3-5)*			
16	WIP, beginning	$ 195,000	$ 160,000	$ 35,000
17	Costs added during period	$ 1,580,000	$ 860,000	$ 720,000
18	**Total costs to account for (Step 3)**	$ 1,775,000	$ 1,020,000	$ 755,000
19				
20	Cost per equivalent unit **(Step 4)**		$ 56.67	$ 45.76

3. The fifth and final step of process costing is to assign costs to completed and in-process units in Row 22. To calculate total transferred-out costs (cell B22), first multiply the equivalent units transferred out by the cost per equivalent unit for each cost category, using the formulas shown in Lab Exhibit 7.1.9. Then, in cell B22, sum cells C22 and D22. Because this plant has a single production process, these costs are transferred to finished goods inventory. After you input the formulas, your spreadsheet should resemble Lab Exhibit 7.1.10.

Lab Exhibit 7.1.9

Microsoft Excel

	A	B	C	D
21				
22	Costs assigned to transferred-out units	=C22+D22	=C9*C20	=D9*D20

Lab Exhibit 7.1.10

Microsoft Excel

	A	B	C	D
21				
22	Costs assigned to transferred-out units	$1,638,788	$ 906,667	$732,121

4. Use the same steps to determine the costs remaining in ending work-in-process in Row 23. For each category, multiply the total ending work-in-process equivalent units (cells C10 and D10) by the cost per equivalent unit (cells C20 and D20). Then total ending work-in-process costs in cell B23. Lab Exhibit 7.1.11 shows the formulas for this step. After you input the formulas, your spreadsheet should resemble Lab Exhibit 7.1.12.

Lab Exhibit 7.1.11

Microsoft Excel

	A	B	C	D
21				
22	Costs assigned to transferred-out units	=SUM(C22:D22)	=C9*C20	=D9*D20
23	Costs assigned to WIP, ending	=SUM(C23:D23)	=C10*C20	=D10*D20
24	**Total costs accounted for (Step 5)**			

	A	B	C	D
21				
22	Costs assigned to transferred-out units	$ 1,638,788	$ 906,667	$ 732,121
23	Costs assigned to WIP, ending	$ 136,212	$ 113,333	$ 22,879
24	**Total costs accounted for (Step 5)**			

Lab Exhibit 7.1.12

Microsoft Excel

5. Sum total costs by cost category in Row 24. Ensure that all costs have been accounted for by comparing Rows 18 and 24 (Lab Exhibit 7.1.13).

	A	B	C	D
15	*Flow of Costs (Steps 3-5)*			
16	WIP, beginning	$ 195,000	$ 160,000	$ 35,000
17	Costs added during period	$ 1,580,000	$ 860,000	$ 720,000
18	**Total costs to account for (Step 3)**	$ 1,775,000	$ 1,020,000	$ 755,000
19				
20	Cost per equivalent unit **(Step 4)**		$ 56.67	$ 45.76
21				
22	Costs assigned to transferred-out units	$ 1,638,788	$ 906,667	$ 732,121
23	Costs assigned to WIP, ending	$ 136,212	$ 113,333	$ 22,879
24	**Total costs accounted for (Step 5)**	$ 1,775,000	$ 1,020,000	$ 755,000

Lab Exhibit 7.1.13

Microsoft Excel

Share the Story

An effective process-costing system allows companies that produce identical items to efficiently determine the amount of costs that remain in a production process (as ending work-in-process) and the amount of costs that have been transferred out of a production process. This work is useful for determining how production inputs change over time, and it is critical to preparing financial statements for reporting and analysis. For Heartwood's production in March, $1,638,788 in cost is transferred out, while $136,212 is assigned to work-in-process inventory. Creating a cost template in Excel or similar programs allows management accountants to quickly determine costs for each reporting period by updating the template with new cost data.

Assessment

1. Take a screenshot of the spreadsheet following the last step in this lab, paste it into a Word document, and label it "Lab 7.1 Submission.docx".
2. Answer the questions in Connect based on your spreadsheet and upload your Lab 7.1 Submission.docx via Connect if assigned.

Assigning Costs to Inventory Accounts Using the Weighted-Average Method (Heartwood)

Keywords

Process Costing, Production Costs, Financial Statements

Required

Given April cost and production data below, replicate the Analysis Tasks in Lab 7.1 Excel using the **Alt Lab 7.1 Data.xlsx** dataset. The data pertain to the same production facility for **Heartwood Cabinets** discussed in Lab 7.1.

Heartwood had 2,000 units in beginning work-in-process inventory on April 1. Costs incurred during March for these units totaled $113,333 for direct materials and $22,879 for conversion costs.

During April, 20,000 additional units were started, and 18,000 units were completed. Costs added to the process in April totaled $1,150,000 in direct materials and $850,000 in conversion costs. The production manager estimates that ending work-in-process inventory is 100 percent complete with respect to direct materials and 30 percent complete with respect to conversion costs.

You have been provided a template for the weighted-average method of process costing.

Assessment

1. Take a screenshot of the spreadsheet at the end of the final Analysis Task, paste it into a Word document, and label it "Alt Lab 7.1 Submission.docx".
2. Answer the questions in Connect based on your spreadsheet and upload your Alt Lab 7.1 Submission.docx via Connect if assigned.

Lab Note: The tools presented in this lab periodically change. Updated instructions, if applicable, can be found in the student and instructor support materials. All Lab Exhibits are available within the eBook and in Connect.

Assigning Costs to Inventory Accounts Using the FIFO Method (Heartwood)

Data Analytics Types: Descriptive Analytics, Diagnostic Analytics

Keywords

Process Costing, Production Costs, FIFO Method

Decision-Making Context

Heartwood Cabinets has a small manufacturing plant in Florida that uses a single manufacturing process to produce a standard bathroom vanity, which is later sold by home-improvement retailers across the United States. The plant uses process costing to assign costs to products. For this lab, assume that Heartwood Cabinets uses the FIFO method of process costing.

Both job costing and process costing can be used to track and record the cost of inventory. Process costing often seems more daunting than job costing because it requires a greater number of steps. However, the steps are relatively straightforward, and process costing is very efficient for companies that produce large quantities of identical units.

Required

1. Use Excel to create a FIFO process-costing template.
2. Calculate WIP inventory and costs transferred out for Heartwood Cabinets.

Ask the Question

Heartwood is compiling month-end financial data. Given cost information for March, how much cost should be assigned to month-end work-in-process inventory and how much cost should be transferred out of production?

Master the Data

Heartwood had 3,000 units in beginning work-in-process inventory on March 1. Costs incurred during February for these units totaled $160,000 for direct materials and $35,000 for conversion costs.

During March, 15,000 additional units were started and 16,000 units were completed. Costs added to the process in March totaled $860,000 in direct materials and $720,000 in conversion costs. The production manager estimates that beginning work-in-process was 100 percent complete with respect to direct materials and 80 percent complete with respect to conversion costs at the start of March. The manager also estimates that ending work-in-process inventory is 100 percent complete with respect to direct materials and 25 percent complete with respect to conversion costs.

You have been provided a template for the FIFO method of process costing.

Open Excel file **Lab 7.2 Data.xlsx**.

Perform the Analysis

Analysis Task #1: Trace the Flow of Units

1. Use the information provided above to complete Step 1 of the process-costing process (measuring physical units of production; see Learning Objective 7.3). To the extent possible, use formulas rather than values so that you may use your template for future months of data. Lab Exhibit 7.2.1 shows the formulas for this step. Ensure that total units accounted for in cell B14 equals total units to account for in cell B7. Lab Exhibit 7.2.2 shows what the spreadsheet will look like after you've entered the formulas.

	A	B	C	D
1				
2		Step 1	Step 2	
3			Equivalent Units	
4	Flow of units (Steps 1-2)	Physical Units	Direct Materials	Conversion Costs
5	WIP, beginning	3000		
6	Started during period	15000		
7	Total Units to Account for	=SUM(B5:B6)		
8				
9	Completed and transferred out			
10	From WIP, beginning[a]	3000		
11	Started and completed	=B12-B10		
12	Total completed and transferred out	16000		
13	WIP, ending[b]	=B14-B12		
14	Total Units Accounted for	=B7		

Lab Exhibit 7.2.1

Microsoft Excel

	A	B	C	D
1				
2		Step 1	Step 2	
3			Equivalent Units	
4	Flow of units (Steps 1-2)	Physical Units	Direct Materials	Conversion Costs
5	WIP, beginning	3,000		
6	Started during period	15,000		
7	Total Units to Account for	18,000		
8				
9	Completed and transferred out			
10	From WIP, beginning[a]	3,000		
11	Started and completed	13,000		
12	Total completed and transferred out	16,000		
13	WIP, ending[b]	2,000		
14	Total Units Accounted for	18,000		

Lab Exhibit 7.2.2

Microsoft Excel

2. The next step is to compute equivalent units of production (Step 2 of the process-costing process). We will do so in Rows 10–14. The FIFO method focuses on the work completed *this period*. In Row 10, we calculate the equivalent units needed to complete beginning work-in-process. To do that, we multiply 3,000 physical units by 0 percent for direct materials (100 percent were completed in February) and 20 percent (80 percent were completed in February).

    By definition, units that were started and completed in March were 100 percent completed *during* the month. For the units in ending work-in-process, we look at footnote *a* to determine how much work was completed by the end of the period. This amount includes 100 percent for direct materials and 25 percent for conversion costs. We multiply these percentages by the physical units to determine equivalent units. We then use the SUM function to determine the total equivalent units of production for both direct materials and conversion costs. Lab Exhibit 7.2.3 shows the formulas for this step. After all the formulas are entered, your spreadsheet should look like Lab Exhibit 7.2.4.

	A	B	C	D
1				
2		Step 1	Step 2	
3			Equivalent Units	
4	Flow of units (Steps 1-2)	Physical Units	Direct Materials	Conversion Costs
5	WIP, beginning	3000		
6	Started during period	15000		
7	Total Units to Account for	=SUM(B5:B6)		
8				
9	Completed and transferred out			
10	From WIP, beginning[a]	3000	0	=B10*0.2
11	Started and completed	=B12-B10	=B11	=B11
12	Total completed and transferred out	16000	=SUM(C10:C11)	=SUM(D10:D11)
13	WIP, ending[b]	=B14-B12	=B13*1	=B13*0.25
14	Total Units Accounted for	=B7	=SUM(C12:C13)	=SUM(D12:D13)

Lab Exhibit 7.2.3

Microsoft Excel

Lab Exhibit 7.2.4

Microsoft Excel

	A	B	C	D
1				
2		Step 1	Step 2	
3			Equivalent Units	
4	Flow of units (Steps 1-2)	Physical Units	Direct Materials	Conversion Costs
5	WIP, beginning	3,000		
6	Started during period	15,000		
7	Total Units to Account for	18,000		
8				
9	Completed and transferred out			
10	From WIP, beginning[a]	3,000	-	600
11	Started and completed	13,000	13,000	13,000
12	Total completed and transferred out	16,000	13,000	13,600
13	WIP, ending[b]	2,000	2,000	500
14	Total Units Accounted for	18,000	15,000	14,100
15	[a]Beginning WIP 100% complete with respect to direct materials and 80% with respect to conversion costs			
16	[b]Ending WIP 100% complete with respect to direct materials and 25% with respect to conversion costs			

Analysis Task #2: Trace the Flow of Costs

1. Next, enter cost information from beginning work-in-process as well as costs added to production. This information is provided above. To complete Step 3 of the process-costing process (summing production costs), sum costs for each cost category. Lab Exhibit 7.2.5 shows the formulas for this step. After you input the formulas, your spreadsheet should resemble Lab Exhibit 7.2.6.

	A	B	C	D
17				
18		Total Costs	Direct Materials	Conversion Costs
19	*Flow of Costs (Steps 3-5)*			
20	WIP, beginning	=C20+D20	160000	35000
21	Costs added during period	=C21+D21	860000	720000
22	**Total costs to account for (Step 3)**	=C22+D22	=SUM(C20:C21)	=SUM(D20:D21)

Lab Exhibit 7.2.5

Microsoft Excel

2. To calculate cost per equivalent unit in Row 24 (Step 4 of the process-costing process), divide costs added to production *this period,* cells C24 and D24, by the equivalent units of production completed *this period,* cells C14 and D14. Lab Exhibit 7.2.7 shows the formulas for this step. After you input the formulas, your spreadsheet should resemble Lab Exhibit 7.2.8.

	A	B	C	D
23				
24	Cost per equivalent unit **(Step 4)**		=C21/C14	=D21/D14
25				

Lab Exhibit 7.2.7

Microsoft Excel

3. The fifth and final step of process costing is to assign costs to completed and in-process units. Transferred-out costs are the sum of costs for beginning work-in-process units and units started and completed in March. For beginning work-in-process units in Row 27, first copy down the costs in beginning work-in-process inventory by setting cells C27 and D27 equal to cells C20 and D20, respectively. Then, for each cost category, multiply the equivalent units of production used to complete these units (cells C10 and D10) by the equivalent cost per unit (cells C24 and D24). Total the production costs in Row 29. Lab Exhibit 7.2.9 shows the formulas for this step. After you input the formulas, your spreadsheet should resemble Lab Exhibit 7.2.10.

	A	B	C	D
26	Costs assigned to transferred-out units			
27	Costs from WIP, beginning	=C27+D27	=C20	=D20
28	Costs to complete WIP, beginning	=C28+D28	=C10*C24	=D10*D24
29	Total costs for WIP, beginning	=C29+D29	=C27+C28	=D27+D28

Lab Exhibit 7.2.9

Microsoft Excel

4. Calculate the cost of units started and completed in March (Row 30) by multiplying started and completed units (cells C11 and D11) by the equivalent cost per unit (cells C24 and D24) for each cost category. Combine started and complete costs with beginning work-in-process costs to calculate total costs transferred out of production in cell B30. Because this plant has a single production process, these costs are transferred to

finished goods inventory. Lab Exhibit 7.2.11 shows the formulas for this step. After you input the formulas, your spreadsheet should resemble Lab Exhibit 7.2.12.

	A	B	C	D
26	Costs assigned to transferred-out units			
27	Costs from WIP, beginning	=C27+D27	=C20	=D20
28	Costs to complete WIP, beginning	=C28+D28	=C10*C24	=D10*D24
29	Total costs for WIP, beginning	=C29+D29	=C27+C28	=D27+D28
30	Cost of started and completed units	=C30+D30	=C11*C24	=D11*D24

Lab Exhibit 7.2.11

5. Use the same steps to determine the costs remaining in ending work-in-process in Row 32. For each category, multiply the total ending work-in-process equivalent units (cells C13 and D13) by the cost per equivalent unit (cells C24 and D24). Total the ending work-in-process costs in cell B32. Lab Exhibit 7.2.13 shows the formulas for this step. After you input the formulas, your spreadsheet should resemble Lab Exhibit 7.2.14.

	A	B	C	D
26	Costs assigned to transferred-out units			
27	Costs from WIP, beginning	=C27+D27	=C20	=D20
28	Costs to complete WIP, beginning	=C28+D28	=C10*C24	=D10*D24
29	Total costs for WIP, beginning	=C29+D29	=C27+C28	=D27+D28
30	Cost of started and completed units	=C30+D30	=C11*C24	=D11*D24
31	Total costs transferred out	=C31+D31	=C30+C29	=D30+D29
32	Costs assigned to WIP, ending	=C32+D32	=C13*C24	=D13*D24

Lab Exhibit 7.2.13

6. Sum total costs by cost category in Row 33. Ensure that all costs have been accounted for by comparing Rows 22 and 33. Lab Exhibit 7.2.15 shows the formulas for this step. After you input the formulas, your spreadsheet should resemble Lab Exhibit 7.2.16.

	A	B	C	D
18		Total Costs	Direct Materials	Conversion Costs
19	*Flow of Costs (Steps 3-5)*			
20	WIP, beginning	=C20+D20	160000	35000
21	Costs added during period	=C21+D21	860000	720000
22	**Total costs to account for (Step 3)**	=C22+D22	=SUM(C20:C21)	=SUM(D20:D21)
23				
24	Cost per equivalent unit **(Step 4)**		=C21/C14	=D21/D14
25				
26	Costs assigned to transferred-out units			
27	Costs from WIP, beginning	=C27+D27	=C20	=D20
28	Costs to complete WIP, beginning	=C28+D28	=C10*C24	=D10*D24
29	Total costs for WIP, beginning	=C29+D29	=C27+C28	=D27+D28
30	Cost of started and completed units	=C30+D30	=C11*C24	=D11*D24
31	Total costs transferred out	=C31+D31	=C30+C29	=D30+D29
32	Costs assigned to WIP, ending	=C32+D32	=C13*C24	=D13*D24
33	**Total costs accounted for (Step 5)**	=C33+D33	=SUM(C31:C32)	=SUM(D31:D32)

Lab Exhibit 7.2.15

Share the Story

An effective process-costing system allows companies that produce identical items to efficiently determine the amount of costs that remain in a production process (as ending work-in-process) and the amount of costs that have been transferred out of a production process. This work is useful for determining how production inputs change over time, and it is critical to preparing financial statements for reporting and analysis. For Heartwood's production in March, $1,634,801 in cost is transferred out, while $140,199 is assigned to work-in-process inventory. Creating a cost template in Excel or similar programs allows management accountants to quickly determine costs for each reporting period by updating the template with new cost data.

Assessment

1. Take a screenshot of the spreadsheet following the last step of this lab, paste it into a Word document, and label it "Lab 7.2 Submission.docx".
2. Answer the questions in Connect based on your spreadsheet and upload your Lab 7.2 Submission.docx via Connect if assigned.

Alternate Lab 7.2   Excel—On Your Own

Assigning Costs to Inventory Accounts Using the FIFO Method (Heartwood)

Keywords

Process Costing, Production Costs, FIFO Method

Required

Given April cost and production data below, replicate the Analysis Tasks in Lab 7.2 Excel using the **Alt Lab 7.2 Data.xlsx** dataset. The data pertain to the same production facility discussed in Lab 7.2.

Heartwood had 2,000 units in beginning work-in-process inventory on April 1. Costs incurred during March for these units totaled $114,667 for direct materials and $25,532 for conversion costs.

During April, 20,000 additional units were started and 18,000 units were completed. Costs added to the process in April totaled $1,150,000 in direct materials and $850,000 in conversion costs. The production manager estimates that beginning work-in-process inventory is 100 percent complete with respect to direct materials and 25 percent complete with respect to conversion costs at the start of April. The production manager also estimates that ending work-in-process inventory is 100 percent complete with respect to direct materials and 30 percent complete with respect to conversion costs.

You have been provided a template for the FIFO method of process costing.

Assessment

1. Take a screenshot of the spreadsheet at the end of the final Analysis Task, paste it into a Word document, and label it "Alt Lab 7.2 Submission.docx".
2. Answer the questions in Connect based on your spreadsheet and upload your Alt Lab 7.2 Submission.docx via Connect if assigned.

Process Costing with Multiple Production Processes

Data Analytics Types: Descriptive Analytics, Diagnostic Analytics

Lab Note: The tools presented in this lab periodically change. Updated instructions, if applicable, can be found in the student and instructor support materials. All Lab Exhibits are available within the eBook and in Connect.

Keywords

Process Costing, Production Costs, Weighted-Average Method

Decision-Making Context

Kenova Inc. recently started manufacturing jeans in a facility in Southeast Asia. Each pair of jeans undergoes three distinct manufacturing processes: cutting, sewing, and dying. The facility uses the weighted-average method of process costing to assign costs to products.

One benefit of process costing is that it can be easily adapted to reflect a business's production processes. For instance, process costing can account for production costs transferred in from earlier manufacturing processes. In addition, a process-costing system can be adapted to reflect assumptions regarding when various costs are added to production.

Required

1. Use Excel to create a weighted-average process-costing template.
2. Use Excel to adapt a weighted-average process-costing template to better reflect a company's manufacturing processes.
3. Calculate WIP inventory and costs transferred out for the sewing department of Kenova Inc.

Ask the Question

Kenova Inc. is implementing a process-costing system, and it must adapt its process-costing system to account for costs transferred in from other departments. Given cost information for Kenova's sewing department in June, how much cost should be assigned to month-end work-in-process inventory and how much cost should be transferred out of production?

Master the Data

Kenova jeans pass through three manufacturing processes before completion: cutting, sewing, and dying. Kenova's sewing department had 12,500 units in beginning work-in-process inventory on June 1. The beginning work-in-process costs for these units include $32,000 of costs transferred in from the cutting department, $8,000 in direct materials, and $12,000 in conversion costs.

During June, Kenova started 125,000 units and 120,000 units were completed. Costs incurred in the sewing department in June included $82,000 in direct materials and $150,000 in conversion costs. In addition, $350,000 of cutting department production costs were transferred in during June.

The production manager notes that transferred-in costs are always considered 100 percent complete (because they are incurred in previous departments). The production manager estimates that the average unit in ending work-in-process inventory is 30 percent complete. Unlike other production departments where all direct materials are assumed to be added at the beginning of the process, the sewing department adds all direct materials to the process (in the form of zippers, buttons, and rivets) when the production is 75 percent complete. Conversion costs are assumed to be added uniformly throughout production.

You have been provided a template for the weighted-average method of process costing. Open Excel File **Lab 7.3 Data.xlsx**.

Perform the Analysis

Analysis Task #1: Trace the Flow of Units

1. Use the information provided above to complete Step 1 of the process-costing process (measuring physical units of production; see Learning Objective 7.3). To the extent possible, use formulas rather than values so that you may use your template for future months of data. Ensure that total units accounted for in cell B11 equals total units to account for in cell B7. Lab Exhibit 7.3.1 shows the formulas and Lab Exhibit 7.3.2 shows what the completed spreadsheet will look like.

	A	B	C	D
1				
2		**Step 1**		**Step 2**
3				**Equivalent Units**
4	Flow of units (Steps 1-2)	Physical Units	Direct Materials	Conversion Costs
5	WIP, beginning	12500		
6	Started during period	125000		
7	**Total Units to Account for**	=SUM(B5:B6)		
8				
9	Completed and transferred out	120000		
10	WIP, ending[a]	=B11-B9		
11	**Total Units Accounted for**	=B7		

Lab Exhibit 7.3.1

Microsoft Excel

	A	B	C	D
1				
2		**Step 1**		**Step 2**
3				**Equivalent Units**
4	Flow of units (Steps 1-2)	Physical Units	Direct Materials	Conversion Costs
5	WIP, beginning	12,500		
6	Started during period	125,000		
7	**Total Units to Account for**	137,500		
8				
9	Completed and transferred out	120,000		
10	WIP, ending[a]	17,500		
11	**Total Units Accounted for**	137,500		

Lab Exhibit 7.3.2

Microsoft Excel

2. Because the sewing department must track transferred-in costs from the cutting department, we must add another column to our table. Right-click on Column C and then click on **Insert** (Lab Exhibit 7.3.3). Next, enter the label "Transferred-in Costs" in cells C4 and C14 (Lab Exhibit 7.3.4). Merge and center cells C2:E2 and C3:E3 (Lab Exhibit 7.3.5).

3. The next step is to compute equivalent units of production (Step 2 of the process-costing process). We do so in Rows 9–11. The weighted-average method focuses on the work completed *to date,* regardless of whether it was started in May or June. All 120,000 units transferred out were completed *to date,* so set cells C9, D9, and E9 equal to B9 (equivalent units equal physical units).

   Determining equivalent units in ending work-in-process requires more thought. Transferred-in costs are always 100 percent complete at the beginning of the period because they occurred in an earlier production process. Thus, we multiply 17,500 physical units by 100 percent to calculate equivalent units for transferred-in costs. We do this by entering =B10*1 in cell C10.

   Often, we make a similar assumption for direct materials because materials are often added at the beginning of the process. However, this is not the case for Kenova jeans. The Decision-Making Context above explains that the sewing department adds all direct materials to the process (in the form of zippers, buttons, and rivets) when the production is 75 percent complete. Because footnote *a* indicates that production is 30 percent complete, direct materials have not yet been added to production in the sewing department for these units. So in cell D10 we multiply 17,500 physical units by 0 percent to calculate equivalent units for direct materials. Because conversion costs are added uniformly throughout the production process, in cell E10 we multiply 17,500 physical units by 30 percent to calculate equivalent units for conversion costs (because production is 30 percent complete).

   Use the SUM function to determine the total equivalent units of production for transferred-in, direct materials, and conversion costs. Lab Exhibit 7.3.6 shows all the formulas. The correct numbers of equivalent units for all three cost categories are shown in Row 11 of Exhibit 7.3.7.

	A	B	C	D	E
1					
2		Step 1		Step 2	
3				Equivalent Units	
4	Flow of units (Steps 1-2)	Physical Units	Transferred-in Costs	Direct Materials	Conversion Costs
5	WIP, beginning	12500			
6	Started during period	125000			
7	Total Units to Account for	= SUM(B5:B6)			
8					
9	Completed and transferred out	120000	=$B$9	=$B$9	=$B$9
10	WIP, ending[a]	=B11-B9	=B10*1	=B10*0	=B10*0.3
11	Total Units Accounted for	=B7	=SUM(C9:C10)	=SUM(D9:D10)	=SUM(E9:E10)
12	[a]Ending WIP production is 30% complete on average				

Lab Exhibit 7.3.6

Microsoft Excel

Analysis Task #2: Trace the Flow of Costs

1. Next, enter cost information from beginning work-in-process as well as costs added to production. This information is provided above. To complete Step 3 of the process-costing process (summing production costs), sum costs for each cost category. All formulas are shown in Lab Exhibit 7.3.8. After you input the formulas, your spreadsheet should resemble Lab Exhibit 7.3.9.

	A	B	C	D	E
14		Total Costs	Transferred-in Costs	Direct Materials	Conversion Costs
15	Flow of Costs (Steps 3-5)				
16	WIP, beginning	=SUM(C16:E16)	32000	8000	12000
17	Costs added during period	=SUM(C17:E17)	350000	82000	150000
18	Total costs to account for (Step 3)	=SUM(C18:E18)	=SUM(C16:C17)	=SUM(D16:D17)	=SUM(E16:E17)

2. To calculate cost per equivalent unit (Step 4 of the production-costing process), divide costs added to production *to date,* cells C18:E18, by the equivalent units of production completed *to date,* cells C11:E11. All formulas are shown in Lab Exhibit 7.3.10. After you input the formulas, your spreadsheet should resemble Lab Exhibit 7.3.11.

	A	B	C	D	E
19					
20	Cost per equivalent unit (Step 4)		=C18/C11	=D18/D11	=E18/E11

3. The fifth and final step of process costing is to assign costs to completed and in-process units. Multiply the equivalent units transferred out by the cost per equivalent unit for each cost category. Total transferred-out costs in cell B22. Because this plant has a single production process, these costs are transferred to Kenova's next production department, in this case the dyeing department. All formulas are shown in Lab Exhibit 7.3.12. After you input the formulas, your spreadsheet should resemble Lab Exhibit 7.3.13.

	A	B	C	D	E
13					
14		Total Costs	Transferred-in Costs	Direct Materials	Conversion Costs
15	Flow of Costs (Steps 3-5)				
16	WIP, beginning	=SUM(C16:E16)	32000	8000	12000
17	Costs added during period	=SUM(C17:E17)	350000	82000	150000
18	Total costs to account for (Step 3)	=SUM(C18:E18)	=SUM(C16:C17)	=SUM(D16:D17)	=SUM(E16:E17)
19					
20	Cost per equivalent unit (Step 4)		=C18/C11	=D18/D11	=E18/E11
21					
22	Costs assigned to transferred-out units	=SUM(C22:E22)	=C9*C20	=D9*D20	=E9*E20
23	Costs assigned to WIP, ending				
24	Total costs accounted for (Step 5)				

4. Use the same steps to determine the costs remaining in ending work-in-process. For each category, multiply the total ending work-in-process equivalent units (cells C10:E10) by the cost per equivalent unit (cells C20:E20). Total the ending work-in-process costs in cell B23. All formulas are shown in Lab Exhibit 7.3.14. After you've input the formulas, your spreadsheet should resemble Lab Exhibit 7.3.15.

	A	B	C	D	E
19					
20	Cost per equivalent unit (Step 4)		=C18/C11	=D18/D11	=E18/E11
21					
22	Costs assigned to transferred-out units	=SUM(C22:E22)	=C9*C20	=D9*D20	=E9*E20
23	Costs assigned to WIP, ending	=SUM(C23:E23)	=C10*C20	=D10*D20	=E10*E20
24	Total costs accounted for (Step 5)				

5. Sum total costs by cost category in Row 24. Ensure that all costs have been accounted for by comparing Rows 18 and 24. All formulas are shown in Lab Exhibit 7.3.16. After you've input the formulas, your spreadsheet should resemble Lab Exhibit 7.3.17.

	A	B	C	D	E
13					
14		Total Costs	Transferred-in Costs	Direct Materials	Conversion Costs
15	Flow of Costs (Steps 3-5)				
16	WIP, beginning	=SUM(C16:E16)	32000	8000	12000
17	Costs added during period	=SUM(C17:E17)	350000	82000	150000
18	Total costs to account for (Step 3)	=SUM(C18:E18)	=SUM(C16:C17)	=SUM(D16:D17)	=SUM(E16:E17)
19					
20	Cost per equivalent unit (Step 4)		=C18/C11	=D18/D11	=E18/E11
21					
22	Costs assigned to transferred-out units	=SUM(C22:E22)	=C9*C20	=D9*D20	=E9*E20
23	Costs assigned to WIP, ending	=SUM(C23:E23)	=C10*C20	=D10*D20	=E10*E20
24	Total costs accounted for (Step 5)	=SUM(C24:E24)	=SUM(C22:C23)	=SUM(D22:D23)	=SUM(E22:E23)
25					

Lab Exhibit 7.3.16

Microsoft Excel

Share the Story

Kenova's total costs transferred during the month are $578,591, while ending work-in-process is $55,409.

We have seen how process costing can be adjusted to reflect firm-specific production processes. Doing so is helpful where companies have multiple production departments, as well as when costs are added to production in different ways. Adapting process costing to address company practices improves the accuracy of cost information and allows for better decisions. It also enables companies to create more accurate financial statements for stakeholders.

Assessment

1. Take a screenshot of the spreadsheet following the final Analysis Task, paste it into a Word document, and label it "Lab 7.3 Submission.docx".
2. Answer the questions in Connect based on your spreadsheet and upload your Lab 7.3 Submission.docx via Connect if assigned.

Alternate Lab 7.3   Excel—On Your Own

Process Costing with Multiple Production Processes

Keywords

Process Costing, Production Costs, Weighted-Average Method

Required

Given June cost and production data for Kenova's third and final production department (the dyeing department), replicate the Analysis Tasks in Lab 7.3 using the **Alt Lab 7.3 Data.xlsx** dataset.

Kenova's dyeing department had 30,000 units in beginning work-in-process inventory on June 1. The beginning work-in-process costs for these units include $152,000 of costs transferred in from the sewing department, $1,700 in direct materials, and $2,800 in conversion costs.

During June, Kenova started 120,000 units and completed 130,000 units. Costs incurred in the dyeing department in June included $8,650 in direct materials and $12,750 in conversion costs. In addition, $578,591 of the sewing department's production costs were transferred in during June.

In the dyeing department, all direct materials are added at the beginning of production and conversion costs are added uniformly throughout production.

Assessment

1. Take a screenshot of the spreadsheet at the end of the final Analysis Task, paste it into a Word document, and label it "Alt Lab 7.3 Submission.docx".
2. Answer the questions in Connect based on your spreadsheet and upload your Alt Lab 7.3 Submission.docx via Connect if assigned.

Boosting Net Income with Process Costing

Data Analytics Types: Descriptive Analytics, Diagnostic Analytics, Prescriptive Analytics

Keywords

Process Costing, Process Costing Methods, Ethics

Decision-Making Context

Family Frames Co. (a fictitious company) produces gilded picture frames using a single production process. The company uses the FIFO method of process costing. Family Frames provides substantial performance bonuses for the executive team if financial performance measures are met. The CEO is interested in how estimates used in process costing can affect reported performance.

   Process costing requires management to estimate equivalent units. These estimates allow for significant judgment, and they can have a significant impact on reported financial performance. It is even possible for companies to defraud investors by using inaccurate estimates. Excel can be used to model the effect of these estimates on financial statements.

Required

1. Use Excel to link process-costing results to Family Frames' financial statements.
2. Determine how estimates change cost per equivalent unit, ending work-in-process, and costs transferred out.
3. Use Excel's Goal Seek function to determine which process costing estimates are required to provide desired financial performance on Family Frames' financial statements.

Ask the Question

Family Frames' CEO receives a substantial bonus if operating income is at least $1,000,000 for the year. How do process-costing estimates affect operating income, and how can these estimates be altered in a way that allows the CEO to achieve her bonus?

Master the Data

Family Frames had 30,000 units in beginning work-in-process inventory at the start of this year. The cost of these units includes $122,000 in direct materials and $45,000 in conversion costs. All direct materials are assumed to be added at the beginning of production, while conversion costs are added uniformly throughout the production process. Family Frames estimates that beginning WIP units are 100 percent complete for direct materials and 50 percent complete for conversion costs.

   During the year, Family Frames started production on 250,000 units and completed 250,000 units. Costs added to the process during the year totaled $1,000,000 in direct materials and $475,000 in conversion costs. Family Frames estimates that ending work-in-process inventory is 100 percent complete for direct materials and 20 percent complete with respect to conversion costs.

   You have been provided a completed template for the Family Frames process-costing report, which uses the FIFO method. You also have been provided with a partially completed income statement.

Lab Note: The tools presented in this lab periodically change. Updated instructions, if applicable, can be found in the student and instructor support materials. All Lab Exhibits are available within the eBook and in Connect.

ETHICS

Open Excel file **Lab 7.4 Data.xlsx**. Process-costing information is found on the **Process Costs** tab.

Perform the Analysis

Analysis Task #1: Create Formulas for Completion Percent

1. The process-costing template is already completed with Family Frames' data. We are interested in examining how management's estimates of completed work-in-process units influence a company's financial statements. Notice that cells C10, D10, C13, and D13 appropriately reflect footnotes *a* and *b* (Lab Exhibit 7.4.1).

2. Select cells C15:D16 and select "%" as the new number format (Lab Exhibit 7.4.2).

3. Change footnote *a* to read "Beginning WIP completion" and change footnote *b* to read "Ending WIP completion". Next, in Columns C and D, enter the percent complete as indicated by the original footnote (Lab Exhibit 7.4.3).

4. Change cells C10 and D10 so that they refer to the beginning WIP completion percentages. When using the FIFO method, we track the work needed to complete beginning work-in-process units. Thus, we must subtract these percentages from 100 percent to calculate the work performed this period. In cell D10, add the formula =B10*(1-D15) (Lab Exhibit 7.4.4). Beginning WIP is 100 percent and 50 percent complete for direct materials and conversion costs, respectively. To complete those units during the current period, Family Frames must finish the remaining 0 percent for direct materials (cell C10) and 50 percent for conversion costs (cell D10).

5. Similarly, change cells C13 and D13 to refer to cells C16 and D16. In cell D13, use the formula =B13*D16. These changes allow us to quickly determine how changes in the estimated completion of units alter process-costing calculations (Lab Exhibit 7.4.5). Notice that the formula is different for ending WIP units than for beginning WIP units. Why? We're focused on the work done this period. For beginning WIP units, we're focused on the work that must be performed this period to complete units started in a prior period. Ending WIP units were started in the current period, so percentages in Row 16 refer to the work done this period.

Analysis Task #2: Determine the Effect of Completion Percent on Income

1. To the right of the process-costing template, you will find a simple income statement for Family Frames. To complete the income statement, you will need to fill in cost of goods sold (COGS) in Row 6.

   For this exercise, we will assume that all costs transferred out of production are completed and sold. Accordingly, set cell G6 equal to cell B31 (Lab Exhibit 7.4.6).

2. Management cannot easily alter beginning WIP completion, which must equal ending WIP completion from the prior period. Because direct materials are added at the beginning of the production process, there is also no judgment involved with direct materials completion percentage. However, management must provide an estimate of the completion percentage for conversion costs. Change cell D15 to determine how this estimate impacts the process-costing template as well as operating income. You should see that a higher estimate increases operating income. After noting the differences, change cell D15 back to "50%".

3. As noted above, the CEO of Family Frames receives a substantial bonus if operating income is at least $1,000,000 for the year. Let's use goal-seek analysis to determine how we can alter the ending WIP completion percent to achieve this goal.

In the **Data** tab, select **What-If Analysis > Goal Seek...** (Lab Exhibit 7.4.7).

In the **Goal Seek** dialog box, set **Set cell** to G9. Set **To value** to $1,000,000. Set **By changing cell** to D16 (Lab Exhibit 7.4.8).

Your analysis should indicate that an estimate of approximately 38 percent is needed for the CEO to achieve her bonus (Lab Exhibit 7.4.9, Row 16). Increasing the percentage completed estimate increases the number of equivalent units, which decreases the cost per equivalent unit. Increasing the percentage also shifts costs from cost of goods sold, which is a current-period expense, to ending work-in-process inventory, which is an asset.

4. Consider the significance of this result. Family Frames has 30,000 frames in ending work-in-process at various stages of completion (see Row 13 of Exhibit 7.4.9). It is probably difficult, and perhaps even impossible, to determine exactly how complete the average unit is at the end of the period, which is why estimates are needed. What would stop a manager who wants to achieve a given target from altering these estimates? Would an auditor know enough about the production of gilded picture frames to challenge this estimate?

Also, note that this boost in income is temporary. By categorizing additional costs as inventory rather than cost of goods sold, Family Frames is deferring expenses to future periods. To continue to increase income in future periods, management will have to increase the estimated completion of ending work-in-process each year. Because a company cannot exceed 100% completion, this method of fudging the numbers is limited. The additional income will be reversed in future periods as inventory is sold. So, although management may be tempted to alter estimates in order to achieve performance targets, this tactic is fraudulent to the extent that it misleads investors, and it will not result in increased profits overall.

Share the Story

We have seen how process costing relies on estimates and how management can strategically alter these estimates to influence accounting performance. By increasing the estimated percentage complete for work-in-process units, companies can recognize a greater proportion of costs as inventory (to be expensed in future periods) rather than cost of finished goods (which are expensed in the current period if sold).

Unfortunately, because of the judgment inherent in these estimates, it can be difficult to determine whether management is accurately reporting performance. However, the extent to which management can use process-costing estimates to mislead investors is limited because all deferred costs will eventually be expensed when inventory is sold in future periods.

Assessment

1. Take a screenshot of the spreadsheet following the final step, paste it into a Word document, and label it "Lab 7.4 Submission.docx".
2. Answer the questions in Connect based on your spreadsheet and upload your Lab 7.4 Submission.docx via Connect if assigned.

Boosting Net Income with Process Costing

Keywords

Process Costing, Process Costing Methods, Ethics

Required

Replicate the Analysis Tasks from Lab 7.4 using the **Alt Lab 7.4 Data.xlsx** dataset, which contains Family Frames' process-costing and income-statement data for another year.

Family Frames had 50,000 units in beginning work-in-process inventory. Costs incurred for these units include $176,000 for direct materials and $70,000 for conversion costs. The production manager estimates that beginning work-in-process inventory is 100 percent complete with respect to direct materials and 30 percent complete with respect to conversion costs.

During the year, 270,000 additional units were started and 240,000 units were completed. Costs added to the process totaled $1,150,000 in direct materials and $538,000 in conversion costs. The production manager estimates that ending work-in-process inventory is 100 percent complete with respect to direct materials and 40 percent complete with respect to conversion costs.

You have been provided a completed template for Family Frames' process-costing report, which uses the FIFO method. You have also been provided with a partially completed income statement.

Assessment

1. Take a screenshot of the spreadsheet following the final step, paste it into a Word document, and label it "Alt Lab 7.4 Submission.docx".
2. Answer the questions in Connect based on your spreadsheet and upload your Alt Lab 7.4 Submission.docx via Connect if assigned.

Identifying Anomalies and Trends with Data Visualizations

Data Analytics Types: Descriptive Analytics, Diagnostic Analytics, Prescriptive Analytics

DATA VISUALIZATION

Keywords

Production Costs, Anomaly Identification, Trend Analysis

Decision-Making Context

Management accountants can use accounting information to identify anomalies in data. It's important to note that anomalies do not necessarily indicate that a problem exists. Rather, anomalies indicate items that merit additional investigation before companies take strategic actions. Thus, anomaly identification is an important first step in data analytics within cost accounting.

Management accountants also use trend analysis to determine whether changes in strategy are necessary. Trend analysis is particularly relevant for cost data.

Enduraplanx (a fictitious company) makes composite decking out of recycled materials. This wood-like material is exceptionally durable as well as environmentally friendly. As a result, Enduraplanx has experienced rapid growth and strong demand for its products. Enduraplanx produces its products in several countries but sells exclusively in the United States. The company has generally expanded production overseas due to lower production costs there, even though producing products internationally substantially increases the time it takes to ship product to customers. All shipping costs are borne by customers. Enduraplanx uses a process-costing system.

Required

Create data visualizations to identify data anomalies and visualize trends in production costs and delivery times.

Ask the Question

Increasing fixed capacity is often associated with increases in conversion costs. Can Enduraplanx use data visualizations to determine months with increased conversion costs that are unrelated to increases in fixed capacity? In addition, what do cost trends in overseas operations suggest about potential production strategies?

Master the Data

Here is the data dictionary for **Lab 7.5 Data.xlsx**.

Data Dictionary

Month	Indicates month and year
Unit Sales	Monthly sales in units. A unit is 1,000 board feet.
Unit Selling Price	Selling price per 1,000 board feet
US_Direct Materials	Direct materials cost per unit of U.S. production

---

US_Conversion Costs	Conversion cost per unit of U.S. production
US_Capacity	Unit capacity in U.S.
US_Lead time	Average days between start of production and delivery in the U.S.
BR_Direct Materials	Direct materials cost per unit of Brazil production
BR_Conversion Costs	Conversion cost per unit of Brazil production
BR_Capacity	Unit capacity in Brazil
BR_Lead time	Average days between start of production and delivery in Brazil

Perform the Analysis

Create data visualizations to identify data anomalies and visualize trends in production costs and delivery times.

Open Tableau and connect to Excel file **Lab 7.5 Data.xlsx**. We're now ready to perform the analysis.

Analysis Task #1: Identify Anomalies Using Scatterplots

1. Double-click on **Sheet 1** and replace the label with "US Capacity and CC".
2. To create the first scatterplot, double-click on **Month** under the **Tables** heading in the **Data** pane. This will place the month pill in the **Columns** shelf. Click the + next to YEAR to see more granular data. Click the + near QUARTER to see monthly data (Lab Exhibit 7.5T.1). The + sign turns into a – sign after it is clicked.
3. Drag the **US Capacity** and **US Conversion Costs** pills to the **Rows** shelf (Lab Exhibit 7.5T.2).
4. Click the **Show Me** tab in the upper-right corner of the screen and select the circle views icon (Lab Exhibit 7.5T.3).

   Notice that as capacity increases, there is a corresponding uptick in per-unit conversion costs (Lab Exhibit 7.5T.4). In other words, when the company invests in excess capacity through larger plants or more equipment, conversion costs immediately increase.
5. Create a new worksheet by clicking on the icon indicated in Lab Exhibit 7.5T.5. Name it "Brazil Capacity and CC".
6. Repeat Steps 1–4 using production data from the Brazilian manufacturing facility. Lab Exhibit 7.5T.6 shows the resulting data visualization.

   Notice that there are several spikes in conversion costs that do not correspond with investments in capacity. These data points merit additional investigation to determine potential causes of increased costs.
7. Create a new dashboard by clicking on the icon shown in Lab Exhibit 7.5T.7. Name the dashboard "Capacity and CC".
8. Drag your two sheets to the dashboard so that you can easily compare the U.S. capacity and conversion costs to the Brazil capacity and conversion costs (Lab Exhibit 7.5T.8).

Analysis Task #2: Create Variables to Calculate Total Cost

1. Create a new worksheet.
2. Our dataset contains direct materials and conversion cost data. To calculate total unit costs, we must create a calculated variable that adds the two together. To calculate

this variable, click on the **Analysis** menu item and then select **Create Calculated Field...** (Lab Exhibit 7.5T.9).

3. Calculate US Unit Cost by adding US Direct Materials and US Conversion Costs, using the formula shown in Lab Exhibit 7.5T.10: [US Direct Materials]+[US Conversion Costs]. The pills on the left of the screen can be dragged to the calculation pane to avoid typing in the variable names. Type the + sign between the variables.

4. Repeat this step to calculate the Brazilian production cost per unit. Name the new variable "BR Unit Cost".

Analysis Task #3: Use Data Visualizations to Analyze Cost Trends

1. Create a new worksheet and name it "Cost Trends".
2. Double-click on **Month**, **US Unit Cost**, and **BR Unit Cost** to add them to the **Columns** and **Measure Values** (Lab Exhibit 7.5T.11).
3. In the **Show Me** pane, select the lines continuous option by clicking on the icon indicated in Lab Exhibit 7.5T.12.
4. Click the + icon next to Year until "Month" is displayed (rather than year, quarter, or week). See Lab Exhibit 7.5T.13.
5. For this visualization, we want the lines to appear in the same pane. This is acceptable because the scale of each variable is similar (that is, they have similar unit costs). To combine these windows, hover over **BR Unit Cost** until a green triangle appears in the upper-left corner (Lab Exhibit 7.5T.14).
6. Click and drag the triangle to the US Unit Cost window. Doing so will combine both variables into a single window (Lab Exhibit 7.5T.15). The resulting visualization is shown in Lab Exhibit 7.5T.16.
7. Analyze the difference in costs between U.S. and Brazilian operations. It appears from the graph that costs are steadily increasing in both countries. However, the rate of cost increase appears to be greater in the United States. These data can help Enduraplanx determine whether it should continue production in the Brazilian facility.

Analysis Task #4: Determine the Average Lead Times for Each Year of U.S. and Overseas Production

1. Create a new worksheet. Name it "Lead time".
2. Double-click on **Month**, **US Lead time**, and **BR Lead time**. (See Analysis Task #3.)
3. As you did in Analysis Task #3, use a continuous line graph and combine the two lines into a single window. Note that for this chart, we want to display data on an annual rather than monthly basis. Lab Exhibit 7.5T.17 shows the data visualization.
4. The default measure is the sum of the lead times. Because we want to analyze average monthly lead times, we must change the measure of the variable. In the **Measure Values** pane, click the triangle next to **BR Lead time**, then click **Measure**, then **Average** (Lab Exhibit 7.5T.18).
5. Repeat Step 4 to determine average US lead time. Lab Exhibit 7.5T.19 shows the result.
    Hovering over either line will display average lead time for country and year.

Share the Story

Our analysis identified months that had increased conversion costs unrelated to increases in fixed capacity. These anomalies require further investigation. If Enduraplanx can determine the cause of the anomalies, it may be able to identify potential solutions to control the increased cost. In addition, our analysis shows a clear and persistent difference in cost between U.S. and Brazilian production, which may indicate that Brazilian production should continue in the future.

Assessment

1. Take screenshots of the Capacity and CC dashboard, the Cost Trends worksheet, and the Lead Time worksheet, and copy each into a Word file. Label each screenshot in the Word file. Save the Word file as "Lab 7.5 Tableau Submission.docx."
2. Answer the questions in Connect and upload your Lab 7.5 Submission.docx via Connect if assigned.

Identifying Anomalies and Trends with Data Visualizations

Data Analytics Types: Descriptive Analytics, Diagnostic Analytics, Prescriptive Analytics

Lab Note: The tools presented in this lab periodically change. Updated instructions, if applicable, can be found in the student and instructor support materials. All Lab Exhibits are available within the eBook and in Connect.

DATA VISUALIZATION

Keywords

Production Costs, Anomaly Identification, Trend Analysis

Decision-Making Context

Management accountants can use accounting information to identify anomalies in data. It's important to note that anomalies do not necessarily indicate that a problem exists. Rather, anomalies indicate items that merit additional investigation before companies take strategic actions. Thus, anomaly identification is an important first step in data analytics within cost accounting.

Management accountants also use trend analysis to determine whether changes in strategy are necessary. Trend analysis is particularly relevant for cost data.

Enduraplanx (a fictitious company) makes composite decking out of recycled materials. This wood-like material is exceptionally durable as well as environmentally friendly. As a result, Enduraplanx has experienced rapid growth and strong demand for its products. Enduraplanx produces its products in several countries but sells exclusively in the United States. The company has generally expanded production overseas due to lower production costs there, even though producing products internationally substantially increases the time it takes to ship product to customers. All shipping costs are borne by customers. Enduraplanx uses a process-costing system.

Required

Create data visualizations to identify data anomalies and visualize trends in production costs and delivery times.

Ask the Question

Increasing fixed capacity is often associated with increases in conversion costs. Can Enduraplanx use data visualizations to determine months with increased conversion costs that are unrelated to increases in fixed capacity? In addition, what do cost trends in overseas operations suggest about potential production strategies?

Master the Data

Here is the data dictionary for **Lab 7.5 Data.xlsx**.

Data Dictionary

Month	Indicates month and year
Unit Sales	Monthly sales in units. A unit is 1,000 board feet.
Unit Selling Price	Selling price per 1,000 board feet
US_Direct Materials	Direct materials cost per unit of U.S. production

US_Conversion Costs	Conversion cost per unit of U.S. production
US_Capacity	Unit capacity in U.S.
US_Lead time	Average days between start of production and delivery in the U.S.
BR_Direct Materials	Direct materials cost per unit of Brazil production
BR_Conversion Costs	Conversion cost per unit of Brazil production
BR_Capacity	Unit capacity in Brazil
BR_Lead time	Average days between start of production and delivery in Brazil

Open Power BI and connect to Excel file **Lab 7.5 Data.xlsx**. We're now ready to perform the analysis.

Perform the Analysis

Create data visualizations to identify data anomalies and visualize trends in production costs and delivery times.

Analysis Task #1: Identify Anomalies Using Scatterplots

1. Double-click on **Page 1** (Lab Exhibit 7.5P.1) and replace the label with "US Capacity and CC".
2. To create the first scatterplot, drag **Month** onto the report canvas (Lab Exhibit 7.5P.2). Deselect **Day** from the **Fields** pane (Lab Exhibit 7.5P.3). Do this step twice. Lab Exhibit 7.5P.4 shows what the screen looks like after you've completed these steps.
3. Drag **US_Capacity** onto one of the **Month** charts in the report canvas (Lab Exhibit 7.5P.5). Drag **US_Conversion Costs** onto the other. Lab Exhibit 7.5P.6 shows the result.
4. Next, select the icon for scatter chart in the **Visualizations** tab (Lab Exhibit 7.5P.7). Make sure **Month** is in the **X-Axis** and **US_Conversion Costs** and **US_Capacity** are in the **Y-Axis** in their respective charts (see bottom of Lab Exhibit 7.5P.7).
5. Right-click on both visualizations and click on **Expand to next level** twice (Lab Exhibit 7.5P.8) to show the scatterplots with a monthly view (Lab Exhibit 7.5P.9).

   Notice that as capacity increases, there is a corresponding uptick in per-unit conversion costs.
6. Create a new worksheet. Name it "Brazil Capacity and CC" (Lab Exhibit 7.5P.10).
7. Repeat Steps 1–5 using production data from the Brazilian manufacturing facility. Lab Exhibit 7.5P.11 shows the resulting scatterplot.

   Notice that there are several spikes in conversion costs that do not correspond with investments in capacity. These data points merit additional investigation to determine potential causes of increased costs.
8. Create a new page and name it "Capacity and CC." Copy and paste all the visualizations into another page so you can easily compare the U.S. to Brazil capacity and conversion costs. Lab Exhibit 7.5P.12 shows the completed dashboard.

Analysis Task #2: Create Variables to Calculate Total Cost

1. Create a new worksheet.
2. Our dataset contains direct materials data and conversion cost data. To calculate total unit costs, we must create a calculated variable that adds the two together. To calculate this variable, click on the **Modeling** menu item and then the **New Column** icon (Lab Exhibit 7.5P.13).

3. Calculate **US Unit Cost** by adding **US Direct Materials** and **US Conversion Costs**. The pills on the left of the screen can be dragged to the **Calculation Pane** to avoid typing in the variable names, but you will have to add the + sign (Lab Exhibit 7.5P.14).

```
✕  ✓  1  US Unit Cost = [US_Direct Materials]+[US_Conversion Costs]
```

Lab Exhibit 7.5P.14

Microsoft Power BI

4. Repeat this step to calculate the Brazilian production cost per unit. Name the new variable "BR Unit Cost" (Lab Exhibit 7.5P.15).

```
✕  ✓  1  BR Unit Cost = [BR_Direct Materials] + [BR_Conversion Costs]
```

Lab Exhibit 7.5P.15

Microsoft Power BI

Analysis Task #3: Use Data Visualizations to Analyze Cost Trends

1. Label your new worksheet "Cost Trends".
2. Select **Month, US Unit Cost,** and **BR Unit Cost**. Deselect **day, month,** and **quarter** to show only **Year** (Lab Exhibit 7.5P.16). The final result is shown in Lab Exhibit 7.5P.17.
3. In **Visualizations** pane, select the **line chart** icon, as shown in Lab Exhibit 7.5P.18.
4. In the **X-axis** field, click the **Month** drop-down and make sure **Month** is selected, not **Date Hierarchy** (Lab Exhibit 7.5P.19).
5. Analyze the difference in costs between U.S. and Brazilian operations. These data can help Enduraplanx identify cost differences and whether they should continue production in the Brazilian facility. Lab Exhibit 7.5P.20 shows the final result.

Analysis Task #4: Determine the Average Lead Times for Each Year of U.S. and Overseas Production

1. Create a new page. Name it "Lead time". Select **Month, US Lead time,** and **BR Lead time** (Lab Exhibit 7.5P.21).
2. As you did in Analysis Task #3, create a line graph. Note that for this chart, we want to display data on an annual rather than monthly basis. Lab Exhibit 7.5P.22 shows the final line graph.
3. The default measure is the sum of the lead times. Because we want to analyze average monthly lead times, we must change the measure of the variable. Select the drop-down of each variable on the **Y-axis** and change it from **Sum** to **Average** (Lab Exhibit 7.5P.23).
4. The final line graph appears in Lab Exhibit 7.5P.24. Hovering over either line will display average lead time for country and year.

Share the Story

Our analysis identified months that had increased conversion costs unrelated to increases in fixed capacity. These anomalies require further investigation. If Enduraplanx can determine the cause of the anomalies, it may be able to identify potential solutions to control the increased cost. In addition, our analysis shows a clear and persistent difference in cost between U.S. and Brazilian production, which may indicate that Brazilian production should continue in the future.

Assessment

1. Take screenshots of the Capacity and CC dashboard, the Cost Trends worksheet, and the Lead Time worksheet, and copy each into a Word file. Label each screenshot in the Word file. Save the Word file as "Lab 7.5 Power BI Submission.docx."
2. Answer the questions in Connect and upload your Lab 7.5 Submission.docx via Connect if assigned.

Alternate Lab 7.5   Tableau/Power BI—On Your Own

Identifying Anomalies and Trends with Data Visualizations

Keywords

Production Costs, Anomaly Identification, Trend Analysis

Using either Tableau or Power BI, apply the same steps in Lab 7.5 to the **Alt Lab 7.5 Data.xlsx** dataset. These data are from the same time period, but they compare U.S. cost data with data from Enduraplanx's Malaysian production facility.

Required

Create data visualizations to identify data anomalies and visualize trends in production costs and delivery times.

Data Dictionary

Month	Indicates month and year
Unit Sales	Monthly sales in units. A unit is 1,000 board feet.
Unit Selling Price	Selling price per 1,000 board feet
US_Direct Materials	Direct materials cost per unit of U.S. production
US_Conversion Costs	Conversion cost per unit of U.S. production
US_Capacity	Unit capacity in U.S.
US_Lead time	Average days between start of production and delivery in the U.S.
MY_Direct Materials	Direct materials cost per unit of Malaysia production
MY_Conversion Costs	Conversion cost per unit of Malaysia production
MY_Capacity	Unit capacity in Malaysia
MY_Lead time	Average days between start of production and delivery in Malaysia

---

Assessment

1. Take screenshots of the Capacity and CC dashboard, the Cost Trends worksheet, and the Lead Time worksheet, and copy each into a Word file. Label each screenshot in the Word file. Save the Word file as "Alt Lab 7.5 Submission.docx".
2. Answer the questions in Connect and upload your Alt Lab 7.5 Submission.docx via Connect if assigned.

Chapter 8

Performance Measurement and Control

A Look at This Chapter

This chapter considers the different management control systems that organizations implement to direct employee behavior and organizational performance. After explaining different organizational structures, the chapter focuses on financial performance measures that organizations can use to evaluate overall performance and to compare the performance of individual business units. It closes by considering how organizations can use transfer pricing to foster coordination among business units, which helps manage organizational performance.

Cost Accounting and Data Analytics

COST ACCOUNTING LEARNING OBJECTIVE	RELATED DATA ANALYTICS LABS	LAB ANALYTICS TYPE(S)
LO 8.1 Describe the purpose of a management control system.		
LO 8.2 Summarize the difference between a centralized organizational structure and a decentralized organizational structure.		
LO 8.3 Describe the different types of responsibility centers.		
LO 8.4 Identify the characteristics of effective performance measures.		
LO 8.5 Calculate ROI, RI, and EVA and describe their use.	**Data Analytics Mini-Lab** Using Data Visualization to Compare Business Segments Based on ROI and Residual Income	Descriptive, Diagnostic
	LAB 8.1 Excel Evaluating Business Units Using ROI	Descriptive

Cost Accounting and Data Analytics (*continued*)

COST ACCOUNTING LEARNING OBJECTIVE	RELATED DATA ANALYTICS LABS	LAB ANALYTICS TYPE(S)
	LAB 8.2 **Tableau** Comparing Different Financial Performance Measures across Business Units	Descriptive, Diagnostic
	LAB 8.3 **Excel** Incentivizing Performance with Budget Plans (Heartwood)	Descriptive, Diagnostic
LO 8.6 Explain how decentralized organizations use transfer pricing.	LAB 8.4 **Excel** Comparing the Effects of Transfer Prices across Tax Jurisdictions	Predictive
	LAB 8.5 **Power BI** Using Visualization to Compare Corporate Tax Rates	Descriptive

Chapter Concepts and Career Skills

Learning About . . .	Helps with These Career Skills
Management control systems	• Motivating and directing employee behavior • Accessing information for strategic decision making
Centralized and decentralized organizations	• Determining who should have decision-making authority in the organization and the implications of those choices
Responsibility centers	• Understanding managers' roles, responsibilities, and incentives
Performance measurement	• Determining whether the organization is meeting its goals • Understanding how incentives motivate employees
Financial performance measures, including return on investment, residual income, and economic value added	• Evaluating the organization's financial performance
Transfer pricing	• Coordinating costs across business units • Minimizing tax obligations in multinational organizations

Decentralized Control at Johnson & Johnson

Johnson & Johnson (J&J) is the world's largest healthcare company.[1] It develops and manufactures a wide variety of consumer health products (for example, Neutrogena and Aveeno products), medical devices (for example, artificial joints), and pharmaceutical products (for example, cancer therapies and a COVID-19 vaccine). It employs approximately 134,500 people across the globe.

J&J is well known for its decentralized structure. While an executive committee oversees the entire organization, senior management is responsible for the strategic plans and operations of each operating company. Thanks to this

[1]"About Johnson & Johnson," Johnson & Johnson, www.jnj.com/about-jnj (accessed May 17, 2021).

Golden Shrimp/Shutterstock

decentralized structure, individual companies under the J&J umbrella are able to make operating decisions that they believe will allow them to provide maximum value to their respective customer bases.[2] J&J believes that the managers who are closest to the customers are in the best position to understand and address those customers' needs, and it has credited its decentralized structure with sparking innovation and insulating itself against economic downturns.[3]

According to the Johnson & Johnson webpage, the company is guided by its "Credo," a management document created by former chairman Robert Wood Johnson.[4] The Credo sets forth J&J's core values and describes the company's responsibilities to the people and communities it serves. A document or philosophy such as Johnson and Johnson's Credo serves as an important informal control in guiding the decisions and behaviors of the company's employees.

Source: Johnson & Johnson, www.jnj.com/.

[2]Johnson & Johnson, *2020 Annual Report,* March 2021, www.investor.jnj.com/annual-meeting-materials/2020-annual-report.
[3]KKing, "Johnson & Johnson," *Digital Initiative,* December 8, 2015, https://digital.hbs.edu/platform-rctom/submission/johnson-johnson/.
[4]"Our Credo," Johnson & Johnson, www.jnj.com/credo/.

MANAGEMENT CONTROL SYSTEMS

As organizations strive to create value, they need explicit rules, processes, performance information, and incentives to direct employees' attention and effort toward the achievement of organizational goals. A **management control system** is a set of rules, activities, and information that an organization uses to make and execute planning and control decisions and to direct employee behavior. The individual control activities that comprise a management control system can vary widely from organization to organization. They are selected on the basis of a variety of factors, including cost, need, and management style.

Formal Controls and Informal Controls

Management controls can be classified several different ways. One common classification is formal controls versus informal controls. **Formal controls** are the explicit rules, procedures, safeguards, and incentive plans employed in the organization. They also include the information systems that provide the data necessary for strategic decision making. These systems include the following:

- The **cost accounting system** aggregates, monitors, and reports information about revenues, costs, and profitability through the use of forms, processes, controls, and reports.
- The **human resources management system** helps the organization manage all aspects of human resources, including compliance with employment laws. It includes information about compensation and benefits, time and attendance, and employee training.
- The **quality management system** records and tracks product quality, including production, defects, and customer service data, such as late deliveries and product ratings.

LO 8.1

Describe the purpose of a management control system.

management control system
A set of rules, activities, and information that an organization uses to make and execute planning and control decisions and to direct employee behavior.

formal controls
The explicit rules, procedures, safeguards, incentive plans, and information systems employed in an organization.

CAREER SKILLS

Learning about management control systems supports these career skills:

- Motivating and directing employee behavior
- Accessing information for strategic decision making

cost accounting system

The system that aggregates, monitors, and reports information about revenues, costs, and profitability through the use of forms, processes, controls, and reports.

human resources management system

The system that helps the organization manage all aspects of human resources, including compliance with employment laws. It includes information about compensation and benefits, time and attendance, and employee training.

LO 8.2

Summarize the difference between a centralized organizational structure and a decentralized organizational structure.

Informal controls are an organization's norms, morals, ethical values, and shared culture, which all guide employees' behavior and strategic decision making. For example, **Workiva**, which provides cloud-based data solutions for its customers, is known for its open communication among employees. Giving and receiving feedback, open and supportive debate, and leadership by example are key aspects of its culture, and employees who exemplify these traits are rewarded with advancement and promotion.[5]

Similarly, **Johnson & Johnson**'s Credo, described in the chapter-opening story, is a key informal control for that organization. For example, the Credo recognizes that J&J has a responsibility to provide quality products to the patients and doctors who use them. This overarching principle guides the company's employees to take care when developing, producing, and distributing products. Employees should not cut corners or ignore safety standards.

Behavior Controls and Output Controls

There are other ways to classify controls. For example, controls can be categorized as behavior controls or output controls. **Behavior controls** direct or restrict the way employees carry out their jobs. For example, some jobs include standard operating procedures that dictate each step that employees must complete in a specific order as they perform their jobs. **Output controls** measure the results of employees' work and evaluate their performance. For example, salespeople are allowed flexibility with how they work with customers to make the sale, but their supervisors review monthly sales reports to determine whether each salesperson made enough sales during the month.

 PROGRESS CHECK

1. What is a management control system? What is its purpose?
2. What is the difference between formal controls and informal controls?
3. Do you think organizations need both formal and informal controls to operate effectively? Defend your answer.

CENTRALIZED VERSUS DECENTRALIZED OPERATIONS

When designing the management control system, managers must consider the structure of the organization. In **decentralized organizations**, senior management delegates a significant amount of decision-making authority and responsibility to business unit (or subunit) managers. That is, business unit managers have **autonomy**, or freedom to make the decisions they think will be best for their business unit. For example, as we saw in the chapter-opening story, **Johnson & Johnson**'s senior management has delegated operating decisions and responsibilities to management of the consumer health products, medical devices, and pharmaceutical products divisions.

In contrast, in **centralized organizations**, senior management maintains decision-making and control responsibilities. Retail organizations often use a centralized management structure.

[5]Bailey Reiners, "21 Company Culture Examples to Get You Inspired," builtin, March 29, 2023, https://builtin.com/company-culture/company-culture-examples; "Who We Are," Workiva, www.workiva.com/about/our-story; Brian Nordli, "Why Workiva Encourages Debate in the Office to Cultivate Teamwork," builtin, April 30, 2018, www.builtincolorado.com/2018/04/30/Workiva-Leadership-Spotlight.

For example, the retail giant **Target** has centralized teams based on specialized expertise (for example, technology, brands, marketing). Major decisions are made at its headquarters in Minneapolis, MN. Target also takes a channel-agnostic approach to sales, meaning that the customer experience is relatively standardized regardless of whether the customer is purchasing online or in-store.[6] The key benefit of a centralized organization is that top management retains control of important decisions, allowing it to leverage its extensive management knowledge and expertise to coordinate activities across the various business units. The primary drawback is that the decisions are made by decision makers who are not close to the customers. If an organization has a diverse customer base, then those decisions may not benefit certain groups of customers.

Organizations choose the extent to which a centralized, decentralized, or hybrid structure works best for their strategy. Exhibit 8.1 shows two possible organizational structures of a fictitious company that develops and manufactures electronic technology. The company has three main lines of business: consumer electronics, automotive, and industrial devices. If it chooses a decentralized organizational structure, each of these sub-units will have its own sales and marketing, research and development, and manufacturing departments. Managers for each sub-unit will make their own decisions about how those departments operate and are controlled.

With a centralized organizational structure, all departments and sub-units report to the president. Operating and controlling decisions are made by the president and executive team. Note, too, that even in a decentralized organization, certain activities such as finance and operations remain centralized under senior management. Why? Senior management may have significantly more knowledge and expertise in these areas, and coordinating activities centrally may improve the opportunities and financing terms available to the entire organization.

Human Dimensions: Benefits and Challenges of Decentralization

As an organization chooses its structure, it must weigh the costs and benefits of each approach. A decentralized organization offers the following benefits:

1. **Business units can be more responsive to customers, suppliers, and employees.** A decentralized structure gives decision-making responsibilities to the managers who are most in tune with the needs and preferences of the company's customers, suppliers, and employees. Not only do business-unit managers know what these parties want, but they can also respond to those needs quickly because decisions do not have to be approved at higher levels of the organization. For example, business-unit managers can set or change the price of products to make a sale to a preferred customer, or they could choose to carry a different brand of product that their customers prefer. Similarly, if business-unit managers find that they cannot hire enough employees at their current hourly wage, they can increase wages to attract new talent.

   Even companies like **McDonald's**, which most of us think of as having a uniform customer experience, can take a decentralized approach. In fact, McDonald's serves different menu items in different regions and countries across the world (Exhibit 8.2). If you travel to Korea, you can try the bulgogi burger. In Spain you can enjoy toast with oil and tomato. When dining in Hawaii, you can order the Spam, rice, and egg plate for breakfast. Marketing and advertising campaigns also differ with locale because local management chooses how best to connect with its customers.

[6]"Target Shares Roadmap to Transform Business," press release, March 3, 2015, https://corporate.target.com/press/releases/2015/03/target-shares-roadmap-to-transform-business.

CAREER SKILLS
Learning about centralized and decentralized organizations supports this career skill:
• Determining who should have decision-making authority in the organization and the implications of those choices

quality management system
The system that records and tracks product quality, including production, defects, and customer service data, such as late deliveries and product ratings.

informal controls
An organization's norms, morals, ethical values, and shared culture, which all guide employees' behavior and strategic decision making.

behavior controls
Control activities that direct or restrict the way employees carry out their jobs.

output controls
Control activities that measure the results of employees' work and evaluate employee performance.

decentralized organization
An organizational structure in which senior management delegates a significant amount of decision-making authority and responsibility to business-unit (or sub-unit) managers.

Decentralized Structure

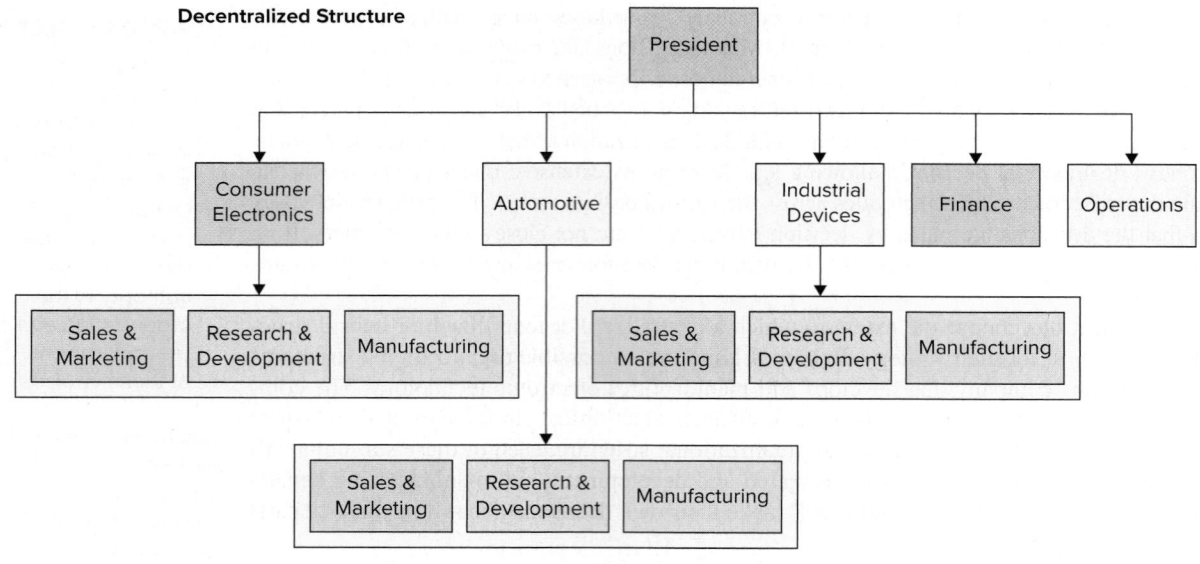

Centralized Structure

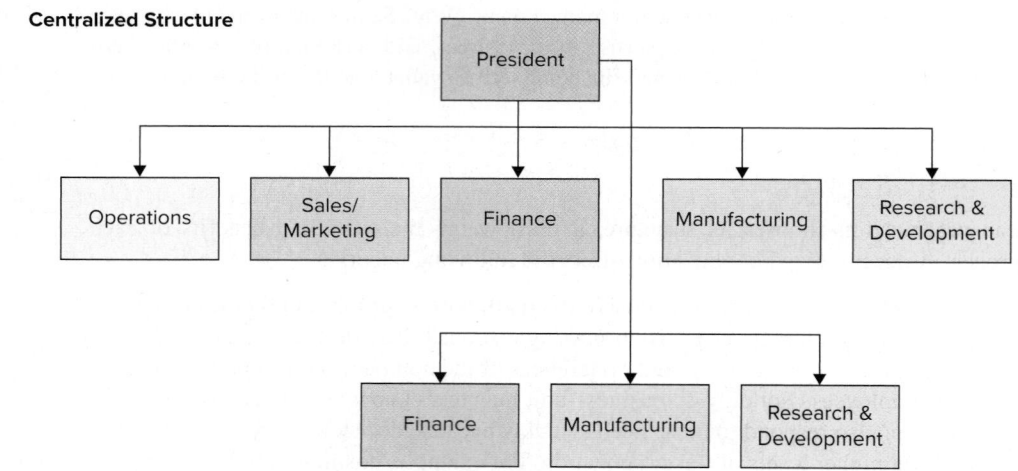

Exhibit 8.1

Examples of Decentralized and Centralized Organization

McGraw Hill

autonomy
Freedom to make
decisions.

**centralized
organization**
An organizational struc-
ture in which senior
management maintains
decision-making and
control responsibilities.

2. **Business-unit managers may be more motivated by performance measures.** As we discuss later in this chapter, organizations use performance measures to evaluate their employees' activities and decisions. Performance measures are most effective in motivating managers to work hard when they are based on activities within the manager's control. When business units are treated as separate operating divisions, the desired outcomes are more likely than when there is centralized control. For this reason, business-unit managers are likely to work harder when the business unit is treated as a separate operating division.

3. **Business-unit managers receive training and advancement opportunities.** Giving business-unit managers the autonomy to make strategic and operational decisions for their business and holding them responsible for the results helps them develop their

Country	Menu Item	Description
Canada	Poutine	French fries with gravy and cheese curds
Hong Kong	Ham N' Egg Twisty Pasta	Bowl filled with pasta, vegetables, ham or sausage, and egg
India	Maharaja Mac	Two vegetarian beef patties with all the fixings
Korea	McChicken Mozzarella	Chicken sandwich topped with fried mozzarella sticks
Japan	Gracoro Burger	Macaroni patty with a breadcrumb crust and a prawn and white sauce
Philippines	Chicken McDo with Spaghetti	Fried chicken drumstick served with a side of spaghetti
Malaysia	Bubu Ayam McD	Porridge made from chicken strips, onions, ginger, chilies, and shallots
Singapore	Samurai Burger	Lettuce and creamy mayonnaise on top of a quarter pound beef patty dipped in teriyaki sauce
United Kingdom	Bacon Roll	Fried bacon on a roll, topped with ketchup or brown sauce

Exhibit 8.2
Menu Offerings at McDonald's around the World

expertise. This autonomy helps them develop the experience that allows them to be promoted to positions in senior management. The whole organization benefits when it promotes managers from within because such promotions help the company retain top talent, knowledge, and company culture. Employee morale improves, too.

4. **Senior management is free to focus on organization-level strategic decisions.** Because business-unit managers are responsible for business-unit decisions, senior management can focus on strategic decisions that affect the organization as a whole.

However, there are several drawbacks to decentralization.

1. **Business units may engage in dysfunctional competition.** In a decentralized organization, business-unit managers may see themselves as being in competition with other business-unit managers. This competition may lead them to prioritize the performance of their business unit over the success of the organization as a whole, and they may be unwilling to help other business units. The result can be **suboptimal decision making**. That is, decisions may benefit one business unit at the expense of the overall organization.

2. **Business units may duplicate activities, causing inefficient redundancies.** In decentralized organizations, some jobs and activities are done in each business unit. For example, each sub-unit will probably have its own IT department and may have its own human resources department. As a result, the overall organization will have more employees dedicated to these activities than it might need if all operations were centralized.

3. **Business units might find it difficult to coordinate activities and data across the organization.** When decisions are centralized, organizations can leverage their knowledge and power to their advantage. For example, larger organizations may have more power to influence the prices they pay vendors for supplies. In a decentralized organization, business-unit managers may not have the knowledge or power to get preferred pricing. Also, when each business unit maintains its own data, it can be more difficult to make decisions that are optimal for the entire organization.

suboptimal decision making
Occurs when a decision benefits one business unit at the expense of the overall organization.

FROM THE FIELD

Keeping Business within the Organization

Recently, the chief information officer (CIO) at a multinational electronics company—let's call it ElectroTech—with a decentralized structure described one interesting drawback to this structure: The company was missing opportunities to cross-sell products to vendors across business units. ElectroTech had vendors from whom it bought component parts for production in Business Unit A, which also purchased and used products that ElectroTech produced and sold from Business Unit B. However, those vendors were not necessarily buying from ElectroTech. They were sourcing their parts elsewhere.

One of the challenges at ElectroTech was that each business unit collected and maintained its own customer and vendor data. So, salespeople in one business unit did not know about potential sales targets who were vendors for other business units. The CIO was working to develop a central solution to this problem. His plan consisted of four steps. First, he compiled a list of all vendors for each business unit. Second, he cross-referenced this list to publicly available data that reports which companies purchase commodities, products, and component parts from *any* vendor. Third, he identified which of ElectroTech's vendors were purchasing component parts from other vendors that ElectroTech could have sold to them. Finally, he provided this list of target customers to salespeople in the appropriate business units.

Thinking Critically

Suppose you work at ElectroTech, and the CIO has asked you to determine whether this new process is successful and worth the effort. What kind(s) of data would you need to collect and analyze to answer his question? What types of analysis would you want to perform? Explain.

⊘ PROGRESS CHECK

4. What is the difference between a centralized organization and a decentralized organization?
5. What are the benefits and drawbacks of decentralization?

LO 8.3

Describe the different types of responsibility centers.

responsibility center
A sub-unit of an organization that has its own goals and responsibilities. May be classified as a cost center, revenue center, profit center, or investment center.

COST, PROFIT, AND RESPONSIBILITY CENTERS

Each sub-unit in an organization can also be described as a **responsibility center**. There are four types of responsibility centers:

1. A **cost center** is a sub-unit that does not generate revenue but supports the business and incurs costs. For example, the customer service department at **Peloton** is a cost center. The manager of a cost center is responsible for the costs but not any of the revenue.
2. A **revenue center** is a sub-unit responsible for sales, which may be defined by the product line or the geographic region served. For example, Peloton may have separate revenue centers for bikes and treadmills. Managers of revenue centers are responsible for the sales from their specific sub-units.
3. In a **profit center**, the manager is responsible for both the costs and the revenues (sales) associated with that sub-unit. However, the manager is not given the authority to invest in capital assets.

4. In an **investment center**, the manager is responsible for the costs, revenues, and investment decisions. **Investments** are the assets or working capital used to generate income.

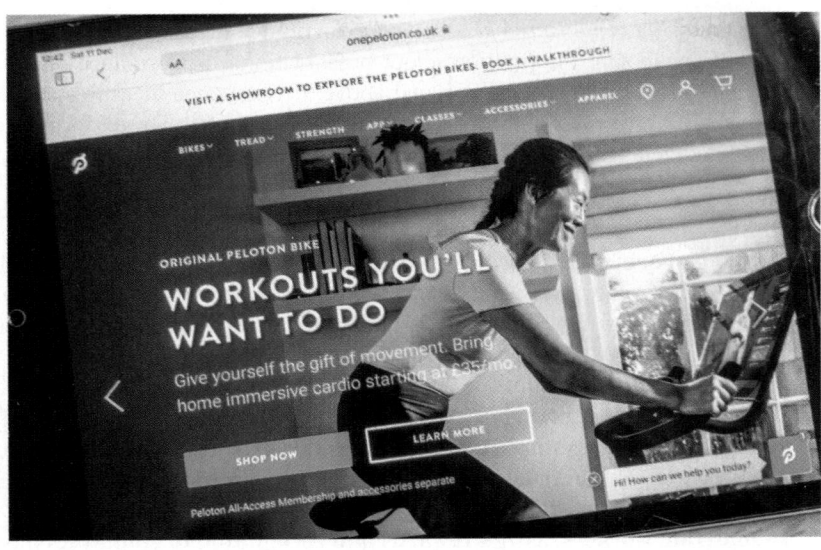

LDNPix/Alamy Stock Photo

cost center
A sub-unit that does not generate revenue but supports the business and incurs costs.

revenue center
A sub-unit responsible for sales, which may be defined by the product line or the geographic region served.

profit center
A sub-unit in which the manager is responsible for revenues and costs.

investment center
A sub-unit in which the manager is responsible for the costs, revenues, and investment decisions.

investments
The assets or working capital used to generate income.

Managers are accountable for activities specific to their responsibility center, and each type of responsibility center will use different performance measures for evaluation. For example:

1. In a cost center, the goal is to minimize costs. Cost-center managers should be evaluated based on whether they meet or fall below the preset target for maximum costs.
2. In a revenue center, managers should be evaluated on their ability to meet or exceed sales targets.
3. In a profit center, managers should be evaluated based on their ability to generate profit. They will have profitability goals, which they may be able to meet either by cutting costs or by increasing sales.
4. In an investment center, managers are also responsible for investment decisions, so their performance measures should include returns on funds invested.

How a responsibility center is classified is likely to have implications for managers' behavior. For example, a profit center's managers are evaluated based on the sub-unit's costs and revenues only, but they are not accountable for their use of assets. Thus, managers have an incentive to use their assets to increase profits. This might mean that a production manager at Peloton overuses a piece of equipment from the assembly line used to produce the bikes, thus degrading the equipment's value and threatening Peloton's ability to maintain production levels in the future. As another example, consider a cost center where managers are primarily evaluated on their ability to keep costs down. This evaluation system creates a disincentive for managers to spend money on improvements that are expensive today but could boost profitability in the future.

CAREER SKILLS

Learning about responsibility centers supports this career skill:

• Understanding managers' roles, responsibilities, and incentives

✓ PROGRESS CHECK

6. What are the four different types of responsibility centers?
7. What performance measures are used to evaluate each responsibility center?

LO 8.4

Identify the
characteristics
of effective
performance
measures.

ENVIRONMENTAL, SOCIAL,
GOVERNANCE

**performance
measurement**
The process of col-
lecting and analyzing
information about orga-
nizational performance
and comparing it to
expectations and goals.

THE IMPORTANCE OF PERFORMANCE MEASUREMENT

It is often said that *what is measured gets done*. **Performance measurement** is the process of collecting and analyzing information about organizational performance and comparing it to expectations and goals. As described above, performance measures should vary depending on the type of responsibility center. Establishing effective performance measures is critical and generally includes four steps:

Step 1. **Identify goals.** Organizations can have many different goals, including earning a profit, embracing sustainability, or achieving high customer-satisfaction scores.

Step 2. **Create performance measures that closely align with goals.** For example, if the goal is profitability, the performance measure may be the amount of sales made by each division. If the goal is high customer satisfaction, the performance measure might be the rating given on a customer satisfaction survey. For a sustainability goal, the organization may measure its energy consumption.

Step 3. **Create specific performance targets for employees related to each performance target (for example, monthly sales targets).** These targets will most likely vary by employee based on the employee's specific job and other factors, such as location or historic performance.

Step 4. **To motivate workers, assign rewards and recognition to employees based on their achievement of these performance targets.** Awards and recognition could include bonuses for achieving sales targets and employee-of-the-month designations.

Human Implications of Performance Measures

Are all performance measures useful? Definitely not! Performance measures are most effective when:

- The organization knows the desired results.
- The results can be clearly measured in a timely manner.
- The results are attainable *and* controllable by the employees responsible for the performance.

For example, at Athens Motors, a fictitious local car dealership, management has determined that its number-one goal is profitability. To meet that goal, the salespeople need to sell a lot of cars. Management uses monthly sales goals to motivate and evaluate its salespeople. Each month, management gives a specific sales target to each salesperson. The target is based on the individual salesperson's historic sales performance during the previous 12 months, as well as the type of car they typically sell (for example, new versus used) and the time of year because, typically, there are two peak auto sales seasons. To motivate salespeople to meet or exceed their targets, management provides financial incentives, including bonus payments and gift cards to local restaurants, as well as awards to publicly recognize the top salespeople. Management has found that this performance-measurement plan works well. The salespeople work hard to meet their targets and are happy to work for Athens Motors.

Across town, at a fictitious competing car dealership, Classic City Toyota, the performance measurement system doesn't work as well. Management has the same goal—profitability—and it also needs its salespeople to sell a lot of cars. However, rather than setting individualized monthly sales goals for its sales staff, the management of Classic City Toyota gives all salespeople the same sales target (based on the top salesperson's

CAREER SKILLS

Learning about
performance mea-
surement supports
these career skills:

- Determining
  whether the
  organization is
  meeting its goals

- Understanding
  how incen-
  tives motivate
  employees

sales from the previous year), and the target stays the same for the entire year. Like the management of Athens Motors, management at Classic City Toyota provides financial incentives and recognition to motivate employees. However, because many salespeople cannot achieve the sales targets, these incentives are not effective motivators. Salespeople at Classic City Toyota are frustrated, rather than motivated, by the incentive program.

FROM THE FIELD

Cash or Prizes?

Would you work harder for cash or a prize? Surveys show that over 80 percent of employers currently use noncash rewards, such as gift cards, to recognize and reward employees, and that percentage is expected to grow.[7] Academic research finds that noncash rewards are more motivating than cash rewards. Why? Employees think of cash rewards as just more salary and generally spend it on typical things like their student loan payments or groceries. Noncash rewards, such as tickets to a baseball game or a gift card to a favorite store, are more fun, special, and memorable.

Thinking Critically

Imagine that the company you work for wants to offer extra vacation days as an employee incentive, instead of end-of-year cash bonuses. The leadership team sees this as a cost-savings initiative because giving an extra vacation day is "cheaper" than giving cash. How would you assess whether this change in incentives is a good idea? Can you think of any costs incurred by extra vacation days?

 PROGRESS CHECK

8. Why is it important to establish effective performance measures?
9. What are the characteristics of effective performance measures? What are the possible consequences of ineffective performance measures?

LO 8.5

Calculate ROI, RI, and EVA and describe their use.

COMMON FINANCIAL PERFORMANCE MEASURES

Financial success is a primary goal of all (for-profit) organizations. In this section, we introduce and explain three of the most common financial performance measures used to evaluate a company's success: (1) return on investment, or ROI; (2) residual income, or RI; and (3) economic value added, or EVA. These measures are commonly used to evaluate the performance of investment centers because each includes a measure of investment. Of course, organizations have other goals, such as customer satisfaction, product quality, and sustainability. These goals are evaluated with other types of performance measures that are discussed in Chapter 12.

CAREER SKILLS

Learning about financial performance measures supports this career skill:

• Evaluating the organization's financial performance

---

[7]Incentive Federation Inc., "Incentive Marketplace Estimate Research Study," July 2016, www.incentivefederation.org/wp-content/uploads/2016/07/Incentive-Marketplace-Estimate-Research-Study-2015-16-White-Paper.pdf.

Return on Investment (ROI)

return on investment (ROI)
A financial performance measure calculated as a measure of profit (or operating income) divided by a measure of investment.

Return on investment (ROI) is a very commonly used measure of short-term financial performance. It is defined as a measure of profit (or operating income) divided by a measure of investment.

$$ROI = \text{Operating income/Investment}$$

Return on investment measures the amount of money made on an investment relative to that investment's cost. The result of the calculation is a percentage or a ratio. A larger percentage means the investment is more worthwhile.

ROI is a popular financial performance measure because it is easy to calculate and includes all the elements of profitability (revenue, costs, and investments). Also, because it is in a percentage form, it is comparable across investments, and it also can be used to compare projects the organization may undertake.

DuPont method
A method for calculating return on investment (ROI) developed in 1912 by the CFO of the DuPont Corporation, Donaldson Brown. This method deconstructs ROI into return on sales and asset turnover, which helps determine how each aspect of the business is performing.

When management uses ROI to evaluate an investment center, the measure of income is usually that sub-unit's operating income. The measure of investment is generally the total assets of the sub-unit. Using the sub-unit's operating income and assets to calculate ROI ensures that the performance measure is generally controllable by the employees being evaluated.

Let's consider an example. **Blast** is a fitness studio that combines treadmill running with strength training during 60-minute group classes. Let's assume that Blast has three locations in the Southeast: Atlanta, Charlotte, and Nashville. Senior management would like to evaluate the ROI for each. Exhibit 8.3 shows the operating income and investments (assets) for each studio and the calculated ROI rounded to the nearest percent.

Exhibit 8.3
ROI for Blast

	Operating Income	÷	**Investment (Assets)**	=	**ROI**
Atlanta	$360,000	÷	$1,100,000	=	33%
Charlotte	$290,000	÷	$1,000,000	=	29%
Nashville	$255,000	÷	$900,000	=	28%

Based on these data, the Atlanta location is showing the highest ROI, indicating that it is making the best use of its investment. However, senior management would be very pleased with the positive ROI for all of these studios. If the managers of these locations wanted to increase their ROI, they could either increase revenues or reduce costs. Either of these steps would increase the operating income used as the numerator in the ROI equation. *Note:* Organizations can define "good" ROI in a variety of ways, depending on the investment that has been made. For example, the ROI gained from an investment in a piece of equipment will be different from the ROI gained from improving the IT infrastructure for an online retail app.

return on sales
The profit earned for each dollar of sales. Calculated as operating profit divided by sales.

ROI can also be calculated via the **DuPont method**, which was originally developed by the chief financial officer of the DuPont Corporation, Donaldson Brown, in 1912. The DuPont method calculates ROI as the product of two other calculations:

asset turnover
Total sales divided by average total assets. A measure of how effectively assets are used to generate sales.

1. **Return on sales**, which is the profit earned for each dollar of sales. Return on sales measures the manager's ability to turn sales into profit. It is calculated by dividing operating profit by sales.
2. **Asset turnover**, which is calculated as the total sales divided by the average total assets of a sub-unit. Asset turnover tells us how effectively the sub-unit is using its assets to generate sales.

By deconstructing ROI into these components, it is easy to tell how each aspect of the business is performing.

$$ROI = \text{Return on Sales} * \text{Asset Turnover}$$
$$ROI = (\text{Profit/Sales}) * (\text{Sales/Average Total Assets})$$

Let's look at Blast again. To calculate ROI from return on sales and asset turnover, we also need the sales data in Exhibit 8.4.

	Sales
Atlanta	$1,500,000
Charlotte	$1,000,000
Nashville	$875,000

Exhibit 8.4
Blast Sales Data by Location

Now that we have operating income, average total assets, and sales for the year, we can calculate ROI using the return on sales and asset turnover ratios, as shown in Exhibit 8.5.

	Return on Sales Operating Income/Sales	Asset Turnover Sales/Assets	ROI Return on Sales * Asset Turnover
Atlanta	360,000 ÷ 1,500,000 = 24%	1,500,000 ÷ 1,100,000 = 1.36	24% * 1.36 = 33%
Charlotte	290,000 ÷ 1,000,000 = 29%	1,000,000 ÷ 1,000,000 = 1.00	29% * 1.00 = 29%
Nashville	255,000 ÷ 875,000 = 29%	875,000 ÷ 900,000 = 0.97	29% * 0.97 = 28%

Exhibit 8.5
Calculating ROI for Blast Using the DuPont Method

Senior management may find it helpful to understand ROI as a function of return on sales and asset turnover because it gives better insight into what is driving the results. At Blast, it appears that, while the Atlanta studio has an overall higher ROI, it has the lowest return on sales (or profit margin), which suggests that this studio has higher costs. Perhaps the managers at this studio should focus on reducing costs in the next period.

Importantly, when using ROI to compare sub-units across the organization, it is necessary that income and investment are calculated the same way by each sub-unit. Also, any measurement decisions need to be fair to all sub-units and not to favor one sub-unit over the others.

LAB CONNECTION

Organizations use ROI to evaluate the performance of their business units and their investments. ROI is often used to compare performance across different business units or projects.

LAB 8.1 EXCEL uses Excel to calculate ROI and compare the performance of a company's business units.

Residual Income

Residual income (RI) is essentially the amount of income earned after the sub-unit has been "charged" to repay the investment made by the organization. This "charge" is known as the **imputed investment cost**. It is the implicit cost of using an asset. The imputed cost is calculated as the desired minimum rate of return multiplied by the investment amount. The **minimum rate of return** (also known as the **required rate of return** or **cost of capital**) is the lowest acceptable amount of earnings from an organization's investment in assets. RI is calculated as income less the imputed investment cost.

$$RI = \text{Operating Income} - (\text{Minimum Rate of Return} * \text{Investment})$$

Let's return to the Blast example and assume that the organization has a desired minimum rate of return equal to 14 percent for each of its studios. Exhibit 8.6 includes the investment in assets made by each location, which is the same as the average total assets shown in Exhibits 8.3 and 8.5. This exhibit shows that the Atlanta studio has the greatest residual income. Like ROI, residual income evaluates short-term performance.

Exhibit 8.6
Residual Income for Blast

	Operating Income	–	Minimum Rate of Return	*	Investment	=	Residual Income (RI)
Atlanta	$360,000	–	14%	*	$1,100,000	=	$206,000
Charlotte	$290,000	–	14%	*	$1,000,000	=	$150,000
Nashville	$255,000	–	14%	*	$900,000	=	$129,000

Comparing Residual Income to ROI

ROI and residual income are both designed to help organizations evaluate the profitability of projects, taking into consideration the investment that the organization must make to implement the project. Often, organizations use these measures when they are considering whether to take on a new project. However, focusing solely on either ROI *or* residual income may cause managers to make different choices about whether to pursue that new venture. Specifically, focusing solely on ROI may give managers a distorted view of the benefits of a new project and make them less inclined to invest in it.

Let's return to our Blast example once again. Exhibit 8.7 focuses only on the Atlanta location. In Column A we see the current results: Blast currently has an ROI of 33 percent and residual income of $206,000. In Column B we see the results of a proposed expansion of the Atlanta location. Local management predicts that if the company spends $500,000 to build a second studio at their current location, the Atlanta division could increase operating income by $100,000 per year. As Column B shows, the prediction with the new investment is an ROI of 29 percent and residual income of $236,000.

Column C shows the trend if this new project goes forward. If the Atlanta management team is incentivized based only on ROI, the downward trend (from 33 percent without the expansion to 29 percent with the expansion) is likely to dissuade them from making the investment. However, if the management team is evaluated based on residual income, then the upward trend in residual income is likely to encourage them to make the investment.

Importantly, notice that even though the trend in ROI with the investment is downward, an ROI of 29 percent still greatly exceeds the required rate of return (14 percent) that Blast has set. Therefore, it IS worthwhile to build a second studio at the Atlanta location! Blast will make more money and exceed the required rate of return even though ROI is going down. Managers who focus only on their ROI may pass on this opportunity because they may perceive that it makes their performance appear weaker.

	[A]	[B]	[C]
	Current Results	**Predicted Results with Expanded Studio**	**Trend**
Operating Income	$ 360,000.00	$ 460,000.00	
Investment	$1,100,000.00	$1,600,000.00	
Required Rate of Return	14%	14%	
ROI	33%	29%	↓
Residual Income	$ 206,000.00	$ 236,000.00	↑

Exhibit 8.7
Considering a New Project at Blast—Atlanta

Most of the time, a new project will decrease ROI, which focuses on the initial investment. Therefore, managers focused on ROI will usually be incentivized to pass on any new project.

The following Mini-Lab uses Excel to walk you through the process of using data visualizations to compare business units on the bases of ROI and residual income.

DATA ANALYTICS MINI-LAB
Using Data Visualization to Compare Business Segments Based on ROI and Residual Income

Data Analytics Types: Descriptive Analytics, Diagnostic Analytics

Lab Note: The tools presented in this lab periodically change. Updated instructions, if applicable, can be found in the student and instructor support materials.

DATA VISUALIZATION

Keywords
ROI, Residual Income, Column Chart

Decision-Making Context
Financial performance measures such as ROI and residual income help organizations evaluate the effectiveness of their investments in assets. In this Mini-Lab, you will use the operating results reported by **Starbucks** for each of its business segments and evaluate their performance based on ROI and residual income. You will use Excel to perform simple calculations and prepare visualizations that allow you to quickly see performance across three years. You will also note that segment performance looks quite different when you use different performance measures.

Required
Exhibit A shows selected financial figures for each Starbucks business segment as described in the company's 2021 annual report. Use this information to calculate ROI and residual income for each segment and use a clustered bar chart visualization to present the comparisons to your stakeholders.

Starbucks Selected Financial Figures for Each Business Segment					
	North America	International	Channel Development	Corporate and Other	Total
2021					
Total Net Revenues	$20,448.00	$ 6,921.60	$1,593.60	$ 97.50	$29,060.70
Depreciation and Amortization Expenses	$ 753.90	$ 544.70	$ 1.20	$ 141.90	$ 1,441.70
Income from Equity Investees	$ —	$ 135.30	$ 250.00	$ —	$ 385.30
Operating Income/(loss)	$ 4,259.30	$ 1,245.70	$ 789.10	$ (1,422.00)	$ 4,872.10
Total Assets	$10,571.80	$10,083.30	$ 125.40	$ 10,612.10	$31,392.60
2020					
Total Net Revenues	$16.296.20	$ 5,230.60	$1,925.00	$ 66.20	$23,518.00
Depreciation and Amortization Expenses	$ 762.00	$ 518.40	$ 1.20	$ 149.70	$ 1,431.30
Income from Equity Investees	$ —	$ 102.30	$ 220.20	$ —	$ 322.50
Operating Income/(loss)	$ 1,801.70	$ 370.60	$ 687.20	$ (1,297.80)	$ 1,561.70
Total Assets	$10,717.40	$ 9,449.70	$ 165.00	$ 9,042.40	$29,374.50
2019					
Total Net Revenues	$18,130.40	$ 6,319.30	$1,992.60	$ 66.30	$26,508.60
Depreciation and Amortization Expenses	$ 696.10	$ 511.50	$ 13.00	$ 156.70	$ 1,377.30
Income from Equity Investees	$ —	$ 102.40	$ 195.60	$ —	$ 298.00
Operating Income/(loss)	$ 3,728.10	$ 1,011.30	$ 697.50	$ (1,359.00)	$ 4,077.90
Total Assets	$ 4,446.70	$ 6,724.60	$ 132.20	$ 7,916.10	$19,219.60

Exhibit A
Selected Financial Figures for Each of Starbucks' Business Segments

Source: https://investor.starbucks.com/.

Ask the Question

Which business segment(s) have the strongest performance based on ROI and residual income?
What are the year-over-year trends in performance based on ROI and residual income?
What are some possible explanations for the observed trends?

Master the Data

Open the data file **Mini-Lab 8 Data.xlsx** to access the data to be used in this mini-lab.

You'll notice that four segments are reported: North America, International, Channel Development, and Corporate and Other. Before you perform the analysis, you should make sure you know what each segment represents. From the 2021 Starbucks Annual Report:[8]

---

[8]Starbucks Corporation, *2021 Form 10-K*, "Note 17: Segment Reporting," p. 79.

We have three reportable operating segments: (1) North America, which is inclusive of the U.S. and Canada; (2) International, which is inclusive of China, Japan, Asia Pacific, Europe, Middle East and Africa, Latin America and the Caribbean; and (3) Channel Development.

North America and International operations sell coffee and other beverages, complementary food, packaged coffees, single-serve coffee products, and a focused selection of merchandise through company-operated stores and licensed stores.

Our North America segment is our most mature business and has achieved significant scale. Channel Development revenues include packaged coffee, tea, food-service products and ready-to-drink beverages to customers outside of our company-operated and licensed stores. Most of our Channel Development revenues are from product sales to and royalty revenues from Nestlé through the Global Coffee Alliance. . . . Non-reportable operating segments such as Evolution Fresh and unallocated corporate expenses are reported within Corporate and Other.[9]

Review the data to confirm that you have all of the data fields you need to perform the following calculations for ROI and residual income:

$$\textbf{ROI} = \text{Operating Income/Investment}$$
$$\textbf{RI} = \text{Operating Income} - (\text{Minimum Rate of Return} * \text{Investment})$$

You'll note that Starbucks' minimum rate of return is not reported in the provided financial results. For this lab, we'll assume that Starbucks' minimum rate of return is 9 percent.

Perform the Analysis

Use the prepared templates for your calculations on the **Calculations** tab of the workbook.

Analysis Task #1: Calculate ROI for Each Business Segment for 2021, 2020, and 2019

In cell B3, enter the formula to calculate ROI for North America in 2021, as shown in Exhibit B.

Exhibit B
ROI Excel Calculation

Microsoft Excel

You can drag that formula across Row 3 into Columns C–F because this ROI template is set up using the same column headers as the selected financial figures from the **Starbucks** tab.

[9]Ibid., p. 6.

Repeat this process for 2020 and 2019. The resulting table will look like Exhibit C.

	A	B	C	D	E	F
1				ROI		
2		North America	International	Channel Development	Corporate and Other	Total
3	2021	40%	12%	629%	-13%	16%
4	2020	17%	4%	416%	-14%	5%
5	2019	84%	15%	528%	-17%	21%

Exhibit C
ROI for Each Business Segment
Microsoft Excel

Analysis Task #2: Calculate Residual Income for Each Business Segment for 2021, 2020, and 2019

In cell B11, enter the formula to calculate residual income for North America in 2021, as shown in Exhibit D.

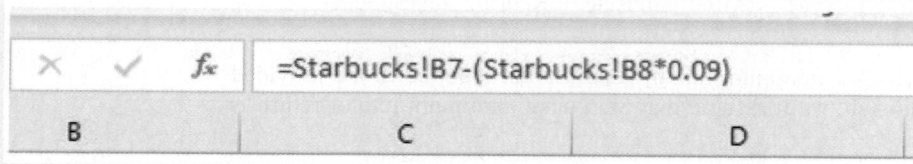

B	C	D
✕ ✔ *fx*	=Starbucks!B7-(Starbucks!B8*0.09)	

Exhibit D
Residual Income Excel Calculation
Microsoft Excel

You can drag that formula across Row 11 into Columns C–F because this Residual Income template is set up using the same column headers as the selected financial figures from the **Starbucks** tab.

Repeat this process for 2020 and 2019. The resulting table will look like Exhibit E.

		North America		International		Channel Development		Corporate and Other		Total
9					Residual Income					
10		North America		International		Channel Development		Corporate and Other		Total
11	2021	$	3,307.84	$	338.20	$	777.81	$	(2,377.09) $	2,046.77
12	2020	$	837.13	$	(479.87)	$	672.35	$	(2,111.62) $	(1,082.01)
13	2019	$	3,327.90	$	406.09	$	685.60	$	(2,071.45) $	2,348.14
14										

Exhibit E
ROI for Each Business Segment
Microsoft Excel

Analysis Task #3: Prepare a Clustered Column Chart Visualization for ROI in 2021, 2020, and 2019

Highlight the table ranging from cells A2:E5 so that you capture the ROI for all four segments (but not the total) for 2021, 2020, and 2019.

Navigate to the **Insert** tab and then select the icon for the **clustered column chart**, as shown in Exhibit F.

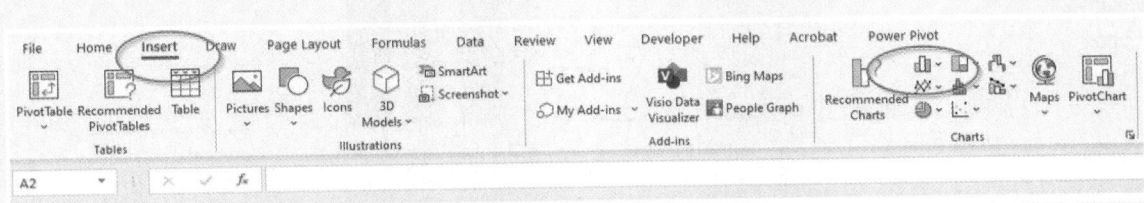

Exhibit F
Navigating to the Clustered Column Chart
Microsoft Excel

The result is a clustered column chart that looks something like the chart shown in Exhibit G.

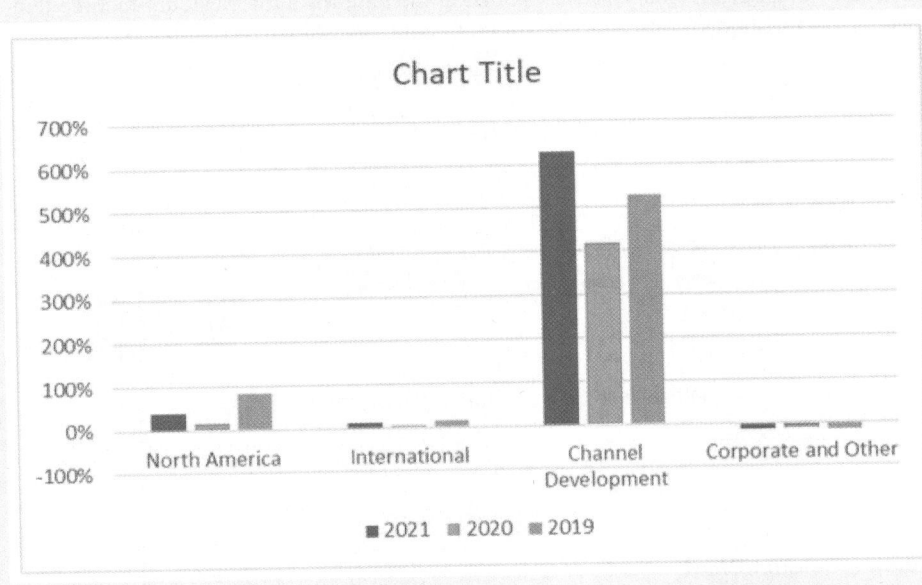

Exhibit G
Basic Clustered Column Chart

Microsoft Excel

You can add a title and make other formatting changes, such as re-ordering the years on the X-axis, as needed. Your finished visualization may look like the one shown in Exhibit H.

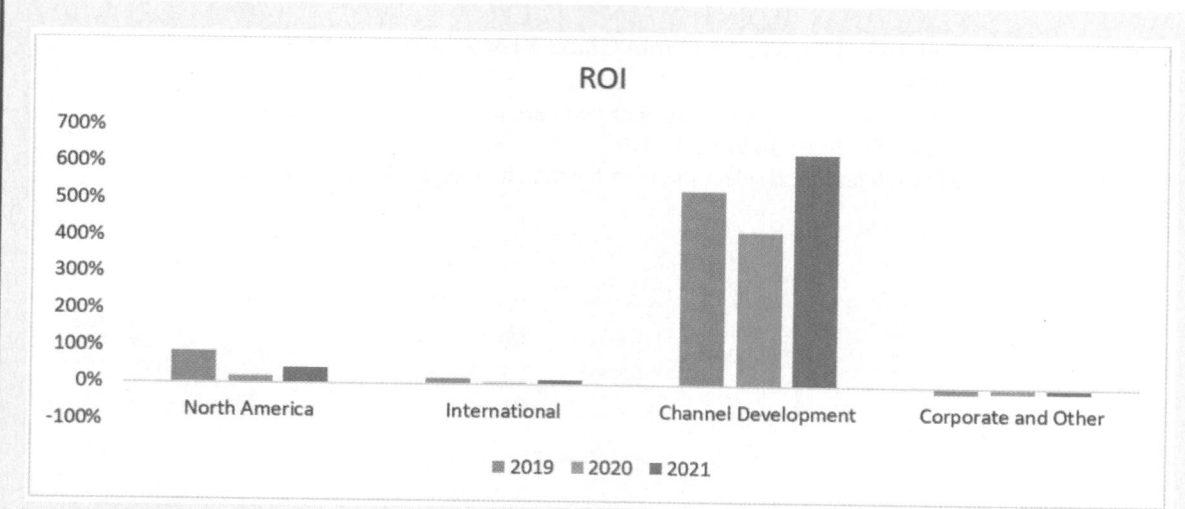

Exhibit H
Formatted ROI Column Chart
Microsoft Excel

Analysis Task #4: Prepare a Clustered Column Chart Visualization for Residual Income in 2021, 2020, and 2019

Repeat the steps from Analysis Task #3 using the data from the Residual Income template. Your finished visualization may look like the one shown in Exhibit I.

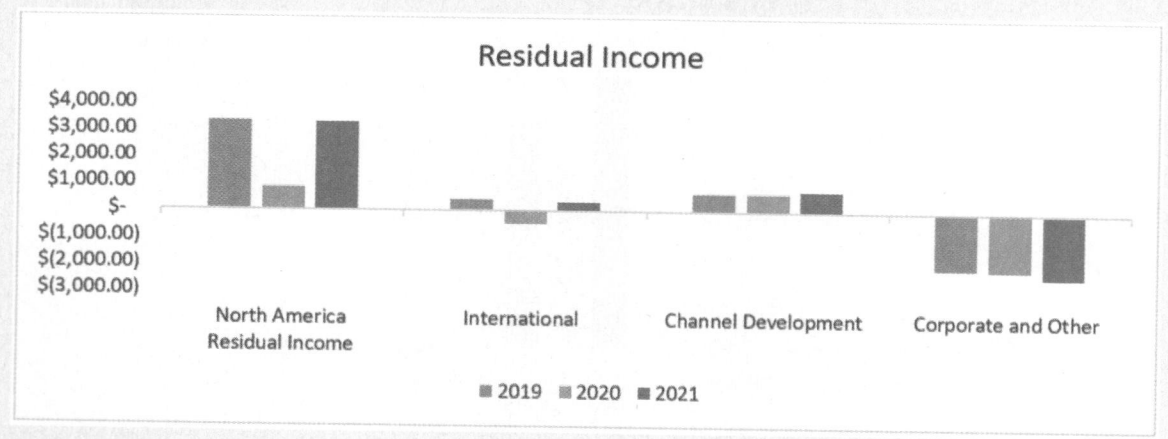

Exhibit I
Formatted Residual Income Column Chart
Microsoft Excel

Share the Story

Now that you've analyzed these data, you can report to the CFO and CEO about the financial performance of each segment. Often, you will prepare a slide presentation that uses visualizations to summarize the results and provide a quick overview of the performance for the executive management team. You will also provide your interpretation of the results, including your understanding of the underlying factors driving performance.

Management was most interested in knowing which business segments have the strongest performance based on ROI and RI, and what the year-over-year trends are. The results reveal that the Channel Development division has had very high ROI consistently over the past three years, as well as positive residual income. This division is responsible for managing the company's retail products sold outside of Starbucks locations; therefore, considerable growth in sales of products such as packaged coffee, tea, and ready-to-drink beverages has contributed to this high ROI. This division also manages the company's e-commerce platform, allowing customers to purchase Starbucks products online and via the Starbucks online mobile ordering app.

North America retail also has positive ROI and RI over the three years observed, suggesting that in-store sales in the North American region have remained strong.

For both of these divisions, we see a noticeable decline during 2020, especially with respect to in-store sales in 2020. This dip is most likely due to the COVID-19 pandemic, when sales dropped.

Mini-Lab Assessment

1. Which segment shows the best performance based on ROI?
2. Which segment shows the best performance based on residual income?
3. What might explain the differences in the top performer when using ROI versus residual income?
4. What trends do you see in the performances of each business unit? What might explain those trends?

Economic Value Added

Economic value added (EVA) focuses on the profit generated by the business unit during a period. Its calculation is very similar to the RI calculation. As with RI, business units do not recognize any return on investment until the cost of capital has been recovered. The primary difference between RI and EVA is how revenue is calculated. EVA uses the after-tax operating income to measure performance. The calculation for EVA is:

$$EVA = \begin{matrix} \text{After-tax} \\ \text{operating} \\ \text{income} \end{matrix} - \left(\begin{matrix} \text{Weighted} \\ \text{average cost of} \\ \text{capital} \end{matrix} * \begin{matrix} \text{Total assets} - \\ \text{Current} \\ \text{liabilities} \end{matrix} \right)$$

The **weighted average cost of capital (WACC)** is the after-tax average cost of all long-term investments.

Let's return to Blast for an example of the EVA calculation. Assume Blast has two sources of capital (funds): (1) long-term debt of $3.0 million with a 20 percent interest rate and (2) equity capital of $5.0 million with a cost of capital of 10 percent. Recall that the WACC is calculated *after tax*. Interest costs (such as the interest on the $3.0 million

economic value added (EVA)
A financial performance measure that focuses on the profit generated during a period. EVA considers the after-tax operating income and the weighted average cost of capital to evaluate performance.

weighted average cost of capital (WACC)
The after-tax average cost of all long-term investments. Used in the calculation of economic value added (EVA) to measure a sub-unit's financial performance.

long-term debt) are tax-deductible, so we must consider the 30 percent tax rate. The cost of financing this debt (1) is calculated as:

(1)   Interest rate $*$ (1 − Tax rate) = 0.20 $*$ (1 − 0.30) = 0.20 $*$ (0.70) = 14%

You use this percentage in your calculation for WACC as follows:

$$\text{WACC} = \frac{(14\% * \text{Market value of debt}) + (10\% * \text{Market value of equity})}{(\text{Market value of debt} + \text{Market value of equity})}$$

$$\text{WACC} = \frac{(0.14 * \$3,000,000) + (0.10 * \$5,000,000)}{(\$3,000,000 + \$5,000,000)}$$

$$= \frac{\$420,000 + \$500,000}{\$8,000,000} = 11.5\%$$

After-tax operating income for each studio is also calculated using the 30 percent tax rate as follows:

Operating income $*$ (1 − Tax rate) = Operating income $*$ (1 − 0.30) = Operating income $*$ (0.70)

Exhibit 8.8 reports the current liabilities for each location and calculates the EVA for the three Blast studios.

Exhibit 8.8
Economic Value Added (EVA) for Blast

	After-Tax Operating Income	−	WACC	*	Total Assets	−	Current Liabilities	=	Economic Value Added (EVA)
Atlanta	$360,000 * 0.70	−	[11.5%	*	($1,100,000	−	$100,000)]	=	$137,000
Charlotte	$290,000 * 0.70	−	[11.5%	*	($1,000,000	−	$150,000)]	=	$105,250
Nashville	$255,000 * 0.70	−	[11.5%	*	($900,000	−	$225,000)]	=	$100,875

From this example, we see once again that each studio has a positive EVA, with the Atlanta studio faring the best and Nashville reporting the weakest performance. To improve this measure, the Nashville studio can try to increase revenue—perhaps by signing up more members or increasing the cost for classes—or by reducing its cost of capital.

⊕ LAB CONNECTION

In **LAB 8.2 TABLEAU** you will use Tableau to compare the performance (ROI, RI, and EVA) across different business segments of a single company. Many companies tie financial performance metrics (for example, ROI) to employee compensation. In **LAB 8.2 EXCEL** you will use Excel to determine if a company's incentive plan is motivating desired employee performance.

✓ PROGRESS CHECK

10. How is ROI calculated? What does a larger ROI indicate?
11. What does the residual income measure represent?
12. How is EVA different from and similar to residual income?

TRANSFER PRICING

Not only do decentralized organizations need effective performance measures to motivate business units to meet goals, they also need to foster coordination between business units. Often, organizations use transfer pricing to coordinate activities across sub-units. A **transfer price** is the price one business unit charges another business unit within the same organization for its product or services. Transfer prices are most commonly used by organizations that are vertically integrated—that is, organizations in which the output from one business unit becomes the input for another unit. For example, **Heartwood Cabinets** very likely uses transfer pricing to coordinate across business units.

Specifically, at Heartwood Cabinets, the cabinet manufacturing division needs to purchase cut lumber from a sawmill. It can purchase that lumber from an outside supplier or Heartwood's own sawmill division. The price that Heartwood's sawmill charges the manufacturing division is the transfer price. The transfer price drives the revenues for the sawmill and the costs for the manufacturing division, and it impacts the operating income for both divisions. Heartwood can use the operating income for each division as part of its performance measurement system.

transfer price
The price one sub-unit charges another sub-unit within the same organization for its product or services.

Nakonechnyi Oleksandr/Shutterstock

Once senior management sets transfer prices, business unit managers can focus on the performance of their sub-unit without considering the effects on the organization as a whole. In general, when establishing transfer prices, the organization's goals are to:

1. Motivate business unit managers to exert a high level of effort.
2. Promote goal congruence, both across the business units and within the organization as a whole.
3. Provide a mechanism for evaluating and rewarding business-unit management for effective decisions.

As we discuss later in this chapter, transfer pricing by multinational organizations also allows them to leverage international locations to minimize tax liabilities.

Calculating Transfer Prices

How does an organization determine its transfer prices? Management can use three different methods for setting its transfer price:

1. In **market-based transfer pricing**, sub-unit management sets a transfer price based on the prices outside suppliers are currently charging.
2. In **cost-based transfer pricing**, management sets a transfer price that allows the sub-unit to recover its costs. The cost-based transfer price could cover the variable production costs, the variable and fixed costs, or the full cost of production.
3. In **hybrid transfer pricing**, the transfer price takes into consideration both the market price and the production costs. Often the price is set through negotiations between the buying and selling sub-units.

When determining which transfer pricing approach to use, the organization must consider whether the transfer price will be beneficial to the organization: Will it motivate an internal or external sale when appropriate? For example, if the sawmill division of **Heartwood Cabinets** sets the transfer price above market, then the manufacturing division will be better off buying its wood from an outside competitor, which may not benefit Heartwood overall.

To set the transfer price, organizations must consider (1) whether there is an external supplier, (2) if the selling division's costs are greater or less than the external supplier's costs, and (3) if the selling division has product to sell, whether it can sell all of its inventory to external parties at a higher price.

Let's see how Heartwood Cabinets sets its transfer prices. The company is currently trying to set its transfer price for the cut pine boards used in some of its most popular cabinet styles. Heartwood does have an external supplier for pine. It frequently buys cut lumber from Buschmore Sawmill in central Florida. Buschmore's price typically varies between $200 and $230 per thousand board feet of pine. Let's assume an average price of $215 in our calculation. Heartwood's sawmill can produce the cut pine for $195 per thousand board feet, and its senior management negotiated a (potential) hybrid price of $205 per thousand board feet, which splits the difference between the sawmill's costs and Buschmore's average sales price. In Exhibit 8.9 you can see the calculation of operating income using each of the potential transfer prices.

As you can see, the Heartwood Sawmill's revenues are higher if the cut pine is sold at the market price of $215 per thousand board feet. In fact, the Sawmill makes $2,000 more on the sale of 100,000 board feet at market than at cost ($10,900 − 8,900). Therefore, if the Sawmill management's only goal is to generate the highest possible income, it would set the transfer price at $215. However, the Manufacturing division is worse off when the transfer price is set at market price, but it is better off, by $2,000, if the transfer price is set at cost rather than market. To help business units set the transfer price that is beneficial to other business units, many organizations evaluate and incentivize managers based on both their business unit's operating income and the operating income of the whole organization.

Tax Implications of Transfer Pricing Decisions

Multinational organizations often use transfer-pricing decisions to reduce the taxes they owe. Taxes are based on the profit earned in each tax jurisdiction. To minimize taxes owed, organizations would rather shift more of their profit to countries with lower tax rates. They can do this by charging high transfer prices for products in high-tax jurisdictions.

Sawmill production: 100,000 board feet Manufacturing sales: 6,250 cabinets @ $250	Market Price = $215 per 1,000 board feet	Full Cost = $195 per 1,000 board feet	Hybrid = $205 per 1,000 board feet
Sawmill Division			
Revenues	$ 21,500	$ 19,500	$ 20,500
Costs			
Sawmill Fixed Costs	3,000	3,000	3,000
Sawmill Purchase Costs ($75 per 1,000 board feet)	7,500	7,500	7,500
Sawmill Variable Costs ($1 per 1,000 board feet)	100	100	100
Total Costs	10,600	10,600	10,600
Sawmill Operating Income	$ 10,900	$ 8,900	$ 9,900
Manufacturing Division			
Revenues (6,250 cabinets at $250 per)	$1,562,500	$1,562,500	$1,562,500
Costs			
Cost of Lumber	$ 21,500	$ 19,500	$ 20,500
Manufacturing Variable Costs ($7 per cabinet)	75,000	75,000	75,000
Manufacturing Fixed Costs	5,000	5,000	5,000
Total Costs	101,500	99,500	100,500
Manufacturing Division Operating Income	$1,461,000	$1,463,000	$1,462,000
Total Operating Income for Both Business Units	$1,471,900	$1,471,900	$1,471,900

Exhibit 8.9
Heartwood Cabinet's Transfer Pricing Calculations

Exhibit 8.10 shows how an organization's overall tax liability changes based on the transfer prices charged between locations with different income tax rates.

	Operating Income			Income Taxes		
	United States	Brazil	Total	United States (26% tax rate)	Brazil (34% tax rate)	Total Income Taxes
Market price	$1,461,000	$10,900	$1,471,900	$379,860	$3,706	$383,566.00
Full cost	$1,463,000	$ 8,900	$1,471,900	$380,380	$3,026	$383,406.00
Hybrid	$1,462,000	$ 9,900	$1,471,900	$380,120	$3,366	$383,486.00

Exhibit 8.10
International Transfer Pricing and Tax Liabilities

As you can see, the operating income for the organization as a whole is the same regardless of the transfer price charged by Brazil to the United States. However, Heartwood owes the lowest amount of taxes if it sets the transfer price at market price. This minimizes the income reported in Brazil, which is the higher-tax jurisdiction.

ETHICS

FROM THE FIELD

THE ETHICS OF TAX HAVENS

Jurisdictions that have relatively low corporate tax rates are known as *tax havens*. The British Virgin Islands, the Cayman Islands, and Bermuda are among the most popular international locations for multinational corporations looking to minimize their tax liability. In the United States, the state of Delaware is an attractive choice for incorporation because Delaware-based companies can avoid corporate taxes even while doing business across state lines.

Some question the ethical considerations of organizations relying heavily on tax havens to reduce their tax liability. Research shows that tax havens cost governments between $500 billion and $600 billion (per year) in lost corporate tax revenue. It is estimated that in 2021 U.S. Fortune 500 companies held $2.6 trillion in profits in offshore tax havens, allowing them to avoid over $700 billion in U.S. federal income taxes.

Let's consider the ethical implications of relying on tax havens. As described previously, tax havens cost governments huge amounts of lost tax revenue. Governments could use this lost revenue to improve infrastructure, education, health care, and so on. Critics of tax-haven use also point to the tremendous wealth amassed by CEOs who rely on this tool. Consider, for example, Stefano Pessina, the CEO of **Walgreens**. He is well known for using transfer-pricing rules and tax havens to his advantage, resulting in a reported $10.2 billion personal fortune. His holdings company is located in the Cayman Islands, which has no tax regime, and in 2008 he received attention for moving the headquarters of **Boots**, the UK-based pharmacy retailer, to a low-tax region in Switzerland, allowing the company to avoid approximately $1.6 billion in taxes.

But, on the flip side, as companies are more profitable, their shareholders are likely to see greater returns on their investments. Greater corporate profits also allow the company to continue operations, employ and pay workers, and provide goods and services to customers.

Thinking Critically

Imagine you work at a multinational corporation, and you've been asked to investigate ways to use transfer pricing and tax havens to reduce your company's corporate tax bill. What information would you collect to make your recommendations?

Ⓠ LAB CONNECTIONS

LAB 8.4 EXCEL uses Excel to analyze the tax implications of transfer-pricing decisions.

LAB 8.5 POWER BI uses Power BI to visualize the tax rates across the world using a mapping tool.

✓ PROGRESS CHECK

13. What is transfer pricing?
14. What are the different methods for determining transfer prices?
15. How do organizations use international transfer pricing to their advantage?

Careers in Management Accounting: Jobs with Financial Performance Measurement Responsibilities

Throughout this chapter we've learned how organizations use performance measures to evaluate current profitability and the potential performance of future investments. Now let's consider the types of careers that rely on the skills you learned in this chapter.

Exhibit 8.11 reproduces a job posting from a site like **Indeed.com** or **LinkedIn.com** for a Senior Finance Analyst at a nonprofit humanitarian organization like the

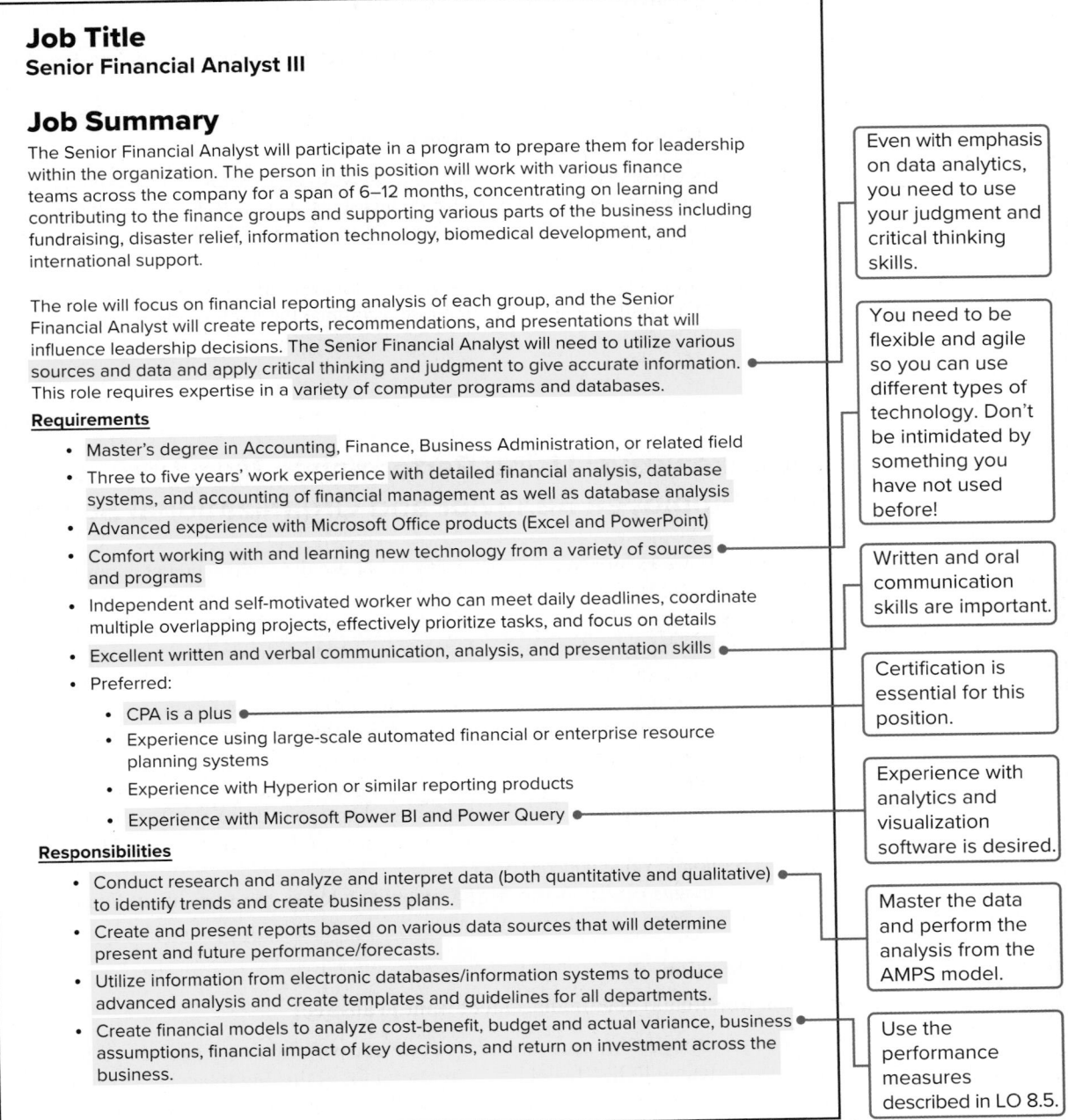

Job Title
Senior Financial Analyst III

Job Summary
The Senior Financial Analyst will participate in a program to prepare them for leadership within the organization. The person in this position will work with various finance teams across the company for a span of 6–12 months, concentrating on learning and contributing to the finance groups and supporting various parts of the business including fundraising, disaster relief, information technology, biomedical development, and international support.

Even with emphasis on data analytics, you need to use your judgment and critical thinking skills.

The role will focus on financial reporting analysis of each group, and the Senior Financial Analyst will create reports, recommendations, and presentations that will influence leadership decisions. The Senior Financial Analyst will need to utilize various sources and data and apply critical thinking and judgment to give accurate information. This role requires expertise in a variety of computer programs and databases.

Requirements
- Master's degree in Accounting, Finance, Business Administration, or related field
- Three to five years' work experience with detailed financial analysis, database systems, and accounting of financial management as well as database analysis
- Advanced experience with Microsoft Office products (Excel and PowerPoint)
- Comfort working with and learning new technology from a variety of sources and programs
- Independent and self-motivated worker who can meet daily deadlines, coordinate multiple overlapping projects, effectively prioritize tasks, and focus on details
- Excellent written and verbal communication, analysis, and presentation skills
- Preferred:
  - CPA is a plus
  - Experience using large-scale automated financial or enterprise resource planning systems
  - Experience with Hyperion or similar reporting products
  - Experience with Microsoft Power BI and Power Query

You need to be flexible and agile so you can use different types of technology. Don't be intimidated by something you have not used before!

Written and oral communication skills are important.

Certification is essential for this position.

Experience with analytics and visualization software is desired.

Responsibilities
- Conduct research and analyze and interpret data (both quantitative and qualitative) to identify trends and create business plans.
- Create and present reports based on various data sources that will determine present and future performance/forecasts.
- Utilize information from electronic databases/information systems to produce advanced analysis and create templates and guidelines for all departments.
- Create financial models to analyze cost-benefit, budget and actual variance, business assumptions, financial impact of key decisions, and return on investment across the business.

Master the data and perform the analysis from the AMPS model.

Use the performance measures described in LO 8.5.

Exhibit 8.11
Senior Financial Analyst Job Opportunity

American Red Cross, UNICEF, or **Doctors Without Borders.** The job responsibilities described for this position include many of the skills that you've learned in this course, including data analytics. In fact, you can see all the steps of the AMPS model described in this job posting. Specifically:

Ask the Question: What are the right performance metrics for the organization? The Senior Finance Analyst is responsible for identifying and developing performance metrics.
Master the Data: The Senior Finance Analyst needs to work with data from a variety of accounting and information systems. Strong ETL (extract, transform, load) skills are a must.
Perform the Analysis: The Senior Finance Analyst needs to produce advanced analysis, identify trends, and perform financial modeling, including variance analysis and ROI. The analyst should also be agile and able to use different technologies, including Excel and Power BI.
Share the Story: The Senior Finance Analyst must use judgment to provide accurate information and needs to be a strong communicator.

Indeed, this job opportunity combines data analytics skills with cost accounting know-how directly related to financial performance measures such as ROI and residual income. This job is also designed to be a steppingstone for advancement into a management career. This upward mobility is possible because someone in this position has a strong knowledge of what makes the organization successful, the costs of and risks associated with doing business, and the ability to analyze data for decision making at all levels.

Key Takeaways: Using Performance Measures to Drive Employee Behavior and Organizational Success

In this chapter, we examined how organizations choose their management control systems and organizational structure to motivate employees and monitor performance. Generally, organizations choose either a centralized structure, in which all decisions are made by senior management, or a decentralized structure, in which lower-level managers in each business unit have the autonomy to make the decisions they think will be best for their business unit. Because the organizational structure influences the incentives that drive the behavior of managers and employees, it also informs the decisions about the types of controls, including performance measures, that the organization should implement.

Organizations can use many different performance measures to motivate employees' behavior on every dimension of their jobs. In this chapter, we described three financial performance measures focused on profitability: return on investment (ROI), residual income (RI), and economic value added (EVA).

Cost accountants can apply the AMPS model to address questions about financial performance using these performance measures.

Ask the Question

■ **What question(s) does management want to answer?**

Management uses performance measures to evaluate performance. Financial performance measures, including ROI, RI, and EVA, are useful for evaluating financial performance (operating income) and considering the size of the investment the organization made to produce that result.

Using these performance measures, management can ask questions such as:
- Which sub-units have the strongest financial performance?
- What are the performance trends over time?
- Should we make an investment in a new project?

Master the Data

■ **Which data are appropriate to address management's questions?**

To address management's questions, cost accountants need financial data, which are pulled primarily from prior-period financial data gathered from the organization's accounting information system. The specific data required include operating income, assets, tax rates, and required rate of return. When considering the profitability of a future project, cost accountants may need to obtain historical data about similar projects implemented at the organization, or external data from other sources. External data may include cost data from potential vendors or suppliers that will be integral in the implementation of the new project, estimates of future revenues based on sales forecasts, and/or comparisons to other companies that have made similar investments.

Perform the Analysis

■ **Which analytics are performed to address management questions?**

When using ROI, RI, or EVA to evaluate financial performance, much of the analysis can be performed using basic calculations in spreadsheet software such as Excel. If these financial performance measures are used to evaluate the current financial performance of business segments, the analytics are **descriptive** or **diagnostic** in nature. When used to evaluate the potential financial performance of a future project, the analytics are **predictive.**

Share the Story

■ **How are the results of the analytics shared with stakeholders?**

ROI, RI, and EVA are powerful tools for evaluating financial performance, comparing performance across business units, and considering future investments. The results of these analyses can be communicated in a variety of ways, but visualizations such as column charts and bar charts may be especially useful for making comparisons.

In this chapter, we also discussed how organizational structure affects how business segments interact with one another. In particular, we considered how profitability goals influence transfer prices, which are the prices that business segments charge each other for the goods and services they provide.

Key Terms

asset turnover	DuPont method	investments	required rate of return
autonomy	economic value added (EVA)	management control system	residual income (RI)
behavior controls			responsibility center
centralized organizations	formal controls	market-based transfer pricing	return on investment (ROI)
cost accounting system	human resources management system	minimum rate of return	return on sales
cost-based transfer pricing	hybrid transfer pricing	output controls	revenue center
cost center	imputed investment cost	performance measurement	suboptimal decision making
cost of capital	informal controls	profit center	transfer price
decentralized organizations	investment center	quality management system	weighted average cost of capital (WACC)

ANSWERS TO PROGRESS CHECKS

1. A management control system is a set of rules, activities, and information that an organization uses to make and execute planning and control decisions and to direct employee behavior.

2. Formal controls are the explicit rules, procedures, safeguards, and incentive plans and information systems employed in an organization. Informal controls are an organization's norms, morals, ethical values, and shared culture, which all guide employee behavior and strategic decision making.

3. Organizations need both formal and informal controls to operate effectively because it is nearly impossible to develop a formal control system to prevent or detect every error or intentional inappropriate action. Further, the design, implementation, and monitoring of formal controls are costly. Therefore, an all-encompassing formal control system would likely be too costly. Informal controls, such as corporate culture and social norms, can substitute for formal controls and direct behavior.

4. In centralized organizations, all decisions are made by the organization's executive management. In decentralized organizations, decision making is delegated to the management of the individual business units.

5. The primary benefits for decentralization include:
   - Business units can be more responsive to customers, suppliers, and employees.
   - Business-unit managers may be more motivated by performance measures because those measures are more directly within their control.
   - Business-unit managers may receive more training and advancement opportunities because the sub-unit has autonomy.
   - Senior management's attention and resources are freed, allowing them to focus on organization-level strategic decisions, rather than sub-unit decisions.

   The primary drawbacks to decentralization include:

   - Business units may engage in dysfunctional competition because there is no coordinated performance measurement system.
   - Business units might duplicate activities, causing inefficiency and redundancies.
   - Business units might find it difficult to coordinate activities and data across the organization.

6. There are four types of responsibility centers: cost centers, revenue centers, profit centers, and investment centers.

7. In cost centers, performance measures are aimed at minimizing costs. In revenue centers, performance measures determine whether managers meet or beat sales targets. In profit centers, managers are evaluated on whether or not they generate profit. In investment centers, performance measures evaluate profits and returns on invested funds.

8. What gets measured gets done. Thus, it is important that an organization establish clear, measurable, and manageable performance measures for each of the priorities it has established for its managers.

9. For performance measures to be effective, the organization must know the results it desires, those results must be cleanly measured in a timely manner, and those results must be attainable and controllable by the employees held responsible. If the organization does not clearly know the results that it is trying to achieve, then employees may make decisions that are not in line with the company's actual objectives. For example, if employees think they are expected to maximize revenue, but the organization really wants them to focus on profit, managers may choose to spend more than necessary on inputs and direct labor. If the company does not provide clear evidence on whether employees have achieved their goals in a timely manner, then the feedback may not be relevant or received in time to allow the managers to make needed changes. Finally, if the performance measures relate to items that are not within the employees' control or are not reasonably attainable, then employees may become discouraged, and the performance measure will no longer motivate the employee to make decisions in line with the organization's overall goals.

10. ROI equals operating income divided by investment. A larger ROI means the investment is more worthwhile.

11. Residual income (RI) is essentially the amount of income earned after a sub-unit has been "charged" to repay the investment made by the organization.

12. When using EVA, business units do not recognize any return on investment until the cost of capital has been recovered. The same holds true for RI. Unlike RI, EVA uses the after-tax operating income to measure performance.

13. Transfer pricing is the method by which business units within an organization charge each other for products and services. Transfer prices are used to coordinate activities across sub-units.

14. There are three commonly used methods for determining transfer prices: (1) Market-based transfer pricing: Sub-unit management sets a transfer price based on the prices that outside suppliers are currently charging. (2) Cost-based transfer pricing: Management sets a transfer price that allows the sub-unit to recover its costs. The cost-based transfer price could cover the variable production costs, the variable and fixed costs, or the full cost of production. (3) Hybrid transfer pricing: The transfer price takes into consideration both the market price and the production costs. Often the price is set through negotiations between the buying and selling sub-units.

15. International transfer pricing can be used to reduce the taxes owed by shifting more profit to countries with lower tax rates.

Multiple Choice Questions   Mc Graw Hill connect

1. (LO8.1) Which of the following describes the policies, procedures, rules, and incentive structure of an organization?

   a. Informal controls

   b. Formal controls

   c. Output controls

   d. Quality management system

2. (LO8.1) The _____ is the system designed to aggregate, report, and monitor data about the organization's revenue and costs.

   a. cost accounting system

   b. human resources system

   c. quality management system

   d. management control system

3. (LO8.2) Acme Co. is a large corporation with four divisions. Management at each division has the autonomy and decision rights to make changes to the product mix and prices offered to its customers. Which organizational structure best describes Acme?

   a. Centralized

   b. Consolidated

   c. Decentralized

   d. Isolated

4. (LO8.2) Summit Co. is a large corporation with four divisions. Senior management makes product mix and pricing decisions centrally so that all customers have the same experience regardless of where they shop. Which organizational structure best describes Summit?

   a. Centralized

   b. Consolidated

   c. Decentralized

   d. Isolated

5. (LO8.2) Which of the following is a challenge associated with decentralized organizational structures?

    a. Competition among business units

    b. Diminished ability to respond to customer needs

    c. Less-sensitive performance measures

    d. Diminished leadership advancement opportunities

6. (LO8.3) A cost center manager is responsible for which of the following?

    a. Revenues

    b. Profitability

    c. Investments

    d. Costs

7. (LO8.4) Which of the following characteristics is NOT necessary for effective performance measures?

    a. Results are provided in a timely manner.

    b. Results are controllable by the employee being evaluated.

    c. Results are attainable by the employee being evaluated.

    d. Results are based on different measures each period.

8. (LO8.5) Au Croissant, a local bakery, has operating income of $175,000, sales of $900,000, and assets valued at $600,000. It expects a 9 percent minimum rate of return and has a 30 percent tax rate. Calculate the ROI for Au Croissant.

    a. 22 percent

    b. 29 percent

    c. $94,000

    d. $121,000

9. (LO8.5) Au Croissant, a local bakery, has operating income of $175,000, sales of $900,000, and assets valued at $600,000. It expects a 9 percent minimum rate of return. Calculate the residual income for Au Croissant.

    a. 22 percent

    b. 27 percent

    c. $94,000

    d. $121,000

10. (LO8.6) Which of the following best defines a hybrid transfer price?

    a. The internal price is set based on the prices available from outside suppliers.

    b. The internal price is set so the sub-unit recovers its fixed costs.

    c. The internal price is set so the sub-unit recovers its fixed and variable costs.

    d. The internal price is set by considering both the costs and outside prices available.

CMA

11. (LO8.5) Return on investment focuses on income as a percentage of investment, while residual income focuses on:

    a. the capital charge.

    b. operating income less a capital charge.

    c. management decisions.

    d. cost of capital times the amount of investment.

CMA

12. (LO8.5) Residual income is often preferred over return on investment (ROI) as a performance evaluation measure because:

    a. the imputed interest rate used in calculating residual income is more easily derived than the target rate that is compared to the calculated ROI.

    b. average investment is employed with residual income while year-end investment is employed with ROI.

c. residual income concentrates on maximizing the amount of income rather than a percentage return as with ROI.

d. residual income is a measure over time, while ROI represents the results for a single time period.

13. (LO8.6) Which one of the following is an *incorrect* description of transfer pricing?

CMA

a. It measures the value of goods or services furnished by a profit center to other responsibility centers within a company.

b. If a market price exists, this price may be used as a transfer price.

c. It measures exchanges between a company and external customers.

d. If no market price exists, the transfer price may be based on cost.

14. (LO8.6) Showtime Incorporated has a decentralized structure with multiple business units, with each unit reporting costs and profits separately. It has several products that are transferred from one business unit to another. Showtime wants to motivate the manager of the selling division to produce efficiently. Assume that all transfer-pricing methods are available. Which is the optimal transfer-pricing method that should be used?

a. Cost-based transfer price that uses actual amounts

b. Cost-based transfer price that uses budgeted amounts

c. Variable cost–based transfer price that uses actual amounts

d. Market-based transfer price

15. (LO8.6) The roasting division of **Jittery Joe's Coffee**, a profit center, sells its products to external customers as well as to other internal profit centers (for example, Jittery Joe's coffee shops). Which one of the following circumstances would justify the roasting division selling to another profit center at a price below the market-based transfer price?

a. The buying unit has excess capacity.

b. The selling unit is operating at full capacity.

c. Routine sales commissions and collection costs would be avoided.

d. The profit centers' managers are evaluated on the basis of unit operating income.

Discussion Questions

1. (LO8.1) Define a cost accounting system, human resource system, and quality management system.

2. (LO8.1) Do you think organizations need to rely primarily on formal controls, informal controls, or a combination of both? How do you think different types of controls affect employees?

3. (LO8.1) What is the difference between behavior controls and output controls? Provide examples of each.

4. (LO8.2) Describe the differences between a centralized organizational structure and a decentralized organizational structure. Summarize their strengths and weaknesses.

5. (LO8.3) Describe the differences among the four types of responsibility centers.

6. (LO8.3) How might managers' behavior be different if their sub-unit is classified as a revenue center instead of a cost center?

7. (LO8.3) How might managers' behavior be different if their sub-unit is classified as a cost center instead of a profit center?

8. (LO8.4) Describe the steps for establishing effective performance measures.

9. (LO8.4) What are the characteristics of effective performance measures?

10. (LO8.5) How are ROI, residual income, and EVA used to evaluate the success of investment centers?

11. (LO8.5) Describe the differences among ROI, RI, and EVA.

12. (LO8.6) What is the purpose of transfer prices? Why might companies charge different prices to internal customers compared to external customers?

13. (LO8.6) Describe the methods management can use to set transfer prices.

14. (LO8.6) How do organizations encourage sub-units to set transfer prices that do not provide the greatest amount of revenue to that sub-unit?

15. (LO8.6) How are transfer prices used to increase profitability?

Brief Exercises Mc Graw Hill connect

1. (LO8.1) Indicate whether each control activity is a formal control or informal control.
   a. Code of ethics
   b. Policy manual
   c. Sales bonus plan
   d. Passwords on data files
   e. Employee evaluations
   f. Company culture
   g. Review of sales trends over time
   h. Mentoring programs

2. (LO8.1) Indicate whether each control activity is a behavioral control or output control.
   a. Code of ethics
   b. Policy manual
   c. Sales bonus plan
   d. Passwords on data files
   e. Employee evaluations
   f. Review of sales trends over time

3. (LO8.2) ChromaCoat is a global paint company that has multiple business segments, including:
   a. Paints and Coatings
   b. Performance Coatings
   c. Consumer Brands
   d. Latin America Coatings
   e. Global Finishes

   It also has the following divisions that support its operations:
   i. Finance
   ii. Legal
   iii. Human Resources
   iv. Information Technology
   v. Marketing
   vi. Research and Development
   vii. Supply Chain

   The entire ChromaCoat organization is run by President and CEO William Raza.

   Required
   a. Draw an organizational chart for ChromaCoat assuming the company has a decentralized structure.
   b. Draw an organizational chart for ChromaCoat assuming the company has a centralized structure.

4. (LO8.6) Match the type of responsibility center to its definition:
   Type of center:
   a. Cost center
   b. Investment center

c. Profit center

d. Revenue center

Definitions:

   i. Sub-unit management is responsible for sales.

   ii. Sub-unit management is responsible for costs, sales, and investment decisions.

   iii. Sub-unit management is responsible for costs.

   iv. Sub-unit management is responsible for costs and sales.

5. (LO8.5) Mountaineer Outfitters, a fictitious company, has locations in Asheville, NC; Lexington, KY; and Charlottesville, VA. Mountaineer's management wants to evaluate and compare performance at each of the three locations. Use the following data to calculate the ROI for each and determine which location had the strongest performance.

	Minimum Rate of Return	Operating Income	Sales	Assets
Asheville, NC	10%	$325,000	$875,000	$800,000
Lexington, KY	10%	$330,000	$910,000	$750,000
Charlottesville, VA	10%	$415,000	$920,000	$825,000

6. (LO8.5) Mountaineer Outfitters, a fictitious company, has locations in Asheville, NC; Lexington, KY; and Charlottesville, VA. Mountaineer's management wants to evaluate and compare performance at each of the three locations. Use the following data to calculate the residual income for each and determine which location had the strongest performance.

	Minimum Rate of Return	Operating Income	Sales	Assets
Asheville, NC	10%	$325,000	$875,000	$800,000
Lexington, KY	10%	$330,000	$910,000	$750,000
Charlottesville, VA	10%	$415,000	$920,000	$825,000

7. (LO8.5) Mountaineer Outfitters, a fictitious company, has locations in Asheville, NC; Lexington, KY; and Charlottesville, VA. Mountaineer's management wants to evaluate and compare performance at each of the three locations. Use the following data to calculate the EVA for each and determine which location had the strongest performance. Note that there is a 30 percent tax rate for all locations, and Mountaineer has two sources of capital: (1) long-term debt of $4 million with a 17 percent interest rate and (2) equity capital of $7 million with a 10 percent cost of capital.

	Minimum Rate of Return	Operating Income	Sales	Assets
Asheville, NC	10%	$325,000	$875,000	$800,000
Lexington, KY	10%	$330,000	$910,000	$750,000
Charlottesville, VA	10%	$415,000	$920,000	$825,000

8. (LO8.6) **Heartwood Cabinets** is setting its transfer price for cut walnut boards used in some of its most popular cabinet styles. Heartwood's external supplier of walnut boards, Appleton Sawmill, charges between $250 and $290 per thousand feet for walnut. Heartwood's sawmill can produce the cut walnut for $235 per thousand board feet. Its senior management negotiated a (potential) hybrid price of $265 per thousand board feet. Assume that Heartwood needs 125,000 board feet to produce enough walnut cabinets to meet anticipated demand. Marketing estimates that Heartwood will sell 5,500 cabinet units at $325 per unit. Assume the manufacturing division has fixed costs of

$7,250 and variable costs of $6.50 per cabinet. Also assume the sawmill has purchase costs of $90 per 1,000 board feet and variable costs of $1.25 per 1,000 board feet.

Determine whether a transfer price based on the market price, cost of manufacturing, or a hybrid yields the best outcome for Heartwood overall, the sawmill division, and the manufacturing division.

9. (LO8.6) Refer to your calculations in Brief Exercise 8 for operating income for the sawmill and manufacturing divisions of **Heartwood Cabinets**. Now assume that the manufacturing division is located in the United States, which has a 26 percent tax rate, and the sawmill is located in Hungary, which has a 9 percent tax rate. Determine which transfer price yields the lower tax obligation.

10. (LO8.5) A company's recent operating results are shown below.

CMA

Operating Results	
Sales	$4,370,000.00
Expenses	$2,728,000.00
Operating income	$1,642,000.00
Total assets	$9,818,000.00
Total liabilities	$7,663,000.00

The company has set a target return on investment (ROI) of 18 percent. Management is evaluating the following two plans.

Plan 1: Invest $1,200,000 in a new location that will produce $3,000,000 in additional sales each year. Operating expenses will increase by $2,781,600 each year.
Plan 2: Reduce company costs by improving technology in the manufacturing process. An equipment investment of $730,000 will reduce annual operating costs by $315,000.

Which plan, if implemented, would result in the company having an ROI at or above the targeted ROI?

11. (LO8.5) Sparky's Chicken Fingers is a (fictitious) regional fast-food restaurant specializing in fried chicken fingers and hot wings. Sparky's CEO has asked the cost accountants to consider purchasing food trucks to set up some mobile locations around town during peak dining times. Brand-new food trucks with a new kitchen will cost Sparky's $150,000 each. The cost accountants obtain data from other food-truck businesses in the area and determine that, on average, each food truck is expected to increase sales by $60,000 per year, but also to increase expenses by $40,000 per year. Sparky's has set a 9 percent minimum rate of return.

Sparky's current financial data is provided:

Sparky's Current Financial Data	
Sales	$2,000,000.00
Expenses	$ 1,250,000.00
Operating income	$ 750,000.00
Total assets	$3,250,000.00
Total liabilities	$ 7,663,000.00

Required:

Use Sparky's current financial data to calculate:

a. Sparky's current residual income.

b. Sparky's residual income if it purchases 1, 2, 3, or 4 new food trucks.

c. How many food trucks should Sparky's purchase to maximize residual income?

12. (LO8.5) ShopTime is a (fictitious) multinational retailer that sells groceries and home goods. Corporate uses EVA to evaluate the financial performance of its regions. Use the data for ShopTime Asia, shown below, to calculate the EVA for this business unit.

Shoptime—Asia	
Total assets	$75,000,000
Total liabilities	$60,000,000
Current liabilities	$48,000,000
Operating profit (before tax)	$22,000,000
Operating profit (after tax)	$17,000,000
Weighted-average cost of capital	12%

13. (LO8.4) Design effective performance measures for each of the following organizations:

   a. **Tifosi Optics** is an eyewear brand offering a wide range of eyewear for various sports, including cycling, running, golf, and baseball. Assume its primary goals are to earn a profit while becoming the chosen eyewear for youth and collegiate athletics. Currently Tifosi is organized such that it has only one responsibility center.

   b. **BlueRidge Chair Works** specializes in producing handcrafted outdoor furniture. Assume its primary goals are to produce durable, unique, high-quality furniture; promote sustainability; and produce high revenues, while maintaining low costs. At BlueRidge Chair Works, the production facilities are a revenue center, while the accounting, human resources, and IT functions are combined into a single cost center.

   c. Assume **General Electric** has three business segments: Power, Aviation, and Renewable Energy. Each segment operates as an investment center.

14. (LO8.2) Use the Internet to research decentralized and centralized organizations.

   a. Identify one (real) manufacturing organization with a decentralized structure and describe its structure. Comment on whether you think this structure is appropriate (or not) and why.

   b. Identify one service organization with a centralized structure and describe its structure. Comment on whether you think this structure is appropriate (or not) and why.

15. (LO8.6) At Anderson Products, the plastics division is a profit center that sells its products to external customers as well as to other internal profit centers. Recently, the sales manager has approved significant sales to another Anderson Products division that is also a profit center for a price that is below the market-based transfer price. Provide a justification for this decision by the sales manager.

Problems   Mc Graw Hill connect

For all answers, round percentages to two decimals.

1. (LO8.5) **Jittery Joe's Coffee Roasters** produces and sells freshly roasted coffee beans. Assume the company sells everything it produces each month. Management expects the following financial and production results for each month in 2023.

Current assets	$ 500,000	
Long-term assets	$1,005,000	
Total assets	$1,505,000	
Production	90,000	cans of roasted coffee per month
Target ROI	25%	
Fixed costs	$300,000	
Variable costs	$5	per can

Required

What is the minimum that Jittery Joe's must charge for each can of coffee to achieve its target ROI?

2. (LO8.5) **Jittery Joe's Coffee Roasters** produces and sells freshly roasted coffee beans. Assume the company sells everything it produces each month. Also assume that it sells each can of coffee for $12.00. Management expects the following financial and production results for each month in 2023.

Current assets	$ 500,000	
Long-term assets	$1,005,000	
Total assets	$1,505,000	
Production	90,000	cans of roasted coffee per month
Target ROI	25%	
Fixed costs	$300,000	
Variable costs	$5	per can
Required rate of return	14%	

Required

Calculate residual income for Jittery Joe's.

3. (LO8.5) Assume that **Marucci Bats** has four production facilities in the United States. The average sales price for each bat is $400. The anticipated financial results for each geographic division (separately) are shown below.

Required

For each production facility, calculate the ROI (rounded to the nearest whole percentage) and residual income (rounded to the nearest whole number) and answer questions a–d.

	North	South	East	West
Current Assets	$ 1,900,000	$ 1,876,000	$ 200,000	$ 1,700,000
Long-Term Assets	$ 3,705,000	$3,900,000	$3,910,000	$3,900,700
Total Assets	$5,605,000	$ 5,776,000	$ 4,110,000	$5,600,700
Production	28,000	30,000	27,000	32,000
Target ROI	25%	25%	25%	25%
Fixed Costs	$ 1,900,000	$ 1,910,000	$1,899,000	$2,300,000
Variable Costs	$ 290	$ 298	$ 276	$ 294
Required Rate of Return	20%	20%	20%	20%

a. Which production facility has the highest ROI?

b. Which, if any, production facilities do not achieve the target ROI?

c. Which, if any, production facilities do not meet the required rate of return?

d. Which production facility has the lowest residual income?

4. (LO8.5) **Phipps Chips** makes artisan potato chips in a variety of flavors. The company sells 12-ounce bags of a variety of flavors in grocery store chains such as **Whole Foods** and **Fresh Market** for $8.00 a bag.

Required

Use the following financial data to calculate the ROI, RI, and EVA for Phipps Chips. (Remember: Interest costs are tax-deductible, so you will need to consider the after-tax cost of financing debt when calculating EVA.) Then answer questions a–c.

Phipps Chips Projected Financial Data	
Current Assets	$ 1,000,000
Long-Term Assets	$2,500,000
Total Assets	$3,500,000
Current Liabilities	$ 950,000
Long-Term Liabilities	$ 1,500,000
Total Liabilities	$2,450,000
Equity	$ 1,050,000
Production units	100,000
Sales Price	$ 8
Target ROI	15%
Fixed Costs	$ 205,000
Variable Costs	$ 1.50
Required Rate of Return	14%
Income Tax Rate	25%
Interest Rate	10%

a. What is Phipps Chips' ROI? Round your answer to two decimal places.

b. What is Phipps Chips' residual income? Round your answer to the nearest dollar.

c. What is Phipps Chips' EVA? For calculations, round numbers to three decimal places (for example, 0.755). Round your answer to the nearest dollar.

5. (LO8.5) Deluxxe Burgers operates four restaurants in the Washington, DC, area.

Required

Use the following data to calculate ROI using the DuPont method to compare the performance of the four restaurants.

	Congress Heights	Dupont Circle	Foggy Bottom	Georgetown
Current Assets	$ 1,650,000	$ 1,815,000	$ 1,850,000	$ 1,900,500
Long-Term Assets	$ 1,900,000	$ 2,125,000	$ 1,600,000	$ 1,760,000
Total Assets	$ 3,550,000	$3,940,000	$3,450,000	$3,660,500
Monthly Sales	$ 1,000,000	$1,250,000	$ 1,250,000	$ 1,250,000
Target ROI	11%	12%	10%	13%
Fixed Costs	$ 800,000	$ 700,000	$ 800,000	$ 750,000
Variable Operational Costs (per $100,000 in sales)	$ 3,000	$ 2,500	$ 3,250	$ 5,000
Required Rate of Return	12%	12%	12%	12%
ROI	5%	13%	12%	12%
Residual Income	$(229,000.00)	$74,075.00	$ 31,937.50	$54,490.00
Income	$ 170,000	$ 518,750	$ 409,375	$ 437,500

6. (LO8.5) Precision Iron Works services large industrial clients in the southwest United States. Annual financial results from last year are as follows:

Precision Iron Works		
	Division A	Division B
Current Assets	$ 1,900,000	$ 1,876,000
Long-Term Assets	$ 3,705,000	$4,000,000
Total Assets	$5,605,000	$5,876,000
Production (units)	28,000	32,500
Target ROI	20%	20%
Fixed Costs	$ 1,900,000	$2,005,500
Variable Costs	$ 290	$ 300
Required Rate of Return	20%	20%
Sales Price per Production Unit	$ 400	$ 400
Operating Income	$ 1,180,000	$ 1,244,500

Executive management has offered each division the opportunity to invest $1.1 million in new equipment that will result in an additional 1,500 units in sales.

Required

Calculate the ROI and RI for each division currently and with the proposed new investment. Then answer the following questions related to which, if any, division will make the investment.

a. Assume division management is incentivized based on trends in ROI only. Explain why each division would or would not choose to invest.

b. Assume division management is incentivized based on RI only. Explain why each division would or would not choose to invest.

c. What do your results reveal about differences between ROI and RI as methods for incentivizing management?

7. (LO8.2) Microdata is a fictitious electronics manufacturing company that specializes in the production of electronic components such as microchips and circuit boards. It has long operated as a centralized organization, with all divisions and operations managed by one central control system. But as the company has grown and increased its international presence, there is growing support for reorganizing with a decentralized structure.

The CEO has turned to you, Microdata's head cost accountant, to prepare a memo explaining the following:

a. The benefits of a decentralized structure.

b. The drawbacks of a decentralized structure.

c. The specific changes that Microdata would have to make to change from a centralized structure to a decentralized structure.

Microdata has significant operations in the United States, Argentina, and Germany, and if the company transforms to a decentralized structure, it will organize around these three geographic locations.

Required

Prepare the memo that the CEO has requested.

8. (LO8.3) Piedmont Pharmaceuticals is a multinational health care products company. The company has four divisions, each with its own research, manufacturing operations, and management teams. Division 1 has its own production facility, located in a major industrial

park near the city of Shenzhen, China. Division 1 produces the generic drugs that Piedmont sells. Division 2 is located near Raleigh, North Carolina, in the United States. Here Piedmont has extensive R & D facilities and focuses on the development of new vaccines and the improvement of existing vaccines. Division 3 is located outside of Tokyo, Japan, and also has an extensive R & D facility that focuses on the development and production of drugs derived from living organisms, such as bacteria or mammalian cells. These drugs are generally used to treat complex medical conditions such as cancers, autoimmune disorders, and genetic diseases. Finally, Division 4 is located near Frankfurt, Germany. Branded prescription drugs and various over-the-counter (OTC) drugs are developed in this facility.

Each division sets its own production schedules and develops performance measures based on cost variances, product quality, sales, and development of new patents, if applicable.

Required

Answer the following questions.

a. Is Piedmont Pharmaceuticals organized with a centralized structure or a decentralized structure?

b. Is each of the four divisions a cost center, revenue center, or profit center?

c. If Piedmont were to restructure such that senior management of the entire company set the production schedules and evaluated each of the divisions using the same performance metrics, how would this change your answers to a and b?

d. Do you think Piedmont Pharmaceuticals should be set up as a centralized organization or as a decentralized organization? Explain your answer.

9. (LO8.4) Caliber Consulting is a fictitious consulting firm headquartered in San Jose, California. It specializes in the tech sector and accepts clients from all industries around the world. It has a centralized structure, but vice presidents oversee operations in each of its four major geographic regions so that it can respond quickly to changing customer needs. You have been tasked with helping Caliber develop an effective performance-measurement program.

Required

Use the four-step plan for establishing effective performance measures to design an effective performance-measurement program for Caliber Consulting.

10. (LO8.1) The following is a list of controls.

Required

Identify whether each control is a formal control or informal control, and whether it is a behavioral control or output control.

Control	Formal Control, Informal Control, or Neither	Behavioral Control, Output Control, or Neither
a. Quality-control procedures		
b. Training and development programs		
c. Code of conduct		
d. Employee incentives		
e. Quality inspections		
f. Customer satisfaction surveys		
g. Inventory tracking systems		
h. Company culture		
i. Open communication		
j. Customer feedback		
k. Standard operating procedures		

11. (LO8.6) NovaTech Innovations is a technology company that produces a variety of "smart" household appliances, including refrigerators and dishwashers that connect to the Internet. NovaTech has a decentralized structure. The Smart Tech Division produces the technology that can be embedded in various household appliances. This technology can be sold to external producers of appliances (such as **GE** or **Whirlpool**) or can be transferred internally to NovaTech's own appliance divisions. Similarly, NovaTech's Appliance Division can buy similar smart tech from an external supplier for $15 per unit. Use the following data to calculate the effects of an internal transfer of technology using a (a) market-based, (b) cost-based, and (c) hybrid transfer price.

- NovaTech sells its smart technology to external customers for $18 per unit.
- NovaTech's Appliance Division's production budget plans for 750,000 appliances sold per year.
- NovaTech's Smart Tech Division produces 1,500,000 smart-technology devices per year.
- The Smart Tech Division has $50,000 in fixed costs, and variable costs average $7.00 per unit.
- The Appliance Division sells appliances for $2,500. Fixed manufacturing costs are $75,000. The cost of the smart technology will vary based on the agreed-upon price. Other variable costs amount to $150 per unit.

Required

Calculate the operating income for the Smart Tech Division, Appliance Division, and NovaTech overall based only on the internal sales between the Smart Tech and Appliance Divisions using the:

a. Market price

b. Full-cost price

c. Hybrid price of $17 per unit

12. (LO8.6) Use the same data provided in Problem 11 to calculate and compare the impact of using the market price, full-cost price, and hybrid price as the transfer price between the Smart Tech and Appliance Divisions. However, now assume that NovaTech is a global enterprise with the Smart Tech Division located in the United States, where there is a 21 percent corporate tax rate, and the Appliance Division located in Germany, where there is a 30 percent corporate tax rate.

Required

Calculate the operating income for the Smart Tech Division, Appliance Division, and NovaTech overall based only on the internal sales between the Smart Tech and Appliance Divisions using the:

a. Market price

b. Full-cost price

c. Hybrid price of $17 per unit

d. Determine which transfer price generates the largest operating income for NovaTech overall when the international tax rates are applied.

13. (LO8.6) Use the same data provided in Problem 11 to calculate and compare the impact of using the market price, full-cost price, and hybrid price as the transfer price between the Smart Tech and Appliance Divisions. However, assume that NovaTech is considering moving its Smart Tech operations to Ireland (with a 12.5 percent corporate tax rate), Dubai (with a 9 percent corporate tax rate), or Mexico (with a 30 percent corporate tax rate). The company has already decided to move the Appliance Division to Mexico.

Required

Consider the impact of the different tax rates on overall operating income for NovaTech using a market price, full-cost price, or hybrid price for the transfer price.

a. Document all results in the following table.

Possible Smart Tech Locations	Market Price	Full Cost	Hybrid
Ireland			
Mexico			
Dubai			

b. Which location and transfer price decision yields the largest overall income?

14. (LO8.5) Assume that Big League Bats has four production facilities in the United States. The average sales price for each bat is $325. The anticipated financial results for each division (separately) are shown below.

Required

Calculate the ROI and residual income for each production facility and answer questions a–f.

	Division 1	Division 2	Division 3	Division 4
Current Assets	$2,000,000	$1,900,000	$2,500,000	$2,250,000
Long-Term Assets	$4,000,000	$4,500,000	$3,595,000	$4,000,000
Total Assets	$6,000,000	$6,400,000	$6,095,000	$6,250,000
Production	45,000	48,000	38,000	52,000
Target ROI	25%	25%	25%	25%
Fixed Costs	$3,000,000	$3,200,000	$3,500,000	$2,980,000
Variable Costs	$250	$225	$215	$265
Required Rate of Return	20%	20%	20%	20%

a. Which production facility has the highest ROI?

b. Which production facility has the lowest residual income?

c. If Big League decides to sell off 25 percent of its long-term assets from Division 4, how does that decision change its ROI and residual income? Assume that long-term assets are reduced by 25 percent but no other balance sheet items are changed. Provide the percentage and dollar value impacts of the change and a written description of why this change affects ROI and residual income in this way.

d. Assume Division 1 management is able to reduce its variable costs by $10 per bat. How does this change its ROI and residual income? Provide the percentage and dollar value impacts of the change and a written description of why this change affects ROI and residual income in this way.

e. Assume Division 2 has production problems and shuts down operations for approximately two weeks, reducing production by 2,000 units. How does this change its ROI and residual income? Provide the percentage and dollar value impacts of the change and a written description of why this change affects ROI and residual income in this way.

f. Assume Division 3 actually has a lower required rate of return than the other divisions. The required rate of return is 9% instead of 10%. How does this change its ROI and residual income? Provide the percentage and dollar value impacts of the change and a written description of why this change affects ROI and residual income in this way.

15. **(LO8.5) Hibo** makes hibiscus-based all-natural energy drinks in a variety of flavors. The company sells four-packs of the beverage at grocery store chains such as **Target** and **EarthFare** for $11 each.

Required

Use the following financial data to calculate the ROI, RI, and EVA for Hibo. (Remember: Interest costs are tax-deductible, so you will need to consider the after-tax cost of financing debt when calculating EVA.) Then answer the following questions.

Hibo Projected Financial Data	
Current Assets	$2,500,000
Long-Term Assets	$3,000,000
Total Assets	$5,500,000
Current Liabilities	$2,500,000
Long-Term Liabilities	$ 1,500,000
Total Liabilities	$4,000,000
Equity	$ 1,500,000
Production units	195,000
Sales Price	$ 11
Target ROI	15%
Fixed Costs	$ 700,000
Variable Costs	$ 3.50
Required Rate of Return	14%
Income Tax Rate	25%
Interest Rate	10%

a. What is Hibo's ROI?
b. What is Hibo's residual income?
c. What is Hibo's EVA?
d. If Hibo reduced its long-term assets by 50 percent, would that action increase, decrease, or have no impact on ROI, residual income, and EVA?

Lab 8.1 Excel

Evaluating Business Units Using ROI

Data Analytics Type: Descriptive Analytics

Lab Note: The tools presented in this lab periodically change. Updated instructions, if applicable, can be found in the student and instructor support materials.

Keywords
ROI, Business Segments, Performance Evaluation

Decision-Making Context
The Sherwin-Williams Company manufactures, develops, distributes, and sells paints, coatings, and related products to professional, industrial, commercial, and retail customers. It sells its product through company-owned stores and mass merchandisers, including **Home Depot**. Sherwin-Williams is organized into three business segments: the Americas Group, Consumer Brands Group, and Performance Coatings Group.

Return on investment (ROI) is a commonly used measure of short-term financial performance. It measures the amount of money made with an investment in assets relative to the cost of that investment. It is popular because it is easy to calculate and easily comparable across business units.

Required
1. Use Excel to calculate and compare the ROI of the three business segments of The Sherwin-Williams Company in 2018, 2019, and 2020.
2. Show results graphically as well as numerically.

Ask the Question
Which business segment has the highest ROI? In which year is the ROI highest for that business unit? Which business segment has the lowest ROI?

Master the Data
The data for this lab have been downloaded from the Securities and Exchange Commission (SEC) to the Excel workbook titled **Lab 8.1 Data.xlsx**. The complete original data can be found online at https://www.sec.gov/ix?doc=/Archives/edgar/data/89800/000008980021000010/shw-20201231.htm.

Perform the Analysis

Analysis Task #1: Build Your Data Table and Calculate ROI

1. On the first tab, labeled **Sherwin Williams Financial Data**, you will find the selected financial figures for each business segment as reported in the Sherwin Williams 2020 financial report (available online).

2. As noted above, in this lab we will calculate the ROI for each reportable business unit from The Sherwin Williams Company in 2018, 2019, and 2020. We will also use Excel's charting function to create visualizations to compare ROI graphically. To do this, first, create a new tab and label it "ROI Results" (Lab Exhibit 8.1.1). You will need to make a table of the ROI data on this page. In cell A1, enter the title "ROI Calculated as Income/Investment". In cells A4, A5, and A6, enter the years "2020", "2019", and "2018", respectively. In cells B3, C3, and D3, enter "The Americas Group", "Consumer Brands Group", and "Protective Coatings Group", respectively. You now have the row and column headers for your ROI table.

Lab Exhibit 8.1.1

Microsoft Excel

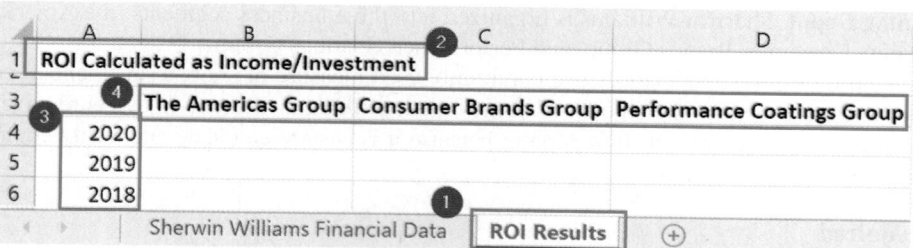

3. Use formulas to calculate ROI and populate the cells in this table. In B4, calculate ROI for The Americas Group in 2020 using the division formula shown in Lab Exhibit 8.1.2:

Cell B4: ='Sherwin Williams Financial Data'!B9/'Sherwin Williams Financial Data'!B15

Do not type the values for segment profit and identifiable assets into this cell. Instead, use cell references to extract these values from the financial data on the previous worksheet. Display ROI rounded to 2 decimals using the **Decrease Decimal** icon on the **Home** tab (see Lab Exhibit 8.1.5). Complete the rest of the table in the same way, using the Excel formulas shown in Lab Exhibit 8.1.2, Lab Exhibit 8.1.3, and Lab Exhibit 8.1.4, as follows:

Cell B5: ='Sherwin Williams Financial Data'!B26/'Sherwin Williams Financial Data'!B32

Cell B6: ='Sherwin Williams Financial Data'!B43/'Sherwin Williams Financial Data'!B49

Cell C4: ='Sherwin Williams Financial Data'!C9/'Sherwin Williams Financial Data'!C15

Cell C5: ='Sherwin Williams Financial Data'!C26/'Sherwin Williams Financial Data'!C32

Cell C6: ='Sherwin Williams Financial Data'!C43/'Sherwin Williams Financial Data'!C49

Cell D4: ='Sherwin Williams Financial Data'!D9/'Sherwin Williams Financial Data'!D15

Cell D5: ='Sherwin Williams Financial Data'!D26/'Sherwin Williams Financial Data'!D32

Cell D6: ='Sherwin Williams Financial Data'!D43/'Sherwin Williams Financial Data'!D49

	A	B
1	ROI Calculated as Income/Investment	
2		
3		The Americas Group
4	2020	='Sherwin Williams Financial Data'!B9/'Sherwin Williams Financial Data'!B15
5	2019	='Sherwin Williams Financial Data'!B26/'Sherwin Williams Financial Data'!B32
6	2018	='Sherwin Williams Financial Data'!B43/'Sherwin Williams Financial Data'!B49
7		

Lab Exhibit 8.1.2
Microsoft Excel

	A	B	D
1	ROI Calculated as Income/Investment		
2			
3			Consumer Brands Group
4	2020		='Sherwin Williams Financial Data'!C9/'Sherwin Williams Financial Data'!C15
5	2019		='Sherwin Williams Financial Data'!C26/'Sherwin Williams Financial Data'!C32
6	2018		='Sherwin Williams Financial Data'!C43/'Sherwin Williams Financial Data'!C49

Lab Exhibit 8.1.3
Microsoft Excel

	A	B	E
1	ROI Calculated as Income/Investment		
2			
3			Performance Coatings Group
4	2020		='Sherwin Williams Financial Data'!D9/'Sherwin Williams Financial Data'!D15
5	2019		='Sherwin Williams Financial Data'!D26/'Sherwin Williams Financial Data'!D32
6	2018		='Sherwin Williams Financial Data'!D43/'Sherwin Williams Financial Data'!D49

Lab Exhibit 8.1.4
Microsoft Excel

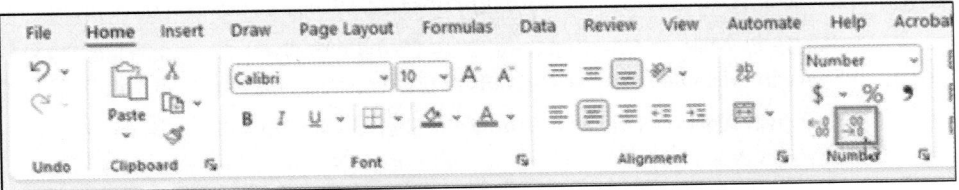

Lab Exhibit 8.1.5
Microsoft Excel

When you are done, your results should resemble Lab Exhibit 8.1.6.

	A	B	C	D
1	**ROI Calculated as Income/Investment**			
2				
3		**The Americas Group**	**Consumer Brands Group**	**Performance Coatings Group**
4	2020	0.43	0.11	0.06
5	2019	0.38	0.07	0.05
6	2018	0.47	0.05	0.05
7				
8				

Lab Exhibit 8.1.6

Microsoft Excel

Analysis Task #2: Recalculate ROI Using the DuPont Method

1. Let's confirm that you can also calculate ROI as a function of Return on Sales and Asset Turnover using the formula ROI = (Profit/Sales) * (Sales/Average Total Assets). To do this, you will create a second ROI table to the right of the first one. In cell F1, enter the title "ROI Calculated as Return on Sales * Asset Turnover". In cells F4, F5, and F6, enter the years "2020", "2019", and "2018", respectively. In cells G3, H3, and I3, enter "The Americas Group", "Consumer Brands Group", and "Protective Coatings Group", respectively.

2. Use formulas to calculate ROI and populate the cells in this table. In cell B4, calculate ROI for The Americas Group in 2020 as ROI = (Segment Profit/Net External Sales) * (Net External Sales/Identifiable Assets). Use the Excel formula shown in Lab Exhibit 8.1.7. Do not type the values for segment profit and identifiable assets into this cell. Instead, use cell references to extract these values from the financial data on the previous worksheet. Display ROI rounded to 2 decimals using the **Decrease Decimal Icon** on the **Home** tab (see Lab Exhibit 8.1.5). Complete the rest of the table in the same way, using the Excel formulas shown in Lab Exhibit 8.1.7:

   2020: =('Sherwin Williams Financial Data'!B9/'Sherwin Williams Financial Data'!B5)*('Sherwin Williams Financial Data'!B5/'Sherwin Williams Financial Data'!B15)

   2019: =('Sherwin Williams Financial Data'!B26/'Sherwin Williams Financial Data'!B22)*('Sherwin Williams Financial Data'!B22/'Sherwin Williams Financial Data'!B32)

   2018: =('Sherwin Williams Financial Data'!B43/'Sherwin Williams Financial Data'!B39)*('Sherwin Williams Financial Data'!B39/'Sherwin Williams Financial Data'!B49)

Lab Exhibit 8.1.7

Microsoft Excel

G	H
ROI Calculated as Return on Sales X Asset Turnover	
	The Americas Group
2020	=('Sherwin Williams Financial Data'!B9/'Sherwin Williams Financial Data'!B5)* ('Sherwin Williams Financial Data'!B5/'Sherwin Williams Financial Data'!B15)
2019	=('Sherwin Williams Financial Data'!B26/'Sherwin Williams Financial Data'!B22)* ('Sherwin Williams Financial Data'!B22/'Sherwin Williams Financial Data'!B32)
2018	=('Sherwin Williams Financial Data'!B43/'Sherwin Williams Financial Data'!B39)* ('Sherwin Williams Financial Data'!B39/'Sherwin Williams Financial Data'!B49)

When you are done, your results should resemble Lab Exhibit 8.1.8.

ROI Calculated as Return on Sales * Asset Turnover			
	The Americas Group	Consumer Brands Group	Performance Coatings Group
2020	0.43	0.11	0.06
2019	0.38	0.07	0.05
2018	0.47	0.05	0.05

Lab Exhibit 8.1.8

Microsoft Excel

Analysis Task #3: Create a Column Chart to Examine Results Visually

1. Create a column chart to visually compare these results. Highlight the first ROI table that you created. (*Note:* Really, you could use either table to create your chart because the results reported in the tables are the same.) Click on the **Insert** tab, then the **Column Chart** icon. Select the first 2-D column chart (Lab Exhibit 8.1.9).

DATA VISUALIZATION

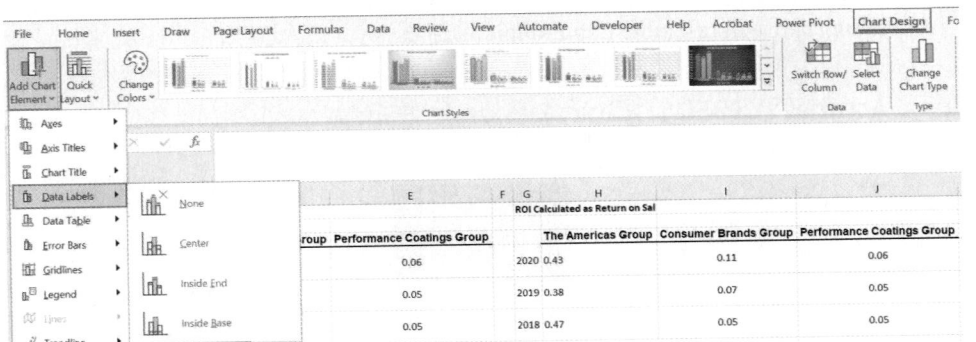

Lab Exhibit 8.1.9

Microsoft Excel

2. Format the bar chart using options on the **Chart Design** tab. Click on the **Add Chart Element** icon, then **Data Labels**, then **Outside End** (Lab Exhibit 8.1.10). This will add the ROI values to the chart at the top of each column. Click the chart so that each of the grid lines is active. Delete the gridlines by right-clicking on them within the chart, and then select **Delete** (Lab Exhibit 8.1.11). Because this is a simple chart, the gridlines are not needed for interpretation. Click the vertical axis and delete this axis

Lab Exhibit 8.1.10

Microsoft Excel

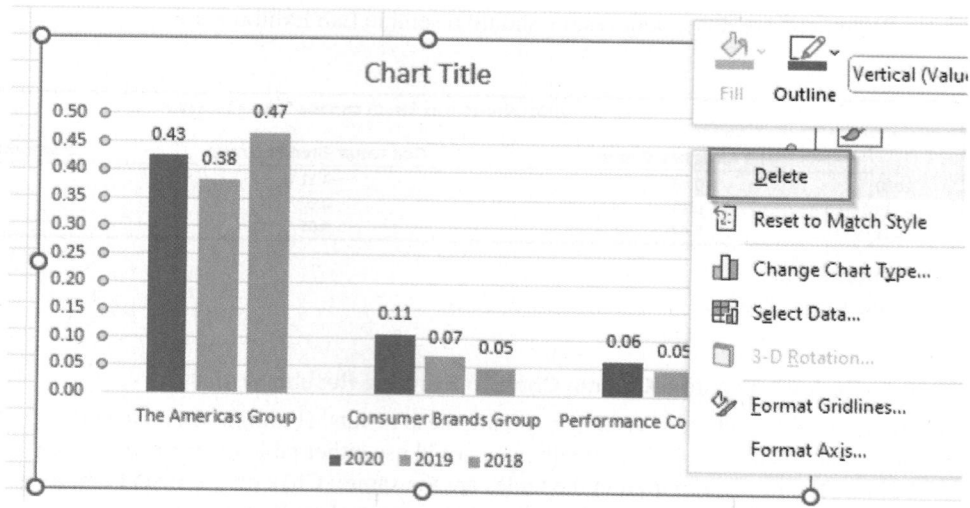

(Lab Exhibit 8.1.12). Because you have added the ROI data labels to the columns, you do not need the numbers on the axis. Click the **Chart Title** and rename the chart "ROI for Business Segments".

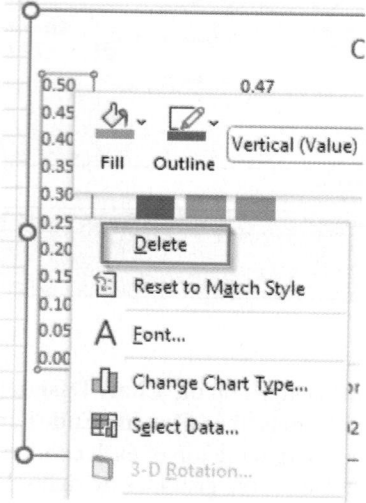

3. By default, the chart may cluster the ROI for each business segment by year. You can change it to cluster ROI for each year by business segment. In the **Chart Design** tab, click the **Switch Row/Column** icon (Lab Exhibit 8.1.13). When you are done, your column chart will resemble Lab Exhibit 8.1.14.

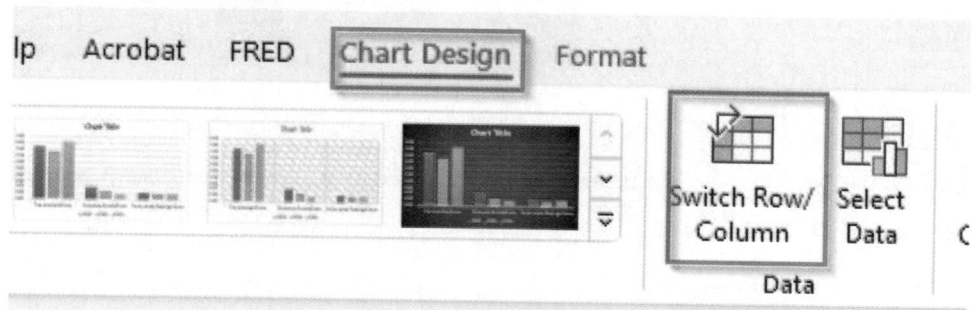

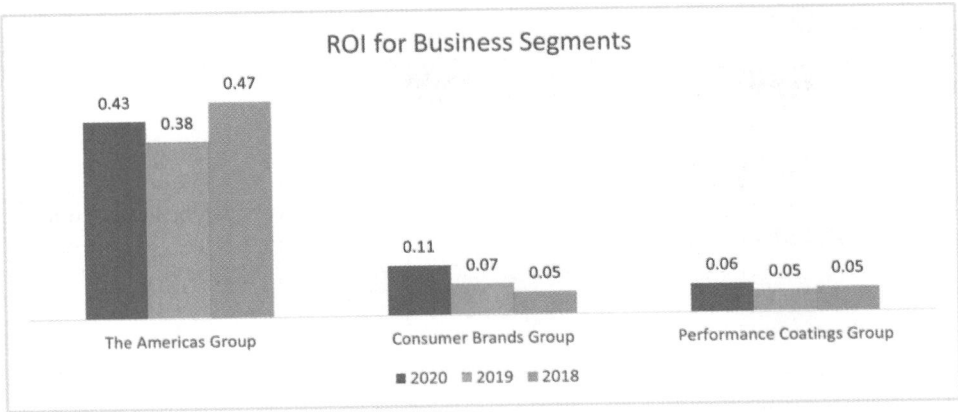

Share the Story

This analysis allows The Sherwin-Williams Company to compare ROI across the three reportable business segments and to evaluate changes in ROI over time. As you can see, ROI increased for all three divisions in 2020, relative to 2019. Furthermore, you can easily tell that The Americas Group is the dominant business segment, as revealed by the significantly greater ROI percentage than for the other two segments. This means that The Americas Group earned a great deal of profits as a result of its investment in assets.

Assessment

1. Take a screenshot of your table and chart, paste it into a Word document, and label it "Lab 8.1 Submission.docx".
2. Use your analysis to answer the questions in Connect and upload your Lab 8.1 Submission.docx via Connect if assigned.

Alternate Lab 8.1   Excel—On Your Own

Evaluating Business Units Using ROI

Data Analytics Type: Descriptive Analytics

Keywords

ROI, Business Segments

Decision-Making Context

Canvas Company is a (fictitious) global leader in the paints and coatings industry. It develops, manufactures, and distributes a broad range of coatings, paints, and related products. It operates in two reportable segments: Coatings and Paints.

Return on investment (ROI) is a commonly used measure of short-term financial performance. It measures the amount of money made with an investment in assets relative to the cost of that investment. It is popular because it is easy to calculate and easily comparable across business units.

Use Excel to calculate and compare the ROI of the two business segments of the Canvas Company in 2018, 2019, 2020, 2021, and 2022. Show your results graphically as well as numerically.

Ask the Question

Which business segment has the highest ROI? In which year is the ROI highest for that business unit? Which business segment has the lowest ROI?

Master the Data

Financial data from each reportable segment for five previous years can be accessed in the file titled **Alt Lab 8.1 Data.xlsx**.

Data Dictionary

You are given a set of segment data from the financial statements of the Canvas Company. The data dictionary includes:

Net Sales	Sales revenue for each business segment
EBIT	Earnings before interest and taxes, which is an indicator of a company's profitability. It is calculated as revenue minus expenses (excluding taxes and interest). It is often called "operating profit."
Identifiable Assets	Value of each business segment's investment in assets.

Share the Story

This analysis allows the Canvas Company to compare ROI across the two reportable business segments and to evaluate changes in ROI over time.

Assessment

1. Take a screenshot of your table and chart, paste it into a Word document, and label it "Alt Lab 8.1 Submission.docx".
2. Use your analysis to answer the questions in Connect and upload your Alt Lab 8.1 Submission.docx via Connect if assigned.

Comparing Different Financial Performance Measures across Business Units

Data Analytics Types: Descriptive Analytics, Diagnostic Analytics

Keywords

ROI, RI, EVA, Tableau

Decision-Making Context

Alpha Conglomerate is a fictional company that is based on **The 3M Company**. It operates in a variety of fields and has four business segments: safety and industrial products, health care, transportation and electronics, and consumer products.

Return on investment (ROI), residual income (RI), and economic value added (EVA) are three commonly used measures of short-term financial performance.

In this lab, we use Excel to calculate and compare the ROI of the four business segments of Alpha Conglomerate in 2023 and 2024.

Required

1. Use Tableau to calculate and compare ROI, RI, and EVA for each of the four business units at Alpha Conglomerate for 2023 and 2024.
2. Illustrate changes in ROI and RI over time for each business segment using an appropriate visualization.

Ask the Question

Which business segment had the highest ROI in 2023? In which year is the ROI highest for that business unit? Which business segment had the lowest RI in 2024? Which business unit saw the biggest performance changes over the two-year period?

Master the Data

The dataset in **Lab 8.2 Data.xlsx** includes all of the relevant financial figures needed to calculate ROI, RI, and EVA for each of the four business segments in 2023 and 2024.

Data Dictionary

Business Unit	The business unit (BU) being evaluated. There are four BUs at Alpha Conglomerate: safety and industrial products, health care, transportation and electronics, and consumer products.
Year	The year associated with the financial data
Net Sales	Sales revenue for each business unit
Operating Income	Profit realized by the business unit
Average Total Assets	Value of the amount invested in assets that are used by the business unit to conduct operations
Revenue	Total amount of money generated by the business unit's operations
Minimum Rate of Return	The lowest acceptable amount of earnings from an organization's investment in assets. It represents the amount required to recover the money spent on the investment.

Lab Note: The tools presented in this lab periodically change. Updated instructions, if applicable, can be found in the student and instructor support materials. All Lab Exhibits are available within the eBook and in Connect.

Tax Rate	Tax rate charged to the organization
Debt	Amount of debt the business unit has accumulated through loans
Equity	Investments made in the business unit that can be used for operations
Interest Rate	The percentage that a lender (for example, a bank) charges the borrower for a loan
Cost of Capital	The return an organization must earn to justify the cost of a capital project (for example, purchasing new equipment, constructing a new warehouse). It is calculated as a percentage of the debt and equity required to complete the project.
Current Liabilities	Debts and obligations that must be repaid within the year

Perform the Analysis

Analysis Task #1: Load the Data

1. Open Tableau. Select **Connect to Data**, then **Microsoft Excel**, then **Lab 8.2 Data.xlsx**.
2. Drag the **Financial Data** tab onto the active data window (Lab Exhibit 8.2.1).
3. Open **Sheet 1**. Before you begin building your visualization, you will need to calculate the various performance measures used to evaluate the business units at Alpha Conglomerate.

Analysis Task #2: Calculate ROI, Residual Income, and EVA

1. Select **Analysis**, then **Create Calculated Field** from the top of the screen (Lab Exhibit 8.2.2).
2. Name this new field "ROI".
3. Drag the required fields into the window to enter the formula for ROI. The formula should appear as displayed in Lab Exhibit 8.2.3. The formula is [Operating income]/[Average Total Assets].

    Once you have calculated this new ROI field, you will see it added to your **Measures** pane on the left side of your screen (Lab Exhibit 8.2.4).
4. Repeat Steps 1–3 to calculate residual income, using the formula shown in Lab Exhibit 8.2.5: [Operating income]–([Required Rate of Return]*[Average Total Assets]).
5. Before you calculate EVA, it may be easiest to calculate a weighted average cost of capital (WACC) field to use in the EVA calculation. Follow Steps 1–3 to calculate WACC using the formula shown in Lab Exhibit 8.2.6: (([Equity]*[Cost of Capital])+([Debt]*[Interest Rate]))/([Debt]+[Equity]).
6. Follow Steps 1–3 to calculate EVA. Use WACC as calculated in Lab Exhibit 8.2.6. See Lab Exhibit 8.2.7 for the formula for EVA: ([Operating income]*(1–[Tax Rate]))–([WACC]*([Average Total Assets]–[Current Liabilities])).

Analysis Task #3: Build a Column Chart Visualization to Compare Business Units on Each Performance Measure

DATA VISUALIZATION

1. Drag **Business Unit** and **Year** to the **Columns** shelf. For this analysis, you want to see how the performance measures change over time within each business unit. So, you'll want to show the business unit pill first on the **Columns** shelf, followed by the year pill (Lab Exhibit 8.2.8).

Note: Depending on how Tableau imported your data, you may have to change the data type for the variable **Year** to be **Date & Time** (see Lab Exhibit 8.2.9).

2. Drag the **ROI**, **Residual Income**, and **EVA** pills to the **Rows** shelf (Lab Exhibit 8.2.10). Tableau defaults to summing these data. Because you have only one data point for each business unit/year combination, it does not matter if you use sum, average, etc.

3. Tableau has defaulted to showing your data as a series of line graphs (because you are analyzing data over time). However, for our purposes, column charts will be more useful. As shown in Lab Exhibit 8.2.11, click on the drop-down box from the **Marks** card to change the type of visualization to bar chart.

4. To make this visualization easier to interpret, drag the **Year** variable (from the **Data** window on the left) to the **Color** marks card on the right (Lab Exhibit 8.2.12). The result appears in Lab Exhibit 8.2.13.

5. Add mark (data) labels to the top of each column to show the total by clicking on the **Analysis** menu and selecting **Show Mark Labels** (Lab Exhibit 8.2.14).

6. Format mark labels appropriately. Right-click on ROI within the visualization and select **Format**. On the pane that opens, select the **Pane** tab and click the drop-down next to **Numbers** and then select **Percentage** and change the **Decimal places** to 0 (see Lab Exhibits 8.2.15 and 8.2.16). The result appears in Lab Exhibit 8.2.17.

7. Format the other mark labels, Residual Income and EVA, appropriately.

8. Once you show the mark labels on each column, you no longer need the tick marks on the Y-axis to interpret the data. To get to the **Edit Axis [ROI]** window (shown in Lab Exhibit 8.2.18), just right-click on the Y-axis. Select **None** under **Major Tick Marks** and **Minor Tick Marks**.

9. Add a title to your visualization, "BU Comparison: ROI, RI, and EVA," by right-clicking on the title at the top of the visualization and then selecting **Edit Title...** (Lab Exhibit 8.2.19). **Center** the title (Lab Exhibit 8.2.20).

The final visualization should look like the one shown in Lab Exhibit 8.2.21.

Share the Story

The visualization you have prepared allows Alpha Conglomerate's management to compare the financial performance of its different business segments across two years. Using it, you can answer each of the questions that management raised at the start of this lab:

Management's Question	Answer Based on Data Analysis
Which business segment had the highest ROI in 2023?	Health Care
In which year is the ROI highest for that business unit?	2023
Which business segment had the lowest RI in 2024?	Consumer
Which business unit saw the biggest performance changes over the two-year period?	Transportation & Electronics saw significant decreases in each performance measure between 2023 and 2024.

Assessment

1. Switch to presentation view. Take a screenshot of your visualization, paste it into a Word document, and label it "Lab 8.2 Submission.docx".

2. Use your analysis to answer the questions in Connect and upload your Lab 8.2 Submission.docx via Connect if assigned.

Comparing Different Financial Performance Measures across Business Units

Data Analytics Types: Descriptive Analytics, Diagnostic Analytics

Keywords

ROI, RI, EVA, Tableau

Decision-Making Context

Beta Conglomerate is a fictional company that is based on **The 3M Company**. It operates in a variety of fields and has four business segments: safety and industrial products, health care, transportation and electronics, and consumer products.

Return on investment (ROI), residual income (RI), and economic value added (EVA) are three commonly used measures of short-term financial performance.

Required

1. Use Tableau to calculate and compare ROI, RI, and EVA for each of the four business units at Beta Conglomerate for 2021 and 2022.
2. Illustrate changes in ROI and RI over time for each business segment using an appropriate visualization.

Ask the Question

Which business segment had the highest ROI in 2021? In which year is the ROI highest for that business unit? Which business segment had the lowest RI in 2022? Which business unit saw the biggest performance changes over the two-year period?

Master the Data

The dataset titled **Alt Lab 8.2 Data.xlsx** includes all of the relevant financial figures needed to calculate ROI, RI, and EVA for each of the four business segments in 2021 and 2022.

Data Dictionary

Business Unit	The business unit being evaluated. There are four BUs at Beta Conglomerate: safety and industrial products, health care, transportation and electronics, and consumer products.
Year	The year associated with the financial data
Net Sales	Sales revenue for each business unit
Operating Income	Profit realized by the business unit
Total Assets	Value of the amount invested in assets that are used by the business unit to conduct operations
Revenue	Total amount of money generated by the business unit's operations
Minimum Rate of Return	The lowest acceptable amount of earnings from an organization's investment in assets. It represents the amount required to recover the money spent on the investment.

Tax Rate	Tax rate charged to the organization
Debt	Amount of debt the business unit has accumulated through loans
Equity	Investments made in the business unit that can be used for operations
Interest Rate	The percentage that a lender (for example, a bank) charges the borrower for a loan
Cost of Capital	The return an organization must earn to justify the cost of a capital project (for example, purchasing new equipment, constructing a new warehouse). It is calculated as a percentage of the debt and equity required to complete the project.
Current Liabilities	Debts and obligations that must be repaid within the year

Share the Story

The visualization you have prepared allows Beta Conglomerate management to compare the financial performance of its different business segments across two years.

Assessment

1. Switch to presentation view. Take a screenshot of your visualization, paste it into a Word document, and label it "Alt Lab 8.2 Submission.docx".
2. Use your analysis to answer the questions in Connect and upload your Alt Lab 8.2 Submission.docx via Connect if assigned.

Lab Note: The tools presented in this lab periodically change. Updated instructions, if applicable, can be found in the student and instructor support materials. All Lab Exhibits are available within the eBook and in Connect.

Incentivizing Performance with Budget Plans (Heartwood)

Data Analytics Types: Descriptive Analytics, Diagnostic Analytics

Keywords

Performance Measures, ROI, Employee Incentives, Heat Map

Decision-Making Context

Several years ago, **Heartwood Cabinets** introduced a countertop division to sell granite, quartz, and marble countertops as a complement to kitchen cabinetry sales. The countertop division has several plants scattered across the United States. To encourage employees to increase profits, Heartwood implemented a bonus plan for the countertop division. Per the bonus plan, employees in the countertop division are awarded 80 percent of their plant's ROI, up to a maximum of 10 percent, as a salary bonus. For example, if a plant records a bonus of 5 percent, then employees of the plant receive a 4 percent bonus (5% * 80%).

ROI depends on operating income and average assets. Due to tax laws, new equipment is depreciated more in the first few years of the life of most assets than in later years.

Depreciation: The reduction in value of an asset as time passes, due to use, wear and tear, or obsolescence.

The corporate controller at Heartwood is concerned that the bonus plan is encouraging behavior that is inconsistent with the company's objectives. Specifically, Heartwood corporate leadership wants increased profits, but not all divisions are experiencing profit growth. You have been asked to analyze basic financial information to gain insight about the bonus structure and recent financial performance of Heartwood's countertop division.

Employees typically respond to incentives, and bonus plans can be an effective way to align employee performance with company goals. However, it can be difficult to design bonus plans, and many bonus plans encourage behavior that is contrary to company goals.

Required

1. Use Excel to calculate ROI for the manufacturing plants in Heartwood's countertop division.
2. Use the Correlation dialog box in Excel to determine whether employee bonuses are correlated with company goals, as measured by important financial ratios. Use conditional formatting to create a heat map from the correlation matrix data.

Ask the Question

Why aren't all countertop plants experiencing high-income growth? Is this outcome related to the company's bonus plan?

Master the Data

For this lab you will use data in the Excel file titled **Lab 8.3 Data.xlsx**.

Data Dictionary

Year	Date of the last calendar year for which data are compiled
Sales	Annual sales, in thousands of dollars
Operating Income	Annual operating income, in thousands of dollars
Average Assets	Average net assets for the year, in thousands of dollars

---

Perform the Analysis

Analysis Task #1: Calculate ROI for the Manufacturing Plants in Heartwood's Countertop Division.

1. Open Excel file **Lab 8.3 Data.xlsx**.
2. Quickly browse the spreadsheet to make sure there isn't any obvious error in the Excel file.
3. We will be using correlations for this lab. To use Excel's **Correlation** dialog box, we make sure our Analysis ToolPak is loaded by looking at the **Data** tab in the **Analysis** group and seeing if the **Data Analysis** add-in has been installed (Lab Exhibit 8.3.1).

   If it has not yet been added, go to **File > Options > Add-Ins** and select the **Analysis ToolPak** (Lab Exhibit 8.3.2). Then select **OK**.
4. To better analyze the data, add five blank rows to the worksheet starting in Row 7. To do so, left-click five rows starting in Row 7. Then, right-click and select **Insert** (Lab Exhibit 8.3.3). As you add data to the table, you may need to format the numbers. Use the **Number** group on the **Home** tab to change the format and the number of decimals displayed on the worksheet (Lab Exhibit 8.3.4).
5. Label Row 7 "Sales growth". In cell C7, insert the following formula: =(C4-B4)/B4. Note that we cannot use this formula in cell B7 because prior-year data are unavailable. Copy the formula over for all columns with data. To do so, click on the bottom-right corner of the cell and drag it to the right until you get to Column K (Lab Exhibit 8.3.5).
6. Label Rows 8–10 "Return on Sales", "Asset Turnover", and "ROI" respectively. You should be familiar with the formulas for these ratios from this chapter, but you can refer to Lab Exhibit 8.3.6 for assistance with the formulas:

   Cell B8: =B5/B4

   Cell B9: =B4/B6

   Cell B10: =B8*B9

Lab Exhibit 8.3.6

Microsoft Excel

Copy the formulas over to the right for all columns.
7. Next, calculate the bonus. Recall that the bonus is equal to 80 percent of ROI, but it cannot be higher than 10 percent. Use this minimum formula in cell B11: =MIN(B10*0.8,0.1) (Lab Exhibit 8.3.7). This will return the lesser of 80 percent of ROI or 10 percent. Copy the formula to the remaining columns.
8. Copy Rows 7 through 11 (Lab Exhibit 8.3.8) and paste them into Row 18 (Lab Exhibit 8.3.9). This will copy all labels and formulas to the Midwest Region's data.

Analysis Task #2: Prepare a Correlation Matrix to Display Correlations between Employee Bonuses and Financial Ratios.

DATA VISUALIZATION

1. Highlight the Southeast Region data (cells A7:K11). On the **Data** tab, select **Data Analysis**, then **Correlation**. Click **OK** (Lab Exhibit 8.3.10). In the **Correlation** dialog box, next to **Grouped By:**, select <u>Rows</u>. Click the box to indicate that there are **Labels in first column**. Select **Output range**, and enter "$M$3" (Lab Exhibit 8.3.11). Use the same steps to create a correlation matrix of the Midwest region in cell M14. The **Correlation** dialog box is shown in Lab Exhibit 8.3.12.

2. Use conditional formatting to color-code the resulting correlations. Select **Conditional Formatting** on the **Home** tab. Then select **Color Scales**, and select the first option, as shown in Lab Exhibit 8.3.13. The resulting visualization uses color to show variation in the values and is known as a heat map.

3. Evaluate the results. One convenient way to summarize information is to highlight a row of data such as Sales Growth for the Southeast Region and examine the bottom-right corner of the worksheet for summary statistics. Notice that average sales growth for the Southeast Region is far less than that of the Midwest Region (1.9 percent vs. 10.5 percent). Despite this fact, the Southeast consistently receives higher bonuses.

Share the Story

Bonus plans can be an effective tool for aligning employee effort with company objectives. However, companies must reevaluate bonus plans and financial performance regularly to determine whether bonus plans are delivering the expected results.

An evaluation of the correlation matrix (Lab Exhibit 8.3.14) reveals that the Southeast plant's bonus is highly correlated with asset turnover but not return on sales. In contrast, the Midwest bonus is correlated with both metrics. Perhaps most troubling is the Southeast Region, where there is a high, negative correlation between average assets and asset turnover, ROI, and bonus. This is very different from the Midwest Region. The results of this analysis may indicate that the bonus plan is not aligned with company goals.

It appears from the data that average assets are declining for the Southeast Region, which dramatically increases the asset turnover each year. This increased asset turnover appears to explain why the Southeast Region receives the maximum bonus, despite a slightly lower return on sales and dramatically lower sales growth than the Midwest Region. These analyses suggest that there is a potential issue with the bonus plan, and more investigation is necessary.

This lab demonstrates how plant managers may hit bonus targets by achieving specified financial metrics in ways that were never intended. In this case, the Southeast Region was able to increase asset turnover by failing to use capital resources to invest in plant, property, and equipment. While this tactic increases short-term ROI, it sacrifices long-term profits as older equipment becomes more costly to repair and less efficient.

Assessment

1. Take a screenshot of the data and correlation table following Step 10, paste it into a Word document, and label it "Lab 8.3 Submission.docx".
2. Answer the multiple-choice questions in Connect using your new spreadsheet and upload your Lab 8.3 Submission.docx via Connect if assigned.

Alternate Lab 8.3   Excel—On Your Own

Incentivizing Performance with Budget Plans (Heartwood)

Data Analytics Types: Descriptive Analytics, Diagnostic Analytics

Keywords

Performance Measures, ROI, Employee Incentives, Heat Map

Decision-Making Context

Several years ago, **Heartwood Cabinets** introduced a countertop division to sell granite, quartz, and marble countertops as a complement to kitchen cabinetry sales. The countertop division has several plants scattered across the United States. To encourage employees to increase profits, Heartwood implemented a bonus plan for the countertop division. Per the bonus plan, employees in the countertop division are awarded 80 percent of their plant's ROI, up to a maximum of 10 percent, as a salary bonus. For example, if a plant records a bonus of 5 percent, then employees of the plant receive a 4 percent bonus (5% * 80%).

ROI depends on operating income and average assets. Due to tax laws, new equipment is depreciated more in the first few years of the life of most assets than in later years.

The corporate controller at Heartwood is concerned that the bonus plan is encouraging behavior that is inconsistent with the company's objectives. Specifically, Heartwood corporate leadership wants increased profits, but not all divisions are experiencing profit growth. You have been asked to analyze basic financial information for the Northwest Region to gain insight about the bonus structure and recent financial performance of Heartwood's countertop division.

Employees typically respond to incentives, and bonus plans can be an effective way to align employee performance with company goals. However, it can be difficult to design bonus plans, and many bonus plans encourage behavior that is contrary to company goals.

Depreciation: The reduction in value of an asset as time passes, due to use, wear and tear, or obsolescence.

Required

1. Use Excel to calculate ROI for the manufacturing plants in Heartwood's Northwest countertop division.
2. Use the Correlation dialog box in Excel to determine whether employee bonuses are correlated with company goals, as measured by important financial ratios. Use conditional formatting to create a heat map from the correlation matrix data.

Ask the Question

Why aren't all countertop plants in the Northwest Region experiencing high income growth? Is this outcome related to the company's bonus plan?

Master the Data

For this lab, you will use data in the Excel file titled **Alt Lab 8.3 Data.xlsx**.

Data Dictionary

Year	Date of the last calendar year for which data are compiled
Sales	Annual sales, in thousands
Operating Income	Annual operating income, in thousands
Average Assets	Average net assets for the year, in thousands

Assessment

1. Take a screenshot of the data and correlation table, paste it into a Word document, and label it "Alt Lab 8.3 Submission.docx".
2. Answer the multiple-choice questions in Connect using your new spreadsheet and upload Alt Lab 8.3 Submission.docx via Connect if assigned.

Lab Note: The tools presented in this lab periodically change. Updated instructions, if applicable, can be found in the student and instructor support materials. All Lab Exhibits are available within the eBook and in Connect.

Comparing the Effects of Transfer Prices across Tax Jurisdictions

Data Analytics Type: Predictive Analytics

Keywords

Transfer Price, Tax Rates, Data Validation, Column Chart

Decision-Making Context

Pharmava, a fictitious U.S.-based drug manufacturer, produces an over-the-counter medication for $80 per bottle. The costs to manufacture a bottle of medication include $75 in variable costs per bottle and $5 in fixed costs per bottle.

Pharmava can sell the medication to a third-party distributor for $110 per bottle, representing a $30 profit per bottle. Pharmava is also considering whether to create a Distribution Division of its own.

Pharmava is considering several locations for its new Distribution Division. Create an analysis in Excel to compare the tax implications of locating the distribution center in different countries under the three different transfer-pricing methods:

- Market price of $110 per bottle
- Cost plus (110 percent)
- Hybrid price of $99 per bottle

Also assume that the Manufacturing Division will transfer 10,000 bottles to the Distribution Division each month and the Distribution Division will sell this entire stock each month for $125 per bottle.

Ask the Question

What are the best location and transfer price for Pharmava, resulting in the greatest overall profits?

Required:

Use the data from the file **Lab 8.4 Data.xlsx** and prepare an analysis in Excel. Your Excel spreadsheet should use the data described above and should include the following:

a. A drop-down box to select the country where the Distribution Division could be located and a cell that shows the tax rate for the chosen country. The selected country from the drop-down box will be used in a **VLOOKUP** function to pull the tax rate from the spreadsheet labeled **Tax Rates**.

Remember, a **VLOOKUP** looks up data from a table based on a value and returns data from that table associated with that value. In this case, the tax rate spreadsheet contains the tax rate (the data) for each country (the value).

For example:

Division	Select Country:	Tax Rate
Distribution Division	Ireland	▼
Manufacturing Division	United States of America	XX

Microsoft Excel

b. A dynamic set of calculations to show the most cost-effective transfer-pricing method based on the countries selected.

c. A column chart providing a visualization to compare the tax implications for each transfer-pricing method. The chart will change based on the country selected.

The final tool will resemble Lab Exhibit 8.4.1.

Master the Data

For this lab you will use data in the Excel file titled **Lab 8.4 Data.xlsx**.

Review the dataset. Note that it contains four worksheets, but only the **Tax Rates** worksheet contains data that you will use in the analysis.

The **Costs**, **Operating Income**, and **Transfer Price Analysis Tool** worksheets are templates for you to complete as you perform your work.

Data Dictionary

Worksheet Tab/Table	Attribute Name	Description	Data Type
Tax Rates	Country	All countries that Pharmava might consider	Text
Tax Rates	Year	The year that the tax rates were effective	General
Tax Rates	TaxRate	The tax rate for each country	Numerical

Perform the Analysis

Analysis Task #1: Complete the Cost Worksheet Using the Data in the Instructions

Enter the relevant data from the instructions into the **Costs** worksheet, as shown in Lab Exhibit 8.4.2.

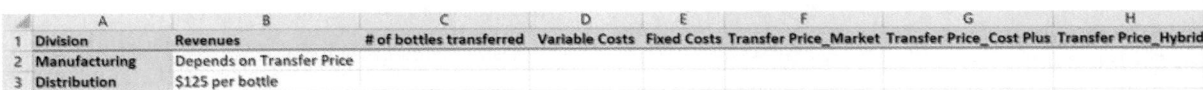

	A	B	C	D	E	F	G	H
1	Division	Revenues	# of bottles transferred	Variable Costs	Fixed Costs	Transfer Price_Market	Transfer Price_Cost Plus	Transfer Price_Hybrid
2	Manufacturing	Depends on Transfer Price						
3	Distribution	$125 per bottle						

Lab Exhibit 8.4.2

Microsoft Excel

Your completed worksheet should look like Exhibit 8.4.3.

	A	B	C	D	E	F	G	H
1	Division	Revenues	# of bottles transferred	Variable Costs	Fixed Costs	Transfer Price_Market	Transfer Price_Cost Plus	Transfer Price_Hybrid
2	Manufacturing	Depends on Transfer Price	10,000	$ 75.00	$ 5.00			
3	Distribution	$125 per bottle	10,000			$ 110.00	$ 88.00	$ 99.00

Lab Exhibit 8.4.3

Microsoft Excel

Analysis Task #2: Complete the Operating Income Worksheet Using the Data in the Instructions

1. Enter the relevant data from the instructions and the cost data from the **Costs** worksheet into the **Operating Income** worksheet. The cost-related data in the **Operating Income** worksheet should be linked to the **Costs** worksheet for you (Lab Exhibit 8.4.4 shows the formulas that have been embedded into the **Operating Income** worksheet).

Lab Exhibit 8.4.4

Microsoft Excel

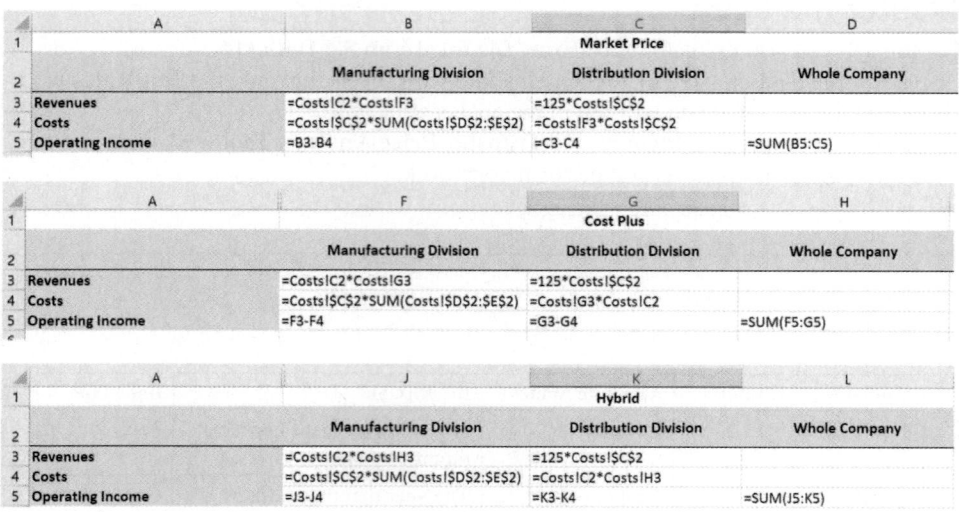

	A	B	C	D
1			Market Price	
2		Manufacturing Division	Distribution Division	Whole Company
3	Revenues	=Costs!C2*Costs!F3	=125*Costs!$C$2	
4	Costs	=Costs!$C$2*SUM(Costs!$D$2:$E$2)	=Costs!F3*Costs!$C$2	
5	Operating Income	=B3-B4	=C3-C4	=SUM(B5:C5)

	A	F	G	H
1			Cost Plus	
2		Manufacturing Division	Distribution Division	Whole Company
3	Revenues	=Costs!C2*Costs!G3	=125*Costs!$C$2	
4	Costs	=Costs!$C$2*SUM(Costs!$D$2:$E$2)	=Costs!G3*Costs!C2	
5	Operating Income	=F3-F4	=G3-G4	=SUM(F5:G5)

	A	J	K	L
1			Hybrid	
2		Manufacturing Division	Distribution Division	Whole Company
3	Revenues	=Costs!C2*Costs!H3	=125*Costs!$C$2	
4	Costs	=Costs!$C$2*SUM(Costs!$D$2:$E$2)	=Costs!C2*Costs!H3	
5	Operating Income	=J3-J4	=K3-K4	=SUM(J5:K5)

2. To calculate the revenues for the Manufacturing Division, multiply the number of units transferred to the Distribution Division (from the **Costs** worksheet) by the market price, cost-plus, and hybrid methods. Lab Exhibits 8.4.5 through 8.4.7 show the formulas that pull the relevant data from the **Costs** worksheet.

Lab Exhibit 8.4.5

Microsoft Excel

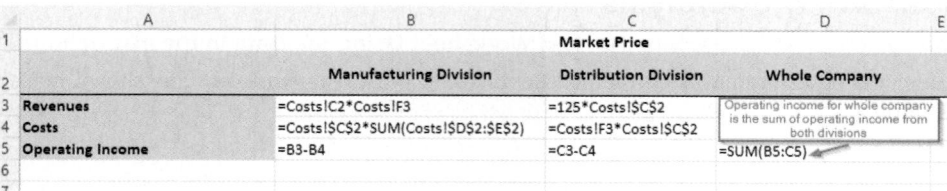

	A	B	C	D	E
1			Market Price		
2		Manufacturing Division	Distribution Division	Whole Company	
3	Revenues	=Costs!C2*Costs!F3	=125*Costs!$C$2	Operating income for whole company is the sum of operating income from both divisions	
4	Costs	=Costs!$C$2*SUM(Costs!$D$2:$E$2)	=Costs!F3*Costs!$C$2		
5	Operating Income	=B3-B4	=C3-C4	=SUM(B5:C5)	
6					

Lab Exhibit 8.4.6

Microsoft Excel

	F	G	H	I
1		Cost Plus		
2	Manufacturing Division	Distribution Division	Whole Company	
3	=Costs!C2*Costs!G3	=125*Costs!$C$2		
4	=Costs!$C$2*SUM(Costs!$D$2:	=Costs!G3*Costs!C2		
5	=F3-F4	=G3-G4	=SUM(F5:G5)	
6				

Lab Exhibit 8.4.7

Microsoft Excel

	J	K	L
1		Hybrid	
2	Manufacturing Division	Distribution Division	Whole Company
3	=Costs!C2*Costs!H3	=125*Costs!$C$2	
4	=Costs!$C$2*SUM(Costs!$D$2:$E	=Costs!C2*Costs!H3	
5	=J3-J4	=K3-K4	=SUM(J5:K5)
6			

3. As Lab Exhibit 8.4.5 shows, you calculate operating income for each division by subtracting the relevant costs from the relevant revenues.
4. Calculate operating income for the whole company by adding the operating income from both divisions (Lab Exhibit 8.4.5). The resulting operating income worksheet should resemble Lab Exhibit 8.4.8.

Analysis Task #3: Create a Drop-Down Box to Select the Country for Each Division

1. Open the **Transfer Price Analysis Tool** worksheet.
2. Click in cell B2. Navigate to the **Data** tab and select the data validation icon in the **Data Tools** section (Lab Exhibit 8.4.9). This will open the **Data Validation** menu (Lab Exhibit 8.4.10).
3. In the **Data Validation** menu, under the **Allow** criteria, select **List**. This means you will be given choices from a predetermined list. Then set the **Source** data for that list by highlighting the list of countries from the **Tax Rates** worksheet (see Lab Exhibit 8.4.10).
4. In cell C2, enter the **VLOOKUP** formula shown at the top of Lab Exhibit 8.4.11, which will pull up the tax rate related to the country you select in cell B2. The formula is =VLOOKUP(B2,'TaxesRates'!A:C,3,FALSE).

C2	⌄ ⋮ ✕ ✓ fx	=VLOOKUP(B2,'Tax Rates'!A:C,3,FALSE)

	A	B	C	D
1	Division	Select Country:	Tax Rate	
2	Manufacturing Divisior	United States of America	26%	

Lab Exhibit 8.4.11

Microsoft Excel

5. Repeat Steps 3 and 4 in Row 3 so that you can select the location for the Manufacturing Division.

Analysis Task #4: Create Dynamic Calculations to Calculate the Tax Implications of Each Transfer Pricing Method

1. Enter the operating income for the Manufacturing Division under each transfer-pricing method by linking cells B7, B8, and B9 to the operating income from the **Operating Income** worksheet. Use the formulas shown in Lab Exhibit 8.4.12.

	A	B	C	D	E	F	G
5			Operating Income				Tax
6	Transfer pricing method	Manufacturing Operating Income	Distribution Operating Income	Total Operating Income	Manufacturing Taxes	Distribution Taxes	Total Taxes
7	Market Price	='Operating Income'!B5	='Operating Income'!C5	=SUM(B7:C7)	=B7*$C$2	=C7*$C$3	=SUM(E7:F7)
8	Cost Plus (110%)	='Operating Income'!F5	='Operating Income'!G5	=SUM(B8:C8)	=B8*$C$2	=C8*$C$3	=SUM(E8:F8)
9	Hybrid Price	='Operating Income'!IJ5	='Operating Income'!K5	=SUM(B9:C9)	=B9*$C$2	=C9*$C$3	=SUM(E9:F9)

Lab Exhibit 8.4.12

Microsoft Excel

2. Repeat Step 1 for operating income for the Distribution Division in cells C7, C8, and C9 using the formulas shown in Lab Exhibit 8.4.12.
3. In cells D7, D8, and D9, calculate the overall operating income for Pharmava using the **SUM** functions shown in Lab Exhibit 8.4.12.
4. In cells E7, E8, and E9, calculate the taxes due for the Manufacturing Division under each transfer-pricing method by multiplying the operating income for the Manufacturing Division by the tax rate shown in cell C2. Lab Exhibit 8.4.12 shows the formulas, and Lab Exhibit 8.4.13 shows the results.
5. In cells F7, F8, and F9, calculate the taxes due for the Manufacturing Division under each transfer-pricing method by multiplying the operating income for the Manufacturing Division by the tax rate shown in cell C3. See Lab Exhibits 8.4.12 and 8.4.13.

6. In cells G7, G8, and G9, calculate the total taxes due for Pharmava by summing the tax implications for each method from the Manufacturing Division and the Distribution Division (see the formulas in Lab Exhibit 8.4.12).

The resulting table should resemble Lab Exhibit 8.4.14.

Analysis Task #5: Create a Column Chart to Visualize the Tax Implications of Each Transfer Price Method

1. Place your cursor in one of the cells showing the total tax implications for each transfer-pricing method (cell G7, G8, or G9). From the **Insert** menu, select the **clustered columns** icon (Lab Exhibit 8.4.15). A default chart will be generated. You will customize this chart in the next steps.

2. In the **Chart Design** tab, click on the **Select Data** icon (Lab Exhibit 8.4.16). This will open the **Select Data Source** dialog box (Lab Exhibit 8.4.17).

3. In the **Select Data Source** dialog box, check to ensure that the chart data range does not include the section headers from Row 5 (for example, Operating Income and Tax). If it does include that row, (1) adjust your chart data range formula as shown in Lab Exhibit 8.4.17. Next, select (2) **Switch Row/Column** so that the different transfer-pricing methods are shown on the horizontal axis. (3) In **Legend Entries (Series)**, uncheck all items except for **Total Taxes** so that only the Total Taxes data show in the chart. (4) Click **OK**.

A default chart similar to that shown in Lab Exhibit 8.4.18 is generated.

4. You can now format the chart. Make the following changes:

   a. Change the title to "Tax Comparison" by clicking into the title on the chart.

   b. Change the colors of each column by clicking on each column separately (so that only one is active at a time). Then right-click on the column to open the **Format** dialog box (Lab Exhibit 8.4.19). Choose **Fill** and select a color for the column. Repeat these steps to assign a different color to the other columns.

   c. Turn off the legend by clicking on the plus sign (+) that shows on the top right of the chart when you click on the chart and then unchecking the **Legend** (Lab Exhibit 8.4.20).

   d. You can widen the columns by clicking on one of the columns, opening the **Format Data Point** dialog box on the right side of the screen, and then adjusting the **Gap Width** so that it is smaller (Lab Exhibit 8.4.21).

Share the Story

Now that we have a tool to calculate the tax implications of each transfer-pricing method in various countries, management can use this information when making decisions about where to locate Pharmava's Distribution Division. Recall that management wanted to know the best location and transfer price, resulting in the greatest overall profits. This tool allows management to vary the possible locations for each division to observe how each possibility affects profit.

Let's assume that Pharmava is considering establishing manufacturing facilities in Mexico and distribution facilities in the United States. The tool reveals that the lowest tax burden is associated with a cost-plus transfer price.

Assessment

1. Take a screenshot of the entire Transfer Price Analysis Tool, paste it into a Word document, and label it "Lab 8.4 Submission.docx".

2. Answer the multiple-choice questions in Connect and upload your Lab 8.4 Submission.docx via Connect if assigned.

Comparing the Effects of Transfer Prices across Tax Jurisdictions

Data Analytics Type: Predictive Analytics

Keywords

Transfer Price, Tax Rates, Data Validation, Column Chart

Decision-Making Context

The headquarters for **Google**'s Asian-Pacific operations is based in Singapore. Imagine that Google is considering locations for a new subsidiary in the region that will handle research services for Google worldwide. Google estimates that the new subsidiary will bring in approximately $275,000,000 in revenue per year for its research services within Google. Further, Google estimates that approximately 30 percent of that business could be attributable to the Asian-Pacific Region. The total cost of the subsidiary's research operations is estimated to be $150,000,000.

Ask the Question

Prepare an Excel tool to estimate the tax implications of locating the research operations in various locations in the Asian-Pacific Region. Your tool should compare the tax implications of locating the distribution center in different countries under the three different transfer-pricing methods:

- Market price of $70,000,000
- Cost plus (110 percent)
- Hybrid price of $57,500,000

Your Excel tool should use the data described above and should include:

a. A drop-down box to select the country where the research division could be located and a cell that shows the tax rate for the chosen country. The selected country from the drop-down box will be used in a **VLOOKUP** function to pull the tax rate from the spreadsheet labeled **Tax Rates**.

b. A dynamic set of calculations to show the most cost-effective transfer-pricing method based on the countries selected.

c. A column chart providing a visualization to compare the tax implications for each transfer-pricing method. The chart will change based on the country selected.

Master the Data

Use the workbook labeled **Alt Lab 8.4 Data.xlsx** for your analysis. Only the worksheet labeled **Tax Rates** has data for your use. The remaining three worksheets contain templates for you to complete and use to build your tool.

Assessment

1. Take a screenshot of the entire Transfer Price Analysis Tool, paste it into a Word document, and label it "Alt Lab 8.4 Submission.docx".
2. Answer the multiple-choice questions in Connect and upload your Alt Lab 8.4 Submission.docx via Connect if assigned.

Lab 8.5 Power BI

Lab Note: The tools presented in this lab periodically change. Updated instructions, if applicable, can be found in the student and instructor support materials. All Lab Exhibits are available within the eBook and in Connect.

DATA VISUALIZATION

Using Visualization to Compare Corporate Tax Rates

Data Analytics Type: Descriptive Analytics

Keywords

Transfer Pricing, Taxes, Mapping

Decision-Making Context

In decentralized companies, managers can use transfer pricing as a tool to shift profits from countries with high corporate tax rates to countries with lower corporate tax rates. In this lab, we use Power BI to create visualizations that illustrate the differences in tax rates across countries and to show the impact of this strategy on the company's overall profitability.

Ask the Question

In what countries are tax rates the lowest or the highest?
1. Use the mapping function in Power BI to generate a visualization that reveals which countries have the lowest and highest corporate tax rates.
2. Use a filter to allow users to review the data easily.

Master the Data

For this lab you will use data in the Excel file titled **Lab 8.5 Data.xlsx**. The data include each country and its corporate tax rate for the year 2020.

Open Excel file **Lab 8.5 Data.xlsx**.

On the first worksheet, labeled **Tax Rates**, we see the country listed in column A, the **Tax Year** in Column B, and the **Tax Rate** in Column C. The data are sorted from the lowest tax rate to the highest.

Data Dictionary

Country	Country
Year	Year the tax rate is effective
Tax Rate	Taxes applied to profits

Perform the Analysis

Analysis Task: Prepare a Filled Map Visualization to Show Variation in Tax Rates Across the World.

1. Open Power BI and select the **Get Data** option (Lab Exhibit 8.5.1).
2. Select the Excel file labeled **Lab 8.5 Data.xlsx**, choose the **Tax Rates** worksheet, and click **Load** (Lab Exhibit 8.5.2).
3. Under **Visualizations**, select the **Filled Map** icon (Lab Exhibit 8.5.3).
4. Drag the **Country** field to **Location** (Lab Exhibit 8.5.4).

5. Go to the **Format visual** tab (**paintbrush** icon) and open the **Fill Colors** menu. Click on the *fx* icon to customize the color (Lab Exhibit 8.5.5).
6. Format by **Color Scale** based on the field Tax Rate. Because each country only has one value, it does not matter how you summarize. Selecting **Average** under **Summarization** will work (Lab Exhibit 8.5.6).
7. Set the **Minimum** as the **Lowest value** to green, the **Middle value** to yellow, and the **Highest Value** to red (Lab Exhibit 8.5.6).
8. Click **OK**. The map should fill and show color variation for each country (see Lab Exhibit 8.5.8).
9. Add **Tax Rate** as a **Filter** so that you can select a specific tax rate to see all the countries that have that same rate (Lab Exhibit 8.5.7).
   Your final visualization should look similar to Lab Exhibit 8.5.8.

Share the Story

Now that we can easily see the variation in tax rates, management can identify which countries should be the primary sources of sales. Based on the map, you can see that the highest tax rates (shown in the reddish/dark orange color) are in central Africa and South America. Asia and Eastern Europe have the lowest tax rates.

Assessment

1. Take a screenshot of the tax rate map, paste it into a Word document, and label it "Lab 8.5 Submission.docx".
2. Answer the multiple-choice questions in Connect and upload your Lab 8.5 Submission.docx via Connect if assigned.

Alternate Lab 8.5   Power BI—On Your Own

Using Visualization to Compare Corporate Tax Rates

Data Analytics Type: Descriptive Analytics

DATA VISUALIZATION

Keywords

Transfer Pricing, Taxes, Mapping

Decision-Making Context

In decentralized companies, managers can use transfer pricing as a tool to shift profits from countries with high corporate tax rates to countries with lower corporate tax rates. In this lab, you will use Power BI to create visualizations that illustrate the differences in tax rates across countries and to show the impact of this strategy on a company's overall profitability.

Lab Note: The tools presented in this lab periodically change. Updated instructions, if applicable, can be found in the student and instructor support materials.

Ask the Question

How does shifting sales from a high-tax jurisdiction to a low-tax jurisdiction affect the company's overall profitability as well as the profitability of each sub-unit?

Master the Data

For this lab, you will use data in the Excel file titled **Alt Lab 8.5 Data.xlsx**, which contains tax rates from 2022 for each country in the world. Perform the same steps as you completed in Lab 8.5.

Required

1. Use the mapping function in Power BI to generate a visualization that reveals which countries have the lowest and highest corporate tax rates.
2. Add a slicer to allow users to review the data easily.

Assessment

1. Take a screenshot of the tax rate map, paste it into a Word document, and label it "Alt Lab 8.5 Submission.docx".
2. Answer the multiple-choice questions in Connect and upload your Alt Lab 8.5 Submission.docx via Connect if assigned.

Chapter 9

Master Budgeting and Flexible Budgets

A Look at This Chapter

This chapter explains the budgeting process that organizations use to set expectations for the upcoming period. It walks through each component of the master budget and discusses the sources of the data used to develop the budget. It also discusses how management uses the budget to motivate and evaluate employee performance, including some of the dysfunctional effects of misused budgets. Finally, it examines other contexts in which organizations frequently use budgeting techniques, such as for environmental, social, and governance (ESG) initiatives.

Cost Accounting and Data Analytics

COST ACCOUNTING LEARNING OBJECTIVE		RELATED DATA ANALYTICS LAB(S)	LAB ANALYTICS TYPE(S)
LO 9.1	Explain the purpose of budgets.		
LO 9.2	Describe the budgeting process.		
LO 9.3	Summarize the process for developing the operating budget, including the individual budgets and forecasts that support it.	**Data Analytics Mini-Lab:** Preparing a Sales Forecast with Excel	Predictive
		LAB 9.1 Excel Forecasting Future Performance: Sales and Earnings	Predictive
		LAB 9.2 Tableau Forecasting Future Performance: Sales and Earnings	Predictive
		LAB 9.3 Power BI Forecasting Future Performance: Sales and Earnings	Predictive
		LAB 9.4 Excel Predicting Product Demand Using Regression Analysis	Diagnostic
		LAB 9.5 Excel Preparing a Master Budget (Heartwood)	Predictive
LO 9.4	Perform a sensitivity analysis and explain how changes to underlying assumptions in the budget affect expectations.	**LAB 9.6 Excel** Performing Sensitivity Analysis with Excel's Scenario Manager	Diagnostic, Predictive

Cost Accounting and Data Analytics (*continued*)

COST ACCOUNTING LEARNING OBJECTIVE	RELATED DATA ANALYTICS LAB(S)	LAB ANALYTICS TYPE(S)
LO 9.5 Describe the difference between a flexible budget and a static budget.		
LO 9.6 Explain the behavioral effects of budgets.		
LO 9.7 Describe the use of budgets for ESG initiatives.		

Chapter Concepts and Career Skills

Learning About . . .	Helps with These Career Skills
The budgeting process	• Understanding how organizations plan and forecast future performance • Providing a benchmark against which future performance can be compared
Human implications of budgeting	• Understanding how budgets can influence employee behavior
Budgeting for ESG	• Understanding the relevance of ESG for organizations and their stakeholder value • Recognizing how the budget process translates to other contexts

REUTERS/Alamy Stock Photo

Smart Budgeting Helps Nissan Save Money

In the summer of 2020, auto manufacturer **Nissan** announced plans to dramatically reduce spending, decrease manufacturing capacity, and even close some of its factories in France. The planned cuts were estimated at more than $2.5 billion over three years. Nissan needed to make these changes because its auto sales had generally not been as strong as expected, and this problem was further exacerbated by the COVID-19 pandemic. How did Nissan's management know what to do? How did it determine where to make the cuts?

Nissan and other companies use an important tool called a *budget* for planning and control. To create a budget, the company estimates expected sales, as well as the costs associated with making those sales. Nissan originally had an aggressive sales growth strategy and estimated that it would sell 14 million cars during the upcoming period. As it became evident it would not sell that many cars, Nissan adjusted the sales estimate down to 10 million.

The budget helps highlight which costs are fixed and which are variable, providing the information that the company needs to identify necessary cuts so it can stay in business. The budget can also show expected sales and costs by division or location, and so it reveals when strategic changes might be necessary, such as determining which manufacturing facilities are too costly and should be closed.

Sources: Sean McLain and Nick Kostov, "Nissan, Renault Prepare Billions of Dollars in Cuts," *The Wall Street Journal,* May 24, 2020, www.wsj.com/articles/nissan-renault-prepare-billions-of-dollars-in-cuts-11590334128?st=sptx6xmgij3nxhd&reflink=article_email_share; Reed Stevenson, Masatsugu Horie, and Tsuyoshi Inajima, "Nissan Said to Plan $2.8 Billion in Cost Cuts, Book Charges," *Bloomberg Business Hyperdrive,* May 20, 2020, www.bloomberg.com/news/articles/2020-05-13/nissan-said-to-plan-2-8-billion-in-cost-cuts-book-charges.

WHAT IS A BUDGET?

A **budget** is an estimate of the activities that will be carried out over a specified future period of time. Generally, budgets estimate the organization's expected revenues and expenses over the next year or so. However, organizations also budget for other aspects of their operations. For example, a company might budget the hours it will take to complete a project or the amount of carbon emissions it will generate next year. In your personal life, you might create a budget to make sure you have enough money to eat and pay your rent for your next school term.

Generally, an organization completes a standard set of three steps to set up a budget:

Step 1. Identify goals and objectives.
Step 2. Determine the activities that will be carried out to meet those goals and objectives.
Step 3. Develop expectations about the activities, income, and cash flows, as well as the market factors that may affect the company's ability to achieve those goals.

Let's consider the budgeting process for the **Athens Area Diaper Bank** (AADB). This nonprofit organization runs a community diaper bank to provide diapers and diaper supplies to families living in poverty in the Athens, Georgia, area. An average monthly supply of diapers costs $80, and most children use diapers for approximately three years. Traditional government assistance programs, such as food stamps and Medicaid, do not provide diapers, so many families experience diaper need.[1]

Nonprofit organizations use the same standard budgeting process that for-profit companies do. The first step in the budgeting process for AADB is to identify its goals and objectives. Its strategic goals include (1) ending diaper need, (2) advancing public policy solutions, and (3) building the capacity for the diaper bank to meet community demand.

The second step is to determine the activities the AADB will execute to meet its goals and objectives. For example, to meet the first goal, the AADB may establish an outreach plan to the 34 percent of community residents who live below the poverty rate. In addition, AADB will likely need to hire employees and engage volunteers to manage the diaper bank and diaper distributions, and it will need to secure facilities to store the diapers. The AADB will also need to run diaper drives and other donation events to collect diapers for distribution to families in need, and it will need to apply for grants to provide additional resources to its clients.

The third step is to develop expectations about the activities, income, and cash flows that may impact the AADB's ability to achieve its goals. The AADB may use the historical data collected since it was established in 2015, as well as data from diaper banks in similar communities, to establish expectations for the next budget period. When establishing expectations for income, the AADB will include both monetary donations and gifts in kind (for example, diapers and wipes). The expected costs will include expenses related to obtaining diaper supplies for distribution, salary paid to employees, rent, maintenance and utilities, storage and office facilities, and marketing.

Purposes of the Budget

Budgets serve several important functions in the organization. First, they provide a benchmark to which the organization can compare performance. As Chapter 10 explains,

LO 9.1

Explain the purpose of budgets.

budget
An estimate of the activities that will be carried out over a specified future period of time.

CAREER SKILLS

Learning about the budgeting process supports these career skills:

- Understanding how organizations plan and forecast future performance
- Providing a benchmark against which future performance can be compared

---

[1]The Athens Area Diaper Bank is part of the National Diaper Bank Network. For more information about the National Diaper Bank Network or to find a diaper bank in your community, see https://nationaldiaperbanknetwork.org/.

Rawpixel.com/Shutterstock

master budget
The overall budget for the organization as a whole.

operating budget
Budget of all the resources needed to execute an organization's operations, including sales, production, purchasing, and marketing.

organizations regularly compare their budgets to actual performance to determine whether they are on track to meet their goals and to identify problems that may be getting in the way.

Second, budgets are used for communication and coordination. As we discuss later in this chapter, the overall budgeting process involves the integration of individual budgets from each business unit. Management can use this process to communicate expectations to each business unit and help each unit see how it fits into the big picture.

Third, budgets are used to motivate employees. Because the budget carefully lays out expectations, employees can understand exactly what goals they need to achieve.

 PROGRESS CHECK

1. What is a budget?
2. What functions do budgets serve for an organization?

THE BUDGET CYCLE

LO 9.2

Describe the budgeting process.

The **master budget** is the overall budget for the organization as a whole. It establishes management's financial and operational plans for the budget period. It also includes budgeted financial statements. Master budgets are made up of operating budgets and financial budgets. **Operating budgets** cover all of the resources needed to execute the organization's operations, including sales, production, purchasing, and marketing. **Financial budgets** describe the sources and uses of funds for planned capital expenditures and the operations anticipated during the period.

financial budget
Budget describing the sources and uses of funds for planned capital expenditures and the operations anticipated during the period.

Exhibit 9.1 provides a graphical overview of the master budget. Each of the rectangles represents a detailed budget that rolls up into the overall master budget for the organization. The operating budgets are shown in green. The financial budgets are shown in yellow. The focus of this chapter is the operating budgets. Cash budgets are covered in Appendix G. Capital budgeting is covered in Chapter 14.

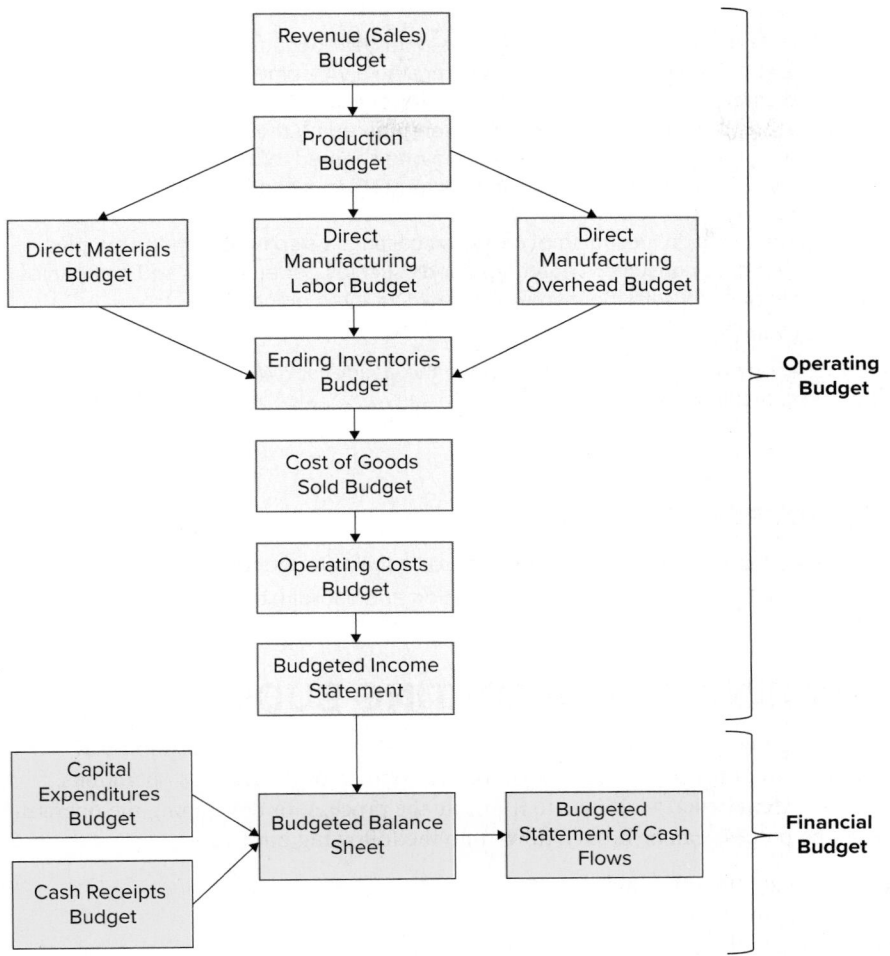

Exhibit 9.1
Overview of Master Budget

The master budget is a **static budget** that the organization sets at the beginning of the period and does not change until the budget period is over.

Budgets can cover any period of time, known as the **budget period**. In most organizations, a budget covers one fiscal year, which can be subdivided into quarters or months.

To develop the master budget, an organization completes the **budget cycle**. The budget cycle generally includes the following four steps:

Step 1. Business units prepare and submit budgets.
Step 2. Senior management approves the budgets.
Step 3. Operations are executed during the budget period.
Step 4. Performance is evaluated and compared to the budget.

static budget
A budget that is set at the beginning of the period and does not change until the budget period is over.

budget period
The period of time that a budget covers.

budget cycle
The process of developing a master budget: (1) Business units prepare and submit budgets, (2) senior management approves the budgets, (3) operations are executed during the budget period, and (4) performance is evaluated and compared to the budget.

FROM THE FIELD

The Business Effects of COVID-19

In 2020, the COVID-19 crisis disrupted businesses across the globe. Although many companies suffered, certain industries experienced unexpected sales boosts that probably made them throw their sales forecasts out the window. For example, retail bike sales increased by 75 percent over the prior year because so many people were stuck at home, and family bike rides became a welcome afternoon adventure. Similarly, **Wayfair**, an online furniture retailer, reported that sales doubled compared to expectations because so many people were upgrading their home offices to make working from home more effective. No one seemed to be prepared for this business disruption, which highlights how external forces can impact the accuracy of an organization's sales forecast.

The pandemic didn't just disrupt sales forecasting; it also impacted the supply chain, which led to consumers hoarding goods such as paper towels and companies extending their order-fulfillment times by weeks or even months.

Thinking Critically

Has your shopping behavior changed since the pandemic? What data do you collect now before making any purchases?

 PROGRESS CHECK

3. What is the master budget, and what are its main components?
4. How can budgets improve communication and coordination within a company?

LO 9.3

Summarize the process for developing the operating budget, including the individual budgets and forecasts that support it.

PREPARING THE OPERATING BUDGETS

The operating budget is part of the master budget shown in green in Exhibit 9.1. It comprises all of the resources needed to carry out the organization's operations. We will use **Heartwood Cabinets** to illustrate the process for developing the operating budget. The process can be broken down into the following nine steps:

Step 1. Prepare the sales budget.
Step 2. Prepare the production budget.
Step 3. Prepare the direct materials cost budget.
Step 4. Prepare the direct manufacturing labor cost budget.
Step 5. Prepare the manufacturing overhead cost budget.
Step 6. Prepare the ending inventories budget.
Step 7. Prepare the cost of goods sold budget.
Step 8. Prepare the operating costs budget.
Step 9. Prepare the budgeted operating income statement.

Note that these nine steps are included in the overview of the master budget shown in Exhibit 9.1.

When developing the operating budget, most organizations start with the sales (or revenue) budget because revenue goals drive the organization's actions. The **sales budget** identifies expected (or forecasted) sales in units and dollars.

The first step in developing a sales budget is creating a **sales forecast**, which is a prediction of the amount of sales that will take place during the budget period. It is very important that management forecasts sales accurately because so many other operating decisions are based on that forecast. Many sources of information must be considered, including:

- Historical sales data.
- Industry and economic trends.
- Competitors' activity.
- Pricing and credit policies.

sales budget
Budget that identifies expected (or forecasted) sales in units and dollars.

sales forecast
A prediction of the amount of sales that will take place during the budget period.

- Marketing and advertising strategies.
- Existing backorders.

Management considers each of these factors and uses its judgment to develop the forecast.

Accountants can use many different tools to generate sales forecasts. For example, computer programs such as Excel can predict future values based on existing (historic) values along a linear trend. Excel uses statistical regression techniques to calculate future value predictions.

Organizations usually need to consider factors beyond historical data when forecasting future sales. For example, if new competitors enter the market, they may steal some sales away. The organization will need to adjust sales forecasts accordingly because the historical data will not account for that external force and the original prediction might therefore overstate expected sales. Alternatively, if the organization's marketing and advertising division introduces a new social media marketing campaign to increase sales, this factor will not be evident in the historical data, and the predicted future sales might therefore be understated.

The following Mini-Lab demonstrates how cost accountants can use the Forecast Sheet function in Excel to create a forecast that predicts sales into the future. In the model shown in the lab, the organization is considering only prior sales to predict future sales. But while you are working with the data, think about what other factors might be interesting to collect and consider to more accurately predict future sales.

DATA ANALYTICS MINI-LAB
Preparing a Sales Forecast with Excel

Data Analytics Type: Predictive

Lab Note: The tools presented in this lab periodically change. Updated instructions, if applicable, can be found in the student and instructor support materials.

Keywords

Sales Forecast, Excel Forecast, Budget

Decision-Making Context

Imagine your university has contracted with **UberEats** to deliver food from its various campus eateries to dorms and offices around campus. The university is interested in forecasting future sales using this distribution channel as it prepares its annual operating budget. Use the prior year data on UberEats sales to forecast next year's sales by month.

Ask the Question

How can Excel use historical data to forecast future sales?

Master the Data

The Excel spreadsheet titled **Mini-Lab 9 Data.xlsx** provides the transaction detail for all sales through UberEats last year. The total number of transactions exceeds 44,000 rows. The data fields provided include the following:

Table	Attribute Name	Description	Data Type
	Transaction ID	Unique identifier for each transaction	Text
	Transaction Date	Date the transaction occurred	Date
	Transaction Location	Type of eatery and location (for example, **Starbucks**–Student Center)	Text
	Transaction Amount	Amount of sale (does not include tax)	Currency
	Transaction Tax	Tax amount (approximately 7% of sale amount)	Currency
	Transaction Description	Sale or Refund	Text

An example of the data is shown in Exhibit A.

	A	B	C	D	E	F
1	Transaction ID	Transaction Date	Transaction Location	Transaction Amount	Transaction Tax	Transaction Description
2	ue-66157953	1/2/2025 7:31	Coffee and Bagels - Student Center | UberEats	3.23	0.24	Sale
3	ue-66160905	1/2/2025 8:20	Starbucks - Union | UberEats	3.83	0.28	Sale
4	ue-66166887	1/2/2025 9:57	Starbucks - Union | UberEats	5.67	$0.42	Sale
5	ue-66187610	1/2/2025 15:22	The Station - Veterinary Medical Center | UberEats	5.39	$0.40	Sale
6	ue-66252855	1/3/2025 9:15	Starbucks - Union | UberEats	2.65	$0.20	Sale
7	ue-66262591	1/3/2025 11:48	Starbucks - Union | UberEats	7.51	$0.56	Sale
8	ue-66339055	1/4/2025 8:28	Starbucks - Union | UberEats	3.83	$0.28	Sale
9	ue-66342150	1/4/2025 9:16	Starbucks - Union | UberEats	5.02	$0.37	Sale
10	ue-66356015	1/4/2025 12:48	Au Bon Pain - College of Business | UberEats	29.87	$2.21	Sale
11	ue-66356185	1/4/2025 12:51	Au Bon Pain - College of Business | UberEats	-29.87	-2.21	Refund

Exhibit A
Example of Transaction Data for UberEats

Microsoft Excel

To generate the forecast for *all* UberEats transactions, you will need only the Transaction Date and the Transaction Amount fields. If you wanted to forecast each location separately, you could do that easily by also considering the Transaction Location field.

Although you can forecast with the individual transaction data, the resulting forecast will be too granular to be very useful. For this reason, it is preferable to summarize the detailed data by month and then use the monthly data to prepare the forecast.

You can summarize the data easily by first adding a Transaction Month field and then creating a pivot table from the data.

To add a Transaction Month field, insert a column to the left of the Transaction Date field and enter the Month formula in cell B2: =MONTH(C2). See Exhibit B.

Exhibit B
Creating a Transaction Date Field

Microsoft Excel

B2 f_x =MONTH(C2)

	A	B	C
1	Transaction ID	Transaction Month	Transaction
2	ue-66157953	1	1/2/202
3	ue-66160905	1	1/2/202
4	ue-66166887	1	1/2/202
5	ue-66187610	1	1/2/2022
6	ue-66252855	1	1/3/202

This formula produces the number associated with the month from the Transaction Date field (for example, January = 1, December = 12).

To create a pivot table, (1) go to the **Insert** tab and (2) select the **Pivot Table** button, as shown in Exhibit C.

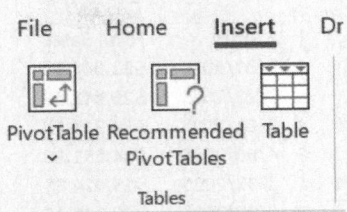

Exhibit C
Pivot Table
Instructions
Microsoft Excel

When the **Pivot Table** menu opens, select the entire table/range and insert into a new worksheet, as shown in Exhibit D.

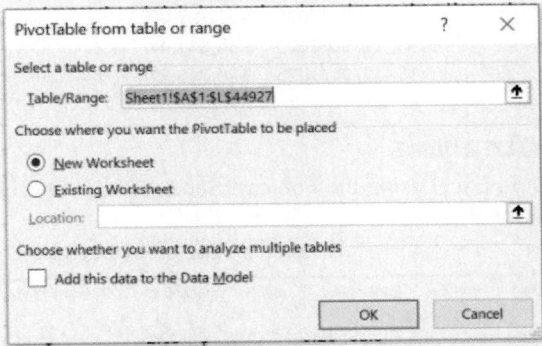

Exhibit D
Insert Pivot Table
Microsoft Excel

When the **PivotTable Fields** dialog opens in a separate worksheet, create a pivot table by assigning (1) the Month field to the Rows and (2) the Transaction Total to the Values, as shown in Exhibit E. *Note:* Because you are interested in the sum of sales for each month, the field values should be set to Sum of Transaction Total.

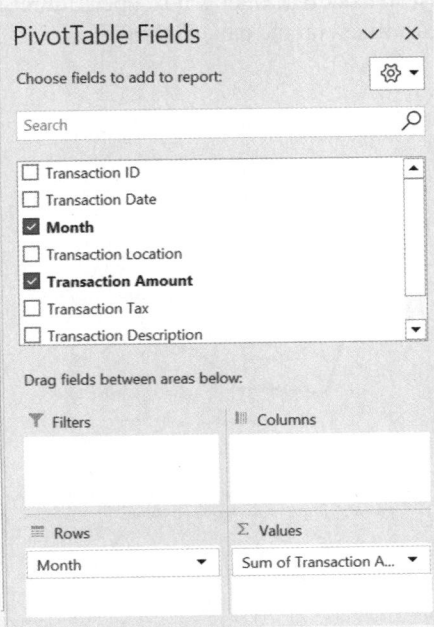

Exhibit E
Preparing the Pivot
Table
Microsoft Excel

The resulting pivot table is shown in Exhibit F.

	A	B
1	**Month**	**Total Sales**
2	1/31/2025	$21,502.13
3	2/28/2025	$29,541.58
4	3/31/2025	$34,315.05
5	4/30/2025	$44,591.30
6	5/31/2025	$19,414.33
7	6/30/2025	$20,388.45
8	7/31/2025	$20,465.71
9	8/31/2025	$29,176.75
10	9/30/2025	$30,114.93
11	10/31/2025	$51,107.00
12	11/30/2025	$34,841.44
13	12/31/2025	$20,746.22

Perform the Analysis

Preparing a forecast in Excel using the Forecast Sheet is very easy. From the **Data** tab, select the **Forecast Sheet** icon, as shown in Exhibit G.

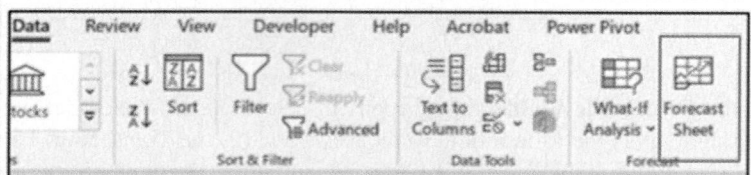

The **Create Forecast Worksheet** dialog box opens immediately and has already prepared a simple forecast based on the data (Exhibit H).

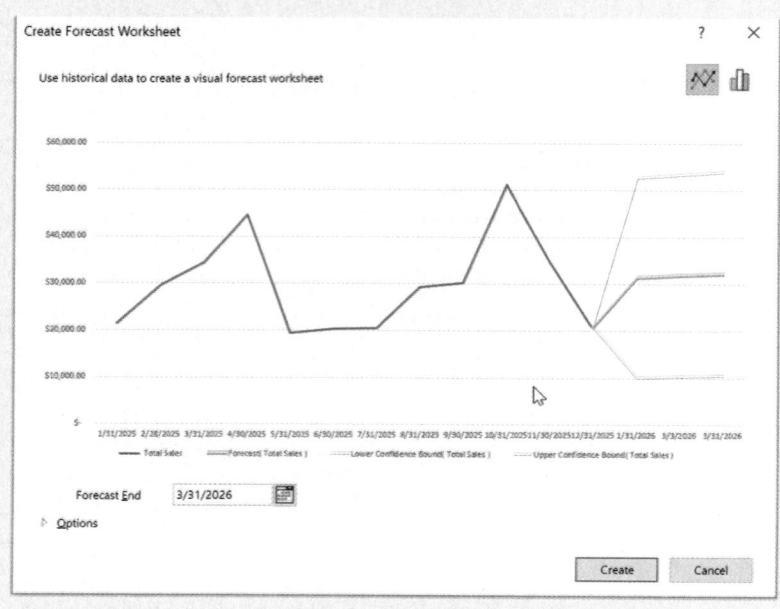

You can make some formatting and analysis selections to alter the forecast to better meet your needs. For example, in Exhibit I we change the forecast so that it ends on June 30, 2026.

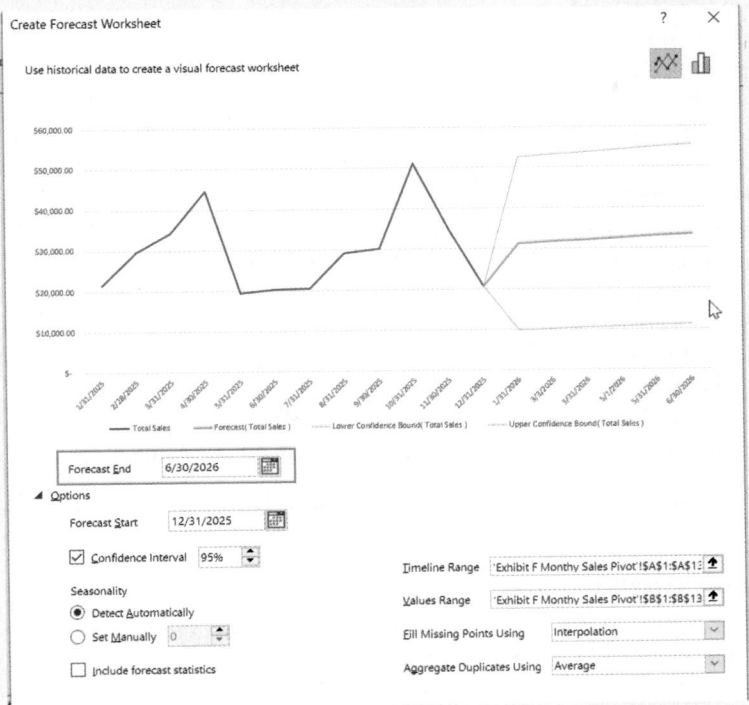

Exhibit I
Changing the End Date of the Forecast
Microsoft Excel

The result of this analysis will be a new worksheet with the sales forecast for the first six months of 2026 and the related forecast statistics, as shown in Exhibit J.

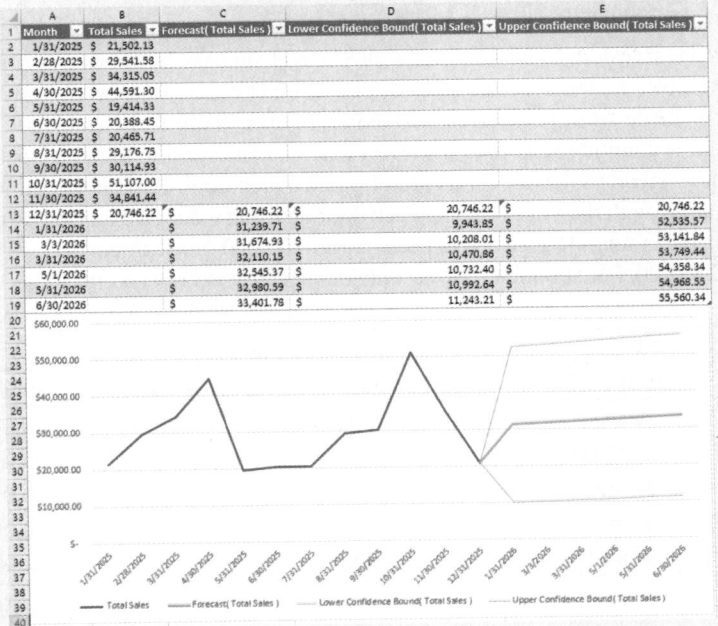

Exhibit J
2026 Sales Forecast
Microsoft Excel

Share the Story

Preparing a forecast like the one shown in Exhibit J is one of the first steps in the budgeting process. This forecast forms the basis for the revenue budget that management will use to predict costs, as well as to develop pro forma financial statements. Also, a forecast like this one shows that there is likely seasonality in the sales activity. You can see that there is a significant dip in sales of food and beverages through UberEats during the summer months. This dip makes intuitive sense because campus activity declines significantly in the summer months.

Mini-Lab Assessment

1. What month in 2026 has the greatest predicted sales?
2. As you can see in Exhibit I, the confidence interval for the forecast is set to 95%. How would the forecast change if the confidence interval were set to 90% instead? What if it were changed to 99%?
3. As shown in Exhibit J, the lower confidence bound for June 2026 is $11,243.21. What does this number represent?
4. If you had the ability to collect other data about UberEats sales at the university, what factors might you also want to consider when forecasting next year's sales?

Ⓠ LAB CONNECTIONS

In **LABS 9.1**, **9.2**, and **9.3** you will use historical sales data to forecast future sales using time series analysis in Excel, Tableau, and Power BI (respectively).

　　LAB 9.4 uses Excel to demonstrate how to use regression analysis to predict product demand based on multiple factors, including economic indicators, weather, and seasonality.

Step 1: Prepare the Sales Budget

Each year, **Heartwood Cabinets** begins the budget process by preparing a sales forecast. For this example, we focus on the sales of pine cabinet doors. Heartwood sells five styles of cabinet door made from pine: Arch, Cathedral, Shaker, Slab, and Beadboard. Heartwood's management accounting staff uses historical data and sales estimates developed by the sales department to predict sales for each type of pine cabinet door. Exhibit 9.2 summarizes these estimates, along with the sales price for each door type and the total expected revenue from the expected sales. In total, Heartwood expects to sell 105,000 pine cabinet doors for a total revenue of $7,250,000. For simplicity, we assume that Heartwood has no other sources of income.

Exhibit 9.2
Heartwood's Revenue (Sales) Budget
Microsoft Excel

Heartwood Sales Budget			
Door Style	Expected Sales	Selling Price	Expected Revenue
Pine - Arch	15,000	$ 50	$ 750,000
Pine - Cathedral	15,000	$ 70	$ 1,050,000
Pine - Shaker	20,000	$ 60	$ 1,200,000
Pine - Slab	25,000	$ 50	$ 1,250,000
Pine - Beadboard	30,000	$ 100	$ 3,000,000
Total	105,000		$ 7,250,000

Step 2: Prepare the Production Budget

Heartwood creates a **production budget** that calculates the total units that must be produced during the budget period to allow the company to meet the expected sales requirements. To calculate this budget, for each door type, Heartwood needs to know the **beginning finished goods inventory**, which is the number of units that have already been produced and are available for sale. Exhibit 9.3 shows the beginning inventory for each cabinet type produced by the Pine division.

production budget
A calculation of the total units that must be produced during the budget period to meet expected sales requirements.

	Beginning Inventoy	Direct Materials Cost Per Unit	Direct Labor Cost Per Unit	Manufacturing Overhead Cost per Unit	Total Cost Per Unit of Output	Total Cost of Finished Goods Beginning Inventory
				Heartwood Beginning Inventories Budget		
Pine - Arch	1,250	$ 25.00	$ 18.75	$ 6.00	$ 49.75	$ 62,187.50
Pine - Cathedral	750	$ 25.00	$ 18.75	$ 6.00	$ 49.75	$ 37,312.50
Pine - Shaker	1,000	$ 20.00	$ 28.75	$ 9.00	$ 57.75	$ 57,750.00
Pine - Slab	1,250	$ 20.00	$ 18.75	$ 6.00	$ 44.75	$ 55,937.50
Pine - Beadboard	1,000	$ 25.00	$ 37.50	$ 12.00	$ 74.50	$ 74,500.00
						$ 287,687.50

Exhibit 9.3

Heartwood's Beginning Inventories Budget

Microsoft Excel

For each door type, Heartwood also must determine the **ending finished goods inventory**, which is the amount of finished goods that the company would like to have left over after all sales are complete at the end of the period. Heartwood uses the following formula to calculate the production budget:

beginning finished goods inventory
The number of units that have already been produced and are available for sale.

ending finished goods inventory
The amount of finished goods that the company would like to have left over after all sales are complete at the end of the period.

Budget production (in units)	=	Budget sales (in units)	+	Target ending finished goods inventory (in units)	−	Beginning finished goods inventory (in units)

Heartwood uses this calculation for each type of cabinet door, as shown in Exhibit 9.4.

	Pine - Arch	Pine - Cathedral	Pine - Shaker	Pine - Slab	Pine - Beadboard
			Heartwood Production Budget (in units)		
Budgeted Sales	15,000	15,000	20,000	25,000	30,000
(Plus) Target Ending Finished Goods Inventory	750	750	1,000	1,250	1,500
Total Required Units	15,750	15,750	21,000	26,250	31,500
(less) Beginning finished goods inventory	1,250	750	1,000	1,250	1,000
Units to be Produced	14,500	15,000	20,000	25,000	30,500

Exhibit 9.4
Production Budget

Microsoft Excel

Note: Total units to be produced = 105,000.

Once the production budget is set, management accountants use it to determine the budgets for production costs, including direct materials costs, manufacturing labor costs, and manufacturing overhead costs.

direct materials cost budget
The budget containing each direct material item and its cost.

Step 3: Prepare the Direct Materials Cost Budget

The **direct materials cost budget** is the budget containing each direct material item and its cost. To create this budget, management accountants start with the **bill of materials (BOM)**

bill of materials (BOM)
A list of all of the raw materials and the quantity of each needed to produce one unit of an item.

for each type of item that will be produced during the budget period. The BOM is a list of all of the raw materials and the quantity of each needed to produce one unit of the item. The accountants will also consult with management to determine whether there will be any changes to the products in the next year that necessitate a change to the bill of materials. For example, perhaps **Heartwood** will use a stainless steel screw instead of a brass screw to attach the door pulls on the Pine–Arch cabinet doors next year. Exhibit 9.5 is an example of a bill of materials for the Pine–Arch cabinet door.

Exhibit 9.5
Bill of Materials for Pine–Arch Style Cabinets
Microsoft Excel

Heartwood Bill of Materials					
Pine - Arch					
Part Number	Part Name	Cost per Unit		Quantity	Total
P27-1244	Panel	$	9	1	$ 9
H14-7589	Handle	$	5	1	$ 5
H99-3622	Hinges	$	2	2	$ 4
L80-5429	Lever	$	3	1	$ 3
L12-9014	Latch	$	4	1	$ 4

After the management accountants review the bill of materials, they will use it to create the direct materials cost budget. To do so, they apply the appropriate costs to each of the raw materials used in production. They also "extend" this cost by multiplying it by the total number of units that must be produced in the budget period to meet the expected demand from the sales forecast. Finally, they deduct the cost and units associated with any finished product that is sitting in beginning inventory left over from the prior period. Exhibit 9.6 shows the direct materials budget for the Pine–Arch cabinet door. The same process is carried out for each of the products Heartwood manufactures.

Exhibit 9.6
Direct Materials Budget for Pine–Arch Style Cabinets
Microsoft Excel

Heartwood Direct Materials Budget				
Pine - Arch				
Part Number	Required Input	Expected Sales	Cost per Unit of Output	Total Cost
P27-1244	1	15,000	$ 9	$ 135,000
H14-7589	1	15,000	$ 5	$ 75,000
H99-3622	2	15,000	$ 4	$ 60,000
L80-5429	1	15,000	$ 3	$ 45,000
L12-9014	1	15,000	$ 4	$ 60,000
Total Direct Materials Required			$ 25	$ 375,000
(Plus) Target Ending Inventory (750 units X $25.00)				$ 18,750
(Less) End Product Available from Beginning Direct Materials Invent (1,200 units X $25.00)				$ 31,250
Direct Materials to be used this Period				$ 362,500

For simplicity, we do not reproduce the BOMs and perform the calculations for each of the other cabinet types here, but instead present the final direct materials budget as shown in Exhibit 9.7.

Heartwood Direct Materials Budget						
	Pine - Arch	Pine - Cathedral	Pine - Shaker	Pine - Slab	Pine - Beadboard	Total
Cost Per Unit	$ 25	$ 25	$ 20	$ 20	$ 25	
Expected Sales	15,000	15,000	20,000	25,000	30,000	105,000
Total Direct Materials Required	$ 375,000	$ 375,000	$ 400,000	$ 500,000	$ 750,000	$ 2,400,000
Target Ending Inventory	750	750	1,000	1,250	1,500	5,250
(Plus) Target Ending Inventory Materials Cost	$ 18,750	$ 18,750	$ 20,000	$ 25,000	$ 37,500	120,000
End Product Available from Beginning Direct Materials Inventory	1,250	750	1,000	1,250	1,000	5,250
(Less) Materials Cost for End Product Available from Beginning Inventory	$ 31,250	$ 18,750	$ 20,000	$ 25,000	$ 25,000	120,000
Direct Materials to be used this Period	$ 362,500	$ 375,000	$ 400,000	$ 500,000	$ 762,500	$ 2,400,000

Exhibit 9.7
Direct Materials Budget for All Pine Cabinets

Microsoft Excel

Step 4: Prepare the Direct Manufacturing Labor Cost Budget

Next, **Heartwood** must consider the labor costs associated with manufacturing its cabinets. To estimate the direct manufacturing labor costs, Heartwood must know the amount of labor required to complete production and employee wages, as well as any changes that may occur during the budget period.

Manufacturing an item usually requires a series of steps carried out by different people. These steps are documented, in order of planned completion, on a **route sheet**. The route sheet identifies the workstation where the work is done, as well as the planned time spent at each station. The route sheet summarizes the planned time required to manufacture each product, but the actual time may deviate from the plan if machines break down, raw materials are defective, or employees are inefficient. Chapter 10 discusses what happens when such deviations occur.

Once the management accountants know the amount of time spent on manufacturing the product, they apply the appropriate employee wage rate to the planned time at each workstation.

As shown in the Direct Manufacturing Labor Cost Budget for Heartwood (Exhibit 9.8), each Pine–Arch door requires 60 minutes of direct labor. Employees' hourly wages range from $15 per hour to $20 per hour. Management accountants need to translate the employees' hourly rates to a per-minute rate to accurately calculate manufacturing labor costs. For example, as shown in Exhibit 9.8, the labor cost for workstation 1 is calculated in two steps:

1. To calculate the labor cost per unit, multiply the hourly wage rate by the percentage of an hour used to complete the task.
2. To calculate total labor cost for a workstation, multiply labor cost per unit by the number of units produced.

So, for workstation 1:

1. Labor cost per unit = $20.00 * (30 minutes/60 minutes) = $10.00
2. Total labor cost at workstation = $10.00 * 14,500 = $145,000

route sheet
Used to summarize a manufacturing process; identifies the workstation where the work is done, as well as the planned time spent at each station.

Heartwood Direct Manufacturing Labor Costs Budget						
Pine - Arch						
Work Station	Activity	Minutes Required (for 1 unit)	Hourly Wage Rate	Labor Cost per Unit	Units to Produce	Total Labor Cost
1	Trim & sand door	30	$20	$ 10.00	14,500	$145,000.00
2	Attach handle	15	$15	$ 3.75	14,500	$ 54,375.00
3	Attach lever and hinges	15	$20	$ 5.00	14,500	$ 72,500.00
Total		60		$ 18.75	14,500	$271,875.00

Exhibit 9.8
Direct Manufacturing Labor Cost Budget for Pine–Arch Style Cabinets

Microsoft Excel

The same process is used to establish the labor cost budget for each product that Heartwood manufactures. For simplicity, we do not reproduce the detailed labor cost calculations for each of the other cabinet types here. Exhibit 9.9 shows the total labor hours required to manufacture a single unit of each cabinet type, as well as the total planned labor hours for all the units planned for production. Note that the units to be produced come from the last line of Exhibit 9.4.

Exhibit 9.9
Direct Labor Hours by Product Type
Microsoft Excel

Heartwood Manufacturing Labor Hours per Unit			
	Units to be Produced	Labor per Unit	Total Planned Labor Hours
Pine - Arch	14,500	1	14,500
Pine - Cathedral	15,000	1	15,000
Pine - Shaker	20,000	1.5	30,000
Pine - Slab	25,000	1	25,000
Pine - Beadboard	30,500	2	61,000
		Total Hours	145,500

Exhibit 9.10 presents the final direct labor-cost budget for all of Heartwood's pine cabinets. Units to be produced come from Exhibit 9.9, and the labor cost for the Pine–Arch cabinet ($18.75) comes from Exhibit 9.8. All the other information is given.

Exhibit 9.10
Direct Labor Cost Budget for All Pine Cabinet Doors
Microsoft Excel

Heartwood Direct Labor Budget						
	Pine - Arch	Pine - Cathedral	Pine - Shaker	Pine - Slab	Pine - Beadboard	Total
Units to Produce	14,500	15,000	20,000	25,000	30,500	105,000
Labor Cost per Unit	$ 18.75	$ 18.75	$ 28.75	$ 18.75	$ 37.50	
Total Labor Cost	$ 271,875.00	$ 281,250.00	$ 575,000.00	$ 468,750.00	$ 1,143,750.00	$ 2,740,625.00

Step 5: Prepare the Manufacturing Overhead Cost Budget

manufacturing overhead
Indirect costs that are essential to the manufacturing of goods.

As you learned in Chapter 4, **manufacturing overhead** refers to the total cost of indirect materials, indirect labor, and all other indirect production costs involved in manufacturing a product or producing a service. Supervisor labor, maintenance personnel, property taxes and rent on the production facilities, and depreciation are all part of manufacturing overhead. Recall that some of these overhead costs are variable, meaning that they increase or decrease as the number of units produced increases or decreases. Other overhead costs are fixed, in that they are incurred regardless of the level of production.

At **Heartwood**, the variable manufacturing overhead costs include glue, polyurethane, materials handling, and indirect labor. Fixed manufacturing overhead costs at Heartwood include factory rent, machine depreciation, utilities, maintenance and repairs, and supervisor labor. Heartwood relies on data from prior years to calculate the total manufacturing overhead.

Heartwood uses direct labor hours as the cost driver for the overhead costs. You can refer back to Chapter 4 (Learning Objective 4.4) for a refresher on how organizations determine the overhead application base. Looking again at Exhibit 9.9, we see that planned production will require 145,500 labor hours. We use these planned labor hours to calculate the variable overhead shown in Exhibit 9.11.

Heartwood Manufacturing Overhead (based on prior year data)			
Units to be produced (From Production budget)		105,000	
Labor hours required for planned production		145,500	
Variable Overhead			
Indirect materials and supplies	$ 3.00	436,500	
Materials handling	$ 1.00	145,500	
Indirect labor	$ 1.25	181,875	
			$ 763,875
Fixed manufacturing overhead			
Factory rent		24,000	
Machine depreciation		13,000	
Supervisor labor		30,000	
Utilities		19,976	
Maintenance and repairs		9,999	
Property taxes		12,150	
			$ 109,125
			$ 873,000
Manufacturing Overhead per Unit			$ 6
($873,000/145,500, rounded to the nearest cent).			

Exhibit 9.11
Manufacturing
Overhead Cost
Calculations
Microsoft Excel

As you review Exhibit 9.11, you will note that variable overhead is calculated by multiplying the overhead rate per labor hour by the total number of labor hours (145,500). If the number of hours required was greater or less than 145,500, the total variable overhead cost would be different. In contrast, total fixed overhead costs are the same regardless of how many units are produced or labor hours are spent. Those numbers, provided by management accountants, are given in Exhibit 9.11.

The total variable overhead costs and total fixed overhead costs are summed, and the total manufacturing overhead cost is determined to be $873,000. To find the per-hour overhead rate, we divide that total by planned labor hours, 145,500. The per-hour overhead rate that Heartwood will apply to production is therefore $6.00.

Now, let's return to the example of Heartwood's Pine–Arch cabinets. Manufacturing a single cabinet requires 60 minutes of direct labor. We apply the predetermined manufacturing overhead rate of $6.00 by multiplying it by the 14,500 units of Pine–Arch planned for production. The result is $87,000, as shown in Exhibit 9.12. The manufacturing overhead is calculated for all cabinet types in the same way, resulting in a total manufacturing overhead of $873,000.

Exhibit 9.12
Manufacturing
Overhead

Microsoft Excel

	Units to Produce	Direct Labor Hours Required for 1 unit	Predetermined Overhead Rate	Overhead per Unit	Manufacturing Overhead
		Heartwood Manufacturing Overhead			
Pine - Arch	14,500	1	$ 6	$ 6	$ 87,000
Pine - Cathedral	15,000	1	$ 6	$ 6	$ 90,000
Pine - Shaker	20,000	1.5	$ 6	$ ✚ 9	$ 180,000
Pine - Slab	25,000	1	$ 6	$ 6	$ 150,000
Pine - Beadboard	30,500	2	$ 6	$ 12	$ 366,000
	105,000	6.5			$ 873,000

Step 6: Prepare the Ending Inventories Budget

Heartwood prepares the ending inventories budget by applying the direct materials cost per unit, the direct labor cost per unit, and the manufacturing overhead cost per unit to the estimated ending inventory, as shown in Exhibit 9.13. Notice where the numbers come from:

- Ending inventory comes from the second row of Exhibit 9.4.
- Direct materials cost per unit comes from the first row of Exhibit 9.7.
- Direct labor cost per unit comes from Exhibit 9.10.
- Manufacturing overhead cost per unit comes from Exhibit 9.12.

Exhibit 9.13
Ending Inventories
Budget

Microsoft Excel

	Ending Inventory	Direct Materials Cost per Unit	Direct Labor Cost per Unit	Manufacturing Overhead Cost per Unit	Total Cost per Unit of Output	Total Cost of Ending Finished Goods Inventory
			Heartwood Ending Inventories Budget			
Pine - Arch	750	$ 25.00	$ 18.75	$ 6.00	$ 49.75	$ 37,312.50
Pine - Cathedral	750	$ 25.00	$ 18.75	$ 6.00	$ 49.75	$ 37,312.50
Pine - Shaker	1,000	$ 20.00	$ 28.75	$ 9.00	$ 57.75	$ 57,750.00
Pine - Slab	1,250	$ 20.00	$ 18.75	$ 6.00	$ 44.75	$ 55,937.50
Pine - Beadboard	1,500	$ 25.00	$ 37.50	$ 12.00	$ 74.50	$ 111,750.00
						$ 300,062.50

Step 7: Prepare the Cost of Goods Sold Budget

cost of goods sold (COGS) budget
The budget used to plan for and track cost of goods sold.

Next, management accountants use the preceding budgets to develop a **cost of goods sold (COGS) budget**, which is the budget used to plan for and track cost of goods sold. Exhibit 9.14 shows the COGS budget for the Pine–Arch cabinet doors only. **Heartwood** will prepare the same estimates for each type of product.

Exhibit 9.14
Cost of Goods Sold
Budget

Microsoft Excel

Heartwood Cost of Goods Sold Budget		
	See budget from exhibit:	
Beginning Finished Goods Inventory	9.3	$ 287,687.50
Direct Materials Used	9.7	$ 2,400,000.00
Direct Manufacturing Labor	9.1	$ 2,740,625.00
Direct Manufacturing Overhead	9.11	$ 873,000.00
Cost of Goods Manufactured		$ 6,013,625.00
Costs of Goods Available for Sale		$ 6,301,312.50
(Less) Ending Finished Goods Inventory	9.13	$ 300,062.50
Cost of Goods Sold		$ 6,001,250.00

Step 8: Prepare the Operating Costs Budget

In addition to incurring manufacturing costs, organizations incur operating costs that are critical to their success. Activities such as marketing, research and development, product development, and product distribution are included in the nonmanufacturing operating costs. Some of these costs, such as marketing or research and development, are likely to be fixed. Others, such as product distribution, are variable and based on the number of units shipped. The operating costs budget is a summary of all of the expenses, including nonproduction costs, that will be required to achieve planned production.

At **Heartwood**, product development costs are fixed at $75,000 per year. Marketing is also fixed at $150,000 per year. Distribution is a variable cost, estimated to be $0.50 per unit sold and shipped. Heartwood's management accountants summarize the estimated operating costs in the operating costs budget shown in Exhibit 9.15.

Heartwood Operating Costs Budget				
	Units Sold	Variable	Fixed	Total Cost
Product Development	105,000		$ 75,000	$ 75,000
Marketing	105,000		$ 150,000	$ 150,000
Distribution	105,000	$ 52,500		$ 52,500
Total Operating Costs				$ 277,500

Exhibit 9.15
Nonmanufacturing Operating Costs Budget

Microsoft Excel

Note: Distribution costs = $0.50 per unit sold * 105,000 units sold = $52,500.

Step 9: Prepare the Budgeted Operating Income Statement

Finally, management accountants, along with management, use all of the prepared budgets to create budgeted financial statements, also known as **pro forma financial statements**. These pro forma statements give a sneak peek into what the organization's financial performance will be if it operates as expected. **Heartwood Cabinetry**'s pro forma operating income statement is shown in Exhibit 9.16.

pro forma financial statements
Financial statements that reflect the organization's performance if it operates as expected.

Heartwood Pro Forma Operating Income Statement		
	See budget from exhibit:	
Revenue	9.2	$ 7,250,000
Cost of Goods Sold	9.14	$ 6,001,250
Gross Margin		$ 1,248,750
Operating Costs		
Production Development	9.15	$ 75,000
Marketing Costs	9.15	$ 150,000
Distribution Costs	9.15	$ 52,500
Operating Income		$ 971,250

Exhibit 9.16
Heartwood's Pro Forma Operating Income Statement

Microsoft Excel

LAB CONNECTION

LAB 9.5 EXCEL asks you to use Excel to build a master budget, including all of the supporting budgets and schedules.

 PROGRESS CHECK

5. How does an organization forecast sales (or revenue in general)?
6. How does an organization determine the amount of product to produce during a budget cycle?
7. How is manufacturing overhead calculated for the budgeting process?

LO 9.4

Perform a sensitivity analysis and explain how changes to underlying assumptions in the budget affect expectations.

sensitivity analysis
A financial modeling tool used to examine how changes to the underlying assumptions in the model may affect the outcome.

SENSITIVITY ANALYSIS

Sensitivity analysis is a financial modeling tool used to examine how changes to the underlying assumptions in the model may affect the outcome. In the case of budgets, management accountants may consider how changes to the expected sales or the costs of raw materials or labor may impact the company's financial performance.

Many organizations use the Scenario Manager tool in Excel to run sensitivity analyses. Scenario Manager is a What-If Analysis found in the Forecasting pane on the Data ribbon in Excel. To operate Scenario Manager, you first enter all of the required data and formulas into a spreadsheet. Then you use the Scenario Manager tool to identify which variables might change and how they might change. When you run the tool, it will calculate how your changes affect the outcome.

Using **Heartwood** again as an example, Exhibit 9.17 reports the key assumptions to calculate budgeted operating income (based on data from the various exhibits throughout this chapter). Heartwood's management and the management accountants will consider the various factors that might affect the assumptions in this financial model. Let's consider the following scenarios:

					Heartwood Sales Budget		
Door Style	**Expected Sales**	**Sales Price**	**Direct Materials Cost**	**Direct Labor Cost**	**Manufacturing Overhead**	**Budgeted Operating Income**	
Pine - Arch	15,000	$ 50.00	$ 25.00	$ 18.75	$ 6.00	$ 3,750.00	
Pine - Cathedral	15,000	$ 70.00	$ 25.00	$ 18.75	$ 6.00	$ 303,750.00	
Pine - Shaker	20,000	$ 60.00	$ 20.00	$ 28.75	$ 9.00	$ 45,000.00	
Pine - Slab	25,000	$ 50.00	$ 20.00	$ 18.75	$ 6.00	$ 131,250.00	
Pine - Beadboard	30,000	$ 100.00	$ 25.00	$ 37.50	$ 12.00	$ 765,000.00	
					Total:	$ 1,248,750.00	

Exhibit 9.17
Key Assumptions for Calculating Budgeted Operating Income
Microsoft Excel

Scenario 1. One of Heartwood's main competitors, **Wellborn Cabinet**, is likely to expand its own sales strategy and begin selling its product at **Lowe's**. Heartwood's management accountants estimate that Wellborn's expansion will result in a 10 percent decrease in the sales of all Heartwood products.

Scenario 2. One of Heartwood's key pine suppliers is likely to offer its loyal customers a discount that will represent a 1 percent savings in direct materials cost for all pine products.

Exhibit 9.18 shows the results generated using the Excel Scenario Manager tool for Scenario 1. Based on this analysis, we see that if sales of each product decrease by 10 percent, the resulting effect on overall income is a decrease of approximately 10 percent.

Exhibit 9.18
Sensitivity Analysis Examining a 10 Percent Decrease in Sales

Microsoft Excel

Scenario Summary		
	Current Values	Scenario 1 - 10% Sales Decrease
Changing Cells:		
$B$3	15,000	13,500
$B$4	15,000	13,500
$B$5	20,000	18,000
$B$6	25,000	22,500
$B$7	30,000	27,000
Result Cells:		
$G$8	$ 1,248,750.00	$ 1,123,875.00

Notes: Current Values column represents values of changing cells at time Scenario Summary report was created. Changing cells for each scenario are highlighted in gray.

Exhibit 9.19 displays the results generated using the Excel Scenario Manager tool for Scenario 2. Based on this analysis, we see that a 1 percent decrease in direct materials cost yields a 2 percent increase in budgeted operating income. This type of sensitivity analysis is useful because it reveals how a change to any part of the operating process could affect operating income.

Scenario Summary			
	Current Values	Scenario 1 - 10% Sales Decrease	Scenario 2 - Direct Materials 1% Discount
Changing Cells:			
$C$4	15,000	13,500	15,000
$C$5	15,000	13,500	15,000
$C$6	20,000	18,000	20,000
$C$7	25,000	22,500	25,000
$C$8	30,000	27,000	30,000
$E$4	$ 25.00	$ 25.00	$ 24.75
$E$5	$ 25.00	$ 25.00	$ 24.75
$E$6	$ 20.00	$ 20.00	$ 19.80
$E$7	$ 20.00	$ 20.00	$ 19.80
$E$8	$ 25.00	$ 25.00	$ 24.75
Result Cells:			
$H$9	$ 1,248,750.00	$ 1,123,875.00	$ 1,272,750.00

Notes: Current Values column represents values of changing cells at time Scenario Summary eport was created. Changing cells for each scenario are highlighted in gray.

Exhibit 9.19
Sensitivity Analysis Examining a 1 Percent Reduction in the Materials Cost for All Pine Cabinets

Microsoft Excel

Q LAB CONNECTION

LAB 9.6 EXCEL asks you to use the Scenario Manager tool in Excel to examine the effects of changes to the budget assumptions on the budgeted operating income.

PROGRESS CHECK

8. What is sensitivity analysis, and how is it used during the budgeting process?

9. Imagine that you are a cost accountant for Blue Dog Merch, a company that produces branded promotional materials like drinkware, apparel, bags, and office supplies. Blue Dog Merch is forecasting operating income for the upcoming year and would like to perform several sensitivity analyses to consider different scenarios. Describe three variables you might change when running what-if analyses in Excel and provide your justification for suggesting those changes.

LO 9.5

Describe the difference between a flexible budget and a static budget.

FLEXIBLE BUDGETS

As we've seen, a static budget is prepared at the beginning of the period and does not change until the next budget cycle. For example, let's imagine that **Champion** expects to sell game-day hoodies at $50 each and Exhibit 9.20 shows its budget for sales of its game-day hoodies in October.

UfaBizPhoto/Shutterstock

Exhibit 9.20
Champion's Budget for Game-Day Hoodies

Microsoft Excel

Champion Budget - Game Day Hoodies	Per Unit	Static Budget
Units Sold		20,000
Revenue	$ 50.00	$ 1,000,000
Variable Costs		
Direct Material	$ 8.00	$ 160,000
Direct Labor	$ 4.00	$ 80,000
Variable Manufacturing Overhead	$ 2.50	$ 50,000
Variable SG&A Costs	$ 2.25	$ 45,000
Total Variable Costs	$ 16.75	$ 335,000
Contribution Margin		$ 665,000
Fixed Costs		
Fixed Manufacturing Overhead	Fixed	$ 100,000
Fixed SG&A Costs	Fixed	$ 50,000
Total Fixed Costs		$ 150,000
Operating Income		$ 515,000

A **flexible budget** is a useful tool that reproduces the budget at various levels of unit sales. It can help organizations prepare for changes in their operating environment and respond to challenges and opportunities more quickly. For example, what would Champion expect income to be if sales are 10 percent or 20 percent higher or lower than expected? Much like sensitivity analysis, a flexible budget can be used to forecast these changes in sales.

To create a flexible budget, revenue and variable expense items must be calculated on a per-unit basis and then multiplied by forecasted sales units, as shown in Exhibit 9.21. Fixed costs remain constant across forecasted sales levels. Flexible budgets are especially helpful when evaluating performance, as they allow for objective comparisons between budgeted and actual results. We return to flexible budgets in Chapter 10.

flexible budget
A tool that reproduces the budget at various levels of unit sales.

Champion Budget - Game Day Hoodies	Per Unit	Static Budget	-20%	-10%	+10%	+20%
Units Sold		20,000	16,000	18,000	22,000	24,000
Revenue	$50.00	$1,000,000	$800,000	$900,000	$1,100,000	$1,200,000
Variable Costs						
Direct Material	$8.00	160,000	$128,000	$144,000	$176,000	$192,000
Direct Labor	$4.00	80,000	$64,000	$72,000	$88,000	$96,000
Variable Manufacturing Overhead	$2.50	50,000	$40,000	$45,000	$55,000	$60,000
Variable SG&A Costs	$2.25	45,000	$36,000	$40,500	$49,500	$54,000
Total Variable Costs	$16.75	335,000	$268,000	$301,500	$368,500	$402,000
Contribution Margin		665,000	$532,000	$598,500	$731,500	$798,000
Fixed Costs						
Fixed Manufacturing Overhead	Fixed	100,000	$100,000	$100,000	$100,000	$100,000
Fixed SG&A Costs	Fixed	50,000	$50,000	$50,000	$50,000	$50,000
Total Fixed Costs		150,000	$150,000	$150,000	$150,000	$150,000
Operating Income		515,000	$382,000	$448,500	$581,500	$648,000

Exhibit 9.21
Champion's Flexible Budget
Microsoft Excel

PROGRESS CHECK

10. How is a flexible budget different from a static budget?
11. What is the purpose of a flexible budget?

HUMAN DIMENSIONS: BEHAVIORAL EFFECTS OF BUDGETS

LO 9.6
Explain the behavioral effects of budgets.

So far we have learned how to create a budget and seen that it is a data-driven, mathematical process. However, budgets have important behavioral effects on the people who create them and those who are held responsible for the organization's performance. In this section, we explore the behavioral effects of budgeting.

Motivation

Because budgets are often used to create performance targets for management, they have strong motivational effects. At the end of the period, management will prepare reports that compare employees' actual performance to the expectations set forth in the budget. Thus, management can use the budget as a tool to encourage employees to work hard by setting challenging but achievable targets, often called **stretch targets**. If targets are too easy, they will not motivate employees to work hard.

CAREER SKILLS
Learning about the human implications of budgeting supports this career skill:
• Understanding how budgets can influence employee behavior

stretch target
A challenging but achievable target; a budget tool used to encourage employees to work hard.

controllability
The extent to which employees have influence over the costs, revenues, and other performance factors that are used to evaluate them.

participative budgeting
Bottom-up budgeting that allows employees who are affected by the budget to be involved in developing it.

authoritative budgeting
Top-down approach to budgeting in which top management makes all budgeting decisions.

negotiated budgeting process
A budgeting process in which employees develop initial budgets based on their knowledge of operations and expectations, which they submit for review and approval from top management.

budgetary slack
A built-in budget cushion that increases the chances of meeting or beating expectations.

When budgets are used for motivational purposes and compared to employees' actual performance, it is important that the employee can control the performance being evaluated. **Controllability** is the extent to which employees have influence over the costs, revenues, and other performance factors that are used to evaluate them. If employees do not believe they can control the factors that impact their evaluation (and as a result their compensation), the budget will have *de*motivating effects.

Participative Budgeting

Many organizations use **participative budgeting**, allowing the employees who are affected by the budget to be involved in developing it. That is, the people who are held accountable for performance help to set the budget numbers. This bottom-up approach contrasts with the top-down approach of **authoritative budgeting**, in which top management makes all of the budgeting decisions.

Participative budgeting allows for better communication and acceptance of performance targets. Employees are more likely to be motivated to perform if they believe that they have had a voice in setting their targets. However, participative budgeting may lead to dysfunctional budgeting behavior, as we discuss in the next section.

Ultimately, organizations are best off if the budget process involves both top management and the individuals held responsible for performance, a practice known as a **negotiated budgeting process**. In negotiated budgeting, employees develop initial budgets based on their knowledge of operations and expectations, which they submit for review and approval from top management. Often, top management will revise and send the budget back to the employees, and this process may continue until a negotiated outcome is reached.

Budgetary Slack

A key function of budgets is to compare actual performance to the plan. Many employees, such as business unit managers, are evaluated on their ability to meet or outperform budgeted expectations. As a result, employees have an incentive to build in a cushion, known as **budgetary slack**, that will increase their chances of meeting or beating expectations. In particular, employees may underestimate expected revenues or overestimate expected costs.

Budgetary slack is problematic for several reasons. First, it gives top-level management a distorted picture of the organization's potential performance, which interferes with planning and resource-allocation decisions. Second, the managers who exploit budgetary slack are engaging in unethical behavior by misrepresenting their own performance.

Organizations can reduce budgetary slack by limiting the number of managers who participate in the budget process. Additionally, organizations can reduce the incentive to create budgetary slack by using the budget only for planning purposes and not for performance evaluation and reward. If employees' compensation and advancement are not tied to their ability to meet or beat budget expectations, they will not have the incentive to create slack.

Overreliance on Comparing Budget to Actual Performance

There are also behavioral effects that organizations need to consider so they do not *over-rely* on comparing budget to actual performance. For example, a focus on meeting budget targets in the current period encourages short-term thinking and **myopia**. Myopia is problematic because it can cause employees to focus on their short-term goals to the detriment of long-term goals. In addition, this short-term thinking can stifle innovation and risk-taking because employees might be unwilling to try something new for fear that it might cause them to miss their targets in the current period. Similarly, it may lead managers to be inflexible and to discourage innovation.

myopia
Decision making that focuses on the short term, often to the detriment of long-term goals.

 PROGRESS CHECK

12. How are budgets used to motivate employees?
13. What is budgetary slack, and why is it a problem?

BUDGETING FOR OTHER ACTIVITIES, INCLUDING ENVIRONMENTAL, SOCIAL, AND GOVERNANCE (ESG) INITIATIVES

LO 9.7

Describe the use of budgets for ESG initiatives.

ENVIRONMENTAL, SOCIAL, GOVERNANCE

Our discussion of budgeting has focused on an organization's financial performance. However, organizations use budgets to forecast and predict all kinds of performance. For example, if you go to work for a public accounting firm, you will compare the hours you spend on each client to the agreed-upon budget your firm established before your work began. If you spend more hours on the client than originally budgeted, that project will not be profitable.

Today, there is increasing pressure for organizations to have an ESG strategy.[2] **ESG** stands for environmental, social, and governance. Organizations are strongly encouraged to consider ESG issues when conducting their operations. When an organization reports on its ESG activities, it presents an evaluation of its overall conscientiousness regarding social and environmental factors.

One key ESG initiative that many organizations have embraced is a reduction of their carbon footprint. To this end, organizations need to quantify their carbon footprint, employing budgeting techniques to estimate how much carbon they currently use to conduct their business and developing targets for their carbon usage in the future. For example, in March 2020, **Delta Air Lines** made a public commitment to become carbon neutral. In the announcement, Delta outlined plans to reduce emissions directly via changes to its fleet and its operations and through the purchase of **carbon offsets**, which are activities that prevent the release of, reduce, or remove carbon emissions from the atmosphere. Specifically, Delta committed to spending $1 billion over the next 10 years to develop clean air-travel technology, reduce carbon emissions and waste, and establish new projects to offset carbon emissions.

To make investors aware of their activities, organizations often publish annual reports of their ESG initiatives and their progress toward their ESG goals. For example, in 2021, Delta offset 13 million metric tons of emissions generated through its air travel during the period March 1–December 31, 2020. This offset is the equivalent of saving 17 million acres of forest.[3]

ESG
Environmental, social, and governance; organizations are strongly encouraged to consider these issues when conducting operations.

carbon offset
An activity that prevents the release of, reduces, or removes carbon emissions from the atmosphere.

---

[2]Camila Domonoske, "Better Late Than Never? Big Companies Scramble to Make Lofty Climate Promises," *NPR,* February 27, 2020, www.npr.org/2020/02/27/806011419/better-late-than-never-big-companies-scramble-to-make-lofty-climate-promises.
[3]From "New Campaign Shines Light on Delta's Carbon Neutrality," video, September 13, 2021, https://news.delta.com/new-campaign-shines-light-deltas-carbon-neutrality (accessed November 30, 2021).

CAREER SKILLS

Learning about budgeting for ESG supports these career skills:

• Understanding the relevance of ESG for organizations and their stakeholder value

• Recognizing how the budget process translates to other contexts

Because ESG activities are so important and investors and consumers pay such close attention to them, it is critical that organizations carefully plan and track their progress toward ESG goals. Budgeting is an effective tool that helps organizations manage their ESG goals.

When organizations budget for ESG activities, they follow a set of steps similar to those described for traditional budgeting:

Step 1. Identify the organization's ESG-related goals. These may include becoming carbon neutral, increasing the world's supply of clean drinking water, or creating an inclusive environment for all employees, clients, and customers.

Step 2. Determine the activities that will be carried out to meet those goals. These activities might include starting new initiatives like reducing water stress in operations through monitoring and tracking,[4] expanding work opportunities for neurodiverse employees,[5] or purchasing carbon offsets. They may also involve careful elimination of harmful practices, such as reducing nonessential travel or encouraging work-from-home arrangements to lower employees' use of personal vehicles.

Step 3. Develop expectations about the costs and financial gains that will result from these activities. The organization also must track the performance toward the goal. For example, if the goal is carbon neutrality, the organization must show the amount of carbon used and offset each period.

 PROGRESS CHECK

14. What is ESG, and why is it important to organizations?
15. What data would an organization, such as **Delta Air Lines**, need to effectively budget and report its progress towards its ESG goals?

Careers with Budgeting Responsibilities

Budgeting is one of the most important job responsibilities a cost accountant has. As described in this chapter, budgets set expectations for performance and are a key tool for measuring performance by employees throughout the organization.

Exhibit 9.22 reproduces a job posting from a site like **Indeed.com** or **LinkedIn.com**. This posting is for a financial analyst position at a global power generation and distribution company like **Siemens**, **Hitachi**, or **Honeywell**. This position is for a highly organized and detail-oriented accountant who can manage multiple projects with detailed budgets and expert data analysis.

[4]Thomas Hundertmark, Kun Lueck, and Brent Packer, "Water: A Human and Business Priority," *McKinsey Quarterly,* May 5, 2020, www.mckinsey.com/capabilities/sustainability/our-insights/water-a-human-and-business-priority.
[5]Ernst & Young, "EY US Launches First Neuro-Diverse Center of Excellence in Boston," press release, April 12, 2021, www.ey.com/en_us/news/2021/04/ey-us-launches-first-neuro-diverse-center-of-excellence-in-boston.

Job Title
Project Controller

Job Summary

We are seeking an experienced and well-rounded individual to join our global team as a key member of our finance group. The Project Controller role utilizes accounting and data analysis skills and works with groups across the company to monitor and report on project profitability and all other commercial aspects of the project. In this role, you will use financial data to identify risks and opportunities and manage schedules and timing changes that may affect overall results. The Project Controller will have a close partnership with operations to analyze key figures and deliver monthly forecasts and reports. In this role, you will work across teams to manage multiple projects at once with minimal supervision, while maintaining a high level of attention to detail.

Qualifications Required:

- BS/BA in Accounting or Finance
- Experience in accounting policies and project management guidelines
- Advanced Excel skills required, including pivot tables, V-lookups, and advanced functions
- ERP system experience (SAP or equivalent)
- Four or more years of experience in financial planning and analysis or cost accounting and budgeting

Preferred:

- MBA or CPA
- Experience creating dashboards using Tableau or other tools
- Self-motivated with excellent organizational skills and the ability to understand and prioritize competing tasks
- Experience and exposure to contract language related to application of proper financial treatment
- Strong communication skills, both written and verbal/presentation
- Ability to work across teams, especially with technical information, to make data-driven decisions in a fast-paced environment
- Experience with financial modeling, strategic thinking, and proven creative problem solving

Responsibilities

- Create and deliver monthly reports and forecasts on revenue, budget, and gross margin for multiple projects and proposals
- Manage logistics for domestic and international projects and coordinate relevant contract requirements
- Create and deliver quarterly reports to project managers and leadership
- Support finance department with reporting on financial close and ensure compliance with GAAP requirements

Callout annotations (right margin):

- This job has many budgeting responsibilities, and data analytics skills are preferred.
- Significant budgeting and forecasting responsibilities
- Preference for an accounting or finance degree
- Proficiency with Excel is a must.
- Certifications and advanced degrees help you stand out.
- Advanced data analytics skills are preferred.
- Soft skills such as creative thinking, multi-tasking, and communication are essential.
- Cost accountants must communicate with technical departments and act as interpreters.

Exhibit 9.22
Financial Analyst Job Opportunity with Budgeting Responsibilities

Key Takeaways: Budgeting in Organizations

In this chapter, we learned about the budget process and its purpose. We gained an understanding of the data and estimates that are used to create a budget and considered how changes to the key assumptions of the budget may influence expectations of operating income. We also learned about several human aspects of budgeting, including its motivational purposes and how employees may try to exploit the budget process for their own gain. Finally, we discussed some of the nonfinancial budget activities commonly performed, such as budgeting for reductions in carbon emissions.

The budgeting process includes all aspects of the AMPS model:

Ask the Question

- **Which question(s) does management want to answer?**

Budgeting can help managers answer many questions, such as: What are our projected revenues and expenses? How much should we produce? How should staffing be adjusted to meet our goals?

Manage the Data

- **Which data are appropriate to address management's questions?**

Many types of data are relevant for the budgeting process, and the data requirements vary based on the focus of the budget (for example, financial vs. carbon emissions). If an organization is budgeting for production, it will need historical sales data, as well data about other economic factors, to forecast future sales. It will also need cost data such as materials costs, labor costs, and overhead.

Perform the Analysis

- **Which analytics are performed to address management questions?**

Much of the basic budget process is based on simple calculations and can be completed using basic tools like Excel. More sophisticated analytics may be necessary if the organization chooses to run a sensitivity analysis or calculate different scenarios. Many organizations use visualizations such as bar charts or line graphs to compare performance to budget.

Share the Story

- **How are the results of the analytics shared with stakeholders?**

Budgets are shared with all employees who are responsible for performance related to the budget. Reports showing comparisons of budgets to actual performance (either numerically or graphically) are distributed periodically and are often used as the basis for performance evaluations.

Key Terms

authoritative budgeting	carbon offset	flexible budget	pro forma financial statements
beginning finished goods inventory	controllability	manufacturing overhead	production budget
bill of materials (BOM)	cost of goods sold (COGS) budget	master budget	route sheet
budget	direct materials cost budget	myopia	sales budget
budget cycle	ending finished goods inventory	negotiated budgeting process	sales forecast
budget period	ESG	operating budget	sensitivity analysis
budgetary slack	financial budget	participative budgeting	static budget
			stretch target

ANSWERS TO PROGRESS CHECKS

1. A budget is an estimate of the activities that will be carried out over a specified future period of time.

2. Budgets serve as an estimate of the expected revenues the organization will earn and expenses it will incur over a specified future time period. Budgets can also be used to plan nonfinancial aspects of an organization's operations, such as expected carbon emissions or hours to complete a project.

3. The master budget is the overall budget for the organization as a whole. Its main components are operating budgets and financial budgets.

4. Organizations use budgets to set expectations for performance. When they are disseminated throughout the organization, they provide a commonly understood set of goals, objectives, and expectations. They help everyone get on the same page and serve as the basis for shared responsibilities.

5. An organization forecasts revenue through predictive analysis that generates future values based on historic values along a linear trend. The organization must also consider other information, such as industry and economic trends, competitors' activity, pricing and credit policies, marketing and advertising strategies, and existing backorders.

6. The organization determines the amount of production by considering the expected sales volume, adding the determined finished goods inventory, and then subtracting beginning finished goods inventory.

7. Manufacturing overhead is the total cost of indirect materials, indirect labor, and all other indirect production costs involved in manufacturing a product or producing a service. The organization will determine an overhead rate and apply it based on some measure, such as labor hours.

8. Sensitivity analysis is a financial modeling tool used to examine how changes to the underlying assumptions in the model may affect the outcome. It could be used during the budgeting process to consider how changes in expected sales or the cost of raw materials may impact a company's financial performance.

9. Blue Dog Merch may consider the following changes when running sensitivity analyses:

    a. A 10 percent decrease in sales because a new competitor from overseas has entered the market

    b. An increase in direct materials costs because supply-chain disruptions have increased the cost of shipping and obtaining raw materials

    c. An increase in direct labor costs because it has been harder to find reliable employees in recent years

    Other correct answers are possible.

10. A flexible budget reproduces the budget at various levels of unit sales, whereas a static budget is set at the beginning of the period and does not change.

11. A flexible budget helps organizations prepare for changes in their operating environment and helps them respond to challenges and opportunities more quickly.

12. Budgets can be used to motivate employees because budgets carefully lay out expectations and employees can understand exactly which goals they need to achieve.

13. Budgetary slack is a budgetary cushion that increases employees' chances of meeting or beating expectations. It's problematic for several reasons. First, it gives top-level management a distorted view of performance. Second, managers who exploit budgetary slack are misrepresenting performance and acting unethically.

14. ESG stands for environmental, social, and governance. Organizations are strongly encouraged to consider ESG issues when conducting their operations. When an organization reports on its ESG activities, it presents an evaluation of its overall conscientiousness regarding social and environmental factors.

15. The necessary data will vary based on the company's ESG goals. **Delta** is particularly interested in reducing its carbon footprint, so data on energy consumption at its training, office, and airport facilities will be critical. Delta will also gather fuel-consumption

per flight (and miles traveled). In addition, if the company has purchased carbon-offset credits, it will include them in the analysis.

Other aspects of ESG can include social issues, such as a focus on diversity and inclusion. The company will quantify the demographic characteristics of its employees as well as any training or inclusivity initiatives in which it is engaged.

For governance, the company will collect and report data about its governance initiatives, and it will specify the makeup of its board of directors and top management. It will also examine executive compensation and lapses in internal control, and it will investigate any potential fraud.

Multiple-Choice Questions McGraw Hill connect

CMA

1. (LO9.1) Which of the following does **not** describe a purpose of a budget?
   a. Provides a benchmark to compare actual performance
   b. Provides a mechanism for communication
   c. Used to motivate employees
   d. Used to prevent negative performance

2. (LO9.3) When preparing an operational budget, in which order are the component budgets commonly prepared?
   a. Sales, production, direct materials purchased, cost of goods manufactured, income statement, capital, cash, and balance sheet
   b. Production, sales, cost of goods manufactured, selling and administrative
   c. Sales, production, cost of goods manufactured, direct materials purchased, administrative
   d. Production, sales, selling and administrative, cost of goods manufactured

3. (LO9.3) Which of the following best describes a budget that expresses the operating and financial plans of management for a fiscal year?
   a. Flexible budget
   b. Rolling budget
   c. Master budget
   d. Strategic budget

4. (LO9.3) Which of the following best describes a budget that includes all of the resources a company needs to execute sales, production, purchasing, and marketing?
   a. Master budget
   b. Operating budget
   c. Financial budget
   d. Materials budget

5. (LO9.3) A company's master budget projected the following information.

Sales (25,000 units)	$250,000
Manufacturing costs (1/3 fixed)	120,000
Other operating costs (all fixed)	100,000

If the company actually sold 27,500 units, the operating income when using a flexible budget will be:
   a. $33,000.
   b. $43,000.
   c. $47,000.
   d. $51,000.

6. (LO9.6) Which of the following is an advantage of participative budgeting?
   a. It minimizes the cost of developing budgets.
   b. It yields information known to management but not to employees.
   c. It encourages acceptance of the budget by employees.
   d. It reduces the effect on the budgetary process of employee biases.

7. (LO9.3) **SoundTrak** produces and sells high-quality noise cancelling headphones. The accountants have used forecasting techniques and predict the following monthly sales:

Date	Sales
1/31/2026	25,000
2/28/2026	27,000
3/31/2026	27,000
4/30/2026	28,000
5/31/2026	28,000
6/30/2026	29,000
7/31/2026	29,000
8/31/2026	30,000
9/30/2026	32,000
10/31/2026	34,000
11/30/2026	35,000
12/31/2026	36,000

Assume that the company's goal is to have 5% of the next month's predicted sales on hand as finished goods inventory. What will be the budgeted production for March 2026?
   a. 27,000
   b. 27,050
   c. 28,000
   d. 29,800

8. (LO9.3) Which of the following is the budget that lists all of the raw materials and their quantities required to produce one unit of an item?
   a. Direct materials cost budget
   b. Bill of materials
   c. Production budget
   d. Manufacturing overhead budget

9. (LO9.3) The sales team at Regional Home Décor Company has prepared the following sales forecast using two years of sales data.

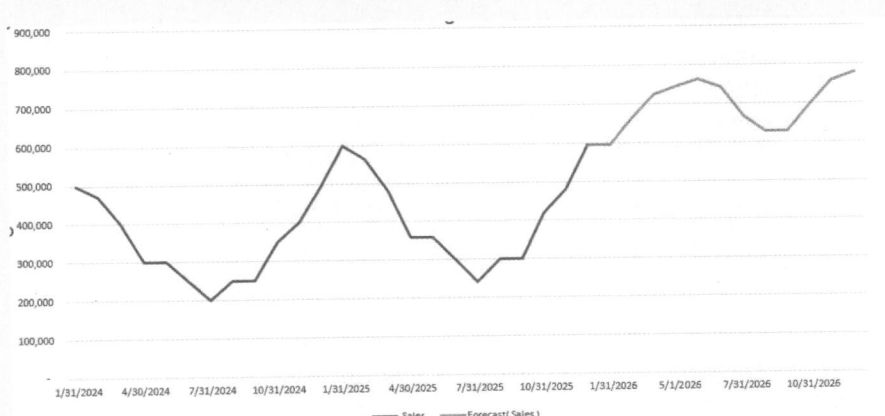

Microsoft Excel

Which of the following best describes the predicted sales based on the forecast?

a. Increasing sales with no clear seasonal trend

b. Increasing sales with a seasonal trend in the winter

c. Increasing sales with a seasonal trend in the summer

d. No predictable trend

10. (LO9.3) Which of the following best describes the data contained on a route sheet?

a. The planned production for the period

b. The cost of materials required for production

c. The employees who will complete each step of the production process

d. The workstation where each step of the production process is performed and the time budgeted for each step

11. (LO9.3) Which of the following is *not* classified as a fixed overhead cost in most organizations?

a. Utilities

b. Rent

c. Indirect materials

d. Supervisor labor

12. (LO9.3) Which of the following is *not* classified as a variable overhead cost in most organizations?

a. Direct labor

b. Indirect labor

c. Indirect materials

d. Materials handling

13. (LO9.3) Which of the following best describes the costs associated with product development (R & D), marketing, and distribution?

a. Operating costs

b. Manufacturing operating costs

c. Nonmanufacturing operating costs

d. Budgeted costs

14. (LO9.3) Which of the following budgets does *not* provide input for the Cost of Goods Sold budget?

a. Beginning inventory budget

b. Direct materials cost budget

c. Direct labor cost budget

d. Nonmanufacturing costs budget

15. (LO9.3) **Heartwood Cabinets** plans to produce 10,000 Walnut–Arch cabinets and budgets the following direct labor costs (per unit):

Heartwood Direct Manufacturing Labor Costs Budget Walnut–Arch			
Workstation	Activity	Minutes Required (for 1 unit)	Hourly Wage Rate
A.1	Trim & sand door	10	$18.00
B.1	Attach handle	5	$15.00
C.1	Attach lever and hinges	12	$21.00

What is the total direct labor cost for the planned production?

a. $84,500

b. $246,000

c. $507,000

d. $5,070,000

16. (LO9.3) TechConnect (a fictitious company) sells copiers, fax machines, and other computer equipment to companies throughout the United States. Management is interested in which factors are associated with the number of sales made each month. TechConnect collects data on several key factors, and its cost accountants have used regression analysis to see which factors are significantly associated with monthly sales. The dependent variable is number of sales per month. The independent variables include the number of sales calls, the season (winter or summer), and whether or not a 50% discount coupon on the first month's cost is available to new customers. Here is a sample of the data:

	A	B	C	D	E
1	Sales Period	Sales Calls	Season	Coupon	Sales Made
2	1/31/2019	30	1	1	35
3	2/28/2019	30	1	1	40
4	3/31/2019	27	1	0	30
5	4/30/2019	33	2	1	38
6	5/31/2019	32	2	0	29
7	6/30/2019	24	2	0	22

Microsoft Excel

The regression output is shown below:

SUMMARY OUTPUT	
Regression Statistics	
Multiple R	0.69
R Square	0.48
Adjusted R Square	0.45
Standard Error	4.37
Observations	60

ANOVA					
	df	SS	MS	F	Significance F
Regression	3.00	988.29	329.43	17.28	0.001
Residual	56.00	1067.68	19.07		
Total	59.00	2055.97			

	Coefficients	Standard Error	t Stat	P-value	Lower 95%	Upper 95%	Lower 95.0%	Upper 95.0%
Intercept	10.39	4.63	2.25	0.03	1.12	19.66	1.12	19.66
Sales Calls	0.65	0.15	4.19	0.02	0.34	0.96	0.34	0.96
Season	−1.50	1.14	−1.31	0.19	−3.79	0.79	−3.79	0.79
Coupon	4.04	1.26	3.20	0.04	1.51	6.57	1.51	6.57

Which of the independent variables is *not* significantly related to the number of sales made?

a. Sales calls

b. Season

c. Coupon

d. All independent variables are significantly related to the number of sales made.

17. (LO9.3) Refer to the regression output prepared by the cost accountants for TechConnect (included in Multiple-Choice Question 16). How can you tell that this regression model provides a good fit for describing the data and that the null hypothesis is rejected?

    a. Multiple R statistic is greater than 0.50.

    b. Standard error is greater than 1.

    c. F statistic has a significance less than 0.05.

    d. P-value for Intercept is less than 0.05.

18. (LO9.3) Refer to the regression output prepared by the cost accountants for TechConnect (included in Multiple-Choice Question 16). How many years of data are used in the regression analysis?

    a. 1

    b. 3

    c. 5

    d. Not enough information is provided to answer this question.

19. (LO9.3) Assume **Toybox 3D Printers** has developed a simple regression model to forecast quarterly sales. The model explains the relationship between the company's sales and the amount it spends on marketing activities. This is the regression equation for the model:

$$s = \$3(m) + \$950,000$$

$$\text{where: } s = \text{sales per quarter}$$

$$m = \text{dollars spent on marketing activities per quarter}$$

If the company has forecasted sales of $989,000 for the next quarter, what amount is it planning to spend on marketing activities in the next quarter?

    a. $13,000

    b. $39,000

    c. $63,000

    d. $113,000

20. (LO9.5) Which one of the following statements is *not* true regarding flexible budgets?

    a. Variable costs must be calculated on a per-unit basis.

    b. Fixed costs vary with predicted sales.

    c. They allow objective comparisons between budget and actual.

    d. Per-unit revenues are multiplied by the expected sales.

21. (LO9.2) Which one of the following budgets covers all of the resources needed to execute the organization's plans?

    a. Master budget

    b. Operating budget

    c. Financial budget

    d. Planned budget

22. (LO9.4) **Heartwood Cabinets** has prepared the following sales budget:

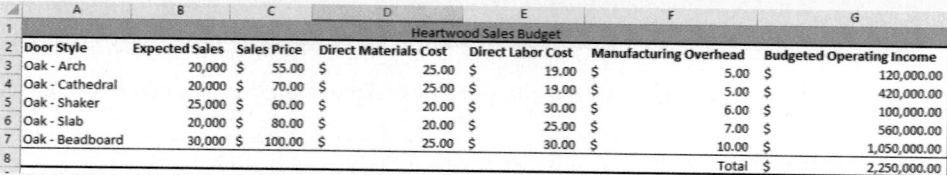

	A	B	C	D	E	F	G
1				Heartwood Sales Budget			
2	Door Style	Expected Sales	Sales Price	Direct Materials Cost	Direct Labor Cost	Manufacturing Overhead	Budgeted Operating Income
3	Oak - Arch	20,000 $	55.00 $	25.00 $	19.00 $	5.00 $	120,000.00
4	Oak - Cathedral	20,000 $	70.00 $	25.00 $	19.00 $	5.00 $	420,000.00
5	Oak - Shaker	25,000 $	60.00 $	20.00 $	30.00 $	6.00 $	100,000.00
6	Oak - Slab	20,000 $	80.00 $	20.00 $	25.00 $	7.00 $	560,000.00
7	Oak - Beadboard	30,000 $	100.00 $	25.00 $	30.00 $	10.00 $	1,050,000.00
8						Total $	2,250,000.00

Microsoft Excel

The cost accountants have run a sensitivity analysis using the **What-If Analysis** function in Excel, which generated the following scenario summary table:

Scenario Summary		
	Current Values	**Scenario 1**
Changing Cells:		
$B$3	20,000	22,000
$B$4	20,000	22,000
$B$5	25,000	27,500
$B$6	20,000	22,000
$B$7	30,000	33,000
Result Cells:		
$G$8	$2,250,000.00	$2,475,000.00

Notes: Current Values column represents values of changing cells at time Scenario Summary Report was created. Changing cells for each scenario are highlighted in gray.

Which of the following most likely describes the change the cost accountants were trying to predict?

a. One of Heartwood's key oak suppliers intends to offer its loyal customers a discount on oak that will reduce direct materials cost by 2%.

b. Heartwood has recently announced a pay increase for all hourly employees.

c. Heartwood is dramatically reducing the cost of its Oak–Beadboard style door.

d. Heartwood intends to increase production of all styles of oak door.

23. (LO9.7) Which of the following components are important considerations for companies that are preparing a budget of their carbon emissions?

    i. ESG-related goals

    ii. Identification of carbon-producing processes/equipment

    iii. Calculation of amount of carbon produced by carbon-emitting processes

    iv. Estimate of financial savings due to emissions-reduction initiatives

    v. Quantification of carbon credits available

      a. ii, v

      b. ii, iii, v

      c. ii, iii, iv, v

      d. i, ii, iii, iv, v

Discussion Questions

1. (LO9.3) Describe the factors that might influence an organization's sales forecasts.

2. (LO9.3) The data available to organizations for budgeting are increasingly precise and diverse. Imagine you are forecasting product demand for a new athletic shoe endorsed by an online fitness influencer. Describe the various types of data you could use to forecast demand.

3. (LO9.5) Describe the flexible budgeting process, including the people involved in the budgeting process and the data they need to prepare accurate budgets.

4. (LO9.5) What is the difference between a static budget and a flexible budget? What different information do they convey?

5. (LO9.4) How is sensitivity analysis used to improve budgeting?

6. (LO9.3) Why do organizations prepare a pro forma operating budget?

7. (LO9.6) Define participative budgeting. What are its benefits and drawbacks?

8. (LO9.6) Describe the unintended consequences that may arise if organizations over-rely on comparing budget to actual performance when evaluating employees.

9. (LO9.7) How do organizations use budgeting for environmental, social, and governance? How does this practice influence the behavior of the organization, its shareholders, and its customers?

10. (LO9.2) Refer back to the regression analysis for TechConnect, provided in Multiple-Choice Question 16. Which other factors, besides those analyzed, could the company include in its regression analysis to predict the number of sales made each month?

11. (LO9.4) **Toybox 3D Printers** manufactures and sells 3D printers that are the perfect size and complexity for beginners and children. Users can 3D-print a wide variety of toys and collectibles using the predeveloped instructions that come loaded in the Toybox app. The marketing and sales departments at Toybox have been working hard to establish contracts with school districts, which could purchase 3D printers for their STEM (science, technology, engineering, and math) labs and media centers.

    Without establishing new contracts with school districts, Toybox estimates it will sell 750,000 units.

    - Materials cost per unit is $75.
    - Labor cost per unit is $24.00.
    - Overhead cost per unit is $8.80.
    - Fixed nonmanufacturing costs are $600,000.

    The cost accountants have used the Excel **Scenario Manager** tool to estimate some potential outcomes if they are able to establish contracts with large school districts in the future. Here is the output from the analysis:

Scenario Summary			
	Current Values	**School District—25%**	**School District—50%**
Changing Cells:			
$B$2	750,000	937,500	1,125,000
Result Cells:			
$B$9	$181,050,000.00	$226,462,500.00	$271,875,000.00

Notes: Current Values column represents values of changing cells at time Scenario Summary Report was created. Changing cells for each scenario are highlighted in gray.

Describe the results of this analysis. Which variables would the accountants have changed for each scenario? Which variables would have remained the same?

12. (LO9.1) Use the three-step process described in Learning Objective 9.1 to develop an annual budget for yourself or your family. Be sure to include:

    a. Your goals and objectives.

    b. The activities you will carry out during each month.

    c. Estimated income and cash flows.

    d. A summary of the factors that will affect your ability to achieve your goals.

13. (LO9.6) Describe budgetary slack, including how it can incentivize dysfunctional behavior.

14. (LO9.6) Many organizations budget for equity and inclusion initiatives within their ESG programs. Search online for information about preparing a budget for racial equity and describe the process, including the challenges and opportunities presented by this process.

15. (LO9.3) Prepare a flowchart of the budgeting process as described in Learning Objective 9.3 of this chapter.

Brief Exercises ![Mc Graw Hill] connect

1. (LO9.3) **Longchamp** manufactures and sells purses, tote bags, wallets, and other accessories. The sales department estimates $525,000 in sales of its Le Pliage original shoulder bag in 2025. The bag retails for $155.00. Beginning inventory at the start of 2025 is 70,000 and the target ending inventory at year-end is 25,000. Compute the number of bags the company intends to produce during the year.

2. (LO9.3) Using the same information from Brief Exercise 1, assume that each bag requires 2 square yards of canvas, 1 metallic (gold) zipper kit, and 0.5 square yard of leather. Assume that at the beginning of the year, **Longchamp** has 150,000 square yards of canvas on hand and 10,000 square yards of leather. Canvas costs $2.50 per square yard and the leather costs $20 per square yard. The company has no zipper kits on hand. Each kit costs $10. Compute the amount Longchamp will spend on canvas purchases during the year to meet its sales demand, including planned ending inventory.

3. (LO9.3) Using the same information from Brief Exercise 2, compute the total cost of materials to be purchased to meet **Longchamp**'s sales demand, including planned ending inventory.

4. (LO9.3) **Rubber Dockie** produces large floating mats for recreational lake use. The company makes two sizes of mat (18 ft. and 9 × 6 ft.) using a closed-cell foam material. The mats are sold by the company online and through brick-and-mortar retailers. In 2024, Rubber Dockie sold 32,340 of its 18 ft. mats and 52,074 of its 9 × 6 mats. The prices were $499.99 and $349.99, respectively. The company expects a 9% increase in sales of both mats in 2025 and another 3% increase in 2026.

   a. Assume no change in sales price for 2025. Prepare a 2025 sales budget for Rubber Dockie based on sales expectations.

   b. Assume a 2% price decrease in 2026. Prepare a 2026 sales budget.

5. (LO9.5) Using the information from Brief Exercise 4, now assume that **Rubber Dockie** intends to have a finished goods inventory of 5% at the end of a production year. Beginning inventory at the start of 2025 was 1,500 units of the 18 ft. mat and 1,750 units of the 9 × 6 mat. Calculate the number of units to be produced in 2025 to meet expected demand.

6. (LO9.3) **Jittery Joe's Coffee**, a coffee company based in Georgia, roasts a wide variety of coffee blends. Assume it uses machine hours as the application base for calculating manufacturing overhead. The following chart provides some production details about five of Jittery Joe's most popular blends. Using the data provided about the quantity of each blend roasted, the number of minutes the machine is used to roast 100 pounds of each blend, and the predetermined overhead rate (applied based on machine hour), calculate the manufacturing overhead for each blend and for all blends in total.

Jittery Joe's Coffee				
Coffee Blends	Pounds of Coffee	Machine Minutes for 100 lbs	Predetermined Overhead Rate (per machine hour)	Manufacturing Overhead (per machine hour)
Morning Ride	38,000	60	$6.50	
Attack the Day	75,000	75	$6.50	
Travelin' Joe	65.000	70	$6.50	
Omoiyari	40,000	60	$6.50	
Summer Brew	50,000	65	$6.50	
Total Manufacturing Overhead				

7. (LO9.3) The Maple division at **Heartwood Cabinets** has prepared the following ending inventories budget:

Heartwood Ending Inventories Budget Maple Cabinets				
	Ending Inventory	Direct Materials Cost per Unit	Direct Labor Cost per Unit	Manufacturing Overhead Cost per Unit
Maple–Arch	800	$25.00	$ 7.50	$3.00
Maple–Cathedral	700	$23.00	$ 7.50	$3.25
Maple–Shaker	1,000	$20.00	$ 7.95	$ 3.10
Maple–Slab	1,000	$24.50	$8.00	$2.90
Maple–Beadboard	1,000	$26.00	$ 7.00	$ 3.15

What is the total cost of ending finished goods inventory for this period?

8. (LO9.3) Kenworth Manufacturing produces light fixtures. The cost accountants have used prior-year data to prepare the following overhead budget. Based on these data, what is the total amount budgeted for manufacturing overhead?

Kenworth Manufacturing Overhead Calculation (based on prior year data)			
Units to be produced (from Production Budget)		100,000	units
Variable overhead			
Indirect materials and supplies	$0.50		
Materials handling	$ 0.75		
Indirect labor	$0.25	_____	_____
Fixed manufacturing overhead			
Factory rent		40,000	
Machine depreciation		20,000	
Supervisor labor		25,000	
Utilities		10,000	
Maintenance and repairs		5,000	
Property taxes		8,000	
Other		2,000	_____
Total manufacturing overhead			========

9. (LO9.4) **Stanley** manufactures and sells drinkware, food storage, coolers and jugs, and camping gear. In recent years, sales of its drinkware have increased significantly, primarily due to viral marketing via online influencers. Assume the following table represents the basic assumptions used to calculate Stanley's overall operating income (ignoring fixed nonmanufacturing costs).

	A	B	C	D	E	F	G
5		Stanley Operating Budget					
6	Drinkware	Expected Sales (in units)	Sales Price	Direct Materials Cost	Direct Labor Cost	Manufacturing Overhead	Budgeted Operating Income
7	Quencher H2.0 Flow State Tumbler	500,000 $	40.00 $	6.00 $	2.25 $	2.50 $	14,625,000.00
8	IceFlow Flip Straw Tumbler	200,000 $	31.00 $	5.00 $	2.25 $	2.50 $	4,250,000.00
9	Wild Imagination Quencher Travel Tumbler	100,000 $	20.00 $	4.50 $	2.25 $	2.50 $	1,075,000.00
10	Wild Imagination IceFlow Flip Straw Tumbler	100,000 $	26.00 $	5.00 $	2.25 $	2.50 $	1,625,000.00
11	Wild Imagination IceFlow Flip Straw Waterbottle	100,000 $	26.00 $	5.00 $	2.25 $	2.50 $	1,625,000.00
12	GO IceFlow Flip Straw Jug	250,000 $	40.00 $	6.00 $	2.25 $	2.50 $	7,312,500.00
13	DayBreak Café Latte Cup & Saucer	75,000 $	50.00 $	3.50 $	2.50 $	2.50 $	3,112,500.00
14	DayBreak Demitasse Cup	75,000 $	20.00 $	3.00 $	2.50 $	2.50 $	900,000.00
15	DayBreak Cappuccino Cup	75,000 $	26.00 $	3.00 $	2.50 $	2.50 $	1,350,000.00
16	AeroLight Transit Bottle	100,000 $	25.00 $	3.00 $	2.25 $	2.50 $	1,725,000.00
17						Total:	$ 23,200,000.00

Microsoft Excel

Stanley is considering the effects of increasing the price of its drinkware by 20%. Management recognizes that this price increase will likely decrease the number of sales, and it estimates an approximate sales decrease of 5%. The cost accountants have used Excel's Scenario Manager to estimate operating income if this price increase goes into effect. The results are shown here:

Scenario Summary				
	Current Values		**Scenario 1—20% Price Increase with 5% sales decrease**	
Changing Cells:				
$B$3		500,000		475,000
$C$3	$	40.00	$	48.00
$B$4		200,000		190,000
$C$4	$	31.00	$	37.20
$B$5		100,000		95,000
$C$5	$	20.00	$	24.00
$B$6		100,000		95,000
$C$6	$	26.00	$	31.20
$B$7		100,000		95,000
$C$7	$	26.00	$	31.20
$B$8		250,000		237,500
$C$8	$	40.00	$	48.00
$B$9		75,000		771,250
$C$9	$	50.00	$	60.00
$B$10		75,000		71,250
$C$10	$	20.00	$	24.00
$B$11		75,000		71,250
$C$11	$	26.00	$	31.20
$B$12		100,000		95,000
$C$12	$	25.00	$	30.00
ResultCells:				
$G$13	$ 23,200,000.00		$28,386,000.00	

Notes: Current Values column represents values of changing cells at time Scenario Summary Report was created. Changing cells for each scenario are highlighted in gray.

What is the estimated percentage change in operating income if prices are increased by 20%, which will decrease sales by 5% for each product?

10. (LO9.4) Consider the same assumptions at **Stanley** as described in Brief Exercise 9. Assume the sales department has proposed discontinuing the DayBreak line of drinkware and instead increasing production (and sales) of the Quencher H2.0 Flow State Tumbler, which is their best seller.

The cost accountants have used Excel's **Scenario Manager** to estimate operating income assuming that all sales of DayBreak items are reduced to zero and sales of the Quencher H2.0 tumblers are increased by 225,000 units (based on the excess capacity left by the discontinuation of the DayBreak line). The results are shown here:

Scenario Summary				
		Current Values		Scenario 2—Discontinue DayBreak Line
Changing Cells:				
$B$3		500,000		725,000
$C$3	$	40.00	$	40.00
$B$4		200,000		200,000
$C$4	$	31.00	$	31.00
$B$5		100,000		100,000
$C$5	$	20.00	$	20.00
$B$6		100,000		100,000
$C$6	$	26.00	$	26.00
$B$7		100,000		100,000
$C$7	$	26.00	$	26.00
$B$8		250,000		250,000
$C$8	$	40.00	$	40.00
$B$9		75,000		—
$C$9	$	50.00	$	50.00
$B$10		75,000		—
$C$10	$	20.00	$	20.00
$B$11		75,000		—
$C$11	$	26.00	$	26.00
$B$12		100,000		100,000
$C$12	$	25.00	$	25.00
Result Cells:				
$G$13		$23,200,000.00		$29,781,250.00

Notes: Current Values column represents values of changing cells at time Scenario Summary Report was created. Changing cells for each scenario are highlighted in gray.

What is the estimated percentage change in operating income if this strategy is used? Would you recommend discontinuing the DayBreak line in favor of producing and selling more Quencher H2.0 tumblers? Why or why not?

11. (LO9.4) Assume **Heartwood Cabinets** uses ABC costing (activity-based costing) to apply overhead to its products. The cost accountants have identified two different cost pools. The first includes all the costs associated with manufacturing cabinets. The second includes all the costs associated with machine setup, as follows:

Heartwood Manufacturing Overhead (based on prior year data)			
Manufacturing Operations Overhead Costs			
Units to be produced (from Production budget)		105,000	
Labor hours required for planned production		145,500	
Variable Overhead			
Indirect materials and supplies	$ 3.00	436,500	
Materials handling	$ 1.00	145,500	
Indirect labor	$ 1.25	181,875	
			$ 763,875.00

(continued)

Heartwood Manufacturing Overhead (based on prior year data)			
Fixed manufacturing overhead			
Factory rent		$ 24,000.00	
Machine depreciation		$ 13,000.00	
Supervisor labor		$ 30,000.00	
Utilities		$ 19,976.00	
Maintenance and repairs		$ 9,999.00	
Property taxes		$ 12,150.00	
			$ 109,125.00
			$ 873,000.00
Machine Setup Overhead Costs			
Labor hours required for machine setup		15,000	
Variable Overhead			
Supplies	$ 10.00	$ 150,000.00	
Indirect labor	$ 25.00	$ 375,000.00	
Utilities	$ 15.00	$ 225,000.00	
			$ 750,000.00
Fixed Overhead			
Depreciation		$ 25,000.00	
Supervision		$ 35,000.00	
			$ 60,000.00
			$ 810,000.00
Total Manufacturing Operations Overhead Cost			$ 873,000.00
Total Machine Setup Overhead Costs			$ 810,000.00
Total Manufacturing Overhead Costs			$1,683,000.00

Use the information above to complete the following table allocating the overhead costs to each type of pine cabinet.

Heartwood Manufacturing Overhead						
	Units to Produce	Direct Manufacturing Labor Hours Required for 1 unit	Predetermined Manufacturing Operations Overhead Rate	Direct Machine Setup Labor Hours Required for 1 unit	Predetermined Machine Setup Overhead Rate	Manufacturing Overhead
Pine–Arch	14,500					
Pine–Cathedral	15,000					
Pine–Shaker	20,000					
Pine–Slab	25,000					
Pine–Beadboard	30,500					
					Total:	$

12. (LO9.2, 9.3) Match the budget with its definition:

BUDGET:	DEFINITION:
a. Master budget	i. Budget consisting of all of the expenses that will be required to achieve planned production.
b. Operating budget	ii. Identifies expected sales in units and dollars.
c. Financial budget	iii. Covers all the resources needed to execute the organization's operations, including sales, production, purchasing, and marketing.
d. Sales budget	
e. Production budget	
f. Direct manufacturing labor-cost budget	iv. Calculates the total units that must be produced during the budget period to allow the company to meet the expected sales requirements.
g. Direct materials cost budget	
h. Direct manufacturing overhead-cost budget	
i. Cost of goods sold budget	v. Uses the planned production amounts to determine the total number of direct labor hours required to achieve production goals.
j. Operating costs budget	
	vi. Contains all of the direct or indirect costs associated with producing the units that have been sold during the budget period.
	vii. Contains each direct material item and its cost.
	viii. Contains a summary of all the manufacturing costs other than the direct materials and direct labor costs.
	ix. Describes the source and use of funds for planned capital expenditures.
	x. Establishes management's financial and operational plans for the budget period.

13. (LO9.1) Your university's entrepreneurship program is conducting a *Shark Tank*–style competition, and the winner will be awarded $25,000 in seed funding to start a business. You and your best friend, Desi, have a great idea for a ride-share program designed for parents who need to transport their children to after-school activities. Desi has not taken any accounting classes, so while she is excited to put together the pitch, she needs your help to develop the budget. In fact, she doesn't even understand what a budget is. Prepare an email to Desi that carefully explains the purpose of a budget and describes the different components that will be necessary to build a proper budget before your meeting with the sharks.

14. (LO9.6) You recently began working as a cost accountant for an insurance company, and the CFO has mentioned that the company is experiencing a high level of turnover in its sales division and is not sure why. The CFO is hoping that you might be able to use your data-analysis skills and expertise in cost accounting to help solve this problem. You start by examining the established sales targets, and you note that the organization uses an authoritative budgeting process in which all of the salespeople are assigned the same sales targets. Based on your experience in the industry, the targets seem high to you, and you review the performance reports for the last 18 months and note that 72% of the workforce is missing the sales target by at least 8%. What advice do you have for the CFO? Defend your answer.

15. (LO9.6) ACD Slicer Company (a fictitious company) produces an all-in-one kitchen tool for prepping produce. Within one handheld gadget, users have a paring knife, vegetable grater, apple corer, potato peeler, and more. The production managers at ACD Slicer are expected to meet or exceed expectations for keeping manufacturing costs low, which are set forth in the budget. A new cost accountant has just joined ACD Slicer and has remarked that this budgetary expectation might have dysfunctional effects. Explain the dysfunctional effects to which the cost accountant may be referring.

Problems

Mc Graw Hill **connect**

1. (LO9.7) Review the 2022 ESG report for **The Coca-Cola Company**, which can be found online at **www.coca-colacompany.com/reports/business-and-sustainability-report**.

   Required

   Identify Coca-Cola's top ESG priorities and the steps the company is taking to meet its goals.

2. (LO9.3) **Toybox 3D Printers** manufactures and sells 3D printers that are small and easy to use—perfect for children. Currently it produces only one model of printer.

   Required

   Use the following spreadsheets and facts to prepare the Cost of Goods Sold budget for Toybox for the year 2025.

   - Expected sales: 750,000
   - Sales price: $350 per printer
   - Target beginning finished goods inventory is always 10% of expected sales.
   - The predetermined overhead rate (which includes variable and fixed costs) is $8.00.

Bill of Materials				
Part Number	**Part Name**	**Cost per Unit**	**Quantity**	**Total**
T–2164	Wifi Component	$ 5.00	1	$ 5.00
T–2331	Digital Component	$20.00	1	$20.00
T–1863	Touchscreen	$ 3.00	1	$ 3.00
M–5273	Screw Kits	$ 1.50	2	$ 3.00
M–1956	Metal Dowel Kits	$ 2.00	1	$ 2.00
P–2776	Nozzel	$ 4.00	1	$ 4.00
P–2875	Printer Food Spool	$ 1.00	1	$ 1.00
P–2193	Platform	$ 8.00	1	$ 8.00
M–7792	Motor	$20.00	1	$20.00
P–5883	Metal Frame	$ 6.00	1	$ 6.00
P–7727	Cord	$ 3.00	1	$ 3.00
Total				$75.00

Toybox 3D printers Route Sheet						
Workstation	**Activity**	**Minutes Required (for 1 unit)**	**Hourly Wage Rate**	**Labor Cost per Unit**	**Units to Produce**	**Total Labor Cost**
1	Install and test digital component	30	$24	$ 12.00	750,000	$ 9,000,000.00
2	Install and test motor	10	$18	$ 3.00	750,000	$ 2,250,000.00
3	Build and install lift platform	5	$15	$ 1.25	750,000	$ 937,500.00
4	Complete metal frame and attach cord	6	$15	$ 1.50	750,000	$ 1,125,000.00
5	Test and calibrate printer	15	$25	$ 6.25	750,000	$ 4,687,500.00
Total		66		$24.00	750,000	$18,000,000.00

Toybox 3D Printers Overhead Calculation (based on prior-year data)			
Units to be produced (from Production Budget)		750,000	units
Variable overhead			
Indirect materials and supplies	$0.50	375,000	
Materials handling	$0.35	262,500	
Indirect labor	$ 0.15	112,500	
			750,000
Fixed manufacturing overhead			
Factory rent		30,000	
Machine depreciation		20,000	
Supervisor labor		40,000	
Utilities		35,000	
Maintenance and repairs		10,000	
Property taxes		5,000	
Other		10,000	
			150,000
Total manufacturing overhead			900,000

Toybox 3D Printers Nonmanufacturing Costs				
	Units Sold	Variable	Fixed	Total Cost
Product Development	750,000		$ 100,000.00	$ 100,000.00
Marketing	750,000		$300,000.00	$300,000.00
Distribution	750,000	$200,000.00		$200,000.00
Total Operating Costs				$600,000.00

3. (LO9.3) **Dyson Limited** manufactures and sells home appliances such as air purifiers, fans, heaters, hand dryers, vacuum cleaners, and hair stylers.

Required

Use the following spreadsheets and facts to develop the pro forma income statement for the Hair Care Division of Dyson Limited for the year 2025.

Dyson Limited Hair Care Division Sales Budget					
Product	Expected Sales	Selling Price	Beginning Inventory	Direct Materials Cost per Unit	Direct Labor Cost per Unit
Dyson Supersonic hair dryers	1,500,000	$450.00	75,000	$40.00	$4.10
Dyson Corrale hair straighteners/stylers	2,000,000	$500.00	100,000	$45.00	$5.45
Dyson Airwrap hair stylers	5,000,000	$600.00	250,000	$50.00	$5.00

Dyson Limited Hair Care Division Nonmanufacturing Costs				
	Units Sold	Variable	Fixed	Total Cost
Product Development	8,500,000		$100,000.00	$100,000.00
Marketing	8,500,000		$200,000.00	$200,000.00
Distribution	8,500,000	$500,000.00		$500,000.00
Total Operating Costs				$800,000.00

- Target ending finished goods inventory is always 5% of expected sales.
- The predetermined overhead rate (which includes variable and fixed costs) is $6.00 per unit.

4. (LO9.5) **Dyson Limited** (described in Problem 3) would like to prepare a flexible budget for its Dyson Supersonic Hairdryers. The static budget is presented below.

Required

Complete the four columns to the right of the static budget to provide a flexible budget if sales are (1) 25% less than expected, (2) 10% less than expected, (3) 10% greater than expected, and (4) 25% greater than expected.

Dyson Limited			Dyson Limited			
			(1)	(2)	(3)	(4)
	Per Unit	Static Budget	−25%	−10%	+10%	25%
Units Sold		750,000				
Revenue	$350.00	$262,500,000				
Variable Costs						
Direct Material	$ 75.00	$ 56,250,000				
Direct Labor	$ 24.00	$ 18,000,000				
Variable Manufacturing Overhead	$ 1.40	$ 1,050,000				
Variable SG&A Costs	$ 0.10	$ 75,000				
Total Variable Costs	$ 16.75	$ 12,562,500				
Contribution Margin		$ 249,937,500				
Fixed Costs						
Fixed Manufacturing Overhead	$ 0.70	$ 525,000				
Fixed SG&A Costs	$ 0.05	$ 37,500				
Total Fixed Costs		$ 562,500				
Operating Income		$ 249,375,000				

5. (LO9.5) **Tifosi Optics** produces high-performance eyewear for cycling, running, hiking, and golfing, as well as fashion frames. You have been given the static budget (below) and asked to prepare a flexible budget for the company.

Required

Complete the 4 columns to the right of the static budget to provide a flexible budget under the following four scenarios:

a. The number of units sold decreases by 1,000.

b. The number of units sold increases by 10%.

c. The number of units sold increases by 25,000.

d. The number of units sold doubles.

Tifosi Optics			Tifosi Optics			
	Per Unit	Static Budget	(1)	(2)	(3)	(4)
Units Sold		100,000				
Revenue	$80.00	$8,000,000				
Variable Costs						
Direct Material	$ 5.00	$ 500,000				
Direct Labor	$ 3.00	$ 300,000				
Variable Manufacturing Overhead	$ 0.15	$ 15,000				
Variable SG&A Costs	$ 0.10	$ 10,000				
Total Variable Costs	$ 8.25	$ 825,000				
Contribution Margin		$ 7,175,000				
Fixed Costs						
Fixed Manufacturing Overhead	$ 0.70	$ 70,000				
Fixed SG&A Costs	$ 0.05	$ 5,000				
Total Fixed Costs		$ 75,000				
Operating Income		$ 7,100,000				

6. **(LO9.3) Tifosi Optics** produces high-performance eyewear for cycling, running, hiking, and golfing, as well as fashion frames. Tifosi has four categories of frames: athletic, fashion, safety, and youth.

Required

Use the following data to prepare the pro forma operating income statement (complete the template provided).

Expected sales and selling price are as follows:

Tifosi Optics Sales Forecast			
Style	Expected Sales	Selling Price	Expected Revenue
Athletic Frames	95,000	$80.00	
Fashion Frames	50,000	$45.00	
Safety Frames	20,000	$ 15.00	
Youth Frames	22,000	$30.00	
Total	187,000		

Beginning and ending finished goods inventory are as follows:

Tifosi Optics Production Budget	Athletic Frames	Fashion Frames	Safety Frames	Youth Frames
Budgeted sales	95,000	50,000	20,000	22,000
(Plus) Target ending finished goods inventory	4,750	2,500	1,000	1,100
Total required units	99,750	52,500	21,000	23,100
(Less) Beginning finished goods inventory	5,000	2,000	2,000	2,000
Units to be produced	94,750	50,500	19,000	21,100

Direct materials cost per unit are as follows:

Tifosi Optics Direct Materials Budget				
	Athletic Frames	Fashion Frames	Safety Frames	Youth Frames
Cost per unit	$8.00	$7.00	$2.50	$6.00

Direct labor cost per unit for each style is calculated using the following data:

Tifosi Optics Direct Manufacturing Labor Costs Budget		
Style	Direct Labor Minutes Required for 1 Unit	Hourly Wage Rate
Athletic Frames	9	$13
Fashion Frames	9	$13
Safety Frames	4	$13
Youth Frames	8	$13

The predetermined overhead rate is $6.00 and is applied based on the number of direct labor hours required.

Assume the company has the following operating costs:

Tifosi Optics	
Operating costs	
Production development	$ 75,000
Marketing costs	$150,000
Distribution costs	$ 54,000

Pro Forma Operating Income Statement template:

Tifosi Optics Pro Forma Operating Income Statement	
Revenue	$ —
Cost of Goods Sold	$ —
Gross Margin	$ —
Operating Costs	
Production Development	$ —
Marketing Costs	$ —
Distribution Costs	$ —
Operating Income	$ —

7. (LO9.3) Pelican Sport produces and sells kayaks for recreational use. The average sales price for a kayak is $250. The company expects to sell 50,000 units this quarter. Ending inventory is planned to be 3% of expected sales, but at the start of this quarter, the company had 1,000 units in stock. Direct materials are $15 per unit. The direct labor rate is $19 per hour and each kayak requires 30 minutes of labor. Overhead is applied using direct labor hours at $6 per hour.

Required

Using the information provided above, prepare the COGS budget (complete the template provided).

COGS template:

Pelican Sport Cost of Goods Sold Budget		
Beginning Finished Goods Inventory		$ —
Direct Materials Used	$ —	
Direct Manufacturing Labor	$ —	
Direct Manufacturing Overhead	$ —	
Cost of Goods Manufactured		$ —
Costs of Goods Available for Sale		$ —
(Less) Ending Finished Goods Inventory		$ —
Cost of Goods Sold		$ —

8. (LO9.6) Hughes Allen owns three car dealerships in Memphis, Tennessee: a Ford dealership, a Honda dealership, and a Kia dealership. You have been given quarterly sales data for the sales agents who work at each dealership as well as their sales targets, as follows:

Dealership	Salesperson	Quarterly Sales Target	Quarterly Sales
Ford	Daniel Martin	60	30
Honda	Erik Andersson	60	33
Ford	Isaiah Thompson	60	33
Kia	Wang Xia	60	45
Ford	Lucy Karlsson	60	48
Honda	Yang Mei	60	48
Kia	Emma Pettersson	60	48
Ford	Marcus Wright	60	48
Honda	Matthew Wilson	60	51
Kia	Nia Turner	60	54
Honda	Elizabeth Clark	60	57
Ford	John Berg	60	63
Honda	Stephanie Lindqvist	60	63
Ford	Emily Nelson	60	63
Honda	Sierra Robinson	60	63
Kia	Liu Chen	60	66

Required

Use these data to prepare the following visualizations and answer the following questions.

a. Use Excel, Tableau, or Power BI to prepare a combo chart that shows each salesperson on the X-axis. Quarterly sales for each salesperson should be represented as columns. Columns should be sorted so that the lowest sales are shown on the left and the highest sales are shown on the right. Each column should be colored to represent the dealership with which the salesperson is associated (that is, there should be three different colors for the columns). Show the sales target using a solid line. Remove unnecessary gridlines. Add the title "Budget to Actual Sales" to your visualization.

b. Do you think Hughes Allen uses participative, negotiated, or authoritative budgeting? Why?

c. Do you think the sales targets are reasonable, controllable, and appropriate? Why or why not?

d. Describe the behavioral effects that you anticipate will be caused by sales targets and sales performance at these dealerships. *Note:* You may describe different effects for different people based on your observations.

e. Do you think Hughes Allen should continue with the current sales targets? If not, what would you recommend? Defend your answer.

9. (LO9.1, 9.2) Budgets are important tools for nonmanufacturing organizations as well as manufacturing organizations. Identify three examples of nonmanufacturing uses for budgets and describe their purpose in that context.

Required

For each, describe the budgeting process and explain how it will be different from that performed in the manufacturing context. Include discussion of which data will be used.

10. (LO9.5) Patty Peterson is the proprietor of Puffy Princess Pastries, a fictional donut shop in Asheville, North Carolina. Customers at the shop select a shape (hearts, stars,

crowns, diamonds) for their donut, which is then fried by the pastry chefs on the spot. Customers then select the color of their icing and choose from an array of fancy toppings, including edible glitter, sprinkles, cookie crumbles, and fresh strawberries. Patty is preparing her budget and has performed several sensitivity analyses to consider different scenarios.

Required

Review the data and output from the What-If analysis from Excel and answer the following questions.

						Puffy Princess Pastries
Pastry	Expected Sales	Sales Price	Direct Materials Cost	Direct Labor Cost	Manufacturing Overhead	Budgeted Operating Income
Donut	50,000	$5.25	$1.00	$0.50	$1.00	$137,500.00
					Total	$137,500.00

Scenario Summary

	Current Values	Scenario 1	Scenario 2	Scenario 3	Scenario 4
Changing Cells:					
$B$5	50000	60000	50000	50000	50000
$C$5	$ 5.25	$ 5.25	$ 6.00	$ 5.25	$ 5.25
$D$5	$ 1.00	$ 1.00	$ 1.00	$ 0.75	$ 1.00
$E$5	$ 0.50	$ 0.50	$ 0.50	$ 0.50	$ 0.25
Result Cells:					
$G$6	$137,500.00	$165,000.00	$175,000.00	$150,000.00	$150,000.00

Notes: Current Values column represents values of changing cells at time Scenario Summary Report was created. Changing cells for each scenario are highlighted in gray.

a. Describe the change that was made to the data for each scenario. (*Note:* Only one change was made to the data in each scenario.)

b. Which change has the biggest effect on operating income?

c. The scenarios modeled in the What-If analysis assume only one change has occurred. In Scenario 2, the sales price is increased without any change in the number of sales. Do you think this is an accurate assumption? As a cost accountant, how would you determine whether this assumption is accurate or not?

11. (LO9.3) Stellar Productions is a fictional electronics manufacturer that produces camera equipment, sound systems, and studio lighting equipment.

Required

Use the following information to
a. Produce a COGS budget.
b. Calculate gross margin.

	Stellar Productions Sales Forecast	
Product Type	Expected Sales	Selling Price
Stellar Cameras	10,000	$350
Stellar Sound Systems	7,500	$400
Stellar Lighting Solutions	9,500	$600

Stellar Productions Production Budget (in units)			
	Stellar Cameras	Stellar Sound Systems	Stellar Lighting Solutions
Budgeted sales	10,000	7,500	9,500
(Plus) Target ending finished goods inventory	500	375	475
Total required units	10,500	7,875	9,975
(Less) Beginning finished goods inventory	450	450	525
Units to be produced	10,050	7,425	9,450

Stellar Productions Direct Materials Budget			
	Stellar Cameras	Stellar Sound Systems	Stellar Lighting Solutions
Direct materials cost per unit	$150.00	$125.00	$200.00

Stellar Productions Manufacturing Labor Costs Budget			
Activity	Minutes Required (for 1 unit)	Hourly Wage Rate	Labor Cost per Unit
Stellar Cameras	36	$25	$15.00
Stellar Sound Systems	24	$25	$10.00
Stellar Lighting	12	$25	$ 5.00

Stellar Productions Manufacturing Overhead Costs Budget		
Activity	Minutes Required (for 1 unit)	Predetermined Overhead Rate (per labor hour)
Stellar Cameras	36	$20
Stellar Sound Systems	24	$20
Stellar Lighting	12	$20

12. (LO9.3) Shampure is a fictitious company that produces sustainably sourced and cruelty-free hair care products. The company has been trying several new techniques to try to increase sales, including (1) offering a 10% pay bonus for team members who exceed sales targets, (2) providing limited-time-only coupons for deep discounts to customers during slower months, and (3) increasing its online marketing budget. The cost accountant has performed a regression analysis to determine which, if any, techniques have been successful and should be considered when forecasting future sales.

Required

Review the regression output below and explain to management what the results tell you about which techniques are (or are not) effective in increasing sales.

SUMMARY OUTPUT Regression Statistics	
Multiple R	0.91
R Square	0.83
Adjusted R Square	0.73
Standard Error	402332.06
Observations	12.00

ANOVA

	df	SS	MS	F	Significance F
Regression	4	5.44083E+12	1.36E+12	8.40	0.01
Residual	7	1.1331E+12	1.62E+11		
Total	11	6.57393E+12			

	Coefficients	Standard Error	t Stat	P-value	Lower 95%	Upper 95%	Lower 95.0%	Upper 95.0%
Intercept	445949.50	1197835.08	0.37	0.72	−2386480.38	3278379.39	−2386480.38	3278379.39
Holiday	1908336.74	383199.08	4.98	0.00	1002214.90	2814458.57	1002214.90	2814458.57
Coupons	656619.08	328502.75	2.00	0.09	−120166.49	1433404.66	−120166.49	1433404.66
Marketing Spend	71.30	81.98	0.87	0.41	−122.56	265.16	−122.56	265.16
Sales Incentive	1634590.24	397899.16	4.11	0.00	693708.25	2575472.24	693708.25	2575472.24

13. (LO9.3) Fire and Flavor produces grilling accessories, most notably cedar plank boards for seasoning and grilling fish. Assume the production facility in Lexington, South Carolina, produces three products: cedar planks, a portable grill set, and a grill accessories kit. The expected sales and selling price for each during the next period are as follows:

Fire and Flavor Sales Forecast		
Product Type	**Expected Sales (in units)**	**Selling Price per unit**
Cedar planks	100,000	$ 15.00
Portable grill set	50,000	$150.00
Grill accessories kit	25,000	$ 55.00
Total	**175,000**	

Planned production to meet demand is as follows:

Fire and Flavor Production Budget (in units)			
	Cedar planks	**Portable grill set**	**Grill accessories kit**
Budgeted sales	100,000	50,000	25,000
(Plus) Target ending finished goods inventory	2,000	1,000	500
Total required units	102,000	51,000	25,500
(Less) Beginning finished goods inventory	1,800	1,200	525

Direct materials cost for each item is summarized in the following table:

Fire and Flavor Direct Materials Budget			
	Cedar planks	**Portable grill set**	**Grill accessories kit**
Cost per unit	$ 2.00	$ 15.00	$ 5.00
Expected sales (in units)	100,000	50,000	25,000
Total direct materials required (in dollars)	$200,000	$750,000	$125,000

A labor rate of $18 per hour is applied to each item, as described in the following table:

Fire and Flavor Manufacturing Labor Costs Budget				
Workstation	Activity	Minutes Required (for 1 unit)	Hourly Wage Rate	Labor Cost per Unit
1	Cedar planks	2	$18	$0.60
2	Portable grill set	8	$18	$2.40
3	Grill accessories kit	6	$18	$1.80

Finally, the predetermined overhead rate is $2 per hour, applied to each unit based on the labor minutes required to produce the item (as shown in the manufacturing labor costs budget).

Required

Using the preceding data, prepare the COGS budget.

14. (LO9.5) **Dagostino** produces and sells handmade pasta. The company specializes in traditional semolina pasta, as well as specialty Louisiana-themed shaped pasta. Dagostino has budgeted to sell 750,000 units, but some uncertainty in the market exists such that the cost accountants believe actual sales could be as much as 10% higher than that, or as little as 10% lower.

Required

a. Use the following format to prepare the static budget:

Dagostino		
	Per Unit	Static Budget
Units Sold		750,000
Revenue	$20.00	
Variable Costs		
Direct Material	$ 1.00	
Direct Labor	$ 0.25	
Variable Manufacturing Overhead	$ 0.10	
Variable SG&A Costs	$ 0.05	
Total Variable Costs	$ 1.40	
Contribution Margin		
Fixed Costs		
Fixed Manufacturing Overhead	$ 0.10	
Fixed SG&A Costs	$ 0.05	
Total Fixed Costs		
Operating Income		

b. Prepare a flexible budget estimating sales under four scenarios: (1) 10% below expectations, (2) 5% below expectations, (3) 5% above expectations, and (4) 10% above expectations.

Dagostino			
(1)	**(2)**	**(3)**	**(4)**
−10%	**−5%**	**+5%**	**+10%**

15. (LO9.6) As described previously, in Problem 9.8, Hughes Allen owns three dealerships, and all salespeople are given a sales target of 60 cars per quarter. You have been given quarterly sales data for the sales agents who work at each dealership as well as their sales targets, as follows:

Dealership	Salesperson	Quarterly Sales Target	Quarterly Sales
Ford	Daniel Martin	60	30
Honda	Erik Andersson	60	33
Ford	Isaiah Thompson	60	33
Kia	Wang Xia	60	45
Ford	Lucy Karlsson	60	48
Honda	Yang Mei	60	48
Kia	Emma Pettersson	60	48
Ford	Marcus Wright	60	48
Honda	Matthew Wilson	60	51
Kia	Nia Turner	60	54
Honda	Elizabeth Clark	60	57
Ford	John Berg	60	63
Honda	Stephanie Lindqvist	60	63
Ford	Emily Nelson	60	63
Honda	Sierra Robinson	60	63
Kia	Liu Chen	60	66

Required

a. Use these data to prepare a pivot table that summarizes the quarterly sales by dealership and calculates the percentage of the target achieved by each dealership. Label this new calculated field "Percent of Target" and format as a percentage.

b. Consider how Hughes Allen may perceive the data when the data are aggregated at the dealership level rather than the individual salesperson level. Comment on your observations.

Lab 9.1   Excel

Lab Note: The tools presented in this lab periodically change. Updated instructions, if applicable, can be found in the student and instructor support materials.

Forecasting Future Performance: Sales and Earnings

Data Analytics Type: Predictive Analytics

Keywords

Predictive Analytics, Forecasting, Time Series

Decision-Making Context

There are many reasons to forecast a firm's future performance. For example, a company may want to predict sales to determine needed manufacturing capacity, or it may want to predict cash flows to determine if it will need a loan. An investor might forecast a company's earnings to determine whether it will be a good investment.

The goal of this lab is to forecast sales and earnings for **Sony Interactive Entertainment** using Excel's Forecast Sheet.

Required

1. Using Excel's Forecast Sheet, forecast future sales for Sony Interactive Entertainment.
2. Using Excel's Forecast Sheet, forecast future income before extraordinary items for Sony Interactive Entertainment.

Ask the Question

What are the company's forecasted 2023 and 2024 quarterly sales and earnings for the given time series data (past quarterly sales and earnings from 2015 to 2022)?

Master the Data

Looking at Sony's financial statements, we accumulate the values of quarterly sales and earnings from 2015 to 2022.

Open Excel file **Lab 9.1 Data.xlsx**.

Data Dictionary

Table	Attribute Name	Description	Data Type
Sony Data	Date	Quarter begin date	Date
Sony Data	Sony Sales	Net sales for Sony Interactive Entertainment during the respective quarter	Currency
Sony Data	Sony Income from Extraordinary Items	Income before extraordinary items for Sony Interactive Entertainment during the respective quarter	Currency

Perform the Analysis

Analysis Task #1: Prepare a Sales Forecast

1. To start the forecast analysis, highlight one of the numbers in Column B (for sales), and then click on the **Data** tab and **Forecast Sheet** (Lab Exhibit 9.1.1).

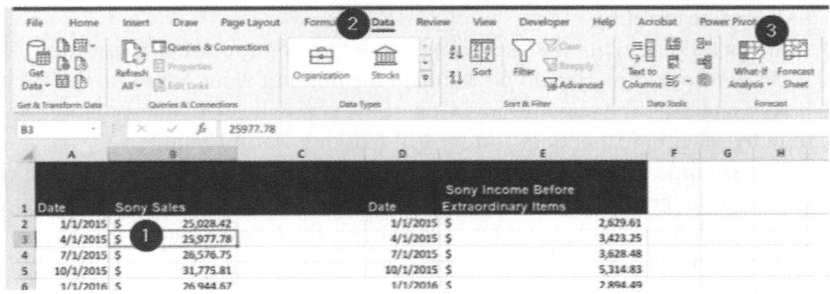

Lab Exhibit 9.1.1

Microsoft Excel

2. The box shown in Lab Exhibit 9.1.2 will open up, allowing us to begin forecasting Sony Interactive Entertainment's sales in 2023 and 2024. The Forecast Sheet is available on PCs but not on Macs. If you use a Mac, you may need to use a computer lab or a virtual desktop to access this functionality.

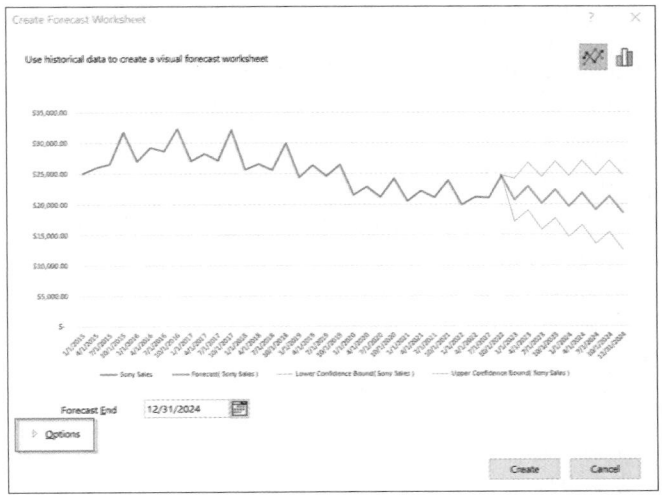

Lab Exhibit 9.1.2

Microsoft Excel

3. Note the seasonality of the data with the reasonably consistent crest and trough over the four quarters of 2023 and 2024. Click on the arrow next to the **Options** near the bottom left (Lab Exhibit 9.1.2).
4. Consider the various options shown in Lab Exhibit 9.1.3, including the start and end dates for the forecast, the confidence interval, the timeline range, the value range, and how missing points and duplicates are handled.

Lab Exhibit 9.1.3

Microsoft Excel

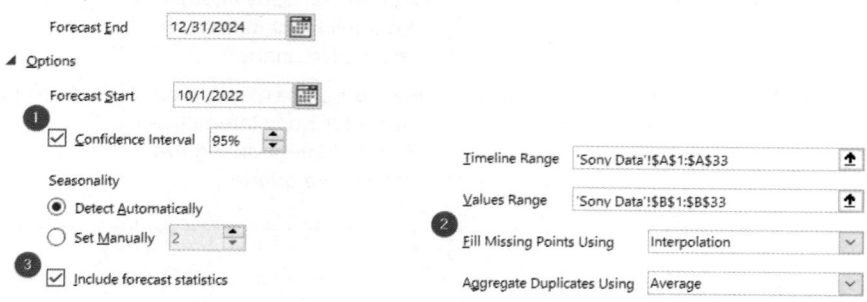

A few notes (see the red circles in Lab Exhibit 9.1.3):

(1) Set the **Confidence interval** to 95%. This means that you can be 95% confident that the range of values that results from your forecast will contain the true performance mean.
(2) You can tell Excel to set any missing value to zero or to use *interpolation.* If you select Interpolation, Excel will estimate the missing value based on the values before and after the one missing. Generally, you will select interpolation, so do so here by selecting **Interpolation** for **Fill Missing Points Using.**
(3) Select **Include forecast statistics** near the bottom left and then click the **Create** button at the bottom. You may have to click the arrow next to **Options** again (see Lab Exhibit 9.1.2) before you can access the **Create** button.
5. A new tab has been created in Excel with forecasts for each quarter in 2023 and 2024. Also note the lower and the upper confidence bounds of the forecast. The forecast sheet suggests that there is a 95% chance that the actual sales will be in the range between the lower and the upper confidence bounds (Lab Exhibit 9.1.4).

Lab Exhibit 9.1.4

Microsoft Excel

	A	B	C	D	E
1	Date	Sony Sales	Forecast(Sony Sales)	Lower Confidence Bound(Sony Sales)	Upper Confidence Bound(Sony Sales)
33	10/1/2022	24683.49	24683.49	24683.49	24683.49
34	1/1/2023		20711.10	17225.81	24196.39
35	4/1/2023		22914.37	19014.58	26814.17

6. The forecast graph should resemble Lab Exhibit 9.1.5.

Lab Exhibit 9.1.5

Microsoft Excel

DATA VISUALIZATION

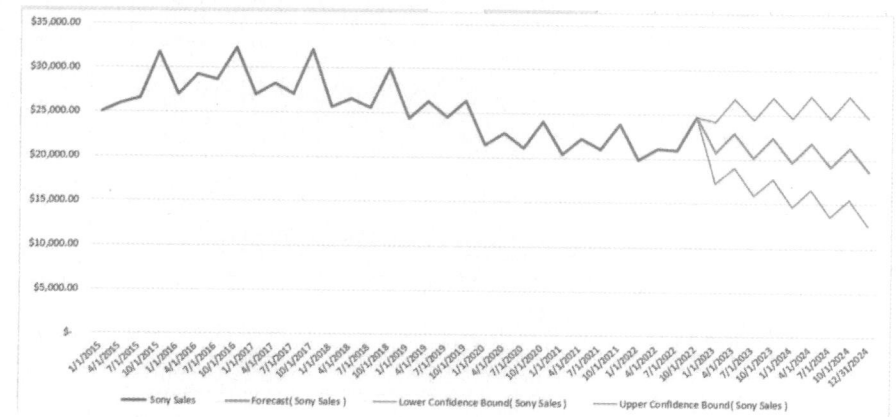

You will also note that the forecast generates a results table (Lab Exhibit 9.1.6).

	A	B	C	D	E	F
1	Date	Sony Sales	Forecast(Sony Sales)	Lower Confidence Bound(Sony Sales)	Upper Confidence Bound(Sony Sales)	Column
2	1/1/2015	25028.42				0.00
3	4/1/2015	25977.78				0.00
4	7/1/2015	26576.75				0.00
5	10/1/2015	31775.81				0.00
6	1/1/2016	26944.67				0.00
7	4/1/2016	29199.27				0.00
8	7/1/2016	28641.92				0.00
9	10/1/2016	32287.17				0.00
10	1/1/2017	27016.94				0.00
11	4/1/2017	28232.39				0.00
12	7/1/2017	27097.97				0.00
13	10/1/2017	32087.88				0.00
14	1/1/2018	25631.76				0.00
15	4/1/2018	26538.42				0.00
16	7/1/2018	25555.11				0.00
17	10/1/2018	29987.67				0.00
18	1/1/2019	24348.42				0.00
19	4/1/2019	26331.47				0.00
20	7/1/2019	24524.72				0.00
21	10/1/2019	26403.74				0.00
22	1/1/2020	21451.05				0.00
23	4/1/2020	22790.24				0.00
24	7/1/2020	21110.51				0.00
25	10/1/2020	24154.61				0.00
26	1/1/2021	20460.08				0.00
27	4/1/2021	22160.61				0.00
28	7/1/2021	21052.47				0.00
29	10/1/2021	23839.25				0.00
30	1/1/2022	19879.73				0.00
31	4/1/2022	21120.36				0.00
32	7/1/2022	20973.63				0.00
33	10/1/2022	24683.49	24683.49	24683.49	24683.49	0.00
34	1/1/2023		20711.10	17225.81	24196.39	6970.58
35	4/1/2023		22914.37	19014.58	26814.17	7799.59
36	7/1/2023		20180.62	15903.47	24457.77	8554.30
37	10/1/2023		22383.90	17760.09	27007.70	9247.61
38	1/1/2024		19650.14	14701.43	24598.85	9897.42
39	4/1/2024		21853.42	16599.86	27106.98	10507.11
40	7/1/2024		19119.67	13575.79	24663.55	11087.76
41	10/1/2024		21322.94	15503.20	27142.68	11639.48

Lab Exhibit 9.1.6

Microsoft Excel

7. Note on the graph the widening between the confidence bounds. Calculate the difference between the lower bound and the upper bound, noting that over time the difference between the lower and upper confidence bounds gets larger because the further we go out in time, the less certain is the outcome (see Lab Exhibit 9.1.6 above).

   (1) At 1/1/2023, the difference between upper and lower confidence bounds is $24,196.39 − $17,225.81 = $6,970.58.
   (2) At 1/1/2024, the difference between upper and lower confidence bounds is $24,598.85 − $14,701.43 = $9,897.42.

Analysis Task #2: Prepare a Forecast for Income before Extraordinary Items

1. Do the same analysis for income before extraordinary items with the data in Sheet 1 in Column E, repeating Steps 1–6 with the new data. We choose income before any possible extraordinary items because predicting extraordinary items is very difficult to do.
2. The graph for the forecast of future income from extraordinary items is shown in Lab Exhibit 9.1.7.

DATA VISUALIZATION

Lab Exhibit 9.1.7

Microsoft Excel

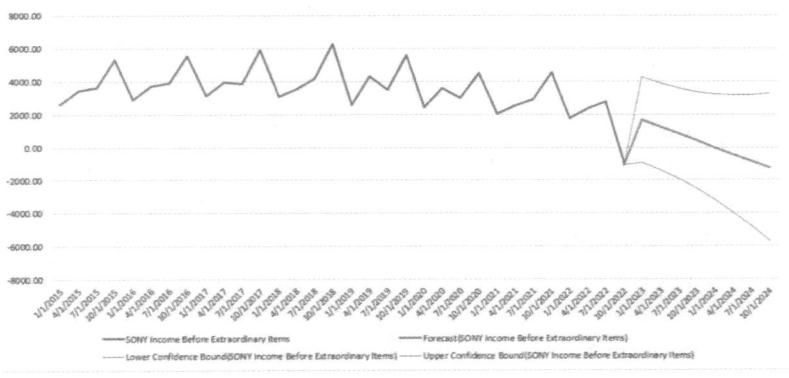

SONY Income Before Extraordinary Items — Forecast(SONY Income Before Extraordinary Items) — Lower Confidence Bound(SONY Income Before Extraordinary Items) — Upper Confidence Bound(SONY Income Before Extraordinary Items)

Share the Story

We have now developed a forecast for future sales and income before extraordinary items for Sony Interactive Entertainment. We see that the forecast for sales has some volatility, but overall we predict decreasing sales. The forecast for income from extraordinary items also predicts an overall decline into the future. Management can use this forecast to make data-driven production decisions for future periods and may also use the information to make changes to the marketing efforts or sales prices if maintaining or increasing sales is a company goal.

Assessment

1. Take a screenshot of the sales forecast and the forecast of income before extraordinary items, paste them into a Word document, and name the document "Lab 9.1 Submission.docx".
2. Answer the multiple-choice questions in Connect and upload your Lab 9.1 Submission.docx via Connect if assigned.

Alternate Lab 9.1 Excel—On Your Own

Forecasting Future Performance: Sales and Earnings

Apply the same steps in Lab 9.1 to the data in **Alt Lab 9.1 Data.xlsx** to forecast sales and earnings for **Nintendo** using Excel's Forecast Sheet.

Required

1. Using Excel's Forecast Sheet, forecast future sales for Nintendo.
2. Using Excel's Forecast Sheet, forecast future income before extraordinary items for Nintendo.

Assessment

1. Take a screenshot of the sales forecast and the forecast of income before extraordinary items, paste them into a Word document, and name the document "Alt Lab 9.1 Submission.docx".
2. Answer the multiple-choice questions in Connect and upload your Alt Lab 9.1 Submission.docx via Connect if assigned.

Forecasting Future Performance: Sales and Earnings

Data Analytics Type: Predictive Analytics

Lab Note: The tools presented in this lab periodically change. Updated instructions, if applicable, can be found in the student and instructor support materials. All Lab Exhibits are available within the eBook and in Connect.

Keywords

Predictive Analytics, Forecasting, Time Series

Decision-Making Context

There are many reasons to forecast a firm's future performance. For example, a company may want to predict sales to determine needed manufacturing capacity, or it may want to predict cash flows to determine if it will need a loan. An investor might forecast a company's earnings to determine whether it will be a good investment.

The goal of this lab is to forecast sales and earnings for **Sony Interactive Entertainment** using Tableau.

Required

1. Using Tableau, forecast future sales for Sony Interactive Entertainment.
2. Using Tableau, forecast future income before extraordinary items for Sony Interactive Entertainment.

Ask the Question

What are the company's forecasted 2023 and 2024 quarterly sales and earnings for the given time series data (past quarterly sales and earnings from 2015 to 2022)?

Master the Data

Looking at Sony's financial statements, we accumulate the values of quarterly sales and earnings from 2015 to 2022.

Open Tableau and connect to Excel file **Lab 9.2 Data.xlsx**.

Data Dictionary

Table	Attribute Name	Description	Data Type
Sony Data	Date	Quarter begin date	Date
Sony Data	Sales	Net sales for Sony Interactive Entertainment during the respective quarter	Currency
Sony Data	Income from Extraordinary Items	Income before extraordinary items for Sony Interactive Entertainment during the respective quarter	Currency

Perform the Analysis

Analysis Task #1: Prepare the Sales Forecast

1. Once you have connected to the data, you will be on the data screen (Lab Exhibit 9.2.1). Because this Excel workbook has only one worksheet, Tableau should automatically load it to your workspace. If it doesn't, drag the sheet "Sony Data" to the workspace on the right. Then click on Sheet 1 to start your visualization.
2. To start the forecast analysis, navigate to the **Data** tab on the left side of the screen. Double-click **Sales** from **Measures**, then double-click **Date** from **Dimensions** (Lab Exhibit 9.2.2).
3. Tableau should have defaulted the visualization type to a line chart, but if it did not, you can change it by clicking on the line chart icon in the **Show Me** tab (Lab Exhibit 9.2.3).
4. Tableau interacts with dates in two ways, as either "Continuous" or "Discrete" (Lab Exhibit 9.2.4). If the variable "pill" is blue, Tableau has treated this as a discrete variable. If it is green, Tableau is treating it as a continuous variable. Regardless of the way Tableau chose to display your dates when you added them to your visualization, you can change the field to the correct display quite easily.

DATA VISUALIZATION

5. From the **Columns** shelf, right-click the **Date** pill. Then select **Quarter Q2 2015** (Lab Exhibit 9.2.5). Doing so will change the date from a discrete variable to a continuous variable, which will allow you to show your visualization as a continuous line. Note that the **Date** pill will change from blue to green.
   The resulting line chart should resemble Lab Exhibit 9.2.6.
6. To expand this line chart to show a Forecast, select **Analysis > Forecast > Show Forecast** (Lab Exhibit 9.2.7).
7. You can now select a variety of options to refine this forecast. From the **Marks** shelf, change the default mark to **Circle** (Lab Exhibit 9.2.8).
8. The line chart has changed, and Tableau has provided whiskers around each of the forecasted data points, as shown in Lab Exhibit 9.2.9.
9. You can also adjust the amount of time you are forecasting. From the **Analysis** tab, select **Forecast > Forecast Options** (Lab Exhibit 9.2.10).
10. Adjust the **Forecast Length** to <u>Exactly 3 Years</u>, as shown in Lab Exhibit 9.2.11.
    As you make the change, you can see how the chart adjusts to provide more data. You can also see that the whiskers around the dates extend as you reach further into the future (Lab Exhibit 9.2.12). The reason is the increasing uncertainty about the outcome.

Analysis Task #2: Prepare a Forecast of Income before Extraordinary Items

1. Create a new sheet and create a forecast for income before extraordinary items, repeating the steps from Analysis Task #1 with the new data. We choose income before any possible extraordinary items because predicting extraordinary items is very difficult to do.
   For this analysis task, leave the visualization in the form of a line chart. (That is, do not change your marks to circles like we did in Analysis Task #1.)
   When you create the forecast line chart, it should resemble Lab Exhibit 9.2.13.
   Note: If you completed Lab 9.1 Excel before this lab, you will notice that the forecast here is quite different. The difference results because Tableau has defaulted to leaving out the last quarter from its analysis.

DATA VISUALIZATION

2. You can adjust the data that Tableau includes in its analysis. Select **Analysis > Forecast > Forecast Options**. (See Lab Exhibit 9.2.10 if you need a refresher of where to find these options.) Adjust the default from 1 to 0 in <u>Ignore Last Quarter</u> (Lab Exhibit 9.2.14).
   Once you have made that change, the resulting visualization should resemble the visualization shown in Lab Exhibit 9.2.15.

DATA VISUALIZATION

Share the Story

We have now developed a forecast for future sales and income before extraordinary items for Sony Interactive Entertainment. We see that the forecast for sales has some volatility, but overall, we predict decreasing sales. The forecast for income from extraordinary items also predicts an overall decline into the future. Management can use this forecast to make data-driven production decisions for future periods and may also consider making changes to the marketing efforts or sales prices if maintaining or increasing sales is a company goal.

Assessment

1. Take a screenshot of the sales forecast and the forecast of income before extraordinary items, paste them into a Word document, and name the document "Lab 9.2 Submission.docx".
2. Answer the multiple-choice questions in Connect and upload your Lab 9.2 Submission.docx via Connect if assigned.

Alternate Lab 9.2   Tableau—On Your Own

Forecasting Future Performance: Sales and Earnings

Apply the same steps in Lab 9.2 to the data in **Alt Lab 9.2 Data.xlsx** to forecast sales and earnings for **Nintendo** using Tableau.

Required

1. Using Tableau, forecast future sales for Nintendo.
2. Using Tableau, forecast future income before extraordinary items for Nintendo.

Assessment

1. Take a screenshot of the forecast of sales and the forecast of income before extraordinary items, paste them into a Word document, and name the document "Alt Lab 9.2 Submission.docx".
2. Answer the multiple-choice questions in Connect and upload your Alt Lab 9.2 Submission.docx via Connect if assigned.

Lab 9.3　Power BI

Forecasting Future Performance: Sales and Earnings

Data Analytics Type: Predictive Analytics

Keywords

Predictive Analytics, Forecasting, Time Series

Decision-Making Context

There are many reasons to forecast a firm's future performance. For example, a company may want to predict sales to determine needed manufacturing capacity, or it may want to predict cash flows to determine if it will need a loan. An investor might forecast a company's earnings to determine whether it will be a good investment.

The goal of this lab is to forecast sales and earnings for **Sephora** using Power BI.

Required

1. Forecast future sales for Sephora using Power BI.
2. Forecast future income before extraordinary items for Sephora using Power BI.

Ask the Question

What are Sephora's forecasted 2024 and 2025 quarterly sales and earnings for given time series data (past quarterly sales and earnings from 2016 to 2023)?

Master the Data

Looking at Sephora's financial statements, we accumulate the values of quarterly sales and earnings from 2016 to 2023.

1. Open Power BI.
2. Select **Get Data > Excel Workbook > Connect > Excel File Lab 9.3 Data.xlsx** (Lab Exhibit 9.3.1).
3. Once you have connected the data, select **Sephora Data** (Lab Exhibit 9.3.2) and click the **Load** button at the bottom right.
4. Power BI opens up the report view, but if you click the data symbol on the left side of the screen (Lab Exhibit 9.3.3), you can review the data you have loaded.
   An example of the data is shown in Lab Exhibit 9.3.4.

Data Dictionary

Table	Attribute Name	Description	Data Type
Sephora Data	Date	Quarter begin date	Date
Sephora Data	Account	Either the Sales or Income Before Extraordinary Items account	Text
Sephora Data	Amount	Dollar amount of sales or income in the given quarter	General

5. From this data view, you can format your Amount field so that it displays as currency. Click in the **Amount** column and then use the menu at the top of the screen (shown in Lab Exhibit 9.3.5) to adjust the settings. Set the **Format** to 2 decimals. (If you don't, Power BI will estimate the forecast with many decimal places.)

   After you have reviewed the data, click back to the report view using the icon shown in Lab Exhibit 9.3.6.

Perform the Analysis

In Power BI, you can build multiple visualizations on one page of the report. For this Lab, you will build two visualizations and add a slicer to your report page. A slicer is a filter that is included as a visual on the dashboard. Slicers allow the user to filter and cut the data on their own so that they can explore and interpret the other visualizations on the dashboard.

You will also format the report with font colors and wallpaper to create a cohesive design for the report. Sephora is a cosmetics company, so you can format the report in a manner that you think represents its brand.

Analysis Task 1: Use a Line Graph to Build a Sales Forecast Visualization

DATA VISUALIZATION

1. Click the **line graph visualization** icon from the **Visualizations** pane (see Lab Exhibit 9.3.7).
2. Click the arrow next to Sephora Data on the **Fields** pane (Lab Exhibit 9.3.8).
3. Select the fields that you will need for your visualization. In this case, you will select the **Amount** and **Date** fields (Lab Exhibit 9.3.9).
4. Drag the **Account** field to the **Filters** pane and drop it in the **Filters on this visual** section (Lab Exhibit 9.3.10).
5. You will need to filter this visualization so that it shows only the values for the sales accounts. If you do not add this filter, Power BI will combine the values for the sales and income before extraordinary items for each quarter.
6. Select **Sales** on the filter (Lab Exhibit 9.3.11).
7. At this point, you should have a visualization that looks like Lab Exhibit 9.3.12.
8. For your visualization, you want the specific values for each quarter as they appear in the Excel workbook, so make sure you are using the **Date** field and not the **Date Hierarchy** field.

   To select only the Date (not Date Hierarchy), click on the down arrow next to the **Date** field on the **Axis** option in the **Visualizations** pane (Lab Exhibit 9.3.13). Then select **Date** (not **Date Hierarchy**) from the drop-down menu (Lab Exhibit 9.3.14).

   Your line graph will now resemble Lab Exhibit 9.3.15.
9. Now you have graphed the existing sales data. Next, add the forecast by clicking on the **Analytics** icon on the **Visualizations** pane (see Lab Exhibit 9.3.16).

   Scroll down to the **Forecast** option and click **+Add** (Lab Exhibit 9.3.17).
10. You can type "Sales Forecast" into the text box at the top of the **Forecast** dialog menu. You want to forecast for 2 years (by quarter), so change the forecast length to 8 quarters. Leave the confidence interval at 95% and allow the seasonality of the data to be determined automatically (default). Click **Apply** at the bottom of the dialog menu (Lab Exhibit 9.3.18).
11. Scroll down further. Leave the **Confidence band style** to be solid **Fill** with 80% **Transparency**. Change the **Color** of the fill to a color of your choice. (Choose a color that fits with the Sephora brand—you will continue to use this theme for your font choices and wallpaper.) See Lab Exhibit 9.3.19.

    Once you have made these changes, your forecast will be added to your visualization, which should now resemble Lab Exhibit 9.3.20.

12. Change the title of the visualization by selecting the **Format** icon on the **Visualization** pane (see Lab Exhibit 9.3.21).
13. Now click on the **Paint Roller** icon, scroll down to the **Title** options, and click on the down arrow (see Lab Exhibit 9.3.22).
    - Change the **Title text** to "Sephora Sales Forecast 2024-2025".
    - Change the **Font color** to the same color you used for your forecast shading.
    - Increase the **Text size** to 20 and center the title using the correct **Alignment** option.
14. You may want to format the axes to remove the titles "Amount" and "Date." This will save a little space, and those titles do not provide information that a user could not glean from the visualization. To remove the axis titles, click the down arrow for each axis and slide the Title to "off." (See Lab Exhibit 9.3.23.)
15. Resize your sales forecast visualization so that it takes up only the top half of the report screen because in Analysis Task #2 you are going to build another visualization below it. Also, navigate to the **Format** menu and center-align the entire visualization by selecting **Align > Align center**, as shown in Lab Exhibit 9.3.24.
    Your report screen should now resemble Lab Exhibit 9.3.25.

Analysis Task #2: Prepare Forecast for Income Before Extraordinary Items

1. Repeat Steps 1–15 from Analysis Task #1 using the Income Before Extraordinary Items account instead of the Sales account in the filter. *Note:* In Step 6, you will select **Income Before Extraordinary Items** instead of Sales in the filter. (See Lab Exhibit 9.3.11 for a review.)

DATA VISUALIZATION

2. Add the new visualization to the bottom half of the report screen. Your report screen should now resemble Lab Exhibit 9.3.26.

Analysis Task #3: Add a Slicer to the Report

Slicers provide another way of filtering a report. When you apply a slicer to a report, it will narrow the portion of the dataset that you are viewing.

1. Click on a blank section of your report screen (top-right corner). Then click on the **slicer** icon on the **Visualizations** pane (Lab Exhibit 9.3.27).
2. Drag the **Date** field to the **Field** space on the **Visualizations** pane (Lab Exhibit 9.3.28).
    You should now see a slider on your report screen that ranges from the first date to the last date of your dataset (Lab Exhibit 9.3.29).
    Move the slider up and down and notice how it changes both of your visualizations. Because our forecast is based on historical data, if you change the dates used as inputs, the forecast will also change.
3. Format the slider by selecting the **Format** icon on the **Visualizations** pane, scrolling down to **Slider**, and changing the **Color** to the same color you previously used for your title font (Lab Exhibit 9.3.30).

Analysis Task #4: Format the Report

Formatting a report can tie it all together. In service industries, such as public accounting, reports are often formatted to match the client's logos and brands. For this lab, you have already added font colors and shadings of your choice. You will now add wallpaper to the background of the report.

1. Click on a blank space on the report screen.
2. Click on the **Format** icon on the **Visualizations** pane. Then scroll down to the **Wallpaper** section and click the down arrow (which will then turn to an up arrow when it expands, showing the embedded options). (See Lab Exhibit 9.3.31.)

3. As shown in Lab Exhibit 9.3.31 (red circle #3), you can set a background **Color** or add a picture. For this lab, you will add a picture. You will need to find a picture online that you would like to use as your wallpaper and save it to your computer. Click **+Add image** and navigate to the picture that you saved. You may need to adjust the image fit so that the picture fills the background. Your final report should resemble Lab Exhibit 9.3.32.

DATA VISUALIZATION

Assessment

1. Take a screenshot of the report page containing both the forecast of sales and the forecast of income before extraordinary items, paste it into a Word document, and name the document "Lab 9.3 Submission.docx".
2. Answer the multiple-choice questions in Connect and upload your Lab 9.3 Submission.docx via Connect if assigned.

Alternate Lab 9.3   Power BI—On Your Own

Forecasting Future Performance: Sales and Earnings

Apply the same steps in Lab 9.3 to the data in **Alt Lab 9.3 Data.xlsx** to forecast sales and earnings for **Dick's Sporting Goods** using Power BI.

Required

1. Forecast future sales for Dick's Sporting Goods using Power BI.
2. Forecast future income before extraordinary items for Dick's Sporting Goods using Power BI.

Assessment

1. Take a screenshot of the report page containing both the forecast of sales and the forecast of income before extraordinary items, paste it into a Word document, and name the document "Alt Lab 9.3 Submission.docx".
2. Answer the multiple-choice questions in Connect and upload your Alt Lab 9.3 Submission.docx via Connect if assigned.

Lab 9.4   Excel

Lab Note: The tools presented in this lab periodically change. Updated instructions, if applicable, can be found in the student and instructor support materials. All Lab Exhibits are available within the eBook and in Connect.

Predicting Product Demand Using Regression Analysis

Data Analytics Type: Predictive Analytics

Keywords

Predictive Analytics, Forecasting, Time Series

Decision-Making Context

Companies forecast future product demand to make sure they have adequate product available for sale.

Marie Callender's Restaurant and Bakery sells frozen cakes and pies through grocery stores and big-box retailers. While you might think any time is a good time for pie, the company actually works very hard to make sure it has the right amount of pie available for sale at the right time.

In this lab, we use regression analysis to predict pie sales based on several variables that are likely to be associated with monthly product demand. Regression analysis also allows us to estimate the impact of each variable.

Required

Using regression, perform a cross-section analysis to determine what drives monthly product demand for frozen pies at Marie Callender's from 2024 to 2027.

Ask the Question

What are the drivers of monthly demand for Marie Callender's frozen pies from 2024 to 2027?

Master the Data

Open the Excel file titled **Lab 9.4 Data.xlsx** and review the data.

Data Dictionary

Table	Attribute Name	Description	Data Type
Product Demand Data	Date	The date that production begins for the month	Date
Product Demand Data	GDP	Gross domestic product, a measure of the size of the overall economy	Currency
Product Demand Data	Temperature	The average temperature (in degrees Fahrenheit) by month of year	Numeric
Product Demand Data	Holiday	A dummy variable coded to 1 for months that include a holiday where people usually serve pie and 0 otherwise	Numeric
Product Demand Data	Demand	Monthly demand for frozen pies	Numeric

614

Perform the Analysis

Analysis Task #1: Develop Hypotheses and Variables to Predict Monthly Demand for Frozen Pies

Let's hypothesize that there might be three predictors of monthly product demand for frozen pies:

- Gross domestic product (GDP), representing the overall economic health of the United States
- Temperature
- Holiday month

It is reasonable to predict that more people will buy frozen pies when the economy is healthy, the temperature is lower, and a food-centric holiday (such as Thanksgiving, Christmas, or the Fourth of July) is coming up. We can summarize our expected relationships as follows:

Independent Variable	Expected Relationship with Monthly Product Demand of Pies
GDP (gross domestic product)	+
Temperature (Avg. Fahrenheit)	−
Holiday Season	+

The regression equation used to describe these relationships is $Y = a + bX$, where

Variable	Definition	Example from Lab 9.4
Y	The dependent variable	Market demand
a	The y-intercept (where the line crosses the Y-axis)	To be calculated
b	Regression coefficient (slope of the regression line)	To be calculated
X	The independent variable(s)	GDP, Temperature, Holiday Season

Because in this lab we expect that three independent variables (GDP, Temperature, Holiday Season) together describe and predict the independent variable (Market Demand), we are actually using *multiple regression*. The basic multiple regression equation to examine the effect of each of these variables on market demand is

$$Y = a + b_1 X_1 + b_2 X_2 + b_3 X_3$$

where X_1 is GDP, X_2 is Temperature, and X_3 is Holiday Month.

However, we may hypothesize that more pies are eaten during July, November, and December because each of these three months includes food-centric holidays that people often associate with pie. July is in a different season than the other two holiday months, so we will also include an *interaction term* that considers the effect of both holiday month *and* temperature, together.

The interaction term is calculated by multiplying the two variables together (which we will see in Analysis Task #3), and the regression equation containing the interaction term is

$$Y = a + b_1 X_1 + b_2 X_2 + b_3 X_3 + b_4 X_2 * X_3$$

Analysis Task #2: Create a Holiday Variable

1. We need to create a holiday variable that indicates whether it is a "Holiday Month" (such as November or December). To do this, insert a column to the right of Column C and label it "Holiday" in cell D1 (Lab Exhibit 9.4.1).

2. Starting with cell D2, insert a "1" for all rows containing the months July, November, or December. Insert a "0" for all other months in the full dataset. You can create this variable in a variety of ways.

One easy way to identify the records that relate to July, November, or December is to use a multiple **IF** function based on the **Month** function, as shown in Lab Exhibit 9.4.2:

=IF(MONTH(A2)=7,1,IF(MONTH(A2)=11,1,IF(MONTH(A2)=12,1,0)))

In this formula, you are telling Excel to enter a 1 in the cell if the date (shown in Column A) is for the month of July (the 7th month), November (the 11th month), or December (the 12th month), and a 0 otherwise.

○ *Note:* When a variable is coded as either 1 for yes or 0 for no, it is known as a dummy (or indicator) variable. Any variable that is either true or false can be represented with a dummy variable.

The resulting spreadsheet should appear as shown in Lab Exhibit 9.4.3.

Analysis Task #3: Calculate Interaction Term

As previously mentioned, because July is in a different season from November and December, it is useful to also consider the interactive effect of holiday month and temperature together. In regression, an interaction effect indicates that the effect of an independent variable on a dependent variable changes depending on the values of another independent variable. This interaction effect will allow the user to determine if the effect of holiday during warm months is different from holiday during cold months.

1. Insert a column to the right of column D and label it "Holiday × Temperature" in cell E1 (Lab Exhibit 9.4.4).
2. In cell E2, enter the formula to multiple Holiday by Temperature (=D2*C2), as shown in Lab Exhibit 9.4.5.
3. Copy this formula down to all rows in Column E. The resulting spreadsheet should appear as shown in Lab Exhibit 9.4.6.

Analysis Task #4: Perform Regression Analysis

1. To perform the regression analysis, click on a cell in the dataset. Select **Data > Data Analysis**, as shown in Lab Exhibit 9.4.7.
2. The dialog box shown in Lab Exhibit 9.4.8 will open. Select **Regression**.
3. The **Regression** dialog box will open. Our dependent variable (Y Range) is Monthly Product Demand. Set the **Input Y Range** as $F$1:$F$49 (see Lab Exhibit 9.4.9).

   Note: Excel will not let you select the entire column because there are blank rows at the end.

4. Next, select the independent variable (X Range). The variables GDP, Weather (Avg Fahrenheit), Holiday, and Holiday × Temperature are the independent variables, so enter $B$1:$E$49 in the **Input X Range** (see again Lab Exhibit 9.4.9).
5. Check the box next to **Labels** to indicate that each column has a label (see again Lab Exhibit 9.4.9). Then click **OK**.
6. The Regression output will open as a new worksheet and should resemble Lab Exhibit 9.4.10.

SUMMARY OUTPUT

Regression Statistics	
Multiple R	0.768052545
R Square	0.589904711
Adjusted R Square	0.551756312
Standard Error	7.233994327
Observations	48

ANOVA

	df	SS	MS	F	Significance F
Regression	4	3236.844736	809.2111841	15.46341989	6.50433E-08
Residual	43	2250.218979	52.33067392		
Total	47	5487.063715			

	Coefficients	Standard Error	t Stat	P-value	Lower 95%	Upper 95%	Lower 95.0%	Upper 95.0%
Intercept	31.60378507	51.83917696	0.609650595	0.545301521	-72.93987871	136.1474488	-72.93987871	136.1474488
GDP	0.890144491	0.517281375	1.720812956	0.092474043	-0.153052822	1.933341804	-0.153052822	1.933341804
Temperature	-0.106671178	0.079884237	-1.335321987	0.188797113	-0.267773094	0.054430739	-0.267773094	0.054430739
Holiday	40.87391021	8.08376993	5.056293111	8.41651E-06	24.57143445	57.17638597	24.57143445	57.17638597
Holiday X Temperature	-0.589979389	0.146707213	-4.021474994	0.000229411	-0.885842681	-0.294116097	-0.885842681	-0.294116097

7. It will be easier to interpret the results if you round the numbers to two decimal places. To do so, highlight the entire sheet and change the format to **Number**, as shown in Lab Exhibit 9.4.11.
8. The final regression results will resemble Lab Exhibit 9.4.12.

	A	B	C	D	E	F	G	H	I
1	SUMMARY OUTPUT								
2									
3	Regression Statistics								
4	Multiple R	0.77							
5	R Square	0.59							
6	Adjusted R Square	0.55 ②							
7	Standard Error	7.23							
8	Observations	48.00							
9									
10	ANOVA								
11		df	SS	MS	F	① Significance F			
12	Regression	4.00	3236.84	809.21	15.46	0.00			
13	Residual	43.00	2250.22	52.33					
14	Total	47.00	5487.06						
15									
16		④ Coefficients	Standard Error	t Stat	③ P-value	Lower 95%	Upper 95%	Lower 95.0%	Upper 95.0%
17	Intercept	31.60	51.84	0.61	0.55	-72.94	136.15	-72.94	136.15
18	GDP	0.89	0.52	1.72	0.09	-0.15	1.93	-0.15	1.93
19	Temperature	-0.11	0.08	-1.34	0.19	-0.27	0.05	-0.27	0.05
20	Holiday	40.87	8.08	5.06	0.00	24.57	57.18	24.57	57.18
21	Holiday X Temperature ⑤	-0.59	0.15	-4.02	0.00	-0.89	-0.29	-0.89	-0.29
22									
23									

Share the Story

We have now performed a regression analysis to determine which factors are significant predictors of product demand.

To interpret the results, we consider several important statistics.

1. This regression model does a good job predicting market demand. We determine this by reviewing the Significance F result (also known as the Omnibus F test). When this statistic is very small, it suggests that there is almost zero probability that market demand cannot be explained by any of the variables in the model. Generally, this result should be below 0.05 for the model to be considered good. Here, the Significance F value is 0.00.

2. The R Square statistic measures how well the model predicts market demand. The adjusted R Square is a value between 0 and 1. An adjusted R Square value of 0 means that the model does not explain the dependent variable at all. An adjusted R Square value of 1 means the model perfectly explains the dependent variable. In this case, the adjusted R Square value is 0.55, which represents a reasonable ability to explain monthly product demand. However, there still are likely to be other, untested, factors that also predict market demand. Marie Callender's should work to identify those factors and add them to the model to improve forecasting in the future.

3. The P-value for each independent variable tests the null hypothesis that each independent variable adds no value to the prediction model (or that the regression coefficient is essentially no different than zero). The P-value is based on the t-stat that is generated by the regression analysis (and is located just to the left of the P-value in the regression output). Independent variables with lower P-values provide a more meaningful addition to the prediction model. Conventionally, only P-values below 0.05 are considered *statistically significant*, meaning their inclusion in the model adds predictive value. Our results show that GDP, Holiday, and Holiday × Temperature (our interaction term) have statistically significant P-values. Temperature, by itself, does not have a significant P-value.

4. The regression coefficients represent the extent to which a one-unit change in a specific independent variable changes the dependent variable (holding all other independent variables constant). The sign of the coefficient indicates whether the change is positive or negative. In our output, we see that GDP has the coefficient 0.89. This indicates that for every one-unit increase in GDP, the market demand for pie increases by 0.89.

5. The regression coefficient on the interaction term is −0.59. This negative coefficient indicates that the effect of holiday month on market demand is less as the temperature rises. Managers can conclude that holiday month has a significant effect throughout the year, but this effect is stronger in the colder months, suggesting there is a larger effect during November and December than in July.

Assessment

1. Take a screenshot of the regression results explaining product demand, paste it into a Word document, and name the document "Lab 9.4 Submission.docx".

2. Answer the multiple-choice questions in Connect and upload your Lab 9.4 Submission.docx via Connect if assigned.

Alternate Lab 9.4—On Your Own

Predicting Product Demand Using Regression Analysis

Decision-Making Context

As organizations gain access to more customer-behavior data, they can make more informed decisions about sales and marketing. Many companies have started using mobile apps to send customers targeted advertisements and coupons based on the individual customer's sales history as well as other customer data, including the customer's current location.

Barb's Big Burger (a fictitious company) started selling smoothies at the beginning of 2023. In 2025, Barb's rolled out an app that includes online ordering and coupons. That same year, Barb's marketing team suggested pushing smoothie coupons out to customers during the cooler months in an effort to boost smoothie sales. Beginning in 2025, customers will receive smoothie coupons in months when the temperature averages between 60 degrees and 70 degrees.

Required

Using the data in Excel file **Alt Lab 9.4 Data.xlsx**, complete the same steps in Lab 9.4 to perform a regression analysis to determine what drives monthly product demand for frozen smoothies at Barb's Big Burger.

Assessment:

1. Take a screenshot of the regression results explaining product demand, paste it into a Word document, and name the document "Alt Lab 9.4 Submission.docx".
2. Answer the multiple-choice questions in Connect and upload your Alt Lab 9.4 Submission.docx via Connect if assigned.

Lab 9.5   Excel

Lab Note: The tools presented in this lab periodically change. Updated instructions, if applicable, can be found in the student and instructor support materials. All Lab Exhibits are available within the eBook and in Connect.

Preparing a Master Budget (Heartwood)

Data Analytics Type: Predictive Analytics

Keywords

Operating Budget, Sales Forecast, Direct Materials Budget, Direct Labor Budget, Overhead Budget, Pro Forma Operating Income Statement

Decision-Making Context

At the beginning of the budget cycle, **Heartwood Cabinets** prepares an operating budget and all of the supporting budgets for the division of the company that produces walnut cabinets.

In this lab, you will create the budgets and the pro forma operating income statement using the sales forecast and cost data provided.

Required

1. Use Excel to build the budgets and operating statements for Heartwood's walnut cabinets.
2. Use formulas and cell references so the numbers flow through the budgets.

Ask the Question

What operating income can Heartwood expect based on its sales forecast?

Master the Data

The Excel workbook **Lab 9.5 Data.xlsx** contains templates for all of the budgets Heartwood will prepare during the master budgeting process:

(1) Sales forecast
(2) Production budget
(3) Beginning inventories budget
(4) Bill of materials for the Arch cabinet
(5) Direct materials budget–Arch
(6) Direct materials budget–All
(7) Route sheet–Labor cost budget–Arch
(8) Labor cost budget–All
(9) Overhead budget
(10) Ending inventories budget
(11) Cost of goods sold budget
(12) Nonmanufacturing costs budget
(13) Pro forma income statement

Some of the data you will need to calculate your budget are given, including sales forecast and beginning inventory.

Open Excel file **Lab 9.5 Data.xlsx** and review the budget templates that have been provided.

Perform the Analysis

Analysis Task #1: Build the Sales Forecast

You have been given the sales forecast from the marketing department. It includes the expected sales and the selling price for each type of walnut cabinet (Lab Exhibit 9.5.1).

1. To calculate expected revenue, add a formula in the Expected Revenue column. The formula is (Expected Sales * Selling Price). Begin in cell E4 with the formula =C4*D4 and copy the formula down to Row 8 to populate the entire column (Lab Exhibit 9.5.2).
2. Use the **SUM** function =SUM(E4:E8) to update the Total in Row 10 (see Lab Exhibit 9.5.2).
3. The resulting table should look like Lab Exhibit 9.5.3.

Analysis Task #2: Build the Production Budget

1. Link the Budgeted Sales row to the Sales Forecast table using an index-match function. Enter the formula in cell C4 as shown in Lab Exhibit 9.5.4. That formula is:

   =INDEX('Sales Forecast'!$C$4:$C$8,MATCH(C$3,'Sales Forecast'!$B$4:$B$8,0),1)

   Note: Index-match can be preferable to VLOOKUP or HLOOKUP because it is flexible enough to work with data configured vertically or horizontally.

Lab Exhibit 9.5.4

Microsoft Excel

- Make sure you've locked your cells, by including "$" signs where appropriate, so that you can drag the formula across to the other types of cabinet.

2. Assume Heartwood wants to have 5 percent of budgeted sales remaining at the end of the budget period. Use a formula to update the Target Ending Finished Goods Inventory row to be an appropriate percentage of the Budgeted Sales row. Enter the formula in cell C5 (=C4*0.05) as shown in Lab Exhibit 9.5.4.
3. Calculate Total Required Units by adding Target Ending Finished Goods Inventory to Budgeted Sales using the formula =SUM(C4:C5). Enter the formula in cell C6, as shown in Lab Exhibit 9.5.4.
4. Update the Beginning Finished Goods Inventory row to reflect last year's ending inventory. Find this information on the Beginning Inventories Budget and use an index-match function to bring the data to the Production Budget. Enter the formula in cell C7 as shown in Lab Exhibit 9.5.5. The formula is:

   =INDEX('Beginning Inventories Budget'!$C$4:$C$8,MATCH(C$3,'Beginning Inventories Budget'!$B$4:$B$8,0),1)

Lab Exhibit 9.5.5

Microsoft Excel

A	B	C
		Heartwood Production Budget (in units)
		Walnut - Arch
	Total Required Units	=SUM(C4:C5)
	(less) Beginning finished goods inventory	=INDEX('Beginning Inventories Budget'!$C$4:$C$8,MATCH(C$3,'Beginning Inventories Budget'!$B$4:$B$8,0),1)
	Units to be Produced	=C6-C7

5. Calculate Units to Be Produced by subtracting Beginning Finished Goods Inventory from Total Required Units. Enter the formula in cell C8 (=C6-C7) as shown in Lab Exhibit 9.5.5.
6. The resulting table should look like Lab Exhibit 9.5.6.

Analysis Task #3: Build the Bill of Materials

1. The Part Number, Part Name, Cost per Unit, and Quantity required per door are given. Calculate the Total column (Column F) with a formula for Cost per Unit * Quantity in cell F4 (=D4*E4) and copy the formula down the column, as shown in Lab Exhibit 9.5.7.
2. The resulting table should look like Lab Exhibit 9.5.8.

Analysis Task #4: Build the Direct Materials Budget

1. The Part Number in cell B4 is given. Link the Required Input using the VLOOKUP formula shown in cell C4 in Lab Exhibit 9.5.9. That formula is =VLOOKUP(B4,BOM!B4:F8,4,0).

Lab Exhibit 9.5.9

Microsoft Excel

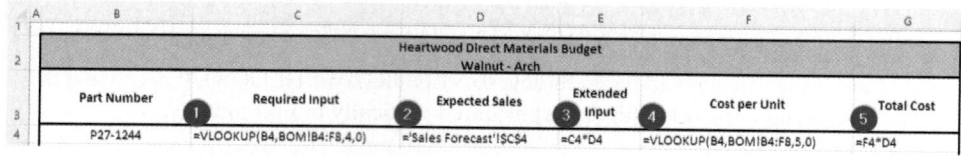

2. Link Expected Sales to the Sales Forecast using a direct link, as shown in cell D4 in Lab Exhibit 9.5.9. The formula is ='Sales Forecast'!$C$4. Remember, this BOM is for the Walnut–Arch cabinet only, so Expected Sales is the number of finished cabinets sold.
3. Calculate the Extended Input column with a formula for Required Input * Expected Sales. In cell E4, input the formula =C4*D4, as shown in Lab Exhibit 9.5.9, and copy the formula down the column.
4. Link the Cost per Unit from the Bill of Materials using the VLOOKUP formula shown in cell F4 in Lab Exhibit 9.5.9. The formula is =VLOOKUP(B4,BOM!B4:F8,5,0).
5. Calculate Total Cost per unit by multiplying Cost per Unit * Expected Sales, as shown in cell G4 in Lab Exhibit 9.5.9. The formula is =F4*D4.
6. Calculate the Total Cost per Unit in cell F9, as shown in Lab Exhibit 9.5.10. The formula is =SUM(F4:F8).

Lab Exhibit 9.5.10

Microsoft Excel

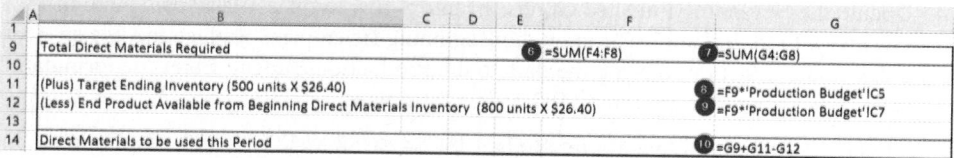

7. Calculate the Total Cost for planned production by summing the Total Cost column in cell G9, as shown in Lab Exhibit 9.5.10. The formula is =SUM(G4:G8).
8. In cell G11, calculate the Materials Cost for Target Ending Inventory as the Ending Inventory Units from the Sales Forecast multiplied by the Total Direct Materials Required for one cabinet (from cell F9). Use the formula shown in Lab Exhibit 9.5.10: =F9*'ProductionBudget'!C5.
9. In cell G12, calculate Materials Cost for Beginning Inventory (from the Beginning Inventories Budget) multiplied by the Total Direct Materials Required for one cabinet (from cell F9). Use the formula shown in Lab Exhibit 9.5.10: =F9*'ProductionBudget'!C7.

10. Now that you have calculated them, add Materials Cost for Target Ending Inventory (cell G11) and subtract Materials Cost for Beginning Inventory (cell G12) from the Total Direct Materials Required (G9). In cell G15, input the formula shown in Lab Exhibit 9.5.10: =G9+G11-G12.
11. The resulting table will look like Lab Exhibit 9.5.11.
12. You have been given the direct materials cost per unit for each type of Walnut cabinet (except for Walnut–Arch) in the Direct Materials Budget–All schedule. Update this schedule with cost per unit of Walnut–Arch (in cell B4) using a direct link to the Direct Materials Budget–Arch, as shown in Lab Exhibit 9.5.12. The formula is ='Direct MaterialsBudget - Arch'!F9.

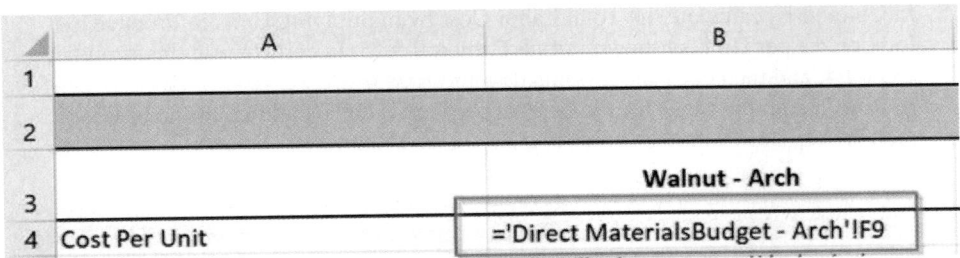

Lab Exhibit 9.5.12
Microsoft Excel

	A	B
1		
2		
3		**Walnut - Arch**
4	Cost Per Unit	='Direct MaterialsBudget - Arch'!F9

13. In Row 5, use index-match to pull the Expected Sales data for each cabinet type from the sales forecast. Use the formula shown in Lab Exhibit 9.5.13: =INDEX('Sales For ecast'!$C$4:$C$8,MATCH(C$3,'Sales Forecast'!$B$4:$B$8,0),1).

Lab Exhibit 9.5.13
Microsoft Excel

	A	B	C
1			Heartwood Direct Mat...
2			Walnut - Al...
3			Walnut - Arch
4		Cost Per Unit	='Direct Materials Budget - Arch'!F9
5		Expected Sales	=INDEX('Sales Forecast'!$C$4:$C$8,MATCH(C$3,'Sales Forecast'!$B$4:$B$8,0),1)
6		Total Direct Materials Required	=C5*C4
7			
8		Target Ending Inventory	=INDEX('Production Budget'!C5:G5,MATCH(C3,'Production Budget'!C3:G3,0),1)
9		(Plus) Materials Cost for Target Ending Inventory	=C8*C4
10		Beginning Inventory	=INDEX('Production Budget'!C7:G7,MATCH(C3,'Production Budget'!C3:G3,0),1)
11		(Less) Materials Cost for Beginning Inventory	=C10*C4
12			
13		Direct Materials to be used this Period	=C6+C9-C11

14. In Row 8, use index-match to pull the Target Ending Inventory data for each cabinet type in from the Production Budget. Use the formula shown in Lab Exhibit 9.5.13: =INDEX('Production Budget'!C5:G5,MATCH(C3,'Production Budget'!C3:G3,0),1).
15. In Row 9, calculate Materials Cost for Target Ending Inventory by multiplying Target Ending Inventory by Cost per Unit for each cabinet type. Use the formula shown in Lab Exhibit 9.5.13: =C8*C4.
16. In Row 10, use index-match to pull the Beginning Inventory from the Production Budget. Use the formula shown in Lab Exhibit 9.5.13: =INDEX('Production Budget'!C7:G7,MATCH(C3,'Production Budget'!C3:G3,0),1).
17. In Row 11, calculate Materials Cost for Beginning Inventory by multiplying Beginning Inventory by Cost per Unit for each cabinet type. Use the formula shown in Lab Exhibit 9.5.13: =C10*C4.
18. In Row 13, add Materials Cost for Target Ending Inventory and subtract Materials Cost for Beginning Inventory from Total Direct Materials Required to calculate Direct Materials to Be Used This Period. Use the formula shown in Lab Exhibit 9.5.13: =C6+C9-C11.
19. The resulting table will look like Lab Exhibit 9.5.14.

Analysis Task #5: Build the Route Sheet and Labor Cost Budget

Open the worksheet Route Sheet & Labor Cost–Arch. The Workstation, Activity, Minutes Required (for one unit), and Hourly Wage Rate required to produce Walnut–Arch are all given.

1. In Column F, calculate the Labor Cost per Unit by dividing Minutes Required by 60 and then multiply by the Hourly Wage Rate, as shown in Lab Exhibit 9.5.15. In cell F4, use the formula =(D4/60)*E4, and then copy the formula down to Row 6.
2. In Column G, link Units to Produce to the data in the Production Budget, as shown in Lab Exhibit 9.5.15. In cell G4, use the formula ='Production Budget'!$C$8, and then copy the formula down to Row 6.
3. In Column H, calculate the Total Labor Cost by multiplying Units to Produce by Labor Cost per Unit, as shown in Lab Exhibit 9.5.15. In cell H4, use the formula =G4*F4, and then copy the formula down to Row 6.
4. In Row 7, sum the totals for Labor Cost per Unit (cell F7) and Total Labor Cost (cell H7) as shown in Lab Exhibit 9.5.15.

Lab Exhibit 9.5.15

Microsoft Excel

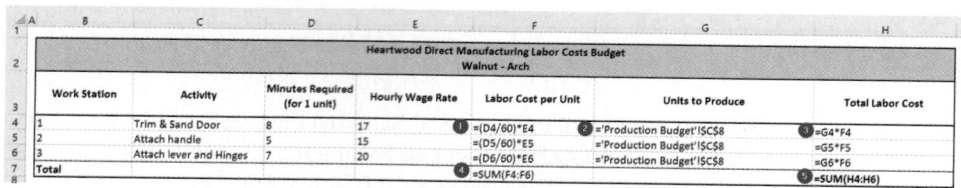

5. The resulting table should look like Lab Exhibit 9.5.16.
6. Open the worksheet labeled Labor Cost–All and complete the direct labor budget for all walnut products. In Row 5, Labor Cost per Unit is given for all cabinet types except Walnut–Arch. Use a direct link from the route sheet to add the Labor Cost per Unit for Walnut–Arch in cell C5. Use the formula shown in Lab Exhibit 9.5.17: ='Route Sheet & Labor Cost- Arch'!F7.

Lab Exhibit 9.5.17

Microsoft Excel

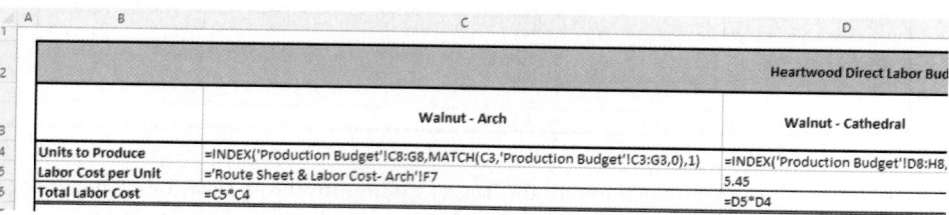

7. In Row 4, use index-match to populate the Units to Produce row with data from the production budget. Use the formula shown in cell C4 in Lab Exhibit 9.5.17: =INDEX('Production Budget'!C8:G8,MATCH(C3,'Production Budget'!C3:G3,0),1).
8. In Row 6, calculate Total Labor Cost by multiplying Units to Produce by Labor Cost per Unit. Use the formula shown in cell C6 in Exhibit 9.5.17: =C5*C4.
9. The resulting table should look like Lab Exhibit 9.5.18.

Analysis Task #6: Build the Overhead Budget

1. In Column C, use index-match to populate the Units to Produce field with data from the production budget, as shown in Lab Exhibit 9.5.19. In cell C4, use this formula: INDEX('Production Budget'!$C$8:$G$8,MATCH($B4,'Production Budget'!$C$3:$G$3,0)). Then copy the formula down to Row 8.

	Heartwood Manufacturing Overhead		Direct Labor Minutes Required for 1 Unit	Direct Labor Hours Required for 1 Unit	Predetermined Overhead Rate	Manufacturing Overhead
	Units to Produce					
Walnut - Arch	=INDEX('Production Budget'!$C$8:$G$8,MATCH($B4,'Production Budget'!$C$3:$G$3,0))		20	=D4/60	6	=C4*E4*F4
Walnut - Cathedral	=INDEX('Production Budget'!$C$8:$G$8,MATCH($B5,'Production Budget'!$C$3:$G$3,0))		20	=D5/60	6	=C5*E5*F5
Walnut - Shaker	=INDEX('Production Budget'!$C$8:$G$8,MATCH($B6,'Production Budget'!$C$3:$G$3,0))		19	=D6/60	6	=C6*E6*F6
Walnut - Slab	=INDEX('Production Budget'!$C$8:$G$8,MATCH($B7,'Production Budget'!$C$3:$G$3,0))		17	=D7/60	6	=C7*E7*F7
Walnut - Beadboard	=INDEX('Production Budget'!$C$8:$G$8,MATCH($B8,'Production Budget'!$C$3:$G$3,0))		18	=D8/60	6	=C8*E8*F8
Total Manufacturing Overhead						=SUM(G4:G8)

2. In Column D, Direct Labor Minutes Required for 1 Unit is given for all cabinet types, as shown in Lab Exhibit 9.5.19.

3. In Column E, calculate Direct Labor Hours Required for 1 Unit by dividing Direct Labor Minutes Required for 1 Unit by 60. Use the formula shown in cell E4 (=D4/60) in Lab Exhibit 9.5.19, and copy it down.

4. Predetermined overhead rate has been set at $6.00 per labor hour, as shown in Column F of Lab Exhibit 9.5.19.

5. In Column G, calculate Manufacturing Overhead by multiplying Units to Produce * Direct Labor Hours Required for 1 Unit * Predetermined Overhead Rate. Use the formula shown in cell G4 of Lab Exhibit 9.5.19, and copy it down. The formula is =C4*E4*F4.

6. Calculate the Total Manufacturing Overhead in cell G9 by summing Column G, as shown in Lab Exhibit 9.5.19.

7. The resulting table looks like Lab Exhibit 9.5.20.

Analysis Task #7: Build the Beginning Inventories Budget

1. Open the worksheet labeled "Beginning Inventories Budget." Beginning Inventory is given. In Column D, use an index-match formula to populate Direct Materials Cost per Unit with data from Direct Materials Budget–All. Use the index-match formula as follows and as shown in Lab Exhibit 9.5.21:

=INDEX('Direct MaterialsBudget - All'!$B$4:$G$4,MATCH(B4,'Direct Materials Budget - All'!$B$3:$G$3,0))

	Beginning Inventory	Direct Materials Cost Per Unit
		Heartwood
Walnut - Arch	800	=INDEX('Direct MaterialsBudget - All'!$B$4:$G$4,MATCH(B4,'Direct MaterialsBudget - All'!$B$3:$G$3,0))

2. In Column E, use an index-match formula to populate Direct Labor Cost per Unit with data from the Labor Cost Budget–All. Use the index-match formula as follows and as shown in Lab Exhibit 9.5.22:

=INDEX('Labor Cost - All'!$C$5:$G$5,MATCH(B4,'Labor Cost - All'!$C$3:$G$3,0))

		Direct Labor Cost Per Unit
Walnut - Arch		=INDEX('Labor Cost- All'!$C$5:$G$5,MATCH(B4,'Labor Cost- All'!$C$3:$G$3,0))

3. In Column F, calculate Manufacturing Overhead Cost per Unit by dividing Manufacturing Overhead by Unit to Produce. Use index-match functions as the numerator and denominator of the equation as follows:

=(INDEX(Overhead!$G$4:$G$8,MATCH('Beginning Inventories Budget'!B4, Overhead!$B$4:$B$8,0),1))/INDEX(Overhead!$C$4:$C$8,MATCH('Beginning Inventories Budget'!B4,Overhead!$B$4:$B$8,0),1)

Also see Lab Exhibit 9.5.23.

Lab Exhibit 9.5.23

Microsoft Excel

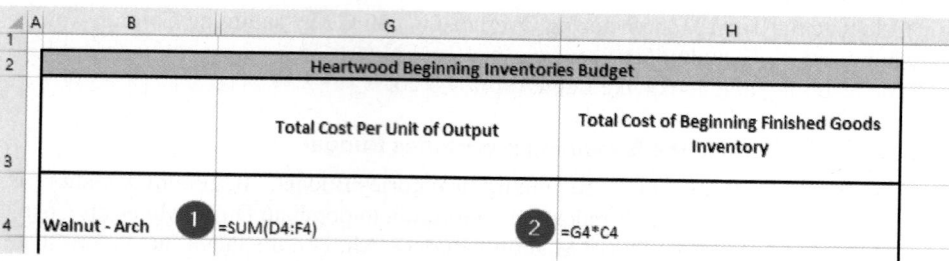

4. In Column G, calculate the Total Cost per Unit of Output by summing Direct Materials Cost per Unit, Direct Labor Cost per Unit, and Manufacturing Overhead Cost per Unit, as shown in Lab Exhibit 9.5.24. The formula is =SUM(D4:F4).

Lab Exhibit 9.5.24

Microsoft Excel

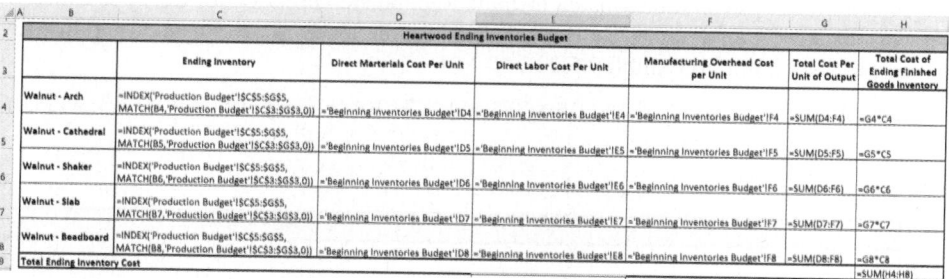

5. In Column H, calculate Total Cost of Beginning Finished Goods Inventory by multiplying Beginning Inventory by Total Cost per Unit of Output, as shown in Lab Exhibit 9.5.24. The formula is =G4*C4.
6. The resulting table looks like Lab Exhibit 9.5.25.

Analysis Task #8: Build the Ending Inventories Budget

1. In Column C, use index-match to populate Ending Inventory with data from the production budget. Use the index-match formula as follows and as shown in Lab Exhibit 9.5.26:

=INDEX('Production Budget'!$C$5:$G$5,MATCH(B4,'Production Budget'!$C$3:$G$3,0)). Then copy the formula to Row 8.

Lab Exhibit 9.5.26

Microsoft Excel

B	C	D	E	F	G	H
			Heartwood Ending Inventories Budget			
	Ending Inventory	Direct Marterials Cost Per Unit	Direct Labor Cost Per Unit	Manufacturing Overhead Cost per Unit	Total Cost Per Unit of Output	Total Cost of Ending Finished Goods Inventory
Walnut - Arch	=INDEX('Production Budget'!$C$5:$G$5, MATCH(B4,'Production Budget'!$C$3:$G$3,0))	='Beginning Inventories Budget'!D4	='Beginning Inventories Budget'!E4	='Beginning Inventories Budget'!F4	=SUM(D4:F4)	=G4*C4
Walnut - Cathedral	=INDEX('Production Budget'!$C$5:$G$5, MATCH(B5,'Production Budget'!$C$3:$G$3,0))	='Beginning Inventories Budget'!D5	='Beginning Inventories Budget'!E5	='Beginning Inventories Budget'!F5	=SUM(D5:F5)	=G5*C5
Walnut - Shaker	=INDEX('Production Budget'!$C$5:$G$5, MATCH(B6,'Production Budget'!$C$3:$G$3,0))	='Beginning Inventories Budget'!D6	='Beginning Inventories Budget'!E6	='Beginning Inventories Budget'!F6	=SUM(D6:F6)	=G6*C6
Walnut - Slab	=INDEX('Production Budget'!$C$5:$G$5, MATCH(B7,'Production Budget'!$C$3:$G$3,0))	='Beginning Inventories Budget'!D7	='Beginning Inventories Budget'!E7	='Beginning Inventories Budget'!F7	=SUM(D7:F7)	=G7*C7
Walnut - Beadboard	=INDEX('Production Budget'!$C$5:$G$5, MATCH(B8,'Production Budget'!$C$3:$G$3,0))	='Beginning Inventories Budget'!D8	='Beginning Inventories Budget'!E8	='Beginning Inventories Budget'!F8	=SUM(D8:F8)	=G8*C8
Total Ending Inventory Cost						=SUM(H4:H8)

2. You can populate Columns D, E, and F using index-match functions, pulling data from the original budgets. However, you should also notice that the Ending Inventories budget contains much of the same data, and uses the same format, as the Beginning Inventories Budget. Therefore, you could just use direct links to the

626

Beginning Inventories Budget to populate these cells, as follows for Columns D, E, and F, respectively, and as shown in Lab Exhibit 9.5.26:

Cell D4: ='Beginning Inventories Budget'!D4

Cell E4: ='Beginning Inventories Budget'!E4

Cell F4: ='Beginning Inventories Budget'!F4

Then copy the formulas down each column to Row 8.

3. In Column G, calculate Total Cost per Unit of Output by summing Direct Materials Cost per Unit, Direct Labor Cost per Unit, and Manufacturing Overhead Cost per Unit (Columns D–F), as shown in Lab Exhibit 9.5.26. Use this formula for cell G4: =SUM(D4:F4). Then copy the formula down to Row 8.

4. In Column H, calculate Total Cost of Ending Finished Goods Inventory by multiplying Ending Inventory by Total Cost per Unit of Output, as shown in Lab Exhibit 9.5.26. In cell H4, use the formula =G4*C4, and then copy the formula down to Row 8.

5. The resulting table looks like Lab Exhibit 9.5.27.

Analysis Task #9: Build the COGS Budget.

Open the worksheet titled "COGS Budget."

Lab Exhibit 9.5.28

Microsoft Excel

1. In cell D4, use a direct link to pull the Total Beginning Finished Goods Inventory from the Beginning Inventories Budget, as shown in Lab Exhibit 9.5.28. The direct link is ='Beginning Inventories Budget'!H9.

2. In cell C5, use the SUM function to calculate Direct Materials Used from the Direct Materials Budget–All, as shown in Lab Exhibit 9.5.28 and reproduced below:

$$=SUM('DirectMaterialsBudget - All'!B13:F13)$$

3. In cell C6, use the SUM function to calculate Direct Manufacturing Labor by summing Total Labor Cost from the Direct Labor Budget, as shown in Lab Exhibit 9.5.28. The formula is =SUM('Labor Cost'!C6:G6).

4. In cell C7, use a direct link to pull Total Manufacturing Overhead from the Overhead Budget, as shown in Lab Exhibit 9.5.28. The link is =Overhead!O9.

5. In cell D8, sum Direct Materials Used, Direct Manufacturing Labor, and Direct Manufacturing Overhead, as shown in Lab Exhibit 9.5.28. The formula is =SUM(C5:C7).

6. In cell D9, sum Cost of Goods Manufactured and Beginning Finished Goods Inventory to calculate Cost of Goods Available for Sale, as shown in Lab Exhibit 9.5.28. The formula is =D8+D4.

7. In cell D10, use a direct link to pull Total Ending Finished Goods Inventory from the Ending Inventories Budget, as shown in Lab Exhibit 9.5.28. The direct link is ='Ending Inventories Budget'!H9.

8. In cell D11, calculate Cost of Goods Sold by subtracting Ending Finished Goods Inventory from Cost of Goods Available for Sale, as shown in Lab Exhibit 9.5.28. The formula is =D9-D10.

9. The resulting table looks like Lab Exhibit 9.5.29.

Analysis Task #10: Build the Nonmanufacturing Costs Budget

Open the worksheet titled "Nonmanufacturing Costs." Note that all variable and fixed costs are given.

1. In Column C, use the **SUM** function to enter the total number of units to be sold (all types). Use the formula shown in cell C4 of Lab Exhibit 9.5.30 and copy it down to Row 6. The formula is =SUM('Sales Forecast'$C$4:$C$8).
2. In Column F, calculate the Total Cost by summing both the Variable and Fixed portions of each expense, as shown in Lab Exhibit 9.5.30. Use the formula =SUM(D4:E4) in cell F4 and copy it down to Row 6. Then, in cell F7, calculate Total Operating Costs with the formula =SUM(F4:F6).

Lab Exhibit 9.5.30

Microsoft Excel

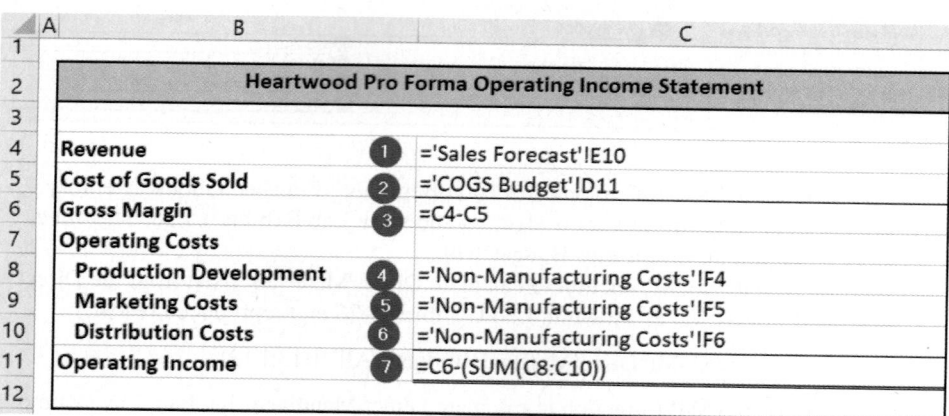

	Units Sold	Variable	Fixed	Total Cost
Product Development	=SUM('Sales Forecast'!$C$4:$C$8)		40000	=SUM(D4:E4)
Marketing	=SUM('Sales Forecast'!$C$4:$C$8)		80000	=SUM(D5:E5)
Distribution	=SUM('Sales Forecast'!$C$4:$C$8)	35000		=SUM(D6:E6)
Total Operating Costs				=SUM(F4:F6)

3. The resulting table looks like Lab Exhibit 9.5.31.

Analysis Task #11: Build the Pro Forma Income Statement

Open the worksheet titled "Pro Forma Income Statement."

Lab Exhibit 9.5.32

Microsoft Excel

Heartwood Pro Forma Operating Income Statement		
Revenue	①	='Sales Forecast'!E10
Cost of Goods Sold	②	='COGS Budget'!D11
Gross Margin	③	=C4-C5
Operating Costs		
Production Development	④	='Non-Manufacturing Costs'!F4
Marketing Costs	⑤	='Non-Manufacturing Costs'!F5
Distribution Costs	⑥	='Non-Manufacturing Costs'!F6
Operating Income	⑦	=C6-(SUM(C8:C10))

1. In cell C4, use a direct link to pull total Revenue from the Sales budget, as shown in Lab Exhibit 9.5.32. The direct link is ='Sales Forecast'!E10.
2. In cell C5, use a direct link to pull COGS from the COGS budget, as shown in Lab Exhibit 9.5.32. The direct link is ='COGS Budget'!D11.
3. In cell C6, subtract COGS from Revenue, as shown in Lab Exhibit 9.5.32. The formula is =C4-C5.
4. In cell C8, use a direct link to pull Production Development costs from the Nonmanufacturing Costs budget, as shown in Lab Exhibit 9.5.32. The direct link is ='Non-Manufacturing Costs'!F4.
5. In cell C9, use a direct link to pull Marketing Costs from the Nonmanufacturing Costs budget, as shown in Lab Exhibit 9.5.32. The direct link is ='Non-Manufacturing Costs'!F5.
6. In cell C10, use a direct link to pull Distribution Costs from the Nonmanufacturing Costs budget, as shown in Lab Exhibit 9.5.32. The direct link is ='Non-Manufacturing Costs'!F6.

7. In cell C11, calculate Operating Income by subtracting the sum of nonmanufacturing costs from Gross Margin, as shown in Lab Exhibit 9.5.32. The formula is =C6-(SUM(C8:C10)).

8. The resulting table looks like Lab Exhibit 9.5.33.

Assessment

1. Take the following screenshots and paste them into a Word document. Name the document "Lab 9.5 Submission.docx."
   - Production Budget
   - Beginning Inventories Budget
   - Bill of Materials
   - Direct Materials Budget–Arch
   - Direct Materials Budget–All
   - Route Sheet and Labor Cost Budget–Arch
   - Route Sheet and Labor Cost Budget–All
   - Overhead Budget
   - Ending Inventories Budget
   - COGS Budget
   - Nonmanufacturing Costs
   - Pro Forma Income Statement

2. Answer the multiple-choice questions in Connect and upload your Lab 9.5 Submission document via Connect if assigned.

Alternate Lab 9.5   Excel—On Your Own

Preparing a Master Budget (Heartwood)

Keywords

Operating Budget, Sales Forecast, Direct Materials Budget, Direct Labor Budget, Overhead Budget, Pro Forma Operating Income Statement

Decision-Making Context

At the beginning of the budget cycle, **Heartwood Cabinets** prepares a master budget and all of the supporting budgets for the division of the company that produces oak cabinets.

In this lab, you will create the budgets and the pro forma operating income statement for the Oak division using the sales forecast and cost data provided in the Excel file **Alt Lab 9.5 Data.xlsx**.

Required

1. Use Excel to build the budgets and operating statements for Heartwood's Oak division.
2. Use formulas and cell references so the numbers flow through the budgets.

Assessment

1. Take the following screenshots and paste them into a Word document. Name the document "Alt Lab 9.5 Submission.docx."
   - Production Budget
   - Beginning Inventories Budget
   - Bill of Materials
   - Direct Materials Budget–Arch

- Direct Materials Budget–All
- Route Sheet and Labor Cost Budget–Arch
- Route Sheet and Labor Cost Budget–All
- Overhead Budget
- Ending Inventories Budget
- COGS Budget
- Nonmanufacturing Costs
- Pro Forma Income Statement

2. Answer the multiple-choice questions in Connect and upload your Alt Lab submission document via Connect if assigned.

Performing Sensitivity Analysis with Excel's Scenario Manager

Data Analytics Type: Predictive Analytics

Lab Note: The tools presented in this lab periodically change. Updated instructions, if applicable, can be found in the student and instructor support materials. All Lab Exhibits are available within the eBook and in Connect.

Keywords

Sensitivity Analysis, Sales Forecast, Product Cost

Decision-Making Context

Rugged Road Outdoors is a start-up company that designs and sells lightweight, high-performing coolers; performance gear; and other outdoor accessories. Products are sold directly to customers through the company's website and through authorized retailers. Because Rugged Road is a start-up, there is a lot of uncertainty around future sales. Sensitivity analysis is particularly important for companies like Rugged Road because it can help management understand the effects of possible or expected changes in operating income.

In this lab, you will perform sensitivity analysis for operating income at Rugged Road.

Required

Use Excel's Scenario Manager to perform sensitivity analyses for operating income at Rugged Road Outdoors assuming:

1. 7 percent increase in sales of coolers.
2. 15 percent decrease in direct labor cost for all products.

Ask the Question

How is Rugged Road's operating income affected by a 7 percent increase in sales of all coolers? How is Rugged Road's operating income affected by a 15 percent decrease in direct labor costs for all products?

Master the Data

The Excel file **Lab 9.6 Data.xlsx** contains the Budgeted Operating Income spreadsheet for Rugged Road with its expected sales for 2027. You see that there are three product categories (Coolers, Apparel, and Accessories) and a total of 18 products for sale. The spreadsheet provides the estimated sales for each product type, as well as the associated sales prices, direct materials costs, and direct labor costs. You will need to use formulas to calculate the Budgeted Operating Income. Then you will use the **Scenario Manager** tool to perform the appropriate sensitivity analyses.

Data Dictionary

Table	Attribute Name	Description	Data Type
Rugged Road Outdoors	Product Category	Quarter begin date	Date
Rugged Road Outdoors	Product Name	Specific product type	Text
Rugged Road Outdoors	Units Sold	Estimated number of units to be sold in the budget period	Numeric
Rugged Road Outdoors	Sales Price	Price for single unit of a given product type	Currency
Rugged Road Outdoors	Direct Materials Cost	Estimated direct materials cost for a single unit of a given product type	Currency
Rugged Road Outdoors	Direct Labor Cost	Estimated direct labor cost for a single unit of a given product type	Currency
Rugged Road Outdoors	Budgeted Operating Income	Estimate of total revenue from sales minus the total cost of direct materials and direct labor required to achieve those sales	Currency

Open Excel file **Lab 9.6 Data.xlsx**. The data will look like Lab Exhibit 9.6.1.

Analysis Task #1: Prepare the Data

1. Use a formula to populate the Budgeted Operating Income column. The appropriate formula is (Units Sold * Sales Price) – (Units Sold * Direct Materials Cost) – (Units Sold * Direct Labor Cost) = Budgeted Operating Income. The formula is shown in cell G3 in Lab Exhibit 9.6.2: =(C3*D3)-(C3*E3)-(C3*F3).

Lab Exhibit 9.6.2

Microsoft Excel

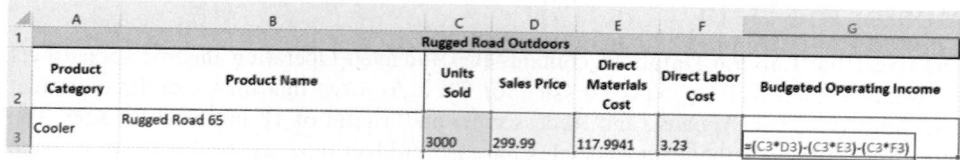

2. Sum the Budgeted Operating Income column at the bottom of the spreadsheet. The resulting table should look like Lab Exhibit 9.6.3.

Analysis Task #2: Use the Scenario Manager

1. Navigate to the **Data > What-If Analysis > Scenario Manager** tool, as shown in Lab Exhibit 9.6.4.
2. Select **Add...**, as shown in Lab Exhibit 9.6.5.
3. Name the scenario "Increase Units Sold - Coolers", as shown in Lab Exhibit 9.6.6.
4. Select cells C3:C5 (the Units Sold cells related to the cooler product category) as the cells that will change, as shown in Lab Exhibit 9.6.6.
5. Enter your name in the comments as shown in Lab Exhibit 9.6.6.

6. Enter the new values for each of the cells in the Units Sold columns and click **OK**, as shown in Lab Exhibit 9.6.7. These new values should correspond with a 7% increase in the amount of each of the cells that are changed. For example, cell C3 will be 3210 (= 3000 * 1.07) and both cells C4 and C5 will be 2410 (= 2000 * 1.07). These correspond to Scenarios 1–3 in Lab Exhibit 9.6.7. Alternatively, you can enter the formulas (so, for cell C3, the formula will be "=3000*1.07").

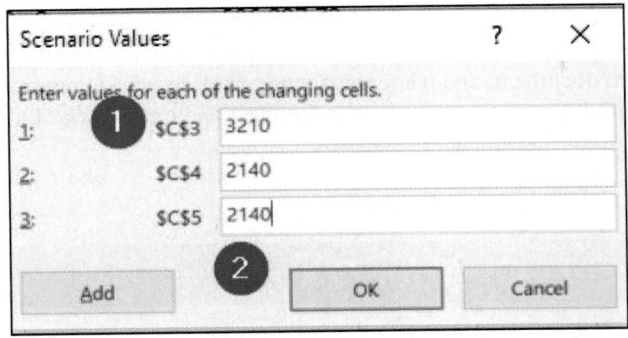

Lab Exhibit 9.6.7

Microsoft Excel

7. The **Scenario Manager** window opens. Select **Summary** (Lab Exhibit 9.6.8).
8. Ensure the **Result cells** field indicates the cell that will be affected by the calculations when you change your inputs, in this case the total budgeted operating income cell (G21). Then click **OK**. (See Lab Exhibit 9.6.9.)
9. View the scenario summary that is generated on a new worksheet in your workbook (see Lab Exhibit 9.6.10).
10. Perform another sensitivity analysis assuming a 15% decrease in direct labor costs for all products. You can use formulas in the **Scenario Manager** to calculate the new values used in the analysis. Lab Exhibit 9.6.11 shows some variations of the formula that will result in a 15% decrease in direct labor costs. (Note that you will need to perform a sensitivity analysis on all of the cooler products. Exhibit 9.6.11 shows five different ways in which you could go about calculating a 15% decrease for each corresponding product.)

Lab Exhibit 9.6.11

Microsoft Excel

Excel will convert your formulas to numbers, as described in the message shown in Lab Exhibit 9.6.12.

The resulting scenario summary should be as shown in Lab Exhibit 9.6.13.

Share the Story

We have now developed sensitivity analyses for Rugged Road Outdoors based on two different scenarios that are likely to occur and could affect budgeted operating income. The analyses show that either scenario will increase operating income. However, increasing the number of units sold results in a 6 percent increase in operating income, while reducing labor costs increases operating income by only 0.44 percent.

Assessment

1. Take a screenshot of the scenario summary containing both sensitivity analyses, paste it into a Word document, and name the document "Lab 9.6 Submission.docx".
2. Answer the multiple-choice questions in Connect and upload your Lab 9.6 Submission.docx via Connect if assigned.

Alternate Lab 9.6   Excel—On Your Own

Performing Sensitivity Analysis with Excel's Scenario Manager

Decision-Making Context

Big Green Egg is one of the world's largest producers and international distributors of the highest-quality ceramic cooking system. The company produces and sells a variety of sizes of its ceramic grill online and through various retail outlets. In this lab, you will perform sensitivity analysis for operating income at Big Green Egg to determine how changes in units sold, sales price, and direct costs are likely to affect operating income.

Required

Use Excel's **Scenario Manager** to perform sensitivity analyses for operating income at Big Green Egg based on data contained in Excel file **Alt Lab 9.6 Data.xlsx**.
   Examine the following three scenarios:

1. 5 percent decrease in sales of large, XL, and 2XL grills as well as a 5 percent increase in sales of medium, minimax, small, and mini grills.
2. A $50 increase in the price of all grills.
3. 5 percent decrease in labor hours for all products and a 2 percent increase in direct materials costs.

To complete this lab, follow the steps in Lab 9.6.

Assessment

1. Take a screenshot of the scenario summary containing all three sensitivity analyses, paste it into a Word document, and name the document "Alt Lab 9.6 Submission.docx".
2. Answer the multiple-choice questions in Connect and upload your Alt Lab 9.6 Submission.docx via Connect if assigned.

Chapter 10

Sales and Direct-Cost Variances

A Look at This Chapter

In this chapter, we use what we know about budgeting to compare budgets to actual performance. First, we learn to calculate static budget variances, which allow companies to examine whether actual performance deviated from expectations set forth in the budget. Next, we investigate why there are deviations between the budget and actual results using two important tools: sales-volume variances and flexible-budget variances. We also discuss how variance analysis is used to motivate and monitor employee performance.

Cost Accounting and Data Analytics

COST ACCOUNTING LEARNING OBJECTIVE	RELATED DATA ANALYTICS LABS	LAB ANALYTICS TYPE(S)
LO 10.1 Explain how organizations establish standard costs.		
LO 10.2 Define variance and explain the different types of variance.		
LO 10.3 Calculate sales variances, price variances, and efficiency variances.	**Data Analytics Mini-Lab:** Analyzing Sales Variances with Tableau	Diagnostic
	LAB 10.1 Excel: Calculating Variance and Using Conditional Formatting	Descriptive, Diagnostic
LO 10.4 Record variances as journal entries using a standard costing system.	**LAB 10.2 Tableau:** Preparing a Sales-Variance Analysis Dashboard (Heartwood)	Diagnostic
	LAB 10.3 Tableau: Preparing a Direct-Cost Variance Analysis Dashboard (Heartwood)	Diagnostic
	LAB 10.4 Power BI: Preparing a Sales-Variance Analysis Dashboard (Heartwood)	Diagnostic
	LAB 10.5 Excel: Preparing a Direct-Cost/ Sales-Variance Analysis Dashboard (Heartwood)	Diagnostic
LO 10.5 Explain how variance analysis is used for performance evaluation and strategic decision making.		

Chapter Concepts and Career Skills

Learning About . . .	Helps with These Career Skills
Standard costs	• Using existing data to establish performance standards
Calculating and analyzing variances	• Understanding the underlying causes of differences between expected and actual performance
Using variances for decision making and control	• Managing and motivating employee performance

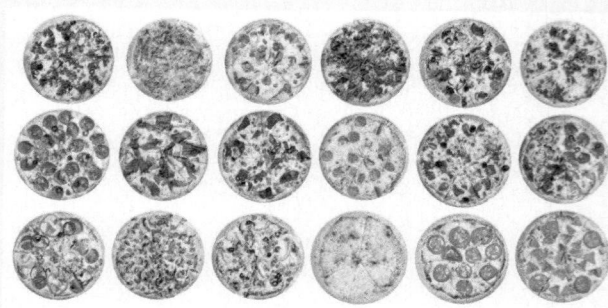

Hihitetlin/Shutterstock

Measuring Variances at Mellow Mushroom

Owning and operating a restaurant is challenging. Profit margins are usually tight, staff turnover is high, and the hours are long. Restaurateurs keep a close eye on food costs and regularly calculate variances—the difference between actual costs and budgeted costs—to improve operating efficiencies and profits.

Consider **Mellow Mushroom**, an Atlanta-based pizza chain. Its menu includes a variety of specialty pizzas, sandwiches, and salads. Like all restaurants, Mellow Mushroom pays close attention to its food costs. It also develops standards for each item it sells, based on the specific measurements of each ingredient for each dish. For example, a large cheese pizza could require:

- 3.5 cups of flour
- 4 teaspoons of yeast
- 2 teaspoons of salt

- 1 tablespoon of olive oil
- 2 tablespoons of parmesan cheese

- 2.5 cups of mozzarella cheese
- 1 cup of pizza sauce

These precise calculations make up the standards for a large cheese pizza. Let's assume the standard cost for this dish totals $2.00. If the pizza chefs follow this recipe exactly, ingredient costs are stable, and there is no waste or shrinkage of ingredients, then the actual cost of preparing one large cheese pizza will be $2.00 and the variance between the standard cost and the actual cost will be $0.

But it is unlikely that everything will always go according to plan. A pizza might be left in the oven too long, and you can't serve a burnt pizza to a customer, so that pizza is scrapped. Maybe, on a busy night, the pizza chef stops using the measuring cup but just sprinkles the cheese on by hand and really uses closer to 3 cups on each pizza. Maybe a member of the kitchen staff trips and spills an entire container of pizza sauce on the floor. These examples of ingredient shrinkage will result in actual food costs exceeding Mellow Mushroom's budget, which is based on the standards prescribed for each menu item. Perhaps, on average, a large cheese pizza really costs $2.55. This 55-cent difference might seem small, but it adds up. If actual costs exceed standard costs by $0.55 per pizza and Mellow Mushroom sells 1,000 pizzas per week, then the difference amounts to $550 in *unexpected* costs per week.

To fix the problem, Mellow Mushroom's management will use variance analysis to identify where actual costs deviate from budgeted expectations. Understanding where problems may be occurring is the first step to improving operations and profitability.

STANDARD COSTS

As described in the Magic Mushroom example, organizations establish standards for the inputs required to produce their products or services. **Standards** are the price, cost, and quantity that the organization has predetermined will be used to produce one unit of output. **Standard costs** are the costs associated with the standard amounts of materials, labor, and fixed and variable overhead required to produce goods and services.

Standard costs are used for:

1. Comparing expected costs with the actual costs associated with production and
2. Planning, controlling, and evaluating performance.

Establishing Standard Costs

Organizations can use a variety of data to determine the standard costs of production, including:

1. Historical data from past periods, including the various factors that were associated with costs in those earlier periods.
2. Data from other companies that produce similar products.
3. Macroeconomic factors, such as inflation, international trade effects, or unemployment.
4. Other factors associated with performance in the past, such as the effects of weather, the political climate, and supply-chain trends.

Importantly, when organizations determine their standards, they are essentially establishing their goals for production. For this reason, management does not simply use the data from prior periods but also considers various circumstances that might affect production. For example, the amount of time it takes to produce a hammock depends on the skill level of the employees involved, the efficiency of the machines, and the quality of the materials. If a machine breaks down, or an employee makes many mistakes, production will likely take longer than if everything is working perfectly. Generally, organizations aim to develop practical standards that are attainable but keep costs as low as possible. These standards allow for some machine downtime and employee rest time, and they are typically based on the effort expected from an efficient but average employee.

Kzenon/Shutterstock

Let's look at a simple example. **Eagles Nest Outfitters (ENO)** produces lightweight, durable outdoor hammocks that are easy to pack and carry with you on your adventures. They have an easy knotless suspension system that allows them to be used almost anywhere. ENO sells direct to customers online and through large retailers such as **Amazon** and **REI**.

ENO calculates the standard costs to produce its hammocks so that it can plan and budget for the appropriate quantity of materials to buy, employees to hire, and time to dedicate to production so that it will meet its expected sales demand.

Exhibit 10.1 shows the total variable costs ENO has calculated to produce each hammock. Total variable costs include direct materials costs, direct manufacturing labor costs, and variable manufacturing overhead costs, as explained in the following paragraphs.

Exhibit 10.1
ENO Standard Variable Cost per Unit

ENO Standard Costs	
Standard Costs	**Variable Cost per Hammock**
Standard Direct Materials Costs	$35.00
Standard Direct Manufacturing Labor Costs	$10.00
Standard Variable Manufacturing Overhead Costs	$12.00
Total Standard Variable Cost	$57.00

To determine standard direct materials costs, ENO uses prior-period data on the amount of material used as well as the cost to purchase these materials from its vendors. Assume that ENO has determined that it needs 4 yards of high-quality nylon fabric to produce a single hammock.

Historically, ENO has paid $8.75 per yard for the fabric, resulting in a standard direct materials cost of:

Standard direct materials cost: 4 yards * $8.75 = $35.00 per hammock

To determine standard direct manufacturing labor costs, ENO uses prior-period data on the amount of time required to produce each hammock and the wages paid to the employees involved in production. ENO has determined that it takes 0.50 hour of employee time to produce a single hammock, and employees are paid $20 per hour. Based on these standards, the standard direct manufacturing labor cost is:

Standard direct manufacturing labor cost: 0.50 hour * $20.00 per hour = $10.00 per hammock

To determine the standard variable manufacturing overhead costs, ENO uses prior-period data on various overhead costs such as utilities, production materials, and wages of nonproduction employees. ENO uses labor hours as the cost driver to apply variable manufacturing overhead and has determined that variable manufacturing overhead is $24.00 per hour. As described previously, each hammock requires 0.50 hour of labor, resulting in a standard variable manufacturing overhead of:

Standard variable manufacturing overhead: 0.50 hour * $24.00 per hour = $12.00

As we'll see in the next section, organizations, including ENO, use these standard costs to evaluate performance by comparing them to the actual costs of producing goods and services.

 PROGRESS CHECK

1. What are standard costs and why do organizations use them?
2. What are the sources of data that organizations use to develop standard costs?
3. What are the benefits of developing accurate standard costs?

DEFINING VARIANCE

In Chapter 9 we learned how organizations use and create budgets to facilitate planning and measure performance. In this chapter, we focus on how organizations compare their budgeted performance to actual performance. A **variance** is the difference between expected performance (from the budget) and actual performance.

How Are Variances Used?

Variance analysis is a form of output control that is used to examine and explain why actual results differ from expected performance, which is based on management-determined standards. Variance analysis is key to helping organizations understand what caused unexpected changes in operating income, whether those factors are controllable, and who should be held accountable.

For example, as the cost of lumber increased dramatically in 2020 and 2021, home-builders saw major decreases in profit. Diminished profits were driven by two key factors: (1) Materials costs were higher than anticipated and (2) revenues decreased because home-owners canceled anticipated projects due to the higher costs. Neither of these variances is easily controlled by the homebuilders. However, after managers have identified why the organization experienced unexpected changes in operating income, they can work to address the underlying issues for the future. In this case, homebuilders could purchase and store a larger supply of extra materials so they do not face shortages in the future, or they could rewrite standard contracts to require larger (nonrefundable) deposits from customers.

Variance Summary

Before we learn how to calculate variances, it is helpful to understand that organizations can examine performance at different levels of disaggregation. The highest level is the least disaggregated and simply compares the difference between the actual and static budget operating income. It answers the following questions: Did our performance meet our expectations? If not, by how much were we off?

Management accountants perform additional analysis to decompose this variance into progressively smaller and smaller components to explore these questions: Where did our performance deviate from our expectations? Why did our performance not meet expectations?

Exhibit 10.2 provides a summary of the variances that management needs to examine. In the following sections, we discuss each of these variance analyses.

> **LO 10.2**
>
> Define variance and explain the different types of variance.

variance
The difference between expected performance (from the budget) and actual performance.

variance analysis
A form of output control that is used to examine and explain why actual results differ from expected performance, which is based on management-determined standards.

CAREER SKILLS
Learning about calculating and analyzing variances supports this career skill:

- Understanding the underlying causes of differences between expected and actual performance

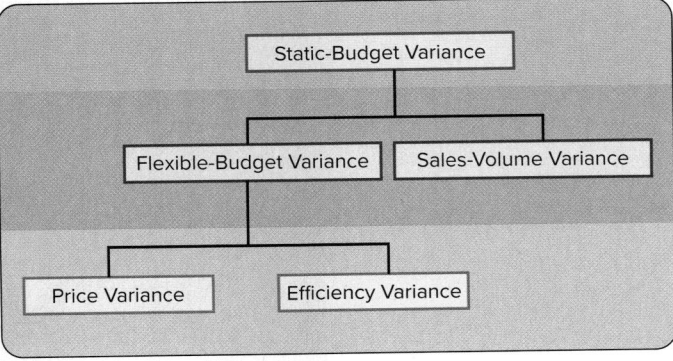

Exhibit 10.2
Variance Summary

Static-Budget Variance Analysis

Recall from Chapter 9 that organizations create a variety of detailed budgets, such as the direct labor budget and materials budget, that roll up to create the master budget. When performing variance analysis, management examines the difference between budgeted and actual performance for each line item on the budgets, as well as the impact of the differences on overall performance.

Organizations are interested in both favorable variances and unfavorable variances. In a **favorable variance**, actual performance is better than the budgeted performance, resulting in a positive impact on operating income. In an **unfavorable variance**, the actual performance is worse than the budgeted performance, resulting in a negative impact on operating income. In the exhibits throughout this chapter, we use **U** to refer to unfavorable variances and **F** to refer to favorable variances.

It is common for organizations to have some favorable variances and some unfavorable variances in the same budget period. For example, the organization may be able to take advantage of sales discounts when purchasing raw materials, resulting in a favorable direct materials budget variance. However, it might also have to pay employees overtime, resulting in an unfavorable direct labor budget variance. The overall impact of all variances on operating income may be positive or negative depending on which variances are larger.

Let's return to our ENO example and assume the following:

1. The only relevant costs are the manufacturing costs (no marketing, shipping, or other costs to consider).
2. All hammocks (units) manufactured are sold during the budget period.
3. There is no beginning or ending direct materials, work-in-process, or finished goods.
4. All types of hammocks require the same amount of materials and labor.

In Chapter 6, you learned that a *cost driver* is a variable that has a causal relationship with cost. In this example, the number of hammocks produced is the cost driver for direct materials, direct manufacturing labor, and variable manufacturing overhead costs. ENO typically sells between 15,000 and 20,000 hammocks per month. Let's consider ENO's budget and actual sales for May of this year:

- Budgeted fixed manufacturing overhead costs for up to 20,000 hammocks $154,000
- Budgeted selling price $99.00 per hammock
- Budgeted production and sales   20,000 hammocks
- Actual production and sales   18,000 hammocks

favorable variance
Occurs when actual performance is better than the budgeted performance, resulting in a positive impact on operating income.

unfavorable variance
Occurs when actual performance is worse than the budgeted performance, resulting in a negative impact on operating income.

Olya Humeniuk/Shutterstock

Recall from Chapter 9 that the master budget is a static budget based on the planned amount of production at the start of the budget period. However, despite an organization's best intentions, results rarely align with plans. There is simply too much uncertainty involved with running a business. The **static-budget variance** is the difference between the actual results and the amounts budgeted in the static budget. Note that the static-budget variance tells us that there is a difference between actual and expected results, but it provides no detailed information about *why* that difference exists.

Exhibit 10.3 compares ENO's budgeted performance (Column 2) with its actual performance (Column 1). The static-budget variance is the difference between these two columns (Column 3).

static-budget variance
The difference between the actual results and the amounts budgeted in the static budget.

ENO Static Budget Variance Analysis May 20XX						
		Actual		Static Budget		Static Budget Variance
Units Sold		18,000		20,000		2,000 U
Revenue	$	1,749,960	$	1,980,000	$	230,040 U
Variable Costs						
Direct Material	$	703,000	$	700,000	$	3,000 F
Direct Labor	$	189,000	$	200,000	$	11,000 F
Variable Manufacturing Overhead	$	220,500	$	240,000	$	19,500 F
Total Variable Costs	$	1,112,500	$	1,140,000	$	27,500 F
Contribution Margin	$	637,460	$	840,000	$	202,540 F
Fixed Manufacturing Overhead	$	167,000	$	154,000	$	13,000 U
Operating Income	$	470,460	$	686,000	$	215,540 U

Exhibit 10.3
ENO Static-Budget Variance Analysis

As the red box in Exhibit 10.3 shows, ENO's operating income shows an unfavorable static-budget variance of $215,540. This overall unfavorable variance is made up of a combination of favorable and unfavorable variances for the various costs and revenues. In particular, revenue has an unfavorable static-budget variance partly because the company sold far fewer units than expected (18,000 hammocks instead of the budgeted 20,000). It will come as no surprise that fewer units sold results in lower operating income.

Also, it appears that the sales price was slightly lower than expected. Budgeted selling price was $99 per hammock. However, when we calculate actual selling price, we see that it was (on average) $97.22.

$$\frac{\text{Revenue}}{\text{Units sold}} = \frac{\$1,749,960}{18,000} = \$97.22$$

You should also notice that ENO has favorable static-budget variances for all the direct variable costs. Why? ENO produced fewer hammocks than expected, and therefore ENO's costs for direct materials, direct labor, and variable manufacturing overhead were lower than expected.

Fixed manufacturing overhead costs (that is, fixed costs) are not sensitive to changes in the number of units produced or sold. However, Exhibit 10.3 shows a difference between actual and standard total fixed costs (13,000 U). Even in the best of circumstances, results may differ from expectations.

Overall, ENO has a $215,540 unfavorable static-budget variance, signifying that actual operating income is $215,540 lower than expected.

 PROGRESS CHECK

4. What is a variance, and how is variance analysis used?
5. Describe the difference between a favorable variance and an unfavorable variance.
6. What circumstances might lead to a positive direct labor variance?

LO 10.3

Calculate sales variances, price variances, and efficiency variances.

USING FLEXIBLE BUDGETS TO UNDERSTAND VARIANCES

The static-budget variance described in the previous section provides high-level analysis to ENO's managers. They can see that operating income was lower than expected and that this outcome was, at least in part, driven by lower-than-expected production and sales prices. But they don't yet have enough information to understand how actual production costs compare to the standards.

flexible budget
A tool that reproduces the budget at various levels of unit sales.

Organizations use flexible budgets to develop a better understanding of *why* cost variances occur. Recall from Chapter 9 that a **flexible budget** calculates expected revenues and costs using the *actual* units produced and sold in a period instead of the *budgeted* units. Flexible budgets allow managers to more accurately compare the actual costs to produce goods or services to the standard costs they had expected.

Let's prepare the flexible budget for ENO using the standard cost data from the previous section, as shown in Exhibit 10.4.

Exhibit 10.4
ENO Hammock Standard Price and Costs

ENO Standards May 20XX	
Total units produced	18,000
Sales price/unit	$99.00
Standard direct materials/unit	4 yards @ $8.75/yd = $35.00
Standard direct labor/unit	0.5 hour @ $20.00/hr = $10.00
Standard variable manufacturing costs	0.5 hour @ $24.00/hr = $12.00
Fixed manufacturing overhead	$154,000.00

Next, Exhibit 10.5 shows the actual results, calculates the flexible budget, and shows the static budget for ENO.

Exhibit 10.5
ENO: Comparison of Budgets to Actual

ENO Actual Results May 20XX		
	Actual Results Calculations	**Actual Results**
Units Sold	Given in Exhibit 10.3	18,000
Revenue	18,000 * $97.22 = $1,749,960	$1,749,960
Variable Costs		—
Direct Materials	Given in Exhibit 10.3	$ 703,000
Direct Labor	Given in Exhibit 10.3	$ 189,000

Variable Manufacturing Overhead	Given in Exhibit 10.3	$ 220,500
Total Variable Costs	Direct Materials Cost + Direct Labor Costs + Variable Manufacturing	$1,112,500
Contribution Margin	Revenue − Total Variable Costs	$ 637,460
Fixed Manufacturing Overhead	Given in Exhibit 10.3	$ 167,000
Operating Income	Revenue − Total Variable Costs − Total Fixed Costs	$ 470,460

ENO Flexible Budget
May 20XX

	Flexible Budget Calculations	Flexible Budget
Units Sold	Given	18,000
Revenue	18,000 * $99.00	$1,782,000
Variable Costs		
Direct Materials	4 yds * $8.75/yd * 18,000 hammocks	$ 630,000
Direct Labor	0.5 hr * $20.00/hr * 18,000 hammocks	$ 180,000
Variable Manufacturing Overhead	0.5 hr * $24.00/hr * 18,000 hammocks	$ 216,000
Total Variable Costs	Direct Materials Costs + Direct Labor Costs + Variable Manufacturing	$1,026,000
Contribution Margin	Revenue − Total Variable Costs	$ 756,000
Fixed Manufacturing Overhead	Given in Exhibit 10.3	$ 154,000
Operating Income	Revenue − Total Variable Costs − Total Fixed Costs	$ 602,000

ENO Static Budget
May 20XX

	Static-Budget Calculations	Static-Budget
Units Sold	Given	20,000
Revenue	20,000 * $99.00	$1,980,000
Variable Costs		
Direct Materials	4 yds * $8.75/yd * 20,000 hammocks	$ 700,000
Direct Labor	0.5 hr * $20.00/hr * 20,000 hammocks	$ 200,000
Variable Manufacturing Overhead	0.5 hr * $24.00/hr * 20,000 hammocks	$ 240,000
Total Variable Costs	Direct Materials Costs + Direct Labor Costs + Variable Manufacturing	$1,140,000
Contribution Margin	Revenue − Total Variable Costs	$ 840,000
Fixed Manufacturing Overhead	Given in Exhibit 10.3	$ 154,000
Operating Income	Revenue − Total Variable Costs − Total Fixed Costs	$ 686,000

Exhibit 10.6 compares the flexible budget to the actual results and the static budget, which allows ENO management to gain a more nuanced understanding of the causes of the $215,540 unfavorable variance.

	Actual Results		Flexible-Budget Variance			Flexible Budget		Sales - Volume Variance		Static Budget
	1		2			3		4		5
Units Sold	18,000		-			18,000		(2,000) U		20,000
Revenue	$ 1,749,960	$	(32,040)	U	$	1,782,000	$	(198,000) U	$	1,980,000
Variable Costs		$	-				$	-		
Direct Material	$ 703,000	$	73,000	U	$	630,000	$	(70,000) F	$	700,000
Direct Labor	$ 189,000	$	9,000	U	$	180,000	$	(20,000) F	$	200,000
Variable Manufacturing Overhead	$ 220,500	$	4,500	U	$	216,000	$	(24,000) F	$	240,000
Total Variable Costs	$ 1,112,500	$	86,500	U	$	1,026,000	$	(114,000) F	$	1,140,000
Contribution Margin	$ 637,460	$	(118,540)	U	$	756,000	$	(84,000) F	$	840,000
Fixed Manufacturing Overhead	$ 167,000	$	13,000	U	$	154,000	$	-	$	154,000
Operating Income	$ 470,460	$	(131,540)	U	$	602,000	$	(84,000) U	$	686,000

ENO Flexible Budget Variance Analysis
May 20XX

1 Flexible budget variance =
$602,000 - $470,460 = $131,540 U

2 Sales volume variance =
$686,000 - $602,000 = $84,000 U

3 Static budget variance = $686,000 - $470,460 = $215,540U

Exhibit 10.6
ENO Flexible-Budget Variance Analysis

As Exhibit 10.6 shows, creating a flexible budget allows ENO to break down the static-budget variance into two components: (1) the flexible-budget variance and (2) the sales-volume variance.

flexible-budget variance
The difference between the actual result and the expected value from the flexible budget.

The **flexible-budget variance** is the difference between the actual result and the expected value from the flexible budget. Remember, to calculate the flexible budget, you use the *actual* number of sales. Therefore, you hold the number of sales constant when calculating the flexible-budget variance. That way, the flexible-budget variance is driven by differences between the actual sales prices and the actual fixed and variable costs, in comparison to the budgeted sales prices, fixed costs, and variable costs.

ENO calculates the flexible-budget variance (Column 2) by subtracting the flexible-budget amounts from the actual results (Column 1 minus Column 3). The flexible-budget variance for operating income is an unfavorable variance of $131,540. Remember, because actual sales are used for both actual results and the flexible budget, flexible-budget variances are caused by per-unit differences between budgeted and actual performance. For instance, in this example, per-unit direct materials and direct labor costs are higher than expected.

sales-volume variance
Calculated by subtracting the static budget from the flexible budget.

Next, consider the **sales-volume variance** (Column 4), which is calculated by subtracting the static budget from the flexible budget (Column 3 minus Column 5). The sales-volume variance holds constant all per-unit costs and revenues at the standard amount. Thus, sales-volume variances are caused entirely by actual sales being higher or lower than budgeted sales. That is, the volume of sales is different from expectations. For ENO, the sales-volume variance for operating income is $84,000, unfavorable.

To reiterate, knowing that ENO has a $215,540 unfavorable static-budget variance for operating income (as calculated at the bottom of Exhibit 10.6) is important, but it provides very little actionable information. Decomposing the static-budget variance into a $131,540 unfavorable flexible-budget variance and an $84,000 unfavorable sales-volume variance provides insight into *why* ENO's performance is different than expected.

Sales Variances

We can apply these same variance analyses to the entire **variable costing income statement** to provide more detailed information to management. This type of income statement allows us to look at variances in revenues (that is, sales variances) and costs separately. Let's start by examining ENO's revenue.

To determine the static-budget variance for revenue, you calculate the difference between actual revenue and the revenue amount in the static budget, as follows:

Static-budget variance for revenue = Budgeted results − Actual results

At ENO:

Static-budget variance for revenue = $1,980,000 − $1,749,960 = $230,040 U

Now that we know that there is an unfavorable variance, we calculate the flexible-budget variance and sales-volume variance to learn more about why actual revenue missed expectations. The flexible-budget variance for revenue is often called the **sales-price variance**. This variance results from differences between the per-unit standard sales price ($99.00) used to calculate the flexible budget for revenue and the actual sales price ($97.22) used to calculate the actual revenue. The sales-price variance is calculated as follows:

Sales-price variance = Actual quantity sold * (Actual price − Standard price)

At ENO:

Sales-price variance = 18,000 * ($97.22 − $99.00) = $32,040 U

It appears that only a small fraction of ENO's static-budget variance for revenue is caused by the lower-than-expected sales price. Therefore, the primary culprit must be lower-than-expected sales, which are indicated by a company's sales-volume variance. Sales-volume variance is calculated as follows:

Sales-volume variance = Standard price * (Actual quantity sold − Budgeted quantity sold)

At ENO:

Sales-volume variance = $99.00 * (18,000 − 20,000) = $198,000 U

Now that ENO has additional information regarding why revenue was lower than expected, its management can try to identify the reason that the sales forecast was inaccurate. There are several possible explanations:

1. The sales team may not have executed the sales plans effectively.
2. Demand for the product may have decreased unexpectedly.
3. Competitors may have entered the market.

variable costing income statement
Income statement that categorizes costs as variable costs or fixed costs and emphasizes contribution margin.

sales-price variance
The flexible-budget variance for revenue; the difference between the per-unit standard sales price and the actual sales price.

In ENO's case, one likely cause is the increasing popularity of ENO outdoor hammocks. As a result, several competitors entered the market, such as **Honest Outfitters** and **Esup**, offering similar products at lower prices. Armed with this information, management can establish a plan to reclaim market share (perhaps with a new marketing campaign) and/or forecast sales more accurately by incorporating its competitors' sales into ENO's sales estimates.

Variance analysis allows management accountants to add value at their employers. Variance analysis provides information that helps companies identify issues and provides insight regarding how performance can be improved. In the following Mini-Lab, you will use Tableau to create visualizations that reveal sales variances at a company that produces fire pits and outdoor stoves.

DATA ANALYTICS MINI-LAB
Analyzing Sales Variances with Tableau

Data Analytics Type: Diagnostic

Lab Note: The tools presented in this lab periodically change. Updated instructions, if applicable, can be found in the student and instructor support materials.

Keywords

Sales Variance, Dashboard

Decision-Making Context

In cost accounting, managers use standards to set expectations for sales and associated revenues for future periods. They compare these standards to actual performance to calculate variances, which help them understand why certain products overperform or underperform.

Assume managers and cost accountants working for **Solo Stoves** want to know how the sales of the company's different fire pit products compared to expectations set forth in the budgets.

Ask the Question

How do actual sales compare to expectations?

Master the Data

The standard and actual cost data are contained in the Excel spreadsheet titled **Mini-Lab 10 Data.xlsx**. It provides the data for each month from July to December 2025. The data fields provided include the following:

Table	Attribute Name	Description	Data Type
Fire Pit Cost Data	Division	Indentifies the division	Text
Fire Pit Cost Data	Product	Identifies the model	Text
Fire Pit Cost Data	Month	Month	Data
Fire Pit Cost Data	Standard Sales Price	Standard price set by management in the static budget	Currency
Fire Pit Cost Data	Standard Units Sold	Number of units expected to be sold during the month	Number
Fire Pit Cost Data	Actual Sales	Actual number of units sold during the month	Number
Fire Pit Cost Data	Actual Sales Price	Actual (average) sales price for units sold during the month	Currency
Fire Pit Cost Data	Standard Units of Input	Standard number of units of raw materials for a single fire pit	Number
Fire Pit Cost Data	Standard Materials Cost per Unit of Input	Standard cost of materials for a single fire pit	Currency
Fire Pit Cost Data	Standard Labor Cost per Hour	Standard labor cost per hour spent in production	Currency
Fire Pit Cost Data	Standard Materials Quantity	Standard quantity of inputs for a single fire pit	Number
Fire Pit Cost Data	Production Budget	Expected number of fire pits to produce during the month	Currency
Fire Pit Cost Data	Standard Labor Hours per Unit	Standard number of labor hours required for a single fire pit	Currency
Fire Pit Cost Data	Actual Production	Actual number of fire pits produced during the month	Number
Fire Pit Cost Data	Actual Materials Quantity	Actual quanitity of inputs used during the month	Number
Fire Pit Cost Data	Actual Materials per Output	Actual quantity of inputs use for a single firepit	Number
Fire Pit Cost Data	Actual Materials Cost per Unit of Input	Actual cost of materials for a single firepit	Currency
Fire Pit Cost Data	Actual Labor Cost per Hour	Actual labor cost per one unit of labor	Currency
Fire Pit Cost Data	Actual Labor Hours per Unit	Actual number of labor hours required for a single fire pit	Number
Fire Pit Cost Data	Actual Labor Hours	Actual number of labor hours used during the month	Number

An example of the data is shown in Exhibit A.

	A	B	C	D	E	F	G	H
1	Division	Product	Month	Standard Sales Price	Standard Units Sold	Actual Sales	Actual Sales Price	Standard Units of Input
2	Fire Pit	Bonfire 2.0	7/1/2025	$ 399.99	75000	88500	$ 250.00	10
3	Fire Pit	Bonfire 2.0	8/1/2025	$ 399.99	75000	73500	$ 275.00	10
4	Fire Pit	Bonfire 2.0	9/1/2025	$ 399.99	75000	82500	$ 300.00	10
5	Fire Pit	Bonfire 2.0	10/1/2025	$ 224.99	80000	64800	$ 224.99	10
6	Fire Pit	Bonfire 2.0	11/1/2025	$ 224.99	85000	96050	$ 224.99	10
7	Fire Pit	Bonfire 2.0	12/1/2025	$ 224.99	85000	79900	$ 224.99	10
8	Fire Pit	Mesa	7/1/2025	$ 129.99	100000	94000	$ 100.00	8
9	Fire Pit	Mesa	8/1/2025	$ 129.99	100000	121000	$ 115.00	8
10	Fire Pit	Mesa	9/1/2025	$ 129.99	100000	109000	$ 115.00	8
11	Fire Pit	Mesa	10/1/2025	$ 129.99	150000	115500	$ 120.00	8
12	Fire Pit	Mesa	11/1/2025	$ 89.99	150000	133500	$ 89.99	8
13	Fire Pit	Mesa	12/1/2025	$ 89.99	150000	126000	$ 89.99	8
14	Fire Pit	Ranger 2.0	7/1/2025	$ 299.99	90000	82800	$ 299.99	6
15	Fire Pit	Ranger 2.0	8/1/2025	$ 299.99	90000	110700	$ 299.99	6

Exhibit A
Example of Sales and Cost Standards and Data for Solo Stove

Microsoft Excel

For this analysis, upload the raw data directly to Tableau. You can do any additional calculations in Tableau.

Perform the Analysis

To analyze the sales variances, create two visualizations.

DATA VISUALIZATION

1. To analyze sales variances, it is useful to first examine the static-budget variance, which is the difference between actual revenue and total revenue.
   - You will first need to create calculated fields for actual revenue and total revenue.
      a. Click on the **Analysis** tab and then select **Create Calculated Field...** from the drop-down menu (as shown in Exhibit B).

Exhibit B
Create Calculated Field

Tableau Software

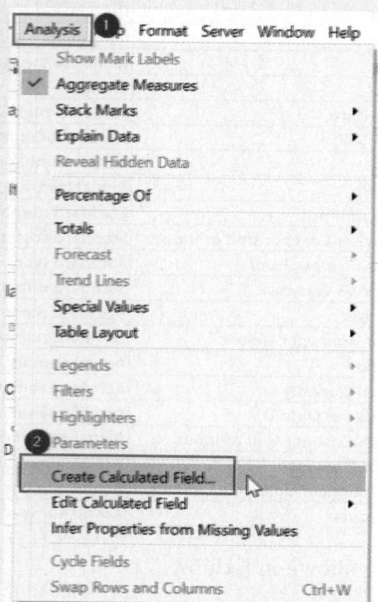

b. Name this new field "Actual Revenue" and enter the following formula in the formula window, as shown in Exhibit C: [Actual Sales]*[Actual Sales Price]. Click **OK**.

Exhibit C
Actual Revenue Calculation

Tableau Software

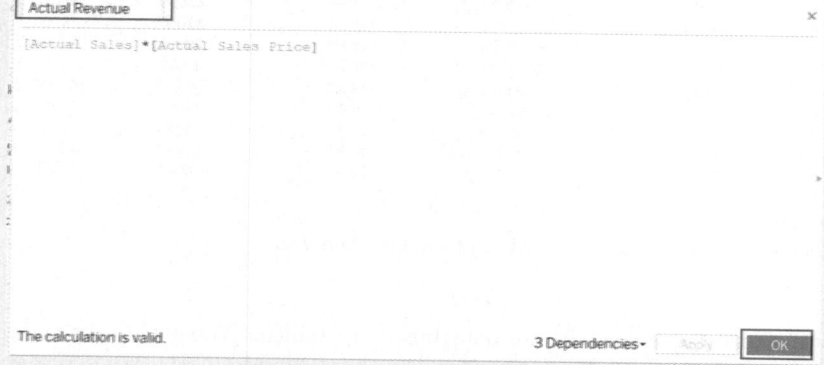

You will see that there is now a new measure on the left side of the screen with a green = sign next to it to signify that it is a calculated field.

c. Repeat this process to create a calculated field for Standard Revenue, as shown in Exhibit D, using the following formula: [Standard Sales Price]*[Standard Units Sold].

Exhibit D
Standard Revenue Calculation

Tableau Software

2. To show the static-budget variance visually, we'll use a bullet graph. Exhibit E shows the first steps for creating a bullet graph.

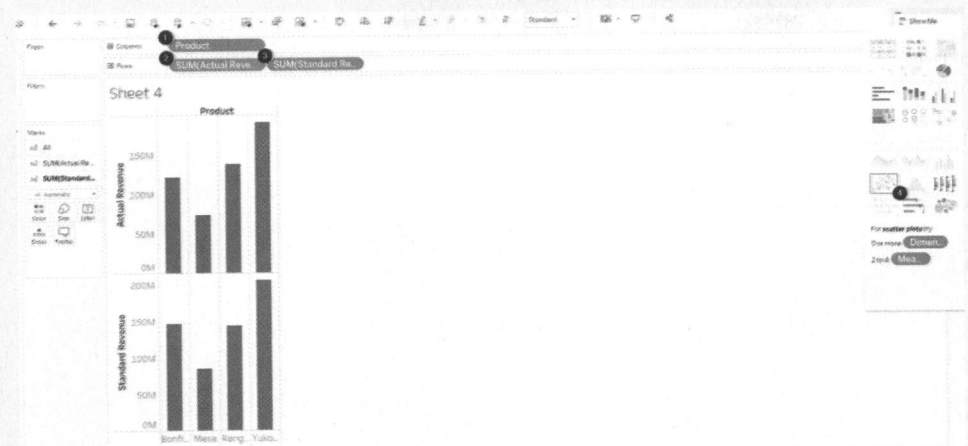

Exhibit E
Standard and
Actual Revenue

Tableau Software

- (1) Drag the **Product** dimension to the **Columns** shelf.
- (2) and (3) Drag **SUM(Actual Revenue)** and **SUM(Standard Revenue)** to the **Rows** shelf.
- (4) Once you have both measures on the **Rows** shelf, the **bullet graph** option will be available for selection from the **Show Me** menu in the upper-right corner of the workspace.
- When you select the bullet graph, Tableau will default to show the actual revenues as the columns with the standard revenues as a target line running horizontally for each column, as shown in Exhibit F. *Note:* You may need to switch rows and columns to make the graph look the way you want.

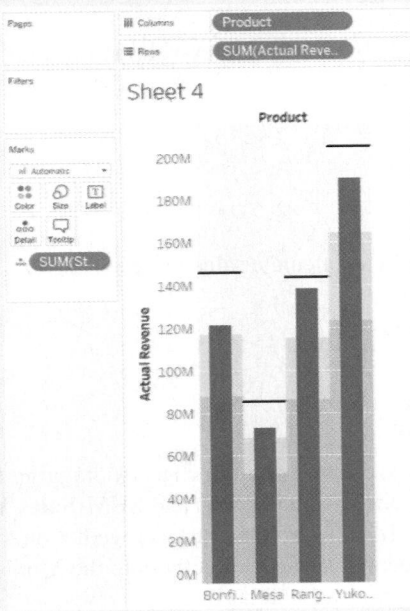

Exhibit F
Bullet Graph for
Static-Budget
Variance

Tableau Software

- You can format the graph as you see fit, changing colors, adding labels, and so on. An example of a finished bullet graph showing the static-budget variance for revenue is shown in Exhibit G.

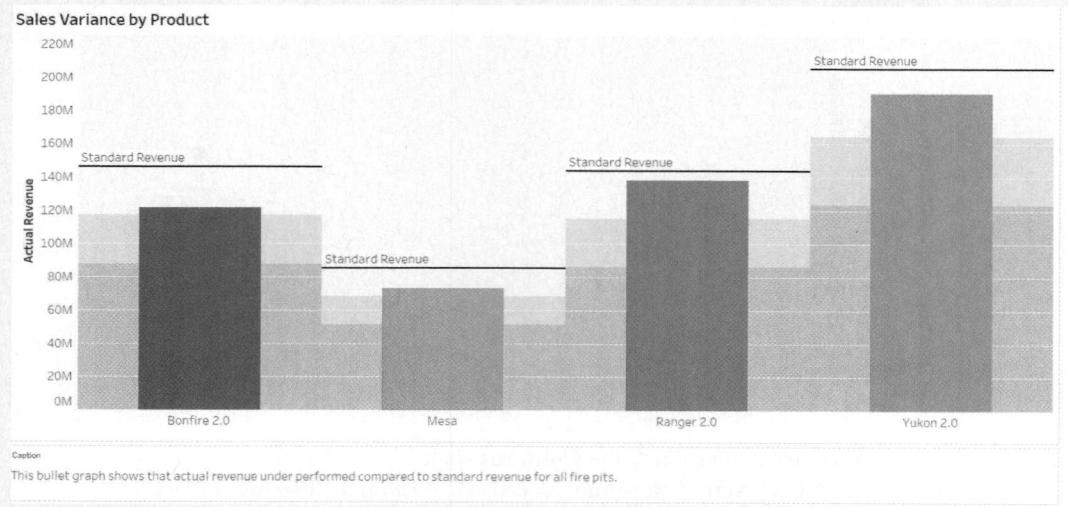

Sales Variance by Product

Caption

This bullet graph shows that actual revenue under performed compared to standard revenue for all fire pits.

Exhibit G
Complete Bullet Graph for Static-Budget Variance

Tableau Software

3. Next, to determine if the unfavorable variances are due to lower-than-planned sales price or sales quantities, examine the sales-price variance and sales-volume variance separately.
   - To examine sales-price variance and sales-volume variance using a visualization, you will need to calculate these variances using Tableau's calculated field function.
   (1) Use this formula to calculate sales-volume variance:

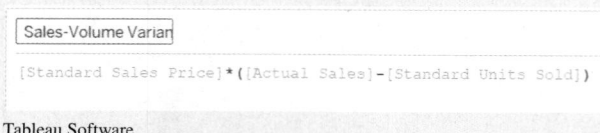

Tableau Software

   (2) Use this formula to calculate sales-price variance:

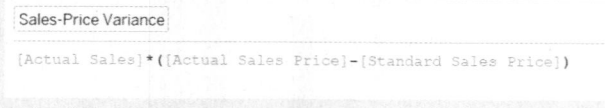

Tableau Software

   - As Exhibit H shows, create a column chart by dragging **Product** to the **Column** shelf and **SUM(Sales-Price)** and **SUM(Sales-Volume)** variances to the **Rows** shelf. To show both variances together on the same graph, drag the pill from the second variance directly onto the Y-axis of the first graph (as shown by the arrow in Exhibit H).

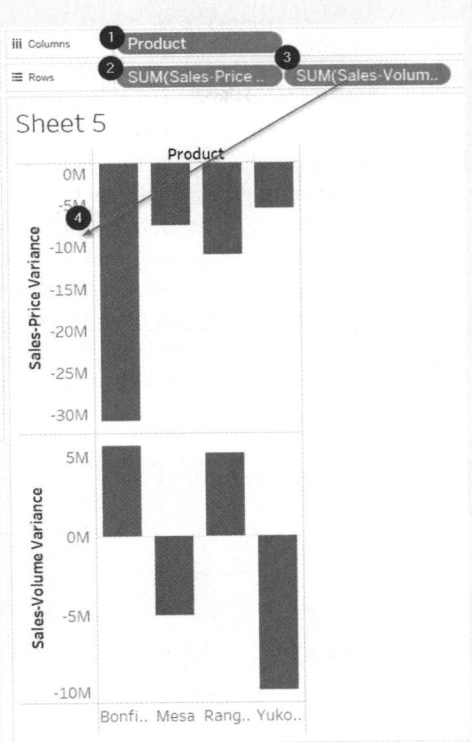

Exhibit H
**Creating a Column
Chart on a Shared
Axis**
Tableau Software

- Format the column chart to show different colors for each variance type and variance totals as needed for clarity. Exhibit I is an example of a finished column chart showing sales-price variance and sales-volume variance.

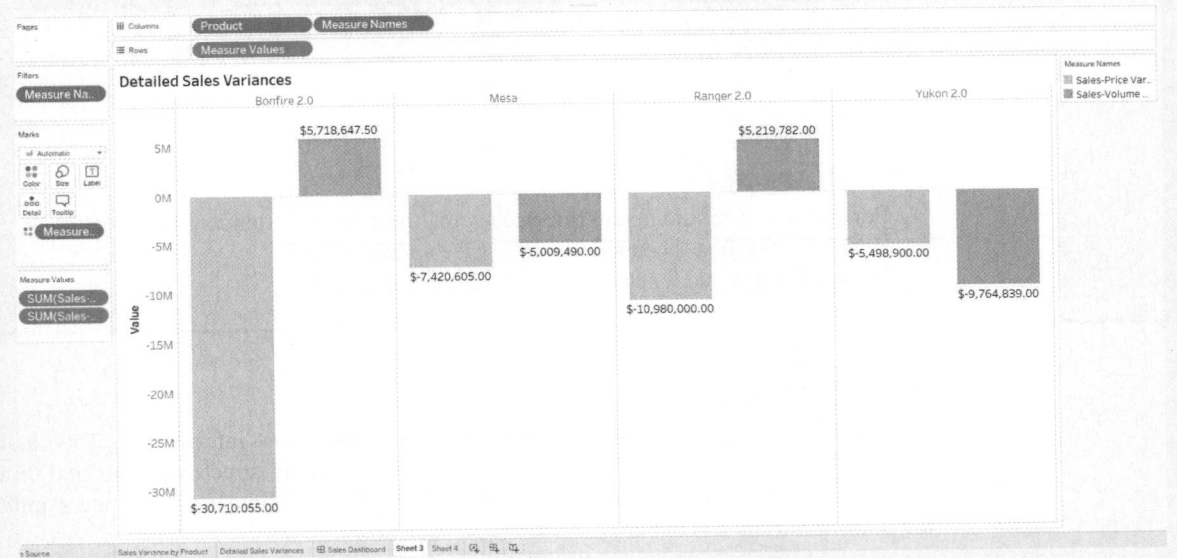

Exhibit I
Sales-Price and Sales-Volume Variance Column Chart
Tableau Software

Share the Story

To share the story, it will be useful to combine both visualizations into a single dashboard like the one shown in Exhibit J. As shown in the Sales Variance by Product visualization, Solo Stoves has an unfavorable static-budget variance for all fire pits. The Detailed Sales Variances visualization shows that this outcome is primarily (but not only) driven by lower-than-standard selling prices for the fire pits, as all models of fire pits have unfavorable sales-price variances. The Bonfire 2.0 and Ranger 2.0, however, reveal favorable sales-volume variances, indicating that they sold more than the expected number of units. The difference in sales prices is reflected on the Solo Stove website, where you can see that many items are discounted during the fall and winter holiday seasons. Lower price points are likely to have been very attractive to customers, as sale numbers have been relatively strong, and Solo Stoves overall boasted a very large increase in sales during the year.

Exhibit J
Final Visualization of Sales Variances

Tableau Software

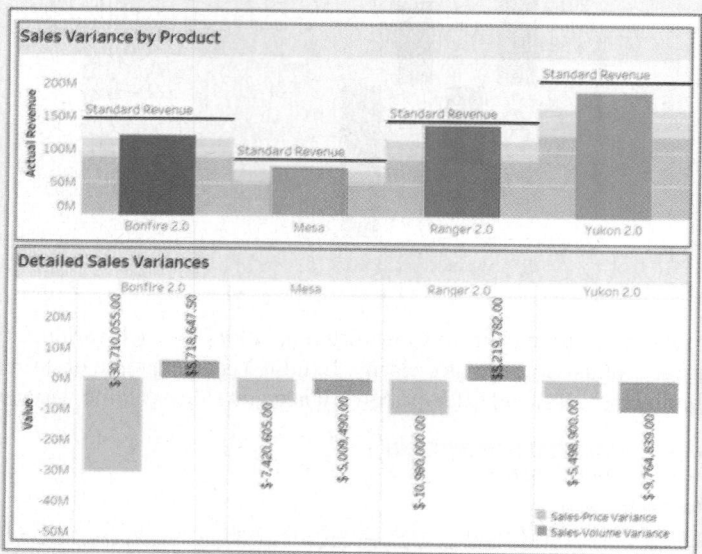

Mini-Lab Assessment

1. For which fire pit did actual revenues come the closest to standard revenues?
2. Which fire pit had the smallest sales-price variance?
3. Which fire pits had a negative sales-volume variance?

Direct-Cost Variances

Companies also use flexible-budget variances to analyze cost information. This analysis is especially important for direct production costs such as direct materials and direct labor. When considering direct-cost variances, management is interested in understanding whether the variance is due to:

- Different-from-expected costs for inputs (for example, higher prices for materials or higher employee wages).
- Different-from-expected use of inputs (for example, more components or labor hours needed to make the product).

Let's examine ENO's direct materials cost. Refer again to Exhibit 10.6. ENO has an unfavorable flexible-budget variance of $73,000 for direct materials. As discussed earlier, this variance is a result of per-hammock differences between the standard costs and the actual results (because the flexible budget is based on actual hammocks sold). For instance, direct materials standards indicate that each hammock should use 4 yards of fabric at $8.75 per yard, for a total cost of $35.00. Actual results indicate a direct materials cost of approximately $39.06 per hammock ($703,000 direct materials costs/18,000 hammocks). Because the amount is higher than the standard, ENO has an unfavorable flexible-budget variance for direct materials. Managers will want to know: Is the problem that ENO's purchase price for raw materials is too high? Or is the problem that ENO is using too much material for each hammock? Maybe inefficient use of material is resulting in **scrap**, which is the term for materials or product that is damaged or deemed unusable during production. Maybe all of these problems are contributing to the cost variance.

scrap
Materials or product that is damaged or deemed unusable during production.

Additional analysis can provide better insight to ENO's managers as they work to investigate this situation and improve future performance. Just as the static-budget variance was decomposed into the flexible-budget and sales-volume variances, the flexible-budget variance for direct materials can be further decomposed into the direct materials price and efficiency variances. Exhibit 10.7 illustrates how these variances are calculated.

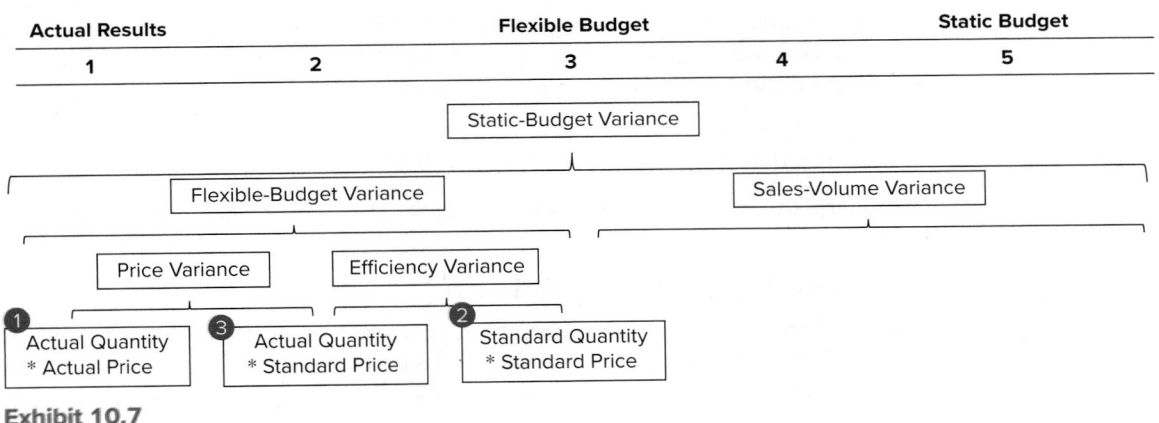

Exhibit 10.7
Calculating Direct Cost Variances
McGraw Hill

In Exhibit 10.7, Columns 1–5 reflect the numbers from the flexible-budget variance analysis shown in Exhibit 10.6. Actual results (red circle 1) are calculated as Actual Quantity * Actual Price, while the flexible budget (red circle 2) is calculated as the Standard Quantity * Standard Price.

To calculate the price and efficiency variances, we can add a box in the column between the actual results and flexible budget (red circle 3), which we calculate by multiplying Actual Quantity by the Standard Price of materials.

Let's examine each variance in turn.

Direct Materials Price Variance

Price variance occurs when the actual price of the inputs to production is different from the budgeted price.

Last period, ENO purchased and used 74,000 yards of material for a total price of $703,000. We can calculate the price per yard at approximately $9.50/yard (= $703,000/74,000).

price variance
Occurs when the actual price of the inputs to production is different from the budgeted price.

As shown in Exhibit 10.7, we calculate the direct materials price variance as:

Direct materials price variance = (Actual quantity purchased * Actual price) − (Actual quantity purchased * Standard price)

This equation can also be written as:

Direct materials price variance = Actual quantity purchased * (Actual price − Standard price)

These are the calculations to determine the direct materials price variance at ENO:

Direct Materials Price Variance Calculations				
Actual quantity		74,000	Actual quantity	74,000
Actual price	$	9.50	Standard price	$ 8.75
		$703,000.00		$ 647,500.00
Direct materials price variance			$55,500.00 U	

Let's examine the direct materials price variance, which is $55,500 unfavorable. This is the difference between the first and second columns in Exhibit 10.7. For this variance, we are holding constant the actual quantity of yards purchased to make ENO's hammocks, and we are allowing the direct materials price to vary. Notice that for this variance, quantity represents *input quantity*, or quantity of yards used. We are not talking about *output* quantity (hammocks), which is always held constant at the actual level of sales.

Because the direct materials cost $9.50 instead of $8.75, we calculate the resulting variance as follows:

Direct materials price variance = 74,000 * ($9.50 − $8.75) = $55,500 unfavorable

We might also refer to the price variance as $0.75 per yard when performing future calculations.

Direct Materials Efficiency Variance

efficiency variance
Occurs when inputs are not used as efficiently as intended.

Efficiency variance occurs when inputs are not used as efficiently as intended. In Exhibit 10.7, the efficiency variance is the difference between Columns 2 and 3. To calculate the efficiency variance, the input price is held constant at the standard price, and the variance is driven by the difference between the actual quantity of inputs used and the standard quantity of inputs that should have been used (see Exhibit 10.4).

Given that ENO produced 18,000 hammocks, the standard quantity of yards of fabric was 72,000 yards (4 yards/unit * 18,000 units). However, in actuality, ENO used 74,000 yards to produce those 18,000 hammocks. This amount is more than was budgeted. This inefficiency results in a $17,500 unfavorable direct materials efficiency variance, as follows:

Direct Materials Efficiency Variance Calculations				
Actual quantity		74,000	Standard quantity	72,000
Standard price	$	8.75	Standard price	$ 8.75
		$647,500.00		$630,000.00
Direct materials efficiency variance			$17,500.00 U	

Because the price per yard of fabric is held constant, the entire difference between these columns is attributable to using more fabric than anticipated.

The direct materials efficiency variance is calculated as follows:

Direct materials efficiency variance = Standard price * (Actual quantity used − Standard quantity)

At ENO:

$$\text{Direct materials efficiency variance} = \$8.75 * (74{,}000 - 72{,}000) = \$17{,}500$$

Referring back to Exhibit 10.6, we see that ENO has a $73,000 unfavorable flexible-budget variance for direct materials. The detailed analyses we just performed reveal an unfavorable price variance of $55,500 and an unfavorable efficiency variance of $17,500. Therefore, it appears that ENO is both paying more than expected for each yard of fabric and using more fabric than anticipated for each hammock.

The same analyses can be used to better understand direct labor costs, as we explain in the next section.

Direct Labor-Price Variance

Exhibit 10.6 shows that ENO has a flexible-budget variance of $9,000 unfavorable for direct labor. Decomposing the flexible-budget variance into its price and efficiency variances provides better information for managers as they seek to understand and improve financial performance.

Last period, ENO used 10,000 hours to produce 18,000 hammocks, for a total cost of $189,000. The standard quantity of hours for 18,000 hammocks is 9,000 (0.5 hour/hammock from Exhibit 10.4) at a cost of $20 per hour. We can use this information to determine the actual price per hour of labor, which is $18.90 (= $189,000/10,000 hours). We can then use these values to determine direct labor-price and efficiency variances, as follows:

Direct Labor-Price Variance Calculation			
Actual quantity	10,000	Actual quantity	10,000
Actual price	$ 18.90	Standard price	$ 20.00
	$189,000.00		$200,000.00
Direct labor-price variance		$11,000.00 F	

The difference between Columns 2 and 3 in Exhibit 10.7 represents the direct labor-price variance. In this case, we are holding constant the quantity of hours used and allowing labor price to vary. The actual cost per hour is $1.10 less than the standard cost per hour, so the resulting $11,000 variance is favorable. The direct labor-price variance is calculated as follows:

$$\text{Direct labor-price variance} = \text{Actual quantity} * (\text{Actual price} - \text{Standard price})$$

At ENO:

$$\text{Direct labor-price variance} = 10{,}000 \text{ hours} * (\$18.90 - \$20.00) = \$11{,}000 \text{ favorable}$$

Direct Labor-Efficiency Variance

Comparing the second and third columns from Exhibit 10.7 allows us to examine the efficiency of direct labor hours while holding constant the cost of labor. ENO's standard quantity of hours needed to produce 18,000 hammocks is 9,000. However, ENO was 1,000 hours over budget, which results in an unfavorable direct labor efficiency variance of $20,000:

Direct Labor-Efficiency Variance Calculation			
Actual quantity	10,000	Standard quantity	9,000
Standard price	$ 20.00	Standard price	$ 20.00
	$200,000.00		$180,000.00
Direct labor-efficiency variance		$20,000.00 U	

The direct labor-efficiency variance is calculated as follows:

Direct labor-efficiency variance = Standard price *
(Actual quantity used − Standard quantity)

At ENO:

Direct labor-efficiency variance = $20.00 * (10,000 − 9,000) = $20,000 unfavorable

This additional analysis indicates that ENO's $9,000 unfavorable flexible-budget variance for direct labor consists of an $11,000 favorable direct labor-price variance and a $20,000 unfavorable direct labor-efficiency variance. While these numbers don't provide precise information regarding the cause of the variance, they do point management in the right direction. Management accountants can speak to the human resources department to determine why average wages are below the standard. It may be the case that less-skilled workers were hired. Speaking with production managers may reveal that less-skilled workers are less efficient than expected, which in turn requires more labor hours than budgeted. Without variances, management would have a much more difficult time determining why labor costs are over budget.

Ⓠ LAB CONNECTIONS

In **LAB 10.1 EXCEL** you will calculate direct-cost variances using an Excel template. You will also apply conditional formatting to automatically set shading to differentiate favorable from unfavorable variances.

✓ PROGRESS CHECK

7. What is the difference between a static budget and a flexible budget?
8. What does the sales-volume variance reflect?
9. What does management learn by deconstructing the flexible-budget variance?

LO 10.4

Record variances as journal entries using a standard costing system.

standard costing system
A costing system in which a standard amount of fixed and variable overhead is allocated to inventory during production.

USING A STANDARD COSTING SYSTEM TO RECORD COSTS AND VARIANCES

A **standard costing system** is a tool (or accounting system) that organizations use to prepare budgets and to record, manage, and control costs. When organizations use standard costing systems, they record transactions based on standard costs, which are the budgeted costs that the organization *expects* to spend as it carries out its activities. Actual costs are also tracked in the standard costing system, and so are the variances that arise when standard cost and actual cost differ.

Organizations use the data from the standard costing system to record journal entries for the cost flows and variances that occur during operations. Standard costing systems use the same types of accounts as regular costing systems.

Let's return to our ENO example to illustrate how journal entries are booked for a company that uses a standard costing system. The general rules are as follows:

- Unfavorable variances are recorded as debits because they decrease operating income.
- Favorable variances are recorded as credits because they increase operating income.

Preparing Journal Entries to Record Direct Materials Price Variance

Recall from our ENO example (refer back to Exhibit 10.4):

- Standard direct materials cost is $8.75 per yard.
- Actual direct materials cost is $9.50 per yard.
- Standard quantity of materials (fabric) for 18,000 units produced is 72,000 yards (18,000 * 4 yards per hammock).
- Actual quantity of materials used is 74,000 yards.

In the first journal entry, the cost accountant will record the cost of the direct materials at the time they are purchased, as follows:

- ENO will debit (increase) the Direct Materials account at the standard price of $8.75 per yard of fabric for the 74,000 yards purchased ($8.75 * 74,000 yards = $647,500).
- ENO will credit (increase) Accounts Payable for the actual price of $9.50 per yard ($9.50 * 74,000 = $703,000).
- ENO will record a debit to Direct Materials Price Variance to reflect the difference of $55,500. Because the actual cost exceeds the standard cost, the result is an unfavorable variance of $3.00 per hammock ($0.75 * 4 yards). Remember, unfavorable variances are always debits because they decrease operating income.

The journal entry is as follows:

Direct Materials Price Variance		
Direct Materials	647,500	
($8.75 per yard * 74,000 yards)		
Direct Materials Price Variance	55,500	
($0.75 per yard * 74,000 yards)		
Accounts Payable		703,000
($9.50 per yard * 74,000 yards)		

Preparing Journal Entries to Record Direct Materials Efficiency Variance

There can be a substantial lag between purchasing raw materials and using those materials in production. For this reason, the direct materials efficiency variance is recorded in a second entry when materials are used.

During the period, ENO used 74,000 yards of fabric to produce 18,000 hammocks. This fabric must be recorded as work-in-process inventory at the standard quantity and the standard cost. ENO should have used 72,000 yards of fabric to produce 18,000 hammocks (18,000 hammocks * 4 yards/hammock). Therefore:

- ENO will debit Work-in-Process for $630,000 (72,000 yards * $8.75 per yard).
- ENO will credit (reduce) Direct Materials by the actual amount of fabric used at the standard price, for a total of $647,500 (74,000 yards * $8.75/yard).
- ENO will record a debit to Direct Materials Efficiency Variance to reflect the unfavorable difference of $17,500.

The journal entry is as follows:

Direct Materials Efficiency Variance		
Work-in-Process	630,000	
($8.75 per yard * 72,000 yards)		
Direct Materials Efficiency Variance	17,500	
($8.75 per yard * 2,000 yards)		
Direct Materials		647,500
($8.75 per yard * 74,000 yards)		

Preparing Journal Entries to Record Direct Labor Variances

Price and efficiency variances are recorded simultaneously for direct labor at the time labor is used. Recall from our earlier example (Exhibit 10.4) that standard labor cost is $20.00 per hour and standard labor hours are 30 minutes per hammock (or 0.5 hour per hammock). In addition:

- Actual direct labor cost for last period was $18.90 per hour.
- Standard quantity of labor (hours) for 18,000 units produced is 9,000 hours (18,000 * 0.5 hour per hammock).
- Actual quantity of labor hours used is 10,000.

The cost accountant will record the cost of direct labor, including the direct labor-price and efficiency variances, at the time it is used as follows:

- ENO will increase the Work-in-Process account with a debit using the standard labor cost (wages) and standard labor hours. Thus, Work-in-Process will be debited for $180,000 (9,000 hours * $20.00/hour).
- ENO will credit Wages Payable for the actual amount owed to workers, for a total of $189,000 (10,000 hours * $18.90/hour).
- ENO will credit Direct Labor-Price Variance for $11,000 to reflect its favorable variance.
- ENO will debit Direct Labor-Efficiency Variance for $20,000 to reflect its unfavorable variance.

ENO records the following entry:

Direct Labor Variance		
Work-in-Process	180,000	
(18,000 units * 0.50 hour * $20.00 per hour)		
Direct Labor-Efficiency Variance	20,000	
(1,000 hours * 20.00 per hour)		
Direct Labor-Price Variance		11,000
(10,000 hours * $1.10 per hour)		
Wages Payable		189,000
($18.90 per hour * 10,000 hours)		

Preparing Journal Entries to Close Out Variances at Period-End

ENO will also record overhead costs and associated variances. We discuss those topics in Chapter 11, so we'll skip them for now.

At the end of production, if most of the production costs are for units that have been completed and sold during the period (which is often the case, and is the case at ENO), cost accountants will need to adjust the cost of goods sold to account for the variances. For example, ENO had unfavorable direct materials variances at the end of the period, which means the COGS was higher than anticipated. Thus, the COGS balance should be increased by the amount of the variances, which will zero out the variances balances at the end of each period.

Also, as we've seen, ENO had a favorable labor-price variance and an unfavorable labor-efficiency variance. Therefore, ENO has some favorable variances and some unfavorable variances during the same time period. Overall, however, the favorable and unfavorable variances net out to require an increase to COGS for the net amount of the variances. ENO will record the following entry to write off the balances to Cost of Goods Sold:

Closing Entries		
Cost of Goods Sold	82,000	
Direct Labor-Price Variance	11,000	
($1.10 per hour * 10,000 hours)		
Direct Materials Price Variance		55,500
($0.75 * 74,000 yards purchased)		
Direct Materials Efficiency Variance		17,500
($8.75 per unit * 2.000 units)		
Direct Labor-Efficiency Variance		20,000
(1,000 hours * 20.00 per hour)		

If, however, a material amount of production costs are still in-process or finished goods, variances should be prorated across WIP inventory, finished goods inventory, and COGS accounts. This prorated approach requires slightly more calculation, but it more accurately accounts for the cost variances that are not associated only with sold units. This approach is similar to the approach used to dispose of overallocated inventory (see Chapter 4).

LAB CONNECTIONS

A variance dashboard is a helpful tool that managers can use to track, analyze, and visualize variances.
- In **LAB 10.2** you will prepare a sales-variance dashboard in Tableau.
- In **LAB 10.3** you will prepare a cost-variance dashboard in Tableau.
- In **LAB 10.4** you will prepare a sales-variance analysis in Power BI.
- In **LAB 10.5** you will prepare a direct-cost/sales-variance analysis dashboard in Excel.

PROGRESS CHECK

10. What does a price variance indicate? Imagine that ENO had a favorable direct materials price variance of $1.00 per hammock. What might be some of the reasons (good and bad) that could explain that variance?
11. What does an efficiency variance indicate? Provide two causes of negative efficiency variances.
12. What is a standard cost?
13. What is a standard costing system, and how is it used to record variances?

HUMAN DIMENSIONS: USING VARIANCE ANALYSIS FOR DECISION MAKING AND CONTROL

We've learned how variance analysis is performed and that it is often one of the initial steps to ensure operating processes are in control. Variances signal that something is not going according to plan. They help management identify the underlying problems that could be occurring and provide a starting point for remediating issues. Overall, variance analysis allows management to look backward to see what has happened and to use that information to make changes in the future.

When Should Management Investigate a Variance?

When organizations have accurate data with which to develop budgets, well-running machines, and efficient personnel, variances may be very small. However, it is unlikely that there will be no difference between the budget and actual numbers for all numbers. So, should management investigate every variance? Probably not. Organizations generally establish thresholds or subjective standards for when a variance is acceptable and when it is out of control and must be examined.

Organizations may set dollar limits or a percentage of budgets that are outside of the acceptable range and therefore trigger an investigation. In addition, they can set different thresholds for investigation for different parts of the budget. For example, a materials variance that exceeds 5 percent of the budgeted cost could trigger an investigation, but any selling-price variance might warrant review. Management sets these thresholds strategically, keeping in mind that it costs time and money to have management accountants and operating employees working to identify the driver of a variance.

Variance Analysis as a Performance Measurement Tool

Generally, unfavorable variances indicate that a process is costing more money and/or taking more time than expected. Favorable variances suggest the company is saving money or working more efficiently. For these reasons, management can use the results of a variance analysis as a key input to a performance evaluation for a division or employee. For example, at **Heartwood Cabinets**, the manager of the Pine division may be evaluated based on his ability to meet or exceed sales targets and keep variable costs low. The results of variance analysis can be a useful input to determining whether he has met performance expectations.

However, reality is more complicated. The fact that the manager has favorable variances does not mean that everything is operating as Heartwood would like. What if the Pine manager has favorable materials cost budgets because he is buying pine from a lower-cost provider whose pine boards are not of the same quality as other suppliers' pine? Maybe the division saves money today—resulting in a favorable variance—but in the long run, if Heartwood's product quality declines, it will make fewer sales as customers become disappointed and purchase from competitors instead.

In short, variance analysis can provide useful insights into how a manager or division is performing, but organizations cannot rely on only one or a few measures for performance evaluations and rewards. Instead, organizations must examine the interactions among the different dimensions of operations to ensure that performance measures are eliciting behavior consistent with the organization's goals. We discuss this topic in more detail when we examine the balanced scorecard in Chapter 12.

Variance Analysis for Strategic Decision Making

Sometimes variances help organizations detect shifts in the economic environment. For example, a negative sales variance for used cars at **Carvana** may suggest an impending recession.

Increased labor costs at **Caterpillar** may suggest that changes in unemployment and other government benefits might be influencing the hourly wage demanded by skilled laborers.

These clues can help organizations identify new programs to implement, potential new or different products to offer, or the need for different suppliers. In other words, variances can help spur strategic decision making as management examines the root causes of the unexpected differences.

Matthew Lloyd/Bloomberg/Getty Images

Variance Analysis for Nonmanufacturing Organizations

Most of the examples in this chapter have described variance analysis in a manufacturing organization. But variance analysis is a useful tool for any organization. Recall that a variance is just the difference between the actual and the expectation. This difference is important for managing the revenues and costs of any organization. For example, at the Big 4 accounting firm **PwC**, each audit partner establishes targets for the revenue to be generated from the audit procedures at each client during the period. This revenue target takes into account a detailed budget of the hours of staff labor that will be used to complete the audit. At the end of each project, or at key milestones during a project, the partner will review the variances between budgets and actuals to determine whether the project is progressing as intended.

FROM THE FIELD

"Eating Time": Underreporting Costs

In service organizations, such as public accounting firms, time budgets are very important tools for managing employee activities and the revenue generated for each job. For repeat clients, managers often use last year's budget to establish expectations and guidelines for this year's job. Audit staff will carefully book each hour they work to specific charge codes that all roll up into the overall budget. For example, one audit staff member may spend 3 hours working on the payroll account on Monday and 8 hours working on accounts payable on Tuesday. If staff charge more than the expected number of hours to a specific charge code, these charges will be easily identified as an unfavorable efficiency variance that will increase

ETHICS

the cost of doing the audit and reduce the profit generated by the job (which may impact the partner's ability to meet her profit targets for her performance review). Sometimes staff members feel pressure *not* to record their time accurately if they take longer than budgeted so that they do not have an unfavorable variance. One of the authors was asked to do this on a consulting engagement for a new client. This underreporting is called "eating time" and, although it allows the job to meet the budget this period, it can create big problems in the future.

Thinking Critically

What types of problems do you think eating time can cause for an auditing firm, and what are the implications when a manager starts with the prior-year budget to create the current-year budget? Do you think it is ethical for staff to eat time? Is it ethical for managers and partners to ask staff to eat time?

DATA VISUALIZATION

Using Data to Improve Budgeting

As we've discussed, sometimes variances occur because of unexpected changes in the cost of or access to labor and materials or unanticipated changes in sales. Organizations can often use data and data analytics to make more accurate budgets, which will improve decision making and operations, and most likely reduce variances in the future.

For example, organizations may want to leverage historical information to identify when *unexpected changes* are really cyclical trends that occur periodically, and can therefore be predicted. Let's look at the dashboard in Exhibit 10.8. These visualizations were created in Tableau using annual cost data tracked in Excel.

Exhibit 10.8
Materials Cost Dashboard

Tableau Software

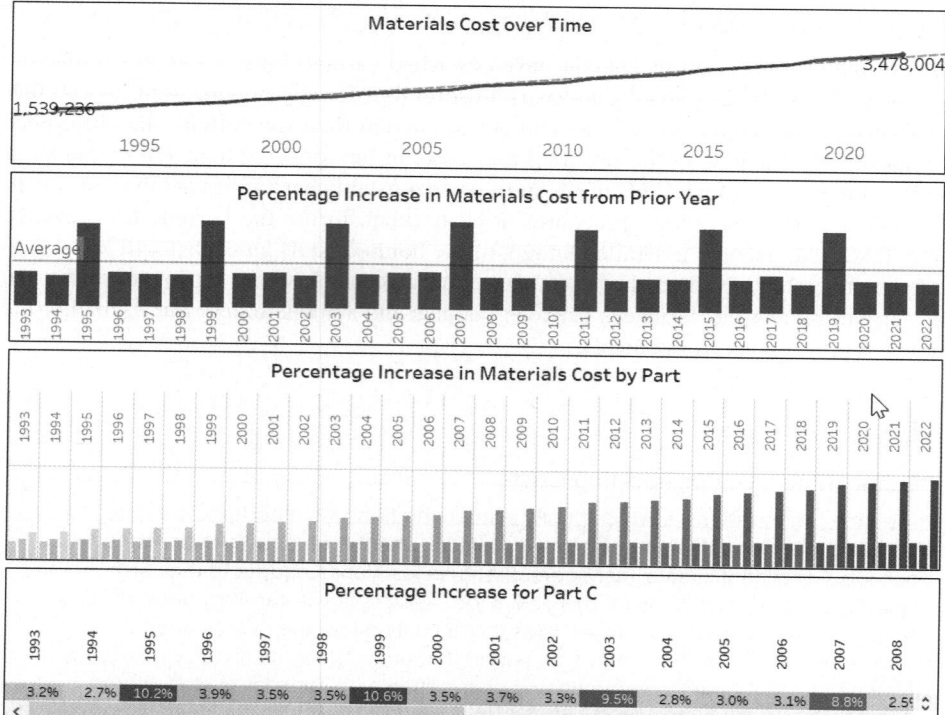

The first visualization is a line graph that shows that materials cost has increased pretty steadily since the start of data collection in 1992. The average increase in materials cost is 2.7 percent per year. Based on this analysis, management will likely estimate an increase in materials cost of approximately 2.7 percent for the next year.

The bar chart in the second visualization illustrates the percentage increase in materials cost in each year and shows a pretty clear pattern, with a much larger increase in materials cost every fourth year. The average line shows that, consistent with our calculations in the first visualization, the average annual increase is about 2.7 percent, but generally the pattern is three years of approximately 2 percent increases and a 5 percent increase every fourth year.

The third visualization disaggregates the data further to investigate materials-cost changes by component part. Here we see that most of the cost increase is driven by part C, shown in blue. While the costs of parts A and B remain relatively stable over time, we see that part C increases over time.

The fourth visualization analyzes part C, in particular, and uses a heat map with variation in color saturation indicating greater percentage increase in cost over time. From this visualization, we can see that the cost for part C has a modest increase in years 1–3 of around 3 percent, followed by a large cost increase (approximately 9 to 11 percent) in the fourth year.

By disaggregating the data and analyzing them carefully, managers can make more precise budgets that provide better control over costs and fewer surprises. Now, instead of simply budgeting for about a 2.7 percent increase in total materials cost each year, and managing the resulting variances, the organization can budget for 2 percent increases in years 1–3 and a 5 percent increase in year 4. Further, the organization may work to reduce the cost of part C, which is the primary driver of materials cost increases.

Organizations may also leverage other features of interactive dashboards that can make them particularly useful. For example:

- Dashboards can be connected to live data so that they are updated in real time, keeping managers apprised of any changes and helping them make decisions based on current information.
- Dashboards can integrate data from a variety of sources and platforms both internal and external to the organization. Integrating data from various sources gives management a comprehensive view of performance and facilitates a holistic analysis.
- Dashboards can be configured with alerts and notifications based on predetermined conditions and benchmarks, allowing management to deal with problems as soon as they occur.
- Dashboards can incorporate forecasting and goal-tracking features that facilitate comparison between actual and desired performance.

Jobs with Variance Analysis Responsibilities

You now understand what variances are and why they are used. But what kinds of jobs have responsibilities related to variances and variance analysis? Many people in an organization are involved in variance analysis. For example, purchasing managers are responsible for identifying materials quantity and labor efficiency variances, and individuals from the sales department have the input necessary to calculate and examine the sales-related variances. Of course, accounting supervisors, including controllers, have oversight responsibilities for all variances and helping the organization make decisions related to improving variances once they are identified.

Exhibit 10.9 reproduces a job posting from a site like **ZipRecruiter.com** or **LinkedIn.com** for a Business Analysis Manager at an international coffee giant like **Starbucks**, **Costa Coffee**, or **Dunkin'**. The employee who is hired for this position will have responsibilities for developing price and cost standards, as well as calculating and evaluating variances. That person is also responsible for communicating this information to others in the organization. As the job listing indicates, the ideal candidate for this position has strong knowledge of cost accounting, as well as keen data-analysis skills. According to **Glassdoor.com**, salaries for positions like these start in the $90,000 range. A job like this might just be the wake-up you need!

Exhibit 10.9
Business Analysis Job Opportunity

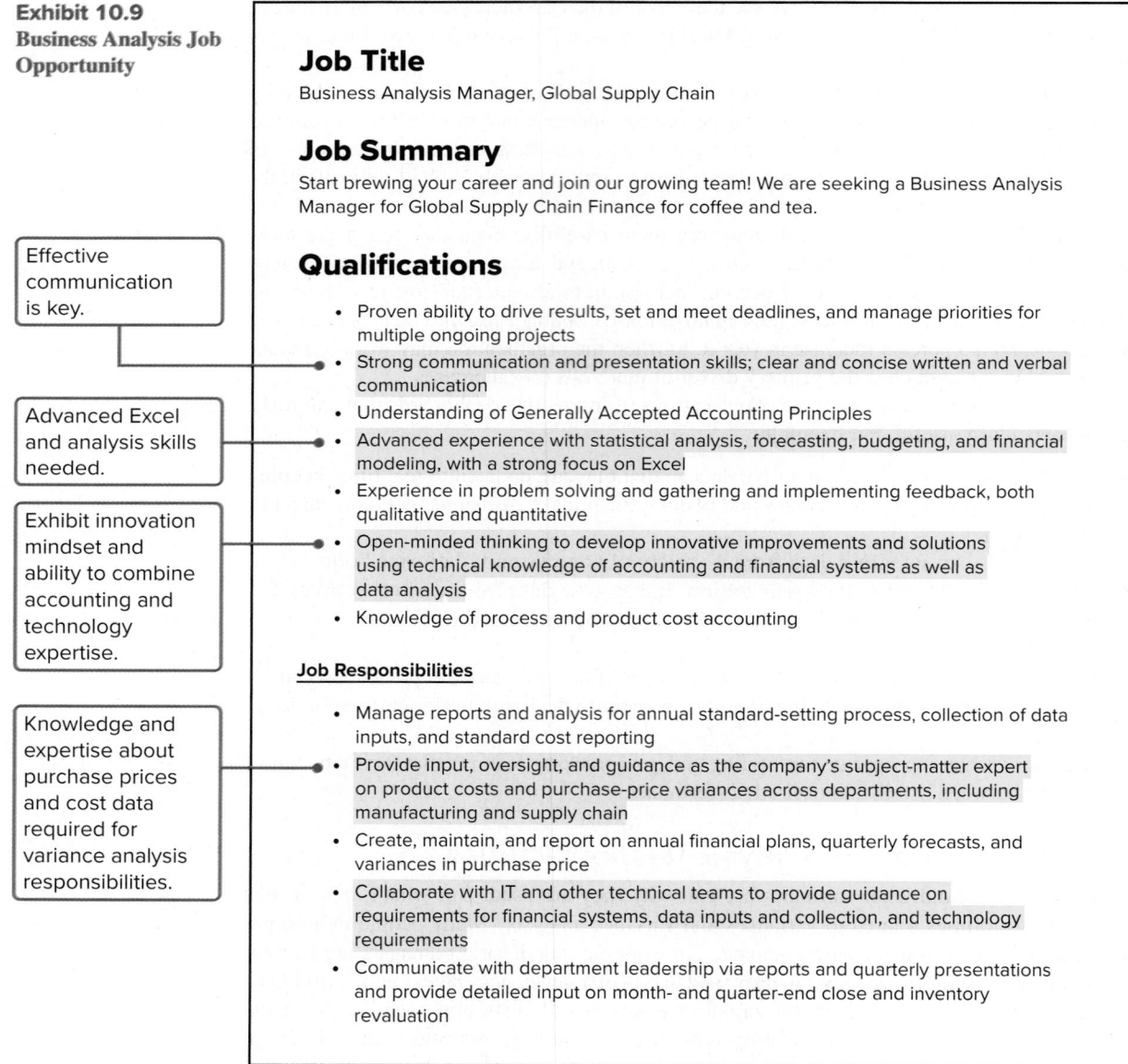

Effective communication is key.

Advanced Excel and analysis skills needed.

Exhibit innovation mindset and ability to combine accounting and technology expertise.

Knowledge and expertise about purchase prices and cost data required for variance analysis responsibilities.

Job Title
Business Analysis Manager, Global Supply Chain

Job Summary
Start brewing your career and join our growing team! We are seeking a Business Analysis Manager for Global Supply Chain Finance for coffee and tea.

Qualifications

- Proven ability to drive results, set and meet deadlines, and manage priorities for multiple ongoing projects
- Strong communication and presentation skills; clear and concise written and verbal communication
- Understanding of Generally Accepted Accounting Principles
- Advanced experience with statistical analysis, forecasting, budgeting, and financial modeling, with a strong focus on Excel
- Experience in problem solving and gathering and implementing feedback, both qualitative and quantitative
- Open-minded thinking to develop innovative improvements and solutions using technical knowledge of accounting and financial systems as well as data analysis
- Knowledge of process and product cost accounting

Job Responsibilities

- Manage reports and analysis for annual standard-setting process, collection of data inputs, and standard cost reporting
- Provide input, oversight, and guidance as the company's subject-matter expert on product costs and purchase-price variances across departments, including manufacturing and supply chain
- Create, maintain, and report on annual financial plans, quarterly forecasts, and variances in purchase price
- Collaborate with IT and other technical teams to provide guidance on requirements for financial systems, data inputs and collection, and technology requirements
- Communicate with department leadership via reports and quarterly presentations and provide detailed input on month- and quarter-end close and inventory revaluation

✓ PROGRESS CHECK

14. What do organizations need to consider if they are using variance analysis for performance evaluations?

15. Explain how variances provide input for strategic decision making.

16. Exhibit 10.8 reveals that by examining more granular data about operations, an organization can improve its budgeting and decision making. In this example, the company learned that materials costs are cyclical by examining the difference in cost year over year. Further, the largest increases are driven by a single input, part C. What other variables might the company consider that could reveal additional insights into how it could better plan for cost changes in the future?

Key Takeaways: Variance Analysis

In this chapter, we learned how to calculate budget variances for revenues and direct costs. We also considered how and why management uses variances for planning and control. Variances are important output controls that help organizations look back at performance to consider what worked well and what went wrong. They can guide decision making as management takes corrective actions to fix inefficiencies or other problems and can help identify strategic decisions that can improve operations in the future.

The process for identifying and evaluating variances includes all aspects of the AMPS model:

Ask the Question

■ **Which question(s) does management want to answer?**

Did our performance meet expectations? Why did actual performance differ from our standards?

Manage the Data

■ **Which data are appropriate to address management's questions?**

Organizations establish standards for the amount of goods or services they intend to produce, as well as the costs for production. They use historical data, industry data, cost data from their suppliers, and salary data from their human resources department to develop these standards. Actual cost and sales data are obtained from operations throughout the period.

Perform the Analysis

■ **Which analytics are performed to address management questions?**

Variance analysis is a relatively simple comparison between budgeted and actual figures. Organizations often establish thresholds for when variances are so large that management should investigate the differences. Data-driven dashboards allow managers to monitor variances to determine whether they have exceeded those thresholds.

Share the Story

■ **How are the results of the analytics shared with stakeholders?**

Employees are often held accountable for meeting the standards set by the organization. Thus, variance analysis is a useful tool to share during performance evaluations. Variance analyses can be used as teaching tools, to help employees see where there may be inefficiencies, as well as to determine whether employees will receive a salary increase and/or a bonus.

Key Terms

efficiency variance	price variance	standard costing system	unfavorable variance
favorable variance	sales-price variance		variable costing income statement
flexible budget	sales-volume variance	standard costs	
flexible-budget variance		standards	variance
	scrap	static-budget variance	variance analysis

⊘ ANSWERS TO PROGRESS CHECKS

1. Standard costs are the costs associated with producing a good or service. Organizations estimate them before the period and use them to evaluate performance. Usually, organizations estimate standard costs for direct labor, direct materials, variable overhead, and fixed overhead.

2. Organizations can use data from various sources to develop standards. Often, organizations use historical data. However, more accurate standards can be developed if organizations use additional data such as data from other companies in the industry, macroeconomic factors, and other factors that have been found to be associated with performance in the past (such as the effects of weather, the political climate, and supply-chain trends).

3. More accurate standards provide effective benchmarks to which organizations can compare performance. Variance analysis is useful for comparing budget to actual performance, but it is meaningful only if the budgets reflect real and attainable goals.

4. A variance is the difference between expected performance and actual performance. It helps management identify where actual costs deviate from budgeted expectations and evaluate its options for saving money.

5. The difference between a favorable variance and an unfavorable variance is the direction of impact on operating income. A favorable variance results in increased operating income, which is a positive impact. An unfavorable variance results in decreased operating income, which is a negative impact.

6. A positive direct labor variance indicates that the organization spent less money on direct labor than expected. Potential reasons include the job taking less time or requiring fewer people than expected. A positive direct labor variance also may arise if employees are paid a lower wage than the company expected.

7. A static budget is set at the beginning of the period and does not change until the budget period is over; a flexible budget reproduces the budget at various levels of unit sales.

8. The sales-volume variance reflects the difference between actual sales and budgeted sales.

9. A flexible-budget variance can be deconstructed into both a price variance and an efficiency variance. Both provide insight into *why* performance is different than expected.

10. A price variance indicates a difference between the per-unit standard sales price and the actual sales price.

   ENO might have a favorable price variance for a variety of reasons. Possible positive explanations include:

   - The purchasing manager may have negotiated a better price with existing suppliers.
   - The purchasing manager may have leveraged quantity discounts.
   - ENO may have found a lower-priced supplier.
   - Direct materials costs may have been reduced due to market or economic factors (such as oversupply).

   Possible negative explanations include:

   - The budgeted figures were not accurate.
   - The direct materials that are now being used are less expensive because they are of lower quality.

   To really understand the cause of a variance (positive or negative), the manager will need to dig into the data and have discussions with the staff to understand what has happened.

11. An efficiency variance indicates that inputs are not used as efficiently as intended. Two causes of negative efficiency variances are (1) damaged materials resulting in scrap and (2) increased required labor to produce a product.

12. A standard cost is the predetermined cost for one unit of output.

13. A standard costing system is a tool or accounting system that organizations use to prepare budgets and to record, manage, and control costs. Organizations record transactions based on standard costs. Actual costs are also tracked, and the variances between standard and actual costs are calculated.

14. When using variance analysis for performance evaluations, organizations must examine the interactions among the different dimensions of operations to ensure that performance measures are eliciting behavior consistent with the organization's goals.

15. Variances can provide input for strategic decision making as management examines the root causes of the unexpected results. For example, a variance can help organizations detect shifts in the economic environment in which they operate.

16. The company could consider the vendors supplying part C. Perhaps the major cost increases are driven by one vendor or a small group of vendors, and the company could achieve cost savings by using a different vendor. The company might also consider the purchasing agent(s) responsible for the purchasing agreements. Perhaps certain negotiation tactics can improve budgeting. The company might be able to lock in a longer-term price with the suppliers of part C that could smooth prices over time.

Multiple-Choice Questions Mc Graw Hill connect

1. (LO10.1) **Phickles Pickles**, a family-owned business, purchases cucumbers, carrots, okra, and other vegetables for pickling from a local farm in northeast Georgia. The standard cost for these raw materials is $6.00 per pound. Phickles usually purchases 1,250 pounds of veggies each spring. Due to drought conditions all winter, the actual price for veggies is $7.50 per pound. Given this information, which variance can you calculate?

   a. Direct labor-price variance

   b. Direct labor-efficiency variance

   c. Direct materials price variance

   d. Direct materials efficiency variance

2. (LO10.2) Using the information from Multiple-Choice Question 1, which of the following represents the variance at **Phickles Pickles**?

    a. $1,875 U

    b. $1,875 F

    c. $7,500 U

    d. $7,500 F

3. (LO10.2) Now assume that **Phickles Pickles** (from Multiple-Choice Question 1) finds a new supplier in the Florida panhandle that has not experienced drought conditions and can supply the vegetables for $5.75 per pound but requires that Phickles purchase 1,500 lbs. Which of the following is the direct materials price variance during this period?

    a. $312.50 U

    b. $312.50 F

    c. $375.00 U

    d. $375.00 F

4. (LO10.2) As described in Multiple-Choice Question 3, **Phickles Pickles** has purchased 1,500 pounds of vegetables from a new supplier for $5.75 per pound. At the start of the year, Phickles budgeted using a standard quantity of 1,250 pounds at $6.00 per pound. Assume that the lower price for the vegetables is associated with slightly lower quality than Phickles is used to, so Phickles used all 1,500 pounds of vegetables even though it was more than the company usually purchases. Calculate the direct materials efficiency variance during the period.

    a. $1,500.00 U

    b. $1,500.00 F

    c. $375.00 U

    d. $312.50 F

5. (LO10.3) Which of the following describes how variances are recorded in journal entries?

    a. Favorable variances are debits; unfavorable variances are credits.

    b. Favorable and unfavorable variances are debits.

    c. Unfavorable and favorable variances are credits.

    d. Unfavorable variances are debits; favorable variances are credits.

6. (LO10.4) When preparing closing entries at the end of the period, assuming most of the products have been produced and sold, which of the following best describes the journal entry?

    a. COGS increases to reflect favorable variances.

    b. COGS increases to reflect unfavorable variances.

    c. COGS decreases to reflect unfavorable variances.

    d. COGS does not change to reflect variances.

7. (LO10.1) In 2022, the Russian invasion of Ukraine significantly increased the price of gasoline in the United States. What type of unexpected variance would this price increase create for **Federal Express**, the shipping company?

    a. Favorable direct materials price variance

    b. Unfavorable direct materials price variance

    c. Favorable direct materials efficiency variance

    d. Unfavorable direct materials efficiency variance

8. (LO10.2) Assume the following data for **Sprouts Market:**

Standard labor hours required	400
Standard labor rate per hour	$9.00
Actual labor hours worked	375
Actual labor rate per hour	$9.25

Given the above information, which of the following represents the direct labor variances?

a. The direct labor-price variance is favorable; the direct labor-efficiency variance is favorable.

b. The direct labor-price variance is unfavorable; the direct labor-efficiency variance is favorable.

c. The direct labor-price variance is favorable; the direct labor-efficiency variance is unfavorable.

d. The direct labor-price variance is unfavorable; the direct labor-efficiency variance is unfavorable.

9. (LO10.2) Using the data in Multiple-Choice Question 8, which of the following accurately represents the direct labor-price variance?

a. $100.00 F

b. $100.00 U

c. $93.75 U

d. $93.75 F

10. (LO10.2) Using the data in Multiple-Choice Question 8, which of the following accurately represents the direct labor-efficiency variance?

a. $225.00 F

b. $225.00 U

c. $231.25 F

d. $231.25 U

11. (LO10.2) A company budgets to sell 5,000 units of its product. Actual sales are 5,500 units. The product has a standard labor price of $55. When analyzing its direct labor flexible-budget variance for the period, the company determines that its direct labor-efficiency variance was an unfavorable variance of $1,000. Which one of the following is closest to the actual price for direct labor if the total direct labor flexible-budget variance was an unfavorable variance of $10,000?

CMA

a. $40

b. $50

c. $53

d. $55

12. (LO10.4) A candle company has purchased 10,000 pounds of clear candle wax this month to create 5,000 designer candles. The wax was purchased for $1.75 per pound, which is $0.25 less than was originally expected when the cost accountants created the budget. Which of the following represents how this variance will be recorded at the time the raw materials are purchased?

a. Credit of $2,500 to Direct Materials Price Variance

b. Debit of $2,500 to Direct Materials Price Variance

c. Credit of $2,500 to Direct Materials Efficiency Variance

d. Debit of $2,500 to Direct Materials Efficiency Variance

13. (LO10.4) Assume that in the next month, the same candle company in Multiple-Choice Question 12 used 15,000 pounds of clear candle wax to create 5,000 designer candles. This is 5,000 pounds more than expected. The wax was once again purchased for $1.75 per pound, which is $0.25 less than was originally expected when the cost accountants created the budget. Which of the following represents how this variance will be recorded at the time the raw materials are purchased?

a. Credit of $10,000 to Direct Materials Price Variance

b. Debit of $10,000 to Direct Materials Price Variance

c. Credit of $10,000 to Direct Materials Efficiency Variance

d. Debit of $10,000 to Direct Materials Efficiency Variance

14. (LO10.2) **Heartwood Cabinets'** Pine division uses the following information to calculate its direct-cost variances for the month of March 2024:

Standard labor hours	30 minutes per cabinet
Actual labor hours	35 minutes per cabinet
Standard labor rate per hour	$15 per hour
Actual labor rate per hour	$14 per hour

Based on this information, which of the following is true?

a. The labor-price and labor-efficiency variances are favorable.

b. The labor-price and labor-efficiency variances are unfavorable.

c. The labor-price variance is favorable and the labor-efficiency variance is unfavorable.

d. The labor-price variance is unfavorable and the labor-efficiency variance is favorable.

15. (LO10.2) **Heartwood Cabinets'** Pine division uses the following information to calculate its direct-cost variances for the month of March 2024:

Standard materials	1 yard per cabinet
Actual materials required	0.75 yard per cabinet
Standard materials cost	$10 per cabinet
Actual materials cost	$11 per cabinet

Based on this information, which of the following is true?

a. The direct materials price and direct materials efficiency variances are favorable.

b. The direct materials price and direct materials efficiency variances are unfavorable.

c. The direct materials price variance is favorable and the direct materials efficiency variance is unfavorable.

d. The direct materials price variance is unfavorable and the direct materials efficiency variance is favorable.

16. (LO10.4) Which of the following statements is incorrect?

a. Unfavorable variances are recorded as credits.

b. Unfavorable variances are recorded as debits.

c. Favorable variances are recorded as credits.

d. All of these statements are correct.

17. (LO10.4) Pauline's Pralines records the following journal entry:

Work-in-Process	500,000	
Direct Materials Efficiency Variance	100,000	
Direct Materials		600,000

Which of the following statements provides a possible explanation for this journal entry?

a. Pauline's used less in praline ingredients than expected.

b. Pauline's purchased materials at a lower-than-expected cost.

c. Pauline's paid more than expected for her materials.

d. Pauline's used more praline ingredients than expected.

18. (LO10.4) Pauline's Pralines records the following journal entry:

Work-in-Process	200,000	
Direct Labor-Efficiency Variance	100,000	
Direct Labor-Price Variance	100,000	
Wages Payable		400,000

Which of the following statements provides a possible explanation for this journal entry?

a. Pauline's labor took more time than expected.

b. Pauline's labor took less time than expected.

c. Pauline's labor was paid a lower wage than expected.

d. Pauline's used more direct materials than expected.

19. (LO10.4) Pauline's Pralines records the following journal entry to close out the journal entries for the period:

COGS	150,000	
Direct Materials Price Variance	150,000	
Direct Materials Efficiency Variance		100,000
Direct Labor-Price Variance		100,000
Direct Labor-Efficiency Variance		100,000

Which of the following statements describes the variances that the organization experienced during the period?

a. Pauline's paid more for direct materials than expected.

b. Pauline's paid less for direct materials than expected.

c. Pauline's labor took less time than expected.

d. Pauline's used less in direct materials than expected.

20. (LO10.5) Which of the following statements describes a problematic explanation for a favorable materials price variance?

a. The purchasing manager is buying substandard materials for a low cost.

b. The purchasing manager has negotiated a lower rate for a multiyear contract to purchase materials from a trusted supplier.

c. The human resources department has hired less-experienced labor that takes longer than expected to complete production.

d. The human resources department has hired more-experienced labor that takes less time than expected to complete production.

Discussion Questions

1. (LO10.1) The static-budget variance at a **Kia** manufacturing facility revealed a $5,000,000 unfavorable variance in operating income. Management wants to do more analysis to understand the cause of this difference. Which data would you need to perform a thorough analysis?

2. (LO10.5) Should management investigate every variance? Explain your answer.

3. (LO10.5) Describe the benefits and challenges associated with using variance analysis to motivate and compensate managers.

4. (LO10.3) A purchasing manager entered into a contract with a new supplier who promised higher quality and lower prices than the company's current supplier. However, at the end of the quarter the cost accountants noted a favorable direct materials price variance and an unfavorable direct materials efficiency variance. Explain this result and its implications for the new supplier.

5. (LO10.3) Suppose you work for a clothing company that has been sourcing its textile manufacturing overseas for many years. Your CEO recently announced a commitment to ethically sourced products. In your industry, this means that you must ensure that products are manufactured in safe environments by workers who are paid fair wages, work legal hours, and have safe and clean working conditions. Cost standards were established last year, months before your CEO made the announcement. Describe how this decision is likely to impact your direct manufacturing and direct labor cost variances.

ENVIRONMENTAL, SOCIAL, GOVERNANCE

6. (LO10.1) Management at Blue Dress Boutique has noted that the sales-volume variance for store revenue has been unfavorable by more than 10% for the past three quarters. The cost accountants have been using historical sales as the primary input for developing sales expectations. Management is concerned that these standards may not be achievable. Which other data could be used to develop more accurate sales forecasts?

Use the following dashboard to answer Discussion Questions 7 and 8.

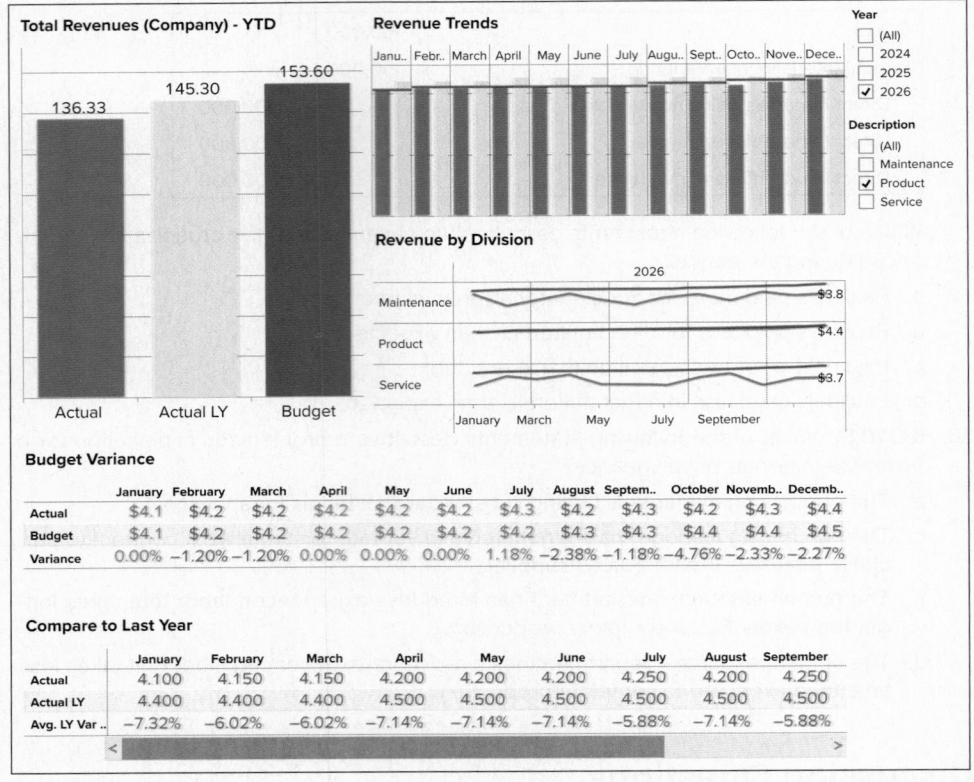

7. (LO10.2) Assume you are the CFO of a multinational company that sells and maintains computer equipment for offices around the world. Your cost accountant has prepared a detailed revenue variance dashboard that includes a variety of visualizations presenting actual performance, actual performance last year (LY), and the budget. Note the filters applied to this dashboard and describe which data are being presented in this report.

8. (LO10.2) Now that you have examined the data analysis in the dashboard (see Discussion Question 7), what feedback would you provide to the managers of the Maintenance, Service, and Product divisions in their annual performance evaluations?

9. (LO10.5) Describe the benefits of using an interactive dashboard for monitoring sales and cost variances.

10. (LO10.3) In a service organization, which do you believe is more important to examine: direct labor variances or direct materials variances? Explain.

11. (LO10.4) Explain why organizations use standard costing systems to record production costs.

12. (LO10.4) At the end of the period, you create a journal entry that increases the COGS balance. What does this indicate for the company's performance during the period?

13. (LO10.3) Explain what a flexible budget is and why it is useful.

14. (LO10.2) Describe the difference between price variances and efficiency variances.

15. (LO10.2) What factors might contribute to a favorable direct labor variance?

Brief Exercises ![McGraw Hill] connect

1. (LO10.2) **Fire & Flavor** produces and sells BBQ accessories, including cedar planks used to infuse meat with flavor while grilling. Assume the company's 2026 static budget and actual performance figures for the Cedar Plank division are as follows:

Fire & Flavor Cedar Grilling Planks Division 2026		
	Static Budget	**Actual**
Units produced and sold	10,000 planks	10,500 planks
Sale price	$18 per plank	$19 per plank
Variable costs	$33,000 total	$3 per plank
Fixed costs	$25,000 total	$24,000 total

Calculate Fire and Flavor's static-budget variance for:

a. revenues.

b. variable costs.

c. fixed costs.

d. operating income.

2. (LO10.2) Use the same data from **Fire & Flavor** as in Brief Exercise 1:

Fire & Flavor Cedar Grilling Planks Division 2026		
	Budget	**Actual**
Units produced and sold	10,000 planks	10,500 planks
Sale price	$18 per plank	$19 per plank
Variable costs	$33,000 total	$3 per plank
Fixed costs	$25,000 total	$24,000 total

Prepare a flexible budget for 2026 and calculate Fire & Flavor's flexible-budget variance for:

a. revenues.

b. variable costs.

c. fixed costs.

d. operating income.

3. (LO10.2) Use the 2026 **Fire & Flavor** data from Brief Exercises 1 and 2 to calculate the sales-volume variance for the revenue of the Cedar Planks division.

4. (LO10.3) Assume the cost accountants at **Fire & Flavor** (see Brief Exercises 1–3) now have more detailed data about variable costs, as follows:

		Standards	**Actual**
Direct labor	Employee pay	$15	$15
	Planks per hour	9	10
Direct materials	Direct materials (per plank)	$1.63	$1.50

Calculate:

a. direct labor-price variance.

b. direct labor-efficiency variance.

c. direct materials price variance.

5. (LO10.4) Using the **Fire & Flavor** data from Brief Exercises 1–4, prepare the journal entries that the cost accountant will use to record:

a. direct materials price variance.

b. direct materials efficiency variance.

c. direct labor variances.

6. (LO10.2) The CFO of **Heartwood Cabinets** intends to evaluate the managers of each division using variance analysis. The cost accountant has collected the following information about the Oak division for March 2026:

	Budgeted	Actual
Sales (cabinets)	2,000	1,900
Sales price per cabinet	$125.00	$119.00
Materials (yards per cabinet)	1.00	1.25
Materials cost (per yard)	$10.00	$11.25
Labor hours per cabinet	0.50	0.40
Labor cost per hour	$15.00	$14.50

Calculate:

a. sales-volume variance.

b. flexible-budget variance.

c. direct materials price variance.

d. direct materials efficiency variance.

e. labor-price variance.

f. labor-efficiency variance.

7. (LO10.4) Using the information in Brief Exercise 6, prepare the journal entries that the cost accountant at **Heartwood Cabinets** will use to record:

a. direct materials price variance for the Oak division.

b. direct materials efficiency variance for the Oak division.

c. direct labor variances for the Oak division.

8. (LO10.2) The CFO of **Heartwood Cabinets** intends to evaluate the managers of each division using variance analysis. The cost accountant has collected the following information about the Maple division for March 2026:

	Budgeted	Actual
Sales (cabinets)	5,000	5,200
Sales price per cabinet	$115.00	$125.00
Materials (yards per cabinet)	1.00	1.00
Materials cost (per yard)	$15.00	$14.00
Labor hours per cabinet	0.50	0.25
Labor cost per hour	$15.00	$15.50
Total hours required	2,500	1,300

Calculate:

a. sales-volume variance.

b. flexible-budget variance.

c. direct materials price variance.

d. direct materials efficiency variance.

e. labor-price variance.

f. labor-efficiency variance.

9. (LO10.4) Using the information about **Heartwood**'s Maple division (from Brief Exercise 8), prepare the journal entries that the cost accountant at Heartwood will use to record:

a. direct materials price variance for the Maple division.

b. direct materials efficiency variance for the Maple division.

c. direct labor variances for the Maple division.

10. (LO10.3) **Saucemoto** produces and sells a dip clip that attaches to a car's air vent to hold fast-food sauce. The clips are made from food-grade plastic and silicon. For November 2026, Saucemoto budgeted that it would produce and sell 24,000 individual dip clip units. Actual production and sales were 25,000 units. Dip clips are sold in pairs and the sale price was budgeted at $12.99 per pair. The sale price was reduced to $10.95 in November for holiday sales. Budgeted variable cost is $1.50 per unit. Budgeted fixed costs are $25,000. Actual variable costs were $1.75 per unit. Actual fixed costs were $24.00.

Prepare a flexible-budget variance analysis (similar to the one shown in Exhibit 10.6 in the text).

11. (LO10.3) **Comfy** developed, produces, and sells a wearable blanket. It looks like an oversized hoodie made from soft microfiber and sherpa materials, with a front pocket big enough for your hands, a book, and some snacks. Comfy has the following data for October 2026.

	Budget	Actual
Units to produce/sell	40,000	45,000
Budgeted sales price (per unit)	$59.99	$55.00
Materials required	4 yards of fleece	4.25 yards of fleece
Cost of materials	$3 per yard	$2.50 per yard
Labor hours per unit	5 minutes	6 minutes
Labor cost per hour	$9.00	$10.00
Variable overhead (per unit)	$0.25	$0.30
Budgeted total fixed costs	$25,000.00	$24,000.00

Compute:

a. sales-volume variance.

b. flexible-budget variance.

c. price and efficiency variances.

12. (LO10.4) Use the October 2026 data from **Comfy** (from Brief Exercise 11) to prepare the necessary journal entries to record the variances and close them out to COGS at the end of the period.

13. (LO10.1) **Shibumi** produces sunshades for the beach. The shades are made from a simple parachute canopy that flows in the wind and aluminum stakes that anchor the shade to the sand.

Assume the following information:

Shibumi Standard Costs		
Standard Direct Materials Costs		
Parachute nylon	6 sq. yards	$4.00 per yard
Aluminum poles	4	$1.00 per pole
Cord	3 yards	$0.10 per yard
Canvas (for carrying case)	1.5 yards	$2.50 per yard
Standard Direct Labor Costs		
Manufacturing wages	0.5 hour	$12 per hour
Standard Variable Manufacturing Costs		
Variable costs		$0.75 per shade

Calculate:

a. the total standard cost for a single sunshade.

b. the total standard cost for a production run of 20,000 sunshades.

14. (LO10.5) The following dashboard is reproduced from Exhibit 10.8 in the chapter:

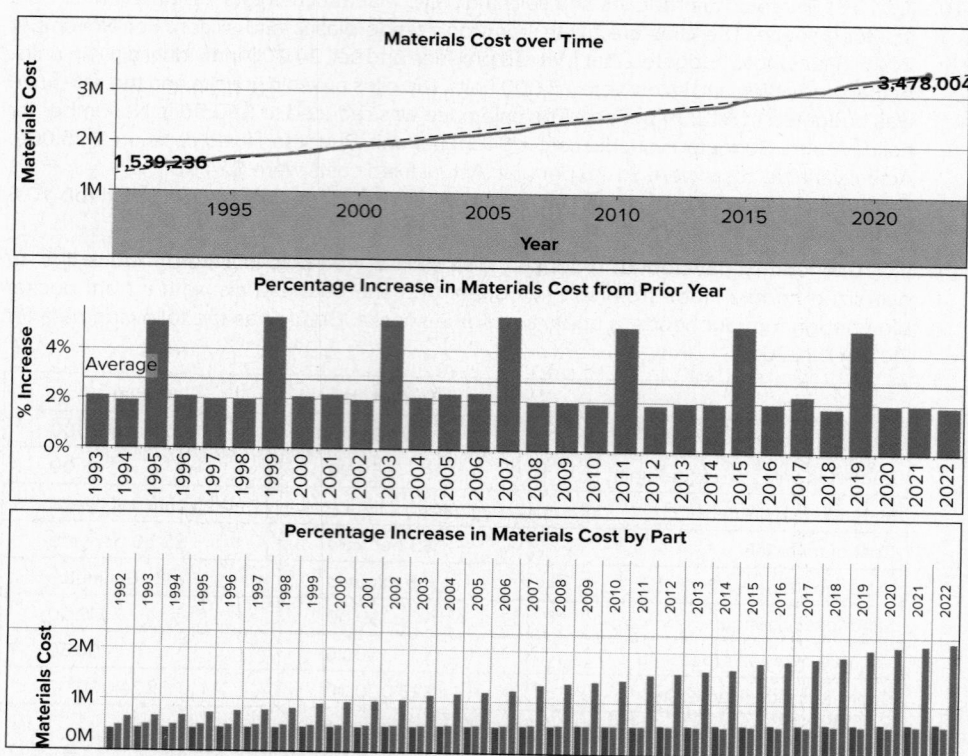

Tableau Software

Based on this dashboard, what feedback would you provide to the purchasing managers of parts 1, 2, and 3 respectively?

15. (LO10.2) Sunstar Microsystems, a fictitious technology company, is popular for its innovative electronics products, especially its line of smart speakers. The company carefully plans its operations each year, including forecasting sales volumes to manage production and inventory effectively.

At the beginning of the year, Sunstar Microsystems forecasted sales of 100,000 units of its flagship smart speaker, Beacon, based on past sales data, market trends, and promotional plans. The budgeted selling price was set at $100 per unit, implying expected revenue of $10 million.

Throughout the year, the company rolled out strategic marketing campaigns, including a successful influencer collaboration and an effective social media marketing drive. Its efforts paid off, and it tapped into the growing trend of smart-home automation, making its smart speakers more popular than ever.

By the end of the year, Sunstar Microsystems had sold 120,000 units of Beacon, 20% higher than the budgeted volume. This increase in sales volume led to a favorable sales-volume variance.

Calculate the sales-volume variance for the Beacon smart speaker and describe the results.

Problems   connect

1. (LO10.3, 10.4) Prepare journal entries to record variances at **Heartwood Cabinets**.
    At Heartwood, the standard direct materials cost per unit for the Pine Arch cabinet is $21.87. In the budget period, Heartwood plans to produce 18,000 units. Assume that the actual cost of materials is $23.25 per unit.

    Required

    a. Assume that Heartwood produces 17,500 units in this period instead of the 18,000 originally budgeted. Prepare the journal entry to record the direct materials efficiency variance.

    b. Prepare the journal entry to record the direct materials price variance.

    c. Standard labor cost is $6.30 per unit and standard labor hours are 21 minutes per unit (or 0.35 hour per unit). Calculate the standard hourly wage for building Pine Arch cabinets.

    d. Calculate the standard amount of time planned to produce 18,000 units.

    e. Assume that it really takes Heartwood 7,000 hours to produce the 17,500 units and that average hourly salary for employees has increased to $19.00. Prepare the journal entry to record the labor-price and labor-efficiency variances.

    f. Assume all variances are immaterial. Prepare the journal entry to write off these balances to cost of goods sold.

2. (LO10.2) Review the variances you calculated in Problem 1.

    Required

    Indicate whether each variance is favorable or unfavorable and explain your answers:

    a. direct materials price variance
    b. direct materials efficiency variance
    c. direct labor-price variance
    d. direct labor-efficiency variance

3. (LO10.5) Review the data and analysis you performed in Problems 1 and 2.

    Required

    Prepare a presentation for management, containing useful visualization(s), to explain your results.

4. (LO10.2) The static-budget variance at a large meat-packing plant revealed an unfavorable variance in operating income of approximately $500,000. Management wants to do more analysis to understand the cause of this difference. Assume that you are the cost accountant for the organization and you have collected the following data:

Standard		Actual	
Units sold	100,000 tons	Units sold	102,000 tons
Units produced	100,000 tons	Units produced	102,000 tons
Sales price	$3,000 per ton	Sales price	$3,150 per ton
Direct materials required	120,000 tons	Direct materials purchased/used	126,300 tons
Direct materials cost	$2,200 per ton	Direct materials cost	$2,250 per ton
Direct labor hours	20,000 hours	Direct labor hours	22,000 hours
Direct labor rate per hour	$12.50	Direct labor rate per hour	$14.00
Variable manufacturing overhead	$1.00 per ton	Variable manufacturing overhead	$1.13 per ton
Fixed costs	$25,000	Fixed costs	$26,000

Required

Prepare a flexible-budget variance analysis using the format from Exhibit 10.6.

	Actual Results	Flexible-Budget Variance	U/F	Flexible Budget	Sales-Volume Variance	U/F	Static Budget
	1	2		3	4		5
Units Sold							
Revenue							
Variable costs							
Direct material							
Direct labor							
Variable manufacturing overhead							
Total variable costs							
Contribution margin							
Fixed costs							
Total fixed costs							
Operating income							

Total static-budget variance:

Flexible-budget variance:

Sales-volume variance:

5. (LO10.3, 10.4) Prepare journal entries to record variances at **Condor Chocolates**, which produces fine chocolates sold direct to consumers and wholesale to retailers and restaurants. The following data reflect the standards and actual sales and costs for May 2025.

At Condor Chocolates, the standard direct materials cost per pound of chocolate candy is $11.99. Planned production during the period is 3,000 pounds of chocolate candy.

Assume that the actual cost of materials is $11.02 per pound and Condor Chocolates produces 2,500 pounds in this period instead of the 3,000 originally budgeted.

Required

a. Prepare the journal entry to record the direct materials efficiency variance.

b. Prepare the journal entry to record the direct materials price variance.

Standard labor cost is $15.00 per hour and standard labor hours are 45 minutes per pound of chocolate candy.

Assume that it really takes Condor Chocolates 55 hours to produce the 2,500 units and that the average salary for employees has increased to $18.00.

c. Prepare the journal entry to record the labor-price and labor-efficiency variances. Round up to the next complete hour if needed.

d. Assume all variances are immaterial to Condor Chocolates. Prepare the journal entry to write off these balances to cost of goods sold.

6. (LO10.1) Velocity Skates is a fictitious company that produces roller skates. As the cost accountants prepare the budget for the upcoming year, they must calculate standard costs. Assume you have received the following bill of materials, which describes the inputs to Velocity Skates' most popular skate, the Speedster:

Skate Boot:		
Leather or synthetic upper material	1	$10.00
Lining material	1	$ 1.50
Insole	1	$ 1.00
Outsole	1	$ 3.00
Heel	1	$ 2.00
Laces	2	$ 0.50
Chassis:		
Aluminum or steel frame	1	$ 7.50
Trucks (pivot points for the wheels)	2	$ 5.00
Cushions (rubber parts within the truck for flexibility)	4	$ 2.00
Wheels:		
Polyurethane wheels	4	$ 3.00
Bearings (allow the wheels to rotate freely)	8	$ 0.50
Toe Stop:		
Rubber stopper	1	$ 2.00
Washer	1	$ 0.50
Nut	1	$ 0.50
Miscellaneous:		
Screws for attaching chassis to boot	4	$ 0.50
Bolts for attaching trucks to the frame	4	$ 0.50
Nuts for securing bolts	4	$ 0.50

Required

a. What is the standard direct materials cost for one pair of Speedster skates?

b. Assume Velocity Skates plans to produce and sell 50,000 pairs of Speedster skates. What is the total standard direct materials cost for the budget?

c. Sales price is $275 per Speedster skate. Assume fixed costs are $70,000 for the period. Labor is paid $9.00 per hour and on average 10 pairs are produced per hour. Calculate Velocity's planned profit.

7. (LO10.2) **Tumi** manufactures and sells high-end suitcases. The static-budget variance is an unfavorable variance in operating income of approximately $10,000,000. Management wants to do more analysis to understand the cause of this difference. Assume that you are the cost accountant for the organization and have collected the following data:

Standard			Actual		
Units sold		1,200,000	Units sold		1,150,000	
Units produced		1,300,000	Units produced		1,250,000	
Sales price		$600	Sales price		$625	
Direct materials required			Direct materials purchased (total)			
• Leather (3 yards)		$12 per yard	• Leather (3 yards)	4,500,000 yards	$58,500,000
• Zipper (5)		$1 per zipper	• Zipper (5)	6,875,000	$ 6,875,000
• Wheels (4)		$1 per wheel	• Wheels (4)	5,005,000	$ 5,005,000
• Handle (1)		$10 per suitcase	• Handle (1)	1,300,000	$ 13,000,000
Direct labor hours		325,000 hours	Direct labor hours	350,000 hours	
Direct labor rate per hour		$12.50	Direct labor rate per hour	$12.00	
Variable manufacturing overhead	$1.00 per suitcase	Variable manufacturing overhead	$0.75 per suitcase	
Fixed costs		$125,000	Fixed costs	$126,000	

Required

Prepare a flexible-budget variance analysis using the format from Exhibit 10.6.

	Actual Results	Flexible-Budget Variance	U/F	Flexible Budget	Sales-Volume Variance	U/F	Static Budget
	1	2		3	4		5
Units Sold							
Revenue							
Variable Costs							
Direct Material							
Direct Labor							
Variable Manufacturing Overhead							
Total Variable Costs							
Contribution Margin							
Fixed Costs							
Total Fixed Costs							
Operating Income							

Total static-budget variance:

Flexible-budget variance:

Sales-volume variance:

8. (LO10.3) **Rocketbook** produces reusable smart notebooks that connect to the cloud so that handwritten notes can be saved and organized digitally. The notebooks are sold online through the Rocketbook website, via other websites (such as **Amazon**), and in retail stores such as **Target** and **Office Depot**.

Cost accountants at Rocketbook have prepared the following estimates to budget for the upcoming year. Use these data to calculate the required variances and journal entries.

	Budget	Actual
Units to produce/sell	18,000,000	18,500,000
Budgeted sales price (per unit)	$36.99	$29.95
Cost of materials	$4.50	$3.95
Units produced per hour	200	185
Labor cost per hour	$12.00	$11.95
Budgeted total fixed costs	$120,000	$135,000

Required

a. Compute the sales-volume variance.

b. Prepare the journal entry to record the direct materials price variance.

c. Prepare the journal entry to record the direct materials efficiency variance.

d. Prepare the journal entry to record the direct labor-price and efficiency variances.

e. Prepare the closing entry to close the variances out to COGS.

9. (LO10.5) Refer back to the **Rocketbook** data in Problem 8. Assume you are the purchasing manager responsible for purchasing direct materials.

Required

a. Prepare a visualization in Excel, Tableau, or Power BI (based on your instructor's preference) that graphically shows the variances.

b. Using the visualization, provide an explanation to management about the company's performance.

10. (LO10.5) Again refer to the **Rocketbook** data and your analysis from Problems 8 and 9.

   Required

   Take management's perspective and provide feedback about the performance of the purchasing manager responsible for direct materials within the broader context of Rocketbook's overall cost performance during the period.

11. (LO10.3, 10.4) **Olipop** produces a soda-style drink made with fiber, prebiotics, and botanicals designed with health in mind. Originally sold in health-food outlets, Olipop is now widely distributed in stores such as **Target** and on websites such as **Amazon.com**.

   The standard unit of Olipop is a four-count package. Olipop plans to sell 20 million standard units, and the standard sales price is $9.50 per unit.

   Cost accountants at Olipop have prepared the following estimates to budget for the upcoming year:

	Budget
Units to produce/sell	20,000,000
Budgeted sales price (per unit)	$9.50
Cost of materials	$1.50 per unit
Units produced per hour	100
Labor cost per hour	$13.50
Budgeted total fixed costs	$25,000.00

   Assume that Olipop produces and sells 22 million units during the year instead of the 20 million units originally budgeted. The company incurred the following actual costs to produce these 22 million units:

	Actual
Units to produce/sell	22,000,000
Budgeted sales price (per unit)	$9.49
Cost of materials	$1.75
Units produced per hour	105
Labor cost per hour	$13.50
Budgeted total fixed costs	$35,000.00

   Required

   a. Prepare the journal entry to record the direct materials efficiency variance.

   b. Prepare the journal entry to record the direct materials price variance.

   c. Prepare the journal entry to record the labor-price and labor-efficiency variances.

   d. Assume these variances are immaterial. Prepare the journal entry to write off these balances to cost of goods sold.

12. (LO10.2, 10.5) Digitize Dynamics is a fictional digital marketing firm that helps clients achieve their goals through various digital marketing strategies, including website optimization, pay-per-click advertising, social media marketing, and website design. Because digital marketing is a service, not a manufactured good, the costs that Digitize Dynamics incurs are somewhat different from those of traditional manufacturing firms. However, the same concepts for direct materials and direct labor variances still apply. Use the data below to calculate variances for Digitize Dynamics. Assume that for the set of required direct materials, Digitize Dynamics purchased the same amount as budgeted.

	Budget	Actual
Direct Materials		
Software and digital tools	$ 825,000	$ 795,000
Stock images and video	$ 25,000	$ 30,000
Online ad spend	$ 40,000	$ 45,000
Website domain and hosting	$ 50,000	$ 35,000
Data and analytics tools	$ 75,000	$ 80,000
Social media influencer	$ 150,000	$ 175,000
Total	$ 1,165,000	$ 1,160,000
Direct Labor		
Combined hourly wage	$ 400	$ 410
Labor Hours Required		
All employees	75,000	78,500
Direct Labor Cost		
All employees	$30,000,000	$32,185,000

Required

Calculate:

a. direct materials efficiency variance.

b. direct materials price variance.

c. direct labor-price variance.

d. direct labor-efficiency variance.

13. (LO10.4) Assume that **Fujifilm** records the following journal entries to record variances. Use the journal entries to complete the data table containing the standard and actual details for production during the month. Assume all of the numbers in the journal entries are rounded to the nearest whole number.

Direct Materials Efficiency Variance		
Direct Materials	72,000	
Direct Materials Price Variance	2,250	
Accounts Payable		74,250

Direct Materials Price Variance		
Work-in-Process	80,000	
Direct Materials Efficiency Variance		8,000
Direct Materials		72,000

Labor-Price and Labor-Efficiency Variances		
Work-in-Process	3,083	
Direct Manufacturing Labor-Price Variance	56	
Direct Manufacturing Labor-Efficiency Variance		1,002
Wages Payable		2,138

Assume all variances are immaterial to Fujifilm. The following journal entry is prepared to write off these balances to cost of goods sold.

Direct Materials Efficiency Variance	8,000	
Direct Materials Price Variance	2,250	
Direct Labor-Efficiency Variance		1,002
Direct Labor-Price Variance		56
COGS		9,192

Required

Identify the missing values in this table:

	Budget	Actual
Units to produce/sell	10,000	(c)
Cost of materials	(d)	$8.25
Minutes to complete 1 unit	(b)	1.50
Hours to complete all units	333	225
Labor cost per unit	$0.31	$0.24
Labor cost per hour	$9.25	(a)

14. (LO10.2) **Stanley** manufactures and sells insulated cups and mugs. The static budget was prepared before an unexpected, viral marketing campaign driven by spontaneous endorsements by online influencers. As a result of this campaign, sales, and therefore production, skyrocketed. Importantly, during the year, purchasing managers renegotiated some materials costs, HR negotiated a higher wage for workers who were now working in higher-pressure conditions, and the organization leased new facilities for production and inventory.

Required

Prepare a flexible budget using the following data:

Standard		Actual		
Units produced & sold	1,000,000	Units produced & sold	20,000,000	
Sales price	$30.00	Sales price	$35.00	
Direct materials required		Direct materials purchased (total)		
• Metal barrel (interior) (1)	$3.00	• Metal barrel (interior) (1)	$2.00	$2,000,000
• External coating (1)	$2.00	• External coating (1)	$1.00	$1,000,000
• Plastic cap (1)	$0.50	• Plastic cap (1)	$0.45	$ 450,000
• Straw (1)	$0.05	• Straw (1)	$0.05	$ 50,000
Total direct materials required per unit	$5.55	Total direct materials required per unit	$3.50	$3,500,000
Direct labor hours	10,000	Direct labor hours	200,000	
Direct labor rate per hour	$9.50	Direct labor rate per hour	$10.50	
Variable manufacturing overhead per DL hour	$1.50	Variable manufacturing overhead per DL hour	$0.08	
Fixed costs	$75,000	Fixed costs	$120,000	

15. (LO10.5) Consider the scenario at **Stanley** described in Problem 14.

Required

a. Prepare a static budget to actual comparison.

b. Describe the importance of the flexible budget in general and in a situation like that experienced by Stanley.

LAB 10.1 **Excel** Calculating Variance and Using Conditional Formatting
LAB 10.2 **Tableau** Preparing a Sales-Variance Analysis Dashboard (Heartwood)
LAB 10.3 **Tableau** Preparing a Direct-Cost Variance Analysis Dashboard (Heartwood)
LAB 10.4 **Power BI** Preparing a Sales-Variance Analysis Dashboard (Heartwood)
LAB 10.5 **Excel** Preparing a Direct-Cost/Sales-Variance Analysis Dashboard (Heartwood)

Lab 10.1   Excel

Lab Note: The tools presented in this lab periodically change. Updated instructions, if applicable, can be found in the student and instructor support materials.

Calculating Variance and Using Conditional Formatting

Data Analytics Types: Descriptive Analytics, Diagnostic Analytics

Keywords

Management Accounting, Direct Materials Variance, Direct Labor Variance

Decision-Making Context

In managerial accounting, the use of standard costs and the calculation of variances are useful in performance evaluation. Why did the costs and usage vary from expectations?

As fans of live sports can attest, more and more stadiums and ballparks are restricting fans' use of handbags and purses. Many stadiums limit the size of bags and allow clear bags only. The goals of the clear-bag policies include increased safety and reduced entry times because gate attendants can inspect clear bags more quickly.

Leigh Ann Barnes Handbags (LABH) designs and produces transparent, stadium-approved handbags with a stylish flair. The bags have removable outer layers of leather and fabric that can be taken off easily when it's game time. The company hires survivors of domestic abuse to produce the bags—helping women in need transform their lives, just as the bags themselves transform.

Assume that the company wants to reduce its costs to become more profitable. It uses standard costing for both direct materials and direct labor to evaluate variances. Because of its mission to help women in need, Leigh Ann Barnes Handbags does not want to cut costs by hiring less expensive labor. Nonetheless, management needs to perform a variance analysis to evaluate its options for saving money.

Remember, a favorable cost variance is present when the actual cost is less than the standard cost. An unfavorable cost variance occurs when the actual cost is greater than the standard cost.

Required

1. Using performance standards for the materials used in the manufacture of handbags, calculate the direct materials variances, including price and quantity variances.
2. Use conditional formatting to identify favorable and unfavorable variances.

Ask the Question

What factors are driving unfavorable variances? Where can management make changes to reduce cost of production?

Master the Data

Open the template we'll use for our analysis in Excel: **Lab 10.1 Data.xlsx**. The template is reproduced in Lab Exhibit 10.1.1.

Lab Exhibit 10.1.1

Microsoft Excel

Note that the direct materials variance calculations are on the upper part of the spreadsheet and the direct labor variance calculations are in the lower part.

Also note that the direct materials variance is composed of a materials price variance and a materials quantity variance. Likewise, note that the direct labor variance is composed of a labor-rate variance and labor-efficiency variance.

LABH will make 6,000 handbags with a standard quantity of leather and clear polyethylene (plastic) per handbag: 21.03 square inches of material @ $0.25/square inch. Actual quantity of materials for those 6,000 handbags produced was 21.53 square inches of materials @ $0.26/square inch. The standard labor is one hour for each handbag with a cost of $8.00/hour. The actual labor used was 1.07 hours at $7.75/hour.

We're now ready to perform the analysis.

Perform the Analysis

Analysis Task #1: Input Actual Quantities and Prices

1. In cell D8, insert the actual quantity of 6,000 handbags * 21.53 square inches/handbag by inputting this formula: =6000* 21.53 (as shown in Lab Exhibit 10.1.2).
2. In cell D9, insert the actual price per square inch of 0.26 by inputting "0.26", as shown in Lab Exhibit 10.1.2.

Lab Exhibit 10.1.2

Microsoft Excel

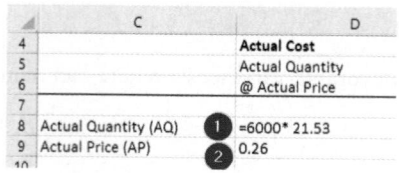

	C	D
4		**Actual Cost**
5		Actual Quantity
6		@ Actual Price
7		
8	Actual Quantity (AQ) ①	=6000* 21.53
9	Actual Price (AP) ②	0.26
10		

3. In cell G8, insert the actual quantity of 6,000 handbags * 21.53 square inches/handbag by inputting this formula: =6000*21.53 (as shown in Lab Exhibit 10.1.3).
4. In cell G9, insert the standard price per square inch of 0.25 by inputting "0.25", as shown in Lab Exhibit 10.1.3.

Lab Exhibit 10.1.3

Microsoft Excel

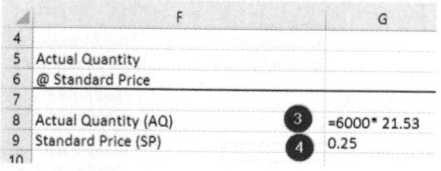

	F	G
4		
5	Actual Quantity	
6	@ Standard Price	
7		
8	Actual Quantity (AQ) ③	=6000* 21.53
9	Standard Price (SP) ④	0.25
10		

5. In cell J8, insert the standard quantity of 6,000 handbags * 21.03 square inches/handbag by inputting this formula: =6000*20.13 (as shown in Lab Exhibit 10.1.4).
6. In cell J9, insert the standard price per square inch of 0.25 by inputting "0.25", as shown in Lab Exhibit 10.1.4.

Lab Exhibit 10.1.4

Microsoft Excel

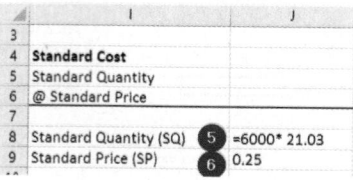

	I	J
3		
4	**Standard Cost**	
5	Standard Quantity	
6	@ Standard Price	
7		
8	Standard Quantity (SQ) ⑤	=6000* 21.03
9	Standard Price (SP) ⑥	0.25

7. In cell D11, to calculate the actual cost by multiplying actual quantity by actual price, input this formula: =D8*D9 (as shown in Lab Exhibit 10.1.5).
8. In cell G11, multiply actual quantity by standard price. Input this formula: =G8*G9 (as shown in Lab Exhibit 10.1.5).
9. In cell J11, to calculate the standard cost by multiplying standard quantity by standard price, input this formula: =J8*J9 (as shown in Lab Exhibit 10.1.5). The results are shown in Lab Exhibit 10.1.6.

Lab Exhibit 10.1.5

Microsoft Excel

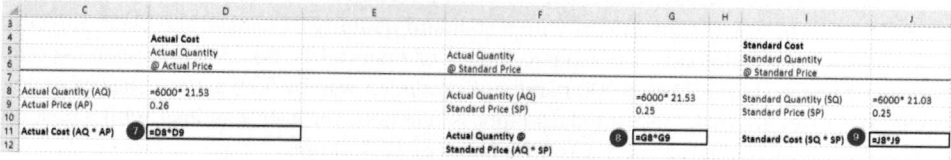

	C	D	E	F	G	H	I	J
3								
4		**Actual Cost**					**Standard Cost**	
5		Actual Quantity		Actual Quantity			Standard Quantity	
6		@ Actual Price		@ Standard Price			@ Standard Price	
7								
8	Actual Quantity (AQ)	=6000* 21.53		Actual Quantity (AQ)	=6000* 21.53		Standard Quantity (SQ)	=6000* 21.03
9	Actual Price (SP)	0.26		Standard Price (SP)	0.25		Standard Price (SP)	0.25
10								
11	Actual Cost (AQ * AP) ⑦	=D8*D9		Actual Quantity @ Standard Price (AQ * SP) ⑧	=G8*G9		Standard Cost (SQ * SP) ⑨	=J8*J9
12								

The spreadsheet should now appear as shown in Lab Exhibit 10.1.6.

Lab Exhibit 10.1.6

Microsoft Excel

	C	D	E	F	G	H	I	J
3								
4		**Actual Cost**					**Standard Cost**	
5		Actual Quantity		Actual Quantity			Standard Quantity	
6		@ Actual Price		@ Standard Price			@ Standard Price	
7								
8	Actual Quantity (AQ)	129,180		Actual Quantity (AQ)	129,180		Standard Quantity (SQ)	126,180
9	Actual Price (AP)	$ 0.26		Standard Price (SP)	$ 0.25		Standard Price (SP)	$ 0.25
10								
11	Actual Cost (AQ * AP)	$ 33,586.80		Actual Quantity @ Standard Price (AQ * SP)	$ 32,295.00		Standard Cost (SQ * SP)	$ 31,545.00
12								

Analysis Task #2: Compute Materials Price and Materials Quantity Variances

Next, we will compute the materials price variance—that is, how much of the variance is due to the change in the materials price from the $0.25/square inch standard cost to the $0.26/square inch actual cost.

1. In cell E16, subtract actual cost from actual quantity at standard price by inserting this formula: =G11-D11 (as shown in Lab Exhibit 10.1.7) to compute the materials price variance. We compute an unfavorable variance of –$1,291.80.

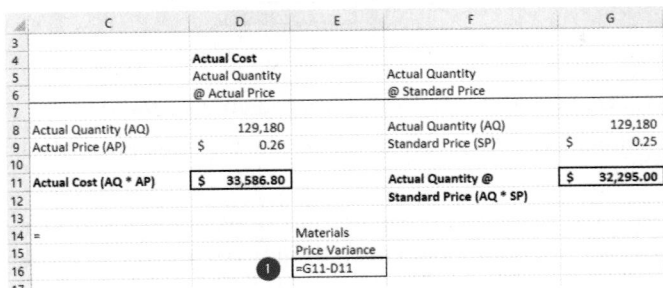

Lab Exhibit 10.1.7

Microsoft Excel

2. In cell H16, subtract actual quantity at standard price by inserting the formula =J11-G11 to compute the materials price variance, as shown in Lab Exhibit 10.1.8. We compute an unfavorable variance of –$750.

Lab Exhibit 10.1.8

Microsoft Excel

3. Compute the total direct materials variance by summing the materials price variance and the materials quantity variance. In cell B16, insert the formula =E16+H16 (see Lab Exhibit 10.1.9).

Lab Exhibit 10.1.9

Microsoft Excel

4. The calculation in Step 3 results in an overall unfavorable direct materials variance of $2,041.80. To check that figure, we'll compare actual cost to standard cost. In cell A17, insert the word "Check". In cell B17, insert the formula =J11-D11 (see Lab Exhibit 10.1.10).

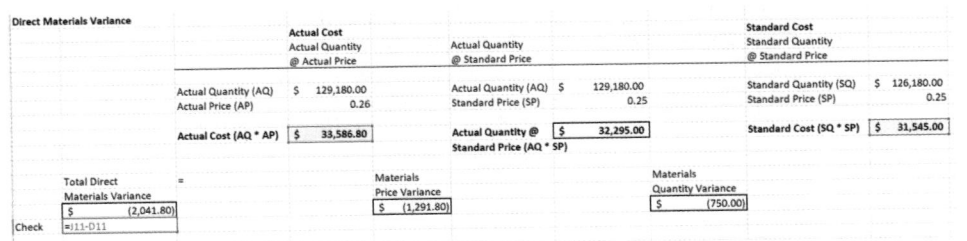

Lab Exhibit 10.1.10

Microsoft Excel

As shown in Lab Exhibit 10.1.11, this check (calculated in cell B17) also results in $2,041.80. This materials variance indicates that LABH both used more quantity than standard (quantity variance) and paid more than it expected (price variance), which resulted in spending more overall than LABH anticipated.

Lab Exhibit 10.1.11

Microsoft Excel

	A	B
13		
14		Total Direct =
15		Materials Variance
16		$ (2,041.80)
17	Check	$ (2,041.80)

Analysis Task #3: Use Conditional Formatting to Evaluate Variances

Next, we will conditionally format each of the cells to highlight favorable and unfavorable variances.

1. Select the cells we would like to conditionally format—specifically, cells B16, E16, and H16—and select **Conditional Formatting > Highlight Cells Rules > Greater Than** in the ribbon, as shown in Lab Exhibit 10.1.12.

Lab Exhibit 10.1.12

Microsoft Excel

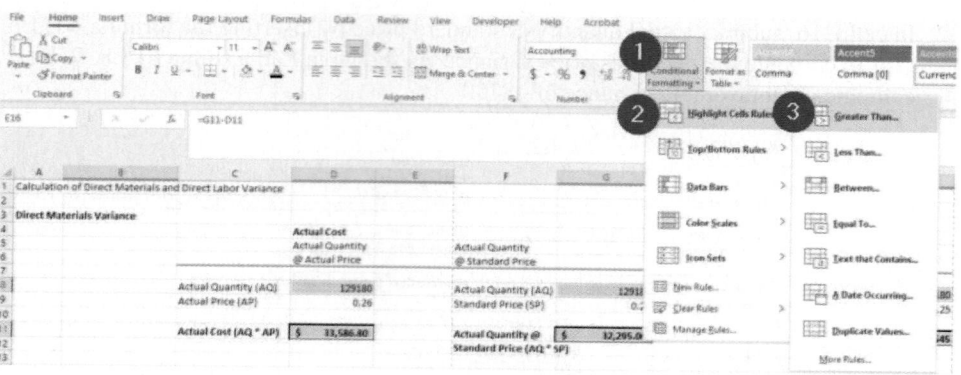

2. Input "0" under **Format cells that are GREATER THAN**. Then select **Green Fill with Dark Green Text** (Lab Exhibit 10.1.13). Then select **OK**. This step will highlight in green any cells that have a positive variance.

Lab Exhibit 10.1.13

Microsoft Excel

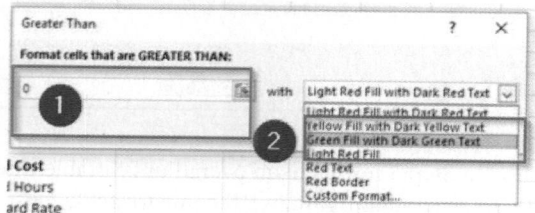

3. Next, to highlight negative variances in red, select the cells to conditionally format—specifically, cells B16, E16, and H16—and select **Conditional Formatting > Highlight Cells Rules > Less Than** in the ribbon, as shown in Lab Exhibit 10.1.14.

Lab Exhibit 10.1.14

Microsoft Excel

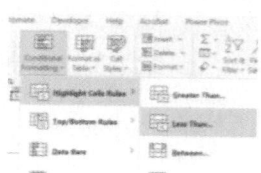

4. Input "0" under **Format cells that are LESS THAN**. Then select **Light Red Fill with Dark Red Text** (Lab Exhibit 10.1.15). Then Select **OK**. This step will highlight in red any cells that have a negative variance.

Given that all of the variances in this analysis are unfavorable, each variance will be highlighted in red, as shown in Lab Exhibit 10.1.16.

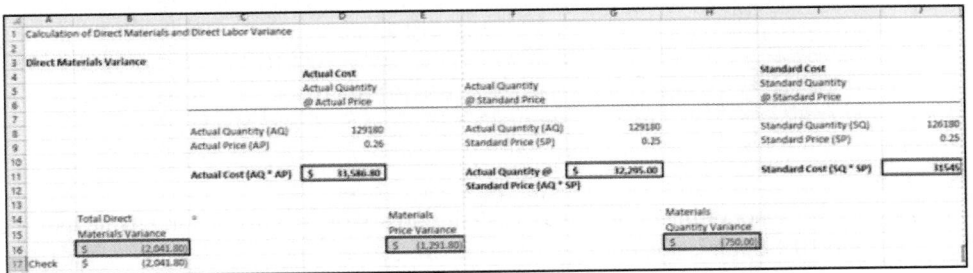

Analysis Task #4: Calculate Direct-Labor Variance and Add Formatting

Apply the steps listed in Analysis Tasks 1–3 above to calculate the direct labor variances. The solution to Analysis Task #4 is shown in Lab Exhibit 10.1.17.

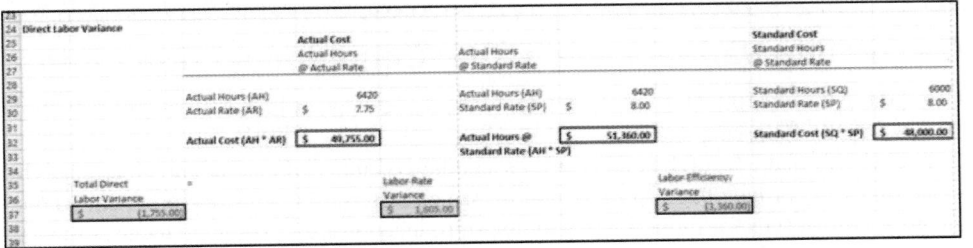

Share the Story

We have computed the variances for direct materials and direct labor. As can be seen in the Excel reports, the total direct materials and total direct labor variances are unfavorable. The only favorable variance we find is a labor-rate variance. This suggests that at LABH, the labor used was less expensive than expected (perhaps the workers required a lower wage). However, there may have been unintended consequences, such as slower production (as shown by the unfavorable labor-efficiency variance) or less expertise using the direct materials (which may have contributed to the unfavorable materials quantity variance).

While not required in this lab, a cost accountant may want to summarize the variances for management using a visualization. One type of visualization, a stacked column chart, can easily illustrate the favorable vs. unfavorable variances and may facilitate

DATA VISUALIZATION

management's decision making. For example, in the following stacked column chart (Lab Exhibit 10.1.18), you can see that the largest contributor to the overall unfavorable variance is the large unfavorable direct-labor variance.

Lab Exhibit 10.1.18

McGraw Hill

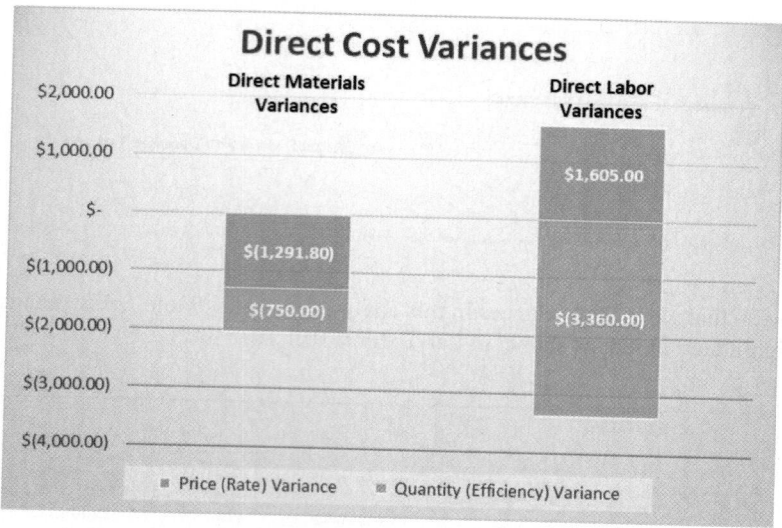

Assessment

1. Take a screenshot of the final output, paste it into a Word document, and name the file "Lab 10.1 Submission.docx".
2. Answer the multiple-choice questions in Connect and upload your Lab 10.1 Submission.docx via Connect if assigned.

Alternate Lab 10.1   Excel—On Your Own

Calculating Variance and Using Conditional Formatting

Using the **Alt Lab 10.1 Data.xlsx** file, apply the same steps in Lab 10.1 to Alternate Lab 10.1, using the following details:

LABH will make 5,500 handbags with a standard quantity of leather and clear polyethylene (plastic) per handbag: 20.25 square inches of material @ $0.31/square inch. Actual quantity of materials for those 5,500 handbags produced was 21.00 square inches of materials @ $0.32/square inch. The standard labor is 1.00 hour for each handbag with a cost of $7.50/hour. The actual labor used was 1.05 hours at $7.75/hour.

Required

1. Using performance standards for the labor utilized in the manufacture of handbags, calculate the direct labor variances, including rate and efficiency variances.
2. Use conditional formatting to identify favorable and unfavorable variances.

Assessment

1. Take a screenshot of the final output, paste it into a Word document, and name the file "Alt Lab 10.1 Submission.docx".
2. Answer the multiple-choice questions in Connect and upload your Alt Lab 10.1 Submission.docx via Connect if assigned.

Preparing a Sales-Variance Analysis Dashboard (Heartwood)

Data Analytics Type: Diagnostic Analytics

Lab Note: The tools presented in this lab periodically change. Updated instructions, if applicable, can be found in the student and instructor support materials. All Lab Exhibits are available within the eBook and in Connect.

Keywords

Sales Variance, Dashboard

Decision-Making Context

In cost accounting, managers use standards to set expectations for sales and associated revenues for future periods. They compare these standards to actual performance to calculate variances, which help them understand why certain products overperform or underperform.

The manager of the Pine division at **Heartwood Cabinets** would like to prepare some detailed variance analysis to evaluate sales performance over the past six months for each product line in her division.

Required

1. Using the monthly sales data and budgeted sales standards, calculate the overall sales variances, the sales-price variances, and the sales-volume variances for each product line.
2. Create a bullet graph visualization to examine the sales variances for each product line.
3. Create a bar chart visualization to examine the sales-price and sales-volume variances to glean more information about the cause of the deviations from expectation.
4. Prepare a dashboard that combines your prepared visualizations into a user-friendly format that will facilitate decision making by management.

Ask the Question

How does actual sales performance compare to expected sales performance? Which product line performed the best compared to expectations? Which product line performed the worst in comparison to expectations? What factors most likely contributed to the deviations?

Master the Data

1. Open the Excel file **Lab 10.2 Data.xlsx**.
2. Review the data in this file to gain an understanding of the variables available for your analysis. Once you are comfortable with the data, close the file.
3. Open Tableau.
4. Navigate to the **Data Source** tab and select **Microsoft Excel** (as shown in Lab Exhibit 10.2.1).
5. Add the file **Lab 10.2 Data.xlsx** as the connection and drag the worksheet **Lab 10.2** to the data pane (Lab Exhibit 10.2.2). Review the view of the data shown at the bottom of your screen to make sure everything has imported correctly.

Perform the Analysis

Analysis Task #1: Prepare a Bullet Graph to Illustrate Sales Variance

A bullet graph is similar to a bar graph, but it provides more information more efficiently. This graph will show a primary measure (in this case, Actual Revenue) as a bar that is compared to a secondary measure (in this case, Budgeted Revenue), which is illustrated with a line placed in relation to the bar. The bullet graph also provides some shading around your primary measure that provides some qualitative assessment of performance (for example, a poor/satisfactory/good range for comparison of budget to actual).

The bullet graph requires you to use multiple measures. For this step, we will use Budgeted Revenues and Actual Revenues. You do not need any dimensions for a bullet graph, but Heartwood would like to understand the sales variance for each product line, so we will use the product dimension.

1. Open a blank worksheet. Recall that your data did not include fields for Standard Revenue, Actual Revenue, or Sales Variance. We will need to create a calculated field for each.
2. To create a calculated field, navigate to **Analysis > Create Calculated Field...** (as shown in Lab Exhibit 10.2.3).
3. When the **Calculated Field** window opens, enter the formula for Standard Revenue as shown in Lab Exhibit 10.2.4, and then click **OK** (at the bottom of the window). The formula is [Standard Sales Price]*[Standard Units Sold].
4. Repeat Step 3 to create a calculated field for Actual Revenue, as shown in Lab Exhibit 10.2.5. The formula is [Actual Sales]*[Actual Sales Price].
5. Repeat Step 3 to create a calculated field for Sales Variance, as shown in Lab Exhibit 10.2.6. The formula is [Actual Revenue] - [Standard Revenue].
   Now that these new fields have been calculated, you can begin building the visualization.
6. Drag the **Product** dimension to the **Columns** shelf (Lab Exhibit 10.2.7).
7. Drag the **Standard Revenue** measure to the **Rows** shelf (see Lab Exhibit 10.2.7).
8. Drag the **Actual Revenue** measure to the **Rows** shelf (see Lab Exhibit 10.2.7).
   We want to combine these two measures on the same chart, but you'll notice that, by default, Tableau creates two separate visualizations side by side.
9. Drag the **Standard Revenue** pill from the **Rows** shelf and drop it onto the axis of the Actual Revenue chart in your workspace (or vice versa). Lab Exhibit 10.2.8 shows what it looks like to create a dual axis so that you can show both measures on the same chart.
10. Select the **Bullet Graph** icon (Lab Exhibit 10.2.9) option from the **Show Me** menu on the right side of your screen.
11. You may find that you have to rearrange the dimensions and measures in the **Rows** and **Columns** shelves to get the graph to look like you want it to look. Ultimately, you want Product in **Columns** and Standard Revenue in **Rows** (as shown in Lab Exhibit 10.2.10).
12. Your bullet graph should look like the one shown in Lab Exhibit 10.2.11.
13. If you notice that the reference lines and bars are backward (that is, the lines reflect the actual revenue and the bars reflect the standards), right-click the Y-axis to **Swap Reference Line Fields** (Lab Exhibit 10.2.12).
14. Make a variety of edits to format the graph:
    - Add a title by renaming the tab at the bottom of the worksheet to read "Sales Variance by Product" (see Lab Exhibit 10.2.13).
    - Add color to the **Product** dimension so that each product has a different color. To do so, drag the **Product** dimension onto the **Color** mark on the **Marks** card (Lab Exhibit 10.2.14).

- Show the Standard Revenue values on the lines by dragging the **Standard Revenue** measure onto the **Label** mark on the **Marks** card (Lab Exhibit 10.2.15).
- We would like to show the measure title (that is, Standard Revenue) on the label as well. To revise the label, double-click on the **Label** icon and then use the dialog box (shown in Lab Exhibit 10.2.16) to format the label to read "Standard Revenue" by adding that in front of the < SUM(**Standard Revenue**)> measure. Then click **OK** (Lab Exhibit 10.2.17).
- Fit the graph to the available space by selecting **Entire View** at the upper right of the menu bar (Lab Exhibit 10.2.18).

15. Add a caption to explain what you see in the visualization, as follows:
- Click on the **Worksheet** menu at the top of the screen, then select **Show Caption** (Lab Exhibit 10.2.19).
- In the **Caption** box that appears at the bottom of the screen, type "This bullet graph shows that actual revenue underperformed compared to standard revenue for all product lines except for Slab" (Lab Exhibit 10.2.20).

Note: An example of the completed Sales Variance by Product visualization is shown in the final dashboard in Lab Exhibit 10.2.42 at the end of this lab.

Analysis Task #2: Prepare a Bar Chart to Analyze the Sales-Price and the Sales-Volume Variances

1. Open a blank worksheet. Recall that your data did not include fields for the sales-price variance and sales-volume variance. We will need to create calculated fields for each.

DATA VISUALIZATION

2. To create a calculated field, navigate to **Analysis > Create Calculated Field...** (Lab Exhibit 10.2.21).
3. When the **Calculated Field** window opens, enter the formula for sales-price variance, as shown in Lab Exhibit 10.2.22. The formula is [Actual Sales]*([Actual Sales Price]−[Standard Sales Price]). Then click **OK** (at the bottom of the window). This action creates a new dimension called Sales-Price Variance.
4. Next, follow the same steps to create the sales-volume variance dimension using the formula shown in Lab Exhibit 10.2.23: [Standard Sales Price]*([Actual Sales]−[Standard Units Sold]). Then click **OK** at the bottom of the window.
5. To create your visualization, drag the **Product** dimension onto the **Columns** shelf (Lab Exhibit 10.2.24).
6. Drag the **Sale-Price Variance** measure onto the **Rows** shelf (see Lab Exhibit 10.2.24).
7. Drag the **Sales-Volume Variance** measure onto the **Rows** shelf (see Lab Exhibit 10.2.24).
8. To show the two variances side by side for each product on the same axis, drag the **Sales-Volume Variance** pill onto the **Sales-Price Variance** axis so that both variances show on the same axis, as shown in Lab Exhibit 10.2.25.
9. Change the colors of the bars so that the sales-price variances are one color and the sales-volume variances are another color. To do this, drag the **Measure Values** measure from the list of measures to the **Color** mark (Lab Exhibit 10.2.26). The **Measure Values** measure is found at the very bottom of the list of measures (Lab Exhibit 10.2.27), and it represents all of the measures you have used in your visualization—in this case, the DM (direct materials) price and DM efficiency variances.
10. To show the variance amounts at the end of each bar, click on the **Analysis** tab at the top of the screen and select **Show Mark Labels** (Lab Exhibit 10.2.28).
11. Format the values by clicking on the down arrow for each dimension on the **Measure Values** pane in the middle of the screen (Lab Exhibit 10.2.29), selecting **Format** and then formatting the number to **Currency (Standard)** when the **Format** pane appears on the left side of the screen (Lab Exhibit 10.2.30).

12. Because you have the legend that shows the color associated with each variance, you can hide the header at the bottom of the screen that repeats sales-price variance and sales-volume variance for each product. To do this, right-click on the header at the bottom of the screen and deselect **Show header** (Lab Exhibit 10.2.31).

13. Fit the graph to the available space by selecting **Entire View** at the top-right of the menu (Lab Exhibit 10.2.32).

14. Add a caption to explain what you see in the visualization, as follows:
    - Click on the **Worksheet** menu at the top of the screen. Then select **Show Caption** (Lab Exhibit 10.2.33).
    - In the caption box that appears at the bottom of the screen, add the caption shown in Lab Exhibit 10.2.34: "By examining the Sales-Price variance and Sales-Volume variance separately, we can see that the unfavorable sales revenue variance is driven by lower-than-expected sales volume, despite higher-than-budgeted sales prices."

15. Add a title to the spreadsheet by renaming the worksheet tab at the bottom of the screen "Detailed Sales Variances" (Lab Exhibit 10.2.35).

    Your final visualization should look like Lab Exhibit 10.2.36.

Analysis Task #3: Prepare a Dashboard to Show Visualizations Together

DATA VISUALIZATION

1. Open a dashboard by clicking on the **Dashboard** icon (⊞) at the bottom of the screen. On the **Dashboard** screen that opens, you will see the two visualizations you have already prepared on the left side of the screen in the **Sheets** area (Lab Exhibit 10.2.37).

2. Drag the **Sales Variance by Product** visualization to the top of the screen and the **Detailed Sales Variances** visualization to the bottom of the screen. By default, Tableau uses a tiled arrangement for the dashboard (Lab Exhibit 10.2.38).

    Note: With a tiled arrangement, as you drag your visualization onto the dashboard, a gray rectangle appears to show you where the visualization will be placed. Each visualization has a designated space, and your visualizations will not overlap. You can resize the visualizations according to your preferences.

    Alternatively, you could use a floating arrangement in which visualizations do not have a designated space but rather "float" in the dashboard space, and you can move them wherever you like. Tableau has online resources that explain how to create a floating arrangement. Lab Exhibit 10.2.39 shows the dialog box that allows you to select the tiled (or floating) layout for your dashboard.

3. You'll notice that the legend from the **Detailed Sales Variances** visualization also shows up in the dashboard and is set into a container that leaves quite a bit of blank, unused space. We can fix this by making the legend "float" and layering it on top of the **Detailed Sales Variances** visualization to which it refers.

    To make the legend float, click on the legend to activate it, and then click on the down arrow to its right. Select **Floating** from the drop-down menu (Lab Exhibit 10.2.40). Now you can drag the legend around the screen and drop it in the bottom-right corner of the **Detailed Sales Variances** visualization.

4. Lab Exhibit 10.2.41 shows the dialog box that allows you to format the layout of the dashboard. This is where you can add and format borders. Add borders around both visualizations on the dashboard by clicking on each visualization and selecting the **Layout** pane from the left of the screen and setting the **Border** to your preferred style and color.

    Your final dashboard should look like Lab Exhibit 10.2.42.

Share the Story

We have calculated sales variances, created visualizations to analyze and interpret the results, and prepared a dashboard to help management understand the results.

Assessment

1. Take a screenshot of the sales dashboard, paste it into a Word document, and name the file "Lab 10.2 Submission.docx".
2. Answer the multiple-choice questions in Connect and upload your Lab 10.2 Submission.docx via Connect if assigned.

Alternate Lab 10.2   Tableau—On Your Own

Preparing a Sales-Variance Analysis Dashboard (Heartwood)

Using the **Alt Lab 10.2 Data.xlsx** file, apply the same steps in Lab 10.2 to Alternate Lab 10.2, using the following details:

The manager of the Walnut division at **Heartwood Cabinets** would like to prepare detailed variance analysis to evaluate sales performance over the past six months for each product line in his division.

Required

1. Using the monthly sales data and budgeted sales standards, calculate the overall sales variances, the sales-price variances, and the sales-volume variances for each product line.
2. Create a bullet graph visualization to examine the sales variances for each product line.
3. Create a bar chart visualization to examine the sales-price and sales-volume variances to glean more information about the cause of the deviations from expectation.
4. Prepare a dashboard that combines your prepared visualizations into a user-friendly format that will facilitate decision making by management.

Assessment

1. Take a screenshot of the final output, paste it into a Word document, and name the file "Alt Lab 10.2 Submission.docx".
2. Answer the multiple-choice questions in Connect and upload your Alt Lab 10.2 Submission.docx via Connect if assigned.

Lab Note: The tools presented in this lab periodically change. Updated instructions, if applicable, can be found in the student and instructor support materials. All Lab Exhibits are available within the eBook and in Connect.

Preparing a Direct-Cost Variance Analysis Dashboard (Heartwood)

Data Analytics Type: Diagnostic

Keywords

Direct Materials Variance, Direct-Labor Variance, Dashboard

Decision-Making Context

In cost accounting, managers use standards to set expectations for direct costs (materials and labor) for future periods. They compare these standards to actual performance to calculate variances, which help them understand why certain products cost more than expected or less than expected.

The manager of the Pine division at **Heartwood Cabinets** would like to prepare some detailed variance analysis to evaluate cost performance over the past six months for each product line in her division.

Required

1. Using the monthly cost data and direct-cost standards, calculate the direct materials and direct labor variances for each product line.
2. Create a text table visualization to examine the direct materials and direct labor variances for each product line.
3. Create visualizations to illustrate direct materials and direct labor variances over time for each product line.
4. Prepare a dashboard that combines your prepared visualizations into a user-friendly format that will facilitate decision making by management.

Ask the Question

How do actual costs compare to expected costs? Which product line performed the best compared to expectations? Which product line performed the worst compared to expectations? What factors most likely contributed to the deviations?

Master the Data

For this lab, we'll use the data from Excel File Lab 10.3.

1. Open the Excel file **Lab 10.3 Data.xlsx**.
2. Review the data in this file to gain an understanding of the variables available for your analysis. Once you are comfortable with the data, close the file.
3. Open Tableau.
4. Navigate to the **Data Source** tab and select **Microsoft Excel** (as shown in Lab Exhibit 10.3.1).
5. Add the file **Lab 10.3 Data.xlsx** as the connection and drag the worksheet **Lab 10.3** to the data pane (Lab Exhibit 10.3.2). Review the view of the data shown at the bottom of your screen to make sure everything has imported correctly.

Perform the Analysis

Analysis Task #1: Prepare a Text Table Visualization to Present Direct Materials Cost Variances

A text table is just a basic table like you would build in Excel. We'll add conditional formatting using the **Color Mark** function on the **Marks** card to make the positive and negative variances easier to distinguish.

DATA VISUALIZATION

1. Open a blank worksheet. Recall that your data do not include fields for the direct materials efficiency or price variance. We will need to create calculated fields for each.
2. To create a calculated field, navigate to **Analysis > Create Calculated Field** (Lab Exhibit 10.3.3).
3. When the **Calculated Field** window opens, enter the formula for DM Efficiency Variance as shown in Lab Exhibit 10.3.4 and then click **OK** (at the bottom of the window). The formula is [Standard Materials Cost Per Unit of Input]*([Actual Materials Quantity] - [Standard Materials Quantity]).
4. Repeat the previous steps to create a calculated field for DM price variance, as shown in Lab Exhibit 10.3.5. The formula is [Actual Materials Quantity]*([Actual Materials Cost per Unit of Input] - [Standard Materials Cost per Unit of Input])
5. To build your text table for the Direct Materials Variance, drag the (1) **DM Efficiency Variance** and (2) **DM Price Variance** measures onto the **Columns** shelf (Lab Exhibit 10.3.6).
6. Tableau will most likely start building a bar chart. Click on the **Text Table** icon under the **Show Me** tab (on the right side of your screen) to select a text table, as shown in Lab Exhibit 10.3.7.
7. Drag the **Product** dimension, which identifies the type of pine cabinet being produced, to the **Rows** shelf (Lab Exhibit 10.3.8).
8. Drag the **Month** dimension to the **Rows** shelf (Lab Exhibit 10.3.9).
   Note: When you drag over the **Month** dimension, because it is a date, you will see that Tableau first adds it as a year. You will need to click the + icon on the left side of the **Year** pill (on the **Rows** shelf) twice so that it will drill down to the Quarter and then the Month. You can remove the Year and Quarter pills from the shelf because you do not need them for this visualization.
   You have now built a text table, and it should resemble Lab Exhibit 10.3.10.
   Next, you can add formatting to better visualize performance by product.
9. To format each variance as currency, click on the down arrow on the **Sum(DM Efficiency Variance)** pill on the **Measures** card. Note, the down arrows only appear when you hover your cursor over the right side of the pill (Lab Exhibit 10.3.11).
   - Select **Format** and then set your formatting to **Currency (Standard)** when the **Format** menu opens up on the left side of the screen (Lab Exhibit 10.3.12).
   - Repeat this process for the DM Price Variance, setting the formatting to standard currency.
10. Next, to add color, we will use the **Color** mark on the **Marks** card. Often, when we add color to a chart, we want to apply the same color rules to all of the values on the chart. However, in this case, we want to set the coloring rules for each column separately. That is, we want to format the DM Efficiency Variance column based on the DM Efficiency Variance values only and the DM Price Variance column based on the DM Price Variance values only. To do this, we need to **Use separate legends**, as described next.
    - Drag the **Measure Values** measure from the list of measures to the **Color** mark. The **Measure Values** measure is found at the very bottom of the list of measures, and it represents all of the measures you have used in your visualization—in this case, the DM price and DM efficiency variances (Lab Exhibit 10.3.13).

- Click on the down arrow on the **Measure Values** pill that is associated with the **Color** mark (not the one associated with the text). See Lab Exhibit 10.3.14.
- Select **Use Separate Legends** from the drop-down menu (Lab Exhibit 10.3.15).
- You'll see that two legends appear on the right side of the screen—one for the DM Efficiency Variance and one for the DM Price Variance (Lab Exhibit 10.3.16).
- Move your cursor to the **DM Efficiency Variance** legend. A drop-down arrow will appear.
- Click the drop-down arrow and select **Edit Colors...**, as shown in Lab Exhibit 10.3.17.

  The **Edit Colors** interface (Lab Exhibit 10.3.18) will appear in the middle of your screen.
- Make the following selections, as shown in Lab Exhibit 10.3.19.
  - Change the color palette to **Red-Green Diverging**.
  - Check **Stepped Color** and change the value to **2** steps.
  - Click on **<< Advanced** to set the parameters for assigning red vs. green coloring.
  - Check **Center**, which means that the color will change at the center that you set, not at the natural median of the numbers.
  - Change the **Center** number to **0** so that you show a different color for a positive vs. negative value.
  - You will also need to check the **Reversed** option because, in this case, positive values mean unfavorable variances, so they should show as red. (Remember: You will rely on your cost accounting knowledge to create visualizations that will help managers, who may not understand the specifics of cost accounting, understand performance easily.)
  - Click **Apply** to apply the changes to the text table.

Lab Exhibit 10.3.19

Tableau Software

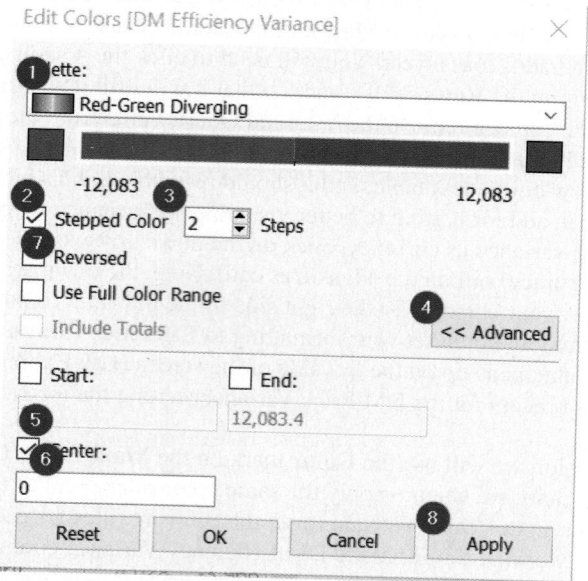

11. Repeat the entire process described in Step 10 to change the text color for the DM Price Variance legend.
12. Add a title by renaming the tab at the bottom of the worksheet as "Direct Materials Variances" (Lab Exhibit 10.3.20).

13. Fit the graph to the available space by selecting **Entire View** in the top-right of the menu (Lab Exhibit 10.3.21).

14. You can remove the legends from the screen because the meaning of the coloring is relatively self-explanatory and you don't want to unnecessarily clutter up your data visualization. To remove legends, click on the drop-down arrow in the upper-right corner of each legend and select **Hide Card** (Lab Exhibit 10.3.22).

15. Add a caption to explain what you see in the visualization, as follows:

- Click on the **Worksheet** menu at the top of the screen. Then select **Show Caption** (Lab Exhibit 10.3.23).
- In the **Caption** box that appears at the bottom of the screen, type the text shown in Lab Exhibit 10.3.24:

   This table shows the direct materials price and efficiency variances for each product line by month. The variances in green are favorable. Those in red are unfavorable. All efficiency variances are unfavorable, indicating that Heartwood is using more materials than expected. The favorable price variances suggest that the materials cost less than expected. Taken together, there is concern that Heartwood is buying poor-quality materials, leading to higher levels of waste during production.

   You may also notice a spike in the unfavorable variance in February - perhaps there was a machine malfunction during this month leading to higher levels of damage to raw materials.

Your final visualization should resemble Lab Exhibit 10.3.25.

Analysis Task #2: Prepare a Line Graph to Visualize the DM Variances over Time

As we began to see in the text table built in Analysis Task #1, there seemed to be a spike in unfavorable variances in February. This spike is somewhat apparent in the text table because the dataset is small enough that we can still see everything on one screen and we can keep the numbers somewhat straight in our heads. But this may not always be the case, so other visualizations can be helpful to supplement our understanding and help us gain more accurate insights.

DATA VISUALIZATION

   Because we are interested in identifying the trends in our variances over time, we will use a line graph, which is generally appropriate for analysis across time.

1. Open a new worksheet.
2. Drag the **Month** dimension onto the **Columns** shelf. As before, Tableau will default to showing date dimensions as a year, and you will need to drill down twice (Lab Exhibit 10.3.26).
   - Click the **+** button on the **Year** pill (see Lab Exhibit 10.3.26) and then the **Quarter** pill to get to the **Month** pill (Lab Exhibit 10.3.27).
   - Because our analysis only covers dates within one year, you can remove the Year and Quarter pills from the shelves and keep only the Month dimension.
3. Drag the **DM Efficiency Variance** and **DM Price Variance** measures to the **Rows** shelf (Lab Exhibit 10.3.28).

   Because you are using a date dimension, Tableau will probably default to a line graph, but if it does not, select the **Line Graph** option from the **Show Me** tab on the right side of the screen (Lab Exhibit 10.3.29).

   Your visualization should resemble Lab Exhibit 10.3.30.

   Note: This visualization is showing the total variances by month for ALL products in the Pine division. This is appropriate based on the goal of this current analysis, which is to see if there are any trends for the Pine division as a whole (based on our findings in Analysis Task #1).

4. To format the visualization to rename the X-axis, right-click on the X-axis and select **Edit axis...**, as shown in Lab Exhibit 10.3.31.
   - From the **Edit Axis** menu, you can change the axis title. Under **Title**, delete "Month of" so that only "Month" shows (Lab Exhibit 10.3.32).
5. Add a caption to explain what you see in the visualization, as follows:
   - Click on the **Worksheet** menu at the top of the screen, then select **Show Caption** (Lab Exhibit 10.3.33).
   - In the **Caption** box that appears at the bottom of the screen, describe the results as shown in Lab Exhibit 10.3.34. The caption should read as follows:

   This table shows the direct materials price and efficiency variances for each product line by month. The variances in green are favorable. Those in red are unfavorable. All efficiency variances are unfavorable, indicating that Heartwood is using more materials than expected. The favorable price variances suggest that the materials cost less than expected. Taken together, there is concern that Heartwood is buying poor-quality materials, leading to higher levels of waste during production.

   You may also notice a spike in the unfavorable variance in February - perhaps there was a machine malfunction during this month leading to higher levels of damage to raw materials.

   Your final visualization should resemble Lab Exhibit 10.3.35.

DATA VISUALIZATION

Analysis Task #3: Prepare a Text Table Visualization to Present Direct Labor Variances

Follow the same steps you completed for preparing the direct materials variance to complete the direct-labor variances.

Your results should resemble Lab Exhibit 10.3.36.

DATA VISUALIZATION

Analysis Task #4: Prepare a Combination Graph That Shows the DL Efficiency and DL Price Variances over Time

As you saw in Analysis Task #3, there appears to be a decrease in unfavorable DL efficiency variances occurring around the same time that unfavorable DL price variances increase—likely due to an increase in employee wages occurring around March.

Next, you will use a combination chart to illustrate both variances together for each product.

1. Drag the **Product** dimension and the **Month** dimension onto the **Columns** shelf (Lab Exhibit 10.3.37).
2. Drag the **DL Efficiency Variance** measure and the **DL Price Variance** measure onto the **Rows** shelf (see Lab Exhibit 10.3.37).
3. Select the **Combination Chart** icon from the **Show Me** pane (Lab Exhibit 10.3.38).
   Refer to Lab Exhibit 10.3.39. You should see that the **Marks** card shows the marks options for **All** (1), **DL Efficiency Variance** (2), and **DL Price Variance** (3).
   By clicking on either the **DL Price Variance** tab or the **DL Efficiency Variance** tab, you can adjust the specific marks for each. This is where you make changes to the colors of the bar or line that you are using, or change which measure is presented as a bar or line (or any other mark that you might want to use depending on your analysis goals).
4. For our analysis, let's show the DL Price Variance as a line graph, in relation to the DL Efficiency Variance, shown as a bar graph.
   - Click on the **DL Price Variance** tab on the **Marks** card. Change the bar to **Line** (Lab Exhibit 10.3.40).
   - Click on the **DL Efficiency Variance** tab on the **Marks** card and confirm that it is set to **Bar**. If it is not, change it to **Bar** using the drop-down menu (boxed in red at the top of Lab Exhibit 10.3.40).

5. Format your visualization so that it does not look cluttered.
   - You can remove the "Month" label from the X-axis by right-clicking on "Months" on the X-axis and clicking on **Show Header** to uncheck it and remove the label (Lab Exhibit 10.3.41). Month will still show on the tool tip when you scroll over the visualization.
6. Add a caption to interpret your results, shown in Lab Exhibit 10.3.42. The caption should read as follows:

   This combination chart shows trends in DL Efficiency Variance and DL Price Variance over time by product line. We see a very clear relationship between the price and efficiency variance illustrating that as pay increases, so does the efficiency of the work. This suggests that Heartwood seems to benefit from hiring more skilled labor.

Your final visualization should resemble Lab Exhibit 10.3.43.

Analysis Task #5: Combine Your Visualizations into a Dashboard to Provide an Overall View of Direct Cost Variances at Heartwood Cabinetry's Pine Division

DATA VISUALIZATION

1. Click the **Dashboard** icon at the bottom of the screen (⊞) to open a blank dashboard page.

   For this dashboard, you will combine all four of the visualizations you have created onto a single dashboard. You can do this using a Tiled layout arrangement (Lab Exhibit 10.3.44). With a tiled arrangement, as you drag your visualization onto the dashboard, a gray rectangle appears to show you where the visualization will be placed. Each visualization has a designated space, and there will not be any overlapping of your visualizations. You can resize the visualizations as you need.

   Alternatively, you could use a floating arrangement in which visualizations do not have a designated space, but rather "float" in the dashboard space, and you can move them wherever you would like. Tableau has online resources that explain how to create a floating arrangement.

As shown in Lab Exhibit 10.3.45:
2. Drag your **Direct Labor Variances** (text table) visualization onto the dashboard and place it in the upper-left corner,
3. Drag your **Direct Materials Variances** (text table) visualization onto the dashboard and place it in the upper-right corner.
4. Drag the **Direct Labor Variances over Time** visualization onto the dashboard and place it in the lower-left corner.
5. Drag the **Direct Materials Variances over Time** visualization onto the dashboard and place it in the lower-right corner.
6. Resize each visualization as needed to show enough of the visualization on the dashboard. You can resize the visualization by moving the cursor to the border of the visualization until the cursor becomes a double-headed arrow. Then drag the border to where you want it.
7. Remove unnecessary details, including the legends, by right-clicking on the items and then pressing **Delete**.
8. Resize fonts as necessary.
9. Add borders around each visualization from the **Layout** tab on the left side of the screen. Click on each visualization, then click the **Layout** tab and select the **Border** type and **Color** that you prefer (Lab Exhibit 10.3.46).

The final dashboard should resemble Lab Exhibit 10.3.47.

Share the Story

We have computed the quantity variance. Once we compute the labor variance, we will be able to decide if hiring less-expensive workers is associated with an unfavorable materials variance. We can also decide what is best both for overall quality as well as for maintaining low costs.

Assessment

1. Take a screenshot of the final output, paste it into a Word document, and name the file "Lab 10.3 Submission.docx".
2. Answer the multiple-choice questions in Connect and upload your Lab 10.3 Submission.docx via Connect if assigned.

Alternate Lab 10.3 Tableau—On Your Own

Preparing a Direct-Cost Variance Analysis Dashboard (Heartwood)

Using the **Alt Lab 10.3 Data.xlsx** file, apply the same steps in Lab 10.3 to Alternate Lab 10.3, using the following details:

The manager for the Pine division at **Heartwood Cabinets** would like to prepare some detailed variance analysis to evaluate cost performance over the past six months for each product line in her division.

Required

1. Using the monthly cost data and direct-cost standards, calculate the direct materials and direct labor variances for each product line.
2. Create a text table visualization to examine the direct materials and direct labor variances for each product line.
3. Create visualizations to illustrate direct materials and direct labor variances over time for each product line.
4. Prepare a dashboard that combines your prepared visualizations into a user-friendly format that will facilitate decision making by management.

Assessment

1. Take a screenshot of the final output, paste it into a Word document, and name the file "Alt Lab 10.3 Submission.docx".
2. Answer the multiple-choice questions in Connect and upload your Alt Lab 10.3 Submission.docx via Connect if assigned.

Preparing a Sales-Variance Analysis Dashboard (Heartwood)

Data Analytics Type: Diagnostic Analytics

Keywords

Sales Variance, Sales-Price Variance, Sales-Efficiency Variance, Dashboard

Decision-Making Context

In cost accounting, managers use standards to set expectations for sales and associated revenues for future periods. They compare these standards to actual performance to calculate variances, which help them understand why certain products overperform or underperform.

   The manager of the Maple division at **Heartwood Cabinets** would like to prepare a detailed variance analysis to evaluate sales performance over the past six months for each product line in her division.

Required

Using the monthly sales data and budgeted sales standards, calculate the overall sales variances, the sales-price variances, and the sales-volume variances for each product line in Power BI.

1. Create a clustered column chart visualization to examine the static-budget variance for revenue (sales) for the entire division.
2. Create a clustered column chart visualization to examine the static-budget variance for revenue (sales) for each product line.
3. Create a clustered column chart visualization to examine the sales-price and sales-volume variances to glean more information about the cause of the deviations from expectation.
4. Show all three visualizations in one Power BI report.

Ask the Question

How does actual sales performance compare to expected sales performance? Which product line performed the best compared to expectations? Which product line performed the worst in comparison to expectations? What factors most likely contributed to the deviations?

Master the Data

1. Open the Excel file **Lab 10.4 Data.xlsx**.
2. Review the data in this file to gain an understanding of the variables available for your analysis. Once you are comfortable with the data, close the file.
3. Open Power BI and select **Get data**, as shown in Lab Exhibit 10.4.1.
4. From the **Get Data** menu, double-click **Excel Workbook** (Lab Exhibit 10.4.2).
5. Select the file **Lab 10.4 Data.xlsx** as the connection and click **Open**.
6. When the navigator opens in Power BI, select the worksheet **Lab 10.4**, then click **Load** (Lab Exhibit 10.4.3).

Lab Note: The tools presented in this lab periodically change. Updated instructions, if applicable, can be found in the student and instructor support materials. All Lab Exhibits are available within the eBook and in Connect.

Perform the Analysis

DATA VISUALIZATION

Analysis Task #1: Prepare a Clustered Column Chart to Illustrate Static-Budget Variance for the Entire Maple Division

1. When the report screen opens, click on the down arrow to the left of sheet **Lab 10.4** in the **Fields** pane (Lab Exhibit 10.4.4). This will allow you to see all the data fields available for your analyses.
2. From the **Visualizations** pane, select the **Clustered Bar Chart Visualization** icon, shown in Lab Exhibit 10.4.5.
3. Add a column for the Actual Revenues and another column for Standard Revenues. You will have to calculate these fields.

   To do so, click on the **Modeling** tab at the top of the screen and then click on the **New Column** icon (Lab Exhibit 10.4.6).
4. In the **Dax Formula Builder** that opens, enter a formula to calculate Actual Revenue. Use the formula shown in Lab Exhibit 10.4.7: Actual Revenue = [Actual Sales Price]*[Actual Units Produced]. This creates a new column in which the actual revenue value is calculated for each row.
5. Repeat Step 4 to create a new column that contains a calculated field for Standard Revenue. Use the formula shown in Lab Exhibit 10.4.8: Standard Revenue = [Standard Sales Price]*[Standard Units Produced].

   You should notice that these new fields have been added to the **Field** pane, as shown in Lab Exhibit 10.4.9. Note that calculated fields show a ▦ symbol.
6. Drag the **Standard Revenue** and **Actual Revenue** fields to the **Values** space in the **Visualizations** pane (see Lab Exhibit 10.4.10).
7. Format the visualization by clicking on the **Paintbrush** icon. To add data labels (specifically, Sum of Actual Revenue and Sum of Standard Revenue), turn the **Data labels** to **On** (Lab Exhibit 10.4.11).
8. Click on the arrow next to the **Title** options on the **Formatting** pane and change the title of the visualization to "Standard vs. Actual Revenue for the Maple Division" (Lab Exhibit 10.4.12).
9. Resize this visualization so that it takes up only the far-left portion of the report screen, as shown in Lab Exhibit 10.4.13. Doing this will allow you to add the next two visualizations to the same report screen.

DATA VISUALIZATION

Analysis Task #2: Prepare a Clustered Column Chart to Illustrate Static-Budget Variance for the Revenue Generated by Each Product in the Maple Division

1. Click on an empty space on the report screen to the right of the visualization you created in Analysis Task #1.
2. Click on the **Clustered Bar Chart** icon on the **Visualizations** pane, as shown in Lab Exhibit 10.4.14.
3. Drag the **Standard Revenue** and **Actual Revenue** fields to the **Values** space in the **Visualizations** pane and drag **Product** to the **Axis** space (Lab Exhibit 10.4.15).

   You should now have a clustered column chart showing the actual and standard revenue for each product, as shown in Lab Exhibit 10.4.16.
4. Format the visualization by clicking on the **Paintbrush** icon. To add data labels (specifically, Sum of Actual Revenue and Sum of Standard Revenue), turn the **Data labels** to **On** (Lab Exhibit 10.4.17).
5. Change the title of the visualization to "Standard vs. Actual Revenue by Product" (Lab Exhibit 10.4.18).

   Because you already have a legend at the top of the first visualization, remove the legend from this visualization to save space. Move the slider next to **Legend** to **Off** (Lab Exhibit 10.4.19).

6. Resize this visualization so that it takes up only the top half of the remaining portion of the report screen, as shown in Lab Exhibit 10.4.20. This will allow you to add the next two visualizations to the same report screen.

Analysis Task #3: Prepare a Column Chart to Illustrate Sales-Price Variance and Sales-Volume Variance for Each Product in the Maple Division

DATA VISUALIZATION

For this analysis, you must calculate the sales-price variance and the sales-volume variance.

1. To create a new column to calculate sales-price variance, click on the **Modeling** tab at the top of the screen and then click on the **New Column** icon (Lab Exhibit 10.4.21).
2. In the **Dax Formula Builder** that opens, enter a formula to calculate Actual Revenue. Use the formula in Lab Exhibit 10.4.22: Sales Price Variance = [Actual Units Produced]*([Actual Sales Price]−[Standard Sales Price]). This creates a new column in which the actual revenue value is calculated for each row.
3. Repeat Step 2 to create a new column that contains a calculated field for Sales Volume Variance. Use the formula shown in Lab Exhibit 10.4.23: Sales Volume Variance = [Standard Sales Price]*([Actual Units Produced]−[Standard Units Produced]).
4. Click on an empty space on the report screen beneath the bottom of the visualization you created in Analysis Task #2.
5. From the **Visualizations** pane, select the icon for the **Clustered Bar Chart** visualization, as shown in Lab Exhibit 10.4.24.
6. Drag the **Sales Price Variance** and **Sales Volume Variance** fields to the **Values** space in the **Visualizations** pane. Also drag **Product** to the **Axis** space, as shown in Lab Exhibit 10.4.25.
7. Format the visualization by clicking on the **Paintbrush** icon. To add data labels (Sum of Actual Revenue and Sum of Standard Revenue), turn the **Data labels** to **On**, as shown in Lab Exhibit 10.4.26.
8. Change the title of the visualization to "Sales Variances by Product" (Lab Exhibit 10.4.27).
9. Remove the title running along the Y-axis to save space (and eliminate redundancy because this information is also contained in the legend). To do so, first click on the **Y Axis** option (Lab Exhibit 10.4.28) and then scroll down until you can move the **Title** slider to **Off** (Lab Exhibit 10.4.29).

Your final report containing three visualizations will resemble Lab Exhibit 10.4.30.

Share the Story

We have now developed a dashboard that shows the revenue-related variances for the Maple division of Heartwood Cabinets for this period. Management can use this information to compare performance across divisions. Further, because the Sales Variances by Product visualization examines the sales-volume and sales-price variances separately, management can see that most of the overall variance is driven by lower-than-expected sales in all divisions, not by sales prices that are below the standard.

Assessment

1. Take a screenshot of the dashboard, paste into a Word document, and name the file "Lab 10.4 Submission.docx".
2. Answer the multiple-choice questions in Connect and upload your Lab 10.4 Submission.docx via Connect if assigned.

Preparing a Sales-Variance Analysis Dashboard (Heartwood)

Apply the same steps in **Lab 10.4** to the data in **Alt Lab 10.4 Data.xlsx** to prepare a dashboard analyzing the sales variances for the Teak division of **Heartwood Cabinets**.

Required

Using the monthly sales data and budgeted sales standards, calculate the overall sales variances, the sales-price variances, and the sales-volume variances for each product line in Power BI.

1. Create a clustered column chart visualization to examine the static-budget variance for revenue (sales) for the entire division.
2. Create a clustered column chart visualization to examine the static-budget variance for revenue (sales) for each product line.
3. Create a clustered column chart visualization to examine the sales-price and sales-volume variances to glean more information about the cause of the deviations from expectation.
4. Show all three visualizations in one Power BI report.

Assessment

1. Take a screenshot of the sales forecast, paste it into a Word document, and name the file "Alt Lab 10.4 Submission.docx".
2. Answer the multiple-choice questions in Connect and upload your Alt Lab 10.4 Submission.docx via Connect if assigned.

Preparing a Direct-Cost/Sales-Variance Analysis Dashboard (Heartwood)

Lab Note: The tools presented in this lab periodically change. Updated instructions, if applicable, can be found in the student and instructor support materials. All Lab Exhibits are available within the eBook and in Connect.

Data Analytics Type: Diagnostic Analytics

Keywords

Direct Materials Variance, Direct Labor Variance, Dashboard

Decision-Making Context

In cost accounting, managers use standards to set expectations for direct costs (materials and labor) for future periods. They compare these standards to actual performance to calculate variances, which help them understand why certain products cost more than expected or less than expected.

The manager of the Cherry division at **Heartwood Cabinets** would like to prepare some detailed variance analysis to evaluate cost performance over the past six months for each product line in her division.

Required

1. Using the monthly cost data and direct-cost standards, calculate the direct materials and direct labor variances for each product line.
2. Create a pivot table to examine the direct materials and direct labor variances for each product line.
3. Prepare combo chart visualizations to illustrate direct materials and direct labor variances over time for each product line.

Ask the Question

How do actual costs compare to expected costs? Which product line performed the best compared to expectations? Which product line performed the worst compared to expectations? What factors most likely contributed to the deviations?

Master the Data

1. Open the Excel file **Lab 10.5 Data.xlsx**.
2. Review the data in this file to gain an understanding of the variables available for your analysis.

Perform the Analysis

Analysis Task #1: Calculate the Direct Materials and Direct Labor Variances for Each Product Line

1. Scroll to the first empty column in your worksheet (Column P). Use Lab Exhibit 10.5.1 to guide you for the next several steps:
2. Label cell P1 as "Direct Labor Price Variance".
3. Label cell Q1 as "Direct Labor Efficiency Variance".
4. Label cell R1 "Direct Materials Price Variance".
5. Label cell S1 "Direct Materials Efficiency Variance".
   Now that you have set up the spreadsheet, you can add your formulas to calculate each variance in the second row of cells.

6. In cell P2, calculate the direct labor-price variance using this formula:

$$\text{Actual Quantity} * (\text{Actual Price} - \text{Standard Price})$$

where Actual Quantity = Actual Units Produced * Actual Labor Hours per Unit. Lab Exhibit 10.5.2 shows the formula: =(F2*O2)*(N2-M2).

7. In cell Q2, calculate the direct labor-efficiency variance using this formula:

$$\text{Standard Price} * (\text{Actual Quantity} - \text{Standard Quantity})$$

where Actual Quantity = Actual Units Produced * Actual Labor Hours per Unit and Standard Quantity = Standard Units Produced * Standard Labor Hours per Unit. Lab Exhibit 10.5.3 shows the formula: =M2*((F2*O2)-(D2*L2)).

8. In cell R2, calculate the direct materials price variance using this formula:

$$\text{Actual Quantity} * (\text{Actual Price} - \text{Standard Price})$$

where Actual Quantity = Actual Units Produced * Actual Direct Materials per Unit. Lab Exhibit 10.5.4 shows the formula: =(F2*J2)*(K2-I2).

9. In cell S2, calculate the direct materials efficiency variance using this formula:

$$\text{Standard Price} * (\text{Actual Quantity} - \text{Standard Quantity})$$

where Actual Quantity = Actual Units Produced * Actual Direct Materials (per Unit) and Standard Quantity = Standard Units Produced * Standard Direct Materials (per Unit). Lab Exhibit 10.5.5 shows the formula: =I2*((F2*J2)-(H2*D2)).

10. Copy each of the formulas down by highlighting cells P2:S2. Grab the square in the bottom-right corner of the highlighted cells and double-click to copy the formula to the rest of the rows (Lab Exhibit 10.5.6).

Analysis Task #2: Create a Pivot Table to Examine the Direct Materials and Direct Labor Variances for Each Product Line

1. Click any cell in the data on the Lab 10.5 worksheet.
2. Click **Insert > PivotTable**, as shown in Lab Exhibit 10.5.7.
3. When the dialog box opens, it should indicate that the entire **Table/Range** is selected, as shown in Lab Exhibit 10.5.8.
4. The pivot table will open on a new worksheet. Rename the worksheet "Pivot Table (1)". To do so, double-click on the tab at the bottom of the screen and type in the new title, as shown in Lab Exhibit 10.5.9.
5. In the **PivotTable Fields** dialog box, drag (1) **Product** and (2) **Month** to the **Rows** shelf. Then drag (3) **Direct Materials Price Variance**, (4) **Direct Materials Efficiency Variance**, (5) **Direct Labor Price Variance**, and (6) **Direct Labor Efficiency Variance** to the **Values** shelf. After you have completed this step, your screen should resemble Lab Exhibit 10.5.10.
6. Your pivot table is now populated. Format the numbers into currency with red font for negative variances by highlighting the entire pivot table, then click the down arrow in the bottom-right corner of the **Currency** options on the **Home** tab (Lab Exhibit 10.5.11).
7. Now navigate to **Currency** and select the option with red font and parentheses for negative numbers, as shown in Lab Exhibit 10.5.12.
8. The completed pivot table is shown in Lab Exhibit 10.5.13.

Analysis Task #3: Prepare a Combo Chart Visualization to Illustrate Direct Materials and Direct Labor Variances over Time for Each Product Line

DATA VISUALIZATION

You can prepare the combo chart directly from the pivot table that you prepared in Analysis Task #2. However, once you start formatting the combo chart and filtering by product, you will make changes to the pivot table itself. So, instead of using the table you completed for Analysis Task #2, you are going to make a copy of the worksheet that contains your pivot table.

1. Right-click on the **Pivot Table (1)** tab to open the menu. Then select **Move or Copy...**, as shown in Lab Exhibit 10.5.14.

2. When the **Move or Copy...** dialog box opens, select **Create a copy** and (**move to end**), as shown in Lab Exhibit 10.5.15.

3. You have now created a new tab at the bottom, and the worksheet contains the same pivot table as your original. Rename this tab "Pivot Table (2)".

4. Click anywhere in the new pivot table.

5. From the **Insert** tab, select the icon for the **Combo Chart**, as shown in Lab Exhibit 10.5.16.

6. A combo chart resembling Lab Exhibit 10.5.17 will be automatically generated using all of the data in the pivot table.

7. Cut/paste the combo chart onto a new worksheet.

8. Label the worksheet "Combo Chart".

9. Using the **Pivot Table Fields** menu on the right side of the screen, deselect the **Direct Labor Price Variance** and the **Direct Labor Efficiency Variance** from the graph so that the dialog box matches Lab Exhibit 10.5.18.
   Now the combo chart includes only the direct materials variances.

10. Navigate to the **Design** tab and then select **Change Chart Type** (Lab Exhibit 10.5.19).

11. Make sure **Combo Chart** is still selected (see Lab Exhibit 10.5.20).

12. Set the **Chart Type** to **Clustered Column** for the Direct Materials Price Variance and to **Line** for Direct Materials Efficiency Variance. Then click **OK**. (See Lab Exhibit 10.5.20.)

13. The combo chart now looks like Lab Exhibit 10.5.21. It shows all variances for each product for each month.

14. The chart is now complete, but you can use the **Filter** in the **Product** button at the bottom-left corner of the graph Product ▾ . Lab Exhibit 10.5.22 shows the **Filter** menu.

15. We also want to create a combo chart to show the direct labor variances. To do so, you will need to repeat Steps 1–14, including copying the pivot table again and labeling your newest pivot table tab "Pivot Table (3)".

16. Cut/paste this combo chart onto the same worksheet as your Direct Materials Variances chart.

17. Format them the same, but change the colors of the bars/lines on the DM variances so that they are different from the DL variances.

18. Your finished DL variance combo chart should look like Lab Exhibit 10.5.23.

19. To make both graphs filter on the same product at the same time, you can add a slicer. Click on your first combo chart. Then click **Insert** and select **Slicer**, as shown in Lab Exhibit 10.5.24.

20. The **Insert Slicers** dialog box will appear. Select **Product** so that you can filter both visualizations by product. Then click **OK** (Lab Exhibit 10.5.25).

21. Find a place on your spreadsheet to place the **Slicer**.

22. Right-click the **Slicer** and select **Report connections**. Doing so opens the **Report Connections** dialog box (Lab Exhibit 10.5.26).

23. The data from the sheet Pivot Table (2) should already be selected. Also select Pivot Table (3) so that it connects the data from your second combo chart to the slicer as well (Lab Exhibit 10.5.26). Click **OK**.

24. Now, when you select any of the products on the **Slicer**, both charts are filtered so you can see visualizations of all variances for that product at the same time. For example, Lab Exhibit 10.5.27 shows both charts filtered on Shaker.

Share the Story

We have calculated direct materials and direct labor variances and created visualizations to analyze and interpret the results. Recall that Heartwood management wanted to understand:

1. How actual costs compare to expected costs.
2. Which product line performed the best compared to expectations.
3. Which product line performed the worst compared to expectations.
4. What factors most likely contributed to the deviations.

The pivot tables and visualizations you have prepared provide insight into each of these questions.

Overall, the Cherry division of Heartwood has a favorable variance, driven by favorable direct materials efficiency variances for all cabinet types.

The Arch cabinet style performed the best compared to expectations. Analysis reveals favorable variances with respect to the efficiency of materials and labor used. The Arch style did, however, experience unfavorable variances for direct materials price and direct labor price. Perhaps higher labor wages or better-quality materials contributed to the favorable efficiency variances.

The Slab cabinet style performed the worst compared to expectations. Analysis reveals a slightly favorable direct materials efficiency variance, but all other variances were unfavorable (and the DM price variance and DL efficiency variance both exceeded $20,000). Examination of the monthly performance compared to target also shows that the favorable variances were small ($1,425 and $750) and only occurred in two out of six months. Overall, these results reveal that during most months, the Slab style cabinets use more materials and labor than expected, and the labor and materials are also more than expected.

Assessment

1. Take a screenshot of the complete pivot table and paste it into a Word.
2. Using the **Slicer**, select the Shaker product line. Take a screenshot of the Combo Charts dashboard, paste it into the same Word document, and name the file "Lab 10.5 Submission.docx".
3. Answer the multiple-choice questions in Connect and upload your Lab 10.5 Submission.docx via Connect if assigned.

Alternate Lab 10.5   Excel—On Your Own

Preparing a Direct-Cost/Sales-Variance Analysis Dashboard (Heartwood)

Using the data in the Excel file **Alt Lab 10.5 Data.xlsx**, apply the same steps in Lab 10.5 to Alt Lab 10.5.

The manager of the Teak division at **Heartwood Cabinets** would like to prepare detailed variance analysis to evaluate cost performance over the past six months for each product line in her division.

Required

1. Using the monthly cost data and direct-cost standards, calculate the direct materials and direct labor variances for each product line.
2. Create a pivot table to examine the direct materials and direct labor variances for each product line.
3. Prepare combo chart visualizations to illustrate direct materials and direct labor variances over time for each product line.

Assessment

1. Take a screenshot of the complete pivot table and paste it into a Word document.
2. Using the **Slicer**, select the Slab product line. Take a screenshot of the Combo Charts dashboard, paste it into the same Word document, and name the file "Alt Lab 10.5 Submission.docx".
3. Answer the multiple-choice questions in Connect and upload your Alt Lab 10.5 Submission.docx via Connect if assigned.

Chapter 11

Indirect Cost Variances

A Look at This Chapter

This chapter continues to explore variances between budgeted and actual performance, with a focus on indirect costs. In addition to describing how organizations plan for and budget fixed and variable overhead, it explains how to calculate the different overhead variances that management uses to understand why results deviate from expectations.

Cost Accounting and Data Analytics

COST ACCOUNTING LEARNING OBJECTIVE	RELATED DATA ANALYTICS LABS	LAB ANALYTICS TYPES
LO 11.1 Understand how organizations budget for indirect overhead costs.		
LO 11.2 Calculate variable overhead spending variance and explain its implication.		
LO 11.3 Calculate variable overhead efficiency variance and explain its implication.		
LO 11.4 Record variable overhead variances as journal entries.		
LO 11.5 Calculate fixed overhead spending variance.		
LO 11.6 Calculate production-volume variance.	**LAB 11.1 Excel:** Graphing Production-Volume Variance	Diagnostic
	LAB 11.2 Power BI: Graphing Production-Volume Variance	Diagnostic
	LAB 11.3 Tableau: Graphing Production-Volume Variance	Diagnostic

Cost Accounting and Data Analytics *(continued)*

COST ACCOUNTING LEARNING OBJECTIVE	RELATED DATA ANALYTICS LAB(s)	LAB ANALYTICS TYPES
LO 11.7 Record fixed overhead variances as journal entries.	LAB 11.4 **Tableau:** Using Data Analytics to Investigate Unusual Overhead Activity (Heartwood)	Diagnostic
	Data Analytics Mini-Lab: Evaluating Overhead Variances Across Divisions Using Tableau Dashboards	Diagnostic
LO 11.8 Examine how organizations can reduce overhead spending.	LAB 11.5 **Tableau:** Evaluating Overhead Variances Across Divisions	Diagnostic

Chapter Concepts and Career Skills

Learning About . . .	Helps with These Career Skills
Budgeting for indirect overhead costs	• Understanding and planning for the costs required to produce goods and services
Calculating overhead variances	• Analyzing and diagnosing causes of deviations from management's expectations
Reducing overhead spending	• Developing creative problem-solving skills and finding innovative solutions

Natee Meepian/Shutterstock

You Paid $5 for That Latte, but What Did It Cost to Produce?

As a customer at your local **Starbucks**, you likely pay about $5.00 for a grande skinny vanilla latte. Have you ever wondered how much it costs the company to produce that cup of coffee?

The retail cost for the coffee, milk, and syrup is about $0.35, and the cost of the cup, lid, and stirrer is about $0.08. So, total direct materials cost is about $0.43. Direct labor cost is about $0.56 for the wages, taxes, and benefits for the baristas and cashiers, bringing direct total costs to $0.99.

There are indirect costs, too. Starbucks management must have a solid understanding of the company's indirect costs so that it can develop an accurate budget and set an appropriate price for customers. At Starbucks, indirect costs include rent, salaries of nonsales personnel, communications, and utilities. Identifying these costs helps the company make strategic decisions that help it meet its profitability goals. In addition, a well-planned budget helps Starbucks set prices for new products, create and implement sales promotions, and make staffing decisions. At Starbucks, indirect costs are approximately 7% of revenues, or about $0.35 per grande skinny vanilla latte.

As with direct costs, sometimes changes in the operating environment affect the indirect cost estimates. For example, the general and administrative expenses at Starbucks recently increased from 6.5% of revenue to 7.1% of revenue. Management attributed some of this increase to higher-than-expected salaries and benefits for employees involved in technology, innovation, and digital platforms (including the Starbucks menu app). Just as direct cost variances occur when direct costs exceed expectations (see Chapter 10), overhead variances occur when overhead costs exceed expectations.

DETERMING STANDARD OVERHEAD COSTS

In Chapter 4, we learned about **indirect costs** such as **manufacturing overhead** and how these costs are allocated to a company's inventory. As a refresher, **overhead costs** are production costs that are not traced back to a specific job performed or product made. Overhead costs can be *variable*, which means they vary with production, or *fixed*, which means they remain the same even if the amount of production increases or decreases. Overhead costs include indirect materials, indirect labor, and other indirect production costs, such as rent and utilities.

Let's think about **Starbucks** again. Some materials, such as the creamer and sugar that patrons can add to their hot beverages, cannot easily be traced back to an individual coffee or sale. For this reason, Starbucks chooses to account for creamer and sugar as indirect materials. Similarly, the salary of the store manager, who sets the employee schedule and places product orders, cannot easily be traced to individual sales, so Starbucks accounts for the manager's salary as indirect labor. Other indirect costs include the rent for the store, the furniture used by patrons, and depreciation and maintenance on the coffee machines, ovens, and refrigerators.

Recall from Chapter 4 that overhead costs are generally applied to specific jobs or activities using a **predetermined overhead rate**, which is calculated based on (1) the total overhead for the reporting period and (2) the allocation base (or cost driver). Recall that an *allocation base,* also called an *application base,* is the basis on which costs are assigned to a cost object. Although companies can choose from a host of allocation bases, the base should be reasonably associated with whatever causes the overhead costs, which is most often direct labor hours or machine hours. Returning to our example, Starbucks has determined that direct labor hours are reasonably correlated with overhead costs and decided to use direct labor hours as an allocation base.

Let's now consider how overhead is incorporated into the budget. As we saw in Chapter 10, many organizations use a **standard costing system**, in which a standard amount of fixed and variable overhead is allocated to inventory during production. A standard costing system is useful because when an organization's results vary from the standard (and they almost always do), variances provide some information about the causes and how managers can improve results.

Determining Standard Variable Overhead Rates

How do organizations, including **Starbucks**, determine the overhead allocation rate? Let's examine variable overhead first. Allocating variable overhead is a three-step process:

1. **Select the cost-allocation bases for allocating variable overhead costs and estimate the quantity of the bases.**
   - The allocation base should be something that is reasonably associated with the cause of the overhead. For example, a manufacturing company might use machine hours for the costs associated with machine usage, including repairs and maintenance. A hotel might use the number of room-nights that the hotel could be occupied.
   - An organization can also use different allocation bases for different **overhead cost pools**, which are the costs associated with performing an activity or task.
   - An organization will estimate the quantity of the allocation base(s) that it expects will be needed for total production during the budget period.
2. **Sum all variable overhead associated with each allocation base.**
3. **Divide the total variable overhead by the standard amount of the allocation base to calculate the variable overhead rate per unit.**

maiva/Shutterstock

Let's look at an example. The **American Accounting Association (AAA)** publishes over 15 journals filled with accounting research conducted by accounting professors from around the world. When preparing the annual budget for variable overhead, AAA likely uses the three-step process described above:

1. **Select the cost-allocation bases for allocating variable overhead costs and estimate the quantity of the bases.**

   The AAA selects page count as the cost-allocation basis. Page count can vary significantly from journal to journal, and even between issues within the same journal, because it depends on the length of the articles submitted by authors. The AAA has guidelines about the length of articles (let's assume that 40 pages is the expected or standard page count), but there are always papers that deviate from that rule. The AAA estimates page count as follows:
   - The AAA publishes 15 journals.
   - The average journal has 3 issues per year.
   - The average issue contains 7 papers.
   - The standard page count for each paper is 40 pages.

   $$15 * 3 * 7 * 40 = 12{,}600 \text{ pages per year.}$$

2. **Sum all variable overhead costs associated with each allocation base.**

   The AAA has a variety of variable indirect costs associated with publishing. These include the energy to run the computers and printers, other office supplies, and maintenance. The AAA uses a single cost pool.
   - Assume that the budgeted overhead costs for the upcoming year are $189,000.

3. **Divide the total variable overhead costs by the standard amount of the allocation base to calculate the variable overhead rate per unit.**

   To calculate the standard variable cost rate for next year, AAA divides total budgeted overhead cost by total (standard) pages.

   $$\$189{,}000/12{,}600 \text{ pages} = \$15 \text{ per page standard variable overhead cost}$$

Now that the AAA has calculated a standard variable cost rate, it can apply that rate to each journal based on the total pages published by that journal in a given year.

FROM THE FIELD

Allocation Bases and Unexpected Consequences

The choice of an allocation base may lead to unexpected consequences. For example, to keep variable overhead cost down at AAA, journal editors might allow fewer pages in each issue. As we've seen, the journals have estimated an average page length (40 pages), but that number is based on typical academic articles containing rigorous statistical analysis and lengthy descriptions. If editors want to save money, they could decrease the total pages per journal. This would likely require either reducing the number of articles published or establishing a strict page limit for each article. These decisions may have the unexpected consequences of preventing important, high-quality, clearly described research from being published. Both solutions may be bad for the authors and readers of the journal.

Thinking Critically

What other solutions might a publisher, such as the AAA, use to keep page counts within the planned range, without sacrificing the quality of the published content?

Determining Standard Fixed Overhead Rates

Fixed overhead costs are overhead costs that do not change as the amount of output increases or decreases. Fixed overhead is a lump sum included in the budget, and the actual amount spent will be the same (or very close to the same) as the budgeted amount, regardless of production or sales. Returning to our AAA publishing example, the amount of fixed overhead will not be affected by the number of pages published.

fixed overhead (costs)
Overhead costs that do not change as the amount of output increases or decreases.

To determine the standard fixed overhead rate, organizations follow the same steps previously described for calculating the variable overhead rate. Let's revisit the publishing process at AAA to illustrate.

1. **Select the cost-allocation bases for allocating fixed overhead costs and estimate the quantity of the bases.**
   - AAA could come up with another cost driver for its fixed overhead costs, but for the sake of simplicity, it likely will use the same cost driver for fixed and variable overhead rates. Therefore, AAA could use the number of pages published per year (12,600) to allocate its fixed overhead costs.
2. **Sum all fixed overhead costs associated with each allocation base.**
   - The AAA has editorial staff, supervisors, and management teams who are all involved to varying extents in the production of each issue of each journal. Many of these wages are categorized as overhead. The AAA also has leasing costs for its office buildings and depreciation on its equipment. In total, the fixed overhead costs for AAA are $252,000.
3. **Divide the total fixed overhead by the standard amount of the allocation base to calculate the fixed overhead rate per unit.**
   - To calculate the standard fixed overhead rate per unit, AAA divides the total fixed overhead costs summarized in Step 2 by the standard number of pages it expects to produce summarized in Step 1. The standard (or budgeted) fixed overhead cost per unit of cost-allocation base is therefore:

$$\$252,000/12,600 = \$20 \text{ per page}$$

As described in the previous section, each article is approximately 40 pages long and each published journal issue contains approximately 7 articles. Therefore, the fixed overhead budgeted for each issue would be:

$$(40 \text{ pages} * 7 \text{ articles}) * \$20 \text{ per page} = \$5,600 \text{ per issue}$$

LO 11.2

Calculate variable overhead spending variance and explain its implications.

CALCULATING VARIABLE OVERHEAD SPENDING VARIANCE

Organizations calculate variances to compare their actual performance to the budget. In Chapter 10 we learned how to calculate and use direct cost variances using **Eagles Nest Outfitters (ENO)** as an example. In the following sections, we continue with the ENO example to calculate overhead variances for the month of May. Exhibit 11.1 shows the same budgeted costs for ENO as described in Chapter 10.

Olya Humeniuk/Shutterstock

CAREER SKILLS

Learning how to calculate overhead variances supports this career skill:

- Analyzing and diagnosing causes of deviations from management's expectations

ENO Hammock Standards	
Total Units Produced (Budgeted)	20,000
Sales Price/unit	$99.00
Direct Materials/unit	4 yards @ $8.75/yd = $35.00
Direct Labor/unit	0.5 hour @ $20.00/hr = $10.00
Direct Labor/hour	$20.00
Variable Manufacturing Overhead/unit	0.5 hour @ $24.00/hr = $12.00
Variable Manufacturing Overhead/hour	$24.00
Total Fixed Costs	$154,000.00

Exhibit 11.1
ENO Standard and Variable Cost per Unit

Microsoft Excel

ENO uses direct labor hours as the allocation base for both fixed and variable overhead. As Exhibit 11.1 shows, the standard variable manufacturing overhead per hour is $24.00, and the cost of direct labor is $20.00 per hour. The standard labor for each hammock is 0.5 hour. Thus, $12.00 in variable overhead will be allocated to each hammock.

Exhibit 11.2 reproduces ENO's actual results, and its flexible and static budgets, which we saw in Chapter 10. Recall that the actual number of units produced is 18,000.

Exhibit 11.2
ENO Comparison of Budgets to Actual Performance

ENO Comparison of Budgets to Actual May 20XX			
	Actual Results	Flexible Budget	Static Budget
Units Sold	18,000	18,000	20,000
Revenue	$ 1,749,960	$ 1,782,000	$ 1,980,000
Variable Costs			
Direct Material	$ 703,000	$ 630,000	$ 700,000
Direct Labor	$ 189,000	$ 180,000	$ 200,000
❶ Variable Manufacturing Overhead	$ 220,500	$ 216,000	$ 240,000
Total Variable Costs	$ 1,112,500	$ 1,026,000	$ 1,140,000
Contribution Margin	$ 637,460	$ 756,000	$ 840,000
Fixed Manufacturing Overhead	$ 167,000	$ 154,000	$ 154,000
Operating Income	$ 470,460	$ 602,000	$ 686,000

Flexible-budget variance calculations for variable overhead are identical to those for direct-cost variances illustrated in Chapter 10. The **variable overhead flexible-budget variance** is the difference between actual variable overhead costs and the flexible budget amounts:

$$\begin{pmatrix} \text{Variable overhead} \\ \text{flexible-budget} \\ \text{variance} \end{pmatrix} = \begin{array}{c} \text{Actual variable} \\ \text{overhead costs} \end{array} - \begin{array}{c} \text{Flexible budget} \\ \text{amount} \end{array}$$

variable overhead flexible-budget variance
The difference between actual variable overhead costs and the flexible budget amounts.

Using the numbers on the Variable Manufacturing Overhead line of Exhibit 11.2 (see ❶), ENO calculates the variable overhead flexible-budget variance as:

$$\$ \; 4,500 \; U \quad = \quad \$ \; 220,500 \quad - \quad \$ \; 216,000$$

Because the actual costs exceeded the budgeted amount, the variance is unfavorable ($4,500 U).

As with the direct-cost variances, ENO managers will want to examine the reasons that ENO spent more than expected in overhead costs. There are many possible causes. For example, maintenance costs may have increased unexpectedly—perhaps a machine broke down in addition to the regular maintenance performed during the period. Maybe the suppliers of indirect materials, such as thread and glue, have increased their prices.

To explore the cause(s) of the unfavorable variance, management can break the flexible-budget variance down into subcomponents using the same mechanics that we saw in Chapter 10 for direct-cost variances. Exhibit 11.3 illustrates how indirect cost variances are calculated. You'll notice that it replicates Exhibit 10.7 in Chapter 10 with one small exception. What was called the *price variance* for direct materials and direct labor is here called the variable overhead *spending variance* (see ❶).

Notice in Exhibit 11.3 that actual results are calculated as Actual Quantity * Actual Price (see column 1). The actual quantity referred to is the quantity of the allocation base, which is direct labor hours for ENO. It may be more natural to think of the "price" of overhead as the rate at which it is incurred and allocated. However, for the sake of consistency, we use the term *price*.

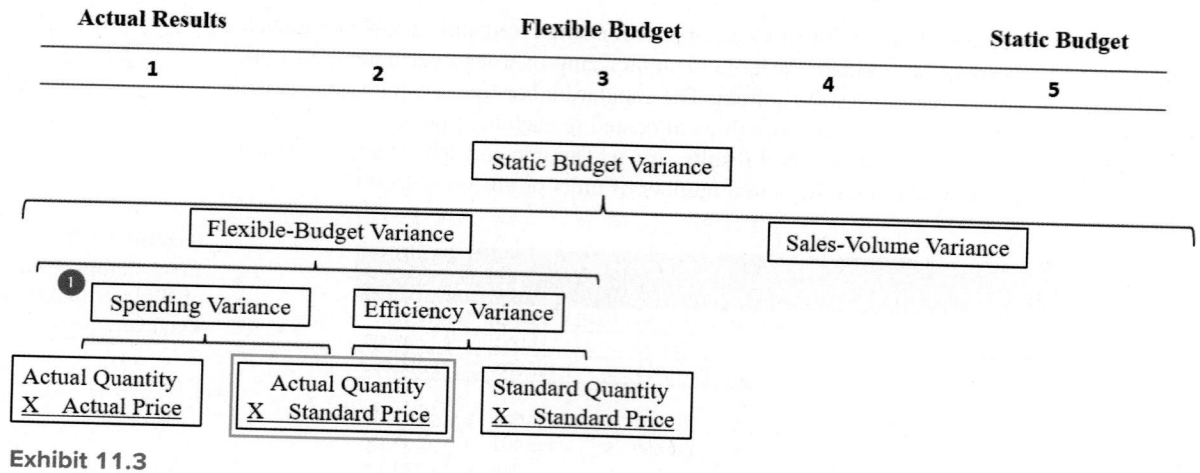

Exhibit 11.3
Calculating Indirect-Cost Variances

The flexible budget (column 3) is calculated as the Standard Quantity * Standard Price of variable overhead. To calculate the price and efficiency variances, we insert a column between the actual results and flexible budget, which we calculate by multiplying Actual Quantity by the Standard Price of variable overhead (see column 2, which outlines the calculation in red).

Now, let's examine each resulting variance in turn.

Variable Overhead Spending Variance

variable overhead spending variance
The difference between the variable production overhead costs and what was budgeted given the activity level.

The **variable overhead spending variance** holds the quantity of the allocation base constant, identifying whether variable overhead spending was greater than or less than it would have been if the standard price of variable overhead had been used. To illustrate, let's examine **ENO**'s variable overhead spending variance.

Last period, ENO produced 18,000 hammocks. ENO used 10,000 hours to produce the hammocks, and variable overhead costs totaled $220,500, as shown in the Variable Manufacturing Overhead row of Exhibit 11.2. The standard quantity of direct labor hours for 18,000 hammocks is 9,000 (0.5 hour/hammock), and the standard variable overhead price is $24 per hour (see Exhibit 11.1).

We can use this information to calculate the actual price of variable overhead per hour of labor (ENO's allocation base), which is $22.05 ($220,500/10,000 hours). We can then plug these values into the formulas from Exhibit 11.3 to determine the variable overhead spending variance, as shown in Exhibit 11.4.

Exhibit 11.4
Calculating Variable Overhead Spending Variance
Microsoft Excel

Variable Overhead Spending Variance Calculation					
From Exhibit 11.3					
Actual Quantity		10,000	Actual Quantity		10,000
Actual Price	$	22.05	Standard Price	$	24.00
	$	220,500.00			$ 240,000.00
Variable Overhead Spending Variance			$	19,500.00 F	

The difference between the values from column 1 and column 2 in Exhibit 11.3 is the variable overhead spending variance. Notice that we hold constant the quantity of hours used (10,000), which allows us to isolate how much of the flexible-budget variance is attributed to the difference between the actual price and the standard price of variable overhead inputs.

The actual price of variable overhead per direct labor hour is $1.95 (= $24.00 − $22.05) less than the standard price per hour, resulting in a $19,500 favorable variance. The variable overhead spending variance can also be calculated as follows:

Variable Overhead Spending Variance = Actual Quantity * (Actual Price − Standard Price)

At ENO:

Variable Overhead Spending Variance = 10,000 hours * ($22.05 − $24.00) = $19,500 F

Now that we've identified this favorable variance, management can investigate further to better understand its causes. One possibility is that the costs of the overhead items, such as utilities and raw materials, may be less than expected.

In the next section, we turn our attention to the variable overhead efficiency variance.

✓ PROGRESS CHECK

4. Provide two possible causes of a favorable overhead spending variance and two possible causes of an unfavorable overhead spending variance.
5. Are favorable spending variances always desirable? Explain.

CALCULATING VARIABLE OVERHEAD EFFICIENCY VARIANCE

The **variable overhead efficiency variance** describes how efficiently the organization uses its allocation base, which for **ENO** is direct labor hours. ENO assumes that as direct labor hours increase, so do variable overhead costs, such as supervisor hours, electricity, and indirect materials. A causal relationship should exist between variable overhead costs and the allocation base. If ENO can use fewer direct labor hours to produce hammocks, then variable overhead costs should also decrease.

In Exhibit 11.5, we use the equations from Exhibit 11.3 to examine how efficiently ENO uses direct labor hours while holding constant the cost of variable overhead. ENO's standard quantity of hours needed to produce 18,000 hammocks is 9,000. However, ENO was 1,000 hours over budget (= 10,000 actual quantity − 9,000 standard quantity), which results in an unfavorable variable overhead efficiency variance of $24,000.

LO 11.3

Calculate variable overhead efficiency variance and explain its implication.

variable overhead efficiency variance The difference between the flexible-budget amount and the amount that would have been incurred if the budgeted rate had been applied to the actual quantity of inputs used for production. It describes how efficiently the organization uses its allocation base.

Variable Overhead Efficiency Variance Calculation				
From Exhibit 11.3	column 2		column 3	
Actual Quantity		10,000	Standard Quantity	9,000
Standard Price	$	24.00	Standard Price	$ 24.00
	$	240,000.00		$216,000.00
Variable Overhead Efficiency Variance	$	24,000.00 U		

Exhibit 11.5
Calculating Variable Overhead Efficiency Variance
Microsoft Excel

The direct labor efficiency variance can also be calculated as follows:

Variable Overhead Efficiency Variance = Standard Price * (Actual Quantity − Standard Quantity)

At ENO:

Variable Overhead Efficiency Variance = $24.00 * (10,000 − 9,000) = $24,000 U

When management identifies an unfavorable variable overhead efficiency variance, its next step is to find the cause and make improvements. In our ENO example, the variance relates to an unexpected increase in the number of hours spent in production. Possible causes for the excessive hours spent include but are not limited to:

1. Machines are running inefficiently.
2. Employees are slower than expected.
3. Production schedules were inefficient.

Once diagnosed, management can address any of these problems. For example:

1. Machines can be serviced more frequently to make sure they are running efficiently. Machines that are chronically in disrepair can be replaced.
2. Employees can receive training to improve their performance. Management also can implement performance incentives to motivate employees to perform high-quality work at the "right" speed. New, more highly skilled people can be hired.
3. Production can be more carefully scheduled to eliminate machine downtime, diminish set-up time, and reduce bottlenecks. These solutions may require the organization to invest in production scheduling software or hire people with production scheduling expertise.

Remember: Management accountants provide important data analysis and insights that can help managers make strategic and operational changes that can help the business achieve its goals. Performing calculations and variance analysis are first steps in ensuring that operations run smoothly.

Exhibit 11.6 summarizes ENO's variable overhead variance analysis, based on the numbers we calculated previously. The $19,500 favorable variable overhead spending variance ❶ and $24,000 unfavorable efficiency variance ❷ combine to create the $4,500 unfavorable flexible-budget variance ❸ we calculated earlier in this chapter. The additional information derived from these variances provides useful insight to managers as they try to improve operations.

Exhibit 11.6
Variable Overhead
Variance Analysis

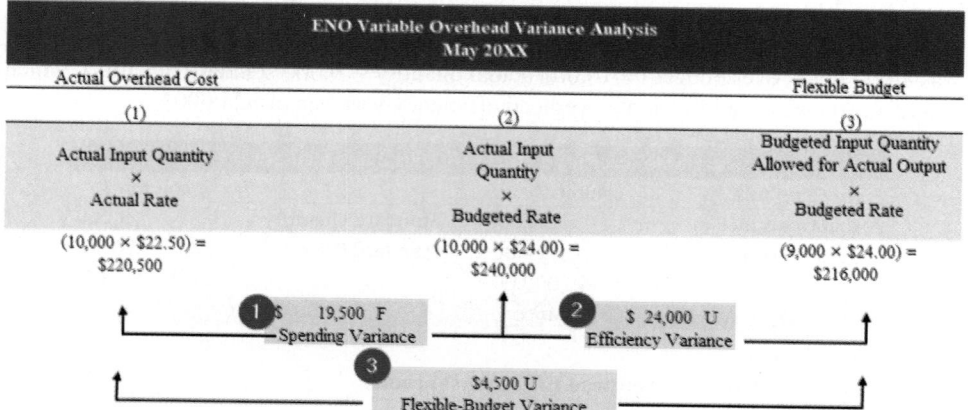

Human Dimensions of Cost Accounting: Variance Analysis

When managers review the results of variance analysis, they must consider the entire picture and the long-term effects of the decision(s) that led to the current variances or lack thereof. Performance measures (such as variances) may cause dysfunctional behavior if employees try too hard to manage them. For example, a plant manager could reduce the cost of manufacturing overhead by purchasing inferior indirect raw materials. This decision might help reduce variances in the short run, but it can have long-term negative implications, such as a lower-quality product that consumers are unwilling to purchase.

 PROGRESS CHECK

6. How is the variable overhead efficiency variance calculated, and what does it tell us about operations?

7. Provide two possible causes of an unfavorable overhead efficiency variance and two possible causes of a favorable overhead efficiency variance.

RECORDING VARIABLE OVERHEAD COSTS AND VARIANCES

LO 11.4

Record variable overhead variances as journal entries.

As with direct-cost variances, organizations prepare journal entries to account for their variances related to overhead. The variances represent the underallocated or overallocated variable overhead costs. Let's examine the entries that **ENO** will record to account for these variances.

To record actual variable overhead cost, ENO prepares the following entry (see Exhibit 11.6):

Variable Overhead	220,500	
Accounts Payable		220,500

To record the allocated variable cost, which is based on the standards, ENO books the following entry:

Work-in-Process	216,000	
Variable Overhead Allocated		216,000

Note that any costs accumulated in the Work-in-Process account will be transferred to Finished Goods when production is complete and subsequently to Costs of Goods Sold when they are sold.

At the end of the accounting period, the variable overhead allocated and variable overhead accounts are zeroed out, and the differences between these accounts are recorded as variances. To record the variances identified during the period, ENO books the following entry:

Variable Overhead Allocated	216,000	
Variable Efficiency Variance	24,000	
Variable Overhead		220,500
Variable Overhead Spending Variance		19,500

Finally, assuming the variable overhead variances are minor, they will be written off to Cost of Goods Sold, as follows:

Cost of Goods Sold	4,500	
Variable Overhead Spending Variance	19,500	
Variable Overhead Efficiency Variance		24,000

If the variances are material, they will be prorated across Work-in-Process Control, Finished Goods Control, and Cost of Goods Sold based on ending balances.

 PROGRESS CHECK

8. Explain why allocated variable cost is recorded using standard values.
9. Explain why organizations record closing entries to account for differences in overhead allocations during the period.

CALCULATING FIXED-OVERHEAD SPENDING VARIANCE

LO 11.5

Calculate fixed overhead spending variances.

Organizations also include fixed overhead costs in their budgets. *Fixed overhead* is a lump-sum amount that does not vary with the amount of output produced. Generally, fixed overhead costs are relatively easy to estimate because they include reasonably stable costs, such as rent on the facilities or depreciation on the machines. However, there are often differences between the actual fixed overhead and the overhead allocated, or applied, to an organization's inventory. To calculate fixed overhead variances, we need three fixed overhead numbers:

1. Actual fixed overhead
2. Budgeted fixed overhead
3. Applied fixed overhead

Exhibit 11.7 summarizes these overhead figures and their associated variance, to which we turn our attention in the following sections.

Exhibit 11.7
Fixed Overhead Summary

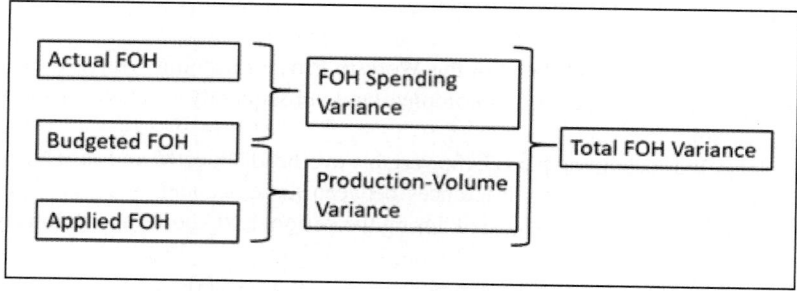

actual fixed overhead
The sum of all fixed overhead costs incurred during the period.

budgeted fixed overhead
The organization's estimate of the fixed overhead for the period.

fixed overhead spending variance
The difference between budgeted and actual fixed overhead.

Fixed Overhead Spending Variance

An organization can easily determine its actual fixed overhead and its budgeted fixed overhead. **Actual fixed overhead** is the sum of all fixed overhead costs incurred during the period, while **budgeted fixed overhead** is the organization's initial estimate of the period's fixed overhead expenses. Note that the static budget and the flexible budget for fixed overhead are equal because, by definition, fixed overhead does not change with production volume. (Refer back to **ENO**'s summary financial information in Exhibit 11.1.)

The **fixed overhead spending variance** is simply the difference between budgeted and actual fixed overhead:

Fixed Overhead Spending Variance = Actual Fixed Overhead − Budgeted Fixed Overhead

To calculate the fixed overhead spending variance at ENO, use the numbers in the Total Fixed Costs line of Exhibit 11.2:

$$\text{Fixed Overhead Spending Variance} = \$167,000 - \$154,000 = \$13,000 \text{ U}$$

Because ENO spent more than budgeted on fixed overhead, the resulting variance is unfavorable. As always, management should investigate any significant variances. Unfavorable fixed overhead variances could be caused by higher-than-anticipated leasing costs for equipment, higher depreciation expenses, or unexpected increases in administrative salaries. In some instances, managers may make changes in their spending behavior to reduce variances in the future. For example, managers may choose to lease equipment to reduce fixed depreciation costs.

⊘ PROGRESS CHECK

10. Generally, fixed overhead is not sensitive to the amount of output produced, but variances can still occur. Identify two possible causes of a favorable fixed overhead spending variance.

11. Identify two possible causes of an unfavorable fixed overhead spending variance.

CALCULATING PRODUCTION-VOLUME VARIANCE

While fixed overhead is independent of the number of units produced, organizations apply fixed overhead as if it were variable. Why? Applying fixed overhead on a per-unit basis allows organizations to spread out fixed costs during the period and provides a better idea of per-unit cost, which is necessary for determining sales price and profitability.

> **LO 11.6**
>
> Calculate production-volume variance.

Let's return to our **ENO** example and the data in Exhibit 11.1. When management developed the budget for ENO, it estimated fixed overhead costs at $154,000 for 20,000 hammocks. Each hammock requires 0.50 labor hour, so total production was estimated to require 10,000 labor hours. Thus, the predetermined fixed overhead allocation rate is $15.40 per direct labor hour (= $154,000/10,000 hours), which equates to $7.70 per hammock.

Throughout the year, this allocation rate of $7.70 is applied to the number of hammocks ENO *actually* produces—even if the number of hammocks produced deviates from the budget. If ENO produces 20,000 hammocks as planned, it will apply $154,000 in fixed overhead (20,000 hammocks * $7.70 per hammock).

A lower production volume of, say, 15,000 hammocks, will result in a lower allocation of $115,500 (15,000 * $7.70) of fixed overhead to production.

Alternatively, a higher production volume will result in a higher allocation. For example, if ENO produces 25,000 hammocks, the company will apply $192,500 (25,000 * $7.70) of fixed overhead to production.

Note that although changes in production should have no bearing on *actual* fixed overhead, they do affect how much fixed overhead is *applied* to inventory.

The difference between the budgeted fixed overhead and applied fixed overhead is called the **production-volume variance**. The formula for production-volume variance is:

production-volume variance
The difference between budgeted fixed overhead and applied fixed overhead.

$$\text{Production-Volume Variance} = \text{Budgeted Fixed Overhead} - \text{Applied Fixed Overhead}$$

At ENO, 18,000 hammocks were produced. Therefore:

$$\text{Production-Volume Variance} = \$154,000 - (18,000 \text{ hammocks} * \$7.70 \text{ standard FOH/hammock})$$

$$= \$154,000 - \$138,600 = \$15,400 \text{ U}$$

Notice that this variance is labeled as unfavorable, which may seem surprising, because the calculation shows that ENO allocated less in fixed costs than budgeted. But remember, fixed costs are a lump sum and are spent regardless of the number of units produced. In this case, the $15,400 unfavorable variance represents the 2,000 hammocks that were budgeted but not produced (= 2,000 hammocks * $7.70 standard fixed overhead, where the standard fixed overhead equals 0.50 hour per hammock * $15.40 per hour). This variance is unfavorable because ENO will have to add more fixed overhead cost to its inventory to account for the underapplied cost.

Exhibit 11.8 illustrates the production-volume variance graphically. Note that it shows the budgeted fixed overhead costs with a solid black horizontal line. This amount does not change, regardless of the number of units produced.[1] Compare that line with the fixed overhead allocated, which is the line that is used for inventory costing. It assumes that fixed overhead will be allocated at $7.70 per unit of output (that is, per hammock). The dashed-and-dotted lines show the amount of overhead allocated based on the actual production, and the shaded part illustrates the difference between the allocated amount and the budgeted fixed costs, representing the production-volume variance.

Exhibit 11.8
Graph of Production-Volume Variance

Microsoft Excel

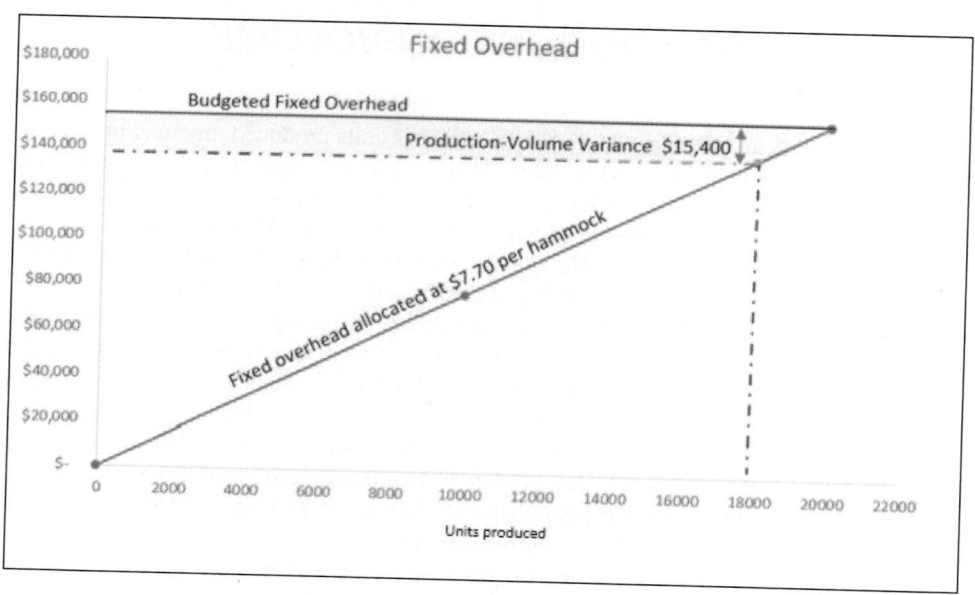

total fixed overhead variance

The difference between actual overhead incurred during the period and overhead applied to inventory.

The **total fixed overhead variance** is the difference between actual overhead incurred during the period and overhead applied to inventory. It is calculated by summing the fixed overhead spending variance and the production-volume variance. Alternatively, it can be calculated as follows:

$$\text{Total Fixed Overhead Variance} = \text{Actual Fixed Overhead} - \text{Applied Fixed Overhead}$$

---

[1]Fixed overhead costs remain fixed within a reasonable range. However, there may be changes if production or capacity needs change greatly. For example, if a new production facility is needed because the organization wants to double manufacturing, there will be additional leasing costs, utilities, and plant management salaries, which will increase fixed costs.

At ENO:

$$\text{Total Fixed Overhead Variance} = \$167,000 - \$138,600 = \$28,400 \text{ U}$$

Note that the $167,000 for Actual Fixed Overhead comes from the Fixed Manufacturing Overhead Costs line of Exhibit 11.2.

Exhibit 11.9 summarizes these fixed overhead figures and the associated variances. ENO incurred $28,400 more overhead than it applied (Total FOH Variance), which will lead to an understatement of work-in-process inventory, finished goods inventory, and cost of goods sold. This understatement is corrected with adjusting entries to cost of goods sold, as described in the next section.

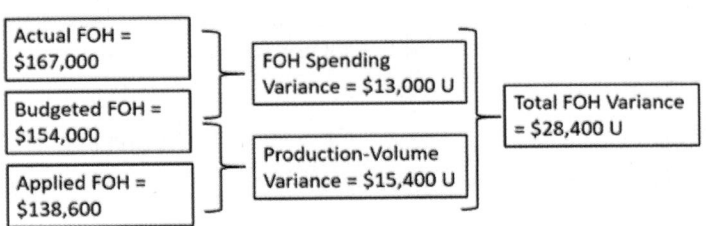

Exhibit 11.9
Fixed Overhead Variance Summary

⊕ LAB CONNECTION

LABS 11.1–11.3 use Excel, Power BI, and Tableau (respectively) to prepare a graph for planning and control that illustrates the production-volume variance.

✓ PROGRESS CHECK

12. Why is it useful for organizations to calculate fixed overhead per unit produced?
13. When budgeted fixed overhead is greater than applied fixed overhead, the result is an unfavorable variance. Why?

RECORDING FIXED OVERHEAD COSTS AND VARIANCES

The journal entries to account for fixed overhead variances follow the same pattern as the variable overhead entries explained earlier in this chapter (see Learning Objective 11.4). **ENO** prepares journal entries to account for its variances related to fixed overhead.

To record fixed overhead costs incurred during the year, ENO books the following entry:

> **LO 11.7**
>
> Record fixed overhead variances as journal entries.

Fixed Overhead	167,000	
Salaries Payable, Accumulated Depreciation, etc.		167,000

To allocate fixed overhead to inventory, ENO makes the following entry:

Work-in-Process	138,600	
Fixed Overhead Allocated		138,600

At the end of the accounting period, the Fixed Overhead Allocated and Fixed Overhead Control accounts are zeroed out. The differences between these accounts are recorded as variances. To record the variances identified during the period, ENO books the following entry:

Fixed Overhead Allocated	138,600	
Fixed Overhead Spending Variance	13,000	
Fixed Overhead Production-Volume Variance	15,400	
Fixed Overhead		167,000

So long as the fixed overhead variances are immaterial at the end of the period, the fixed overhead variances are written off to COGS to correct the underapplication of fixed overhead.

Cost of Goods Sold	13,000	
Fixed Overhead Spending Variance		13,000
Cost of Goods Sold	15,400	
Production-Volume Variance		15,400

ETHICS

FROM THE FIELD

Overhead Accounts and Fraudulent Activity

Overhead accounts are at risk for fraudulent activity. Although organizations generally like to keep overhead costs down, in actuality these costs are typically large. They include salaries of high-level management; rent and utilities for production facilities, offices, and warehouses; and the costs of large quantities of raw materials and tools. As a result, overhead accounts can easily be used to hide fraudulent transactions among the many journal entries posted during the period. Furthermore, because overhead is allocated based on a predetermined rate, variances are expected and are easily explained as the result of misapplied overhead. Thus, fraudulent entries that contribute to variances are unlikely to raise suspicion.

Organizations can use data analytics techniques to scrutinize overhead variances to identify fraud. The use of data analytics will increase the likelihood of identifying suspicious entries, and if such analysis becomes a routine, it will deter potential fraudsters from trying to hide fraud in these previously unexamined accounts.

Thinking Critically

What types of fraud should a company be concerned about if there is an unfavorable fixed overhead spending variance?

Human Dimensions of Cost Accounting: Using Overhead Variances as Performance Measures

As described in Chapter 10, organizations use variance analysis to evaluate past performance and to make informed decisions for the future.

Because variance analysis compares past performance to expectations, it allows management to reflect on the operational and financial decisions that managers and employees made in the prior period. Individual employees, such as division managers, and even entire business units can be evaluated based on their ability to keep unfavorable variances to a minimum. Management may even prefer that favorable variances be kept limited because high, or repeated, favorable variances indicate that the organization did a poor job setting expectations with the budget. They also may suggest that managers do not really understand the factors that affect performance and that resources should be reallocated to other areas in the organization.

The following Data Analytics Mini-Lab asks you to use Tableau dashboards to evaluate overhead variances across a company's divisions.

 LAB CONNECTION

Fraudsters can use overhead accounts to hide fraudulent transactions. **LAB 11.4 TABLEAU** uses data analytics techniques to perform variance analysis that can help identify anomalous transactions, including some that are potentially fraudulent.

 PROGRESS CHECK

14. Describe the effect on COGS of unfavorable overhead variances during the period. How should these unfavorable overhead variances be booked at the end of the period?

15. Explain how overhead variances are used as performance measures and why it is useful for organizations to track overhead variances over time as a performance measure. How might an organization respond to consistently favorable variances? To consistently unfavorable variances?

DATA ANALYTICS MINI-LAB
Evaluating Overhead Variances Across Divisions Using Tableau Dashboards

Data Analytics Types: Descriptive, Diagnostic

Lab Note: The tools presented in this lab periodically change. Updated instructions, if applicable, can be found in the student and instructor support materials.

DATA VISUALIZATION

Keywords

Fixed Overhead Spending Variance, Production-Volume Variance, Variable Overhead Spending Variance, Variable Overhead Efficiency Variance, Performance Evaluations, Tableau

Decision-Making Context

We have discussed the different overhead variances that management uses to understand how the organization is managing its overhead costs. Now, let's apply what we have learned and consider how management can use visualizations to monitor and compare variances across time and among divisions to evaluate performance.

PowerVR is a fictitious company that designs and manufactures virtual reality (VR) headsets and other equipment. It has three production divisions. Each division manufactures various models of VR headsets.

Haiyin Wang/Alamy Stock Photo

Management wants to understand how the company's different divisions are managing their overhead costs. The cost accounting team has pulled data from sales, production, and accounting for each division from 2022 to 2027. Now the team wants to prepare several interactive Tableau dashboards that will help management compare performance.

Ask the Question

How is each division of PowerVR managing its overhead costs?

Master the Data

The data used to prepare these dashboards are stored in an Excel workbook titled **Mini-Lab 11 Data.xlsx**. It provides the data for the years 2022–2027. The data fields provided include those shown in Exhibit A.

Exhibit A

Table	Attribute Name	Description	Data Type
Variance Data	Division	Identifies the division	Text
Variance Data	Date	Identifies the performance year ranging from 2022–2027	Date
Variance Data	Budgeted Units of Output	Budgeted (standard) units of output planned for production during the year	Number
Variance Data	Machine Hours per Unit	Number of machine hours required to produce one unit	Number
Variance Data	Actual Units of Output	Actual units produced during the year	Number
Variance Data	Actual Quantity of Machine Hours	Total number of machine hours required for production	Number
Variance Data	Actual Price	Actual price (rate) of variable per machine hour	Currency
Variance Data	Standard Price	Budgeted (standard) price for unit of variable overhead per machine hour	Currency
Variance Data	Standard Quantity of Machine Hours	Budgeted (standard) number of machine hours expected for planned production	Number

Table	Attribute Name	Description	Data Type
Variance Data	VOH Flexible Budget Variance	Actual Variable Overhead Costs – Flexible Budget Costs	Currency
Variance Data	VOH Spending Variance	Calculated as Actual Quantity of Machine Hours * (Actual Price – Standard Price)	Currency
Variance Data	VOH Efficiency Variance	Calculated as Standard Price * (Actual Quantity of Machine Hours – Standard Quantity of Machine Hours)	Currency
Variance Data	Actual FOH	Actual fixed overhead costs during the year	Currency
Variance Data	Budgeted FOH	Budgeted (standard) fixed overhead expected for the year	Currency
Variance Data	FOH Spending Variance	Actual FOH – Budgeted FOH	Currency
Variance Data	FOH Rate per Machine Hour	Budgeted FOH/Standard Quantity of Machine Hours	Currency
Variance Data	FOH Rate per Unit of Output	Budgeted FOH/(Budgeted Units of Output * Machine Hours per Unit)	Currency
Variance Data	Applied FOH per Unit	FOH Rate per Unit of Output * Actual Units of Output	Currency
Variance Data	Production Volume Variance	Budgeted FOH – Applied FOH	Currency
Variance Data	Total FOH Variance	Actual FOH – Applied FOH	Currency

Exhibit B shows an example of the data.

Division	Date	Budgeted Units of Output	Machine Hours per Unit	Actual Units of Output	Actual Quantity of Machine Hours	Actual Price	Standard Price	Standard Quantity of Machine Hours	VOH Flexible Budget Variance	VOH Spending Variance	VOH Efficiency Variance	Actual FOH	Budgeted FOH	FOH Spending Variance	FOH Rate per Machine Hour	FOH Rate per Unit of Output	Applied FOH per Unit	Production-Volume Variance	Total FOH Variance
Div 1	2022	12,000	0.5	11,000	5500	$ 3.75	4	6,000	$ (3,375.00)	$ (1,375.00)	$ (2,000.00)	12,750	12,000	750	2	1	11,000	1,000	1,750
Div 1	2023	12,000	0.5	11,500	5750	$ 4.00	4	6,000	$ (1,000.00)	$ -	$ (1,000.00)	13,200	12,000	1,200	2	1	11,500	500	1,700
Div 1	2024	12,000	0.5	11,700	5850	$ 4.00	4	6,000	$ (600.00)	$ -	$ (600.00)	13,200	12,000	1,200	2	1	11,700	300	1,500
Div 1	2025	12,000	0.5	11,800	5900	$ 4.25	4	6,000	$ 1,075.00	$ 1,475.00	$ (400.00)	13,200	12,000	1,200	2	1	11,800	200	1,400
Div 1	2026	12,000	0.5	11,900	5950	$ 4.35	4	6,000	$ 1,882.50	$ 2,082.50	$ (200.00)	13,200	12,000	1,200	2	1	11,900	100	1,300
Div 1	2027	12,000	0.5	12,100	6050	$ 4.50	4	6,000	$ 3,225.00	$ 3,625.00	$ 200.00	14,400	12,000	2,400	2	1	12,100	(100)	2,300
Div 2	2022	24,000	0.5	23,000	11500	$ 4.10	4	12,000	$ (850.00)	$ 1,150.00	$ (2,000.00)	14000	12,000	2,000	1	0.5	11,500	500	2,500
Div 2	2023	24,000	0.5	23,000	11500	$ 4.10	4	12,000	$ (850.00)	$ 1,150.00	$ (2,000.00)	14000	12,000	2,000	1	0.5	11,500	500	2,500
Div 2	2024	24,000	0.5	23,500	11750	$ 4.20	4	12,000	$ 1,350.00	$ 2,350.00	$ (1,000.00)	12600	12,000	600	1	0.5	11,750	250	850
Div 2	2025	24,000	0.5	24,000	12000	$ 4.20	4	12,000	$ 2,400.00	$ 2,400.00	$ -	13200	12,000	1,200	1	0.5	12,000	-	1,200
Div 2	2026	24,000	0.5	24,250	12125	$ 4.20	4	12,000	$ 2,925.00	$ 2,425.00	$ 500.00	12600	12,000	600	1	0.5	12,125	(125)	475
Div 2	2027	24,000	0.5	24,500	12250	$ 4.20	4	12,000	$ 3,450.00	$ 2,450.00	$ 1,000.00	12600	12,000	600	1	0.5	12,250	(250)	350
Div 3	2022	12,000	0.5	11,750	5875	$ 4.25	4	6,000	$ 968.75	$ 1,468.75	$ (500.00)	11000	12,000	-1,000	2	1	11,750	250	(750)
Div 3	2023	12,000	0.5	12,100	6050	$ 4.10	4	6,000	$ 805.00	$ 605.00	$ 200.00	11880	12,000	-120	2	1	12,100	(100)	(220)
Div 3	2024	12,000	0.5	11,500	5750	$ 4.00	4	6,000	$ (1,000.00)	$ -	$ (1,000.00)	11880	12,000	-120	2	1	11,500	500	380
Div 3	2025	12,000	0.5	11,000	5500	$ 4.00	4	6,000	$ (2,000.00)	$ -	$ (2,000.00)	11400	12,000	-600	2	1	11,000	1,000	400
Div 3	2026	12,000	0.5	11,000	5500	$ 4.00	4	6,000	$ (2,000.00)	$ -	$ (2,000.00)	13200	12,000	1,200	2	1	11,000	1,000	2,200
Div 3	2027	12,000	0.5	10,750	5375	$ 4.00	4	6,000	$ (2,500.00)	$ -	$ (2,500.00)	11760	12,000	-240	2	1	10,750	1,250	1,010

Exhibit B

Microsoft Excel

Perform the Analysis

The cost accounting team has prepared the following three interactive dashboards in Tableau to allow management to review the overhead variances for each division (Exhibits C, D, and E). In Lab 10.5 at the end of this chapter, you will learn how to build similar dashboards in Tableau.

Exhibit C

Tableau Software

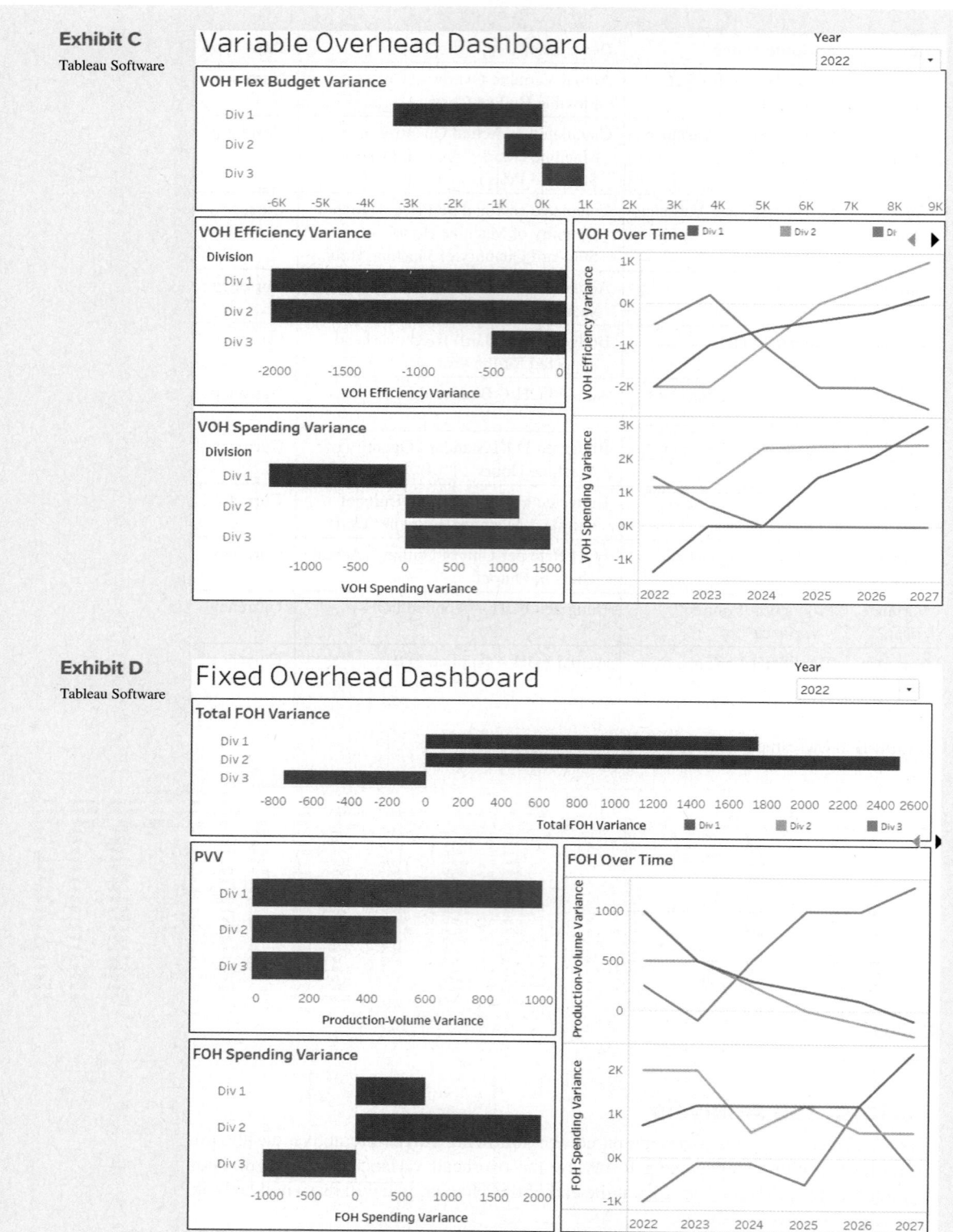

Variable Overhead Dashboard

Year: 2022

VOH Flex Budget Variance
- Div 1, Div 2, Div 3
- Scale: -6K to 9K

VOH Efficiency Variance (by Division)
- Div 1, Div 2, Div 3
- Scale: -2000 to 0

VOH Spending Variance (by Division)
- Div 1, Div 2, Div 3
- Scale: -1000 to 1500

VOH Over Time (Div 1, Div 2, Div 3)
- VOH Efficiency Variance: -2K to 1K
- VOH Spending Variance: -1K to 3K
- Years: 2022–2027

Exhibit D

Tableau Software

Fixed Overhead Dashboard

Year: 2022

Total FOH Variance
- Div 1, Div 2, Div 3
- Scale: -800 to 2600

PVV
- Div 1, Div 2, Div 3
- Production-Volume Variance: 0 to 1000

FOH Spending Variance
- Div 1, Div 2, Div 3
- Scale: -1000 to 2000

FOH Over Time (Div 1, Div 2, Div 3)
- Production-Volume Variance: 0 to 1000
- FOH Spending Variance: -1K to 2K
- Years: 2022–2027

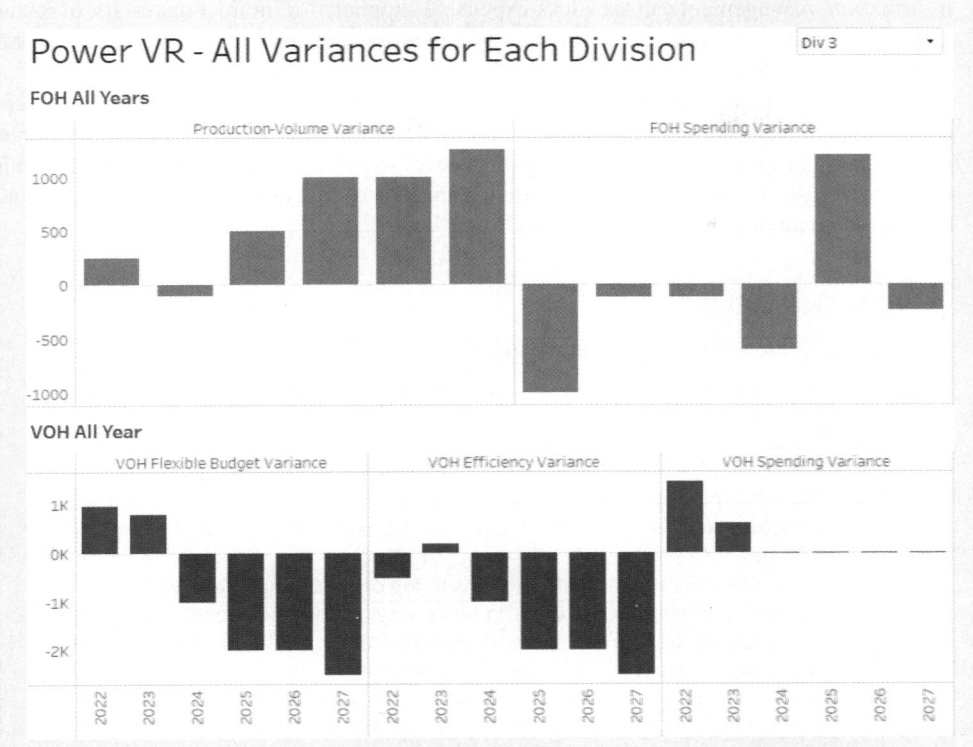

Power VR - All Variances for Each Division

Div 3

Exhibit E

Tableau Software

Share the Story

By using interactive dashboards, PowerVR's managers and cost accounting team are able to compare the company's three different divisions on the management of overhead costs.

Mini-Lab Assessment

1. In 2022, which variance was unfavorable in all three divisions?
2. Consider the performance of Division 3 over time. For which variances has the division experienced increasingly favorable variances in recent years?
3. Consider the performance of Division 3 in 2026. Use the variance analyses to explain its performance.
4. Describe how these interactive dashboards allow management to compare performance across divisions.

USING VARIANCE ANALYSIS TO REDUCE OVERHEAD COSTS

LO 11.8

Examine how organizations can reduce overhead spending.

When variance analysis shows that overhead costs deviate from expectations, organizations can use data to identify specific costs that are unfavorable. With this information, they can make changes in the way they conduct business to reduce these costs.

For example, unfavorable variable overhead spending variances indicate that the organization is spending more on supplies or indirect labor than anticipated. Based on this information, management can seek less-expensive suppliers for indirect materials, or it can eliminate jobs with administrative or support functions that are not directly related to the production of goods or services.

Importantly, organizations should review overhead frequently. Many companies perform variance analysis monthly to make sure there are no big surprises that might force the company to take unexpected, drastic measures. Modern enterprise resource planning (ERP) systems can produce real-time variance analysis so that managers can monitor overhead costs on an ongoing basis.

FROM THE FIELD

Decreasing Overhead Costs at Swiggy

When a company's profits take an unexpected downturn, overhead is the first place it looks to improve financial performance. Consider **Swiggy,** a food-delivery company that operates in India. Swiggy found it difficult to accurately predict demand for food delivery; consumer preferences and behavior were inconsistent as the effects of the COVID-19 pandemic receded. The company also found that it had overinvested in infrastructure, and it had hired more employees than it needed to meet declining demand.

In January 2023, Swiggy announced plans to lay off 380 employees who were doing work that was already being done in other ways within the organization. Some of the laid-off employees were drivers who were no longer needed and office workers who did not work efficiently. In his letter to employees, Swiggy's CEO, Sriharsha Majety, directly discussed the company's efforts for reducing overhead. Although he noted that Swiggy had sufficient cash reserves to weather the storm, he also pointed to the importance of decreasing the company's indirect costs, including infrastructure, office/facilities, and human resources, in order to increase its profitability.[2] He also described how overhead had increased due to strategic decisions the company had made in the past, and he noted that the company now needed to improve the efficiency of operations by streamlining the organization. To read Majety's full statement, please refer to the article referenced in footnote 2 below.

Thinking Critically

Reducing overhead costs through layoffs is never easy. What other changes could Swiggy have made to reduce overhead spending?

 LAB CONNECTION

Organizations are interested in keeping overhead costs as low as possible. Managing overhead costs can be an important performance metric, and organizations may choose to compare performance across different divisions. **LAB 11.5 TABLEAU** uses data analytics techniques to compare overhead spending across divisions of an organization.

Leveraging Big Data to Reduce Overhead

Artificial intelligence (AI) can help organizations reduce overhead by predicting when maintenance is needed, which allows the organization to schedule maintenance ahead of time—when it won't disrupt operations—thus reducing downtime.

[2]Kahekashan, "Why Is Swiggy Laying Off 380 Employees? Find Details," *Hans India,* January 20, 2023, www.thehansindia.com/technology/tech-news/why-is-swiggy-laying-off-380-employees-find-details-778402.

Along with robotic process automation, AI can also be used to make workflows more efficient by automating mundane, routine tasks, which gives human employees more time to focus on more important or judgment-based tasks. Back-office job functions such as marketing, customer service, purchasing, payroll, and billing include many activities that are good candidates for automation, and because these tasks do not relate directly to the product, they are all considered overhead expenses.

Phonlamai Photo/Shutterstock

Labor costs aren't the only type of overhead that organizations can reduce by leveraging Big Data, technology, and analytics. Utilities are another major overhead expense. As an example, think about a supermarket. Some of its biggest expenses are overhead lighting, air conditioning, and refrigeration. Or consider a big office building—all those lights left on all night make for a nice outside photo but cost the company a lot of money. Organizations can collect and analyze data about energy consumption and determine when they are spending money unnecessarily. When the data reveal wasted consumption, the organization can make educated, strategic decisions about changes that could help reduce overhead costs. In the case of lights, many organizations have invested in motion-activated lighting. Sometimes it might mean the lights go out while you are sitting quietly at your desk reading, but it saves the organization in overhead expenses in the long run.

rbrigant44/123RF

Reducing Overhead with Flexible Work Arrangements

Overhead costs include advertising, accounting fees, rent, equipment repairs, utilities, travel, and telecommunications. For many companies, especially nonmanufacturing companies, flexible work arrangements and the shift to online meetings have provided opportunities to significantly reduce overhead costs. For example, at the height of the COVID-19 pandemic and afterwards, many companies allowed employees to work from home, dramatically reducing the amount of time they spend in the office. As a result, some office buildings sit empty, copy machines are idle, lights are off, and custodial staff have less to clean. Companies can adjust to this "new normal" by making strategic changes. For example, the next time the lease contract is due, **EY** may reduce the number of floors it occupies in downtown Chicago. Instead, it might encourage staff who want to work in the office to reserve a desk (a practice known as "hoteling"). It might also reduce the number of copy machines and other office equipment. These types of equipment are generally leased and subject to costly repairs and routine maintenance, which are all part of overhead expense.

Business-related travel expenses are another large overhead cost that can be reduced with innovative ways of working. Training sessions, travel to clients, and meetings can often be conducted via online platforms such as **Zoom** and **Microsoft Teams**. Reducing employees' travel can dramatically decrease overhead spending.

Alexander Spatari/Moment/Getty Images

Cost Accounting Careers Involving Overhead Variance Analysis

You may be wondering what kinds of jobs involve analysis of overhead variances. There are many job opportunities for accounting and finance graduates with the skills you have learned in this chapter. Exhibit 11.10 shows one example: You could work as Manager of Finance Overhead at a movie studio like **Paramount Pictures, Universal Studios**, or **Warner Brothers** in Los Angeles, California. In this position, you will use many of the skills you've learned throughout this cost accounting course, including tracing information through various sources and computer systems and then conducting various analyses.

You'd also be responsible for developing and managing the overhead budgets and performing variance analysis. You can't make movie magic without keeping a keen eye on the budget!

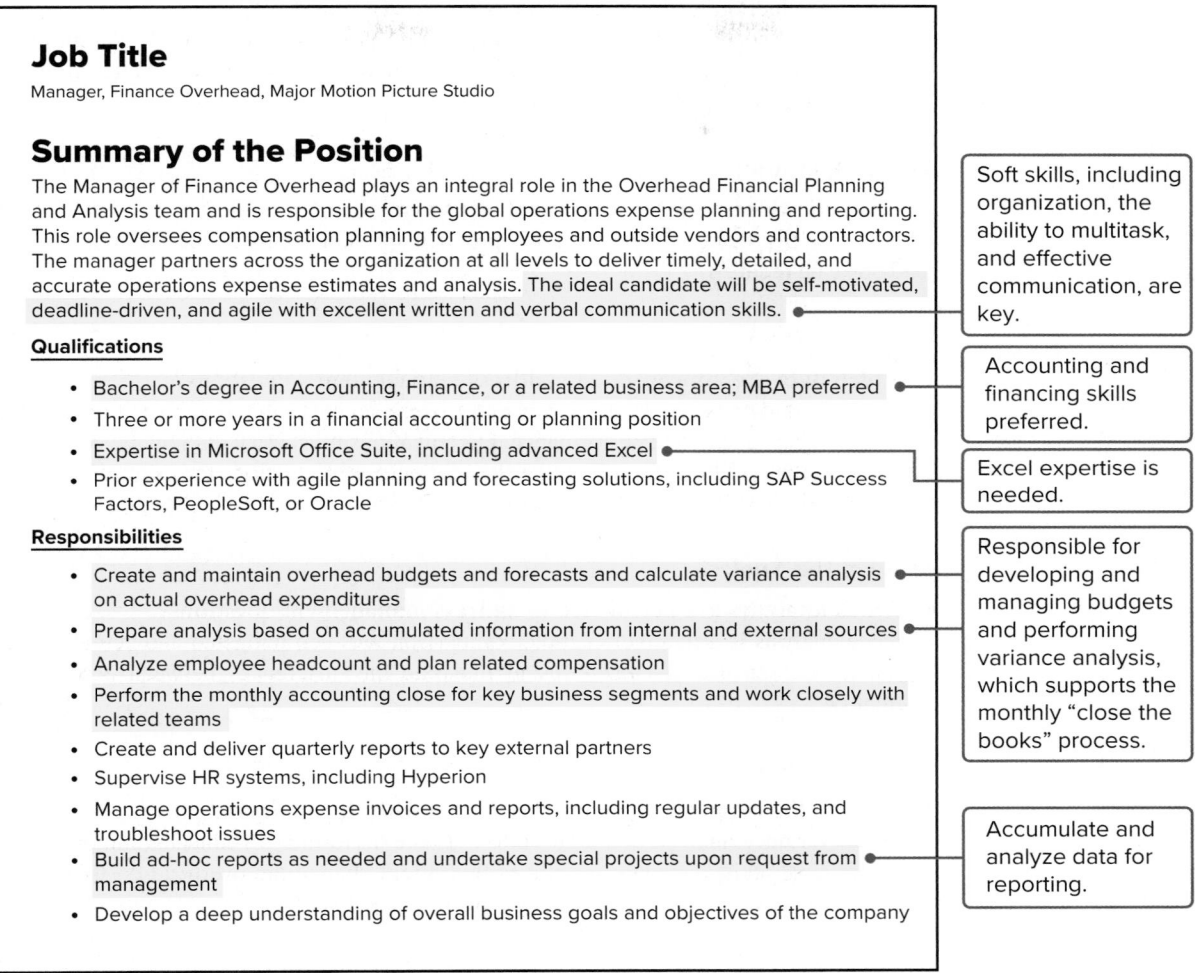

Job Title
Manager, Finance Overhead, Major Motion Picture Studio

Summary of the Position
The Manager of Finance Overhead plays an integral role in the Overhead Financial Planning and Analysis team and is responsible for the global operations expense planning and reporting. This role oversees compensation planning for employees and outside vendors and contractors. The manager partners across the organization at all levels to deliver timely, detailed, and accurate operations expense estimates and analysis. The ideal candidate will be self-motivated, deadline-driven, and agile with excellent written and verbal communication skills. ●━━ Soft skills, including organization, the ability to multitask, and effective communication, are key.

Qualifications
- Bachelor's degree in Accounting, Finance, or a related business area; MBA preferred ●━━ Accounting and financing skills preferred.
- Three or more years in a financial accounting or planning position
- Expertise in Microsoft Office Suite, including advanced Excel ●━━ Excel expertise is needed.
- Prior experience with agile planning and forecasting solutions, including SAP Success Factors, PeopleSoft, or Oracle

Responsibilities
- Create and maintain overhead budgets and forecasts and calculate variance analysis on actual overhead expenditures ●━━ Responsible for developing and managing budgets and performing variance analysis, which supports the monthly "close the books" process.
- Prepare analysis based on accumulated information from internal and external sources ●
- Analyze employee headcount and plan related compensation
- Perform the monthly accounting close for key business segments and work closely with related teams
- Create and deliver quarterly reports to key external partners
- Supervise HR systems, including Hyperion
- Manage operations expense invoices and reports, including regular updates, and troubleshoot issues
- Build ad-hoc reports as needed and undertake special projects upon request from management ●━━ Accumulate and analyze data for reporting.
- Develop a deep understanding of overall business goals and objectives of the company

Exhibit 11.10
Major Movie Studio Job Opportunity

✓ PROGRESS CHECK

16. Identify a major overhead cost that companies may be able to reduce after carefully analyzing data. What kind of data will they need to collect and analyze to determine whether cost savings are available?
17. Sometimes companies have to spend money to save money. As a cost accountant, how would you convince the CFO of your organization that investments in technologies, such as AI, or other strategic changes, such as engaging a remote workforce, are worth the investment?

Key Takeaways: Analyzing Overhead and Variances

Organizations have overhead costs associated with their operations. Variable overhead increases or decreases as production changes, while fixed overhead generally remains the same regardless of how much is produced. During the budgeting process, organizations estimate variable overhead costs based on planned production. They also estimate fixed overhead. As with direct costs, organizations compare the actual overhead costs associated with production to the budget and calculate variable and fixed overhead variances. Once these variances are identified, organizations can probe their data to determine the underlying causes of the discrepancies and make changes in the future to better align performance with expectations.

Ask the Question

- **What question(s) does management want to answer?**

What are the overhead costs necessary to produce our goods and services? Can those overhead costs be reduced?

Master the Data

- **Which data are appropriate to address management's questions?**

Many different data types are used to plan for overhead costs and to analyze the variances between budgets and actual performance. Organizations must track data on the cost allocation base(s) they will use for allocating the cost across production (for example, machine hours, labor hours, square footage), as well as detailed cost and production data.

Perform the Analysis

- **Which analytics are performed to address management questions?**

Variance analysis is a relatively simple comparison between budgeted and actual figures. Organizations can use visualizations to illustrate the differences between expectations and reality.

Share the Story

- **How are the results of the analytics shared with stakeholders?**

Overhead variance analysis can be used to evaluate performance, educate employees, and make strategic decisions about initiatives that might change the overhead costs incurred. Often, variances are tracked with visualizations in dashboards.

Key Terms

actual fixed overhead	manufacturing overhead	standard costing system	variable overhead flexible-budget variance
budgeted fixed overhead	overhead cost pools	total fixed overhead variance	variable overhead spending variance
fixed overhead costs	overhead costs	variable overhead efficiency variance	
fixed overhead spending variance	predetermined overhead rate		
indirect costs	production-volume variance		

ANSWERS TO PROGRESS CHECKS

1. Variable costs vary with production and fixed costs do not vary with production. Two examples of a variable cost are indirect labor and indirect materials. Two examples of a fixed cost are rent for the manufacturing facility and the manufacturing manager's salary.

2. Organizations calculate budgeted variable overhead as follows:

   • Select the cost-allocation bases for allocating variable overhead costs and estimate the quantity of the bases.
   • Sum all variable overhead associated with each allocation base.
   • Divide the total variable overhead by the standard amount of the allocation base to calculate the variable overhead rate per unit.

   Organizations calculate budgeted fixed overhead as follows:

   • Select the cost-allocation bases for allocating fixed overhead costs and estimate the quantity of the bases.
   • Sum all fixed overhead costs associated with each allocation base.
   • Divide the total fixed overhead by the standard amount of the allocation base to calculate the fixed overhead rate per unit.

3. Relevant allocation bases are as follows:

   a. A relevant allocation base for manufacturing golf carts is machine hours.

   b. A relevant allocation base for building custom closets is direct labor hours (or, possibly, a combination of direct labor hours and machine hours).

   c. A relevant allocation base for raising and selling free-range chickens is direct labor hours.

   d. A relevant allocation base for providing home-based health care to older adults could be miles driven or direct labor hours.

4. Two potential causes of an unfavorable overhead variable spending variance are:

   • An unexpected increase in the prices of indirect materials.
   • An unexpected increase in indirect labor wages.

   Two potential causes of a favorable variance are:

   • A decrease in the cost of variable manufacturing utilities.
   • A decrease in factory supplies costs.

5. Favorable variances are not always desirable because they may motivate employees to work in ways that are ultimately dysfunctional to the organization. For example, to have a favorable spending variance, employees are motivated to keep the actual costs of indirect materials lower than the standard. They may therefore purchase lower-quality materials that may result in an inferior product.

6. The variable overhead efficiency variance is calculated as:

   Standard price * (Actual Quantity − Standard Quantity)

   The variable overhead efficiency variance sheds light on the efficiency with which the organization uses its resources to produce its goods or service.

7. Possible causes of an unfavorable overhead efficiency variance include:

   • Machines are running inefficiently.
   • Employees are slower than expected.
   • Production schedules were inefficient.

   Possible causes of a favorable overhead efficiency variance include:

   • New machines were used, and they are more efficient than machines used in prior periods.
   • More-skilled employees are motivated to work faster and more efficiently.

8. Allocated variable costs are recorded using standard values because standard values allow the accounting system to monitor deviations from expectation easily.

9. Overhead should be included in the COGS at an organization. Therefore, any variances (favorable or unfavorable) will affect the total COGS and should be reflected in that amount recorded. These adjustments are typically made at the end of the period.

10. Possible causes of a favorable fixed overhead spending variance include:
    - A human resources manager left the firm and was not replaced immediately.
    - The organization began following a new policy to reduce travel and training expenses.

11. Possible causes of an unfavorable fixed overhead spending variance include:
    - There was a heat wave last fall and the company had to spend more than expected on air conditioning to keep the workers comfortable during their shifts.
    - Due to increased demand, the company leased additional warehouse space.

12. It is useful for organizations to calculate fixed overhead per unit produced so that they can appropriately set their price to ensure a profit.

13. When budgeted fixed overhead is greater than applied fixed overhead, the result is an unfavorable variance because there are fewer units across which to disperse the fixed costs.

14. Unfavorable overhead variances should increase COGS and therefore should be reflected as a credit to COGS at the end of the period.

15. Overhead variances can be used as performance measures to help the organization evaluate how efficiently and effectively it is using its overhead resources. Tracking variances over time allows the organization to identify trends and make data-guided adjustments to improve performance.

    If overhead costs are consistently higher than budgeted, the organization should work to identify opportunities for cost savings. If overhead costs are consistently lower than budgeted, the organization may be able to reallocate resources to other areas of the business.

16. Office space is a major overhead cost, and organizations will save a lot of money if they can reduce it. Many organizations learned during the COVID-19 pandemic that employees can work from home, and they are reevaluating their use of expensive real estate. Organizations can perform data analysis on space utilization to determine whether they can reduce their footprint. To do this analysis, accountants will need data on headcount, square footage of office space, cost per square foot, utilization records, and possibly data from employee surveys about work from home versus office preferences.

17. To make a compelling argument for investing in technology and/or strategic or infrastructure changes today to reduce overhead costs in the long term, the cost accountant should provide a quantitative cost-benefit analysis to the CFO. This analysis should include:
    - An accurate estimate of the overhead costs in the current and future periods based on existing practices.
    - An estimate of the cost to implement the new technology/strategy/change.
    - An estimate of the overhead costs given that change for the same future periods estimated based on existing practices.

    In addition, it may be useful to describe the other benefits of the suggested change. For example, using AI to replace inefficient human activities may benefit the organization by improving the quality or consistency of the work (for example, no mistakes from human error). Additionally, the use of AI may increase employee morale because it may allow employees to do more interesting, meaningful work instead of mundane tasks.

Multiple-Choice Questions

1. (LO11.1) Which of the following is the most appropriate allocation base for a company that manufactures running shoes?
   a. Number of machine set-ups
   b. Machine hours
   c. Direct labor hours
   d. Square footage of facilities

2. (LO11.1) Which of the following is the most appropriate allocation base for a company that provides janitorial services to corporations?
   a. Number of machine set-ups
   b. Machine hours
   c. Direct labor hours
   d. Square footage of facilities

3. (LO11.1) Which of the following is not included in fixed manufacturing overhead costs?
   a. Depreciation on machinery
   b. Rent on the production facility
   c. Advertising costs
   d. Manufacturing manager's salary

4. (LO11.2) Which of the following will not be included in variable overhead costs for a hospital?
   a. Bandages
   b. MRI machines
   c. Laundry
   d. Medication

5. (LO11.2) Estimated variable manufacturing overhead costs are $425,000 and actual variable manufacturing overhead costs are $450,000. The standard allocation base is 70,000 labor hours and the actual allocation base in labor hours is 68,000 hours. What is the standard predetermined variable manufacturing overhead rate?
   a. $6.07
   b. $6.43
   c. $6.25
   d. $6.62

6. (LO11.2) Estimated variable manufacturing overhead costs are $350,000 and actual variable manufacturing overhead costs are $325,000. The standard allocation base is 50,000 machine hours and the actual allocation base in machine hours is 48,000 hours. What is the standard predetermined variable manufacturing overhead rate?
   a. $6.50
   b. $6.77
   c. $7.00
   d. $7.29

7. (LO11.5) Which of the following is not a step for calculating the standard fixed overhead rate?
   a. Choose the appropriate cost-allocation base.
   b. Divide total fixed overhead costs by the actual amount of the allocation base.
   c. Determine an estimate of the quantity of the base.
   d. Sum all fixed overhead costs for each allocation base.

8. (LO11.2) Actual overhead costs are $85,000. The flexible budget amount is $78,000. The standard budget amount is $79,500. Estimated overhead costs are $89,000. Calculate the variable overhead flexible-budget variance.

   a. $7,000 unfavorable

   b. $11,000 unfavorable

   c. $7,000 favorable

   d. $11,000 favorable

9. (LO11.2) What is the equivalent of the price variance, used for direct costs, for variable overhead?

   a. Sales volume variance

   b. Efficiency variance

   c. Spending variance

   d. Flexible-budget variance

10. (LO11.3) What is the equation for calculating the variable overhead efficiency variance?

    a. (Standard quantity * Actual price) – (Standard quantity * Standard price)

    b. (Standard quantity * Standard price) – (Standard quantity * Actual price)

    c. (Actual quantity * Actual price) – (Actual quantity * Standard price)

    d. (Actual quantity * Standard price) – (Standard quantity * Standard price)

11. (LO11.2) What is the equation for calculating the variable overhead spending variance?

    a. (Standard quantity * Actual price) – (Standard quantity * Standard price)

    b. (Standard quantity * Standard price) – (Standard quantity * Actual price)

    c. (Actual quantity * Actual price) – (Actual quantity * Standard price)

    d. (Actual quantity * Standard price) – (Standard quantity * Standard price)

12. (LO11.2) Which variance is included in the variable overhead flexible-budget variance?

    a. Spending variance

    b. Variable overhead spending variance

    c. Sales volume variance

    d. Flexible rate variance

13. (LO11.2) An organization has a $25,000 unfavorable variable overhead flexible-budget variance and a $14,000 favorable spending variance. What is its efficiency variance?

    a. $11,000 F

    b. $11,000 U

    c. $39,000 F

    d. $39,000 U

14. (LO11.3) An organization has a $5,000 unfavorable variable overhead efficiency budget variance and a $12,000 favorable spending variance. What is its flexible-budget variance?

    a. $17,000 F

    b. $17,000 U

    c. $7,000 F

    d. $7,000 U

15. (LO11.2) Which of the following scenarios will cause an unfavorable variable overhead spending variance?

    a. The actual quantity of hours used in production is 8,000 hours. The expected quantity of hours was determined to be 9,500 hours. The actual price is $15, while the standard price is $12.

    b. The actual quantity of hours used in production is 12,000 hours. The expected quantity of hours was determined to be 13,000 hours. The actual price is $10, while the standard price is $13.50.

c. The actual quantity of hours used in production is 15,000 hours. The expected quantity of hours was determined to be 12,000 hours. The actual price is $8.45, while the standard price is $9.50.

d. The actual quantity of hours used in production is 50,000 hours. The expected quantity of hours was determined to be 43,000 hours. The actual price is $12.50, while the standard price is $15.00.

16. (LO11.3) What information does the variable overhead efficiency variance provide to management?

   a. How efficiently the organization is using its office supplies and tools

   b. How efficiently the organization is using its allocation base

   c. How efficiently the organization is depreciating its machinery

   d. How efficiently the organization is using direct materials

17. (LO11.3) Which of the following could be a solution to an unfavorable variable overhead efficiency variance?

   a. Machines can be serviced on a more regular basis to ensure they are running efficiently.

   b. Employees can receive training to improve performance.

   c. Production scheduling could be more carefully performed.

   d. Common errors could be addressed and corrected.

   e. All of the above

18. (LO11.4) **FiServ**, a financial services firm, budgeted $115,000 for variable overhead. Actual variable overhead was $127,000. When recording the appropriate journal entries, what amount does FiServ debit to Work-in-Process?

   a. $115,000

   b. $127,000

   c. $12,000

   d. $0

19. (LO11.5) **Bogg Bag** produces beach bags in various sizes and colors. The company estimated fixed overhead to be $575,000 for the year. Actual fixed overhead was $572,500. The company uses machine hours as a cost-allocation base and estimates that each bag takes 0.25 hour of machine time. Planned production was 2,000,000 bags. Actual production was 1,950,000 bags. What is the fixed overhead spending variance?

   a. $2,500 F

   b. $2,500 U

   c. $8,125 F

   d. $8,125 U

20. (LO11.6) **Bogg Bag** produces beach bags in various sizes and colors. The company estimated fixed overhead to be $575,000 for the year. Actual fixed overhead was $572,500. The company uses machine hours as a cost-allocation base and estimates that each bag takes 0.25 hour of machine time. Planned production was 2,000,000 bags. Actual production was 1,950,000 bags. What is the production-volume variance?

   a. $8,125 F

   b. $8,125 U

   c. $14,375 F

   d. $14,375 U

21. (LO11.7) Which of the following statements best describes the correct method for recording fixed overhead variances?

   a. Actual fixed overhead is credited to a fixed overhead account.

   b. Actual fixed overhead is debited to a fixed overhead account.

   c. Work-in-process is debited to offset the fixed overhead spending variance.

   d. Work-in-process is debited to offset the fixed overhead efficiency variance.

22. (LO11.8) Which of the following statements is true regarding using variance analysis to reduce overhead costs?

   a. Variance analysis is used to determine the actual overhead costs incurred during a period.

   b. Variance analysis compares the actual overhead costs to the budgeted overhead costs.

   c. Variance analysis is useful only for determining the causes of unfavorable variances.

   d. Variance analysis is not useful for identifying areas where overhead costs can be reduced.

CMA

23. A company has a plant capacity of 200,000 units per month. Unit costs at capacity are shown below.

Direct materials	$4.00
Direct labor	$6.00
Variable overhead	$3.00
Fixed overhead	$1.00
Fixed marketing	$7.00
Variable distribution costs	$3.60

   Monthly sales are 190,000 units at $30 each. A customer has contacted the company about purchasing 2,000 units at $24 each. Current sales will not be affected by the one-time-only special order. What will be the total variable overhead variance, also known as the flexible-budget variance, if the company accepts this one-time-only special order?

   a. $10,800
   b. $14,800
   c. $22,000
   d. $33,200

CMA

24. A company has a plant capacity of 200,000 units per month. Unit costs at capacity are shown below.

Direct materials	$4.00
Direct labor	$6.00
Variable overhead	$3.00
Fixed overhead	$1.00
Fixed marketing	$7.00
Variable distribution costs	$3.60

   Monthly sales are 190,000 units at $30 each. A customer has contacted the company about purchasing 2,000 units at $24 each. Current sales will not be affected by the one-time-only special order. What will be the total fixed overhead variance if the company accepts this one-time-only special order?

   a. $0
   b. $2,000
   c. $14,000
   d. $16,000

Discussion Questions

1. (LO11.1) Imagine you work for **Oakley**, a company that designs and manufactures sunglasses. What fixed overhead costs does your company have? What variable costs does your company have?

2. (LO11.1) Refer back to your answer in Discussion Question 1. How will **Oakley**'s management team *plan and budget* for the fixed and variable overhead costs you identified?

3. (LO11.1) Refer back to your answer in Discussion Question 1. Which data could **Oakley**'s management use to determine the actual fixed and overhead costs at the company for conducting variance analysis?

4. (LO11.1) Why is it important to conduct variance analysis of fixed overhead costs? Why might actual fixed overhead costs deviate from budgeted overhead costs?

5. (LO11.2) What is the difference between a variable overhead spending variance and a variable overhead efficiency variance?

6. (LO11.1) Imagine that you are a cost accountant for **Blue Bell Ice Cream**, a creamery headquartered in Brenham, Texas. Management has asked you to identify the best cost-allocation base to use to calculate the overhead rate per unit. What cost-allocation base do you suggest? Provide an explanation that includes the criteria you used to identify the appropriate base.

7. (LO11.2) You are a cost accountant for a midsized manufacturing company that produces office furniture. After calculating the company's variable overhead spending variance, you find an unfavorable variance of approximately $25,000. Provide an explanation to management about what the overhead spending variance represents in general, and conjecture what could have caused this variance at your company.

8. (LO11.2) You are a cost accountant for a midsized manufacturing company that produces office furniture. After calculating the company's variable overhead efficiency variance, you find a favorable variance of approximately $9,000. Provide an explanation to management about what the overhead efficiency variance represents in general, and conjecture what could have caused this variance at your company.

9. (LO11.6) You are a cost accountant for a midsized manufacturing company that produces office furniture. Budgeted fixed overhead is $250,000. Applied fixed overhead is $245,000. You calculate the production-volume variance and report to management that you have an unfavorable variance. Why is this variance unfavorable?

10. (LO11.1) You are a cost accountant for a hospital. Select an appropriate cost-allocation base for the fixed and variable overhead costs. Defend your answer.

11. (LO11.1) You are a cost accountant for a technology company that maintains computer servers for clients around the United States and Canada. Select an appropriate cost-allocation base for the fixed and variable overhead costs. Defend your answer.

12. (LO11.5, 11.6) Describe each of the fixed cost variances. What data does the cost accountant need to evaluate them?

13. (LO11.8) Organizations can reduce cost, including overhead costs, by engaging in sustainability efforts. Suggest several ways a manufacturing company can cut overhead costs while also focusing on sustainability.

ENVIRONMENTAL, SOCIAL, GOVERNANCE

14. (LO11.3) You are a cost accountant for **Weber Grills**. The company uses machine hours as the cost-allocation basis for variable overhead. You find a $75,000 unfavorable efficiency variance at the end of the period. What are three possible reasons for this variance? What are some potential management responses that could reduce this unfavorable efficiency variance in the future?

15. (LO11.2) You are a cost accountant for **Weber Grills**. The company uses machine hours as the cost-allocation basis for variable overhead. You find a $25,000 favorable spending variance at the end of the period. What are three possible reasons for this variance? Describe the potential positive and negative implications of each of those three reasons.

16. (LO11.6) Is there an efficiency variance for fixed overhead costs? Why or why not?

Brief Exercises   ![Mc Graw Hill] connect

1. **(LO11.1)** Consider the following data from **ENO**:
   - Total budgeted variable overhead is $240,000.
   - Standard labor hours are 0.5 hour per hammock.
   - Budgeted production is 20,000 hammocks.

   Required
   a. Calculate the budgeted variable overhead per hour.
   b. Calculate the budgeted variable overhead per hammock.

2. **(LO11.1, 11.5, 11.6)** Consider the following data from **ON Running Shoes**:
   - Budgeted fixed overhead for 2025 is $400,000.
   - Fixed overhead costs are allocated based on labor hours.
   - The company budgeted 25,000 labor hours to manufacture 100,000 pairs of shoes.
   - Actual pairs of shoes manufactured were 99,750.
   - Actual fixed costs were $402,000.

   Required
   a. Calculate the fixed overhead rate for 2025.
   b. Calculate the fixed overhead spending variance for 2025.
   c. Calculate the production-volume variance for 2025.

3. **(LO11.1, 11.2, 11.3)** **Brooklyn Kayak Co.** manufactures kayaks. The 2023 operating budget estimates production of 50,000 units using 1.5 machine hours per kayak. The standard variable overhead per hour is $20. Actual production in 2023 was 48,000 units using a total of 76,800 hours. Actual variable costs were $22 per machine hour.

   Required
   a. Calculate budgeted variable overhead for 2023.
   b. Calculate the variable overhead spending variance.
   c. Calculate the variable overhead efficiency variance.

4. **(LO11.4)** Using the data from **Brooklyn Kayak Co.** (in Brief Exercise 3 above), prepare the journal entries to record these variances and to write off the difference to COGS.

5. **(LO11.4)** **Torani** produces flavored syrups for coffee and other beverages. The company's budget and actual variable costs for the month of March are as follows:

   Actual variable overhead costs incurred: $250,000
   Budgeted variable overhead costs: $260,000

   At the end of the month, the cost accountants post the following entries to write off the balances in the variance accounts to Cost of Good Sold:

Costs of Goods Sold	10,000	
Variable Overhead Spending Variance	10,000	
Variable Overhead Efficiency Variance		20,000

   Which entry or entries were made previously in the period to result in this closing entry?

6. **(LO11.7)** **Torani** produces flavored syrups for coffee and other beverages. The company's actual and allocated fixed overhead costs during the month are as follows:

   Actual fixed overhead: $515,000
   Allocated fixed overhead: $480,000

At the end of the month, the cost accountants post the following entries to write off the balances in the variance accounts to Cost of Good Sold:

Costs of Goods Sold	15,000	
Fixed Overhead Spending Variance		15,000

Which entry or entries were made previously in the period to result in this closing entry?

7. (LO11.6) **Magic Spoon** is a company that develops and produces healthier alternatives to your favorite breakfast cereals. In the last quarter:
   - Budgeted fixed overhead was $50,000.
   - Planned production was 1,000,0000 units.
   - Actual production was 990,000 units.

   Calculate the production-volume variance and indicate if it is favorable or unfavorable. Provide a potential explanation for the variance.

8. (LO11.6) **Magic Spoon** is a company that develops and produces healthier alternatives to your favorite breakfast cereals. In the last quarter:
   - Budgeted fixed overhead was $50,000.
   - Planned production was 1,000,0000 units.
   - Actual production was 1,020,000 units.

   Calculate the production-volume variance and indicate if it is favorable or unfavorable. Provide a potential explanation for the variance.

9. (LO11.5) **Dyson** produces specialty hair-care products, including the Dyson Airwrap dryer. In May of 2025, Dyson produced 105,000 Airwrap dryers and had the following budget and results:

	Actual Result	Flexible-Budget Amount
Output units	105,000.00	105,000.00
Machine hour per output unit	0.15	0.10
Machine hours (total)	15,750.00	10,500.00
Variable overhead costs	$141,750.00	$140,000.00
Variable overhead costs per machine hour	$9.00	$13.33
Variable overhead costs per unit	$1.35	$1.33

Calculate the variable overhead flexible-budget variance and provide an explanation for the results.

10. (LO11.3) **Dyson** produces specialty hair-care products, including the Dyson Airwrap dryer. In May of 2025, Dyson produced 105,000 Airwrap dryers and had the following budget and results:

	Actual Result	Flexible-Budget Amount
Output units	105,000.00	105,000.00
Machine hours per output unit	0.15	0.10
Machine hours (total)	15,750.00	10,500.00
Variable overhead costs	$141,750.00	$140,000.00
Variable overhead costs per machine hour	$9.00	$13.33
Variable overhead costs per unit	$1.35	$1.33

Calculate the variable overhead efficiency variance and provide an explanation for the results.

11. **(LO11.2) Dyson** produces specialty hair-care products, including the Dyson Airwrap dryer. In May of 2025, Dyson produced 105,000 Airwrap dryers and had the following budget and results:

	Actual Result	Flexible-Budget Amount
Output units	105,000.00	105,000.00
Machine hour per output unit	0.15	0.10
Machine hours (total)	15,750.00	10,500.00
Variable overhead costs	$141,750.00	$140,000.00
Variable overhead costs per machine hour	$9.00	$13.33
Variable overhead costs per unit	$1.35	$1.33

Calculate the variable overhead spending variance and provide an explanation for the results.

12. **(LO11.4, 11.7)** Using the data and your answers from Brief Exercises 9, 10, and 11, generate the following journal entries for **Dyson**:

   a. Record the actual variable overhead costs incurred.

   b. Record variable overhead costs allocated.

   c. Record the variance(s) for the accounting period.

   d. Close the entries to COGS.

13. **(LO11.8) Dyson** is exploring several initiatives to reduce overhead costs while also sup- porting its ESG goals. In particular, the company is considering installing solar panels on the roof of its headquarters building. The solar panels are expected to reduce variable overhead costs by $300 per month. Calculate the VOH spending and efficiency vari- ances for Dyson assuming that the company has implemented the new solar panels, resulting in a $300 per month decrease in variable overhead costs. Assume the rest of the flexible budget and actual results are the same as in Brief Exercise 11. Provide an explanation for your results and explain how the solar panel installation affects each variance.

14. **(LO11.5) Marucci Bats** is a company that develops and produces baseball bats. In the last month:

   • Budgeted fixed overhead was $20,000.

   • Actual fixed overhead was $22,000.

   • Planned production was 1,000,0000 units.

   • Actual production was 1,010,000 units.

   Calculate the fixed overhead spending variance and indicate if it is favorable or unfavorable. Provide a potential explanation for the variance.

15. **(LO11.7)** Use the data and your answer(s) from Brief Exercise 14 about **Marucci Bats** and generate the following journal entries.

   a. Record actual fixed overhead costs incurred.

   b. Record fixed overhead costs allocated.

   c. Record variances for the last month.

   d. Close the entry to COGS.

Problems   Mc Graw Hill connect

1. **(LO11.6)** As a cost accountant for a company that manufactures cell phone cases, you prepare the following production-volume variance graph.

DATA VISUALIZATION

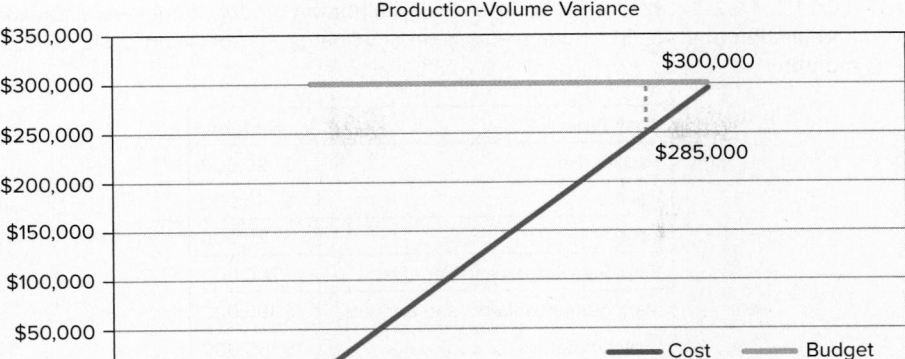

Production-Volume Variance

$300,000

$285,000

Cost — — Budget

100,000

Required

Interpret and describe these results for your senior management. Assume management does not know much about cost accounting and does not understand what production-volume variance represents.

2. (LO11.1, 11.2, 11.3, 11.4, 11.5, 11.6, 11.7) One division of **Heartwood Cabinets** anticipates the following costs for the next year:

Cost	Budget
Facilities rent	$ 72,000
Utilities	$ 28,000
Taxes	$ 17,000
Wages for production workers	$555,000
Management salaries and benefits	$320,000
Wages for shipping and handling workers	$256,000
Direct materials for cabinets	$350,000
Supplies	$ 38,000
Indirect materials	$ 120,000
Equipment rental	$ 32,000
Advertising	$ 25,000
Repairs and maintenance	$ 36,000
Travel	$ 95,000

The company uses machine hours as the sole cost driver of variable overhead. Based on prior years, Heartwood estimates it will take 0.30 machine hour per cabinet produced. Budgeted output is 75,000 cabinets. Actual output is 73,000 cabinets and it really takes 0.40 machine hour to produce one cabinet. Actual variable overhead costs are $474,500. Actual fixed overhead costs are $600,000.

Required

Round all answers to two decimal points.

a. Calculate budgeted variable overhead for the year.
b. Calculate the variable overhead spending variance.
c. Calculate the variable overhead efficiency variance.
d. Calculate the fixed overhead spending variance.
e. Calculate the production-volume variance.
f. Create the journal entries to record the variable overhead variances and include a description of what each journal entry does.
g. Create the journal entries to record the fixed overhead variances.

3. (LO11.1, 11.2, 11.3, 11.4, 11.5, 11.6, 11.7) **Calphalon** produces cookware, appliances, and kitchen utensils. Its cookware division anticipates the following costs for the next month:

Cost Type	Budget
Facilities rent	$ 90,000
Utilities	$ 48,000
Taxes	$ 25,000
Employee wages and benefits	$700,000
Management salaries and benefits	$300,000
Direct materials for cookware	$265,000
Supplies	$ 145,000
Equipment rental	$ 30,000
Advertising	$ 65,000
Repairs and maintenance	$ 50,000
Travel	$ 95,000

The company uses machine hours as the sole cost driver of variable overhead. Based on prior production periods, Calphalon estimates 0.25 machine hour per unit produced. Budgeted output is 200,000 units. Actual output is 220,000 units. Actual variable costs were 3% less than anticipated due to some cost savings on repairs and maintenance and equipment rental costs. Actual fixed overhead was $580,000.

Required
Round all answers to two decimal points.

a. Calculate budgeted variable overhead for the year.
b. Calculate the variable overhead spending variance.
c. Calculate the variable overhead efficiency variance.
d. Calculate the fixed overhead spending variance.
e. Calculate the production-volume variance.
f. Create the journal entries to record the variable overhead variances.
g. Create the journal entries to record the fixed overhead variances.

4. (LO11.5, 11.6) The cost accountants from **Costa Del Mar** sunglasses prepared the following column chart to display the FOH spending and production-volume variances over time. Assume budgeted fixed overhead for Division 2 is $135,000.

DATA VISUALIZATION

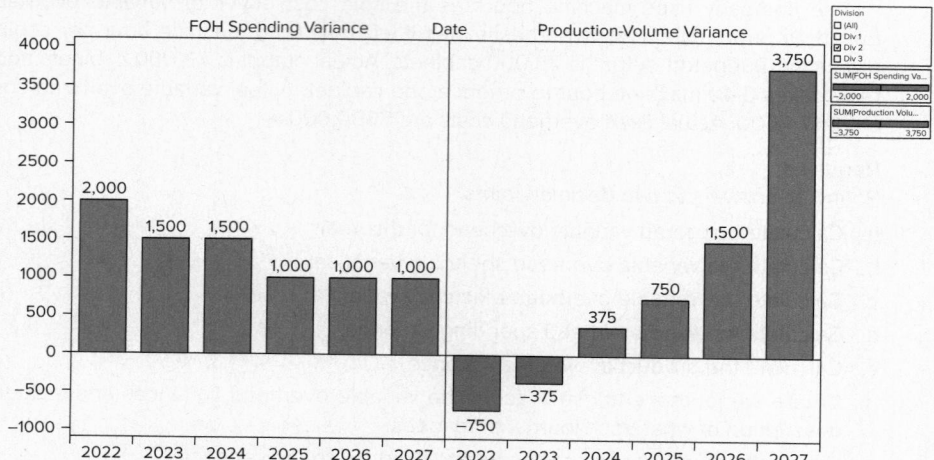

Required

a. Calculate the actual fixed overhead costs incurred by Costa del Mar for 2026.
   Hint: FOH spending variance = Actual costs incurred − Flexible budget amount.

b. Calculate the amount of fixed overhead Costa del Mar applied to fixed overhead during 2026.
   Hint: Production-volume variance = Budgeted FOH − Fixed overhead allocated for actual units produced.

c. Describe what management learns about FOH based on the results from 2026.

d. Describe what management learns about FOH when evaluating the trend in FOH variances over time.

5. (LO11.1, 11.2, 11.3, 11.4, 11.5, 11.6, 11.7) **Delta Air Lines** is a major airline carrier based in the United States. The company anticipates the following costs for the next year (in millions):

Item	Overhead Cost	Budgeted Overhead
A.	Aircraft leases and financing costs	$90,000,000
B.	Airport fees and charges	$10,000,000
C.	Catering costs	$ 300,000
D.	Crew expenses	$ 3,000,000
E.	Fuel costs	$ 11,500,000
F.	Ground handling costs	$ 500,000
G.	Information technology costs	$ 340,000
H.	Insurance premiums	$ 260,000
I.	Landing and take-off fees	$ 2,000,000
J.	Maintenance costs	$ 2,000,000
K.	Marketing and sales expenses	$ 100,000
L.	Navigation fees	$ 150,000
M.	Rent and utilities	$ 600,000
N.	Salaries and benefits	$ 12,000,000

Assume Delta uses the number of passengers as the sole cost driver of overhead costs. Based on prior years, Delta estimated it would have approximately 150,000,000 passengers. Actual number of passengers for the year was 166,000,000. Actual fixed overhead costs are $125,000,000.

Required

a. Which of the costs listed above should be classified as variable overhead costs?

b. Which of the costs listed above should be classified as fixed overhead costs?

c. Calculate budgeted variable overhead for the year.

d. Calculate budgeted fixed overhead for the year.

e. Calculate the budgeted variable overhead costs per passenger based on the passenger estimate prepared by Delta (round to two decimal places).

f. Calculate the budgeted fixed overhead costs per passenger based on the passenger estimate prepared by Delta (round to two decimal places).

g. Use the budgeted FOH cost calculated in part f and calculate the production-volume variance for Delta.

h. Use the budgeted FOH cost calculated in part f and calculate the fixed overhead spending variance for Delta.

6. (LO11.1, 11.2, 11.3, 11.4, 11.5, 11.6, 11.7) **Power Wheels** produces electric toy vehicles that look like real cars and trucks. The cost accountants at Power Wheels summarized the following data about the static budget and actual production for the last year.

	Actual	Static Budget
Units produced	220,000	200,000
Machine hours required to produce one unit	1.40	1.50
Variable overhead	$585,200	$600,000
Fixed overhead	$62,000	$66,000

Required

Use the information in the table above to calculate the following variances and to post the requisite journal entries.

a. Calculate the variable overhead flexible-budget variance.

b. Calculate the variable overhead spending variance.

c. Calculate the variable overhead efficiency variance.

d. Calculate the fixed overhead spending variance.

e. Calculate the production-volume variance.

f. Create the journal entries to record the variable overhead variances.

g. Create the journal entries to record the fixed overhead variances.

7. (LO11.1, 11.2, 11.3, 11.4, 11.5, 11.6, 11.7) **Coach** produces handbags, wallets, shoes, clothing, and other leather accessories. Its manufacturing facilities are located in Cambodia, Vietnam, and the Philippines. Coach estimates the following costs for production at one of its facilities in Cambodia, where its larger handbags are manufactured.

Facilities rent	$ 105,000
Utilities	$ 65,000
Taxes	$ 34,000
Production employee wages	$1,600,000
Indirect wages	$ 800,000
Management salaries and benefits	$ 400,000
Direct materials	$1,800,000
Supplies	$ 650,000
Equipment rental	$ 30,000
Advertising	$ 250,000
Repairs and maintenance	$ 150,000

Coach uses labor hours as the sole cost driver of variable overhead. Based on prior production periods, Coach estimates 0.75 hour per unit produced. Budgeted output is 500,000 units. Actual output is 495,000 units.

Actual fixed costs for the year were:

Facilities rent	$ 105,000
Taxes	$ 33,000
Management salaries and benefits	$400,000
Advertising	$250,000

Actual labor hour per unit produced was 0.80. Actual variable overhead costs were 10% higher than anticipated.

Required

Round all answers to two decimal points.

a. Calculate budgeted variable overhead for the year.

b. Calculate the variable overhead spending variance.

c. Calculate the variable overhead efficiency variance.

d. Calculate the fixed overhead spending variance.

e. Calculate the production-volume variance.

f. Create the journal entries to record the variable overhead variances.

g. Create the journal entries to record the fixed overhead variances.

8. (LO11.1, 11.2, 11.3, 11.5, 11.6) You are the cost accountant for Porch Perfection, a fictitious company that manufactures porch swings. You have summarized the following manufacturing overhead data for the last period.

	Actual Costs Incurred	Flexible Budget	Cost Allocation
Variable overhead	$ 93,500.00	$ 92,000.00	$ 90,000.00
Fixed overhead	$355,000.00	$350,000.00	$355,000.00

Budgeted number of output units	1,400
Planned allocation rate (machine hours per unit)	1.50
Actual number of machine hours used	2,450
Static-budget variable manufacturing overhead costs	$92,000.00

Required

Calculate each of the following items.

a. Budgeted machine hours.

b. Budgeted fixed manufacturing overhead costs per machine hour.

c. Budgeted variable manufacturing overhead costs per machine hour.

d. Actual number of swings produced.

e. Budgeted number of machine-hours allocated for actual number of swings produced.

f. Actual number of machine-hours used per swing.

9. (LO11.1, 11.2, 11.3, 11.4, 11.5, 11.6, 11.7) MotoMingle is a fictional scooter company that produces environmentally friendly scooters. MotoMingle uses labor hours as the sole cost driver of variable overhead.

Based on prior production periods, MotoMingle estimates it will take 3.25 labor hours per unit produced. Budgeted output is 100,000 units per month. Budgeted variable overhead costs for the year were $3,600,000.

Actual labor hours required were 3.50 per unit produced. Actual output for the year was 1,000,000. Actual variable overhead costs for the year were $3,380,000. MotoMingle budgeted $800,000 for fixed overhead costs during the year. Actual fixed overhead costs were $750,000.

Required

Round all answers to two decimal points.

a. Calculate the variable overhead spending variance.

b. Calculate the variable overhead efficiency variance.

c. Calculate the fixed overhead spending variance.

d. Calculate the production-volume variance.

e. Create the journal entries to record the variable overhead variances.

f. Create the journal entries to record the fixed overhead variances.

10. (LO11.1, 11.2, 11.3, 11.4, 11.5, 11.6, 11.7) Galactic Gaming produces handheld gaming devices. The company plans for production of 200,000 units per quarter. At the beginning of the year, Galactic Gaming estimates that the following quarterly costs will be incurred for the planned production:

Cost	Quarterly Estimate
Facilities rent	$ 90,000
Utilities	$ 54,000
Taxes	$ 25,000
Production employee wages	$700,000
Shipping and handling employee wages and benefits	$200,000
Management salaries and benefits	$300,000
Direct materials for gaming devices	$265,000
Supplies	$ 145,000
Equipment rental	$ 30,000
Advertising	$ 65,000
Repairs and maintenance	$ 50,000
Travel	$ 95,000

Budgeted machine hours are 0.50 per unit.
Actual production results and costs per quarter are as follows:

	Q1	Q2	Q3	Q4
Actual production	200,000	205,000	180,000	190,000
Actual machine hours per unit	0.5	0.6	0.75	0.70
Facilities rent	$ 90,000.00	$ 90,000.00	$ 90,000.00	$ 90,000.00
Utilities	$ 50,000.00	$ 58,000.00	$ 62,000.00	$ 49,000.00
Taxes	$ 25,000.00	$ 26,500.00	$ 26,500.00	$ 26,500.00
Production employee wages	$ 710,000.00	$ 816,500.00	$825,000.00	$ 810,000.00
Shipping and handling employee wages and benefits	$ 198,000.00	$ 199,000.00	$ 199,000.00	$ 210,000.00
Management salaries and benefits	$300,000.00	$325,000.00	$325,000.00	$325,000.00
Direct materials for gaming devices	$270,300.00	$262,350.00	$ 267,597.00	$ 267,597.00
Supplies	$ 142,000.00	$ 140,000.00	$ 141,000.00	$ 144,000.00
Equipment rental	$ 20,000.00	$ 20,000.00	$ 40,000.00	$ 25,000.00
Advertising	$ 65,000.00	$ 65,000.00	$ 65,000.00	$ 65,000.00
Repairs and maintenance	$ 30,000.00	$ 30,000.00	$ 75,000.00	$ 60,000.00
Travel	$ 90,000.00	$ 90,000.00	$ 90,000.00	$ 90,000.00

Required

Calculate the VOH efficiency variance, VOH spending variance, FOH spending variance, and production-volume variance for each quarter. Comment on the trend(s) you observe in the variances.

11. (LO11.1, 11.2, 11.3, 11.4, 11.5, 11.6, 11.7) Use the data in Problem 10 to prepare a graph in Excel to visualize the trends in variances and production by quarter.

DATA VISUALIZATION

Required

Use a combo chart to display each variance by quarter in a clustered column and the units produced as a line on the same chart.

12. (LO11.8) **Stanley** has been producing thermoses and drinkware since 1913. In the early 2020s, one of its newest offerings, a 40-ounce insulated tumbler that fits in a car's cup holder, went viral when it was featured by prominent online influencers. As a result, Stanley increased production significantly. In 2025, Stanley's estimated and actual production figures were as follows:

	Estimate	Actual
Production	2,000,000	2,020,000
Sales Price per Unit	$45.00	$45.00
Expected Revenue	$90,000,000.00	$90,900,000.00
VOH	$1,800,000.00	$1,900,500.00
FOH	$500,000.00	$600,000.00
Machine hour per unit	0.05	0.04

Assume Stanley wants to be true to its mission to help build a more sustainable world, and it is exploring some new green production initiatives that are likely to change the overhead costs associated with production. The changes and their anticipated effect on overhead costs are as follows:

Change	Expected Effect
Installing motion-detecting lights in all office buildings	Decrease utilities cost by 1%
Reducing all nonessential corporate travel	Decrease travel cost by 20%
Using more eco-friendly packaging for shipping product	Increase packaging costs by 1%

Required

a. Calculate the VOH efficiency variance, VOH spending variance, FOH spending variance, and production-volume variance for 2025.

b. For each variance, indicate whether the suggested change will make the variance more favorable, will make it less favorable, or have no effect.

13. (LO11.1, 11.2, 11.3, 11.4, 11.5, 11.6, 11.7) **Vitamix** produces high-quality blenders that are used in the home and in restaurants. The cost accountants at Vitamix anticipate the following costs for the next year:

Cost Type	Budget
Facilities rent	$ 100,000
Utilities	$ 50,000
Taxes	$ 50,000
Employee wages and benefits	$2,000,000
Management salaries and benefits	$ 750,000
Direct materials for blenders	$ 1,500,000
Supplies	$ 375,000
Equipment rental	$ 125,000
Advertising	$ 1,000,000
Repairs and maintenance	$ 150,000
Travel	$ 300,000

The company uses machine hours as the sole cost driver of variable overhead. Based on prior production periods, Vitamix estimates 0.25 machine hour per unit produced. Budgeted output is 1,650,000 units. Actual output is 1,650,000 units. Actual variable costs were 5% more than anticipated. Actual fixed overhead was $2,000,000.

Required

Round all answers to two decimal points.

a. Calculate budgeted variable overhead for the year.
b. Calculate the variable overhead spending variance.
c. Calculate the variable overhead efficiency variance.
d. Calculate the fixed overhead spending variance.
e. Calculate the production-volume variance.
f. Create the journal entries to record the variable overhead variances.
g. Create the journal entries to record the fixed overhead variances.

Required

Review the dashboard and describe your insights to Ms. Navarro.

14. (LO11.2, 11.3, 11.4, 11.5, 11.6, 11.7) Monica Navarro, the CFO of XYZ Company, has asked her cost accounting team to prepare a visualization to summarize the trends in overhead costs over time. The team has prepared the following combo chart to display the budgeted and actual units produced (lines) and the overhead variances (columns) for the past four years.

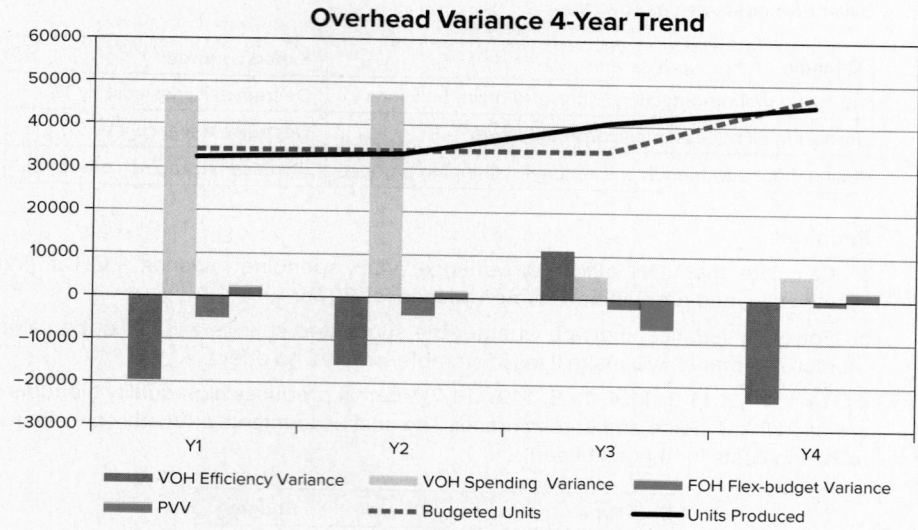

Overhead Variance 4-Year Trend

Required

Review the dashboard and describe your insights to Ms. Navarro.

15. (LO11.8) Kascade Kayaks manufactures kayaks and related equipment. For 2026, Kascade's cost accountants provide the following estimates:

ENVIRONMENTAL, SOCIAL, GOVERNANCE

	Estimate	Actual
Production	175,000	172,000
Sales price per unit	$600.00	$600.00
Expected revenue	$105,000,000.00	$103,200,000.00
VOH	$3,000,000.00	$3,300,000.00
FOH	$1,500,000.00	$1,470,000.00
Direct materials	$25,000,000.00	$29,000,000.00
Direct labor	$35,000,000.00	$36,000,000.00
Expected profit	$75,500,000.00	$69,430,000.00
Machine hours per unit	0.5	0.6

Kascade Kayaks budgeted the same amounts for 2027. However, after the budgeting was complete, Kascade implemented several important initiatives aimed at becoming a more eco-friendly company and achieving overhead cost reduction. These changes had the following effects in 2027:

Change	Effect
Installing motion-detecting lights in all office buildings	Decrease utilities cost by $25,000
Reducing all nonessential corporate travel	Decrease travel cost by $150,000
Using more eco-friendly packaging for shipping product	Increase packaging costs by $55,000
Implement robotic processing for invoicing and payment processing, reducing the number of back-office personnel required	Decrease office staff salaries by $175,000

Required

a. Calculate the VOH efficiency variance, VOH spending variance, FOH spending variance, and production-volume variance for 2026. Round to the nearest dollar.

b. Assume that Kascade Kayaks used the same budget in both 2026 and 2027 and that all actual results were the same *except* for the changes described above. Calculate the VOH efficiency variance, VOH spending variance, FOH spending variance, and production-volume variance for 2027. Round to the nearest dollar.

Lab 11.1 Excel

Lab Note: The tools presented in this lab periodically change. Updated instructions, if applicable, can be found in the student and instructor support materials.

Graphing Production-Volume Variance

Data Analytics Types: Diagnostic Analytics

Keywords

Production-Volume Variance, Excel, Line Graph

Decision-Making Context

You are the cost accountant for Voltage Wheels, a (fictitious) company that produces electric scooters. Budgeted fixed overhead is $984,000 for the year. Budgeted production is 180,000 units for the year. Budgeted machine hours are 0.75 hour per unit. Actual units produced during the year were 162,000.

Required

1. Calculate the production-volume variance.
2. Graph the production-volume variance in Excel.

Ask the Question

Is the company using its fixed overhead efficiently?

Master the Data

For this lab, you will create the data, based on the information about Voltage Wheels, in a blank Excel workbook.

Perform the Analysis

Analysis Task #1: Prepare the Data

For Analysis Task #1, you will enter the data you need to calculate the production-volume variance. Follow along with Lab Exhibit 11.1.1 as you complete the following steps.

1. In cell A1, enter the header "Budgeted Fixed Cost".
2. In cell A2, enter the amount of fixed overhead budgeted for the year at Voltage Wheels, $2,970,000.
3. In cell B1, enter the header "Hours".

4. In cell B2, enter 0.75, which is the number of hours required to produce a single electric scooter.
5. In cell C1, enter the header "Budgeted Annual Production".
6. In cell C2, enter 180,000, which is the budgeted annual production of scooters.
7. In cell D1, enter the header "Actual Annual Production".
8. In cell D2, enter the actual annual production, 162,000.
9. In cell E1, enter the header "Budgeted Fixed Overhead Cost per unit of cost-allocation base".
10. In cell E2, calculate the budgeted fixed overhead cost per unit of cost allocation base. Remember, the cost allocation base is hours.

	A	B	C	D	E
1	Budgeted Fixed Cost	Hours	Budgeted Annual Production	Actual Annual Production	Budgeted Fixed Overhead Cost per unit of cost-allocation base
2	$ 2,970,000	0.75	180,000	162,000	$ 22.00
3					

Lab Exhibit 11.1.1

Microsoft Excel

11. Use cell references to enter the formula that represents Budgeted Fixed Cost/ (hours * budgeted annual production). The Excel expression is =A2/(B2*C2), as shown in Lab Exhibit 11.1.2.

	E
1	Budgeted Fixed Overhead Cost per unit of cost-allocation base
2	=A2/(B2*C2)

Lab Exhibit 11.1.2

Microsoft Excel

Analysis Task #2: Prepare Data for Graphing

Your final product should be a line graph similar to Exhibit 11.8 in the text. You'll need lines representing (1) budgeted fixed cost, (2) allocated fixed cost for all possible amounts of production, and (3) the allocated fixed cost for the actual amount of production. You will also need to calculate the production-volume variance. Follow along with Lab Exhibit 11.1.3 as you complete the following steps.

1. In cell A4, enter the header "Units Produced". Under this header, you will enter the range of possible production in separate cells as described next. We will use this range as the start and end points for the line representing allocated fixed cost for all possible amounts of production.
2. In cell A5, enter 0, which represents the smallest amount of production possible.
3. In cell A6, use a cell reference to enter the highest amount of production (the total budgeted annual production) that you entered manually into cell C2. The cell reference is =C2.
4. In cell B4, enter the header "Allocated Fixed Overhead".
5. In cell B5, use cell references to enter the formula that represents: Allocated fixed overhead per units produced = Budgeted fixed overhead cost per unit of cost-allocation base * Units produced.
   - The Excel expression is =$E$2*A5. (Note the use of the $ sign to lock the cells.)
6. Copy that formula down to cell B6.
   - The Excel expression is =$E$2*A6.
7. In cell C4, enter the header "Budgeted Fixed Overhead Cost".

8. In cell C5, use a cell reference to enter the budgeted fixed overhead cost that you entered manually into cell A2. The cell reference is =$A$2.
   - *Note:* Because this amount is budgeted fixed costs, you will use the same value from cell A2 for the lowest and highest number of units produced. Therefore, you can lock the cells using the $ sign before the column and row references.
9. Copy the formula in cell C5 down to cell C6.
10. In cell D4, enter the header "Allocated Fixed Cost for Actual Production".
11. In cell D5, enter the formula to calculate allocated fixed cost for actual production, but allow this cell to be dynamic based on the actual production amount that you will enter in cell F5 later. Use cell references to enter the formula that calculates allocated fixed cost for actual production:
    - Actual production * Budgeted fixed overhead cost per unit of cost-allocation base * Hours per unit. The Excel expression is =(F$5*E$2*B$2).
    - Copy the formula in cell D5 down to cell D6.
12. In cell F4, enter the header "Actual Production".
13. In cell F5, insert the Excel expression to reference cell D2, which contains the Actual Production for the year. The Excel expression is =D2.
    - Note that after you make the graph, you can change this Actual Production value entered in cell D2. The allocated cost line will shift based on the production value you enter.
    - Highlight F5 in yellow to indicate that you can change this value later if actual production changes.
14. In cell E4, enter the header "Production-Volume Variance".
15. In cell E5, use cell references to enter the formula that represents the production volume variance: Budgeted annual production − Actual annual production. The Excel expression is =C5-D5.

    Lab Exhibit 11.1.3 shows the formulas for the prepared spreadsheet, and Lab Exhibit 11.1.4 shows the values based on these formulas.

	A	B	C	D	E	F
4	Units Produced	Allocated Fixed Overhead	Budgeted Fixed Overhead Cost	Allocated Fixed Cost for Actual Production	Production-Volume Variance	Actual Production
5	0	=$E$2*A5	=$A$2	=(F$5*E$2*B$2)	=C5-D5	=D2
6	=C2	=$E$2*A6	=$A$2	=(F$5*E$2*B$2)		
7						

Lab Exhibit 11.1.3

Microsoft Excel

Lab Exhibit 11.1.4

Microsoft Excel

	A	B	C	D	E	F
4	Units Produced	Allocated Fixed Overhead	Budgeted Fixed Overhead Cost	Allocated Fixed Cost for Actual Production	Production-Volume Variance	Actual Production
5	0	$ -	$ 984,000	$ 885,600.00	$ 98,400.00	162,000
6	180,000	$1,312,000.00	$ 984,000	$ 885,600.00	$ 98,400.00	

DATA VISUALIZATION

Analysis Task #3: Prepare the Line Graph

1. As shown in Lab Exhibit 11.1.5, highlight cells A4:D6.
2. Click the **Insert** tab at the top of the screen.

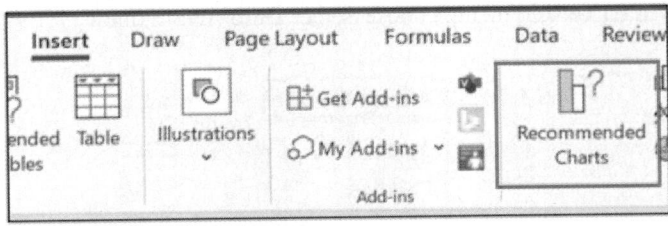

3. Click **Recommended Charts** (Lab Exhibit 11.1.6).

4. As shown in Lab Exhibit 11.1.7, choose the **All Charts** tab.
5. Select a **Combo** chart.

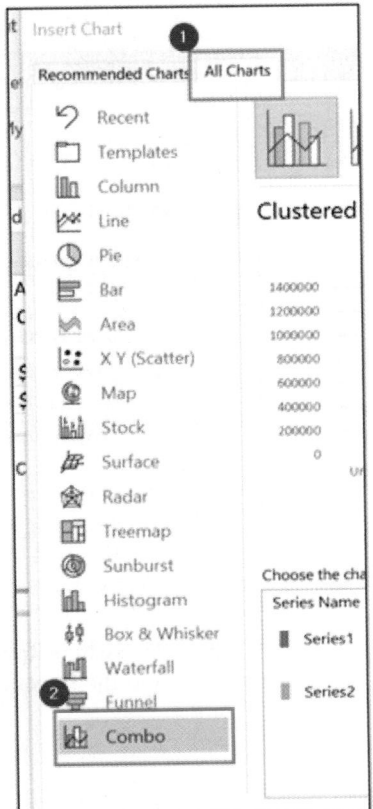

6. Click on the custom combo chart option at the top (the one with the pencil; see Lab Exhibit 11.1.8).

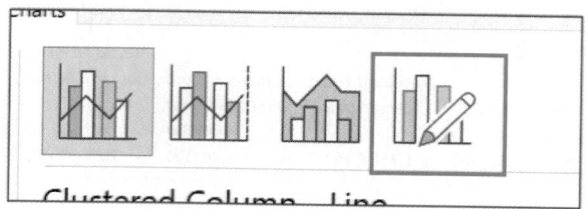

7. Click **OK** at the bottom right of the dialog box. The chart shown will not look anything like Exhibit 11.8 in the chapter. We have to do some custom formatting.
8. From the **Chart Design** menu, choose **Select Data** (Lab Exhibit 11.1.9).

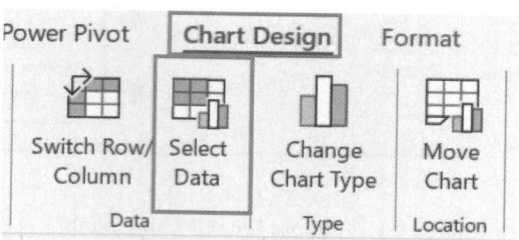

9. The dialog box shown in Lab Exhibit 11.1.10 will open.

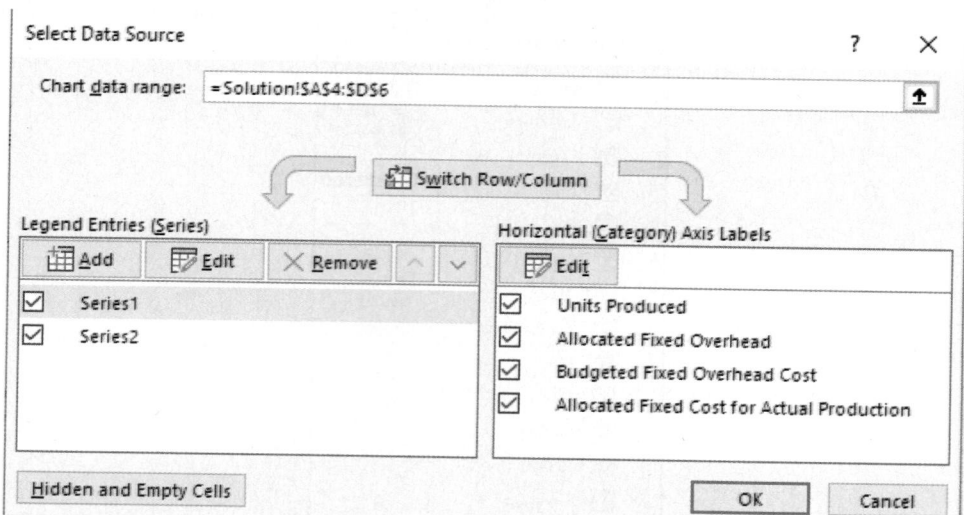

10. Make the following adjustments:
    - As shown in Lab Exhibit 11.1.11, click the **Switch Row/Column** button so that the variables we want to graph are shown as the **Legend Entries (Series)**.

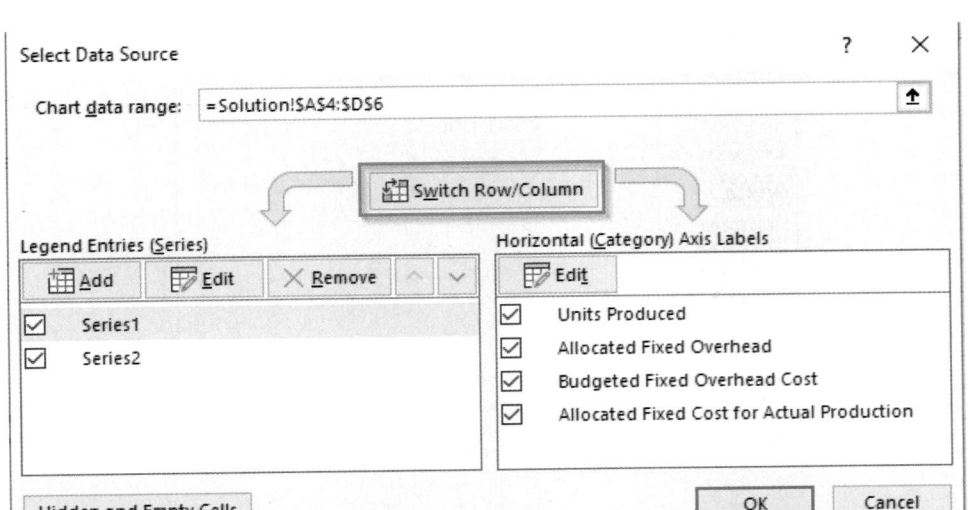

- As shown in Lab Exhibit 11.12, remove **Units Produced** completely. To do so, click the red **X Remove** button. Then click the **Edit** button under **Horizontal (Category) Axis Labels**.

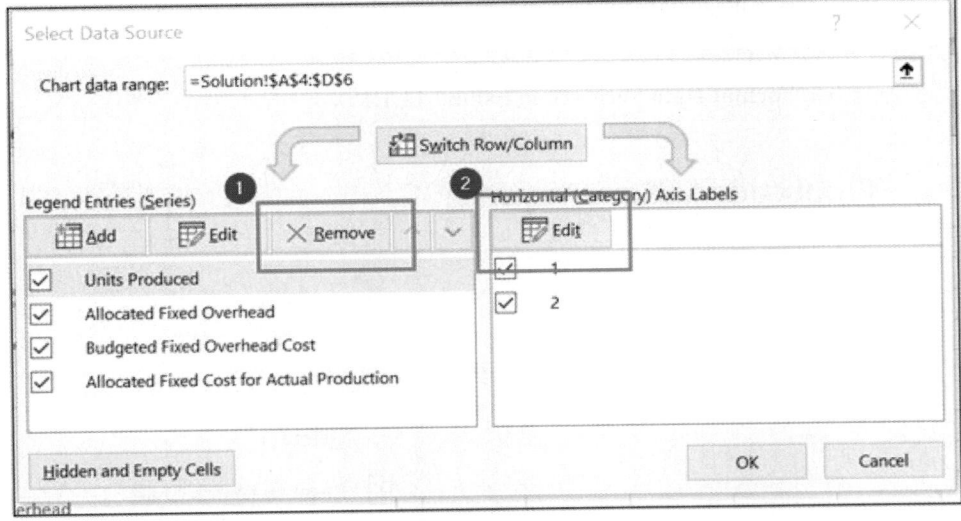

- The **Axis Labels** dialog box will appear (Lab Exhibit 11.1.13). Enter the cell references for the values of possible units produced here so that the units produced will become your X-axis. *Note:* Select only the actual values. Do not include the header or select the entire column.
  - The Excel expression for the range is =Sheet1!$A$5:$A$6.
- Click **OK**.

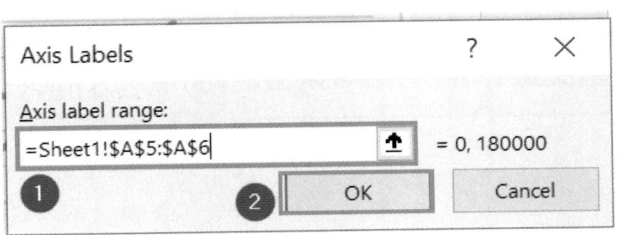

Your chart should now look like Lab Exhibit 11.1.14.

Lab Exhibit 11.1.14

Microsoft Excel

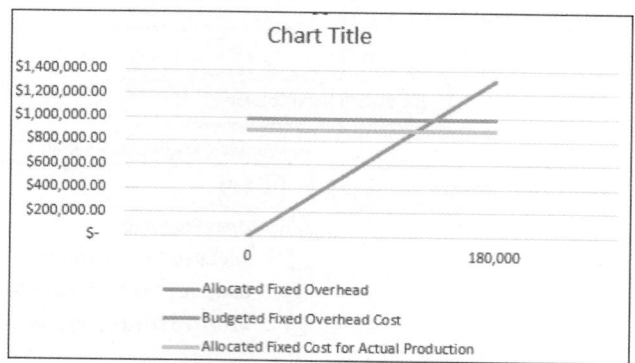

11. You can now make various formatting changes that will improve the usability of your graph.
    - Click on the "Chart Title" at the top of your chart and change the title to "Production-Volume Variance".
    - Remove the gridlines by right-clicking any of the lines and then selecting **Delete**.
    - Make the "Allocated Fixed Cost for Actual Production" line into a dotted line to further differentiate it from the other lines.
      ○ Right-click on the line to highlight it.
      ○ Click **Format Data Series** (Lab Exhibit 11.1.15).

Lab Exhibit 11.1.15

Microsoft Excel

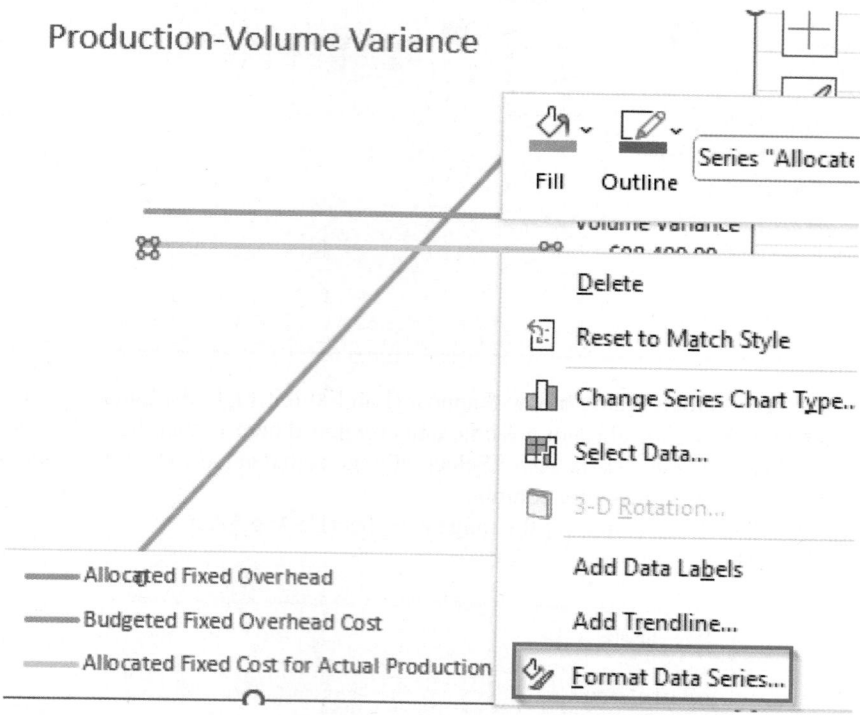

- As shown in Lab Exhibit 11.1.16, click the fill & line option (the **paint can** icon). Then change the dash type to a dotted line.

Lab Exhibit 11.1.16

Microsoft Excel

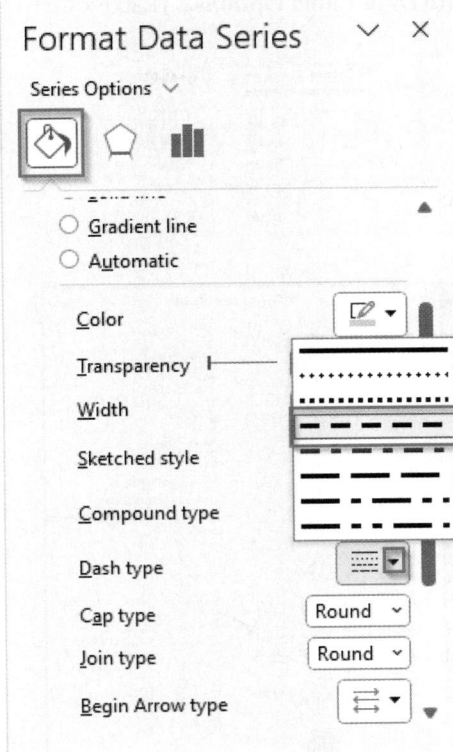

The graph will now appear as shown in Lab Exhibit 11.1.17.

Lab Exhibit 11.1.17

Microsoft Excel

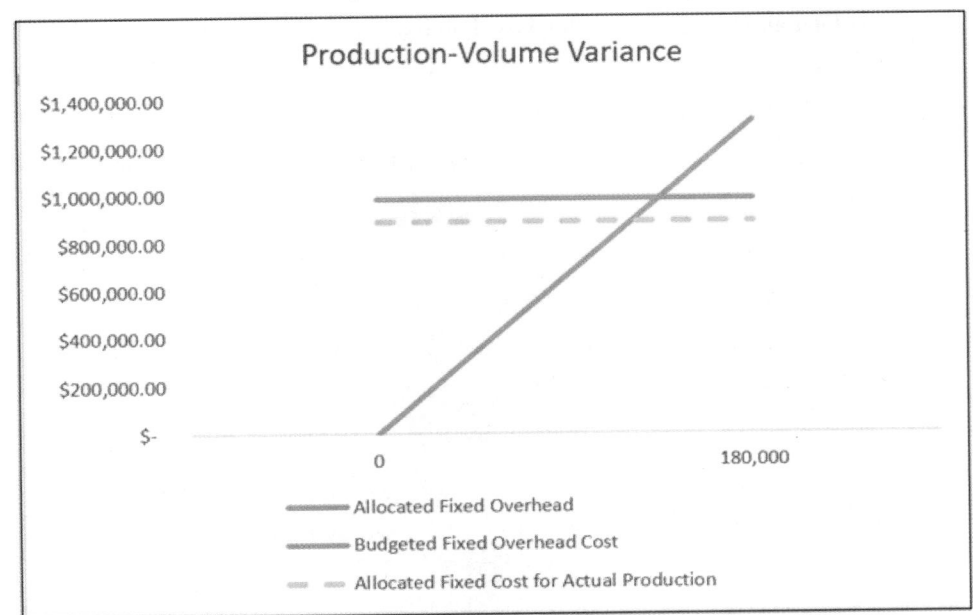

In Excel, there is no easy way to add shading to represent the production-volume variance. But we can add the calculated difference from our worksheet as a chart element.

12. From the **Chart Design** tab (Lab Exhibit 11.1.18), select **Add Chart Element > Data Labels > More Data Label Options...** (Lab Exhibit 11.1.19).

Lab Exhibit 11.1.18

Microsoft Excel

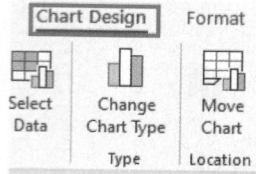

Lab Exhibit 11.1.19

Microsoft Excel

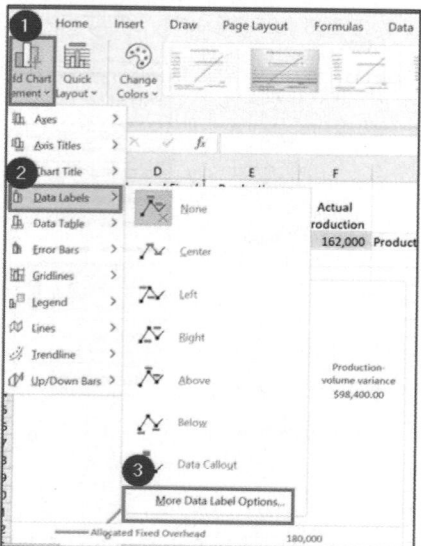

The **Format Data Labels** dialog box (Lab Exhibit 11.1.20) opens on the right of the screen.

Lab Exhibit 11.1.20

Microsoft Excel

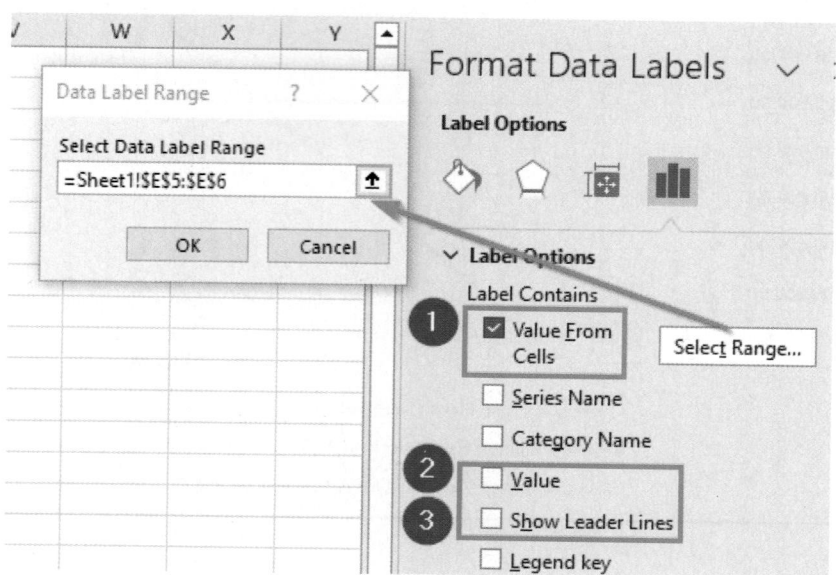

13. Check the box next to **Value From Cells**, and then enter the cell reference for your calculated production-volume variance (E5) and the header (E4). As shown in Lab Exhibit 11.1.20, the formula that will show once you select your range is =Sheet1!$E$4:$E$5, where "Sheet1!" is the name of the current worksheet. Next:

   - Uncheck **Value**.
   - Uncheck **Show Leader Lines**.
   - Click **OK**. Now you will see two new labels on your chart: "Production-Volume Variance" and the calculated variance ($98,400.00 in this case). Your line graph should resemble Lab Exhibit 11.1.21.

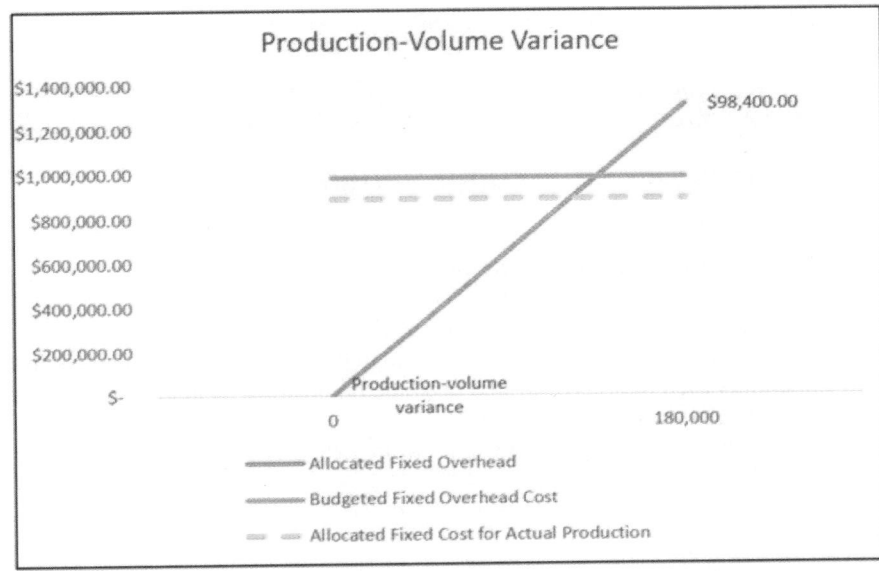

Lab Exhibit 11.1.21

Microsoft Excel

14. As shown in Lab Exhibit 11.1.22, drag the new labels to the section of the chart that represents the production-volume variance.

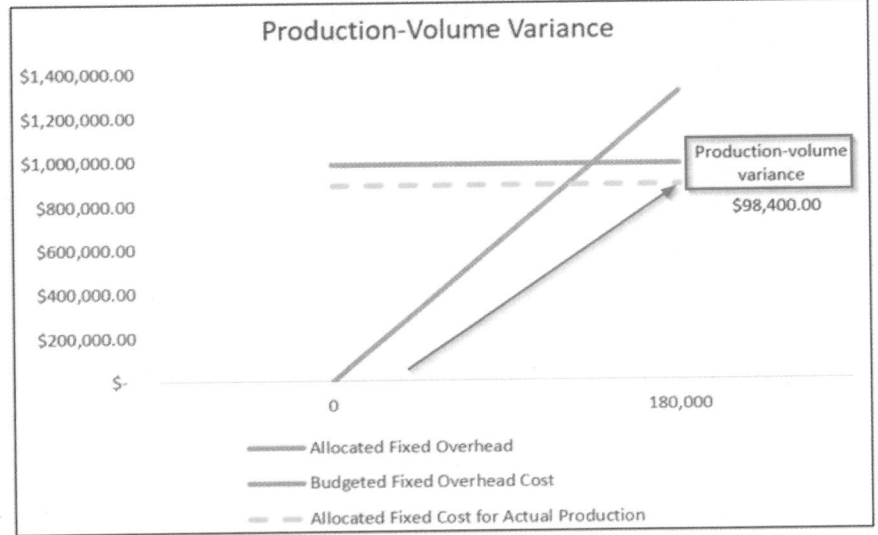

Lab Exhibit 11.1.22

Microsoft Excel

Share the Story

We have prepared a graph of the production-volume variance. This graph allows a user to see the difference between the budgeted fixed overhead cost and the allocated fixed overhead based on the calculated fixed overhead allocation rate.

Assessment

1. Take a screenshot of the final output and paste it into a Word document named "Lab 11.1 Submission.docx".
2. Answer the questions in Connect and upload your Lab 11.1 Submission.docx via Connect if assigned.

Alternate Lab 11.1 Excel—On Your Own

Graphing Production-Volume Variance

Keywords

Production-Volume Variance, Excel, Line Graph

You are the cost accountant for Voltage Wheels, a (fictitious) company that produces electric scooters. Budgeted fixed overhead is $1,050,000 for the year. Budgeted production is 19,500 units each month. Budgeted machine hours are 1.25 hours per unit. Actual units produced during the year were 235,000.

Use the data above and perform the steps from Lab 11.1 to complete the following requirements:

Required

For this lab, you will create the data, based on the information about Voltage Wheels, in a blank Excel workbook.

1. Calculate the production-volume variance.
2. Graph the production-volume variance in Excel.

Assessment:

1. Take a screenshot of the final output and paste it into a Word document named "Alt Lab 11.1 Submission.docx".
2. Answer the questions in Connect and upload your Alt Lab 11.1 Submission.docx via Connect if assigned.

Graphing Production-Volume Variance

Data Analytics Types: Diagnostic Analytics

Lab Note: The tools presented in this lab periodically change. Updated instructions, if applicable, can be found in the student and instructor support materials. All Lab Exhibits are available within the eBook and in Connect.

Keywords

Production-Volume Variance, Excel, Line Graph

Decision-Making Context

You are the cost accountant for Voltage Wheels, a (fictitious) company that produces electric scooters. Budgeted fixed overhead is $1,000,000 for the year. Budgeted production is 250,000 units per year. Budgeted machine hours are 1.50 hours per unit. Actual units produced during the year were 235,000.

Required

1. Graph the production-volume variance (PVV) in Power BI.
2. Include a parameter that allows you to enter the amount of actual output so you can evaluate the PVV at different levels of production.

Ask the Question

What is the production-volume variance for the year?

Master the Data

Open the Excel file labeled **Lab 11.2 Data.xlsx**.

In this file you will work with only one worksheet, labeled FOH [Fixed Overhead] Data, which includes the very simple chart shown in Lab Exhibit 11.2.1.

The Data Dictionary follows.

Data Dictionary

Table	Attribute Name	Description	Data Type
FOH Data	Units of Output	Range of units of output that could be produced during the period	Numeric
FOH Data	Budgeted FOH Rate per Unit	Budgeted FOH rate per unit based on total FOH budget and budgeted output of 250,000 units	Numeric
FOH Data	Cost	Applied FOH based on Actual Units of Output * Budgeted FOH Rate	Numeric
FOH Data	FOH Budget	Total FOH budgeted for the year	Numeric

Once you have reviewed and understand the data in the Excel table, import it into Power BI.

1. Once you have opened Power BI, select **Get data** and then choose **Excel Workbook** and **Connect**, as shown in Lab Exhibit 11.2.2. Then select the Excel file labeled **Lab 11.2 Data.xlsx**.
2. Select the **FOH Data** worksheet and then click **Load**, as shown in Lab Exhibit 11.2.3.

Perform the Analysis

DATA VISUALIZATION

Analysis Task #1: Create the Basic Line Graph

1. Select the line graph visualization from the **Visualizations** tab by selecting the icon indicated in Lab Exhibit 11.2.4.
2. Drag $\sum$ **Units of Output** to the **X-Axis** field and $\sum$ **Cost** to the **Y-Axis** field, as shown in Lab Exhibit 11.2.5.
3. Add $\sum$ **FOH Budget** to the **Y-Axis** field, as shown in Lab Exhibit 11.2.6.
4. You have now created the basic line graph showing the cost if the budgeted amount of units is produced. The line graph (produced so far) should resemble Lab Exhibit 11.2.7.

Analysis Task #2: Create a Parameter to Enter Actual Output

In this analysis task, you will create a form field, called a parameter, which will be placed on the report page next to your visualization. It allows the user to enter any value for the actual output. Later, you will use this parameter in your calculations to show the allocated FOH.

1. From the **Modeling** tab, select **New parameter**, as shown in Lab Exhibit 11.2.8.
2. The **What-if parameter** dialog box will open. Make the following selections, as shown in Lab Exhibit 11.2.9:
   (1) Change the **Name** to Actual Output.
   (2) Set the **Maximum** to some value equal to or above the total budgeted amount. In this case, enter 250000.
   (3) Set the **Increment** to 1000.

   Note that in Power BI, what-if parameters are not designed to use really large ranges, so if you set your increment to 1 or 10, when you enter your number in the form field, it will *sample* the values and may change your input to a number less than, but close to, the number you entered. You can guard against this to some extent by selecting a large enough increment.

   (4) Click **OK**.
3. This new parameter will now be added (as a slicer) to your page. You can move it around if you need to. With the parameter slicer active (that is, you have clicked on it), select the formatting tool to format the parameter. To do so, select the icon shown in Lab Exhibit 11.2.10.
   a. Turn the slicer off, as shown in Lab Exhibit 11.2.11.
   b. Make the font on the numeric inputs larger by selecting a **Text size** of 14 points, as shown in Lab Exhibit 11.2.12.
4. Notice that in the **Fields** pane (on the right side of the screen), you now have a second set of fields labeled **Actual Output**, as shown in Lab Exhibit 11.2.13.
5. As shown in Lab Exhibit 11.2.14, enter the number 240000 in your new Actual Output parameter field on your report screen. This number indicates that the company produced 240,000 units.

Analysis Task #3: Create a New Measure Using the Actual Output Parameter

1. To show the amount of FOH allocated to the units of actual output, you need to create a new measure that uses the actual output. Click on the **FOH Data** table in the **Fields** pane to activate that table so that you can add the new measure to that table. See Lab Exhibit 11.2.15.
2. From the **Modeling** tab, select **New Measure**, as shown in Lab Exhibit 11.2.16.
3. When the measure field opens, enter the calculation for the allocated overhead as shown in Lab Exhibit 11.2.17. You have to use the average of the budgeted FOH rate because both fields used in the calculation must be aggregated. Because the rate is the same for every row in the table, the average will be equal to the rate. The calculation is:

Allocated FOH = [Actual Output Value]&(Average('FOH Data' [Budgeted FOH Rate]))

```
1 Allocated FOH = [Actual Output Value]&(AVERAGE('FOH Data'[Budgeted FOH Rate]))
```

Lab Exhibit 11.2.17

Microsoft Power BI

4. **Allocated FOH** is now showing as a field in the FOH Data table in the **Fields** pane (on the right side of the screen), as shown in Lab Exhibit 11.2.18.
5. Activate your line chart by clicking on it.
6. Drag the **Allocated FOH** field you just created to the **Values** field in the **Visualizations** pane, as shown in Lab Exhibit 11.2.19.
7. The visualization now shows a new line representing Allocated FOH, as shown in Lab Exhibit 11.2.20.

Analysis Task #4: Calculate PVV and Add to the Tooltip

The difference between the Allocated FOH line and the FOH Budget line represents the production-volume variance (PVV). Now you will calculate this amount and include the PVV value in the tooltip so it is visible when a user scrolls over the Allocated FOH line.

1. Activate the FOH Data table (by clicking on it in the **Fields** pane) so that your new measure will be contained within that table.
2. Create a new calculation by clicking the **Modeling** tab and selecting **New Measure**, as shown in Lab Exhibit 11.2.21.
3. When the Measures calculation field opens, enter the equation for PVV, as shown in Lab Exhibit 11.2.22. The calculation is PVV = average('FOH Data' [FOH Budget])-[Allocated FOH].

```
1 PVV = average('FOH Data'[FOH Budget])-[Allocated FOH]
```

Lab Exhibit 11.2.22

Microsoft Power BI

4. PVV now appears as a new field in the **Fields** pane, as shown in Lab Exhibit 11.2.23.
5. Now drag **PVV** to the **Tooltips**, as shown in Lab Exhibit 11.2.24.
6. Now when you scroll over the Allocated FOH line, the tooltip shows the PVV (as well as the other fields used in this analysis), as shown in Lab Exhibit 11.2.25.
7. Your final visualization will resemble Lab Exhibit 11.2.26.

Share the Story

We have prepared a graph of the production-volume variance. This graph allows a user to see the difference between the budgeted fixed overhead cost and the allocated fixed overhead based on the calculated fixed overhead allocation rate. It can be included in a presentation to management to show the extent to which Voltage Wheels is efficiently using its fixed overhead capacity.

Assessment

1. Take a screenshot of the final output and paste it into a Word document named "Lab 11.2 Submission.docx".
2. Answer the questions in Connect and upload your Lab 11.2 Submission.docx via Connect if assigned.

Alternate Lab 11.2 Power BI—On Your Own

Lab Note: The tools presented in this lab periodically change. Updated instructions, if applicable, can be found in the student and instructor support materials.

Graphing Production-Volume Variance

Data Analytics Types: Descriptive Analytics, Diagnostic Analytics

Keywords

Production-Volume Variance, Excel, Line Graph

You are the cost accountant for Voltage Wheels, a (fictitious) company that produces electric scooters. Budgeted fixed overhead is $750,000 for the year. Budgeted production is 150,000 units per year. Budgeted machine hours are 1.0 hour per unit. Actual units produced during the year were 148,000.

For this lab, you will create the data, based on the information about Voltage Wheels, in a blank Excel workbook.

Use the data above and perform the steps from Lab 11.2 to complete the following requirements:

Required

1. Graph the production-volume variance (PVV) in Power BI.
2. Include a parameter that allows you to enter the amount of actual output so you can evaluate the PVV at different levels of production.

Assessment

1. Take a screenshot of the final output and paste it into a Word document named "Alt Lab 11.2 Submission.docx".
2. Answer the questions in Connect and upload your Alt Lab 11.2 Submission.docx via Connect if assigned.

Graphing Production-Volume Variance

Data Analytics Types: Diagnostic Analytics

Lab Note: The tools presented in this lab periodically change. Updated instructions, if applicable, can be found in the student and instructor support materials. All Lab Exhibits are available within the eBook and in Connect.

Keywords

Production-Volume Variance, Excel, Line Graph

Decision-Making Context

You are the cost accountant for Voltage Wheels, a (fictitious) company that produces electric scooters. Budgeted fixed overhead is $300,000 for the year. Budgeted production is 15,000 units. Voltage Wheels uses machine hours as the cost-allocation basis for fixed overhead. Budgeted machine hours are 1.0 hour per unit. Actual units produced during the year were 14,500.

Required

1. Graph the production-volume variance (PVV) in Tableau.
2. Include a parameter that allows you to enter the amount of actual output so you can evaluate the PVV at different levels of production.

Ask the Question

What is the production-volume variance for the year?

Master the Data

1. Open the Excel file titled **Lab 11.3 Data.xlsx**.

   This file includes only one worksheet, labeled FOH [Fixed Overhead] Data, which includes a very simple chart, as shown in Lab Exhibit 11.3.1.

Data Dictionary

Table	Attribute Name	Description	Data Type
FOH Data	Units of Output	Range of units of output that could be produced during the period	Numeric
FOH Data	Budgeted FOH Rate	Budgeted FOH rate per unit based on total FOH budget and budgeted output of 15,000 units	Numeric
FOH Data	Cost	Applied FOH based on Actual Units of Output * Budgeted FOH Rate	Numeric
FOH Data	FOH Budget	Total FOH budgeted for the year	Numeric

---

2. Once you have reviewed and understand the data in the Excel table, import it into Tableau.
3. Once you have opened Tableau, select **Connect to Data**, as shown in Lab Exhibit 11.3.2.
4. Select the Excel File labeled **Lab 11.3 Data.xlsx**. The data source pane in Tableau will open and you should see the one worksheet, **FOH Data**, loaded. If it is not, drag the worksheet into the center pane, as shown in Lab Exhibit 11.3.3.
5. As shown in Lab Exhibit 11.3.4, click on **Sheet 1** at the bottom of the screen to begin building your graph.

Perform the Analysis

DATA VISUALIZATION

Analysis Task #1: Build a Line Graph to Show the PVV

1. You'll notice that all of the variables from your table have been imported as measures, as shown in Lab Exhibit 11.3.5.
2. However, the line graph we need to create has the units of output along the X-axis. Therefore, units of output need to be changed from a measure to a dimension. Click on the down arrow on the right side of the Actual Units of Output variable. Then select **Convert to Dimension**, as shown in Lab Exhibit 11.3.6.
3. As shown in Lab Exhibit 11.3.7 (numbers **1** and **2**), drag **Units of Output** to the **Columns** shelf. Drag **Cost** to the **Rows** shelf. You'll notice that Tableau is starting to build a visualization and has assumed that you want a column chart. Click on **Automatic** on the **Marks** card (as shown in Lab Exhibit 11.3.7, number **3**).
4. Change the mark from **Automatic** to **Line**, as shown in Lab Exhibit 11.3.8.
5. Your graph will now be a line graph, as shown in Lab Exhibit 11.3.9. You can format it to fill the entire screen by making adjustments to the view, which is currently set to **Standard**. From that menu, select **Fit Width**.
6. Next, you will add the budgeted FOH to the graph by dragging the **FOH Budget** variable onto the Y-axis of your current graph, as shown in Lab Exhibit 11.3.10. This will drop it onto the same graph you are already building. If you do not drag the **FOH Budget** variable to the existing Y-axis, and instead just place it on the shelf, the software will create a separate line graph for FOH Budget only.
7. You now have a graph that looks like Lab Exhibit 11.3.11.

Analysis Task #2: Create a Parameter to Allow Users to Input the Level of Actual Output Produced

1. From the **Data** pane on the left side of the screen, click on the down arrow and then select **Create Parameter...**, as shown in Lab Exhibit 11.3.12.
2. When the **Create Parameter** dialog box opens, set the criteria as shown in Lab Exhibit 11.3.13.
   (1) Name the parameter "Actual Output".
   (2) Change the **Data type** to **Integer**.
   (3) Set the **Current value** to 15,000 (the budgeted output).
   (4) Click **OK**.
3. This new parameter (Actual Output) will appear at the bottom of the **Data** pane, as shown in Lab Exhibit 11.3.14.
4. Show the Actual Output parameter on the sheet by right-clicking on the **Actual Output** parameter pill and then selecting **Show Parameter** in the menu that appears (Lab Exhibit 11.3.15).

The parameter—including the blank where the user can enter the amount of the actual output—will appear on the right side of the screen. See Lab Exhibit 11.3.16.

Analysis Task #3: Create a Calculated Field to Calculate Allocated Fixed Overhead

Next, create a calculated field that uses the Actual Output parameter to calculate the allocated fixed overhead.

1. As shown in Lab Exhibit 11.3.17, open the **Analysis** tab and then select **Create Calculated Field...** from the drop-down menu.
2. When the **Calculated Field** dialog box opens, enter Allocated FOH as the name of the new variable at the top of the dialog box. Then enter the formula for Allocated FOH as shown in Lab Exhibit 11.3.18: [Actual Output]*[Budgeted FOH Rate]. Then click **OK**.

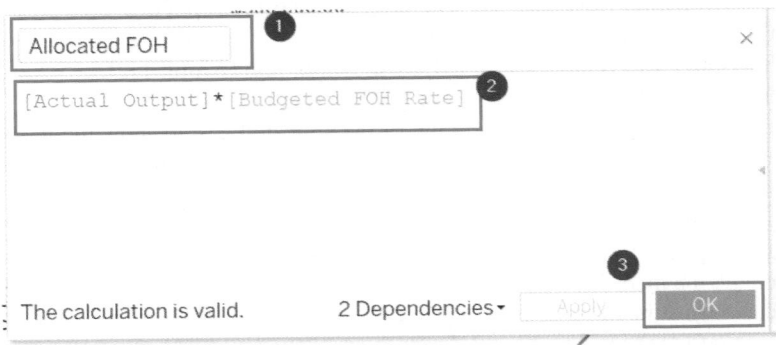

Lab Exhibit 11.3.18

Tableau Software

3. As shown in Lab Exhibit 11.3.19, drag the **Allocated FOH** variable to the graph to show the value of the allocated FOH at the production level indicated in the Actual Output parameter.

Note: If your Actual Output is set to 15,000, when you drag Allocated FOH to the graph, it will be on top of the FOH Budget line because these two values are the same. If you change the Actual Output value in the parameter box to any other value, the line will shift down or up.

Analysis Task #4: Create a Calculated Field to Calculate the Production-Volume Variance

1. As shown in Lab Exhibit 11.3.20, open the **Analysis** tab and then select **Create Calculated Field...** from the drop-down menu.
2. When the **Calculated Field** dialog box opens, enter PVV as the name of the new variable at the top of the dialog box. Then enter the formula for PVV as shown in Lab Exhibit 11.3.21: [FOH Budget]-[Allocated FOH]. Then click **OK**.

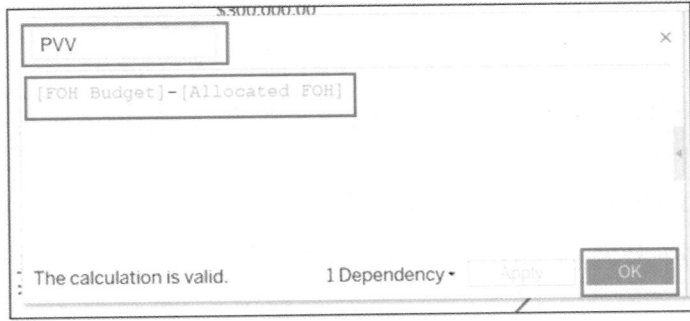

Lab Exhibit 11.3.21

Tableau Software

3. Add the PVV as a tooltip by dragging the **PVV** measure (that you just created) to the **Tooltip** mark on the **Marks** card, as shown in Lab Exhibit 11.3.22. Now when you roll the mouse over any point on either of the lines on the graph, it will show the PVV for that amount of production.

   Note: Because we made this graph with only the two endpoints, it will not show any values between those endpoints. However, if we had used data for all production amounts between 0 and the total, we would be able to see the accurate values anywhere along the graph.

4. Now we can do some formatting to improve our ability to interpret the results. First, add mark labels to show the values of the graph. As shown in Lab Exhibit 11.3.23, click **Analysis** and then select **Show Mark Labels**.

5. Change the default formatting for the values to be in currency by clicking the down arrow by the **Cost** variable. Then select **Default Properties**, then **Number Format...** (as shown in Lab Exhibit 11.3.24).

   Then select **Currency (Standard)** as shown in Lab Exhibit 11.3.25.

6. Repeat Step 5 for the FOH Budget and PVV variables.

7. Add an annotation next to the endpoint of the allocated cost to show the PVV. To do this, right-click on the endpoint. Then select **Annotate** and **Mark...** as shown in Lab Exhibit 11.3.26.

8. When the **Mark** dialog box opens, delete all of the data (by highlighting and backspacing) except for the PVV. Then click **OK** (see Lab Exhibit 11.3.27).

9. By default, the mark will appear right next to the endpoint (see Lab Exhibit 11.3.28). You can format the mark and move it around so that it doesn't overlap with the endpoint.

10. Add a title to the visualization: "Voltage Wheels Production-Volume Variance". Double-click in the current title (that reads Sheet 1). When the **Edit Title** dialog box opens, change the title and then click **OK** (see Lab Exhibit 11.3.29).

11. The final visualization will resemble Lab Exhibit 11.3.30.

Share the Story

We have prepared a graph of the production-volume variance. This graph allows a user to see the difference between the budgeted fixed overhead cost and the allocated fixed overhead based on the calculated fixed overhead allocation rate. It can be included in a presentation to management to show the extent to which Voltage Wheels is efficiently using its fixed overhead capacity.

Assessment

1. Take a screenshot of the final output and paste it into a Word document named "Lab 11.3 Submission.docx".

2. Answer the questions in Connect and upload your Lab 11.3 Submission.docx via Connect if assigned.

Alternate Lab 11.3 Tableau—On Your Own

Graphing Production-Volume Variance

Data Analytics Types: Descriptive Analytics, Diagnostic Analytics

Keywords

Production-Volume Variance, Excel, Line Graph

You are the cost accountant for Voltage Wheels, a (fictitious) company that produces electric scooters. Budgeted fixed overhead is $450,000 for the year. Budgeted production is 75,000 units. Voltage uses machine hours as the cost allocation basis for fixed overhead. Budgeted machine hours are 1.0 hour per unit. Actual units produced during the year were 81,000.

Required

Using the Excel File named **Alt Lab 11.3 Data.xlsx**, follow the same process outlined in Lab 11.3 to complete the following requirements:

1. Graph the production-volume variance (PVV) in Tableau.
2. Include a parameter that allows you to enter the amount of actual output so you can evaluate the PVV at different levels of production.

Assessment

1. Take a screenshot of the final output and paste it into a Word document named "Alt Lab 11.3 Submission.docx".
2. Answer the questions in Connect and upload your Alt Lab 11.3 Submission.docx via Connect if assigned.

Lab 11.4 Tableau

Lab Note: The tools presented in this lab periodically change. Updated instructions, if applicable, can be found in the student and instructor support materials. All Lab Exhibits are available within the eBook and in Connect.

DATA VISUALIZATION

Using Data Analytics to Investigate Unusual Overhead Activity (Heartwood)

Data Analytics Types: Diagnostic Analytics

Keywords

Production-Volume Variance, Tableau, Line Graph

Decision-Making Context

You have been hired as a cost accountant for **Heartwood Cabinets**. Management has asked you to examine overhead costs to determine if the company's allocated overhead rate is appropriate. Overhead rates have not been evaluated in several years. Additionally, overhead costs have been increasing, even though Heartwood has maintained stable production levels. Management would like you to investigate any anomalies and provide insights to help manage these costs in the future.

You have three years of cost data, including payroll, in an Excel file, and you intend to use Tableau to investigate the activity. The following is additional information for your consideration:

- Budgeted production is stable at 2,000,000 cabinets per year.
- The allocation base is machine hours. Each cabinet takes 0.75 machine hour.
- Budgeted fixed overhead is $10,000,000.
- Budgeted variable overhead is $6,000,000.
- Actual production was 2,000,000 in 2023; 1,990,000 in 2024; and 1,950,000 in 2025.

Required

Use Tableau to prepare:

1. A tabular analysis of all costs for the years 2023, 2024, and 2025.
2. A pie chart of overhead costs with a filter for each year.
3. A heat map of the amounts spent with each supplies vendor by year.
4. A listing of the transactions with any questionable vendors.
5. A dashboard of the relevant visualizations that will help detect anomalies.

Ask the Question

Are there any anomalies in spending that management should investigate?

Master the Data

For this lab, you will connect your Excel data into Tableau.

Open the Excel file labeled **Lab 11.4 Data.xlsx**. Your data are contained in the worksheet labeled "Cost Data". An example of the data is shown in Lab Exhibit 11.4.1.

The data dictionary follows.

Data Dictionary

Table	Attribute Name	Description	Data Type
Cost Data	Transaction	Unique identifier for each transaction	Text
Cost Data	Date	Date transaction occurred	Date
Cost Data	Vendor	Name of vendor or payee	Text
Cost Data	Amount	Total amount of transaction	Currency
Cost Data	Account	Specific general ledger account	Text
Cost Data	Account Type	Designates account as direct or overhead cost	Text
Cost Data	Cost Type	Designates account as fixed or variable cost	Text

Once you have reviewed and understand the data in the Excel table, import it into Tableau.

1. Open Tableau and select **Connect to Data**, as shown in Lab Exhibit 11.4.2.
2. Select the Excel file labeled **Lab 11.4 Data.xlsx** and drag the worksheet labeled "Cost Data" to the middle of the data pane, as shown in Lab Exhibit 11.4.3.
3. Click on **Sheet 1** at the bottom of the screen to begin building your first graph (see Lab Exhibit 11.4.4).

Perform the Analysis

Analysis Task #1: Prepare a Tabular Analysis of All Costs for the Years 2023, 2024, and 2025

1. As shown in Lab Exhibit 11.4.5, drag the **Account Type**, **Cost Type**, and **Account** dimensions to the **Rows** shelf. The order in which you add these dimensions to the shelf dictates the way the graph is displayed. For this analysis, you want the Account to be nested within the Cost Type and both to be nested within the Account Type. If you accidentally drag the dimensions to the shelf in a different order, you can always move them around on the shelf so that the chart displays as you intended.
2. Drag the **Date** dimension to the **Columns** shelf. For this analysis, we will leave the date as Year. Your screen should appear as in Lab Exhibit 11.4.6.
3. As shown in Lab Exhibit 11.4.7, drag the **Amount** measure to the center of the graph. The sum of the amount for each account type during the year will appear on the graph. Notice the **SUM(Amount)** mark that shows on the **Marks** card to indicate that a text mark is being used.
4. Next, we want to add a field that displays the percentage change in cost for each account across the years. To do this, we need to create a quick table calculation on the **Amount** measure. However, because you already have that measure in your table, Tableau might not let you easily drag it onto the graph a second time. We'll work around that by dragging it onto the **Color** mark on the **Marks** card for now, as shown in Lab Exhibit 11.4.8.

5. As shown in Lab Exhibit 11.4.9, click on the down arrow on the right of the **SUM(Amount)** measure (on the **Color** mark on the **Marks** card). Then select **Quick Table Calculation** and **Percent Difference** from the drop-down menus that appear.

6. Now that you have created that quick table calculation, drag the measure onto the **Text** mark so that the numerical graph displays on the chart (Lab Exhibit 11.4.10).

7. Now, as shown in Lab Exhibit 11.4.11, drag the **SUM(amount)** (from the **Measure Values** section of the **Color** mark on the **Marks** card with the new % difference) measure onto the graph itself so that both the total amount and the percentage difference appear on the chart in the same rows.

    You will also notice that the **Marks** card has changed to indicate that all **Measure Values** are in text, and the **Measure Names** dimension is now showing on the **Columns** shelf, to indicate that there are column headers for each of the measures showing in the chart (see again Lab Exhibit 11.4.11).

    You may also notice that when you drag the measure onto the chart, the cursor has the "Show Me" label on it. This label indicates that you are dragging the measure directly onto the body of the visualization.

8. You would like to show both the amount and the percentage change nested within the year columns, so you need to move the **YEAR(Date)** dimension to be the first dimension on the **Columns** shelf, as shown in Lab Exhibit 11.4.12.

9. Similarly, you want the amount to display before the percentage, so you need to make sure that the **SUM(Amount)** measure value is listed before the **SUM(Amount)** table calculation on the **Measures** card. The table calculation is indicated by a triangle icon. See Lab Exhibit 11.4.13.

10. Add color to the graph so that it shows changes in spending as positive (green) or negative (red).

    a. Just like in the previous steps, drag the **Amount** measure to the **Color** mark on the **Marks** card.

    b. Create a quick table calculation to show percent difference.

    c. You may need to edit the calculation to ensure that it is calculating the percent difference *across* the table, not down the table. Select **Edit Table Calculation...** and then select **Table across** under **Compute Using** (see Lab Exhibits 11.4.14 and 11.4.15). This horizontal format will compare the current costs to last year's costs. If Tableau is calculating *down* the table (vertically), it would be comparing, for example, direct materials to direct labor (in the same year). In that case, you will probably notice that some of the percentages calculated seem to be pretty nonsensical.

    d. To change the way the color is displayed, click the down arrow in the **Color** legend (on the right of the screen) and select **Edit Colors...**, as shown in Lab Exhibit 11.4.16.

    e. Change the color palette to **Red-Green Diverging**, as shown in Lab Exhibit 11.4.17.

    f. Follow the next several steps by referring to Lab Exhibit 11.4.18.

        (1)   Select **Reversed** so that the color will show red when the costs have increased from one year to the next.

        (2) and (3)   Select **Stepped Color** and set **Steps** to 2. These selections will mean that there is no variation to show the size of the difference from 0, just red vs. green. If you wanted to show variation, you could leave **Stepped Color** unchecked.

        (4) and (5)   **Center** the divergence at zero so that any negative difference will show in green and any positive difference will show in red.

        (6)   Click **OK**.

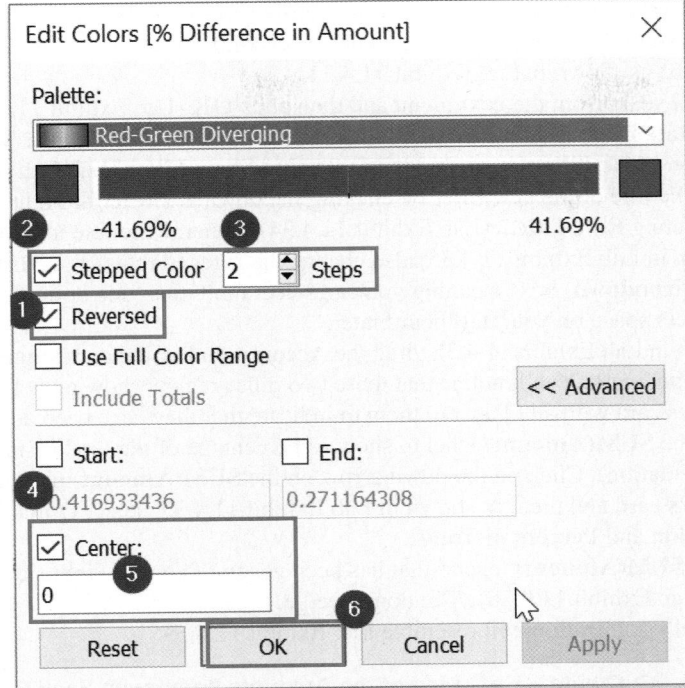

11. Label the page "Costs by Type and Year." This will become your title of the worksheet as well (see Lab Exhibit 11.4.19).

12. Let's do some formatting to make the visualization easier to fit and use on a dashboard.
    a. As shown in Lab Exhibit 11.4.20, set the fonts for all of the worksheets by navigating to **Format** and then **Workbook...**.

    When the worksheet formatting pane opens on the left side of the screen, change the **Worksheet Titles** to be 10 points and select a blue color, as shown in Lab Exhibit 11.4.21.

    Change the Worksheets font to be 6 points, as shown in Lab Exhibit 11.4.22.
    b. Remove the color legend. You don't need it because it is fairly self-explanatory what the colors mean on this chart. Right-click on the corner of the legend and then select **Hide Card** (Lab Exhibit 11.4.23).
    c. Change the name of the Percentage Difference column header so that it fits better. As shown in Lab Exhibit 11.4.24, right-click on a column header, then select **Edit Alias...**.

    Change the Name to "Percent Change" in the **Edit Alias** dialog box, as shown in Lab Exhibit 11.4.25.

13. Your final visualization should resemble Lab Exhibit 11.4.26.

Analysis Task #2: Create a Pie Chart of Overhead Costs with a Filter for Each Year

1. Open a new worksheet and label it "Overhead Costs Pie Chart" (see Lab Exhibit 11.4.27).
2. As shown in Lab Exhibit 11.4.28, drag the **Account** dimension to the **Rows** shelf and drag the **Amount** measure to the chart.

   Select the **pie chart** icon (Lab Exhibit 11.4.29) from the **Show Me** pane on the right side of the screen.

3. Change your view to the entire screen by choosing **Entire View** (Lab Exhibit 11.4.30).
4. Drag the **Date** dimension to the filter and select **Years** from the **Filter Field [Date]** dialog box, as shown in Lab Exhibit 11.4.31.
5. Select **All** years from the next menu and then click **OK** (Lab Exhibit 11.4.32).
6. Set the **Date Filter** to show by right-clicking on the down arrow on the **YEAR(Date)** dimension in the **Filters** card, and then selecting **Show Filter** (Lab Exhibit 11.4.33).
7. Change the title of the new filter by clicking the down arrow to the right of the filter, then selecting **Edit Title...** (Lab Exhibit 11.4.34). Rename the title to be "Year".
8. As shown in Lab Exhibit 11.4.35, also change the filter so that it is a **Multiple Values (dropdown)** box (meaning you can select more than one option). This will take up less space on your dashboard later.
9. As shown in Lab Exhibit 11.4.36, drag the **Account** dimension and **Amount** measure to the **Label** mark. You'll notice that these two pills are now showing at the bottom of the **Marks** card with a [T] next to them to indicate that they have been added as labels.
10. Change the **SUM(Amount)** label to show as percentage of the total (using a quick table calculation). Click on the down arrow on the **SUM(Amount)** measure on the **Marks** card and then, as shown in Lab Exhibit 11.4.37, select **Quick Table Calculation** and **Percent of Total**.
11. Hide the **SUM(Amount)** legend that has been generated on the right side of the screen (Lab Exhibit 11.4.38). You don't need it.
12. Your final visualization will resemble Lab Exhibit 11.4.39.

Analysis Task #3: Create a Heat Map of the Amounts Spent with Each Supplies Vendor by Year

Your analyses in Task #1 and Task #2 have revealed interesting increases in Supplies costs. You would like to investigate further to see whether these increases are attributable to specific vendors (suppliers).

Open a new worksheet and label it "Supplier Heat Map", as shown in Lab Exhibit 11.4.40. For Steps 1–4, refer to Lab Exhibit 11.4.41.

1. Drag **YEAR(Date)** to the **Columns** shelf.
2. Drag **Vendor** to the **Rows** shelf.
3. Drag **Amount** to the middle of the chart.
4. Drag **Account** to the **Filters** area. Then, as shown in Lab Exhibit 11.4.42, in the **Filter [Account]** dialog box, select **Supplies** and click **OK**.
5. Change the formatting of **SUM(Amount)** to currency. Click the down arrow on the **SUM(Amount)** measure in the **Marks** card and then select **Format...**, as shown in Lab Exhibit 11.4.43.

   Then, as shown in Lab Exhibit 11.4.44, set the **Default** font from the **Pane** tab to **Currency (Standard)**.
6. Apply color to the entire graph so that it displays as a heat map by selecting the **heat map** icon from the **Show Me** pane (Lab Exhibit 11.4.45).
7. The final visualization should look like the one displayed in Lab Exhibit 11.4.46.

Analysis Task #4: Prepare a Listing of the Transactions with Any Questionable Vendors

Based on the analysis from Analysis Task #3, you see that two vendors appear to be outliers in the supplies costs. Create a visualization that summarizes the costs and number of transactions associated with these two vendors by quarter for each year.

1. Open a new worksheet and label it "Amount & Count for Key Vendors" (see Lab Exhibit 11.4.47).
2. Drag the **Date** dimension to the **Rows** shelf and click on the [+] icon on the left side of the icon to show the quarters as well so that it changes to the [-] icon, as shown in Lab Exhibit 11.4.48.

3. Drag **Amount** to the middle of the chart.
4. Format **Amount** as you did in Analysis Task #3 so that it shows as currency.
5. Drag **Vendor** to the **Columns** shelf to display the amount for all vendors. Your screen should appear as shown in Lab Exhibit 11.4.49.
6. Drag **Vendor** to the **Filter** and check **Howard, Inc.** and **Piper Industries** to select those two vendors for your chart (see Lab Exhibit 11.4.50). Then select **OK**.
7. As shown in Lab Exhibit 11.4.51, drag the **Cost Data (Count)** measure to the chart to display the number of transactions for each of these vendors by quarter by year.
   Notice that the **CNT(Cost Data)** measure is now listed as a **Measure Value**, and **Measure Names** is showing on the **Columns** shelf. Also, **Measure Values** is shown as a label on the **Marks** card.
8. The final visualization looks like the one shown in Lab Exhibit 11.4.52.

Analysis Task #5: Combine the Visualizations into a Single Dashboard

You want to combine the visualizations that are most relevant to management into one dashboard. In this case, the visualizations you prepared in Analysis Tasks #1, #3, and #4 tell the most important story.

1. Open a new Dashboard and label it "Overhead Cost Analysis" (see Lab Exhibit 11.4.53).
2. As shown in Lab Exhibit 11.4.54, drag the **Costs by Type and Year** visualization onto the dashboard screen. It will take up the entire screen at first.
3. Then, as shown in Lab Exhibit 11.4.55, drag and drop the **Supplier Heat Map** onto the bottom half of the dashboard.
4. When you add the supplier heat map, it also adds the related legend, but you do not need it for this dashboard, so remove it by clicking on the down arrow and selecting **Remove from Dashboard** (see Lab Exhibit 11.4.56). If Tableau prompts you, agree that you also want to remove the containers.
5. As shown in Lab Exhibit 11.4.57, drag the **Amount & Count for Key Vendors** visualization to the bottom right of the dashboard.
6. Add borders around each visualization by clicking on each visualization (individually) and then selecting the **Layout** pane and then the solid border (see Lab Exhibit 11.4.58).
7. Show the title of the dashboard by clicking on the **Dashboard** tab and then **Show Title**. Leave the other items checked as they automatically appear (Lab Exhibit 11.4.59).
8. Your final dashboard will look like the one shown in Lab Exhibit 11.4.60.

Share the Story

Because management wants to know whether there are any anomalies in overhead spending, you will need to look at all of the evidence from your various analyses to consider whether there are any suspicious patterns of behavior. Using the dashboard that you completed in Analysis Task #5, you might describe your findings to senior management as follows:

- In the Costs by Type and Year table, in the respective "Percent Change" columns, we see that there have been increases in Administration salaries (up 10% from 2023 to 2024), Office Supplies (up 27% between 2024 and 2025), Indirect Supplies (up 14% between 2023 and 2024, and another 6% between 2023 and 2024), and Rent (up 10% in 2024 and 8% in 2025).
- The increase in Office Supplies costs is likely best explained by the significant *decrease* that had occurred between 2023 and 2024.
- Increases in Administration salaries and Rent are easily verified.
- The increases in indirect supplies (shown in the Costs by Type and Year table in the Variable Overhead section) are more concerning and should be reviewed more closely.

These increases are especially curious because production has not increased over these periods. They suggest that vendors are charging more for these supplies than in previous years, or the company is using more supplies than in the past (which could be caused by lower-quality supplies, less-skilled workers, or employees stealing supplies, also known as *shrinkage*).

- The Supplier Heat Map reveals two vendors with much higher invoice totals than the rest: Howard Inc. and Piper Industries. There may be many good reasons for this—perhaps the supplies purchased from these vendors are more specialized than those purchased from other vendors, or perhaps these suppliers use higher-quality materials. However, it is worth investigating these vendors more closely.
- In the analysis of the Amount & Count [of invoices] for Key Vendors, we see that the invoices from Piper are relatively consistent in number and value. However, Howard Inc. showed a dramatic increase in Q4 2023 and has been quite high ever since. In addition, invoice amounts were very high in Q4 2024 ($62,732) and Q4 2025 ($49,000), with a relatively small number of invoices in each (13 and 7, respectively). Also in Q4 2025, notice that the total invoice amount is a round number ($49,000), which is unusual and is a red flag suggesting the amounts were fabricated.

Based on this analysis, you should recommend a thorough review of all of Howard, Inc. invoices.

Assessment

1. Take a screenshot of the tabular analysis of all costs, paste it into a Word document named "Lab 11.4 Submission.docx", and label the screenshot Submission 1.
2. Take a screenshot of the Overhead Costs pie chart, paste it into your Word document named "Lab 11.4 Submission.docx", and label the screenshot Submission 2.
3. Take a screenshot of the heat map, paste it into your Word document named "Lab 11.4 Submission.docx", and label the screenshot submission 3.
4. Take a screenshot of the list of transactions with questionable vendors, paste it into your Word document named "Lab 11.4 Submission.docx", and label the screenshot Submission 4.
5. Take a screenshot of your dashboard, paste it into your Word document named "Lab 11.4 Submission.docx", and label the screenshot Submission 5.
6. Answer the questions in Connect and upload your Lab 11.4 Submission.docx via Connect if assigned.

Alternate Lab 11.4 Tableau—On Your Own

DATA VISUALIZATION

Using Data Analytics to Investigate Unusual Overhead Activity (Heartwood)

Data Analytics Types: Descriptive Analytics, Diagnostic Analytics

Keywords

Production-Volume Variance, Tableau, Line Graph

You have been hired as a cost accountant for **Heartwood Cabinets**. Management has asked you to examine overhead costs to determine if the company's allocated overhead rate is appropriate. Overhead rates have not been evaluated in several years. Additionally, overhead costs have been increasing, even though Heartwood has maintained stable production levels. Management would like you to investigate any anomalies and provide insights to help manage these costs in the future.

You have three years of cost data, including payroll, in an Excel file, and you intend to use Tableau to investigate the activity. Additional information for your consideration:

- Budgeted production is stable at 2,000,000 cabinets per year.
- The allocation base is machine hours. Each cabinet takes 0.75 machine hour.
- Budgeted fixed overhead is $12,000,000.
- Budgeted variable overhead is $8,000,000.
- Actual production was 3,000,000 in 2023; 2,800,000 in 2024; and 2,950,000 in 2025.

Required

Use the Excel file **Alt Lab 11.4 Data.xlsx** and follow the same steps you performed in Lab 11.4 to prepare the following analyses in Tableau:

1. A tabular analysis of all costs for the years 2023, 2024, and 2025.
2. A pie chart of overhead costs with a filter for each year.
3. A heat map of the amounts spent with each supplies vendor by year.
4. A listing of the transactions with any questionable vendors.
5. A dashboard of the relevant visualizations that will help detect anomalies.

Assessment

1. Take a screenshot of the tabular analysis of all costs, paste it into a Word document named "Alt Lab 11.4 Submission.docx", and label the screenshot Submission 1.
2. Take a screenshot of the Overhead Costs pie chart, paste it into your Word document named "Alt Lab 11.4 Submission.docx", and label the screenshot Submission 2.
3. Take a screenshot of the heat map, paste it into your Word document named "Alt Lab 11.4 Submission.docx", and label the screenshot Submission 3.
4. Take a screenshot of the list of transactions with questionable vendors, paste it into your Word document named "Alt Lab 11.4 Submission.docx", and label the screenshot Submission 4.
5. Take a screenshot of your dashboard, paste it into your Word document named "Alt Lab 11.4 Submission.docx", and label the screenshot Submission 5.
6. Answer the questions in Connect and upload your Alt Lab 11.4 Submission.docx via Connect if assigned.

Lab 11.5 Tableau

Lab Note: The tools presented in this lab periodically change. Updated instructions, if applicable, can be found in the student and instructor support materials. All Lab Exhibits are available within the eBook and in Connect.

DATA VISUALIZATION

Evaluating Overhead Variances Across Divisions

Data Analytics Types: Diagnostic Analytics

Keywords

Fixed Overhead Spending Variance, Production-Volume Variance, Variable Overhead Spending Variance, Variable Overhead Efficiency Variance, Performance Evaluations, Tableau

Decision-Making Context

You are the cost accountant for Voltage Wheels, a (fictitious) company that produces electric scooters. Budgeted fixed overhead is $1,000,000 for the year. Budgeted production is 250,000 units per year. Budgeted machine hours are 1.50 hours per unit. Actual units produced during the year were 235,000.

Required

Use Tableau to prepare three interactive dashboards to compare fixed and variable overhead across the three divisions of Voltage Wheels.

1. Dashboard 1: Shows all variable overhead variances for each division and can be filtered by year.
2. Dashboard 2: Shows all fixed overhead variances for each division and can be filtered by year.
3. Dashboard 3: Shows all variances over time and can be filtered by division.

Ask the Question

Are overhead allocation rates appropriate given the recent transaction activity? Are there any anomalies in spending that management should investigate?

Master the Data

For this lab, you will use the data contained in the Excel file named **Lab 11.5 Data.xlsx**. All of the relevant data are contained in one worksheet, labeled "Variance Data."

1. Open the Excel file labeled **Lab 11.5 Data.xlsx**.
   This file contains only one worksheet, labeled FOH Data. Lab Exhibit 11.5.1 shows an excerpt from the worksheet.

Data Dictionary

Table	Attribute Name	Description	Data Type
Variance Data	Division	Identifies the division	Text
Variance Data	Date	Identifies the performance year ranging from 2022–2027	Date
Variance Data	Budgeted Units of Output	Budgeted (standard) units of output planned for production during the year	Number
Variance Data	Machine Hours per Unit	Number of machine hours required to produce one unit	Number
Variance Data	Actual Units of Output	Actual units produced during the year	Number
Variance Data	Actual Quantity of Machine Hours	Total number of machine hours required for production	Number
Variance Data	Actual Price	Actual price (rate) of variable per machine hour	Currency
Variance Data	Standard Price	Budgeted (standard) price for unit of variable overhead per machine hour	Currency
Variance Data	Standard Quantity of Machine Hours	Budgeted (standard) number of machine hours expected for planned production	Number
Variance Data	VOH Flexible Budget Variance	Actual Variable Overhead Costs – Flexible Budget Costs	Currency
Variance Data	VOH Spending Variance	Calculated as Actual Quantity of Machine Hours * (Actual Price – Standard Price)	Currency
Variance Data	VOH Efficiency Variance	Calculated as Standard Price * (Actual Quantity of Machine Hours – Standard Quantity of Machine Hours)	Currency
Variance Data	Actual FOH	Actual fixed overhead costs during the year	Currency
Variance Data	Budgeted FOH	Budgeted (standard) fixed overhead expected for the year	Currency
Variance Data	FOH Spending Variance	Actual FOH – Budgeted FOH	Currency
Variance Data	FOH Rate per Machine Hour	Budgeted FOH/Standard Quantity of Machine Hours	Currency
Variance Data	FOH Rate per Unit of Output	Budgeted FOH/(Budgeted Units of Output * Machine Hours per Unit)	Currency
Variance Data	Applied FOH per Unit	FOH Rate per Unit of Output * Actual Units of Output	Currency
Variance Data	Production Volume Variance	Budgeted FOH – Applied FOH	Currency
Variance Data	Total FOH Variance	Actual FOH – Applied FOH	Currency

2. Once you have reviewed and understand the data in the Excel table, import it into Tableau using the **Connect to Data** function, as shown in Lab Exhibit 11.5.2.
3. Select the Excel File labeled **Lab 11.5 Data.xlsx**. The data source pane in Tableau will open. Drag the worksheet labeled **Variance Data** into the center pane, as shown in Lab Exhibit 11.5.3.
4. Click on **Sheet 1** at the bottom of the screen to begin building your graph (Lab Exhibit 11.5.4).

Perform the Analysis

Analysis Task #1: Prepare Visualizations for the VOH (Variable Overhead) Flexible Budget Variance, VOH Efficiency Variance, and VOH Spending Variance

1. The date field was imported as a number, not a date. You will need to change the format of this field to date. Click on the down arrow on the right side of the **Date** field, then select **Change Data Type**, and then select **Date** (see Lab Exhibit 11.5.5).
   After you make this change, the **Date** field moves to the **Dimensions** section of the data pane (see Lab Exhibit 11.5.6).
2. Drag the **VOH Flexible Budget Variance** to the **Columns** shelf and **Division** to the **Rows** shelf, as shown in Lab Exhibit 11.5.7. You'll notice that the **VOH Flexible Budget Variance** field shows as a sum once you drag it to the **Columns** shelf. This indicates that Tableau has aggregated the field by adding all of the VOH Flexible Budget Variances in the dataset.
3. Drag the **Date** field to the **Filters** area, as shown in Lab Exhibit 11.5.8.
4. Select **Years** from the **Filter Date** dialog box, as shown in Lab Exhibit 11.5.9. Then click **Next**.
5. When the **Filter** dialog box opens, select **All**, and then click **OK** (Lab Exhibit 11.5.10).
6. The date field now shows as **YEAR(Date)** to indicate that you can filter by year. Click on the down arrow on the right side of the **YEAR(Date)** field in the **Filters** pane (see Lab Exhibit 11.5.11).
7. Select **Show Filter** from the drop-down menu (Lab Exhibit 11.5.12). This will make the filter appear on the right side of the visualization.
8. The bar graph visualization should look like the one shown in Lab Exhibit 11.5.13.
9. Drag the **VOH Flexible Budget Variance** to the **Color** mark on the **Marks** card, as shown in Lab Exhibit 11.5.14.
10. To format the colors of the visualization to improve interpretability, click on the down arrow on the right corner of the **VOH Flexible Overhead** color legend on the right side of the screen and then click **Edit Colors**, as shown in Lab Exhibit 11.5.15.
11. Remember that for the VOH flexible budget analysis, if the actual costs incurred are greater than the flexible budget amount, the result is an unfavorable variance because the actual costs exceeded the expectations. Therefore, a variance that exceeds zero is unfavorable. Format the colors of the visualization to show as red if there is an unfavorable variance (greater than zero) or green if there is favorable variance (less than zero). Refer to Lab Exhibit 11.5.16 as you complete the following steps:
    (1) Use the drop-down box to select the **Red-Green Diverging** color scheme.
    (2) Set the color to change in discrete steps (vs. gradual change) by clicking the box next to **Stepped Color**.
    (3) Set the number of **Steps** to 2 so that the color shows only as red or green.
    (4) Because a positive number is an unfavorable variance, check the box next to **Reversed**.
    (5) Click on **<<Advanced** to expand the dialog box.
    (6) Click the box next to **Center** to designate where the color changes based on the values.
    (7) Set the center of the visualization to 0 to designate where the color changes based on the values.

12. Click on the tab labeled Sheet 1 at the bottom of the screen (see Lab Exhibit 11.5.17) to rename your sheet (and add a title to your visualization).

13. Enter "VOH Flexible Budget Variance" in the tab. This will change the title of the sheet as well. Lab Exhibit 11.5.18 shows the finished visualization.

14. You can adjust the formatting to facilitate creating a clean dashboard (which you will create in Analysis Task #3):

    a. Remove the **Colors** legend from the screen (because you have enough information in the visualization without it). Click the down arrow in the top-right corner of the **Colors** legend, then select **Hide Card** (Lab Exhibit 11.5.19).

    b. Change the **Years** legend so that it takes up less space. Click the down arrow in the right corner of the legend and then select the **Multiple Values (dropdown)** format, as shown in Lab Exhibit 11.5.20.

    c. Change the title of the legend to "Year" instead of YEAR(Date). Click the down arrow in the right corner of the legend and then **Edit Title...** (Lab Exhibit 11.5.21).

    d. Remove the title "Division" from the Y-axis. Right-click the title of the Y-axis (that is, **Division**). Select **Hide Field Labels for Rows** from the drop-down menu (Lab Exhibit 11.5.22).

    e. Change the font of the worksheet title for ALL worksheets in the workbook. Select **Format > Workbook**, as shown in Lab Exhibit 11.5.23.

       When the workbook format pane opens, set all of the workbook titles to be size 11 font and boldface. Also select a color (see Lab Exhibit 11.5.24). This step sets all of the titles to be the same (and to be smaller than the default font).

       Set all of the worksheet fonts to 8, as shown in Lab Exhibit 11.5.25. This setting will make the other (non-title) fonts smaller.

       Now, the visualization should look like the one shown in Lab Exhibit 11.5.26.

15. Now that you have created a visualization for the VOH Flexible Budget Variance, follow the same steps to create a visualization for the VOH Spending Budget Variance and the VOH Efficiency Budget Variance. You will need to open new worksheets for each. Your finished visualizations should look like those shown in Lab Exhibits 11.5.27 and 11.5.28.

Analysis Task #2: Prepare a Visualization for the VOH Budgets Over Time

For this visualization, you will create two line graphs showing the variances over time for each division. You can build both of these line graphs on the same worksheet.

Begin by opening a new worksheet. Name it "VOH Variances Over Time." For Steps 1–3 below, refer to Lab Exhibit 11.5.29.

1. Drag **Date** to the **Columns** shelf.
2. Drag **VOH Spending Variance** to the **Rows** shelf.
3. Drag **VOH Efficiency Variance** to the **Rows** shelf.
4. Drag **Division** to the **Color Mark** (Lab Exhibit 11.5.30) so that each division is a different color on the line graph.
5. Right-click on the X-axis at the bottom of the worksheet to remove the "Year of Date" title from the axis. As shown in Lab Exhibit 11.5.31, uncheck **Show Header**.

You can see the completed visualization in the dashboard in Figure 11.5.39.

Analysis Task #3: Prepare a Dashboard Combining the VOH Visualizations Built in Analysis Tasks #1 and #2

1. Open a blank dashboard by clicking the **dashboard+** icon at the bottom of the screen (Lab Exhibit 11.5.32).
2. The worksheets that have already been created are listed on the **Dashboard** pane on the left side of the screen (Lab Exhibit 11.5.33).

3. Drag **VOH Flexible Budget** to the top of the dashboard screen, as shown in Lab Exhibit 11.5.34.

   The visualization will take up the entire screen when you first drop it in, as shown in Lab Exhibit 11.5.35.

4. Format the legend so that it is floating. This will allow you to layer it on top of your FOH Flexible Budget Variance visualization so it will not take up room on the dashboard. Click on the down arrow and then select **Floating**, as shown in Lab Exhibit 11.5.36.

5. The container that the legend was in will still be on your dashboard, so you will want to remove it from the dashboard. Click on the down arrow and then select **Remove from Dashboard**, as shown in Lab Exhibit 11.5.37.

6. Use your cursor as a double-headed arrow to resize the Flexible Budget Variance visualization so that it takes up only about one-third of the screen (Lab Exhibit 11.5.38).

7. As shown in Lab Exhibit 11.5.39, drag **VOH Spending Variance** to the bottom of the screen, and then drag **VOH Efficiency Variance** beneath it. Drag the **VOH Variances Over Time** visualization to the right side of those variances.

   Note: If any additional date legend containers open up, just remove them from the dashboard as you did previously.

   However, you do want the Division legend to show for the VOH Variances Over Time visualization. Set this to a floating legend, but also arrange it as a single line. To do so, right-click on the legend and go to **Arrange Items** and then select **Single row** (as shown in Lab Exhibit 11.5.40). Also select **Floating** so it is checked and then move the legend to be near the VOH Variances Over Time visualization.

8. Fit each visualization to its allotted space on the dashboard by clicking on the down arrow to the right of the visualization, then selecting **Fit** and **Entire View** (see Lab Exhibit 11.5.41).

9. Allow the VOH Flexible Budget Variance visualization to act as a filter for the entire dashboard so that if you click on any dimension, the other visualizations focus on the same division. Click on the down arrow next to the visualization and select **Use as Filter**, as shown in Lab Exhibit 11.5.42.

10. You can add borders around each individual visualization from the **Layout** tab. You must click on the visualization for which you would like to add a border, then click the down arrow under **Border**, then select your border of choice (see Lab Exhibit 11.5.43).

    Add borders to all of the visualizations.

11. Add a title to the dashboard by clicking **Dashboard**, then **Show Title** (as shown in Lab Exhibit 11.5.44). Name the **Dashboard** "Variable Overhead Variance Analysis".

Analysis Task #4: Prepare Visualizations for the Total FOH Variance, FOH Spending Variance, and Production-Volume Variance

Follow the same sets of steps from Analysis Task #1 to prepare FOH visualizations.

Analysis Task #5: Prepare Visualization for the FOH Budgets Over Time

Follow the same sets of steps from Analysis Task #2 to prepare FOH visualizations.

Analysis Task #6: Prepare a Dashboard Combining the FOH Visualizations You Built in Analysis Tasks #4 and #5

Follow the same set of steps from Analysis Task #3 to prepare an FOH dashboard. The final dashboard should resemble the one shown in Lab Exhibit 11.5.45.

Analysis Task #7: Prepare a Column Chart Visualization That Shows the VOH Spending and VOH Efficiency Variances for Each Division Over Time

Open a new worksheet and name it "VOH by Division Over Time".

   For Steps 1–3, refer to Lab Exhibit 11.5.46.

1. Drag the **Date** field to the **Columns** shelf.

2. Drag the **VOH Spending Variance** to the **Rows** shelf.
3. Drag the **VOH Efficiency Variance** to the **Rows** shelf.
4. Using the **Show Me** function on the right side of the screen, select the **column chart** icon (Lab Exhibit 11.5.47).
5. You may have to reorder your **Column** shelf variables so that **Measure Names** precedes **YEAR(Date)**. In this case, Measure Names refers to the VOH Spending and VOH Efficiency variances, and you want your visualization to group the variances by Type first and then by Date, as shown in Lab Exhibit 11.5.48.
6. Tableau may have defaulted to putting **Measure Names** on the **Marks** card, as shown in Lab Exhibit 11.5.49. If so, remove it.
7. As with the earlier visualizations, we want to use color to show if each year had a positive or negative variance. To do this, you need *separate legends* for each measure.
   a. Drag **Measure Values** to the **Color** mark on the **Marks** card, as shown in Lab Exhibit 11.5.50.
   b. Right-click on the **Measure Values** pill on the **Marks** card and select **Use Separate Legends** from the drop-down menu (Lab Exhibit 11.5.51).
   c. Two legends will appear to the right of the screen, as shown in Lab Exhibit 11.5.52.
   d. Format each legend just like you did on the VOH Spending Variance and VOH Efficiency Variance dashboards in Analysis Task #1. You can hide the legends when you are done because you do not need them to interpret the graphs.
8. Drag **Division** onto the **Filters** card. Select **All** from the **Filter** dialog box. Then click **OK**. (See Lab Exhibit 11.5.53.)
9. Select **Show filter** so you have the ability to choose which division is displayed.
10. You can remove the titles from the X-axis and Y-axis to save space on the visualization.
11. You can also change the view to "Fit Width" at the top of the screen (see Lab Exhibit 11.5.54).
12. Your final visualization should resemble Lab Exhibit 11.5.55.

Analysis Task #8: Prepare a Column Chart Visualization That Shows the FOH Spending and Production-Volume Variances for Each Division Over Time

Perform the same steps as you did in Analysis Task #7 using the FOH variances.

Analysis Task #9: Prepare a Dashboard That Displays the Visualizations from Analysis Tasks #7 and #8 to Show All Detailed Variances Over Time for a Division

Perform similar steps to those completed in Analysis Tasks #3 and #6 to create the dashboard. The final dashboard should resemble Lab Exhibit 11.5.56.

Share the Story

The dashboards you created in Analysis Tasks #3, #7, and #9 provide management with a snapshot of overhead variance performance for each of its three divisions. The dashboard shows the variances over time for the entire company, but management can look at individual divisions using the filter.

When considering the company as a whole, management can see that the FOH spending variance is always unfavorable, and is becoming more unfavorable as time goes on. The production volume variance, on the other hand, is favorable. This indicates that the organization is using its available FOH capacity reasonably efficiently, but the cost to acquire that overhead is consistently more than anticipated. This may mean that there are many unexpected FOH costs, but also perhaps the budgeting process should be revisited. Perhaps the cost accountants are not using the most up-to-date information available when setting their expectations.

According to the dashboard of the whole company, VOH efficiency variances are consistently favorable and, although the VOH spending variance was unfavorable for several years, it has trended favorable in more recent years. In previous years, when VOH spending was favorable but VOH efficiency was unfavorable, it may have suggested that the company was cutting costs on materials or labor; inexperienced labor or low-quality materials may lead to more rework, making the production process more inefficient. However, the favorable trends in both variances are a positive signal.

Assessment

1. Take a screenshot of the VOH Variance Analysis dashboard, paste it into a Word document named "Lab 11.5 Submission.docx", and label the screenshot Submission 1.
2. Take a screenshot of the FOH Variance Analysis dashboard, paste it into your Word document named "Lab 11.5 Submission.docx", and label the screenshot Submission 2.
3. Take a screenshot of the Overhead Variances Over Time dashboard, paste it into your Word document named "Lab 11.5 Submission.docx", and label the screenshot Submission 3.
4. Answer the questions in Connect and upload your Lab 11.5 Submission.docx via Connect if assigned.

Alternate Lab 11.5 Tableau—On Your Own

Evaluating Overhead Variances Across Divisions

Data Analytics Types: Descriptive Analytics, Diagnostic Analytics

Keywords

Fixed Overhead Spending Variance, Production-Volume Variance, Variable Overhead Spending Variance, Variable Overhead Efficiency Variance, Performance Evaluations, Tableau

Decision-Making Context

You are the cost accountant for Voltage Wheels, a (fictitious) company that produces electric scooters. Budgeted fixed overhead is $1,000,000 for the year. Budgeted production is 250,000 units per year. Budgeted machine hours are 1.50 hours per unit. Actual units produced during the year were 235,000.

Required

Upload the file **Alt Lab 11.5 Data.xlsx** into Tableau and follow the same steps as in Lab 11.5 to prepare three interactive dashboards to compare fixed and variable overhead across the three divisions of Voltage Wheels.

1. Dashboard 1: Shows all variable overhead variances for each division and can be filtered by year.
2. Dashboard 2: Shows all fixed overhead variances for each division and can be filtered by year.
3. Dashboard 3: Shows all variances over time and can be filtered by division.

Assessment

1. Take a screenshot of the VOH Variance Analysis dashboard, paste it into a Word document named "Alt Lab 11.5 Submission.docx", and label the screenshot Submission 1.
2. Take a screenshot of the FOH Variance Analysis dashboard, paste it into your Word document named "Alt Lab 11.5 Submission.docx", and label the screenshot Submission 2.
3. Take a screenshot of the Overhead Variances Over Time dashboard, paste it into your Word document named "Alt Lab 11.5 Submission.docx", and label the screenshot Submission 3.
4. Answer the questions in Connect and upload your Alt Lab 11.5 Submission.docx via Connect if assigned.

Chapter 12

Strategy and the Balanced Scorecard

A Look at This Chapter

This chapter introduces strategy maps and the balanced scorecard, which many organizations use to supplement backward-looking tools such as variance analysis. The balanced scorecard incorporates strategic goals and nonfinancial measures, such as customer satisfaction, that drive future performance.

Cost Accounting and Data Analytics

COST ACCOUNTING LEARNING OBJECTIVE	RELATED DATA ANALYTICS LABS	LAB ANALYTICS TYPE(S)
LO 12.1 Describe how an organization identifies its strategy.		
LO 12.2 Describe the purpose of the balanced scorecard and explain its four dimensions.		
LO 12.3 Explain the purpose of strategy maps and how they are developed.		
LO 12.4 Identify key performance indicators that relate to the balanced scorecard dimensions.	**LAB 12.1 Excel:** Tracking Key Performance Indicators (KPIs)	Descriptive
	LAB 12.2 Excel: Evaluating Key Performance Indicator (KPI) Effectiveness with Regression	Predictive
LO 12.5 Understand how organizations use strategy maps and balanced scorecards to evaluate success.	**LAB 12.3 Excel:** Creating a Balanced Scorecard Dashboard to Track Performance	Descriptive, Prescriptive
	LAB 12.4 Tableau: Creating a Balanced Scorecard Dashboard to Track Performance	Descriptive, Prescriptive
	LAB 12.5 Power BI: Creating a Balanced Scorecard Dashboard to Track Performance	Descriptive, Prescriptive
LO 12.6 Understand how organizations apply data analytics to the balanced scorecard framework.	**Data Analytics Mini-Lab:** Building a Balanced Scorecard Dashboard	Descriptive, Prescriptive

Chapter Concepts and Career Skills

Learning About . . .	Helps with These Career Skills
Mission and vision statements	• Understanding the organization's purpose, core values, and aspirations
Organizational strategy	• Making decisions to help the organization achieve its strategic goals in line with its mission and vision
The balanced scorecard	• Understanding links between performance on four different dimensions and how they affect the organization's ability to achieve its strategic goals
Strategy maps	• Understanding how the organization's strategic goals interact
Integrating environmental, social, and governance (ESG) goals into strategy maps and the balanced scorecard	• Understanding the importance of ESG to stakeholders
Key performance indicators	• Measuring performance toward organizational goals

The National Marrow Donor Program

Every year, thousands of people, including many children, are diagnosed with leukemia, blood cancers, and other life-threatening diseases. Many of them will die unless they receive a bone marrow or cord blood transplant. Over 70 percent of these patients do not have a matching donor in their family and must rely on unknown donors. The **National Marrow Donor Program (NMDP)** and **Be The Match Foundation**[1] are nonprofit organizations that help patients in need of bone marrow or umbilical cord blood transplants receive the care they need.

Like all organizations, these nonprofits need to set strategic goals and develop and monitor performance metrics to achieve those goals. In the mid-2000s, NMDP set an aggressive goal of delivering 10,000 transplants per year by 2015. Management adopted a *balanced scorecard* approach to better facilitate progress toward this goal.

The first step was to revise NMDP's mission statement. The new statement is "*We save lives through cellular transplantation—science, service, and support.*" Second, the organization developed four strategic themes: (1) global access and acceptance, (2) excellent stakeholder experience, (3) research, and (4) cultural excellence. Third, for each strategic theme, management teams developed strategic goals and measures to assess whether each objective was met. The end result was a "Vision into Action" strategy map that included 13 strategic goals and 46 strategic measures (Exhibit 12.1). This strategic performance management tool was presented to and approved by the board of directors and later shared more broadly with the entire organization.

Each department within NMDP has used the strategy map to develop its own objectives to support the entire organization's strategic goals. The map is also a meaningful communication and coordination tool because it gives all NMDP departments a shared understanding of the metrics that are used to determine the organization's success. In addition, managers use the map as part of their employees' professional development and performance appraisals.

The "Vision into Action" map facilitates an ongoing assessment of organizational success. All departments input their results into an online reporting system, which color-codes the results to identify areas that may need attention, corrective action, or more resources. Importantly, NMDP also uses the map to identify and celebrate successes and outstanding performance.

---

[1]The National Marrow Donor Program® (NMDP), a nonprofit organization, is the global leader in providing bone marrow and umbilical cord blood transplants to patients in need. As Be The Match®, it operates the Be The Match Registry®, the world's largest listing of potential marrow donors and donated cord blood units. It also raises funds to help provide transplants to patients through the Be The Match Foundation®. It matches patients with donors, educates health care professionals, and conducts research through its research arm, the Center for International Blood and Marrow Transplant Research® (CIBMTR), so more lives can be saved. For more information, or to join the registry, see https://bethematch.org/support-the-cause/donate-bone-marrow/join-the-marrow-registry/. You could literally save a life.

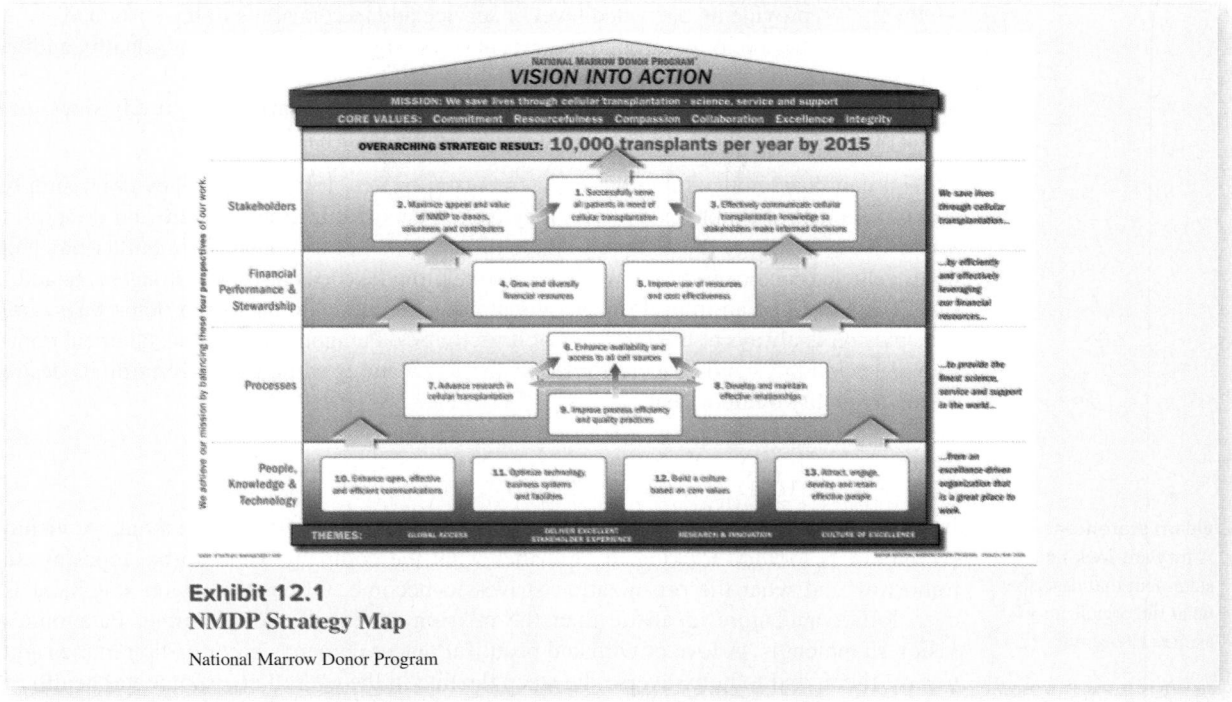

Exhibit 12.1
NMDP Strategy Map

National Marrow Donor Program

SETTING ORGANIZATIONAL STRATEGY

In Chapter 1, we learned that companies exist to create value. Management must make strategic decisions about how the company can best create that value. Creating value often begins with the development of a mission statement and a vision statement.

Developing a Mission Statement

Before a company can create value, management must first determine what the organization strives to be and do. What are its goals and objectives? Many organizations start with a **mission statement**, a succinct statement that captures the organization's purpose. It provides insight into the principles that guide the organization, and it forms the basis on which the organization develops its strategic goals and strategic plan.

When developing a mission statement, the organization should answer the following questions:

- What challenges does this organization solve?
- Why are we in business?
- What is our purpose?
- Who are our customers?
- What are our customers' values?
- What image do we want to convey to the world?
- What differentiates us from our competitors?

After answering these questions, management will let the marketing team take over to ensure the statement is catchy and will connect with the public.

Most mission statements are no longer than three sentences. Here are some examples of mission statements.

- **Jet Blue**: "To inspire humanity—both in the air and on the ground."
- **Tesla**: "To accelerate the world's transition to sustainable energy."

- **PwC**: "To provide an unrivaled level of service and to contribute to the sustained growth of the economy through the execution of vigorous, fair, and high-quality audits based on clear leadership and creative teamwork."
- **Patagonia**: "Build the best product, cause no unnecessary harm, [and] use business to inspire and implement solutions to the environmental crisis."

You may have noticed that these statements all reflect lofty ideals. They don't simply communicate profit motives. Instead, they reflect the organization's culture and principles while also referring to the company's type of business. For example, Tesla builds cars and other vehicles, so the use of the word *accelerate* provides nice car-related imagery. In addition, Tesla has had an impact on the global use of sustainable energy in other ways, and this mission is always at the forefront of its activities. Patagonia's mission statement communicates kindness and concern for Earth and its creatures while also specifying its desire to create quality outdoor gear.

Developing a Vision Statement

vision statement
A forward-looking statement that describes what the organization aspires to become.

In addition to a mission statement, organizations create a vision statement. A **vision statement** is forward looking. It describes what the company wants to be, focusing on tomorrow and what the organization strives to become. Often, the vision statement is even loftier and more idealistic than the mission statement. For example, Patagonia's vision statement is "A love of wild and beautiful places demands participation in the fight to save them, and to help reverse the steep decline in the overall environmental health of our planet."

core values
An organization's defining features that form the basis of its mission statement and vision statement and shape its culture.

In developing the mission and vision statements, organizations consider their **core values**, which are the organization's defining principles. Core values support the organization's vision, represent its standards, and shape its culture. Patagonia's core values are:

- Build the best product.
- Cause no unnecessary harm.
- Use business to protect nature.
- Embrace new ways of thinking.

strategy
A plan of action for achieving a company's mission.

As described on its website, Patagonia's core values "reflect those of a business started by a band of climbers and surfers, and the minimalist style they promoted."

Defining Organizational Strategy

strategic goals
The objectives that must be accomplished to implement an organization's strategy.

After the organization has identified and defined its core values and written its mission and vision statements, it develops its strategy to align with its ideals. An organization's **strategy** is its plan of action for achieving its mission, and it is generally composed of **strategic goals**, which are the objectives that must be accomplished to implement the strategy. Later in this chapter, we will see that the organizations tie their performance measures to their strategic goals.

All organizations have a variety of strategic goals. Often these goals are organized into four categories or dimensions:

- Financial
- Customer
- Internal processes
- Learning and growth

Many of these goals interact, such that certain goals may be achievable only if other goals are also achieved. We discuss the cause-and-effect relationships among goals later in this chapter.

THE BALANCED SCORECARD

Setting goals is important, but achieving them is more important. How can an organization achieve its goals?

Managers need tools to help them translate their mission into measurable actions and achievable metrics. Given the complex nature of the business environment and the fact that most organizations are managing multiple goals, they also need a framework for strategic management.

In the early 1990s, Harvard University professors Robert Kaplan and David Norton developed the **balanced scorecard**.[2] To do so, they worked with 12 companies over the course of many years studying the adage "You get what you measure." They recognized that, at the time, most companies almost exclusively measured past financial performance, which can cause managers to make decisions that are short-term oriented. In other words, managers often engaged in **myopic decision making**.

Managerial myopia can be problematic because managers may make decisions that optimize or improve performance in the present or immediate future with no regard for how those decisions will affect the organization's long-term success. Traditional management accounting tools such as budgets and variance analysis can exacerbate myopia because they focus managers on meeting or beating performance targets.

This tendency toward myopic decision making does not result solely from the tools used to measure performance. It also stems from the organizational culture and goals. Fortunately, organizations can use tools such as the balanced scorecard to shift the organizational culture toward more forward-looking decision making.

In their original article, Kaplan and Norton compare the balanced scorecard to the instruments in an airplane flight deck.[3] Pilots need a lot of information to fly a plane effectively. For example, they need to know the plane's speed, altitude, direction, and fuel level, and they need to be aware of other factors, too, including the weather and the weight of the passengers and cargo. If pilots considered only one measure, such as speed, the result could be disastrous. Similarly, organizations cannot survive if they consider only one measure of performance, such as profitability.

With the balanced scorecard, organizations consider not only short-term measures but also future performance indicators on the four dimensions summarized in Exhibit 12.2: financial, customer, internal processes, and learning and growth. Let's look more closely at each dimension.

LO 12.2

Describe the purpose of the balanced scorecard and explain its four dimensions.

balanced scorecard
A strategic management tool that divides an organization's goals into four dimensions (financial, customer, internal, and learning and growth) and defines the performance measures that should be used to assess the organization's performance in each dimension.

myopic decision making
Decision making that focuses on the short term.

	Dimension	Key Question	Horizon	Financial/ Nonfinancial
1.	Financial	How do we appear to shareholders?	Short term	Financial
2.	Customer	How do our customers see us?	Long term	Nonfinancial
3.	Internal processes	What must we excel at?	Long term	Nonfinancial
4.	Learning and growth	Can we continue to improve and add value?	Long term	Nonfinancial

Exhibit 12.2
Four Dimensions of the Balanced Scorecard

[2]Robert S. Kaplan and David P. Norton, "The Balanced Scorecard: Measures That Drive Performance," *Harvard Business Review* 83, no. 7 (2005), p. 172.
[3]Robert S. Kaplan and David P. Norton, "The Balanced Scorecard—Measures That Drive Performance," *Harvard Business Review,* January–February 1992, https://hbr.org/1992/01/the-balanced-scorecard-measures-that-drive-performance-2.

1. **Financial dimension: How do we appear to shareholders?** When assessing the organization on the financial dimension, managers evaluate whether their strategies are profitable and provide value to shareholders. Organizations use traditional financial metrics, such as profit and revenue growth, to evaluate themselves on the financial dimension. These metrics help answer many important questions, including:
   - Are revenues growing?
   - Are we managing costs effectively?
   - Is revenue growth (or decline) occurring in certain segments of the organization?

2. **Customer dimension: How do our customers see us?** When assessing the organization from a customer dimension, managers measure its responsiveness to customers' needs using metrics such as new-customer acquisition and current-customer retention. To gather information, they often use customer satisfaction surveys and other marketing research. When considering the customer dimension, the organization wants to answer questions such as:
   - Are we meeting or exceeding customers' needs and expectations?
   - Are we gaining new customers?
   - Are we losing customers?
   - Do customers have a positive experience when interacting with us?

3. **Internal process dimension: What must we excel at?** When evaluating the organization on the internal process dimension, managers are interested in acquiring information that will help them develop internal processes to meet the company's financial goals and its customers' needs, such as lower-cost production or a smaller environmental footprint, as shown in Patagonia's hypothetical strategy map (see Exhibit 12.4 later in this chapter). When improving internal processes, organizations keep an eye on what their customers value. Focusing on the internal process dimension involves answering questions such as:
   - Do our products meet quality standards?
   - Is our cycle time appropriate to meet customer demands?
   - Are our factories operating at capacity?
   - What is our inventory turnover rate?

4. **Learning and growth dimension: Can we continue to improve and add value?** An organization's ability to innovate is critical to its ability to compete and survive. For an organization to succeed financially and meet its customers' needs, it must respond, grow, and evolve. It must be able to develop and launch new products, create customer value, improve marketing efficiencies, and expand into new markets. When evaluating itself on the learning and growth dimension, an organization might choose to focus on process innovation and then measure the number of or success of new innovations. A focus on learning and growth requires managers to answer important questions about employees, including:
   - Do employees receive adequate training?
   - Do employees' performance evaluations indicate that they are meeting expectations?
   - Are employees developing new ideas to improve our product/service or the customer experience?

FROM THE FIELD

The Importance of Innovation

Recently, many organizations have signaled their commitment to innovation by creating the role of chief innovation officer (CIO). The CIO is primarily responsible for managing innovation within the organization by identifying new strategies, business opportunities, technologies, and partnerships.

Even the most traditional organizations are constantly striving to innovate and meet evolving customer needs. Jay Henry was the CIO for **Shaw Industries**, a company that has been designing and manufacturing flooring for over 50 years. At a recent lecture, he described flooring innovations focused on environmental sustainability and smart surfaces, including flooring that can detect when a nursing home resident has fallen and alert caregivers.

Mr. Henry noted, "The customer is not the same as they were five years ago or ten years ago. They're certainly not the same as they were 55 years ago. We have to meet those changing expectations, and we can't do it by being the same company that we've always been. We are focused on being the most customer-centric company in our industry."[4] In addition, he noted that the same customers who are now streaming entertainment on their smartphones, arranging rides through **Uber**, staying in **Airbnb** rentals, and buying cryptocurrencies are shopping for flooring from Shaw Industries—so the company has to evolve to meet these customers' expectations.

Critical Thinking

How can a company measure innovation? What performance measures would be useful for evaluating performance with respect to innovation?

lagging indicator

A performance metric that reports how the organization has performed in the past. Financial metrics are lagging indicators because they report on financial performance that has already occurred. Lagging indicators are easy to measure and are generally accurate.

leading indicator

A performance metric that provides information about potential future performance. Leading indicators such as customer satisfaction and employee training can help organizations predict the company's future performance.

The balanced scorecard contains both leading indicators and lagging indicators. Most financial measures are **lagging indicators** that tell us the financial results of the organization's past performance. Because they are easy to measure and generally accurate, organizations have historically relied on them. **Leading indicators** provide information about potential future performance. For example, customer satisfaction scores are leading indicators because they suggest how the organization will perform in the future: Happier customers are likely to result in greater future sales. Compared to lagging indicators, leading indicators are harder to identify, but they *can* be influenced to improve future performance.

Benefits of the Balanced Scorecard

The balanced scorecard has five primary benefits:

1. It aligns the organization by focusing individual departments and employees on their role in accomplishing the organization's strategic goals.
2. It helps managers focus on what is really important in the long run.
3. It broadens the organization's focus by considering the needs of its various stakeholders, such as customers.
4. It makes the organization more forward-looking.
5. It facilitates performance evaluations and discussions about professional development.

Many proponents of the balanced scorecard also note that it is implemented as part of a larger strategic initiative in which the organization thinks critically about its goals and how they relate to one another. Exhibit 12.3 illustrates a balanced scorecard that Patagonia might use. You will notice that front and center is the organization's mission statement, which drives the strategy. Surrounding the mission are the four dimensions of the balanced scorecard and the related objectives.

When building a balanced scorecard and identifying the right metrics to measure performance (discussed later in this chapter), it is crucial to understand the cause-and-effect relationships among the different strategic goals and measures, as illustrated by the double-headed arrows connecting all of the dimensions in Exhibit 12.3. The effectiveness of the

CAREER SKILLS

Learning about the balanced scorecard supports this career skill:

- Understanding links between performance on four different dimensions and how they affect the organization's ability to achieve its strategic goals

---

[4]Merritt Melancon, "Innovation Speaker: If We Don't Disrupt Ourselves, Someone Else Will," University of Georgia, Terry College of Business, November 15, 2021, www.terry.uga.edu/news/stories/2021/innovation-speaker-if-we-dont-disrupt-ourselves-someone-else-will.

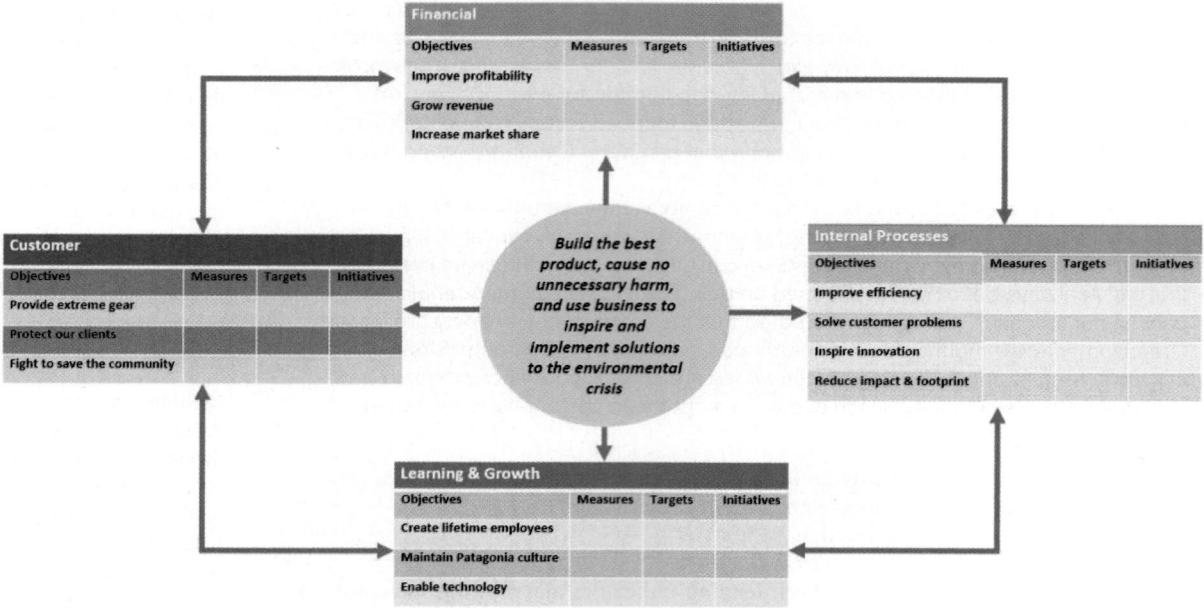

Exhibit 12.3
A Possible Balanced Scorecard for Patagonia

balanced scorecard hinges on the assumption that nonfinancial aspects of the business, such as customer satisfaction and loyalty, will predict and influence future financial performance. Thus, managers must always keep these relationships in focus.

Sometimes managers include performance measures that lack a cause-and-effect relationship, which may lead them to rely on performance indicators that have no bearing on financial success and may lead to dysfunctional employee behavior and suboptimal organizational performance. Consider Adventigo, a fictitious company that offers adventures and experiences to companies looking to foster team-building, innovation, and adaptability. It is likely that Adventigo wants to measure the success of its marketing efforts in terms of increasing its customer base because getting new customers is likely to directly affect revenue. A great deal of data is available to motivate and measure the effectiveness of marketing efforts.

Imagine that Adventigo has established guidelines that encourage marketers to send frequent text blasts promoting its new virtual reality programs. On first glance, it might seem like a good idea to encourage the marketing department to spread the word via text messages. However, the cause-and-effect link between number of texts sent and profit is tenuous at best. Here, marketing is incentivized to send texts without regard for the number of texts that actually reach viable customers. In addition, sending a text doesn't mean the potential target *reads* the text before deleting it! The messages may not be reaching potential customers at all. (Think about how many texts you delete without reading them.) In this example, the marketing department may be meeting its management-imposed text requirements every period, with no financial results to show for it. In fact, the marketing department may be doing wasteful things, such as purchasing lists of contact information for companies or individuals that would never realistically become paying customers.

This example makes it clear that management needs to put a process in place to evaluate the effectiveness of its performance measures for predicting success. For example, management may perform regression analysis to understand the relationships among its performance measures. We'll see an example of regression analysis later in this chapter.

⊘ **PROGRESS CHECK**

3. Describe the four dimensions of the balanced scorecard and the key question that each answers for the organization.

4. What is the difference between leading indicators and lagging indicators? Why is it important for the organization to consider both types of indicators when assessing performance?

5. Universities want to provide students with an excellent education. Achieving this objective helps keep applications high and increases revenues. University faculty are often evaluated on the basis of course evaluations written by students. Do you think that evaluating faculty based on student evaluations aligns with the strategic goal of providing students with an excellent education? Why or why not? Describe some positive and negative features of using course evaluations as a measure of instructor quality.

strategy map
An illustration that succinctly describes an organization's strategies and shows how different strategic goals interact in cause-and-effect relationships.

DEVELOPING STRATEGY MAPS

Many organizations use **strategy maps** to succinctly describe their organizational strategies and to show how the organization's different strategic goals interact in cause-and-effect relationships. Strategy maps help everyone in the organization visualize how their actions and responsibilities support the organization's overarching strategic goals. Exhibit 12.4 shows a hypothetical strategy map that could be implemented at Patagonia.

LO 12.3

Explain the purpose of strategy maps and how they are developed.

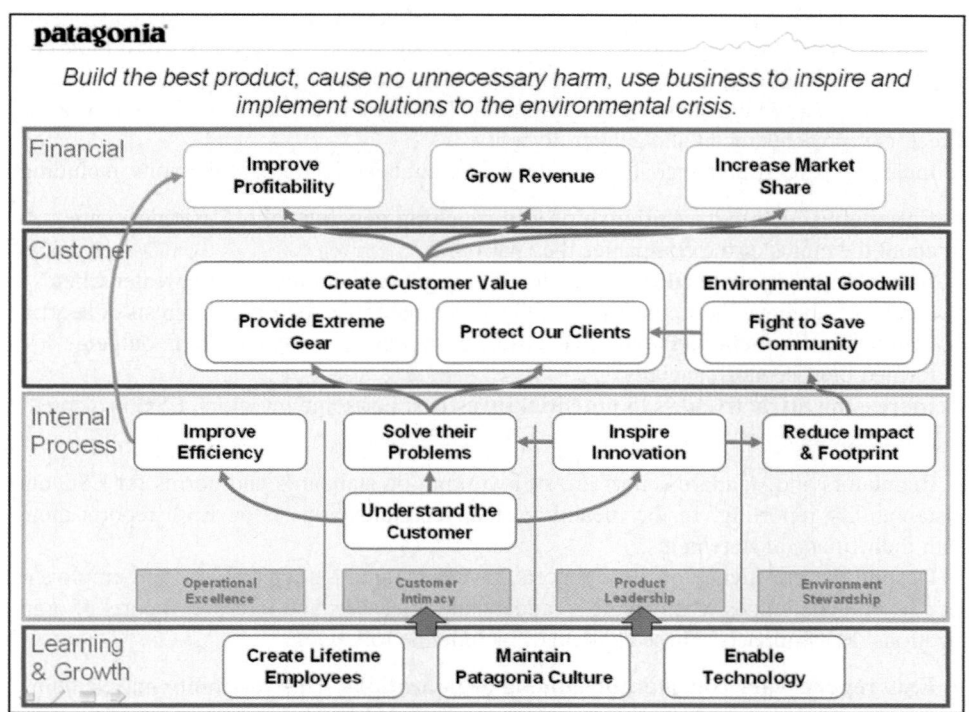

Exhibit 12.4
Hypothetical Patagonia Strategy Map

PureStone Partners LLC

You can see that the strategy map is divided into the four categories or dimensions that are used for the balanced scorecard. Importantly, there is at least one strategic goal related to each dimension.

Notice how the strategic goals in each dimension of the organization affect goals in the same dimension, as well as other dimensions. The arrows in Exhibit 12.4 illustrate the cause-and-effect relationships that exist among the strategic goals. For example, because Patagonia knows its customers, it believes it will create financial value if it can address their need for protection against the elements when they are engaging in outdoor activities. Simultaneously, Patagonia is working to reduce the company's environmental footprint, which will also benefit its community of customers.

By focusing on the cause-and-effect relationships among strategic goals, the organization can understand (and communicate) how the achievement of one goal impacts the achievement of other goals, allowing the organization to identify the key drivers of its success and prioritize its efforts accordingly. Based on the relationships shown in Exhibit 12.4, Patagonia would need to prioritize understanding the customer (a strategic goal in the internal process dimension) because success there is necessary for Patagonia to achieve most of its other goals.

The cause-and-effect relationships depicted in the strategy map are the relationships that the organization believes are most significant. These are the relationships that best help the organization achieve its goals. It is likely that many other cause-and-effect relationships that occur within the organization are not depicted on the strategy map.

ENVIRONMENTAL, SOCIAL, GOVERNANCE

Incorporating Environmental, Social, and Governance Goals into the Strategy Map and Balanced Scorecard

Many stakeholders, including standard-setters, company management, customers, and shareholders, recognize that organizations can help to improve societal problems such as environmental degradation, inequality, and poverty. This recognition has led many organizations to incorporate environmental, social, and governance (ESG) goals into their corporate strategies. Some examples of common ESG initiatives that organizations consider are reducing carbon emissions, engaging in fair labor practices, and ensuring the board of directors represents racial and gender diversity.

Including ESG strategic goals generates important benefits for organizations, including:

- **Enhancing customer relationships and reaching new markets.** Customers care about the ethics of the companies they patronize.
- **Improving corporate culture.** Employee engagement and loyalty are greater when employees believe their company is ethical and that it has their best interests at heart.
- **Improving financial performance.** Historically, ethical companies have outperformed their peers financially.
- **Increasing attractiveness to potential investors.** For some investors, ESG is a core consideration.

Regulators and standard setters are still working on standards and norms for ESG and sustainability reporting. In the meantime, many organizations issue ESG reports along with their financial statements.

Despite the prevalence of these reports, investors, analysts, customers, and employees face several challenges when trying to understand, measure, and interpret reports of organizations' ESG impacts. These challenges include the following:

- **ESG reports vary considerably among organizations.** This variability makes them difficult to compare. Because there is no single global ESG reporting standard or framework, companies have great flexibility in what and how they report.
- **ESG regulations are still evolving.** Current regulations vary considerably across different countries. In 2021 the International Sustainability Standards Board (ISSB) was created; its goal is to develop comprehensive global sustainability–related disclosure standards.

- **ESG impact is difficult to measure and quantify.** In fact, many aspects of ESG cannot be easily defined in terms of dollars and cents. For example, how should a company quantify the financial impact of increasing diversity on the board of directors?
- **ESG reporting is susceptible to greenwashing. Greenwashing** is the practice of misrepresenting the environmental or social impact of production, such that it appears more favorable than it is.

greenwashing
The practice of misrepresenting the environmental or social impact of production, such that it appears more favorable than it is.

These same challenges exist for the organizations that are incorporating ESG goals into their strategic plan. Strategy maps and the balanced scorecard provide useful tools to help organizations overcome these challenges. As previously described, a strategy map helps management understand the cause-and-effect relationships among the different strategic goals. By leveraging the four dimensions of the balanced scorecard framework, management can better understand the impact of ESG goals across the entire organization.

Let's consider an example. Suppose that **Heartwood Cabinets** develops a strategic goal to use only sustainably sourced wood so as to minimize its impact on forests and native wildlife. This choice may impact all four of the balanced scorecard dimensions, as follows:

- **Financial dimension.** Heartwood's decision to use only sustainably sourced wood is likely to increase Heartwood's cost of manufacturing cabinets.
- **Customer dimension.** Heartwood's decision may attract new customers who appreciate Heartwood's commitment to the environment.
- **Internal process dimension.** Heartwood's decision may increase the length of time required to receive the materials from the suppliers, thus increasing the time taken to manufacture the end product.
- **Learning and growth dimension.** Heartwood's decision may improve employee loyalty and pride in the company.

Importantly, when ESG goals are included in strategy maps, balanced scorecards, and stakeholder reports, management accountants must identify, collect, and analyze new and different data sources. Often, these data are unstructured, so they must be transformed into a machine-readable format. Further, these data often come from external sources, so they must be verified to ensure that they are true and can be relied upon. And, of course, management accountants must be able to share the story with the executives who are making strategic decisions, so they must be able to understand and interpret the relationships among these diverse data sets.

⊘ PROGRESS CHECK

6. Why is it important to consider the cause-and-effect relationships among goals in different business dimensions?
7. Imagine that you are building a strategy map for **Visa**, the credit card company. It has three strategic goals in the financial dimension: increase shareholder value, decrease costs, and increase revenue. Identify two or three strategic goals for each of the customer, internal processes, and learning and growth dimensions that relate to those financial goals.

DEFINING KEY PERFORMANCE INDICATORS FOR THE BALANCED SCORECARD

LO 12.4
Identify key performance indicators that relate to the balanced scorecard dimensions.

Strategy maps and the balanced scorecard help an organization articulate how achieving its various strategic goals supports its mission. The balanced scorecard also helps the organization measure and assess performance. To this end, management identifies specific

CAREER SKILLS

Learning about key performance indicators supports this career skill:

• Measuring performance toward organizational goals

performance metrics that can be tracked and evaluated for each strategic goal. These measures are called **key performance indicators**, or **KPIs**.

A KPI is a metric that provides evidence of the success or failure of a strategic goal over a specific amount of time. Managers must be able to measure the KPI and compare it to the established standards. In addition, KPIs should focus on results and use results-oriented language so that managers can focus on the precise goal they want to achieve.

Sometimes managers develop KPIs that focus on activities rather than results, which is not an effective management practice. For example, a manager may specify the KPI *implement a sales plan.* Although you can measure whether a plan has been implemented, simply implementing a plan does not help the organization determine if the plan was successful in terms of the ultimate goal of increased sales. A more effective KPI is *implement a sales plan that reduces the number of days taken to convert a qualified sales lead into an actual sale from 15 days to 10 days.* Exhibit 12.5 provides some other examples of KPIs that organizations commonly use. Note that these KPIs run the gamut of business activities.

Business Area	Purpose	Examples	Goal
Financial	To measure financial performance	Increase revenue growth	↑
		Increase net profit margin	↑
		Increase net sales growth	↑
		Increase operational cash flow	↑
		Increase earnings before interest, taxes, depreciation, and amortization (EBITDA)	↑
		Increase inventory turnover	↑
Customer	To understand the customer	Increase percentage of market share	↑
		Increase number of customers retained	↑
		Decrease average time to convert lead to a customer	↓
		Increase net promoter score (NPS)[a]	↑
		Increase customer satisfaction survey score	↑
Operational	To gauge operational performance	Decrease order fulfillment time	↓
		Decrease time to market	↓
		Decrease inventory shrinkage rate	↓
		Decrease project cost variance	↓
Marketing	To evaluate marketing efforts	Increase monthly website traffic	↑
		Increase keywords in Top 10 search engine results	↑
		Increase number of qualified leads	↑
Environmental, Social, and Governance (ESG)	To measure environmental and sustainability performance	Decrease carbon footprint	↓
		Decrease energy consumption	↓
Employee	To assess employee performance	Increase employee satisfaction rating	↑
		Decrease employee churn (i.e., turnover) rate	↓
		Increase revenue per employee	↑
		Increase 360-degree feedback score	↑

Exhibit 12.5
Commonly Used KPIs (Key Performance Indicators)

[a]Net promoter score (NPS) is a marketing tool for measuring the customer experience and customer loyalty. It relies on customers' response to the question: "How likely are you to recommend the brand to a friend or colleague?" NPS will be discussed in more detail later in this chapter.

How many KPIs should an organization have? If the organization has too few KPIs, it is likely missing key information about its performance. In contrast, too many KPIs can overwhelm the human brain, and managers will selectively focus on just a few of them. Most organizations identify between 10 and 20 KPIs divided among the four dimensions of the balanced scorecard, but this number is tied directly to the overall number of strategic goals. Each strategic goal should have at least one KPI.

The following table summarizes some KPIs that Patagonia might use:

Dimension	Strategic Goal	KPI
Financial	Improve profitability.	Increase sales revenue by 15% this year.
Customer	Create customer value.	Increase net promoter score (NPS) by 2 points over last year.
Internal processes	Reduce impact and footprint.	Decrease carbon emissions from shipping processes by 25% this year.
Learning and growth	Create lifetime employees.	Reduce turnover rate by 20% this year.

key performance indicators (KPIs) Measures used to evaluate factors that are important to the organization's success; provide evidence of the success or failure of a strategic goal over a specific amount of time.

What makes a good KPI? Effective KPIs are "SMART":

1. *Specific.* They include specific information, such as percentages of improvement, to allow managers to determine success or failure.
2. *Measurable.* They are quantifiable so that managers can determine success or failure.
3. *Achievable.* They are ambitious but within the reasonable range of outcomes.
4. *Relevant.* They are related to key business objectives.
5. *Time-bound.* Success or failure is determined based on a length of time.

You'll notice that our example KPIs for Patagonia meet all of these criteria. For example, Patagonia has the strategic goal of creating customer value. The related KPI uses the **net promoter score (NPS)**, a respected marketing tool for measuring the customer experience and customer loyalty. It relies on the responses to a simple question asked of customers: "How likely are you to recommend the brand to a friend or colleague?" Responses are coded on a scale from 0 to 10, with responses coded as 9 or 10 identified as "promoters." Responses coded as 7 or 8 are considered "passives," and those below 7 as detractors. The summary measure subtracts all detractors from all promoters, yielding an NPS that ranges from −100 to 100. Let's review how the NPS KPI for Patagonia meets all five criteria for an effective KPI:

net promoter score (NPS) A tool for measuring the customer experience and loyalty. The NPS is based on customers' responses to the question "How likely are you to recommend the brand to a friend or colleague?"

1. It is *specific* in that it seeks to increase the NPS by 2 points.
2. It is *measurable* because it is an objective, easily quantifiable measure.
3. It is *achievable* because it is a reasonable increase. (Generally, an organization can rely on historical trends to ensure that a target is achievable.)
4. Increasing the NPS is *relevant* because it is a known measure of customer loyalty that relates to customers' perceptions of the brand.
5. It is *time-bound* in that it compares this year's performance to last year's performance.

FROM THE FIELD

Implementing the Balanced Scorecard Effectively

The balanced scorecard has many benefits, but those benefits do not accrue if the scorecard is not implemented effectively.

When organizations do not clearly articulate their strategic goals, do not specify how those goals relate to one another, measure the wrong performance metrics, or do not understand the cause-and-effect relationships between the strategic goals and related performance measures, the balanced scorecard won't be an effective tool. Problems can also occur if the organization is trying to measure too many performance metrics rather than focusing on true KPIs. Finally, if the organization develops a scorecard but does not use it to inform decisions and strategic thinking, it won't help propel the organization to success.

Accounting academics have published over 100 studies on the balanced scorecard, with many of these studies focusing on its shortcomings. Results from these studies reveal that many organizations have been a bit unsophisticated in their implementation of their balanced scorecard, thus hindering its effectiveness.

Research on the balanced scorecard continues, with academics and practitioners together investigating factors that can facilitate or inhibit successful implementation of the scorecard in organizations. Factors such as organizational culture, employee participation, and resource constraints have all been considered. While many factors play a role in the successful use of the balanced scorecard, having support from top management, as well as employee participation and buy-in on the strategic goals and KPIs, is especially important. Also, organizations with a culture that encourages thoughtful strategic planning and embraces continuous improvement are more likely to be effective in their balanced scorecard implementation.

Thinking Critically

One of the most important benefits of the balanced scorecard is that it can provide a shared vision and language for everyone in the organization. But what happens if the organization is acquired or merges with another organization? What happens if there is turnover in the management team and the new executives do not have the same vision as the previous team?

 LAB CONNECTIONS

Organizations can track KPIs at a point in time and also review trends over time. In **LAB 12.1**, you will use Excel to compare performance to an organization's target for a number of KPIs. You will use conditional formatting to highlight when organizations are meeting or exceeding their targets, and when they are falling short.

In **LAB 12.2**, you will perform regression analysis in Microsoft Excel to evaluate whether an organization's customer, internal process, and learning and growth KPIs are related to its financial performance.

 PROGRESS CHECK

8. Why does an organization focus on only a small number of KPIs?
9. Search online for **Airbnb**'s mission statement. Based on that mission statement, identify a strategic goal and relevant KPI for each of the four dimensions in the balanced scorecard for Airbnb.
10. Describe the benefits of a balanced scorecard if implementation is effective.
11. What challenges do organizations face when developing and implementing a balanced scorecard?

LO 12.5

Understand how organizations use strategy maps and balanced scorecards to evaluate success.

USING THE BALANCED SCORECARD FOR PERFORMANCE MEASUREMENT

After the organization has developed the balanced scorecard by identifying and categorizing its strategic goals and developing effective KPIs, it can use the scorecard to evaluate organizational performance.

Human Dimensions: Using the Balanced Scorecard for Performance Measurement

Many companies tie employee compensation and rewards to the balanced scorecard measures, believing that this link will increase both employee motivation and the likelihood of organizational success. For example, some organizations use a pay-for-performance compensation program in which executives' and employees' pay is linked to meeting specific goals on the relevant balanced scorecard measures.

However, tying compensation to the balanced scorecard can be complicated. Anytime an organization uses multiple measures in its compensation program, it must assign weights to the different measures. Determining the appropriate weights requires careful consideration. Experts, including Norton and Kaplan, recommend that organizations assign relative weights that best reflect the organization's overall business model and strategic goals. Thus, managers may need to prioritize the strategic goals while keeping in mind the cause-and-effect relationships among the goals. The assigned weights should reflect the organization's priorities because employees are likely to focus their attention on the more highly weighted measures.

When an organization assigns weights to multiple performance measures to determine compensation, it creates a formula-driven compensation program. One potential risk in a formula-driven compensation program is that employees may try to game the system, focusing their attention on the measures that help them achieve their own personal goal (for example, earning a bonus) even if those measures do not help the organization achieve its strategic goals. For example, if employees can earn most of their bonus by signing up new customers, they may focus their energies on customer acquisition, even if those customers make only one purchase and do not turn into profitable long-term customers. This measure has focused on increasing the number of customers at the possible expense of the company not meeting financial targets. As a result, the organization may compensate employees for *un*balanced performance.

Whether or not the organization uses the balanced scorecard in its compensation practices, the tool provides meaningful insight about the performance of the organization as a whole and of individual employees. The balanced scorecard is also a critical communication tool, allowing managers and employees to assess performance on a regular basis. Organizations should communicate the results of the balanced scorecard as frequently as they can.

Using Data Analytics to Build a Balanced Scorecard Dashboard

DATA VISUALIZATION

Often, organizations develop dashboards to track balanced scorecard measures. Exhibit 12.6 shows a very simple balanced scorecard dashboard for a fictitious company.

The four balanced scorecard dimensions are listed on the left side of this dashboard, and the current status of each is shown using the red/yellow/green stoplight method. While we don't know exactly how this fictitious organization, The Modern Company, establishes its summary measure for each balanced scorecard dimension, we can see that the organization is not performing well on the financial dimension because it is colored red. Based on the yellow indicator, the internal processes and customer dimensions appear to be doing okay, and the organization is performing strongly on learning and growth, as indicated by green. In the "Monthly Trend" column of this summary visualization, The Modern Company tracks the trend in performance for each dimension. Even though internal processes are performing okay currently, they are declining from the prior period, which may be a cause for concern.

On the right side of this dashboard, we see some of the most important KPIs for The Modern Company: sales by month, gross revenue, customer retention, on-time delivery, and

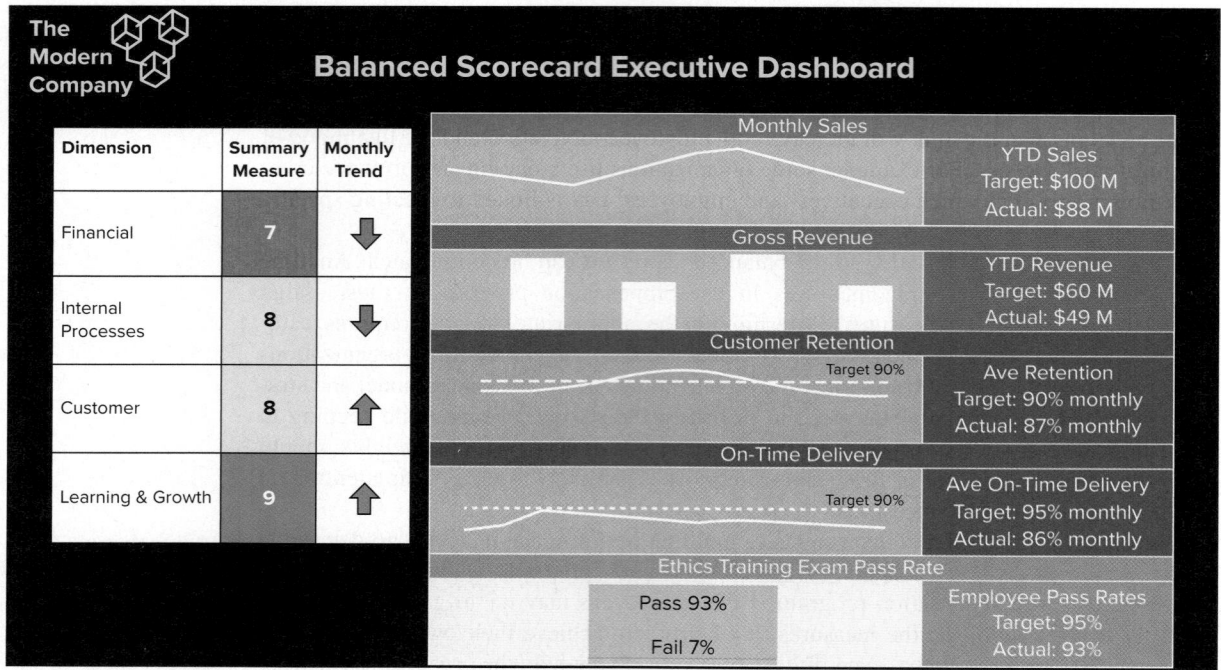

Exhibit 12.6
Sample Balanced Scorecard Indicators Dashboard

ethics training exam pass rate. These visualizations provide a quick snapshot that management can review to see how the organization is performing in a variety of important areas.

To build a dashboard like this one, the management accountants at The Modern Company apply the AMPS model as follows:

Ask the Question: How is The Modern Company performing on each KPI?

Manage the Data: In Chapter 2 we discussed the different systems that make up an organization's enterprise resource planning (ERP) system. The management accountants at The Modern Company will pull the appropriate data from these systems to answer the questions related to each KPI. For example, to answer the questions about monthly sales and revenue, they access sales and cost data from the financial reporting system (FRS). To answer questions about customer retention, they pull data about customer purchase history from the customer relationship management (CRM) system. On-time delivery data are found in the supply chain management system (SCMS), and employee ethics exam score data are found in the human resources management system (HRMS). Once the data are accessed, they may need to be reorganized, formatted, and cleaned before they are uploaded into the organization's preferred data analytics tool.

Perform the Analysis: Each of the visualizations in the dashboard represents the results of descriptive analytics. For example, for monthly sales, the management accountant uses a line graph to chart total sales per month. Although the axes are not shown in the visualization, you can tell that the month of the year is charted on the X-axis and total sales are on the Y-axis. For the customer retention, on-time delivery, and monthly summary data, the visualization also includes the target so the user can see months in which the organization has fallen short of those goals. For customer retention, it has been short of the 90 percent monthly goal for much of the year. When examining the results of employee ethics exams, it makes sense to consider the percentage of employees who passed versus those who failed. To present this information, the management accountants use a stacked bar chart that shows the relative percentage of each category (pass or fail), where the total always equals 100 percent. A pie chart or a donut chart can show the same data equally effectively.

In addition to the specific analytics shown on the right in Exhibit 12.6, management accountants can use conditional formatting to change the colors shown in the summary measures and to add the up or down arrows in the summary table on the left.

Share the Story: To share the story, the management accountants built and distributed this dashboard to the appropriate decision makers.

Of course, Exhibit 12.6 is just a very basic example, and organizations can and do customize their dashboards.

 PROGRESS CHECK

12. Describe the pros and cons of using the balanced scorecard for compensating employees.

13. Based on the balanced scorecard dashboard in Exhibit 12.6, what do you think management will be most concerned about? Least concerned about?

BUILDING A BALANCED SCORECARD DASHBOARD

> **LO 12.6**
>
> Understand how organizations apply data analytics to the balanced scorecard framework.

Our discussion of the balanced scorecard has thus far focused on the big picture. Now, in the following Data Analytics Mini-Lab, let's get into a detailed example to see how strategic goals are measured, evaluated, analyzed, and summarized using data analytics and visualizations.

DATA ANALYTICS MINI-LAB
Building a Balanced Scorecard Dashboard

Data Analytics Type: Descriptive

Keywords
KPIs, Balanced Scorecard, Dashboard

Decision-Making Context
Organizations have an enormous amount of data they can use to track KPIs and progress toward their goals. Selecting the right measures and finding the right data to evaluate those measures are critical. In consultation with cost accountants and operations personnel, management will select a set of KPIs that are keenly focused on the strategic goals. For this Data Analytics Mini-Lab, we return to the example at the start of this chapter: the National Marrow Donor Program (NMDP).

Lab Note: The tools presented in this lab periodically change. Updated instructions, if applicable, can be found in the student and instructor support materials.

Review the NMDP strategy map in Exhibit 12.1. These strategic goals are also presented in Exhibit A below. Let's now use the AMPS model to analyze NMDP's performance related to each of its strategic goals using the balanced scorecard framework.

Required

Complete the table shown in Exhibit A by identifying appropriate KPIs (Column 3) and their data sources (Column 4) for each strategic goal. You'll see that Column 1 contains the four balanced scorecard dimensions and Column 2 identifies NMDP's strategic goals. Use the KPI choices and Data choices given below to complete the table. The first strategic goal for each dimension has been completed for you.

Exhibit A
Possible Strategic Goals for the National Marrow Donor Program (NMDP)

(1) Dimension	(2) Strategic Goals	(3) KPIs	(4) Data Sources
Financial	1. Grow and diversify financial resources	C	3
	2. Improve use of resources and cost effectiveness		
Stakeholders[a]	3. Successfully serve all patients in need of cellular transplant	D	5
	4. Maximize appeal and value of NMDP to donors, volunteers, and contributors		
	5. Effectively communicate cellular transplantation knowledge so patients can make informed decisions		
Internal processes	6. Advance research in cellular transplantation	H	9
	7. Develop and maintain effective relationships		
	8. Improve process efficiency and quality practices		
Learning and growth	9. Enhance open, effective, and efficient communications	A	10
	10. Optimize technology, business systems, and facilities		
	11. Build a culture based on core values		
	12. Attract, engage, develop, and retain effective people		

[a]NMDP uses the term *stakeholders* instead of *customers* because the people it serves include patients and donors, rather than traditional customers.

Ask the Question

What KPI should NMDP use to monitor performance for each strategic goal?

For each strategic goal, select one KPI that NMDP could use to measure achievement toward that goal. Choose from the following list, and place your answers in Column 3 of Exhibit A. You will use each choice only once.

KPI choices*:

A. Average employee satisfaction rating of 4 out of 5 each quarter (or an upward trend over time).

B. Decrease employee turnover rate by 2 percent each year.

C. Increase revenue from individual and corporate donors by 2 percent on average each year.

D. Increase frequency of patient and donor match by 5 percent each year.

*KPIs included in this Mini-Lab are hypothetical.

E. Monthly contact with hospitals in all major metropolitan areas and each state within 5 years.

F. Reduce facilities maintenance costs by 2 percent each period.

G. Decrease COGS (cost of goods sold) by 1 percent each year.

H. Increase number of research grants fulfilled by 5 percent each year.

I. Reduce number of lapsed donors to below 30 percent each year.

J. Reduce patient acquisition cost by 5 percent by year-end.

K. Reduce research-funding processing time by 5 percent each quarter.

L. 20 employee training hours completed by at least 90 percent of employees each year.

Manage the Data

Next, the NMDP will need to identify the appropriate data source for each KPI. Note that the KPIs address activities throughout the organization. Therefore, data will come from many different sources, including financial systems, human resources systems, and marketing records. Management accountants will perform a critical function when they consolidate and transform the data coming in from these different sources, perform analytics, and then present the results in a dashboard that is easily understood by management.

For each KPI, select the most appropriate source of data that NMDP could use to measure performance. Choose from the following list, and place your answers in Column 4 of Exhibit A. You will use each data choice only once.

Data Choices:

1. Employee records, including hiring and termination dates (if applicable), from the human resources (HR) department.

2. Financial donor lists, including lifetime donations, number of donations, and frequency of donations.

3. Revenue records based on donations and grants.

4. Employee evaluations.

5. Records of patients included on the registry, including date added, treatment required, and current status.

6. Stakeholder surveys.

7. Records of operational costs, such as salaries, overtime, and property, plant, and equipment.

8. Marketing records, including communication channels, data on distribution of materials, and contacts with physicians and hospitals.

9. Records of medical research funded and status of completed and ongoing research.

10. Employee satisfaction surveys.

11. Building maintenance cost records.

12. Process-mapping software output showing processes and time taken for research funding.

Perform the Analysis

NMDP will use the available data to prepare a series of visualizations that will eventually be presented in a balanced scorecard dashboard. Exhibit B describes the types of visualization that NMDP could prepare to examine many of its KPIs. Note that not all KPIs are included in this example balanced scorecard analysis.

DATA VISUALIZATION

Dimension	Strategic Goals	Types of Visualization Created
Financial	• Grow and diversify financial resources	• Column chart to show donations by month for each donor type (individual vs. corporate) separately • Column chart to show average monthly donation amount for each donor type
	• Improve use of resources and cost effectiveness	• Line graph to display sum of expenses by type (for example, compensation expense, rent expense) over time
Stakeholders	• Successfully serve all patients in need of cellular transplant	*No data were available for analysis.*
	• Maximize appeal and value of NMDP to donors, volunteers, and contributors	• Text tables to show donors by number of donations and total donation amount
	• Effectively communicate cellular transplantation knowledge so patients can make informed decisions	*No data were available for analysis.*
Internal processes	• Advance research in cellular transplantation	• Text tables to summarize global research grants by country showing number of grants and total funding amounts • Map visualization to show relative research funding amount by state
	• Develop and maintain effective relationships	*No data were available for analysis.*
	• Improve process efficiency and quality practices	*No data were available for analysis.*
Learning and growth	• Enhance open, effective, and efficient communications	• Column chart to show results of employee satisfaction survey over time • Column chart to display average employee satisfaction over multiple years
	• Optimize technology, business systems, and facilities	*No data were available for analysis.*
	• Build a culture based on core values	• Column chart to show results of employee satisfaction survey over time • Column chart to display average employee satisfaction over multiple years
	• Attract, engage, develop, and retain effective people	• Column chart to show the number of active employees in different tenure ranges

Exhibit B
Potential Analyses for Performance Related to KPIs

Share the Story

Recall that management can use a dashboard, like the one shown in Exhibit C, to continuously monitor organizational performance on the four key performance dimensions. The dashboard can also be used as a communication tool throughout the relevant areas of the organization because it helps each department focus on the KPIs that are most critical to organizational success.

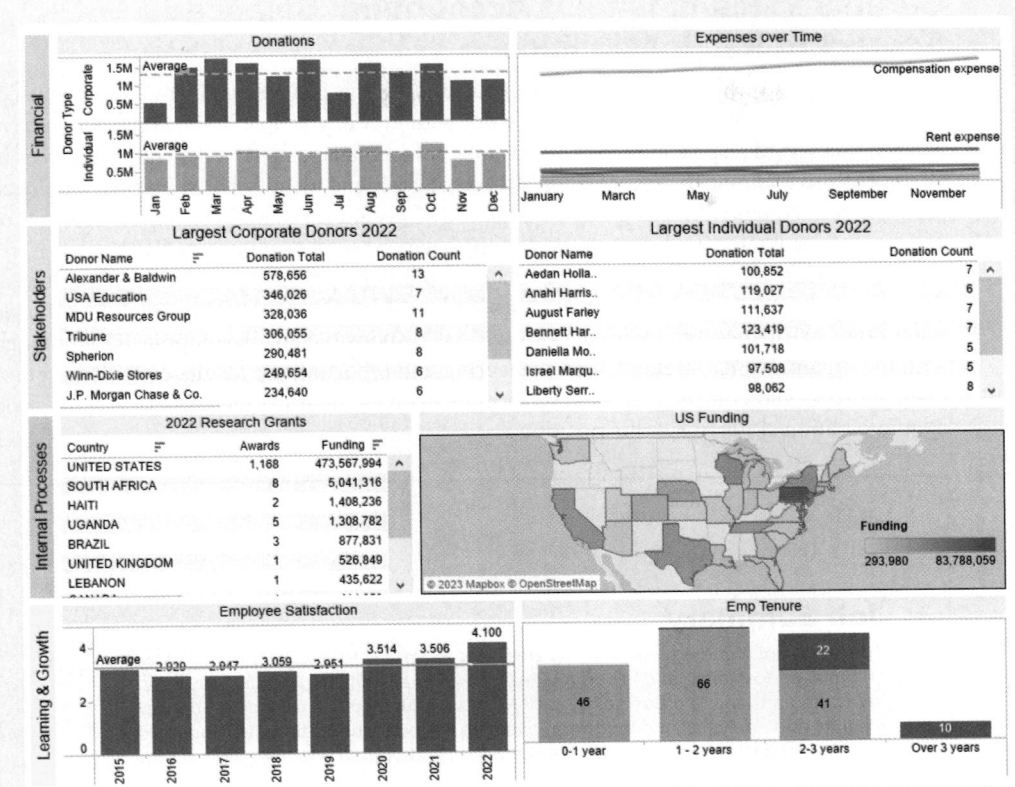

Exhibit C
NMDP Balanced Scorecard

Microsoft Power BI

Mini-Lab Assessment

Based on Exhibit C, answer the following questions:

1. What other KPIs could NMDP use to evaluate its ability to attract, engage, develop, and retain effective employees?
2. Based on the balanced scorecard dashboard, which type of expense represents the most significant cost to NMDP? Is that expense increasing, decreasing, or staying the same?
3. For each dimension, do you think that NMDP is succeeding in its strategic goals or failing to meet its goals, or can you not tell based on the dashboard view?

🔍 LAB CONNECTIONS

In **LABS 12.3–12.5**, you will use data related to the four dimensions of the balanced scorecard to prepare visualizations that will be used to evaluate whether the organization is meeting its targets for each KPI. Then you will combine these visualizations into one dashboard that displays the entire set of measures that comprise the balanced scorecard.

- **LAB 12.3** uses Excel.
- **LAB 12.4** uses Tableau.
- **LAB 12.5** uses Power BI.

Careers in Management Accounting: Balanced Scorecard Responsibilities

Now that you've seen what a balanced scorecard is, how it is developed, and how it is used, let's think about what types of employees work with it. Many people in the organization have balanced scorecard responsibilities. For example, senior management works with employees in all dimensions to define the organization's strategic goals and identify KPIs. Further, employee performance is often evaluated using the balanced scorecard KPIs. In short, most employees of an organization interact with some aspect of the balanced scorecard on a regular basis.

Exhibit 12.7 is a job posting for a financial planning and analysis business partner at a fast-food chain like **Krispy Kreme**, **Dunkin'**, or **Tim Horton's**. This position is for an accounting or finance professional who will be responsible for developing KPIs aligned with the organization's strategy, then measuring and reporting the results of KPIs to senior management. The company is looking for a tech-savvy, detail-oriented person with good communication skills to fill this position.

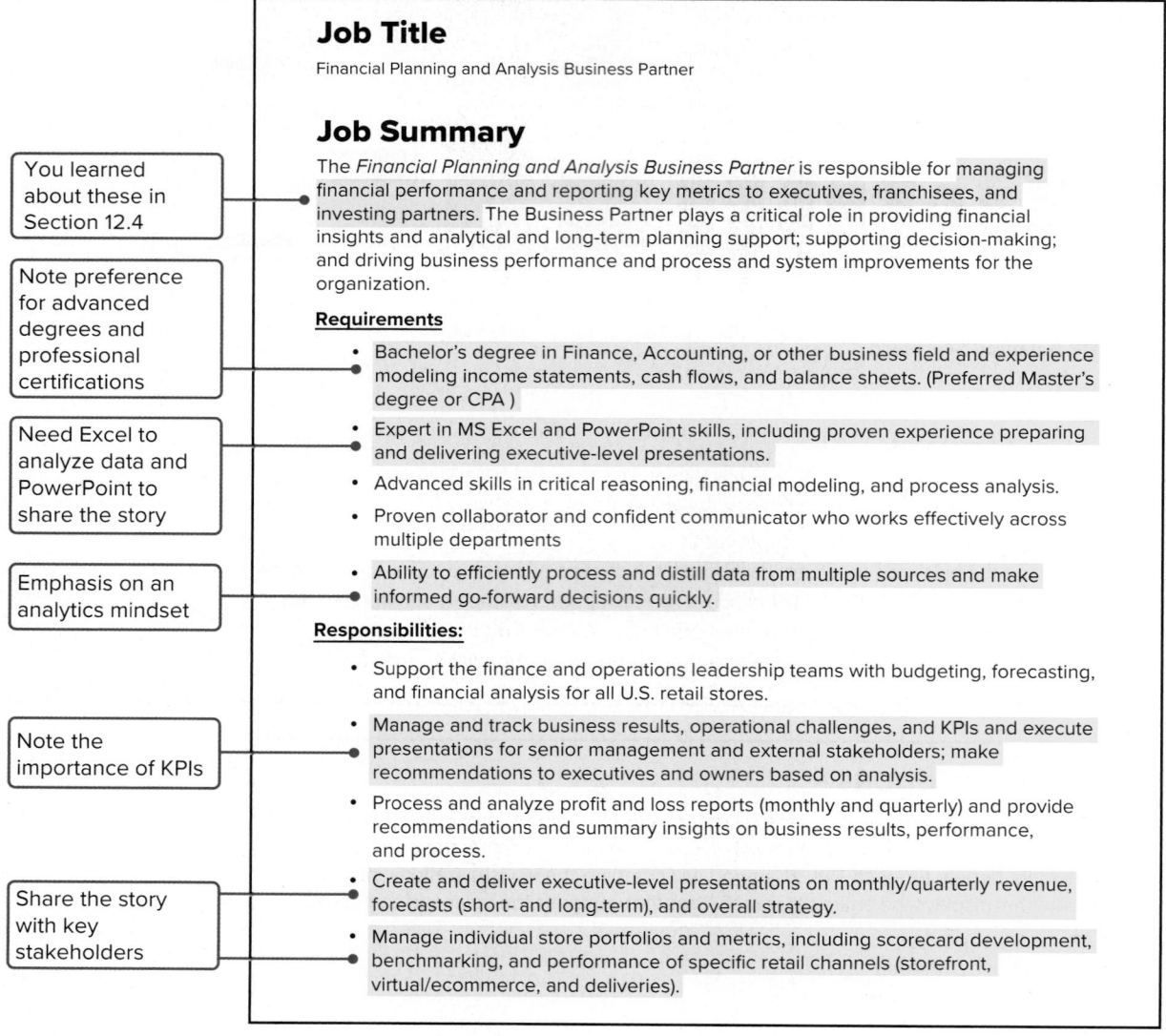

Exhibit 12.7
Financial Planning and Analysis Business Partner Job Opportunity

Key Takeaways: Strategy Maps and the Balanced Scorecard

Organizations use strategy maps and the balanced scorecard to guide strategic decision making. These tools help the organization understand the interactions among its various goals and identify the appropriate performance metrics that will help the organization monitor its progress toward those goals. The balanced scorecard serves as a communication tool, aligning the activities of all departments and employees with the organization's strategic goals. The balanced scorecard includes carefully considered key performance indicators (KPIs) that facilitate performance evaluation, which is often used as a critical input in compensation programs.

Using strategy maps and the balanced scorecard approach includes all aspects of the AMPS model:

Ask the Question

■ **What question(s) does management want to answer?**

When using strategy maps and a balanced scorecard approach, management is interested in measuring organizational and financial performance across several dimensions of the business: financial, customer, internal processes, and learning and growth.

Manage the Data

■ **Which data are appropriate to address management's questions?**

Data from many areas of the organization are accumulated, transformed, and prepared for analysis, including financial data, customer data, employee data, and operations data.

Perform the Analysis

■ **Which analytics are performed to address management questions?**

The balanced scorecard approach includes a combination of descriptive, diagnostic, and prescriptive analytics.

Share the Story

■ **How are the results of the analytics shared with stakeholders?**

The results of the analyses can be presented together in a dashboard that allows management to easily monitor performance across multiple dimensions of the organization. The dashboard can be shared throughout the organization, giving everyone a shared understanding of the organization's goals and performance.

Key Terms

balanced scorecard

core values

greenwashing

key performance indicators (KPIs)

lagging indicator

leading indicator

mission statement

myopic decision making

net promoter score (NPS)

strategic goals

strategy

strategy map

vision statement

ANSWERS TO PROGRESS CHECKS

1. A mission statement captures the organization's purpose while also providing insight into the organization's guiding principles. An organization's strategic goals and plans are based on the mission statement. In contrast, a vision statement is forward- and future-looking. The mission statement is focused on the here and now, whereas the vision statement is focused on progress and the future.

2. The mission statement informs an organization's strategic goals by guiding the development of the organizational strategy. An organization's strategy is its plan of action for achieving its mission. Strategic goals are objectives that must be accomplished to implement the strategy.

3. The four dimensions of the balanced scorecard are:

    a. Financial. The financial dimension of the balanced scorecard aids in management's evaluation of strategies, helping to determine whether these strategies are profitable and provide value to shareholders. The critical question that the financial dimension aims to answer is "How do we appear to shareholders?" (See Exhibit 12.2.)

    b. Customer. The customer dimension of the balanced scorecard aids in the measurement of the organization's responsiveness to customer needs. The critical question that the customer dimension aims to answer is "How do our customers see us?"

    c. Internal processes. The internal process dimension of the balanced scorecard aids in the development of internal processes that will better serve customer needs and meet financial goals. The key question that the internal process dimension aims to answer is "What must we excel at?"

    d. Learning and growth. The learning and growth dimension of the balanced scorecard seeks to encourage and measure process innovation and the creation of new efficiencies. The key question that the learning and growth dimension aims to answer is "Can we continue to improve and add value?"

4. Lagging indicators provide information about the organization's past financial performance, whereas leading indicators provide information about potential future performance. It is important for the organization to consider both types of indicators because doing so will help the organization better understand its past performance and devise ways to improve its future performance.

5. There may be better options than course evaluations to determine an excellent educator because one educator's methods may work extremely well for one group of students but not for a different group of students. Additionally, the evaluations may not be specific enough to enable the deans or department heads to determine faculty success or failure. Students may also penalize a professor of a particularly difficult and complex subject with lower evaluation scores just because the students had to work harder to achieve good course grades. Performance measures must be able to compare the results to the optimal outcome, which may be impossible given the idiosyncrasies of educating. One positive aspect of using student evaluations to evaluate faculty performance is that they are time-specific and relevant because they apply to a certain quarter/trimester/semester and have the potential to provide direct and useful feedback.

6. It is important to consider the cause-and-effect relationships among goals in different business dimensions because these relationships show how the achievement of one goal can impact the achievement of another. Top-level goals, such as revenue generation, cannot be achieved unless sublevel goals from different dimensions (for example, internal processes, customer, or learning and growth) are also achieved. By identifying the cause-and-effect relationships, employees can determine where to prioritize their efforts to ensure success at the higher levels.

7. The following examples would be likely strategic goals for Visa (other answers are possible):

   a. Customer

      i. Make our products easy to use.

      ii. Protect our customers' identity and other personal information.

      iii. Team up with customer-chosen charities to provide philanthropy.

   b. Internal processes

      i. Streamline internal processes to gain efficiencies.

      ii. Strive to understand customer needs and which products are most important to them.

      iii. Become an early adopter in the technology space to provide the most up-to-date products to customers.

   c. Learning and growth

      i. Provide internal training and education to help employees become more familiar and comfortable with the company.

      ii. Empower individuals to adopt and embrace technological advancements.

8. If an organization implements too many KPIs, those in charge of managing and achieving these KPIs may be overwhelmed or lost in a sea of goals. Setting a smaller number of KPIs allows managers to focus efforts more directly on what will bring the most value to the organization. Most organizations identify between 10 and 20 KPIs divided among the four dimensions of the balanced scorecard, but this number is tied directly to the overall number of strategic goals.

9. The following are likely strategic goals and relevant KPIs for Airbnb. (Other correct answers are possible.)

   a. Customer

      i. Strategic goal: Create customer trust.

      ii. KPI: Increase customer satisfaction survey scores.

   b. Financial

      i. Strategic goal: Increase shareholder value.

      ii. KPI: Increase net income, leading to larger shareholder value.

   c. Internal processes

      i. Strategic goal: Increase brand loyalty of hosts.

      ii. KPI: Increase host survey satisfaction through app and website updates and modifications.

   d. Learning and growth

      i. Strategic goal: Retain hosts and increase host loyalty.

      ii. KPI: Increase host outreach and provide homeowner training, tips, and tricks.

10. Benefits of a balanced scorecard include:

- Organizational alignment: By implementing a balanced scorecard effectively, the organization is able to better align employees' and managers' efforts to achieve the goals that the organization has set.
- Focused efforts by managers: Managers are asked to focus on many things in their day-to-day operations. A balanced scorecard provides them with specific goals and KPIs. Based on these goals and KPIs, managers can focus their efforts to achieve the organization's most important goals.
- Broadened organizational focus: Using a balanced scorecard, high-level management can more easily identify the organization's various stakeholders and carefully consider the impacts of each business decision on each type of stakeholder. Having a broader view also allows the organization to identify new areas of opportunity and future growth by identifying potential customers and upcoming changes in trends and forecasts.

- Forward-looking organization: A balanced scorecard helps an organization focus on the factors that promote the organization's longevity. By identifying upcoming challenges and opportunities, the organization can more effectively prepare today for what may come tomorrow.
- Evaluations and professional development: The balanced scorecard can help identify the skills that are important for employees to obtain and develop. The company can then focus training and development in these areas, creating longer-tenured employees and promoting a beneficial work environment.

11. Challenges for implementing the balanced scorecard include:

- Understanding the business: One main challenge in developing a balanced scorecard relates to understanding the organization. It is important to understand all aspects of a business and their various dimensions. Balanced scorecard goals and KPIs may not always provide the best results for all groups within an organization and may need to be modified for each group.
- Predicting future trends: Try as they might, organizations cannot foresee the future. They cannot always accurately predict the future and coming trends. Therefore, when creating forward-looking goals and KPIs, managers should allow for the possibility of revisions, as the circumstances in which the organization operates can change frequently.

12. Pros and cons of using the balanced scorecard for compensating employees include:

- Pros: One major benefit of using a balanced scorecard to compensate employees is the ease of use once the objectives are established. They provide a simple and objective method for management to evaluate and compensate those who have performed exceptionally.
- Cons: Compensating employees based on a balanced scorecard can be complicated and require significant consideration by management. Managers need to determine which factors are most relevant for employees to focus on and give more weight to these factors. This way, employees will be motivated to focus on the objectives that are most relevant to the company's success and growth.

13. Based on Exhibit 12.6, it appears the main factors that management will be concerned about are:

- Sales
- Gross revenue
- Customer retention

Management will be most concerned about the financial dimension, which is currently a "red" measure and has experienced a downward trend during the past month. Internal processes are also declining, but they are currently still at a "medium" status. The organization appears to be performing well in the learning and growth category.

Multiple-Choice Questions   Mc Graw Hill connect

1. (LO12.1) Which of the following does an organization use to articulate its purpose?
   a. Mission statement
   b. Vision statement
   c. Strategic goals
   d. Core values

2. (LO12.1) Which of the following might be a vision statement used by a fast-food chain?
   a. To make delicious food for everyone
   b. We put our customers and people first.
   c. To serve the needs of our people
   d. To be the world's best quick-service restaurant

3. (LO12.1) Which best describes the difference between an organization's mission and its vision?

   a. The mission guides the organization's employees; the vision guides the organization's managers.

   b. The mission focuses on the details; the vision focuses on the big picture.

   c. The mission describes the organization's purpose today; the vision describes the organization's purpose for the future.

   d. The mission is only communicated internally; the vision is communicated to all stakeholders.

4. (LO12.2) Which of the following is not one of the dimensions of the balanced scorecard?

   a. Internal process dimension

   b. Strategic dimension

   c. Learning and growth dimension

   d. Financial dimension

5. (LO12.2) Which of the following is a leading indicator of future performance?

   a. Return on assets

   b. Revenue growth

   c. Customer satisfaction

   d. Debt ratio

6. (LO12.2) Which of the following is not typically included in a balanced scorecard?

   a. Performance measures

   b. Strategic goals

   c. Organization's mission

   d. Employee compensation

7. (LO12.2) What is a leading performance indicator?

   a. An indicator that anticipates future performance

   b. An indicator that describes past performance

   c. An indicator that builds on another performance measure

   d. An indicator that describes an organization's goals

8. (LO12.2) Which of the following is an example of a lagging indicator?

   a. Customer service calls about hardware malfunctions

   b. Quarterly sales

   c. Number of customers renewing warranties

   d. Customer satisfaction scores

9. (LO12.2) Which of the following is not a benefit of the balanced scorecard?

   a. Focusing on long-term goals

   b. Increasing myopic decision making

   c. Aligning an organization's employees toward stated goals

   d. Facilitating communication, performance evaluations, and professional development

10. (LO12.3) Which of the following describes a strategy map?

    a. It is an illustration of who in the organization is responsible for each strategic goal.

    b. It is an illustration of the business processes used to fulfill strategic goals.

    c. It is an illustration of the causal links between strategic goals.

    d. It is an illustration of the organization's achievement of strategic goals.

11. (LO12.4) Which of the following KPIs would be used to measure financial performance at a retail organization such as **Target** or **Aldi**?
    a. Return on innovation investment
    b. Gross profit margin
    c. Market growth rate
    d. Conversion rate

12. (LO12.4) Which of the following KPIs would be used to evaluate success from the learning and growth dimension at a manufacturing organization?
    a. Six Sigma level
    b. Capacity utilization rate
    c. Market growth rate
    d. Employee engagement level

13. (LO12.4) Which of the following KPIs would be used to evaluate success from the customer dimension at a public accounting firm?
    a. Project schedule variance
    b. Time to market
    c. Market growth rate
    d. Employee engagement level

14. (LO12.4) Assume that one of the strategic goals at **Netflix** is to focus on quality movies, TV shows, and stand-up comedy. In 2022, Netflix reported annual revenue of over $31 billion. If Netflix is using a balanced scorecard, one of its KPIs related to the financial dimension could be to have revenue equal to or greater than $33 billion. Which one of the principles of effective KPIs does this KPI violate?
    a. Time-bound
    b. Achievable
    c. Specific
    d. Measurable

15. (LO12.4) Measures of employees' skills, expertise, and satisfaction are included in which of the balanced scorecard dimensions?
    a. Financial
    b. Internal processes
    c. Customer
    d. Learning and growth

16. (LO12.4) Measures of the efficiency with which goods are manufactured are included in which of the balanced scorecard dimensions?
    a. Financial
    b. Internal processes
    c. Customer
    d. Learning and growth

17. (LO12.4) Measures related to the costs associated with facilities maintenance are included in which of the balanced scorecard dimensions?
    a. Financial
    b. Internal processes
    c. Customer
    d. Learning and growth

18. (LO12.3) Which of the following summarizes the cause-and-effect relationships between an organization's strategic goals?
    a. The balanced scorecard
    b. Strategy maps
    c. Strategic goals
    d. Key performance indicators

19. (LO12.6) Which of the following types of data analysis can be used to determine which of an organization's leading indicators is associated with financial performance?

    a. Sensitivity analysis

    b. Correlation analysis

    c. SWOT analysis

    d. Regression analysis

20. (LO12.5) A sign of the successful implementation of a balanced scorecard is the presence of cause-and-effect relationships showing how performance in different dimensions of the organization impact financial performance. An example of this success for a hotel is meeting the target of:

    a. decreasing a customer's check-in time, which increases the number of implemented employee suggestions.

    b. increasing employee training hours, which increases employee compensation.

    c. increasing profit, which increases employee job satisfaction ratings.

    d. receiving more 5-star ratings from customers, which increases profit.

CMA

21. (LO12.5) An example of an item that would fall under the customer dimension on the balanced scorecard of an airline is

    a. customer complaints will decrease by 10%.

    b. bags will be unloaded and available to passengers no longer than 25 minutes after the plane has reached its destination.

    c. 90% of the flights will arrive on time.

    d. three new in-flight meals will replace existing offerings that are unpopular with customers.

CMA

Discussion Questions

1. (LO12.1) Look up the mission and vision statements for **Nike** (https://about.nike.com/). Develop four to eight strategic goals, at least one for each of the balanced scorecard dimensions.

2. (LO12.4) Based on the strategic goals for **Nike** you described in Discussion Question 1, identify two or three KPIs for each goal to create a balanced scorecard.

3. (LO12.3) Develop a strategy map for **Nike** based on the balanced scorecard you prepared in Discussion Question 1.

4. (LO12.1) Core values, mission statements, vision statements, and strategic goals aren't just for companies. You can develop them for yourself as well. Identify four of your core values, and write a mission statement and vision statement that best describe you. Create three to eight strategic goals that will help you achieve your mission and vision.

5. (LO12.4) Keeping in mind the strategic goals you created for yourself in Discussion Question 4, identify two KPIs to help you gauge whether you are meeting your goals in support of your personal mission.

6. (LO12.2) Assume you are in the cost accounting department at **On**, the rapidly growing running shoe company. You have been asked to prepare a presentation to management about whether to implement a balanced scorecard at the company. Include in your presentation:

    • A description of the key benefits of a balanced scorecard in general.

    • How it could be beneficial for On.

    • Examples of KPIs for each of the four dimensions that might be useful for On to incorporate in its balanced scorecard.

7. (LO12.2) **Hibo** produces energy drinks using hibiscus and natural flavors. Assume that the company has a strategic (financial) goal to increase its revenue mix. The company intends to implement a balanced scorecard. Describe two leading indicators in each of the customer, internal processes, and learning and growth dimensions that would be useful to include in the balanced scorecard.

8. (LO12.5) Describe how the use of visualization enhances or detracts from the usability of a balanced scorecard framework.

9. (LO12.5) Your company has recently implemented a balanced scorecard and hopes that it will help you (1) identify areas of improvement, (2) monitor progress toward strategic goals, (3) align company resources with its activities and initiatives, and (4) facilitate communication and collaboration among employees. Describe how a balanced scorecard can be an effective tool for achieving each of these goals.

10. (LO12.6) Use the AMPS model to describe how organizations use data analytics to develop and update their balanced scorecard.

11. (LO12.1) Why is it important for an organization's strategic goals to align with its mission and vision statements? What could go wrong if they are not aligned?

12. (LO12.1) Describe myopic decision making and explain how the use of a balanced scorecard helps to reduce this behavior.

ENVIRONMENTAL, SOCIAL, GOVERNANCE

13. (LO12.3) Because many different stakeholders have emphasized the importance of environmental, social, and governance factors, organizations often include some ESG goals in their strategic plan and frequently report their initiatives to the world. To what extent do an organization's ESG initiatives influence you as a consumer? An investor? An employee? Use examples of your experiences with specific companies, if possible.

DATA VISUALIZATION

14. (LO12.6) Review the following KPIs and related performance for Make Stuff, a fictitious manufacturing organization. How would you describe Make Stuff's performance over the past two years? What advice would you give to management for improving performance going forward?

KPI	Defintion	Goal	Target	12/31/2020	12/31/2021	Trend
Sales	Total sales per year	Above	$ 650,000	$ 487,000	$ 600,000	↑
Average order size	Average order size is the amount a customer typically spends on a single order.	Above	$ 35	$ 24	$ 28	↑
Cost of goods sold (COGS)	Average COGS for a single order.	Below	$ 28	$ 23	$ 26	↑
Gross profit	Gross Profit = Average Order Size – COGS	Above	$ 7	$ 1	$ 2	↑
Average margin	Average Margin = Gross Profit/Average Order Size	Above	20%	4%	7%	↑
Number of transactions	This is the total number of sales transactions.	Above	18500	12,500	16,000	↑
Conversion rate	The conversion rate is the rate at which users on ecommerce site are converting (or buying products). Calculated as the total number of visitors divided by the number of sales	Above	50%	30%	35%	↑
Shopping cart abandonment rate	The number of users that add products to their shopping cart but do not check out.	Below	15%	22%	17%	↓
Percent of repeat customers	Percent of customers who make more than one purchase.	Above	25%	19%	25%	↑
Total available market relative to a retailer's share of market	Percent of market share.	Above	25%	8%	11%	↑
Customer lifetime value (CLV)	How much the average customer is worth to your business over the course of their relationship with your brand.	Above	$ 140	$ 80	$ 110	↑
Customer acquisition cost (CAC) per customer	The amount the organization spends to acquire a new customer. Calculated as Total Marketing Spend/# of Customers	Below	$ 50	$ 56	$ 50	↓
Site traffic	Total number of visits to the website.	Above	40,000	33,259	41,143	↑
Time on site (in seconds)	Average number of seconds users spend on the website.	Above	180	76	123	↑
Bounce rate	The percent of users that exit the website after viewing only one page.	Below	14%	21%	15%	↓
Pageviews per visit	Pageviews per visit refers to the average number of pages a user will view on your site during each visit.	Above	3	1.20	1.70	↑
Texting subscribers	Newer to digital marketing than email, ecommerce brands can reach consumers through SMS-based marketing. Texting subscribers refers to the number of customers on your text message contact list.	Above	25,000	18,543	19,947	↑
Email open rate	This KPI tells you the percentage of subscribers that open your email.	Above	10%	3%	7%	↑
Email click-through rate (CTR)	Click-through rate tells you the percentage of those who actually clicked on a link after opening.	Above	45%	12%	12%	↔
Unsubscribes	Rate of unsubscribers to the email list.	Below	10%	23%	19%	↓
Number and quality of product reviews	Customer reviews of the products.	Above	30,000	14,250	24,783	↑
Customer satisfaction (CSAT) score	Average Customer Satisfaction Score (out of 5 stars)	Above	4.5	3.10	3.74	↑
Net promoter score (NPS)	Average Net Promotor Score for the year.	Above	9	6.70	7.20	↑
Overall equipment effectiveness (OEE)	OEE describes how well manufacturing equipment is performing.	Above	0.9	0.78	0.82	↑
Overall labor effectiveness (OLE)	OLE describes how productive the staff operating the machines are.	Above	0.9	0.65	0.77	↑
Number of noncompliance events or incidents	Number of reported violations of regulation or organizational policies.	Below	5	28	22	↓

15. (LO12.3) ESG reporting regulations are still evolving. As a result, there is risk that organizations will engage in greenwashing, the practice of conveying a false impression or providing misleading information about the environmental impact of the organization's operations. Research some companies that have been accused of greenwashing and describe the allegations. Explain how challenges related to data collection, verification, quantification, and standardization may have contributed to the company's alleged greenwashing.

ETHICS

Brief Exercises   connect

1. (LO12.5) Executives at **Hydroflask**, the water bottle company, could use the following dashboard to monitor the key performance indicators on their balanced scorecard. Which dimension requires the most immediate attention by management? Describe why management should focus on this dimension even though the company is performing at a high level on the financial dimension.

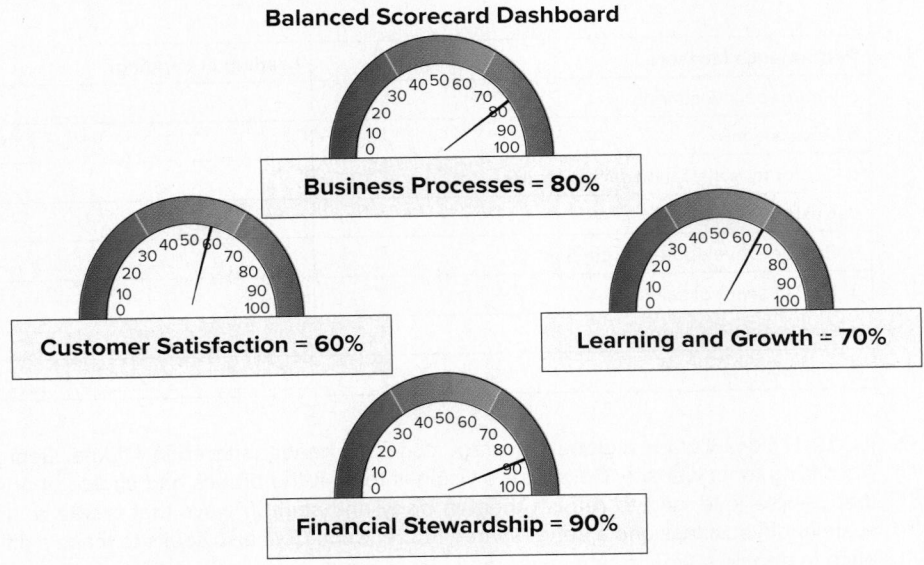

Balanced Scorecard Dashboard

Business Processes = 80%

Customer Satisfaction = 60%

Learning and Growth = 70%

Financial Stewardship = 90%

2. (LO12.2) Imagine that you have recently been hired by the City of Pawnee, Indiana, as a strategic business consultant. Tomorrow you will make a presentation to the city manager and the city council to recommend that they implement a balanced scorecard approach. Describe the benefits of the balanced scorecard and how it could help Pawnee achieve greatness. Include a description of the challenges that some organizations face when implementing a balanced scorecard and how Pawnee can overcome them.

3. (LO12.4) In 2016 **Wells Fargo** was fined approximately $185,000,000 for creating millions of fraudulent savings and checking accounts for existing customers without their consent. Unsuspecting customers were saddled with unexpected and unexplained fees, and they received unrequested debit cards, credit cards, and/or lines of credit. Employees alleged that they were encouraged to create these fraudulent accounts because one of the main KPIs used to measure their performance was "products per household," with a target of eight accounts or other banking products per customer household. This example illustrates why organizations must consider the potential for

ETHICS

employees to meet targets and goals through unethical means. How could Wells Fargo have designed a better KPI to diminish the likelihood that employees would commit fraud to meet their targets?

4. (LO12.3) While many companies have focused their initial ESG efforts on environmental impact, ESG also includes social goals and initiatives. Download **Boeing**'s 2022 Global Equity, Diversity & Inclusion Strategy and review its initiatives. For each of the nine goals, identify a performance measure that would allow Boeing to determine whether the company has achieved the goal.

5. (LO12.1) **Marucci Bats** specializes in producing baseball bats, apparel, and equipment. The company was started in the early 2000s by two former Major League Baseball players and their athletic trainer, handcrafting bats in their garage. Since then, it has captured one of the largest shares in the baseball bat market. Assume its core values are (1) making a commitment to quality, (2) displaying an authentic passion for baseball, (3) providing excellent customer service, (4) exhibiting strong teamwork, (5) developing the most innovative equipment and apparel, and (6) succeeding with integrity. Write a vision statement and mission statement for Marucci Bats based on those core values.

6. (LO12.2) Classify each of the following measures as either a leading indicator or a lagging indicator:

Performance Measure	Leading or Lagging?
a. Return on investment	
b. Revenue mix	
c. Customer satisfaction survey results	
d. Customer retention	
e. Product development cycle time	
f. Market share of sales	
g. Employee goal alignment	
h. Employee satisfaction	

7. (LO12.1) **Coca-Cola** is a global beverage company headquartered in Atlanta, Georgia. According to its website, Coca-Cola's vision is to craft the brands and choice of drinks that people love, and to refresh them in body and spirit in ways that create a more sustainable business and a better shared future. Coca-Cola also seeks to make a difference in people's lives, communities, and planet Earth.

Based on its vision statement, what are four core values that Coca-Cola is likely to have?

8. (LO12.2) **Crumbl Cookie** is a chain of cookie shops that offer a rotating menu of freshly baked cookies. Assume Crumbl Cookie has a goal of increasing monthly sales for each region. For each balanced scorecard dimension, identify and describe a leading indicator and a lagging indicator that could provide information about the likelihood of success in achieving this goal.

Balanced Scorecard Dimension	Leading Indicator	Lagging Indicator
Financial		
Customer		
Internal processes		
Learning and growth		

9. (LO12.4) Assume **Audi**, the car manufacturer, monitors the following list of KPIs. Classify each KPI in the appropriate balanced scorecard dimension.

KPI	Balanced Scorecard Dimension (Financial, Customer, Internal Processes, or Learning and Growth)
a. Warranty claims rate	
b. Revenue growth percentage	
c. Customer satisfaction rate	
d. Market share percentage	
e. Product development cycle time	
f. Cost reduction percentage	
g. Environmental impact reduction percentage	
h. Employee satisfaction rate	
i. Return on investment (ROI)	
j. Number of complaints received	
k. Gross profit margin	
l. Net profit margin	
m. Adoption rate of new technologies	
n. Employee retention rate	
o. Net promoter score (NPS)	
p. Innovation rate (number of new products/services introduced)	
q. Training and development hours per employee	
r. Production efficiency rate	
s. Quality control measures	
t. Customer retention rate	

10. (LO12.6) **Havertys Furniture** has strategic goals to grow market share and increase revenues. Havertys uses a balanced scorecard and has included product quality ratings from customers as a KPI related to internal processes. The goal is for quality ratings to exceed 4.5.

You have been given an Excel file, labeled **BriefExercise10.xlsx**, that contains the ratings for 255 unique products. The data dictionary is as follows:

Attribute	Description
Product ID	Unique product identifier
Category	Category of furniture
Price	Average price
Average Rating	Average rating by customers for product
Qty_Ratings	Number of ratings received for product

a. Use the Excel file to perform an analysis to determine whether Havertys has met its product-quality goal.

b. Prepare a pivot table to report the average rating per category. (Round the PivotTable values to 2 decimal places.)

c. Provide an explanation to management to provide insights on Havertys' achievement (or nonachievement) of its product-quality goal.

DATA VISUALIZATION

11. (LO12.6) **Havertys Furniture** has strategic goals to grow market share and increase revenues. Havertys uses a balanced scorecard and has included product quality ratings from customers as a KPI related to internal processes. The goal is for quality ratings to exceed 4.5.

You have been given an Excel File, labeled **BriefExercise11.xlsx**, that contains the ratings for 255 unique products. The data dictionary is as follows:

Attribute	Description
Product ID	Unique product identifier
Category	Category of furniture
Price	Average price
Average Rating	Average rating by customers for product
Qty_Ratings	Number of ratings received for product

a. Import the Excel file to Tableau to perform an analysis to determine whether Havertys has met its product-quality goal.

b. Prepare a column chart visualization to report the average rating per category.
1. Show the average rating per category as data labels on the chart.
2. Sort the columns from highest to lowest rating.
3. Add a constant line (at 4.5) to reflect Havertys' KPI goal for product quality. This line will allow you to see which products are helping or hurting the company's ability to achieve the goal.

c. Provide insights to management on Havertys' achievement (or nonachievement) of its product-quality goal.

12. (LO12.6) Assume Epicurean Essentials sells high-end cooking products like pots and pans, knives, etc. The company's strategic goals include growing market share and increasing revenues. Epicurean Essentials uses a balanced scorecard and has included product quality ratings from customers as a KPI related to internal processes. The goal is for quality ratings to exceed 4.0.

You have been given an Excel File, labeled **BriefExercise12.xlsx**, that contains the ratings for 255 unique products. The data dictionary is as follows:

Attribute	Description
Product ID	Unique product identifier
Category	Category of kitchen tool
Price	Average price
Average Rating	Average rating by customers for product
Qty_Ratings	Number of ratings received for product

a. Import the Excel file into Power BI to perform an analysis to determine whether Epicurean Essentials has met its product-quality goal.

b. Prepare a column chart visualization to report the average rating per category.
1. Show the average rating per category as data labels on the chart.
2. Sort the columns from highest to lowest rating.
3. Add a constant line (at 4.0) to reflect Epicurean's KPI goal for product quality. This line will allow you to see which products are helping or hurting the company's ability to achieve the goal.
4. Add an average line to display the overall average product-quality ratings for the company.

c. Provide insights to management on the company's achievement (or nonachievement) of its product-quality goal.

13. **(LO12.4) Shield Insurance Company** currently uses the following KPIs in its balanced scorecard:

BSC Dimension	KPI	KPI Description
Financial	Net income	Financial measure of the difference between revenue and COGS
Customer	Customer retention rate	Percentage of customers that are retained from previous quarters
Customer	Customer satisfaction score	Results of customer satisfaction survey (scale from 1 to 10)
Customer	Net promoter score (NPS)	Results of net promoter score survey (scale from 1 to 10)
Internal processes	Claims settlement rate	Percentage of insurance claims settled during the period
Internal processes	Market share of new products	Percentage of market share for new products rolled out
Learning and growth	Employee retention rate	Percentage of employees staying with the company each quarter
Learning and growth	Employee engagement score	Results of an employee satisfaction survey (scale from 1 to 10)

The cost accounting team at Shield Insurance is interested to learn whether the various customer, internal processes, and learning and growth KPIs predict financial performance, so they used regression analysis, which yielded the following output.

SUMMARY OUTPUT

Regression Statistics	
Multiple R	0.993793203
R Square	0.98762493
Adjusted R Square	0.944312183
Standard Error	64046.4544
Observations	10

ANOVA

	df	SS	MS	F	Significance F
Regression	7	6.547E+11	9.353E+10	2.280E+01	0.043
Residual	2	8.204E+09	4.102E+09		
Total	9	6.629E+11			

	Coefficients	Standard Error	t Stat	P-value	Lower 95%	Upper 95%
Intercept	17282122.82	3217160.09	5.37	0.03	3439800.17	31124445.47
Customer retention rate	13241310.12	3948868.60	3.35	0.08	−3749300.17	30231920.40
Customer satisfaction score	−1648748.02	569821.39	−2.89	0.10	−4100491.57	802995.54
Net promoter score	−1700519.05	291939.76	−5.82	0.03	−2956634.46	−444403.65
Claims settlement rate	−1032504.30	524296.93	−1.97	0.19	−3288371.90	1223363.30
Employee retention rate	−979211.67	735105.66	−1.33	0.31	−4142116.06	2183692.72
Employee engagement score	292793.98	48077.83	6.09	0.03	85931.75	499656.21
Market share of new products	5977669.67	1069959.54	5.59	0.03	1374005.33	10581334.01

Microsoft Excel

Review the output and explain which KPIs provide insights that are useful for predicting financial performance. Explain how you arrived at your conclusions.

14. **(LO12.5) Carmichael Industrial Products** manufactures pumps, valves, and other component parts. It sells to downstream manufacturers around the globe. Carmichael is implementing a strategy map and balanced scorecard. Its strategies for each dimension are shown below, but the company has not yet identified the cause-and-effect relationships among the different strategies.

		Financial
Financial	Increase Market Share in New Segments	Increase Profits	Reduce Costs
Customer	Foster Customer Loyalty	Personalized Customer Experience	Leverage Customer Data
Internal Processes	Expand Product Offerings	Growth through Mergers and Acquisitions	Gain Efficiencies through Automation	Become Industry Leader in Sustainability
Learning and Growth	Strengthen Employee Expertise	Develop Servant Leaders	Establish a Strong Mentorship Culture	Continuous Improvement and Innovation

For each strategy, identify the direct cause-and-effect relationship(s) that follow.

- If a strategy leads to multiple direct effects, list all of the effects. Note that the items in the "Cause" column can also be effects.
- If a strategy has no direct effects, leave the "Effect" column blank.

The first answer is provided for you: An increase in market share in new markets has the effect of increasing profits (B).

	Cause	Effect
A	Increase market share in new segments	B
B	Increase profits	
C	Reduce costs	
D	Foster customer loyalty	
E	Personalized customer experience	
F	Leverage customer data	
G	Expand product offerings	
H	Growth through merger and acquisition	
I	Gain efficiencies through automation	
J	Become industry leader in sustainability	
K	Strengthen employee expertise	
L	Develop servant leaders	
M	Establish a strong mentorship culture	
N	Continuous improvement and innovation	

15. (LO12.1) In recent years, many companies have tried to implement ESG strategies as part of their business.

   a. Why is it important to align new ESG strategies with the company's mission statement and core values?

   b. Imagine that you are a consultant that has been hired by Big Soda, a fictional beverage company. Big Soda's current mission statement is "To maximize shareholder value by achieving strong financial performance and growth, while maintaining a competitive edge in our market and being every family's favorite beverage." However, the company has decided to revise this statement in light of some recent ESG strategies it has implemented, including reducing its carbon footprint, improving access to clean water, promoting a diverse and inclusive workforce, and encouraging a healthy lifestyle. Write a new mission statement that incorporates Big Soda's strategic goals related to ESG in addition to its financial and market-focused goals.

ENVIRONMENTAL, SOCIAL, GOVERNANCE

Problems [Mc Graw Hill] connect

1. (LO12.4) **Shein** is an online fashion retailer that sells direct to customers and focuses on "fast fashion" at an accessible price. Assume Shein is just starting to implement a balanced scorecard and has identified the following KPIs as potentially relevant. Match each KPI with the balanced scorecard dimension to which it relates. The first answer in each category is provided. (Note that these KPIs do not fit the SMART criteria. Problem 2 asks you to rewrite the KPIs to make them SMART.)

Dimension	KPI
Financial **o—ROI**	a. Average order price b. Average response time c. Churn rate (rate at which customers stop doing business with the organization) d. Customer acquisition rate
Customer **e—Customer satisfaction**	e. Customer satisfaction f. Employee diversity rate g. Earnings per share h. Employee participation
Internal processes **j—Equipment effectiveness**	i. Employee satisfaction j. Equipment effectiveness k. Gross profit margin l. Health promotion
Learning and growth **i—Employee satisfaction**	m. Inventory turnover n. Machine setup o. Return on investment (ROI) p. Website traffic

2. (LO12.4) Rewrite the KPIs for **Shein** listed in Problem 1 using the SMART framework. The first answer is provided for you.

Original KPI	SMART KPI
a. Average order price	Average order price is $70 by fiscal year-end.
b. Average response time	
c. Churn rate	
d. Customer acquisition rate	
e. Customer satisfaction	
f. Employee diversity rate	
g. Earnings per share	
h. Employee participation	
i. Employee satisfaction	
j. Equipment effectiveness	
k. Gross profit margin	
l. Health promotion	
m. Inventory turnover	
n. Machine setup	
o. Return on investment (ROI)	
p. Website traffic	

3. (LO12.6) You work on the cost accounting team for Snack-Attack, a (fictitious) company that produces gourmet snack chips. You conducted a regression analysis to determine whether your current set of leading indicators is associated with revenue. The analysis yielded the following result:

SUMMARY OUTPUT

Regression Statistics	
Multiple R	0.895433
R Square	0.801801
Adjusted R Square	0.702701
Standard Error	118383.2
Observations	16

ANOVA

	df	SS	MS	F	Significance F
Regression	5	5.67E+11	1.13E+11	8.090851	0.002737837
Residual	10	1.4E+11	1.4E+10		
Total	15	7.07E+11			

	Coefficients	Standard Error	t Stat	P-value	Lower 95%	Upper 95%
Intercept	668099.88	682406.47	0.98	0.35	−852396.49	2188596.24
Customer Satisfaction	0.23	0.11	2.18	0.05	−0.01	0.47
Employee Training	16328.47	7516.23	2.17	0.05	−418.72	33075.66
Employee Turnover	−3785.35	10761.44	−0.35	0.73	−27763.33	20192.62
Machine Downtime	−41347.63	18005.81	−2.30	0.04	−81467.07	−1228.18
Product Quality Score	−39661.12	163849.06	−0.24	0.81	−404739.57	325417.33

Use these results to answer the following questions:

a. Overall, is this model significant?

b. What statistic do you use to determine overall model significance?

c. What does it mean if this model is significant overall?

d. How much of the variation in revenue is explained by this set of KPIs?

e. Which of the KPIs are significantly associated with revenue?

f. Does the sign of the relationship for each KPI make sense? If not, explain.

g. Identify the balanced scorecard dimension to which each of the KPIs in the model relates.

4. (LO12.3) **Apex Athleisure** is an online athletic apparel company that has developed the following strategy map.

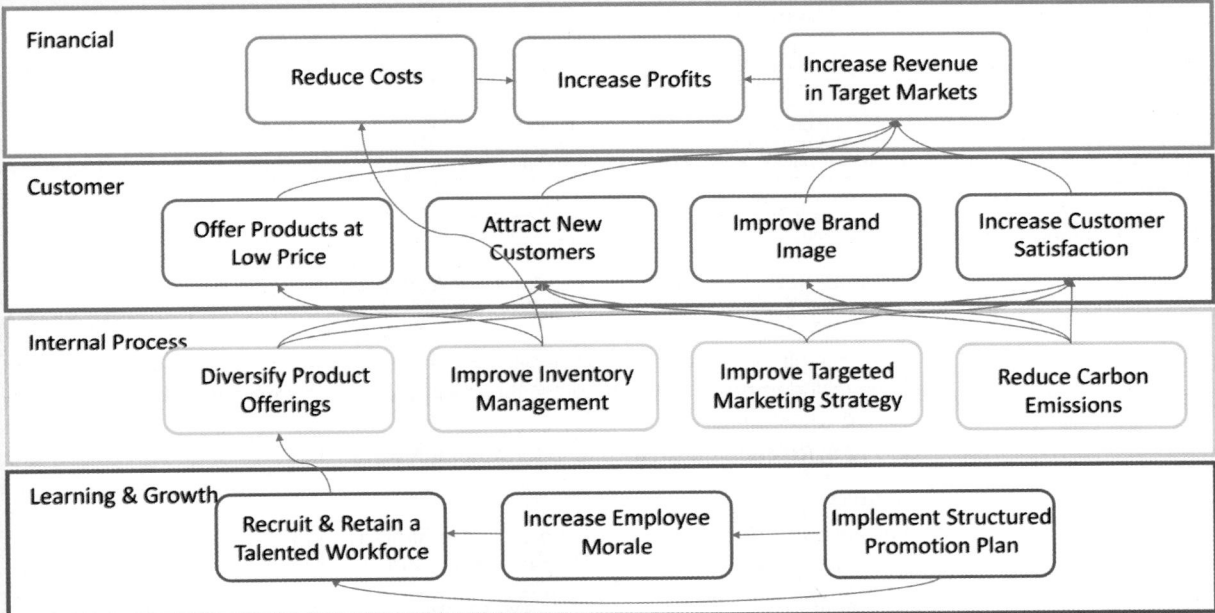

Required

The arrows represent the anticipated relationships among the different strategic goals. Assume you are a management accountant for Apex and the CEO has asked you to assess these relationships. For each relationship, indicate whether the predicted relationship is likely, unlikely, or uncertain and provide an explanation for your response. The first answer is provided for you.

Relationship	Likely, Unlikely, or Uncertain?	Explanation
a. A structured promotion plan will increase employee morale.	Likely	Employees will appreciate the clarity of their career path and will have a good idea of what steps they must complete to achieve their personal goals.
b. A structured promotion plan will increase employee recruitment and retention.		
c. Increased employee morale will improve employee recruitment and retention.		

Relationship	Likely, Unlikely, or Uncertain?	Explanation
d. Recruiting and retaining a talented workforce will improve product diversification.		
e. Diverse product offerings will help attract new customers.		
f. Diverse product offerings will increase customer satisfaction.		
g. Improved inventory management will lower product prices to customers.		
h. Improved inventory management will reduce overall costs.		
i. Improved targeted marketing strategy will attract new customers.		
j. Improved targeted marketing strategy will increase customer satisfaction.		
k. Reducing carbon emissions will increase customer satisfaction.		
l. Reducing carbon emissions will improve the brand image.		
m. Reducing carbon emissions will attract new customers.		
n. Offering products at a low price will increase revenue in target markets.		
o. Attracting customers will increase revenue in target markets.		
p. Improving the brand image will increase revenue in target markets.		
q. Increasing customer satisfaction will increase revenue in target markets.		
r. Increasing revenue in target markets will increase profits.		
s. Reducing costs will increase profits.		

5. (LO12.3) Refer to the strategy map for **Apex Athleisure in** Problem 4.

   Required

   Determine if there are any relationships among strategic goals that management should have included but did not. If so, list them and provide an explanation for your hypothesized relationship(s).

6. (LO12.5) Refer to the strategy map for **Apex Athleisure** in Problem 4.

   Required

   For each of the strategic goals shown in the strategy map, provide a SMART KPI and describe the data you could use to measure the KPI. (The first answer is provided for you.)

Strategic Goal	SMART KPI	Potential Data
a. Reduce costs	Reduce production and distribution costs by 5% by the end of the year.	Cost data from the FRS
b. Increase profits		
c. Increase revenue in target markets		
d. Offer products at low prices		
e. Attract new customers		
f. Improve brand image		
g. Increase customer satisfaction		
h. Diversify product offerings		
i. Improve inventory management		
j. Improve targeted marketing strategy		
k. Reduce carbon emissions		
l. Recruit and retain a talented workforce		
m. Increase employee morale		
n. Implement structured promotion plan		

7. (LO12.5) **Carmichael Industrial Products** manufactures pumps, valves, and other component parts. It sells to downstream manufacturers around the globe. Carmichael is

implementing a strategy map and balanced scorecard. Its strategies for each dimension are shown below.

Financial	Increase Market Share in New Segments	Increase Profits	Reduce Costs	

Customer	Foster Customer Loyalty	Personalized Customer Experience	Leverage Customer Data

Internal Processes	Expand Product Offerings	Growth through Mergers and Acquisitions	Gain Efficiencies through Automation	Become Industry Leader in Sustainability

Learning and Growth	Strengthen Employee Expertise	Develop Servant Leaders	Establish a Strong Mentorship Culture	Continuous Improvement and Innovation

Required

For each strategy listed in the strategy map, identify a smart KPI that Carmichael could use to evaluate performance. (The first answer is provided for you.)

Strategy	Smart KPI
a. Increase profits	Increase profits 5% from the previous quarter
b. Increase market share in new segments	
c. Reduce costs	
d. Foster customer loyalty	
e. Personalized customer experience	
f. Leverage customer data	
g. Expand product offerings	
h. Growth through mergers and acquisitions	
i. Gain efficiencies through automation	
j. Become leader in sustainability	
k. Strengthen employee expertise	
l. Develop servant leaders	
m. Establish a strong mentorship culture	
n. Continuous improvement and innovation	

8. (LO12.2) **EcoPet** has been in business for five years and has established itself as a leading retailer in the eco-friendly pet products and natural pet foods space. The company operates a chain of 105 stores across the country, with a focus on selling products that are environmentally friendly and sustainably sourced. EcoPet sources its products from a variety of local and international suppliers who meet its standards for eco-friendliness and sustainability.

EcoPet's mission statement is: "At EcoPet, we believe that pets are important members of our families, so our mission is to provide pet owners with eco-friendly and sustainable products that promote the health and happiness of their pets while also protecting our planet."

Required

Prepare a strategy map and balanced scorecard with SMART KPIs for EcoPet. Include at least 3 strategies for each dimension.

9. (LO12.6) **Magic Spoon** is a company that produces healthy alternatives to your favorite cereals. Most of Magic Spoon's customers order cereal through its online store.

Assume the company has recently implemented a balanced scorecard to track its performance and made the following observations:

- One of Magic Spoon's KPIs for internal processes is "average order fulfillment time." The company has set a target of 2 days for this KPI, but the actual average order fulfillment time is currently 3.5 days. The company wants to improve its order fulfillment time to meet its target and improve customer satisfaction.

- One of Magic Spoon's KPIs for the customer perspective is the net promoter score (NPS). In recent months, NPS has been declining, and the company wants to understand the reasons behind this trend and take corrective action.

Required

Describe how Magic Spoon might take action to improve performance on the dimensions described above. What data would be necessary to effectively identify problems and initiate solutions?

10. (LO12.6) The balanced scorecard framework relies on accurate, relevant, and timely data to measure and monitor an organization's performance.

Required

Explain how using inaccurate or irrelevant data can undermine the effectiveness of a balanced scorecard.

11. (LO12.1) Review the following description of **GameX**:

GameX is a video game development company that produces high-quality video games for a range of platforms, including consoles, PCs, and mobile devices. The company was founded in 2010 by a group of gamers who dropped out of the computer science program at a prominent university. Their goal was to create engaging and innovative video games that will entertain and challenge players around the world.

GameX produces action, adventure, role-playing, simulation, and strategy games. Its most popular game is *Galaxy Warriors*, a science-fiction action game with fast-paced combat, immersive storytelling, and collaborative strategy. GameX's target market includes players of all ages, and its games appeal to a wide range of players, from casual to hardcore gamers, of varying ages. The company's marketing strategy focuses on building a strong brand identity through social media and community engagement. The company leverages popular social media platforms such as TikTok, Instagram, and Facebook to showcase its latest games, engage with fans, and generate excitement around upcoming releases. GameX also partners with popular gaming influencers and content creators to promote its games and reach a wider audience.

GameX has an organizational culture that emphasizes collaboration, creativity, and innovation. The company's development team is divided into smaller groups that work on specific games. Each group is led by a project manager who oversees the development process and ensures that the game meets the company's quality standards. The company also has a marketing team that focuses on promoting and distributing the games, as well as a customer support team that provides assistance to players who encounter issues while playing the games.

GameX values creativity, innovation, and collaboration. The founder, Skyler Wilkins, has told stakeholders, "The best video games are created when they have input from everyone—developers, artists, and players."

Required

Prepare the following for GameX:

a. A vision statement
b. A mission statement
c. Identify 2 strategic goals and an associated SMART KPI for each BSC dimension.

Lab 12.1 Excel

Tracking Key Performance Indicators (KPIs)

Data Analytics Type: Descriptive Analytics

Lab Note: The tools presented in this lab periodically change. Updated instructions, if applicable, can be found in the student and instructor support materials.

Keywords

KPI, Excel

Decision-Making Context

Dan-O's Seasoning manufactures and sells all-natural, low-sodium seasonings online and in retail stores. Dan-O's managers have just established a long list of KPIs that they would like to monitor, and you have been assigned to develop a spreadsheet to track them. You have decided that you can add some conditional formatting to an Excel spreadsheet to really make it obvious where Dan-O's is meeting expectations and where it is missing the mark.

Required

1. Apply conditional formatting to the 2020 and 2021 performance data in the Excel file to indicate whether performance was meeting the targets for each performance measure.
2. Add a column to indicate whether the performance was trending up or down across the two periods.

Ask the Question

For which KPIs is Dan-O's missing its performance targets? How is Dan-O's performance trending over time?

Data Dictionary

Worksheet Tab/Table	Attribute Name	Description	Data Type
KPI Tracker	KPI	Key performance indicator. Each row represents a different KPI.	Text
KPI Tracker	Definition	Description of KPI	Text
KPI Tracker	Goal	Indicates whether the company wants performance to be above or below this KPI	Text
KPI Tracker	Target	KPI value to compare to performance	Numerical
KPI Tracker	12/31/2020	Performance related to this KPI in 2020	Numerical
KPI Tracker	12/31/2021	Performance related to this KPI in 2021	Numerical

Master the Data

For this lab you will use data in the Excel file titled **Lab 12.1 Data.xlsx**. This data file provides the list of Dan-O's KPIs, their definitions, and the targets, as well as the company's performance for the years ended 12/31/2020 and 12/31/2021. The Data Dictionary below describes the data contained in the dataset.

Perform the Analysis

Analysis Task #1: Apply Conditional Formatting to Shade Cells Based on Performance Compared to Target for Each KPI

1. Highlight Column E, which includes the performance figures for 2020 (Lab Exhibit 12.1.1).

Lab Exhibit 12.1.1

Microsoft Excel

	D	E	F
1	**Target**	**12/31/2020**	**12/31/2021**
2	$ 650,000	$ 487,000	$ 600,000
3	$ 35	$ 24	$ 28
4	$ 28	$ 23	$ 26
5	$ 7	$ 1	$ 2
6	20%	4%	7%
7	18500	12,500	16,000

2. Click on the **Conditional Formatting** icon at the top of the screen (Lab Exhibit 12.1.2).

Lab Exhibit 12.1.2

Microsoft Excel

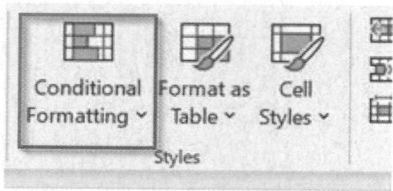

3. Select **New Rule...**, which opens the **New Formatting Rule** dialog box (Lab Exhibit 12.1.3).

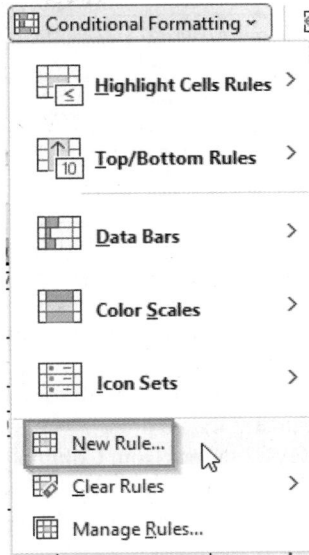

4. Select **Use a formula to determine which cells to format** (Lab Exhibit 12.1.4).

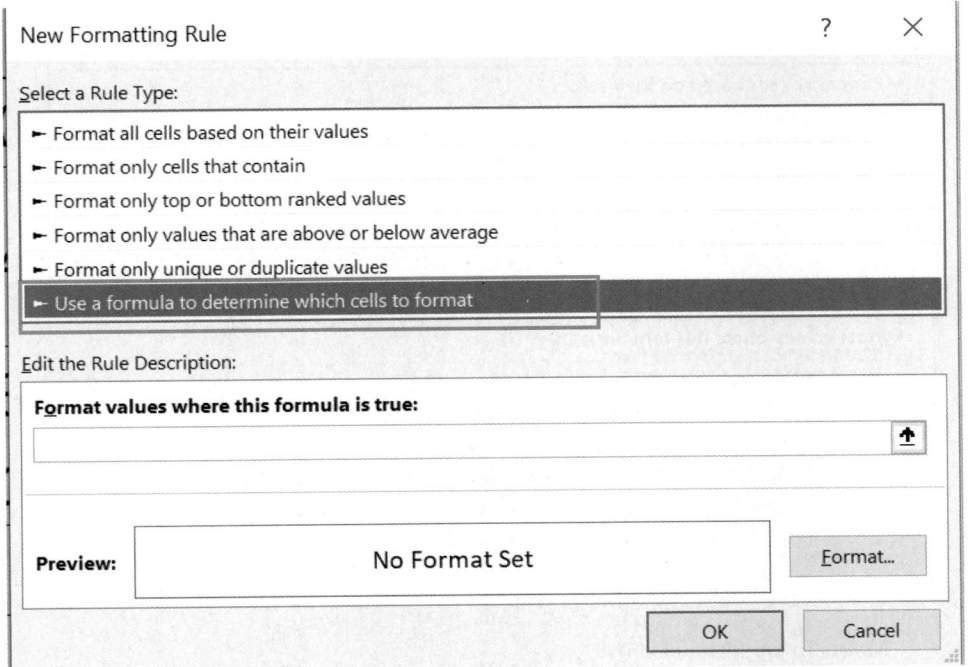

5. In the **Edit the Rule Description:** section (Lab Exhibit 12.1.5), enter a conditional formula (provided below) that will assign the conditional formatting based on several criteria:
   a. Whether the target is a minimum goal (performance should be Above that goal) or a maximum goal (performance should be Below that goal). This information is provided in Column C.
   b. The organization's performance compared to the target.

You will classify performance into three categories as follows:

	Goal (Relative to target)	And	Conditional Formatting
	From Column C	*Comparing Column D to Column E (for 2020) or Column F (for 2021)*	
1	Above	Performance >= Target	Green
2	Above	Performance < Target, but >= 75% of Target	Yellow
3	Above	Performance < 75% of Target	Red
4	Below	Performance <= Target	Green
5	Below	Performance > Target, but <= 1.25% of Target	Yellow
6	Below	Performance > 1.25% of Target	Red

Green is considered positive. Yellow is considered neutral (between 75% and 125% of target). Red is considered negative.

6. The first conditional format you will prepare will format the cells in Column E to have green fill and dark green text if:
   - The KPI should be "ABOVE" target (from Column C) and
   - 2020 Performance > Target (comparing Column E to Column D)

   The formula that achieves this is =AND($C1="Above",$E1>=$D1), as shown in Lab Exhibit 12.1.5.

Lab Exhibit 12.1.5

Microsoft Excel

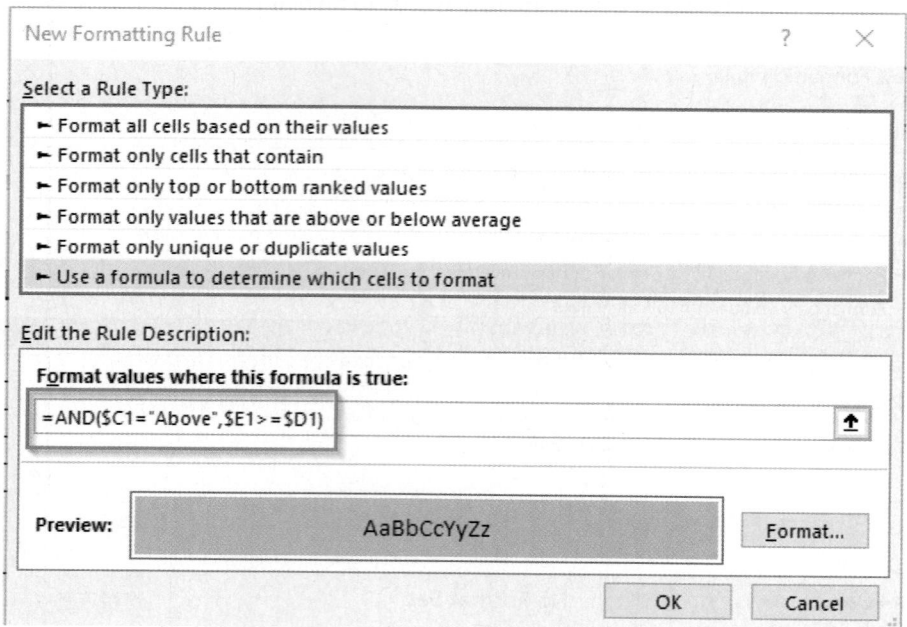

Notes: In the formula above,
- "Above" is in quotation marks because it is a text field.
- The "$" in front of the column labels locks the formula to refer only to the specified column (specifically, Columns C, E, and D in this formula) so that even if this formula is copied to another column, it will still refer to those specific columns.
- "And" indicates that you are testing multiple conditions. In this case, you are testing whether the goal of the KPI is to exceed the target (that is, is Above) and performance actually is above target.

7. To change the formatting to green fill with green text, click the **Format...** button (Lab Exhibit 12.1.6) and make the appropriate selections in the **Format Cells** dialog box (Lab Exhibit 12.1.7).

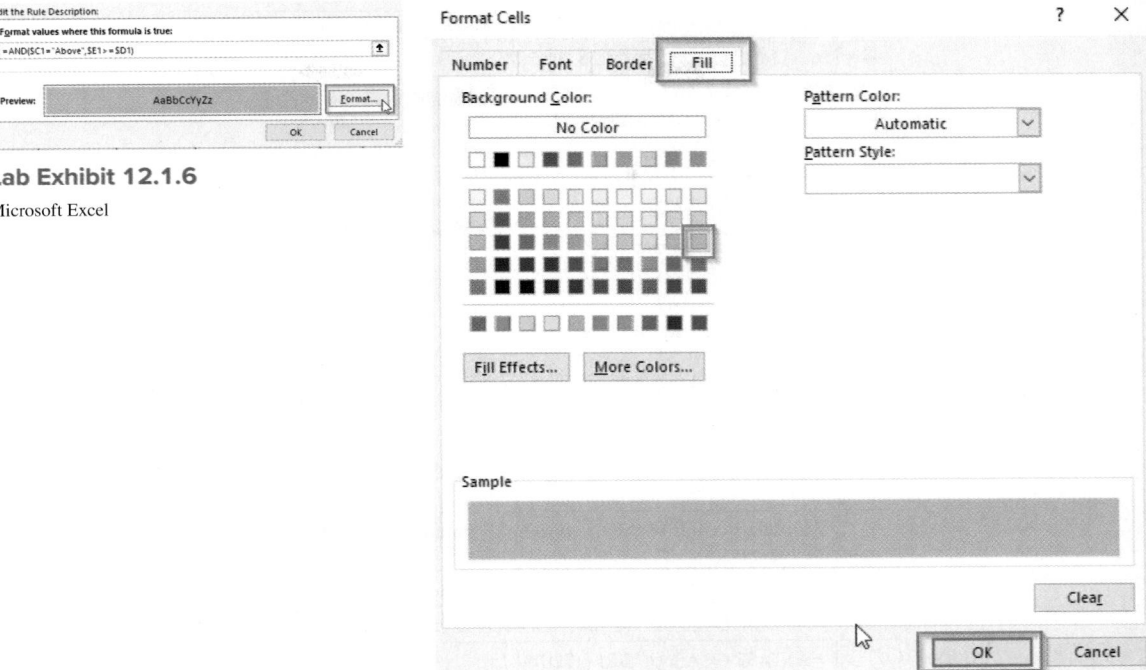

Lab Exhibit 12.1.6

Microsoft Excel

Lab Exhibit 12.1.7

Microsoft Excel

8. Now that you have completed the first conditional format, you can create the additional five conditional formats by using the **Manage Rules...** function in the **Conditional Formatting** dialog box.
   - Click on **Conditional Formatting** from the home tab again (as shown previously in Lab Exhibit 12.1.2), but this time select **Manage Rules...** (Lab Exhibit 12.1.8).

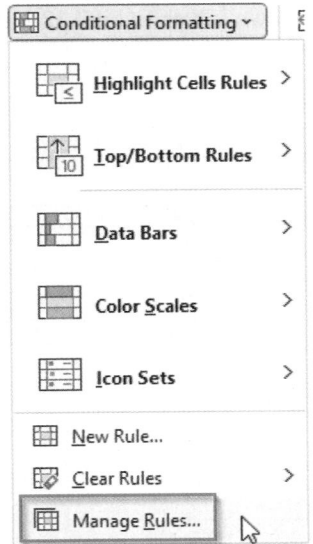

Lab Exhibit 12.1.8

Microsoft Excel

- Click on the **Duplicate Rule** button and edit the formulas as needed (Lab Exhibit 12.1.9).

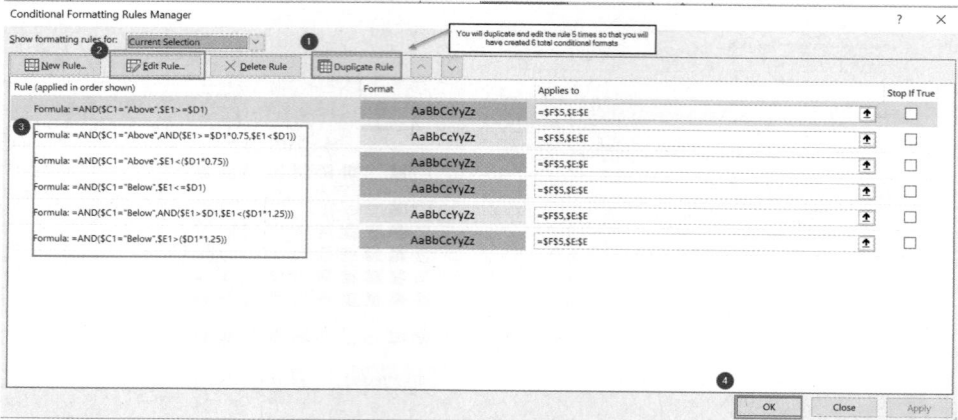

- The formulas that you will use (as shown in Lab Exhibit 12.1.9) are as follows:

	Formula to enter in the Conditional Formatting Rules Manager dialog box	Conditional Formatting
1	=AND($C1="Above",$E1>=$D1)) [from Step 6]	Green
2	=AND($C1="Above",AND($E1>=$D1*0.75,$E1<$D1))	Yellow
3	=AND($C1="Above",$E1<($D1*0.75))	Red
4	=AND($C1="Below",$E1<=$D1)	Green
5	=AND($C1="Below",AND($E1>$D1,$E1<($D1*1.125)))	Yellow
6	=AND($C1="Below",$E1>($D1*1.125))	Red

9. To assign conditional formatting to Column F, you will highlight Column F and then navigate to **Conditional Formatting** (as shown previously in Lab Exhibit 12.1.2), and once again select **Manage Rules...** (as shown in Lab Exhibit 12.1.8).
10. Again, you will duplicate and edit the rules you have previously created. When you edit the rules, you will be comparing 2021 performance (from Column F) to the target (from Column D) as shown in Lab Exhibit 12.1.10. Click **OK** when finished adding all 6 new conditional formats.

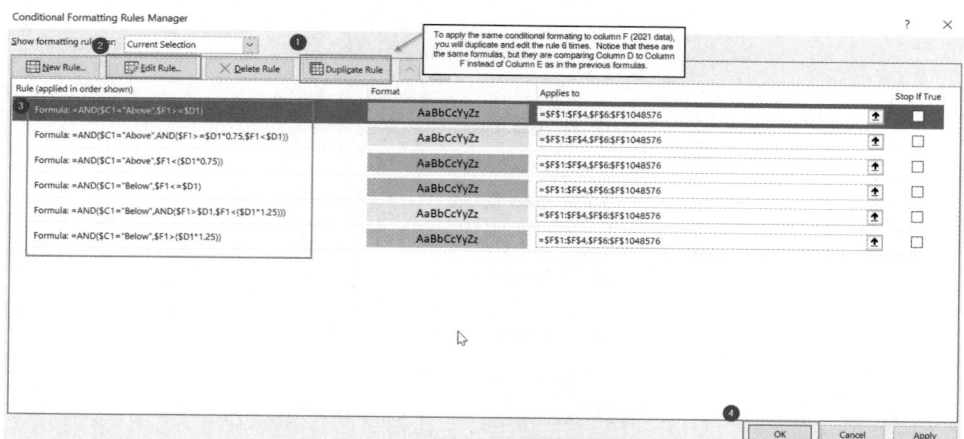

- The formulas that you will use (and are shown in Lab Exhibit 12.1.10) are as follows:

	Formula to enter in the Conditional Formatting Rules Manager dialog box	Conditional Formatting
1	=AND($C1="Above",$F1>=$D1))	Green
2	=AND($C1="Above",AND($F1>=$D1*0.75,$F1<$D1))	Yellow
3	=AND($C1="Above",$F1<($D1*0.75))	Red
4	=AND($C1="Below",$F1<=$D1)	Green
5	=AND($C1="Below",AND($F1>$D1,$F1<($D1*1.125)))	Yellow
6	=AND($C1="Below",$F1>($D1*1.125))	Red

11. Once you click **OK**, the spreadsheet will update. A sample of the formatted data is shown in Lab Exhibit 12.1.11.

	A KPI	B Defintion	C Goal	D Target	E 12/31/2020	F 12/31/2021
1	KPI	Defintion	Goal	Target	12/31/2020	12/31/2021
2	Sales	Total sales per year	Above	$ 650,000	$ 487,000	$ 600,000
3	Average order size	Average order size is the amount a customer typically spends on a single order.	Above	$ 35	$ 24	$ 28
4	Cost of goods sold (COGS)	Average COGS for a single order.	Below	$ 28	$ 23	$ 26
5	Gross profit	Gross Profit = Average Order Size - COGS	Above	$ 7	$ 1	$ 2
6	Average margin	Average Margin = Gross Profit/Average Order Size	Above	20%	4%	7%
7	Number of transactions	This is the total number of sales transactions.	Above	18500	12,500	16,000

Lab Exhibit 12.1.11

Microsoft Excel

Analysis Task #2: Add a Symbol to Show the Trend in Performance over Time for Each KPI

Excel has built-in indicator symbols (for example, arrows) that can be used for conditional formatting. However, these cannot be applied when comparing cells. They can be used only with actual numbers as thresholds. So, we are going to work around this limitation by using **Symbols**, **Special Characters**, and **Conditional Formatting**.

a. In Column G, label the column header "Trend" (Lab Exhibit 12.1.12).

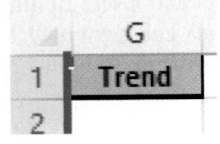

Lab Exhibit 12.1.12

Microsoft Excel

b. Create a generic if/then function that compares performance in 2021 to 2020. The formula is shown in Lab Exhibit 12.1.13: =IF(E2>D2,"x",IF(E2=D2,"y","z")).

Lab Exhibit 12.1.13

Microsoft Excel

MEDIAN	: ✕ ✓ fx	=IF(E2>D2,"x",IF(E2=D2,"y","z"))

	D Target	E 12/31/202	F 12/31/202	G Trend	H	I	J
1	Target	12/31/202	12/31/202	Trend			
2	$ 650,000	$ 487,000	$ 600,000	=IF(E2>D2,"x",IF(E2=D2,"y","z"))			
3	$ 35	$ 24	$ 28				

Note: We are going to replace the "x", "y", and "z" with arrows from the **Symbol** keyboard.

c. Click on a blank cell to the right of your new Column G. Then click on the **Symbol** icon on the **Insert** ribbon (Lab Exhibit 12.1.14).

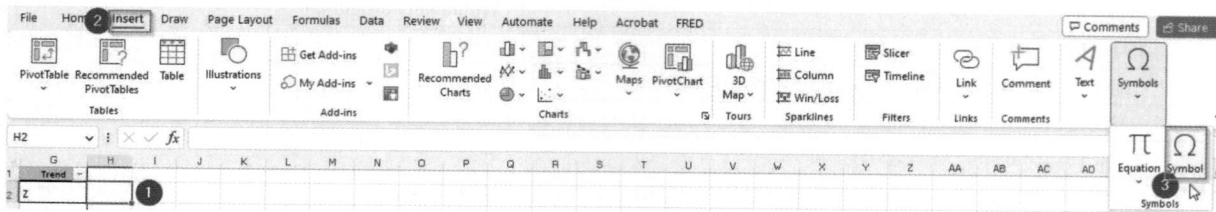

Lab Exhibit 12.1.14

Microsoft Excel

d. This action will bring up the special **Symbol** keyboard shown in Lab Exhibit 12.1.15. You may have to search for the arrows.

Lab Exhibit 12.1.15

Microsoft Excel

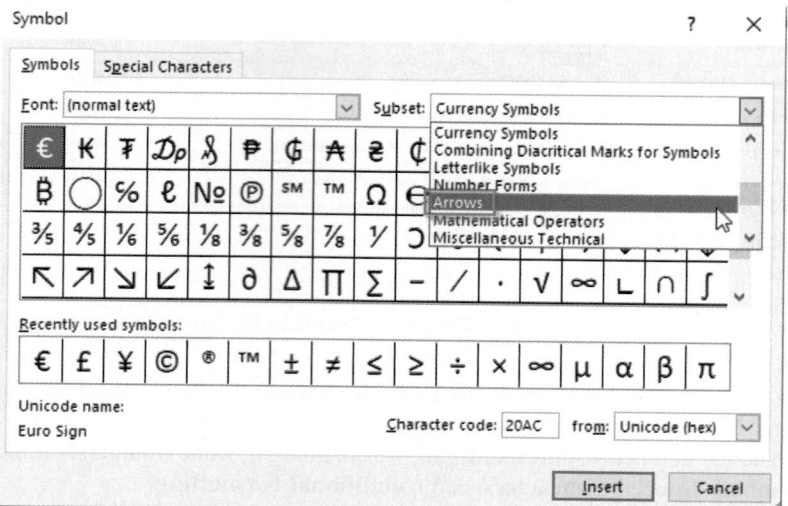

e. It will be easiest if you just select and insert all three of the arrows you will want to use in your formula into this blank cell right now, so select the up, down, and two-sided arrows and then click **Insert** (Lab Exhibit 12.1.16).

Lab Exhibit 12.1.16

Microsoft Excel

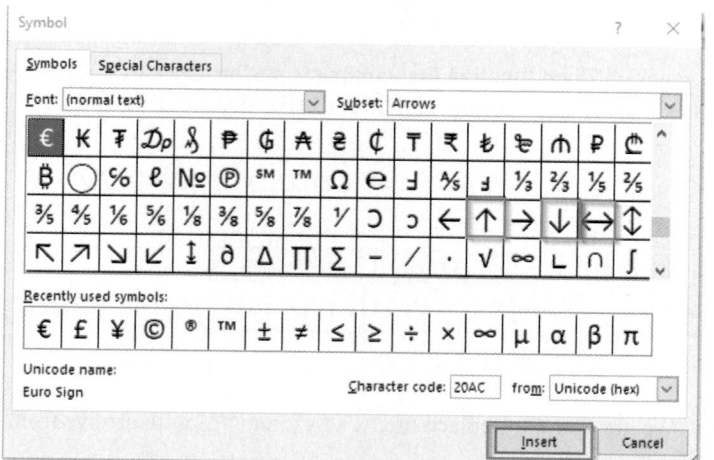

f. Now go back into your if/then formula and replace the "x" with the up arrow, the "y" with the two-sided arrow, and the "z" with the down arrow, using the formula shown in Lab Exhibit 12.1.17: =IF(E2>D2,"↑",IF(E2=D2,"↔","↓")).

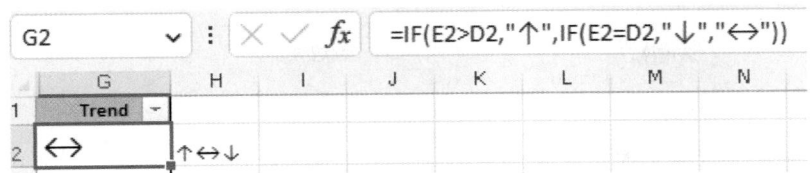

Lab Exhibit 12.1.17

Microsoft Excel

g. Now you can apply conditional formatting following similar logic to the previous analysis task. Create rules to make the down arrow Red, the up arrow Green, and the two-sided arrow Gray. Follow the steps as shown in Lab Exhibits 12.1.18 through 12.1.21). *Note:* For the neutral (two-sided) arrow, we use gray because it is easier to see than yellow font.

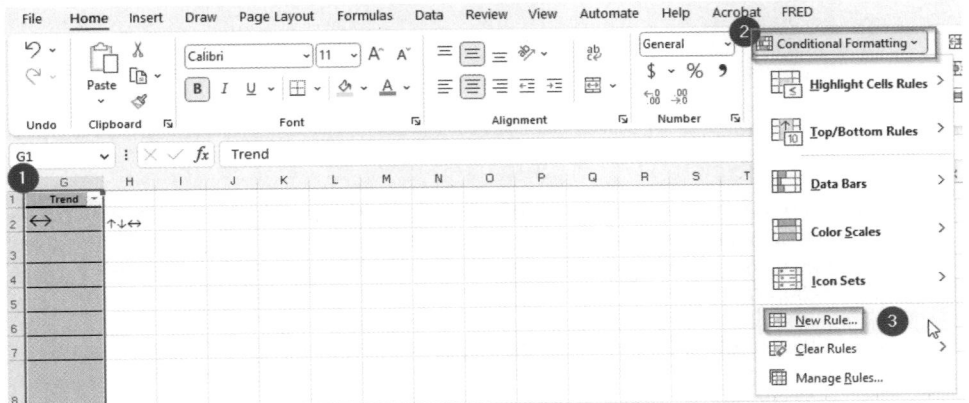

Lab Exhibit 12.1.18

Microsoft Excel

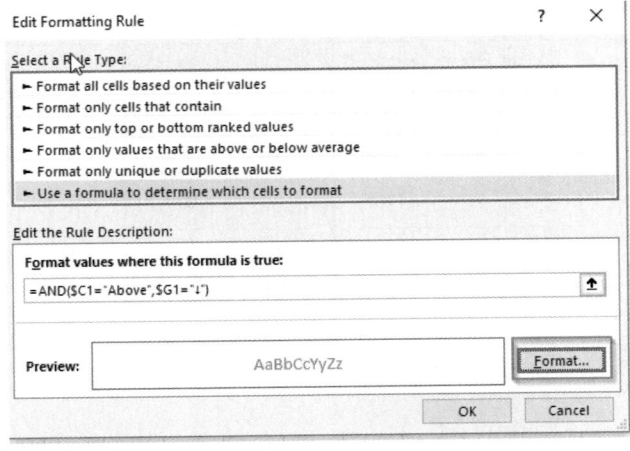

Lab Exhibit 12.1.19

Microsoft Excel

Lab Exhibit 12.1.20

Microsoft Excel

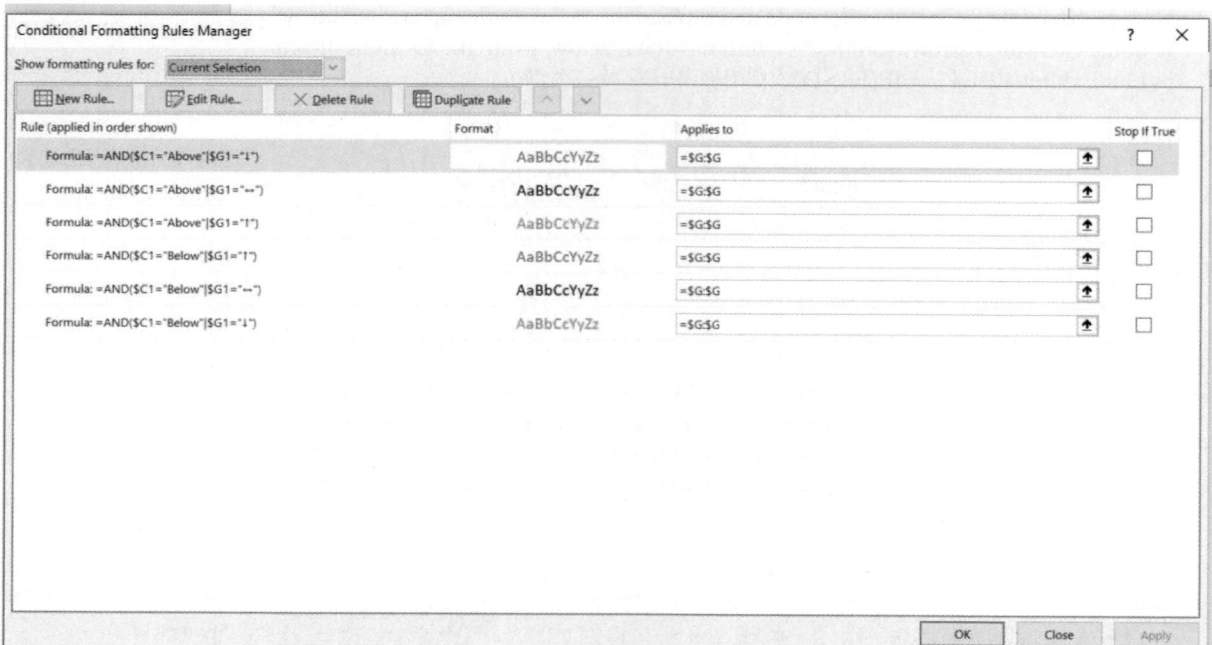

Lab Exhibit 12.1.21

Microsoft Excel

h. Notice that in the conditional formatting shown above, the color of the arrow depends on whether the goal is to exceed or stay below the target. This system allows us to see the trend in each KPI over time, and also to see whether that trend is desirable (green) or undesirable (red).

A sample of the conditionally formatted data is shown in Lab Exhibit 12.1.22.

	A	B	C	D	E	F	G
1	KPI	Defintion	Goal	Target	12/31/2020	12/31/2021	Trend
2	Sales	Total sales per year	Above	$ 650,000	$ 487,000	$ 600,000	↑
3	Average order size	Average order size is the amount a customer typically spends on a single order.	Above	$ 35	$ 24	$ 28	↑
4	Cost of goods sold (COGS)	Average COGS for a single order.	Below	$ 28	$ 23	$ 26	↑
5	Gross profit	Gross Profit = Average Order Size - COGS	Above	$ 7	$ 1	$ 2	↑
6	Average margin	Average Margin = Gross Profit/Average Order Size	Above	20%	4%	7%	↑
7	Number of transactions	This is the total number of sales transactions.	Above	18500	12,500	16,000	↑
8	Conversion rate	The conversion rate is the rate at which users on ecommerce site are converting (or buying products). Calculated as the total number of visitors divided by the number of sales	Above	50%	30%	35%	↑
9	Shopping cart abandonment rate	The number of users that add products to their shopping cart but not checking out.	Below	15%	22%	17%	↓
10	Percent of repeat customers	Percent of customers who make more than one purchase.	Above	25%	19%	25%	↑
11	Total available market relative to a retailer's share of market	Percent of market share.	Above	25%	8%	11%	↑
		How much the average customer is worth to your business over the					

Lab Exhibit 12.1.22

Microsoft Excel

Share the Story

DATA VISUALIZATION

Once you have applied all the conditional formatting, you have a spreadsheet resembling Lab Exhibit 12.1.23 that you can give to Dan-O's managers so they can track performance easily.

KPI	Defintion	Goal	Target	12/31/2020	12/31/2021	Trend
Sales	Total sales per year	Above	$ 650,000	$ 487,000	$ 600,000	↑
Average order size	Average order size is the amount a customer typically spends on a single order.	Above	$ 35	$ 24	$ 28	↑
Cost of goods sold (COGS)	Average COGS for a single order.	Below	$ 28	$ 23	$ 26	↑
Gross profit	Gross Profit = Average Order Size – COGS	Above	$ 7	$ 1	$ 2	↑
Average margin	Average Margin = Gross Profit/Average Order Size	Above	20%	4%	7%	↑
Number of transactions	This is the total number of sales transactions.	Above	18500	12,500	16,000	↑
Conversion rate	The conversion rate is the rate at which users on ecommerce site are converting (or buying products). Calculated as the total number of visitors divided by the number of sales	Above	50%	30%	35%	↑
Shopping cart abandonment rate	The number of users that add products to their shopping cart but do not check out.	Below	15%	22%	17%	↓
Percent of repeat customers	Percent of customers who make more than one purchase.	Above	25%	19%	25%	↑
Total available market relative to a retailer's share of market	Percent of market share.	Above	25%	8%	11%	↑
Customer lifetime value (CLV)	How much the average customer is worth to your business over the course of their relationship with your brand.	Above	$ 140	$ 80	$ 110	↑
Customer acquisition cost (CAC) per customer	The amount the organization spends to acquire a new customer. Calculated as Total Marketing Spend/# of Customers	Below	$ 50	$ 56	$ 50	↓
Site traffic	Total number of visits to the website.	Above	40,000	33,259	41,143	↑
Time on site (in seconds)	Average number of seconds users spend on the website.	Above	180	76	123	↑
Bounce rate	The percent of users that exit the website after viewing only one page.	Below	14%	21%	15%	↓
Pageviews per visit	Pageviews per visit refers to the average number of pages a user will view on your site during each visit.	Above	3	1.20	1.70	↑
Texting subscribers	Newer to digital marketing than email, ecommerce brands can reach consumers through SMS-based marketing. Texting subscribers refers to the number of customers on your text message contact list.	Above	25,000	18,543	19,947	↑
Email open rate	This KPI tells you the percentage of subscribers that open your email.	Above	10%	3%	7%	↑
Email click-through rate (CTR)	Click-through rate tells you the percentage of those who actually clicked on a link after opening.	Above	45%	12%	12%	↔
Unsubscribes	Rate of unsubscribers to the email list.	Below	10%	23%	19%	↓
Number and quality of product reviews	Customer reviews of the products.	Above	30,000	14,250	24,783	↑
Customer satisfaction (CSAT) score	Average Customer Satisfaction Score (out of 5 stars)	Above	4.5	3.10	3.74	↑
Net promoter score (NPS)	Average Net Promotor Score for the year.	Above	9	6.70	7.20	↑
Overall equipment effectiveness (OEE)	OEE describes how well manufacturing equipment is performing.	Above	0.9	0.78	0.82	↑
Overall labor effectiveness (OLE)	OLE describes how productive the staff operating the machines are.	Above	0.9	0.65	0.77	↑
Number of noncompliance events or incidents	Number of reported violations of regulation or organizational policies.	Below	5	28	22	↓

Lab Exhibit 12.1.23

Microsoft Excel

Assessment

1. Take a screenshot of the output, label it Submission 1, and paste it into a Word document named "Lab 12.1 Submission.docx".
2. Answer the questions in Connect and upload your Lab 12.1 Submission.docx via Connect if assigned.

Alternate Lab 12.1 Excel—On Your Own

Tracking Key Performance Indicators (KPIs)

Data Analytics Type: Descriptive Analytics

Keywords

KPI, Excel

Decision-Making Context

Bol and Branch manufactures and sells bedding made from all-natural, organic cotton. Customers order bedding online, and Bol and Branch relies heavily on podcasts, online, and social media for advertising. The company has just established a long list of KPIs to monitor, and you have been assigned to develop a spreadsheet to track them. You have decided that you can add some conditional formatting to an Excel spreadsheet to really make it obvious where Bol and Branch is meeting expectations and where it is falling asleep on the job.

For this lab you will use data in the Excel file titled **Alt Lab 12.1 Data.xlsx**. This data file provides the list of Bol and Branch's KPIs, their definitions, and the targets, as well as the company's performance for the years ended 12/31/2023 and 12/31/2024. The Data Dictionary below describes the data contained in the dataset.

Data Dictionary

Worksheet Tab/Table	Attribute Name	Description	Data Type
KPI Tracker	KPI	Key performance indicator. Each row represents a different KPI.	Text
KPI Tracker	Definition	Description of KPI	Text
KPI Tracker	Goal	Indicates whether the company wants performance to be above or below this KPI	Text
KPI Tracker	Target	KPI value to compare to performance	Numerical
KPI Tracker	12/31/2023	Performance related to this KPI in 2023	Numerical
KPI Tracker	12/31/2024	Performance related to this KPI in 2024	Numerical

Required

1. Apply conditional formatting to the 2023 and 2024 performance data in the Excel file to indicate whether performance was meeting the targets for each performance measure.
2. Add a column to indicate whether the performance was trending up or down across the two periods.

Assessment

1. Take a screenshot of the conditionally formatted Excel table, label it Submission 1, and paste it into a Word document named "Alt Lab 12.1 Submission.docx".
2. Answer the questions in Connect and upload your Alt Lab 12.1 Submission.docx via Connect if assigned.

Evaluating Key Performance Indicator (KPI) Effectiveness with Regression

Data Analytics Type: Predictive Analytics

Keywords

KPI, Balanced Scorecard, Regression, Excel

Decision-Making Context

Organizations have considerable flexibility when identifying KPIs to use for measuring performance on the four balanced scorecard dimensions. Statistical tools, such as regression, can be useful to determine if the KPIs used to measure the customer, internal processes, and learning and growth dimensions do in fact predict financial performance.

Let's use **Netflix** as an example. We can find publicly available data regarding Netflix's quarterly revenues, the number of paid memberships, and the size of its content portfolio (original, branded streaming content). Let's assume that Netflix uses the following KPIs in its balanced scorecard:

Balanced Scorecard Dimension	KPI(s)
Financial	• Revenue
Customer	• Average paid memberships • Average stream time per day
Internal processes	• Content assets
Learning and growth	• Employee satisfaction

Required

Use multiple regression to determine which KPIs will be useful to Netflix in predicting financial success.

Ask the Question

Do the KPIs related to the customer, internal processes, and learning and growth dimensions predict revenue?

Master the Data

For this lab, we'll use the data in the Excel file titled **Lab 12.2 Data.xlsx**.

Open **Lab 12.2 Data.xlsx**, then review the data to confirm that the spreadsheet has columns representing each of the KPIs described above.

Perform the Analysis

Using regression analysis to determine which KPIs are most likely to predict positive financial performance is an example of *predictive analytics*.

1. Navigate to the **Data** tab and click on the **Data Analysis** icon (Lab Exhibit 12.2.1).
   Note: If you do not have this **Data Analysis** icon, then you will need to activate it. To do so, proceed as follows (Lab Exhibits 12.2.2 and 12.2.3):
   - Click **File** (in the top-left corner of your screen).
   - Click **More**.
   - Click **Options**.
   - Select **Add-ins** from the list.
   - Select **Analysis ToolPak** from the list.
2. Select **Regression**, as shown in Lab Exhibit 12.2.4.
3. For Steps 3–7, refer to Lab Exhibit 12.2.5. In the **Regression** dialog box (❶) enter the revenue data from Column C ($C$1:$C$10) for your Y Range. This is your dependent variable. It is what you intend to predict with your other KPIs.
4. Enter the range of all other KPIs from Columns D through G ($D$1:$G$10) as your X range (❷). These are your independent variables.
5. Click on **Labels** (❸) so that Excel knows that your columns have headers.
6. Click on **Confidence Level** (❹). You can adjust that percentage if you'd like, but 95% confidence level is a good choice.
7. Click **OK** (❺).

Lab Exhibit 12.2.5

Microsoft Excel

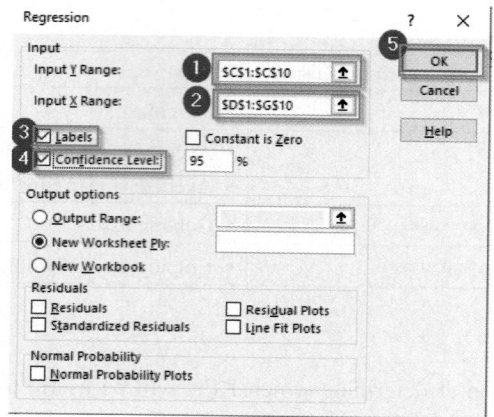

Your output will appear on a separate worksheet and should look like Lab Exhibit 12.2.6.

Lab Exhibit 12.2.6

Microsoft Excel

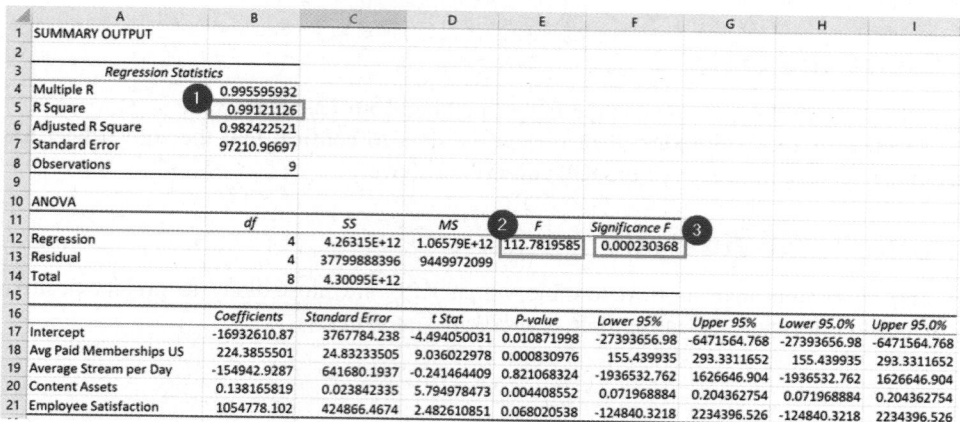

Let's dig into these results.

First, we review the regression statistics and see that the R Square (❶) is quite high (0.99). This means that our four independent variables (the leading KPIs) explain *most* of the variation in revenue.

Second, we can see from the F statistic (❷) in the ANOVA results that, in general, these leading indicators predict revenues well. This conclusion is evident from the very significant F value (❸). That is, $F < 0.05$.

Third, if we look at the coefficients, t stats, and p-values for the individual KPIs we can learn more about the relationships between the specific KPIs and revenue. For example, from the results table, we see that Average Paid Memberships US has a positive coefficient (224.38), meaning that it has a positive effect on revenue. That is, the more paid memberships Netflix has, the more revenue it makes. We see that the t stat is pretty large (9.03) and that the associated p-value is very small—below the conventional value of 0.05, which researchers agree means that the relationship is significant. Thus, changes in the Average Paid Memberships do influence the annual revenues.

The results for each of the independent variables are summarized in the following table:

Balanced Scorecard Dimension	KPI	Relationship to Revenue
Customer	• Average paid memberships • Average stream time per day	• Positive and significant • Negative and marginally significant
Internal processes	• Content assets	• Positive and significant
Learning and growth	• Employee satisfaction	• Not significant

Share the Story

If we were to go to Netflix management to explain these results, what would we say? We will need to provide an interpretation of the results that makes sense to the average shareholder, who is likely not experienced in statistics.

In an executive summary of the results, we could write the following:

> Our KPIs for the customer and internal process dimensions predict future revenues well, but our KPI for learning and growth does not relate to revenue. Therefore, we may need to find a more useful KPI than employee satisfaction for the learning and growth dimension.

> Also, our results indicate that the number of paid memberships in the United States is a key indicator of future financial success. That is, more paid customers lead to revenue growth. The negative relationship between average hours of streaming per day and revenue is somewhat curious, however, if we consider the time period of our data. Those data include the peak of the COVID-19 pandemic, when most people were stuck at home and streaming content more than usual. Finally, the positive relationship between content assets and revenue suggests that more original content available on the Netflix platform is associated with higher revenues.

Assessment

1. Take a screenshot of the output, label it Submission 1, and paste it into a Word document named "Lab 12.2 Submission.docx".
2. Answer the questions in Connect and upload your Lab 12.2 Submission.docx via Connect if assigned.

Evaluating Key Performance Indicator (KPI) Effectiveness with Regression

Data Analytics Type: Predictive Analytics

Keywords

KPI, Balanced Scorecard, Regression, Excel

Decision-Making Context

Lyft, Inc. specializes in transportation as a service and is primarily known for peer-to-peer ride-sharing. Publicly available data regarding Lyft's quarterly revenues, costs, number of active riders, and the revenue per active rider for 2017–2021 are available online.

Assume that Lyft uses the following KPIs in its balanced scorecard:

Balanced Scorecard Dimension	KPI
Financial	• Increase revenue • Decrease cost
Customer	• Increase number of active riders • Increase revenue per active rider
Internal processes	• Decrease customer wait time
Learning and growth	• Average driver rating 4.5 or above

Required

Replicate the tasks in Lab 12.2 using the **Alt Lab 12.2 Data.xlsx** dataset to run a regression analysis in Excel to examine the relationship among financial performance (that is, revenue) and the other KPIs at Lyft.

Assessment

1. Take a screenshot of the output, label it Submission 1, and paste it into a Word document named "Alt Lab 12.2 Submission.docx".
2. Answer the questions in Connect and upload your Alt Lab 12.2 Submission.docx via Connect if assigned.

Creating a Balanced Scorecard Dashboard to Track Performance

Data Analytics Type: Descriptive

Keywords

Balanced Scorecard, KPI

Decision-Making Context

Managers use the balanced scorecard to evaluate organizational performance on multiple dimensions. Key performance indicators (KPIs) from the financial dimension provide insight into the firm's financial performance and provide a look back. KPIs related to customers, the internal processes of the organization, and the learning and growth of employees provide additional insight into how the organization may fare in the future.

   You work for an oceanside restaurant called Castaways. The executive chef has recently implemented a balanced scorecard approach and has asked you to summarize the data using Excel. She would like you to create a snapshot summary of the balanced scorecard in Excel so that she can easily see where Castaways stands on each of the four dimensions.

Required

Determine if Castaways is meeting expectations on all four dimensions of the Balanced Scorecard.

Ask the Question

Is Castaways meeting expectations on all four dimensions? To answer this question, refer to the following strategic measures and objectives:

KPI	Target
Financial	
Increase revenue	Increase over time
Decrease COGS	Decrease over time
Increase profit	Increase over time
Customer	
Positive net promoter score (NPS)	• At least 75% "promoters" (that is, 75% of responses are 9 or 10) • Less than 10% detractors (that is, less than 10% of responses are 6 or less) • NPS increases (or remains stable) over time
Internal Processes	
Minimize time required to serve a meal	Average time to table should be below 18 minutes
Optimize table turnover	Average mealtime should be less than 90 minutes
Learning and Growth	
Positive employee satisfaction	• At least 80% of scores greater than 4 • Increase employee satisfaction score over time
Improve employee training	75% of employees have completed 20 hours of training

Lab Note: The tools presented in this lab periodically change. Updated instructions, if applicable, can be found in the student and instructor support materials. All Lab Exhibits are available within the eBook and in Connect.

DATA VISUALIZATION

Master the Data

For this lab, we'll use the data in the Excel file titled **Lab 12.3 Data.xlsx**.

Notice that this Excel workbook has multiple tabs. Review the tabs to familiarize yourself with the data:

Worksheet (Tab)	Description
Sales Records	Detailed sales records from the year
COGS	COGS entries made during the year
Profit	Sales minus COGS for each month
Customer	Individual net promoter score (NPS) data from customers throughout the year
Time to Serve	Daily average time to serve tables
Table Turnover	Daily average table turnover time
Employee Satisfaction	Employee satisfaction scores from two employee surveys (September and June)
Training	Employee training records

Note that Castaways' fiscal year (FY) runs from July 1 to June 30, which means the data span two calendar years. The data provided are for FY 2026, which runs from July 1, 2025, to June 30, 2026. You will need to keep this in mind when running analyses over time.

Perform the Analysis

A balanced scorecard uses descriptive analytics from a variety of KPIs and combines them into one dashboard so that management can easily review and interpret the results. It provides a useful overview of the state of the organization and can be used to make strategic decisions for the future.

Analysis Task #1: Prepare an Area Chart to Show Sales, COGS, and Profit over Time

Summarize Sales

1. Open the **Sales Records** tab.
2. Create a new column to indicate the year for each sale.
    a. Insert two columns to the right of the **Transaction Date** column.
    b. Use the **Text** function to populate the first column with the month and the second column with the year.
       - =TEXT(B3,"MMM") will give you a 3-letter abbreviation for the month.
       - =TEXT(B3,"YYYY") will give you a 4-digit year.
3. With your cursor somewhere within your data, click the **Insert** tab at the top of the screen and select the **PivotTable** icon (Lab Exhibit 12.3.1).
    a. Select **Table/Range**. Excel should automatically select all of your (contiguous) data. If it does not, then you can enter the correct columns/rows in the **Table/Range** field in the dialog box (see Lab Exhibit 12.3.2).
    b. Click the indicator button to place the pivot table in an **Existing Worksheet**.
    c. Click in the **Location** field, and then click in a cell to the right of your data, at the top of your screen (for example, cell G1). Doing so will place your pivot table to the right of your data set on this same worksheet. See again Lab Exhibit 12.3.2.
4. Build your pivot table using the field list to the right of your screen.
    a. Add the Year and Month to the **Rows** (Lab Exhibit 12.3.3).
       If you don't include Year, Excel will still summarize by month correctly, but your pivot table and any related charts will assume that your data represent a normal calendar year and will order your data from January to December even though the calendar year is not the fiscal year for Castaways.
    b. Add Sales to the **Values** (Lab Exhibit 12.3.4).

Excel should default to Sum. If it does not, you can change the summarization method by clicking the down arrow to the right of the **Sales** value in the **Value Field Settings** list (Lab Exhibit 12.3.5).

This option opens the **Value Field Settings** dialog box, where you can select Sum (❶ in Lab Exhibit 12.3.6). *Note:* Doing so changes the **Custom Name** to "Sum of Sales" to indicate that you are summing sales (❷). From this dialog box you can also change the number format to show currency by clicking on the **Number Format** button (❸). When you are done, click **OK** (❹).

5. Your resulting pivot table will look like Lab Exhibit 12.3.7.

Summarize COGS

6. Use the same methodology on the **COGS** tab to summarize COGS into a pivot table.
7. Your resulting pivot table should look like Lab Exhibit 12.3.8.

Combine Summarized Sales and Summarized COGS to calculate Profit on a new worksheet

8. Insert a new worksheet after the COGS worksheet and label it "Profit".
9. Beginning in cell A1, enter the column and row headers shown in Lab Exhibit 12.3.9 to prepare your spreadsheet.
10. Use cell reference formulas to pull Sales and COGS data from the relevant spreadsheets. For example, to get the value for July 2025 sales, enter this formula: ='Sales Records'!H3. To get the value for July 2025 COGS, enter this formula: =COGS!J3. See Lab Exhibit 12.3.10.

	A	B	C	D
1	Month	Year	Sales	COGS
2	Jul	2025	='Sales Records'!H3	=COGS!J3
3	Aug	2025		
4	Sep	2025		

Lab Exhibit 12.3.10

Microsoft Excel

Note: If you try to link the cells by clicking in the pivot table and then copying the formula down, it won't work. If you try it, you'll notice that the formula that Excel pulls is from the specific row/column of the pivot table (for example, =GETPIVOTDATA("Sales"|'Sales Records'!$G1|"Month"|"Jul"|"Year"|"2025"). These cell references would be cumbersome to change.

11. In the Profit column, calculate Profit by subtracting COGS from Sales for each month. For example, in cell E2 enter =C2-D2 (Lab Exhibit 12.3.11).

	A	B	C	D	E
1	Month	Year	Sales	COGS	Profit
2	Jul	2025	='Sales Records'!H3	=COGS!J3	=C2-D2
3	Aug	2025			
4	Sep	2025			
5	Oct	2025			

Lab Exhibit 12.3.11

Microsoft Excel

Create an area chart to show changes in Sales, COGS, and Profit over time

12. Highlight the Sales, COGS, and Profit data (that is, Columns C, D, and E). Click **Insert > Recommended Charts** and then select the **Histogram** option (Lab Exhibits 12.3.12 and 12.3.13). If the Histogram is not showing under recommended charts, click the tab for **All Charts** and select it from there.
13. By default, your chart will resemble Lab Exhibit 12.3.14.
14. Now let's format the chart. Click on **Chart Title** and change the name to "Financial Summary".

15. To reorder the chart so that Sales is on top, COGS is in the middle, and Profit is at the bottom, click on the **Select Data** icon at the top of the screen in the **Chart Design** tab (Lab Exhibit 12.3.15).

16. Use the arrows for the **Legend Entries (Series)** to reorder your measures, as shown in Lab Exhibit 12.3.16.

Lab Exhibit 12.3.16

Microsoft Excel

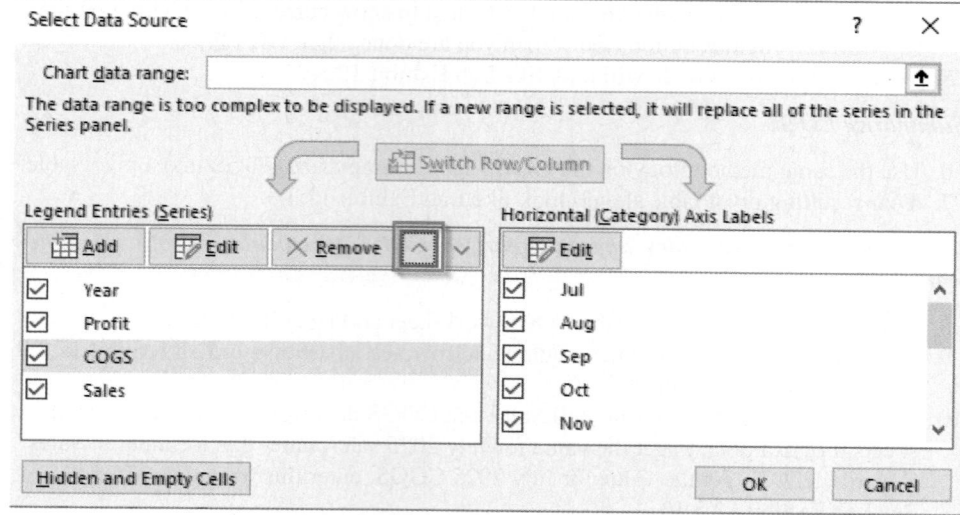

17. To change the color of each measure, click in the colored section of your graph. Doing so will open the **Format Data Series** options on the right of your screen (Lab Exhibit 12.3.17). Ensure that **Solid fill** is selected, and change the color for Profit to blue.

18. To change the color of Sales to green and the color of COGS to Gray, you'll need to click on each of those sections of the chart and change the colors accordingly.

19. You can add data labels to the chart by right-clicking on one of the data points in each series (for example, for Sales) and selecting **Add Data Labels** (Lab Exhibit 12.3.18).
    - Once you have added the data label, you can edit the one all the way to the right to read "Sales" instead of the value. Then delete the other data labels so that you have only one label, "Sales," all the way to the right.
    - Repeat for COGS and Profit.
    - You can now remove the legend at the bottom of your chart because you already have that information showing as a data label on the chart.

Your finished area chart will look something like Lab Exhibit 12.3.19.

Analysis Task #2: Prepare Visualizations to Assess KPIs Related to the Customer Dimension

Prepare a pie chart to illustrate the percentage of customers classified as promoters, passives, and detractors

1. Open the **Customer** tab.
2. Create a new column to indicate the year for each sale.
   a. Insert two columns to the right of the **Date** column.
   b. Use the **Text** function to populate the first column with the month and the second column with the year.
      - =TEXT(B3,"MMM") will give you a 3-letter abbreviation for the month.
      - =TEXT(B3,"YYYY") will give you the 4-digit year.
3. Populate column F using an if/then function to categorize each customer response into an NPS category. NPS of 9 or 10 is a promoter, 7 or 8 is a passive, and 0 to 6 is a detractor. The function is:

$$=IF(E2 > 8, \text{"Promoter"},IF(E2 < 7,\text{"Detactor"}, \text{"Passive"}))$$

When you are done, your data will resemble Lab Exhibit 12.3.20.

4. In our chart showing NPS over time, we will want to display the target score of 9 (that is, the minimum promoter score) as a reference point, so we need to add it as a column in our data.

Label column G "Promoter Score" and enter 9 in every cell in the column (Lab Exhibit 12.3.21).

5. Create a pivot table to calculate the percentage of customers in each NPS category.

   a. Insert this pivot table into your current spreadsheet to the right of your data (for example, in cell I2) by following Steps 1–4 as shown in Lab Exhibit 12.3.22.

   b. In your **PivotChart Fields** window, drag NPS Category to **Axis (Categories)** and drag Sum of ResponseID to **Values** (Lab Exhibit 12.3.23).

   c. Click the drop-down arrow to the right of **Sum of ResponseID** (Lab Exhibit 12.3.24). In **Value Field Settings**, change **Custom Name** to Count of ResponseID and **Summarize Values By** field by selecting **Count**. Then click **OK** (Lab Exhibit 12.3.25).

   d. Also within the **Value Field Settings** dialog box, click the **Show Values As** tab and change **Show values as** to **% of Grand Total** and change **Base field** to **Year**. Then click **OK** (Lab Exhibit 12.3.26).

6. Click on any cell inside the pivot chart. Click on the **Pie Chart** icon in the **Charts** section of the **Insert** tab to create a pie chart, as shown in Lab Exhibit 12.3.27.

7. Select the **2-D pie** icon shown in Lab Exhibit 12.3.27. By default, your pie graph will resemble Lab Exhibit 12.3.28.

8. Format your pie graph as follows:

   a. When you hover over (or click into) the graph, a green cross (**+**) will appear to the right. You can select some data elements by clicking on that cross.

     i. Uncheck the **Legend** to remove the legend from your chart (Lab Exhibit 12.3.29).

     ii. Check **Data Labels** to add the percentages to your chart and then select the right arrow next to **Data Labels** and then **More Options** to do more formatting (Lab Exhibit 12.3.29).

     iii. These actions open the **Format Data Labels** window on the right (Lab Exhibit 12.3.30). Click on **Category Name** to show the category with the percentage. And, in the drop-down box labeled **Separator**, change the option to a space instead of a pipe (|). You should notice on your chart that there will no longer be a vertical line between the category name and the percentage.

   b. To change the color of the pie slices, click on any slice. Doing so opens the **Format Data Series** window on the right (Lab Exhibit 12.3.31). Click on the **paint can** icon at the top left to format color. Make sure **Vary colors by slice** is clicked, and then you can change the color. You will do this for each slice. Change "Promoters" to green, "Passives" to yellow, and "Detractors" to red.

   c. To separate your pie pieces a bit, you can click on the **Series Options** icon in the **Format Data Series** window and change the pie explosion percentage to 10%, as shown in Lab Exhibit 12.3.32.

   d. Change the title of your graph to "Net Promoter Score".

   e. You can remove the gray value button that says **Count of ResponseID** by right-clicking on it and selecting **Hide All Field Buttons on Chart** (Lab Exhibit 12.3.33). These options make your visualization cleaner and give you more room.

Your finished pie chart should resemble Lab Exhibit 12.3.34.

Prepare a combo chart to illustrate Average NPS overtime

9. While still on the **Customer** worksheet, create a new pivot chart. Insert this one on the customer worksheet as well, in the space below your previous pivot chart.

10. Build your pivot chart by placing Year and Month in the **Rows** column and Average NPS and Average Promoter Score in the **Values** column (Lab Exhibit 12.3.35). You'll see that the image shows "Values" in the Columns section. Excel does that on its own because you have added multiple values to the Values area. It knows that each value will need its own column. You will need to use the **Value Field Settings** dialog box again (as you have in previous steps) to change the aggregation of the NPS and Promoter Score fields to **Average**.

11. Click a cell in the pivot table, and then select the **Recommended Charts** icon from the **Insert** tab (Lab Exhibit 12.3.36).

12. Choose **Combo chart**. We want to show the average NPS per month as columns. We also want to show the target value of 9 (the lowest score classified as a promoter) as a reference.

13. You will want to change the chart type and axis so that the Average Promoter Score is shown as a line and the Average NPS is shown as a clustered column. To do so, use the **Chart Type** drop-down menus, as shown in Lab Exhibit 12.3.37.

14. Now we will format the combo chart.
    a. To remove the gray buttons showing on the chart, click on the **PivotChart Analyze** tab on the ribbon. Then click the **Field Buttons** icon and select **Hide All** (Lab Exhibit 12.3.38).
    b. Click on the green **+** to the right of the chart to select which chart elements to turn on and off.
        i. Turn off **Legend** (Lab Exhibit 12.3.39).
        ii. Turn on **Chart Title** (Lab Exhibit 12.3.39).
        iii. Change the title to "NPS Over Time".
    c. To add the variable name to the far-right values on the graph, click on the single data point to the very right on the Average Promoter Score line. Click **Add Data Label** and then change the label to "Promoter" (Lab Exhibit 12.3.40). You can drag this text box up a little so that you can see it more clearly.
    Your finished chart should resemble Lab Exhibit 12.3.41.

Analysis Task #3: Prepare Combo Charts to Assess KPIs for Internal Processes

Prepare combo chart to compare average time to serve by month to the goal of less than 18 minutes

1. Open the **Time to Serve** tab.
2. Create a new column to indicate the month and year for each date.
    a. Insert two columns to the right of the Transaction Date column.
    b. Use the **Text** function to populate the first column with the month and the second column with the year.
        • =TEXT(A2,"MMM") will give you a 3-letter abbreviation for the month.
        • =TEXT(A2,"YYYY") will give you the 4-digit year.
3. Because we want to compare monthly averages to the goal (18 minutes), add a column to the right of the existing data and label it "Goal". Then enter "18" in all of the cells below.
    When you are done, your data will resemble Lab Exhibit 12.3.42.
4. With your cursor somewhere within your data, click the **Insert** tab at the top of the screen and select the **PivotTable** icon (Lab Exhibit 12.3.43).
    a. Select **Table/Range**, which should automatically select all of your (contiguous) data. If it does not, you can enter the correct columns/rows in the **Table/Range** field in the dialog box (Lab Exhibit 12.3.44).
    b. Click the indicator button to place the pivot table in an **Existing Worksheet**. Click in the **Location** field, and then click in a cell to the right of your data, at the top of your screen (for example, cell G1). Doing so will place your pivot table to the right of your dataset on this same worksheet (Lab Exhibit 12.3.44).

c. Create your pivot table with the Year and Month in the **Rows** area. In the **Values** area, include the Average Goal and the Average Daily Time to Serve (Lab Exhibit 12.3.45).

5. Click a cell in the pivot table, and then select the **Recommended Charts** icon from the **Insert** tab (Lab Exhibit 12.3.46).

6. Choose **Combo chart**. We want to show the average Time to Serve as columns. We also want to show the target value of 18 minutes as a reference.

7. You will want to change the chart type and axis so that the Average Goal is shown as a line and the Average Daily Time to Serve is shown as a clustered column. Use the drop-down menus under **Chart Type** to make those selections (Lab Exhibit 12.3.47).

8. Now we will format the combo chart.
   a. To remove the gray buttons showing on the chart, click on the **PivotChart Analyze** tab on the ribbon. Then click the **Field Buttons** icon and select **Hide All** (Lab Exhibit 12.3.48).
   b. Click on the green **+** to the right of the chart to select which chart elements to turn on and off.
      i. Turn off **Legend** (Lab Exhibit 12.3.49).
      ii. Turn on **Chart Title** (Lab Exhibit 12.3.49).
      iii. Change the title to "Average Time to Table".
   c. To add the variable name to the far right values on the graph, click on the single data point to the very right on the Average Goal line. Click **Add Data Label** and then change the label to "Goal" (Lab Exhibit 12.3.50). You can drag this text box up a little so that you can see it more clearly.
   d. To delete the gridlines, click on them and then hit **Delete**.
   Your finished chart should resemble Lab Exhibit 12.3.51.

Prepare combo chart to compare time customers spend enjoying their meal by month to the goal of less than 90 minutes

9. Open the **Table Turnover** tab.
10. To prepare this visualization, you will perform all of the same steps that you just performed to create the Average Time to Table visualization. Your finished visualization will look like Lab Exhibit 12.3.52.

Analysis Task #4: Prepare Visualizations to Assess KPIs for the Learning and Growth Dimension

Prepare pie chart to show percentage of employees with different employee satisfaction scores on the most recent employee satisfaction survey

1. Open the **Employee Satisfaction** tab.
2. Create a pivot table from the existing data. Place the pivot table to the right of your data. Follow the steps in Lab Exhibit 12.3.53.
3. When creating the pivot table, place the June Score in the **Rows** area and the Employee ID in the **Values** area (Lab Exhibit 12.3.54).
   a. Select **Value Field Settings** and then change the field values for the Count of Employee ID to **Count**. Then click **OK** (Lab Exhibits 12.3.55 and 12.3.56).
   b. For **Show values as**, indicate **% of Grand Total** and use June Score as the **Base field**. Then click **OK** (Lab Exhibit 12.3.57).
4. You'll notice that you have a row for every different employee satisfaction score in your data set. That is too much detail to be useful, so we'll use the grouping function to create bins of a reasonable size so we can gain the necessary insights from our data.
   a. Right-click on one of the row labels in your pivot table.
   b. Select **Group...** from the drop-down menu.
   c. The **Grouping** dialog box opens and you can enter the parameters of your groups. As Lab Exhibit 12.3.58 shows, the parameters will provide groups of 1 full value from 1 to 5.

5. The resulting pivot table will resemble Lab Exhibit 12.3.59.
6. Now you can edit the Row labels. The row for scores "< 1" are employees who were no longer employed at Castaways at the time of the June survey, so you can change the label to "Terminated". To change the label, simply type in the cell where the label you want to change is currently located.

   Change all of the row labels as shown in Lab Exhibit 12.3.60.
7. Now, create a pie chart using these pivot table data. You will make the pie chart following the same methodology you used in creating the NPS in Analysis Task #2. Click on any cell inside the pivot chart. Then click on the **Pie Chart** icon in the **Charts** section of the **Insert** tab to create your pie chart (Lab Exhibit 12.3.61).
8. Select a 2-D pie chart. By default, your pie graph will resemble Lab Exhibit 12.3.62.
9. Format your pie graph as follows.
   a. When you hover over (or click into) the graph, a green cross (**+**) will appear to the right. You can select some data elements there.
      i. Uncheck **Legend** to remove the legend from your chart (Lab Exhibit 12.3.63).
      ii. Check **Data Labels** to add the percentages to your chart and then select the right arrow next to **Data Labels** and then **More options...** to do more formatting (Lab Exhibit 12.3.63).
      iii. The **Format Data Labels** window opens on the right. Click on **Category Name** to show the category with the percentage. In the drop-down box next to **Separator**, change the option to a space instead of a pipe (Lab Exhibit 12.3.64). You should notice on your chart that there will no longer be a vertical line between the category name and the percentage.
   b. To change the color of the pie slices, click on any slice. The **Format Data Point** window opens on the right. Click on the **paint can** icon at the top to format color. Make sure that **Vary colors by slice** is checked, and then you can change the color for each slice. Change "4 and above" to green, "3 to 3.99" to yellow, "2 to 2.99" to orange, "Below 2" to red, and "Terminated" to gray (Lab Exhibit 12.3.65).
   c. Remove the gray value button by right-clicking on it and selecting **Hide All Field Buttons on Chart**. This makes your visualization cleaner and more spacious.
   d. Change the title of your pie chart to "Average Employee Satisfaction - June". Your finished pie chart will resemble Lab Exhibit 12.3.66.

Prepare column chart to show the percentage of employees that have completed their training hours

10. Open the **Training** tab.
11. Create a pivot table using the existing data and place it on the same worksheet to the right of your data.
12. Build your pivot table by placing Training Hours in the **Rows** area and Employee ID in the **Values** area (Lab Exhibit 12.3.67). Change the **Employee ID** field to **Count** and **Show Values as % of Grand Total**.
13. Use the **Grouping** function to create bins that group employees into meaningful buckets based on the number of training hours they have completed.
    a. Make bins that start at 0 and go to 19 in increments of 10 (Lab Exhibit 12.3.68). Doing so will force anyone with 20 hours (that is, anyone who has completed all of their hours) into a separate bucket.
    b. Change the row labels in your pivot table as shown in Lab Exhibit 12.3.69.
14. Next, create a column chart from your pivot table data. Select the **Column Chart** icon from the **Insert** tab, and select the first icon under **2-D Column** (Lab Exhibit 12.3.70).
15. The default column chart should resemble Lab Exhibit 12.3.71.

16. Now you can format the column chart as needed.
    a. Use the green **+** on the side of the chart to turn chart elements on and off (Lab Exhibit 12.3.72):
        i. Turn off **Legend**.
        ii. Turn on **Chart Title**. Change the title to "Training Hours".
        iii. Turn on **Axis Titles**.
            1. Change the Y-axis title to "Percent of Employees".
            2. Change the X-axis title to "Training Hours Completed".
        iv. Turn on **Data Labels**.
        v. Turn off **Gridlines**.
    b. Click on the Y-axis and delete it (Lab Exhibit 12.3.73).
17. Your finished chart should resemble Lab Exhibit 12.3.74.

Analysis Task #5: Build Your Dashboard

Now that you have created all of the visualizations that illustrate Castaways' performance related to its KPIs, you can combine them in one central location.

1. Insert a new worksheet and label it "Dashboard" (Lab Exhibit 12.3.75).
2. You can format this dashboard a variety of ways. For this example, we'll create four horizontal sections, one for each balanced scorecard dimension.
3. Change the page orientation to **Landscape** in the **Page Layout** tab (Lab Exhibit 12.3.76).
4. In cell A1, enter the title "Castaways' Balanced Scorecard Dashboard". Highlight cells A1:B1 and click the **Merge and Center** icon at the top of the screen (Lab Exhibit 12.3.77).
5. Drag the right edge of the B column all the way to the end of the page. If you cannot tell where the page ends, use the **Page break preview** from the **View** tab (Lab Exhibit 12.3.78).
6. Highlight Rows 2:5. Right-click and select **Row Height...** Set the row height to 175 (Lab Exhibits 12.3.79 and 12.3.80).
7. In cell A2, type "Financial". Then, click on the little down arrow in the **Alignment** section of the **Home** ribbon (Lab Exhibit 12.3.81).

    Then change the alignment of the text to 90 degrees using the **Format Cells > Alignment > Orientation** dialog box, as shown in Lab Exhibit 12.3.82.

    Also, change the font size to 18 and fill the cell with light green paint (Lab Exhibit 12.3.83). Repeat this process for the other three dimensions.
8. Highlight cells A2:B2 and add a dark black border (Lab Exhibit 12.3.84).
9. Repeat Steps 7–8 for the other three balanced scorecard dimensions so that you have the shell of a dashboard that looks like Lab Exhibit 12.3.85.
10. To add each visualization to this dashboard, you will move each one from its individual worksheet to this dashboard worksheet. To do so, navigate to one of your visualizations and right-click on it. Select **Move Chart...** from the dialog box (Lab Exhibit 12.3.86).
11. Next, indicate that you want to move the chart to be an **Object in:** the Dashboard worksheet (Lab Exhibit 12.3.87).
12. Now the chart will be removed from its existing sheet and dropped onto the dashboard. You can move the chart into the position you prefer on the dashboard worksheet. When you move the chart (rather than copying and pasting), the chart is still linked to the underlying data. This means that when you make any changes to the underlying data, they will flow through to your visualization on the dashboard.
13. Repeat Steps 10–12 for all of your visualizations.
14. You can resize all of your visualizations so that they fit into the parameters you have set by clicking on all of the visualizations and then setting the shape **Height** and **Width** in the **Size** section of the **Format** tab (Lab Exhibit 12.3.88).

15. Set the height to about 2.15 for all shapes. (Excel will make minor adjustments based on the actual shape of your visualizations, so they won't all remain at precisely 2.15″.)
16. You can align the shapes within their containers by highlighting any on the same row and then selecting **Align** in the **Arrange** area in the **Shape Format** tab (Lab Exhibit 12.3.89).
    a. Align them in the center horizontally so that they line up evenly in the row.
    b. If you also want to align across rows/in columns, highlight the visualizations you wish to align and then align them in the center vertically.

Share the Story

Once you have completed all of these steps, your finished dashboard will resemble Lab Exhibit 12.3.90.

Assessment

1. Take a screenshot of the dashboard, label it Submission 1, and paste it into a Word document named "Lab 12.3 Submission.docx".
2. Answer the questions in Connect and upload your Lab 12.3 Submission.docx via Connect if assigned.

Alternate Lab 12.3 Excel—On Your Own

Creating a Balanced Scorecard Dashboard to Track Performance

Data Analytics Type: Descriptive

Keywords

Balanced Scorecard, KPI

DATA VISUALIZATION

Decision-Making Context

Managers use the balanced scorecard to evaluate organizational performance on multiple dimensions. Key performance indicators (KPIs) from the financial dimension provide insight into the firm's financial performance and provide a look back. KPIs related to customers, the internal processes of the organization, and the learning and growth of employees provide additional insight into how the organization may fare in the future.

You work for an oceanside restaurant called Castaways. The executive chef has recently implemented a balanced scorecard approach and has asked you to summarize the data using Excel. She would like you to create a snapshot summary of the balanced scorecard in Excel so that she can easily see where Castaways stands on each of the four dimensions.

Required

Apply the same steps in Lab 12.3 to the **Alt Lab 12.3 Data.xlsx** dataset and prepare a balanced scorecard dashboard that can answer the question.

Ask the Question

Is Castaways meeting expectations on all four dimensions?

Refer to the following strategic measures and objectives shown in the table below. To prepare your dashboard, you will first produce the visualizations shown in the third column of the table:

KPI	Target	Visualization Type
Financial		
Increase revenue	Increase over time	Area chart showing all three measures over time
Decrease COGS	Decrease over time	
Increase profit	Increase over time	
Customer		
Positive net promoter score	• At least 75% "promoters" (that is, 75% of responses are 9 or 10) • Less than 10% detractors (that is, less than 10% of responses are 6 or less) • NPS increases (or remains stable) over time	• Pie chart showing percentage of customers in each NPS category • Column chart showing average NPS per month with a reference line showing promoter goal
Internal Processes		
Minimize time required to serve a meal	Average time to table should be below 18 minutes	Column chart showing average time required to serve tables with a reference line showing KPI goal
Optimize table turnover	Average mealtime should be less than 90 minutes	Column chart showing average mealtime with a reference line showing KPI goal
Learning and Growth		
Positive employee satisfaction	• At least 80% of scores greater than 4 • Increase employee satisfaction score over time	Pie chart showing percentage of employees reporting different levels of satisfaction
Improve employee training	75% of employees have completed 20 hours of training	Column chart showing percentage of employees completing different amounts of training hours (0–9, 10–19, 20)

Assessment

1. Take a screenshot of the dashboard, label the screenshot Submission 1, and paste it into a Word document named "Alt Lab 12.3 Submission.docx".
2. Answer the questions in Connect and upload your Alt Lab 12.3 Submission.docx via Connect if assigned.

Lab Note: The tools presented in this lab periodically change. Updated instructions, if applicable, can be found in the student and instructor support materials. All Lab Exhibits are available within the eBook and in Connect.

DATA VISUALIZATION

Creating a Balanced Scorecard Dashboard to Track Performance

Data Analytics Type: Descriptive

Keywords

Balanced Scorecard, KPI

Decision-Making Context

Managers use the balanced scorecard to evaluate organizational performance on multiple dimensions. Key performance indicators (KPIs) from the financial dimension provide insight into the firm's financial performance and provide a look back. KPIs related to customers, the internal processes of the organization, and the learning and growth of employees provide additional insight into how the organization may fare in the future.

You work for an oceanside restaurant called Castaways. The executive chef has recently implemented a balanced scorecard approach and has asked you to summarize the data using Tableau software. She would like you to create a snapshot summary using the Tableau dashboard function so that she can easily see where Castaways stands on each of the four dimensions.

Required

1. Prepare visualizations for each of the KPIs available to you.
   a. Financial
      i. Revenue
      ii. COGS
      iii. Profit
   b. Customer
      i. Net promoter score
   c. Internal Processes
      i. Meals served time
      ii. Table turnover
   d. Learning and Growth
      i. Employee satisfaction score
      ii. Employee training
2. Prepare a dashboard that combines your prepared visualizations in a user-friendly format that will facilitate decision making by the executive chef and her management team.

Ask the Question

Is Castaways meeting expectations on all four dimensions? To answer this question, refer to the following strategic measures and objectives:

KPI	Target
Financial	
Increase revenue	Increase over time
Decrease COGS	Decrease over time
Increase profit	Increase over time
Customer	
Positive net promoter score	• At least 75% "promoters" (that is, 75% of responses are 9 or 10) • Less than 10% detractors (that is, less than 10% of responses are 6 or less)
Internal Processes	
Decrease meals served time	Time to table should be below 18 minutes
Table turnover	Total mealtime should be less than 90 minutes
Learning and Growth	
Increase employee satisfaction score	At least 80% of scores are greater than 3.5
Improve employee training	90% of employees have completed 20 hours of training

Master the Data

For this lab, we'll use the data in the Excel file titled **Lab 12.4 Data.xlsx**.

1. Open Tableau.
2. Navigate to the **Data Source** tab.
3. Add the Excel file **Lab 12.4 Data.xlsx** as the connection (Lab Exhibit 12.4.1).

   Note: You will notice that you have several worksheets in your data set. They do not all relate to one another, so it does not make sense to join them. This situation is common when you are examining data from different dimensions of the organization. We will discuss how to import additional (unrelated) worksheets as needed.

Perform the Analysis

Analysis Task #1: Prepare an Area Chart Visualization to Summarize the Financial Measures

1. Open a new worksheet. You will need to add a new data source to analyze data related to the time it takes to serve each table. Select the **Add Data** icon at the top of the screen (Lab Exhibit 12.4.2).
2. Connect to **Lab 12.4 Data.xlsx** (Lab Exhibit 12.4.3).
3. On the **Data Source** page, drag the **Sales Records** worksheet to the **Data** pane. Review the view of the data shown at the bottom of your screen to make sure everything has imported correctly (Lab Exhibit 12.4.4).
4. Rename the **Sheet 1** worksheet tab "Financial_Summary" (Lab Exhibit 12.4.5).
5. To add color to the tab to differentiate the different BSC (balanced scorecard) dimensions, right-click on the tab. Select **Color**, then choose **Green** (Lab Exhibit 12.4.6).
6. First, create an area graph that shows sales over time.
   a. Drag the **Transaction Date** dimension to the **Columns** shelf (Lab Exhibit 12.4.7). Using the boxed plus sign, expand the date so that you can see the months, as shown in Lab Exhibit 12.4.8.
   b. Drag the **Sales** measure to the **Rows** shelf (Lab Exhibit 12.4.9).
   c. Select the **Area** graph visualization from the **Marks** card (Lab Exhibit 12.4.10).
7. Second, add the COGS data to this visualization.

a. You will need to add a new data source to analyze data related to the time it takes to serve each table. Select the **Add Data** icon at the top of the screen (Lab Exhibit 12.4.11).

b. Connect to **Lab 12.4 Data.xlsx**.

c. Drag the **COGS** worksheet to the **Data** pane (Lab Exhibit 12.4.12). Now you'll see that you have both the **COGS** and the **Sales Records** worksheets showing as options in the **Data** pane on the left side of your Tableau worksheet (Lab Exhibit 12.4.13).

d. If you try to add the COGS data to the existing area graph, either you will get an error message or your data will look obviously wrong. (For example, the COGS may have the same value for every month.) Why? The data sets are not connected.

e. To connect the COGS data with the Sales data, you will need to blend the data sets using the date (month). Proceed as follows:
   • Click on the **Data** tab at the top of the screen. Then select **Edit Blend Relationships...** (Lab Exhibit 12.4.14).
   • In the **Blend Relationships** dialog box, set the **Primary data source** as the **Sales Records** and the **Secondary data source** as **COGS**. Then click **Custom** and **Add...** (Lab Exhibit 12.4.15).
   • Choose the **MONTH** dimension from each data set for your blend. Then click **OK** (Lab Exhibit 12.4.16).

f. Now you can drag the COGS dimension onto your data visualization.

g. To show both Sales and COGS on the same graph, drag the **COGS** pill and drop it on the Y-axis of the Sales area graph (Lab Exhibit 12.4.17).

8. Third, you must calculate profit by creating a calculated field that subtracts COGS from Sales.

a. Click on the **Analysis** tab at the top of the screen.

b. Click on **Create Calculated Field...** (Lab Exhibit 12.4.18).

c. Name the new field "Profit".

d. Enter this calculation:

$$SUM([Sales]) - SUM([COGS (Lab 12.4 Data)].[Cogs])$$

   • *Note:* Recall that you are pulling data from two different spreadsheets.
   • The calculation assumes you are adding the **Profit** field to the **Sales Records** worksheet. To do this, you must have the **Sales Records** spreadsheet highlighted when you create the calculated field, as shown in Lab Exhibit 12.4.19.
   • If you were creating this field on the COGS sheet, the formula would be:

$$SUM([Cogs]) - SUM([Sales Records (Lab 12.4 Data)].[Sales])$$

Lab Exhibit 12.4.19

Tableau Software

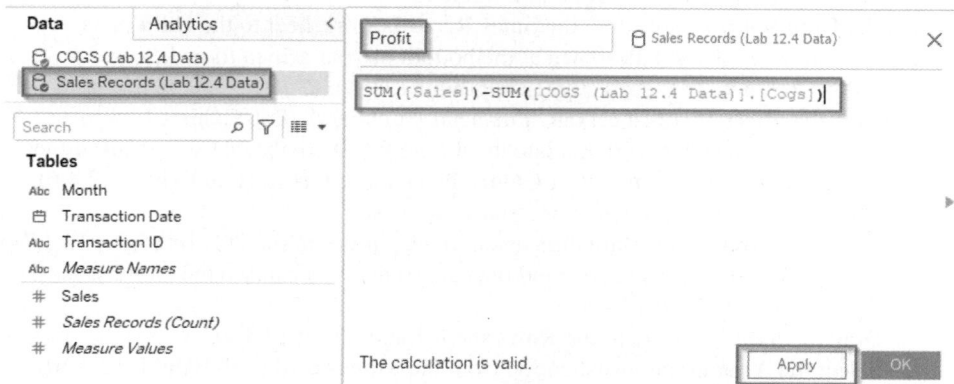

e. Once you have calculated the profit, drag the **Profit** measure onto the Y-axis of the data visualization (Lab Exhibit 12.4.20).

f. You should now have a visualization that resembles Lab Exhibit 12.4.21.

g. To change the colors of the different measures, drag the dimension **Measure Names** to the **Color** mark on the **Marks** card (Lab Exhibit 12.4.22). This will change the colors of the different measures and bring up the color legend.

h. You can edit the colors from the drop-down arrow on the color legend. Format the colors so that Profit is green, Sales is blue, and COGS is yellow (Lab Exhibit 12.4.23).

i. From the **Measure Values** window to the left of the graph, rearrange the values so that the layers of the area graph show Sales as the largest amount, COGS in the middle, and Profit on the bottom, as shown in Lab Exhibit 12.4.24.

j. Edit the title to read "Financial Summary" and change the font size to 9 by right-clicking on the existing title and selecting **Edit title** (Lab Exhibit 12.4.25). *Note:* You will need to highlight the text when you change the font size so that it applies the change. Click **OK**.

k. Edit the X- and Y-axes to delete the title to remove the label. Leave the dates showing on the X-axis and the $ value on the Y-axis (Lab Exhibits 12.4.26 and 12.4.27).

l. Label the areas on the graph using the **Annotate** function.
   - Right-click on the area.
   - Select **Annotate** and then **Area...** (Lab Exhibit 12.4.28).
   - Type the appropriate label, left justify, and set to 6 point font (Lab Exhibit 12.4.29).
   - The result is a box around the label, as shown in Lab Exhibit 12.4.30.
   - To remove the box, right-click on it and adjust the **Shading** to None via the **Format...** menu. Also set the **Border** to None (Lab Exhibits 12.4.31 and 12.4.32).
   - Now that you have annotated, you can hide the legend by clicking the down arrow on the upper-right corner of the legend and selecting **Hide Card** (Lab Exhibit 12.4.33).
   - The final visualization should resemble Lab Exhibit 12.4.34.

Analysis Task #2: Prepare a Line Graph to Summarize the Difference in Financial Measures during the Time Period

1. Open a new worksheet.
2. Rename the worksheet tab "Financial_Change" (Lab Exhibit 12.4.35).
3. To add color to the tab to differentiate the different BSC dimensions, right-click on the tab. Select <u>C</u>olor, then choose **Green** (Lab Exhibit 12.4.36).
4. With the **Sales Records** data source highlighted on the **Data** pane, drag **Transaction Date** to the **Columns** shelf (Lab Exhibit 12.4.37). Expand so that **Month** is showing (Lab Exhibit 12.4.38).
5. Drag **Sales** onto the **Rows** shelf (Lab Exhibit 12.4.39).
6. On the **Marks** card, select the line graph visualization by clicking the drop-down arrow next to **Automatic** and then choosing **Line** (Lab Exhibit 12.4.40).
7. Drag **Profit** onto the Y-axis of the sales line graph (Lab Exhibit 12.4.41).
8. Click on the **COGS** data source so that the COGS fields are active (Lab Exhibit 12.4.42).
9. Drag **COGS** onto the Y-axis (Lab Exhibit 12.4.42). Now you should have all three measures showing on your line graph, as shown in Lab Exhibit 12.4.43.

10. Click on the **Sales Records** data source again and drag **Transaction Date** into the **Filters**. Choose **Months** as your method of filtering. Then click **Next >** (Lab Exhibit 12.4.44).
11. Choose the first and last months of your data to see the change over the period. In this case, because Castaways has a June 30 year-end, select **July** (beginning) and **June** (end) and then click **OK** (Lab Exhibit 12.4.45).
12. Now you will have a smooth line. Show the values by clicking on **Analysis** and **Show Mark Labels** (Lab Exhibit 12.4.46).
13. Format the axes to remove the titles (Lab Exhibits 12.4.47 and 12.4.48).
14. From the legend, click on the drop-down arrow and edit colors so that the colors of this graph match the area graph you made in Analysis Task #1. Profit is green, Sales is blue, and COGS is yellow (Lab Exhibit 12.4.49).
15. Edit the title to read "Financial Changes" and change the font size to 9 by right-clicking on the existing title and selecting **Edit Title** (Lab Exhibit 12.4.50). The final data visualization should resemble Lab Exhibit 12.4.51.

Analysis Task #3: Prepare a Line Chart Visualization to Summarize the Net Promoter Score (NPS) Obtained from Customers over Time

1. Drag the **Customer** worksheet to the data pane, as shown in Lab Exhibits 12.4.52 and 12.4.53. Review the view of the data shown at the bottom of your screen to make sure everything has imported correctly.
2. Rename the worksheet tab "Customer_NPS Over Time".
3. To add color to the tab to differentiate the different BSC dimensions, right-click on the tab. Select **Color**, then choose **Purple**.
4. Drag the **NPS** measure to the **Rows** shelf. To summarize the NPS as an average, click on the down arrow to the right of the measure pill on the **Rows** shelf. Select **Measure (Sum)** and then **Average** (Lab Exhibit 12.4.54).
5. Add the **Date** dimension to the **Columns** shelf. Click on the **+** icon on the date dimension pill twice to expand the date so that it shows the **Month** (Lab Exhibit 12.4.55). (Drag the **Quarter** dimension off the shelf so that quarter does not show on your visualization.)
6. Right-click on the Y-axis to change the axis so that it shows from 0 to 10 (the entire NPS scale). Within the **Edit Axis** dialog box, select the **Fixed** range and change the **Fixed end** to 10. You can remove the axis titles (to save room on your visualization) by deleting the title shown under **Axis Titles** (Lab Exhibit 12.4.56).
7. Add constant lines to show that NPS of 9 and 10 are promoters, and 6 and below are detractors. Click on the **Analytics** tab. Drag **Constant Line** to the pane and select **Add a Reference Line to Table** (Lab Exhibit 12.4.57). Right-click on the line to edit it. Change the **Value** to 9. Change the **Label** to Custom. Enter "Promoter" as the label (Lab Exhibit 12.4.58). Repeat these same steps to create a constant line at a value of 6 to show the Detractors.
8. Edit the title to read "NPS Over Time" and change the font size to 9 by right-clicking on the existing title and selecting **Edit Title**.
9. Right-click on the Detractor constant line again. Select **Format** and change the color of the reference line to red (Lab Exhibit 12.4.59).
10. Right-click on the Promoter constant line. Select **Format** and change the color of the reference line to green. The final visualization should resemble Lab Exhibit 12.4.60.

Analysis Task #4: Prepare a Stacked Column Chart Visualization to Summarize the Percentage of Customers Based on the NPS Measure

1. Add a new worksheet and rename the worksheet tab "Customer_NPS".
2. To add color to the tab to differentiate the different BSC dimensions, right-click on the tab. Select **Color**, then choose **Purple**. (For a refresher, see Lab Exhibit 12.4.6.)

3. Create groups from the NPS measure to assign NPS scores of 9–10 as "promoters," 7–8 as "neutral," and all others as "detractors."
   - Click on the down arrow on the **NPS** pill. Then select **Create** and then **Group...** (Lab Exhibit 12.4.61).
   - Select scores of 0–6 and click **Group** (Lab Exhibit 12.4.62). Change the name to "Detractors" by right-clicking on the default title.
   - Select scores of 7–8 and click **Group**. Change the name to "Neutral" by right-clicking on the default title.
   - Select scores of 9–10 and click **Group**. Change the name to "Promoters" by right-clicking on the default title.
4. Drag the **NPS (group)** measure to the **Rows** shelf. To summarize the NPS as an average, click on the down arrow to the right of the measure pill on the **Rows** shelf (Lab Exhibit 12.4.63).
5. Drag **Customer (count)** to the worksheet as the value (Lab Exhibit 12.4.63).
6. Change the value so that the count of customers giving each score is shown as the percent of total. To do so, click on the down arrow on the **CNT(Customer)** pill on the **Marks** card (Lab Exhibit 12.4.63).
   - Select **Quick Table Calculation**.
   - Select **Percent of Total**.
7. Change the visualization type to a stacked column by selecting the icon shown in Lab Exhibit 12.4.64.
8. Show the percentage of total in the visualization by clicking on the **Analysis** tab at the top of the screen. Then select **Show Mark Labels** (Lab Exhibit 12.4.65).
9. To show the label on the visualization as well, drag the **NPS (group)** dimension onto the **Label** mark. The **Marks** card should resemble Lab Exhibit 12.4.66.
10. Remove the Y-axis by right-clicking on the Y-axis and unchecking **Show Header** (Lab Exhibit 12.4.67). You do not need the Y-axis header because you are showing the values on the stacked column.
11. Hide the **Legend** card by right-clicking on the down arrow and selecting **Hide card** or by clicking on the **Analysis** tab, selecting **Legends**, and unchecking **Color legend** (as shown in the previous steps).
12. Edit the title to read "Customer NPS" and change the font size to 9 by right-clicking on the existing title and selecting **Edit Title**. The final visualization should resemble Lab Exhibit 12.4.68.

Analysis Task #5: Prepare a Text Table with Conditional Formatting to Summarize the Average Time Required to Deliver Food to Table over Time

1. Open a new worksheet. You will need to add a new data source to analyze data related to the time it takes to serve each table. Select the **Add Data** icon at the top of the screen.
2. Connect to **Lab 12.4 Data.xlsx**.
3. Drag the **Customer** worksheet to the **Data** pane. Review the view of the data shown at the bottom of your screen to make sure everything has imported correctly.
4. Rename the worksheet tab "Internal_Time to Table".
5. To add color to the tab to differentiate the different BSC dimensions, right-click on the tab. Select **Color**, then choose **Blue**. (For a refresher, see Lab Exhibit 12.4.6.)
6. Add the date dimension to the **Columns** shelf. Click on the **+** icon on the date dimension pill twice to expand the date so that it shows the **Month**. (Drag the **Quarter** dimension off the shelf so that quarter does not show on your visualization.)
7. Drag the measure **Daily Time to Serve** to the **Rows** shelf. Use the drop-down arrow on the **Daily Time to Serve** pill to change the summarization to **Average** (Lab Exhibit 12.4.69).

8. Change the visualization type to a text table by clicking on the icon shown in Lab Exhibit 12.4.70.
9. You can reformat the average to show only two decimals by clicking on the down arrow on the **AVG(Daily Time to Table)** pill on the **Marks** card. Select **Format...** and then adjust the numbers, as shown in Lab Exhibits 12.4.71 and 12.4.72.
10. Format the values in the table so that the text is in green if the value is less than 18 minutes (the target established by management) and red if the value is greater than 18 minutes.
   a. Drag the measure **Daily Time to Serve** to the **Color** mark on the **Marks** card (Lab Exhibit 12.4.73).
   b. Change the measure to **Average**.
   c. Click on the down arrow on the legend and select **Edit Colors...** (Lab Exhibit 12.4.74).
   d. Change the **Palette** to **Red-Green Diverging** (Lab Exhibit 12.4.75).
   e. Select the red color and change the **Stepped Color** number to **2** Steps (Lab Exhibit 12.4.75).
   f. Select **Reversed** (so that the table shows lower values as green). See again Lab Exhibit 12.4.75.
   g. Select **<<Advanced** and set the **Center** to **18**. The dialog box should look like Lab Exhibit 12.4.75.
   h. Click **OK**.
   i. Hide the legend.
   j. Right-click on the year and click **Show Header** to hide the year (to save space on your visualization). See Lab Exhibit 12.4.76.
   k. Change the title to "Time to Table". Change the font size to 9.
   l. The final visualization should resemble Lab Exhibit 12.4.77.

Analysis Task #6: Prepare a Text Table with Conditional Formatting to Summarize the Average Table Turnover Time

1. Open a new worksheet. You will need to add a new data source to analyze data related to table turnover time. Select the **Add Data** icon at the top of the screen.
2. Connect to **Lab 12.4 Data.xlsx**. Drag the **Table Turnover** worksheet to the **Data** pane.
3. Review the view of the data shown at the bottom of your screen to make sure everything has imported correctly.
4. Rename the worksheet tab "Internal_Table Turnover".
5. To add color to the tab to differentiate the different BSC dimensions, right-click on the tab. Select **Color**, then choose **Blue**. (See Lab Exhibit 12.4.6.)
6. This visualization is similar to the one you prepared in Analysis Task #5 except that you use the **Daily Turnover** measure as your value.
7. Instead of a text table, use the **Highlights Table** visualization by selecting the icon shown in Lab Exhibit 12.4.78.
8. Edit the colors of the highlights by clicking the right arrow on the legend and then **Edit Colors**. The final set of selections should match Lab Exhibit 12.4.79.
9. Hide the legend.
10. Hide the **Field Labels for Columns** (to remove the word "Date" from the top of your visualization).
11. Click **Show Header** so that the year does not show at the top of your visualization.
12. You can change the way the month appears so that it shows only the abbreviation. To do so, right-click on the month at the top of your table and then select **Format**.
13. When the **Format** dialog pane opens to the left of the screen, change the date format to **Abbreviation** (Lab Exhibit 12.4.80).
14. Change the title to "Table Turnover" and change the font size to 9.
15. The final visualization should resemble Lab Exhibit 12.4.81.

Analysis Task #7: Prepare a Pie Chart to Summarize the Employee Satisfaction Scores

1. Open a new worksheet. You will need to add a new data source to analyze data related to employee satisfaction scores. Select the **Add Data** icon at the top of the screen.
2. Connect to **Lab 12.4 Data.xlsx**. Drag the **Employee Satisfaction** worksheet to the **Data** pane. Review the view of the data shown at the bottom of your screen to make sure everything has imported correctly.
3. Rename the worksheet tab "Learning_EmpSat".
4. To add color to the tab to differentiate the different BSC dimensions, right-click on the tab. Select <u>C</u>olor, then choose **Yellow**. (See Lab Exhibit 12.4.6.)
5. Create groups for the employee satisfaction score to differentiate the low scores (3.5 and below) from the high scores (above 3.5). Start by clicking on the **June Score** variable and then follow the path shown in Lab Exhibits 12.4.82 and 12.4.83.
6. Drag the **June Score (group)** dimension to the **Rows** shelf.
7. Drag the **Count of Employee ID** as the value in the middle of the visualization.
8. You'll notice that there are employees who have an employee satisfaction score of 0. These employees left Castaways before they completed the Employee Satisfaction Survey in June. Exclude these from the analysis by right-clicking on the **0** and selecting **Exclude**.
9. Use a quick table calculation to change the value to the percent of the total. To do so, click on the down arrow on the **CNT(Employee Satisfaction Score)** pill on the **Marks** card.
10. Change the visualization type to a pie chart (Lab Exhibit 12.4.84).
11. Show **Marks** labels. Drag the labels onto the visualization. You may want to lighten the color of the pie chart by editing the color from the **Marks** card. Set the **Opacity** to **75%** (Lab Exhibit 12.4.84).
12. Add the Group name to the visualization by dragging the **June Score (group)** dimension onto the **Label** mark.
13. Change the colors to **Red** for low and **Green** for high by clicking the **Color** mark on the **Marks** card and then editing the colors.
14. Hide the legend.
15. Change the title to "Employee Satisfaction Scores" and change the font size to 9.
16. The final visualization should resemble Lab Exhibit 12.4.85.

Analysis Task #8: Prepare a Bar Chart to Summarize the Completed Employee Training

1. Open a new worksheet. You will need to add a new data source to analyze data related to employee training. Select the **Add Data** icon at the top of the screen.
2. Connect to **Lab 12.4 Data.xlsx**. Drag the **Training** worksheet to the **Data** pane. Review the view of the data shown at the bottom of your screen to make sure everything has imported correctly.
3. Rename the worksheet tab "Learning_Training".
4. To add color to the tab to differentiate the different BSC dimensions, right-click on the tab. Select <u>C</u>olor, then choose **Yellow**. (See Lab Exhibit 12.4.6.)
5. Create bins for the number of training hours in 5-hour increments. Click on the down arrow on **Training Hours**. Select **Create**. Select **Bins**, and set the **Size of bins** to 5 (Lab Exhibits 12.4.86 and 12.4.87).
6. Drag **Training Hours (bin)** to the **Columns** shelf.
7. Drag **Employee ID** to the **Rows** shelf and change the summarization to **Count (Distinct)** by following the path shown in Lab Exhibit 12.4.88a.
8. Use the **Quick Table Calculation** (see Lab Exhibit 12.4.88a) to change the calculation type to **Percent of the Total** (Lab Exhibit 12.4.88b).

9. Change the alias for the bins at the bottom of your column chart by right-clicking on the label and then selecting **Edit Alias** (Lab Exhibit 12.4.89). Change the aliases to 0-4, 5-9, and 10-14.
10. From the **Analysis** tab at the top of the screen, select **Show Mark Labels**.
11. Click the Y-axis and select **Show Header** to remove the header (Lab Exhibit 12.4.89). You do not need it because you have shown the Marks labels on the visualization.
12. Change the title to "Employee Training" and change the font size to 9.
13. The final visualization should resemble Lab Exhibit 12.4.90.

Analysis Task #9: Summarize All Visualizations into a Dashboard for Executive Management

You are going to create a single dashboard, separated into four parts (one for each dimension). Within each part, you will have two visualizations. Due to the nature of some of the visualizations in your set, it will be best to format the dashboard so that you have four horizontal compartments.

1. Click on the **Dashboard** icon at the bottom of your screen to create a new dashboard (Lab Exhibit 12.4.91).
2. Make sure your dashboard is set to **Tiled** and drag a vertical object to the dashboard screen (Lab Exhibit 12.4.92).
3. Drag a second vertical compartment onto the screen so that your screen is split in half horizontally, as shown in Lab Exhibit 12.4.93.
4. You will repeat this process two more times to get a total of four bands on the dashboard. It may be helpful to add borders around each so that you can see what you are doing spatially. (Creating dashboards can be challenging if you are working without seeing where the containers are.) To add a border, click the **Layout** tab, and then select/format the **Border**, as shown in Lab Exhibit 12.4.94.
5. Once you've done this and have all four containers, you will see that the item hierarchy (on the layout tab) shows four vertical containers, as shown in Lab Exhibit 12.4.95.
6. Now we will fill each container with the visualizations relating to each dimension.
   a. Financial
      • On the **Layout** screen, make sure **Vertical** on the **Item hierarchy** is selected, and change the **Background** color to green. Set the opacity to about **20%**. This action will make the top band green and will help differentiate the financial performance measures from the others (Lab Exhibit 12.4.96).
      • Click back to the **Dashboard** tab.
      • Drag the **Financial Summary** visualization onto the dashboard and situate it *inside* the top container. The screen will turn gray to show where the visualization is going to fit (Lab Exhibit 12.4.97).
      • Drag the **Financial Change** visualization on the dashboard to the right of the summary visualization, still within the top container.
      • Drag a text object into the container as well. Align it all the way to the left and adjust the size so that it is narrow (approximately 30 pixels if you use the **Edit width** option when you right-click on the text box). Type "Financial" in the text box, then click **OK** (Lab Exhibit 12.4.98).
         • Right-click on the text box. Select **Format text**. In the **Format Text** pane on the left, click the drop-down arrow on the alignment box to turn the text sideways (Lab Exhibit 12.4.99).
      • At this point, your financial container should resemble Exhibit 12.4.100.
      • You will need to make formatting adjustments to make your data visualization more legible. It is easiest to do this back on the original visualization. You may want to change font size, delete headers or titles, and so on.

Note: You'll want to make formatting changes consistent. For example, if you change the title size on one dimension, you'll want to do the same for all dimensions.

b. Customer
- On the **Layout** screen, make sure the second layout container on the **Item hierarchy** is selected, and change the **Background** color to purple. Set the opacity to **20%**.
- Drag **Customer NPS** into the container.
- Drag **NPS Over Time** into the container to the right of Customer NPS.
- Resize as needed. For this dimension, you will probably want NPS Over Time to take up about 75 percent of the container.
- Add the text box showing "Customer" to the left.
- Format as needed.
- This result will resemble Lab Exhibit 12.4.101.

c. Internal Processes
- On the **Layout** screen, make sure the third layout container on the **Item hierarchy** is selected, and change the **Background** color to blue. Set the opacity to **20%**.
- Drag **Time to Table** into the container.
- Drag **Table Turnover** into the container just below Time to Table. (The orientation of these visualizations makes this layout better.)
- Resize as needed.
- Add the text box showing "Internal Processes" to the left.
  - You may find that you cannot fit this text box into the same container, and instead it creates its own container to the left of the Internal Processes container.
  - If so, you can still format and orient as you did previously, but this is now acting as a separate object in your item hierarchy. You will need to add a background color to match the rest of your dimension.
  - Also adjust the inner and outer padding (also in the **Layout** screen) to zero, as shown in Lab Exhibit 12.4.102.
- Format as needed.
- This dimension will resemble Lab Exhibit 12.4.103.

d. Learning and Growth
- On the **Layout** screen, make sure the fourth layout container on the **Item hierarchy** is selected, and change the **Background** color to yellow. Set the opacity to **20%**.
- Drag **Employee Satisfaction Scores** into the container.
- Drag **Employee Training** into the container to the right of Employee Satisfaction Scores.
- Resize as needed. For this dimension, you will probably want Employee Training to take up about 75% of the container.
- Add the text box showing "Learning & Growth" to the left.
- Format as needed.
- This dimension will resemble Lab Exhibit 12.4.104.

The finished dashboard will resemble Lab Exhibit 12.4.105. Rename your dashboard "Castaways BSC".

Assessment

1. Take a screenshot of the dashboard, label it Submission 1, and paste it into a Word document named "Lab 12.4 Submission.docx".
2. Answer the questions in Connect and upload your Lab 12.4 Submission.docx via Connect if assigned.

DATA VISUALIZATION

Creating a Balanced Scorecard Dashboard to Track Performance (Heartwood)

Data Analytics Type: Descriptive

Keywords

Balanced Scorecard, KPI

Decision-Making Context

Managers use the balanced scorecard to evaluate organizational performance on multiple dimensions. Key performance indicators (KPIs) from the financial dimension provide insight into the firm's financial performance and provide a look back. KPIs related to customers, the internal processes of the organization, and the learning and growth of employees provide additional insight into how the organization may fare in the future.

Heartwood Cabinets has just implemented a balanced scorecard and has asked you to summarize the data using Tableau software. Follow the methodology in Lab 12.4 to create a snapshot summary using the Tableau dashboard function so that you can assess Heartwood's performance on all four dimensions.

Required

Apply the same steps in Lab 12.4 to the **Alt Lab 12.4 Data.xlsx** dataset and:

1. Prepare visualizations for each of the KPIs available to you.
   a. Financial
      i. Revenue
      ii. COGS
      iii. Profit
   b. Customer
      i. Net promoter score
   c. Internal Processes
      i. Changeover time (amount of time spent between production)
      ii. Overtime rate (% of overtime hours as a function of regular hours)
   d. Learning and Growth
      i. Employee satisfaction score
      ii. Supervisor evaluations
      iii. Employee training
2. Prepare a dashboard that combines your prepared visualizations in a user-friendly format that will facilitate decision making by the Heartwood management team.

Ask the Question

Is Heartwood meeting expectations on all four dimensions?

To answer this question, refer to the following strategic measures and objectives. The third column tells you which type of visualization(s) to create to evaluate performance for each dimension.

KPI	Target	Visualization
Financial		
Increase revenue	Increase over time	• Area chart showing all three measures
Decrease COGS	Decrease over time	• Bar graph showing calculated difference by quarter for each measure
Increase profit	Increase over time	
Customer		
Positive net promoter score	• At least 50% "promoters" (50% of responses of 9 or 10) • Less than 10% detractors (less than 10% of responses of 6 or less)	• Stacked bar chart • Line graph spanning each month of 2012
Internal Processes		
Changeover time	Changeover time (in minutes) should be less than 5% of total available time (in minutes)	• Highlights table showing Changeover Time Percent for each month (2012 only) • Changeover % = (Net Available Time – Production Time)/(Net Available Time)
Overtime rate	Overtime rate should not exceed 2%	• Highlights table showing Overtime Rate as a percent for each month (2012 only) • Overtime Rate = Overtime Hours/Regular Hours
Learning and Growth		
Increase employee satisfaction score	At least 80% of scores greater than 3.5	• Pie chart showing percent of employees with high and low scores
Increase employee evaluation score	• At least 30% of employees with scores of 8 or above • Fewer than 10% of employees below 5	• Column chart showing % of employees receiving each evaluation score
Improve employee training	50% of employees have completed 20 hours of training	• Pie chart showing groups of 10 or less, 11–19, and 20

Assessment

1. Take a screenshot of the dashboard, label it Submission 1, and paste it into a Word document named "Alt Lab 12.4 Submission.docx".
2. Answer the questions in Connect and upload your Alt Lab 12.4 Submission.docx via Connect if assigned.

DATA VISUALIZATION

Creating a Balanced Scorecard Dashboard to Track Performance

Data Analytics Type: Descriptive

Keywords

Balanced Scorecard, KPI

Decision-Making Context

Managers use the balanced scorecard to evaluate organizational performance on multiple dimensions. Key performance indicators (KPIs) from the financial dimension provide insight into the firm's financial performance and provide a look back. KPIs related to customers, the internal processes of the organization, and the learning and growth of employees provide additional insight into how the organization may fare in the future.

You work for an oceanside restaurant called Castaways. The executive chef has recently implemented a balanced scorecard approach and has asked you to summarize the data using Power BI software. She would like you to create a snapshot summary using the Power BI dashboard function so that she can easily see where Castaways stands on each of the four dimensions.

Required

1. Prepare visualizations for each of the KPIs available to you.
   a. Financial
      i. Revenue
      ii. COGS
      iii. Profit
   b. Customer
      i. Net promoter score
   c. Internal Processes
      i. Meals served time
      ii. Table turnover
   d. Learning and Growth
      i. Employee satisfaction score
      ii. Employee training
2. Prepare a dashboard that combines your prepared visualizations in a user-friendly format that will facilitate decision making by the executive chef and her management team.

Ask the Question

Is Castaways meeting expectations on all four dimensions? To answer this question, refer to the following strategic measures and objectives:

KPI	Target
Financial	
Increase revenue	Increase over time
Decrease COGS	Decrease over time
Increase profit	Increase over time
Customer	
Positive net promoter score	• NPS $\geq$ 9 • At least 60% "promoters" (that is, 60% of responses are 9 or 10) • Less than 10% detractors (that is, less than 10% of responses are 6 or less)
Internal Processes	
Decrease meals served time	Time to table should be below 18 minutes
Table turnover	Total mealtime should be less than 90 minutes
Learning and Growth	
Increase employee satisfaction score	• Average employee satisfaction $\geq$ 3.5 • At least 80% of scores greater than 3.5
Improve employee training	90% of employees have completed 20 hours of training

Master the Data

For this lab, we'll use the data in the Excel file titled **Lab 12.5 Data.xlsx**.

Notice that this Excel workbook has multiple tabs. Review the tabs to familiarize yourself with the data:

Worksheet (Tab)	Description
Customer	Individual net promoter score (NPS) data from customers throughout the year
Sales Records	Detailed sales records from the year (2024)
COGS	COGS entries made during the year
Time to Serve	Daily average time to serve tables
Table Turnover	Daily average table turnover time
Employee Satisfaction	Employee satisfaction scores from two employee surveys (September and June)
Training	Employee training records

Note that Castaways' fiscal year (FY) runs from Jan 1 to Dec 31. The data provided is for FY 2024.

To import the data into Power BI, proceed as follows:

1. Open Power BI and select **Get data**, as shown in Lab Exhibit 12.5.1.
2. From the **Get Data** dialog box, select **Excel Workbook** and click **Connect** (Lab Exhibit 12.5.2)
3. Navigate to your data and select **Lab Data 12.5.xlsx**.
4. When the **Navigator** dialog window opens, select each of the worksheets because you will include them all in your analysis (Lab Exhibit 12.5.3). Then click **Load**.
5. Once the data are loaded, you will see the list of tables (worksheets) available for your analysis in the **Fields** section of your **Power BI Report** screen, as shown in Lab Exhibit 12.5.4.

Perform the Analysis

In Power BI you can create multiple visualizations on the same report tab. We will use a different tab for each balanced scorecard dimension before combining all visualizations into a single dashboard report. At the end of your work, you will have five tabs total.

Analysis Task #1: Prepare Visualizations Related to the Financial Dimension

For the financial dimension, you will make two visualizations:

- An area chart showing sales, COGS, and profit by month.
- A line graph showing sales, COGS, and profit by month.

1. Rename the first tab "Financial" at the bottom of your report screen, as shown in Lab Exhibit 12.5.5.

Calculate monthly profit from sales and COGS

2. Profit is a function of sales and COGS. However, these two fields are in separate tables and there is not a direct connection between them in the data. Therefore, to calculate profit, you will need to create a new measure using the sum of sales and the sum of COGS to find profit.
3. To create a new measure, click on the **Modeling** tab at the top of the screen and select **New measure** (Lab Exhibit 12.5.6).
4. When the **Measure** tab opens, enter the formula for Profit in the formula bar at the top of the screen. Use the formula shown in Lab Exhibit 12.5.7: Profit = sum('Sales Records'[Sales])-sum([COGS]).

Lab Exhibit 12.5.7

Microsoft Power BI

Note: When you enter a formula, the syntax shows the table from which the field is pulled in single quotes ('Table') and the field name in square brackets ([Field]). In Lab Exhibit 12.5.7, you should notice that the COGS field does not show the table name. Power BI defaulted to putting the new profit measure in the COGS table, so you do not need to tell it which table to look to in order to find the field. If you had clicked the **Sales Record** table before opening the **Measures** tab (from Step 3 above), the formula would have looked a little different because you would not need 'Sales Records' to precede [Sales].

Don't worry, though, when you are creating a new formula. All you really need to do is start typing the field name, and Power BI will open a list of fields from which you can select the right one, as shown in Lab Exhibit 12.5.8.

5. You will now see that **Profit** has been added to the list of available fields in the **Fields** list (see Lab Exhibit 12.5.9).

Create an area chart to show changes in Sales, COGS, and Profit over time

6. Click on the **stacked area chart** icon in the **Visualizations** tab on the right side of your report screen (see Lab Exhibit 12.5.10) to start building this visual.

7. Drag the **COGS**, **Profit**, and **Sales** fields to the **Values** shelf in the **Visualizations** tab, as shown in Lab Exhibit 12.5.11.

8. Open the **Date Hierarchy** in the **COGS** table in the **Fields** tab by clicking on **Transaction Date**, then **Date Hierarchy**, and then **Month** (as shown in Lab Exhibit 12.5.12). Then, in the **Visualizations** tab, drag the **Month** to the **Axis** shelf.

9. You will notice that the visualization is being built in the report screen to the left. But, so far, it shows almost the same amount of sales and COGS each month as evidenced by the straight lines representing sales and COGS (see Lab Exhibit 12.5.13). This is because the two tables are not yet related to each other. We will fix this problem in the next steps.

10. Let's look at the data model to see how to relate these two tables. Click on the **Modeling** icon on the left side of the report screen to open up the **Modeling** screen (Lab Exhibit 12.5.14). COGS and Sales Records do not really have any fields in common. Although both have **Transaction Date**, we know that there is not a straightforward relationship between individual sales transactions (which are entered immediately) and COGS entries (which are summarized and booked periodically).

11. To relate these two tables, we are going to create a Month field (column) in the **COGS** table and the **Sales Records** table. Then we will be able to connect the data using the Month field to aggregate the individual transactions.

12. Navigate back to the report screen by clicking on the **report** icon on the left side of the screen (see Lab Exhibit 12.5.15).

13. Click on the **Modeling** tab, then make sure you've clicked to activate the **COGS** table (so that you will place the new column in the **COGS** table) and then click **New column**.

14. In the formula bar that opens up, you will enter a **Format** formula to create a field that extracts the month from the Transaction Date field and creates a text field that spells out the month name. As shown in Lab Exhibit 12.5.16, this formula is Month = FORMAT ([Transaction Date], "MMMM"). In this formula, "MMMM" tells the program to return the full name for the month.

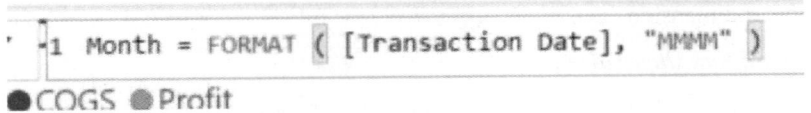

Lab Exhibit 12.5.16

Microsoft Power BI

15. Repeat Steps 13 and 14, but this time make sure you have clicked on the **Sales Records** table so that the Month column will be added to the Sales Records table.

16. Now that you have a month field in each table, return to the **Modeling** tab by clicking the **Modeling** icon on the left of the screen (Lab Exhibit 12.5.17).

17. Drag the **Month** field from the **COGS** table to the **Sales Records** table, as shown in Lab Exhibit 12.5.18.

18. You'll see that a connection is now made between the two tables. Also, the **Edit relationship** dialog box opens up (as shown in Lab Exhibit 12.5.19). In this case, you do not have to make any changes. Just click **OK**.

19. Now when you navigate back to the report screen by clicking on the **Report** icon on the left, you will see that the area graph has changed and you can now see variation in the values for each month. Your visualization should resemble the one shown in Lab Exhibit 12.5.20.

20. Now let's format this chart. Make sure your cursor has clicked in your visualization to activate it. Then click on the **paint roller** icon (Lab Exhibit 12.5.21) in the **Visualizations** tab to start formatting.

21. Click on the **Data colors** option and then change the colors using the drop-down boxes for each measure so that Sales is blue, COGS is yellow, and Profit is green (Lab Exhibit 12.5.22).

22. Next, we do not need the title "Month" on the X-axis. It is obvious that this axis represents month because we have the individual month names showing. To remove this axis title, navigate to the **X axis** option, and then scroll down and toggle the **Title** option to **Off** (as shown in Lab Exhibit 12.5.23).

23. The final visualizations should resemble Lab Exhibit 12.5.24.

Create a line graph to show Sales, Profit, and COGS over time

The line graph will be very similar to the area graph you just created. However, we will not put the data in the same order as shown in the area graph, which will allow us to focus more on the trend in the individual measures rather than their relationships to one another.

24. Because these charts are so similar, instead of creating the new visualization from scratch, you can copy and paste the area graph just below the original area graph. Then select the **line graph** icon from the **Visualizations** tab (Lab Exhibit 12.5.25).

25. You'll see that the entire line graph is created automatically, as shown in Lab Exhibit 12.5.26. If necessary, you could format this graph now, but in this case you do not need to make any additional modifications.

Analysis Task #2: Prepare Visualizations Related to the Customer Dimension

For the customer dimension, you will make three visualizations:

- A card that shows the overall NPS.
- A pie chart that shows the percentage of customers in each NPS category.
- A line graph that shows average NPS by month.

1. Open a new tab by clicking on the orange + sign at the bottom of the screen (see Lab Exhibit 12.5.27) and name it "Customer" to begin preparing visualizations for the customer dimension.

Create a card that shows overall NPS

2. Click on the **card visualization** icon in the **Visualizations** pane, as shown in Lab Exhibit 12.5.28.

3. In the **Visualizations** pane, click open the **Customer** table from the **Fields** pane, select **NPS**, and drag NPS to the **Fields** shelf (Lab Exhibit 12.5.29).

4. By default, the **NPS** field will be set to **Sum**. Change it to **Average** by clicking on the down arrow on the **NPS** field and selecting **Average**, as shown in Lab Exhibit 12.5.30.

5. The card on your report screen will now show **Average of NPS**, as shown in Lab Exhibit 12.5.31.

6. Format the card so that the background color is red if the average NPS is below 6 (that is, detractors), yellow if it is between 6 and 8 (that is, passives), and green if it is above 8 (that is, promoters). To format the background color, click on the **paintbrush** icon in the **Visualizations** pane, then select **Background** and click the *fx* button under **Color** (Lab Exhibit 12.5.32).

7. Once you open the **Color** *fx* dialog box, set **Format by** to **Rules**, as shown in Lab Exhibit 12.5.33.

8. Change the **Summarization** of the **Based on field** option to **Average**, as shown in Lab Exhibit 12.5.34.

9. In the **Rules** section, create three conditional formatting rules. For the first, change the color to green if the average NPS is above 8.5, indicating that on average customers are promoters. Use the drop-down arrow in the first box (shown in Lab Exhibit 12.5.35) to indicate an **is greater than** rule. Enter the number **8.5** in the second box. This rule requires a second condition, so in this case, select **is less than** from Box 3 and enter **11** in Box 4 because NPS only ranges to 10, so this will include any average 9 or above. In Box 5, use the drop-down arrow to select the green color. Then click **New rule** to create the next rule.

10. Follow similar logic to create the two additional rules as shown in Lab Exhibit 12.5.36. Click **OK** when done with both rules.

11. Even after you click **OK**, the background color will not update because the transparency is set to 0 by default (meaning you cannot see the color). Increase the transparency by moving the slider to 75% in the **Background** section of the **Visualizations** pane, as shown in Lab Exhibit 12.5.37.

12. The completed card will resemble Lab Exhibit 12.5.38.

Create a pie chart that shows the percentage of customers in each NPS category

13. To categorize customers into NPS categories (promoter, passive, or detractor), click on the three dots to the right of the **NPS** field in the **Fields** pane, as shown in Lab Exhibit 12.5.39.

14. Select **New group** from the drop-down menu, as shown in Lab Exhibit 12.5.40.

15. When the **Groups** dialog box opens, change the **Group type** to **List** (as shown in Lab Exhibit 12.5.41)

16. In the **Groups** dialog box, you will now see a list of all of the possible values in the NPS field in the **Ungrouped values** window. You will select the values that apply to each group and then click **Group**, which will move those values over to the **Groups and members** window (Lab Exhibit 12.5.42).

17. For the first group, select values 0,1,2,3,4,5,6; group them; and rename their group "Detractors", as shown in Lab Exhibit 12.5.43.

18. Repeat this step for Passives (values 7, 8) and Promoters (values 9, 10). You will be left with no values in the **Ungrouped values** window. Then click **OK**. See Lab Exhibit 12.5.44.

19. You will see a new field has been created called **NPS (groups)** in the **Customer** table on the **Fields** pane (Lab Exhibit 12.5.45).

20. Now, select the **pie chart** icon from the **Visualizations** pane (Lab Exhibit 12.5.46).

21. The pie chart should reflect the percentage of total customers categorized as promoters, passives, and detractors, so you need to use a field that captures each individual response. In this case, use ResponseID. In the **Visualizations** pane, drag **ResponseID** to the **Values** shelf (Lab Exhibit 12.5.47).

22. Then, to show each slice of the pie, drag **NPS (groups)** to the **Legend** shelf (Lab Exhibit 12.5.48).

23. Your pie chart will now look like the one shown in Lab Exhibit 12.5.49.

24. Format the pie chart by changing the colors to reflect the red/yellow/green shading used in the previous NPS-related visualizations. Click on the **paintbrush** icon to open the **Format** pane. Then select **Data colors** and change the colors of each category (Lab Exhibit 12.5.50).

25. Next, change the data label on the chart by opening the **Data labels** tab. Then change the **Label style** to **Category, percent of total**, as shown in Lab Exhibit 12.5.51.

26. Scroll down and change the **Label position** to **Inside** (this will save room by placing the category and % of total inside the chart). You may need to change the font color back to black after the position change so that you can see all of the labels. See Lab Exhibit 12.5.52.

27. Because you have the labels on the chart, you can turn off the legend (see in Lab Exhibit 12.5.53).
28. Change the title of the chart. Click on **Title**, and then type "% of Customers in each NPS Category" in the **Title text** space. Finally, center the **Alignment** (Lab Exhibit 12.5.54).
29. Your final chart will look like the one shown in Lab Exhibit 12.5.55.

Create a line graph that shows average NPS by category by month

30. From the **Visualizations** pane, select the icon for the line graph visualization (Lab Exhibit 12.5.56).
31. Drag **NPS** to the **Values** shelf and change the field **Values** to **Average**, then drag the **Month** field (from **Date Hierarchy**) to the **Axis** shelf by following the steps in Lab Exhibit 12.5.57.
32. Your line graph should look like the one shown in Lab Exhibit 12.5.58.
33. We now want to add two reference lines to the chart so that users can easily visualize average NPS relative to promoter (9–10) or detractor (0–6) scores. For Steps 34–39, follow along with Lab Exhibit 12.5.59.
34. Click on the **Analytics** icon on the **Visualizations** tab.
35. Click on **Y-Axis Constant Line 1**.
36. Change the name to "Detractor" in the **Label** field.
37. Change the **Value** to **6** (so that the line shows on the graph at a constant value of 6).
38. Change the **Color** to red (to reflect the negative evaluation).
39. Set the **Line style** to **Dashed**.
40. Continue formatting this constant line by turning on the **Data label**, setting the label **Color** to red, setting the label **Text** to **Name and value**, and moving the label to the **Right** side of the visualization. These steps are summarized in Lab Exhibit 12.5.60.
41. You now have a constant line that represents the detractor score for reference, as shown in Lab Exhibit 12.5.61.
42. Repeat steps 34–41 to add a green reference line for Promoters at a value of 9.
43. You should now have two constant lines on your line graph, which should resemble the line graph shown in Lab Exhibit 12.5.62.
44. You can remove the axis titles from the X- and Y-axes because they are self-explanatory.
    a. Click on the **paintbrush** icon, select **X axis**, and slide **Title** to **Off** (Lab Exhibit 12.5.63).
    b. Repeat the steps in part a, this time using the **Y axis** options (as shown in Lab Exhibit 12.5.64).
45. Your final line graph should look like the one shown in Lab Exhibit 12.5.65.

Analysis Task #3: Prepare Visualizations Related to the Internal Processes Dimension

For the internal processes dimension, you will make two visualizations:

- A matrix table with conditional formatting showing the average time required to turn tables.
- A matrix table with conditional formatting showing the average time to serve customers.

1. Open a new tab by clicking on the orange **+** sign at the bottom of the screen (as shown in Lab Exhibit 12.5.66) and name it "Internal Processes" to begin preparing visualizations for the internal processes dimension.

Create matrix table with conditional formatting showing the average time required to turn tables

2. From the **Visualizations** pane, select the **matrix table** icon (Lab Exhibit 12.5.67).

3. Open the **Table Turnover** table from the **Fields** pane. Drag **Month** (from the **Date Hierarchy**) to the **Columns** shelf in the **Visualizations** pane. Drag **Daily Turnover** to the **Values** shelf. Change the aggregation of **Daily Turnover** to average by clicking on the down arrow on the field and selecting **Average**. Lab Exhibit 12.5.68 summarizes these steps.

4. You now have a matrix table that shows the average time to turn a table by month, as shown in Lab Exhibit 12.5.69.

5. Next, apply conditional formatting by clicking on the **paintbrush** icon and scrolling down to **Conditional formatting**. Open the **Conditional formatting** tab, slide **Background color** to **On**, and select **Advanced controls** (as shown in Lab Exhibit 12.5.70).

6. When the **Advanced controls** dialog box opens, set the **Format by** to **Rules**. For **Based on field**, select **Average of Daily Turnover**. Under **Summarization** select **Average**. Then set rules in the same manner you did when creating the background color for the **Average NPS** card in Analysis Task #2. However, in this case, the color should be green if the average time to turn tables is less than 75.5 minutes and red if it is greater than or equal to 75.5 minutes (as shown in Lab Exhibit 12.5.71). Click **OK** when finished.

   Note: Because Power BI requires both a less than and a greater than value, set the high end of the red values to be very high (for example, 500 minutes) so that it captures all values.

7. Add a title by clicking on the **paintbrush** icon, opening the **Title** tab, changing the **Title text** to **Average Time to Turn Tables**, and then centering the title using the **Alignment** options (as shown in Lab Exhibit 12.5.72).

8. You now have a matrix table that is conditionally formatted and resembles the one in Lab Exhibit 12.5.73.

Create a matrix table with conditional formatting showing the average time to serve customers

9. From the **Visualizations** pane, select the **matrix table** icon (as shown in Lab Exhibit 12.5.74).

10. Click open the **Time to Serve** table from the **Fields** pane. Drag the **Month** field (from the **Date Hierarchy**) to the **Columns** shelf of the **Visualizations** pane. Drag the **Daily Time to Serve** field to the **Values** shelf of the **Visualizations** pane. Change the field value by clicking on the down arrow and selecting **Average** from the drop-down menu. Lab Exhibit 12.5.75 summarizes these steps.

11. Use conditional formatting to change the font color to red or green based on the criteria set forth by Castaways. First, click on the **paintbrush** icon, then open the **Conditional formatting** tab, slide the **Font color** slider to **On**, and click **Advanced controls** (see Lab Exhibit 12.5.76).

12. When the **Advanced controls** dialog box opens, you will set the conditions following the same steps as you did when formatting the background color of the **Table Turnover** visualization. As shown in Lab Exhibit 12.5.77, set the **Format by** option to **Rules** and the **Summarization** option to **Average**. Then create two rules. For the first, any values less than or equal to 18 should be colored green. For the second, any values greater than 18 (and less than a large number like 60) should be colored red. Then click **OK**.

13. Add a title by sliding the **Title** slider to **On**. In the **Title text** box, enter the title "Average Time to Serve" and set the **Alignment** to center (as shown in Lab Exhibit 12.5.78).
14. You now have a finished matrix table visualization that looks like Lab Exhibit 12.5.79.

Analysis Task #4: Prepare Visualizations Related to the Learning and Growth Dimension

For the learning and growth dimension, you will make three visualizations:

- A card that shows the average employee satisfaction.
- A donut chart showing changes in employee satisfaction.
- A column chart showing the training hours completed by employees to serve customers.

1. Open a new tab by clicking on the orange **+** sign at the bottom of the screen (as shown in Lab Exhibit 12.5.80) and name it "Learning and Growth" to begin preparing visualizations for the learning and growth dimension.

Create a card that shows the average employee satisfaction

2. On the **Visualizations** pane, click on the **card** icon, as shown in Lab Exhibit 12.5.81.
3. As shown in Lab Exhibit 12.5.82, open the **Employee Satisfaction** table in the **Fields** pane. Drag **June Score**, which is the most recent employee satisfaction survey, to the **Fields** shelf (on the **Visualizations** pane) and change the field value to average by clicking on the drop-down arrow and selecting **Average** from the drop-down menu.
4. Add conditional formatting to the background of the card (similar to what you did in Analysis Task #2) such that the background is red if the average employee satisfaction score is less than or equal to 3.5 and green if the score is between 3.5 and 6. As shown in Lab Exhibit 12.5.83, click on the **paintbrush** icon to open the **Formatting** pane, move the **Background** slider to **On**, and click the *fx* button to open the **Conditional formatting** dialog box.
5. When the **Conditional formatting** dialog box opens, set it to **Format by Rules**, based on the **Average of June Score**, and set the **Rules** so that it is red if the average employee satisfaction score is greater than or equal to 0 and less than or equal to 3.5, and green if the score is between 3.5 and 6 (as shown in Lab Exhibit 12.5.84). Click **OK** when done.
6. Add a title by sliding the **Title** slider to **On** (as shown in Lab Exhibit 12.5.85). Then enter the title "Current Average Employee Satisfaction" in the **Title text** field and set the **Alignment** to center.
7. Turn off the category label on the card so that it does not show "average of June score" under the value by sliding the **Category** slider to **Off** (as shown in Lab Exhibit 12.5.86).
8. You now have a completed card visualization that looks like the one shown in Lab Exhibit 12.5.87.

Create a donut chart showing changes in employee satisfaction

9. To create a chart showing the changes in employee satisfaction, you must first calculate the change in employee scores. To do so, you will create a new column titled "Change" for the **Employee Satisfaction** table.
10. Make sure you have clicked in the **Employee Satisfaction** table (Lab Exhibit 12.5.88).
11. Select **New column** from the top of the report screen (Lab Exhibit 12.5.89).

12. In the bar, enter the formula shown in Lab Exhibit 12.5.90 to calculate the change for employee satisfaction between the January survey and the June survey. The formula is Change = [January Score] - [June Score].

```
1  Change = [January Score]-[June Score]
```

13. You will see that the new column has been added to the **Employee Satisfaction** table, as shown in Lab Exhibit 12.5.91.
14. Next, create a change category field that will classify each employee as having an Increase, Decrease, or No Change in their satisfaction rating between the two surveys. Also, create a category for new employees who do not have a January survey. The formula is shown in Lab Exhibit 12.5.92 and is described below.

```
Change Category = IF(Not(Isblank([January Score])), If([January Score]<[June Score], "Increase", if ([January Score]>[June Score], "Decrease", "No Change")),"New Employee")
```

Lab Exhibit 12.5.92

Microsoft Power BI

- IF(Not(Isblank([January Score]))) → tells the program to only apply the subsequent **IF** formulas to the employees for whom the **January Score** field has a value. Otherwise, it would categorize all new employees as Increase.
- If([January Score]<[June Score], "Increase" → categorizes any employee whose January score was less than their June score as an increase.
- If([January Score]>[June Score], "Decrease" → categorizes any employee whose January score was greater than their June score as a decrease.
- "No Change" → categorizes everyone else (who has a January score) as "No Change".
- "New Employee" → categorizes everyone who does not have a January score as a new employee.

Next, we'll use the new category field we created in our donut chart.

15. In the **Visualizations** pane, click on the **donut** icon (Exhibit 12.5.93).
16. As shown in Lab Exhibit 12.5.94, drag **Employee ID** to the **Values** shelf. Click on the down arrow and click on **Show value as** and **Percent of grand total**.
17. Drag **Change Category** to the **Legend** shelf, as shown in Lab Exhibit 12.5.95.
18. Now you should have a donut chart that looks like the one shown in Lab Exhibit 12.5.96.
19. Change the **Detail labels** on the donut graph so that it shows only the **Percent of total** for each category (Lab Exhibit 12.5.97)
20. Change the title of the chart by sliding the **Title** slider to **On**. Then enter the title "Change in Employee Satisfaction" in the **Title text**. See Lab Exhibit 12.5.98.
21. Change the legend so that it shows at the bottom of the chart and takes less space. To do so, slide the **Legend** slider to **On** and change the **Position** to **Bottom Center**, as shown in Lab Exhibit 12.5.99.
22. Your final donut chart will look like the one shown in Lab Exhibit 12.5.100.

Create a column chart showing the training hours completed by employees to serve customers

23. You need to create bins to categorize the number of training hours each employee has completed. To do this, click on the ellipses (3 dots) on the right side of the **Training Hours** field in the **Training** table. See Lab Exhibit 12.5.101.
24. From the drop-down menu that opens, select **New group** (Lab Exhibit 12.5.102).

25. This time you will create groups using bins of equal size. When the **Groups** dialog box opens, make sure the **Group type** is set to **Bin**, and the **Bin size** is set to **5**. This will place individuals in a group based on the number of training hours they have completed (0–5, 6–10, and so on). Click **OK**. See Lab Exhibit 12.5.103.

26. In the **Field** pane, you will now see a new field, **Training Hours (bins)**, in the **Training** table (Lab Exhibit 12.5.104).

27. To begin creating your visualization, click on the **clustered column chart** icon on the **Visualizations** pane, as shown in Lab Exhibit 12.5.105.

28. Drag the **Training Hours (bins)** field to the **Axis** and the **Employee ID** field to the **Values** shelf. Then click the down arrow in the **Count of Employee ID** under **Values** (Lab Exhibit 12.5.106).

29. From the drop-down menu, click **Show value as** and then select **Percent of grand total**, as shown in Lab Exhibit 12.5.107.

30. Show the percentages on the chart by clicking on the **paintbrush** icon and then sliding the **Data labels** slider to **On** (as shown in Lab Exhibit 12.5.108).

31. Your column chart should look like the one shown in Lab Exhibit 12.5.109.

32. Change the color of the bins so that the column representing employees with 20 hours is green, those columns representing 10 and 15 hours are yellow, and the column showing 5 hours is red. To do this, click on the **paintbrush** icon. Then open the **Data colors** tab and slide the **Show all** slider to **On** (see Lab Exhibit 12.5.110).

33. Change the color for each bin as shown in Lab Exhibit 5.12.111.

34. Change the **Title text** of the graph to "Training Hours Completed", as shown in Lab Exhibit 12.5.112.

35. Your finished column chart should look like the one shown in Lab Exhibit 12.5.113.

Analysis Task #5: Prepare the Balanced Scorecard Dashboard

For this dashboard, you will create four bands (using shapes formatted with different colors) on the report screen to represent the different dimensions. Then you will place visualizations that you created previously within the appropriate band.

1. Open a new tab at the bottom of the report page, and label it "Dashboard".

2. Click the **shapes** icon in the upper-right corner of the screen and select a rectangle shape from the drop-down menu, as shown in Lab Exhibit 12.5.114.

3. A rectangle will appear on your screen, as shown in Lab Exhibit 12.5.115.

4. Fit this rectangle so that it takes up approximately the top ¼ of the screen. Then format the color of the rectangle so that it is light green. To do so, click on the **Format shape** pane, then slide the **Fill** slider to **On**, change the **Fill** color to green, and set the **Transparency** to **75%** (so that this background color is not too overpowering). See Lab Exhibit 12.5.116.

5. Repeat this process three times. Make the fill colors purple for the second band, blue for the third band, and yellow for the fourth band. Your dashboard should look like Lab Exhibit 12.5.117 when you are done.

6. Now you will just copy your visuals and paste them onto the dashboard in the appropriate place. To copy the visual, right-click on your visual, then select **Copy** and **Copy visual** (as shown in Lab Exhibit 12.5.118)

7. Resize and move your visuals around so that they fit on the screen. When you are done, your dashboard should resemble Lab Exhibit 12.5.119.

8. Add labels for each dimension on the left side of the screen (in each rectangle layer) by first clicking on the **Insert** tab (Lab Exhibit 12.5.120).

9. Click **Shapes** and then select the rectangle from the drop-down menu (Lab Exhibit 12.5.121).

10. From the shape formatting space, slide the **Fill** to **Off**. Slide the **Text** to **On** and enter "Financial Dimension" in the **Text** box. Also change the **Font color** to black (see Lab Exhibit 12.5.122).

11. Click on the **Rotation** option and set the **Text rotation** to **270 degrees** so that the text is aligned vertically (Lab Exhibit 12.5.123).
12. Resize and move the label to fit it to the left of the **Financial Dimension** visualizations, as shown in Lab Exhibit 12.5.124.
13. Repeat this process for the other three dimensions. Your final dashboard should resemble Lab Exhibit 12.5.125.

Share the Story

Castaways' balanced scorecard dashboard shows that financial performance is increasing over the year. While performance on the other three dimensions is more mixed, the internal process dimensions show improvements in internal processes, such as serving customers in a timely fashion and turning tables over so that more customers can be served. Employee satisfaction is also above a neutral point (that is, above 3) and has improved over the year. The NPS (customer satisfaction score) has been relatively stable, and while it is, on average, in the detractor range, it is close to the passive (or neutral) rating. In summary, it seems that there is room for improvement in all dimensions, but Castaways' performance is steady or improving, which seems to be reflected in the increasing sales.

Assessment

1. Take a screenshot of the dashboard, label it Submission 1, and paste it into a Word document named "Lab 12.5 Submission.docx".
2. Answer the questions in Connect and upload your Lab 12.5 Submission.docx via Connect if assigned.

Alternate Lab 12.5 Power BI—On Your Own

Creating a Balanced Scorecard Dashboard to Track Performance (Heartwood)

DATA VISUALIZATION

Data Analytics Type: Descriptive

Keywords

Balanced Scorecard, KPI

Decision-Making Context

Managers use the balanced scorecard to evaluate organizational performance on multiple dimensions. Key performance indicators (KPIs) from the financial dimension provide insight into the firm's financial performance and provide a look back. KPIs related to customers, the internal processes of the organization, and the learning and growth of employees provide additional insight into how the organization may fare in the future.

Heartwood Cabinets has just implemented a balanced scorecard and has asked you to summarize the data using Power BI software. Use the data contained in the Excel file labeled **Alt Lab 12.5 Data.xlsx** and follow the methodology in Lab 12.5 to create a snapshot summary report so that you can assess Heartwood's performance on all four dimensions.

Required

1. Prepare visualizations for each of the KPIs available to you.
    a. Financial
        i. Revenue
        ii. COGS
        iii. Profit

b. Customer
    i. Net promoter score
c. Internal Processes
    i. Changeover time (amount of time spent between production)
    ii. Overtime rate (% of overtime hours as a function of regular hours)
d. Learning and Growth
    i. Employee satisfaction score
    ii. Supervisor evaluations
    iii. Employee training

2. Prepare a dashboard that combines your prepared visualizations in a user-friendly format that will facilitate decision making by the Heartwood management team.

Ask the Question

Is Heartwood meeting expectations on all four dimensions?

To answer this question, refer to the following strategic measures and objectives. The third column tells you which type of visualization(s) to create to evaluate performance for each dimension:

KPI	Target	Visualization
Financial		
Increase revenue	Increase over time	• Area chart showing all three measures
Decrease COGS	Decrease over time	• Bar graph showing calculated difference by quarter for each measure
Increase profit	Increase over time	
Customer		
Positive net promoter score	• At least 50% "promoters" (50% of responses of 9 or 10) • Less than 10% detractors (less than 10% of responses of 6 or less)	• Stacked bar chart • Line graph spanning each month of 2012
Internal Processes		
Changeover time	Changeover time (in minutes) should be less than 5% of total available time (in minutes)	• Highlights table showing Changeover Time Percent for each month (2012 only) • Changeover % = (Net Available Time – Production Time)/(Net Available Time)
Overtime rate	Overtime rate should not exceed 2%	• Highlights table showing Overtime Rate as a percent for each month (2012 only) • Overtime Rate = Overtime Hours/Regular Hours
Learning and Growth		
Increase employee satisfaction score	• At least 80% of scores greater than 3.5	• Pie chart showing percent of employees with high and low scores
Increase employee evaluation score	• At least 30% of employees with scores of 8 or above • Fewer than 10% of employees below 5	• Column chart showing % of employees receiving each evaluation score
Improve employee training	50% of employees have completed 20 hours of training	• Pie chart showing groups of 10 or less, 11–19, and 20

Assessment

1. Take a screenshot of the dashboard, label it Submission 1, and paste it into a Word document named "Alt Lab 12.5 Submission.docx".
2. Answer the questions in Connect and upload your Alt Lab 12.5 Submission.docx via Connect if assigned.

Chapter 13

Strategic Decision Making

A Look at This Chapter

Management accountants provide relevant information to decision makers regarding alternative courses of action, especially in the presence of changing conditions and resource constraints. This chapter uses prescriptive analytics to evaluate data and provide insights for strategic decision making. These prescriptive analytics techniques include differential analysis, goal-seek analysis, scenario analysis, sensitivity analysis, and optimization. As always, management accountants must perform their work ethically and professionally.

Cost Accounting and Data Analytics

COST ACCOUNTING LEARNING OBJECTIVE	RELATED DATA ANALYTICS LABS	LAB ANALYTICS TYPE
LO 13.1 Explain the types of prescriptive analytics that are useful in decision making.		
LO 13.2 Apply differential analysis techniques to make-or-buy decisions.		
LO 13.3 Use goal-seek analysis to address management questions.	**LAB 13.1 Excel:** Using Goal-Seek Analysis: Calculate Break-Even Sales	Prescriptive
LO 13.4 Use scenario analysis to evaluate the possible outcomes of changing conditions.	**LAB 13.2 Excel:** Scenario Analysis: Identifying the Expected Impact of a Trade War	Prescriptive
LO 13.5 Use sensitivity analysis to address management questions.	**LAB 13.3 Excel:** Sensitivity Analysis: Using an Excel Data Table to Analyze Profitability under Changing Volume, Sales Price, and Fixed and Variable Costs	Prescriptive

Cost Accounting and Data Analytics (*continued*)

COST ACCOUNTING LEARNING OBJECTIVE	RELATED DATA ANALYTICS LABS	LAB ANALYTICS TYPE
LO 13.6 Apply optimization techniques to pricing and product-mix decisions.	**Data Analytics Mini-Lab #1:** Using Excel Solver to Optimize Price	Prescriptive
	LAB 13.4 Excel: Using Excel Solver to Optimize Pricing	Prescriptive
	Data Analytics Mini-Lab #2: Using Excel Solver to Optimize Product Mix	Prescriptive
	LAB 13.5 Excel: Using Excel Solver to Optimize Product Mix (Heartwood)	Prescriptive

Chapter Concepts and Career Skills

Learning About . . .	Helps with These Career Skills
Differential techniques	• Analyzing the financial implications of potential decisions
Goal-seek analysis	• Understanding which inputs are required to achieve an expected outcome
Scenario analysis	• Determining possible outcomes and the probability of each outcome
Sensitivity analysis	• Understanding the extent to which outcomes may change if we vary our assumptions and estimates
Optimization	• Optimizing outcomes (such as profits) in the presence of constraints

jetcityimage/Getty Images

Tesla

Tesla's CEO Elon Musk recently announced the company's plans to drastically reduce the cost of the battery cells and packs used in its electric cars. This cost reduction is key to dropping the price of a Tesla car to $25,000. Management accountants at Tesla continuously run what-if analyses, including sensitivity analysis and scenario analysis, to help Elon Musk and other managers make decisions regarding Tesla's level of production and profitability, which to a large degree may be determined by battery costs. The cost of the battery packs of the future will have a dramatic impact not only on Tesla but also on all other manufacturers of electric cars.

Source: Andrew J. Hawkins, "Tesla's Elon Musk Said a $25,000 Electric Car with Next-Gen Battery in the Works," *The Verge,* September 22, 2020, www.theverge.com/2020/9/22/21450916/tesla-battery-pack-elon-musk-price-kilowatt-hour-ev-cost-tabless.

LO 13.1

Explain the types of prescriptive analytics that are useful in decision making.

SUPPORTING DECISION MAKING USING PRESCRIPTIVE ANALYTICS

In Chapter 1, we defined a **management accountant** as one who analyzes accounting-related data to help an organization make effective business decisions. Decision making often involves choices among alternative courses of action. Management accountants help managers understand the possible or likely impact of these different courses of action.

To do so, they often use **prescriptive analytics**, which are analytics that help managers make decisions in the face of resource constraints and/or changing conditions.

While *predictive* analytics (see Chapter 9) forecasts future performance, *prescriptive* analytics takes those predictions one step further by addressing the questions "What should we do, based on what we expect will happen?" and "How do we optimize our performance based on potential resource constraints or changing conditions?"

Resource Constraints

All companies face resource constraints. Scarce or limited resources include capital, cash, time, employees, parts, supplies, computer chips, ideas, factory capacity and availability, and raw materials such as cobalt, lithium, and uranium. Because firms don't have access to unlimited capital resources, they must optimize the resources that they can access. Optimization models, explained later in this chapter, specifically address the resource constraints that a company faces.

Changing Conditions

Companies regularly face changes in cost structure, technology, availability of supplies, manufacturing technologies, machinery breakdowns, consumer preferences, tax laws, interest rates, risk levels, exchange rates, and demand for employees and their expertise. **Disruptive technologies** are major innovations in technology that significantly alter the way that companies, industries, or consumers operate. These changing conditions require the company to continuously react, re-analyze, and adjust operations. Prescriptive analytics techniques can provide the information needed to help managers address these changing conditions. Adapting to these changing conditions better than its competitors can provide a company with a competitive advantage.

Exhibit 13.1 lists some of the disruptive trends in the automotive industry and how these changing conditions and resource constraints impact automakers. These changing conditions and resource constraints necessitate prescriptive analytics.

Disruptive Technology	Changing Condition	Potential Resource Constraint	Impact on Automakers
The connected car	Over time, technology/ sensors (computer chips) have become increasingly important components of automobiles.	Automakers need sources and a sufficient supply of computer chips.	Automakers must make sourcing and supply of technology/computer chips a key priority.
Autonomous vehicles	Autonomous driving vehicles are increasingly desirable.	Automakers need to hire highly skilled and trained computer programmers.	Autonomous vehicles require continuous software updates.
Environmentally friendly vehicles	Auto buyers are increasingly demanding electric vehicles.	Automakers need sources and a sufficient supply of electric car batteries at a reasonable cost.	Automakers must make sourcing and supply of electric car batteries a key priority.
Cutting-edge production	3D printers are now widely used in production processes.	Automakers need access to 3D printers.	Automakers must continue to innovate their production techniques and facilities.

management accountant
An accountant who analyzes accounting-related data to help an organization make effective business decisions.

prescriptive analytics
Analytics that identifies best possible options given constraints or changing conditions.

disruptive technologies
Major innovations in technology that significantly alter the way that companies, industries, or consumers operate.

Exhibit 13.1
Disruptive Trends in the Automotive Industry

Source: https://industrywired.com/top-10-disruptive-trends-that-are-shaping-the-automobile-industry/. Accessed August 2022.

what-if analysis
A set of prescriptive analytics techniques evaluating how changes in the amounts of various inputs affect related outputs, or how changes in desired output affect the required level of inputs.

differential analysis
A prescriptive analytics technique to determine the change in profit typically associated with the differences in revenues and costs among alternative courses of action.

make-or-buy analysis
A prescriptive analytics technique that helps a company determine whether to manufacture a product in-house or purchase it externally.

goal-seek analysis
A what-if prescriptive analytics technique that determines the required input or actions needed to reach a desired outcome, output, or result.

scenario analysis
A what-if prescriptive analytics technique that evaluates the impact of potential future events by considering their possible outcomes. Scenario analysis does not try to predict one possible outcome, but rather a range of alternative outcomes to evaluate the expected value (or weighted average) of the impact.

sensitivity analysis
A what-if prescriptive analytics technique that evaluates outcomes based on uncertainty regarding inputs.

Based on Exhibit 13.1, we can ask: How will a chip shortage, an example of both changing conditions and a resource constraint, affect decision making at automakers such as **Toyota**? Which plants will they idle? Which car models will they prioritize if they must decrease production due to the chip shortage? Which factors will management accountants consider when recommending the best course of action? In the future, how will the company source and maintain an adequate supply of chips?

Prescriptive Analytics Techniques

Using prescriptive analytics, management accountants examine a variety of scenarios to provide data-driven insights to decision makers. The following are the most commonly used types of prescriptive analytics. This chapter describes each one in detail.

1. **What-if analysis** is a set of prescriptive analytics techniques evaluating how changes in the amounts of various inputs affect related outputs, or how changes in desired output affect the required level of inputs. There are four main types of what-if analysis.

   a. **Differential analysis** is a prescriptive analytics technique to determine the change in profit typically associated with the differences in revenues and costs among alternate courses of action. Differential analysis can take many different forms, such as:

      i. **Make-or-buy analysis** is an application of differential analysis to help a company determine whether to manufacture a product in-house or to purchase it externally. For example, should **Cisco** manufacture its routers in-house, or should it purchase routers from other manufacturers?

      ii. *Add-or-drop product line* is an application of differential analysis to determine whether a company should add or drop a product line. For example, should **Ford** drop a particular van from its vehicle offerings because it doesn't seem to be profitable?

      iii. *Add-or-drop customer* is an application of differential analysis to determine whether a company should add or drop a customer. For example, should **PWC** take on **Tyson** as an audit client even though doing so will require PWC to hire a bigger auditor team (and perhaps a more expensive one as well)?

      iv. *Lease-or-buy equipment* analysis is an application of differential analysis to determine whether to buy equipment (such as a truck or a building) outright or lease it from another company. There are many factors to consider here, such as whether to tie up available cash in an asset and what the overall cost of ownership might be. On a more personal level, is it better to lease an iPhone or buy it outright?

   b. **Goal-seek analysis** is a what-if prescriptive analytics technique that determines the required input or actions needed to reach a desired outcome, output, or result. For example, what level of sales (input) is needed for the company to break even on its operations, or what would be needed to achieve a target cost or target profit?

   c. **Scenario analysis** is a what-if prescriptive analytics technique that evaluates the impact of potential future events by considering their possible outcomes. For example, what is the expected impact of a possible trade war with another country on the company's profitability based on different possible scenarios?

   d. **Sensitivity analysis** is a what-if prescriptive analytics technique that evaluates outcomes based on uncertainty regarding inputs. For example, how will changing product volume, sales price, and/or fixed and variable costs affect profits?

2. **Optimization models** seek the best feasible solution based on a goal (also called an *objective function*), decision variables, and business constraints. For example, what is the optimal product mix for the company based on certain constraints? What is the optimal price to charge for each product that will maximize profitability?

3. **Capital budgeting** is a prescriptive analytics technique that uses different metrics to evaluate the return on potentially large investments based on the amounts, timing, and uncertainty (risk) of expected cash flows. Specifically, we prioritize different capital expenditures using metrics such as net present value, internal rate of return, accounting rate of return, payback, and discounted payback. (Capital budgeting is the subject of Chapter 14.)

Exhibit 13.2 provides a summary of these predictive analytics techniques, the types of questions they address, and the specific types of tests conducted. We explain the most common uses of these techniques in the management accounting space both in this chapter and in Chapter 14. We begin with a discussion of differential analysis.

optimization model
A prescriptive analytics technique used to find the best feasible solution based on an objective function (goal), decision variables, and business constraints.

Exhibit 13.2
Predictive Analytics Techniques, Examples, and Specific Tests Employed

capital budgeting
A prescriptive analytics technique that uses different metrics to evaluate the return on potentially large investments based on the amounts, timing, and uncertainty (risk) of expected cash flows.

Prescriptive Analysis Technique	Addresses Changing Conditions or Resource Constraints?	Example Question	Specific Test to Address the Question
Differential analysis: A prescriptive analytics technique to determine the change in profit typically associated with the difference in revenues and costs among alternate courses of action. It examines the costs and revenues (benefits) associated with specific business decisions.	Changing conditions	Should **Heartwood Cabinets** make and sell one additional unit of product?	Compare the relevant costs of additional production to the relevant revenue from the additional sale.
Make-or-buy analysis: A differential analysis technique to determine the change in profit typically associated with manufacturing a product in-house or buying it externally.	Changing conditions	Should **Apple** manufacture or outsource the production of its iPads?	Estimate and compare the financial implications of two scenarios: (1) make iPads in-house or (2) outsource iPad production to another party.
Add-or-drop product line: A differential analysis technique to determine whether a company should add or drop a product line.	Changing conditions	Should **YouTube** drop its TV streaming service, YouTube TV?	Estimate the cost savings of dropping the service and compare those savings to the lost revenues from selling the streaming service.
Add-or-drop customer: A differential analysis technique to determine whether a company should add or drop a customer.	Changing conditions	A plumbing contractor provides services to a hospital, but the hospital is consistently late in paying. Should the plumber drop the hospital as a customer?	Estimate the cost savings of dropping the customer and compare those savings to the lost revenues from servicing the customer.

(continued)

Exhibit 13.2
(*continued*)

Prescriptive Analysis Technique	Addresses Changing Conditions or Resource Constraints?	Example Question	Specific Test to Address the Question
Goal-seek analysis: A what-if technique that evaluates the required input needed to reach a desired outcome, output, or result.	Changing conditions	For **McGraw Hill**, how many copies of this textbook must be sold for the company to break even?	Perform a break-even analysis to calculate the needed level of sales.
Scenario analysis: A what-if technique that evaluates the impact of potential future events by considering their possible outcomes.	Changing conditions	How does **Walmart** respond to various scenarios of increased tariffs imposed by another country?	Analyze potential scenarios to determine the overall potential impact of each one.
Sensitivity analysis: A what-if technique that evaluates outcomes based on uncertainty regarding inputs.	Changing conditions	If the percentage of visitors to **Amazon**'s website who buy products increases from 25% to 30%, what is the impact on Amazon's sales and profits?	Test the sensitivity of Amazon's profits to changing assumptions regarding those who visit Amazon's website and purchase items (also known as conversion rates).
Optimization: A prescriptive analytics technique used to find the best feasible solution based on an objective function, decision variables, and business and resource constraints.	Resource constraints	Pricing: How should we price our products to maximize short-term and/or long-term profits? For example, what is the right price for **Delta Air Lines** to charge for a trip from Atlanta to Milan?	Using optimization models and considering various resource constraints, determine the optimal flight pricing that maximizes company profits.
	Resource constraints	Product mix: Should **Coca-Cola** focus its product mix on all of its beverages, or only on its most profitable beverages?	Using optimization models and considering various resource constraints, determine the optimal product mix that maximizes company profits.
Capital budgeting: A prescriptive analytics technique that uses different metrics to evaluate the return on potentially large investments based on the amounts, timing, and uncertainty (risk) of expected cash flows. (This topic is covered extensively in Chapter 14.)	Resource constraints	What are the cash flows associated with an investment in a new piece of equipment at **Boeing**, or a new truck at **J.B. Hunt**?	Estimate and evaluate the amounts, timing, and risk (uncertainty) associated with the predicted cash flows of investing in new equipment using cash-flow analysis techniques to evaluate potential investments.

1. What is the difference between predictive analytics and prescriptive analytics?
2. Which prescriptive analytics technique might be used to identify the break-even level for a proposed new product?

DIFFERENTIAL ANALYSIS

As defined above, differential analysis is a prescriptive analytics technique to determine the change in profit typically associated with the difference in revenues and costs among alternate courses of action. It examines the associated costs and revenues (benefits) of specific business decisions. If the differential revenues are greater than the differential costs, then additional production is recommended. In conducting differential analysis, it is particularly important to identify which costs and revenues are relevant to the decision at hand and which are not.

Relevant Costs and Relevant Revenues

When analyzing various courses of action, it is important to consider the costs and revenues that differ among the alternatives. Specifically, we must consider both **relevant costs** (expected future costs that differ among alternative courses of action) and **relevant revenues** (expected future revenues that differ among alternative courses of action). At the same time, we recognize that **sunk costs**, which are past costs spent that cannot be recovered regardless of the future course of action, are not relevant costs. Similarly, any costs that do not differ between alternative courses of action are not relevant.

Let's now illustrate the importance of understanding relevant costs using an outsourcing decision as an example.

Outsourcing Decisions: Make or Buy?

As defined above, a make-or-buy analysis helps managers address the question of whether to manufacture a product in-house or to outsource it (purchase it externally). Many experts believe that a company should outsource any process or function that is not part of its core competency—that is, the specific area where it has a competitive advantage or creates business value. For example, while **Apple** is expert at designing iPhones (which is arguably a source of Apple's competitive advantage), it generally outsources all production of its smartphones to other companies, such as **FoxConn**. Similarly, many companies outsource specialized services, such as marketing, payroll, or legal work, so that they can focus on what they do best or where they hold a competitive advantage.

How do managers make outsourcing decisions? The essence of the decision is how best to use the company's available resources. Let's go back to our Apple example. Should Apple manufacture its iPhones or outsource manufacturing to FoxConn?

Assume that the cost for Apple to manufacture the latest version of the iPhone is $490.50 per phone, which is the full absorption cost (as discussed in Chapter 3) that includes all fixed and variable costs and manufacturing overhead. FoxConn is willing to produce the iPhones for $500 per phone. To help make the decision, Apple could consider **quantitative factors**, or measurable decision outcomes such as relevant costs and relevant revenues. For example, how does Apple's variable manufacturing cost per unit compare to the price offered by the outsourcer?

While the full absorption of the manufacturing cost ($490.50/phone) saved is less than the cost to outsource the product ($500/phone), Apple must conduct a deeper evaluation of the iPhone's full cost, which is shown in Exhibit 13.3.

LO 13.2

Apply differential analysis techniques to make-or-buy decisions.

CAREER SKILLS

Learning about differential techniques supports this career skill:

• Analyzing the financial implications of potential decisions

relevant costs
Expected future costs that differ among alternative courses of action.

relevant revenues
Expected future revenues that differ among alternative courses of action.

sunk costs
Past costs spent that cannot be recovered regardless of the future course of action chosen.

quantitative factors
Measurable decision outcomes, such as relevant costs and relevant revenues.

Exhibit 13.3
**Expected
Per-Unit Cost of
Manufacturing
iPhone**

Source: The Cost of
Making an iPhone (https://
www.investopedia.com/
financial-edge/0912/the-
cost-of-making-aniphone.
aspx#:~:text=Depending%20
on%20the%20storage%20
size,phone%20amounts%20
to%20approximately%20
%24490.50.)

Cost Components	Expected Per-Unit Cost of 1 iPhone
Direct materials	$309.50
Variable direct manufacturing labor	81.00
Variable manufacturing overhead	30.00
Mixed (variable and fixed) batch-level materials handling and setup manufacturing overhead	50.00
Fixed manufacturing overhead costs (plant lease, insurance, administration)	20.00
Total manufacturing cost for 1 iPhone	**$490.50**

Because the fixed manufacturing overhead costs are sunk costs (at least in the short run), they are not relevant in this decision and are not considered in the make-or-buy analysis. Exhibit 13.4 summarizes the relevant costs in this make-or-buy analysis. The analysis of the quantitative factors, namely the relevant costs of production, suggests a $29.50-per-unit savings if Apple makes the iPhone itself.

Exhibit 13.4
**Relevant Costs of
Making or Buying
iPhones**

	Relevant Cost per Unit	
	Make (Apple Manufactures iPhones)	Buy (iPhone Manufacturing Outsourced to FoxConn)
Outside manufacturing of iPhones by FoxConn		**$500.00**
Direct materials	$309.50	
Variable direct manufacturing labor	81.00	
Variable manufacturing overhead	30.00	
Mixed (variable and fixed) batch-level materials handling and setup manufacturing overhead	50.00	
Total relevant manufacturing costs	**$470.50**	
Per-unit difference in favor of Apple manufacturing iPhones itself	**$ 29.50**	

The variable costs are relevant costs to Apple, which will have to incur those costs to manufacture the iPhones itself. So are the mixed (variable and fixed) costs. However, the fixed manufacturing overhead costs are not relevant because they will be the same regardless of whether Apple makes the iPhones or outsources the manufacturing to another company.

Despite these cost savings, we know that in the real world, Apple has chosen to outsource some or all of the manufacturing of its iPhones. Why? Apple might also be considering **qualitative factors**, which are decision outcomes that are difficult to measure. In considering qualitative factors, Apple will consider many questions, including:

qualitative factors
Decision outcomes that
are difficult to measure.

- If Apple doesn't manufacture its own products, will its freed-up capacity allow it to pursue other promising projects that are consistent with its core product design and other competencies?
- If Apple decides to outsource, should it engage multiple companies as outsourcing partners rather than just one (FoxConn)?

- Can Apple trust outsourcing partners to protect its intellectual property? What safeguards does Apple need to put in place?
- If FoxConn faces financial or political problems (such as accusations of poor working conditions or enforced child labor), how will those problems affect Apple and its stakeholders?
- Can Apple trust FoxConn to manufacture iPhones in accordance with important environmental standards? If FoxConn is revealed to be a major polluter, what will happen to the sales of Apple iPhones?
- Are other contract manufacturers available to do the high-quality work required by Apple but at a lower cost than FoxConn?

ENVIRONMENTAL, SOCIAL, GOVERNANCE

In short, a large number of both quantitative factors and qualitative factors may influence important, potentially strategic decisions. Before making any decision, a company needs to consider all factors holistically. For example, a firm's calculations may suggest that outsourcing has a lower financial cost, but if the manufacturing is a key strategy capability, then the company likely should keep manufacturing in-house. In contrast, if manufacturing is a more generic process, then outsourcing may make more sense.

Add or Drop Product Line or Customers

A different type of differential analysis evaluates whether to add or drop a product line. As in other types of differential analysis, companies must consider the relevant revenues and costs, including sales revenue lost, direct costs, variable overhead, and direct fixed overhead. However, allocated fixed overhead is irrelevant here because allocated fixed overhead will not be eliminated if the product line is dropped.

Differential analysis is also used to consider whether to add or drop a customer. This type of analysis closely considers the differential relevant revenues and costs.

Lease-or-Buy Analysis

Yet another type of differential analysis seeks to determine whether to buy equipment (such as a truck or a building) outright or lease it from another company, such as a financing company. There are many factors to consider here, such as whether to tie up available cash in an asset (versus other investments), how long the company expects to hold the asset, whether the asset is going obsolete or changing frequently, and the overall cost of ownership. On a more personal level, is it better to lease a **Tesla** car or buy it outright?

⊘ PROGRESS CHECK

3. Why are sunk costs ignored in make-or-buy analysis? How do sunk costs differ from relevant costs?

4. Why are the qualitative factors associated with a make-or-buy analysis often just as important as the quantitative factors?

GOAL-SEEK ANALYSIS

Goal-seek analysis is a form of what-if analysis that determines the needed input or actions to reach a desired outcome, output, or result. To perform goal-seek analysis, management accountants start with the desired result and work backwards to understand potential paths (including inputs) needed to achieve that output.

LO 13.3

Use goal-seek analysis to address management questions.

Exhibit 13.5 provides examples of how goal-seek analysis might be used in various settings. Notice that the desired output is specified first (in the left-hand column), followed by the level of the inputs required to achieve that desired output.

Exhibit 13.5
Examples of Goal-Seek Analysis in Business and Everyday Life

ENVIRONMENTAL, SOCIAL, GOVERNANCE

Desired Output (or Outcome or Result)	Corresponding Level of Required Inputs
Monthly principal and loan payment that does not exceed $1,200	Maximum amount of small business loan at the prevailing interest rate
Break even: No profit, where total expenses equal total revenues	Minimum level of sales required to break even
Become carbon neutral at our corporate location by 2035	Needed level of use of green technology and carbon offsets
Target profit of $1,000,000	Minimum level of sales required to reach target profit of $1,000,000
Adequate labor resources to fill factory orders	Minimum number of employees needed to fill factory orders
An "A" as a final grade in this Cost Accounting class	Minimum necessary score on the midterm and final exams to reach the desired grade in this Cost Accounting course
Pass all parts of the CPA exam in one sitting with a 75% passing score	Minimum number of hours of study needed to pass all parts of the CPA exam, assuming each hour spent studying increases the probability of passing by about 2%

CAREER SKILLS

Learning about goal-seek analysis supports this career skill:

• Understanding which inputs are required to achieve an expected outcome

A natural type of goal-seek analysis in management accounting is the computation of break-even sales—that is, the sales revenue required to break even or achieve exactly $0 in profits. Recall from Chapter 3 that the *break-even point* is the point at which total revenues equal total expenses. The break-even sales point helps a company understand the nature and extent of its variable and fixed costs, as well as the contribution margin earned on each dollar of sales. (The *contribution margin* is the selling price per unit minus the variable cost per unit. It tells us how much a particular product contributes to the company's overall profit.) Goal-seek analysis can also be used to determine the necessary conditions for hitting a target profit.

⊙ LAB CONNECTION

LAB 13.1 EXCEL uses Excel's goal-seek functionality to help you determine a company's level of break-even sales. The generated input (or the "goal" of the analysis) is the amount of sales required to obtain the output of zero profitability (when revenues exactly equal expenses). Goal-seek analysis can also be used to identify the necessary conditions for achieving target profit objectives, where the outcome is the target profit level.

✓ PROGRESS CHECK

5. How is determining the level of sales needed to break even similar to determining the amount of sales needed to achieve a target profit?

6. A car dealer might ask you what level of monthly payment you desire to help determine the level of car you can afford. How is the car dealer's question consistent with goal-seek analysis?

SCENARIO ANALYSIS

Scenario analysis is a what-if technique that evaluates the impact of potential future events by considering their possible outcomes. Scenario analysis does not try to predict one possible outcome, but rather a range of alternative outcomes to evaluate the expected value (or weighted average) of the impact.

Let's use an example to better understand scenario analysis. Assume the Arkansas General Assembly is debating a reduction in the corporate income tax rate from 8 percent to either 6 percent or 4 percent. This reduction will have a direct impact on **Tyson** and other Arkansas-based corporations. At the same time, in the upcoming year Tyson might have a 5 percent increase in taxable income, might have neither an increase nor a decrease in taxable income, or might have a 5 percent decrease in taxable income.

Exhibit 13.6 shows the range of taxes owed (that is, tax burden) based on each of the potential scenarios. Note that the three possible tax rates and three possible taxable-income scenarios give us nine potential scenarios. This scenario analysis will help Tyson understand how changes in the tax rate affect taxes owed under different scenarios.

Income Scenarios	Taxable Income	Taxes Owed If Tax Rate = 8%	If Tax Rate = 6%	If Tax Rate = 4%
Income increases by 5%	$2,100,000	$168,000	$126,000	$84,000
Income remains unchanged	$2,000,000	$160,000	$120,000	$80,000
Income decreases by 5%	$1,900,000	$152,000	$114,000	$76,000

Exhibit 13.6
Taxable Income and Taxes Owed, Based on Average Before-Tax Earnings of $2,000,000

Exhibit 13.7 identifies the *change* in tax burden under different corporate income-tax proposals as compared to the base $160,000 tax (= $2,000,000 taxable income * 8%). Negative values (in parentheses) represent tax savings.

Income Scenarios	Taxable Income	Change in Taxes Owed If Tax Rate = 8%	If Tax Rate = 6%	If Tax Rate = 4%
Income increases by 5%	$2,100,000	$ 8,000	$(34,000)	$(76,000)
Income remains unchanged	$2,000,000	—	$(40,000)	$(80,000)
Income decreases by 5%	$1,900,000	$(8,000)	$(46,000)	$(84,000)

Note: Negative values represent tax savings.

Exhibit 13.7
The Change in Tax Burden Based on the Different Taxable-Income and Tax-Rate Scenarios in Exhibit 13.6

The next step is for the management accountant, in consultation with Tyson management, to establish the probability of each scenario occurring. (Each scenario is shown in one of the nine cells.) In Exhibit 13.8, note that the sum of all possible scenarios totals 100 percent. Also note that you can sum the columns or the rows to get to 100 percent.

		Likelihood of Each Scenario			
	Taxable Income	If Tax Rate = 8%	If Tax Rate = 6%	If Tax Rate = 4%	Sum
Income increases by 5%	$2,100,000	0.05	0.10	0.15	0.30
Income remains unchanged	$2,000,000	0.15	0.20	0.15	0.50
Income decreases by 5%	$1,900,000	0.10	0.05	0.05	0.20
Sum		0.30	0.35	0.35	1.00

Exhibit 13.8
Joint Probabilities of Changes in Tax Rate and Change in Taxable Income

With these probabilities calculated, we now need to use the probability of each of the nine scenarios to determine the likely impact of the two changes indicated by each cell (income, tax rate). We multiply the change in taxes in Exhibit 13.7 by the joint probabilities in the same cell of Exhibit 13.8 to get the expected value of each scenario, as shown in Exhibit 13.9. So, for example, in the scenario where the tax rate stays at 8 percent and income increases by 5 percent, taxes will increase by $8,000 (from the green-highlighted cell in Exhibit 13.7). There is a 0.05 probability of this happening (from the green-highlighted cell in Exhibit 13.8). Multiply $8,000 by 0.05 to get the expected increase in taxes of $400, as shown in the green-highlighted cell in Exhibit 13.9. This same calculation needs to be performed for the other eight cells. The results are shown in Exhibit 13.9.

	Taxable Income	8% Tax Rate	6% Tax Rate	4% Tax Rate	Sum of Expected Savings
Income increases by 5%	$2,100,000	$ 400	$ (3,400)	$(11,400)	$(14,400)
Income remains unchanged	$2,000,000	—	$ (8,000)	$(12,000)	$(20,000)
Income decreases by 5%	$1,900,000	$(800)	$ (2,300)	$ (4,200)	$ (7,300)
Sum of expected savings		$(400)	$(13,700)	$(27,600)	$(41,700)

Note: Negative values represent tax savings.
Exhibit 13.9
Expected Value of Each of the Scenarios

The total expected value of all the potential scenarios is a tax savings of $41,700, which is the sum of the individual expected values or sum of the expected savings (see yellow-highlighted cell in the bottom-right corner of Exhibit 13.9). This is the sum of expected savings after considering all possible scenarios.

Using scenario analysis allows decision makers to see the overall potential impact of changes in tax rates across multiple scenarios. This model relies heavily on assumptions that drive each scenario, such as the initial earnings before tax, the expected change in earnings, and the possible tax rates. Data analytics helps to confirm or refine the details guiding the scenarios. In this example, the analysis of before-tax income and other external factors can help determine the probability estimates. Likewise, an analysis of legislative proceedings can help determine the likelihood of a change in the corporate tax rate.

 LAB CONNECTION

LAB 13.2 EXCEL asks you to use scenario analysis to evaluate the expected impact of a potential trade war with another country.

✅ PROGRESS CHECK

7. How could scenario analysis be used to assess the expected impact of changing lumber prices on the prices of new houses?

8. Refer to the chapter-opening story about decreasing battery prices for electric cars. How could **Tesla** use scenario analysis to evaluate the impact of battery prices on its electric car sales and its company profitability?

SENSITIVITY ANALYSIS

As defined above, *sensitivity analysis* is a prescriptive analytics technique that evaluates outcomes based on uncertainty regarding inputs. Management accountants use sensitivity analysis to understand how input variables (such as fixed and variable costs, pricing, and estimated sales volume) might affect outcomes (such as expected revenues, profit, and cash flows). Here are a few examples of questions that sensitivity analysis might address:

- If the variable cost and fixed cost structure changes from the original assumptions made for a potential new product at **Mattel**, will that change affect the company's decision to sell the new product? Will it affect the level of sales needed for Mattel to break even?
- How sensitive are profits to changes in sales price or sales volume at **Nintendo**?
- If fuel prices increase or decrease by 10, 15, or 20 percent, what will be the impact on net income for **Southwest Airlines**?
- If exchange rates between the Chinese RMB (yuan) and the U.S. dollar increase or decrease 10, 20, or 30 percent, how will that change affect the overall profitability of **General Motors Company (GM)**? (In 2022, GM sold more cars in China than in the United States.)

By examining how sensitive profitability is to the changing assumptions, management can make more informed decisions on pricing, expenses, and profit margins.

LO 13.5

Use sensitivity analysis to address management questions.

CAREER SKILLS

Learning about sensitivity analysis supports this career skill:

- Understanding the extent to which outcomes may change if we vary our assumptions and estimates

An Example of Sensitivity Analysis Using Excel's Data Table

As an example of sensitivity analysis, let's assume that **Nintendo** is considering introducing a new Pokémon plush toy. Because sales and costs are uncertain at this point, management accountants would like to know the assumptions or conditions under which the product will not be profitable. This sensitivity analysis will help company management determine whether to produce the new product and offer it for sale.

To perform the sensitivity analysis, the management accountants can use an Excel what-if analysis tool called a data table. A **data table** is a what-if analysis tool that allows the analyst to evaluate the impact of one or two changing inputs (parameters) on a related output. To start their analysis of the new Pokémon plush toy, they establish what they assume is the most likely scenario of revenues and costs, or the **base case scenario**, as follows:

data table
A what-if analysis tool in Excel that allows the analyst to evaluate the impact of one or two changing inputs (parameters) on a related output.

base case scenario
In sensitivity analysis, the most likely scenario of revenues and costs.

Base Case Scenario:			
Sales price per unit	$ 28	Variable cost per unit	$20
Units sold	300	Total variable costs	$6,000
Total revenue	$8,400	Total fixed costs	1,500
		Total costs	$7,500

Profit ($8,400 – $7,500) = $900

DATA VISUALIZATION

heat map
Representation of data in the form of a table where data values are illustrated using colors such as red (poor outcome), yellow (moderate outcome), or green (positive outcome).

The what-if analysis performed in Excel's data table allows managers to evaluate how either one or two varying inputs affect an output. Because management is uncertain of the production costs and the marketing department is uncertain how many of the new toys will sell at a price of $28, management would like to evaluate the profitability (outcome) at (1) different levels of variable cost per unit and (2) different numbers of total units sold (the inputs), while holding all of the other parameters (sales price per unit and total fixed costs) constant.

Exhibit 13.10 provides an illustration of the sensitivity analysis using the data table in Excel. It uses a data visualization technique called a **heat map**, which represents data in the form of a table where data values are illustrated with colors. Here, the most extreme losses are in red, and the highest levels of income are in green. Often, heat maps use the colors of a traffic signal. Shades of red mean a poor outcome, shades of yellow mean a moderate outcome, and shades of green indicate a positive outcome. The worst outcome is the deepest red; the best outcome is the deepest green.

Let's now look more closely at Exhibit 13.10:

❶ From Columns H:Q, we allow the variable cost per unit to vary between $4 and $40.

❷ In Rows 4:14, we allow the number of units sold to vary between 50 and 550 units.

❸ We highlight the base case with profitability of $900 (corresponding to the base case of $20 variable cost per unit and 300 units sold; see cell L9). Based on this sensitivity analysis, we note that total profit varies all the way from a loss of $8,100 (in deep red at the lower right) to net income of $11,700 (in deep green at the lower left).

❹ In Column N, we note a case where all of the outcomes are −$1,500. This is the case where the price per unit ($28) exactly equals the variable cost per unit ($28), so the −$1,500 reflects the fixed costs. All other things equal, we note that as the variable costs increase, overall profitability falls. We also note that when the variable cost per unit goes up, the losses increase as the units sold increase.

	E	F	G	H	I	J	K	L	M	N	O	P	Q
1							❶			❹			
2				Variable Cost per Unit									
3			$ 900.00	$ 4.00	$ 8.00	$ 12.00	$ 16.00	$ 20.00	$ 24.00	$ 28.00	$ 32.00	$ 36.00	$ 40.00
4			50	-300.00	-500.00	-700.00	-900.00	-1100.00	-1300.00	-1500.00	-1700.00	-1900.00	-2100.00
5	Units Sold		100	900.00	500.00	100.00	-300.00	-700.00	-1100.00	-1500.00	-1900.00	-2300.00	-2700.00
6		❷	150	2100.00	1500.00	900.00	300.00	-300.00	-900.00	-1500.00	-2100.00	-2700.00	-3300.00
7			200	3300.00	2500.00	1700.00	900.00	100.00	-700.00	-1500.00	-2300.00	-3100.00	-3900.00
8			250	4500.00	3500.00	2500.00	1500.00	500.00	-500.00	-1500.00	-2500.00	-3500.00	-4500.00
9			300	5700.00	4500.00	3300.00	2100.00 ❸	900.00	-300.00	-1500.00	-2700.00	-3900.00	-5100.00
10			350	6900.00	5500.00	4100.00	2700.00	1300.00	-100.00	-1500.00	-2900.00	-4300.00	-5700.00
11			400	8100.00	6500.00	4900.00	3300.00	1700.00	100.00	-1500.00	-3100.00	-4700.00	-6300.00
12			450	9300.00	7500.00	5700.00	3900.00	2100.00	300.00	-1500.00	-3300.00	-5100.00	-6900.00
13			500	10500.00	8500.00	6500.00	4500.00	2500.00	500.00	-1500.00	-3500.00	-5500.00	-7500.00
14			550	11700.00	9500.00	7300.00	5100.00	2900.00	700.00	-1500.00	-3700.00	-5900.00	-8100.00

Note: This figure comes from Lab 13.3 Excel.

Exhibit 13.10
Sensitivity Analysis: Examining How Changes in Variable Cost per Unit and Units Sold Affect Profitability
Microsoft Excel

As you can see, sensitivity analysis helps decision makers evaluate which levels are profitable and which levels are not. Using a color scheme, the heat map helps to visualize areas of profitability and loss. This analysis will help Nintendo's management decide whether to offer this product for sale or not.

LAB CONNECTION

LAB 13.3 EXCEL asks you to evaluate how changing volume sold, sales price, and fixed and variable costs affects firm profitability. In that lab, you will use Excel's data table to perform what-if sensitivity analysis and create a heat map to visualize the differing levels of profitability.

 PROGRESS CHECK

9. Poultry feed prices are highly volatile and affect the choice of feed options. How might **Tyson** (a large beef, poultry, and other protein producer) use sensitivity analysis to support its choice of feed options?

10. How will interest rates, which are often volatile, affect the profitability of **Wells Fargo Bank**? Why is it important for a bank to perform sensitivity analysis to prepare for and respond to changing interest rates?

OPTIMIZATION MODELS

Optimization, via an *optimization model*, is a prescriptive analytics technique used to find the best feasible solution based on an objective function (goal), decision variables, and business constraints. Recall that the goal of prescriptive analytics is to help management make the best decision subject to resource constraints and/or changing conditions. Optimization models specifically emphasize the best decision in the presence of resource constraints.

LO 13.6

Apply optimization techniques to pricing and product-mix decisions.

CAREER SKILLS

Learning about optimization supports this career skill:

• Optimizing outcomes (such as profits) in the presence of constraints

Imagechina Limited/Alamy Stock Photo

Optimization techniques are used in many business functions, such as pricing optimization, product-mix optimization, and project management, to increase efficiency and minimize the downtime between processes.

Setting Up an Optimization Model

To set up an optimization model, management accounts must follow a five-step process. We define each step and provide examples below. Our goal is to answer the question, "What is the optimal price to charge for a one-day ticket to **Disneyland Hong Kong**?"

objective function

The function (or mathematical expression) that management would like to optimize (by either minimizing it or maximizing it).

Step 1. **Identify the objective function.** The **objective function** is the function or mathematical expression that the company would like to optimize (by either minimizing it or maximizing it). That is, the objective function identifies the goals the company wants to achieve via optimization. The most common objective function is to maximize profits. Often, though, the question arises whether the best objective function is to (1) maximize short-term profits, (2) maximize long-term profits, or (3) choose a scenario that may eventually lead to long-term profit maximization (such as maximizing sales to grab market share in the short term).

Disney: We'll assume that Disney wishes to maximize its long-term profits, which serves as its objective function.

decision variables

Input into the optimization model that the decision maker controls.

Step 2. **Define decision variables.** **Decision variables** are the input into the optimization model that the decision maker controls. For example, in a pricing optimization, the decision variable is the price to charge for a product or service.

Disney: We'll assume the decision variable is the price charged for a one-day ticket purchased at the ticket booth at Disneyland Resort in Hong Kong.

optimization constraints

Real-world limits on an optimization that a solution to an optimization must satisfy.

Step 3. **Identify all relevant constraints.** **Optimization constraints** are real-world limits on an optimization that a solution to an optimization must satisfy. For example, in a pricing optimization, two constraints are the change in product demand and the change in product consumption in relation to a change in its price. For example, we could increase the price of a donut to $1 million, but no one would buy one (and so demand would be zero).

Disney: In the case of Disney, we'll assume the relevant constraints are other substitute theme parks and attractions in Hong Kong. In addition, as the price of a one-day ticket to Disneyland Hong Kong increases, demand for park attendance falls.

Step 4. **Write the objective function and constraints as mathematical equations (expressions).** Because the software tools use math to run their models, the objective function and the constraints need to be written as mathematical expressions. For example, in a pricing optimization, a management accountant will express the company's objective function as a mathematical equation that calculates profits, including revenues impacted by pricing decisions, variable costs as a function of both price and volume of product sold, and total fixed costs. Here, the mathematical expression is: Profits = (Revenue per unit * Number of units sold) − (Variable cost per unit * Number of units sold) − Total fixed costs. Also, in a pricing optimization, a management accountant will express the relationship between product price and product demand as a mathematical equation.

Disney: We can express long-term profits (Disney's objective function) as revenues minus variable costs and fixed costs.

Step 5. **Run the optimization model, obtain the result, and use data-driven insights to make decisions.** When the optimization model is run, it will identify the value of the decision variable that optimizes the objective function. While this input is important, decision makers generally consider other quantitative and qualitative factors before making a final determination. For example, in a pricing optimization, the optimization model will identify the price that maximizes profit (the objective function). However, if a company believes it is more important to grab market share (maximize sales) in the short run to give the company the best chance of maximizing long-term profits, it may choose a different objective function in the short term. Qualitative factors that may be considered in a pricing decision include the (market) price of a similar product being offered by competitors or the market price of similar products in the company's own product line.

Disney: A pricing optimization will reveal the Hong Kong Disneyland gate ticket price that optimizes Disney's long-term profits subject to constraints. Decision makers may also consider qualitative factors.

Optimizing Price (Pricing Decisions)

One of management's key tasks is to set the price for each of its products in such a way as to maximize profits. One way to evaluate pricing is to use price optimization, setting the price at exactly the level that maximizes profits. One critical element of pricing is knowing the extent to which product demand adjusts as the price changes.

Price Elasticity of Demand

All other things equal, a decline in price is generally associated with an increase in demand, and vice versa. The constraint associated with pricing decisions is the extent to which demand will fall when price increases. The **price elasticity of demand** is a measure of the change in consumption of (or demand for) a product in relation to a change in its price. A price elasticity of demand of 2 means that if prices increase by 1 percent, then demand will fall by 2 percent, and if prices decrease by 1 percent, then demand will increase by 2 percent. Likewise, a price elasticity of demand of 3 means that if prices increase by 1 percent, then demand will fall by 3 percent, and if prices decrease by 1 percent, then demand will increase by 3 percent.

The price elasticity of demand is the primary constraint in the pricing decision because every increase in price is associated with a decrease in demand. Often, the marketing department works to measure the price elasticity of demand for each product.

As we think about optimizing product prices, we must recognize that market determines price, not the level of costs. Exhibit 13.11 reprints Douglas Hicks' Second Law of Pricing, which indicates the importance of basing product price on market demand rather than on costs.

price elasticity of demand
A measure of the change in consumption of (or demand for) a product in relation to a change in its price.

> **Law #2–Cost does not determine price; the market determines price. Cost determines whether or not a company wants to sell at the market price**. When an organization quotes business by rolling up its estimated cost and adding a profit margin, it develops a subconscious, but nonexistent, link between cost and price. Such organizations regularly lie to themselves by artificially manipulating costs so that they can reduce a price to meet the market and still show a targeted profit on a product or service they're trying to sell. They're then surprised when they win the job and it doesn't earn them the targeted profit. In cases where the organization is especially efficient in producing its product or providing its service, it often ends up winning the business at price below market and losing out on potential profits. This law highlights the importance of both a solid understand of "what price the market will bear" and a valid, causality-based cost model to an organization that wants to maintain a profitable portfolio of business.

Exhibit 13.11
Hick's Second Law of Pricing

Source: Douglas T. Hicks, "Hicks' Three Laws of Pricing," Profitability Analytics, April 26, 2021, www.profitability-analytics. org/forum/profitability-analytics/hicks-three-laws-of-pricing.

Excel Solver
A tool that finds the values of the decision variables that satisfy the constraints and maximize the objective function.

The following Mini-Lab uses Excel Solver to help a fictional producer of cell-phone covers optimize its pricing decision. **Excel Solver** is a tool that finds the values of the decision variables that satisfy the constraints and maximize the objective function.

DATA ANALYTICS MINI-LAB #1
Using Excel Solver to Optimize Price

Data Analytics Type: Prescriptive Analytics

Lab Note: The tools presented in this lab periodically change. Updated instructions, if applicable, can be found in the student and instructor support materials.

Keywords

Price Optimization, Maximize Profits, Prescriptive Analytics

Decision-Making Context

We will use the five-step optimization model, demonstrating how it is performed in Excel Solver, a tool that finds the values of the decision variables that satisfy the constraints and maximize the objective function.

Gorilla Cases, Inc., is a fictitious company that sells phone covers for both iPhones and Android phones. The company has asked you to find the price that maximizes profits for its iPhone 15 covers.

Ask the Question

What is the optimal price Gorilla should charge for its iPhone 15 covers?

Master the Data

Open the Excel file **Pricing Optimization Data.xlsx**. Prior data analysis suggests the price elasticity of demand for Gorilla's customers is 2. We also note that as a starting point, at a price of $12 for a Gorilla iPhone 15 cover, there is a demand for 10,000 Gorilla Cases covers (or units).

Perform the Analysis

Let's now go through the steps of setting up the optimization model.

Step 1.   **Identify the objective function**. We want to maximize current-period profits.

Step 2.   **Define decision variables**. The product price is the decision variable.

Step 3.   **Identify all relevant constraints**. Price elasticity of demand is the constraint. As noted above, the price elasticity of demand for the product is 2. That is, if price rises by 1 percent, then product demand will decrease by 2 percent.

Step 4.   **Write the objective function and constraints as mathematical equations (expressions)**. These are the relevant mathematical equations:
   Objective function: Total revenues (Product price * Product demand) − Total Expenses (Fixed costs + (Product demand * Per-unit variable cost)) in the current period.
   Product demand function: Demand = f(Price), or demand is a function of price.

Step 5.   **Run the optimization model, obtain the result, and use data-driven insights to make decisions**. The result of the model calculation is the price that maximizes current-period profit. The management of Gorilla Cases can then decide whether to apply this pricing or not.

If you haven't already done so, you'll want to make sure to add the Excel Solver to Excel's main menu. To do so, go to **File > Options > Add-Ins > Manage Excel Add-ins** and then put a check mark next to "Solver Add-In" (Exhibit A). The Solver will then be available in **Data > Analyze > Solver**.

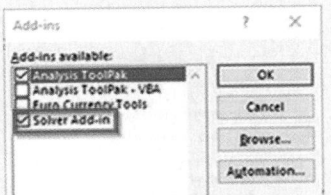

Exhibit A

Microsoft Excel

Exhibit B illustrates the pricing optimization using Excel Solver. (You will see a similar exhibit in Lab 13.4.) It shows the spreadsheet on the left, Excel Solver on the right, and the optimized result after the algorithm is run. Follow Exhibit B as you read through the following steps.

1. Cell B1 references the calculation of total profit. Maximizing this objective function is the goal of this pricing optimization.
2. The formula for cell B1 is =(B5*B3)-(B7+(B5*B8)), which calculates total revenues (B5*B3) less total fixed costs (B7) and total variable costs (B5*B8).
3. In **Set Objective**, we input the cell, $B$1, that represents the objective function. It is the total profit cell that we are trying to maximize.
4. The decision variable is the pricing variable. We are using this optimization to determine the price for this product.
5. In Excel Solver, we input the cell that represents the decision variable in the field titled **By Changing Variable Cells**. The decision variable is price in cell $B$3.
6. The constraint on this pricing equation is the price elasticity of demand. Demand is a function of price, which we get in the graph at the bottom-left of Exhibit B.
7. The formula shown in the graph, y = −1641.7x + 29700, allows us to graph demand as a function of price. The variable y represents the demand and x represents the price. We input this formula in cell B5 as =29700-1641.7*B3.

8. In Excel Solver we select the solver method as **GRG Nonlinear**, and we set the unconstrained variables to be non-negative by checking the box next to **Make Unconstrained Variables Non-Negative**. The method specifies which algorithm we tell Solver to follow to optimize the unconstrained variables.

9. Finally, in Excel Solver we click on **Solve** and let Excel Solver find the price that will optimize the objective function and maximize the result.

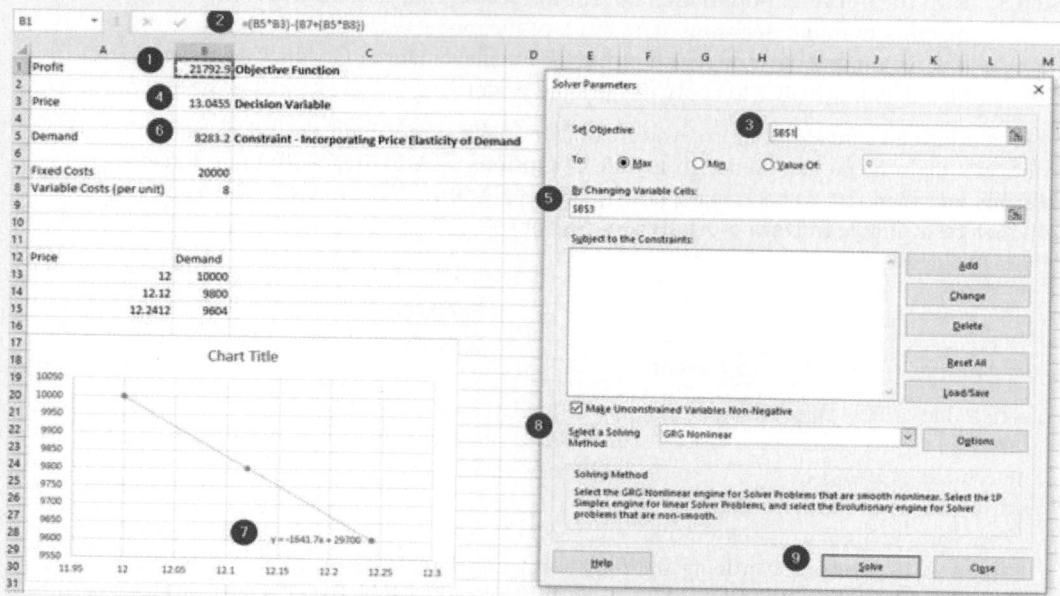

Exhibit B

Microsoft Excel

Share the Story

Gorilla Cases is now in a position to decide, based on this optimization analysis and other factors, what price it will charge for its iPhone 15 cover. While earlier marketing studies suggest that a reasonable starting price to consider is $12 per cover, the optimization analysis suggests that a price of $13.05 (see cell B3 in Exhibit B) will maximize total profit at $21,792.90 (cell B1 in Exhibit B).

Mini-Lab Assessment

1. Why can't companies just continue to raise prices on their products? Why does the price elasticity of demand serve as a constraint on product pricing?

2. Do all companies want to maximize income? What do not-for-profit companies maximize instead?

3. Is $13.0455 a realistic price? Is $13.05 better? Why do we often see prices like $12.99 instead?

LAB CONNECTION

LAB 13.4 EXCEL asks you to use Excel Solver to conduct a pricing optimization for razors. It walks step by step through the process of performing a pricing optimization in Excel Solver.

FROM THE FIELD

Setting Prices for Air Travel

One international airline operates 1,000 flights per day, with an average of 20 ticket prices per flight. It sets prices daily on each flight starting one year in advance of departure, which translates to more than 2.6 billion pricing decisions a year.

Thinking Critically

How can prescriptive analytics using optimization help automate the process of setting prices at this airline?

Optimizing Product Mix

To create value, a company must develop products that are both appealing to customers and profitable for the company. Once a company has a set of potential product offerings, it must determine its **product mix**—that is, which products to offer, the price of each product, and how many of each product to produce.

For example, **Coca-Cola** uses a formal process to continuously evaluate its product mix, reshaping its beverage portfolio (or product mix) to position itself for growth and economies of scale. For example, Coca-Cola discontinued Tab diet soda and Zico coconut water in the United States in order to focus on the brands with the greatest potential for growth and profit.[1] Management accountants use optimization to identify the product mix that maximizes profits.

In the following Mini-Lab, we follow the five-step optimization model detailed above to optimize the product mix.

product mix
The products offered by a company, along with the price of each product and how many of each product are produced.

DATA ANALYTICS MINI-LAB #2
Using Excel Solver to Optimize Product Mix

Data Analysis Type: Prescriptive Analytics

Lab Note: The tools presented in this lab periodically change. Updated instructions, if applicable, can be found in the student and instructor support materials.

Keywords
Maximize Profit, Product Mix

---

[1] "Coca-Cola Reshapes Beverage Portfolio for Growth and Scale," The Coca-Cola Co., October 16, 2020, www.coca-colacompany.com/news/coca-cola-reshapes-beverage-portfolio-for-growth-and-scale.

Decision-Making Context

Clipit is a fictitious company that offers a range of self-propelled lawn mowers. It is working to identify the mowers that maximize the company's profitability. Exhibit C provides an illustration of the product mix optimization using Excel Solver. It shows the spreadsheet on the left, Excel Solver on the right, and the optimized result that maximizes profit after the optimization algorithm is run. You will see a similar spreadsheet in Lab 13.5. (For information on ensuring that Excel Solver is installed, refer to Data Analytics Mini-Lab #1.)

Ask the Question

What is the right product mix for Clipit models S, X, E, and Z?

Master the Data

Open the file **Product Mix Solution.xlsx**. While you won't actually run the analysis here, you will be able to follow the optimization process and see and interpret the result.

Perform the Analysis

We now work through the optimization problem using the five steps in the optimization problem:

1. Identify the objective function.
2. Define decision variables.
3. Identify all relevant constraints.
4. Write the objective function and constraints as mathematical equations (expressions).
5. Run the optimization model, obtain the result, and use data-driven insights to make decisions.

For more information on each of these steps, or if you'd like to review each step in more detail, refer back to Data Analytics Mini-Lab #1.

Exhibit C shows the components of our analysis that are also shown in the file Product Mix Solution.xlsx. Note that the various numbers in Exhibit C correspond to the numbers in the following list.

1. Cell G6 references the calculation of total profit. Maximizing this objective function is the goal of this product-mix optimization.
2. The formula for cell G6 is =SUMPRODUCT(C5:F5,C6:F6), or the sum of the quantity of each product produced multiplied by the profit obtained from each specific product.
3. In Excel Solver we input $G$6 under **Set Objective**. This value represents the objective function, the goal of the optimization, which is the total profit cell that we are trying to maximize.
4. The quantity to produce is the decision variable. We are using this optimization to determine the quantity of each different product to produce (which we call the product mix).
5. In Excel Solver, under **By Changing Variable Cells**, we input the cells that represent the decision variables, which is the quantity of each product to produce in cells $C$5:$F$5.

6. The constraint on this product mix is the available resources for each business process (cells I11:I13).
7. In Excel Solver we insert the constraints into the model in the **Subject to the Constraints** box. It says that the amount of hours used of each business process (cells H11:H13) must be less than or equal to available resources (cells I11:I13). Also, the decision variables in cells $C$5:$F$5 must be integers (so that we do not have partial products).
8. In Excel Solver, we select the solver method as **Simplex LP**, and we set the unconstrained variables to be non-negative by checking the box next to **Make Unconstrained Variables Non-Negative**. The method specifies which algorithm we tell Solver to follow to optimize the unconstrained variables.
9. Finally, in Excel Solver we click on **Solve** and let Excel Solver find the product mix that will optimize the objective function and maximize the result.

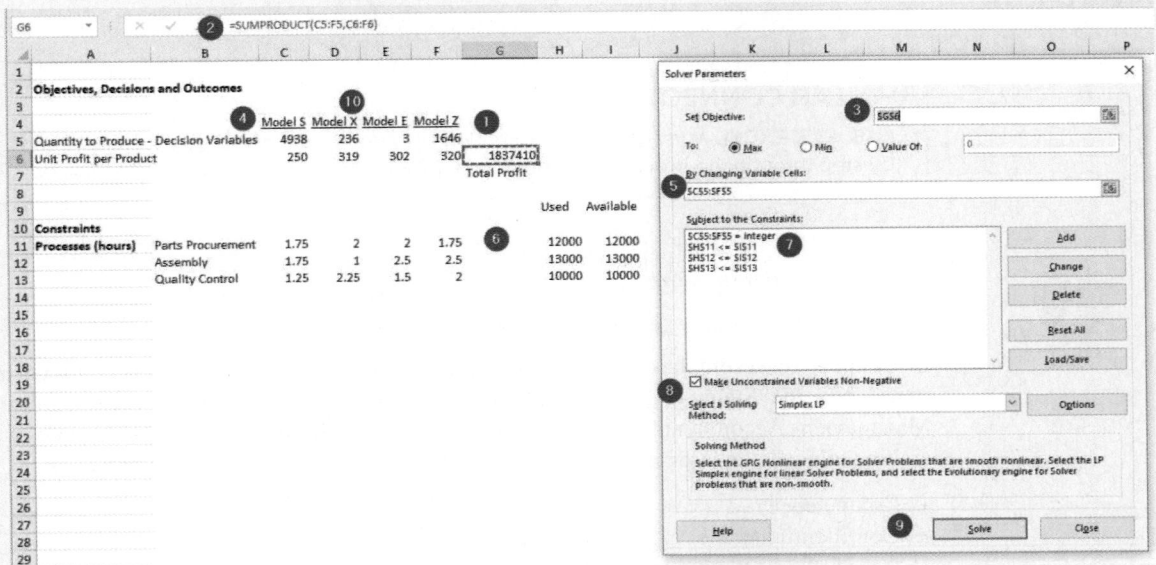

Exhibit C

Microsoft Excel

Share the Story

As a result of this analysis, Clipit has determined its optimal product mix: 4,938 of Model S, 236 of Model X, 3 of Model E, and 1,646 of Model Z. (See Row 5 of Exhibit C.) There may be other quantitative and qualitative factors that might affect the optimal product mix both now and in the future. Based on this analysis and other factors, Clipit will determine the product mix it will offer to its customers.

We also note that Clipit used all of its available capacity. A further analysis might suggest whether additional capacity should be built to increase profitability in the future.

Just like Clipit, a company like **Tesla** uses optimization techniques to determine how many of each of its popular models to produce, as determined by its objective function (current-year profitability or long-term profitability). Tesla will also have to answer these questions: What are its business constraints (batteries, semiconductor chips, factory capacity)? What other qualitative factors (reputation, future products, full product line) should be considered before making the final decision?

Mini-Lab Assessment

1. Which processes end up being the constraint? For which process is there slack when the optimal solution is calculated?
2. Could a similar optimization be used to determine which products to produce in China, in Mexico, or in the United States? How would the decision variables be different?
3. Why do we require that the decision variable be integers, instead of allowing decimal points?

 LAB CONNECTION

LAB 13.5 EXCEL asks you to use Excel Solver to optimize product mix. It walks step by step through the process of performing a product-mix optimization in Excel Solver.

ETHICS

Human Dimensions of Prescriptive Analytics: Ethical Standards and Decision Making

In Chapter 1, we emphasized the importance of ethics in management accounting and introduced the Statement of Ethical Professional Practice, issued by the Institute of Management Accountants (IMA). The statement (see Exhibit 1.15) emphasizes four overarching ethical standards that should be displayed by management accountants:

- Competence
- Confidentiality
- Integrity
- Credibility

This chapter describes the types of analysis performed by management accountants to assist managers in making strategic, data-driven decisions. In performing their jobs, they (and all other types of accountants) must exhibit a strong degree of integrity and adhere to a strict code of ethics. That is, management directly takes information provided by management accountants and assumes that the management accountant is competent, is appropriately trained, maintains confidentiality, exhibits integrity, and has credibility. It also presumes that when a **conflict of interest** arises—that is, when a management accountant has a competing personal or financial interest that makes it challenging to fulfill their duties fairly—it is fully and faithfully disclosed.

conflict of interest
A situation in which an employee has a competing personal or financial interest that makes it challenging to fulfill their duties fairly.

Management Accounting Careers

Increasingly, the profession is expecting a certain level of skills, including the prescriptive analytics skills addressed in this chapter. As an example, consider the summary of *The Finance 2020 Workforce* (Exhibit 13.12), which showcases the needed skills, and note how many of them emphasize prescriptive analytics discussed in this chapter.

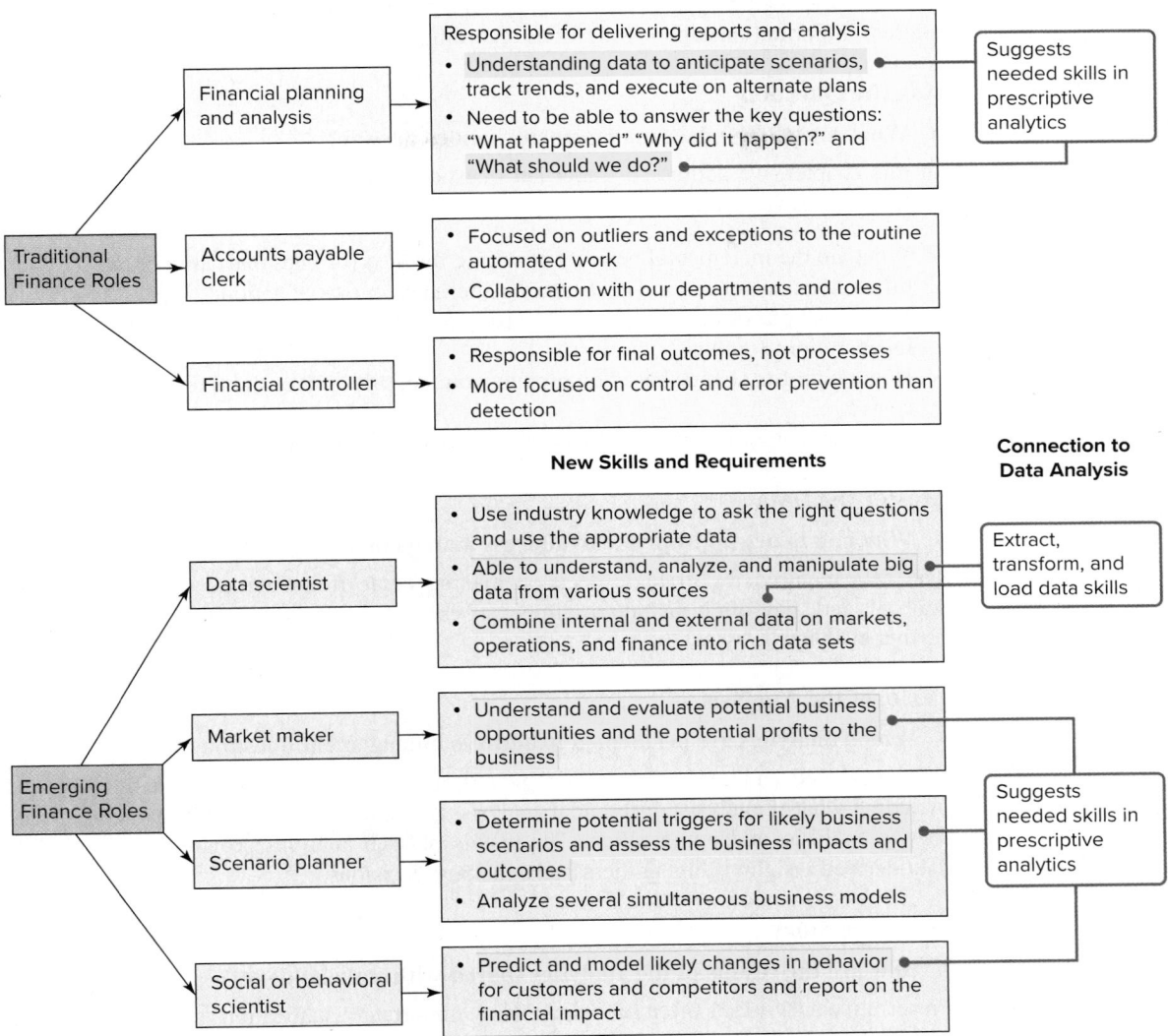

Exhibit 13.12
The Finance 2020 Workforce

(✓) **PROGRESS CHECK**

11. How would you show the relationship between product price and product demand in a mathematical expression? Why is there a negative association between price and demand?

12. What is the trade-off between an objective function (or goal) that maximizes short-term profits and an objective function that maximizes long-term profits? How might this trade-off affect managers' behavior?

Key Takeaways: Strategic Decision Making

Let's use the AMPS model to review how the information in this chapter can be used to address important managerial questions regarding strategic decision making.

<u>A</u>sk the Question

■ **What question(s) does management want to answer?**

In this chapter, we addressed important questions related to strategic decision making, including:

- What are the incremental benefits of selling the next (or marginal) unit, or the difference in revenues and costs among alternate courses of action?
- What level of sales (input) does a company need to achieve in order to break even in its operations (output)?
- How do profits change based on product volume, sales price, and fixed and variable costs?
- What is the optimal price to charge for any given product to maximize profitability?

<u>M</u>aster the Data

■ **Which data are appropriate to address management's questions?**

The data required for strategic decision making come from internal and external data sources, and they often include a number of estimates and assumptions that need to be further evaluated.

<u>P</u>erform the Analysis

■ **Which analytics are performed to address management questions?**

We introduced and explained several prescriptive analytics techniques in this chapter, including what-if analysis, differential analysis, goal-seek analysis, scenario analysis, sensitivity analysis, and optimization. The results of such analyses provide managers with data-derived insights, helping them make the best decisions.

<u>S</u>hare the Story

■ **How are the results of the analytics shared with stakeholders?**

Prescriptive analytics is often accompanied by important visualizations such as heat maps, which show the likely effects of changing conditions and resource constraints.

Key Terms

base case scenario	Excel Solver	optimization constraints	quantitative factors
capital budgeting	goal-seek analysis	optimization model	relevant costs
conflict of interest	heat map	prescriptive analytics	relevant revenues
data table	make-or-buy analysis	price elasticity of demand	scenario analysis
decision variables			sensitivity analysis
differential analysis	management accountant	product mix	sunk costs
disruptive technologies	objective function	qualitative factors	what-if analysis

ANSWERS TO PROGRESS CHECKS

1. Predictive analytics forecast what might happen in the future. Prescriptive analytics help determine what course of action should be taken based on what is expected to occur.

2. To determine the break-even level for a proposed new product, management accountants might use goal-seek analysis, which will identify the inputs needed to reach the desired outcome, output, or result. In the case of a break-even analysis, the desired outcome is the level of new product sales at which the new product sales revenue exactly equals the costs of producing and selling the new product.

3. Sunk costs are past costs spent that cannot be recovered regardless of the future course of action. In contrast, relevant costs differ among alternative courses of action.

4. Qualitative factors involved in the make-or-buy decision may include an assessment of a company's available capacity, the quality of outsourced work, and financial or political issues related to outsourcing. In making a make-or-buy decision, these factors may be just as important as the quantitative factors such as relevant costs and relevant revenues.

5. Goal-seek analysis requires a management accountant to identify the desired output to determine the needed input. In the case of the break-even level of sales, the management accountant specifies a target profit of zero. In the case of the target profit, the desired output is the specific level of profit to be achieved.

6. Goal-seek analysis requires management accountants to identify the desired output to determine the needed input. In this case, the outcome is a certain level of monthly payment, and goal-seek analysis can be used to determine the maximum price you can afford to pay for a new car.

7. Scenario analysis evaluates the impact of potential future events by considering their possible outcomes. In this case, management accountants could evaluate various potential lumber price scenarios and their impact on the prices of new houses.

8. Scenario analysis can be used to evaluate what **Tesla**'s electric car sales and/or company profitability may be based on certain projections of decreasing battery prices due to factors such as changes in technology or economies of scale.

9. **Tyson** could use sensitivity analysis to assess the point at which one feed source is preferred to another based on profitability.

10. Because a bank's profitability is often based on variable and volatile interest rates, sensitivity analysis may help managers evaluate and plan for expected interest rate volatility in the future (including plans to evaluate interest rate hedges and interest rate swaps).

11. Pricing optimization requires a mathematical expression of demand as a function of price. The expression should reflect the fact that the higher the price, the lower the demand. Generally, the higher an item is priced, the lower the demand for that item. This is the law of demand in economics.

12. Short-term profitability may be at the expense of long-term profitability. To maximize bonuses or keep their jobs, managers may pursue short-term profitability and set it as the objective function in a pricing, product-mix, or other type of optimization.

Multiple-Choice Questions   Mc Graw Hill connect

1. (LO13.1) Which type of prescriptive analytics evaluates outcomes based on uncertainty regarding the inputs?
   a. Goal-seek analysis
   b. Scenario analysis
   c. Sensitivity analysis
   d. Optimization

2. (LO13.1, 13.2, 13.3, 13.4, 13.5) An assessment regarding which large investment to invest in is typically called:

   a. cash flow analysis.

   b. net present value analysis.

   c. what-if analysis.

   d. capital budgeting.

3. (LO13.1, 13.2, 13.3, 13.4, 13.5) Which analysis helps managers decide whether to out-source certain aspects of producing a product or service?

   a. Sensitivity analysis

   b. Make-or-buy analysis

   c. Scenario analysis

   d. Financial modeling

4. (LO13.1, 13.2, 13.3, 13.4, 13.5) Which prescriptive analytics technique evaluates the average expected impact of potential future events by considering their potential outcomes?

   a. Sensitivity analysis

   b. Goal-seek analysis

   c. Scenario analysis

   d. Financial modeling

5. (LO13.5) Which software tool is used to perform sensitivity analysis regarding the impact of varying one or two inputs (assumptions) to evaluate the output?

   a. Data table

   b. Excel Solver

   c. Optimization

   d. Goal seek

6. (LO13.6) Price elasticity of demand is:

   a. a measure of the change in consumption of or demand for a product relative to a change in price.

   b. a measure of the change in price due to a change in demand.

   c. a measure of the change in price due to a change in the underlying cost.

7. (LO13.6) A price elasticity of demand of 4 suggests that _____.

   a. if price increases four percent, demand will fall by one percent.

   b. if price increases one percent, demand will fall by four percent.

   c. if price decreases one percent, demand will fall by four percent.

   d. if price decreases four percent, demand will fall by four percent.

8. (LO13.6) If a company is trying to maximize its profits through its product pricing, what is the objective function?

   a. Maximize the sales of its products

   b. Maximize profits associated with its products

   c. The price of its products

   d. The price elasticity of demand

9. (LO13.6) If a company is trying to maximize its profits by adjusting its product mix, what is a common constraint of the optimization?

   a. Maximize profits associated with the product mix

   b. The price of its products

   c. The resources available to produce or offer its products

   d. The quantity of each product sold

10. (LO13.1, 13.6) Which technique may work to maximize profits by varying product prices subject to certain constraints?

   a. Optimization

   b. Cash flow analysis

   c. Sensitivity analysis

   d. Goal-seek analysis

11. (LO13.1, 13.6) The decision variable in a product pricing optimization is:

   a. level of profits.

   b. price of product.

   c. price elasticity of demand.

   d. variety of products for sale.

12. (LO13.1, 13.3) Break-even analysis is performed using the prescriptive analytics tool of:

   a. optimization.

   b. cash flow analysis.

   c. sensitivity analysis.

   d. goal-seek analysis.

13. (LO13.6) The objective function of a product mix decision is to _____ subject to constraints?

   a. maximize revenues

   b. maximize profits

   c. minimize expenses

   d. maximize products manufactured

14. (LO13.2) What is a prescriptive analytics technique to determine the change in profit typically associated with the differences in revenues and costs among alternate courses of action?

   a. Optimization

   b. Cash flow analysis

   c. Sensitivity analysis

   d. Differential analysis

15. (LO13.1) Which of the following is an example of a changing condition in the automotive industry?

   a. 3D printers are now widely used in production processes.

   b. Automakers need sources and a sufficient supply of computer chips.

   c. Autonomous vehicles require continuous software updates.

   d. Automakers must continue to innovate their production techniques and facilities.

16. (LO13.2) In make-or-buy analysis, all of the following are key inputs to the decision except:

   a. avoidable fixed costs.

   b. sunk costs.

   c. cost by the contract manufacturer.

   d. direct costs

17. (LO13.6) According to Douglas Hicks' Second Law of Pricing, the market determines the price of the product, and cost determines:

   a. the profit of the product sold.

   b. whether or not the company wants to sell at the market price.

   c. the amount of product sold.

   d. the competitor price for a similar product.

913

18. (LO13.6) Which Excel software tool is used to optimize product mix?
    a. Excel data table
    b. Excel Solver
    c. Excel what-if analysis
    d. Excel forecast sheet

19. (LO13.7) In Accenture's *Meet the Finance 2020 Workforce* document, the company suggests that accountants should be able to answer "What Shall We Do"-type questions. Which analytics type does that category correspond to?
    a. Descriptive analytics
    b. Diagnostic analytics
    c. Predictive analytics
    d. Prescriptive analytics

Discussion Questions

1. (LO13.1) Given resource constraints, which prescriptive analytics technique might be used to maximize profits by focusing either on a company's mix of products considering all potential product offerings or by focusing only on the most profitable products?

2. (LO13.1) Using Exhibit 13.2 as a guide, describe each prescriptive analytics technique and the questions each addresses.

3. (LO13.1) How do businesses cope with limited resources? Which prescriptive analytics technique might they use to address resource constraints?

4. (LO13.1) How does capital budgeting address resource constraints?

5. (LO13.2) Why are fixed costs not considered to be relevant costs in a make-or-buy decision? How do variable costs differ from fixed costs?

6. (LO13.2) Why are sunk costs not considered to be relevant costs? When are other costs considered to be relevant or not relevant?

7. (LO13.3, 13.5) What is the difference between goal-seek analysis and scenario analysis? What is the objective of each of these prescriptive analytics techniques?

8. (LO13.3) How can determining the needed level of sales to reach a target profit of $2 million be considered goal-seek analysis? What is the desired output? What is the input?

9. (LO13.3) How does determining the needed grade on the final exam to get a certain grade in a class be considered goal-seek analysis? What is the desired output? What is the input?

10. (LO13.4) Which prescriptive analytics technique would you use to evaluate the impact of rising fuel prices on **J.B. Hunt** (a trucking company)? Which technique would you use to evaluate the outcomes based on uncertainty of future fuel prices?

11. (LO13.5) Why is sensitivity analysis a powerful tool for predicting the impact of different possible inputs on the output?

12. (LO13.5) Trying to understand the impact of volatile exchange rates between the Chinese RMB (yuan) and U.S. dollar on **Microsoft**'s profitability is an example of sensitivity analysis, which evaluates the outcomes based on uncertainty regarding the inputs. In this example, what are the inputs and the outputs?

13. (LO13.5) According to Hicks' Second Law, discovering the appropriate product price is based on market demand rather than on costs. Why is Hicks' Second Law consistent with price optimization that considers the constraint based on the product's price elasticity of demand?

14. (LO13.6) Optimization models often have an objective function to maximize profits. What are the trade-offs between considering short-term profits (with the short term defined as less than a year) and long-term profits (with the long term defined as one year or longer)? Are long-term profits always better (or worse) than short-term profits? Explain.

15. (LO13.6) Why is the price elasticity of demand considered to be a constraint in a pricing decision? Why are product demand and product price negatively related to each other (that is, negatively correlated)?

Brief Exercises   Mc Graw Hill connect

1. (LO13.1) Match each prescriptive analytics technique to its description.

Description	Prescriptive Analytics Technique (What-if analysis, Make-or-buy analysis, Optimization model, Goal-seek analysis, Sensitivity analysis, Scenario analysis)
a. Evaluates outcomes based on uncertainty regarding the inputs	
b. Evaluates the impact of future events by considering potential outcomes	
c. Finds the best feasible solution based on an objective function, decision variables, and business constraints	
d. A form of what-if analysis that tells us what needs to be done (or assumed) in order to reach a desired outcome, output, or result	
e. Determines whether to manufacture a product in-house or purchase it (or outsource it) externally	
f. Evaluates how changes in the values of various inputs affect outputs	

2. (LO13.2) Match each differential analysis term to its definition.

Definition	Differential Analysis Term (Sunk costs, Relevant costs, Relevant revenues, Make-or-buy analysis, Qualitative factors, Quantitative factors)
a. Expected future costs that differ among alternative courses of action	
b. Decision outcomes that are difficult to measure	
c. Past costs spent that cannot be recovered regardless of the future course of action chosen	
d. Prescriptive analytics technique to determine whether to manufacture a product in-house or purchase it externally	
e. Expected future revenues that differ among alternative courses of action	
f. Measurable decision outcomes	

3. (LO13.6) Match the optimization term with each aspect of the product-mix decision.

Product Mix Decision	Optimization Term (Objective function, Decision variable, Constraint)
a. Maximize total long-term profits	
b. The quantity of each product must be an integer	
c. The quantity of each product to manufacture	
d. Only the amount of resources available to manufacture the products may be used	
e. Maximize total short-term profits	

4. (LO13.1) Match the appropriate prescriptive analytics techniques with its example.

Prescriptive Analytics Example	Prescriptive Analytics Technique (Differential analysis, Financial modeling, Make-or-buy analysis, Sensitivity analysis, Scenario analysis)
a. Should **FedEx** hire more full-time drivers or ask its current drivers to work overtime?	
b. How sensitive is net income to a 2, 3, or 5 percent increase in gross domestic product (GDP) for the overall economy?	
c. How will three different possible tariff scenarios with a major trading partner affect our company's overall performance?	
d. What is the financial impact of three different possible tax-law changes on **Cisco**'s earnings?	
e. Should **GM** manufacture small cars or buy them from an automaker in China and sell them as GM cars?	

5. (LO13.6) At a price of $20, 10,000 units of product are demanded. If price increases to $20.20 at a price elasticity of 3, what is the level of product demand? What is the total revenue as a result of the price increase? What other information is needed to determine whether profit increases or decreases as a result of the price increase?

6. (LO13.6) At a price of $10, 20,000 units of product are demanded. If price decreases to $9.90 at a price elasticity of 2, what is the level of product demand? What other information is needed to determine whether profit increases or decreases as a result of the price decrease?

7. (LO13.3) How would you set up a goal-seek analysis to determine what grade you need to get on the final exam in order to receive an "A" in this course? What is the desired outcome? What input is needed to get the "A" desired in this course? How does this goal-seek analysis compare/contrast with a break-even analysis?

8. (LO13.4) Suppose that a local bank in Arkansas, **Arvest Bank**, decides to perform scenario analysis. It believes the prime interest rate for business loans will change from the current 4 percent to either 5 percent or 3 percent in the next year. There will be no change in its $3,000,000 annual income at the 4 percent interest level, but net income will fall to $1,000,000 if the interest rate falls to 3 percent and increase to $4,000,000 if the interest rate increases to 5 percent. Arvest predicts a 25 percent probability of a 4 percent interest rate, a 25 percent probability of a 3 percent interest rate, and a 50 percent probability of a 5 percent interest rate.

What is the expected financial impact on net income of changing interest rates given all the potential interest-rate scenarios at Arvest Bank?

9. (LO13.4) First Provo Bank is conducting a scenario analysis. It believes that its source of funds (the Federal Reserve) will soon increase the cost of loans (that is, the interest rate charged). In fact, First Provo Bank expects the interest rate to change from the current 2 percent interest to either 3 percent or 4 percent in the next year. There will be no change in its $2,000,000 annual income at the 2 percent interest level, but net income will fall to $1,000,000 if the interest rate increases to 3 percent and decrease to $100,000 if the interest rate increases to 4 percent. First Provo Bank predicts a 10 percent probability of a decrease to a 2 percent interest rate, a 50 percent probability of an increase to a 3 percent interest rate, and a 40 percent probability of an increase to a 4 percent interest rate.

What is the expected financial impact on net income of changing interest rates given all the potential interest-rate scenarios at First Provo Bank?

10. (LO13.7) Answer the following questions regarding management accountants' ethical standards.

   a. Refer to the opening story in Chapter 1, regarding **Tesla**'s solar roofs. Which management accounting ethical standard appears to be in question: competence, confidentiality, integrity, or credibility? Explain.

   b. If a management accountant at **Netflix** tries to steer a production contract to a distant cousin, which management accounting ethical standard appears to be in question: competence, confidentiality, integrity, or credibility? Explain.

   c. If a management accountant made mistakes running analysis in Power BI due to a lack of training, which management accounting ethical standard appears to be in question: competence, confidentiality, integrity, or credibility? Explain.

   d. If a management accountant doesn't secure her laptop when she leaves work, which management accounting ethical standard appears to be in question: competence, confidentiality, integrity, or credibility? Explain.

11. (LO13.7) Answer the following questions regarding management accountants' ethical standards.

   a. If a management accountant shows bias in his analysis "because he's been around a long time and knows what is best for the company regardless of the data analysis," which management accounting ethical standard appears to be in question: competence, confidentiality, integrity, or credibility? Explain.

   b. If a management accountant fails to download all of the data from the financial reporting system needed for the analysis, which management accounting ethical standard appears to be in question: competence, confidentiality, integrity, or credibility? Explain.

   c. If a management accountant intentionally creates an incomplete data analysis to please one member of the executive team, which management accounting ethical standard appears to be in question: competence, confidentiality, integrity, or credibility? Explain.

   d. If a management accountant provides fake information about his education and college degree in order to get hired, which management accounting ethical standard appears to be in question: competence, confidentiality, integrity, or credibility? Explain.

12. (LO13.6) Price elasticity of demand is an important constraint in a pricing optimization. If the price elasticity of demand suddenly increased from 1 to 2 due to the increasing availability of substitutes, what would a company do to determine if raising prices is optimal? How important will an understanding of the fixed costs and variable costs be? If variable costs were 60 percent of the total sales price, what does that mean for overall profits? Would the company be more likely to increase prices or decrease prices? Provide the intuition that suggests what will happen when prices increase and what will happen when prices decrease.

13. (LO13.3) Consider Exhibit 13.5, which provides a number of examples of goal-seek analysis. Suppose your desired output is to reduce your company's employee turnover from 10 percent annually to 5 percent annually. Brainstorm some ideas for the required inputs to achieve that goal. What will need to be done? To get a goal-seek function to work, you will need a formula. What kind of formula would you use? For example, every day per week you let people work remotely, overall employee turnover is reduced by 1 percent annually. What other relationships would you propose?

14. (LO13.5) Evaluate each of the following cases and answer the accompanying questions.

   a. *Case 1:* What do you think is the key input in plastic production to evaluate with respect to sensitivity analysis? What is plastic made of?

   b. *Case 2:* With recent news that most plastic is not recyclable, suppose that the Environmental Protection Agency asks Congress to pass a "plastic tax" of 2 percent, 4 percent, or 6 percent? Which type of analysis will management accountants perform: scenario analysis or sensitivity analysis?

   c. *Case 3:* A company wants to achieve a net-zero carbon output. Which prescriptive analytics technique could be used to evaluate the needed inputs? What type of inputs might be relevant here?

15. (LO13.5) Evaluate each of the following cases and answer the accompanying questions.

   a. *Case 1:* In an inflationary environment in which prices increase each year, which prescriptive analytics technique will be used to evaluate how the nominal and real effects of inflation on variable costs affect company profits?

   b. *Case 2:* In an inflationary environment in which product prices change frequently, how could optimization be used to set the right price each time it changes?

   c. *Case 3:* In an inflationary environment in which input prices change frequently, how could optimization be used to find the right product mix? How often would you optimize? Is capacity measured in units of capacity or in prices of those units of capacity?

Problems   connect

1. (LO13.4) The legislature is considering changing tax rates from 7 percent to either 6 percent or 5 percent. Pathways Landscaping Equipment is trying to understand the impact of these changes and is using scenario analysis to assess the expected value of the impact. Before any changes are made, the base case scenario is $1,000,000 in annual taxable income at a tax rate of 7 percent.

   The following table summarizes the expected financial impact of each scenario, assuming that taxable income increases or decreases by 5 percent and either no changes are made in the 7 percent tax rate or the tax rate decreases to either 6 percent or 5 percent.

Income Scenario	Taxable Income	If Tax Rate = 7%, Taxes Owed =	If Tax Rate = 6%, Taxes Owed =	If Tax Rate = 5%, Taxes Owed =
Income increases by 5%	$1,050,000	$ 3,500	$ (7,000)	$(17,500)
Income remains unchanged	$1,000,000	0	$(10,000)	$(20,000)
Income decreases by 5%	$ 950,000	$(3,500)	$(13,000)	$(22,500)

   Based on Pathways' assessment of the probability of the tax-law changes and potential changes in its own taxable income, here are the joint probabilities of the changes in tax rate and taxable income.

		Likelihood of Each Scenario		
		If Tax Rate = 7%, Taxes Owed =	If Tax Rate = 6%, Taxes Owed =	If Tax Rate = 5%, Taxes Owed =
	Taxable Income	If Tax Rate = 7%	If Tax Rate = 6%	If Tax Rate = 5%
Income increases by 5%	$1,050,000	0.05	0.05	0.15
Income remains unchanged	$1,000,000	0.2	0.2	0.1
Income decreases by 5%	$950,000	0.05	0.1	0.1

   Required

   Based on the expected changes in taxable income and the change in tax rate, what is the value of the expected impact on Pathways' tax burden? Show your work.

2. (LO13.4) Use the same scenario from Problem 1, but now assume that the tax rates are expected to change to 8 percent, 7 percent, and 6 percent with the same probabilities as Problem 1.

Required

Compute the value of the expected impact of the changes in tax rates on Pathways' tax burden. Show your work.

3. (LO13.5) Given the base case scenario in the table below, which is based on the decision to evaluate the variable cost per unit, evaluate the differing levels of profitability shown in the accompanying heat map.

Base Case Scenario:

Sales price per unit	$ 28
Units sold	300
Total revenue	$8,400
Variable cost per unit	$20
Total variable costs	$6,000
Total fixed costs	1,500
Total costs	$7,500
Profit	$ 900

		Variable Cost per Unit									
	$ 900.00	$ 4.00	$ 8.00	$ 12.00	$ 16.00	$ 20.00	$ 24.00	$ 28.00	$ 32.00	$ 36.00	$ 40.00
Units Sold	50	-300.00	-500.00	-700.00	-900.00	-1100.00	-1300.00	-1500.00	-1700.00	-1900.00	-2100.00
	100	900.00	500.00	100.00	-300.00	-700.00	-1100.00	-1500.00	-1900.00	-2300.00	-2700.00
	150	2100.00	1500.00	900.00	300.00	-300.00	-900.00	-1500.00	-2100.00	-2700.00	-3300.00
	200	3300.00	2500.00	1700.00	900.00	100.00	-700.00	-1500.00	-2300.00	-3100.00	-3900.00
	250	4500.00	3500.00	2500.00	1500.00	500.00	-500.00	-1500.00	-2500.00	-3500.00	-4500.00
	300	5700.00	4500.00	3300.00	2100.00	900.00	-300.00	-1500.00	-2700.00	-3900.00	-5100.00
	350	6900.00	5500.00	4100.00	2700.00	1300.00	-100.00	-1500.00	-2900.00	-4300.00	-5700.00
	400	8100.00	6500.00	4900.00	3300.00	1700.00	100.00	-1500.00	-3100.00	-4700.00	-6300.00
	450	9300.00	7500.00	5700.00	3900.00	2100.00	300.00	-1500.00	-3300.00	-5100.00	-6900.00
	500	10500.00	8500.00	6500.00	4500.00	2500.00	500.00	-1500.00	-3500.00	-5500.00	-7500.00
	550	11700.00	9500.00	7300.00	5100.00	2900.00	700.00	-1500.00	-3700.00	-5900.00	-8100.00

Heat Map: Sensitivity Analysis Examining Changes in Variable Cost per Unit and Units Sold on Profitability

Microsoft Excel

Required

Refer to the heat map to answer the following questions.

a. What is the profit at $36 variable cost and 100 units sold?

b. Why is the result −$1,500.00 profit for each number of units sold in the $28 variable cost per unit column?

c. Reconstruct the profit of $11,700 at a variable cost of $4 and 550 units sold by constructing an income statement using relevant information (the fixed costs and sales price) above.

d. Estimate the profitability at a variable cost of $6 and sales of 550. Beyond reconstructing a complete income statement, is there an easier way of determining profitability?

4. (LO13.5) The following heat map results from a sensitivity analysis that might be performed by management accountants. It evaluates the changing profitability based on two important inputs: (1) the level of total fixed costs and (2) the sales price. The sales price ranges from $35 to $53 (as shown in the columns) and the fixed costs range from

$500 to $3,000 (as shown in the rows). The colored columns are the total profits based on the changing input parameters.

Sales Price

Fixed Costs	$ 35.00	$ 37.00	$ 39.00	$ 41.00	$ 43.00	$ 45.00	$ 47.00	$ 49.00	$ 51.00	$ 53.00
500	4000.00	4600.00	5200.00	5800.00	6400.00	7000.00	7600.00	8200.00	8800.00	9400.00
750	3750.00	4350.00	4950.00	5550.00	6150.00	6750.00	7350.00	7950.00	8550.00	9150.00
1,000	3500.00	4100.00	4700.00	5300.00	5900.00	6500.00	7100.00	7700.00	8300.00	8900.00
1,250	3250.00	3850.00	4450.00	5050.00	5650.00	6250.00	6850.00	7450.00	8050.00	8650.00
1,500	3000.00	3600.00	4200.00	4800.00	5400.00	6000.00	6600.00	7200.00	7800.00	8400.00
1,750	2750.00	3350.00	3950.00	4550.00	5150.00	5750.00	6350.00	6950.00	7550.00	8150.00
2,000	2500.00	3100.00	3700.00	4300.00	4900.00	5500.00	6100.00	6700.00	7300.00	7900.00
2,250	2250.00	2850.00	3450.00	4050.00	4650.00	5250.00	5850.00	6450.00	7050.00	7650.00
2,500	2000.00	2600.00	3200.00	3800.00	4400.00	5000.00	5600.00	6200.00	6800.00	7400.00
2,750	1750.00	2350.00	2950.00	3550.00	4150.00	4750.00	5350.00	5950.00	6550.00	7150.00
3,000	1500.00	2100.00	2700.00	3300.00	3900.00	4500.00	5100.00	5700.00	6300.00	6900.00

Heat Map: Sensitivity Analysis Examining Changes in Variable Cost per Unit and Units Sold on Profitability

Microsoft Excel

Required

Refer to the heat map to answer the following questions.

a. As sales price increases, what happens to the estimated profitability?

b. As total fixed costs increase, what happens to the estimated profitability?

c. If the sales price is $53 and total fixed costs are $3,000, what is the estimated profitability?

d. If the sales price is $45 and total fixed costs are $500, what is the estimated profitability?

e. Which has more impact on profitability: a $2 increase in sales price or a $250 decrease in total fixed costs?

f. How does conditional formatting help you to visualize the impact of these two important inputs on estimated profitability?

5. (LO13.5) The following heat map results from a sensitivity analysis that might be performed by financial analysts. It evaluates the two most important inputs to determine the estimated stock price: (1) the cost of capital and (2) sales growth in the future. Sales growth varies from 1 percent to 10 percent (as shown in the columns), and the cost of capital varies from 4 percent to 14 percent (as shown in the rows). The colored columns are the estimated stock prices based on the changing input parameters.

DATA VISUALIZATION

Horizon Period Sales Growth

Cost of Capital	1%	2%	3%	4%	5%	6%	7%	8%	9%	10%
4%	156.64	161.90	167.31	172.87	178.60	184.48	190.54	196.76	203.15	209.71
5%	118.33	122.07	125.91	129.86	133.93	138.11	142.41	146.82	151.36	156.02
6%	95.35	98.18	101.09	104.08	107.16	110.33	113.58	116.92	120.35	123.87
7%	80.03	82.26	84.56	86.92	89.34	91.83	94.40	97.03	99.73	102.50
8%	69.09	70.90	72.76	74.67	76.63	78.65	80.73	82.86	85.04	87.29
9%	60.88	62.38	63.92	65.50	67.12	68.79	70.50	72.26	74.06	75.92
10%	54.50	55.76	57.05	58.37	59.73	61.13	62.57	64.04	65.55	67.10
11%	49.40	50.46	51.56	52.68	53.84	55.02	56.24	57.49	58.77	60.09
12%	45.22	46.14	47.07	48.04	49.02	50.04	51.08	52.15	53.24	54.37
13%	41.75	42.53	43.34	44.17	45.02	45.89	46.79	47.71	48.66	49.62
14%	38.80	39.49	40.19	40.90	41.64	42.40	43.18	43.97	44.79	45.63

Heat Map: Sensitivity Analysis Examining Changes in Variable Cost per Unit and Units Sold on Profitability

Microsoft Excel

Required

Refer to the heat map to answer the following questions.

a. As the cost of capital increases, what happens to the estimated stock price?

b. As sales growth decreases, what happens to the estimated stock price?

c. If sales growth is 4 percent and the cost of capital is 14 percent, what is the estimated stock price?

d. If sales growth is 10 percent and the cost of capital is 4 percent, what is the estimated stock price?

e. Which has more impact on stock price: a 1 percent increase in sales growth or a 1 percent increase in cost of capital?

f. How does conditional formatting help you to visualize the impact of these two important inputs on estimated stock price?

6. (LO13.6) The following exhibit shows the optimized result for a company's product mix. After performing Lab 13.5 and based on this Excel output, answer the following questions related to product mix.

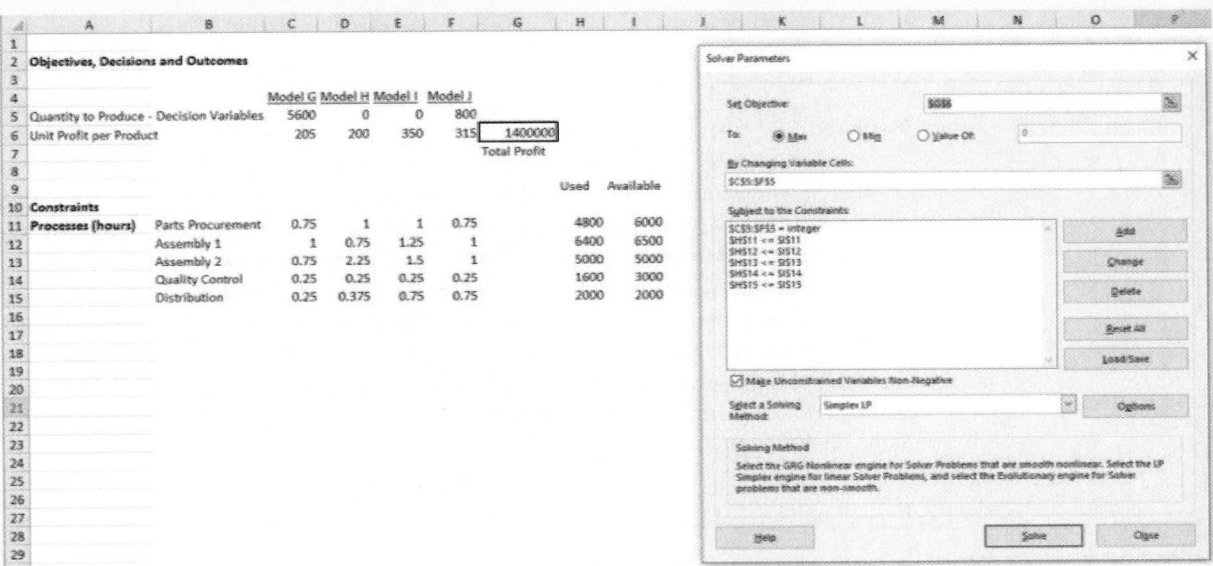

Microsoft Excel

Required

a. Which cell has the objective function? Why is that objective function chosen?

b. Which cells have the decision variables?

c. Where are the six constraints?

d. What would happen if the unit profit changed for just one product? When would that change affect the product mix?

7. (LO13.6) The following exhibit shows the optimized result for a company's product mix. After performing Lab 13.5 and based on this Excel output, answer the following questions related to product mix.

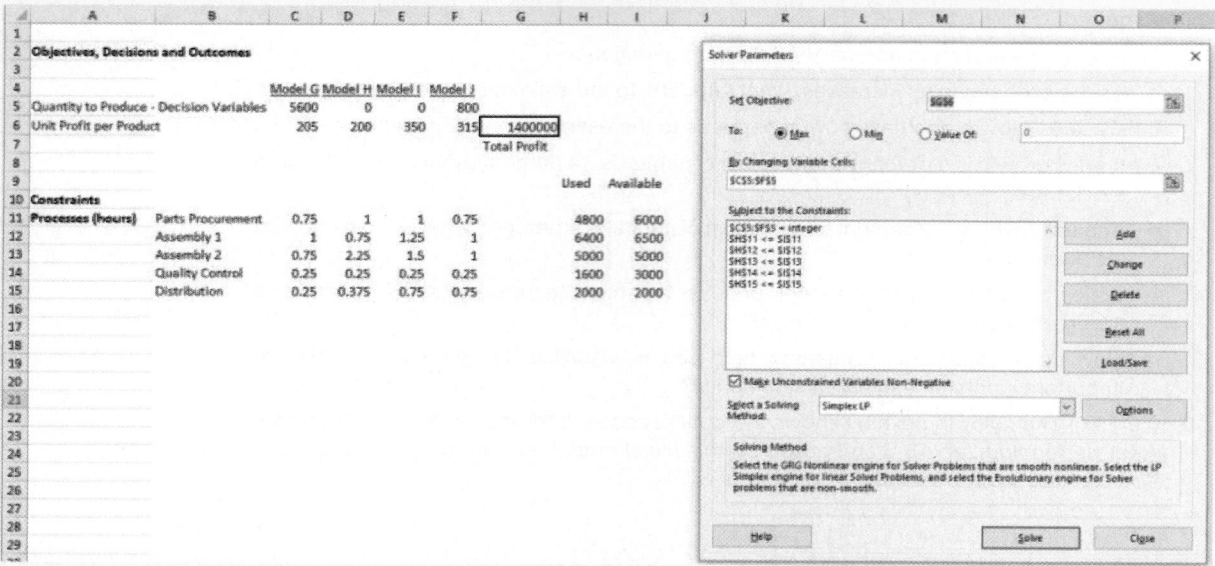

Microsoft Excel

Required

a. According to the optimization, the maximized profit is $1,400,000. How is that number computed? (*Hint:* Consider all of the revenues and expenses.)

b. Recreate the use of available resources of Assembly 2 and Distribution because the production of Model G and Model J seems to exhaust all available resources.

c. Given that Assembly 2 and Distribution have exhausted all resources, why can we assume that there is no production of Model H? (*Hint:* Consider Model H's profit as well as Model H's expected usage of Assembly 2 and Distribution processes.)

8. (LO13.6) The following exhibit shows the optimized result for a company's product mix. After performing Lab 13.5 and based on this Excel output, answer the following questions related to product mix.

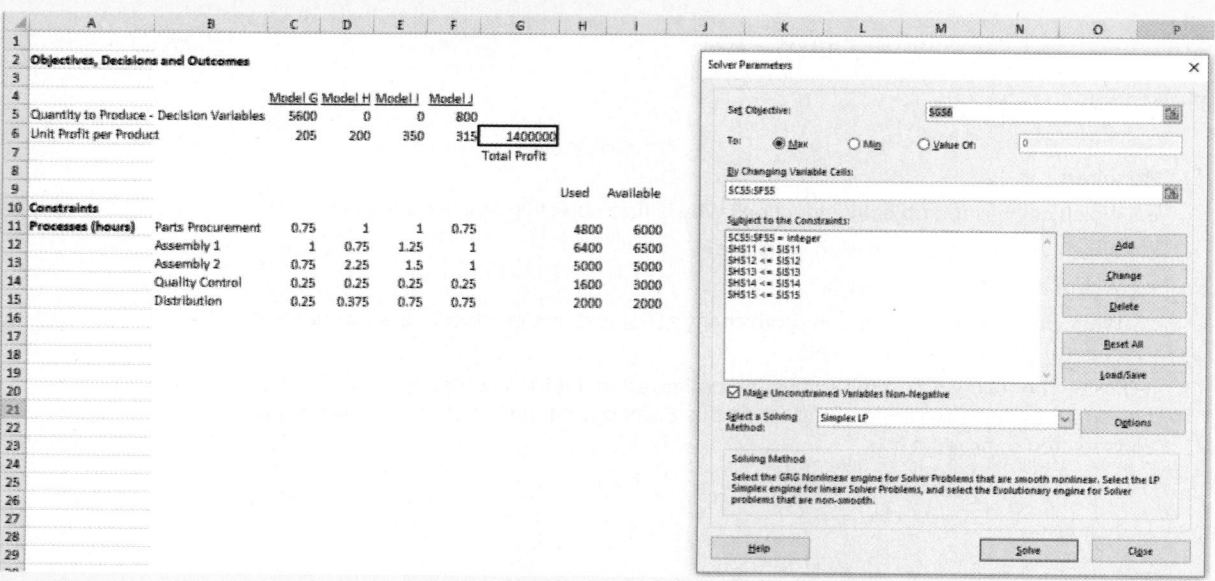

Microsoft Excel

Required

a. Given that Assembly 2 and Distribution have exhausted all resources, why can we assume that there is no production of Model I? (*Hint:* Consider Model I's profit as well as Model I's expected usage of Assembly 2 and Distribution processes.)

b. Which process has the most slack in its constraints? To help compute the amount of slack, note the difference between the amount used and the amount available.

c. Why are the number of products (Models) produced required to be integers? Why is that a constraint?

9. (LO13.6) The following exhibit shows the optimized result for a company's product pricing. After performing Lab 13.4 and based on this Excel output, answer the following questions related to optimizing price.

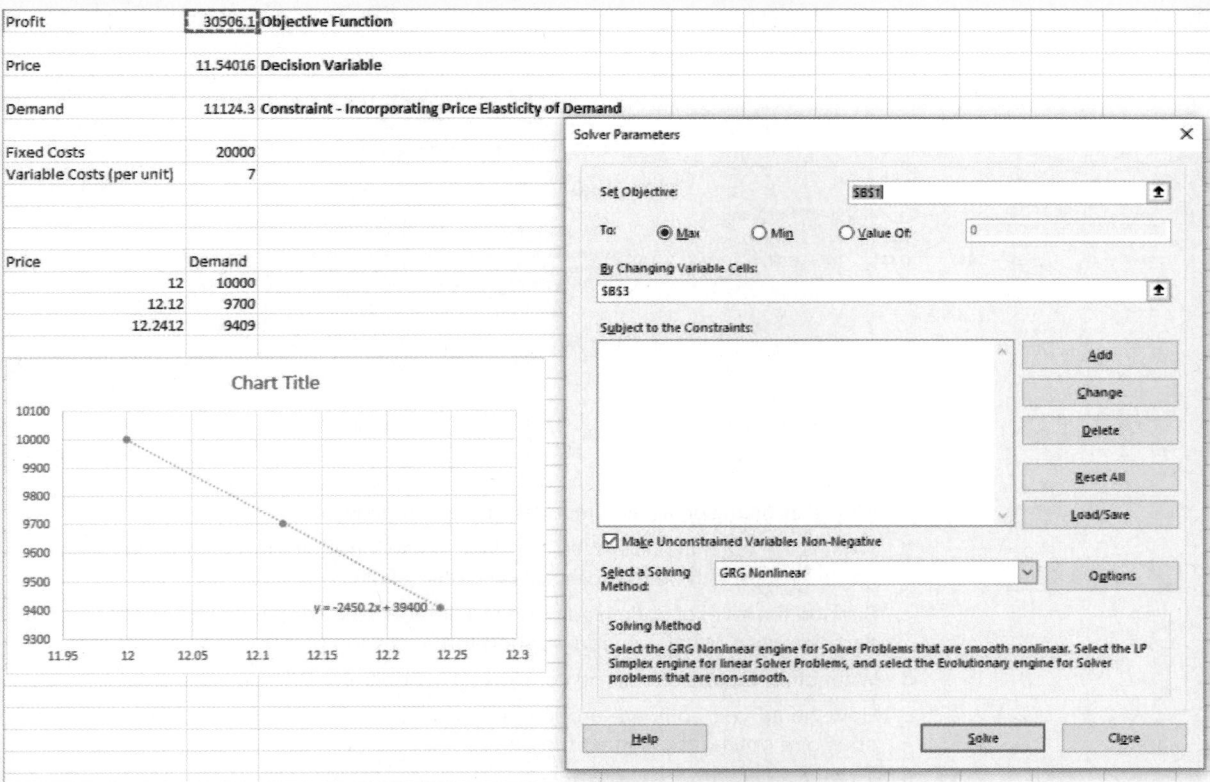

Microsoft Excel

Required

a. What is the price elasticity of demand? How is it computed?

b. How was the demand curve determined?

c. How is the optimized product pricing determined?

10. (LO13.6) The following exhibit shows the optimized result for a company's product pricing. After performing Lab 13.4 and based on this Excel output, answer the following questions related to optimizing price.

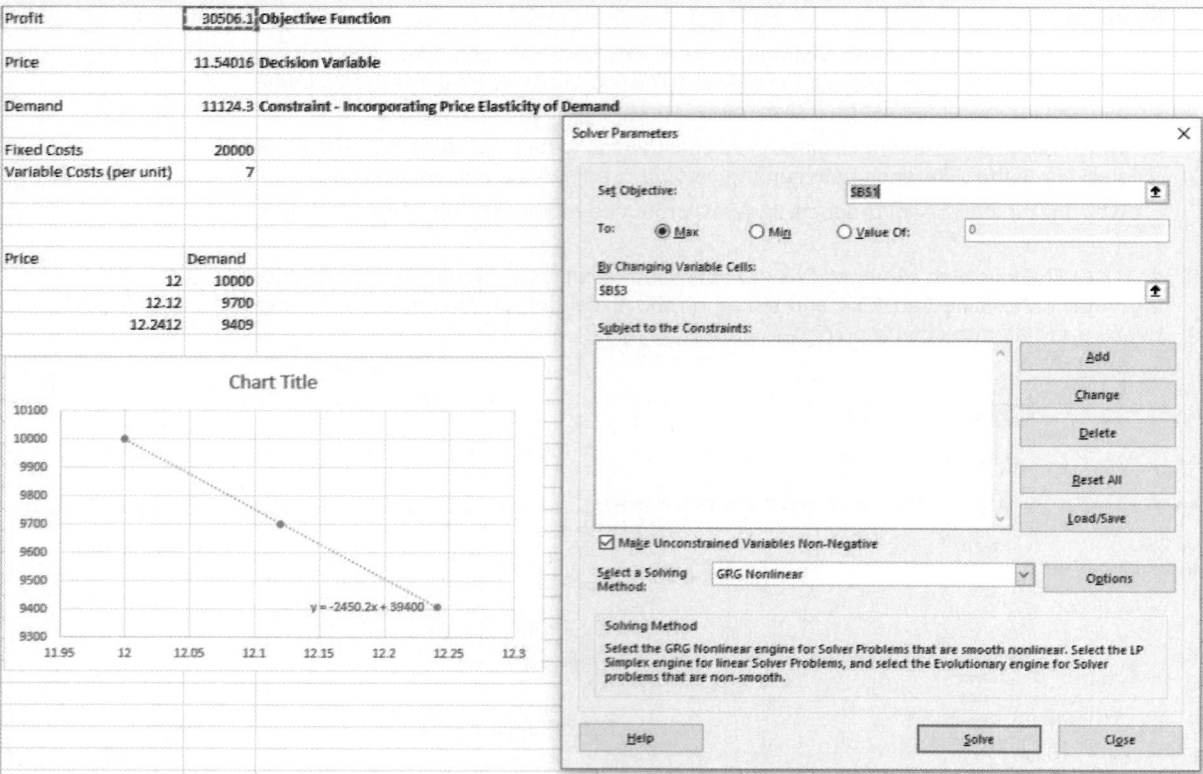

Microsoft Excel

Required

a. Why is profit maximization important for a company?

b. What is the optimal price? Would it make sense to require this number to be an integer or require it to be rounded to two digits? Explain.

c. Support the level of optimized profit of $30,506.10 by determining level of revenues and expenses. What numbers support the optimized profit?

d. What other factors should be considered in addition to the optimized result?

e. How would you compare a price optimization to a product-mix optimization? How does one optimization affect the other?

11. (LO13.2) Assume that **Gillette** faces a make-or-buy decision for its 12-pack razors. Given the cost details below, what would you recommend?

	Cost per Unit	
	Make (Gillette makes own razors)	**Buy** (Hua Mfg.)
Outside purchase of 12-pack razors from Hua Mfg.		$21
Direct materials	$9	
Variable direct manufacturing labor	$4	
Variable manufacturing overhead	$5	
Mixed (variable and fixed) batch-level materials handling and setup manufacturing overhead	$4	
Fixed manufacturing overhead costs (plant lease, insurance, administration)	$5	

Required

a. Calculate the relevant costs of Gillette making the razors.

b. Compare the "make" vs. "buy" of the razors. From a quantitative perspective, which decision should be made?

c. If Gillette completely outsources its razor production, how would that decision affect its strategy for designing and selling razors or related products in the future?

12. (LO13.6) Consider the summary depiction of Accenture's *Meet the Finance 2020 Workforce* in Exhibit 13.12. Note how strongly the document emphasizes the prescriptive analytics discussed in this chapter.

Required

a. Which prescriptive analytics technique is used to "anticipate alternative scenarios"?

b. What type of analytics (descriptive, diagnostic, predictive, or prescriptive) is required to "Not just answer the 'what happened' and 'why did it happen' questions but also answer the 'what should we do' questions"?

c. Why does diagnostic analytics fulfill the expectation of "focusing on exceptions"?

13. (LO13.6) Consider the summary depiction of Accenture's *Meet the Finance 2020 Workforce,* reproduced in Exhibit 13.12. Note how strongly the document emphasizes the prescriptive analytics discussed in this chapter.

Required

a. Why do ETL skills (see Chapter 2), which are part of the Master the Data step in the AMPS model, work as a descriptor for "Ability to understand and manipulate massive volumes of data from internal and external sources"?

b. Which prescriptive analytics technique addresses determining "the business impact of each scenario"?

c. Which prescriptive analytics technique addresses "the ability to analyze new business opportunities"?

d. Which prescriptive analytics technique addresses "the ability to model changes in customer and competitor behavior and describe the financial implications"? (*Hint:* Note the word "changes" used in the descriptor.)

14. (LO13.5) The **Husqvarna Group** is a Swedish company that manufactures outdoor power products including robotic lawn mowers, chainsaws, trimmers, and garden tractors.

   In the exhibit below, we see the sensitivity of changing exchange rates between the Swedish krona and either the U.S. dollar or the euro on Husqvarna Group's operating income. We also see the impact of a one percent change in interest rates, and the impact of a 10 percent change in the price of steel, aluminum, or plastics, on Husqvarna's operating income. These details came from the company's annual financial report, and they are included in the annual report every year.

Required

a. Why would Husqvarna calculate the sensitivity of its operating profits based on its currency, raw materials, and interest rates?

b. Why would Husqvarna share this information with its shareholders?

c. If raw materials steel prices increase by 10 percent, will operating profits go up or down? Will the impact be symmetric if steel prices decrease by 10 percent? Why or why not?

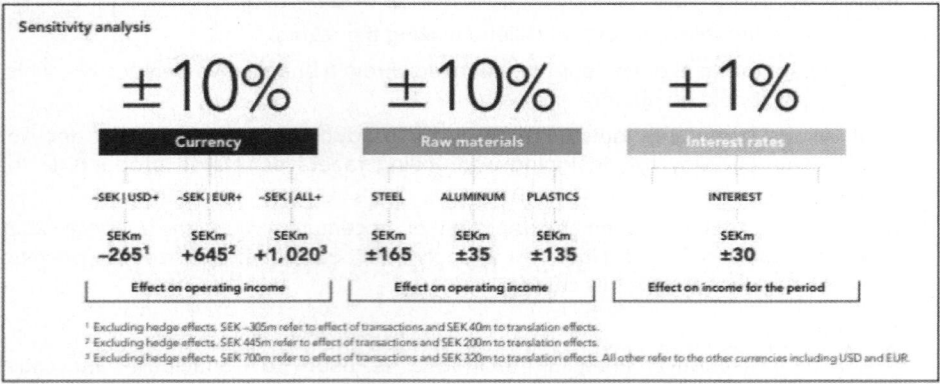

Source: Husqvarna Group, *Annual Report 2021* (2022), p. 51, www.husqvarnagroup.com/sites/default/files/pr/202203162196-1.pdf.

15. (LO13.5) The **Husqvarna Group** is a Swedish company that manufactures outdoor power products including robotic lawn mowers, chainsaws, trimmers, and garden tractors. In the exhibit shown in Problem 14, we see the impact of changing exchange rates between the Swedish krona and either the U.S. dollar or the euro on Husqvarna Group's operating income. We also see the impact of a one percent change in interest rates and a 10 percent change in the price of steel, aluminum, or plastics on Husqvarna's operating income. These details came from the company's annual financial report, and they are included in the annual report every year.

Required

a. Why would the company analyze a 1 percent change in interest rates but a 10 percent change in currency?

b. What does inclusion of raw materials in this sensitivity analysis say about Husqvarna's business model?

c. How important would it be to Husqvarna to include the volatile price of fuel for its customers? Are there any other items you think should be included here?

d. What does the inclusion of currency in this sensitivity analysis say about Husqvarna's customers and suppliers?

Lab 13.1   Excel

Using Goal-Seek Analysis: Calculate Break-Even Sales

Data Analytics Type: Prescriptive Analytics

Lab Note: The tools presented in this lab periodically change. Updated instructions, if applicable, can be found in the student and instructor support materials.

Keywords

What-If Solver, Break-Even, Goal Seek

Decision-Making Context

Managers use historical data to predict costs and prices of products. What-if analysis helps managers estimate the break-even point, which sets the threshold for positive net income and the goal for minimum sales.

In this lab, we use the what-if solver in Excel to estimate the break-even point.

Required

Use Excel Solver to determine the break-even point.

Ask the Question

What is the company's break-even point given its costs and sales prices?

Master the Data

Jing LCC is a fictitious food company. The costs of ingredients for food production vary by season. Using costs and sales prices for 2025, Jing LLC's management wants to estimate the break-even point for product A in each month in 2026 to set up minimum sales targets. For this lab you will use data in the Excel file titled **Lab 13.1 Data.xlsx**.

Data Dictionary

Price	The unit price of product A
Unit Sales	The expected unit sales of product A per month
Variable Cost per Unit	The variable costs of product A per month
Total Fixed Costs	The fixed costs of each month
Total Variable Costs	Total variable costs of product A per month
Total Costs	The total costs of product A per month
Total Sales Revenue	Total sales revenue of product A per month
Net Income	The net income of product A per month

Perform the Analysis

Analysis Task # 1: Compute Net Income

1. Open Excel file **Lab 13.1 Data.xlsx**.
2. Browse the spreadsheet very quickly to make sure there isn't any obvious error in the Excel file.
3. Calculate the total variable costs of product A in January, using the formula Total Variable Costs = Unit Sales * Variable Cost per Unit, or =B3*B4, as shown in Lab Exhibit 13.1.1.

Lab Exhibit 13.1.1

Microsoft Excel

VLOOKUP	▼	⋮	✕	✓	*fx*	=B3*E

◢	A	B	C
1		Jan	Feb
2	Price	7.00	7.00
3	Unit Sales	300.00	300.00
4	Variable Cost per Unit	4.50	3.80
5	Total Fixed Costs	1000.00	1000.00
6	Total Variable Costs	=B3*B4	
7	Total Costs		
8	Sales Revenue		
9	Net Income		

4. Calculate the total cost of product A in January, using the formula Total Costs = Total Variable Costs + Total Fixed Costs, or =B5+B6, as shown in Lab Exhibit 13.1.2.

	A	B
1		Jan
2	Price	7.00
3	Unit Sales	300.00
4	Variable Cost per Unit	4.50
5	Total Fixed Costs	1000.00
6	Total Variable Costs	1350.00
7	Total Costs	=B5+B6

Lab Exhibit 13.1.2

Microsoft Excel

5. Calculate the sales revenue of product A in January using the formula Sales Revenue = Price * Unit Sales, or =B2*B3, as shown in Lab Exhibit 13.1.3.

	A	B
1		Jan
2	Price	7.00
3	Unit Sales	300.00
4	Variable Cost per Unit	4.50
5	Total Fixed Costs	1000.00
6	Total Variable Costs	1350.00
7	Total Costs	2350.00
8	Sales Revenue	=B2*B3
9	Net Income	

Lab Exhibit 13.1.3

Microsoft Excel

6. Calculate net income of product A in January, using the formula Net income = Sales revenue − Total costs, or =B8-B7, as shown in Lab Exhibit 13.1.4.

Lab Exhibit 13.1.4

Microsoft Excel

	A	B
1		Jan
2	Price	7.00
3	Unit Sales	300.00
4	Variable Cost per Unit	4.50
5	Total Fixed Costs	1000.00
6	Total Variable Costs	1350.00
7	Total Costs	2350.00
8	Sales Revenue	2100.00
9	Net Income	=B8-B7

Analysis Task # 2: Calculate the Break-Even Point Using Goal-Seek Analysis

1. In cell B9, estimate the break-even for revenue and total costs using the what-if solver. Click on the **Data** tab in the ribbon. In the **Forecast** section, click **What-If Analysis** (Lab Exhibit 13.1.5). In the submenu, click **Goal Seek...** (Lab Exhibit 13.1.6).

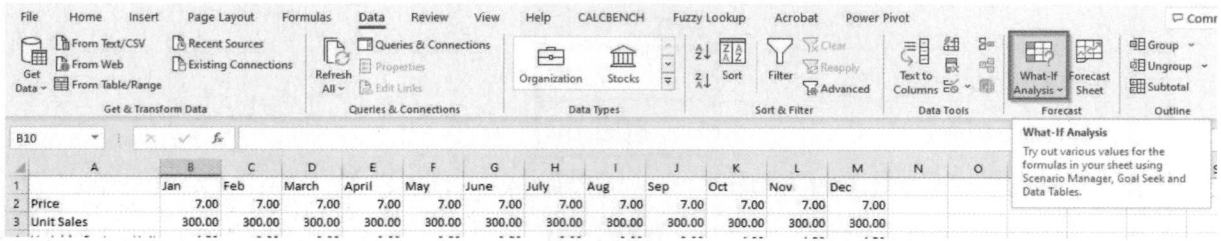

Lab Exhibit 13.1.5

Microsoft Excel

Lab Exhibit 13.1.6

Microsoft Excel

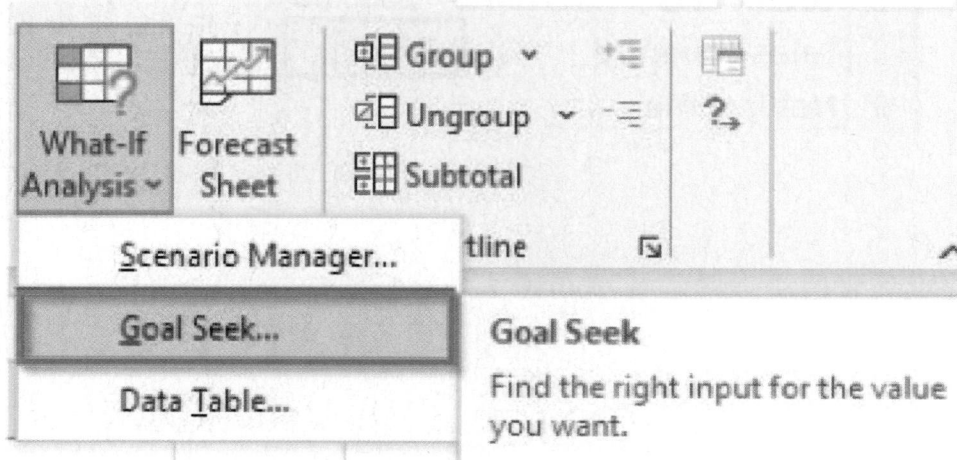

2. Estimate the unit sales when net income is equal to zero. In the **Goal Seek** window, in the box next to **Set cell**, select **Net income** in the January column (data under a condition). Type "0" (the condition) in the box next to **To value**. Then, in the box next to **By changing cell**, select **Unit Sales** in the January column. Click **OK**. Your screen will resemble Lab Exhibit 13.1.7.

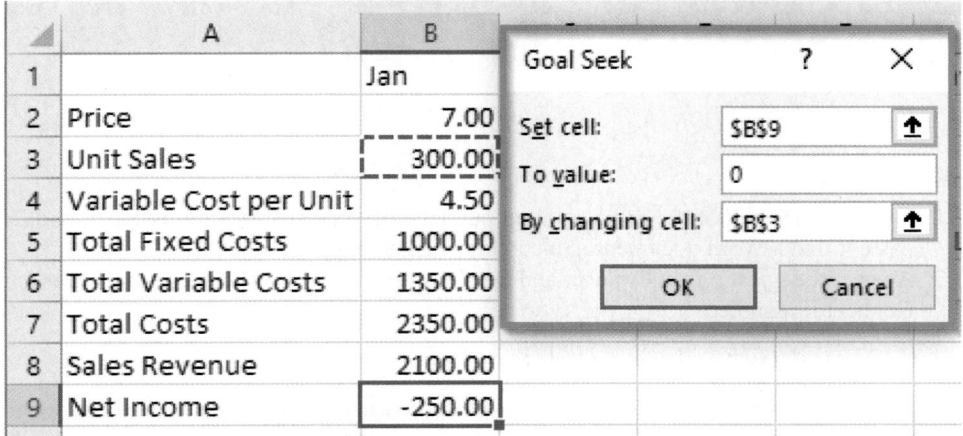

3. Click **OK** in the **Goal Seek Status** window. Once you press **OK**, notice that the number of units in B3 changes to 400, which is the estimated units of sales in January that will result in net income equal to zero, or the break-even point (Lab Exhibit 13.1.8).

	A	B	C	D	E	F
1		Jan				
2	Price	7.00				
3	Unit Sales	400.00	Goal Seek Status	?	X	
4	Variable Cost per Unit	4.50	Goal Seeking with Cell B9 found a solution.	Step		
5	Total Fixed Costs	1000.00		Pause		
6	Total Variable Costs	1800.00	Target value: 0			
7	Total Costs	2800.00	Current value: 0.00	OK	Cancel	
8	Sales Revenue	2800.00				
9	Net Income	0.00				

4. To identify the number of units sold in order to result in a net income equal to zero, follow all the steps in Task Analysis #1 and #2 for each month.

Share the Story

Using what-if analysis, managers can identify the required unit sales to achieve break-even net income. Lab Exhibit 13.1.9 shows the break-even unit sales for each month. Managers can set the minimum unit sales as the threshold for profitability and adjust sales strategies accordingly.

	Jan	Feb	March	April	May	June	July	Aug	Sep	Oct	Nov	Dec
Price	7.00	7.00	7.00	7.00	7.00	7.00	7.00	7.00	7.00	7.00	7.00	7.00
Unit Sales	400.00	312.50	312.50	312.50	285.71	285.71	250.00	250.00	250.00	333.33	400.00	400.00
Variable Cost per Unit	4.50	3.80	3.80	3.80	3.50	3.50	3.00	3.00	3.00	4.00	4.50	4.50
Total Fixed Costs	1000.00	1000.00	1000.00	1000.00	1000.00	1000.00	1000.00	1000.00	1000.00	1000.00	1000.00	1000.00
Total Variable Costs	1800.00	1187.50	1187.50	1187.50	1000.00	1000.00	750.00	750.00	750.00	1333.33	1800.00	1800.00
Total Costs	2800.00	2187.50	2187.50	2187.50	2000.00	2000.00	1750.00	1750.00	1750.00	2333.33	2800.00	2800.00
Sales Revenue	2800.00	2187.50	2187.50	2187.50	2000.00	2000.00	1750.00	1750.00	1750.00	2333.33	2800.00	2800.00
Net Income	0.00	0.00	0.00	0.00	0.00	0.00	0.00	0.00	0.00	0.00	0.00	0.00

Lab Exhibit 13.1.9

Microsoft Excel

Assessment

1. Take a screenshot of the break-even output, label the screenshot Submission 1, and paste it into a Word document named "Lab 13.1 Submission.docx."
2. Answer the questions in Connect and upload your Lab 13.1 Submission.docx via Connect if assigned.

Alternate Lab 13.1   Excel—On Your Own

Using Goal-Seek Analysis: Calculate Break-Even Sales

Keywords

What-If Solver, Break-Even, Goal Seek

Apply the same steps in Lab 13.1 to the **Alt Lab 13.1 Data.xlsx** dataset, which includes sales information on products A, B, C, D, E, F, and G in 2025. Estimate the break-even point of unit sales for each product when net income equals zero.

Required

Use Excel Solver to determine the break-even point.

Assessment

1. Take a screenshot of the break-even output, label the screenshot Submission 1, and paste it into a Word document named "Alt Lab 13.1 Submission.docx."
2. Answer the questions in Connect and upload your Alt Lab 13.1 Submission.docx via Connect if assigned.

Scenario Analysis: Identifying the Expected Impact of a Trade War

Data Analytics Type: Prescriptive Analytics

Keywords

What-If Scenarios, Trade War Impact

Decision-Making Context

What-if scenario analysis considers potential outcomes by analyzing future events. It does not try to predict one possible outcome. Instead, it presents a range of alternative outcomes to understand the overall impact of possible future events.

In this lab, we assume that there is a possibility of a trade war with another country that may have no effect (no trade war), a 10 percent decrease in company income, or a 25 percent decrease in company income. At the same time (and unrelated to the trade war), the company might have a potential increase in domestic demand that will cause income to either increase by 5 percent, be neutral (net income remains unchanged), or decrease by 5 percent. The CFO has asked you to evaluate the expected value of the potential impact of all these potential scenarios on income.

Required

Calculate the expected dollar impact of the various potential trade war scenarios based on the dollar impact and probability of each scenario occurring.

Ask the Question

How will a possible trade war impact expected income?

Master the Data

SticksOfJoy is a small (fictitious) company that manufactures and sells joysticks. Your task is to evaluate the impact of a potential trade war on the company's profits. For this lab you will use the data in the Excel file titled **Lab 13.2 Data.xlsx**. Open this file, which provides a template for our analysis. Browse the spreadsheet quickly to make sure there isn't any obvious error in the Excel file. The data file should appear as shown in Lab Exhibit 13.2.1.

Perform the Analysis

Analysis Task: Calculate the Impact of Each Scenario

1. All in all, there are nine possible scenarios measuring the impact of the possible trade war. If there is no trade war with another country, there will be no impact on the company's net income. There will be a 10 percent decrease in income if there is a moderate trade war and a 25 percent decrease in income if there is a severe trade war.

   Using cell B5 as the base case, calculate the change in income from the base case ($B$5) for each of the nine scenarios using the correct formulas in cells C4:E6 and C13:E15. Lab Exhibit 13.2.2 provides the formulas.

Lab Note: The tools presented in this lab periodically change. Updated instructions, if applicable, can be found in the student and instructor support materials. All Lab Exhibits are available within the eBook and in Connect.

⁄	A	B	C	D	E
1	Change in Income under each scenario				
2			No Trade War	Moderate Trade War	Severe Trade War
3	Income Scenarios	Income	0	-0.1	-0.25
4	Domestic Demand Increases Income by 5%	=(1+0.05)*B5	=$B$5*(1+0.05)*(1-$C$3)	=$B$5*(1+0.05)*(1+$D$3)	=$B$5*(1+0.05)*(1+$E$3)
5	Domestic Demand Doesn't Change	2000000	=$B$5*1*(1-$C$3)	=$B$5*1*(1+$D$3)	=$B$5*1*(1+$E$3)
6	Domestic Demand Decreases Income by 5%	=(1-0.05)*B5	=$B$5*(1-0.05)*(1+$C$3)	=$B$5*(1-0.05)*(1+$D$3)	=$B$5*(1-0.05)*(1+$E$3)
7					
8					
9	The change in income based on scenario above:				
10					
11			No Trade War	Moderate Trade War	Severe Trade War
12	Income Scenarios	Income	0	-0.1	-0.25
13	Domestic Demand Increases Income by 5%	=(1+0.05)*B14	=C4-$B$5	=D4-$B$5	=E4-$B$5
14	Domestic Demand Doesn't Change	2000000	=C5-$B$5	=D5-$B$5	=E5-$B$5
15	Domestic Demand Decreases Income by 5%	=(1-0.05)*B14	=C6-$B$5	=D6-$B$5	=E6-$B$5

Lab Exhibit 13.2.2

Microsoft Excel

The result is as shown in Lab Exhibit 13.2.3.

2. Next, we need to estimate the probability of each scenario occurring. After talking to management, we estimate the expected impact of each scenario. Input these probabilities in cells C20:E22, as shown in Lab Exhibit 13.2.4. Then sum up both the row totals and the column totals to make sure they equal 100%.

Probability of the scenario occurring:		No Trade War	Moderate Trade War	Severe Trade War
Income Scenarios	Income	0%	-10%	-25%
Domestic Demand Increases Income by 5%	2,100,000	0.05	0.20	0.25
Domestic Demand Doesn't Change	2,000,000	0.05	0.15	0.10
Domestic Demand Decreases Income by 5%	1,900,000	0.10	0.05	0.05

Lab Exhibit 13.2.4

Microsoft Excel

3. We are now ready to calculate the expected impact of each individual scenario. We do so by multiplying the expected dollar change in income by the probability of that scenario occurring. For example, in cell C28, we multiply cell C13 by cell C20. We then sum the expected impact to come up with the result shown in Lab Exhibit 13.2.5.

Share the Story

According to our scenario analysis, the expected impact of the trade war on income is a decrease in income of $256,500 (see cell F31 in Exhibit 13.2.5). Management can use this information to evaluate the expected impact of a possible trade war on profitability and plan accordingly.

Assessment

1. Take a screenshot of the completed spreadsheet, label the screenshot Submission 1, and paste it into a Word document named "Lab 13.2 Submission.docx."
2. Answer the questions in Connect and upload your Lab 13.2 Submission.docx via Connect if assigned.

Scenario Analysis: Identifying the Expected Impact of a Trade War

Keywords

What-If Scenarios, Trade War Impact

Peters Engineering, a fictional company, has income of $3,000,000 with a potential increase or decrease of 10 percent due to possible changes in domestic demand. Evaluate the expected change in income based on a possibility of no trade war, moderate trade war (income decrease of 5 percent), and severe trade war (income decrease of 30 percent).

Following the example of Lab 13.2, apply the same scenario analysis to this Lab.

The probability of each tax scenario occurring is summarized in this table:

	Income	No Trade War	Moderate Trade War	Severe Trade War
Domestic demand increases income by 10%	3,300,000	0.10	0.05	0.10
Domestic demand doesn't change	3,000,000	0.10	0.20	0.10
Domestic demand decreases income by 30%	2,700,000	0.15	0.05	0.15

Apply the same steps in Lab 13.2 to the **Alt Lab 13.2 Data.xlsx** dataset.

Required

Calculate the expected dollar impact of the various potential trade war scenarios based on the dollar impact and probability of each scenario occurring.

Assessment

1. Take a screenshot of the completed spreadsheet, label the screenshot Submission 1, and paste it into a Word document named "Alt Lab 13.2 Submission.docx."
2. Answer the questions in Connect and upload your Alt Lab 13.2 Submission.docx via Connect if assigned.

Sensitivity Analysis: Using an Excel Data Table to Analyze Profitability under Changing Volume, Sales Price, and Fixed and Variable Costs

Data Analytics Type: Prescriptive Analytics

Keywords

Sensitivity Analysis, Cost-Volume-Profit, Conditional Formatting, Changing Assumptions

Decision-Making Context

Profitability is a function of number of units sold, price, and fixed and variable costs.

What happens if we change the assumptions we make? For example, how sensitive are the results to changes in the number of units sold or the variable cost per unit? How much will profit change?

By examining how sensitive profitability is to the changing assumptions, managers can make more informed decisions on pricing, manufacturing, and margins.

This lab is an example of prescriptive analytics, evaluating the impact of changing conditions or changing assumptions. Specifically, in this lab we evaluate how changes in volume sold, sales price, and fixed and variable costs will affect a firm's profitability. We also use conditional formatting to visualize the differing levels of profitability.

The company is selling Sleep Sound white noise machines, which help those suffering from insomnia and anxiety to fall asleep. The company is trying to determine the profitability based on various inputs.

Required

1. Determine how profit will respond to changing assumptions regarding the number of units sold and level of variable costs per unit.
2. Apply conditional formatting to the differing levels of profitability in the resulting data table.

Ask the Question

How sensitive are company profitability levels given different assumptions regarding inputs?

Master the Data

For this lab we will use a blank Excel file.

Perform the Analysis

Analysis Task #1: Prepare the Excel File for Analysis

1. Open a new file in Excel. There is no other data file provided. For Steps 2–5, follow along with Lab Exhibit 13.3.1.
2. In cell A1, type "Assumptions:" and then boldface and underline it.
3. In cell A2, type "Price". In cell B2, enter the number 28.
4. In cell A3, type "Units Sold". In cell B3, enter the number 300.

5. In cell A4, type "Total Revenues". In cell B4, enter the formula =B2*B3. Your screen should resemble Lab Exhibit 13.3.1.
6. For Steps 6–10, follow along with Lab Exhibit 13.3.2. In cell A5, type "Variable Cost per Unit". In cell B5, enter the number 20.
7. In cell A6, type "Total Variable Cost". In cell B6, enter the formula =B3*B5.
8. In cell A7, type "Total Fixed Costs". In cell B7, enter the number 1500.
9. In cell A8, type "Total Costs". In cell B8, enter the formula =B6+B7.
10. In cell A9, type "Profit". In cell B9, enter the formula =B4-B8, which equals Total Revenue minus Total Costs. At this point, the spreadsheet should resemble Lab Exhibit 13.3.2.

Analysis Task #2: Input the Range of Assumptions

1. Let's now assess how profitability changes based on changes in the assumptions regarding the variable cost per unit and the number of units sold.
2. In cell H2, type "Variable Cost per Unit".
3. In cell H3, type $4 (including the dollar sign). In cells I3:Q3, input from $8 to $40, increasing by $4 in each cell, as shown in Lab Exhibit 13.3.3.
4. In cell E5, type "Units Sold".
5. In cell G4, input 50. In cells G5:G14, input from 100 to 550 in increments of 50 down the column, as shown in Lab Exhibit 13.3.4.
6. In cell G3, insert the formula =B9. That link references the total profits, and it is the result that will change based on different assumptions in the data table. In this table, we will see the impact of changing assumptions on variable cost per unit and number of units sold.
7. Highlight cells G3:Q14 and go to **Data > What-If Analysis > Data Table...**, as shown in Lab Exhibit 13.3.5.
8. In the **Data Table** dialog box, input $B$5 for **Row input cell**, suggesting the row input varies by variable cost. Input $B$3 for **Column input cell**, suggesting that column input varies by the number of units sold, as shown in Lab Exhibit 13.3.6. Select **OK**.
9. The output showing the total profits in each scenario appears in a data table. Note the base case scenario, outlined in green in Lab Exhibit 13.3.7, with a $20 variable cost and 300 units sold. The base case scenario gives a profit of $900.
10. Next, we will visualize the trends using conditional formatting. Highlight cells H4:Q14 and then go to **Home > Conditional Formatting > Color Scales**. Click on **Green-Yellow-Red Color Scale**, as shown in Lab Exhibit 13.3.8.

DATA VISUALIZATION

Share the Story

We have now completed an analysis that will help us assess basic profitability levels based on a set of alternate assumptions. We can use this analysis to help with decision making.

The company now knows where profitability lies based on units sold and variable cost per unit. This information will help them determine basic profitability and understand how the company's costs map into profitability.

Assessment

1. Take a screenshot of your completed profitability analysis, label the screenshot Submission 1, and paste it into a Word document named "Lab 13.3 Submission.docx."
2. Answer the questions in Connect and upload your Lab 13.3 Submission.docx via Connect if assigned.

Sensitivity Analysis: Using an Excel Data Table to Analyze Profitability under Changing Volume, Sales Price, and Fixed and Variable Costs

Keywords

Sensitivity Analysis, Cost-Volume-Profit, Conditional Formatting, Changing Assumptions

Apply the same base scenario in Lab 13.3 to Alternate Lab 13.3, but now vary the fixed costs from $500 to $3,000 (in increments of $250) and vary sales price from $5 to $50 (in increments of $5) to determine how profitability varies. There is no additional data file for this lab because we're building on the Lab 13.3 data.

Required

1. Determine how profit will respond to changing assumptions regarding the number of units sold and level of variable costs per unit.
2. Apply conditional formatting to the differing levels of profitability in the resulting data table.

Assessment

1. Take a screenshot of your completed profitability analysis, label the screenshot Submission 1, and paste it into a Word document named "Alt Lab 13.3 Submission.docx."
2. Answer the questions in Connect and upload your Alt Lab 13.3 Submission.docx via Connect if assigned.

Using Excel Solver to Optimize Pricing

Data Analytics Type: Prescriptive Analytics

Lab Note: The tools presented in this lab periodically change. Updated instructions, if applicable, can be found in the student and instructor support materials. All Lab Exhibits are available within the eBook and in Connect.

Keywords

Profit Maximization, Pricing

Decision-Making Context

One important management task is setting the price for each of the company's products in such a way as to maximize profits. One way to evaluate pricing is to use price optimization, setting price at exactly the point that maximizes profits. One critical element of pricing is knowing the extent to which product demand adjusts as the price changes.

All other things equal, a decline in price is generally associated with an increase in demand. As defined in this chapter, the price elasticity of demand is a measure of the change in consumption of (or demand for) a product relative to a change in price. This constraint is used in pricing decisions.

This lab demonstrates optimization techniques for maximizing profits in a pricing scenario for **Gillette** razors. With cheaper alternative razors available, pricing is of critical importance to Gillette.

Required

Identify the price that maximizes profits on the sale of razors.

Ask the Question

What is the optimal price for razors that maximizes profits?

Master the Data

For this lab, you will use the data in the Excel file titled **Lab 13.4 Data.xlsx**, which provides a template for the analysis. Open the spreadsheet and browse it quickly to make sure there isn't any obvious error in it.

Perform the Analysis

Analysis Task # 1: Determine the Price Elasticity of Demand

1. The fixed production costs for these razors are $20,000. Insert 20000 in cell B7. The variable production costs are $8 per unit. Insert 8 in cell B8 (see Lab Exhibit 13.4.1).
2. The decision variable for this pricing lab is price. The optimization will ultimately tell us the optimal price, but we need to guess what number that will be. For now, insert 15 in cell B3, as shown in Lab Exhibit 13.4.1.
3. Next, we need to determine the price elasticity of demand. That is, we need to determine the extent to which product demand falls when prices go up. Our research suggests that the firm has a price elasticity of demand equal to 2. That is, for every 1 percent increase in price, there is a 2 percent decrease in product demand.
4. In cell A13, insert 15, denoting a $15 product price. In cell B13, insert 10000 to represent a demand of 10,000 units sold at a price of $15. In cell A14, formulate and insert the formula for price increases by 1 percent: =A13*1.01. In cell B14, insert the formula for demand falling by 2 percent: =B13*(1-0.02). In cell A15, formulate and

insert the formula for price increases by another 1 percent: =A14*1.01. In cell B15, insert the formula for demand falling by another 2 percent: =B14*(1-0.02). Formula details and results should be as shown in Lab Exhibit 13.4.2.

Lab Exhibit 13.4.2

Microsoft Excel

	A	B	C
3	Price	15	**Decision Variable**
4			
5	Demand		**Constraint - Incorporating Price Elasticity of Demand**
6			
7	Fixed Costs	20000	
8	Variable Costs (per unit)	8	
9			
10			
11			
12	Price	Demand	
13	15	10000	
14	15.15	=B13*(1-0.02)	
15	15.3015	9604	

5. Next we will work to determine the demand function that will serve as a constraint by following these four steps: (**1**) Highlight cells A13:B15. (**2** and **3**) Insert a scatterplot by selecting **Insert > Scatter** to show the scatterplot (labeled **4**), as shown in Lab Exhibit 13.4.3.

6. Click on one of the data points in the scatterplot, then right-click and select **Add Trendline...**. Select **Linear** and **Display Equation on chart**. Lab Exhibit 13.4.4 shows the result.

7. Using the trendline just derived, insert the formula for demand into cell B5 as follows: =29700-(1313.4*B3). This equation relates price to demand, representing the constraint imposed by the price elasticity of demand.

Analysis Task # 2: Calculate the Optimal Price

1. In cell B1, we need to write our objective function, which is to maximize profits (total product revenues minus the costs of those products). Insert the following equation in cell B1: =(B5*B3)-(B7+(B5*B8)). In this formula, note that revenues equal total demand (B5) multiplied by price (cell B3) minus the fixed costs (B7) and variable costs (B5*B8).

2. We now have what we need to use the Solver. In the **File > Options > Add-ins** menu, select **Manage: > Excel Add-ins > Go...** and add the **Solver Add-in**. Ask your instructor for assistance if needed. The Solver will then appear in the **Data > Analysis > Solver**. Select **Solver**.

3. Under **Set Objective:** insert $B$1 and set optimization to **Max**. Under **By Changing Variable Cells:**, insert $B$3. Select **GRG Nonlinear** under **Select a Solving Method** and ensure that the **Make Unconstrained Variables Non-Negative** has a checkmark. Select **Solve**. Your screen should resemble Lab Exhibit 13.4.5.

4. The result is a price of $15.30653, which will yield a profit of $50,116.41, which maximizes profit.

Share the Story

Using optimization and the given costs and price elasticity, Gillette has determined the optimal price to maximize profits.

1. Take a screenshot of the completed spreadsheet with optimized price, label the screenshot Submission 1, and paste it into a Word document named "Lab 13.4 Submission.docx."
2. Answer the questions in Connect and upload your Lab 13.4 Submission.docx via Connect if assigned.

Alternate Lab 13.4 Excel—On Your Own

Using Excel Solver to Optimize Pricing

Keywords

Profit Maximization, Pricing

Start with your solution to Lab 13.4. All of the input variables are the same as Lab 13.4, except for the following:

- Variable costs are now $7 and
- Price elasticity of demand is now 3.

Rerun the Solver analysis and identify the price that maximizes profits.

Required

Identify the price that maximizes profits on the sale of razors.

Assessment

1. Take a screenshot of the completed spreadsheet with optimized price, label the screenshot Submission 1, and paste it into a Word document named "Alt Lab 13.4 Submission.docx."
2. Answer the questions in Connect and upload your Alt Lab 13.4 Submission.docx via Connect if assigned.

Lab Note: The tools presented in this lab periodically change. Updated instructions, if applicable, can be found in the student and instructor support materials. All Lab Exhibits are available within the eBook and in Connect.

Using Excel Solver to Optimize Product Mix (Heartwood)

Data Analytics Type: Prescriptive Analytics

Keywords

Profit Maximization, Product Mix, Pricing

Decision-Making Context

One important management task is determining the appropriate product mix in a way that takes into account various resource constraints and optimizes profit. In this lab, we use optimization techniques to determine the appropriate product mix.

    Heartwood may potentially produce decking product, railing product, doors, and windows. Its managers can use optimization to determine the quantity of each product (decision variable) that will maximize profits (objective function). For this reason, they will go through the product-mix optimization to determine the appropriate mix that will maximize profits.

Required

Identify the product mix that maximizes profits of various wood products.

Ask the Question

What is the optimal product mix that maximizes profits?

Master the Data

For this lab, we will use the data in the Excel file titled **Lab 13.5 Data.xlsx**, which provides a template for our analysis. Open the spreadsheet and browse it quickly to make sure there isn't any obvious error in it.

Perform the Analysis

Analysis Task # 1: Input the Constraints

1. The decision variable is the quantity of each of the products to produce. These appear in cells C5:F5. Insert "1" in each cell, C5:F5. See Lab Exhibit 13.5.1.
2. The unit profit per product sold appears in cells C6:F6. To determine the overall profitability (the objective function), we need to calculate total profit. In cell G6, insert this formula: =SUMPRODUCT(C5:F5,C6:F6). This formula multiplies the quantity of each product by the profit per product, producing a sum total to calculate total profit.
3. In cells C11:F14, note the number of hours needed for the business processes of each product. In cells I11:I14, notice the total number of hours available in each business at Heartwood. Each of these business processes will serve as a constraint. We next need to calculate how many hours we use in each process. In cell H11, insert this formula: =SUMPRODUCT($C$5:$F$5,C11:F11). This equation multiplies the number of each product produced by cutting process hours required.
4. Copy the formula from cell H11 to cells H12:H14. The spreadsheet should appear as shown in Lab Exhibit 13.5.1.

Analysis Task # 2: Calculate the Optimal Product Mix Using Excel's Solver

1. In the **File > Options > Add-ins** menu, select **Manage: > Excel Add-ins > Go...** and add the **Solver Add-in**. Ask your instructor for assistance if needed. The Solver will then appear in the **Data > Analysis > Solver**. Select **Solver**.

2. Under **Set Objective:** insert $G$6 and set optimization to **Max**. Under **By Changing Variable Cells:**, insert $C$5:$F$5, as shown in Lab Exhibit 13.5.2.

3. We'll now set the constraints. We are going to require that each of the decision variables, the quantity of each product produced, be an integer. To do so, click on **Add** under **Subject to the Constraints**. For cell reference, insert $C$5:$F$5 and select "int" for integer, as shown in Lab Exhibit 13.5.3.

    We'll next require that the process hours used are less than or equal to those available. For the cutting process, for example, add the constraint shown in Lab Exhibit 13.5.4.

    Also, add a similar constraint for the sanding, gluing, and finishing processes requiring that the amounts used are less than or equal to the amounts available.

4. Click **Simplex LP** under **Select a Solving Method** and ensure that there is a checkmark in the box next to **Make Unconstrained Variables Non-Negative**. Then select **Solve** (Lab Exhibit 13.5.5).

Share the Story

The result of the optimization is maximizing profit at $169,403 and producing 0 decking products, 2,648 railing products, 569 doors, and 1,997 windows. Using optimization, Heartwood determines the optimal product mix to maximize profits. Heartwood can assess its constraints, make sure they represent reality, and then decide to follow (or not follow) the recommendations.

Assessment

1. Take a screenshot of the completed spreadsheet with optimized product mix, label the screenshot Submission 1, and paste it into a Word document named "Lab 13.5 Submission.docx."

2. Answer the questions in Connect and upload your Lab 13.5 Submission.docx via Connect if assigned.

Alternate Lab 13.5   Excel—On Your Own

Using Excel Solver to Optimize Product Mix (Heartwood)

Keywords

Profit Maximization, Product Mix, Pricing

Start with your solution to Lab 13.5. All of the input variables are the same as Lab 13.5, except for the following:

1. We are required to produce a minimum of 20 decking products. This is an additional constraint.

2. The numbers for available processing hours are as follows:
    a. Cutting: 6,000 hours
    b. Sanding: 5,000 hours
    c. Gluing: 6,000 hours
    d. Finishing: 8,000 hours

3. Change the inputs within the Solver and rerun the optimization.

Required

Identify the product mix that maximizes profits from production and sales of the various wood products.

Assessment

1. Take a screenshot of the completed spreadsheet with optimized product mix, label the screenshot Submission 1, and paste it into a Word document named "Alt Lab 13.5 Submission.docx."
2. Answer the questions in Connect and upload your Alt Lab 13.5 Submission.docx via Connect if assigned.

Chapter 14

Capital Budgeting

A Look at This Chapter

This chapter evaluates capital budgeting decisions using predictive and prescriptive analytics. It considers various metrics useful in prioritizing different capital expenditures, including net present value, internal rate of return, accounting rate of return, payback, and discounted payback. Because capital budgeting analysis uses many assumptions and estimates (such as the size and timing of future cash flows and expected rates of return), management accountants use the prescriptive analytics technique of sensitivity analysis to assess how prioritizing different capital expenditures may change as the underlying assumptions change. Finally, this chapter considers additional qualitative factors related to company strategy that might also impact capital budgeting decisions.

Cost Accounting and Data Analytics

COST ACCOUNTING LEARNING OBJECTIVE	RELATED DATA ANALYTICS LABS	LAB ANALYTICS TYPE(S)
LO 14.1 Define capital expenditures and capital budgeting, and explain their impact on firm strategy.		
LO 14.2 Explain how predictive analytics (forecasting) and prescriptive analytics (cash flow evaluation) assist with capital budgeting decisions.		
LO 14.3 Use discounted cash flow techniques (net present value and internal rate of return) to evaluate capital expenditures.	**Data Analytics Mini-Lab:** Capital Budgeting Using Internal Rate of Return (IRR) in Excel	Prescriptive
	LAB 14.1 Excel: Capital Budgeting: Calculating Net Present Value and Internal Rate of Return (Heartwood)	Predictive, Prescriptive
LO 14.4 Use the payback and discounted payback methods to evaluate capital expenditures.		

Cost Accounting and Data Analytics (*continued*)

COST ACCOUNTING LEARNING OBJECTIVE	RELATED DATA ANALYTICS LABS	LAB ANALYTICS TYPE(S)
LO 14.5 Use the accrual accounting rate-of-return methods to evaluate capital expenditures.	**LAB 14.2 Excel:** Capital Budgeting: Calculating Payback, Discounted Payback, and Accrual Accounting Rate of Return	Predictive, Prescriptive
LO 14.6 Use and evaluate sensitivity analysis to determine the impact of different input assumptions on the expected financial outcome.	**LAB 14.3 Excel:** Sensitivity Analysis of the Net Present Value Method: Using an Excel Data Table to Evaluate the Impact of Assumptions Related to the Returns to Capital Expenditures	Prescriptive
	LAB 14.4 Excel: Sensitivity Analysis of the Internal Rate of Return Method: Using an Excel Data Table to Evaluate the Impact of Assumptions Related to the Returns to Capital Expenditures	Prescriptive
	LAB 14.5 Excel: Sensitivity Analysis of the Internal Rate of Return Method: Assessing the Timing of Cash Inflows from Capital Expenditures	Prescriptive
LO 14.7 Explain the qualitative factors related to capital budgeting decisions.		

Chapter Concepts and Career Skills

Learning About . . .	Helps with These Career Skills
Capital expenditures and capital budgeting	• Applying prescriptive analytics to a firm's investment decisions
Forecasting and evaluating future cash flows	• Determining the amounts, timing, and uncertainty of future cash flows
Sensitivity analysis regarding capital budgeting	• Evaluating the impact of varying assumptions on decision making
Qualitative factors that affect capital budgeting decisions	• Complementing the quantitative metrics of performance with qualitative factors

Amazon Plans to Build a Second Headquarters Building

After a nationwide frenzy that included receiving 238 proposals from cities around the country, **Amazon** announced plans to build a second headquarters building (nicknamed HQ2) in Arlington, Virginia. Following the COVID-19 pandemic, when working from home became common, some may question the benefits of a second headquarters space. How can we quantify the benefits of Amazon's proposed $2.5 billion capital expenditure? For example, will HQ2 give

Amazon access to new markets or new products that will increase its revenues? Will HQ2 create cost savings among employees by creating synergies? Which methods can we use to compare the expected quantitative benefits of HQ2 with other potential capital expenditures Amazon might be considering? This chapter uses predictive analytics to determine the resulting cash inflows or cash savings from capital expenditures and prescriptive analytics to assess whether capital expenditures pay off quantitatively. It also discusses the possible qualitative benefits of capital expenditures.

Source: Eva Fedderly, "Amazon Unveils Nature-Infused HQ2 Design That Includes 'The Helix,'" *Architecture + Design*, February 3, 2021, www.architecturaldigest.com/story/amazon-unveils-nature-infused-hq2-design-includes-helix.

The Washington Post/Getty Images

CAPITAL BUDGETING DECISIONS AND COMPANY STRATEGY

Capital expenditures are large investments, typically in land, machinery, and/or buildings. Because capital is scarce, companies cannot invest in every potential expenditure opportunity they consider. Instead, based on quantitative and qualitative factors, they prioritize which capital expenditures they will make. For example, **Amazon** had to evaluate the best use of a $2.5 billion expenditure. Is the new headquarters building the best use of its capital? What process did Amazon's management use to evaluate the many alternatives available to the company? Which quantitative and qualitative factors were most important in its final evaluation?

Capital budgeting is a prescriptive analytics technique used to evaluate capital expenditures based on quantitative factors such as the amounts, timing, and riskiness of expected cash flows. Capital budgeting is the process of (1) determining the returns and other benefits that are expected to accrue to different capital expenditures and then (2) deciding which capital expenditures to pursue. Capital budgeting often takes into account relevant qualitative factors, including the extent to which capital expenditures affect and align with company strategy. Capital budgeting helps a company prioritize the risk and return associated with the various capital expenditure alternatives a company might potentially make. Because capital is scarce, management accountants help decision makers prioritize some expenditures over others in a process called **capital allocation**, which is the process of allocating financial resources to different capital and other expenditures to increase efficiency and maximize profits.

LO 14.1
Define capital expenditures and capital budgeting, and explain their impact on firm strategy.

CAREER SKILLS
Learning about capital expenditures and capital budgeting supports this career skill:

- Applying prescriptive analytics to a firm's investment decisions

capital expenditure
A large investment, typically in land, machinery, and/or buildings.

capital budgeting
A prescriptive analytics technique that uses different metrics to evaluate the return on potentially large investments based on the amounts, timing, and uncertainty (risk) of expected cash flows.

✓ PROGRESS CHECK

1. Why is it important for companies to evaluate and prioritize potential capital expenditure alternatives as part of capital allocation?

2. How might **Amazon**'s strategy to sell products via e-commerce affect its evaluation of appropriate capital expenditures?

capital allocation
The process of allocating financial resources to different capital and other investments to increase efficiency and maximize profits.

LO 14.2

Explain how predictive analytics (forecasting) and prescriptive analytics (cash flow evaluation) assist with capital budgeting decisions.

---

time value of money
Financial concept that money today is worth more than money received in the future due to its ability to make a profit now.

persistence
The repeatability, continuity, and durability of past outcomes (such as profits, sales, and cash flows) in future outcomes over time.

USING PREDICTIVE AND PRESCRIPTIVE ANALYTICS TO EVALUATE CAPITAL BUDGETING DECISIONS

In addition to evaluating the profits and payback of capital expenditures, we can evaluate the subsequent cash flows considering the time value of money. The **time value of money** is a financial concept that money today is worth more than money received in the future due to its ability to make a profit now.

To evaluate a capital expenditure, we need to assess the amounts, timing, and uncertainty (risk) of the related future cash inflows and cash outflows. In terms of cash flows, we may ask these questions:

Amounts. How much cash does the capital expenditure require? How much cash will the capital expenditure generate in terms of either revenue enhancement or cost savings?
Timing. In what time period (month, quarter, or year) will each year's cash flow be invested or received?
Uncertainty/Risk. How likely or unlikely are we to receive this future cash flow? Is it at greater risk or uncertainty than other cash flows that the company receives?

Predictive Analytics: Forecasting the Amounts and Timing of Future Cash Flows

In Chapter 9, we used predictive analytics (including time series analysis) to forecast future sales and operations for budgeting purposes. Similarly, capital budgeting decisions require us to predict the amounts and timing of future cash flows of a new project, whether they are cost savings or new incremental revenues and their associated profits. To do so, we again employ predictive analytics, using past financial performance to forecast future cash flows.

To understand the relationship between the past and the future, we must measure the persistence between the past and the future. **Persistence** is the repeatability, continuity, and durability of past outcomes (such as profits, sales, and cash flows) in future outcomes over time. Simply, persistence is an estimate of whether the trends of past financial performance are expected to continue into the future. Persistence helps analysts and decision makers understand the extent to which they can feel comfortable extrapolating past trends to the future. In conducting their analysis, they may ask questions like these:

- Have we made similar capital expenditures in the past, and can we expect similar cash flows from the new expenditure alternatives that we are considering?
- How did prior expenditures pay off in terms of cost savings and/or new, incremental revenues and profits?
- Were previous predictions accurate?

Understanding the level of persistence and accurately predicting future outcomes help us forecast the amounts, timing, and uncertainty of future cash flows for the capital expenditures under current consideration.

Prescriptive Analytics: Evaluating Future Cash Inflows and Outflows

To evaluate future cash flows, we use prescriptive analytics to evaluate the expected returns on expenditures, given the forecasted cash flows from predictive analytics. As we've seen throughout this book, prescriptive analytics addresses the questions "What should we do, based on what we expect will happen?" and "How do we optimize our performance based on potential resource constraints or changing conditions?" Two common prescriptive analytics techniques are discounted and nondiscounted cash flow analysis, discussed in the next section.

Expected future net cash inflows and outflows may come from a variety of sources. Once the opportunities for improvement are identified and alternative solutions are proposed, the project team assesses the potential benefits of each alternative. A benefit is a positive consequence that should be measurable in financial terms:

1. *Revenue enhancement*—creating all-new sales opportunities, such as using e-commerce capabilities to expand the firm's market.
2. *Revenue protection*—protecting existing revenue streams. For example, a new capabilities system may protect against the loss of customer data and encourage customers to share their data.
3. *Cost savings*—modifying business processes to reduce low-value-added or manually intensive activities, to better manage assets, to increase efficiencies, and/or to reduce errors. For example, improving the supply chain allows reduced inventory investments.
4. *Cost avoidance*—changing business processes to avoid cost increases in the future, for example, by modifying assets when required to accommodate needed changes in strategy and business processes.

Relevant costs include the incremental cash flows of developing, implementing, and operating the proposed capital project over its useful life. The total *acquisition cost* includes all direct and indirect costs required to acquire and deploy the asset. The total *operation cost* includes all direct and indirect costs of operating, maintaining, and administering the asset over its expected life. These costs might include purchases of assets, sale of assets, tax effects, and increases in working capital (receivables, inventory, and payables).

Because the specific future payoff of capital expenditures is not known with a high degree of certainty, sensitivity analysis—another prescriptive analytics technique—is particularly useful in determining how decisions about various capital expenditures may change as the assumptions also change. This sensitivity analysis serves as a useful input for decision makers. We explain sensitivity analysis in detail later in this chapter.

Evaluating Returns Based on Four Capital Budgeting Methods

In the following sections, we explain the following four capital budgeting methods:

- Net present value.
- Internal rate of return.
- Payback and discounted payback methods.
- Accrual accounting rate of return (or accounting rate of return).

Each has different ways of expressing the quantitative returns to capital expenditures.

✓ PROGRESS CHECK

3. Compare and contrast the role of predictive analytics and prescriptive analytics in capital budgeting. What do they do differently?
4. How can the payoffs of prior capital expenditures influence the expected payoffs to current capital expenditure alternatives?

LO 14.3

Use discounted cash flow techniques (net present value and internal rate of return) to evaluate capital expenditures.

DISCOUNTED CASH FLOW METHODS

Discounted cash flow (DCF) methods measure all expected future cash flows accruing to a project discounted to the present value. DCF methods rely on the *time value of money*, defined above as the financial concept that money today is worth more than money received in the future due to its ability to make a profit now. If you receive money today, you can immediately put it to use (or invest it) to earn a return, making it more valuable today than in the future. Exhibit 14.1 shows the decreasing value of one dollar over time and by discount (or interest) rate, illustrating the value of money over time.

CAREER SKILLS

Learning about forecasting and evaluating future cash flows supports this career skill:

• Determining the amounts, timing, and uncertainty of future cash flows

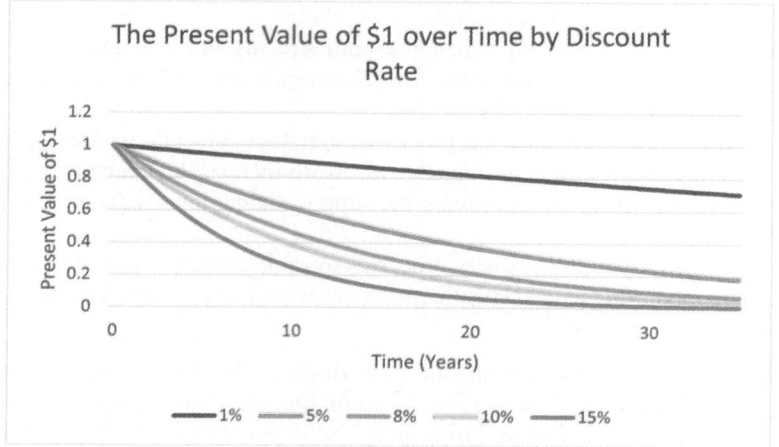

Exhibit 14.1
The Present Value of $1 over Time by Discount Rate
Microsoft Excel

discounted cash flow (DCF) method
An analysis that assesses all expected future cash flows accruing to a project discounted to the present value.

required rate of return (RRR) (cost of capital, discount rate, or hurdle rate)
The minimum acceptable annual rate of return on an investment.

net present value (NPV)
The present value of cash inflows minus the present value of cash outflows; used to evaluate the feasibility and profitability of a capital expenditure.

To help compare the value today of future cash flows, we discount those future cash flows using DCF methods (also called discounted cash flow analysis). To discount the future cash flows a company expects to receive in the future and to estimate their present (or current) value, companies use a **required rate of return (RRR)**, which is the minimum acceptable annual rate of return on an investment. The RRR is also called the **discount rate**, **cost of capital**, or **hurdle rate**.

Two common DCF methods used to evaluate capital budgets are net present value and internal rate of return.

1. *Net present value (NPV)* uses the required rate of return to discount all cash flows to their present value. That is, it calculates the present value of all cash flows. The computed net present value provides a summative dollar value today for each capital expenditure alternative.
2. *Internal rate of return (IRR)* analysis identifies the rate of return at which the present value of the expected cash outflows is exactly equal to the present value of the expected cash inflows. The company then compares the IRR to the required rate of return.

Net Present Value

Net present value (NPV) is calculated as the present value of cash inflows minus the present value of cash outflows. The present value of each inflow and outflow is calculated, as follows:

$$\text{Present value} = CF_t/(1 + r)^t$$

where

CF_t = cash flows for period t (usually year).
r = the required rate of return (typically an annual rate of return).

Assume **J.B. Hunt**, one of the largest transportation and logistics companies in North America, is considering an expenditure in a semitruck at a cost of $100,000 today (that is, in Year 0). This expenditure is expected to return $25,000 per year for seven years. At the end of the seven years, the truck is scrapped with no **salvage value**, which is the estimated book (or resale) value of the asset at the end of its useful life after depreciation is complete.

salvage value
The estimated book (or resale) value at the end of an asset's useful life after depreciation is complete.

Assuming the required rate of return is 10 percent annually, the NPV is calculated as shown in Exhibit 14.2.

Exhibit 14.2
Calculation of Net Present Value

Year 0	Present value =	$-\$100,000/(1.10)^0$	=	$-\$100,000.00$
Year 1	Present value =	$\$25,000/(1.10)^1$	=	$\$22,727.27$
Year 2	Present value =	$\$25,000/(1.10)^2$	=	$\$20,661.16$
Year 3	Present value =	$\$25,000/(1.10)^3$	=	$\$18,782.87$
Year 4	Present value =	$\$25,000/(1.10)^4$	=	$\$17,075.34$
Year 5	Present value =	$\$25,000/(1.10)^5$	=	$\$15,523.03$
Year 6	Present value =	$\$25,000/(1.10)^6$	=	$\$14,111.85$
Year 7	Present value =	$\$25,000/(1.10)^7$	=	$\$12,828.95$
Sum of present values of cash flows, or NPV				$\$21,710.47$

Note that a cash outflow, like the $100,000 upfront payment (or expenditure), is included in the NPV analysis as a negative number: here, −$100,000. Cash inflows are included in the analysis as positive numbers, as reflected by the $25,000 revenue for each of Years 1–7. When the same amount is received or paid each year or each period, it is called an **annuity**. The $25,000 received each year in Exhibit 14.2 is an annuity. In contrast, a **lump-sum payment** occurs when all future payments (usually a large sum) are made at once.

annuity
A series of fixed payments or receipts, perhaps monthly or annually.

The analysis in Exhibit 14.2 indicates that the sum of the present value of the cash flows, or net present value, of the semitruck is $21,710.47.

lump-sum payment
A large sum that is paid in one single payment.

Exhibit 14.3 shows how Excel formulas can be used to calculate NPV. Note that the net present value of $21,710.47 matches the analysis above.

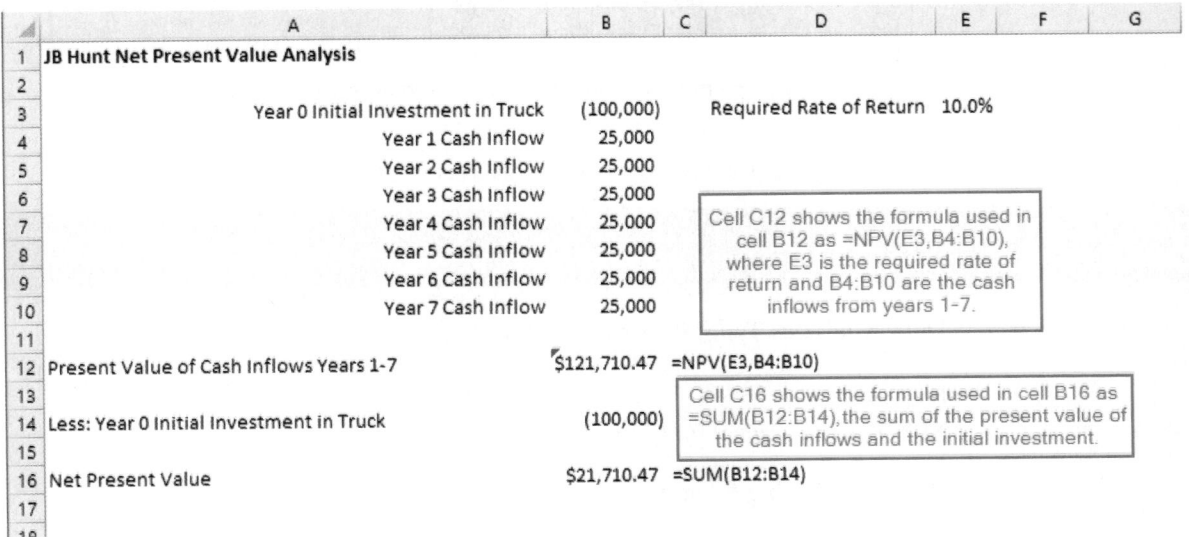

Exhibit 14.3
J.B. Hunt Truck Net Present Value Analysis in Excel

The analysis suggests that at a required rate of return of 10 percent, the net present value is a positive $21,710.47, suggesting that the present value of the cash inflows is greater than the present value of the cash outflow (initial investment). Decision makers can compare this net present value to other potential capital expenditures to prioritize the company's investment opportunities.

Internal Rate of Return

internal rate of return (IRR)
The rate of return that makes a project's net present value equal to zero (that is, the present value of the cash outflows equals the present value of the cash inflows). Used to evaluate the feasibility and profitability of a capital expenditure, and typically computed as an annual rate.

A second way to analyze the returns to capital expenditures uses the **internal rate of return (IRR)**, which is the rate of return that makes the project's net present value equal to zero (where the present value of the cash outflows equals the present value of the cash inflows). Although there is no exact mathematical formula to compute the internal rate of return, financial calculators and Excel use an iterative technique to input various rates of return until an NPV of exactly "zero" is reached.

All other things equal, if the internal rate of return is greater than the required rate of return, then the expenditure is generally viewed in a positive light. Companies also use the internal rate of return to rank various proposed capital expenditures in terms of their potential payoffs.

Exhibit 14.4 shows how the internal rate of return analysis is computed using the **IRR()** function in Excel, along with the needed formulas. Note that the computed internal rate of return is 16.3 percent, which the company will compare to the 10 percent required rate of return. This analysis suggests that the **J.B. Hunt** truck expenditure of $100,000 will return more than the required rate of return.

Exhibit 14.4
Internal Rate of Return Analysis in Excel

Microsoft Excel

	A	B	C	D	E	F
1	JB Hunt Internal Rate of Return Analysis					
2						
3	Year 0 Initial Investment in Truck	(100,000)				
4	Year 1 Cash Inflow	25,000				
5	Year 2 Cash Inflow	25,000				
6	Year 3 Cash Inflow	25,000				
7	Year 4 Cash Inflow	25,000				
8	Year 5 Cash Inflow	25,000				
9	Year 6 Cash Inflow	25,000				
10	Year 7 Cash Inflow	25,000				
11						
12	Internal Rate of Return	16.3%	=IRR(B3:B10)			
13						

Cell C12 shows the formula used in cell B12 as =IRR(B3:B10), with B3:B10 representing all of the cash inflows and outflows for JB Hunt's capital expenditure in a truck.

The following Data Analytics Mini-Lab asks you to use Excel to calculate IRR.

DATA ANALYTICS MINI-LAB
Capital Budgeting Using Internal Rate of Return (IRR) in Excel

Lab Note: The tools presented in this lab periodically change. Updated instructions, if applicable, can be found in the student and instructor support materials.

Data Analytics Type: Prescriptive Analytics

Keywords
NPV(), IRR(), Capital Budgeting

Decision-Making Context
Managers can use several methods to evaluate the profitability of potential expenditures, including the internal rate of return (IRR), which is the rate of return that makes

the net present value of all cash flows from an expenditure or project equal to zero. It is the interest rate at which the present value of cash outflows exactly equals the present value of cash inflows.

In this lab, **Cory Stanford Consulting** is looking at various software expenditures. Its required rate of return (or cost of capital) is 8 percent.

Ask the Question

What is the internal rate of return for three possible software investments?

Master the Data

Open Excel file **Mini-Lab Data 14**.xlsx.

Cory Stanford Consulting is evaluating three possible expenditures in software. If it makes financial sense to do so, the company may well invest in all three. Each potential expenditure costs a different amount and has a different profit payoff structure over its expected four-year life.

The analysis suggests the string of cash flows shown in Exhibit A. Note that Year 0 is today, or the date of the expenditure. Years 1–4 are years when profits from the investment are realized.

	A	B	C	D	E
1	Year		Investment 1	Investment 2	Investment 3
2	Year 0 (today)	Buy New Software	(8,000)	(10,000)	(12,000)
3	Year 1	Increased Profits	2,500	3,000	4,000
4	Year 2	Increased Profits	2,500	3,000	4,000
5	Year 3	Increased Profits	2,500	3,000	4,000
6	Year 4	Increased Profits	2,500	3,000	4,000

Exhibit A

Microsoft Excel

Perform the Analysis

Analysis Task #1: Calculate the Net Cash Flows

1. In cell A8, insert the title "Net Cash Flows over Life (not discounted)".
2. In cell C8, sum the cash flows from cells C2:C6. Copy the contents of cell C8 to cells D8:E8.
3. Note that the original investment is shown as a negative number because cash is being paid out instead of being received. As Row 8 of Exhibit B shows, potential Investments 1 and 2 pay a net of $2,000 back, while Investment 3 pays back a net of $4,000.

	A	B	C	D	E
1	Year		Investment 1	Investment 2	Investment 3
2	Year 0 (today)	Buy New Software	(8,000)	(10,000)	(12,000)
3	Year 1	Increased Profits	2,500	3,000	4,000
4	Year 2	Increased Profits	2,500	3,000	4,000
5	Year 3	Increased Profits	2,500	3,000	4,000
6	Year 4	Increased Profits	2,500	3,000	4,000
7					
8	Net Cash Flows over Life (not discounted)		2,000	2,000	4,000
9					
10	Internal Rate of Return (IRR)		=IRR(C2:C6)		

Exhibit B

Microsoft Excel

Analysis Task #2: Calculate the Internal Rate of Return

The internal rate of return (IRR) allows managers to compare the profitability of potential expenditures by evaluating the amounts and timing of cash flows. We will use the Excel **IRR()** function to evaluate the internal rate of return for these expenditures.

1. As shown in Exhibit B, in cell A10 insert the words "Internal Rate of Return (IRR)".
2. In cell C10, insert the following formula: =IRR(C2:C6).
3. Use the same **IRR()** function for Investments 2 and 3 by copying the contents of cell C10 to cells D10:E10. Your completed spreadsheet should resemble Exhibit C.

Exhibit C

Microsoft Excel

	A	B	C	D	E
1	Year		Investment 1	Investment 2	Investment 3
2	Year 0 (today)	Buy New Software	(8,000)	(10,000)	(12,000)
3	Year 1	Increased Profits	2,500	3,000	4,000
4	Year 2	Increased Profits	2,500	3,000	4,000
5	Year 3	Increased Profits	2,500	3,000	4,000
6	Year 4	Increased Profits	2,500	3,000	4,000
7					
8	Net Cash Flows over Life (not discounted)		2,000	2,000	4,000
9					
10	Internal Rate of Return (IRR)		9.56%	7.71%	12.59%

The internal rate of return is higher for Investment 3 (12.59 percent) than it is for the other investments. Why? Cory Stanford Consulting gets more cash flows back from Investment 3 (as identified by the net cash flow in Row 8), and it receives a larger amount sooner from Investment 3 than it does from Investments 1 and 2. The time value of money suggests that the sooner we get the money, the sooner we can reinvest it in other investments or use it for other purposes.

What we have not factored in here is the different amount of risk (or uncertainty) for each of these investments. In general, higher-risk investments generally require a higher rate of return.

Share the Story

We have calculated the internal rate of return to evaluate the profitability of Investments 1, 2, and 3. The cost of capital at Cory Stanford Consulting is 8 percent. If Cory Stanford Consulting has available funds, it will invest in Investments 1 and 3, which return 9.56 percent and 12.59 percent respectively. It will not invest in Investment 2, which returns only 7.71 percent.

Mini-Lab Assessment

1. If the required rate of return is 10 percent, which software investments will Cory Stanford Consulting make?
2. What would happen if the payoff to the various investments all appeared in Year 4 instead of evenly over Years 1–4? Would that change Cory Stanford's decision? Why or why not?
3. Does the internal rate of return incorporate the time value of money? Explain.

LAB CONNECTION

LAB 14.1 EXCEL asks you to evaluate a range of capital expenditures based on net present value, internal rate of return, and required rate of return. These methods assist managers in prioritizing a capital expenditure based on the amounts and timing of expected cash flows.

Uneven Cash Flows and Nonstandard Cash Flow Dates

Thus far, we have provided examples of even cash flows (that is, the same amount each year) that arrive at a regular cadence (for example, at the beginning or end of the year). But not all cash flows come that way. Excel formulas can accommodate uneven cash flows, as shown in Exhibit 14.5.

Amount	Year	Description		
-20000	2024	Investment	Cost of Capital	10%
3000	2025	Return		
2000	2026	Return		
1000	2027	Return		
25000	2028	Return		
13.41%	IRR	=IRR(A2:A6)		
2,206.82	NPV	=NPV(E2,A3:A6)+A2		

Exhibit 14.5
Illustrating IRR and NPV for Uneven Cash Flows

Microsoft Excel

To evaluate IRR and NPV using uneven cash flows and nonstandard dates, Excel uses the **XNPV()** and **XIRR()** functions. In Exhibit 14.6, note the uneven cash flows and nonstandard dates. The **XIRR()** and **XNPV()** functions reference both the cash flows (cells A2:A6) and the nonstandard dates (cells B2:B6) in their calculations.

	A	B	C	D	E
1	Amount	Year	Description		
2	-20000	1/1/2024	Investment	Cost of Capital	10%
3	3000	2/1/2025	Return		
4	2000	3/1/2026	Return		
5	1000	4/1/2027	Return		
6	25000	5/1/2028	Return		
7					
8					
9	12.31%	IRR	=XIRR(A2:A6,B2:B6)		
10	1,605.39	NPV	=XNPV(E2,A2:A6,B2:B6)		

Exhibit 14.6
Calculating IRR and NPV for Uneven Cash Flows and Nonstandard Dates Using XIRR() and XNPV() Excel Functions

Microsoft Excel

FROM THE FIELD

Using Excel's MIRR() Function

Sometimes managers want to see the results of DCF analyses that use different assumptions or estimates. For example, the IRR calculation assumes that profits are reinvested at same rate as the IRR, which may not be realistic. A *modified internal rate of return* is used to test these different assumptions. Specifically, Excel uses the **MIRR()** function, which computes the internal rate of return assuming a user-specified reinvestment rate, allowing the analyst to see the impact of different reinvestment rates on the overall return calculation.

Suppose an expenditure with an initial cash outflow of $100,000 is expected to pay off each year over the next five years. The return to those cash inflows over those subsequent five years will be different if we reinvest the money we receive each year at 2 percent as opposed to 10 percent, resulting in a major impact on the overall return. Lab 14.1 provides an example of **MIRR()** and an illustration of how the internal rate of return changes depending on the various assumptions made.

Thinking Critically

How sensitive are the results to different assumptions? If the company is able to reinvest the money received at 2 percent, instead of 10 percent, how might its decision differ?

Comparing and Contrasting NPV and IRR DCF Metrics

In the above example, both DCF analysis metrics—NPV and IRR—suggest that J.B. Hunt should invest in the truck. Note, however, the differences between the methods:

1. While the NPV reports the financial consequences of a capital expenditure in terms of dollar impact, IRR reports the results in percentage terms.
2. The IRR method makes it difficult to compare capital expenditures that have unequal lives (lengths of time when cash flows are incoming or outgoing). While the IRR calculations assume that the cash flows from the capital expenditure can be reinvested at the capital expenditure's rate of return (which may not be realistic), the NPV method assumes that those cash flows are reinvested at the required rate of return.

 PROGRESS CHECK

5. How does IRR analysis incorporate a required rate of return?
6. If you wanted to evaluate the financial implications of a capital expenditure, which would you use, NPV or IRR? Explain.

LO 14.4

Use the payback and discounted payback methods to evaluate capital expenditures.

PAYBACK AND DISCOUNTED PAYBACK METHODS OF EVALUATING CAPITAL EXPENDITURES

All other things being equal, companies will choose the investments with the shortest payback periods. **Payback methods** calculate the length of time required to earn back the amount of the initial outlay for a capital expenditure. In the following sections, we explain the payback method and discounted payback method in more detail.

Payback Method

Companies use the payback method to evaluate the feasibility, profitability, and liquidity associated with a capital expenditure. The goal is to identify when the invested money will be earned back and available for reuse. For example, **J.B. Hunt** may use the payback method to evaluate its initial $100,000 investment in a truck that returns a uniform $25,000 in profits each year for the first seven years following the investment. As Exhibit 14.7 shows, the payback method suggests a payback period of four years:

$$\$100,000 \div \$25,000 = 4.0$$

Year	Cash Inflows	Net Initial Investment Not Yet Recovered
0		$100,000
1	$25,000	75,000
2	25,000	50,000
3	25,000	25,000
4	25,000	0
5	25,000	
6	25,000	
7	25,000	

payback method
Method of evaluating potential investments according to the length of time required to earn back the amount of the initial outlay for a capital expenditure.

Exhibit 14.7
Illustration of Payback Method

Discounted Payback Method

The payback method does not incorporate the time value of money in its calculations. To incorporate the time value of money, we can use the **discounted payback period** to discount future cash flows and determine the length of time required to earn back the initial investment.

Exhibit 14.8 uses the discounted cash flows from our earlier computations in Exhibit 14.4, using a 10 percent required rate of return.

discounted payback period
The length of time required to earn back the amount of the initial investment, obtained by discounting future cash flows and taking into account the time value of money.

Year	Cash Savings	Discounted Cash Inflows	Net Initial Investment Not Recovered
0			$100,000.00
1	$25,000	$22,727.27	77,272.73
2	25,000	20,661.16	56,611.57
3	25,000	18,782.87	37,828.70
4	25,000	17,075.34	20,753.36
5	25,000	15,523.03	5,230.33
6	25,000	14,111.85	
7	25,000		

Exhibit 14.8
Illustration of Discounted Payback Method

According to Exhibit 14.8, at the end of Year 5 there is still $5,230.33 that needs to be recovered in the fifth year of cash inflows. We calculate the discounted payback period to be 5.37 years as follows:

Discounted payback period = 5 years + (5,230.33/14,111.85) = 5.37 years

Note that the payback period without discounting is four years (as shown in Exhibit 14.7), but it is 5.37 years (an additional 1.37 years, or 5.37 − 4.00 years) with discounting. In other words, it takes an additional 1.37 years to pay back the initial $100,000 investment using the discounted payment method. Given the time value of money, we expect the discounted payback period to always be greater than the undiscounted payback period.

 PROGRESS CHECK

7. Why will the discounted payback period always be longer than the (undiscounted) payback period?

8. What information do the payback and discounted payback methods provide that might be important before a company makes the decision to invest?

<table>
<tr><td>**LO 14.5**</td></tr>
<tr><td>Use the accrual accounting rate-of-return methods to evaluate capital expenditures.</td></tr>
</table>

ACCRUAL ACCOUNTING RATE OF RETURN

Another method of evaluating capital expenditures uses the **accrual accounting rate of return (AARR)**, which is the average percentage rate of return expected on a capital expenditure based on an increase in expected average annual after-tax operating income. Sometimes the accrual accounting rate of return is called simply the *accounting rate of return.*

accrual accounting rate of return (AARR) The average percentage rate of return expected on a capital expenditure based on an increase in expected average annual after-tax operating income; used to evaluate the feasibility and profitability of a capital expenditure and typically computed as an annual return. Sometimes called the *accounting rate of return.*

$$\text{Accrual accounting rate of return (AARR)} \atop \text{on initial capital expenditure} = \frac{\text{Increase in expected average annual after-tax operating income}}{\text{Net initial capital expenditure}}$$

$$\text{Accrual accounting rate of return (AARR)} \atop \text{on average capital expenditure} = \frac{\text{Increase in expected average annual after-tax operating income}}{\text{Net average capital expenditure over life}}$$

As noted above, J.B. Hunt's $100,000 investment in a new truck provides $25,000 in increased profit each year. As with other income, taxes must be paid on returns to capital expenditures. The truck's annual depreciation on a straight-line basis is computed as the $100,000 initial investment divided by seven years, or $14,285.71 per year. At a tax rate of 20 percent, the total taxes for this investment each year are computed as ($25,000 − $14,285.71) * 0.20 = $2,142.86. The increase in expected average annual after-tax income is therefore $25,000 (operating cash flows) minus $14,285.71 depreciation minus $2,142.86 in taxes, or $8,571.43.

To compute the AARR, we have two choices for a denominator. We can use either the initial investment of $100,000 or the average investment of $50,000 over the life of the investment, which equals ($100,000 initial investment + $0 salvage value)/2. Depending on which denominator we choose, the AARR ranges from 8.57 percent ($8,571.43/$100,000) to 17.14 percent ($8,571.43/$50,000), as Exhibit 14.9 shows.

Human Dimensions: Manager Evaluation and Accrual Accounting Rate of Return

Given the NPV, IRR, and payback metrics, why do companies also consider AARR? The AARR allows a company to evaluate the impact of an investment on its reported net income as shown in the financial statements, where they are reported on an accrual basis (as opposed to a cash basis). The performance of a company's managers is often assessed based on the accrual-basis net income reported to shareholders, and this evaluation may

Year	Additional Operating Cash Flows as a Result of the Investment	Less: Annual Depreciation ($100,000/7 years)	Less: 20% Taxes	Increase in Expected Average Annual After-tax Operating Income
1	$25,000	$14,285.71	$2,142.86	$8,571.43
2	25,000	14,285.71	2,142.86	8,571.43
3	25,000	14,285.71	2,142.86	8,571.43
4	25,000	14,285.71	2,142.86	8,571.43
5	25,000	14,285.71	2,142.86	8,571.43
6	25,000	14,285.71	2,142.86	8,571.43
7	25,000	14,285.71	2,142.86	8,571.43

Accrual Accounting Rate of Return Calculation:

AARR assuming $100,000 initial investment   8.57%

AARR assuming $50,000 average investment over truck useful life   17.14%

Exhibit 14.9
Computation of Accrual Accounting Rate of Return

determine if the manager gets a raise, a bonus, or stock options. If company management evaluates capital expenditures on the basis of cash flows using NPV, IRR, or payback, that method may not be consistent with how they are evaluated as managers. In short, AARR helps sync up the evaluation of capital expenditures and the performance metrics (such as net income) most often considered in manager evaluation.

 LAB CONNECTION

LAB 14.2 EXCEL uses the payback, discounted payback, and accrual accounting rate of return methods to evaluate capital expenditures. Payback methods allow an evaluation of the feasibility, profitability, and liquidity of various capital expenditures. Estimating after-tax accrual-basis operating income is helpful in prioritizing various capital expenditures.

 PROGRESS CHECK

9. Why does the accrual accounting rate of return deduct depreciation expense?

10. Why does the accrual accounting rate of return deduct taxes?

SENSITIVITY ANALYSIS OF THE ASSUMPTIONS IMPACTING CAPITAL BUDGETING

LO 14.6

Use and evaluate sensitivity analysis to determine the impact of different input assumptions on the expected financial outcome.

Recall that sensitivity analysis is a prescriptive analytics technique that evaluates possible outcomes based on uncertainty regarding inputs. In the case of capital budgeting, the amounts and timing of cash flows are based on uncertain inputs (or assumptions) that affect the outcomes. Therefore, we need to evaluate the outputs (including NPV, IRR, payback, discounted payback, and AARR metrics) based on a range of the uncertain inputs.

Uncertainty Related to the Amounts of the Cash Inflows from a Capital Expenditure

Rarely is there a high level of certainty as to the exact cash flows accruing to the capital expenditure. While the cash outflow, or initial investment, can be determined with reasonable certainty, the incoming cash flows coming at some point in the future do not exhibit that same level of certainty. Although sensitivity analysis allows us to examine different levels of initial cash outflows and cash inflows, we'll emphasize the uncertainty associated with the amount of cash inflows in subsequent years.

Uncertainty Related to the Timing of the Cash Inflows

Recall that according to the time value of money concept, money that a company receives today is worth more than money it receives in the future. If more cash inflows arrive sooner than expected or later than expected during the life of the capital expenditure, there can be a dramatic impact on the net present value and the internal rate of return metrics used. Exhibit 14.10 comes from Lab 14.5, which asks you to analyze five different scenarios with different timing of cash inflows for a software investment. Scenario 4 receives the highest level of cash inflows, $4,000, the soonest, and thus it has the highest internal rate of return among the five scenarios (13.48 percent).

Year		Scenario 1	Scenario 2	Scenario 3	Scenario 4	Scenario 5
Year 0 (today)	Buy New Software	(8,000)	(8,000)	(8,000)	(8,000)	(8,000)
Year 1	Cash Inflows	1,000	-	1,000	4,000	1,000
Year 2	Cash Inflows	2,000	-	1,000	1,000	1,000
Year 3	Cash Inflows	4,000	5,500	4,500	1,000	1,000
Year 4	Cash Inflows	4,000	5,500	4,500	5,000	8,000
Net Cash Flows over Life (not discounted)		3,000	3,000	3,000	3,000	3,000
Internal Rate of Return (IRR)		11.40%	9.56%	10.85%	13.48%	9.80%

Exhibit 14.10
Sensitivity Analysis Regarding the Timing of Cash Flows (from Lab 14.5 Excel)

Microsoft Excel

 LAB CONNECTION

LAB 14.3 EXCEL asks you to perform sensitivity analysis in Excel for the different timing of cash inflows for a single investment.

Uncertainty Related to the Acceptable Rate of Return

Recall that the required rate of return is the minimum acceptable rate of return for the firm. But some projects have more uncertainty or risk than others, and they may therefore need to be evaluated at a higher (lower) discount rate, consistent with the notion that the higher (lower) the amount of risk taken on, the higher (lower) the expected return. In other words, the uncertainty generally takes the form of an interest rate (also called *discount rate* or *required rate of return*) that reflects the risk of the cash flows not arriving. Sensitivity analysis allows management accountants to use different discount rates to evaluate the uncertainty regarding the prioritization of different capital expenditures.

Visualizations Used to Highlight the Range of Possible Outcomes Using Sensitivity Analysis

DATA VISUALIZATION

Visualizations such as heat maps and conditional formatting are often helpful in highlighting and interpreting the differing outcomes in a sensitivity analysis. In fact, 91 percent of people prefer visual content over written content.[1] Why? The brain processes images 60,000 times faster than text, and 90 percent of information transmitted to the brain is visual.[2]

Exhibit 14.11 provides an example of a heat map that shows the results of a sensitivity analysis. It shows the expected net present value for differing levels of required rate of return and annual cash inflows for a specific capital expenditure. This heat map is conditionally formatted using Excel's green-yellow-red color scale, with green being the most positive and red being the least positive. (See Lab 14.3 Excel for more details.)

Net Present Value		Annual Cash Inflow (Years 1-7)						
	($2,106.97)	8000	9000	10000	11000	12000	13000	14000
Required Rate of Return	8.0%	-8349.0395	-3142.67	2063.701	7270.071	12476.44	17682.81	22889.18
	8.5%	-9051.8918	-3933.38	1185.135	6303.649	11422.16	16540.68	21659.19
	9.0%	-9736.3773	-4703.42	329.5284	5362.481	10395.43	15428.39	20461.34
	9.5%	-10403.102	-5453.49	-503.878	4445.734	9395.347	14344.96	19294.57
	10.5%	-11685.579	-6896.28	-2106.97	2682.329	7471.631	12260.93	17050.24
	11.0%	-12302.43	-7590.23	-2878.04	1834.159	6546.355	11258.55	15970.75
	11.5%	-12903.72	-8266.68	-3629.65	1007.385	5644.42	10281.46	14918.49
	12.0%	-13489.948	-8926.19	-4362.43	201.3219	4765.078	9328.835	13892.59
	12.5%	-14061.593	-9569.29	-5076.99	-584.69	3907.611	8399.912	12892.21

Exhibit 14.11
Sensitivity Analysis Showing the Net Present Values Obtained from Differing Annual Cash Flows and Required Rates of Return Using Excel's Data Table and Heat Maps (from Lab 14.3 Excel)

Microsoft Excel

⊙ LAB CONNECTION

LABS 14.3 EXCEL, 14.4 EXCEL, and **14.5 EXCEL** ask you to conduct sensitivity analysis by evaluating the amounts and timing of subsequent cash flows and required rates of return used to evaluate capital expenditures. These labs use heat maps (a type of conditional formatting) to visualize the differing levels of net present value across the different assumptions.

---

[1]Zohar Dayan, "Visual Content: The Future of Storytelling," *Forbes,* April 2, 2018, www.forbes.com/sites/forbestechcouncil/2018/04/02/visual-content-the-future-of-storytelling/?sh=6517bfbe3a46.

[2]Harry Eisenberg, "Humans Process Visual Data Better," *Thermopylae Sciences + Technology,* September 15, 2014, www.t-sciences.com/news/humans-process-visual-data-better#:~:text= Visualization%20works%20from%20a%20human,to%20the%20brain%20is%20visual.

PROGRESS CHECK

11. Why do management accountants conduct sensitivity analysis? Which assumptions in a capital budgeting analysis should be considered in a sensitivity analysis?

12. How does a heat map help decision makers visualize a sensitivity analysis?

LO 14.7

Explain the qualitative factors related to capital budgeting decisions.

CAREER SKILLS

Learning about qualitative factors that affect capital budgeting decisions supports this career skill:

• Complementing the quantitative metrics of performance with qualitative factors

QUALITATIVE FACTORS ASSOCIATED WITH CAPITAL BUDGETING

Not all benefits of capital expenditures can be quantified. To the extent capital expenditures align with company strategy, or create or enhance a company's competitive advantage, qualitative factors should be considered alongside quantitative factors in evaluating a capital expenditure. The following are good examples of capital expenditures that align with company strategy and create business value:

• To compete with **Amazon**, **Walmart** needed to reduce delivery times. To achieve this goal, Walmart bought **DroneUp**, which allows it to deliver products with drones. Walmart will continue to make capital expenditures in other delivery options.
• Amazon bought **MGM Studios** to create movies to support the value created by its Amazon Prime offering.
• An important component of **Tesla**'s business model is the capability and cost of its electric-car batteries. For this reason, Tesla invested in an energy storage company, **Maxwell Technologies**, to improve its batteries and lower the costs of battery production.
• **Apple** considers the automobile to be a technology product. As a worldwide leader in technology, it decided to acquire vehicle startup **Drive.ai** to support its strategic foray into the automotive market.

In many cases, strategic investments like these are made even if they do not make sense from a strictly quantitative perspective.

Additional Qualitative Factors to Consider: The Case of Amazon

The story at the start of this chapter provided an example of **Amazon**'s capital expenditure in a new (second) headquarters building. Why did Amazon choose to build it in Arlington, Virginia? Amazon may have been able to find cheaper (and perhaps better) locations for its headquarters in different places around the country. Alternatively, Amazon might have chosen to rent an existing building instead of building an all-new headquarters building. Indeed, Amazon may have had other options for capital expenditures that have a greater net present value, payback, or rate of return than its $2.5 billion capital expenditure in its second headquarters building.

However, qualitative factors likely affected the decision regarding its second headquarters building. These factors may have included the following.

1. **The building's location allows enhanced access to a high-quality workforce**. Arlington, Virginia, is close to Washington, DC, which is home to an educated and highly qualified workforce. A high-quality workforce can help Amazon become even more successful.

2. **Arlington offers easy access to the federal government**. As Amazon grows its profits and market share, it will be subject to increased scrutiny from the federal government. Having a major headquarters close to Washington, DC, may help Amazon develop relationships with lawmakers that lead to reduced taxes or reduced regulation in the long run.

3. **The new headquarters' building design meets Amazon's unique needs**. Amazon will soon be the largest retailer in the world. A headquarters building designed to meet Amazon's exact specifications may better match its unique needs than existing buildings. For example, in the new building, certain business functions, such as marketing and supply chain, may be located close to each other to allow careful coordination.

4. **The new headquarters building helps Amazon reduce its environmental impact**. The new headquarters building follows the latest environmental standards and helps the company reach its goal of a zero net carbon footprint. Although the capital expenditure required to reach this goal is greater, making the IRR and NPV lower, it helps Amazon meet its overall company ESG goals.

ENVIRONMENTAL, SOCIAL, GOVERNANCE

 PROGRESS CHECK

13. What are some other quantitative factors that might affect **Amazon**'s decision to invest in a new headquarters building?

14. Why would **Tesla** consider making a long-term capital expenditure in technology to manufacture better and cheaper batteries that may not pay off in the short term?

Careers in Management Accounting

Companies make a large number of capital expenditures each year, and management accountants assist in the capital budgeting process of prioritizing investments. Exhibit 14.12 is an example of a cost accounting position advertised recently at a site like **LinkedIn.com** or **Indeed.com**. It highlights the need for the cost accountant to perform capital budgeting using sophisticated data analytics and other critical tasks, particularly in companies that have large capital expenditures, such as commodity chemicals, natural resources, and engineered building supplies.

Job Title

Cost Accountant

Job Summary

Join our team at one of the largest privately owned and family-run companies in the United States. We are proud to be a global supplier of specialty and commodity chemicals, natural resources, and engineered building supplies, working with customers across a myriad of industries in more than 15 countries.

We are looking for a dedicated cost accountant to provide services to our dedicated chemicals strategic business unit. This position supports the annual finance and budget process as well as key projects across the organization. Responsibilities include management of product costing, detailed financial reporting, pricing and cost analysis, and partnering across the management organization to make data-driven business decisions.

Salary:

$115,000–135,000 (with benefits)

Qualifications and Requirements:

- Minimum four-year degree in Accounting or Finance
- Three-plus years of experience working in a cost accounting position or related field
- Microsoft Office-certified ●
- Experience using Oracle SAS highly desired ●
- Deep knowledge and experience in cost accounting, capital budgeting, project ● accounting, forecasting, computer modeling, and corporate policies and procedures

Software tools and ERP system (Oracle) knowledge

Capital budgeting and forecasting skills

Job Responsibilities:

- Create and distribute month-end closing reports, including balance sheet accounts and journal entries. Create and maintain new analysis reports on spending and plant efficiencies. Provide operating and expense reports for plant-related expenses and analysis of variances.
- Responsible for setting and maintaining standard costs for key products using Oracle costing system. Costs will be based on understanding of operations management, production processes, and engineering needs.
- Create and maintain forecasting reports and capital budget tracking system. ●
- Ensure inventory systems are accurate, up-to-date, and relevant and utilize systems and plant operations to relay information to senior management.
- Work cross-functionally to support daily accounting responsibilities.
- Create new business and accounting reports as needed to inform senior leadership on decision making.
- Coordinate communication between finance, accounting, plant managers, and leadership to aid in operations success.

Standard costing and diagnostic analysis

Capital appropriations (budgeting) knowledge

Exhibit 14.12
Cost Accounting Job Listing

Key Takeaways: Capital Budgeting

Let's review our key takeaways for this chapter using the AMPS model.

Ask the Question

- **What question(s) does management want to answer?**

Important capital budgeting questions include:

- How can decision makers prioritize the company's possible capital expenditures?
- What metrics are used to evaluate capital expenditures?
- How do management accountants incorporate varying qualitative characteristics of each potential investment into the capital budgeting process?

Master the Data

- **Which data are appropriate to address management's questions?**

The projections of cash outflows (the investment) and the cash inflows come from past experience, predictive analytics, and engineers and other experts. The required rate of return (or cost of capital) typically comes from the chief financial officer (CFO) or finance department.

Perform the Analysis

- **Which analytics are performed to address management questions?**

Prescriptive analytics techniques are used to evaluate the projected cash flows accruing to each investment. Cash flow analysis, a prescriptive analytics technique, allows decision makers to evaluate the amounts, timing, and uncertainty of the estimated future cash flows. Because many assumptions and estimates are used in a capital budgeting analysis (such as the size and timing of the future cash flows and expected rates of return), we can employ sensitivity analysis to assess how the prioritizing of different capital expenditures may change as (and if) the underlying assumptions change.

  Qualitative factors that are aligned with company strategy or other company priorities may also ultimately impact capital budgeting decisions. Qualitative analysis complements the quantitative analysis, incorporating many factors beyond the financial metrics (such as NPV and IRR). Many times, the qualitative factors are just as important as, or even more important than, the quantitative factors.

Share the Story

- **How are the results of the analytics shared with stakeholders?**

Using payback, discounted payback, NPV, IRR, and/or AARR helps analysts rank-order all possible investments. Conditional formatting and heat maps can help to tell the story of how the various assumptions affect management decisions.

Key Terms

accrual accounting rate of return (AARR)

annuity

capital allocation

capital budgeting

capital expenditure

discounted cash flow (DCF) method

discounted payback period

internal rate of return (IRR)

lump-sum payment

net present value (NPV)

payback method

persistence

required rate of return (RRR) (cost of capital, discount rate, or hurdle rate)

salvage value

time value of money

ANSWERS TO PROGRESS CHECKS

1. In the presence of scarce resources, companies must prioritize their capital expenditures based on quantitative factors (such as expected financial return) and qualitative factors (such as expected impact on firm strategy).

2. Evaluation of capital expenditures is conducted in tandem with the setting and implementation of company strategy. Both support present competencies while building additional competencies that may give the company a competitive advantage in the future.

3. While predictive analytics forecasts the amounts and timing of cash inflows and cash outflows, prescriptive analytics evaluates the future cash flows and helps managers decide which capital expenditures to make.

4. Understanding how prior investments paid off in terms of future cost savings and/or new, incremental revenues and profits is helpful in predicting the returns to possible new capital expenditures. This information is particularly helpful in determining the amounts and timing of future cash flows.

5. Internal rate of return (IRR) analysis reports a percentage return to a capital expenditure. To determine whether a company should invest in that opportunity, decision makers compare that return to the required rate of return.

6. Net present value and internal rate of return measure different aspects of the capital budgeting decision. The net present value analysis output is a dollar return based on a required rate of return. The internal rate of return is a percentage return that can be compared to the required rate of return.

7. According to the time value of money concept inherent in discounting future cash flows, the money that a company receives in the future is worth less than the money it receives today. Therefore, a discounted payback will take longer to return the initial investment than an undiscounted payback.

8. The payback methods help decision makers evaluate the feasibility, profitability, and liquidity associated with a capital expenditure, addressing when the money will be earned back and available for reuse. Knowing whether and when an investment is expected to pay off is critical in determining the impact on companywide cash flows.

9. As reported on an accrual basis, depreciation expense is deducted as an expense from net income, but it does not affect the amount of cash inflows or cash outflows.

10. As with other income earned by the company, taxes must be paid on returns to capital expenditures.

11. Sensitivity analysis allows management accountants to evaluate the metrics associated with capital expenditures based on uncertainty regarding the inputs (including assumptions relating to the amount and timing of cash flows as well as the rates of return).

12. A heat map is helpful in visualizing gradations associated with different financial outcomes depending on the inputs assumed. The brain processes images 60,000 times faster than text (and 90 percent of information transmitted to the brain is visual).

13. Answers will vary. Some possible answers: The new **Amazon** headquarters building in the Washington, DC, area may have received tax credits from local governments; it is centrally located on the East Coast, with a large number of customers close by; it may be close to a set of critical Amazon suppliers; and/or it may have easier access to expertise that is not available at its main headquarters building in Seattle.

14. **Tesla** is a pioneer in the manufacture and sale of electric automobiles. Innovation in batteries is now and will continue to be important to Tesla's strategy, regardless of the quantitative performance factors associated with any specific capital expenditure.

Multiple-Choice Questions

1. (LO14.3) The _____ is the present value of cash inflows minus the present value of cash outflows.
   a. net present value
   b. internal rate of return
   c. accounting rate of return
   d. discounted payback

2. (LO14.7) When a company's capital budgeting includes an analysis of the extent to which capital expenditures affect and align with company strategy, that company is incorporating _____ factors into its analysis.
   a. quantitative
   b. qualitative
   c. financial
   d. monetary

3. (LO14.3) The discount (or interest) rate at which the present value of cash inflows equals the present value of cash outflows is the _____.
   a. required rate of return
   b. internal rate of return
   c. accounting rate of return
   d. discounted payback

4. (LO14.5) The accrual accounting rate of return _____ cash outflows and cash inflows.
   a. discounts
   b. does not discount
   c. is the difference between
   d. is the sum of

5. (LO14.4) The time value of money suggests that for an evaluation of a capital expenditure, the payback period will always be _____ the discounted payback period.
   a. greater than
   b. less than
   c. equal to
   d. preferable to

6. (LO14.3) All other things equal, the greater the initial capital expenditure (or greater initial cash outflow), the _____ the overall net present value of the capital expenditure.
   a. lower
   b. greater
   c. greater the volatility of
   d. less relevant

7. (LO14.2) _____ is the repeatability, continuity, and durability of past outcomes (such as profits, sales, and cash flows) in future outcomes over time.
   a. Permanence
   b. Persistence
   c. Relativity
   d. Forecastability

8. (LO14.6) In a sensitivity analysis of capital expenditures, the greater the _____, the greater the computed internal rate of return.

   a. required rate of return

   b. annual cash inflows

   c. initial capital expenditure

   d. payback period

9. (LO14.3, 14.4, 14.5) Which capital budgeting metric should you use if you want to determine whether a capital expenditure will increase the net income reported?

   a. Internal rate of return

   b. Accrual accounting rate of return

   c. Discounted payback

   d. Net present value

10. (LO14.3, 14.6) All other things equal, the sooner the cash flows come in the life of the investment, the greater the internal rate of return.

    a. True

    b. False

11. (LO14.3) A payment that is made all at once, at one time, is a(n) _____.

    a. annuity

    b. lump-sum payment

    c. sunk cost

    d. capital payment

12. (LO14.1) The decision regarding which big project(s) to invest in is called _____.

    a. cash flow analysis

    b. net present value analysis

    c. internal rate of return

    d. capital budgeting

13. (LO14.3) What is the internal rate of return for the stream of cash flows for a $32,000 investment (−$32,000) and cash inflows of $9,000 per year for years 1 through 4?

    a. 3.25 percent

    b. 4.88 percent

    c. 7.18 percent

    d. 2.39 percent

14. (LO14.2) Persistence is most important for which type of analytics?

    a. Descriptive analytics

    b. Diagnostic analytics

    c. Predictive analytics

    d. Prescriptive analytics

15. (LO14.3) What is the net present value for the stream of cash flows for a $32,000 investment (−$32,000) and cash inflows of $9,000 per year for years 1 through 4, assuming a 3 percent cost of capital?

    a. −$1,312.66

    b. $1,453.89

    c. $1,312.66

    d. −$1,453.89

16. (LO14.3) What is the Excel formula to compute the internal rate of return for the stream of cash flows for a $32,000 investment and cash inflows of $10,000 per year for years 1 through 4?

   a. =IRR(32000,-10000,-10000,-10000,-10000)

   b. =IRR(-10000,-10000,-10000,-10000,32000)

   c. =IRR(10000,10000,10000,10000,-32000)

   d. =IRR(-32000,10000,10000,10000,10000)

17. (LO14.3) What is the Excel formula to compute the net present value for the stream of cash flows for an initial $50,000 investment and cash inflows of $18,000 per year for years 1 through 4 with a 10% cost of capital?

   a. =NPV(0.1,18000,18000,18000,18000)-50000

   b. =NPV(0.1,+50000,-18000,-18000,-18000,-18000)

   c. =NPV(0.1, 18000,18000,18000,18000,-50000)

   d. =NPV(18000,18000,18000,18000)-50000

18. (LO14.3, 14.4, 14.5) Which one of the following should *not* be considered when completing a project cash flow analysis?

   a. Increased sales related to the project

   b. Lease payments on previously existing equipment

   c. Increased depreciation expense

   d. The effect of inflation

CMA

19. (LO14.6) Which one of the following is the best example of using sensitivity analysis in the valuation of future cash flows?

   a. Dividing the average annual income by net initial investment

   b. Measuring the time to recoup the initial investment

   c. Using discount rates that are higher in the later years

   d. Varying inputs to the net present value calculation

CMA

20. (LO14.4) After calculating both the simple payback period and the discounted payback period for a project, the discounted payback period is:

   a. shorter because the time value of money raises the value of the cash flows.

   b. longer because the time value of money raises the value of the cash flows.

   c. shorter because the time value of money lowers the value of the cash flows.

   d. longer because the time value of money lowers the value of the cash flows.

CMA

Discussion Questions

1. (LO14.1) How does capital allocation use capital budgeting to prioritize different capital expenditures to increase efficiency and maximize profits?

2. (LO14.3) Explain how discounted cash flow analysis works. What does it try to achieve?

3. (LO14.2) What are four different ways to think of the benefits (or cash flows) associated with capital expenditures?

4. (LO14.2) How do predictive analytics and prescriptive analytics work together? Which is an important prerequisite to the other?

5. (LO14.3, 14.4, 14.5) Why do you deduct taxes and depreciation to assess the impact of a new capital expenditure when computing the accrual accounting rate of return?

6. (LO14.3) If the underlying risk for some capital expenditures is dramatically different than it is for other capital expenditures, should a different discount rate (or cost of capital or minimum required rate of return) be used to evaluate the investment? Explain.

7. (LO14.5) Why is the accrual accounting rate of return considered the most appropriate metric for managers to use if their performance is evaluated on the basis of net income?

8. (LO14.3) Why is discounted cash flow analysis the most appropriate metric for managers to consider if their performance is evaluated on the basis of operating cash flows?

9. (LO14.7) In which situations should qualitative factors be weighed as part of the capital budgeting process? Does quantitative analysis generally weigh more in a decision than qualitative factors?

10. (LO14.6) Why are heat maps and conditional formatting helpful in visualizing different outcomes? Which visualization types are particularly useful in presenting the results of a sensitivity analysis?

11. (LO14.5) Should depreciation of a capital asset be considered as part of capital budgeting? Why or why not?

12. (LO14.2) The payback method does not incorporate the time value of money in its analysis. Should this fact eliminate this method from consideration in capital budgeting?

13. (LO14.7) What does it mean when a capital expenditure has an IRR that is below the required rate of return? Why should the company consider making this capital expenditure, even if there are no prevailing qualitative reasons to consider it?

14. (LO14.2) Why is persistence important in predicting future cash flows for an investment? Why is experience important in making accurate forecasts of the future?

15. (LO14.2) Why does NPV report the financial consequences of a capital expenditure in terms of dollar impact, but IRR reports the results in percentage terms?

Brief Exercises   Mc Graw Hill connect

1. (LO14.1, 14.2, 14.3) Match the capital budgeting term to its definition.

Term	Definition
a. Net present value	a. Analysis performed that identifies the best possible options given constraints or changing conditions
b. Internal rate of return	b. A large sum that is paid in one single payment
c. Annuity	c. A series of fixed payments, perhaps monthly or annually
d. Lump-sum payment	d. The discount rate that makes the present value of the cash inflows equal to the present value of the cash outflows
e. Prescriptive analysis	e. The present value of the cash inflows minus the present value of the cash outflows
f. Predictive analysis	f. Forecast of the cash flows accruing to a particular investment

2. (LO14.1, 14.3, 14.4, 14.5, 14.6) Match the capital budgeting term to its definition.

Term	Definition
a. Accrual accounting rate of return	a. A prescriptive analytics technique used to evaluate potential large investments based on quantitative factors such as amounts, timing, and riskiness of expected cash flows
b. Capital budgeting	b. A what-if prescriptive analytics technique that evaluates outcomes based on uncertainty regarding inputs
c. Payback method	c. Method of evaluating potential investments according to the length of time required to earn back the amount of the initial outlay for a capital expenditure
d. Required rate of return	d. The minimum acceptable annual rate of return on an investment
e. Sensitivity analysis	e. A large investment, typically in land, machinery, and/or buildings
f. Capital expenditure	f. The average percentage rate of return expected on a capital expenditure based on an increase in expected average annual after-tax operating income

3. (LO14.3) What is the net present value of cash flows of a capital expenditure of $12,333 in year 0, annual cash inflows of $5,100 each year for four years, and a minimum required rate of return of 7.5 percent?

Required

a. Compute calculations by hand.

b. Compute by using the **NPV()** function in Excel (or a financial calculator).

4. (LO14.3) Using the capital expenditure scenario in Brief Exercise 3, compute the internal rate of return. Is the IRR greater than the minimum required rate of return of 7.5 percent? All other things equal, will the company invest?

5. (LO14.4) Using the capital expenditure scenario in Brief Exercise 3, compute the payback and discounted payback (assuming a minimum required rate of return of 7.5 percent). All other things equal, will the company invest?

6. (LO14.5) Using the capital expenditure scenario in Brief Exercise 3, compute the accrual accounting rate of return assuming four-year straight-line depreciation and a 15 percent tax rate. Calculate the return on both a $12,333 initial investment as well as a $6,166.50 average investment.

7. (LO14.3) What is the net present value of cash flows of a capital expenditure of $26,573 in year 0; annual cash inflows of $9,200, $10,300, $11,400, and $10,300; and a minimum required rate of return of 10 percent?

Required

a. Compute NPV calculations by hand.

b. Compute by using the **NPV()** function in Excel (or a financial calculator).

c. Are the answers to (a) and (b) the same? What does each method assume about the timing of the cash flows? Were cash inflows and cash outflows received at the end of the year or at the beginning of the year? Why does it matter?

8. (LO14.3) Using the capital expenditure scenario in Brief Exercise 7, compute the internal rate of return. Is the IRR greater than the minimum required rate of return of 10 percent? All other things equal, will the company invest?

9. (LO14.4) Using the capital expenditure scenario in Brief Exercise 7, compute the payback and discounted payback assuming a minimum required rate of return of 7.5 percent. All other things equal, will the company invest?

10. (LO14.5) Using the capital expenditure scenario in Brief Exercise 7, compute the accrual accounting rate of return assuming four-year straight-line depreciation and a 20 percent tax rate. Calculate the return on both a $26,573 initial investment as well as a $13,286.50 average investment.

11. (LO14.3) If you hope to retire in 20 years with $3 million saved, expect to get a 12 percent annual return, and have nothing currently saved, how much will you need to save each year? Use the Excel **PMT()** function to calculate how much you need to save each year. (*Hint:* As part of the Excel **PMT()** function, assume that PV = $0 and FV = $3,000,000.)

12. (LO14.3) If you hope to retire in 40 years with $4 million saved, expect to get a 10 percent annual return, and have $20,000 currently saved, how much will you need to save each year? Use the Excel **PMT()** function to calculate how much you need to save each year. (*Hint:* As part of the Excel **PMT()** function, assume that PV = $20,000 and FV = $4,000,000.)

13. (LO14.3) Use the Excel **NPV()** function to calculate the maximum loan you can expect to receive if you promise to pay back five years of $12,000 payments at 5 percent interest.

14. (LO14.3) Assume that you are a lender. Use the Excel **NPV()** function to calculate the maximum loan you would be willing to give today to a borrower who will make eight years of $18,000 annual payments at 10 percent annual interest.

15. (LO14.4) Assume that an investment is made in farming equipment that costs $75,000 in year zero and increases net income by $12,000 each year for 10 years. Assume the tax rate is 15 percent. What is the accrual accounting rate of return, assuming a useful life on the farming equipment over 10 years on a straight-line basis?

16. (LO14.7) **Tyson Chicken** is determining whether to invest in a chicken processing plant in China. Beyond the quantitative metrics used in this chapter, what are some qualitative factors that also should be considered? Consider political environment, sales in Asia, new markets, and other relevant factors.

Problems connect

1. (LO14.3) **Amazon** is considering the purchase of some new packaging equipment. Calculate the net present value for Amazon assuming a required rate of return of 10.5 percent and the cash flows.

	A	B
1	**Amazon Packaging Equipment Net Present Value**	
2		
3	Year 0 Initial Investment in Packaging Equipment	(50,000)
4	Year 1 Cash Inflow	10,000
5	Year 2 Cash Inflow	10,000
6	Year 3 Cash Inflow	10,000
7	Year 4 Cash Inflow	10,000
8	Year 5 Cash Inflow	10,000
9	Year 6 Cash Inflow	10,000
10	Year 7 Cash Inflow	10,000

Microsoft Excel

Required

Calculate the net present value in the following ways:

a. By hand, using the formula present value = $CF_t/(1 + r)^t$, where CF_t = cash flows for period t and r = the required rate of return.

b. Using the **NPV()** function in Microsoft Excel.

c. Did you get the same answer with both methods?

d. Given the net present value calculated, would you recommend Amazon invest in this new packaging equipment? What qualitative factors should be considered as well?

2. (LO14.3) Use the cash flows shown in Problem 1 related to **Amazon**'s proposed $50,000 capital expenditure in packaging equipment.

Required

a. Calculate the internal rate of return.

b. Is the internal rate of return higher or lower than the required rate of return of 10.5 percent?

c. Would you recommend investing in this capital expenditure?

3. (LO14.4) Use the cash flows shown in Problem 1 related to **Amazon**'s proposed $50,000 capital expenditure in packaging equipment.

Required

a. Calculate the payback period and the discounted payback period assuming a required rate of return of 10 percent.

b. Calculate the accrual accounting rate of return assuming a seven-year straight-line depreciation and 20 percent tax rate.

4. (LO14.3) Evaluate the capital expenditure using net present value (using an 8 percent cost of capital) for a **Walmart** truck with an initial investment of either $80,000 or $90,000 in year zero and annual cash inflows of $22,000, $25,000, or $30,000 each year over five years. You may choose to complete this problem after completing Lab 14.3 Excel.

Required

a. Evaluate the possible net present values for the six different scenarios using sensitivity analysis (using Excel's data table).

b. Assuming that an initial investment of $80,000 and annual cash inflow of $22,000 are most likely, would you recommend that Walmart make this capital expenditure?

5. (LO14.3) Evaluate the capital expenditure using internal rate of return for a **Walmart** truck with an initial investment of either $80,000 or $90,000 in year zero and annual cash inflows of $22,000, $25,000, or $30,000 each year over five years. You may choose to complete this problem after completing Lab 14.4 Excel.

Required

a. Evaluate the possible internal rates of return for the six different scenarios using sensitivity analysis (using Excel's data table).

b. Assuming that an initial investment of $90,000 and annual cash inflow of $22,000 are most likely, would you recommend that Walmart make this capital expenditure?

6. (LO14.4) Evaluate the capital expenditure using the discounted payback (using an 8 percent cost of capital) for a **Walmart** truck with an initial investment of either $80,000 or $90,000 in year zero and annual cash inflows of $22,000, $25,000, or $30,000 each year over five years. You may choose to complete this problem after completing Lab 14.4 Excel.

Required

a. Evaluate the possible discounted paybacks for the six different scenarios using sensitivity analysis (using Excel's data table or any means possible).

b. Assuming that an initial investment of $90,000 and annual cash inflows of $22,000 are most likely, would you recommend that Walmart make this capital expenditure?

7. (LO14.6) Evaluate the sensitivity analysis of a calculation of the net present values of a specific capital expenditure using the following Excel data table and heat map. Assume the initial investment is made in year zero.

DATA VISUALIZATION

Net Present Value		Annual Cash Inflow (Years 1-7)						
	($2,106.97)	8000	9000	10000	11000	12000	13000	14000
Required Rate of Return	8.0%	-8349.0395	-3142.67	2063.701	7270.071	12476.44	17682.81	22889.18
	8.5%	-9051.8918	-3933.38	1185.135	6303.649	11422.16	16540.68	21659.19
	9.0%	-9736.3773	-4703.42	329.5284	5362.481	10395.43	15428.39	20461.34
	9.5%	-10403.102	-5453.49	-503.878	4445.734	9395.347	14344.96	19294.57
	10.5%	-11685.579	-6896.28	-2106.97	2682.329	7471.631	12260.93	17050.24
	11.0%	-12302.43	-7590.23	-2878.04	1834.159	6546.355	11258.55	15970.75
	11.5%	-12903.72	-8266.68	-3629.65	1007.385	5644.42	10281.46	14918.49
	12.0%	-13489.948	-8926.19	-4362.43	201.3219	4765.078	9328.835	13892.59
	12.5%	-14061.593	-9569.29	-5076.99	-584.69	3907.611	8399.912	12892.21

Microsoft Excel

Required

a. What is the net present value for this investment if there are annual cash flows of $12,000 each year over Years 1–7 and a 12.5 percent required rate of return?

b. What are the required rate of return and annual cash flow when the net present value is −$2,106.97?

c. What is the heat map trying to communicate? Why are the red and green colors used? What do they signify? Is there another color scheme you think might work better? Explain.

d. For every conceivable required-rate-of-return scenario given in the sensitivity analysis, which is the first annual cash flow shown in the sensitivity analysis in which the net present value is greater than zero? How does that information help managers decide when to invest and when not to invest? How can IRR help with this decision?

e. For every conceivable annual cash inflow scenario in the sensitivity analysis, in which cases is the net present value negative? How does that information help managers decide when to invest and when not to invest?

8. (LO14.6) Evaluate the sensitivity analysis of a calculation of the net present values of a specific capital expenditure using the following Excel data table and heat map. Assume the initial investment is made in year zero, and the annual cash inflows are $10,000.

Net Present Value		Initial Investment						
	($2,106.97)	40,000	45,000	50,000	55,000	60,000	65,000	70,000
Required Rate of Return	8.0%	12063.701	7063.701	2063.701	-2936.3	-7936.3	-12936.3	-17936.3
	8.5%	11185.135	6185.135	1185.135	-3814.86	-8814.86	-13814.9	-18814.9
	9.0%	10329.528	5329.528	329.5284	-4670.47	-9670.47	-14670.5	-19670.5
	9.5%	9496.1222	4496.122	-503.878	-5503.88	-10503.9	-15503.9	-20503.9
	10.5%	7893.0261	2893.026	-2106.97	-7106.97	-12107	-17107	-22107
	11.0%	7121.9626	2121.963	-2878.04	-7878.04	-12878	-17878	-22878
	11.5%	6370.3501	1370.35	-3629.65	-8629.65	-13629.6	-18629.6	-23629.6
	12.0%	5637.5654	637.5654	-4362.43	-9362.43	-14362.4	-19362.4	-24362.4
	12.5%	4923.0091	-76.9909	-5076.99	-10077	-15077	-20077	-25077

Microsoft Excel

Required

a. Would you make this capital expenditure if the initial investment is $55,000 or higher?

b. What are the required rate of return and annual cash flow when the net present value is −$20,077?

c. Give two reasons why you would not make the capital expenditure even if the initial investment is $40,000. Include both qualitative and quantitative reasons.

d. For every conceivable required-rate-of-return scenario, which is the first annual cash flow shown in the sensitivity analysis in cases when the net present value is greater than zero? How does that information help managers decide when to invest and when not to invest?

e. For every conceivable initial investment scenario in the sensitivity analysis, in which cases is the net present value negative? How does that help managers decide when to invest and when to not invest?

9. (LO14.6) Evaluate the sensitivity analysis of a calculation of the internal rate of return to a specific capital expenditure scenario using the following Excel data table and heat map. The required rate of return is 10 percent.

Internal Rate of Return				Initial Investment			
	9.20%	40000	50000	60000	70000	80000	90000
Annual Cash Inflows	8000	9.20%	2.92%	-1.70%	-5.29%	-8.20%	-10.63%
	10000	16.33%	9.20%	4.01%	0.00%	-3.23%	-5.92%
	12000	22.93%	14.95%	9.20%	4.78%	1.23%	-1.70%
	14000	29.16%	20.34%	14.02%	9.20%	5.35%	2.18%
	16000	35.14%	25.46%	18.58%	13.35%	9.20%	5.79%
	18000	40.92%	30.38%	22.93%	17.30%	12.84%	9.20%
	20000	46.56%	35.14%	27.12%	21.08%	16.33%	12.45%

Microsoft Excel

Required

a. What is the internal rate of return for this investment if there are annual cash inflows of $8,000 and an initial investment of $90,000?

b. What are the annual cash inflows and initial investment for a 16.33 percent internal rate of return?

c. What is the heat map trying to communicate? Why are the red and green colors used? What do they signify?

d. For every conceivable annual cash-inflow scenario, which is the first internal rate of return shown in the sensitivity analysis where the internal rate of return is greater than the required rate of return? How does that information help managers decide when to invest and when not to invest?

10. (LO14.6) Evaluate the timing of cash inflows and cash outflows for each of the five scenarios.

	A	B	C	D	E	F	G
			Scenario 1	Scenario 2	Scenario 3	Scenario 4	Scenario 5
1	Year						
2	Year 0 (today)	Buy New Software	(8,000)	(8,000)	(8,000)	(8,000)	(8,000)
3	Year 1	Cash Inflows	1,000	-	1,000	4,000	1,000
4	Year 2	Cash Inflows	2,000	-	1,000	1,000	1,000
5	Year 3	Cash Inflows	4,000	5,500	4,500	1,000	1,000
6	Year 4	Cash Inflows	4,000	5,500	4,500	5,000	8,000
7							
8	Net Cash Flows over Life (not discounted)		3,000	3,000	3,000	3,000	3,000
9							
10	Internal Rate of Return (IRR)		11.40%	9.56%	10.85%	13.48%	9.80%

Microsoft Excel

Required

a. The net cash inflows over the life of each investment scenario are the same (+$3,000). What is different between each of these five scenarios?

b. For internal-rate-of-return purposes, is receiving cash inflows sooner associated with a higher IRR or a lower IRR?

c. In your estimation, which of these scenarios will have the greatest net present value? How would you test your decision? What decision would you make if the required rate of return is 15 percent?

11. (LO14.6) Evaluate the timing of cash inflows and cash outflows for each of the five scenarios.

	A	B	C	D	E	F	G
			Scenario 1	Scenario 2	Scenario 3	Scenario 4	Scenario 5
1	Year						
2	Year 0 (today)	Buy New Software	(8,000)	(8,000)	(8,000)	(8,000)	(8,000)
3	Year 1	Cash Inflows	1,000	-	1,000	4,000	1,000
4	Year 2	Cash Inflows	2,000	-	1,000	1,000	1,000
5	Year 3	Cash Inflows	4,000	5,500	4,500	1,000	1,000
6	Year 4	Cash Inflows	4,000	5,500	4,500	5,000	8,000
7							
8	Net Cash Flows over Life (not discounted)		3,000	3,000	3,000	3,000	3,000
9							
10	Internal Rate of Return (IRR)		11.40%	9.56%	10.85%	13.48%	9.80%

Microsoft Excel

Required

a. If the required rate of return is 10 percent, and each of these five scenarios is equally likely as a return to the new software purchase, would you invest or not invest?

b. Assume a Scenario 6, where the initial investment is −$8,000, but the annual cash inflows are $2,750 each year. Would you invest if the required rate of return is 11 percent?

c. Assume a Scenario 7, where the initial investment is −$8,000, but the first-year annual cash inflow is $8,000 and the fourth-year annual cash inflow is $3,000. Would you invest if the required rate of return is 12 percent?

d. Come up with an investment scenario (and label it as Scenario 8) that has an initial investment of $8,000 and payoff over the next four years of $11,000 in total. Would you invest if the required rate of return is 9 percent? Would you invest if the required rate of return is 11 percent?

12. (LO14.3) Use Microsoft Excel to assess the internal rate of return for a capital investment in information technology. Suppose the initial investment is $60,000 in year zero. The returns on investment in dollars for the following five years are (1) $10,000, (2) $12,000, (3) $15,000, (4) $21,000, and (5) $26,000.

Required

a. Use the **IRR()** function to compute the internal rate of return after two, four, and five years.

b. Next, assume that the loan for the initial $70,000 is at 8 percent (finance rate) and you are earning 16 percent (reinvest rate) on the annual returns. Use the **MIRR()** Excel function to calculate the internal rate of return and insert finance and reinvest rates.

c. Is the annual rate of return higher when using the **MIRR()** function than the **IRR()** function? Under what circumstances would it be lower?

13. (LO14.3) Evaluate the returns to the following investment, which has uneven cash flows and nonstandard dates.

	A	B	C	D
1	Amount	Date	Description	Cost of Capital
2	-20000	1/1/2024	Investment	11%
3	3337	3/1/2025	Cash inflow	
4	2122	6/1/2026	Cash inflow	
5	1932	8/1/2027	Cash inflow	
6	1702	10/1/2028	Cash inflow	
7	26666	5/1/2029	Cash inflow	

Microsoft Excel

Required

a. Use Excel's **XNPV()** function to determine the net present value.

b. Use Excel's **XIRR()** function to determine the internal rate of return.

c. If the cost of capital is 11 percent, would you recommend going ahead with the investment?

14. (LO14.7) Respond to each of the following scenarios and questions:

a. Your company is considering a capital expenditure in R&D equipment. There is little likelihood that the investment will pay off in terms of cash inflows within the next five years, but it may be critically important to the long-term sustainability of the company's intellectual property. How do you justify this investment to management?

b. What should you do if the payback method and the discounted payback method result in different outcomes? Should you still make the investment? Will the discounted payback time period be longer or shorter than the payback method time period? Should you always include the time value of money in this calculation? Why or why not?

c. You have been asked to evaluate a possible investment for which the expected cash inflows are really just a guesstimate because the capital expenditure is a brand new one with which the company doesn't have any experience. How would you go about evaluating the investment if you are uncertain of its prospects? How much weight would you give the qualitative aspects of this investment? How might you use sensitivity analysis for the quantitative portion of the analysis to assist in the evaluation?

15. (LO14.7) Bob has been a management accountant for Jones High-Pressure Gauges for many years. Given his experience, he believes he knows which capital expenditure will be best for the company overall. And because no one knows with any certainty what the actual timing of the cash flows will be, he figures he might as well be optimistic about the timing of the cash inflows to make the IRR come out the way he expects, and to help the decision maker choose Bob's preferred capital expenditure.

ETHICS

Required

a. Is Bob's behavior ethical? Why or why not?

b. What types of analysis could be performed in an unbiased way that might show that, in fact, Bob's preferred alternative is the best one?

16. (LO14.7) Sally is a management accountant for Clawson Logistics and Trucking. Given her degree, work experience, and training as a management accountant, she believes she knows which capital expenditure will be best for the company overall. And because no one knows with any certainty the true risk of the cash flows, she argues that her preferred capital expenditure is less risky and thus merits a lower required rate of return than the alternatives. She acts on her belief accordingly.

ETHICS

Required

a. Is Sally's decision ethical? Why or why not?

b. What types of analysis could be performed in an unbiased way that might show that, in fact, Sally's preferred alternative is the best one?

LAB 14.1 **Excel:** Capital Budgeting: Calculating Net Present Value and Internal Rate of Return (Heartwood)

LAB 14.2 **Excel:** Capital Budgeting: Calculating Payback, Discounted Payback, and Accrual Accounting Rate of Return

LAB 14.3 **Excel:** Sensitivity Analysis of the Net Present Value Method: Using an Excel Data Table to Evaluate the Impact of Assumptions Related to the Returns to Capital Expenditures

LAB 14.4 **Excel:** Sensitivity Analysis of the Internal Rate of Return Method: Using an Excel Data Table to Evaluate the Impact of Assumptions Related to the Returns to Capital Expenditures

LAB 14.5 **Excel:** Sensitivity Analysis of the Internal Rate of Return Method: Assessing the Timing of Cash Inflows from Capital Expenditures

Lab 14.1   Excel

Lab Note: The tools presented in this lab periodically change. Updated instructions, if applicable, can be found in the student and instructor support materials.

Capital Budgeting: Calculating Net Present Value and Internal Rate of Return (Heartwood)

Data Analytics Types: Predictive Analytics, Prescriptive Analytics

Keywords

NPV(), IRR(), Capital Budgeting

Decision-Making Context

Managers use several tools to evaluate the returns on potential capital expenditures. The net present value (NPV) equals the present value of expected cash inflows minus the cost of cash outflows minus the costs of acquiring the investment. We use the company's required rate of return as the benchmark for the costs of acquiring the investment. In general, if the present value of cash flows is not greater than the costs of acquiring the investment, then there is no strictly financial reason to pursue that investment. Internal rate of return (IRR) is the rate of return that makes the project's net present value equal to zero (where the present value of cash outflows equals the present value of cash inflows).

Net present value and internal rate of return also help decision makers rank various competing capital expenditures. Although investors don't know the future, they will use all of the information they have at their disposal, including the net present value, to evaluate potential investments.

In this lab, we take the perspective of an investor looking at three different potential investment scenarios and consider their expected cash flows.

Required

1. Calculate the net cash flows over the life of each investment.
2. Calculate net present value to evaluate the potential capital expenditures.
3. Calculate the internal rate of return to evaluate the potential capital expenditures.

Ask the Question

How do we calculate net present value and internal rate of return and use them to evaluate potential capital expenditures?

Master the Data

For this lab, you will use data in the Excel file titled **Lab 14.1 Data.xlsx**.

Heartwood Cabinets is evaluating three possible capital expenditures in software. If it makes sense to do so, the company will make all three investments. Each potential investment costs a different amount and has a different profit payoff structure over its expected four-year life.

Heartwood's required rate of return is 9 percent.

All of the analyses suggest that the string of cash flows shown in Lab Exhibit 14.1.1 will result from the investments. Note that Year 0 is today, or the date of the investment. Years 1–4 are years when cash inflows are received.

	A	B	C	D	E
1	Year		Investment 1	Investment 2	Investment 3
2	Year 0 (today)	Buy New Software	(8,000)	(10,000)	(12,000)
3	Year 1	Increased Profits	2,500	3,000	4,000
4	Year 2	Increased Profits	2,500	3,000	4,000
5	Year 3	Increased Profits	2,500	3,000	4,000
6	Year 4	Increased Profits	2,500	3,000	4,000

Lab Exhibit 14.1.1

Microsoft Excel

Perform the Analysis

Analysis Task #1: Calculate the Net Cash Flows over the Life of the Capital Expenditure

1. In cell A8, insert the words "Net Cash Flows over Life (not discounted)."
2. In cell C8, sum the cash flows from cells C2:C6. Copy the contents of cell C8 to cells D8:E8.
3. In cell F1, insert the column heading "Required Rate of Return."
4. In cell F2, insert the number "9%," which is the required rate of return for capital expenditures for this company.

Note that the initial investment is shown as a negative number because cash is being paid out instead of received. Investment 1 pays back a net of $2,500 annually; Investment 2, a net of $3,000 annually; and Investment 3, a net of $4,000 annually.

We can use the net present value (NPV) to compare the profitability of these potential investments by evaluating the amounts and timing of cash flows.

As Lab Exhibit 14.1.2 shows, we can use the **NPV()** Excel function to evaluate the return for these investments. More details about the required formula are provided in the next step.

	A	B	C	D	E	F
1	Year		Investment 1	Investment 2	Investment 3	Required Rate of Return
2	Year 0 (today)	Buy New Software	(8,000)	(10,000)	(12,000)	9%
3	Year 1	Increased Profits	2,500	3,000	4,000	
4	Year 2	Increased Profits	2,500	3,000	4,000	
5	Year 3	Increased Profits	2,500	3,000	4,000	
6	Year 4	Increased Profits	2,500	3,000	4,000	
7						
8	Net Cash Flows over Life (not discounted)		2,000	2,000	4,000	
9						
10	Net Present Value (NPV) of Expected Future Cash Inflows		=NPV($F$2,C3:C6)			
11						

Function Arguments ? ✕

NPV

Rate $F$2   = 0.09

Value1   C3:C6   = {2500;2500;2500;2500}

Value2   = number

= 8099.299693

Returns the net present value of an investment based on a discount rate and a series of future payments (negative values) and income (positive values).

Rate: is the rate of discount over the length of one period.

Formula result = $8,099.30

Help on this function   OK   Cancel

Lab Exhibit 14.1.2

Microsoft Excel

Analysis Task #2: Calculate the Net Present Value of Each Capital Expenditure Scenario

Follow Lab Exhibit 14.1.3 as you complete the following steps.

1. In cell A10, insert the words "Net Present Value (NPV) of Expected Future Cash Inflows." The **=NPV()** function requires information regarding the rate used to denote the cost of acquiring the funds or the required rate of return as well as the string of cash flows.
2. In cell C10, insert this formula: =NPV($F$2,C3:C6). Note that $F$2 refers to the required rate of return and C3:C6 refers to the string of cash flows. We use an absolute reference to $F$2 so that it will stay referenced to the required rate of return as we copy to other cells. See again Lab Exhibit 14.1.2.
3. We use the same NPV function for Investments 2 and 3 by copying the contents of cell C10 to cells D10:E10.

After you've completed these steps, your spreadsheet should resemble Lab Exhibit 14.1.3.

Lab Exhibit 14.1.3

Microsoft Excel

	A	B	C	D	E	F
1	Year		Investment 1	Investment 2	Investment 3	Required Rate of Return
2	Year 0 (today)	Buy New Software	(8,000)	(10,000)	(12,000)	9%
3	Year 1	Increased Profits	2,500	3,000	4,000	
4	Year 2	Increased Profits	2,500	3,000	4,000	
5	Year 3	Increased Profits	2,500	3,000	4,000	
6	Year 4	Increased Profits	2,500	3,000	4,000	
7						
8	Net Cash Flows over Life (not discounted)		2,000	2,000	4,000	
9						
10	Net Present Value (NPV) of Expected Future Cash Inflows		$8,099.30	$9,719.16	$12,958.88	

Follow Lab Exhibit 14.1.4 as you complete the following steps.

4. In cell A11, insert the title "Less: Initial Investment."
5. In cell C11, insert this formula: =C2.
6. In cell A12, insert the title "Net Present Value (NPV) of Investment."
7. In cell C12, insert this formula: =SUM(C10:C11).
8. Copy the results from cells C11:C12 to cells D11:E12. The results are as shown in Lab Exhibit 14.1.4.

	A	B	C	D	E	F
1	Year		Investment 1	Investment 2	Investment 3	Required Rate of Return
2	Year 0 (today)	Buy New Software	(8,000)	(10,000)	(12,000)	9%
3	Year 1	Increased Profits	2,500	3,000	4,000	
4	Year 2	Increased Profits	2,500	3,000	4,000	
5	Year 3	Increased Profits	2,500	3,000	4,000	
6	Year 4	Increased Profits	2,500	3,000	4,000	
7						
8	Net Cash Flows over Life (not discounted)		2,000	2,000	4,000	
9						
10	Net Present Value (NPV) of Expected Future Cash Inflows		$8,099.30	$9,719.16	$12,958.88	
11	Less: Initial Investment		(8,000)	(10,000)	(12,000)	
12	Net Present Value (NPV) of Investment		$99.30	($280.84)	$958.88	

Lab Exhibit 14.1.4

Microsoft Excel

We find that the net present value is higher for Investment 3 (at $958.88) than for the other two investments. Why? Compared to Investments 1 and 2, Investment 3 gets more cash flows back (as evidenced by the net cash flows), and Heartwood receives a larger amount sooner. The time value of money suggests that the sooner we get the money, the sooner we can reinvest it or use it for other purposes.

Analysis Task #3: Calculate the Internal Rate of Return and Modified Rate of Return of Each Capital Expenditure Scenario

Follow Lab Exhibit 14.1.5 for steps 1–3.

1. In cell A14, insert the title "Internal Rate of Return."
2. In cell C14, insert this formula: =IRR(C2:C6).
3. Copy the results from cell C14 to cells D14:E14.

	A	B	C	D	E	F
1	Year		Investment 1	Investment 2	Investment 3	Required Rate of Return
2	Year 0 (today)	Buy New Software	(8,000)	(10,000)	(12,000)	9%
3	Year 1	Increased Profits	2,500	3,000	4,000	
4	Year 2	Increased Profits	2,500	3,000	4,000	
5	Year 3	Increased Profits	2,500	3,000	4,000	
6	Year 4	Increased Profits	2,500	3,000	4,000	
7						
8	Net Cash Flows over Life (not discounted)		2,000	2,000	4,000	
9						
10	Net Present Value (NPV) of Expected Future Cash Inflows		$8,099.30	$9,719.16	$12,958.88	
11	Less: Initial Investment		(8,000)	(10,000)	(12,000)	
12	Net Present Value (NPV) of Investment		$99.30	($280.84)	$958.88	
13						
14	Internal Rate of Return		9.56%	7.71%	12.59%	

Lab Exhibit 14.1.5

Microsoft Excel

4. Let's further assume that the increased profits each year are immediately reinvested at a 12 percent rate of return. To determine the impact on the internal rate of return, we use the modified internal rate of return function in Excel, **MIRR()**. In cell A15, insert the title "Modified Internal Rate of Return" (Lab Exhibit 14.1.6).
5. In cell G1, insert the title "Reinvestment Rate" and in cell G2, the percentage, 12%.
6. In cell C15, calculate the MIRR by inserting the formula =MIRR(C2:C6,$F$2,$G$2), using the Required Rate of Return as the finance_rate and Reinvestment Rate as the reinvest_rate. See again Lab Exhibit 14.1.6.
7. Copy the result from cell C15 to cells D15:E15. Format the cells to show two digits.

	A	B	C	D	E	F	G
1	Year		Investment 1	Investment 2	Investment 3	Required Rate of Return	Reinvestment Rate
2	Year 0 (today)	Buy New Software	(8,000)	(10,000)	(12,000)	9%	12%
3	Year 1	Increased Profits	2,500	3,000	4,000		
4	Year 2	Increased Profits	2,500	3,000	4,000		
5	Year 3	Increased Profits	2,500	3,000	4,000		
6	Year 4	Increased Profits	2,500	3,000	4,000		
7							
8	Net Cash Flows over Life (not discounted)		2,000	2,000	4,000		
9							
10	Net Present Value (NPV) of Expected Future Cash Inflows		$8,099.30	$9,719.16	$12,958.88		
11	Less: Initial Investment		(8,000)	(10,000)	(12,000)		
12	Net Present Value (NPV) of Investment		$99.30	($280.84)	$958.88		
13							
14	Internal Rate of Return		9.56%	7.71%	12.59%		
15	Modified Internal Rate of Return		=MIRR(C2:C6,$F$2,$G$2)				

Lab Exhibit 14.1.6

Microsoft Excel

8. The final result is shown in Lab Exhibit 14.1.7. We note the increase in MIRR for Investments 1 and 2, where the original IRR was below the reinvestment rate, and the decrease in MIRR for Investment 3, where the original IRR was above the reinvestment rate. This shows the importance of how funds are reinvested (or used) once new profits are received.

	A	B	C	D	E	F	G
1	Year		Investment 1	Investment 2	Investment 3	Required Rate of Return	Reinvestment Rate
2	Year 0 (today)	Buy New Software	(8,000)	(10,000)	(12,000)	9%	12%
3	Year 1	Increased Profits	2,500	3,000	4,000		
4	Year 2	Increased Profits	2,500	3,000	4,000		
5	Year 3	Increased Profits	2,500	3,000	4,000		
6	Year 4	Increased Profits	2,500	3,000	4,000		
7							
8	Net Cash Flows over Life (not discounted)		2,000	2,000	4,000		
9							
10	Net Present Value (NPV) of Expected Future Cash Inflows		$8,099.30	$9,719.16	$12,958.88		
11	Less: Initial Investment		(8,000)	(10,000)	(12,000)		
12	Net Present Value (NPV) of Investment		$99.30	($280.84)	$958.88		
13							
14	Internal Rate of Return		9.56%	7.71%	12.59%		
15	Modified Internal Rate of Return		10.55%	9.43%	12.35%		

Lab Exhibit 14.1.7

Microsoft Excel

Share the Story

We have used the capital budgeting techniques of net present value and internal rate of return to evaluate the profitability of Investments 1, 2, and 3. Due to its required rate of return of 9 percent, Heartwood will make Investments 1 and 3, but it will not make Investment 2. (Note that we are considering only quantitative factors here. We have not considered any possible qualitative issues, such as whether some investments offer critical functionality to the rest of the business that allow increased profits or capabilities.)

The internal rate of return gives us a percentage return that we can use to compare to the required rate of return.

Assessment

1. Take a screenshot of the NPV analysis, paste it into a Word document named "Lab 14.1 Submission.docx," and label the screenshot Submission 1.
2. Take a screenshot of the IRR analysis, paste it into a Word document named "Lab 14.1 Submission.docx," and label the screenshot Submission 2.
3. Answer the questions in Connect and upload your Lab 14.1 Submission.docx via Connect if assigned.

Alternate Lab 14.1   Excel—On Your Own

Capital Budgeting: Calculating Net Present Value and Internal Rate of Return

Keywords

NPV(), IRR(), Capital Budgeting

Apply the same steps in Lab 14.1 to the **Alt Lab 14.1 Data.xlsx** dataset.

Vern Richardson is trying to evaluate the profitability of three capital expenditures. Use the Excel **NPV()** and **IRR()** functions to evaluate the potential investments, using a 7 percent required rate of return (or cost of capital). Note that at the end of the investment, the capital expenditure is sold for its salvage value.

When computing the marginal internal rate of return, assume the reinvestment rate is 5 percent.

Required

1. Calculate the net cash flows over the life of each investment.
2. Calculate net present value to evaluate the potential capital expenditures.
3. Calculate the internal rate of return to evaluate the potential capital expenditures.

Open Excel file **Alt Lab 14.1 Data.xlsx** and perform the NPV and IRR analyses.

Assessment

1. Take a screenshot of the NPV analysis, paste it into a Word document named "Alt Lab 14.1 Submission.docx," and label the screenshot Submission 1.
2. Take a screenshot of the IRR analysis, paste it into a Word document named "Alt Lab 14.1 Submission.docx," and label the screenshot Submission 2.
3. Answer the questions in Connect and upload your Alt Lab 14.1 Submission.docx via Connect if assigned.

Lab Note: The tools presented in this lab periodically change. Updated instructions, if applicable, can be found in the student and instructor support materials. All Lab Exhibits are available within the eBook and in Connect.

Capital Budgeting: Calculating Payback, Discounted Payback, and Accrual Accounting Rate of Return

Data Analytics Types: Predictive Analytics, Prescriptive Analytics

Keywords

Capital Budgeting, Payback, Accrual Accounting Rate of Return

Decision-Making Context

Managers can use several tools to evaluate the returns to potential capital expenditures, including an assessment of payback, discounted payback, and accrual accounting rate of return. Both payback methods are used to evaluate the feasibility, profitability, and liquidity associated with a capital expenditure. In contrast, the accrual accounting rate of return shows the impact of the investment on the company's accrual-basis net income.

In this lab, we take the perspective of a company using these three metrics to consider a capital expenditure.

Required

1. Calculate and evaluate the payback period for a potential capital expenditure.
2. Calculate and evaluate the discounted payback period for a potential capital expenditure.
3. Calculate and evaluate the accrual accounting rate of return for a potential capital expenditure.

Ask the Question

How can we use payback, discounted payback, and accrual accounting rate of return to evaluate potential capital expenditures?

Master the Data

For this lab, you will use data in the Excel file titled **Lab 14.2 Data.xlsx**.

FedEx is evaluating the purchase of a hydrogen truck for its fleet. Company management wants to evaluate this potential investment on the basis of payback, discounted payback, and accrual accounting rate of return.

FedEx's required rate of return for its capital expenditures is 7 percent.

All of the analyses suggest that this investment will result in the string of cash savings shown in Lab Exhibit 14.2.1. Note that Year 0 is today, or the date of the initial investment of $90,200. Years 1–7 are years when cash savings (cash inflows) are received.

Perform the Analysis

Analysis Task #1: Calculate the Payback Period

1. In cell C6, insert "90200" to reflect the Year 0 initial investment.
2. In cell C7, insert the formula =C6-B7 to reflect the payback of the first year's cash flows. Your screen should resemble Lab Exhibit 14.2.2.
3. Copy the contents of cell C7 to cells C8:C10. Note that once the initial investment is paid off, the number in cell C10 turns negative. Also note that the payback seems to be complete between Years 3 and 4.

4. To calculate the payback period, we take the three years and add the portion of the fourth year until payback is complete. To do so, insert this formula in cell C16: =3+C9/B10. The result is shown in Lab Exhibit 14.2.3.

Analysis Task #2: Calculate the Discounted Payback Period

1. We next calculate the discounted payback period, noting that the required rate of return is 7 percent. In cell J6, insert "7%," reflecting the required rate of return. See Lab Exhibit 14.2.4.
2. Recall the formula for discounting the annual cash flows to the present is $CF_t/(1 + r)^t$

   where

   > CF_t = cash flows for period t, typically annually as year t
   > r = the required rate of return (typically an annual rate of return)

   To discount the annual cash flow for Year 1, in cell H7 insert the equation =G7/(1+$J$6)^F7 to discount the cash savings for one period at a 7 percent rate. Note that we use an absolute reference for the required rate of return at $J$6, as shown in Lab Exhibit 14.2.4.
3. Use the same discounted cash savings calculation for this investment by copying the contents of cell H7 to cells H8:H13. In cells I7:I13, calculate the net investment not recovered.

   Note that once the initial investment is paid off, the net investment not recovered number turns negative. Also note that the discounted payback seems to be complete between Years 3 and 4.
4. To calculate the discounted payback period, we take the three years and add the portion of the fourth year until the discounted payback is complete. To do so, insert this formula in cell I16: =3+I9/H10. After you've added the formula, your screen should resemble Lab Exhibit 14.2.5.

Analysis Task #3: Calculate the Accrual Accounting Rate of Return

1. Next, we calculate the accrual accounting rate of return. The annual depreciation expense reduces the income each year. Using the straight-line method of depreciation and assuming no salvage value, the annual depreciation is $90,200 divided by seven years. In cell N7, insert the equation =90200/7 to calculate the depreciation expense in Year 1.

   Next, copy the contents of cell N7 to cells N8:N13.
2. First, we calculate the operating income net of the 15 percent tax to calculate our increase in expected average annual after-tax operating income. In cell O7, insert the equation =(M7-N7)*0.85, as shown in Lab Exhibit 14.2.6. The number 0.85 reflects the net amount left after paying the taxes ($0.85 = 1 - 0.15$). Copy the contents of cell O7 to cells O8:O13.
3. Our final step is to compute the accrual accounting rate of return by either the initial investment of $90,200 or the average investment over the life of the investment ($90,200 divided by 2, or $45,100).

   To compute the accrual accounting rate of return by the initial investment, we take the average return over the seven-year period and divide by the initial investment. To do so, in cell O16, insert the equation =AVERAGE(O7:O13)/90200.

   To compute the accrual accounting rate of return by the average investment, we take our average return over the seven-year period and divide by the initial investment. To do so, in cell O17, insert the equation =AVERAGE(O7:O13)/45100.

   The resulting Accrual Accounting Rate of Return is shown in Lab Exhibit 14.2.7.

Share the Story

We have completed three related analyses that tell us how long it takes to pay back the initial investment using nondiscounted or discounted cash flows, along with the impact on the accrual-based operating income using the accrual accounting rate of return.

Each of these metrics helps us compare different capital expenditures and decide whether to invest in them. Which metric is more important? How will qualitative characteristics change the analysis or make us prioritize one investment over another despite the analyses we've conducted?

Assessment

1. Take a screenshot of the payback analysis, paste it into a Word document named "Lab 14.2 Submission.docx," and label the screenshot Submission 1.
2. Take a screenshot of the discounted payback analysis, paste it into a Word document named "Lab 14.2 Submission.docx," and label the screenshot Submission 2.
3. Take a screenshot of the accrual accounting rate of return analysis, paste it into a Word document named "Lab 14.2 Submission.docx," and label the screenshot Submission 3.
4. Answer the questions in Connect and upload your Lab 14.2 Submission.docx via Connect if assigned.

Alternate Lab 14.2   Excel—On Your Own

Capital Budgeting: Calculating Payback, Discounted Payback, and Accrual Accounting Rate of Return

Keywords

Capital Budgeting, Payback, Accrual Accounting Rate of Return

Apply the same steps in Lab 14.2 to the **Alt Lab 14.2 Data.xlsx** dataset.

Note the initial $145,000 investment, a 20 percent tax rate, and the cash savings summarized in Lab Exhibit 14.2.8. The required rate of return is 7.3%.

Lab Exhibit 14.2.8

Microsoft Excel

Year	Cash Savings
0	
1	41996
2	45336
3	31986
4	44821
5	61735
6	31118
7	23560

Required

1. Calculate and evaluate the payback period for the potential capital expenditure.
2. Calculate and evaluate the discounted payback period for the potential capital expenditure.
3. Calculate and evaluate the accrual accounting rate of return for the potential capital expenditure.

Assessment

1. Take a screenshot of the payback analysis, paste it into a Word document named "Alt Lab 14.2 Submission.docx," and label the screenshot Submission 1.
2. Take a screenshot of the discounted payback analysis, paste it into a Word document named "Alt Lab 14.2 Submission.docx," and label the screenshot Submission 2.
3. Take a screenshot of the accrual accounting rate of return analysis, paste it into a Word document named "Alt Lab 14.2 Submission.docx," and label the screenshot Submission 3.
4. Answer the questions in Connect and upload your Alt Lab 14.2 Submission.docx via Connect if assigned.

Lab Note: The tools presented in this lab periodically change. Updated instructions, if applicable, can be found in the student and instructor support materials. All Lab Exhibits are available within the eBook and in Connect.

Sensitivity Analysis of the Net Present Value Method: Using an Excel Data Table to Evaluate the Impact of Assumptions Related to the Returns to Capital Expenditures

Data Analytics Type: Prescriptive Analytics

Keywords

Sensitivity Analysis, Net Present Value, Heat Map

Decision-Making Context

Management accountants use various metrics, including net present value, to prioritize different capital expenditures. Because many assumptions and estimates are used in this type of analysis (such as the size and timing of the future cash flows and expected rates of return), we use the prescriptive analytics technique of sensitivity analysis to assess how the prioritizing of different capital expenditures may change as (and if) the underlying assumptions change.

In this lab, we consider the varying levels of required rates of return and annual cash flows for **Amazon**, which is considering an investment in packaging equipment.

Required

1. Determine how net present value changes with different assumptions of the required rate of return and annual cash flows.
2. Apply conditional formatting/heat mapping to the differing levels of net present value calculated using an Excel data table.

Ask the Question

How sensitive is net present value to changing assumptions about the required rate of return and annual cash flows?

Master the Data

For this lab, you will use a blank Excel file. You will enter the data and follow the steps outlined below.

Perform the Analysis

Analysis Task #1: Prepare the Spreadsheet

1. Open a new file in Excel. There is no other data file provided. Follow Lab Exhibit 14.3.1 as you complete steps 2–6.
2. In cell A1, type the words "Amazon Packaging Equipment Net Present Value" and then boldface them.
3. In cell A3, type the words "Year 0 Initial Investment in Packaging Equipment," and in cell B3, enter the number −50,000. (Don't forget the negative sign.)
4. In cell D3, type the words "Required Rate of Return," and in cell E3, insert 10.5%.

5. In cell A4, type the words "Annual Cash Inflows Years 1-7 (each year)," and in cell B4 enter the number 10,000.

6. In cell A6, type the words "Present Value of Cash Inflows Years 1-7," and in cell B6 enter the formula =PV(E3,7,-B4,FALSE) to calculate the present value. Your spreadsheet should now resemble Lab Exhibit 14.3.1.

7. Follow Lab Exhibit 14.3.2 as you complete steps 7–9. In cell A8, type the words "Less: Year 0 Initial Investment in Packaging Equipment," and in cell B8 insert the formula =B3.

8. In cell A10, type the words "Net Present Value," and in cell B10 enter the formula =SUM(B6:B8).

9. Note the base case shows a net present value of −$2,106.97, as shown in Lab Exhibit 14.3.2.

Analysis Task #2: Input the Range of Assumptions

We must now assess how net present value changes based on changes in the assumptions regarding the annual cash inflows and the required rate of return.

1. In cell D15, input the words "Net Present Value."
2. In cell F15, input the words "Annual Cash Inflow (Years 1-7)."
3. In cell F16, input 8000. In cells G16:L16, input from 9000 to 14000, increasing by 1,000 in each cell, as shown in Lab Exhibit 14.3.3.
4. In cell D17, input the words "Required Rate of Return," as shown in Lab Exhibit 14.3.4.
5. In cell E17, input 8.0%. In cells E18:E26, input from 8.5% to 12.5% in increments of 0.5% down the column, as shown in Lab Exhibit 14.3.4.

Analysis Task #3: Create a Data Table in Excel to Evaluate Sensitivity to Different Assumptions

DATA VISUALIZATION

1. In cell E16, insert the formula =B10. That link references the net present value, and it is the result that will change based on different assumptions in the data table (specifically, the assumptions regarding the annual cash inflows and the required rate of return).

2. Highlight cells E16:L26 and go to **Data > What-If Analysis > Data Table...**, as shown in Lab Exhibit 14.3.5.

3. In the **Data Table** dialog box, input $B$4 for **Row input cell**, suggesting the row input varies by annual cash inflow (see Lab Exhibit 14.3.6). Input $E$3 for **Column input cell**, suggesting that column input varies by the required rate of return. Select **OK**.

4. The output will appear as shown in Lab Exhibit 14.3.7, representing the total profits in each of these scenarios. Note the base-case scenario (outlined in green) with $10,000 annual cash inflows and a 10.5% required rate of return.

5. Next, we will visualize the trends in intrinsic value using conditional formatting. Highlight cells F17:L26 and then go to **Home > Conditional Formatting > Color Scales** and click on **Green-Yellow-Red Color Scale**, as shown in Lab Exhibit 14.3.8.

Share the Story

We have now completed the analysis that will help us assess capital expenditure levels based on a set of alternate assumptions. Lab Exhibit 14.3.9 summarizes the outcomes that we can expect when the assumptions change, helping us decide whether or not to invest.

1. Take a screenshot of the net present value analysis showing the sensitivity analysis, paste it into a Word document named "Lab 14.3 Submission.docx," and label the screenshot Submission 1.
2. Answer the questions in Connect and upload your Lab 14.3 Submission.docx via Connect if assigned.

Alternate Lab 14.3   Excel—On Your Own

Sensitivity Analysis of the Net Present Value Method: Using an Excel Data Table to Evaluate the Impact of Assumptions Related to the Returns to Capital Expenditures

Keywords

Sensitivity Analysis, Net Present Value, Heat Map

Apply the same base scenario in Lab 14.3 to Alternate Lab 14.3 (note that there is no alternate dataset), but now vary the annual cash inflows from $10,000 to $12,000 (in increments of $250) and vary the required rate of return from 9.5 percent to 11.5 percent (in increments of 0.25 percent) and determine how net present value varies.

Required

1. Determine how sensitive the net present value is to changing assumptions of the required rate of return and annual cash flows.
2. Apply conditional formatting/heat mapping to the differing levels of net present value calculated using an Excel data table.

Assessment

1. Take a screenshot of the net present value analysis, paste it into a Word document named "Alt Lab 14.3 Submission.docx," and label the screenshot Submission 1.
2. Answer the questions in Connect and upload your Alt Lab 14.3 Submission.docx via Connect if assigned.

Sensitivity Analysis of the Internal Rate of Return Method: Using an Excel Data Table to Evaluate the Impact of Assumptions Related to the Returns to Capital Expenditures

Data Analytics Type: Prescriptive Analytics

Lab Note: The tools presented in this lab periodically change. Updated instructions, if applicable, can be found in the student and instructor support materials. All Lab Exhibits are available within the eBook and in Connect.

Keywords

Sensitivity Analysis, Internal Rate of Return, Heat Map

Decision-Making Context

Management accountants use various metrics, including the internal rate of return, to prioritize different capital expenditures. Because many assumptions and estimates are used in this type of analysis (such as the size and timing of the future cash flows and expected rates of return), we employ the prescriptive analytics technique of sensitivity analysis to assess how the prioritizing of different capital expenditures may change as (and if) the underlying assumptions change.

In this lab, we consider the varying levels of the initial investment and annual cash inflows for **Kraft Heinz**, which is considering investing in packaging equipment.

Required

1. Determine how internal rate of return changes with different assumptions of the required rate of return and annual cash flows.
2. Apply conditional formatting/heat mapping to the differing levels of internal rate of return calculated using an Excel data table.

Ask the Question

How sensitive is internal rate of return to changing assumptions about the required rate of return and annual cash flows?

Master the Data

For this lab you will use a blank Excel file. You will enter the data and follow the steps outlined below.

Perform the Analysis

Analysis Task #1: Prepare the Spreadsheet

Follow Lab Exhibit 14.4.1 as you proceed through steps 1–13.

1. Open a new file in Excel. There is no other data file provided.
2. In cell A1, type the words "Kraft Heinz Packaging Equipment Internal Rate of Return" and then boldface them.
3. In cell A3, type the words "Year 0 Initial Investment in Packaging Equipment," and in cell B3 enter the number 50,000.

4. In cell A4, type the words "Annual Cash Inflow," and in cell B4 enter the number 10,000.
5. In cell A6, type the words "Cash Outflow Year 0," and in cell B6 enter the formula =−B3.
6. In cell A7, type the words "Cash Inflow Year 1," and in cell B7 enter the formula =B4.
7. In cell A8, type the words "Cash Inflow Year 2," and in cell B8 enter the formula =B4.
8. In cell A9, type the words "Cash Inflow Year 3," and in cell B9 enter the formula =B4.
9. In cell A10, type the words "Cash Inflow Year 4," and in cell B10 enter the formula =B4.
10. In cell A11, type the words "Cash Inflow Year 5," and in cell B11 enter the formula =B4.
11. In cell A12, type the words "Cash Inflow Year 6," and in cell B12 enter the formula =B4.
12. In cell A13, type the words "Cash Inflow Year 7," and in cell B13 enter the formula =B4.
13. In cell A15, type the words "Internal Rate of Return," and in cell B15 enter the formula =IRR(B6:B13) to calculate the internal rate of return for this cash flow. The resulting analysis should appear as shown in Lab Exhibit 14.4.1.

Analysis Task #2: Input the Range of Assumptions

1. We need to assess how internal rate of return changes based on changes in the assumptions for the varying levels of the initial investment and annual cash inflows for Kraft Heinz.
2. In cell D3, input the words "Internal Rate of Return" (Lab Exhibit 14.4.2).
3. In cell H3, input the words "Initial Investment."
4. In cell F4, input 40000. In cells G4:K4, input from 50,000 to 90,000, increasing by 10,000 in each cell, as shown in Lab Exhibit 14.4.2.
5. In cell D5, input the words "Annual Cash Inflows" (Lab Exhibit 14.3.3).
6. In cell E5, input "8000." In cells E6:E11, input from 10,000 to 20,000 in increments of 2,000 down the column, as shown in Lab Exhibit 14.4.3.
7. The completed preparation for the sensitivity analysis is shown in Lab Exhibit 14.4.4.

DATA VISUALIZATION

Analysis Task #3: Create a Data Table in Excel to Evaluate Sensitivity to Different Assumptions

1. In cell E4, insert the formula =B15. That link references the computed internal rate of return, and it is the result that will change based on different assumptions in the data table (specifically, changes in the assumptions regarding the annual cash inflows and the initial capital expenditure).
2. Highlight cells E4:K11 and go to **Data > What-if Analysis > Data Table...**, as shown in Lab Exhibit 14.4.5.
3. In the **Data Table** dialog box, input $B$3 for **Row input cell**, suggesting the row input varies by initial investment (see Lab Exhibit 14.4.6). Input $B$4 for **Column input cell**, suggesting that column input varies by the annual cash inflows. Select **OK**.
4. The output appears as in Lab Exhibit 14.4.7, representing the total profits in each of these scenarios. Note the base-case scenario (outlined in green) with $10,000 annual cash inflows and a $50,000 initial investment.

5. Next, we will visualize the trends in intrinsic value using conditional formatting. Highlight cells F5:K11 and then go to the **Home > Conditional Formatting > Color Scales** and click on **Green-Yellow-Red Color Scale**, as shown in Lab Exhibit 14.4.8.

Share the Story

The completed sensitivity analysis is shown in Lab Exhibit 14.4.9.

We have now completed the analysis that will help us assess capital expenditure levels using IRR based on a set of alternate assumptions. We can use these to help with decision making or refine further with additional assumptions or along with qualitative factors that should be considered as well.

Assessment

1. Take a screenshot of the completed sensitivity analysis, paste it into a Word document named "Lab 14.4 Submission.docx," and label the screenshot Submission 1.
2. Answer the questions in Connect and upload your Lab 14.4 Submission.docx via Connect if assigned.

Alternate Lab 14.4   Excel—On Your Own

Sensitivity Analysis of the Internal Rate of Return Method: Using an Excel Data Table to Evaluate the Impact of Assumptions Related to the Returns to Capital Expenditures

Keywords

Sensitivity Analysis, Internal Rate of Return, Heat Map

Apply the same base scenario in Lab 14.4 Excel to Alternate Lab 14.4 Excel, but now vary the annual cash inflows from $12,000 to $20,000 (in increments of $1,000) and the initial investment from $40,000 to $60,000 (in increments of $2,500) and determine how internal rate of return varies. There is no additional data file for this alternate lab.

Required

1. Determine how sensitive the internal rate of return is to changing assumptions of the required rate of return and annual cash flows.
2. Apply conditional formatting/heat mapping to the differing levels of internal rate of return calculated using an Excel data table.

Assessment

1. Take a screenshot of the completed sensitivity analysis, paste it into a Word document named "Alt Lab 14.4 Submission.docx," and label the screenshot Submission 1.
2. Answer the questions in Connect and upload your Alt Lab 14.4 Submission.docx via Connect if assigned.

Sensitivity Analysis of the Internal Rate of Return Method: Assessing the Timing of Cash Inflows from Capital Expenditures

Data Analytics Type: Prescriptive Analytics

Keywords

Sensitivity Analysis, Internal Rate of Return, Timing of Cash Flows

Decision-Making Context

Management accountants use various metrics, including the internal rate of return, to prioritize different capital expenditures. Many assumptions, such as the size and timing of the future cash flows and expected rates of return, are used in this type of analysis. But how much does the timing of cash flows actually matter?

In this lab, we consider the impact on internal rate of return of an investment that has the same net cash flows over its life, but the cash inflows arrive at different times in each scenario.

Required

1. Calculate the net cash flows over the life of the capital expenditure (nondiscounted) for all five scenarios.
2. Calculate the internal rate of return for all five capital-expenditure scenarios.

Ask the Question

How sensitive is the internal rate of return to changing assumptions regarding the timing of incoming cash flows?

Master the Data

For this lab, you will use data in the Excel file titled **Lab 14.5 Data.xlsx**.

Perform the Analysis

Analysis Task #1: Calculate the Net Cash Flows over the Life of the Scenario

1. Open **Lab 14.5 Data.xlsx** and browse its contents. Note the five different scenarios, as shown in Lab Exhibit 14.5.1.
2. In cell A8, input the words "Net Cash Flows over Life (not discounted)."
3. In cell C8, calculate the net cash flows over the life of the investment by inserting this formula: =SUM(C2:C6).
4. Copy the results of cell C8 into cells D8:G8. Note the same value of net cash flows were returned over the life of the capital expenditure.

Analysis Task #2: Calculate the Internal Rate of Return

1. In cell A10, input the words "Internal Rate of Return (IRR)."
2. In cell C10, calculate the internal rate of return by inserting this formula: =IRR(C2:C6).
3. Copy the results of cell C10 into cells D10:G10.
4. The final result appears in Lab Exhibit 14.5.2. Note the differing internal rate of return calculated even though the nondiscounted cash flows are identical in each case.

Share the Story

We have now completed the analysis that will help us assess capital expenditure levels based on differing timing of cash inflows. While the net cash flows are the same in each scenario ($3,000 net cash inflow), we see the impact of the time value of money by the timing of cash inflows in the various scenarios.

Assessment

1. Take a screenshot of the completed internal rate of return analysis, paste it into a Word document named "Lab 14.5 Submission.docx," and label the screenshot Submission 1.
2. Answer the questions in Connect and upload your Lab 14.5 Submission.docx via Connect if assigned.

Alternate Lab 14.5   Excel—On Your Own

Sensitivity Analysis of the Internal Rate of Return Method: Assessing the Timing of Cash Inflows from Capital Expenditures

Keywords

Sensitivity Analysis, Internal Rate of Return, Timing of Cash Flows

Apply the same analysis in Lab 14.5 Excel to **Alt Lab 14.5 Data.xlsx**, noting the all-new scenarios as shown in the Alt Lab 14.5 Data spreadsheet.

Required

1. Calculate the net cash flows over the life of the capital expenditure (nondiscounted) for all five scenarios.
2. Calculate the internal rate of return for all five capital expenditure scenarios.

Assessment

1. Take a screenshot of the completed internal rate of return analysis, paste it into a Word document named "Alt Lab 14.5 Submission.docx," and label the screenshot Submission 1.
2. Answer the questions in Connect and upload your Alt Lab 14.5 Submission.docx via Connect if assigned.

Excel Tutorial (Formatting, Sorting, Filtering, and Pivot Tables)

You may already have a basic understanding of Excel from your other classes. As a review, and to gain a few more skills, we offer this basic tutorial, which has the following elements:

1. Basic formatting for an income statement using Excel function **SUM()**.
2. Basic data manipulation (filters, sorts, pivot tables).

A note to Mac users: Excel for Mac is different than Excel for Windows. While most of the features and keystrokes are similar, sometimes you'll note differences. If necessary, contact your instructor for suggested workarounds. The instructions, screen shots, and videos in this text are all based on Excel for Windows.

Basic Formatting for an Income Statement Using Excel Function SUM()

A company's income statement summarizes its sales (revenues), expenses, and profit or loss for a particular period, such as a quarter or a year. Suppose we want to put the following data into the appropriate income-statement format:

Revenues	50,000
Expenses	
Cost of Goods Sold	20,000
Research and Development Expenses	10,000
Selling, General, and Administrative Expenses	10,000
Interest Expense	3,000

Required

1. Add a comma as a 1,000 separator for each number.
2. Insert the words "Total Expenses" below the list of expenses.
3. Calculate subtotal for Total Expenses using the **SUM()** command.
4. Insert a single bottom border under Interest Expense and under the Total Expenses subtotal.
5. Insert the words "Net Income" and calculate Net Income (Revenues – Total Expenses).
6. Format the top and bottom numbers of the column with a $ currency sign.
7. Insert a bottom double border to underline the final Net Income total.

Solution

1. Open **Appendix_A_Data_1.xlsx** in Excel. Highlight the column with all the numbers. Right-click on **Format Cells...** to open the dialog box, shown in Exhibit A1.
   Click on **Number** and set decimal places to zero. Click on **Use 1000 Separator (,)** and click **OK**.

Source: Vernon J. Richardson and Marcia Weidenmier Watson, *Introduction to Business Analytics* (New York: McGraw Hill, 2024), Appendix A, pp. 860–867.

2. Insert the words "Total Expenses" below the list of expenses.

3. Calculate the subtotal for Total Expenses using the **SUM()** command, as shown in Exhibit A2. Use the **SUM()** command to sum all the expenses. The resulting output appears in Exhibit A3.

4. Insert a single bottom border under Interest Expense and under the Total Expenses subtotal. Use the **border** icon located in the **Font** toolbar on the **Home** tab to add the bottom border (as shown in Exhibit A4).

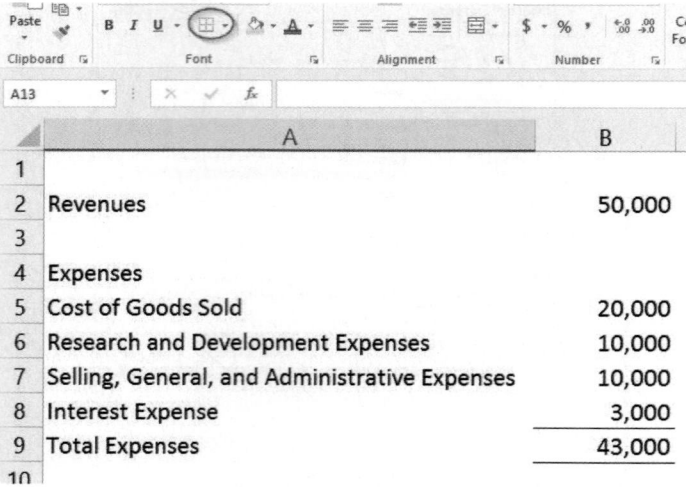

5. Insert the words "Net Income" and calculate Net Income (Revenues – Total Expenses). Type "Net Income" at the bottom of the spreadsheet. Calculate net income by inserting the correct formula in the cell (=B2-B9), as shown in Exhibit A5.

	A	B
1		
2	Revenues	50,000
3		
4	Expenses	
5	Cost of Goods Sold	20,000
6	Research and Development Expenses	10,000
7	Selling, General, and Administrative Expenses	10,000
8	Interest Expense	3,000
9	Total Expenses	43,000
10		
11	Net Income	=B2-B9

6. Format the top and bottom numbers of the column with a $ currency sign. Right-click on each number and choose **Format Cells**, then select **Currency** under the **Number** sign and zero decimal places (as shown in Exhibit A6).

Format Cells   ? ✕

| Number | Alignment | Font | Border | Fill | Protection |

Category:

General
Number
Currency
Accounting
Date
Time
Percentage
Fraction
Scientific
Text
Special
Custom

Sample

$50,000

Decimal places: 0

Symbol: $

Negative numbers:

-$1,234
$1,234
($1,234)
($1,234)

Currency formats are used for general monetary values. Use Accounting formats to align decimal points in a column.

OK   Cancel

7. Insert a bottom double border to underline the final Net Income total. Place your cursor on the cell containing Net Income (7,000). Then select **Bottom Double Border** from the **Font > Borders** menu.

The final project is shown in Exhibit A7.

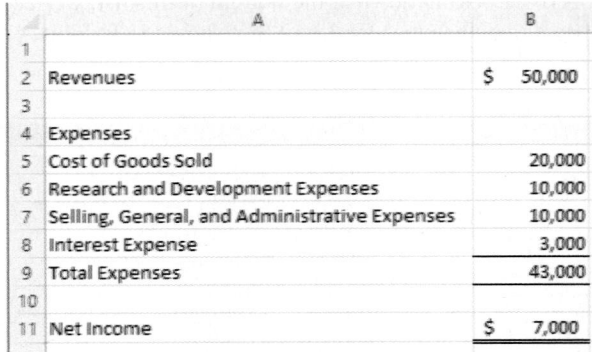

	A	B
1		
2	Revenues	$ 50,000
3		
4	Expenses	
5	Cost of Goods Sold	20,000
6	Research and Development Expenses	10,000
7	Selling, General, and Administrative Expenses	10,000
8	Interest Expense	3,000
9	Total Expenses	43,000
10		
11	Net Income	$ 7,000

BASIC DATA MANIPULATION (SORTS, FILTERS, AND PIVOT TABLES)

1. Open **Appendix_A_Data_2.xlsx**.
2. Look at the data.

Sorting the Data

3. Sort the data. To do so, select **Data > Sort & Filter > Sort** (as shown in Exhibit A8).

Exhibit A8

Microsoft Excel

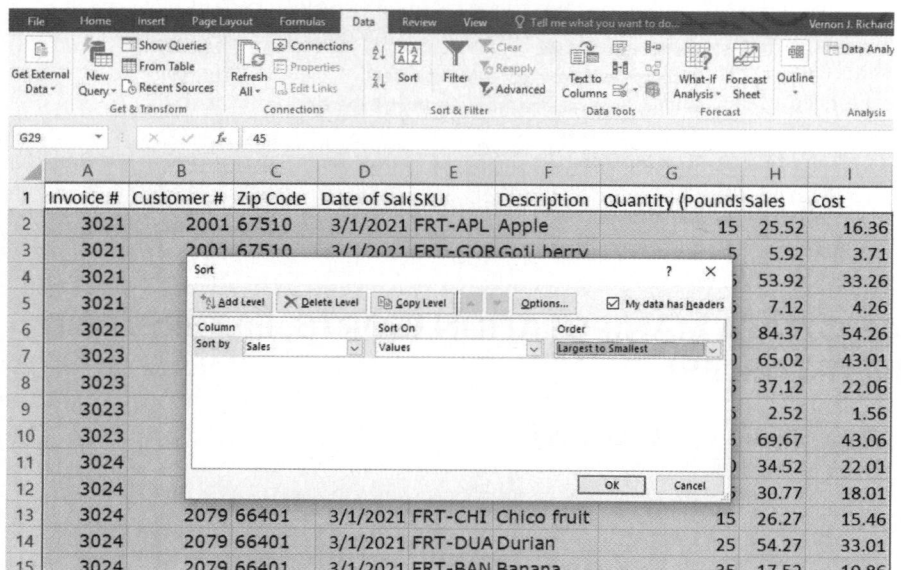

	A	B	C	D	E	F	G	H	I
1	Invoice #	Customer #	Zip Code	Date of Sale	SKU	Description	Quantity (Pounds	Sales	Cost
2	3021	2001	67510	3/1/2021	FRT-APL	Apple	15	25.52	16.36
3	3021	2001	67510	3/1/2021	FRT-GOR	Goji berry	5	5.92	3.71
4	3021	2001	67510	3/1/2021	FRT-OLV	Olive	35	53.92	33.26
5	3021	2001	67510	3/1/2021	FRT-REN	Redcurrant	5	7.12	4.26
6	3022	2091	67621	3/1/2021	FRT-FII	Fig	35	84.37	54.26
7	3023	2021	67511	3/1/2021	FRT-JUR	Juniper ber	50	65.02	43.01
8	3023	2021	67511	3/1/2021	FRT-PAY	Papaya	35	37.12	22.06
9	3023	2021	67511	3/1/2021	FRT-BAN	Banana	5	2.52	1.56
10	3023	2021	67511	3/1/2021	FRT-PEO	Persimmon	35	69.67	43.06
11	3024	2079	66401	3/1/2021	FRT-SAM	Satsuma	50	34.52	22.01
12	3024	2079	66401	3/1/2021	FRT-MII	Miracle frui	15	30.77	18.01
13	3024	2079	66401	3/1/2021	FRT-CHI	Chico fruit	15	26.27	15.46
14	3024	2079	66401	3/1/2021	FRT-DUA	Durian	25	54.27	33.01
15	3024	2079	66401	3/1/2021	FRT-BAN	Banana	35	17.52	10.86

4. Sort by sales price from largest to smallest. Select Sales from the drop-down list in the **Sort** by box, select **Largest to Smallest** in the **Order** box, and click **OK** (as shown in Exhibit A9). The highest sales price appears to be apricots at a cost of $140 (Exhibit A10). Looking down at the bottom of this list, we see that the lowest sales price appears to be bananas for $2.52 (not shown in Exhibit A10).

Exhibit A9

Microsoft Excel

	A	B	C	D	E	F	G	H	I
1	Invoice #	Customer #	Zip Code	Date of Sale	SKU	Description	Quantity (Pounds	Sales	Cost
2	3069	2047	67838	3/4/2021	FRT-APO	Apricot	50	140	88.01
3	3026	2088	67004	3/1/2021	FRT-FII	Fig	50	120.5	77.51
4	3043	2087	67731	3/2/2021	FRT-TAN	Tamarind	50	109.5	69.01
5	3028	2086	67416	3/1/2021	FRT-COU	Coconut	45	108.5	69.31
6	3046	2064	67732	3/2/2021	FRT-SOO	Soursop	45	108	65.71
7	3039	2060	67518	3/2/2021	FRT-PLT	Plumcot (or	50	105	62.01
8	3067	2072	66736	3/4/2021	FRT-LYE	Lychee	50	100.5	62.51
9	3069	2047	67838	3/4/2021	FRT-BIT	Bilberty	50	100	58.51
10	3068	2046	67035	3/4/2021	FRT-LEO	Lemon	40	98.42	59.21
11	3048	2031	67626	3/2/2021	FRT-SOO	Soursop	40	96.02	58.41

Filtering the Data

Next, filter the data to look at only the banana transactions.

5. To sort the data, select **Data > Sort & Filter > Filter**.
6. An upside-down triangle (called a *chevron*) will appear. Click the chevron in cell F1, click **Select All** to unselect all, and then select only the word "Banana." The resulting data should appear as shown in Exhibit A11.

Invoice #	Customer #	Zip Code	Date of S	SKU	Description	Quantity (Poun	Sales	Cost
3041	2066	66408	3/2/2021	FRT-BAN	Banana	50	25.02	15.51
3025	2099	66710	3/1/2021	FRT-BAN	Banana	45	22.52	13.96
3055	2081	66014	3/3/2021	FRT-BAN	Banana	45	22.52	13.96
3028	2086	67416	3/1/2021	FRT-BAN	Banana	40	20.02	12.41
3054	2088	66842	3/2/2021	FRT-BAN	Banana	40	20.02	12.41
3069	2047	67838	3/4/2021	FRT-BAN	Banana	40	20.02	12.41
3024	2079	66401	3/1/2021	FRT-BAN	Banana	35	17.52	10.86
3048	2031	67626	3/2/2021	FRT-BAN	Banana	35	17.52	10.86
3049	2043	66840	3/2/2021	FRT-BAN	Banana	25	12.52	7.76
3048	2031	67626	3/2/2021	FRT-BAN	Banana	15	7.52	4.66
3050	2084	66936	3/2/2021	FRT-BAN	Banana	15	7.52	4.66
3061	2024	66937	3/3/2021	FRT-BAN	Banana	15	7.52	4.66
3023	2021	67511	3/1/2021	FRT-BAN	Banana	5	2.52	1.56

7. Alternatively, we could filter based on date to get all transactions on 3/2/2021. We first need to clear the filter in cell F1 by clicking on the **Filter** symbol and selecting **Select All**.
8. Click the chevron in cell D1, click **Select All** to unselect all, and then select **2021**, then **March**, then **2**. The sorted results are as shown in Exhibit A12.

	A	B	C	D	E	F	G	H	I
1	Invoice #	Customer #	Zip Code	Date of S	SKU	Description	Quantity (Poun	Sales	Cost
4	3043	2087	67731	3/2/2021	FRT-TAN	Tamarind	50	109.5	69.01
6	3046	2064	67732	3/2/2021	FRT-SOO	Soursop	45	108	65.71
7	3039	2060	67518	3/2/2021	FRT-PLT	Plumcot (or	50	105	62.01
11	3048	2031	67626	3/2/2021	FRT-SOO	Soursop	40	96.02	58.41
12	3045	2100	66226	3/2/2021	FRT-PEA	Pear	50	91.52	53.51
14	3043	2087	67731	3/2/2021	FRT-CUE	Cucumber	50	91.02	54.51
15	3053	2032	66414	3/2/2021	FRT-JAU	Jambul	45	87.77	50.86
16	3043	2087	67731	3/2/2021	FRT-APL	Apple	50	85.02	54.51
26	3046	2064	67732	3/2/2021	FRT-FEO	Feijoa	40	79.22	52.01

Pivot Tables

gross margin
Net sales less the cost of goods sold. It is the amount of money a company retains after deducting the direct costs of producing a good or service.

Let's compute the accumulated gross margin for bananas, apricots, and apples. We will take a few steps to get the data ready for pivot tables.

9. First, unclick the filter at **Data > Sort & Filter > Filter** by clicking on and unselecting **Filter**.

10. Next, compute the gross margin for each line item in the invoice. In cell J1, input the words "Gross Margin". Underline Gross Margin with a bottom border. In cell J2, input the formula =H2-I2 and hit **Enter**. See Exhibit A13.

	A	B	C	D	E	F	G	H	I	J
1	Invoice #	Customer #	Zip Code	Date of Sale	SKU	Description	Quantity (Pounds	Sales	Cost	Gross Margin
2	3069	2047	67838	3/4/2021	FRT-APO	Apricot	50	140	88.01	=H2-I2
3	3026	2088	67004	3/1/2021	FRT-FII	Fig	50	120.5	77.51	
4	3043	2087	67731	3/2/2021	FRT-TAN	Tamarind	50	109.5	69.01	

Exhibit A13

Microsoft Excel

11. Copy the result from cell J2 to cells J3:J194.

12. Now it is time to use a pivot table, which summarizes selected columns in a spreadsheet but doesn't change the spreadsheet itself. Recall we are trying to summarize the accumulated gross margin for bananas, apricots, and apples.

   Select **Insert > Tables > PivotTable**.

Analytics Tool: Excel Pivot Tables

PivotTables allow you to quickly summarize large amounts of data. In Excel, select **Insert** > **PivotTable**, choose your data source, and then click the check mark next to or drag your fields to the appropriate boxes in the **PivotTable Fields** pane to identify filters, columns, rows, or values. You can easily move attributes from one pane to another to quickly "pivot" your data. Here is a brief description of each section.

Rows: Show the main item of interest. You usually want master data here, such as customers, products, or accounts.

Columns: Slice the data into categories or buckets. Most commonly, columns are used for time (for example, years, quarters, months, dates).

Values: This area represents the meat of your data. Any measure that you would like to count, sum, average, or otherwise aggregate should be placed here. The aggregated values will combine all records that match a given row and column.

Filters: Placing a field in the Filters area will allow you to filter the data based on that field, but it will not show that field in the data. For example, if you want to filter based on a date, but you don't care to view a particular date, you could use this area of the field list. More recent versions of Excel offer improved methods for filtering, but this legacy feature is still functional.

---

13. Make sure all data are selected as follows in **Table/Range** and click **OK** (as shown in Exhibit A14).

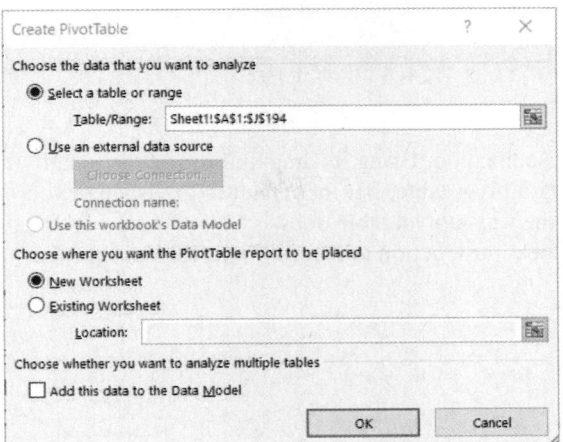

14. The empty pivot table will open in a new worksheet, ready for the pivot table analysis. Alternatively, you can select **Existing Worksheet** so that your pivot table appears in your current worksheet. To build a report, choose fields from the pivot table field list.

Inputs into Pivot Table
_____

Columns:
Rows: [Description]
ΣValues: [Gross Margin]

Drag **[Description]** from PivotTable Fields into the Rows and **[Gross Margin]** from FIELD NAME into **ΣValues** fields in the pivot table. The **ΣValues** will default to "Sum of Gross Margin."

The resulting pivot table will look as shown in Exhibit A15. The analytics suggest that the gross margin for apples is $140.39; for apricots, $78.02; and for bananas, $77.08.

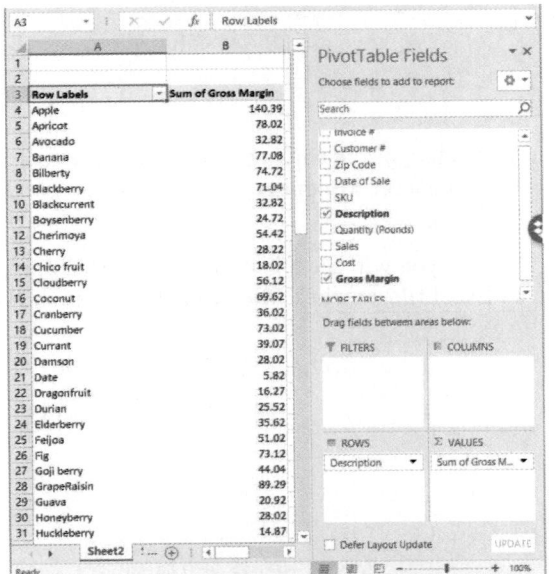

Unless otherwise credited screenshots: Source: Microsoft Excel
Design Elements: (Vector Scales): K3Star/Shutterstock; Checkmark icon, (Briefcase icon): McGraw Hill; (Set of flat icons): PureSolution/Shutterstock; (Arrow logo): Nada design/Shutterstock; (Circular icons): miakievy/DigitalVision Vectors/Getty Images.

Tableau Tutorial

Tableau is a tool for data visualization. Using its drag-and-drop functionality to showcase your data is similar to using a pivot table, but its default is to visualize your data, not to show it in a tabular format the way a pivot table does.

Exhibit B1 provides a quick introduction to pieces of the Tableau canvas.

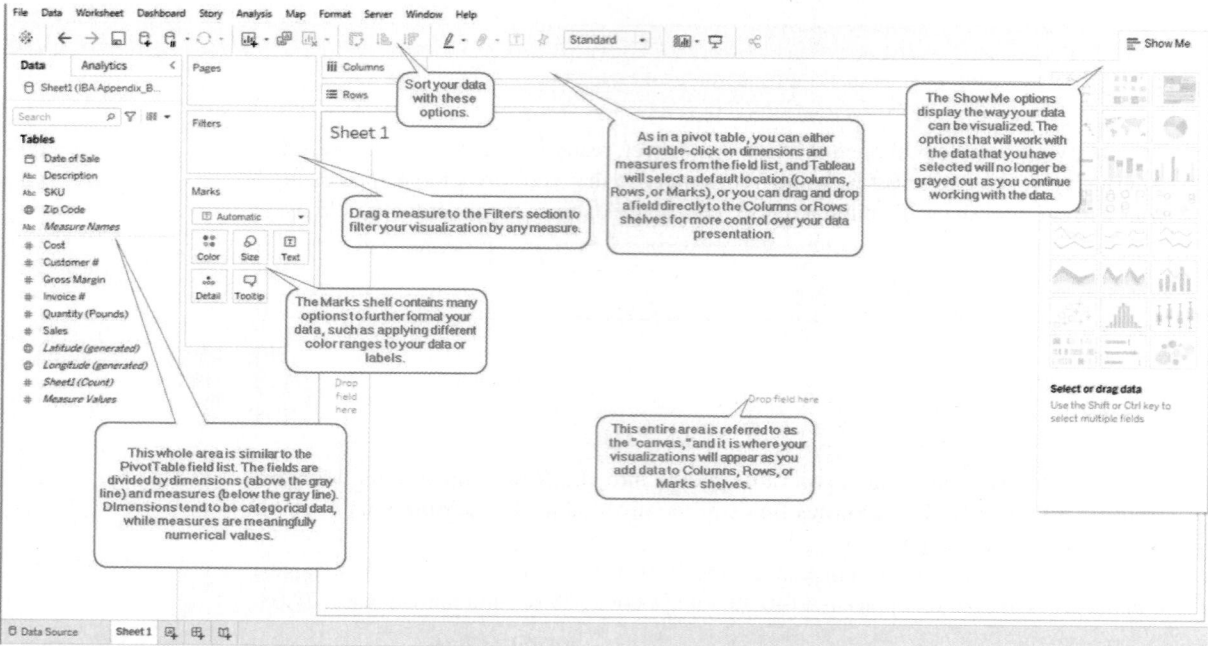

Exhibit B1

Tableau Software

Tableau can connect to a variety of data types, including data housed in Excel, Access, and SQL Server. We will connect to the data set **Appendix_B_Data.xlsx**.

1. Open Tableau.
2. Immediately upon opening Tableau, you will see a list of file types that you can connect to. We'll connect to an Excel file, so click **Microsoft Excel** (as shown in Exhibit B2).

Source: Vernon J. Richardson and Marcia Weidenmier Watson, *Introduction to Business Analytics* (New York: McGraw Hill, 2024), Appendix B, pp. 868–871.

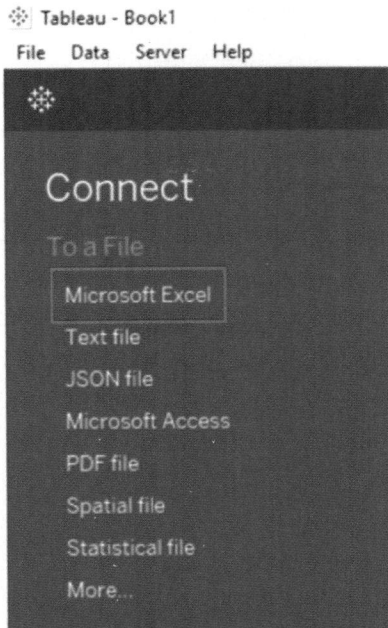

Exhibit B2

Tableau Software

3. Navigate to where your file is stored, highlight the file, and click **Open**.

Tableau automatically detects the data types of the attributes you import. In this data set, the attributes probably all imported as the data type you would expect. Notice that the first two, Invoice # and Customer #, imported as numbers. Continue looking at the attributes, and you will notice the **globe** icon above Zip Code (Exhibit B3). This is Tableau showing you one of its best features: The Zip Code data were imported as geographic data, which will allow you to create maps.

Exhibit B3

Tableau Software

# Sheet1 **Invoice #**	# Sheet1 **Customer #**	⊕ Sheet1 **Zip Code**	📅 Sheet1 **Date of Sale**	Abc Sheet1 **SKU**	Abc Sheet1 **Description**
3,069	2,047	67838	3/4/2021	FRT-APO	Apricot
3,026	2,088	67004	3/1/2021	FRT-FII	Fig
3,043	2,087	67731	3/2/2021	FRT-TAN	Tamarind

4. To begin working with the data, click **Sheet 1** at the bottom left (as shown in Exhibit B4).

Exhibit B4

Tableau Software

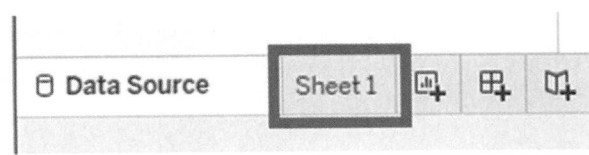

5. Now double-click on the measure **Gross Margin** (as shown Exhibit B5).

Exhibit B5

Tableau Software

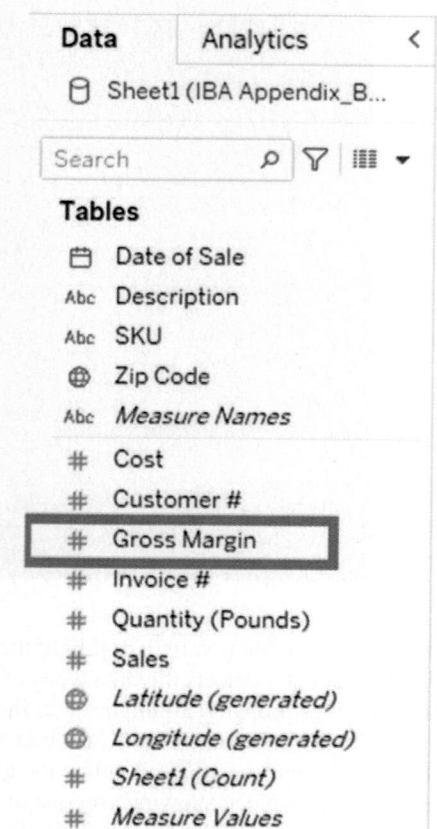

Immediately you will see that Tableau interacts with data differently than Excel because it has defaulted to displaying a bar chart. This isn't a very meaningful chart as it is, but you can add meaning by adding a dimension.

6. Double-click **Description** from the dimensions and it will appear as a column. You find the same numbers that you find in the analytics in Appendix A: apples with a gross margin of $140.40, apricots with a gross margin of $78.00, and so on.

7. To make these data easier to interpret, you can sort them. Click the **Sort Descending** icon (Exhibit B6) to sort the data.

Exhibit B6

Tableau Software

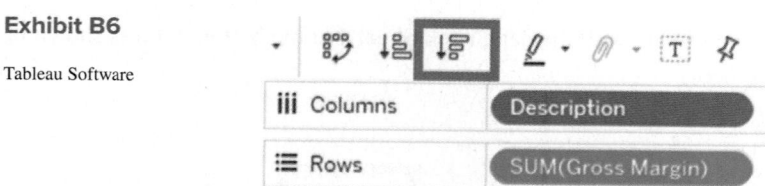

8. Instead of summing the gross margin for each product, we can also get the average or median gross margin by clicking on the chevron next to gross margin in the **Rows** shelf (see Exhibit B6) and changing to the desired measure.

9. You can continue adding attributes to the **Columns** or **Rows** shelves and changing the method of visualization by using the **Show Me** tab to further familiarize yourself with Tableau.

Introduction to Power BI Desktop

Power BI Desktop is a Microsoft tool that is useful for visualizing data, creating dashboards, or just exploring data. It is very similar to Tableau. However, if you will ultimately want to run statistical tests such as hypothesis testing or regression analysis, it's best to work within Excel directly, and then use Power BI to supplement those analyses with visualizations to facilitate sharing the story.

Power BI allows you to create visualizations that are very similar to those you can create in Tableau (see Appendix B), but the path to getting there is different. Power BI defaults to a report mode (similar to Tableau's Dashboard mode) so that as you create visuals, they appear as tiles that you can resize and rearrange around the canvas. This means that Power BI allows you to prepare multiple visuals on the same report screen, rather than preparing them on separate workspaces and then moving them to a dashboard.

The Report View

Exhibit C1 provides an overview of the Report View, which is the main screen you will use to build your visualizations in Power BI.

Let's summarize what you see on the Report View in Exhibit C1.

❶ Report Mode. The first option, represented by an icon that looks like a bar chart, is for Report mode. This is the default view, where you can build your visualizations and explore your data.

❷ Data Mode. The second option, represented by an icon that looks like a table or a spreadsheet, is for Data mode. When you click this icon, you can view the raw data that you have imported into Power BI. You can also create new measures or new columns from this mode.

❸ Model Mode. The third option, which looks like a database diagram, is for Model mode. When you click this icon, you enter PowerPivot. From this mode, you can edit the table and attribute names or edit relationships between tables.

❹ Visualizations. You can drag any of these options over into the canvas to begin designing a visualization. Once you have tiles on your report, you can change the type of visualization being used by clicking the tile, then selecting any of the visualization options to change the way the data are presented.

❺ Fields. This section is similar to the PivotTable field list in Excel. You can expand the tables to see the attributes that are within each. Placing a check mark in the fields will add them to an active tile.

❻ Values, Filters, etc.: This section will vary based on the tile and the fields you are actively working with. Anytime you add a field to a visualization, that field gets automatically added to the filters, which eliminates the need to manually add filters or slicers to your PivotTable.

❼ Ribbon: Immediately above the canvas is the familiar ribbon that you can expect from Microsoft applications. Four of the tabs—**Home**, **View**, **Modeling**, and **Help**—stay consistent across the three different modes (Report, Data, and Model), but the options that you can select will vary based on the mode in which you are working.

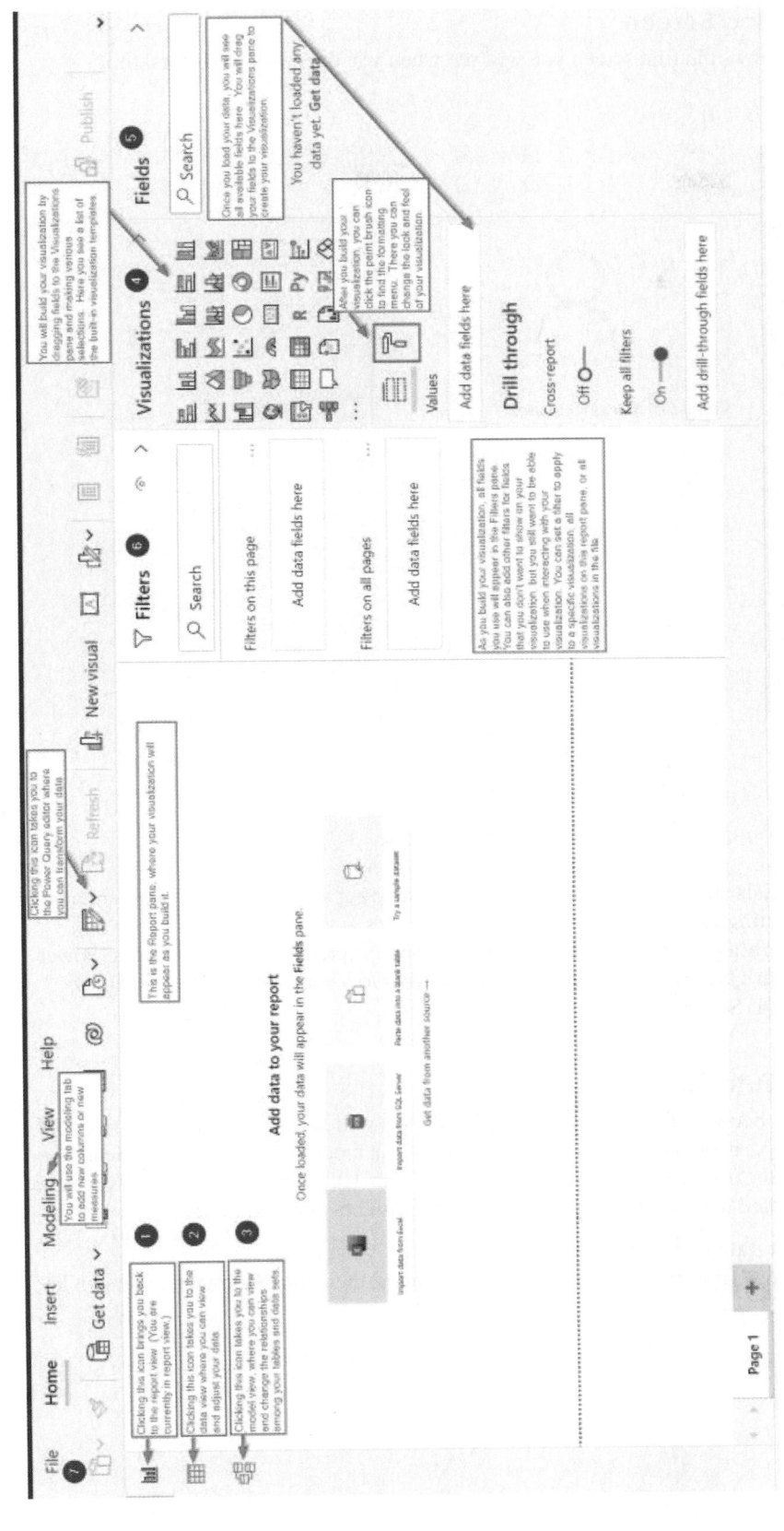

Exhibit C1
Power BI Desktop Report View

Microsoft Power BI

The Opening Screen

Exhibit C2 shows the first screen you will see when you open Power BI Desktop.

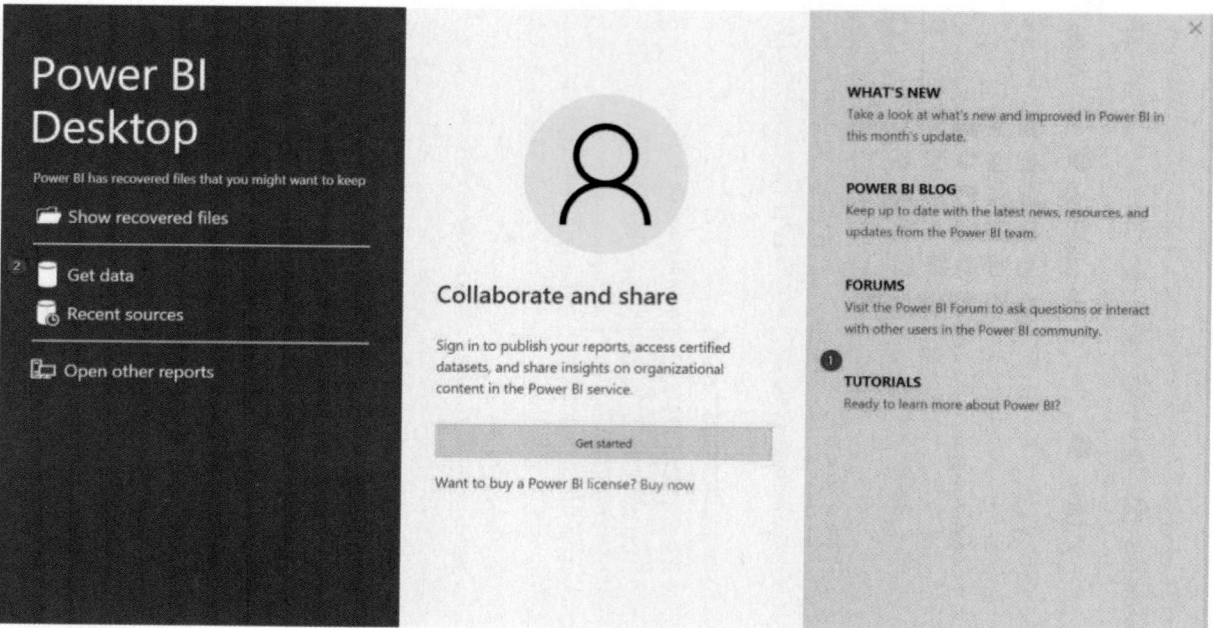

Exhibit C2
Power BI Opening Screen

Microsoft Power BI

❶ The tutorials and other training resources on the right of the start-up screen are helpful for getting started with Power BI.

❷ The **Get data** button on the left side of the start-up screen will bring you into Power BI's Power Query tool. You can use it to connect to a variety of sources (such as Excel, SQL Server, and Access).

Power BI Tutorial

To help you become familiar with Power BI, we will use the data file **Power BI_ Appendix.xlsx**, available in the Connect Library. It is a modified version of the Heartwood Maple Division file that you might work with in Lab 10.4. The data are a subset of the sales data related to a cabinet manufacturer named **Heartwood Cabinets**.

1. Click **Get data** on the start-up screen.
2. Select **Excel** from the list of possible data sources, then click **Connect**, as shown in Exhibit C3.

Get Data

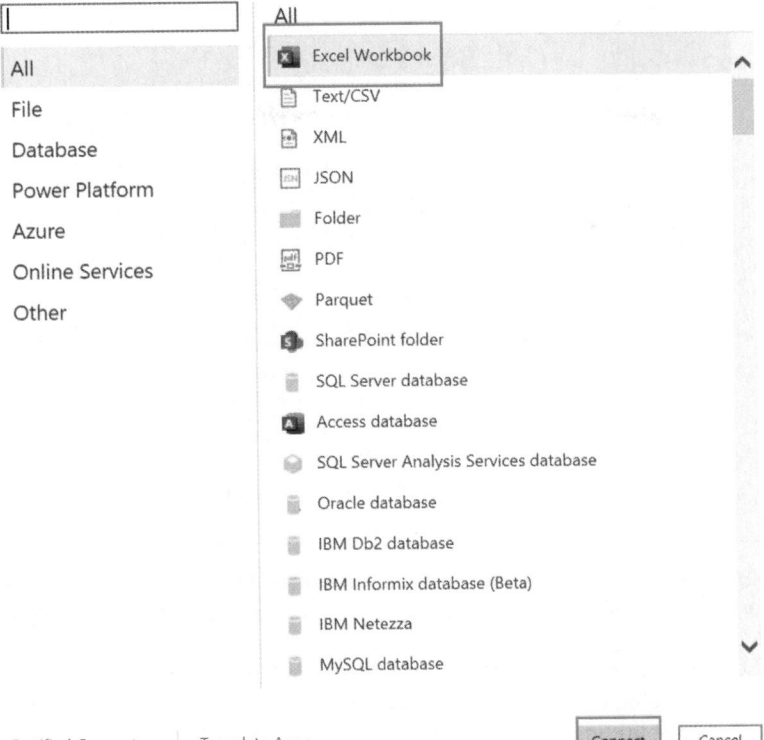

All

- All
- File
- Database
- Power Platform
- Azure
- Online Services
- Other

All

- Excel Workbook
- Text/CSV
- XML
- JSON
- Folder
- PDF
- Parquet
- SharePoint folder
- SQL Server database
- Access database
- SQL Server Analysis Services database
- Oracle database
- IBM Db2 database
- IBM Informix database (Beta)
- IBM Netezza
- MySQL database

Certified Connectors | Template Apps

Connect Cancel

3. Browse to the file location for **Appendix_C_Data.xlsx** and open the file.
4. There is only one spreadsheet in the file, **Maple Data**, so the Navigator screen provides only the option to select that spreadsheet. Place a check mark in the square to the left of Maple Data.
   - *Note:* If your file had multiple spreadsheets, each would be listed and you would need to place a check mark in the square for each spreadsheet you intend to use to build your visualizations.
5. You are also given an option to either Load or Transform the data. If you click **Transform**, you will enter the Power Query window and have the ability to add columns, split columns, pivot data, and so on. These data do not need to be transformed, so click **Load**.
   - *Note:* You can also transform the data later from the **Power Query** icon on the report pane.
6. Once the data are loaded, you will see a blank report pane on which you can build a report. You will see that the Maple Data have been loaded and the fields are available to you in the **Fields** pane on the right side of the screen. See Exhibit C4.

Exhibit C4

Fields Pane

Microsoft Power BI

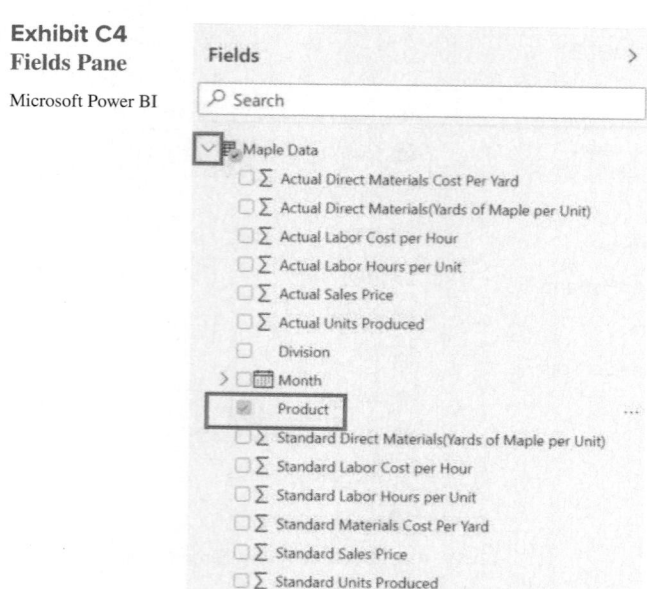

7. To begin working with the data, expand the **Maple Data** table by clicking on the arrow to the left of the title, Maple Data, and place a check mark in the **Product** field, as shown in Exhibit C4.

8. You will see that the **Product** field has now populated the **Values** in the **Visualizations** pane, and the list of products is shown on the **Report** pane as Power BI has begun building a table visualization. See Exhibit C5.

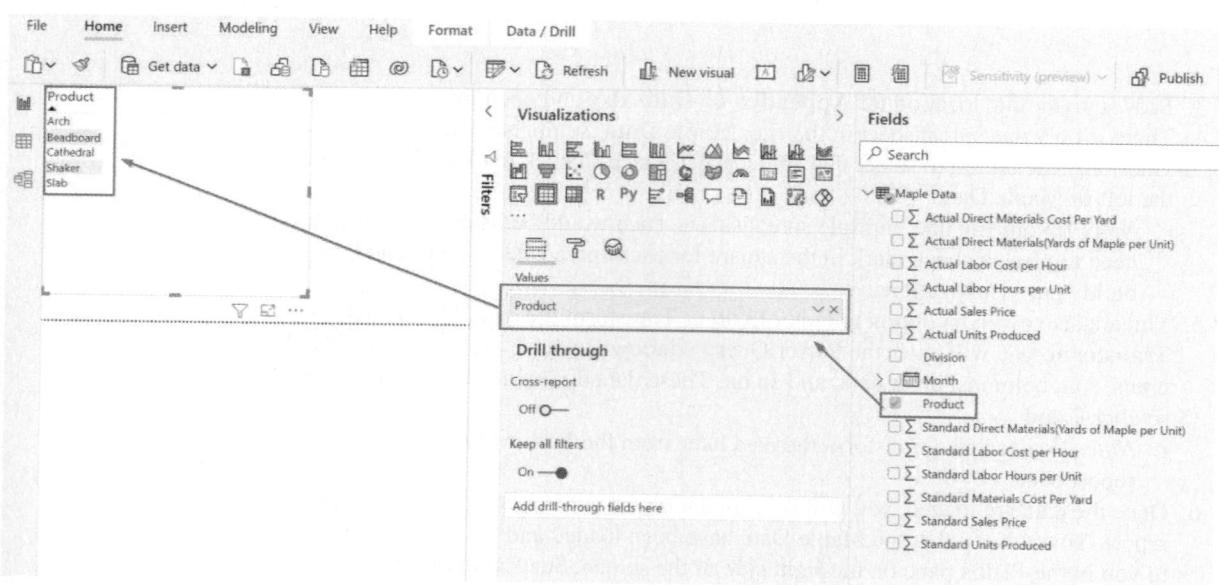

Exhibit C5

Selecting Fields

Microsoft Power BI

9. Next, click **Actual Units Produced**, and you will see that this field is also added to the **Visualizations** pane and in your new table in the **Report** pane. See Exhibit C6.

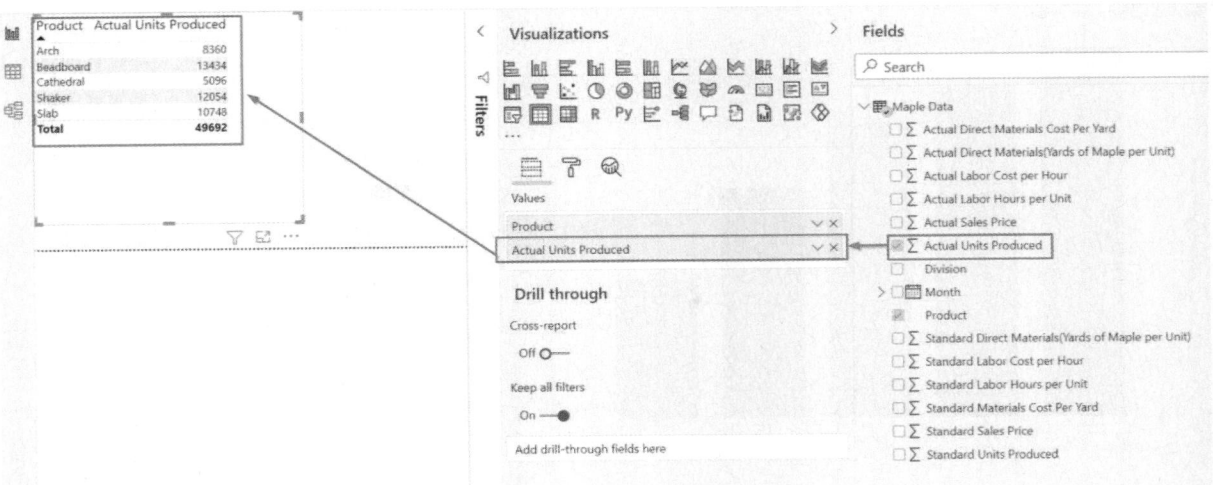

Exhibit C6
Adding Additional Fields

Microsoft Power BI

10. If you click to expand **Actual Units Produced** (or any numerical field), you will see that the default aggregation method is to sum the data. You can change the aggregation from this drop-down menu (shown in Exhibit C7) to average, minimum, maximum, and so on. However, for this tutorial, you can just leave it as **Sum**.

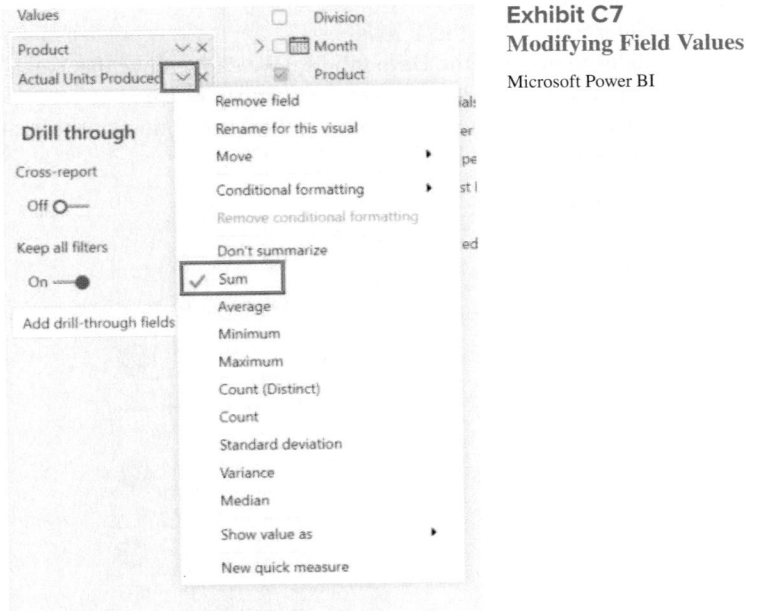

Exhibit C7
Modifying Field Values

Microsoft Power BI

11. While Power BI has defaulted to creating a table visualization, you can change the type of visualization by selecting a different visualization from the icons at the top of the **Visualizations** pane. For this example, select a column chart by clicking the icon shown in Exhibit C8.
    - You'll see that the **Product** field has moved to the **Axis**, meaning that each product will be shown at the bottom of the visualization.
    - The **Actual Units Produced** field has moved to the **Values**, meaning that this field will be represented by the height of the columns.

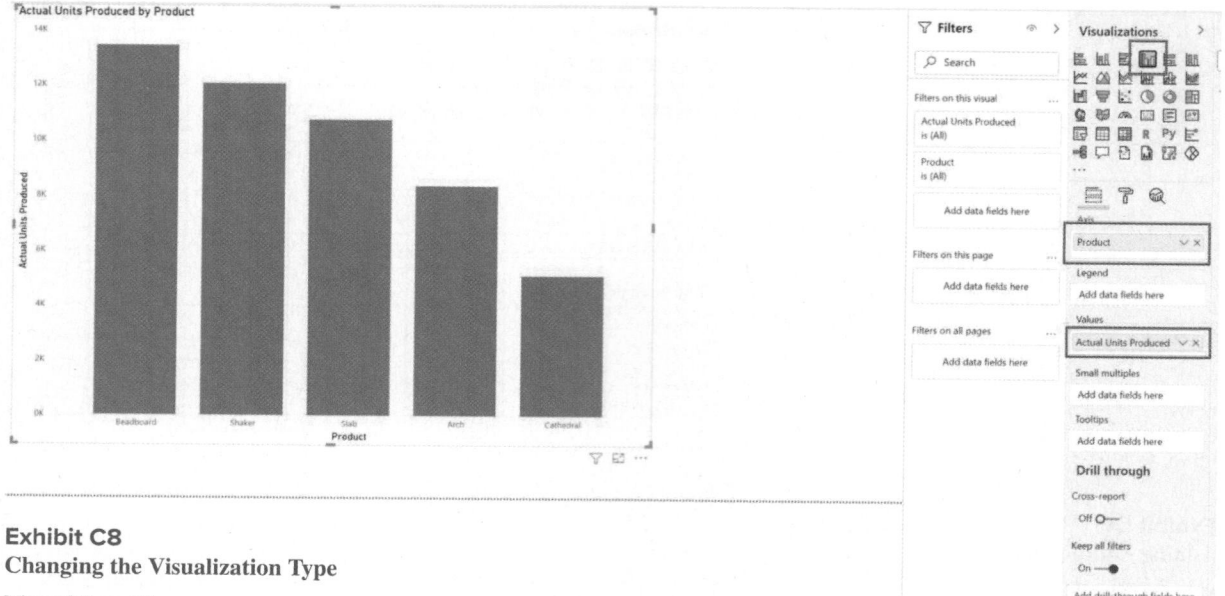

Exhibit C8
Changing the Visualization Type

Microsoft Power BI

12. If you want to format this visualization, you can click on the **paint brush** icon, which opens the **Formatting** menu (as shown in Exhibit C9). Here you can change the color, format the axes, add data labels, format the titles, and so on. For this tutorial, let's make the following changes:

❶ Use the slider to turn **Off** the **Y axis**.

❷ Use the slider to turn **On** the **Data labels**. (We can remove the Y-axis because it is redundant now that we've added the data labels.)

❸ Align the Title in the center by expanding the **Title** option and selecting the **center** icon (shown at the bottom of Exhibit C9).

Exhibit C9
Formatting the Visualization

Microsoft Power BI

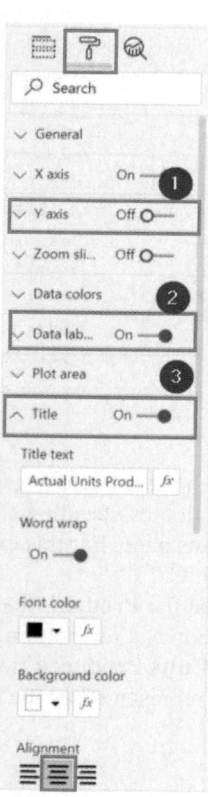

Your visualization should now resemble Exhibit C10.

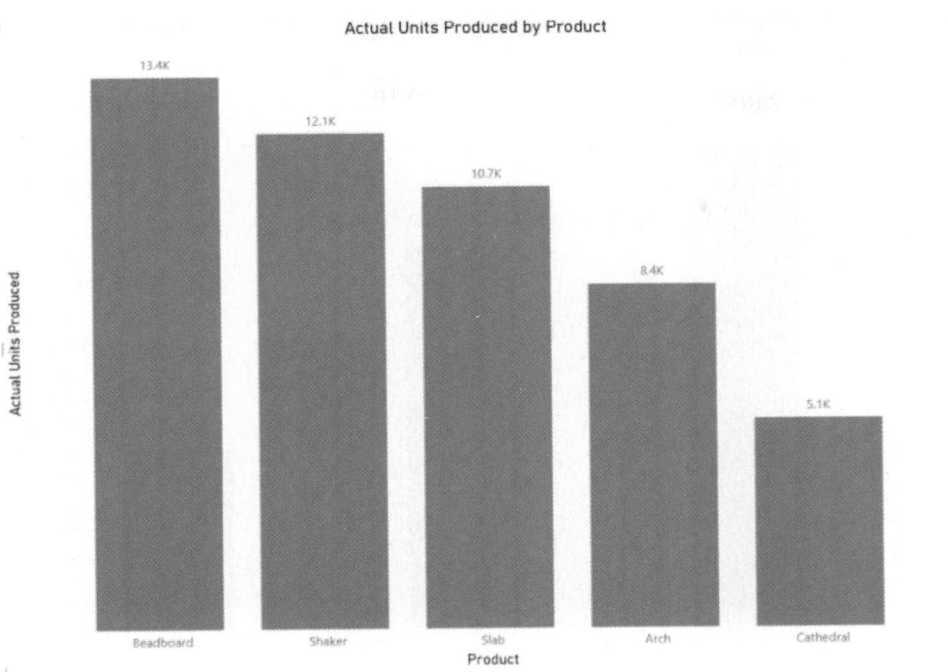

Actual Units Produced by Product

Exhibit C10
Formatted
Visualization

Microsoft Power BI

13. You can add some basic analytics to your visualization by clicking on the **Analytics** icon (as shown at the top of Exhibit C11) and opening the **Analytics** menu.

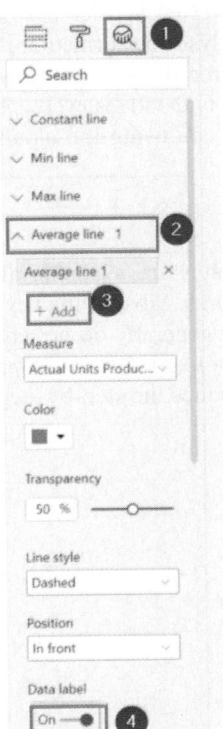

Exhibit C11
Adding Basic Analytics Elements

Microsoft Power BI

14. As Exhibit C11 shows, this menu allows you to add simple elements to the visualization, such as a constant line or an average line. Let's add an average line by expanding the **Average Line 1** option and then selecting **+Add**. Also turn the **Data label** to **On** so that the visualization will show the average number of units produced. Exhibit C12 shows the visualization with this average line.

Exhibit C12
Completed Visualization with Average Line

Microsoft Power BI

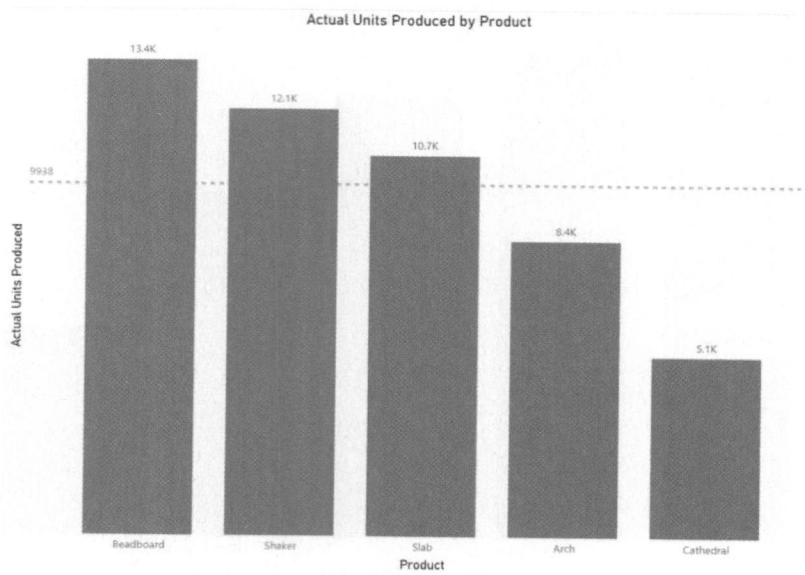

Power BI Service

Power BI is also available as a cloud-based solution. This version is relatively similar to Power BI Desktop. Both versions allow users to create reports and visualizations. The primary differences relate to collaboration, and Power BI Service is somewhat limited in its modeling capabilities. However, the types of analyses performed in this text should all be manageable in either Power BI Desktop or Power BI Service. However, please note that all step-by-step lab instructions, screenshots, and videos were prepared in Power BI Desktop, so minor differences may exist if you are using the cloud-based Power BI Service application.

New Releases of Power BI

Power BI Desktop is updated frequently, and updates are available almost monthly to respond to customer feedback and provide new features. Most of the key functionalities—especially those used in this text—are standard and generally do not change from month to month. But there may be minor changes to the look and feel of the program if you are using a different version than the version used to produce the step-by-step lab instructions, screenshots, and videos in this book.

Installing Excel's Data Analysis ToolPak Add-In

Excel's Data Analysis ToolPak Add-In allows you to execute predefined analytics such as Descriptive Statistics and Regression analysis.

Task #1: Determine If the ToolPak Is Installed

1. Open Excel.
2. From the menu, select **Data > Analyze**. If Excel looks like Exhibit D1, the ToolPak has been installed, and you are done! If the **Data Analysis** menu option is missing, the ToolPak needs to be installed. Follow the instructions below to install.

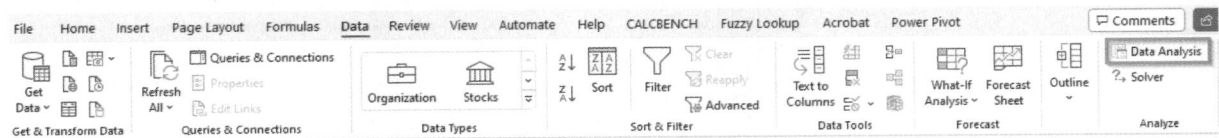

Exhibit D1

Microsoft Excel

Task #2: Install the ToolPak

1. From the menu, select **File> Options** (at the bottom left of the screen, as shown in Exhibit D2).

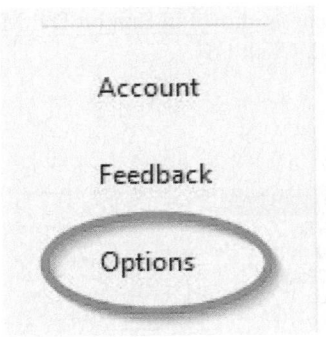

Exhibit D2

Microsoft Excel

2. The **Excel Options** dialog box should open, as shown in Exhibit D3. Select **Add-Ins**.

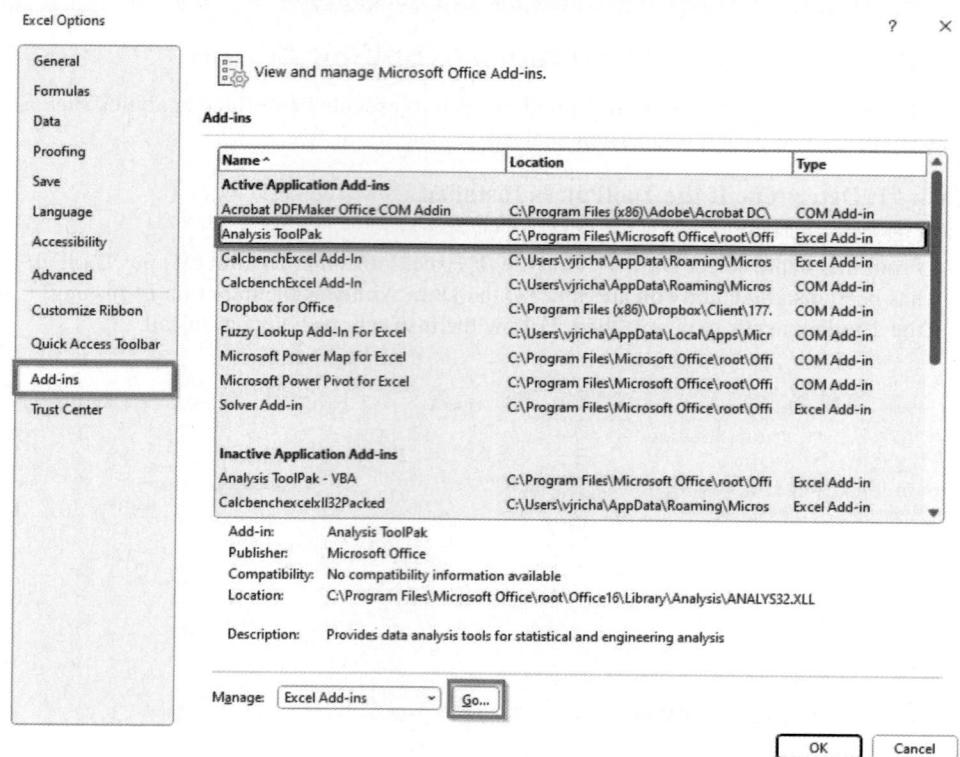

3. Select the **Analysis ToolPak** add-in.
4. Click **Go...**.
5. The **Add-ins** dialog box should appear as shown in Exhibit D4. Make sure the **Analysis ToolPak** Add-in is checked. Click **OK**.

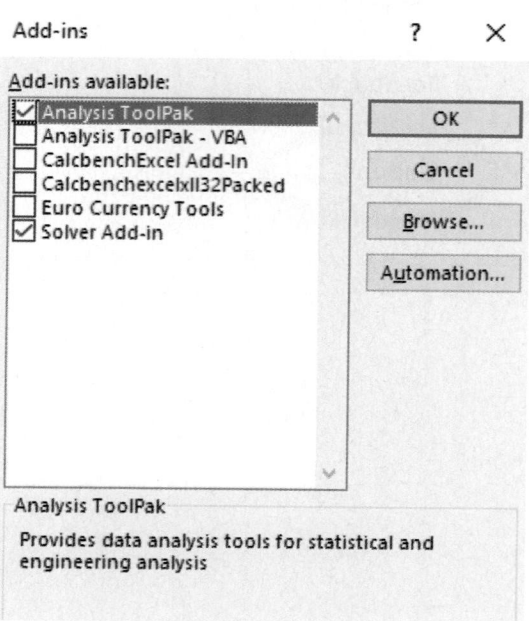

6. From the menu, click the **Data** tab to see **Data Analysis** in the **Analyze** group, as shown in Exhibit D5. You are now ready to use the Analysis ToolPak.

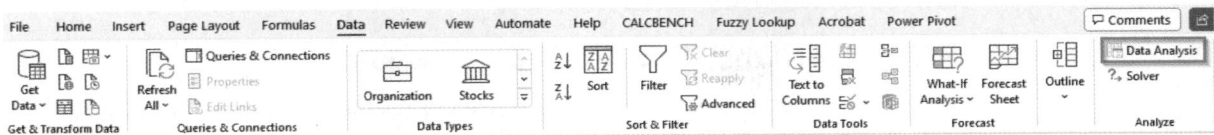

Exhibit D5

Microsoft Excel

Basic Statistics Tutorial

POPULATION VS. SAMPLE

Restaurant stores such as **Chick-fil-A** and retail stores such as **Target** often face the decision of whether to stay open on Sunday. Why? Many retail owners and restaurant owners like to close on Sunday to allow their employees to spend time with families or simply to take a break for the day.

What percentage of restaurants and retail stores close on Sunday? We'd love to ask a survey question on **SurveyMonkey** or **Qualtrics** and get every retail/restaurant owner to respond. In that case, we'd have a set of results that reflect the entire *population* of restaurants and retail stores. However, because it is virtually impossible to get every owner to respond to our survey, we often draw a *random sample* (that is, a subset of the data collected from members of the population) expecting that the results of that sample are representative of the total population.

In a cost setting, we could ask a sample of companies their level of sales on Saturday as compared to Sunday to help address the "Should we close on Sundays?" question. We could also ask a sample of companies if they use activity-based costing to assist them in allocating overhead. If the sample queried is representative of the population, we will be able to infer these results for the population overall.

PARAMETERS VS. STATISTICS: WHAT IS THE DIFFERENCE?

Whereas a *parameter* comes from a population, a *statistic* comes from a sample. For example, the population average of stores closed on Sunday might be 24 percent. However, because we're able to survey only a sample, the result of surveying the sample will be the sample statistic average x-bar, or $\bar{x}$. If we don't know the true population average, μ, then we will use the sample average to make inferences about the true population average.

DESCRIBING THE SAMPLE BY ITS CENTRAL TENDENCY, THE MIDDLE, OR MOST TYPICAL, VALUE

It is often helpful to use a summary variable to describe the sample. Generally, we use a measure of **central tendency**, which is a measure of the center point in the data. The mean, median, and mode are three common measures of central tendency.

The sample arithmetic **mean** is the sum of all the data points divided by the number of observations. The **median** is the midpoint of the data and is especially useful when the numbers are skewed one way or another. The **mode** is the observation that occurs most frequently. If a dataset has data points with values of 5, 6, 6, 7, 8, 9, 12, then the mean is 7.57, the median is 7, and the mode is 6.

DESCRIBING THE SPREAD (OR VARIABILITY) OF THE DATA

The next step after describing the central tendency of the data is to assess its spread, or variability. This might include considering the maximum and minimum values and the difference between those two values, which we define as the **range**.

The most common measures of spread or variability are **standard deviation** and **variance**, where each ith observation in the sample is x_i, and the total number of observations is N. The standard deviation, represented by the Greek letter sigma, σ, is computed as follows:

$$\sigma = \sqrt{\frac{1}{N}\sum_{i=1}^{N}(X_i - \bar{x})^2}$$

The standard deviation is a measure of dispersion or spread of the values in a dataset from the mean. The standard deviation equals the square root of the variance.

The variance, σ^2, is computed as follows:

$$\sigma^2 = \frac{1}{N}\sum_{i=1}^{N}(X_i - \bar{x})^2$$

The variance is the measure of variability around the mean of a dataset. It tells us the average degree to which the values in the dataset differ from the mean.

The greater the sample standard deviation or variance, the greater the variability.

If a dataset has data points with values of 5, 6, 6, 7, 8, 9, and 12, then the standard deviation is 2.37 and the variance is 5.62.

PROBABILITY DISTRIBUTIONS

There are three primary probability distributions used in statistics, accounting, and data analytics: the normal distribution, the uniform distribution, and the Poisson distribution. Managers can use probability distributions to better understand their data and set expectations for future outcomes.

Normal Distribution

A normal distribution is arguably the most important probability distribution because it fits so many naturally occurring phenomena in and out of accounting—from the distribution of return on assets on the sales of chicken sandwiches to the IQ of the human population.

The normal distribution is a bell-shaped probability distribution that is symmetric about its mean, with the data points closer to the mean more frequent than the data points further from its mean. As shown in Exhibit E1, data within one standard deviation (+/− one standard deviation) include 68 percent of the data points; within two standard deviations, 95 percent of the data points; within three standard deviations, 99.7 percent of the data points.

A z-score is computed to tell us how many standard deviations (σ) a data point (or observation), x_i, is from its population mean, μ, using the formula $z = (x_i - \mu)/\sigma$. A z-score of 1 tells us that the observation is one standard deviation above its mean. A z-score of −2 tells us that the observation is two standard deviations below its mean.

Many of the statistical tests employed in data analysis are based on the normal distribution and how many standard deviations a sample observation is from its mean.

Uniform Distribution and Poisson Distribution

The uniform distribution is a probability distribution where all outcomes are equally likely. For example, in a fair coin toss, the coin is equally likely to come up heads or tails. A deck of cards has an equal distribution of hearts, clubs, diamonds, or spades. Likewise, a deck of cards has an equal distribution of queens and 3s. A Poisson distribution is a distribution that has a low mean and is highly skewed to the right. An example of the Poisson distribution might be the number of patients who arrive at the emergency room between 2 and 3 a.m.

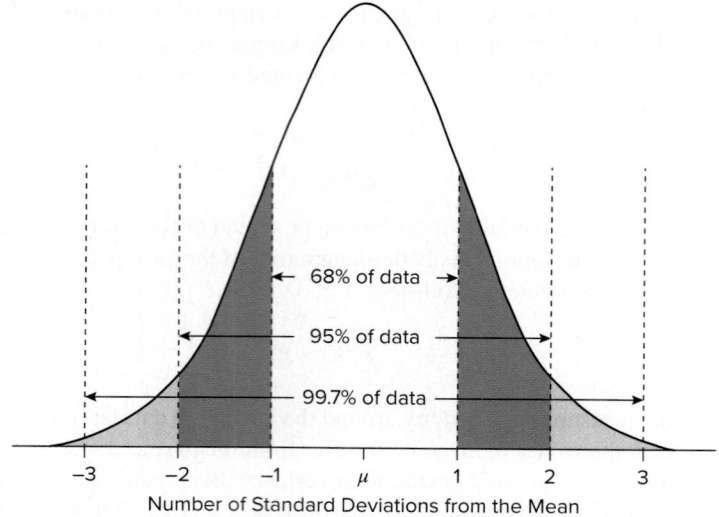

HYPOTHESIS TESTING

Data by themselves are not really that interesting. It is using data to answer, or at least address, questions posed by management that makes them interesting.

Managers might pose a question in terms of a hypothesis or prediction—for example, their belief that sales at their stores are higher on Saturdays than on Sundays. Perhaps they want to know this information to decide if they will need more staff to support sales (such as cashiers, shelf stockers, and parking lot attendants) on Saturday as compared to Sunday. In other words, management holds an assumption that sales are higher on Saturdays than on Sundays.

Usually hypotheses are paired: the null hypothesis and the alternate hypothesis.

The first hypothesis is the base case, often called the **null hypothesis**, and it assumes the hypothesized relationship does not exist. In this case, the null hypothesis is stated as follows:

Null hypothesis: H_0: Sales on Saturday are less than or equal to sales on Sunday.

The **alternate hypothesis** is the case that management believes to be true:

Alternate hypothesis: H_A: Sales on Saturday are greater than sales on Sunday.

For the null hypothesis to hold, we would assume that Saturday sales are the same as (or less than) Sunday sales. Evidence for the alternate hypothesis occurs when the null hypothesis does not hold and is rejected at some level of statistical significance. In other words, before we can reject or fail to reject the null hypothesis, we need to do a statistical test of the data with sales on Saturdays and Sundays and then interpret the results of that statistical test.

STATISTICAL TESTING

Scientists use many different statistical tests to test their hypotheses, including *t*-tests and regressions, which we cover later in this appendix. First, though, we need to review two important statistical concepts: the *p*-value and confidence intervals.

The *p*-Value

We describe a finding as statistically significant by interpreting the *p*-value.

A statistical test of a hypothesis returns a *p*-value. The *p*-value is compared to a threshold value, called the **significance level** (or **alpha**). A common value used for alpha is 5 percent or 0.05.

A result is statistically significant when the *p*-value is less than alpha. This signifies a change was detected: that the default hypothesis can be rejected.

If *p*-value > alpha: Fail to reject the null hypothesis (not significant result).
If *p*-value <= alpha: Reject the null hypothesis (significant result).

For example, if we are performing a test of whether Saturday sales are greater than Sunday sales and the test statistic is a *p*-value of 0.09, we would state, "The test found that Saturday sales are not different than Sunday sales, and we fail to reject the null hypothesis at a 5 percent level of significance."

This statistical result should then be reported to management.

The Confidence Interval

The **confidence interval** tells us how confident we can be that the result that we've found would be found again in a different set of data. The significance level can be computed by subtracting alpha (α) from 1 to give a confidence level of the hypothesis given the statistical test of the data.

For example, if the confidence level is 95 percent, then alpha is 5 percent. In Exhibit E2, the 95 percent portion of the figure represents the confidence interval—we are 95 percent confident that the true population parameter of Saturday and Sunday sales falls somewhere in that area.

Therefore, we can make the following statement:

With a *p*-value of 0.09, the test found that Saturday sales are not different than Sunday sales, and we fail to reject the null hypothesis at a 95 percent confidence level.

This statistical result should then be reported to management.

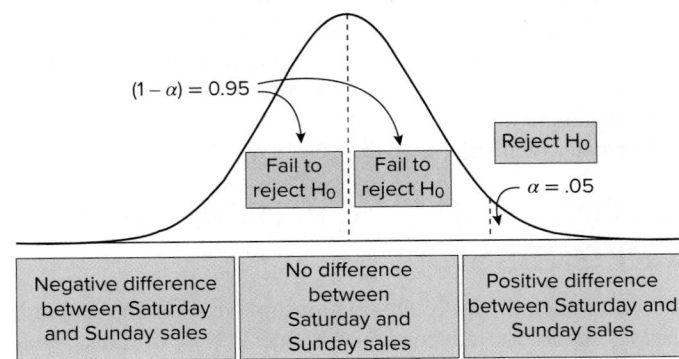

Exhibit E2
Statistical Testing Using Alpha, *p*-Values, and Confidence Intervals

INTERPRETING THE STATISTICAL OUTPUT FROM A SAMPLE *t*-TEST OF A DIFFERENCE OF MEANS OF TWO GROUPS

A sample *t*-test is a statistical test used to compare the means of two sets of data observations.

For example, it might be comparing means of two independent groups, perhaps comparing the total sandwich sales on Saturday as compared to Sunday to see if one is statistically greater than the other.

Let's suppose that a company is trying to understand if its rate of sandwich sales is different on Saturday and Sunday. To assess whether the sales are different, a *t*-test is performed in Excel between sales on Saturday and sales on Sunday. After performing the *t*-test, Excel returns the following statistical output:

t-Test: Two-Sample Assuming Equal Variances		
	Saturday Sandwich Sales	*Sunday Sandwich Sales*
Mean	1046.87533	1027.483204
Variance	653.3064817	677.3542673
Observations	104	104
Pooled Variance	665.3303745	
Hypothesized Mean Difference	0	
df	206	
t Stat	5.42136216	
P(T<=t) one-tail	8.2337E-08	
t Critical one-tail	1.652284144	
P(T<=t) two-tail	1.64674E-07	
t Critical two-tail	1.971546669	

Microsoft Excel

The *t*-test output indicates that over the 104-week period, Saturday sales were $1,046.88 and Sunday sales were $1,027.48. The question is whether those two numbers are statistically different from each other. The *t*-stat of 5.42 and the *p*-value [shown as "P(T<=t) one-tail"] is 8.2337E-08 (a tiny number that is well below 0.01 percent), suggesting the two sample means are significantly different from each other.

The *t*-test output notes the difference in crucial *p*-values for a one-tailed *t*-test and a two-tailed *t*-test. A one-tailed *t*-test is used if we hypothesize that Saturday sales are significantly greater (or significantly smaller) than Sunday sales. A two-tailed *t*-test is used if we expect the two sample means will be different from each other, but we don't predict which one will be greater or smaller than the other.

INTERPRETING THE STATISTICAL OUTPUT FROM A REGRESSION

Regressions are used to help measure the relationship between one output (or dependent) variable and various inputs (or independent variables). We can think about this in terms of an algebraic equation where y is the dependent variable and x is the independent variable, where $y = f(x)$. As an example, we hypothesize a model where y (or total weekend sandwich sales) $= f$(factors potentially predicting weekend sandwich sales, including the independent variables of rainy weather and the summer season). In other words, we hypothesize that total weekend sandwich sales (the output or dependent variable) depend on rain and the season (the input or independent variables).

Through regression analysis, we can assess if the total weekend sandwich sales are statistically related to the weather (rain) and season (summer). The Rain variable is marked as a "1" if it is a rainy day and "0" otherwise. The summer variable is coded as a "1" during the summer season and "0" otherwise.

Let's suppose we are considering the relationship between total weekend sandwich sales and our two hypothesized predictors of sales.

Here is a regression output considering the relationship (generated by Excel's Data Analysis ToolPak):

SUMMARY OUTPUT

Regression Statistics	
Multiple R	0.873
R Square	0.762
Adjusted R Square	0.757 (2)
Standard Error	17.905
Observations	104

ANOVA (1)

	df	SS	MS	F	Significance F
Regression	2	103564.76	51782.38	161.52	3.42052E-32
Residual	101	32379.84	320.59		
Total	103	135944.60			

	Coefficients	Standard Error	t Stat	P-value	Lower 95%
Intercept	2055.7	3.5	585.4	0.0	2048.7
Rain	(4) -28.0	5.1	-5.5 (3)	0.0	-38.2
Summer	47.1	4.3	11.0	0.0	38.6

Microsoft Excel

There are many things to note about the regression results:

❶ The overall regression model did better than chance at predicting the total weekend sandwich sales, as shown by the **F score**. The p-score represented under **Significance F** is very small, almost zero, suggesting there is virtually zero probability that the weekend sandwich scores can be better explained by a model with no independent variables than by a model with independent variables. This is exactly the situation we want, as we are interested in identifying the factors that help to explain total weekend sandwich sales.

❷ The **Adjusted R Square** statistic measures how well the overall regression model predicted the dependent variable of total weekend sandwich sales. In general, the Adjusted R Square is a value between 0 and 1. An Adjusted R Square value of 0 represents the model's complete inability to explain the dependent variable, and an Adjusted R Square value of 1 represents the model's perfect ability to explain the dependent variable. In this case, the Adjusted R Square value is 0.757, which represents the model's reasonably high ability to explain the changes in sandwich sales.

❸ The statistics also report that both the rain and summer variables help predict total weekend sandwich sales. The **t Stat** column shows a value of −5.5 for rain, which is greater than 2 (or less than −2) for rain, and the accompanying p-value of 0.00 is less than an alpha of 0.05. A t-stat with an absolute value of greater than 2 indicates that the independent variable helps to predict the dependent variable.

❹ Given the negative coefficient on the t-stat, it appears that total weekend sandwich sales decrease by $28 if there is rain, as noted in the **Coefficients** column.

This regression also evaluates sales that occurred during the summer. The t-stat for summer is 11, which is greater than 2 (or less than −2), and the p-value of 0.00 is less than an alpha of 0.05. Given the positive coefficient, it appears that total weekend sandwich sales increase by $47.10 during the summer season.

Fundamentals of Data Visualization

Management accountants prepare visualizations so they can effectively "share the story" with management and with other stakeholders in and around their organization. But creating a chart or graph should not be a mechanical process. Instead, you must think carefully about how to prepare a visualization that it is clear, attractive, and easily understood.

WHAT IS DATA VISUALIZATION?

When applying the AMPS model, you may create a data visualization during the Perform the analysis step, and the completed visualization is often an important component of "sharing the story." Data visualization provides a graphical representation of the data and information that you have analyzed.[1] Visualization allows you to communicate the results of your analysis clearly and concisely, enabling decision makers to make informed decisions.[2]

WHO IS YOUR AUDIENCE?

Before you begin, you will want to think about the stakeholders or audience that will use your visualization, and the question(s) that they will answer by using it. For example, if your audience is a high-level manager or executive (such as the CFO), they will probably have limited time to review your work and will want to draw accurate conclusions from it quickly. In contrast, a business analyst may want to focus on it intensely to gain a detailed understanding of the data and insights.

SELECTING THE RIGHT VISUALIZATION

You can use many different types of visualizations to communicate with stakeholders. Exhibit F1 reproduces the **Show Me** pane from Tableau, which shows all of the readily available visualizations that the software makes possible. When you hover your cursor over each image, the name of the visualization appears at the bottom of the **Show Me** pane.

Only the visualizations that make sense given the fields you have moved to the **Columns** or **Rows** shelf will be active. However, if you hover your cursor over a grayed-out visualization icon, you will see what field types (for example, dimensions or measures) you will need to add to use that visualization.

[1]"What Is Data Visualization? Definition, Examples, and Learning Resources," Tableau, **www.tableau.com/learn/articles/data-visualization**.
[2]Ryan Lasker, "Data Visualization: A Picture Worth 1,000 Numbers," AICPA & CIMA, December 1, 2022, **www.aicpa-cima.com/resources/article/data-visualization-a-picture-worth-1-000-numbers**.

Exhibit F1

Tableau Show Me Pane

Tableau Software

F Show Me

For **scatter plots** try

0 or more (Dimensions)

2 to 4 (Measures)

Depending on the characteristics of your data and the questions you are trying to answer, certain types of visualizations are more useful than others in terms of communicating your story.

Exhibit F2 summarizes the most common types of visualizations.

Exhibit F2
Summary and Examples of Common Data Visualizations

Tableau Software

Type of Visualization	Definition	Example Image	Description of Example
Area map	Values are distributed across a map to show the location of data. Values can be represented as shapes (for example, as circles in the map to the right), or counties/ states/countries can be filled in with color or shading to indicate concentration. • Good choice when you want to understand the distribution of values across geographical locations.		Compares the total value of cabinets Heartwood sent to customers by zip code during the previous calendar year. The larger dots represent greater sales to that zip code. The map also shows concentration of sales in regions when dots are clustered together.
Bar chart	Data are displayed as horizontal bars. The length of each bar represents the value. • Good choice when you want to compare values.		Summarizes the actual revenues for each product line from the Heartwood Pine division.

Type of Visualization	Definition	Example Image	Description of Example
Box-and-whisker plot	Boxes show the distribution of values. The box shape represents the middle 50% of the data. The whiskers represent the minimum and maximum data points. Longer whiskers indicate that there is a wider distribution of values. • Good choice when you want to show the distribution of variables and easily identify outliers.		Shows the distribution of actual revenue results for each month from the Heartwood Pine division. You can see that one product line consistently has lower revenues than the others.
Bubble chart	Bubbles represent the value for three different measures. The location of the bubble represents its value relative to two measures, and its size represents the third measure. • Good choice when you want to show the relationship between three variables.		Displays each product in the Heartwood Pine division based on actual labor hours (Y-axis), actual quantity of materials used (X-axis), and actual production (size).

Exhibit F3 (*continued*)

Type of Visualization	Definition	Example Image	Description of Example
Bullet graph	A bar (or column) chart shows progress toward a goal. • Good choice when you want to compare values and determine whether a goal has been met.		Compares the actual revenue to the standard revenue estimated for each product line produced by the Heartwood Pine division.
Column chart	Data are displayed as vertical columns. The height of each column represents the value. • Good choice when you want to compare values.		Summarizes the actual revenue for the Heartwood Pine division by product line.
Combo chart	Different types of marks appear in the same visualization to represent different dimensions of the data, allowing the user to see how the different datasets relate to each other. • Good choice when you want to compare different data simultaneously.		Shows the actual revenue (line) in combination with the actual labor hours (columns) for each product in the Heartwood Pine division. Reveals how the pattern of revenue closely resembles the pattern of labor hours, perhaps because the most expensive products require more time to produce.

Type of Visualization	Definition	Example Image	Description of Example
Donut chart	A circular chart with segments shows data as a percentage of a whole, but the middle of the circle is removed, so the chart resembles a donut. When the center of the circle is removed, users focus on the length of the arc for comparison. • Good choice when you want to show the composition of the whole.	 20.93% 19.02% 24.95% 10.92% 24.18%	Shows the actual revenue for each product line as a percentage of the entire revenue for the Heartwood Pine division.
Heat map	A text table displays variation in the values by using color-coding. • Good choice when you want to summarize data across categories and want to compare the individual values quickly.	See table below	Summarizes actual revenue for each product in the Heartwood Pine division. Uses color to show variation in the values. Darker colors represent higher values.
Highlight table	A text table uses color to categorize data. • Good choice when you want to summarize data across categories and make the categories particularly salient.	See table below	Summarizes actual revenue for each product in the Heartwood Pine division, but shows each product category in a different color for easy identification.
Histogram	A bar chart splits a continuous measure into different bins to allow the user to easily analyze the distribution of values. • Good choice when you want to show a distribution.		Shows customer-satisfaction scores separated into bins.

Heat map example:

	January	February	March	April	May	June
Arch	1,400	1,393	1,425	1,235	1,444	1,463
Beadboard	2,228	2,295	2,205	2,318	2,205	2,183
Cathedral	916	800	880	800	800	900
Shaker	1,960	1,960	2,058	1,960	2,058	2,058
Slab	1,798	1,800	1,780	1,760	1,820	1,790

Highlight table example:

	January	February	March	April	May	June
Arch	1,400	1,393	1,425	1,235	1,444	1,463
Beadboard	2,228	2,295	2,205	2,318	2,205	2,183
Cathedral	916	800	880	800	800	900
Shaker	1,960	1,960	2,058	1,960	2,058	2,058
Slab	1,798	1,800	1,780	1,760	1,820	1,790

Exhibit F3 (*continued*)

Type of Visualization	Definition	Example Image	Description of Example
Line graph	A graph shows data, depicted as a line, over time. • Good choice when you want to compare values over time.	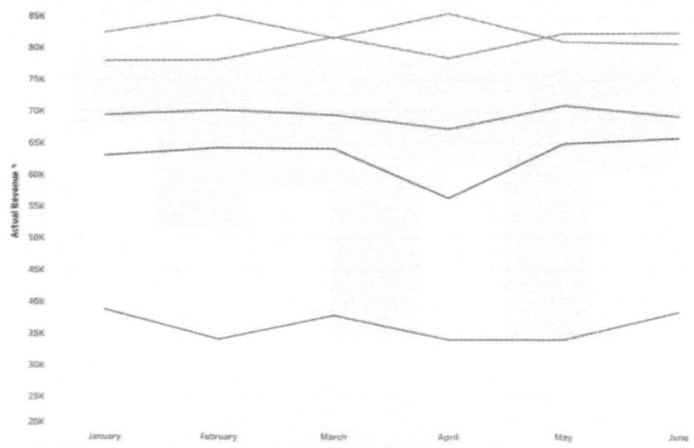	Shows the actual revenue for each product line of the Heartwood Pine division (indicated by line color), over time.
Pie chart	A circular chart with triangular segments shows data as a percentage of a whole. • Good choice when you want to show the composition of the whole.	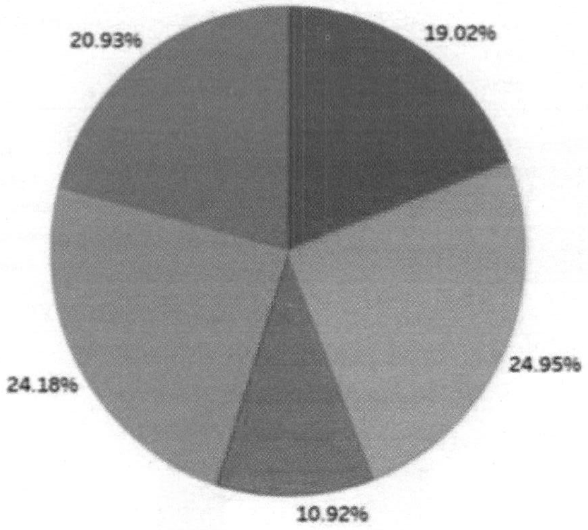	Shows the actual revenue for each product line as a percentage of the entire revenue for the Heartwood Pine division.

Type of Visualization	Definition	Example Image	Description of Example
Scatterplot	Dots (or another discrete symbol) represent the value for two different measures. Can be useful when fitting a regression line to estimate the relationships between the measures. • Good choice when you want to show the relationship between two variables. • Good choice when you want to show the distribution across two variables.		Displays each product in the Heartwood Pine division based on actual labor hours and actual quantity of materials used.
Table	Data are summarized visually in a tabular format (similar to a spreadsheet view). • Good choice when you want to summarize data across categories.		Summarizes actual revenue for each product in the Heartwood Pine division.
Treemap	The values of different, related dimensions are shown as rectangles nested together. The size of each rectangle represents relative value within a category. • Good choice when you want to summarize data within categories.		Shows the relative size of the actual revenue of each product in the Heartwood Pine division nested within the month.

Table example image data:

	January	February	March	April	May	June
Arch	1,400	1,393	1,425	1,235	1,444	1,463
Beadboard	2,228	2,295	2,205	2,318	2,205	2,183
Cathedral	916	800	880	800	800	900
Shaker	1,960	1,960	2,058	1,960	2,058	2,058
Slab	1,798	1,800	1,780	1,760	1,820	1,790

SEVEN DESIGN PRINCIPLES FOR PREPARING DATA VISUALIZATIONS

When preparing a data visualization, keep the following seven design principles in mind. Visualizations designed according to these principles will help your users understand and use the visualizations effectively.

1. **Focus on the data.**
   Always remember that the data are the star of your visualization. Keep the visualization simple and limit (or eliminate) unnecessary embellishments. Visualization design experts refer to the data-to-ink ratio[3] and recommend that you remove "non-data ink" or "redundant ink." These are features of the chart that do not add value or increase understandability. Follow these basic guidelines:
   - Do not apply color to a graph if it does not help you communicate.
   - Remove redundant legends.
   - Remove gridlines or borders if they are unnecessary.
   - Remove axes if you can effectively communicate values as mark labels.
   - Remove titles, headers, and axis labels if possible. For example, if you show months by name across the X-axis, you can omit the axis label "Months."
   - Remove unnecessary background color.

2. **Use color effectively.**
   Color is a very powerful tool in your visualization toolbox. It can be used to differentiate among categories, highlight key data, and represent relative quantities. However, color should be used with care. Too many colors can be distracting or confuse the user. Too much color can lead to cognitive overload.
   The following tips can help you use color effectively:
   - Certain colors have inherent meaning to most users. For example, in the United States, red often means stop or bad, while green means go ahead or good. You can leverage this common understanding to make your visualization powerful. At the same time, you must be careful not to use common colors in ways that will confuse your user.
   - If you are preparing multiple visualizations for use together, apply color consistently so that users can follow it through the entire presentation.
   - Remember that approximately 300 million people in the world are color-blind. The most common type of color blindness is red-green, and those who experience this type of color blindness have limited (or no) ability to discriminate colors along the red-green axis. Blue-yellow is the second most common type of color blindness. Strive for maximum readability and accessibility when you are selecting your colors.

3. **Exploit hierarchy and scale.**
   The use of hierarchy and scale can guide the user's eye towards the most important part of the visualization, especially when you prepare a dashboard combining multiple visualizations on one screen. Larger elements of the dashboard will draw the user's attention, as will elements at the top left of the screen.
   Always use an appropriate scale. Changing the scale of a visualization can distort or misrepresent the data. For example, if you change the endpoints on the Y-axis to be closer together, small differences between data points will seem larger, which may mislead the user. It is especially important to use consistent scales if you want your user to compare values across different visuals.

4. **Attend to balance and proportion.**
   Your visualization should be balanced, and its elements should be proportional according to their importance. For example, you would not want to create a histogram

---

[3]E. R. Tufte, *The Visual Display of Quantitative Information,* 2nd ed. (Cheshire, CT: Graphics Press, 2001).

using bins of vastly different sizes, which could mislead the user. Carefully consider the size and the placement of the visual elements on any visualization that you create.

5. **Maintain consistency.**

Consistency is especially important if you are preparing multiple visualizations for your user. You should work to keep color, fonts, and symbols consistent across all of your visualizations to help users understand and interpret the data. Often, organizations establish a preferred color palette—one that likely coordinates with company colors—to simplify the preparation of consistent visualizations.

6. **Ensure accessibility.**

Your visualizations should be accessible to all likely users. As noted above, many people have some degree of color blindness, but color blindness is only one type of visual limitation. To ensure that your visualizations are as accessible as possible, carefully consider the font size, contrasting colors, and complexity of your visualization.

Also, keep in mind that some users may view your visualization on a computer screen, while others may be using a mobile device such as a mobile phone or an iPad. Some may even print it out on paper! The user's choice will affect their experience with your visualization, and you will want to keep this in mind while you are designing your graphics.

7. **Use interactive elements.**

Many visualizations prepared in data-visualization software can be designed to be interactive. For example, users can often drill down from summary visuals to see more granular data, or they can use filters or slicers to narrow the data analysis to specific dimensions of the graph. For example, users reviewing a sales dashboard from the Pine division at **Heartwood** can filter the visual so that only the "Arch" style cabinet is shown, or only the June sales are visible.

When making your visualization interactive, keep the user's experience in mind. The interaction needs to be intuitive; the user should know exactly what to click and how the visual is likely to change once they have clicked. In addition, not everything needs to be interactive—again, a focus on what really matters to the user is key. Also note that interactive visualizations often require more resources than static visualizations. Thus, they may take up more space on your computer, require more memory to run, and can sometimes be a bit slow, especially if they are designed to have a live connection to real data that are updated when the visualization is refreshed.

INTERPRETING DATA ANALYTICS OUTPUT AND DATA VISUALIZATIONS

How do you interpret data analytics output and data visualizations accurately, using them to help guide your thinking and decision making? Keep the following guidelines in mind.

1. **Understand the basics.**

Make sure you understand the type of visualization that is presented and its strengths and weaknesses. For example, a pie chart should not be used to show sales over time. Also, make sure you understand which data are used in the visualization—do you know what all of the variables represent?

2. **Read the labels and legends.**

All axes, legends, titles, and data points should be clearly labeled (unless they are otherwise obvious). Make sure you understand all of the elements of the visualization before you draw insights from the data.

3. **Consider contextual information**

Consider the source and the context of the data. Ask yourself:
- Where did the data come from?
- Who collected the data?
- How were the data collected?

- When were the data collected?
- How were the data summarized?
- Are the data potentially biased?

Even the most beautiful visualization is useless if it is based on bad data. So, make sure you understand the data before you create the visualization.

4. **Consider the scale.**

Pay attention to the scales used on the axes. A change in scale can dramatically affect how the data appear. Always be aware of whether axes start from zero or not.

5. **Identify patterns and trends.**

Look for general trends or patterns in the data. Does it appear that one variable increases as another increases? Are there clear groups or clusters? Are there any outliers? Does the variable change over time? Answering questions like these will help you draw initial conclusions about the data.

6. **Consider how color is used.**

Consider how color is used in the visualization. For example, colors might be used to represent different categories, indicate a continuum of values, or highlight specific data points.

7. **Understand the purpose.**

Understand what message the visualization is trying to convey. In a management accounting context, and as described by the AMPS model, data visualizations are usually prepared to help answer important questions. Keep those questions in mind as you review and interpret the visualization.

8. **Maintain professional skepticism.**

Don't take every data visualization at face value. When applicable, question the data and the methods used to create the visualization. Misleading data visualizations can be created intentionally or unintentionally, so always approach them with a critical eye and a healthy dose of skepticism. Trust, but verify!

9. **Get to know the interactive elements.**

Interactive features can often provide deeper insights into the data. Be sure to understand what each interactive feature does and how it affects the display of the data. Learn how to activate (and deactivate) the features. Also, make sure you know whether filters and slicers used on specific visualizations carry through to other visualizations in the presentation.

10. **Check for consistency.**

Verify that design elements, such as symbols and colors, are used consistently throughout the visualization. Inconsistencies can cause confusion or misinterpretation and may lead to faulty decision making.

Index